"A JOURNALISTIC MILESTONE ...
Randy Shilts may change a few minds."
—*Time*

"The accounts of lawless, senseless and secret persecutions of lesbian and gay soldiers are chilling. . . . *Conduct Unbecoming* is about what happened to individuals: about their being rousted out of bed, informed against, punished without trials, hounded, set up, brutalized to nervous and physical collapse and rewarded for loyal and able service with disgrace."
—Los Angeles Times Book Review

"*Conduct Unbecoming* is both history-making and history-changing: After this book, readers will find it inconceivable that the ban on homosexuals in the military could possibly be upheld."
—San Francisco Chronicle

"*Conduct Unbecoming* journeys from Europe and Vietnam to all corners of the United States, from battlefield to bedroom . . . Shilts takes the reader inside the mind of a gay soldier in Vietnam who hoped to catch a bullet in the head or heart because death would be easier than owning up to his homosexuality in a hostile world. He takes the reader inside the interrogation rooms where military inquisitors have treated gays and lesbians with the kind of contempt usually reserved for cold-blooded killers and rapists."
—Detroit Free Press

"A convincing and readable narrative on gay life in uniform . . . By maintaining that the present policy is unbecoming for a mature nation, *Conduct Unbecoming* expands the boundaries of the debate and makes a strong contribution to our knowledge."
—The New York Times

"POWERFUL . . . EPIC . . . ENGROSSING . . .

Conduct Unbecoming is at its heart a patriotic book, full of respect for the men and women who are good soldiers and sailors."

—*Los Angeles Times*

"The writing is fast-paced . . . Told through episodes, mini-biographies, portraits and pictures, *Conduct Unbecoming* is a history of the military's long record of expelling homosexuals. The text follows the homosexual in uniform from the end of World War II through McCarthyism to Eisenhower's presidency and the revolutionary '60s. It twists and turns through the civil rights movement to the advent of black power, through women's rights and feminism. It follows the anti-war, anti-military and anti-authority movements as well as the student revolution. It traces Kent State, the end of the draft, Roe v. Wade and gay pride before bringing us to the present day."

—*The Washington Post Book World*

"Encyclopedic in scope and enthralling in execution, *Conduct Unbecoming* should be on every congressional desk . . . Alas, truth and politics are uncommon bedfellows while ignorance and hate are inseparable kin."

—*The Virginian Pilot & Ledger Star*

"A masterful job . . . This country always has had its share of super patriots willing to give their life on battlefields. This book is about some of them. The gay ones."

—*Anderson Independent-Mail*

"Compelling . . . Stunning . . . Must reading . . . A chilling portrait of the toll the gay ban has taken on all-too-human lives, *Conduct Unbecoming* not merely laments the loss of expertise and experience, it indicts a system of military justice that has gone amok."

—*Lexington Herald Leader*

"STUNNING ... A MONUMENTAL ACHIEVEMENT ...

[*Conduct Unbecoming*] ought to make citizens of this country, especially those who served in the military, doubtful about both the military's and government's commitment to the Constitution."

—*Denver Post*

"[A] hard-hitting exposé . . . Shocking . . . *Conduct Unbecoming* rips the secrecy from the military's methods of implementation to reveal the policy's human—and political—costs. . . . Shilts has written a book about the abuse of power, about totalitarian practices and a totalitarian ethic in the midst of a democratic society. Everything about the stories he recounts is offensive—deeply so—and their implications are dangerous."

—*The Nation*

"This powerful book illustrates beyond any doubt that the debate isn't about gay people, it's about heterosexuals' reactions to gay people."

—*Greensboro News & Record*

"Remarkable . . . Shilts examines many individual cases with both compassion and investigative zeal. Those often compelling personal stories thread together this unrelenting narrative of discrimination. Because Shilts' focused passion is so evident, *Conduct Unbecoming* is both readable and persuasive. I don't know how any reader—politician or otherwise—could come away from this book without feeling that the persecution of homosexuals in the American military is terribly wrong."

—*Playboy*

"This work merits recognition as a classic of advocacy writing. . . . His descriptions of witch-hunts based on denunciations evoke McCarthyism at its worst and demonstrate the need for a comprehensive overhaul of the armed forces' investigative services. . . . A valuable resource."

—*Library Journal*

CONDUCT UNBECOMING

GAYS AND LESBIANS IN THE U.S. MILITARY

Randy Shilts

FAWCETT COLUMBINE·NEW YORK

A Fawcett Columbine Book
Published by Ballantine Books

Copyright © 1994 by the Estate of Randy Shilts
Copyright © 1993 by Randy Shilts

Grateful acknowledgment is made to Henry Holt and Company, Inc., Jonathan Cape Limited, and the Estate of Robert Frost for permission to reprint an excerpt from "Stopping by Woods on a Snowy Evening" from *The Poetry of Robert Frost* edited by Edward Connery Lathem. Copyright 1923, © 1969 by Henry Holt and Company, Inc. Copyright © 1951 by Robert Frost. Reprinted by permission of the publishers, Henry Holt and Company, Inc. and Jonathan Cape Ltd.

This edition published by arrangement with St. Martin's Press, Inc.

Library of Congress Catalog Card Number: 93-91047

ISBN 0-449-90917-4

Cover design by Andrew Baris
Cover photo © Tony Stone International

Manufactured in the United States of America

First Ballantine Books Edition: June 1994

10 9 8 7 6 5 4 3 2 1

*To Linda Alband,
a very good friend,*

*and of course to Barry Barbieri,
more than a friend*

Contents

BOOK FIVE:
LESBIAN VAMPIRES OF BAVARIA (1981–1985) 373

BOOK SIX: HOMOVAC (1986–1990) 515

ACKNOWLEDGMENTS

MY CAREER AS AN AUTHOR is due almost solely to the assistance of one person, my editor at St. Martin's Press, Michael Denneny. Neither of my earlier books would have been published except for him; this third book reflects his ongoing confidence and support. The second crucial figure has been my literary agent Fred Hill, who prodded me to do this book and has been unfailing in his support.

My independent editor Doris Ober helped me fine-tune the manuscript, making me look much smarter than I really am. I would also like to acknowledge my brothers, Reed and Gary, for their ongoing support.

This book marked the first time I was afforded the luxury of researchers, who helped make this book both timely and thorough. Steve Robin assisted me with interviews around the country while Jennifer M. Finlay performed miracles in libraries and archives, ferreting out written material. I'm also grateful to Judy Miller, Gart Zeebregts, who helped with the European research, and Sam Gallegos, who followed down leads in Colorado.

Many libraries and archives were invaluable in helping assemble the material for this book, including the Lesbian and Gay Archives of San Diego, Gay and Lesbian Historical Society of Northern California Archives, *San Francisco Chronicle* library, International Lesbian & Gay Association, University of California at Berkeley Library, San Francisco State University library, National Archives, California State Library, Stanford University library, Hastings College of Law, and the Smithsonian Institution's Department of Naval History. Of particular help were Linda M. Finlay, Jim Kepner and the International Gay and Lesbian Archives in Los Angeles, Don Michaels of the *Washington Blade* and Linda Wheeler of the Hoover Institution Library.

A number of people generously shared their files and research with me for this book, including Howard Wallace, William Lederer, Vaughan Taylor, Patricia Davis, Linda Grant De Pauw, Charles Thompson of *60 Minutes*, Peter Cary of *U.S. News & World Report*, Howard Bragman, Benjamin Schatz, Marc Wolinsky, Diana Shaw, and especially Dr.

Rhonda Rivera of Ohio State University Law School. Other figures prominent in the issue of gays in the military also gave me an extraordinary amount of time, even though the structure of the book did not permit me to record their stories completely. These people include Jim Woodward, Mary Newcombe, Miriam Ben-Shalom, Michael Patton, Karen Stupsky, Bill Woods, Ted Werner, Bridget Wilson, Robert Adams, and especially Kate Dyer. I'm also grateful to the National Gay and Lesbian Task Force for helping me contact gay and lesbian veterans, as well as the many gay newspapers that carried my request for interviews.

Although I drew on many other written accounts for background, I am particularly indebted to three for their influence in shaping my attitudes on this subject. Allan Bérubé's definitive account of gays in World War II, *Coming Out Under Fire,* pioneered research into gays in the military and set forth a number of themes repeated in this work. Also crucial in formulating my thoughts were two essays, Dr. Kenneth Karst's "The Pursuit of Manhood and the Desegregation of the Armed Forces," first published in the *UCLA Law Review,* and "Military Women in Nontraditional Job Fields: Casualties of the Armed Forces War on Homosexuals" by Michelle M. Benecke and Kirstin S. Dodge, first published in the *Harvard Women's Law Journal.*

Thanks to the friends of Bill Wilson, who helped sustain me through this arduous project with their experience, strength, and hope. I remain indebted to the support of my film agent Ron Bernstein, my lecture agent George Greenfield, and to Annie & Barry Biderman, Pamela Vevea, Lisa Calpadini, Dale Jenkins, and Pam Pryal for their help. I am blessed with many very good friends who have always been there for me. They include Bill Cagle, Janie Krohn, Cindy Hirsh, Will Pretty, Dan Yoder, Danny Richter, Rebecca Geil, Ann Neuenschwander, and Robert Tan.

A reporter can only be as good as his sources. The people who most assisted me were the 1,100 people who took the time to share their experiences and knowledge with me. I'm grateful to the many people within the Defense Department and the military who gave me background briefings not only on Pentagon personnel policies but on the military subculture. Many of my interviews were with active-duty and Reserve personnel who worried that their cooperation might cost them their military careers. Yet they were there for me just the same. They cannot be publicly identified; you know who you are, and I thank you.

AUTHOR'S NOTE

THE SUBJECT OF LESBIANS AND GAYS in the military is one about which many people have opinions though few have any facts. The debate has been driven by clichés, stereotypes, and misconceptions. For the past quarter century, however, a vast gay subculture has existed in the United States military, and no informed debate can be conducted on this issue without an understanding of that culture's history.

This history takes place during a time when the rest of the nation, like the U.S. military itself, is undergoing wrenching and still uncompleted changes over how to define the roles of women and men in our society. One story cannot be told without the other.

This book is a piece of investigative reporting, employing standard journalistic corroboration. Over the past five years, I have interviewed 1,100 people for this book, including military personnel, their families, and their lawyers, as well as political activists and government officials involved with this issue. Through more than fifty requests under the Freedom of Information Act, I have accumulated nearly 15,000 pages in previously unreleased documents that offer a behind-the-scenes look at the investigations and policy-making concerning homosexuals in the armed forces. My research has also taken me around the world to examine how other countries handle the presence of lesbians and gay men in their military organizations.

This book is written in a narrative nonfiction style, so I sometimes employ such phrases as "he thought" or "she believed" in ascribing ideas and views to various people. When such notations are used, they have been corroborated either by contemporary documentation or interviews from others present at the time. Because of the military's exhaustive record-keeping, the reportage on hearings, investigations, and courts-martial is drawn from transcripts and military records, which are noted in the Notes on Sources. I have endeavored to identify all names, dates, times, and places of the incidents I document in this work, but approximately 150 of the women and men I have interviewed for this book are still members of the military. Any identification of their names or in some circumstances of their duty stations could be damaging to their careers. Because of that, I have shielded the identities of a small number of people and places recounted here. In such cases, however, I have obscured names and sites rather than substitute false information. In this book, there are no pseudonyms or fictionalized anecdotes.

This new Ballantine edition contains not only all the original material from the hardcover version of this book, but a new ending that covers the period from 1990 until early 1994. Most notably, the new edition includes the involvement of lesbian and gay soldiers in Operation Desert Storm, and the debate that consumed the country in 1993 over changing the military's homosexual policies.

That debate, sparked by President Clinton's inclination to change the gay policies, became a complex political story about which an entire book could be written. It is not a book that I would want to write, however. My goal has not been to provide news flashes on the latest twists and turns concerning this issue. Rather, I wanted to use the subject of lesbians and gays in the military to illustrate changing gender roles in the armed services and, more significantly, within the broader society. For the past generation, conflicts over changing views of sexuality and gender have been building toward the time when the new and the old would explode. That this would happen first and most prominently in the U.S. military was inevitable, given the military's role as the last bastion of traditional heterosexual male values. The dissension here is virtually archetypal. It is also inevitable that similar conflict would be fought in every sector of society, as lesbians and gay men become further entrenched as a minority asserting their political perogatives.

These young social movements seem strange and frightening to many people. It is my hope that an accurate account of the evolution of these issues can make for a more informed public, eradicate the fear attendant to these issues, and advance the traditional American values of justice, equality, and freedom.

—RANDY SHILTS
Guerneville, California
January 1994

. . . Truth is great and will prevail if left to herself.

—Thomas Jefferson
Virginia Statute of Religious Freedom

THE DANGEROUS DIFFERENCE

(1778–1954)

After a while you'll think no thought the others do not think. You'll know no word the others can't say. And you'll do things because the others do them. You'll feel the danger in any difference whatever—a danger to the crowd of like-thinking, like-acting men. . . . Once in a while there is a man who won't do what is demanded of him, and do you know what happens? The whole machine devotes itself coldly to the destruction of his difference. They'll beat your spirit and your nerves, your body and your mind, with iron rods until the dangerous difference goes out of you. And if you can't finally give in, they'll vomit you up and leave you stinking outside—neither part of themselves, nor yet free. . . . They only do it to protect themselves. A thing so triumphantly illogical, so beautifully senseless as an army can't allow a question to weaken it.

—John Steinbeck
East of Eden

The Dangerous Difference

THE HISTORY OF HOMOSEXUALITY in the United States armed forces has been a struggle between two intransigent facts—the persistent presence of gays within the military and the equally persistent hostility toward them. All the drama and controversy surrounding the demand for acceptance by lesbians and gay men in uniform represent the culmination of this conflict, one that dates back to the founding of the Republic.

Over the past twenty years, as the gay community has taken form in cities across the nation, a vast gay subculture has emerged within the military, in every branch of the service, among both officers and enlisted. Today, gay soldiers jump with the 101st Airborne, wear the Green Beret of the Special Forces, and perform top-level jobs in the "black world" of covert operations. Gay Air Force personnel have staffed missile silos in North Dakota, flown the nuclear-armed bombers of the Strategic Air Command, and navigated Air Force One. Gay sailors dive with the Navy SEALS, tend the nuclear reactors on submarines, and teach at the Naval War College. A gay admiral commanded the fleet assigned to one of the highest-profile military operations of the past generation. The homosexual presence on aircraft carriers is so pervasive that social life on the huge ships for the past fifteen years has included gay newsletters and clandestine gay discos. Gay Marines guard the President in the White House honor guard and protect U.S. embassies around the world.

Gay military personnel are among the graduates of Annapolis, West Point, and the Air Force Academy in Colorado Springs. At least one gay man has served in the astronaut program. Recent gay general-staff officers have included one Army four-star general, renowned in military circles, who served as head of one of the most crucial military missions of the 1980s. In the past decade, gay people have served as generals in every branch of the armed forces. The Marine Corps has also had at least one gay person at four-star rank since 1981, and at least one gay man has served on the Joint Chiefs of Staff in that time.

Never before have gay people served so extensively—and, in some cases, so openly—in the United States military. And rarely has the military moved so aggressively against homosexuality. The scope and sweep of gay dragnets in the past decade have been extraordinary. Their aim is to coerce service personnel into revealing names of other homosexuals. If investigators are successful, the probes turn into purges in which scores of people are drummed out within weeks. The pressure to cooperate is so fierce that lovers sometimes betray their partners and friends turn against one another.

Separation hearings and courts-martial follow the investigations. But finding witnesses for the defense can be a problem. In the recent purge of lesbians at the Parris Island Marine Corps Recruit Training Depot, two Marines who stepped forward as character witnesses for an accused lesbian were reduced in pay, demoted, and received negative job evaluations. Their superiors openly admitted the Marines' testimony was the reason for the poor ratings. The accused lesbian was quickly dispatched to prison, and lawyers for later defendants found it very difficult to solicit character witnesses. An administrative board in a related case recommended a less than honorable discharge for a Marine captain because she had a civilian lesbian friend. In another case, a senior Navy officer was consistently passed over for promotion after testifying on behalf of an accused gay ensign. Though the ensign was his own son, in the Navy, fathers are expected to turn against their children if their children are accused of homosexuality.

The ruthlessness of the investigations and hearings serves a central purpose: to encourage lesbian and gay soldiers to resign from the military, to accept passively an administrative discharge or, if they are officers, to leave quietly under the vague rubric of "conduct unbecoming." Such quiet separations help conceal the numbers of lesbians and gay men the military turns out of the service, as many as two thousand a year during the past decade.

In the past decade, the cost of investigations and the dollars spent replacing gay personnel easily amount to hundreds of millions. The human costs are incalculable. Careers are destroyed; lives are ruined. Under the pressure of a purge, and in the swell of rumors that often precedes one, despairing men and women sometimes commit suicide.

The military's policies have had a sinister effect on the entire nation: Such policies make it known to everyone serving in the military that lesbians and gay men are dangerous to the well-being of other Americans; that they are undeserving of even the most basic civil rights. Such policies also create an ambience in which discrimination, harassment, and even violence against lesbians and gays is tolerated and to some degree encouraged. Especially for lesbians, the issues are far more complex than simple homophobia, because they also involve significant features of sex-based discrimination.

There are many men who never wanted women in *their* Army or *their*

Navy in the first place, and the military regulations regarding homosexuality have been the way to keep them out for the past decade. Until proven otherwise, women in the military are often suspected of being lesbian. Why else, the logic goes, would they want to join a man's world? Many of these women take jobs that have traditionally been held by men. If they are successful, they are suspect for not being womanly enough; if they fail, they are harassed for not being man enough to do the job.

The way women can prove themselves to be nonlesbians is to have sex with men. Thus antigay regulations have encouraged sexual harassment of women. Those who will not acquiesce to a colleague's advances are routinely accused of being lesbian and are subject to discharge. Some women have allowed themselves to be raped by male officers, afraid that the alternative would be a charge of lesbianism. Those who do complain of sexual harassment often find themselves accused: Their commands are far more intrigued with investigating homosexuals than with investigating sexual harassment. Several investigations of suspected lesbians in the 1980s presaged waves of pregnancies on various installations, as women became pregnant in order to avoid suspicion that they were gay.

There is a saying among gay women in the military: One accusation means an investigation. Two accusations mean guilt. And when a woman mutters, "I'm under investigation," she rarely has to say what for. The branches of the service most resistant to allowing women in their ranks—the Navy and Marines—are the branches that drum out the most women for being gay. The Navy releases twice as many women as men on grounds of homosexuality. In the Marine Corps, the figure is seven times higher for women than men.

Of course, sex discrimination in the military's enforcement of anti-homosexual regulations since 1981 mirrors deeper conflicts. We are a nation in transition when it comes to attitudes toward gender roles and sexuality in general, and homosexuality in particular. Military service was once considered a rite of male passage. This clearly was the case during the early years of the Vietnam conflict; and it remains so among those who were trained during that era of military history—the people who are at the top of the military's chain of command today. In different ways, the presence of women and gays in the ranks challenges the traditional concept of manhood in the military, just as the emergence of women and gays in other fields has done in society at large.

The profound victimization of lesbians in the military has less to do with homophobia than with sexual discrimination and harassment, the kind faced by women breaking into occupations once reserved for men. Meanwhile, the presence of gay men—especially so many who are thoroughly competent for military service—calls into question everything that manhood is supposed to mean. For both women and men, the story of gays in the military is a story about manhood. For generations, after all, the military has been an institution that has promised to do one thing, if nothing else, and that is to take a boy and make him a man. The military's gay policy crisis in the past decade reflects the turmoil of a nation thrust into conflict over our society's changing definition of manhood.

Strikingly, the new aggression against homosexuals in uniform during the 1980s came at a time when just about everyone in the military, from the Secretary of Defense on down, seemed aware that these policies would be abolished. During the Vietnam War, the military had slowed the enforcement of its gay regulations when it appeared that the proscriptions on gay soldiers might interfere with manpower needs. When the next major war broke out a generation later in the Persian Gulf, the armed forces once again curtailed enforcement of policies excluding gays, at least until the exigencies of war were behind them.

What is clear is that the military is far less concerned with having no homosexuals in the service than with having people think there are no homosexuals in the service. Time and again, if a military staffer is someone whom the service needs, his or her discharge is lost or delayed. The military always needs physicians, for example, so it has sometimes taken as long as two years for the gay-related discharge of a doctor, even though such paperwork is routinely completed in two weeks for less valued service members. More than one general and admiral in the armed forces' medical branches have commented privately that if they really went after all the gay doctors and medics, the military would have to close down its medical centers, because there aren't enough heterosexuals in the military medical fields to staff them all.

The candor with which government lawyers and top military men have privately admitted the policies' flaws has surprised civil liberties advocates. In 1982, lawyers took a deposition from a two-star general who made an impassioned defense of the gay exclusion for the court record in a gay-rights court case, but then, over lunch, unofficially admitted he expected that the regulations would fall within a few years. He added, while he would deny saying this in court, that the change would be fine with him, because he knew many fine gay soldiers. That general, Norman H. Schwarzkopf, led U.S. troops in the Persian Gulf and later reaffirmed his public opposition to allowing gays in the military. By then, however, a staff officer with the Joint Chiefs had already drafted the regulations to allow gays to serve in the armed forces.

The report that follows reflects the upheaval in the sexual psyche of this nation for the past generation, as we struggle with profound questions about what it means to be a man and what it means to be a woman in the modern world. The emergence of the contemporary gay movement is one unfolding part of this story. The discomfort of the heterosexual majority with this movement points up its own insecurities over changes in sexual roles that have come too quickly for many to absorb.

In truth, homosexuals in this time and in this culture have very little control over many of the most crucial circumstances of their lives. Control resides with the heterosexual majority, which defines the limits of freedom for the homosexual minority. The story of homosexual America is therefore the story of heterosexual America.

The record that follows poses the question: What kind of nation will we be? In the most narrow sense, it asks us to define the purpose of our military institutions and the hundreds of billions of dollars spent every year to finance them. Is the purpose of the armed forces primarily to offer men an opportunity to define their manliness? Or does our military exist to provide the nation with the most cost-effective means of national defense?

EVEN BEFORE THE ARMED FORCES of the United States were formally organized, gays were bearing arms for the yet unborn nation. The United States might never have become a nation, in fact, were it not for the services of one particular gay general in the first difficult years of the American Revolution.

In 1777, the rebellion was going badly. General George Washington made a dashing figure on horseback and was revered by his troops, but he had little background in the art of military drills and training. Thirteen disparate and mutually suspicious colonies had contributed soldiers for what were, in effect, thirteen different armies. Though all fought under the fraying banner of the Continental Army, they were not yet one unified and disciplined force. The army desperately needed training, and in Paris, Benjamin Franklin plotted to supply the one man he believed could save them: Baron Frederich Wilhelm Ludolf Gerhard Augustin von Steuben, one of Europe's leading military prodigies.

Steuben was the son of a Prussian army officer of high enough rank to be able to secure King Frederick William I as the godfather for the infant. At sixteen, young Steuben followed his father into the army, and distinguished himself in the Seven Years War, in which he was taken prisoner by the Russians. While a prisoner, history records, Steuben became a favorite of Czar Peter III and Peter's ambitious wife, who soon overthrew her husband and became Czarina Catherine the Great. After his release, Steuben was a particularly valuable aide to the greatest military genius of his era, King Frederick II of Prussia.

Steuben's acceptance into Frederick's all-male court was the first historical suggestion of his homosexuality. Frederick was Europe's most notorious gay ruler at the time and had been known as such since his youth. From his earliest days, Frederick had evinced an interest in poetry, music, and art that enraged his overbearing, militaristic father. When he had attempted to escape his father's public beatings by running off to England with his lover, Lieutenant Hans Hermann von Katte, the son of an important Prussian general, King Frederick William had both his son and his lover court-martialed and sentenced to death. The king ordered a scaffold erected outside the window of his son's prison cell, and guards forced the crown prince to watch while an executioner chopped off his lover's head. Frederick blew the lieutenant a kiss and shouted his oath of love as the executioner's sword fell. Ultimately, the king granted his son clemency and sent a soldier to be his valet, but those two also apparently became lovers. Once Frederick became king, he banished women from his palace and surrounded himself not only with handsome soldiers and pages but with the greatest cultural figures of his day, most notably Voltaire.

In the following years, Frederick turned to military matters and soon emerged as one of the most brilliant strategists in European history. His prowess transformed Prussia from a weak backwater to the strongest military power in Europe and made the Prussian army the most feared fighting machine on the Continent. The king also set about to formalize the instruction of his officers. He personally directed the military tutelage for thirteen handpicked officers, among them Steuben. His education, at the forerunner of the famous Kriegs Akademie, made Steuben a charter member of the royal "Great General Staff" and perfected his military skills. In 1763, for reasons never made public, Steuben abruptly left the Prussian service and spent the next years as chief minister for the prince of Hohenzollern-Hechingen, who named him a baron in 1771.

Benjamin Franklin was convinced that the Prussian penchant for order and discipline was precisely what the American forces needed if they were to prevail in their uphill fight against the well-trained British army. His first meeting with Steuben in Paris, however, proved unsuccessful. The Continental Congress was already bridling at having two major generals of foreign birth, Lafayette and De Kalb, and were reluctant to commission a third, so Franklin could not guarantee Steuben a commission in the Continental Army, or even a salary. Steuben could accept that; when Franklin indicated the Americans could not even pay travel expenses across the Atlantic, however, Steuben declined Franklin's entreaties and instead took a position with another royal family in Baden. But as he was returning to Germany, he heard news that sent him back for another meeting with Franklin.

The identity of the author of the crucial letter was later lost to history, but it is known that it arrived at the desk of the prince of Hohenzollern-Hechingen in August 1777. "It has come to me from different sources that M. de Steuben is accused of having taken familiarities with young boys which the law forbids and punishes severely," the letter said. The dispatch further noted that "the clergy. . . . intend to prosecute him by law as soon as he may establish himself anywhere." That Steuben would be hounded for homosexuality during the reign of Frederick was no small irony, as was noted even by his contemporaries. A newspaper article in 1796 commented, the "abominable rumor which accused Steuben of a crime the suspicion of which, at another more exalted court of that time (as formerly among the Greeks) would hardly have aroused such attention." Still, the impending scandal forced Steuben out of Europe. As his biographer, John McAuley Palmer, wrote, "Whether true or false, it is certain the charge was made and that it was a final determining influence in sending Steuben to America."

The scandals that exiled Steuben did not receive broad circulation in Europe until more than a decade after the Revolutionary War, and it is unlikely that the Americans knew of them when Franklin negotiated an arrangement with Steuben. The French government secretly agreed that it would compensate Steuben for his services if the Continental Congress did not.

There remained the delicate test of promoting the baron to the Americans. Though Steuben had risen only to the rank of captain in the Prussian army, Franklin did not think this position grand enough to impress the Continental Congress, so he spread word that Steuben was a lieutenant general. Silas Deane, who served with Franklin as a Colonial commissioner to France, wrote Congress that Steuben had left behind the "certificates of service" that attested to his status as a lieutenant general when he departed Germany, and that it would take too long to retrieve them. But, Deane said, he had seen the certificates himself and could attest to Steuben's credentials. Never one to question his own importance, the garrulous Steuben went along with the ruse, though keeping his stories about his past straight would cause him no small amount of difficulty in his later life. Before leaving France, Steuben had Parisian designers sew a set of impressive-looking uniforms that were largely of his own invention. If he was going to be a lieutenant general, he wanted to look the part.

When Steuben arrived in America, it was in the company of a handsome seventeen-year-old French nobleman who served as his secretary and interpreter. The pair was entertained by Governor John Hancock in Boston and was immediately the toast of the revolutionary leadership. With his long, thin patrician nose and erect bearing, the forty-seven-year-old Steuben looked like everything a European military genius was supposed to be. He also had a self-deprecating wit that charmed even the most skeptical colonist. To the Continental Congress, Steuben suggested that he be paid only if he actually helped the Americans win some battles, a proposal the cash-strapped Congress enthusiastically accepted.

Great expectations greeted Steuben when he arrived at George Washington's encampment at Valley Forge on February 23, 1778, in the last months of the Continental Army's most bitter winter. The American cause was imperiled. The British occupied Philadelphia, and the Americans had sustained losses at Brandywine and Germantown. The colonists' lines of supply were ravaged, and the army was scarcely clothed and even less disciplined. Washington asked Steuben to review his troops and offer his frank suggestions for improvement. Communication was difficult; Steuben's teenage protégé quickly proved to be so ignorant of military ways that he was an inept interpreter, so Washington assigned Steuben two French-speaking colonels from his own staff, twenty-year-old Alexander Hamilton and twenty-four-year-old John Laurens.

The assignment was uniquely appropriate. Hamilton was Washington's most trusted aide and Laurens was the son of Henry Laurens, president of the Continental Congress. The pair was inseparable, to the point that some later historians have surmised they were lovers. Their letters to each other swore undying love and included numerous double entendres, such as Hamilton complaining that during a separation their written correspondence was "the only kind of intercourse now in my power." (Laurens was later killed in a minor skirmish with the British.) At Valley Forge, both Laurens and Hamilton became close friends of Steuben and his most effusive admirers.

After his first review of Washington's troops, Steuben was discouraged. There was no uniformity among the regiments. Some drilled in the French style, others in the English, others in the Prussian. He set about writing a drill book. Every day, he issued new chapters in French, which were translated and then laboriously hand-copied for each brigade and regiment and company in the Army. Once the first chapter was completed, General Washington ordered one hundred top soldiers selected from the fourteen infantry brigades to form a model training brigade.

The first uniform drills of the Continental Army began on the morning of March 19, 1778. Steuben led them himself. Though he knew no English, he had memorized the words for each drill and shouted the orders—load musket, fix bayonet, and charge—eliminating the Prussian flourishes so the American Army would use the minimum number of motions.

The fact that Steuben led the drills himself greatly impressed the enlisted men, since American officers, like their English counterparts, did not perform such menial tasks. When the training went poorly, Steuben swore in French and German, with frequent *goddamn*s, the only English oath he knew. He asked his translator to put the better profanities in English for the sake of the troops. All this made Steuben immensely popular. This was no effete European adventurer, but a military man who was going to win battles.

Three days after the first drills were performed in what would become the United States Army, General Washington was impressed enough that he ordered Steuben's training be extended to his entire command. No general in the Continental Army would do any more drills, he added, until they had Steuben's specific instructions. Two days later, the whole army at Valley Forge was drilling under Steuben's guidance. Members of the model brigade became the drill masters who trained other drill masters as they had been trained. Five weeks after the first drill, Washington appointed Steuben the first Inspector General of the Army. Six days after that, Congress commissioned him a major general at a salary of $166.67 a month. A year later, Congress enacted Steuben's "Regulations for the Order and Discipline of the Troops of the United States." In 1780, he received his coveted field command, and was a division commander during the war's final siege at Yorktown.

His impact on the Revolutionary cause was incalculable. Some historians have counted Steuben, along with General Washington, as one of only two men whose services were "indispensable" to the success of the Revolution. When the American cause was won at Yorktown and Washington issued his congratulatory order, Steuben was one of only three commanders he singled out for praise. In 1783, General Washington's last official act as Commander in Chief of the Continental Army was to write a letter thanking Steuben. As Colonel Hamilton later wrote, "Tis unquestionably to his efforts we are indebted for the introduction of discipline in the Army."

THE ACCEPTANCE OF GENERAL STEUBEN and his contributions to the fledgling American military did not mean there was even tacit acceptance of homosexuality. On March 11, 1778, just sixteen days after Steuben arrived at Valley Forge, drums and fifes assembled on the Grand Parade in the brisk morning air to conclude the punishment ordered by a general court-martial and approved by General Washington himself. On that morning, Lieutenant Gotthold Frederick Enslin became the first known soldier to be dismissed from the U.S. military for homosexuality.

Enslin had arrived in the United States on September 30, 1774, aboard the ship *Union,* which had sailed from Rotterdam to Philadelphia. He was in his late twenties or early thirties. He arrived alone, according to the ship's records, suggesting that he was single. Three years later he enlisted in the Continental Army; within a few months, he was serving as an officer in Colonel William Malcolm's regiment.

Though little is known of Enslin's earlier life, the exacting penmanship he used on his company's muster sheets and his command of the English language indicate that he was an educated man of some financial means. The Continental Army preferred its officers to be educated and able to provide their own supplies.

Under the bunking arrangements at Valley Forge, enlisted men lived in communal barracks while officers resided in small cabins with officers of similar rank. It was in Enslin's cabin that Ensign Anthony Maxwell apparently discovered the lieutenant with Private John Monhart. Maxwell reported this to his commanding officer, Lieutenant Colonel Aaron Burr. Enslin responded that Maxwell was lying in an attempt to impugn his character.

On February 27, 1778, the company commander being in New York, Burr presided first at a court-martial of Ensign Maxwell, charged with "propagating a scandalous report prejudicial to the character of Lt. Enslin." In his orderly book, Burr later wrote, "The court after mature deliberation upon the evidence produced could not find that Ensign Maxwell had published any report prejudicial to the character of Lt. Enslin further than the strict line of his duty required and do therefore acquit him of the charge."

Eleven days later, on March 10, Burr presided over Enslin's court-martial, in which the lieutenant was found guilty of sodomy and perjury, the latter presumably stemming from his charges against Maxwell. According to General Washington's general order of March 14, Enslin was ". . . to be dismiss'd with Infamy. His Excellency the Commander in Chief approves the sentence and with Abhorrence and Detestation of such Infamous Crimes orders Lieutt. Enslin to be drummed out of the Camp tomorrow morning by all the Drummers and Fifers in the Army never to return; The Drummers and Fifers to attend on the Grand Parade at Guard mounting for that Purpose."

Drumming a soldier out of the Army was a dramatic event in those times. According to custom, an officer's sword was broken in half over the head of the disgraced soldier, while drummers played a very slow tattoo. So did Lieutenant Enslin leave the Continental Army on that cold morning in March, trudging away alone on the deeply rutted and muddy road out of Valley Forge, not far from where Major General von Steuben was shouting orders in broken English.

Some observers have suggested that Enslin's sentence is evidence that Washington held a lenient view of homosexuality, since such transgressions could have been punishable by imprisonment or even death in the conventions of the day. (Thomas Jefferson demonstrated his liberalism by proposing a year earlier that sodomy be punished by castration instead of death in the new penal code that would replace Virginia's Colonial charter.) This, however, remains speculation.

PROSCRIPTIONS AGAINST HOMOSEXUALITY did not alter the presence of gays among the armed forces, possibly including some of the most celebrated American military heroes. In the United States' next war, against the Barbary pirates, Stephen Decatur and Richard Somers became two of the nation's earliest Naval heroes. Decatur and Somers had been fast friends since grade school and were commissioned together in 1798 as third and fourth midshipmen in the new United States Navy. They shared a berth on their first ship assignment, the USS *United States*. James Fenimore Cooper, who served as a midshipman in the early Navy, wrote that "they loved each other as brothers." Both distinguished themselves early in their careers, and in 1803 Decatur took command of the USS *Enterprise*.

It was the Barbary pirates' demands that American ships pay tithes in the pirate-controlled portion of the Mediterranean that brought Decatur's ship and several other Naval ships to the shores of Tripoli. There, Decatur performed a number of daring feats as both a ship's commander and in hand-to-hand combat with Tripolitan pirates. In one such battle he captured a Tripolitan ketch, which the Navy rechristened the *Intrepid*. Though Decatur was only twenty-five, President Jefferson ordered him promoted to the rank of captain, then the highest rank in the Navy. Decatur became the youngest person ever to achieve this rank. Then Somers's heroism in a gunboat attack on Tripoli won him his captain's epaulets, albeit posthumously.

The seminal event of the Barbary conflicts occurred on the night of September 4, 1804, when Somers and a dozen other sailors volunteered to sail the *Intrepid,* disguised to look like a Tripolitan ship and loaded with 100 barrels of gunpowder and 150 charged shells, into Tripoli harbor. The plan was to slip into the harbor and ignite a fifteen-minute fuse, long enough to allow Somers and his crew to escape. When the ship exploded, it would destroy a good number of the Barbary pirate ships, as well as the Tripolitan fortifications.

Moments before boarding the *Intrepid,* Somers gave Decatur a gold ring. Decatur slipped the band on his finger as he watched Somers sail away.

Just what happened to the *Intrepid* became the source of much speculation. Perhaps the fuse malfunctioned; perhaps the ruse was spotted by Tripolitan sailors who fired upon the ketch, setting it ablaze. Some historians have suggested that Somers and his crew may have ignited the ship themselves; they had sworn they would die rather than let the huge cache of explosives fall into enemy hands. What is certain is that one hour and forty-seven minutes after Somers left, a huge flash lit up the harbor and an explosion echoed over the sea. Outside the harbor, Stephen Decatur stood on the deck of his ship and waited for a sign of Somers and his crew.

Naval historians record that Decatur fell into inconsolable grief after Somers's death. "For a time there was little satisfaction for him in his promotion to the captaincy," according to one. Decatur became one of the early Navy's most acclaimed heroes, most notably for his service during the War of 1812, in which he commanded the USS *United States.* He retired from the Navy at the rank of commodore, though he continued to sit on the nation's Naval Advisory Committee, which met at the Washington Naval Yard not far from the monument erected to Somers and the other Navy crewmen who lost their lives in the Barbary wars.

All his life, Decatur wore the ring that Somers had given him, inscribing the legend *Tripoli 1804* on the outside of the band and *R.S. to S.D. 1804* on the inside. The issue of the two men's relationship has been treated gingerly by biographers, when it has been discussed at all. At the age of twenty-seven, Decatur married a woman he had never met, who had fallen in love with his picture. Decatur is reported to have told his wife that his first mistress would always be the sea and his country—not she. The couple never had any children. James Fenimore Cooper reported with some bemusement that Somers was never known to have relationships with women. "Although it is scarcely possible that a warm hearted young man, like Somers, should not have felt a preference for some persons of the opposite sex, it is now known that he had a serious attachment when he lost his life," Cooper wrote, adding poetically, "Glory appears to have been his mistress."

After leaving the Navy, Decatur demonstrated a flair for design and decoration, and devoted much of his energy to the Federal-style home he had built across the street from Lafayette Square in Washington, D.C., just one block from the White House, where Decatur frequently dined with his friends President James and Dolley Madison. Decatur was killed in 1820 at the age of forty-one in a duel with a former Naval officer who felt he had been mistreated by a commission that had included the commodore.

———

AS THE AMERICAN MILITARY'S SIZE GREW in the generations that followed, so did the presence of gays in uniform. Numerous documents cite the service of homosexual soldiers during the Civil War. While living in Washington, D.C., in 1862 and 1863 poet Walt Whitman recorded in his diaries that he "slept with" a soldier named Daniel Spencer, a "somewhat feminine" man from the Second New York Light Artillery, as well as soldiers from two other regiments, one of whom he met at Fort Greene. That war also records the first apparent lesbians documented to have served in the U.S. military. In his memoirs, Union General Philip Sheridan wrote of two women disguised as men who fought in the Fifteenth Missouri Regiment. Sheridan learned of the pair after they got drunk on applejack one day and nearly drowned in the Stone River. The soldiers who resuscitated them discerned the truth. "An intimacy had sprung up between" the women, Sheridan wrote, adding that one was so masculine as to be able to pass as a man with ease while the other was much more "prepossessing." Both women were transported behind friendly lines.

The Confederate Army also appeared to have a celebrated gay general in Major General Patrick Ronayne Cleburne, a daring fighter whose attacks on the western fronts of the Civil War made him known as the "Stonewall Jackson of the West." A native of Cork, Ireland, Cleburne served in the British army before emigrating to Arkansas, where he became a successful attorney. The lifelong bachelor enlisted as a private in the Confederate Army when war broke out. He soon became captain of his company and then colonel of his regiment. The drilling and organization skills he had learned in the British army made him a valuable asset to the Confederacy, and by 1862 he was promoted to brigadier general and later to major general.

Cleburne's relationship with his twenty-two-year-old adjutant, Captain Irving Ashby Buck, drew the notice of the general's colleagues. Cleburne's biographer John Francis Maguire wrote that the general's "attachment" to Buck "was a very strong one" and that Buck "for nearly two years of the war, shared Cleburne's labors during the day and his blankets at night." Buck himself wrote that the pair were "close and confidential. I habitually messed with him and shared his tent and often his blankets."

When Buck was wounded in September 1864, Cleburne ordered the surgeons at his hospital to give him special care because "he is the best adjutant general in the Army." Buck survived his wounds, but he never saw his general again. On November 30, 1864, Cleburne was killed while leading his troops against the Union front line in the Battle of Franklin, Tennessee.

––––––––––

WHEN THE CIVIL WAR ended and the Army's concerns shifted to battling the Indians, stories of gay soldiers moved westward. There was, for example, the story of Mrs. Nash, who, according to writer Don Rickey, Jr., lived with "a succession of soldier-husbands" between 1868 and 1878 in western forts. Though her husbands left the service, Mrs. Nash stayed at the Army fort and would marry another soldier. In 1878, Mrs. Nash was married to a corporal in General George Armstrong Custer's Seventh Cavalry stationed at Fort Meade, Dakota Territory. While the corporal was on a prolonged campaign, Mrs. Nash passed away. As other soldiers' wives prepared her body for burial, they discovered that Mrs. Nash was a man. When her husband returned and the story became public, he shot himself with his Army revolver.

Gays also served in World War I, in all the armies involved. Author Radclyffe Hall memorialized the work of British lesbian ambulance drivers on the Allied front in her book *The Well of Loneliness,* now considered the earliest lesbian novel. Poet Wilfred Owen, a British soldier, wrote homoerotically of other male soldiers before his death at the front in France in 1918. The German sex researcher Dr. Magnus Hirschfeld documented the stories of a number of gay soldiers who performed heroics for the German army during that conflict.

It was during World War I that the punishment of homosexual soldiers was first codified in American military law. The Articles of War of 1916, which became effective the next year, included assault with the intent to commit sodomy as a felony crime. This law, the first revision of the Articles of War in more than a century, did not name sodomy itself as a crime, but a new revision of the Articles of War three years later did, for the first time, include sodomy as a specific felony, the crime now being the sexual act itself, whether it involved assault or was consensual. Through the 1920s and 1930s, homosexuality was dealt with as a criminal act, a move that saw huge numbers of gay sailors and soldiers imprisoned.

The idea of excluding people for having a homosexual orientation, as opposed to punishing only those who committed homosexual acts, was born during World War I, and advanced by practitioners in the fledgling field of psychiatry. After San Francisco police found a number of soldiers during a raid on a gay club, a San Francisco psychiatrist, Dr. Albert Abrams, wrote in September 1918 that while "recruiting the elements which make up our invincible army, we cannot ignore what is obvious and which will militate against the combative prowess of our forces in this war. . . . From a military viewpoint, the homosexualist is not only dangerous, but an ineffective fighter. . . . It is imperative that homosexualists be recognized by the military authorities."

It was in this period that the first attempt to purge an installation of homosexuals was recorded. Upon his assignment to the Naval Training Station in Newport, Rhode Island, in 1919, Chief Machinist's Mate Ervin Arnold, who had been a police investigator in civilian life before enlisting in the Navy, decided to launch his own investigation of gays in the Navy there. He eventually secured approval for the plan from superiors, and then persuaded seven enlisted men to entrap suspected gays, largely at the local YMCA. After three months, Arnold expanded his investigation, until a number of presumably gay sailors had been caught, court-martialed for sodomy, and sentenced to prison terms, usually of five to six years.

Civilians were caught up in Arnold's investigation, too, most notably the Reverend Samuel Neal Kent, who had been commended by the Army for his work in tending ailing soldiers during the deadly Spanish influenza outbreak a year earlier. The charges brought Newport's clergy to Neal's defense, which provoked national press coverage of the purge. Rather than siding with the Navy, newspaper editorials questioned why sailors were being dispatched to have sex with others. Two courts of inquiry investigated the operation. The latter censured Arnold, who was soon discharged, and the Navy officials who approved the operation.

A Senate subcommittee held hearings in 1920. With a Republican majority, the Senate was particularly interested in the involvement of Assistant Navy Secretary Franklin D. Roosevelt, who had approved the operation and who was the Democratic nominee for Vice President that year. The subcommittee condemned the probe and called upon the Navy to offer better treatment to those accused of "perverted acts," including an end of imprisonment of gays. "Perversion is not a crime in one sense, but a disease that should properly be treated in a hospital," the senators concluded. The report, however, marked the last time that the government would condemn a purge of homosexuals in the military for the next seventy years.

———

THE MOVE TO TRANSFORM HOMOSEXUALITY from crime to illness occurred during the great mobilization of World War II. The armed forces were faced with the gargantuan task of enlisting 16 million soldiers and sailors between 1941 and 1945, and turned to the field of psychiatry to help establish guidelines that would help winnow out those who might not be fit to be soldiers. For psychiatry, a relatively new field still held in disrespect in many scientific circles, this task was a mark of its legitimization. Since almost all psychiatrists, from the days of Freud on, had viewed homosexuality as a pathology, the psychiatrists helped formulate regulations that banned all those with "homosexual tendencies" from the military. In 1942, the first regulations instructing military psychiatrists to discriminate between the homosexual and the "normal" person were promulgated, with the notation that "persons habitually or occasionally engaged in homosexual or other perverse sexual practices" were "unsuitable for military service." In 1943, the final regulations were declared, banning homosexuals from all branches of the military, and they have remained fundamentally unchanged in the half century since then. Though the exclusions would lead to untold injustices and horrors in later years, they were initially written as an enlightened and even compassionate treatment of homosexuality.

FROM THE START, the regulations—and rationale offered for them—were clearly designed to bend with the needs of the time. When the Army needed more men by the end of the war, for example, new edicts allowed for the military to retain "reclaimable" homosexuals, after an appropriate time of hospitalization. Though the policy remained the same over the years, the rationale for it changed to reflect prevailing attitudes. During the anti-Communist hysteria of the McCarthy era, for example, "national security" was advanced as the central reason for keeping gays out of government service. In more recent years, when the notion that gays are potential traitors has seemed less plausible, the most often articulated reason for excluding homosexuals from the military is that their presence would undermine the "good order, discipline and morale" of the fighting forces.

For all the talk against them, gays remained a significant component of the U.S. armed forces. In fact, the refusal of homosexual recruits to declare their "tendencies" had brass in World War II worrying for the first time about the problem of the "reverse malingerer." There has not been a military operation in the last half century in which gay soldiers have not played a part, very often with honor.

In World War II, gay soldiers died on the decks of the USS *Arizona* in Pearl Harbor and spilled their blood on the sands of innumerable South Pacific islands. They died at Inchon and in the rice paddies of Vietnam. In more recent years, they parachuted into Grenada, suffocated in the rubble of Marine barracks in Beirut, and dug foxholes in the shifting sands of Saudi Arabia, Iraq, and Kuwait.

THE FATE OF LIEUTENANT ENSLIN, the first man known to be cashiered from the American military for homosexuality, remains a mystery. His name does not appear on any of the young nation's census rolls from 1790, 1800, or 1810, indicating that he probably abandoned whatever dreams he might have had for a new life in America and returned to Germany.

History seemed determined to tie together the disparate stories of early war heroes in the American military. Decatur's first achievements in the Barbary wars, for example, were overshadowed in the United States by the news that Vice President Aaron Burr, who had presided over the first court-martial of a gay American soldier, had killed Alexander

Hamilton, the presumably homosexual colonel who had befriended the nation's first gay general. A monument commemorating the service of Baron von Steuben now sits in Lafayette Square, directly across the street from the redbrick home Stephen Decatur took such pains to redecorate in his last years.

After the Revolution, and after the Continental Army became the United States Army, Steuben retired to a farm in upstate New York and a government pension, but he still had ambitious plans for the American military. His proposals led to the creation of the United States Military Academy at West Point. The blue book he authored was the Army's official drilling manual until the War of 1812.

He remained devoted to two young captains who had served as his aides-de-camp, and his last will named them his "adopted children" and only heirs. When he died at the age of sixty-four in 1794, one of those captains laid his body in an unmarked grave in a forest near Utica, New York. By then, he was a national hero. The key Army post in the new territory of Ohio was named for him, Fort Steuben, and the nearby town was called Steubenville. Near the general's grave, a bronze plaque was fixed on a granite boulder with the inscription "Indispensable to the Achievement of American Independence."

BOOK ONE

THE SANCTION OF THE VICTIM

(1954–1969)

Almighty God has created the mind free, so that all attempts to influence it by temporal punishments or burdens, or civil incapacitations, tend only to beget habits of hypocrisy and meanness. . . .

—Thomas Jefferson
Virginia Statute of Religious Freedom

— I —

What Tom Dooley Really Wanted: A Prologue to Vietnam

AUGUST 1954

ON A BALMY AUGUST MORNING in 1954, it was not only the story of Tom Dooley's life that lay beyond the bow of the USS *Montague,* it was the story of the next quarter century of American history. But this was not what Dooley saw as he stood at the rail, contemplating his Temporary Assignment Duty (TAD) as medical officer of the *Montague.* Ahead, shimmering in the morning sun like an emerald, was a country few Americans had heard of then, a place variously called Tonkin or Annam or Cochin China, but which in the past dozen or so years had become known by a new name, Vietnam.

A twisted tale lay behind Dooley's abrupt transfer from his job in the American military hospital at Yokosuka, Japan, but the twenty-seven-year-old was not aware of it at the time. When orders for the first TAD of his career came through for the *Montague,* Dooley had taken them to be propitious, since his initials were TAD. Friends credited Dooley with an uncanny kind of prescience: Dooley claimed to know two things about his future—that he was meant to accomplish some great task in his lifetime and that he would die young.

Dozens of small gray landing craft pulled alongside the *Montague.* Slowly, hundreds of weary Vietnamese took their first steps up the gangplank. Within a few hours, the ship held more than two thousand refugees, clutching their belongings close while they warily eyed the strange American sailors. Operation Passage to Freedom had begun.

The division of Vietnam had been announced, carving out one Vietnam that would be comprised of two "zones of temporary political influence" divided by the 17th parallel. In the north, the Vietminh would run things "temporarily"; in the south, the government would be aligned with the West. The plan called for free elections in both sectors by 1956, and a reunited Vietnam.

The West had reneged on numerous promises to their colonials, so the Vietminh never believed they would willingly let go of South Vietnam.

And the Communists had as bad a record for providing free elections, so the West never believed they would willingly let go of North Vietnam. Therefore, a lot of people in the new "temporary zone" of North Vietnam were eager to flee to South Vietnam. This was particularly true of anyone who had links to the French, whom the Vietminh detested.

Catholics were especially nervous, since they were suspect to the nationalists for having taken up the colonizers' religion. The Catholic solution was Operation Virgin Mary, a campaign coordinated by the U.S. Central Intelligence Agency and the Catholic Church in which priests told their congregations that the Virgin Mary was leaving the north to live in the south, and if they wanted to be saved they had better go south, too. Getting all these people south became the mission of the United States Navy's Operation Passage to Freedom.

One million refugees were expected to board the handful of Navy ships supplied for the task. The Navy quickly converted the cargo holds of a half dozen auxiliary cargo attack, or AKA, ships into huge warehouses with food, sleeping, and toilet facilities for their human cargo. They did not anticipate the miserable health problems that attended their passengers. Tending these health problems became the job of the *Montague*'s health officer, Lieutenant (junior grade) Tom Dooley.

As he watched the first refugees crawl over the gang rail of the USS *Montague* on the morning of August 14, 1954, he was stunned to see how many were diseased. Though he had not been a stellar medical student, he soon recognized symptoms of tropical maladies he had studied just two years before at St. Louis University medical school: yaws and small-pox, leprosy and elephantitis, malaria, and, of course, malnutrition. The voyage from Haiphong to the mouth of the Saigon River took two days. Among the 2,061 refugees, Dooley recorded four births and two deaths. In his meticulous diaries, he also recorded many worries. The operation threatened to expose American sailors to a panoply of microbes to which they had no immunity. As more Catholics crowded into Haiphong, their squalid living conditions were bound to create even more health problems. Already 150,000 had come to Haiphong to board the American transports; hundreds of thousands more were expected. The prospects of epidemics of bubonic plague and cholera headed the list of Dooley's fears.

At the end of the first voyage, he pleaded for better medical screening of refugees before they were loaded onto ships from the south. The admiralty saw the wisdom of the suggestion and appointed Dooley medical officer for Task Force 90, the unit that would monitor the refugees' health conditions. Dooley set up his medical shop at the refugee camps and burst into a flurry of activity that astounded his Navy colleagues and would leave him revered for decades by hundreds of thousands of Vietnamese.

Deciding it was his job to define his mission, Dooley resolved that no refugee should leave Haiphong until he or she had been thoroughly screened for all tropical diseases and appropriately treated. He wrote to American pharmaceutical companies for cases of antibiotics. Pan American

Airlines sent ten thousand bars of soap. Seeing the publicity value in helping the young doctor, corporations across the country soon began donating supplies. To ensure that the pesky chain of command did not interfere with his plans, Dooley always sent his requests and solicitations through Red Cross mail runs rather than by military mail delivery.

Every time a new American ship entered Haiphong harbor, Dooley launched out to greet it, demanding every available bandage, hemostat, and medication. Dooley's most effective tool was his chutzpah. If he needed equipment that a ship commander was reluctant to turn over, Dooley blustered that he spoke for the admiral and *that* was an order— whether it was true or not.

Though the Navy had intended for Dooley to run a single processing station, he quickly established a network of clinics that treated between three and four hundred people a day. At his various camps, a population of fifteen thousand refugees was always waiting for vaccinations, antibiotic treatments, and screening for communicable diseases. Before long, Dooley insisted on offering surgery to those refugees in need of urgent treatment. Meanwhile, he directed his staff to collect stool samples, insects, and even rats for laboratory studies of indigenous diseases. The United States "never knew where it had to fight next," he said, and the studies of local ailments could benefit troops in the future.

To give the entire effort a patriotic spin that the military brass would have to endorse, Dooley repeated the same phrase with each pill he dispensed and every disease he cured: *Dai la My-quoc Viet-tro.* "This," he told his patients, "is American aid." To the Vietnamese, he became known simply as *Bac Sy My,* "the American doctor."

In his off-hours, Dooley also started writing long letters about his work to his widowed mother in St. Louis, who passed a few of them on to local newspapers. His easy style and dramatic flair soon caught the attention of newspaper editors nationwide, as well as Navy Commander William Lederer, who was working as public-affairs aide to Admiral Felix Stump. When he stumbled across Dooley in Haiphong, he suggested the young lieutenant keep a diary of his Vietnam experiences and stop by Lederer's home in Honolulu on his way back to the United States. There might be a book in Dooley's experience.

Haiphong was to be an "open zone," allowing debarkation only until May 1955, and with each month the area in which the Vietminh would allow Americans to operate grew smaller. In the last months, Dooley was down to three Navy corpsmen to tend the thousands of ailing Vietnamese under his care. After supervising the treatment of 610,000 refugees in nine months, Dooley left on one of the last boats out of Haiphong, with his diary and the Vietnamese who now venerated him.

By now, the Navy realized that it had gained a precious public-relations asset with *Bac Sy My.* Operation Passage to Freedom had failed to garner the publicity the U.S. government had expected, but the memoirs of the young Navy doctor offered a rare chance to recoup. Dashingly handsome, with a square jaw, sparkling blue eyes, and thick black hair, Dooley also made a striking appearance when giving public lectures and on the new medium of television.

On a visit to South Vietnam before returning to the United States, President Ngo Dinh Diem awarded Dooley the highest honor South Vietnam could bestow on a foreigner, the "Officier de l'Ordre National de Vietnam." The only other two Americans so honored were a general and an admiral, the commanders of Operation Passage to Freedom. On the tarmac of Hickam Air Force Base in Honolulu, Dooley received the Legion of Merit, the youngest doctor in Navy history to be so honored. Navy Surgeon General Lamont Pugh wrote what was for Dooley the most meaningful praise: "It is my earnest hope that some day you may become Surgeon General of the Navy, not merely because you say that is what you want to be, but because I will leave that office soon with a sense of contentment that it will be in the most worthy and 'can do' hands if it ever reaches yours."

In Hawaii, Lederer, who would gain greater fame a few years later as coauthor of *The Ugly American*, helped Dooley fashion his diary into a book, *Deliver Us from Evil*. Early drafts did not please the publisher, who complained they were not dramatic enough, so later drafts included colorful embellishments. Dooley's devout Catholicism also influenced the book. Refugees streamed into the harbor in little sampans that flew the golden-keyed flag of the Vatican, Dooley wrote. As biographer Diana Shaw later noted, Dooley's readers could come away from his writing with the impression that the Vietnamese were overwhelmingly Catholic.

Even more troubling were the book's unsubstantiated allegations of Communist atrocities. According to one story, Vietminh soldiers crammed chopsticks into the ears of children who had heard a priest recite the Lord's Prayer, tearing their eardrums. In another account, Dooley related that Catholic teachers who had taught the Gospel had had their tongues pulled out with pliers.

All these episodes were news to everyone who had worked with Tom Dooley. As people associated with the refugees' medical treatment later pointed out, the tales of atrocity were inarguably fiction.

They were fiction, however, that played very well in the frenzied anti-Communist mood of the mid-1950s. Few words could have been more pleasing to the American Catholic establishment, which was, to a large extent, the domestic American patron of President Diem. Dooley soon struck up a personal relationship with New York's Francis Cardinal Spellman, the most vociferously anti-Communist cleric in the nation. More than promoting anticommunism and rhapsodizing about heroic Vietnamese Catholics, the book was a paean to the United States Navy. "Everything we did because the Navy made it possible for us to do," Dooley wrote in the book's afterword. "A finer lot of men cannot be found on this earth."

The Navy reciprocated the admiration. Chief of Naval Operations

Admiral Arleigh Burke wrote in his foreword to the book, "Today's naval traditions have been built by men like young Dr. Dooley who have served their country well under arduous and challenging circumstances. . . . It is a story of which the United States Navy is proud."

After being excerpted in *Reader's Digest, Deliver Us from Evil* shot up the best-seller list. Dooley made the Gallup poll's list of the men most admired in the United States. Much in demand as a speaker, he repeated the stories of Communist aggression in hundreds of personal appearances around the country, but he offered his own, very nonmilitary prescription for solving them. Only American kindness could "wash away the poisons of Communist hatred," he argued. The efforts in Haiphong had built "a quiet pride in our hearts at being American. . . . We brought not bombs and guns, but help and love."

These recommendations were rather sentimental for the cold warriors in the Pentagon, and such ideas were easily overlooked. Many were girding, even then, for an armed confrontation with Communist aggressors in Southeast Asia. From their point of view, President Roosevelt had given away Eastern Europe at Yalta, and President Truman had "lost" China to the Communists. Korea had been saved, but aggression continued in Laos and Vietnam. Vietnam was the place to draw the line against the enemy, and most Americans had heard of Vietnam by now because of Tom Dooley.

And this was what made the events in the first months after Tom Dooley's return from Vietnam so problematical.

Dooley's friend Navy Lieutenant Commander Ted Werner had seen the paperwork on the desk of the crusty old admiral who headed the military hospital in Yokosuka. Homosexuality was running rampant on the medical staff and an investigation was demanded. The admiral wanted nothing to do with the messy business of a homosexual purge. Rather than have such revelations come to light on his watch, he proceeded to transfer the suspects elsewhere, where somebody else would have to deal with it. That was how one of the suspects, Tom Dooley, had ended up on the USS *Montague*.

Once Dooley was back from Vietnam, however, the rumors surfaced again. Though a stirring speaker, Dooley was, in private, extraordinarily effeminate. Rumors streamed into the Office of Naval Intelligence that the famous young doctor was homosexual, and this time a very thorough investigation followed. Of course, it had to be handled delicately. This was a man who, according to what the Chief of Naval Operations said in a book now a best-seller, was the epitome of what was good in the U.S. Navy. Any publicity would be as embarrassing to the Navy as to the doctor himself.

The Navy fretted over how to rid itself of Dooley without bringing undue attention to the circumstances. The Office of Naval Intelligence suggested two possible routes of obtaining his severance from the Navy. First, the Navy could attempt to obtain a straightforward confession.

"While there is always the possibility that interrogation will fail to bring forth a confession of guilt, past experience indicates that few homosexuals refuse to admit their activities when skillfully interrogated," the ONI said. The other option was to plant an ONI agent at the hotel bar where Dooley was staying so he could be solicited by the doctor. "A trained and skillful agent, carefully avoiding any possibility of entrapment or homosexual involvement, would be a capable witness to verbal statements and overt actions by subject . . . (which) would most probably result in the latter's complete confession of homosexual tendencies and activities."

The details of the confrontation between the ONI and Tom Dooley have been lost to history. Within two weeks, however, Dooley announced that he was resigning his commission in the Navy to return to Southeast Asia and continue his work tending the sick. He arranged a mission with the Laotian government and the Navy flew medical supplies to the remote outpost of Muong Sing, where Dooley opened his first hospital.

Tom Dooley's story did not end with his forced resignation from the Navy; it had only begun. In the following years, he would become more famous than he had ever been in the service, much to the chagrin of the military, which always worried that the secret of his resignation might become public. Dooley worried about it, too, and he worried that others might learn of the words spelled out, all in capital letters, on his separation papers: UNDESIRABLE DISCHARGE. Changing these words and getting his discharge upgraded to honorable became a crusade for the rest of his life.

LIKE SO MANY OTHERS of his generation, Tom Dooley had done everything he could to overcome the singular defect that in his eyes made him less than human. His entire life, it seemed, was an effort to compensate for this, and everything good and everything evil that he did can be traced back to the shame he carried over his homosexuality. The Catholic Church had said he could not see the face of God because of his sin, so he struggled to be the best Catholic he could be, performing acts of kindness and obediently following the ideology of the Church. He had been told he could not be a good sailor if he was homosexual, so he set out to be a great sailor, and, it seemed, nearly succeeded. He had been told he could not be a great American, so he had tried to be the best American he could, fighting his country's enemies and gaining the United States new friends. He would even lie if his lies would be good for the country, and lie he did. He did all of this—for his God, for the Navy, and for his country—and, in the end, it did not help.

Perhaps that is why in his final years he struck out on a more independent path. He no longer repeated the tales of Communist atrocities he had told in the mid-1950s. Now he grew sharply critical of U.S. policies that were drawing Southeast Asia closer and closer to war. The U.S. military seemed to care only for the political credentials of Asian leaders, not for whether they were actually improving the lot of their citizens. In files from the Central Intelligence Agency and the Federal Bureau of Investigation, government agents complained that Dooley had become "extremely disparaging of U.S. propaganda techniques and their results" and "highly critical of the official American community . . . [and] particularly of official lack of interest in 'the Laotian people.' "

Dooley's old friend Ted Werner, who had left his commission as a Navy fighter pilot to fly Dooley between his hospitals, remembered that on the doctor's last trip to Asia, in late 1960 when tensions were rising, he had met with embassy officials to warn against considering a ground war in that region. The basis of American infantry power, the tank, would be useless on this terrain, he had said. The enemies here would not fight like European ground armies but, rather, would take to the jungle once they had inflicted casualties. And the United States would be fighting for governments that did not have popular support. These were governments that did not care for their people, Dooley said, only for their own power.

But by now, everyone in the Asian capitals knew that the CIA and the military brass were pushing for war. All through the Eisenhower years, the numbers of military advisers in Vietnam had been climbing. The embassy officials listened politely to Dooley, but Werner could see they had no intention of heeding his advice. It did not jell with American policy. The United States had never lost a war in its nearly two-hundred-year history, and it did not intend to lose one to a bunch of rice-growing, slant-eyed peasants barely out of the Stone Age.

Besides, everybody knew, Tom Dooley was dying. The brass were seeing him only as a courtesy—and less as a courtesy to Dooley than to the Asians who worshiped him.

— 2 —

Manhood

BULLETS TORE OUT of a thick green cluster of bamboo, ripped through the young Marine's dark green camouflage, and smashed into his flesh. A blossom of crimson spread across his back as he fell.

I'm going to die. It's for the best.

A second Marine crumpled. They were two of a squad of young men. They came from ranch homes in New Jersey, from small frame houses in Iowa cornfields, from the affluence and comfort of America. How did they end up here, under a punishing tropical sun, fighting a ghostlike enemy that was even now firing its automatic weapons *rat-a-tat-tat, rat-a-tat-tat* with impersonal, gruesome efficiency?

A third Marine screamed out, falling to the marshy ground, blood gurgling in his throat, strangling the last words he tried to speak as he stared up into the leafy canopy. Hospital corpsman Jess Jessop splinted the leg of the first Marine but saw he was losing blood fast; he died on the stretcher. The gunfire had pierced the second Marine in his heart. He was dying, too. The third Marine was crying out in pain, but Jess ran past him, toward the machine-gun nest. He saw everything clearly, finally.

I'll die, of course. The best way out.

Behind him, the rest of the squad watched him race toward the very front of the ill-defined line of combat as the air around them echoed with the screams of their dying buddies. There went their faithful Navy corpsman, seemingly unconcerned for his own safety, racing to save the dying Marines. This is what Navy corpsmen do. This is why Marines love their corpsmen.

Jess Jessop, hospital corpsman second class, deserved his Marines' love and respect. He was among the best of corpsmen, with performance ratings to prove it, but this day he was not thinking about the wounded and dying as he raced toward the deadly bamboo thicket. Jess was thinking about himself: that it would be good to die, that it was the way out.

IT WAS NOT AN ENDING he had anticipated when he volunteered for duty in Vietnam. In fact, as senior corpsman in his squad with the First Battalion, Ninth Marines, Third Marine Division, he had always told his medics that they were not combatants. This was not a job for dime-store heroes. The corpsman's job was to stay alive, help the wounded, and, if necessary, comfort the dying—be they American or Vietnamese, friend or foe.

Even that day, he was not running to be a hero: Jess Jessop was running to escape the fate that some capricious God had cast upon him. He was running for his manhood. And if he could not achieve that, then he would die, which, it seemed, was the best alternative—for his kind.

To his friends and family, Jessop was full of life and good humor. Born in 1939, the second of four children in a blue-collar family in Baltimore, Robert Hall Jessop was a fanatic about rock 'n' roll. He knew every lyric to every pop song—whether by Elvis or Little Richard, Fats Domino or Buddy Holly—and could sing them in exacting impersonation of their performers. Even as he was rated the life of any party, his secret haunted him.

When his preadolescent friends in Baltimore huddled over a purloined copy of the *National Geographic* to ogle photos of bare-breasted African native women, Jesse's eyes darted toward the photos of the all-but-naked men. Later, when his buddies on the Towson High School varsity cross-country team cracked about one or another cheerleader, Jessop laughed wickedly with them, though he had no genuine interest. What did interest him, deeply, were the lean, muscular bodies of his teammates. He tried to fight his attraction, but to no avail.

Every adolescent knows fear and insecurity, but Jessop's secret created a dimension of anxiety that few of his friends would comprehend. For Jess, his every sexual thought was evidence that something dreadful, something satanic inhabited him. Furthermore, he had no control over his inclination; if he could control it, he would be out popping girls in the backseats of '57 Bel Airs like all his friends, and laughing about it in the locker room on Monday morning. Christ, how he wanted to fit in, to be a man. He did not want to be a queer.

After high school, he went to work at a Montgomery Ward warehouse. He tried dating girls, but his true crushes were on other guys. In dreams, he sometimes reached out to touch one of them, and then his shame would wash over him in a furious, bitter wave, instructing him again that God had chosen him to be among the outcasts and the damned.

By the spring of 1961, the idea for resolving his struggle was almost fully formed. There was a way to prove to the world he was a man. Nobody would call him queer if he was defending his country. That's what men did.

Jess visited his local Navy recruiting station. As he sat filling out his enlistment application, he came across the box that asked whether he had "homosexual tendencies." He felt a stab in the pit of his stomach. They must know his secret. Why else would it be on the form? He paused and then quickly checked *no*. Nobody challenged him. On November 21, 1961, Jessop was accepted into the United States Navy. He set out to become the best sailor he could.

He did a pretty good job of it, too, making the honor roll in all three training schools to which he was sent, advancing in grade as quickly as Navy regulations allowed. For three years running, he was named outstanding hospital corpsman at Moffett Field Naval Air Station in California.

Though he expected that such success would make him feel more secure, Jess's inner torment deepened. His secret longings continued. Though he never acted on them or expressed them in any way, they ran through him as a deep, strong current and no matter how much he prayed, or how good a sailor he became, they persisted. He feared these urges would defeat everything he had accomplished.

There was never a day in the Navy when he did not think, if they knew my secret, I would be drummed out and disgraced. There was never a day he did not think, *I'm the world's greatest fraud.*

Jessop's enlistment ended in 1965 as excitement mounted throughout the military over the growing U.S. presence in Vietnam. In February, after the Vietcong killed seven U.S. advisers to the South Vietnamese army in a mortar attack on the U.S. barracks, President Johnson announced an air war against North Vietnam and the introduction of American ground troops to aid South Vietnam. In the Army, Marines, and Air Force, officers too young to have served in Korea began volunteering for Vietnam service, eager for the experience and the promotions that only the battlefield offers. At the service academies, young cadets and midshipmen in the freshman and sophomore classes cursed their luck. The war would undoubtedly be over before they even got out of school. Juniors and seniors were cautiously optimistic. They just might make it to Vietnam for the tail end of the fighting.

The Navy desperately needed corpsmen to attach to Marine units being dispatched to carry the brunt of the ground war. For Jessop, facing the end of his service, the demand for corpsmen touched something even deeper than his sense of duty. They needed him, and he still had something to prove. He extended his enlistment fifteen months and volunteered for assignment to Vietnam with the Fleet Marine Force.

Even as Jessop saw the aspects of war they didn't put in the John Wayne movies, the carnage and horror, he also learned the truth of a central cliché of war: Combat builds bonds among men as does no other situation. As the medic for his Marine squad, Jessop also bore the veneration that Marines heap upon their Navy "Doc." Jessop was his men's physician, their nurse, their counselor and father confessor.

Jessop was close to six feet tall, with light brown hair combed straight back from his forehead and black-frame Navy-issue glasses. Sexually, Jessop's experience with the Marines was an exercise in complete and total repression. He was attracted from time to time, but he suppressed his feelings; he maintained his lie. Still, for all his efforts at hiding, someone noticed something that didn't look right. Jessop never knew who reported to the Office of Naval Intelligence, which probed errant behavior among sailors and Marines, that he had seen Jessop touch another man. It could have been during any of the many late-night talks with any of the young men who thought of him as a mentor. Jessop had occasionally touched a man's shoulder. Twice, he had put his arm around someone who was particularly distraught.

No one ever claimed Jessop had had sex or made any sexual advances toward another soldier, but real men, everyone knew, did not touch one another unless they were in a fistfight or a football game or some other manly pursuit. An investigation began.

Rumors that the ONI was checking to see whether the senior corpsman was queer sped through the base camp. Suddenly, Jessop's best friends did not want to have anything to do with him. Even those friends who were not particularly uptight about gays worried about the people who were, and what those people might think if they hung out with a suspected faggot.

Jess answered the investigation by doing what he had always done about his homosexuality—he lied. "No, I'm not a fucking queer," he told the ONI. And a few buddies had the courage to step forward, too, and talk about what a good corpsman Jess was and how he had boosted the morale of the company. Jess was grateful. Their testimony was protecting him, he knew, but it pained him to hear his friends say, in effect, that he could not be a faggot because he was a good sailor. Eventually, the combination of his stellar record and his staunch stonewalling led the ONI to conclude that there was "insufficient evidence" to bring formal charges against him, and the investigation ended.

Still, Jessop was tortured. He believed he had betrayed the Marines. They had trusted him, respected him, handed their lives to him, and in truth he *was* a queer and therefore less than a man. He did not deserve their respect.

Days after the investigation ended, when his Marine company was walking up a narrow road under a heavy Vietnamese sky, they were suddenly barraged with machine-gun fire, and Jessop saw his chance. Rather than live a queer, he would die a man.

Shoot me now.

Jessop ran toward the machine-gun nest, imagining what would follow his death in that muggy Southeast Asian jungle. Everybody would say he was a hero, he died a man.

Directly ahead of him, a fourth Marine screamed, clutching his head as he went down. As the man alongside him turned, gunfire hit him in the throat. *Now*, Jessop thought, as he crashed through the thicket.

Suddenly, he was face-to-face with the gunner, a very young, sinewy Vietcong with thick black hair and piercing eyes. There was a second of frozen shock before the gunner leapt out of his nest. At the same moment, another Marine burst into the thicket after Jessop.

Jess did not feel present. He was in some other place, watching the next few moments unfold like a movie, watching himself pull his .45 pistol from his holster. There was no sound, only visuals. The VC machine gunner was unarmed; he threw his hands over his face.

Jess shot him in the heart. The gunner crumpled to the ground while Jessop fired again, at the head, and again at the chest. Dazed, he stared at the corpse that bled for a long time into the dark Vietnamese soil.

THERE ARE MANY REASONS why young men go to war. Some go because they are forced to by conscription or the expectations of families and society. Others go to escape something, an unhappy home, a broken love affair, or simply for adventure. But for many thousands of years, there has been another reason, which in all probability dwarfs all the others combined. Boys go to war to prove they are men. Some anthropologists and psychologists have gone so far as to assert that this is one reason why wars exist in the first place: so men can have a venue in which to prove their manliness.

Though the call for such avowal was strong throughout American culture and, therefore, throughout the U.S. military, there was one group of soldiers for whom this desire was most pronounced, particularly in those early years of the Vietnam War. The people who most need to prove something, after all, are the people who are most in doubt. Where proof of manliness is concerned, this meant young men who thought they might be queer.

"I went to Vietnam to prove I was a man." Years later, gay veterans of that conflict repeated those words endlessly, with a kind of wry bemusement that did not altogether mask the pain they felt at what had so often proved a futile effort.

From the start of the Vietnam buildup, military psychiatrists marveled about this phenomenon. In a survey of twenty-four "confirmed homosexuals" by the Army's Mental Hygiene Consultation Service, Dr. Richard Druss noted later in *Psychiatric Quarterly*, only two "were described as being in any way effeminate; the others were indistinguishable in manner and dress from the general group of soldiers seen at this facility. Many of them said that they had hoped the army would be a salubrious and perhaps even curative experience for them with its discipline and emphasis on virile behavior." (Druss also wrote that Army psychiatrists should disregard normal concerns of patient confidentiality and report all gay clients, since kicking them out of the military was good not only for the military but for their own psychological well-being.)

The futility of trying to establish virility through military service is obvious when one probes the notion of manhood in all its thoroughly nonbiological implications. Manhood is an entirely social construct. Even within the military, over time, definitions keep changing. In the days of Sparta, the greatest warrior nation of the ancient world, a real man spent his adolescence as the sexual partner of an older man, usually a friend of the family. In those armed forces, the most respected soldiers had an intimate male partner; these men made love together, marched together, and in the heat of battle died to defend one another. The Greek regimen produced one of the most fearsome, and thoroughly homosexual, corps of soldiers in the history of warfare, the Sacred Band of Thebes. As the popular saying of the time went, "An army of lovers can never be defeated."

Manhood looked quite different in the days of the American Revolution, when a role model like George Washington carefully powdered his shoulder-length hair and pulled on silk tights before galloping off to fight the British.

In succeeding years, *real men* continued to change with the fashions. Until 1948, male African Americans in the United States were not considered real men, which is why *boy* was a favored southern epithet for blacks, and why blacks were denied combat roles in the United States military and confined to segregated units, usually acting as servants, mess cooks, or menial laborers. The subtext was clear. If a black man could engage in combat, what good was war at proving to a white soldier that *he* was a man? Harry Truman's need to win black votes in the 1948 presidential elections changed this. Now, blacks could spend the Korean War and early Vietnam years proving they, too, were men.

None of this should suggest that the need to prove manliness and the connection of this proof to war are altogether fallacious. There are few proving grounds so sure as combat. War challenges the human ability to perform and succeed against the most dire of circumstances. Fears are overcome in moments that define courage. Self-confidence may be established with a certainty that is elusive in civilian peacetime. War cements the bonding between a person and his or her nation. If the combat carries some overriding ideological purpose, it weds one to some higher good. Participation in war, therefore, can cause one resolutely to shed childhood insecurities and can create a place for the individual in the broader network of community, nation, and even God.

But this process does not establish manhood so much as personhood. However, in the United States in the middle of the twentieth century, to be a person meant to be a man.

On the broad cultural level, people were beginning to be aware, in the early 1960s, even if unconsciously, that the accepted concept of manliness was fallacious. This made the idea of manhood doubly revered. Cultures, like individuals, labor most vigorously to defend what they most doubt.

For no group of warriors embarking to Vietnam was this imperative more forceful than for those who sensed that they held a secret that, if known, would forever deprive them of manhood. Their psychic syllogisms were simple. Soldiers are real men. Queers are not real men. Therefore, a soldier cannot be a queer.

Today such theory sounds simplistic. Remember that this was the early 1960s—another time, another world, really. The generation that marched off to Vietnam had little notion that the secret some kept had any relevance to civil rights or irrational social prejudice. For this minority there was no sense of rights at all, just shame, embarrassment, and the knowledge that this one aspect of their character could humiliate their families, threaten their community, be subversive to their nation, and prove an abomination to their God.

In all of the United States, among the 200 million people who lived in this country in 1967, there were perhaps only one or two thousand who had ever publicly expressed an opinion to the contrary, though this in a country where surveys, such as the Kinsey Report in 1948, found that one in ten adults was gay. About the most liberal statement made publicly in support of homosexuals, and one only recently utterable, was: "Maybe they're not criminals. Maybe they're just sick." Just about everywhere in this country, gays were treated like criminals, with their sexual relations strictly prohibited by felony laws first written by Englishmen during the reign of Henry VIII. The idea that homosexuals should not be imprisoned but given compassionate medical treatment instead was still rather novel. Such outlandishly progressive voices were hardly heard, of course, because homosexuality was such a horrible thing that decent people did not discuss it publicly. The word was not printed in the newspapers, there were no stories about gays on television, and the subject was not mentioned in normal conversation. There was just silence.

The generation of homosexuals coming of age in this time kept that silence and repressed their sexual urges and sexual thoughts. It was how most of the young gay soldiers in Vietnam coped with the knowledge of themselves in those years. They simply did not express it to anyone, not even to themselves.

This whole cloth of prejudice was so seamless, it was impossible to tell where one aspect ended and another began. It was not just that a young man's family might reject him, or that he would never find a job in his hometown, or that his government would give him a dishonorable discharge, or that his God condemned him. It was the totality of the stigma that was so entirely frightening. One would do anything to keep from veering toward an abhorrent identity.

Some resolved it would be better not to live than to face the collective revulsion of an entire culture. And some went to Vietnam for just that reason: to die. It was not the first war in which this had occurred. One earlier study of homosexual veterans, for example, concluded, "Among the causes which drive homosexuals to war perhaps the most tragic one is that wish or hope, expressed by more than one of their number, that a bullet might put an end to their life. . . . Driven by this feeling, many a [gay] officer exposed himself to the thickest rain of bombs and the most deadly attacks. Only recently a flier whom I had congratulated on his distinctions replied that in truth, his disregard of death was nothing more than disgust with life." This report referred not to Americans but to German homosexuals fighting in World War I.

In the process, some soldiers would claim their personhood without dying. They would return to the United States to follow their sexual attractions without shame. Others would continue to live through years of conflict, but even some of them would emerge as central players in the movement that grew out of their pain. And the new movement they helped create would call into question not only the place of homosexuals in the United States and what it meant to be a man, but the entire culture's carefully defined structures of male and female roles. For there were many, even in those years, getting a first glimpse that there was something wrong in the way these structures were established.

JESS JESSOP DID NOT KNOW how long he stood there staring at the Vietnamese man who had died so Jess could prove his manhood. Suddenly, there was sound again and he was yanked back into the moment by the screams of one of his fallen Marines. He turned toward the sound. He saw the man had a head wound, and then, in slow motion, Jessop watched a hand grenade roll under the man's shoulder. When had the pin on the grenade been pulled? When would it explode?

The split second of waiting felt like an eternity. When the grenade detonated, it tore into the wounded man's back. A flak jacket had saved his torso but not his arm, which was now attached by only a thin strand of ligament.

Jessop knelt to inject the man with morphine. This done, he could see the head wound was serious. But the man remained conscious. *If I had gotten to him sooner,* Jess thought, *I might have saved him.* Gunfire burst overhead and the dying Marine's head dropped backward. Explosion after explosion followed. It seemed incredible that the firefight could escalate. With each round of fire, the young Marine jerked again, sometimes staring deeply into Jess's eyes. The jungle was alive, swarming with Marines and Vietcong, with mortar and bullets, with explosions and the acrid smell of spent gunpowder. And Jess and the Marine stared into each other's eyes, totally alone.

Finally, it stopped. The gunfire ended, the young Marine lay dead in Jess's arms, and Jess clearly was a real man. The guys who had been avoiding him since the gay investigation were at his side again, slapping his back, shaking his hand, and congratulating him on his courage.

When Jess was finally alone, he vomited. That night, he could not sleep, wondering whether he might have saved that last Marine if he had not taken the time to pump those three bullets into the Vietcong gunner.

Had he killed one of his own men in his frantic need to prove himself? All night he cried, wishing there was somebody around to hold him in the darkness of his desolation.

The company commander and two Marines who had been on the scene wrote Jessop up for a Silver Star, but Jessop declined consideration for the honor. As he wrote to his cousin, "The gesture is nice, but it's the last thing I want." He had proved his manhood, all right, with an act that had no honor attached to it and for which he would always try to atone.

— 3 —

Rules

DE KALB'S MAJOR SOURCE of pride was the fact that barbed wire was invented there. The inventor lived in a mansion that has long since been carved into little apartments for students at Northern Illinois University. It was from one of these apartments that Danny Flaherty's journey to Vietnam began, on a sunny morning in May, on the first day of final examinations for spring semester. He was still asleep at 8:00 A.M., having stayed up all night to cram for his History of Western Civilization final, when two campus police knocked on his door. They asked Flaherty to come with them.

Still groggy, Danny responded that he had an exam to take in a couple of hours.

"Cooperate and you'll be out in time," one of the two men replied.

Minutes later, Danny was seated in a campus security office, listening to the calm pronouncement: "We have reason to believe you are a homosexual."

Flaherty understood immediately what those words meant on a campus tucked snugly among miles of cornfields, not far from the tiny hamlet where he had been raised. Homosexuality was considered as foreign and potentially menacing as communism. He felt his stomach sink. They left him alone in a room with a pen, a paper, and a ticking clock. All they wanted were names of other homosexuals.

He could not believe it was happening. He had always played by the rules. That Danny was gay was never in doubt. It was one of the first truths he knew about himself, and he had known it as a child playing under the maple and oak trees along the rolling banks of the Illinois River. Not that anybody in Spring Valley, Illinois, the town of five thousand where Danny's family had lived since 1900, ever talked about homosexuality. And it was not even a sexual issue at first; Danny had just known from as early as he could remember that he was . . . different. Later, he understood that this difference had something to do with sexuality.

The fact that no one talked about homosexuality was a way of denying that it existed. Most folks in Spring Valley preferred to think that there were no homosexuals in their town. Maybe a handful in Chicago. Maybe even one or two in Aurora or Joliet, but not in Spring Valley. Danny, however, was an observant child, and he could tell fairly soon that he was not the only different person in town.

Every morning on his paper route, for example, he threw a copy of the *Lasalle-Peru Daily Tribune* on the doorstep of George the Town Queer. George lived on St. Paul Street and some folk seemed to know he was a homo—the wry smiles and obscure jokes that were never entirely clear to Danny said as much.

When the kids gathered at Kirby Park on hot summer evenings for Pony League games, George would be there, parked across Devlin Street with the town queer from Granville, an even smaller hamlet on the other side of the Illinois River. The two watched the boys from their car, but they never approached anybody. Since they kept up their end of the rules—never talked about being queer and never made anybody have to acknowledge it—they survived. Nobody beat George up, at least as far as Danny knew; when they didn't make harmless jokes about him, George was clearly a man viewed with pity rather than hatred. Maybe those people aren't criminals; maybe they're just sick: The condescension of such compassion convinced Danny that he did not want to end up like George the Town Queer.

Once he began taking courses at Lasalle-Peru-Oglesvy Community College, Danny became aware that violating the rules could have serious consequences. He noticed occasional stories in the Chicago papers about police raiding gay bars. The stories included the names and places of employment for people arrested at such "establishments catering to homosexuals," as they were called then. Individuals so listed were almost always fired, since few businesses would knowingly employ a homosexual. Danny realized that he must adhere to a second rule: Don't get caught. Be very, very careful.

This required subterfuges. In Spring Valley and at community college, it meant dating girls and keeping up appearances. It also meant a great deal of sexual frustration. By the time Danny packed up and drove the sixty miles to De Kalb for his first semester at Northern, he had still never engaged in what Dr. Kinsey called a homosexual experience to the point of orgasm. It did not seem likely he would. There was no university in the United States at this time with a campus gay group. But Danny soon discovered the next best thing—the Drama Club.

It made perfect sense that people who spent much of their lives acting like someone else would be attracted to theater. Before long, Danny fell in with Bill, a member of the debating team. Together, they kept up appearances by double-dating with girls. After a movie, they'd drop off the girls and have sex in Bill's Ford. Neither of them ever spoke about these interludes. *Don't talk about it. It doesn't exist.* But within a few days, they would be planning their next double date.

Danny began to learn that there were many more homosexuals than he had ever imagined. He heard about gay bars in Chicago and began visiting them. Like other establishments catering to homosexuals in this era, these were not wholesome places. Most were run-down and Mafia-owned, since decent people wouldn't operate such businesses. For Danny, however, they were a revelation—places you could be homosexual without being the town queer.

Even in these nights of freedom in the Chicago bars, the rules were always in effect. No one touched. Same-sex couples could dance, but the lights switching on and off signaled that the vice squad had entered the bar, so men could change partners with the nearest pair of lesbians.

Danny also learned more about the penalties for violating the rules when he met four sailors from the Great Lakes Naval Training Center in nearby Waukegan. They had been found out as gay and were being housed in a special barracks while they were being processed out. Two of the young men talked darkly about a war that looked as if it was gearing up in Southeast Asia. They were just as glad to be out of the military. The other two wanted to stay in. The Navy was their life. Danny could see the emptiness of their future in their eyes, even as they tried to maintain their bravado and pick up guys. They had gotten caught; they had violated the rules.

Danny came to understand the rules better: You had to make it by the police, pass as straight to your boss, and not let anybody know. It was a dangerous lifestyle. Psychologists said that homosexuals liked to flirt with danger—more evidence that they were sick. No one ever said homosexuals flirted with danger because heterosexuals had made the world a very dangerous place for them.

Altogether, the rules defined the one road it was safe for homosexuals to walk in America; and the discrimination, police harassment, religious denunciations, and all-around disdain functioned as discernible walls to keep them on that road. If most Americans seemed blithely unaware of such walls, it was only because they had never been inclined to step off their own path and so had never bumped into one. When you did run up against the walls, you never forgot it.

SCORES OF FRIGHTENED YOUNG STUDENTS like Danny Flaherty would never forget being brought into a room on campus and asked to give names. Many were offered the same deal: Name other homosexuals at the university and you can simply withdraw from classes. Don't and flunk out. In May 1965, just two months after President Johnson committed ground troops to Vietnam, flunking out meant more than the end of one's college career. It was also an end to one's student deferment from the draft. Next came a notice from the local draft board to report for a preinduction physical.

Flaherty looked at the paper in front of him, glanced at the clock, and tried to figure out who had betrayed him. He had had sex with only two men at NIU: Bill, his boyfriend, and Ted, a rich kid from Barrington, Illinois, who had spent the past semester partying. Danny had spent the previous evening with Bill and everything had seemed normal. It must have been Ted. Danny took his pen and started writing his woeful tale. He had gotten drunk. Ted offered to give him a blowjob. Danny was just experimenting, he wrote. Normal curiosity. The campus police seemed satisfied with the letter and released Danny in time to let him take his examination.

From the stories he heard around the Drama Club afterward, Danny pieced together what had happened. Ted had been flunking out. He had gone to the school psychiatrist and explained that he could not study because he was so confused over being a homosexual. The university made him a deal: If Ted gave names, he could withdraw from classes rather than fail outright. From the names he had given, campus authorities had been able to draw still more names.

According to one count, as many as two hundred students were under investigation. Across the campus, graduating seniors were being told they couldn't take their finals.

Danny finished his tests and was packing for home when his mother called to say she had opened a letter for him from the university informing him that he would not be allowed to return because of his "sexual misconduct." A quarter of a century later, when the university denied having any records about what had happened to Danny Flaherty in May 1965, Danny could recite the last sentence of that letter verbatim: "We hope this investigation has given you the impetus to seek the professional help you need so badly."

Danny knew then that he would soon be on his way to Vietnam. There was no question of whether he would go into the Army once called. He would never say he was gay to get out of the service. One of his grandmother's best friends was the clerk of the local draft board. Word would be all over town in fifteen minutes. Danny loved his family and would never embarrass them—not to mention that going into the Army was his patriotic duty. Like most young people in small towns across America, that, too, was never in question. Though Danny had read about antiwar protesters in places like Berkeley, California, and New York City, they might as well have been on another planet. They were certainly a long way from Spring Valley, where Dan's dad was a loyal member of the Catholic War Veterans and the American Legion.

Indeed, after living a year in California, where he met a new boyfriend, Danny got his draft notice and was inducted and sent to Vietnam.

SOME PEOPLE ACCEPT what they are told by their friends, families, leaders, and church as the *truth*. Others accept such edicts as the *rules*. The difference defines two distinctly separate ways to approach being homosexual in American culture. Truths are things one believes, absorbs, and attempts to obey in thought and deed. Rules are strictures imposed from the outside that one may or may not accept as valid. One may obey them, or reject them, or, for the most comfortable life, simply try to navigate around them.

Jess Jessop accepted what he had learned about homosexuality as the truth. Since the truth was incongruous with what he knew about himself, he was destined to years of internal strife. People who accept others' truths end up being the most tortured, because their primary concern is not that they will fail others but that they will fail themselves. Daniel Joseph Flaherty had never internalized what he learned of homosexuality as the truth. He suffered no particular shame or embarrassment. Instead, he learned a complex set of rules by which he must play.

Surely, most homosexuals serving in the military during the early part of the Vietnam War struggled through their service like Jessop, accepting society's truths and repressing their sexuality. But others, like Danny Flaherty, simply played by the rules. And since the rules for the military reflected the rules of society, it was not so tough an adjustment for those who had already figured out the game.

JUNE 1966
BIEN HOA, SOUTH VIETNAM

THE HEAT FELT TO DANNY like 49,000 degrees when he stepped off the plane. To the west, clouds clung to the mountains, as in those Oriental paintings: the clouds white and light gray, the mountains lush green.

When Danny wrote of his impressions of Vietnam, and of his loneliness, to Gary Peterson, the lover he had left behind in Sausalito, he addressed his letters to "Peggy." Changing "Gary" to "Peggy" was just part of the coding process he had adopted years earlier. Being gay meant being bilingual. And when Gary wrote back or sent gifts and books, he signed his name the same way. He was Peggy Peterson. You never knew who was going to read your mail. *Don't get caught.*

Peggy was the reason Danny didn't visit the whores in Saigon on weekends. Slowly, however, Danny became aware of signals from other men like himself, each adapting the rules to his own disposition. Some of the most flamboyant were sailors from the USS *Constellation,* who called themselves "The Connie Girls." Always testing the limits of what passed for discretion, the Connie Girls answered admonishments from more cautious gays by chortling, "What are they going to do to us? Shave our heads, put us on a boat, and ship us off to Vietnam?"

The men who had it best were known as REMFs—rear-echelon mother fuckers. These were officers and senior enlisted who stayed far back from the bloody front lines, enjoying the air-conditioned luxury of life in military headquarters. They ate real food, not C-rations, and swigged cold drinks with real ice cubes, unheard-of luxuries for the grunts in the mud.

The air base at Da Nang saw considerable action that was not particularly warlike during these early days in Vietnam. The veranda of the officers' club at China Beach was a favorite place for REMF gay cruising. And the swimming pool at any Army or air base also became a cruising zone as the numbers of troops swelled in 1965 and 1966. Most organized gay life, however, was in Saigon, a cosmopolitan city that had long considered itself the Paris of the East.

Saigon's best pickup spot was the bar at the Continental Hotel, which had been a favorite gay meeting place since the days of Tom Dooley, where a casual visitor might not even notice the subplots being played out between five and seven every evening. Here, large numbers of handsome young officers gathered to strike up convivial conversations before pairing off for dinner.

A few blocks from the Presidential Palace were the Louis Pasteur Scientific Baths, where a gentleman could usually spot like-minded companions. If no assignation occurred here, one might make a trip to Tu Do Street, a honky-tonk thoroughfare with rooftop bars and restaurants that served thick American steaks. Rooftops made the bars fairly safe from random hand grenades thrown by passing Vietcong bicyclists, and, at night, tanked up with plenty of beer, one could watch U.S. Air Force bombing raids on suspected enemy supply routes, the explosions lighting up the horizon like fireworks on the Fourth of July.

Curfews complicated cruising. You had to pick up early enough to get your business over with in time to return to the barracks, or you had to be sure you could spend the night. Curfews also presented a cover. Army intelligence officer Lieutenant Dave Dupree learned this one morning when eyebrows raised over his having spent the night in the room of an Army major with whom he was having an affair. He had gotten drunk and missed curfew, Dave explained, and everybody understood, because under the pressure of the fighting and dying just about everybody got drunk at one time or another and missed curfew.

After a night of cruising the Continental, the Pasteur Baths, and Tu Do Street, Lieutenant Jerry Rosanbalm was rather amused to hold top-secret briefings for general-staff officers he had seen the night before in these same places. Rosanbalm had "come out" as a gay man in his early twenties in the less inhibited atmosphere of Southern California and had learned the rules well. By the time officers or the occasional senior enlisted men were old enough to make it to these briefings, they knew the rules, too. No one ever mentioned a word about the night before, even alone with one another. *Don't talk about it.*

Though no one spoke of it, there were rumors. Rumor had it that the most elite staff of all, General William Westmoreland's own, was among those rife with gay officers, according to several officers who served at the general's headquarters. It started with one gay staffer recommending his own gay replacement and continued with other recommendations, until a significant share of the staff was gay. Westmoreland's insistence that his staff be spit-shined and polished also appealed to and attracted homosexual officers; gay men, it seemed, tended to care more than straight men about personal appearance.

Being homosexual was still a risky business. The safest way to make contact with gay people was through private friendship networks. Civilian expatriates, most notably the French, were usually at the center of such networks, having lived in country longer than the one-year stint required of most U.S. servicemen. In villas throughout Vietnam, lavish parties welcomed and bid farewell to a stream of handsome young American soldiers.

One such party to which Rosanbalm was invited took place in a luxurious villa across from the Presidential Palace in Saigon. The guest list included a number of American servicemen in drag. It was the same night that Vice President Hubert Humphrey arrived at the palace to pay respects to the president of Vietnam. Throughout the evening, limousines carrying prominent American officials and high-ranking military officers sped past drag queens in exquisite wigs and gowns, some of whom would attend intelligence briefings the next day for the Vice President and military brass.

LIFE WAS MUCH TOUGHER at the front lines, because the field offered so few opportunities for privacy and because the soldiers at the front tended to be younger and less confident in skirting the rules. The Vietnam experience was far less libidinous for the typical gay soldier than was later fantasized in homophile fiction and erotic filmmaking.

Danny Flaherty, for instance, had only one homosexual experience in Vietnam, with his first sergeant's effeminate driver in the back of a truck. There was, however, a near encounter a few months later, as Danny was smoking pot with a heterosexual sergeant. As Danny took a deep drag of marijuana, he saw that his friend had opened his zipper and was glancing toward him. Danny was extremely stoned; it took a moment to appreciate what was going on. It was a moment too long. The next thing he knew, the zipper was closed. The two of them continued smoking and joking, and neither of them acknowledged that anything out of the ordinary had happened.

For thousands of gay soldiers in Vietnam, overtures from heterosexual colleagues were the most confusing experiences of their service careers.

Though there were indeed some brazenly gay troops who were not reluctant to put the make on anybody, it was also true that the most sexually aggressive soldiers in the field tended to be heterosexual, usually married, and clearly intent on resuming their heterosexual proclivities once they returned to the United States.

A sexual subtext was rarely absent from these gatherings of men. The longer the war continued, the more distant the notions of purpose and victory, the deeper the current ran, because there was not much else to think about.

SPECIALIST GARY MILO was drafted into the Army when the Pentagon yanked draft exemptions from graduate students. Once in country, he was struck by how bluntly and frequently the straight men talked about masturbation. Milo thought his buddies, the elite paratroopers of the 101st Airborne Division, should change their nickname from the "Screaming Eagles" to the "Screaming Queens." All these men talked about night and day was jacking off, often adding suggestive glances and comments that they would prefer not to do it alone. Every hooch seemed to have at least one guy walking around naked with a hard-on, sometimes saying with a wink, "I sure wish somebody would help me out with this."

If there was any hint that a soldier really was gay, he was often subject to scores of advances. Straight guys would never say, "Let's have sex," of course. That would be queer. But if they believed somebody would be receptive, they might suggest something appropriately mechanical and impersonal, such as "Let me put my dick in your mouth."

Straight guys had a hundred reasons why such behavior did not make them queer. They were just horny. Years later, scores of gay Vietnam veterans recounted the rationalizations: As long as they were not having sex with a woman, they were staying faithful to their wives. Getting a blowjob from a guy wasn't real sex, anyway. Besides, American men would not give them gonorrhea like the hookers in Saigon.

The fact that they discussed it proved to many of the gay soldiers that these adventurers were certainly not homosexual. They did not know the rules. *Don't talk about it.* Male-male sex was just something they thought of when they found themselves in a strange country without any Caucasian women. Psychologists call it "facultative homosexuality."

Married men in particular exuded a cavalier confidence, because everyone knew you couldn't be queer and be married. In the 101st, for example, there were two soldiers who jerked each other off every night in a jeep behind the barracks. It raised few eyebrows. They were not queer, Gary Milo was told: They both had wives at home.

So while most genuinely homosexual soldiers utterly repressed their sexuality or only cautiously engaged in a rare encounter, the straight guys made out like Casanovas, usually unaware of any danger.

FOR MILITARY WOMEN serving in Vietnam, life was very different. To be female in the military at this time was unusual; to be among the few hundred women who served in the war zone was extraordinary. Virtually all women assigned to Vietnam were nurses; nursing was one of the only jobs open to women in the military, anyway. Though their medical chores put them in proximity to doctors, who were some of the best educated personnel in the service, the women still had to contend with male attitudes that defined them solely in terms of whether they could fulfill the men's sexual needs. If they could not, they must be lesbians.

First Lieutenant Mary Hall had learned of the Army's obsession with its lesbian members a decade before her assignment to Vietnam, back in 1956, when she first enlisted in the Women's Army Corps. Even after a dozen broken engagements to men, she had not considered herself a lesbian; she just thought she had a hard time finding a man to whom she could relate.

Mary was statuesque, with thick dark hair and a smooth Texas accent. She did not conform to the tough lesbian stereotype. And she could explain her WAC service as a family tradition: Her grandfather had been a captain in the Union Army during the Civil War, her father an enlisted man in World War I, and her uncle a Naval Academy graduate.

In her early assignments, therefore, Mary's colleagues never considered that she might be a lesbian, and they spoke to her openly. These were the days, just a decade after the massive mobilization of women in World War II, when "members of the church," as lesbian WACs called themselves, still occupied a huge share of both the WAC's upper echelons and its enlisted ranks, which made it resemble an exclusive lesbian sorority. The male officers seemed preoccupied with changing that. At her first assignment at Valley Forge Army Hospital, for example, a gay medic told Mary that his gay friend's principal job in the Criminal Investigation Division was ridding the hospital of lesbians. He had to do a good job at it, too, or the brass would become suspicious of him and he might be kicked out. But the medic's friend had some scruples and so only went after those who by his judgment were so indiscreet as to get caught.

At Mary's next duty station at Camp Zama in Japan, she met a large group of lesbian WACs who were anything but discreet. They held parties at which they wore men's clothes and smoked cigars. These were the days when lesbians related to one another as butches or femmes. Mary felt no affinity for either category and breathed a sigh of relief at her introduction to this lesbian subculture. She was not like them; therefore, she must not be a lesbian. The Army conducted regular investigations of these women, eavesdropping on their rooms, even tapping their phones, and many were discharged.

By the time she reentered the Army in 1966 as an officer, Mary had a surer sense that her sexual identity was not heterosexual, after all; she also knew she must be very careful, and she was. In Vietnam, her best friend became a gay male nurse named Jerry. She had met him at Fort Ord shortly before both were sent to the Twenty-fifth Infantry's Twelfth Evacuation Hospital at Cu Chi.

The physical setting, with its tents and Quonset huts, was not unlike the set that later become familiar to Americans from the television show "M*A*S*H," except that there was more jungle, and the constant sound of incoming rocket and mortar fire. Mary handled the night duty, tending the wounded and preparing the worst of them for transportation to the better hospitals in Japan and the Philippines. Everybody was busy all the time. And now that there were women around, the men were busier than ever.

There was the issue of territoriality: Men from an engineer unit built air-conditioned rooms for the new women, a rare luxury in the stifling tropical climate. This infuriated the doctors in Mary's unit, who told the nurses matter-of-factly that if they were going to have sex with men in Vietnam, it should be only with the doctors in their unit. Meanwhile, some of Jerry's heterosexual colleagues had figured out that he was gay and began to make advances on him.

That male homosexuality was accepted in the war setting became most clear to Mary when she went on an R and R to Bangkok. The military-organized trips had long included briefings on where soldiers could pick up bar girls, but the one Mary sat in on included new advice. Although the Marine briefer looked embarrassed talking about it in front of Mary and the other female officer with whom she was traveling, he nevertheless advised the rest of the passengers, "All of you have been fighting for your country. If you don't like girls, we have something for you, too," and he went on to tell them where a GI could hire a boy.

— 4 —

The Spy

VIETCONG WRITHING *on the ground, wounded but clearly alive.* It was the sight Danny Flaherty would always describe first, even decades later, when he talked about Operation Cedar Falls. That sight and one other: of the tanks running over the wounded men, crushing them, because everybody was so angry and frustrated and the brass had decided to take no prisoners at this phase of the operation. Later, plow blades were attached to the front of their trucks to push the bodies into piles and shove them into a hastily dug trench.

This was not the way they were supposed to be conducting a war, Danny thought; it was not what they portrayed in John Wayne movies or sang about in the "Ballad of the Green Beret." He had never seen so many dead bodies in one place. He had seen them lined up after a firefight, lying by the side of the road awaiting official body counts. But those were ten bodies at a time, maybe. These were hundreds of bodies. All day, under the hot sun, Danny and his unit threw them like sacks of potatoes into mass graves.

As Danny watched the bodies pile up, the thought occurred to him that these were all people, fathers and sons with mothers and sisters, and he was drawn to them and started pulling out their wallets. There he was, six feet tall, his dark hair falling over his forehead, wandering among the heaps of Vietcong and plucking out their wallets. He could not read the Vietnamese writing, but, leafing through the contents, he found photos that looked like pictures of wives and children, mothers and fathers. He gathered the wallets and gave them to his first sergeant. Somebody would want to know that these men had died, Danny said; somebody cared about them.

OPERATION CEDAR FALLS, one of the most massive military missions mounted in 1967, embodied all the mistakes of the war in Vietnam.

For years, the Iron Triangle area just northwest of Saigon had been an impenetrable bastion of Vietcong strength. A million pounds of American bombs had failed even to dent Communist support there. Finally, General William Westmoreland vowed to root out the insurgents with a massive ground operation pinpointed against the village of Ben Suc, a key center of civilian support for the insurgents. The crude solution: Destroy the village and move out all the people.

The coordinated land-air assault of the area was flawless, everybody later agreed. They had taken the village completely by surprise, discovered huge caches of weapons and food, and retrieved numbers of important documents. Within days, they had rounded up thousands upon thousands of villagers and deported them to refugee camps that flew the cheerful banner "Welcome to the reception center for refugees fleeing Communism."

Once the people were out of the way, jets showered the jungle with napalm to incinerate the foliage that had sheltered and fed Communist troops. Some suspected Vietcong were killed, though it was never clear whether the victims were actually Communist fighters or hapless villagers who had gotten in the way. As one soldier explained to a newspaper reporter, "Anything that moves around here is automatically considered Vietcong and bombed or fired on."

The cleanup phase of Operation Cedar Falls went on for weeks. Entire plains of the Iron Triangle had been planted with mines, so it fell to Danny Flaherty and his buddies in the Thirty-fourth Armored Division to ensure that the fields were safe for more infantry troops. Slowly, their tanks progressed into the clearings, with ten soldiers between each tank, scanning the ground for the deadly Claymore mines. From the driver's seat of his armored personnel carrier, Danny watched the men with whom he had served throughout his stint in Nam. He had met some of them at the Oakland Induction Center on the day he was drafted. And then the explosions began.

The mines were being detonated from somewhere over the field, perhaps that small mound overgrown with bamboo toward the end of the clearing, but even that was not certain. The tanks started racing toward the mound, to crush it and whoever might be in it, and then Danny felt a stinging in his shoulder—a burning. Blood gushed from his wound, soaking through his shirt, making it stick to his arm. Before long, the helicopters droned overhead to carry away the bodies and the wounded, and Danny was on a stretcher being pulled into the chopper's belly. His journey back to the United States had begun.

———————

As DANNY LAY IN THE HOSPITAL, his wound kept open for fear of infection, Operation Cedar Falls concluded with confident pronouncements from the generals that it had been an astounding success. New charts reported the numbers of installations destroyed, the amount of food seized, and the crucial intelligence documents that had been discovered. Major General William DePuy, an architect of U.S. military strategy in the war, called Cedar Falls "a decisive turning point" that represented "a tremendous boost to the morale of the Vietnamese government and army, and a blow from which the VC in this area may never recover."

The much-touted success at Ben Suc, however flawless militarily, was also problematical. Rather than stand up and fight, the Vietcong had simply melted into the jungle and disappeared. Once interrogators started quizzing villagers in order to unearth the Vietcong support network, it was clear that they *all* cooperated with the enemy. It was a difficult concept: The United States saw itself as fighting to save these villagers from the monstrous international Communist conspiracy. For the villagers, the monster looked like the U.S. Army, which had just destroyed their homes and uprooted them from a village they had farmed peacefully for centuries. Their experience with the Americans at Ben Suc only reaffirmed their nationalist sympathies and strengthened their commitment to the Communist cause.

SPRING 1967
FORT MASON, SAN FRANCISCO

THE NEED FOR MEN AND SUPPLIES for Vietnam overwhelmed the services' ability to fly and ship them, particularly in the early years of the buildup. This made plenty of work for private ships working in the Military Sea Transportation Service, the merchant marine. When their ships were required for secret missions, their civilian crews needed security clearances. In San Francisco at Fort Mason, it was the job of Lieutenant (junior grade) Jim Spahr to do the footwork for the Office of Naval Intelligence and conduct the necessary background checks.

Usually, this meant little more than looking into the crews' police records. Barring some serious crime, approval was routine. It was while looking into such records, however, that Spahr began running across police accounts of individuals who had been observed at a "known homosexual gathering place." Under regulations, this meant the crewman could not be cleared for work: He might be queer and a security risk. To keep the government's business, the shipping company must fire the crewman.

Like most people in the mid-1960s, Spahr's knowledge of homosexuality was limited. There had been a little fairy kid who had lived down the street in Tarentum, Pennsylvania, where Spahr had grown up. Jim had given him a bloody nose once and been the big hero on the block for it. In high school, a scandal had erupted over a pedophile scoutmaster. The man was driven from town, and not a moment too soon as far as

most of the townspeople were concerned. These experiences told Jim
Spahr what queers were: small-town fairies and child molesters.

After Jim joined the Navy and completed Officer Candidate School,
his preconceptions were challenged. One assignment was on the USS *Stone
County.* There, he met a shipfitter first class named Welby, an openly
gay man who lived by his own rules. Welby had his own little love nest,
a storeroom he had painted in soft pastels and lighted with red lights.
There was even a stereo setup that played romantic music when the ship
was in port and Welby had friends on board. If somebody banged on the
door when Welby was entertaining one of his friends, sometimes he would
answer, sometimes not. So the crew got the message not to knock when
Welby was pouring on the charm. All this was against regulations, of
course, but Welby was a terrific welder, so nobody made trouble for him.
Good welders were hard to find.

Welby was of particular interest to Spahr, not because Spahr had ever
felt the inclination to be gay—in fact, he was happily married now—but
because his wife, Jane, talked so much about her close friendships with
other women. Although he had never asked her specifically, Jim believed
these close friendships might be more than platonic. In an effort to find
out more, Jim read everything he could on the subject of homosexuality, but there was not much around. He picked up some medical texts
describing case histories of sociopathic people who flirted with danger.
He had seen a few magazine stories about the shadowy denizens of a
dark subculture. None of them were remotely like Jane or Welby,
but that was all there was to read. Welby, he figured, could clear
things up.

In conversations when nobody else was around, Spahr tried to draw
Welby out on the subject, but the shipfitter would not speak directly
about homosexuality. Spahr did not understand the other man's reluctance, but, then, he did not know the rules.

Jim loved his wife, even if she was a lesbian. It might have been
difficult for other men of his generation to understand, but she was a
good mother to their two sons and a wonderful human being. Spahr also
knew she was not a security risk. Welby, too, was one of the best sailors
Jim had ever met. He certainly was not a security risk, either. Welby did
not hide what was going on. How could he ever be blackmailed?

At his job at Fort Mason, Spahr was mired in an ethical quandary.
At first, he simply could not authorize yanking a crewman's security
clearance just because he was homosexual. But the way Jim later recalled
it, his assistant was zealous. When Jim dropped such an application in
the pile marked TO CLEAR, his assistant would announce tartly, "I'm going
to appeal," which was a military way of saying, "I'm going to tell on
you."

Spahr knew that nobody was at greater risk for an investigation than
an investigator. If he was investigated, his wife's secret could be discovered. What, then, would his superiors think of him? Who would marry

a lesbian but a gay man? He could lose his military career and whatever career lay beyond his military service. Jim knew it was wrong but felt he had little choice. Under the smug smile of his assistant, he moved the questionable application to the pile marked NOT CLEARED.

In San Francisco, this was not a small pile. As Jim learned his job better, he was astounded at the variety of intelligence gathered on homosexuals by the police and government. The FBI followed people to gay bars, checked license numbers of cars parked outside, and followed people home to see with whom they had made an assignation. The San Francisco police, like police in many other cities, freely shared with the FBI and military police files of men and women they arrested in raids on gay bars, so that everyone had up-to-date lists of deviates.

Not a month went by when somebody wasn't removed from a ship because he was gay. One man was married and had an impeccable background, but he had been busted in a gay bar; he was officially branded a threat to his nation. One after another were labeled *not cleared*. The process became so routine that Jim stopped remembering their names.

Any doubts about possible exceptions were also cleared up at that time by a memorandum from the Chief of Naval Personnel to the commanding officer of fleet intelligence in San Francisco. The complete exclusion of anyone who had any evidence of even one homosexual experience was necessary, the memo stated, "because of the coexistence of homosexual activity with emotional immaturity, instability and related impulsivity, defects in judgment and the like. . . . They are emotionally immature and unstable, talk too much and are highly susceptible to flattery. It follows that a heterosexual who has committed only one act or so may be even more dangerous from a blackmail standpoint. His act may have been repulsive to him. He cannot stand the fear of being exposed to his family and friends, being ostracized, being subject to possible discharge, and finding a new job." Barring a security clearance was not only good for the country but good for the homosexual himself, the memo stated, because that way he would never have to worry about being blackmailed.

Jim Spahr was also struck by the fact that hardly anybody fought back. One man had tried to appeal but gave up, probably afraid of the publicity and what further damage there could be.

With every man Jim got fired for being gay, he grew a little more sick with himself. He made up his mind to leave the Navy once his obligation was up. Until then, he bore the knowledge of a terrible prejudice that prevailed around him. Everyone else seemed oblivious to it and to the great harm it caused, but it was there, almost like a living thing demanding tribute. And Jim was obliged to honor it.

IT WAS NOT A TIME when most people questioned things. There were certain truths and certain rules. That certainty made for a kind of confidence among Americans, an arrogant confidence perhaps. In the waning months of 1967, there was no better evidence of this hubris than the conflict in Vietnam.

The United States government was building troop strength, certain that push after push of young American troops and the daily pounding of American air power would force the Communists to submit. And submit they would, the generals all said. The buildup from February 1965 into the summer of 1967 was a prelude to another triumph for the United States.

In August 1967, President Johnson ordered a public-relations offensive to reinforce this confidence. Officials took to the TV news shows with new kill ratios indicating that the Vietcong and North Vietnamese were being mauled by American firepower. General Westmoreland solemnly told the National Press Club, "I am absolutely certain that whereas in 1965 the enemy was winning, today he is certainly losing." And public opinion polls showed that support for the war surged.

A handful of newspaper reporters in the field were doubtful. A few stories about the elusive enemy, inflated body counts, and sporadic rumors of American massacres made it home. Back in the great media centers of Washington and New York, however, such reports were disbelieved and neither printed nor aired by senior editors who were in direct contact with the very top echelon at the Pentagon. They had the assurances of the four-stars, the Defense Department's civilian whiz kids, and even the President that we were on the brink of winning, and that is what they passed on in sublime confidence to the American public.

Because of the Vietnam War, however, and campaigns such as Operation Cedar Falls, those days when no one questioned authority were about to end abruptly.

LATE 1967
SAIGON

ARMY LIEUTENANT JERRY ROSANBALM recognized that unmistakable mouth immediately. It was Martha Raye, here to entertain the troops. Unfortunately, she also recognized him.

"Dear, I remember you from somewhere," she said. "I'll remember."

Rosanbalm was hoping she would not. They had met at a gay bar in Laguna Beach when Jerry was running with some guys in the entertainment industry. Before Raye could remember, Jerry slipped out the back door of the officers' club in Saigon.

Fortunately, Jerry had a job that allowed him plenty of mobility. He was a spy. He hadn't planned on intelligence work, but he had seen a Military Occupation Specialty (MOS) called "area studies," and he thought this meant he would be studying exotic areas of the world, such as Yugoslavia or Fiji, so he checked the box. When given MOS number 9668, he learned what area studies really meant: intelligence.

In advanced training school, young Lieutenant Rosanbalm learned how to break into buildings, crack safes, and take photos surreptitiously. In orientation, he learned about the brutal tactics enemies employed on prisoners of war, particularly those thought to hold important information: ripping off toenails, wiring testicles. There were insidious psychological ploys, as well. A POW might be told his parents would suffer, or that his comrades had turned against him. To get information, enemies might threaten that the people the soldier loved most would be harmed, or would betray him, depending on which version was most plausible under the circumstances. It was chilling. After they were briefed, Rosanbalm's class was asked to write an essay describing how they would respond to such tactics. Rosanbalm had decided by now he did not want to spy, so he wrote, "Under such circumstances, I'd tell them anything they wanted to know."

It was the correct answer. These tactics were employed because they nearly always worked. The correct answer got Jerry assigned to Vietnam, where he arrived just weeks after the wrap-up of Operation Cedar Falls. His first assignment was a project called ICEX, which became more famous under its later name, Phoenix. The goal of the operation was to identify the North Vietnamese infrastructure in the south and either get them to work for the United States or discredit them—or, if these pacifist options failed, "terminate with prejudice."

It was exciting work, briefing colonels and generals and enjoying the Saigon gay nightlife. And then sometimes, like the night he ran into Martha Raye, Jerry remembered he had another enemy in Vietnam, the Army. He was on the Army's side in the war, of course, but he knew the Army would never be on his side if they knew the truth about him. His career would be over, with untold consequences for the rest of his life.

So a few months after seeing Raye, Jerry was relieved when he got an assignment to spy for the Army away from Saigon. As it was, he was feeling guilty for having such a comfortable life as a REMF. He had gotten off easy. Many of his OCS graduating class were dead by now. He gladly accepted reassignment to an undercover intelligence job at the remote outpost of Quang Ngai: near the Laotion border.

He was given a new name, Jerry Rusk, chosen in honor of the then Secretary of State, Dean Rusk; given a new identity as a civilian soil expert for the Department of Agriculture; and set up in a four-bedroom colonial villa with a large staff of servants. His assignment was the daily collection of raw intelligence for the headquarters in Saigon. He paid his agents from a drawer full of cash in his study.

There was only one problem with the assignment. Rosanbalm had met Donald Winn while Jerry was going through basic training at Fort Ord. It was an attraction of opposites: Rosanbalm was tall, with dark hair and dark eyes, a carefree guy from Southern California. Winn was sandy-haired, blue-eyed, and from Kansas, his feet planted firmly on the ground.

Within a few weeks of their meeting, Rosanbalm knew he would prefer an officer's life to that of an infantry ground-pounder. He applied to Officer Candidate School and was accepted. At night, Jerry would sneak away from his barracks to make love with Winn, creeping back in the early morning before his scheduled bunk check. After Jerry went to OCS, the pair maintained their relationship and were ultimately shipped to Vietnam at the same time.

On liberty together, as they prepared to leave Fort Ord, they spent a weekend in San Francisco and bought four-leaf-clover medallions at Fisherman's Wharf, upon which they imprinted each other's initials. Once in Nam, they wore the medallions with their dog tags. But Jerry had wanted something more substantial to mark their commitment, and he had bought a pair of wedding bands. Since people would ask questions if they wore them on their ring fingers, they wore them on their little fingers. The last letter Jerry got from Don before assuming the identity of Jerry Rusk included a photo of Don in his fatigue-green beret, giving his big all-American-boy grin to the Instamatic, wearing the wedding band on his little finger. On the back, he had written, "Jerry, notice it is where it has been since you saw me last & it will stay there!"

Getting Winn to Jerry's remote outpost for a visit was no mean task. Nobody in Quang Ngai was supposed to know Jerry's true identity, so Winn had to think of some ruse for going on an in-country R and R to the rather obscure town. By the first weeks of January 1968, Winn had figured it out, however, and Rosanbalm looked forward to a reunion with the man with whom he had every intention of spending the rest of his life.

It was January 1968. The radios were blaring assurances that American victory was at hand, but Rosanbalm's field agents noticed something odd. The units of Vietcong guerrillas and North Vietnamese regulars were all celebrating the New Year early. Asians take their lunar New Year celebrations very seriously, so Rosanbalm suspected this break in tradition meant something serious connected with the New Year, the holiday the Vietnamese call Tet.

— 5 —

A Name on the Wall

JANUARY 30, 1968
QUANG NGAI, SOUTH VIETNAM

IT BEGAN AS A STINGING, became a long, deep burn, and then went beyond pain. How did a surfing kid from California end up here, about to die? He knew he was losing blood. By now, he knew American troops were being killed all over. Had he told Don he loved him the last time they saw each other?

He kept thinking, *I want to be conscious when I die, to truly experience it.*

Rosanbalm had been convinced something was going to happen. He had been up late on the eve of Tet, eve of the Year of the Monkey, warning local officials, but it had been too late. He had woken the next morning to the sound of artillery and mortar rounds bombarding the town and his staff banging on the door of his room. Lights flashed and flared behind the louvered shutters of his window. He filled his pockets with the grenades he kept on his nightstand, holstered his Army-issue Colt .45, and loaded his "grease gun," an old-fashioned World War II assault weapon. Through the door, the cook shouted, "VC, VC!"

A group of Red Cross nurses bedded down in his living room were now up and frantic. Jerry spoke to them, trying to appear calm, and then went to his study to call headquarters at Da Nang. As a senior spy in the area, he enjoyed top-priority evacuation. At headquarters, his contact laughed out loud at the thought of sending a chopper to Quang Ngai. Ellsworth Bunker, the American ambassador to the whole country, was pinned down by fire in some bunker in Saigon; the whole country was locked in battle.

"Buddy," Rosanbalm's contact said, "you're on your own."

Jerry knew that the VC always slipped back into the forests at daybreak. They attacked ferociously but never tried to hold anything, blending back into the jungle once they lost the advantage of darkness. Rosanbalm glanced at his watch. Dawn would come in an hour; meanwhile, he and his staff and the frightened nurses hugged the floor of the villa, listening to machine-gun fire and shrapnel bouncing off the tile roof and counting the seconds until it would end.

When sunrise came and the fighting droned on, Rosanbalm and the Red Cross nurses crept out of the villa and made it to the citadel. Twenty minutes later, a column of North Vietnamese regulars put a rocket through his compound's wall, and captured and killed Rosanbalm's entire staff and their families.

At the police station, the rumor was that Vietcong were summarily executing any government troops who tried to surrender. Rosanbalm rounded up a group of South Vietnamese troops who were milling around in terror at the news, and the lot of them headed for the local Catholic high school, where there was supposed to be a concentration of Communist strength.

Snipers fired at them from rooftops as they approached the school. Through a mortar hole in the wall, Rosanbalm and the others could see military activity inside the compound. The rustling movement from the rear told them the Communists might be flanking from behind. There was no hesitation; the group leapt through the breach in the wall to get inside the compound. The Vietnamese captain who jumped through first was shot dead, as was the officer who ran in behind him. Rosanbalm was the first to make it through alive; within seconds he was up tight against the wall of the school, slipping past each door, pulling the pins from his grenades, *one-one thousand, two-one thousand, three-one thousand,* and tossing them into the rooms.

Two Vietcong burst out of the last door. Rosanbalm shot them, but then he was surprised by other VC, who got off a round from their AK-47s that tore into Rosanbalm's right arm. Now his arm dangled uselessly, all wrapped up in the leather strap of his assault rifle. He was very vulnerable. He had to get away, back through the breach in the wall through which he had come. He raced across the courtyard, ducking machine-gun fire, running toward the hole. Then he felt a burning sensation in his back, another in his shoulder, then a large thump in the back of his head.

On the other side of the wall, he could hear American soldiers, saw them watch him fall backward into the dusty courtyard. Then he heard Don's voice. Don Winn had made it to Quang Ngai the night before. Just in time for this, to watch his lover die.

Jerry watched the machine-gun fire press back the men who would have rescued him. And then one soldier dared it; Jerry saw Don leap through the wall, and then he heard machine-gun fire and saw Don fall.

Stay conscious, Jerry thought. He had no pain. His body felt only incredible confusion. To stay conscious, he concentrated on the sun, the wind, and the bursts of machine-gun fire that kept kicking up gravel around him.

"It was a day, a day like all other days," Walter Cronkite used to say. "Except you are there." A day like all other days, Jerry thought.

The day Jerry Rosanbalm dies. The end of my program. The only thing left is the credits.

Funny thoughts pass through your mind when you are dying. Jerry thought about all the money his dad had spent sending him to prep schools. How ironic: A guy from Beverly Hills, prep schools and Whittier College, killed by some kid who could not read or write in his own language.

Jerry noticed blood pumping out of his arm, oozing through his green jacket. An artery. He put his hand through the hole in his jacket, pressing on his artery, holding it tightly, and stared into the sky. He wondered whether Don was dead. The sun was directly overhead, pure white ethereal light. But it was still very early in the morning; the sun could not be overhead. Yes, there was the sun off to his side, as well. Gradually, he felt himself float out of his body toward the light above. He saw himself lying on the ground; he saw the Americans huddled by the hole in the wall; and there was Don Winn lying on the ground, apparently bleeding from the head. As he rose toward the light, Jerry was determined to keep his presence of mind so that he would notice when something about the light changed. That would be the moment he died.

———————

THE LIGHT WAS SO CLOSE. Suddenly, Jerry Rosanbalm felt a jerk and he was inside himself again. He looked up at the soldier everybody called Ray Charles, because he was black and wore black sunglasses. Ray had grabbed him by the collar and was dragging him through the hole in the wall. Someone brought a jeep around and lay Jerry's body across the vehicle. From a South Vietnamese aid station, he was taken to the American compound, then medivacced under fire to a field hospital in Chu Lai.

While Rosanbalm was being admitted to the Chu Lai hospital, Mary Hall worked furiously at the hospital in Cu Chi. When the first mortar fire had struck that morning, Mary was working in the intensive-care unit. The doctor had dropped his tray of medical instruments and run out of the hospital for a bunker. Mary got in the way of another doctor, a major running for cover, who grabbed her by the collar and yanked her out of the way so he could get by.

All day, the helicopters brought in the wounded and dying. After sixteen-hour shifts, the doctors and nurses took turns sleeping on air mattresses on the hospital's cement floor while rockets continued to burst overhead. It was only a few hundred yards from where Jerry Rosanbalm had watched Bob Hope's Christmas show a few weeks before. The VC were so close that patients were ordered to sleep under their hospital beds and given pistols in the event they needed to defend themselves in hand-to-hand combat.

The next morning, Jerry was moved to Cam Rahn Bay, where another attack from the Vietcong came within one hundred yards of the field hospital in which he and mounting numbers of wounded lay. It was proving to be the most aggressive assault the Communists had launched since Dien Bien Phu in 1954. Generous amounts of morphine had dulled Rosanbalm's senses; the fighting took on a dreamlike quality, as did his evacuation to Clark Air Base in the Philippines, and later the flight to Kadina Army Hospital in Japan, where he underwent extensive surgery on his mutilated right arm, shoulder, and back.

At the hospital in Japan, Rosanbalm and other wounded officers shared their memories of the disastrous morning of Tet. Together, they pieced together the offensive's military significance. The war, they realized, would not be over soon. If anything, it was only beginning. And it was not at all certain who would win.

THE DAYS OF THE TET OFFENSIVE have been recorded as the turning point of the Vietnam War. One day they may also be remembered as a national watershed. For nearly a century, the United States had ridden an uninterrupted ascendancy in world power, never knowing defeat and always growing stronger. But on January 30, 1968, that era came to an end.

The scale of the attacks was as awesome as it was audacious. Within hours of 3:00 A.M., firefights had spread throughout the country. In their most impertinent move, a seventeen-man Communist guerrilla squad burst into the new and supposedly impregnable American embassy and held parts of it throughout the night. The 101st Airborne was called in to reclaim the embassy while General William Westmoreland hid in a windowless command center.

The embassy's seizure alone signaled how vulnerable the United States was in a war it claimed to be decisively winning, but that story soon became a subplot in the larger story of coordinated assaults throughout the country—on the Army airfield at Cam Ranh Bay, considered the most secure area in the country; on the airfields at Tan Son Nhut, Bien Hoa, and Long Binh. Twenty-eight of South Vietnam's forty-four provincial capitals fell under attack. As *Time* magazine observed days later, "The mighty U.S. suddenly seemed as impotent as a beached whale."

For days, the firefights continued; for days, more Americans died. In the United States, news of Tet crowded every other story off the front pages, including the announcement that former Vice President Richard Nixon was going to run for President. President Johnson quickly launched a public-relations counteroffensive to try to minimize the significance of the attacks. The Tet offensive had been "a complete failure," Johnson said, even as fighting continued to rage just one mile from the center of Saigon.

But this time, most Americans were not believing. The government suffered from what Defense Department officials called a "credibility gap." In the following weeks, support for the war plummeted. Those describing themselves as hawks fell in the polls by 19 percent. While 50 percent had believed the United States was "making progress" against the

Vietcong in August 1967 during the administration's last prowar PR campaign, only 18 percent believed that in the days after the Vietcong's Tet offensive. To any but the most gung ho, it was clear that the United States was going to lose its first war.

One might say the country lost its innocence in the firefights over Vietnam in those days of January and February of 1968. Much of the population understood, for the first time, that sometimes the government of the United States lied; never again would Americans so blithely believe their government.

The antiwar cause, which had been building since 1965, exploded with new activism and began to take the shape of a national mass movement. And that was only the beginning: As faith in the government waned, so did faith in nearly every institution of what became known as the Establishment. The counterculture, born a few months earlier in San Francisco's Summer of Love in 1967, now became a major social phenomenon and spread across the country. The generation gap became a chasm. Everyone questioned everything: how people related to their work, their lives, and, of course, to sex. New movements were about to be born. Though the decade was already eight years old, these days marked the beginning of the sixties, the years that would shape the nation for the rest of the century.

Tet also marked a turning point for the United States military. As Vietnam turned into an unpopular war, the military saw its currency sink to the lowest level in its history. Nobody wanted to enlist anymore, and the growing reliance on conscription only made the military more unpopular. "Join the Army if you fail," wrote Bob Dylan in the anthem "Subterranean Homesick Blues," reflecting the widely held belief that the only people who voluntarily joined the military were those who could not make it anywhere else. The Tet offensive marked a watershed from which the military would try to redeem itself for the next generation.

IN JAPAN, Army doctors wanted at first to amputate Jerry Rosanbalm's right arm, but Rosanbalm begged them to wait to see if it would mend, and in time it did. He was sent to Letterman Army Hospital at the Presidio in San Francisco for a long recuperation.

He had heard Don Winn was dead. Twenty-three years later, he learned that Winn had survived that firefight. Of course, Don had not been able to find Jerry. According to the Army, Jerry Rosanbalm had never been at Quang Ngai. He was Jerry Rusk, a civilian soil expert. And within a few months, Jerry would be in Europe on another spy mission. Don could never have tracked him down.

Don had survived the Tet offensive, but he did not survive the war. He died in Vietnam on January 1, 1971, according to the records in Washington; and his name is inscribed on the twentieth slab of a long, low wall of polished black granite—DONALD D. WINN—one of the many gay men named on the Vietnam Veterans Memorial.

— 6 —

Convenience of the Government
(Part 1)

PERRY WATKINS WALKED across Pacific Avenue toward the front door of the federal building for his induction into the United States Army. Mounting the staircase outside, he happened upon a dozen other young men, including five former classmates from Lincoln High School, all there for the same purpose. The group had been talking but stopped, stunned, when Perry joined them.

Finally, one said, "What are you doing here?"

"I've been drafted," Watkins said.

"Didn't you tell them?"

Of course he had told them; he always told anybody who asked.

Word spread quickly inside the induction hall, according to Perry's recollection of the day. Many of the young men knew Watkins by reputation, if not personally. Tacoma was still a small town. Everyone stared.

During the induction physical at Fort Lewis, the doctor looked up from Perry's paperwork, stared at him oddly, and asked, "Has anything changed in your life since you filled this out?"

Watkins knew what the doctor was talking about. It was the *yes* box Watkins had checked regarding "homosexual tendencies." He knew how uncomfortable the truth made people, especially when the subject was homosexuality, so he was not surprised that the doctor talked around it.

"No," Watkins said. "Nothing has changed."

The doctor turned back to the form. Watkins, he wrote, was "qualified for military service."

The doctor probably figured Watkins would be drafted, go to Vietnam, get killed, and nobody would ever hear about it again. At least that was how Watkins sized up the situation years later with a wry chuckle.

Ola Delores Watkins was born in Doyline, Louisiana, in 1928, the great-granddaughter of freed slaves, and had been brought up proud. She had high cheekbones and penetrating brown eyes and never wore makeup. Her dad was a determined preacher who had built the first black Southern Baptist church in Joplin, Missouri, the segregated town he had brought his family to in 1945 and where he opened a small grocery, one of the only black-owned stores in town. After a brief marriage, Ola divorced and looked for work to support herself, her daughter, and her three-year-old son, Perry James Henry Watkins. About the only work a black woman could find in those days in Joplin was as a domestic for families in the white part of town, but Ola knew this would not provide her a decent income. Though no Negro had ever been allowed into Joplin's nursing school before, Ola strode into the admissions office just the same, knowing that being rejected could not be any worse than being a domestic all her life. She was accepted, and she worked her way through nursing school by washing dishes and later as a nurse's aide at the local Catholic hospital.

As an African American woman in the South, Ola had grown up knowing what it was like to be despised, and she had concluded that you just had to ignore it. Once you did that, she believed, you could do anything you wanted if you put your mind to it. These observations led her to a short list of truths, which she taught her children:

Don't give a hoot what anybody thinks about you.
You can do anything and be anybody you want.
Be responsible for who you are.
Take the punishment when you are wrong and you will get the rewards when you are right.

There was also one final commandment that Ola rigorously enforced: Never lie. There was only one way to tell the truth, she said, but many ways to lie. Lying was confusing, and you could never get your stories straight, so it was just easier to tell the truth.

Everybody commented on how much alike Perry and Ola were. It was not just the physical resemblance, which was striking; their similarity also lay in their straightforward personalities. Other kids rebelled against their parents, but Perry idolized his mother, and she respected his individuality.

This was remarkable considering the unusual interests Watkins began to demonstrate at a rather early age. Playing with dolls was perhaps the first. Perry never had much use for the team sports that so intrigued other boys. He preferred styling the hair on his sister's dolls and dressing them in their fabulous tiny satin gowns, or playing jacks with the other girls. The guys watched "Combat" and "Gunsmoke" on TV, but Perry preferred the June Taylor Dancers every Saturday night on "The Jackie Gleason Show."

In some households, it might have been a problem; but for Perry's, consisting of himself, his mother, sister, grandmother, and two aunts, it was not. And Perry figured if his family could accept him the way he was, then he really did not care if other people could not.

Perry was in junior high school when Ola married a buck sergeant she had known since high school. When the sergeant was transferred to Fort Lewis in Tacoma, Ola packed up her two children and moved.

Perry's first days in Franklin B. Gault Junior High were a bore. He hated wood-shop classes, now that he knew his true ambition was to be a ballet dancer. In mechanical-drawing class, however, one of his classmates suggested they have sex. Perry had had some marginal sexual experiences in Joplin and had no doubts about where his sexual interests lay. He was happy to comply.

The next day, another boy approached Perry in the school auditorium and asked whether it was true that he'd sucked off their classmate. "Are you queer?" the boy asked.

Perry stared at his interrogator, remembering "Never lie," and "Be responsible," and "Don't give a hoot what anybody thinks," and he said he was.

The other boy was speechless. First he looked surprised, then a little scared, and then he quickly backed away. This informed Watkins of the power of telling the truth. Giving people the answer they did not expect gave you the upper hand. Maybe it scared people. You would suffer more from being homosexual if you lied about it, he realized. He resolved never to lie about being homosexual.

From that moment on, nobody ever picked on Perry Watkins and nobody ever called him a faggot to his face. From that moment, he became one of a very small number of gay men in the mid-1960s who lived entirely by their own rules.

Of course, word spread throughout Gault Junior High, and later Abraham Lincoln High, that Perry was queer. His black schoolmates were the most outspoken about not liking fags, especially this fag who had perfect elocution and talked like a white person. A lot of other students, however, were privately asking to meet him after school, maybe to study or something.

Meanwhile, Perry studied dance at the Tacoma City Ballet Company, participated in and won speech tournaments, and even made the finals for the cheerleading squad. He did not make the team, but no black person had ever made the cheerleading team at Lincoln. Not long after Perry's high school graduation in 1966, his stepfather transferred to Germany and invited Perry to go along. It was a chance to see Europe, and the best place to study ballet. Perry figured he had the time, since he was not worried about being drafted. He was gay and he knew the Army did not take gays.

It was in Germany, in August 1967, that Perry was summoned to the U.S. Army Ninety-seventh General Hospital in Frankfurt and given his draft physical. In the course of filling out the forms, right after checking *no* to the questions about drugs or alcohol, Perry checked *yes* to the question about homosexual tendencies.

Watkins would later be asked to recall what happened next, and no one would ever step forward to challenge his recollections. The Army psychiatrist wanted to know precisely which sexual acts Watkins performed with men.

"Oral and anal sex," Perry answered evenly.

"I can't accept that answer," the psychiatrist said.

Watkins rephrased it. "I like to suck dick and get fucked in the ass," he said.

"Do you ever date women?" the psychiatrist asked.

Perry thought it was strange that when he talked about having sex with men the doctor wanted to know about precise acts but when he talked about sex with women he referred to it as "dating." The psychiatrist, a lieutenant colonel, pressed further, trying to dissuade Watkins from his admission—to no avail.

Perry was sent to another psychiatrist, with no explanation on the accompanying paperwork as to why he was there. But Perry took a number-two pencil and wrote in big block letters in the space provided, "I'm here because I checked 'homosexual tendencies.' "

"Why did you do that?" asked the second psychiatrist.

"Because it's the truth."

"Do you want to go in the Army?"

"I don't object to going in the Army," Watkins said. He was not trying to get out of the draft; he was simply telling the truth.

"Do you want to go to Vietnam?" the psychiatrist asked.

"I wouldn't object to going to Vietnam."

"Why did you check the box?"

"Because it was the truth."

The psychiatrist then wrote on Perry's form: "This 19 year old inductee has had homosexual tendencies in the past. . . . Patient can go into Military service—qualified for induction." And May 1968 saw Perry Watkins, an acknowledged gay man, inducted into the United States Army.

Though Perry did not want an Army career, he did have a strong sense of patriotism. For all its faults—and having grown up in the segregated South, he knew those faults intimately—America was still the best thing going, Watkins believed, and he believed he owed his country something. He was willing, if not thrilled, to do his service. As for being gay, he just figured they had changed the rules somewhere along the way. When he explained the whole story to Ola, she agreed.

A few months later, in advanced training at Fort Dix to become a clerk/typist, Perry was talking about the local gay hangouts with another gay draftee. Perry suggested they go barhopping the next weekend.

"I won't be here next week," the recruit said.

When Perry asked why, the young man said, "Because I'm gay."

He had not even engaged in any sexual acts in the Army, he said. He had just told his commanding officer he was gay and they had started the paperwork to kick him out.

Perry marched into his commander's office and explained that he was homosexual and that he wanted to be discharged. For a month, Perry did not hear anything. Then he was told that he could not be discharged for being gay, because he could not really *prove* he was gay. In order to do that, he would have to be caught in a sexual act.

Perry contemplated this odd treatment. There was one difference between the draftee being bumped for being gay and himself, Perry observed. The other man was white. One other black friend of Perry's had also checked the *yes* box, Perry learned later, and was denied exemption; this young man had stopped the induction process finally by complaining to his congressman. It was interesting, but Perry didn't have any grudge against the military; he did not fight his induction.

"GREETING."

By the mid-1960s, this was the most feared salutation to appear on a letter. It was how the U.S. Selective Service System opened its draft notice. Not "Dear Mr. Watkins," or even "Greetings."

"Greeting. You are hereby ordered to report . . ."

By 1968, more Americans were being so addressed than at any time since World War II. Within six months of the first escalation of the war in early 1965, the Selective Service was calling up 27,500 men a month for the Army, the largest draft call of any month since 1953. Within three months of that, the call rose to over forty thousand a month. By March 1968, when General Westmoreland asked President Johnson for 200,000 more troops to bolster the sagging effort in Vietnam, draft calls for troops increased to nearly 300,000. While military manpower typically maintained 2.4 million troops through the 1950s and early 1960s, the draft had bloated the number of American men in uniform to 3.5 million by 1969.

The United States had gone through most of its history without a large standing peacetime Army and without conscription. But facing superpower responsibilities in the post–World War II era, the Truman administration instituted a peacetime military draft in 1948. By the late 1960s, the biased nature of the Selective Service System's selectivity had become more apparent. College students got their 2-S deferments; divinity students got their 4-D deferments. Men whose parents were well connected could get a coveted slot in the National Guard. This meant the draft boards did a lot of selecting on the basis of class, among people who could not afford college or did not have the right family ties. A low-income high school dropout had a 70 percent chance of going to Vietnam. That was only the beginning of the inequities. Draftees were far more likely to get the dangerous grunt duty on the front lines of Vietnam than those who enlisted. Though conscripts accounted for 39 percent of the Army in Vietnam, they comprised 55 percent of the deaths.

Such distinctions also had profound racial overtones. Between 1961 and 1966, when 8 percent of the U.S. military was black, African American soldiers comprised 16 percent of those killed in Vietnam. In 1966, blacks accounted for 23 percent of combat deaths there. Blacks did not get much sympathy from draft boards. In 1967, only 1.3 percent of 16,632 draft-board members nationally were African American; draft boards in seven states had no black members at all.

Such statistics partially explain how Perry Watkins, a black man from a working-class background, would be drafted into the United States Army, even though he had openly stated he was gay. The inclusion of Perry Watkins, and thousands of others like him, represents one of the most intriguing though seldom-discussed aspects of the military's per-sonnel policies in Vietnam. Despite regulations and public protestations to the contrary, the military needed able-bodied men to fight its war and was quite ready to look the other way if some of them were homosexual.

As early as 1966, when Vietnam manpower needs first mounted, the Pentagon issued a directive to local draft boards requiring that potential draftees claiming homosexuality be required to submit "proof," according to later reports from gay organizers. The Defense Department later said a search of files turned up no such directive, but from that year onward, draft boards clearly did begin demanding evidence of homosexuality for gay claimants, either signed affidavits from sex partners or the sworn statement of a psychiatrist. The catch, of course, was that in forty-nine of the fifty states, confessing to a homosexual act also meant confessing to a felony, one that was sometimes punishable by twenty years in prison.

When publicly pressed to state its policy on admitting gays, the De-fense Department asserted that it would not allow homosexuals to serve because, as Colonel M. P. DiFusco wrote at the time, "The presence of homosexuals would seriously impair discipline, good order, morals and the security of our armed forces."

———————

IN LOS ANGELES, Don Slater monitored the local induction centers in the weeks after the Tet offensive. Slater was a feisty little man with a gravelly voice and a thick shock of sandy brown hair beginning to turn white. In 1968, he was one of a handful of Americans who could be called a full-time gay activist. At the time, the entire gay movement of the United States could comfortably fit in one medium-sized living room. Most gay organizations in existence then were outgrowths of the few Mattachine Society chapters that had slowly formed in major cities since the early 1950s. After a purge of early organizers who drew their political heritage from the American Communist party's heyday of the 1930s, these groups of "homophiles," as they politely called themselves, devoted their efforts to producing gentle educational materials—pamphlets and various news-letters—that not very many people outside their own memberships read.

From his office on Cahuenga Boulevard near the old Universal Studio lots, Slater had launched a new crusade, in opposition to the military's policies: the Committee to Fight Exclusion of Homosexuals from the Armed Forces. He took his cause, the first that specifically concerned gays in the military, to the National Planning Conference of Homosexual Organizations in Kansas City in April 1966. The conference included all of forty gay leaders from fifteen gay groups who agreed that, with the war growing, the military's ban on gays could be an issue around which they might mobilize gays.

Of course, hardly anyone took homosexual organizing very seriously back in the mid-1960s. The conference received a polite write-up in *The New York Times*, focusing on the military issue, but few efforts after that, including a series of demonstrations planned for Armed Forces Day in 1966, attracted much attention. Gay demonstrations in that era were lucky if they drew more than a dozen picketers.

Nevertheless, Slater pushed his cause ahead, issuing advertisements in the growing number of underground newspapers. These ads, offering free draft counseling to gays, put Slater in touch with the draft-resistance network, which taught him what was going on in induction centers in Southern California. Within four weeks of the Tet offensive, it was clear that the Selective Service would draft anybody they could, queer or not. By Slater's count, in Los Angeles alone, at least a dozen openly homosexual men had been drafted or classified 1-A during the previous two months.

Slater's committee issued an angry press release on February 28, 1968: "Because of the growing need for manpower in Vietnam, the Defense Department, while publicly paying lip-service to the idea that homosexual persons are unfit for military service, has quietly instructed induction centers to make discreet 'exceptions' to the rule—the case of homosexuals who are not the 'obvious' types."

The Committee to Fight Exclusion did not object to the war or to service in it, Slater wrote, just to the hypocrisy of publicly saying gays could not serve in the military while privately drafting them. "If homosexuals are to be drafted, we insist that it be done under a publicly acknowledged policy change regarding their fitness, and that it be conducted according to uniform national standards rather than under the secret and divergent judgments of local induction center personnel."

At this point, Slater changed his strategy from merely fighting the ban on gays in the military to helping to keep gays out of the military until the armed forces openly accepted them. In ads in underground papers, Slater warned that "homosexuals are secretly being drafted into the Armed Forces even though they do not 'measure up' to the medical, mental and moral standards established by the Defense Department. . . . Every homosexual has a right and a duty to refuse induction."

THE TOUGHER STAND by the Selective Service System was more than just hypocrisy. To a large extent, the policy was a response to the fact that a lot of people who were not gay were claiming to be so in order to get out of the draft. As the war grew increasingly unpopular, particularly among those of draft age, the problem of "gay deceivers" turned into a major Selective Service headache. Across the country, growing numbers of draft counselors added detailed advice for gay poseurs to their standard draft-resistance manuals.

"Dress very conservatively. Act like a man under tight control," advised one pamphlet. "Deny you're a fag, deny it again very quickly, then stop, as if you're buttoning your lip. But find an excuse to bring it back into a conversation again and again, and each time deny it and quickly change the subject. And maybe twice, no more than three times over a half-hour interview, just the slightest little flick of the wrist."

Draft Help, a San Francisco group, advised that "overt feminine behavior or drag costume or affected mannerisms may convince the psychiatrist that one is trying to evade the draft through pretense." And they warned, "The journey to the psychiatrist may be punctuated by a few derisive remarks from doctors or other personnel along the way, and perhaps from other registrants, but everyone has his mind on other things, and a man is not likely to be submitted to extensive humiliation."

An article in the radical magazine *The Realist* asserted that being a "hoaxosexual" was the best way out of military service. "Trick knees, bad backs, migraines, etc. are so hackneyed by now that they're generally ignored altogether by the time-wizened staff physicians. . . . Homosexuality is the bomb that unhinges the escape hatch for any and all disgruntled draftees who are determined enough to take advantage of its somewhat inviting provisions." Among those taking advantage of such advice was an aspiring actor and comedian named Chevy Chase.

At one point in 1967, between thirty and forty men a day were claiming "homosexual tendencies" at the Los Angeles Examination and Entrance Station, according to an officer there. It seemed that heterosexuals were far more likely to say they were gay than gays themselves. Heterosexuals were also far more naïve about the lasting stigma of being branded gay in those days.

Gay groups commenting on the gay exemption were less cavalier about using confessional statements as a means to avoid military service. In San Francisco, the Society for Individual Rights issued a 1967 brochure that cautioned, "If you wish to serve you may do so knowing that countless homosexuals have, but you must at the same time weigh the real danger that you may receive a less-than-honorable discharge that will create serious difficulties for you in obtaining employment." It went on to outline the lack of confidentiality of records at local draft boards, as well as the problems one would face in getting any type of Civil Service employment after such a declaration.

Ironically, authentically gay men also tended to be less successful than the gay deceivers in convincing draft boards they really were gay. The trick to convincing the Army psychiatrist, after all, rested not in behaving the way gay men actually behaved but in acting the way the psychiatrist imagined they did. Fulfilling the heterosexual fantasies of homosexuality was, of course, an easier task for a heterosexual than for someone gay.

Army efforts to thwart gay deceivers, however, violated regulations meant to eject anyone gay or with "homosexual tendencies," whether or not these tendencies had been acted upon. But at this time, it was not for "the convenience of the government"—as the informal military phrasing went—to enforce these regulations against feigning or bona fide homosexuals alike.

During the Vietnam era, of 5 million men exempted from military service because of their draft physicals, only 1 percent was deferred because of a "moral defect." Gay men who realized their orientation only after they joined the service also discovered by the late 1960s that the U.S. military had sometimes achieved a newfound acceptance of homosexuality—at least in the foxholes for the duration of the war.

———————

ARMY PRIVATE DARRYL WEST was on his last leave before going to Vietnam when a group of high school friends took him to his first gay bar, allowing him to accept what he had long denied about himself—that he was gay. Convinced he would be killed if he went to war, West wrote President Johnson and explained that he was gay. Although he wrote that he did not object to Army service in the United States, he worried how he would resist temptation in Vietnam, when there were only men around. West hoped the letter would save him from Vietnam, but it did not.

After West had been in Vietnam several months, CID agents burst into his hooch and took him off for interrogation. The agents held up the letter West had written the President and demanded that West sign a statement saying that he was heterosexual and had just written the letter to get out of going to Vietnam. West refused. After threats of informing his parents failed to secure a recantation, one of the CID agents pulled out his service revolver and put it against West's head. According to West's recollection, the agent said, "We can shoot you and tell your parents you were killed in action." Or West could sign a statement saying that he was not homosexual.

West signed. The agents seemed satisfied and sent West back to his company, where he continued his military service uneventfully.

———————

FEW VIETNAM-ERA VETERANS have such extreme stories of coercion, but a surprising number of active-duty personnel relate instances of commanders overlooking the most blatant homosexual behavior.

Army Private First Class Dennis Seely broadcast "Lover's Concerto" by The Toys over his military field radio and dedicated it to Steve, another private. Seely was busted back to E-1 for the infraction, not for directing a romantic song to another man but because his commanding officer was miffed that he had endangered the lives of troops by disobeying a military radio ban with the love song.

During basic training at Fort Leonard Wood, when Army recruit Herb Lotz confided to the chaplain that he was worried about being put in barracks with men only, the chaplain told him to "hang in there," and that Lotz would be able to relieve his sexual tensions by getting away to gay bars on weekends.

Airman Jeff Boler was in his first day of basic training at Lackland Air Force Base when he checked *yes* on a form that asked about "homosexual tendencies." He did so because his sergeant had warned that if airmen were not honest in filling out all their forms, the truth would catch up with them later. Boler had checked *yes* on his enlistment form as well, but his Air Force recruiter said that since Boler was still a virgin he could not really say he had any sexual tendencies yet. The recruiter then changed the answer to *no*.

Now, standing in formation with the other new recruits, Boler did not know what to expect when the ugliest master sergeant in creation shouted out, "Boler, get up here." Once in front of the assembled recruits, the sergeant shouted again: "Boler, you say here you're a queer. Do you suck dick?"

Everybody laughed. Boler blushed with embarrassment. The master sergeant boomed at him, "You wanna suck my dick?"

"Good God, no," Boler answered truthfully.

"Then you ain't queer," the sergeant yelled.

NONE OF THIS could possibly have happened, of course—at least not according to Department of Defense regulations. "Personnel who voluntarily engage in homosexual acts . . . will not be permitted to serve in the armed forces, in any capacity, and their prompt separation is mandatory," read the Army's regulation. "Homosexuality is a manifestation of a severe personality defect, which appreciably limits the ability of such individuals to function effectively in a military environment."

The Navy's official regulations were no less insistent. "Homosexuals and other sexual deviates are military liabilities who cannot be tolerated in a military organization. Their prompt separation from the naval service is essential." And the Air Force publicly maintained, "Participation in a homosexual act, or proposing or attempting to do so, is considered a very serious misbehavior."

But the military's own statistics offer the most compelling evidence that the exigencies of wartime overrode the military's usual antipathy for those with nonconforming sexual orientations. Between 1963 and 1966, for example, the Navy discharged between 1,600 and 1,700 enlisted members a year for homosexuality. From 1966 to 1967, however, the number of gay discharges dropped from 1,708 to 1,094. In 1968, the Navy ejected 798 enlisted men for homosexuality. In 1969, at the peak of the Vietnam buildup, gay discharges dropped to 643. A year later, only 461 sailors were relieved of duty because they were gay. These dramatic reductions occurred during the period of the service's highest membership since World War II.

THE FLEXIBLE ENFORCEMENT of the antihomosexual regulations was not without precedent. From their adoption in 1943, implementation of such rules has been almost entirely dependent on the manpower needs of the services at any particular time. In his research on gays in World War II, Allen Bérubé discovered that during the height of the final European offensive against Germany in 1945, Secretary of War Harry Stimson ordered a review of all gay discharges during the previous two years, with an eye toward reinducting gay men who had not committed any in-service homosexual acts. At the same time, orders went out to "salvage" homosexuals for the service whenever necessary. The War Department also considered releasing convicted "sodomists" to fight in separate combat units with other freed prisoners. The Army's official history of psychiatry in World War II reports that in the Thirty-eighth Division, commanders often merely reassigned to different regiments those soldiers who made passes at other men. In these cases, the history records, "this was the last that was heard of the case."

Overlooking homosexuality sometimes required great effort. In his book, Bérubé describes a gay torpedo officer who frequently walked around the decks in a bathrobe, hair net, and slippers. This surely would not have been tolerated on many ships, but by all accounts the man was the best torpedo officer in the Seventh Fleet, and good torpedo officers were hard to find. The ship's captain squashed any gossip that the sailor was gay and, during his subsequent service, personally pinned the Silver Star on the man's uniform.

The Korean War also saw a dramatic plunge in gay-related discharges. In the fifteen years before Vietnam, for example, the Navy, the service that kept the only records on the issue, typically meted out 1,100 undesirable discharges a year to gay sailors. In 1950, at the height of the Korean War, that number was down to 483. The next year, it was 533. But in 1953, when the armistice was signed at Panmunjom, the Navy cracked down again with vigor, distributing 1,353 gay-related undesirable discharges in that year alone.

IN CONFLICT after conflict—from World War II to Desert Storm—the paradox has persisted: during World War II, Korea, Vietnam, and a generation after Vietnam, when the United States went to war again in 1991. The gay exclusion policies were enacted ostensibly to ensure good order and discipline in the military. At no time is order and discipline more essential than in combat. History also demonstrates that at no time are the regulations banning homosexuality more routinely sidestepped. What made things different a generation later was that the world changed immensely between 1968 and 1991—and life changed profoundly for people who were homosexual. The first signs of those changes were already visible in certain places in the United States in 1968.

Days of Future Passed

JUNE 1968
GOLDEN GATE PARK
SAN FRANCISCO

IN THE CRUSH of people, Jerry Rosanbalm worried that his wounded right arm, still in a brace and badly aching even after five months, would be jostled. He tried to protect himself, at the same time trying to make out the words everybody in the crowd was so enthusiastically singing along with Country Joe and the Fish while he sang his antiwar anthem with its famous chorus: "One-two-three what are we fighting for?"

The song confused Army Lieutenant Rosanbalm. Were they *for* Communists? Do you just let the Reds overrun another country?

The scene was as exotic as anything Rosanbalm had seen in Da Nang or Saigon. The young women were barefoot and wore calico dresses and flowers in their hair. The young men dressed in brightly patched blue jeans and tie-dyed shirts and cinched rags around their waists for belts. Everyone had uniformly long hair and painted faces and wore love beads. They smiled a lot and said "far out." People carried radios that played songs entirely unlike the pop music Jerry once listened to: "All You Need Is Love," "Light My Fire," "White Rabbit," "San Francisco (Be Sure to Wear Flowers in Your Hair)"—songs about sex and drugs and love and peace.

His recuperation at Letterman had been slow and painful. Once he was well enough, because of his officer's status, Jerry was allowed to move off the base and into San Francisco. He got an apartment on Broadway Boulevard overlooking the Golden Gate Bridge. After his daily physical-therapy sessions, he would venture into San Francisco, where he discovered the wild "happenings" going on in the Haight-Ashbury neighborhood.

Those afternoons were electric with excitement. Once he had stumbled on a performance by a band from Los Angeles named The Doors. They were great, and Jerry found himself swaying to their music with the rest of the hippies, caught up with them in what the papers called the Youth Revolution.

It was strange and kinetic, like a Fellini movie but infinitely sweeter, and it touched Jerry. But the songs against the war and the government challenged and confused him. When he heard Country Joe singing, "Feel-Like-I'm-Fixin'-to-Die Rag," and everybody sang along to "what are we fighting for?" Jerry thought he could get up onstage and tell them precisely what they were fighting for. They were fighting to contain communism: Communism was wrong; political power should not come from the barrel of a gun. Communism should not be permitted to expand; it must be stopped. Obviously, these people had never heard the explanation, and Rosanbalm felt betrayed.

He was not the only one. Lying there with their arms and legs blown off, their heads bashed in, watching TV, the other guys in the Letterman ward shared their disbelief that the media had turned against them. Where was the support? Why did somebody not ask *them* what *they* thought? To a man, all sixty soldiers on Jerry's ward had believed in what they were doing in Nam, no matter what it had cost them personally.

The feeling of betrayal cut deep. Prominent on Jerry's nightstand was an autographed photo of Lyndon Johnson, taken at the President's home on the banks of the Pedernales River. "I'm very proud of your fine record in Vietnam," Johnson had written. "The example of your courage, your convictions and your awareness of the vital role that America must play in the defense of Southeast Asia are an encouragement to all who persevere in search of peace."

Days after arriving at Letterman and receiving the letter, Jerry had turned on the TV set to watch LBJ decline to seek reelection. Everyone knew it was because of the unpopularity of the war. The ward was stunned. Jerry cried. Suddenly, the men could feel their country moving somewhere, and it was leaving them behind.

Despite his sense of dislocation, Jerry was nonetheless drawn toward the vibrant, strange scene in San Francisco, and he looked forward to his afternoon excursions to Golden Gate Park. There was an openness about people, a sense of acceptance that gradually led him to think in new ways about his homosexuality.

———

WHEN HISTORIANS later reviewed the era, most agreed that no decade of the twentieth century would change the United States more than the 1960s, and no year of that decade would have greater impact than 1968. Most of what happened over the next generation was either because of or in reaction to the social forces let loose in that turbulent year.

By 1968, the attitudes of the counterculture had permeated the nation and had inspired millions of young people, not merely intellectual malcontents in coastal cities and college towns. And this had happened because of the draft. Because at this time, any male under twenty-seven might be sent off to die in a country nobody had heard of a few years before and for reasons that were never clearly defined. The questions this raised set off a chain reaction of other questions.

So many contradictions in American life had so long been endured that some type of massive cultural paroxysm may have been inevitable. In the United States, everyone was created equal, but that equality did not seem to extend to nonwhites. The United States was supposed to be a godly nation, but the post–World War II prosperity had clearly mired the culture in the grossest materialism to be found anywhere in the world. People talked about peace on earth at Christmas, but nobody thought twice about escalating the war, with Presidents holding their obligatory prayer sessions with the Reverend Billy Graham before sending thousands more to die in Vietnam. The hypocrisy was so blatant that it was difficult not to take note. A counterphilosophy to the mainstream culture emerged, rejecting materialism, violence, prejudice, and hypocrisy in favor of vaguely defined precepts of universal love and peace, brotherhood and liberation. The split in the cultures left the nation more polarized than at any time since the Civil War, people of color against white, parents against children. Every passing week in 1968 seemed to exacerbate the tension.

After a young peace activist named Gerry Studds organized Senator Eugene McCarthy's near victory over Johnson in the New Hampshire Democratic primary came Johnson's decision in late March not to seek reelection. Senator Robert F. Kennedy chose to run, inspiring some with the dream of a new Camelot. That April, the assassination of the Reverend Martin Luther King, Jr., unleashed fierce race riots across the country. A few weeks later, striking students seized the Columbia University campus. Six weeks after that, Senator Robert F. Kennedy was shot and fatally wounded, moments after claiming victory in a bitter California primary that might have carried him to the Democratic presidential nomination and the White House. This event, perhaps more than any other, resounded like a call to war among the newly political youth.

In August, the Republicans nominated Richard Nixon and Spiro Agnew for President and Vice President and riots erupted near the Miami convention site. George Wallace selected former Air Force Chief of Staff Curtis LeMay as his running mate in what was shaping up as the century's second strongest third-party challenge for the presidency. Three weeks later, open warfare erupted in the streets of Chicago at the Democratic National Convention when Hubert Humphrey, who had barely won any primaries in the Democratic presidential campaign, was nominated in an electoral process dominated by party bosses. On television, the world watched police brutally beat the protesters. In the same days, the Beatles released their new song "Revolution." The country was coming apart.

All the changes came as very bad news for the U.S. military and a sign of much worse to come. The military represented all that was dehumanizing, conformist, and violent in American society. For generations, the lure of the military was that it would make boys into men, but suddenly being a man, in the conventional sense, was not considered all that desirable anymore. Under almost every hippie's black light was the popular poster: JOIN THE ARMY—TRAVEL TO EXOTIC, DISTANT LANDS, MEET EXCITING UNUSUAL PEOPLE, AND KILL THEM!

There were other changes that were to affect the military in years to come. Even women were acting crazy. In Atlantic City, just days after the Chicago riots, female protesters picketed the Miss America pageant, decrying inequitable treatment of women in society. They called them-selves by a new name—*feminists*—and they talked about something called sexism. As the young black militants had iconoclastically adopted the name of the Vietcong resistance—the National Liberation Front—and called themselves the Black Liberation Front, so had the feminists an-nounced the Women's Liberation Front.

The best-selling novel in the United States was *Myra Breckenridge,* the story of a cheerful transsexual, by Gore Vidal. And for the first time, homosexuality was discussed publicly in a presidential campaign. In his short, ill-fated bid for the Republican nomination, California governor Ronald Reagan called homosexuality "a tragic disease" and said it should be kept illegal. Allusions to homosexuality, however, were rare in 1968. That it was addressed even in passing by Reagan, whom nobody outside the state of California took even remotely seriously as a presidential can-didate, was a measure of what an utterly trivial issue it was.

The 1968 presidential campaign was dominated by an agenda largely written by young activists. Former Vice President Nixon favored lowering the voting age to eighteen and pledged "a generation of peace" by ending the war, though he didn't say how. Nixon also adopted a platform that had long been a dream of libertarian-oriented Republicans: the abolition of the military draft. Though polls showed that most Americans supported conscription, Nixon maintained that the armed forces could be better staffed by a professional, all-volunteer Army. In any case, few took the pledge seriously, given the fact that it was, after all, a campaign promise. Certainly, with the cities burning in race riots, campuses in rebellion over the war, and every traditional value in question, the call to end the draft received far less attention than the Republican campaign's promise to bring law and order to the United States.

ORDER.

It was what Leonard Matlovich, Jr., a young sergeant in the Air Force, wanted more than anything else. The rest of the country may have been rejecting tradition, but Matlovich was trying to find a tradition by which to live. He was looking for structure, for something larger than himself— for the security of knowing just where he fit. It was why he had joined the military as soon as he could.

His father had had something to do with it. Leonard Matlovich, Sr., was a career Air Force man who had enlisted in the Army Air Corps in

1939 and served thirty-two years before retiring. These were the years during which U.S. air power was built from the ground up. The military hospital near the air base at Savannah, Georgia, was so new that when Vera Matlovich gave birth in July 1943, her son, Leonard Phillip Matlovich, Jr., had the distinction of being the first male child born there.

Leonard senior was a strict, chief master sergeant and he raised his son with a no-nonsense approach. The family lived the military life, moving from base to base around the world. When his dad was stationed in Guam, Leonard sometimes took boat trips to the tiny uninhabited islands nearby, their beaches still littered with the rusting shells of Japanese landing craft. Leonard fantasized about landing on the islands with World War II fighting men, all working together to take the islands back. Later, when the Matloviches moved to Charleston, South Carolina, Leonard's fantasies turned to fighting alongside the Confederate soldiers at Gettysburg. In his daydreams, young Lenny was the hero whose courage earned the respect and approval of one and all.

Matlovich's dreams and fantasies were always male-dominated. They nearly always took place in a military setting, where the absence of women was routine, and that made them permissible. But as Lenny entered his early teens in the mid-1950s, he began to feel the first urges of his sexuality and he understood his fantasies were no longer acceptable.

Being tall, skinny, and loquacious, the young Matlovich stood out among his classmates. Maybe they noticed that he paid more attention to other guys than to girls, Matlovich later told his biographer, Mike Hippler. In any case, by the sixth grade, Leonard was taunted daily with shouts of queer and faggot. At night, he got down on his knees and prayed to the crucifix he kept in his room, like all good Catholic kids. He begged God to change him, but, as he said later, the harder he prayed, the queerer he got.

Leonard graduated from high school in 1962. On May 7, 1963, with his dad at his side, he was accepted into the United States Air Force. He was now part of a great order in which you could read everyone's entire career in the medals and ribbons on their chest; a structure in which you knew exactly where you fit in.

More than anything, Leonard hoped that the military orderliness would enable him to overcome his homosexuality. He had read that it was just a phase people went through and outgrew, and he figured the quickest way to outgrow it, to prove his manhood, was to go to war. He immediately volunteered for Vietnam. He waited out his first year, however, at Travis Air Force Base, working as an electrician, worried that the war was going so well, it might be over before he could get there. He became involved in Republican party politics during this time, serving as president of the county Young Republicans and campaigning for Barry Goldwater—until somebody pointed out this violated the Hatch Act's ban on political activities by federal employees.

Leonard was by then, however, a staunch conservative Republican.

The Catholic Church had betrayed him with the radical reforms of Vatican II. Nuns no longer wore habits, you did not have to eat fish on Friday, and they did not even say Mass in Latin anymore, he fumed to friends. Where was tradition? Thank goodness for the Republican party, which stood for tradition in Leonard's mind, and whose platform complemented his fervent patriotism.

Matlovich arrived for his first tour of Vietnam on Thanksgiving Day, 1965. He was assigned to "Little Alamo," a remote and embattled base ten miles south of the demilitarized zone. Soon he went to work creating a new system of perimeter lighting that warded off nighttime sniper attacks from the Vietcong. One night, heavy fire knocked out the lights and Matlovich went out to repair the damage, crawling from light to light on his belly, replacing and repairing the wiring, under heavy machine-gun fire. For his performance, the Air Force awarded him their Commendation Medal and the Bronze Star in March 1966, a rare achievement for a mere airman first class.

Matlovich had demonstrated his courage and earned the respect of one and all, but he had not fulfilled his fondest hope—to get over his deep longings. He was always getting crushes on his buddies. Now his fantasies were that someday one would reciprocate. Unfortunately, he was drawn to people who shared his conservative political and religious views—the very people most likely to reject him.

By July 1968, when Matlovich flew into Cam Rahn Bay for his second tour of Vietnam, there was nothing he wanted more than a lover—someone who would make a place for him in his world. That was still the fundamental problem, he realized: He had not found his place.

Then, in the summer of 1968 in Vietnam, Matlovich listened to a Mormon missionary and learned about the Mormon celestial hierarchy that extended from the upper reaches of heaven, to earth, and into hell. Like Catholicism, Mormonism was an authoritarian religion, which appealed to Matlovich, as did the belief that the United States was a divine nation destined to help solve the problems of the world. Even his military service was part of a godly plan in supporting America's destiny, according to the Book of Mormon. Matlovich believed he had found the answer, and in the warm blue waters of the South China Sea, he was baptized a member of the Church of Jesus Christ of Latter-Day Saints.

MARY HALL RETURNED from her nursing duty in Vietnam to Fort Sam Houston in San Antonio in July 1968, thoroughly drained. Not long after, her gay friend Jerry also came home. Jerry ordered his lover *not* to meet him at the airport. When he saw him for the first time, Jerry wanted to be able to hold him; he knew he would probably cry. And he could not do any of that in front of other Army people.

Jerry's lover had planned a big party for him and invited many of the gay medical personnel with whom he worked. Mary was invited, of course, but she declined to come. Guest lists at gay parties sometimes wound up in the hands of the Criminal Investigation Division.

"You know I love you," Mary told Jerry, "but I've got too many years invested in the Army to go to your party." She felt sheepish but also felt she had no choice. She was a captain now and had a Bronze Star for her work under fire, but she was not out of danger.

In spite of that, her deep affection for Jerry, the kind of affection you have only for someone with whom you have shared the ordeal of combat, took hold. She could not stay away, though she came late, after everybody else had left.

AT THE PRESIDIO in San Francisco, at about the same time that Leonard Matlovich shipped out for his second tour in Vietnam, Sergeant Daniel Flaherty was seeing his last days in the United States Army, assigned to the Military Police unit at Fort Scott. Danny even had a regular boyfriend, another MP, Rick Kellogg, also Army. The two spent most weekends off the base, attending psychedelic concerts at the Avalon Ballroom and Winterland, becoming part of San Francisco's counterculture.

It was beginning to affect the way they viewed the Army and the war. When Kellogg was assigned to guard prisoners who were mainly conscientious objectors, he handed his rifle to his first sergeant, saying that if any of them tried to escape he could not in good conscience shoot them. The Army was starting to have these kinds of problems all over the world now.

The sixties had changed a lot for both young men, but it had not yet profoundly affected the way they lived their lives as gay people. So when Danny packed up his Purple Heart, folded his uniform, and prepared to return to civilian life, he returned to the same kind of hiding he had known in Spring Valley and in the Army. At his first job at Levi Strauss, he pretended to be talking to his girlfriend when Rick called.

He did know he could never return to Spring Valley. He understood who he was now and he realized there was no place for him in Illinois. Danny stayed in San Francisco, even though he was not much more open about being gay in California than he had been in Bureau County, Illinois. It would be a few years before this changed.

— 8 —

Home Front

SEPTEMBER 1968
FORT HAMILTON
BROOKLYN, NEW YORK

AFTER BASIC TRAINING Perry Watkins chose the job of chaplain's assistant as his Military Occupation Specialty. On his second day at the United States Army Chaplain's School, however, the commandant called Perry into his office.

"You have a statement on your record that you're a homosexual," the commandant said bluntly.

Perry said it was true.

Then it was not possible for Perry to become a chaplain's assistant, the commandant said.

"I think that's the dumbest motherfucking thing I've ever heard," Perry answered. "I'm too queer to be a chaplain's assistant, but I'm not too queer to be in the Army."

Watkins demanded to be discharged immediately. The commandant seemed amenable, and sent Watkins to an Army psychiatrist as part of the initial screening for a discharge. The psychiatrist was one of the most effeminate men Perry had ever met, so much so that Watkins was never sure whether he was for real or merely being satirical. In any case, he began the interview by quizzing Watkins about his sex life. Perry said he was gay, but declined to give the names or dates of his sexual contacts. "Whom I sleep with is none of your business," he said.

Army records confirm that once the interview was over, Watkins was pulled from classes and assigned to a small cleanup detail, mopping floors and tidying rooms with other soldiers who were waiting to get out. Watkins's discharge never came through. Instead, he was informed that it could not be established that he was indeed homosexual, at least not enough to warrant a discharge. He would not be allowed to be a chaplain's assistant, however, since he had said he was gay; instead, he would be reassigned to Fort Belvoir, Virginia, and trained as a personnel clerk.

WATKINS WAS ONLY ONE of hundreds of gay soldiers who were learning the anomalies of military service during the Vietnam era. In the war zone, gays could sometimes live relatively open lives, but once out of Vietnam they could look forward only to the same bias gays faced in peacetime.

Roberto Reyes-Colon, an Air Force sergeant from a Puerto Rican neighborhood in New York City, was learning this well now. He had lived openly at the Little Alamo near the demilitarized zone—the same post where Airman Leonard Matlovich had served. On one very drunken evening, Reyes-Colon had staggered off the base in full view of Military Police while hanging on to a Marine corporal, kissing and carrying on.

The next day, the base commander called Reyes-Colon into his office, Reyes-Colon later recalled. Two MPs from the night before were present; they accused him of leaving the camp, a violation of base security. "And we saw you guys kissing," one of the MPs said, staring at him.

Reyes-Colon shrugged, noted that he had been off duty, and said, "This is a war."

Later, alone, the base commander, a major, took the report on the incident and threw it away. It was the last Reyes-Colon ever heard of it.

When he was reassigned to work with the II Corps in the central highlands south of Pleiku, Reyes-Colon found the environment even more accepting of gay soldiers. He and other gay friends double-dated and even turned a small hooch into a makeshift gay bar where they danced with their boyfriends to the latest Temptations albums. The straight soldiers had their own hooch for boozing it up and dancing. Nobody cared.

But back in the United States, where Reyes-Colon was assigned to work intelligence at Lowry Air Force Base, people cared.

There were gay bars in nearby Denver, so it was easy for him to meet other gay service personnel. Within months of arriving at Lowry, there were about twenty gay friends in two squadrons with whom he palled around. But then, in early 1968, Reyes-Colon's friends started disappearing. He did not think much of it at first. There was a war going on and Reyes-Colon was working intelligence now, meaning anybody could get twenty-four-hour orders that would dispatch them anywhere in the world without the time to say good-bye to friends.

He began to understand otherwise on the morning that two agents from the Office of Special Investigations, the agency that investigated wrongdoing among Air Force personnel, walked into the class where Reyes-Colon was giving a briefing on penetrating Polish air defenses. The two men ordered him out of the classroom.

They took him to a small room. Their opening comment was, "We're agents of the OSI and we want to talk to you about being queer."

Reyes-Colon denied it. The larger of the two agents said they knew he was queer anyway, and that he could make it easy on himself by giving them the names of other queers. Reyes-Colon refused.

The OSI then revealed it had been confiscating all Reyes-Colon's letters and postcards mailed by Air Force friends around the world. Which were queers? Where did the queers hang out? Who else was queer around there? Reyes-Colon could be court-martialed, they reminded him. He could go to the stockade.

Reyes-Colon would not talk.

The OSI agents then marched Reyes-Colon to his barracks room, where they commenced a search of his locker and drawers. They tore apart his shoes, looking for contraband in the soles. They insisted the frightened sergeant explain every possession. At every opportunity, the agents used the words *queer* and *fag*. And then they found a book that confirmed he was queer—a copy of *Naked Lunch* by the homosexual author William S. Burroughs.

Reyes-Colon, who had just reenlisted, was terror-stricken. He was twenty-two years old, and suddenly his life seemed over. The only life he had known since he was seventeen was the United States Air Force. Aside from his indiscretions in Vietnam, he had played by the rules and been a star performer; he had won the Bronze Star before he was even old enough to vote. The Air Force had been his ticket out of poverty, and now it was all falling apart because he was queer. It was the kind of humiliation and disgrace he had always feared, ever since he had first suspected he was different from other boys. Now he was on his way to prison.

Reyes-Colon asked for a lawyer and was sent to a counsel for the Judge Advocate General. The JAG attorney advised him to tell the OSI the truth. The worst that could happen was that he would be kicked out. But Reyes-Colon did not want to be kicked out, and he would not give names, so he refused to confess.

Day after day, the OSI called him in for grueling interrogations. Usually, there was one harsh agent and one nice one. The questions were always the same, though: Who were the other homos? Did he want to go to the stockade? Somebody had turned him in, so why didn't he return the favor? Still, Reyes-Colon would not confess to anything or give names. As the interrogations continued, his base commander yanked Reyes-Colon out of the training course he was about to complete, canceled his graduation, confiscated his passport, confined him to his barracks, and ordered him to report to the charge of quarters every two hours. Meanwhile, OSI agents fanned out across the country to interrogate Reyes-Colon's friends. Civilians were usually contacted at their jobs in an apparent effort to maximize the potential for embarrassment. Reyes-Colon's mother called, frantic, one night because OSI agents had come to question her at the factory where she worked as a seamstress in New York's garment district. She had told him where they could stuff their investigation, but she was worried for Roberto. What was going on? Reyes-Colon was too humiliated to tell her.

Finally, the Air Force made a deal. Reyes-Colon did not have to submit a list or admit to anything; if he waived his right to a hearing, he would be discharged. Otherwise, he would be court-martialed and possibly sent to prison. He signed. Seven months after he had been pulled from his classes, an airman knocked on his door and told him he had twenty-four hours to leave the base. Reyes-Colon could not imagine returning home, so he bought a plane ticket to Los Angeles, where he would try to disappear—like the others.

———

THE INVESTIGATIONS SOMETIMES took strange turns. Air Force Second Lieutenant Jeff Boler, fresh from Officers' Training School, found himself caught up in one such OSI investigation while he was based in Orlando producing and directing Air Force films that documented flight exercises and training at various bases in Florida and the Caribbean.

Though he had ventured into the gay community only a year earlier, Boler was by now a regular at the Cactus Room, the local gay bar. Here he had met two sergeants from nearby McCoy Air Force Base, one of whom had been tipped off by a gay clerk in the OSI that a close friend of his was under investigation. The subject of the investigation, another buck sergeant, was currently stationed at an air base in the Philippines. Boler's drinking buddy wanted to warn his friend before the OSI got to him. But the OSI had already started interrogations of the sergeant's friends at McCoy. By now, they figured all their phones were tapped. For the OSI, tapping phones was like intercepting mail—it was not supposed to happen, but any gay airman ever caught up in an investigation knew it did. The warning phone call needed to come from some base other than McCoy, and at that time Boler was working at the Naval Training Center in Orlando.

Boler made the call but was too late. OSI agents had already pulled the sergeant in. A few days later, OSI agents were in Boler's office, too. The sergeant had written Jeff's name and number down on his desk blotter. Did Jeff know this man? Did he know whether the man was a homosexual? Was he sure? Why had he called? Did Jeff know any homosexuals at all?

"Homosexuals?" Jeff asked in amazement. "Not that I am aware of," he said. As for the call to the Philippines, he said he had called about a film in production. How could he know on whose office blotter his name would end up?

The intensity of the investigation mystified Boler, until he heard why the OSI was so interested in this particular buck sergeant. His lover, it was said, was a four-star general in a top command position in one of the most strategically important branches of the U.S. Air Force. Indeed, a few weeks earlier, Boler heard that the general had abruptly retired.

NOVEMBER 17, 1968
FORT BELVOIR, VIRGINIA

IT WAS A SLOW SUNDAY afternoon in the barracks. Private Perry Watkins was alone. Echoing through the deserted barracks, Watkins heard a group of men approaching his area. There were five of them, cooks from the floor above. They wanted blowjobs.

Perry said he was not interested. When the soldiers could not persuade Watkins to get interested, they tried to force him.

The rape attempt quickly turned into a noisy melee, with Perry leaping over lockers and shoving over bunks to protect himself. The soldiers grabbed him occasionally, but Perry discovered that terror gave him a strength he did not know he had, and even five men could not keep him down. Eventually, they tired of trying and sauntered away. Watkins was badly frightened. People got hurt in rapes; sometimes they got killed. The next morning, Perry was back in front of his supervisor.

"I want out of this motherfucker Army and I want out today," he ranted. "You put me in here knowing I'm gay, and it's your job to protect me."

Records from the CID indicate that the official investigation started four days later. It was not, however, an investigation of the assault against Watkins in the barracks. It was an investigation of Watkins himself. If he wanted out of the Army, the CID insisted, he would have to prove he was gay and give them names of at least two people with whom he had had sex—one prior to his induction and one after. Watkins gave the names of two civilians. He also wrote out the names of the five men who had assaulted him in the barracks. He wanted them investigated, too, he said. The CID said it would get back to him on that.

Nearly two months passed. It was January 16, 1969, just four days before President Nixon's inauguration, when Perry heard from the CID again. Both men Watkins named denied ever having sex with him. Therefore, the CID had concluded, "There is insufficient evidence to prove or disprove that Watkins committed acts of sodomy."

Perry would stay in the Army. As to the men who had tried to rape him, the CID had never pursued that investigation, had not so much as spoken to any one of them.

Clearly, Watkins was stuck in the Army, and he would have to figure out his own way to cope, because he believed the Army would not help him one bit. A few days later, Perry asked his field officer to spread a simple message: If anybody ever tried to rape him again, he would not fight, he would take it. Sometime, whoever messed with him would have to go to sleep; when he did, Perry would rearrange his head with a bunk adapter—one of the steel rods that held barracks beds in place. The threat seemed to work; he was not bothered again.

———

TWO DAYS AFTER Nixon's inauguration, nine senators introduced legislation to abolish the military draft and institute an all-volunteer Army. Nixon was eager to cool down the potential for the kind of antiwar protests that had crippled his predecessor's presidency and to fulfill his campaign promise to end conscription. Within a week, the new Defense Secretary, Melvin Laird, announced that President Nixon had ordered him to devise a "detailed plan," due at the end of the year, to replace the draft with a professional Army.

Meanwhile, antimilitary sentiment was spreading. The same day as the Laird announcement, the Yale University faculty voted to deny course credit in the Reserve Officers' Training Corps (ROTC). And, by faculty vote, ROTC instructors, who were mainly military officers assigned to the college, were no longer to be considered full professors at the university, as they had been in the past. A proponent of the move called it in keeping with "the temper of the times." The military was furious at the civilian encroachment into a program that had long provided a majority of its officers. At the Pentagon, Brigadier General Clifford Hannum fumed, "Universities have a responsibility to do this job for their country." But antiwar protesters argued the faculty had not gone far enough, that ROTC should be kicked off campus altogether.

The debate spread. ROTC buildings soon became a focus for peace-movement demonstrators across the country. Here was a thoroughly military institution right in their own backyard, one that could be held accountable to civilian values. It was the first time ROTC found itself the target of campus attacks for policies that were out of synch with the rest of the country. It would not be the last.

Two weeks after the Nixon administration launched its study on how to create a professional military, a small band of women walked into the Oak Room at the Plaza Hotel, one of the most prestigious dining rooms in Manhattan. The head waiter and the maître d' did their best to stop them. Women were not allowed in the Oak Room at lunchtime. However, the women would not be turned away. Dressed in their best fur coats and heels, they strode across the burgundy carpet and seated themselves at two large, round tables. They asked for service. They were refused. They asked again, and were refused again. They waited, unserved, for a half hour and then went back outside for interviews with a mob of reporters. The demonstration, said members of a three-year-old group called the National Organization for Women (NOW), served notice that women would challenge discrimination against women wherever it existed in the United States.

There was more bravado to the protest than actual challenge. Few women were sympathetic to the cause. Writing about the incident in the *New York Post* two days later, columnist Harriet Van Horne asserted, "Women lose so much—beginning with charm, dignity and a certain mystery—when they carry on like strumpets in foolish causes. . . . A sexual ban in this context can hardly be termed illegal or immoral. It is simply the way of the world at lunchtime."

Though the antiwar movement had spawned a New Left that challenged capitalistic ideology, there was little sympathy for redefining gender roles. At the "counterinaugural" protesting Nixon's inauguration, participants booed off the stage those women who attacked male chauvinism. Still, challenging conventional male/female roles was so audacious it seized the nation's attention. And it seemed that every day another sacrosanct cultural institution came under attack. A radical offshoot of New York City's NOW, called the Feminists, picketed the city's marriage bureau, claiming that marriage demeaned women. Another new women's group, the Redstockings, began holding public hearings on the issue of abortion, advancing the notion that abortion should be legalized. A high school student sued the New York Board of Education because she was refused permission to enroll in a metal-shop class. Though it was not clear at the time, this new assertion of the right of women to participate fully in society would inspire dramatic changes in the U.S. military in the decades to come.

FEBRUARY 6, 1969
SHORT STOP DISCO
MUNICH, WEST GERMANY

GAY LIFE IN EUROPE was more exciting than Jerry Rosanbalm could have imagined: ski weekends in the Tirol and the Alps, exploring the gay bars in Innsbruck, meeting glamorous jet-setters. He had even dined with a gay German prince. Work was going well, too. In January, he had received his promotion to captain, and his officer-evaluation reports showed good performance in his intelligence mission. And then on an early February night at the Short Stop, a gay disco in Munich, he met Karel Rohan and fell in love. Tall and handsome, with sandy blond hair and blue eyes, the nineteen-year-old Rohan had fled Czechoslovakia five months earlier when Russian tanks had crushed his country's brief attempt at liberalization known as the "Prague Spring." It had been more than a year since Jerry had seen Don Winn fall from snipers' bullets in Quang Nagh, and he was ready for love again.

GREENWICH VILLAGE
NEW YORK CITY

ROBERTO REYES-COLON finally found the courage to write to his mother about what had happened in the Air Force. Ana gathered her other six children together and explained to them: Roberto had not done anything illegal, and, no matter what, he was still part of the family. Roberto's six brothers and sisters agreed on that, and Ana dispatched Roberto's sister Carola to Los Angeles to check up on her younger brother. By Christmas 1968, Roberto was back in New York with his family and getting ready to go to college.

It was during the holidays that some of his friends took him down to Christopher Street, the gay strip in Greenwich Village. It seemed a wonderful time to be gay in New York, in spite of certain strictures. Most owners of gay bars, for example, enforced the rule that patrons at the bar could not face away from the bartender. The New York State Liquor Authority had ruled that homosexuals looking away from the bar were guilty of "accosting" with their eyes, an activity that, if permitted, could lose the bar its license. Homosexuals could not walk around in a bar, either, since they might use that opportunity to "accost" other men with their eyes. If someone at the bar wanted to join his friends at a table, therefore, the bartender accompanied him, carrying his drink.

There was a new place on Sheridan Square, however, a private club that charged a two-dollar membership fee and offered unparalleled freedom. You could walk around and cruise, and even dance, something few gay bars anywhere in the country allowed. The bar at 53 Christopher Street drew a party crowd of drag queens and a lot of young Puerto Rican men like Reyes-Colon. On just about any weekend night in the early months of 1969, you could find Roberto there, at the Stonewall Inn.

The Sanction of the Victim

MEMORANDUM
MUNICH STATION, 766TH MILITARY INTELLIGENCE DETACHMENT
66TH MILITARY INTELLIGENCE GROUP
UNITED STATES ARMY, EUROPE

> On 10 March 1969, Munich Station 766th MID, 66th MI Gp
> was informed by the Munich Office of the 13th CID that [an
> informant] had indicated that he had knowledge of homosexuals
> assigned to the 66th MI Gp, but would not disclose the informa-
> tion to the CID. Munich Station contacted [the informant] and,
> after five hours of discussion [the informant] admitted he had
> seen [Captain Gerald Lynn Rosanbalm] participate in anal so-
> domy with a Czechoslovakian male national. . . .

On March 18, 1969, a secret cable was sent from Captain Jerry Rosanbalm's commanding officer to the deputy chief of staff for intelligence for
the United States Army in Europe:

> This headquarters is presently conducting a Limited Counterin-
> telligence Investigation to confirm or refute allegations of a seri-
> ous nature against Captain Gerald Lynn Rosanbalm, 05 336
> 692, a member of this Group. The allegations concern Captain
> Rosanbalm's moral turpitude, financial responsibility and contin-
> uing association with foreign nationals who may be of question-
> able character with interest inimical to the United
> States. . . . Request that this headquarters be authorized to con-
> duct a Subject Interview of Captain Rosanbalm and, if he is
> willing, a polygraph examination.

Within hours, the interview was authorized.

THE NEXT AFTERNOON as Jerry Rosanbalm lay in bed with Karel Rohan, he heard noises—someone was trying to force his way into the apartment. Naked and armed with a tennis racket, Jerry leapt into the hallway to investigate, when the door burst open and a cadre of military police crashed in. With guns drawn and cameras ready, military police shouted their disappointment at not having caught the two in bed. Karel made a vain attempt to hide under the covers as agents pressed into the bedroom and then tried to force Rosanbalm onto the bed for the photographer. After Rosanbalm fought off the agents with his tennis racket, somebody yelled, "Screw it—just arrest him." The agents dragged both men naked out of the bedroom and pronounced Captain Gerald Lynn Rosanbalm under arrest for espionage against the United States.

The 727-page dossier on the investigation that followed does not record the content of the interviews between Rosanbalm and his interrogators, but it corroborates the substance of what Rosanbalm recalls in great detail. His first stop was his commanding officer's desk, where the colonel told him what the Army believed it knew: Jerry was a traitor to his country and had become an agent for the Soviet Union. They had known this for months, the colonel said. They had been following him for months. They had tapes, photographs, witnesses, and all the evidence they needed to lock up Jerry for life. In a war zone he would be facing a firing squad. He said Jerry could make it easier on himself by admitting right now, "that you're a queer and a Commie spy."

Counterintelligence agents joined the colonel to question Rosanbalm. Military intelligence officers such as Rosanbalm—and his CO, for that matter—had little use for their counterintelligence colleagues. Military intelligence, which collected raw data through the glamorous business of espionage, considered counterintelligence personnel to be bimbos capable only of keeping filing cabinets locked. Counterintelligence thought members of military intelligence were prima donnas who believed they were better than everyone else. They clearly relished the opportunity to badger an MI officer, and a "queer" one at that. They used the word constantly. "You queer, you Commie spy queer," they repeated ad nauseam, Rosanbalm recalled later. "Make it easy on yourself, you Commie queer, and tell us everything—who are your KGB handlers? Who are your Soviet contacts? Who else is a spy?"

Rosanbalm refused to talk. He knew they were lying. If they had suspected for months that he was involved in anything wrong, he would never have received his promotion to captain just six weeks earlier, and he would never have continued to have access to virtually all the classified Army intelligence in Europe.

When the first round of questioning failed, Jerry and Karel were taken to adjacent rooms in the Munich station of the Sixty-sixth Military Intelligence Group. Rosanbalm tried to cut short his interrogation by asking for a lawyer. This was a national-security matter: Rosanbalm could not see a lawyer, counterintelligence agents informed him.

Then, according to the Army's account, Karel Rohan freely gave a statement that he and Rosanbalm repeatedly engaged in "anal and oral sodomy." Rosanbalm suspected the statement was not voluntary, because he could hear the sounds of somebody being beaten in the next room. Karel was shouting for help, and more shouts and scuffling ensued, and then more cries from Karel.

Jerry could make it easier on his "queer boyfriend," his inquisitors said, even if he would not do it for himself. Rohan was an illegal refugee in Germany, fleeing a government that was not going to come to his defense, the agents reminded Jerry. They could beat him, they could even kill him, and nobody would care. They offered Rosanbalm a written confession that he was a Communist agent. "Sign it now," they said. Jerry refused.

After a short break, MP interrogators resumed the questioning, focusing on gay issues. "Who else is queer?" they asked. He must know other queers in the Army, in intelligence. They would find out, anyway. He faced life in prison, they reminded him.

Rosanbalm refused to talk any more and the interrogation ended, after seventeen hours. Army intelligence records show that after about ten hours of questioning, Karel Rohan signed a statement saying he had participated in acts of sodomy with Captain Gerald Rosanbalm.

The next day, Rosanbalm was confined to his quarters. At the same time, cables flew across the Atlantic between Rosanbalm's commander, the Commander in Chief of the U.S. Army in Europe, and the Pentagon in Washington. "Subject's foreign service tour is curtailed and he will be returned to CONUS [continental United States] ASAP. . . . This action is necessary to prevent possible defection and/or to limit his opportunities to continue as a definite security risk." Another cable warned, "Because he has occupied several extremely sensitive positions, his continued presence in the command could seriously jeopardize the accomplishment of the intelligence mission of this organization."

The orders were given to bring Rosanbalm home immediately and for his diplomatic passport to be seized in order to prevent him from traveling elsewhere. Two days after his arrest, handcuffed and escorted by two captains, Jerry boarded a train in Munich bound for Frankfurt. In Frankfurt, a jeep loaded with armed guards took him directly to a commercial jet on the airport tarmac. Armed guards walked him to his seat, with the rest of the plane gaping at the drama. Jerry would be met in New York City by more guards, they told him, and they left.

Through the entire flight, Rosanbalm contemplated his uncertain future. Less than fourteen months after he had nearly died for his country in Vietnam, he was branded a traitor and faced jail time, not because of any evidence that he had done wrong but because it was assumed a homosexual was a Judas and that any homosexual contact with any citizen from behind the Iron Curtain entailed espionage. His record against Communists in Vietnam did not matter; his Purple Heart and his wounds did not matter. If they could not get him on the espionage charges, they would nail him for sodomy. Under the Uniform Code of Military Justice, that meant five years in the military prison at Fort Leavenworth.

When his plane landed at Kennedy Airport, there was no military escort to greet him. Rosanbalm collected his luggage and reported to Fort Hamilton, New York, as per his orders.

The commanding officer looked quizzical when Rosanbalm appeared in his office. No one had alerted him to expect the captain. He could tell by Rosanbalm's MOS number 9668 that he was military intelligence, and he knew military intelligence personnel trained in area studies were not supposed to be in the continental United States. But that was all he knew. He assigned Rosanbalm to officer's quarters to wait for further orders.

MAY 1969
CHARLESTON NAVAL STATION
CHARLESTON, SOUTH CAROLINA

JESSE HELMS HAD A WAY of talking out of the side of his mouth and he carried himself with a rigidity that people noticed, even then. But to young television reporter Armistead Maupin, Helms, the executive vice president of WRAL-TV in Raleigh, where Maupin worked, was downright fatherly, and Maupin was clearly Jesse's golden boy.

Maupin had made a small name for himself in conservative circles with a column he had written for the *Daily Tarheel,* the campus newspaper of the University of North Carolina. The feature poked fun at the foibles of antiwar protesters and other assorted college lefties in a style that crossed the satire of Art Buchwald with the rock-ribbedness of William F. Buckley, Jr. Helms railed publicly at many of the same people in his five-minute televised commentaries every day. Some people even thought Jesse Helms ought to get into politics, in spite of the fact that he was a Republican in a state of "yellow-dog" Democrats—those who would vote for any yellow dog as long as he was a Democrat. Maupin, for one, believed this would change. By now, in the 1960s, it was the Republicans who addressed the issues of states rights, which the South held so dear. States rights was another issue upon which Helms and Maupin could see eye-to-eye.

But there was an issue on which they would never agree, an issue that emerged when Maupin was assigned to do a story on the marriage of a black man to the daughter of Secretary of State Dean Rusk. Maupin had interviewed the Imperial Wizard of the Ku Klux Klan, who said flatly of the Secretary of State, "What else could you expect from a man who is a practicing homosexual?" Maupin ran back to Helms with the quote, wondering whether to use it. Helms despised Rusk, Maupin knew, but still refused even to consider airing the film clip. "That's the worst thing you can say about anybody," Helms said solemnly. Maupin could tell Helms thought the issue should not even be discussed, because by now Maupin knew the rules: *Don't talk about it.*

But in early 1969, at his first duty station at Charleston Naval Station in Charleston, South Carolina, Navy Ensign Armistead Maupin needed to talk about it. He had always known. He had had mad crushes on boys since he was thirteen. And all through college, his sexual fantasies were of other men, the strapping country boys he would see working in the tobacco fields. But the issue came to a head once he was out of Officer Candidate School and assigned to the USS *Everglades,* a destroyer tender. He had gone walking one night on the city's old Battery, where the first shots of the Civil War had been fired. He had stopped and was looking into the cool black water of Charleston Harbor when he noticed a very effeminate-looking man watching him. After a while, the man walked over to him and asked the time.

"I'm not what you're looking for," Maupin said brusquely.

The man quickly apologized and left. Maupin continued staring into the water, knowing that indeed he was what the man was looking for. He caught up with the fellow, apologized, and brought him back to the carriage house he had rented for his off-base housing. At twenty-five, he had sex for the first time.

Afterward, Maupin worried because his officer's cap had been in full view on his dresser. What if the man appeared on ship the next day to blackmail him? He had always heard that homosexuals got blackmailed. Still, he awoke the next morning feeling exhilarated, as if he had gone over the brink. The radio was playing the song "Good Morning Girl" by the group Neon Philharmonic: "Things look different now. . . ."

The panic only set in later. It lasted for days. He was a homosexual. Would they notice? Could he accept it?

He went back to the Battery after that, to more sexual encounters, and more guilt and confusion. He was not ready for the humiliation and disgrace. Nothing in his life had prepared him for that; he was the great-great-grandson of a respected Confederate general, Lawrence O'Bryan Branch. His distinguished family had been steeped in southern tradition for generations. He did not want to spend his life as an outcast. There was, he thought, one solution. Maupin's father had always believed that history provided every generation of southern males with a war in which they could prove their manhood. Maupin could move beyond his guilt and prove he was a man: He would volunteer for Vietnam.

JUNE 28, 1969
53 CHRISTOPHER STREET
NEW YORK CITY

ROBERTO REYES-COLON was sitting on a stoop on Greenwich Avenue with some other young men when they heard a commotion a few blocks away near Sheridan Square. The group ambled toward Christopher Street. It was warm and the moon was full. At the Stonewall Inn, a crowd had gathered around a group of policemen who were trying to haul some drag queens out of the bar and into paddy wagons.

The raids were routine; there had been five on gay Village bars in the last three weeks alone; but the reaction on the streets was anything but routine on this night. The queers were fighting back.

They started chanting: "Christopher Street belongs to the queens / Christopher Street belongs to the queens." Somebody threw something— a can, then a bottle, then a rock. The police looked mystified at first. When the crowd surged toward them menacingly, the police barricaded themselves inside the Stonewall and called for reinforcements.

Reyes-Colon felt his anger grow as new units of police arrived to rescue their comrades from the marauding drag queens. It was the same feeling of anger that had replaced his shame and humiliation over the Air Force discharge a year before. He was a decorated Vietnam veteran and had risked his life for his country, but in New York City he faced arrest if he did not sit on a bar stool facing the bartender. It felt exhilarating to pick up a rock and throw it at the police, who so personified the prejudice that had shaped the past few years of his life.

Rocks shattered the window of a jewelry store next to the Stonewall, but there was no looting. This demonstration was not about looting; it was about rage. It was about people insisting on their rights. It was not only the first gay riot; it was the beginning of a powerful new movement.

ACCORDING TO AUTHORITIES, the Stonewall Inn was raided that night because the establishment had been selling liquor without a license. That the Stonewall lacked a license was true, but it had been selling liquor without a license just a few blocks from the Sixth Precinct station house for some time. Most people assumed the real reason for the raid was that the bar owners had fallen behind in their payoffs to the police department.

As Donn Teal recounted in his book *The Gay Militants*, protesters gathered for four nights thereafter to face off against the police. It was not your typical police/rioter confrontation. Tactical squads approaching Sheridan Square came up against the "Stonewall Girls," who formed a kick line against them. As word of the riots spread through Manhattan, college students and political activists already familiar with the rhetoric of revolution from the antiwar movement joined the cause. By the last night, the Stonewall Inn had become something of a tourist attraction.

Older gays fretted that nothing good would come of it, but others sensed the opposite. As poet Allen Ginsberg marveled to a *Village Voice* reporter, "They've lost that wounded look that fags all had ten years ago."

It was in those nights that the words *gay power* were first heard. Roberto Reyes-Colon came back every night to join in the low-intensity guerrilla warfare. Also there every night was Army Captain Jerry Rosanbalm, still on hold in Brooklyn at Fort Hamilton. The past three months had been the most painful and humiliating he had ever endured. He got the most embarrassing assignments the brass could dream up. He was put in charge of cleaning a warehouse, for example—alone. They insisted he be done with the sweeping in fifteen minutes, though it was a job that would clearly take two days. When he was not finished in the allotted time, he was written up for insubordination. He spent his days raking leaves and sweeping warehouses and waiting. No charges had yet been filed. Slowly, his humiliation was turning to anger, too.

That was why he had gone back to Sheridan Square every night, though he went with trepidation. Someone could be following him; he could be at risk here. But he could not pull himself away from what was happening. As the nights passed, Rosanbalm saw the street fighters increasingly made up of radicals and antiwar activists, and Rosanbalm was neither radical nor against the war. But he still responded to what was going on here. Something was changing.

WHAT FOLLOWED in the next weeks was an explosion of activism and organizing. Ten days after the first rock was thrown at the Stonewall, the first "gay power meeting" of young radicals wrote its first manifesto: "What Homosexuals Want." From a twenty-plus-year perspective, some of the demands read like anachronisms of the time, such as a demand for the reform of the New York State Liquor Authority. Others were issues that would dominate gay organizing for the next generation, such as a demand for the repeal of sodomy laws and the enactment of gay civil rights protections. The substance of the manifesto, however, was less remarkable than its style. These were not polite homosexuals with discreet names such as the Mattachine Society. These were angry, in-your-face militants who were out to rock the boat. As one flier proclaimed, "Do you think homosexuals are revolting? You bet your sweet ass we are."

Within weeks of the Stonewall riot, newborn Gay Liberation Front (GLF) chapters had sprung up in every major city in the United States, holding encounter groups modeled on the consciousness-raising groups of the new women's movement. Leaders in other radical movements were wide-eyed at the fervor and seeming potential of these new activists. As the radical *San Francisco Free Press* observed, "Every homosexual is a potential revolutionary."

But few mainstream newspapers found reason to cover the Stonewall riots and even in New York the organizing of homosexuals afterward

received practically no media attention. So much else was happening—
Easy Rider and *Butch Cassidy and the Sundance Kid,* for instance. Actress
Sharon Tate had died in a strange cultlike murder in Los Angeles. And
the first man had walked on the moon. It would be years before the
broader culture took notice.

AUGUST 17, 1969
DA NANG, SOUTH VIETNAM

AIR FORCE SERGEANT Leonard Matlovich was a good Mormon, but it
had not helped him contain his homosexual attractions. He had developed
a crush on another airman in the Red Horse Battalion, to which he had
been assigned. Like a lot of military buddies, they became an inseparable
pair and Leonard wondered whether maybe his buddy felt the same way
he did—until one day, the other airman started talking about faggots and
queers. Lord, how he hated faggots, he said. Matlovich could not bear
it; he asked to be reassigned to Da Nang.

He had tried so hard. He had prayed so fervently. Here he was twenty-
six years old and he had never made love to another person. Sometimes
he thought it would be better to die.

He wondered years later whether this was not what he had sought
that early August, just weeks before his second Vietnam tour was to end,
when he volunteered to clear a heavily mined area near Da Nang.

It was an agonizingly hot afternoon. After a few hours of digging,
Leonard stuck his shovel in the ground and prepared to sit—except the
shovel hit something hard. Leonard tried pushing it again, harder.

Later, Matlovich remembered watching the explosion rise out of the
ground. His next memory was of thinking, *My lung. Where is my lung?*
He knew he still had all his limbs, because every inch of his body was in
excruciating pain. He told himself to remain conscious. If he slipped into
shock, he knew he might never come back. After a while, he realized that
he could take the pain. As he lay there, he discovered it was almost easy
to accept, compared to the suffering he had felt in his soul. And for the
first time he knew, truly, how much pain he had been in.

IN THE MONTHS during which Sergeant Leonard Matlovich was recovering
from his wounds, Gay Liberation Front chapters were forming across the
United States and shaping an ideology. By November, four months after
the Stonewall Inn riots, a central article of faith had emerged from the
new movement: Self-hatred was more crippling than the hatred of others.
And something else became clear: Gay libbers would not respect society's
taboo, *Don't talk about it.* They were going to talk about it whenever
they could. As Craig Schoonmaker advised in *Homosexual Renaissance,*
one of scores of gay papers that appeared almost overnight, "Homosexuals

can effectively demand respect from others only if we first respect ourselves—as homosexuals. That requires that we admit to ourselves that we are homosexual; that we affirm it, understand it, realize it in all its implications. I am homosexual. Say it! aloud; 'I am homosexual.' Shout it, whisper it. Laugh it, cry it. State it, proclaim it, confess it in sobs, but *say* it. . . . Not 'Leonardo da Vinci was homosexual,' but 'I am homosexual.' "

This demand for openness also created a tension among gays that would persist for the rest of the century. Not only was a heterosexual establishment to be fought, but so were gays who would not come out, the gay libbers believed. Closeted gay men, activists argued, tacitly consented to society's prejudice. Cultural prejudice had not only succeeded in making most heterosexuals hate gays; it had succeeded in making most gay people hate themselves. This, more than anything else, was what the new movement was determined to change. Hence, gay pride became a movement watchword. "Coming out," or acknowledging one's homosexuality—either privately to oneself or publicly—became like a born-again experience to the new gay activists.

In the first issue of the Gay Liberation Front's newspaper—*Come Out!*—the group declared, "The passive acceptance of homosexuality as a perversion or emotional illness IN YOUR OWN MIND plays into the hands of your persecutors. This is called THE SANCTION OF THE VICTIM."

THE NEW GAY MOVEMENT quickly merged its aims with the panoply of liberation movements asserting themselves in that era. Committed GLFers, therefore, not only demonstrated for gay rights but were ideologically inclined to demonstrate for black rights, women's rights, Third World countries, and farm workers. Some of these alignments—with women's right to privacy in the abortion issue, for example—made sense, but others lacked much intellectual consistency. As Donn Teal later noted, gay libbers joined their leftist comrades cutting Cuban sugar in the Venceremos Brigade, despite the fact that Fidel Castro himself locked up Cuban gays in concentration camps. Gay lib leaders solemnly quoted Chairman Mao's wisdom from their own little red books, though Mao's Red Guards were known to castrate "sexual degenerates" publicly. GLFers handed out FREE BOBBY SEALE posters alongside Black Panthers, even though black liberation guru Malcolm X had commented, "All white men are blond, blue-eyed faggots." Gays who had once been Uncle Toms to the Establishment were now Uncle Toms to the New Left.

The trend allied Gay Liberation to the crusade against the war in Vietnam, as well. Since the people who marched in the GLF protests were largely the same people who for the past two or three years had been attending antiwar pickets, the affiliation was natural. By November, at the second Moratorium Against the War, a contingent of fifteen thousand gay protesters joined the massive antiwar march in San Francisco. Heterosexual marchers shouted the then-routine chant:

Ho Ho Ho Chi Minh
Dare to struggle, dare to win.

While one gay contingent offered:

Ho Ho Homosexual
The status quo is ineffectual.

Favored GLF signs at such events included SOLDIERS—MAKE EACH OTHER—NOT WAR and SUCK COCK TO BEAT THE DRAFT.

The progay but antiwar alignment would have repercussions for decades to come, particularly for those Americans who were gay and chose to serve in the U.S. military. The gay movement was against all forms of oppression, but it wanted nothing to do with the anguish of gays in uniform. In late August 1969, a week after a land mine blew Leonard Matlovich apart, the radical Youth Committee of the North American Conference of Homophile Organizations meeting in Kansas City resolved, "The homophile movement must totally reject the insane war in Vietnam and refuse to encourage complicity in the war and support of the war machine, which may well be turned against us. We oppose any attempts by the movement to obtain security clearances for homosexuals since they contribute to the war machine."

An editorial in the *San Francisco Free Press* agreed: "Homosexuals should not fight in a war propagated by a society that fucks us over in all its institutions. We will not fight in an army that discriminates against us . . . that rapes us and gives us less than honorable discharges."

From the start, there were dissenters. When the New York City Gay Liberation Front collapsed amid internal ideological struggles, the Gay Activists Alliance took over its place, and a former Air Force sergeant named Roberto Reyes-Colon became one of its earliest members. He was a pacifist now and wore love beads, long hair, and bell-bottoms, but he sometimes argued that groups like the GAA should not turn their backs on gay soldiers. The Air Force had been his way out of New York's mean streets; a way of easing the burden on his mother, who would die young, working three jobs to make sure all her seven children got a college education, a way for a better life.

GAA activists listened sympathetically and agreed that no matter what Reyes-Colon might have done to help the war machine in Vietnam, he had been a victim of the system rather than a despoiler. But at a time when the military represented everything that idealists in all the liberation movements wanted to change, few could muster much enthusiasm for helping anybody associated with the armed forces. Efforts for equal rights for gays would not extend to gays in uniform. The discrimination against them would, in effect, have the sanction of the gay movement for many years to come.

To say that these attitudes were dominant among gay Americans would be vastly inaccurate. At this point, gay libbers comprised only a fraction of a percent of gays, but, because they were the only people talking out loud about homosexuality, their voices were the only ones heard. For most gay Americans at the dawning of the 1970s, life continued to be lived as it had been for generations, in silence and in hiding.

IN THE AUTUMN of 1969, during his long recuperation, Leonard Matlovich was the hero he had always wanted to be. His parents doted on him. Nurses took special care of him. He would soon receive his Purple Heart. Once he was well enough to be back in the barracks, he finally felt as if he fit in. He even went to great lengths to mock an airman who was caught with a gay porn magazine. *Stupid little fairy.*

Anybody suspected of being queer could expect a good razzing from Mat. He had proven his manhood. He was one of the guys at last.

BOOK TWO

INTERROGATIONS

(1969–1975)

"If you mean confessing," she said, "we shall do that, right enough. Everybody always confesses. You can't help it."

—George Orwell, *1984*

— 10 —

National Security

FOR NEARLY SIX MONTHS, Jerry Rosanbalm sweated out his future at Fort Hamilton. In July, the Army told him he would be discharged if he submitted his resignation and left quietly. Rosanbalm proffered the necessary letter, with the proviso that he be granted an honorable discharge. A month later, the Army replied that it would not accept such a conditional resignation. By the end of the summer, Jerry still faced a court-martial for espionage and homosexuality, but no charges had been lodged against him and none seemed forthcoming. Twice a month, he picked up his paycheck, then returned to his demeaning duties. The Army was playing hardball. Since it had no case against him for espionage, it seemed the Army might be trying to build some other case against him by piling on reports of insubordination and poor performance. There were also the sodomy charges to worry about. His only relief came on weekends when he escaped to Fire Island or Greenwich Village.

Military intelligence, meanwhile, was in a quandary. The case was deemed sensitive enough to be handled at the highest levels of intelligence commands in Europe and Washington. Nearly a quarter of a century later, extensive portions of the records on the probe would still be classified. But the CID's records reveal that it kept close tabs on Jerry's Czech lover, Karel Rohan, interrogating him regularly and intercepting every note and letter Rosanbalm sent to him in Europe. The letters asked Karel to live with Jerry in the United States. They confirmed what intelligence analysts had already decided: Rosanbalm was no threat to national security.

According to Army documents, agents sought interviews throughout Europe and Vietnam with everyone who had had contact with Rosanbalm during his Army career. They found colleagues who considered him overbearing, overly opinionated, and overly fond of telling Vietnam War stories, but they found none who thought he would betray his country. As one investigator wrote, "Subject was proud to be an officer in the US Army and a citizen of the United States, had a high appraisal of his position, and probably would not downgrade it by deliberately collaborating with representatives of a hostile or potentially hostile nation." Another report concluded, "Numerous interviews with US co-workers and associates of subj failed to reveal any evidence of disloyalty. Subject's knowledge of 430th mission and ops is extensive and if revealed to hostile intel, would cause real damage. The possibility of blackmail appears remote in view of overt knowledge of subj's homosexual activities, which he had informed his parents of according to his letters." The earlier allegation that an informant had seen Rohan and Rosanbalm have sex proved to be a complete fabrication.

After six months of interviewing, which resulted in ninety reports, the CID finally stopped badgering Karel, "based upon the assessment that [he] is a hippie type, psychologically devoted homosexual whose main interest is gratification of his sexual desires with his paramour of the moment. Prolonged interrogation failed to reveal any indication of hostile intelligence control." And polygraph tests found that Rosanbalm had betrayed no state secrets to the young Czech.

Not only had Rosanbalm done nothing to compromise national security; recent court rulings would disqualify much of the evidence the Army had accumulated to support a charge of sodomy. Despite these conclusions, the Army was not letting him go. Though Rosanbalm had no way of knowing it at that time, the only impediment to his release was his demand that he receive an honorable discharge.

Jerry believed his service merited an honorable discharge, no matter his sexual orientation, but there was also a practical consideration in wanting it—anything but an honorable discharge would deny him Veterans Administration benefits. Rosanbalm remained partially disabled from wounds suffered in the 1968 Tet offensive. He had regained only 50 percent of his strength in his right arm and was frequently racked by pain. Life would be tough without the medical and educational benefits the VA provided.

This fear, along with the accumulated humiliation he suffered every day at Fort Hamilton, prompted Rosanbalm into audacious action in early September. It seemed no riskier than doing nothing and ending up in prison.

The first part of his plan involved a letter to President Nixon, ostensibly to plead his case. "I felt I owed a lot to this country of ours and found the meaning of true patriotism," he wrote, but now "I want out of the Army but with an honorable discharge. I have a good position waiting for me in civilian life, but if the Army gives me anything other than an Honorable Discharge, my future has been greatly affected. I will feel that my country has betrayed me, making it impossible for me to find work or enjoy the other rights that should be afforded me. . . . I can not believe that our country, Mr. President, can be so cruel to me after I have so zealously supported and served America."

The phrase about feeling his country had "betrayed" him was, Rosanbalm knew, sure to send up red flags in the intelligence community. Except for money, the number-one reason that bona fide spies betrayed their country was because they felt betrayed on some level by it. To make sure nobody missed the point, Rosanbalm also inserted a paragraph in the letter alluding to all the top-secret information he knew, such as the names of every American spy in Eastern Europe, the workings of the American unilateral spying operation in Vietnam, and "many things that one picks up in working daily in intelligence." His descriptions included a number of military intelligence acronyms hot enough to designate the six-page letter CONFIDENTIAL as soon as the White House forwarded it to the Army.

A few days after mailing the letter, Rosanbalm put into effect the next, more incendiary phase of his plan: a visit to the Soviet Mission to the United Nations on Sixty-seventh Street in Manhattan. He had no business there, of course, but he knew the FBI routinely photographed every person who walked in and out of the building and that he would be photographed that day, too, if he were not already being followed. Rosanbalm walked in the door and then walked out again.

The ploy worked. After months of waiting for some official word on the case, the Defense Department lurched into action. Just a few days later, Jerry received a phone call from the Pentagon instructing him that a car would pick him up shortly for a drive to Washington. No record of the Washington meeting exists in the official files of Rosanbalm's investigation, but phrasing that Rosanbalm says he made there—and that exists in no other official documents prior to that time—suddenly began appearing in every subsequent Pentagon memorandum pertaining to his case.

Jerry remembers that he was met at the door of the Pentagon by a WAC major who directed him to General Staff Briefing Room 1. At least eight field- and general-grade officers were present. They asked what Rosanbalm meant by his letter to the President.

He meant exactly what he said, Rosanbalm told them. He was being railroaded out of the Army with a less than honorable discharge. It would destroy his future and it was unconscionable.

The assembled generals and colonels asked the familiar questions about whether he had compromised national security. As he had for months, Rosanbalm offered to take a lie-detector test; once that was done, however, he also wanted out of the Army—with an honorable discharge. "I should not be court-martialed for being homosexual," he said.

That was Army regulation, he was told. He should have admitted he was homosexual and never gone into the Army in the first place.

That kind of admission could dog him for the rest of his life, Rosanbalm answered. A gay deferment would have deprived him of any number of jobs on the outside. None of this mattered anyway, because they were talking about today, and all he wanted today was his honorable discharge so he could get on with his life.

The entire conversation was very cordial. After a few hours, the generals said they would review the matter and Jerry was free to return to Fort Hamilton.

According to Army records, a flurry of official activity followed the meeting. Within days, intelligence offices in Europe, Vietnam, and the United States issued their final assessments of the security risk Rosanbalm might pose to ongoing intelligence operations and what should be done with him. Most of the communiqués included an addendum: "Case is of White House interest and request response as soon as possible."

Military intelligence clearly did not know what to make of a decorated Army officer who was so nonchalant about discussing his homosexuality. "Concern here is if subject is released under other than honorable conditions or even honorable conditions, what will his actions be?" asked one memorandum from the chief of central intelligence for the Army's European operations. "Will he return to Europe and possibly behind [Iron] Curtain? Is he subject for possible pressure to pass classified information? . . . This office feels there are definite security complications in the case and request your reply and comments as soon as possible."

The questions remained unresolved weeks later when Rosanbalm received orders to report to Valley Forge General Hospital in Pennsylvania for medical evaluation. In November 1969, with antiwar moratoriums still dominating public discussion, the captain reported to Valley Forge, expecting a thorough going-over of his shoulder wounds. Instead, he was thrown into a locked ward for psychotics.

Jerry was first inclined to see himself as a dissident cast into a Soviet-style confinement. But that scenario did not add up. Soon he realized the Army really just wanted to know whether it could trust him once he got out. He would show the Army it could.

IF CAPTAIN JERRY ROSANBALM had been an artillery officer or an infantry commander, his story undoubtedly would have been much simpler. If the separations of officers in comparable cases are any indication, he would have been given the chance to resign for "the convenience of the government." An especially draconian commander might have tried to push a sodomy court-martial, but cooler heads higher in the chain of command probably would have prevailed. What made Rosanbalm's case different was that he was an intelligence officer. His problems rested on the very foundation of the military's ban on homosexuals, the notion that gays were a threat to national security.

By the last days of 1969, it still seemed self-evident that foreign powers could blackmail homosexuals into betraying their country. Though the systematic exclusion of anyone with "homosexual tendencies" from the military began in 1943, its creation was never justified on the grounds of national security. In fact, the words *security risk* do not appear associated with homosexuality until the late 1940s and early 1950s, during the McCarthy era.

The move to link homosexuality and treason dates back to 1950, when the Senate Committee on Expenditures in the Executive Department, an august group that included Senator Joseph R. McCarthy of Wisconsin, authorized its investigations subcommittee to prepare a report on homosexuals in government. The subcommittee, chaired by Senator Clyde Hoey of North Carolina, proceeded to interview leading experts on the issue of homosexuality, which at that time meant physicians, psychiatrists, law enforcement, and military officials. To avoid a "circus atmosphere," questioning occurred in closed executive session. The resulting report, "Employment of Homosexuals and Other Sex Perverts in Government," found gays to be generally "unsuitable" for government employment because of weakened "moral fibre" and the "corrosive influence upon his fellow employees," but more dangerous by far and at the crux of the study was the consideration of "Sex Perverts as Security Risks." The consensus was that "the pervert is easy prey to the blackmailer" and that espionage agents could use homosexuality as leverage to extort confidential information from a gay government employee.

On paper, the argument carried some merit. Most homosexuals in the 1950s clearly would have preferred not to be publicly identified as such. But it was a great leap of faith—for which there was no evidence—to assert that this preference for privacy would cause gay Americans to betray their country.

Though it was eager to buttress the contention that gays were prima facie threats to national security, the Senate subcommittee had to reach back to the days of the Hapsburg dynasty of the Austro-Hungarian Empire to find an example of any homosexual anywhere who had been successfully blackmailed into double-crossing his own government. The report carefully recounted the story of Colonel Redl, chief of Austrian counterintelligence service in 1912, whom Russian agents threatened on the eve of World War I and blackmailed into destroying Austrian intelligence reports of czarist war plans. Redl was exposed after the outbreak of the Great War in 1914 and committed suicide.

Redl's may have been the only documented case, but the report insisted that blackmailing homosexuals was something the Communists *wanted* to do. The other evidence that gays represented a threat to national security came from military intelligence agents who assured the committee that "perverts are vulnerable to interrogating by a skilled questioner and they seldom refuse to talk about themselves."

In spite of these assurances, no one produced a single case of Russian agents attempting extortion—much less succeeding. A handful of cases of homosexual British spies during the Cold War were linked not to their sexual practices but to their earlier pro-Communist ideological leanings. The lack of facts, however, did not dampen enthusiasm for launching an all-out effort to rid the government of gays. For all the attention that has subsequently been devoted to McCarthyism, there has been little said about the antihomosexual purges that swept the government at this time. In the Hoey report, the Senate subcommittee took credit for prodding the Truman administration into action. While praising the "firm and aggressive attitude" of the military toward eliminating gays, the report decried the Civil Service Commission's "slipshod manner" in ferreting out "sex perverts."

The antigay campaign in various federal departments was awesome in its scope and impact. Between the first of January 1947 and April 1950, the report said, only 192 homosexuals had been fired from government jobs. But under pressure of the Senate investigation, the Civil Service Commission booted out 382 gays between April and October 1950. In its first round of State Department investigations before the Senate hearings, ninety-one lost their jobs, either for being gay or associating with gays. Of sixty-six State Department employees fired in 1950 under tightened anti-Communist security regulations, fifty-four were gay. In 1951, 119 of 154 State Department employees fired for national-security reasons were homosexual. The next year, gays constituted 134 of the 204 State Department employees so terminated. The sweep extended to congressional employees, from clerks at the Library of Congress to the pruners at the botanical gardens. *New York Post* columnist Max Lerner dubbed the sweeps "the purge of the perverts," while Illinois senator Everett Dirksen complained that the work was "no picnic."

To keep gays out of state and local jobs, legislatures in twenty-one states enacted bills requiring the registration of anyone convicted of a gay-related crime. Loyalty oaths required for many state jobs, most notably teaching, were amended to include a pledge that the swearer was not guilty of "moral turpitude." Few states would grant any sort of licenses—for lawyers, doctors, veterinarians, or even hairstylists—to anyone on these lists. Historian Allan Bérubé calculated that official regulations banning the employment of homosexuals finally encompassed 12 million jobs—or about 20 percent of the nation's work force. Under new policies, the names and fingerprints of anyone arrested on even the suspicion of a gay-related offense would be passed along to the Federal Bureau of Investigation in order to assure that such people would never find federal employment.

LATER, WHEN THE COUNTRY'S OBSESSION with internal subversion became a national embarrassment, the official sanction against gays remained, as well as its corollary assumption that homosexual people posed a threat to national security.

One of two men who ensured the perpetuation of equating homosexuality and political subversion was FBI director J. Edgar Hoover. More than forty years after the Senate subcommittee investigation of "sex perverts," Defense Department security experts were struck by his impact on the official view of gay Americans. According to their 1991 report analyzing the history of "Homosexuality and Personnel Security," "Without citing evidence, Hoover declared that homosexuals are security risks and should be separated from government service. Over 600 'security separations' were reported for a 16-month period beginning in 1953. The charge was 'perversion' and included employees from such nonsensitive agencies as the Post Office and the Department of Agriculture." Even in the 1990s, the Defense Department report acknowledged, homosexual citizens battled "Hoover's legacy of combining homosexuality and disloyalty."

Dwight D. Eisenhower was the other man to transform temporal political winds into a policy that persisted for decades. Ike's contribution to institutionalized discrimination against gay people was Executive Order 10450, signed within the first one hundred days of his assuming office in 1953. The order dealt with tightening security regulations to meet the demands of a public whose paranoia of domestic Communist infiltration was at a fever pitch. Another clause delineated "sexual perversion" as the basis for terminating and not hiring federal employees.

It is intriguing that neither Hoover nor Eisenhower was swept up in the dementia of their times; both of them were public figures making calculated moves to exploit fears and political trends that they *knew* were wholly unjustified.

In gay veterans' circles, WAC Sergeant Johnnie Phelps became legendary for a conversation she had with Eisenhower when she served on the general's staff during the postwar occupation of Europe. Phelps admired Eisenhower as a soldier's soldier who genuinely cared for his troops and would never order them to do something he would not do himself. Out of respect for Eisenhower, Phelps would never have lied to him, which was why she knew how to answer the day he called her into his office and said he had heard reports that there were lesbians in the WAC battalion. He wanted a list of their names, he said, so he could get rid of them. That, Phelps suspected, would be a tall order, since she estimated 95 percent of the WAC battalion of nine hundred women at that headquarters was lesbian.

"Yes, sir," Phelps said to the general, according to her later account. She would make the list, if that was the order. Then she reminded Eisenhower that the WAC battalion at his headquarters was one of the most decorated in the Army. It performed superbly, had the fewest unauthorized absences, the least number of venereal-disease cases, and the most infrequent number of pregnancies of any WAC group anywhere. Getting rid of the lesbians would mean losing competent file clerks, typists, and a large share of the headquarters' key personnel. "I'll make your list," Phelps concluded in her crackling North Carolina accent, "but you've got to know that when you get the list back, my name's going to be first."

Eisenhower's secretary, also in the room, corrected the sergeant. "Sir," the secretary said, "if the General pleases, Sergeant Phelps will have to be second on the list. I'm going to type it. My name will be first."

According to Phelps, Eisenhower looked at her, looked at the secretary, shook his head, and said, "Forget that order. Forget about it."

If the general allowed an acknowledged lesbian to hold a desk right outside his office door and a battalion of lesbians to hold key office jobs when he was a five-star general, it is doubtful that he believed that homosexuals were intrinsically traitorous and deserving of wholesale dismissal by the federal government. Clearly, the motivating factor for Executive Order 10450 was the prevailing politics of the early 1950s, when the order was made.

The Republican party had lost five out of five presidential elections prior to 1952. One of its only successful political issues in the dawning post–World War II era advanced the notion that Communists were subverting the nation from within. The issue was used successfully against President Truman to blame soft Democrats for everything from "losing" China to the Communists to allegedly allowing homosexuals to take over the State Department. Even though Eisenhower himself did not have much stomach for the excesses of McCarthyism, he certainly was not going to surrender a political agenda that generated badly needed Republican votes. In these years, Joe McCarthy was a hero to many Americans, and he was, after all, a Republican. Homosexuals were an even easier target than suspected Communist infiltrators, since no one would stand up for them. Even the American Civil Liberties Union gave the brush-off to gays who contacted them for help against the government purges. So Eisenhower played the subversive and the homosexual-subversive issues for votes, and permanently sealed the "gays as security risk" ethos into federal law. Politics. It was just politics.

HOOVER'S MOTIVES were far murkier, although few administrators in Washington history played public fears and private Capitol corridors as skillfully to advance a political agenda. Hoover's power exceeded even those Presidents who vainly wished to topple him, essentially making him director of the FBI for life. What started his twenty-year intensive investigation of groups advancing gay civil rights was a veiled reference in a November 1955 issue of "One," the publication of One, Inc., one of the earliest gay organizations in Los Angeles, that homosexuals occupied "key positions" in the FBI. Both One, Inc., and the FBI knew precisely which "key positions" were implied—Hoover's own and that of his long-time companion, Clyde Tolson, the FBI's associate director. Newspaper accounts politely referred to Tolson as the director's "alter ego"; in Southern California gay circles, he was known as Hoover's lover.

Early gay organizers such as Harry Hay, a founder of the Mattachine

Society, based their speculation on reports from gay friends in San Juan Capistrano, where Hoover and Tolson vacationed every year to attend the Del Mar races. Del Mar was popular among well-heeled gay men in the 1950s, and at the races Hoover and Tolson functioned as a typical middle-aged gay couple. Nor was such speculation restricted to gay circles in Southern California; it had been a major topic of Washington gossip. The two bachelors were inseparable both on the job and in their personal lives, vacationing together, taking lunch together every day at the Mayflower Hotel, and dining together in the city's best restaurants almost every night. Though they did not live together, Hoover's limousine picked up Tolson at his small apartment every morning on the director's way to work.

In 1953, shortly after President Eisenhower issued his executive order about subversives and sex perverts, Hoover sent copies to his various field offices, instructing them to investigate the dozen or so homosexual organizations in existence at that time. Virtually every resulting field report noted that there was no evidence of any links with Communist organizations. As one special agent summarized in early 1954, talk of "subversive ramifications" was "unfounded in fact." The issue died there—until November 1955, when Hoover was alerted to the "One" magazine story about homosexuals in high positions at the FBI. FBI memoranda record a meeting in which Associate FBI Director Tolson said: "I think we should take this crowd on and make them 'put up or shut up.' " Hoover answered, "I concur."

Although the magazine had a paid circulation of fewer than two thousand, Hoover responded by launching a two-year investigation of the article's author and of One, Inc., and of its sister group, the Mattachine Society. The memos reveal that FBI agents spied on a wide array of Mattachine leaders, interviewing their neighbors, watching their homes, recording license numbers of cars parked in their driveways, and obtaining birth records, college transcripts, motor-vehicle records, and other information concerning their early lives. These investigations turned up no evidence of subversive or illegal activities.

By then, however, Hoover had personally launched an expanded campaign of illegal domestic surveillance of all gay organizations. In memos to the Justice Department, Hoover justified the probes by calling them "internal security" investigations, citing Executive Order 10450, which deemed perverts subversive per se.

The scope of the investigations was remarkable. FBI special agents hired informants, tape-recorded meetings, collected lists of members of gay organizations, photographed participants in early homosexual-rights marches, and investigated advertisers in gay publications. Newsletters from Mattachine, the Daughters of Bilitis, and other groups were meticulously catalogued both in various FBI field offices and at FBI headquarters in Washington. Agents secretly tape-recorded Mattachine Society lectures in their entirety, and regularly enlisted informants to attend all

Mattachine meetings and conventions and collect names of those in attendance. The lists were forwarded to Washington. A twenty-two-page file on the 1959 Mattachine convention in Denver, for example, shows that informants at the convention furnished copies of the conference minutes, financial reports, and even the group's luncheon and dinner menus. Names culled from the minutes were passed to local FBI field offices for further investigations.

The FBI's analysis of all this intelligence sometimes bordered on the comical. The special agent in charge of Seattle's FBI office confidently wrote Hoover in 1962 that gays could be identified because they all wore "a diamond ring on the little finger of the right hand." This secret sign, he wrote, was "especially true in the eastern part of the United States." The same agent provided a long glossary of gay slang, including such terms as *butch*, *drag*, and *mad queen*. A long political analysis offered by a San Francisco FBI agent in the early 1960s concluded that it was inconceivable that the "limp-wrist population" could ever achieve political power despite their nascent attempts at political organizing, because "homosexuals as a group are not interested in elections generally."

Hoover's obsession with homosexuals raised eyebrows at the Justice Department, where the FBI director's sexual orientation was a subject of considerable discussion. When Clyde Tolson went to the hospital for surgery, for example, Attorney General Robert Kennedy jokingly asked whether it was for a hysterectomy.

None of this diminished Hoover's determination to thwart any group that might publicly link him to homosexuality. When gay activist Frank Kameny began including Hoover on the mailing list for the Mattachine Society's newsletter, FBI agents personally visited Kameny at his home and demanded that the director's name be dropped from further mailings. That was when Kameny realized the FBI files were extensive. They had come directly to him, even though his name appeared nowhere on the newsletter.

In the mid-1960s, when Kameny escalated his protests against federal discrimination, Hoover directed his agents to escalate their monitoring of the nascent gay movement. FBI records came to include the license-plate numbers of every participant in a 1965 picket of the Pentagon, with the notation that the field office would "endeavor to identify" a marcher whose car carried a congressional staff license plate.

Through Hoover's prodigious investigations, the government began amassing impressive lists of gays that proved useful to other agencies engaged in the business of hunting homosexuals—to the Civil Service Commission, for instance, and to various military branches running background checks on job applicants. Intelligence agencies for the Air Force, Army, and Navy appeared to be so impressed with the FBI results that they began working with local law enforcement to compile their own homosexual lists. In October 1960, the Army initiated Project 220, whereby it gathered the names of 220 men arrested by San Francisco police for homosexual activity in the five previous months. Of these, fifteen people had security clearances or served as civilian or uniformed personnel in the armed forces. The Army was so pleased with these results, it instigated Project 440, expanding its search through police records to Salt Lake City, Portland, San Diego, and San Francisco. This effort uncovered one agent of the Central Intelligence Agency, three sailors, three members of the Air Force, ten Army recruits, and five civilian employees of industrial firms with security clearances; their names were promptly turned over to government authorities, according to FBI files.

As the influence of moderate gay groups such as Mattachine and Daughters of Bilitis waned in 1969, FBI surveillance of the proliferating chapters of the radical Gay Liberation Front increased dramatically. Within six weeks of the Stonewall riot, Hoover directed the FBI's New York field office to "identify officers, aims and objectives" of the "Fag Liberation Front." The order spread nationally, ultimately targeting twenty-five GLF chapters for FBI surveillance. These investigations into the GLF and its successor organizations were such a well-established beat within the FBI that they continued until 1975, three years after Hoover's death.

By the 1960s, the FBI could no longer claim national security to justify their investigations. As early as 1962, the special agent in charge of the Seattle FBI office had written Hoover that it was inappropriate to classify the probes as "security" investigations because "evidence of the existence of subversive activity, etc., appears to be almost totally lacking." But scores of internal FBI memoranda showed that the probes continued nonetheless, personally directed by Hoover, without legal justification. The case of J. Edgar Hoover may be the first case of the American gay movement gaining a powerful enemy not by offending heterosexuals but by offending a homosexual.

BY THE TIME Jerry Rosanbalm was put under observation at Valley Forge General Hospital in the last days of 1969, questions were beginning to arise about the wisdom of denying security clearances to all homosexuals. In those same weeks, Frank Kameny, the gay activist who so vexed Hoover, was promoting a federal-court challenge to the security regulations. The case involved Benning Wentworth, a thirty-five-year-old employee of a firm doing government business that required security clearances for its employees. In interviews for his clearance, Wentworth had acknowledged having sex with between seventy-five and one hundred men in the fourteen years since 1955. His interrogators asked for all the details: Did he engage in oral or anal sex? Who put what where? In hearings before federal security panels, Kameny noted that such detailed questions were virtually never asked of heterosexuals.

Wentworth had hardly kept his homosexuality secret. It was difficult to argue that Soviet agents could get far with Wentworth by threatening to expose his homosexuality; he had already discussed it in *The New York Times,* *The Wall Street Journal,* and *The Washington Post.* The security clearance board, however, maintained that whatever the specifics of Wentworth's case, he was still part of a group "amenable" to blackmail. The courts agreed. In January 1970, the U.S. Court of Appeals ruled to uphold Judge Carl McGowan's opinion that the Defense Department regulations "include ample indication that a practicing homosexual may pose serious problems . . . emotional instability and possible subjection to sinister pressures and influences which have traditionally been the lot of homosexuals living in what is, for better or worse, a society still strongly oriented towards heterosexuality." Denying clearances, McGowan ruled, was consistent with "an overall common-sense view of the particular situation."

Gay organizers were optimistic nonetheless. "With Joshua blowing his horns outside the walls of Jericho, it would not be surprising if they [the Pentagon] did give in," opined *The Advocate,* a gay newspaper. Besides, the courts had been getting more liberal for the last decade; ultimately, the judges would see the rightness of the homosexual cause.

What gay advocates could not know then was that in 1969 and 1970 the courts were as liberal as they would probably be for the rest of the century; the walls of Jericho were safe for the moment.

————————

NEARLY FORTY YEARS after the antihomosexual regulations on national security became official federal policy, the Pentagon's own agency on personnel security matters, the Defense Personnel Security Research and Education Center, conducted a lengthy study that found that there was no justification for the conclusion that homosexuals were security risks. Moreover, it added, there had never been any justification. The notion was merely an anachronism attributable to the nationwide excesses of the McCarthy era, and to the more personal eccentricities of one FBI director.

"Once begun, bureaucratic policies and procedures are resistant to change," the report concluded. "Although no empirical data have been developed to support any connection between homosexuality and security, it is reasonable to assume that Hoover's beliefs have continued to influence more recent security practice. . . . Whatever the basis of Hoover's beliefs, he was not privy to the wealth of scientific information currently available."

It is a tribute to bureaucratic resistance that even when this report was written in 1991, the Department of Defense declined to change a single word in its official policies that assumed gay servicemen would create "breaches in the national security." And it is a tribute to the tenacity of politics and prejudice that the antihomosexual regulations enacted in a period of national hysteria in the 1950s would reach across four decades to darken the careers and aspirations of thousands of Americans.

11

Endings

OVERHEAD, HELICOPTERS with loudspeakers blasted Christmas carols, the melodies distorted by the *chop-chop-chop*. A strangely dissonant "Silent Night" was barely audible over the constant sound of gunfire. Red and green Army flares burst above the canal to mark the approaching holiday, but to Navy Lieutenant (junior grade) Armistead Maupin the sight was garish, the flares mingling with the flashes of real firefights over the Vinh Te Canal separating Vietnam from Cambodia.

Maupin had been looking for danger when he volunteered to go to Vietnam earlier that year. Assigned to a protocol office in Saigon, he appealed personally to his boss, Admiral Elmo Zumwalt, for a combat assignment. He envied those who wore the Combat Action Ribbon for having been fired upon. He wished a sniper would take a potshot at him— and miss, of course—but come close enough to earn Armistead that ribbon.

His job in Chau Doc was to make sure the Navy did not fire on the Army, and the Army did not fire on the Navy, and that none of them fired on innocent civilians transporting their crops across the small canal. Most evenings he spent at an old terra-cotta-colored French Foreign Legion post with open porches, high ceilings, and spacious rooms with geckos crawling on the walls. The building headquartered the Construction Brigade, and at night they showed movies like *Gone With the Wind* while bats flew around the room.

Those were the images he kept from Vietnam years: red and green flares during a Christmas Eve firefight, and bat shadows over the white colonnades of Tara. As for the subtext that had brought him to Vietnam in the first place, it remained a subtext. He was busy with the business of war and of staying alive. He wrote colorful letters home portraying hardship, and then cavalierly dismissing the danger with a quip. He knew the stories would terrify his mother and make his father secretly proud.

To a large degree, the war succeeded in putting Maupin's conflicts about his manhood on a back burner.

And that is where they remained a week after Christmas Eve, on the night of December 31, 1969, when the Construction Brigade decided to make honorary Seabees out of Maupin and a young Army lieutenant—after subjecting them to the appropriate initiation. With much beer and cajoling, the Seabees first made the two lieutenants kneel at a chopping block, where they were given axes and sheets of paper to chop up. After a few minutes of practice, the two lieutenants were ordered to take off their shirts and, blindfolded, to chop away. The Seabees cheered wildly while the two men hatcheted furiously. When their blindfolds were removed, they discovered they had not been chopping paper but their own shirts. They were expected to wear their tattered shirts the rest of the night; it was part of the joke.

As the New Year's Eve celebration wore on, the two initiates began wrestling, much to everyone's amusement. In the grappling, tumbling about on the tile floors, they ripped the torn shirts off each other and continued their playful fight, clinging to each other and pushing each other away at the same time. And in the blackness of the Asian sky there were flares and gunshots, decreeing the New Year and an end to the decade of the 1960s.

TO THE IDEALISTS of that time, the decade passing into history was a time of great beginnings: It was the dawning of the Age of Aquarius, a time when the Woodstock Nation would displace the gray-flannel dwarfs of the Establishment. Few on the greener side of the generation gap doubted that this was inevitable, if not for the clear superiority of the flower children's values of peace and love, than because the older generation, and all the materialistic conformity it fostered, would eventually die out.

While the sixties still had much drama to play out, particularly in the turbulent months ahead in 1970, this watershed ultimately marked less a time of beginnings than an epoch of endings. The sixties would have a lasting impact on the culture, not because it created the template for the future but because it marked the conclusion of values of the recent past.

Before this, individuals strove to merge with, or at least emulate, society's shared ideas of God and country. In the era that was beginning, people would seek to distinguish themselves, test other ideas, discover individuality. Individuality did not inevitably make people hippies, as the hippies learned in the following years, much to their distress, but it did make the conformist-oriented values born of the fifties and early sixties passé.

The past had ended, but the future did not have a shape. Perhaps no public-policy quandary reflected this better than the Vietnam War. A year into the Nixon presidency, it was plain there had been no secret plan to end the war. Nobody liked the war, it seemed; the peace movement had scored that victory. But nobody knew what else to do, either. President Nixon would not simply withdraw all the troops, because that would look as if the United States would not stand up to an enemy. Instead, there was now talk of Vietnamization of the war: training the Vietnamese to take over American jobs during a long, gradual withdrawal process. This allowed the United States to preserve a staunch masculine image while still getting itself off the firing line. In those last days of the 1960s, the United States was in Vietnam for much the same reason Armistead Maupin and so many others were—to prove manhood.

While the rule of manhood as the dominant cultural imperative was being reconsidered, as was everything conventional in American life at that time, it was not at all clear what would replace masculinity as a guiding national principle. What was apparent was that women and gays would no longer sublimate their own identities and aspirations to unjust principles prescribed by a biased culture. By January 1, 1970, a careful observer could see that the old days were over, although few, even a score of years later, could predict what social configuration might eventually assimilate the hopes of these people.

AT CHAU DOC, after the New Year was properly seen in, Lieutenant Maupin's initiation partner invited him to his hooch not far from the Seabee brigade headquarters. There, the lieutenant showed Maupin a copy of *Avant-Garde* magazine, a cutting-edge periodical considered quite racy where Armistead came from because of its explicit discussion of sex. The lieutenant turned to a W. H. Auden poem entitled "A Day for a Lay," which described a protracted blowjob. Finally, the lieutenant showed Maupin an audiotape a friend had made of the newly released movie *The Boys in the Band.* Maupin wondered briefly whether the lieutenant was trying to tell him something, but only briefly—he still believed that he was one of a handful of homosexuals on the planet and that homosexuals were derelicts who populated boweries and back alleys. The battlefront would be the last place to find a homosexual, Maupin thought. It never occurred to him that the lieutenant might be like himself, in Vietnam to prove something. So after the show-and-tell, Maupin excused himself, returned to his hooch, and steeled himself to greet the first morning of the 1970s with a hangover.

JANUARY 1970
VALLEY FORGE GENERAL HOSPITAL
PHOENIXVILLE, PENNSYLVANIA

AT THE UPPER ECHELONS of United States Army military intelligence, decisions were being made to end Jerry Rosanbalm's long ordeal. "This ofc interposes no objection to issuing sub an honorable discharge," one priority memo instructed. "It is suggested that the issuance of such discharge be used as a bartering point to influence subj to submit to poly exam regarding the security aspects of this case." Apparently concerned about the implications of a court-martial showing that a well-placed spy in both Europe and Vietnam was happily homosexual and ready to discuss it publicly, the deputy director of counterintelligence for the Army in Europe suggested, "Subject should be released from service under honorable conditions. This would facilitate expeditious release with least amount of publicity."

Jerry Rosanbalm knew he had won on the day that an employee of the Department of Defense showed up at Valley Forge General Hospital and hooked Jerry up to a polygraph machine.

Two days later, Jerry got word that he would receive a medical retirement with benefits to allow him job retraining, because the physical disabilities from the Tet offensive precluded him from doing any serious physical labor. The Army wanted him to stay at Valley Forge to continue physical therapy on his shoulder for a few months and he agreed.

FEBRUARY 1970
WESTOVER AIR FORCE BASE
CHICOPEE, MASSACHUSETTS

IF ANY FOREIGN AGENT CAME to Rich McGuire and threatened to expose him as a homosexual, McGuire had long ago decided that he would go to the Office of Special Investigations and turn himself in. Long ago, in this case, being a relative time, since, in the winter of 1970, Airman First Class Richard Joseph McGuire was just six months past his twentieth birthday.

That his line of work required such contemplations had become clear to McGuire when the Air Force sent a press release to his hometown newspaper, which printed that upon completion of basic training McGuire would be assigned to Lowry Air Force Base in Colorado. Rich's mom proudly clipped the story, along with its accompanying picture of the dark-haired airman in his crisp new uniform. McGuire never set foot on Lowry and the Air Force had never intended to send him there. Instead, he was assigned to cryptographic school at Lackland Air Force Base in San Antonio, where he learned how to encode the most secret of military information.

The school was the highest of high-security operations. No book or paper ever left the building where classes were held and at the end of each day every book was inventoried and every page of every book was counted to assure enemy eyes would never see American encryption methods. Even though its students were selected from the crème de la crème of Air Force recruits, the school had a high washout rate. Men who did not make the grade became food-service workers in the enlisted men's mess.

After his tech school, McGuire went to work at the Combat Operations Center at Westover Air Force Base for the Eighteenth Communications Squadron with the Ninety-ninth Bomb Wing of the Eighth Air Force. The Combat Operations Center, or COC, was a five-story office building contained entirely in a mountain on the eastern edge of the Berkshires adjacent to Westover. From the beginning, McGuire's superiors impressed upon him the importance of maintaining the utter secrecy of his work. Any comment, no matter how innocuous, could be pieced together with another comment to undermine national security. You had to be careful. You did not want to end up at the military prison at Fort Leavenworth. Such talk impressed Rich McGuire and sometimes kept him awake at night with thoughts about what he would do if he was threatened with blackmail.

Everything in Rich's routine informed him of the clandestine world he now inhabited. There was, for example, Hotel Juliet, code name for the daily ritual of breaking the international Air Force teletype circuit and inserting a new punch card to feed the computers new secret codes. Air sorties, bombing missions, and, presumably, the end of the world through mutually assured nuclear destruction relied on these codes for approval. They were issued from the extraordinarily high-tech COC command room, which looked like a set from *Dr. Strangelove,* and were linked directly to Washington and Vietnam, Germany and the Strategic Air Command Headquarters near Omaha. Even the procedure was announced in code. Noncommissioned officers curtly intoned "HJOM," which meant "Hotel Juliet, Old Man," the signal for all but the highest-classified personnel to skedaddle so that Hotel Juliet could be fulfilled.

Such responsibilities were heady stuff for a young man who had never spent more than a few days outside Newark (pronounced New-Ark), Delaware. It affirmed that he had been right to join the Air Force rather than wait to get drafted as some brainless infantry ground-pounder in the Army. He had never really considered college. His dad worked the docks for the Tidewater Oil refinery and, like all the working-class Catholic kids he knew, Rich believed that everybody served their time. That McGuire served his time in a job he loved so much was especially lucky, he thought.

Except for one thing—the secret thing he kept carefully encrypted in his deepest thoughts—the secret of his difference. He had heard that some people went through phases of this sort and so he waited for his phase to be finished, at which time he expected to become attracted to girls. Then he would go steady, get married, have kids, and move to the suburbs like everybody else.

But it never happened. In Air Force technical school, an instructor sometimes mentioned homosexuality, usually in the context of security risks. "If any of you are cocksuckers, watch out," one instructor joked. Everyone laughed raucously. Rich felt his temperature rising and his ears ring, and he prayed no one could see the blood rushing to his face.

Perhaps there were other homosexuals in the United States Air Force, he thought, but he would not have been surprised to learn authoritatively that he was the only one. It felt that lonely.

McGuire had never had a real sexual encounter, but once he had come close to fulfilling his fantasies. It had been on a weekend in tech school when Rich and three other airmen had driven to Corpus Christi to drink beer, watch TV, and cruise chicks. Not having much money, the four men shared two single rooms and slept two to a bed. Late on the last night of the weekend, Rich lay awake while his buddy slept. He glanced over at the other man, who was turned away from him, and gently laid his hand on the other man's thigh. The airman mumbled, "No," but immediately turned over, displaying evidence that at least part of him was aroused by the advance. Rich had heard what homosexuals do and he slipped down on the man. It tasted as if he was sucking his thumb. It was not at all enjoyable. Rich stopped immediately. The whole episode lasted only seconds, during which time the other airman appeared thoroughly asleep and unaware of what was happening.

The next morning, as they loaded Rich's car for the trip back to Massachusetts, the other airman pointed toward a young woman walking by and observed, "That's what I want."

"But that's not what I want," Rich answered, startled at his own candor.

"But that's what I want," his friend said.

And that was all that was ever said or done. That Rich McGuire's sexual history was so slight would prove ironic, considering all that was about to happen to him.

FEBRUARY 21, 1970
THE WHITE HOUSE
WASHINGTON, D.C.

WITH PRESIDENT NIXON beside him, former Defense Secretary Thomas Gates delivered the final report of the commission the President had established nearly a year before to study whether the draft could be ended.

"We unanimously believe that the nation's interests will be better served by an all-volunteer force, supported by an effective stand-by draft, than by a mixed force of volunteers and conscripts," the report concluded, "that steps should be taken promptly to move in this direction and that the first indispensable step is to remove the present inequity in the pay of men serving their first term in the armed forces."

The Gates Commission believed the draft could be ended by June 1971 largely by adding economic incentives. To build an all-volunteer force of 2.5 million, the armed forces should recruit about 325,000 soldiers a year, the report advised. Though 500,000 were enlisting every year during the late 1960s, strategists estimated that only about half were true

volunteers and that the other half volunteered only to get better assignments than those typically given to draftees. Gates's plan increased the
pay for junior enlisted personnel and officers. In lieu of a standing Army
as massive as it was in 1969, about 3.5 million men, the ready Reserves
and state National Guard would shoulder a larger share of military responsibilities during a crisis. Projecting for an all-volunteer force of 2.5
million, about the size of the pre-Vietnam military, the annual added cost
would be $3.3 billion for the next fiscal year.

The plan immediately provoked a maelstrom of controversy, not the
least of which occurred in the military itself. Senior Pentagon officials
were distraught at the prospect of losing their legions of new soldiers.
Even Nixon's defense secretary, Melvin Laird, commented that he could
not imagine many people volunteering for duty that might take them to
Vietnam. Nevertheless, both Nixon and Laird made their positions clear:
There would be an all-volunteer Army.

The push for "a professional Army," as Nixon liked to call it, was
dictated as much by politics as by military considerations. The Gates
Commission's report capped a year during which the administration had
worked furiously to defuse antiwar sentiment on college campuses. Draft
calls were slashed dramatically from levels earlier projected. To alleviate
some of the many inequities of Selective Service, Nixon was paring away
at various deferments, which tended to allow the more affluent to avoid
military service while forcing the less prosperous into uniform. But none
of this did much to calm protests, as the next few months demonstrated
dramatically.

———

ABOUT A WEEK AFTER the Gates press conference, Airman First Class Rich
McGuire received orders for temporary duty at McCoy Air Force Base
in Orlando. An entire bomb wing, the 306th, had been dispatched to
Asia, putting the base in dire need of cryptographers. McGuire was in a
plane on the way to Florida even before his CO had issued his orders.
There was no time for formalities. Some escalation of the bombing in
Southeast Asia was afoot, McGuire knew, and it involved an awesome
number of airplanes. Like everybody else, however, he had to read the
newspapers to learn about the invasion of Cambodia.

MAY 1, 1970
VALLEY FORGE GENERAL HOSPITAL
PHOENIXVILLE, PENNSYLVANIA

"YOU ARE NOT A HOMOSEXUAL," the psychiatrist told Jerry Rosanbalm
confidently. "You're neurotic."

According to the doctor, whatever homosexual feelings the Army captain may have had were merely the aftereffects of the trauma he had suffered during the Tet offensive. With therapy, he would be cured.

With this pronouncement, the psychiatrist signed off on Jerry Rosanbalm's last physical in the United States Army. It was a strange conclusion, Rosanbalm thought. His file was full of his open affirmations of his homosexuality, but he saw the military logic behind it. If homosexuals were security risks and bad soldiers, as the Army insisted, then a decorated war veteran who, by their own barrage of polygraph tests, was not a threat to national security could not be a homosexual. That ruling allowed Rosanbalm to retire like an ordinary wounded soldier at 50 percent disability. The word came down on May 1, one day after President Nixon announced the invasion of Cambodia and one day before Rosanbalm's twenty-ninth birthday.

Jerry felt relief but no jubilation. It had been more than a year since counterintelligence agents had broken through his door in Munich, and he had spent every moment since then on red alert. Though he believed he had beaten the system, he still felt fundamentally violated as he packed his belongings for his final exit from the Army. He knew that if he had been lying in bed with a Czech girl that March morning a year earlier, none of the ensuing trauma would have happened. Rosanbalm had entered the Army believing in his country. In college, he had earned a degree in government; but once he was a civilian again, he could never believe that politics really mattered. It would be another twenty years before he would vote in an election. The government had taken a year of his life and forever dyed it the color of misery in his memory, and that was bad enough. But the Army had also robbed him of his faith in America.

Rosanbalm drove away from the Army in a green Ford Fairlane he had bought when he was in Officer Candidate School four years earlier. In the Army, he had learned to pack light, and everything fit nicely in the car. He was leaving for a life as a college student in New York. He would lose himself in the city, a more bitter man than he had ever imagined he would be.

FEW WEEKS IN AMERICAN HISTORY defined disillusion more than the days following President Nixon's announcement of the invasion of Cambodia. The President justified the assault by American and South Vietnamese troops as necessary to deprive the North Vietnamese of their sanctuaries and supply lines. Privately, the administration hoped it would encourage North Vietnam to negotiate more earnestly at the Paris peace talks, thereby allowing the United States to withdraw more quickly. To the peace movement and to many moderates, however, the invasion represented another escalation of war at a time when the government should have been seeking peace.

Within days, fierce protests spread to almost every college campus in the nation. At Kent State University, a blue-collar commuter campus near Cleveland, students burned the campus ROTC building while chanting, "One-two-three-four, we don't want your fucking war." ROTC structures had been favorite targets of protesters for several years, so the arson, by the standards of the times, was not too unusual, nor was the decision by Ohio's Governor Rhodes to call out National Guard troops, who had become fixtures on many college campuses by this time. What was unusual was the decision, on the afternoon of May 4, to fire live ammunition into a crowd of antiwar protesters, wounding nine and killing four. Those shots turned the generation gap into a war.

The killings at Kent State and the slaying of two more students at Jackson State College in Mississippi days later electrified the nation's campuses. One-third of the students throughout the country boycotted classes in a student strike that drew broad support from college staff and professors. Protesting was so fierce that many administrators contemplated simply ending classes and shutting down campuses a month before school was due to close for the summer. With authorities ready to kill people who protested government policy, the leftists' calls for revolution did not seem so farfetched anymore.

The forces of reaction unified, as well. Hard hats marched through the streets of Manhattan in support of Nixon and the Cambodian invasion. The group that the President had a few months earlier dubbed "the Silent Majority" was beginning to get noisy. Vice President Spiro Agnew launched bitter attacks on the media and on the "radical liberals," or the radiclibs, who were corrupting the nation.

The violence, coming after years of race rioting, political assassinations, and general social disruptions genuinely scared people. Nothing seemed safe anymore. The United States was becoming a polarized nation. Where once politicians had won elections by capitalizing on Americans' fears about outsiders, such as Communists, now they played on the fears of one American for another. It was a potent political formula, particularly for the Republican party, and one guaranteed to be successful, given that most people prefer the status quo to change. In 1970, those who demanded change were radiclibs and antiwar protesters. In decades to come, politicians would use other groups to appeal to the nation's fear and to try to win elections.

MAY 1970
MCCOY AIR FORCE BASE
ORLANDO, FLORIDA

WHILE MUCH OF HIS GENERATION mutinied, Rich McGuire was having the time of his life in Florida. He had sneaked back to Delaware for a weekend to retrieve the "Gray Whale," his silver-gray '61 Thunderbird with white sidewalls and a hot 390 engine. He had an aunt in Daytona, so every weekend Rich cruised over to the beach with his AM radio blasting the top-ten hits on WLOF-AM: "American Woman" and "Bridge Over Troubled Water," "Woodstock" and "Spirit in the Sky." The Beatles had just announced they were breaking up, and the group's two current hits, "Let It Be" and "Long and Winding Road," played endlessly on the radio. They were wonderful songs to sing along with as he sped down Highway 4 to Daytona in his starched tan uniform, the wind blowing through his dark hair. Driving through Volusia County, it seemed as though God had personally scented the air for him with the blossoming orange groves that lined the highway.

Rich had never seen anything like Daytona's beach subculture, populated with tanned beach boys who had worked every muscle group at the gym before oiling up and heading for the surf. Rich did not dare attempt an assignation, but he did make a discovery at an adult bookstore in Daytona: nudist magazines with pictures of naked men. He also purchased a few copies of *After Dark,* an entertainment magazine clearly marketed for gay men but that studiously avoided any overt references to homosexuality. These magazines represented the sum total of Rich's sex life.

McGuire's temporary assignment ended with the return of the 306th Bomb Wing from its air-support mission in the Cambodian invasion. He went back to Westover with an envelopeful of commendations for his cryptographic work. According to all of his evaluations, Rich McGuire was the best of the best, and, on June 1, the Air Force rewarded him with sergeant's stripes.

He had not been back in Massachusetts for more than a week when, according to Air Force documents, on the night of June 11, he was awakened in the middle of the night by a loud pounding on his door. He knew immediately what it was: a shakedown. Drugs were a growing problem in the Air Force, and the brass had ordered surprise inspections to uncover contraband. McGuire had started groggily toward the door when he remembered the nudist magazines that he kept in his briefcase. He dashed to his locker and pulled out the cache. There was no place to hide it. He ran to the window and pushed it out.

"I'll take that," said a voice outside. "What room are you in?"

His heart plummeting to his stomach, Rich gave his room number.

NCOs completed the inspection without saying a word about the briefcase. The next morning, sick to his stomach with fear, Rich went to work at the COC as usual.

Everything was normal.

After a few hours, Rich went into the bathroom and threw up. He recalled that he was sitting in a stall recovering his composure when two airmen came into the bathroom discussing some guy who had gotten caught during the previous night's shakedown.

"Was he queer?" one of them asked. McGuire was surprised he did not hear a note of disapprobation in the question, just curiosity.

"Who knows?"

"What's going to happen?" the other asked.

Sitting on the commode, staring at the cool gray wall of the stall, Sergeant McGuire wondered the same thing.

12

Interrogations

JUNE 12, 1970
WESTOVER AIR FORCE BASE
CHICOPEE, MASSACHUSETTS

IN ACCORDANCE WITH the Fifth Amendment of the United States Constitution, the Uniform Code of Military Justice forbids any branch of the military from forcing soldiers to incriminate themselves for any violation of military law. Military regulations specify that statements acquired by the "use of coercion (physical or psychological pressure)" or "unlawful inducement (empty promises)" are inadmissible as evidence into any military proceeding. Because of these regulations, the investigative agencies of each branch of the armed forces all have written policies banning coercion during interviews.

Each branch of the service adamantly denies that it ever engages in such tactics. However, every branch of the service routinely resorts to every form of psychological pressure in order to coerce statements from suspected homosexuals. The practices are so routine as to appear to be official policy, even though such a policy is officially forbidden. As a practical matter, one can understand why coercion is necessary. Consider the dilemma for investigators. They can only rarely find evidence of homosexuality in a soldier's service record. Rarely do aggrieved "victims" volunteer as witnesses. Nor are investigators likely to find direct proof that homosexual deeds actually took place. Given this, illegal coercive interrogations are not an unfortunate side effect of antigay regulations; they are virtually the only way to execute the work that the regulations demand.

As soon as the antihomosexual regulations went into effect in the early 1940s, military investigators learned that the only sure way to prove their cases against gays was to force suspects into supplying the self-incriminating evidence. The nature of the interrogations changed little from the 1940s to the 1970s; they would change little from the 1970s to the 1990s. The procedures, after all, worked. They tended to be indelicate, though, and, to the uninitiated, terrifying.

This was what Sergeant Rich McGuire was going to find out on the morning after the shakedown inspection, when his sergeant told him he was wanted at headquarters. There, two agents from the Office of Special Investigations escorted Rich to the backseat of a nondescript blue Plymouth Valiant with black-walled tires. As the car sped away, Rich noticed there were no handles on the insides of the back doors.

THE MILITARY MANUALS on criminal investigations agree that choosing the proper interview site is crucial. The manual for the Army Criminal Investigation Division, for example, suggests that friendly witnesses should be interviewed at their homes or wherever they are most comfortable. "With suspects and hostile witnesses," the manual continues, "it is best to conduct the questioning in a proper interrogation room . . . or in any other available location where the investigator enjoys the psychological advantage."

The car did not drive to the lawyers' offices, where McGuire thought such an interview would take place. Instead, it drove to the Stonybrook Nuclear Arsenal in a remote corner of the base and pulled in front of a quaint New England–style wooden frame house with shutters. The agents ushered McGuire into the house, down a flight of stairs and into a large subterranean basement room lined with cinder blocks and cement. To Rich, the expansive basement seemed the size of a warehouse, certainly much larger than the house above. Its air was damp and musty. Rich was not a large man, and he felt even smaller here.

In the center of the huge chamber was a small, thickly padded cell. McGuire was guided inside. The cell contained only one table, two chairs, and a very bright light.

It was a room where OSI agents definitely enjoyed psychological advantage. More than twenty years later when Rich tried to obtain the government records of his interrogations under the Freedom of Information Act, the OSI insisted it did not have a single piece of paper with his name on it. In fact, they maintained, there was no record of anybody named Richard Joseph McGuire in any file of any security agency of the United States. It was an odd assertion, considering McGuire's copious documentation of security questionnaires he had filled out for his top-secret clearance in the Air Force. What follows, therefore, is McGuire's account of his interrogation, buttressed by Air Force documentation that the service moved to investigate him for homosexuality in those very days. More significantly, however, McGuire's account is corroborated by several hundred other gay soldiers who have cited interrogations so utterly identical that they appear to be completely scripted, chapter and verse.

OSI agents read McGuire his rights. He did not have to answer questions and he could demand a lawyer right then. The two investigators looked angry. Rich did not want to get them any more pissed off than they already were. Besides, he had not done anything wrong. Should he get a lawyer? They suggested he should do an "interview" now; Rich thought they knew what was best.

———————————

CRIMINAL-INVESTIGATION MANUALS propose three principal means of interrogation. For friendly witnesses, the indirect method is suggested, more of a rambling conversation than a question-and-answer session, designed to make the witness comfortable, and induce him to supply maximum information. For the suspects most likely to be guilty, there is the direct approach. According to the Army manual: "In using this approach, the investigator assumes an air of confidence with regard to, and stresses the evidence or testimony indicative of the guilt of the suspect. In the direct approach, the investigator behaves in an accusatory manner displaying complete belief in the suspect's guilt and strives to learn why the suspect did what he did rather than if the suspect did that of which he was suspected."

The third method is called "logic and reasoning" and is employed for the most nefarious criminal suspects. "The habitual criminal who feels no sense of wrongdoing in having committed a crime must normally be convinced by the investigator that his guilt can be easily established or is already established by testimony or available evidence. The investigator should point out to the suspect the futility of denying his guilt. The suspect should be confronted at every turn with testimony and evidence to refute his alibis, that his guilt is definitely a matter against which no lies will defend."

Interrogation techniques in the Army, Air Force, Marines, and Navy all indicate that homosexuals are dealt with as the worst kind of criminal suspects, almost always deserving of direct interview techniques, and, when this fails, logic and reasoning. The tact of subjecting homosexuals to interrogation techniques reserved for "habitual criminals" is odd considering that the offense in question is not a violation of a criminal statute but an administrative regulation against homosexuals. Only in instances of copulation proved beyond a shadow of a doubt can criminal charges of sodomy be pressed in a court-martial, which is why most gays are not court-martialed but, rather, administratively processed out of the military. The tougher interrogative style cannot be justified by military law, but it does reflect the military's position, at least during those times when the military chooses to enforce its regulations. And the harshest techniques were to be employed that day, June 12, 1970, against a very frightened twenty-year-old named Rich McGuire.

By McGuire's account, one OSI agent stood in front of him and one stood behind. One was kind and understanding; the other was harsh and confrontational. They alternated; the tough agent began. They knew McGuire was part of an entire network of homosexuals in the Air Force, he said. There was no denying it. They already had the evidence. McGuire could make it easy on himself if he helped them flesh out their case. They needed names, a list of other gays.

McGuire insisted he knew no other homosexuals. He had never had sex himself.

"If you help us, we'll help you," the other, more sympathetic OSI agent said.

There was nothing he could do to help, McGuire said. He did not know any other gays.

The OSI agents then proceeded to tell Rich whom he spent time with, who his friends were, what he did in his spare time. To the young sergeant, it seemed as if there had been an OSI agent whose only duties consisted of following him. "So you see," the agent concluded, "we already know practically everything about you, and we *will* find out the rest. You could save us a lot of trouble by telling us the rest now."

When this tack did not work, the tough agent pulled out the briefcase McGuire had shoved through the window the previous night. Gingerly, he held out each magazine and started thumbing the pages, pointing at pictures of men.

"Do you like that? Does that turn you on? Is that cute?"

It was the first time in McGuire's life that he had ever discussed his sexuality. His code was broken. He broke down and told them what he believed they knew already, about the night at the motel in Texas with the other airman. The agents seemed very pleased. "Did the airman ejaculate?" the nicer agent asked solicitously.

"No," McGuire replied. Neither of them had. He had never ejaculated with anybody else.

Neither agent believed that, and they demanded Rich repeat the story. Then they demanded he repeat it again, and again, and again; and they tore into every detail of it, trying to get Rich to change any part of the story. But he could not, because he told them the truth.

Up to this point, the questioning had been entirely within the law. The agents did not really have proof of a homosexual ring in the Air Force, nor did they have any evidence on McGuire other than a few magazines, which would not have been enough to support even an Article 15 nonjudicial punishment. Rich didn't know this. He believed that agents of the United States government would never lie to him. But there is no rule that investigators have to tell the truth when conducting an interrogation. As the Army's *Manual of Law Enforcement Investigations* states, "Trickery and deceit . . . will not render [a statement] inadmissible unless the tactics amount to coercion in and of themselves."

What followed next, however, elevated trickery and deceit to the level of coercion. By McGuire's account, the tough agent spoke gravely: "The punishment for what you've done is a twenty-thousand-dollar fine and life imprisonment at hard labor," he said. If Rich could not pay the fine, the government could seize his parents' home to secure the money. Did his parents know he was queer? Did they know they were about to lose their home because of their queer son?

It would be so much easier if Rich just told them what he knew now, the nicer agent said. Just get it all off his chest. All they wanted were the names of other homosexuals. Rich insisted he had told them everything.

Where would his parents live, they asked, once they lost their home?

And one more thing. Rich was to tell no one of this investigation, or even that he was being questioned. If he told, he could go to prison for obstruction of justice. This was a national security investigation.

McGuire was shattered by the time the OSI agents had finished and led him back up the flight of stairs. This time, a slightly overweight brown-haired woman sat waiting at a typewriter. Rich cringed when she took the OSI agents' handwritten notes about the details of his sex life and began typing them up.

"Don't worry," the nicer agent said to him kindly. "She types a hundred and twenty words a minute. She's not even reading it."

Minutes later, Rich signed the statement, which included the routine assertion that the OSI had done nothing to coerce him into making his confession. It had been morning when the OSI agents first took him into the little house at the weapons arsenal; it was dark when he left.

IF RICH HAD KNOWN names of other homosexuals, he surely would have given them up to the OSI by the end of the interrogation. Most did. By a conservative estimate, that is how at least 80 percent of the gays who were ejected from the military services were discovered from the 1970s through the early 1990s. Even as OSI agents at Westover interviewed Rich McGuire, other OSI personnel at Offutt Air Force Base were going great guns on a gay investigation instigated by an intercepted letter to a twenty-five-year-old staff sergeant. As Staff Sergeant Richard Burchill later told *The Advocate*, the OSI had threatened him with criminal prosecution and imprisonment if he did not give the names of all the homosexuals he knew. If he did cooperate, the OSI would drop prosecution and allow him to stay in the Air Force. Burchill, who had entered the Air Force at the age of eighteen, worked as a security policeman with the Strategic Air Command. The son of a thirty-one-year Air Force veteran, Burchill had planned to make the Air Force his career and he was desperate to stay in the service. Believing both the threats and the promises, he gave the OSI a sixty-two-page statement, including numerous names of gays in all branches of the military.

OSI agents fanned out from there and continued investigating those whom Burchill had named. By April 1970, they had the names of 270 suspected homosexuals, according to a story in *Air Force Times*, although many were only nicknames or first names. Ultimately, the list included fifty-five military personnel and seventy-six civilians. At Offutt alone, nineteen airmen were discharged, most with undesirable discharges. One major was allowed to resign. By May, Burchill told *The Advocate*, the Air Force had gathered nearly seven hundred names to investigate, presumably by taking other young airmen into small rooms and threatening them with prison. For all his assistance, Burchill was rewarded with a discharge—and an uncertain future.

HIS STOMACH KNOTTED and cramped after his interrogation, Rich McGuire returned to his room and curled into a fetal position on his bed. He left the bed only to throw up. He was so afraid of what people would say if they saw him in the mess hall that he did not eat for the next week.

Rich's security clearance was immediately revoked, so he lost his job. He was assigned to be a bay orderly, which essentially meant cleaning barracks bathrooms, scrubbing behind the post's Pepsi machines, and mowing lawns.

Off the job, he was, in effect, under house arrest and was not permitted to leave an area within a certain small radius of Westover. Whenever he left his barracks, he noticed that the two OSI agents who had questioned him followed him. When he finally decided to duck back to his parents' home in Delaware for a weekend, a nondescript blue Plymouth Valiant with black-walled tires followed him there.

At unpredictable times, they hauled him back to the same interrogation chamber at the nuclear-weapons arsenal and questioned him again.

They knew he was queer and that he had fucked with half the guys on the base, the harsh one said. Did he want to go to prison? Did he want his parents to lose their home? It would be so much easier if he just told them what they knew already, the nice one said. Hard labor could take a lot out of a man—especially if he had to do it for the rest of his life.

JUNE 30, 1970
NEAK LUONG, CAMBODIA

WHEN PRESIDENT NIXON ANNOUNCED the invasion of Cambodia on April 30, he had promised that the troops would be out within two months, which was why, on June 30, Lieutenant (junior grade) Armistead Maupin and his crew were chugging down the Mekong River toward the Vietnamese border, the last boat in the "Brown Water Armada" the Navy had deployed for the invasion. Though the crew had spent most of their time in Cambodia in cutoffs, they wore their camouflaged fatigues accessorized with hand grenades and jungle knives for the benefit of the cameras recording the first televised retreat in the history of modern warfare. Nobody complained about shoving off from the riverbank twice so the cameraman could get the right angles from another boat. As the flotilla chugged along, however, somebody fired at them. To make matters worse, the Navy public-affairs man was wounded when a sniper's bullet ricocheted off his beer can.

Maupin's boat went to General Quarters, which was when he noticed his was the last boat in the flotilla. He knew he'd be off duty about a half hour before the boat reached the border between the two countries. If he happened to be nonchalantly showering on the boat's fantail as it passed out of Cambodia, he would be the last person on the last boat leaving the country.

When the historic moment approached and Maupin was stripped down to take his shower, he noticed the ranking officer, a lieutenant commander, walking aft and then loitering in the stern, behind Maupin. Seeing his place in history slipping away, Maupin set aside his soap and walked to the anchor winch at the very rear of the boat. He saluted the commander as he walked past, then climbed out on the winch. The commander, seeing his own historic distinction usurped by a mere lieutenant, grabbed a line and began to lower himself off the stern so he would trail behind the boat, making *him* the last American sailor in Cambodia. Maupin crawled farther out on the winch, his hands slipping on the oily metal. If he fell in and drowned, how would the Red Cross explain this in the obligatory letter to his family? he wondered. Nevertheless, he inched out farther and just before the Vietnamese flagpole that marked the border slid abeam he arched his back and shoved his left leg out behind him, his big toe just surpassing the commander.

That was how a young Navy lieutenant, who in a few years would become the most celebrated gay fiction writer in America, became the last American sailor to leave Cambodia, naked and trailing soapsuds.

JUNE 1970
WESTOVER AIR FORCE BASE
CHICOPEE, MASSACHUSETTS

"WHY THE HELL did you sign this?" the Air Force lawyer asked Rich McGuire.

McGuire explained that the OSI had said it would be easier for him if he did.

"And you believed them?" the lawyer asked incredulously. "Why didn't you ask for an attorney?"

McGuire said he did not believe he had done anything wrong, so he did not think he needed a lawyer. The attorney sighed and laid out the bad news. By signing the statement, McGuire had admitted to homosexual tendencies, which was all the Air Force needed to kick him out. All the lawyer could do was try to get a decent grade of discharge.

McGuire looked pale and wan. He had never been robust. In the weeks since the interrogations started, he had shrunk from 145 to 120 pounds. Both his sergeant and a colonel had taken him aside and given him their home numbers to call if he had any . . . personal emergencies. "If you get to feeling really bad," the colonel said, "don't do anything dumb."

Nobody ever said, "Don't commit suicide." But it was what they were thinking, Rich knew. It was what Rich was thinking, too.

13

Indoctrination

AUGUST 1970
FORT LEONARD WOOD
JEFFERSON CITY, MISSOURI

"YOU FAGGOT. You little girl. You stupid sissy."

The drill sergeant looked serious shouting his taunts at the ninety-eight-pound weakling who struggled with his heavy pack during the physical training. The sergeant looked as if he wanted to kill him. Temperatures were in the nineties and it was still morning. Gilbert Baker had never known this kind of exertion before, having spent his years in high school doing everything he could to avoid gym class.

"Get moving, you little girl. You're such a sissy, can't you move it?"

Gilbert struggled a few minutes more, lying on the ground far behind the rest of his platoon. Then his eyes rolled toward the cloudless sky and he collapsed. The drill sergeant revived him with a whiff of amyl nitrate. The men crouching over him came into focus: the fierce face of the drill instructor, shouting something still unintelligible, the equally angry expressions on the faces of his squad, aware they would all be doing extra push-ups under the punishing Missouri sun because of this gay sissy in their squad.

"You stupid little faggot," the sergeant shouted. "You're nothing but a turd. Get your ass up and get moving."

———

GILBERT BAKER'S PARENTS had been greatly relieved when they learned their son was going into the Army. They knew it would make a man out of him. This was no small concern. Their worries had begun in 1956 when Gilbert, just five years old, had watched that year's Miss America pageant on television with a special rapture and then launched into a frenzy of drawing. He drew Lee Meriwether in lavish gowns, flowing ballroom dresses, and elaborate hairstyles. There was no denying that Gilbert had talent, but there was also something wrong with the direction his talent was taking. When he went off to work in the morning, his dad stopped kissing him good-bye; he came home with building blocks and Erector sets for the boy. The senior Baker, a former Army drill sergeant, had dreamed of his son going to West Point. Instead, he suffered the indignity of coming home one day to discover Gilbert in the basement, naked with another boy.

By high school, when Gilbert had still failed to become interested in normal teenage pursuits, his dad had made him tear up his fashion drawings and break the records of his goddess, Barbra Streisand, and his idol, Mick Jagger. He would be a man, goddamnit, whether he liked it or not.

So when the draft notice came in early 1970, the entire Baker family rejoiced. His parents saw it as his deliverance into manhood; Gilbert saw his deliverance from Chanute, Kansas. What it turned out to be was his worst nightmare. The Army was determined to make a man out of him, the military way.

When veterans wax poetic about their Army experience having made them men, they often mean that they learned some profound truths about themselves during the rigors of combat; they speak of strengths gained and insecurities lost. The way a typical Army drill instructor goes about making a man is less abstract. The first weeks in basic training represent not only the creation of a soldier but an elemental indoctrination into the ideology of masculinity.

The idea is to shear the recruit of any personal identity except for remnants that can be refashioned toward making him an interchangeable component in a massive fighting machine. This is a sensible and even necessary goal of introductory military training. The lessons on manhood, however, focus less on creating what the Army wanted than on defining what the Army did not want. This is why calling recruits faggots, sissies, pussies, and girls had been a time-honored stratagem for drill instructors throughout the armed forces. The context was clear: There was not much worse you could call a man.

This was also why at the firing range, when Gilbert Baker could not pull the trigger on his M-16 and keep his eyes open at the same time, the drill sergeant called him "a stupid girl." Baker still could not open his eyes, but he started blasting away in the direction of the target.

"You stupid faggot," the drill sergeant yelled. "Everybody here is going to do push-ups until he gets it right."

Afterward, Baker still could not get it right. The drill instructor put a watermelon out on the firing range so the men could get an idea of what their bullets would do to a human body. When Baker saw the watermelon skull explode and the red juice spray through the air, he wanted to throw up. He could not bring himself to pull the trigger at all now.

"Shoot like a man," the sergeant shouted while the rest of the platoon did push-ups again. "You're nothing but a turd, you little sissy."

No matter how hard Gilbert tried, he couldn't get over his fear of guns. And as the other troops all did push-ups, they began to talk about punching out that stupid faggot good. This was another part of the indoctrination for the recruits: Sissies got you in trouble; they made your life miserable. Not only did you not want to be one; it was appropriate to despise them.

Every taunt from the drill sergeant told these young men that Gilbert Baker was less than a man, which meant he was less than human, so you didn't even have to treat him the way you treat normal people. Every taunt and bit of ridicule told the recruits that you could call a sissy just about anything and mete out any punishment, because he deserved it.

AT OFFICERS' TRAINING SCHOOL at Lackland Air Force Base, five hundred prospective Air Force officers took seats in a large auditorium. The lights dimmed, and on a screen hovering over the front stage was projected just one word, all in black capital letters on a red background: HOMOSEXUAL. For ten minutes, the instructors said nothing. There was just that word and complete silence. For Bill Oyler, who was on his way to pilot training and eagerly looking ahead to his bombing missions in Vietnam, those ten minutes seemed to last a year. Did they know about him?

A very solemn-looking officer then took the podium. The Air Force had nothing against homosexuals as people, the man said, but the Air Force was an inappropriate place for them. If anyone in the room was a homosexual, he should just get up and leave now. There would be no shame and no one would ever know. Just get up, leave, and you would be processed out quietly.

The speech was so genuine and so emotional that Bill almost got up. He thought he detected movement elsewhere in the auditorium, but the lights were so dim that he could not see. Oyler did not rise, because he believed the Air Force was going to make him heterosexual; this was his chance to change.

At the Recruit Training Command for Women in Bainbridge, Maryland, the lecture for young WAVEs was more pointed. A matronly captain delivered what had become known as her "Tootsie Belle" lecture. There were women, she said, who might stare too long at a recruit in the shower. This kind of woman might gawk at the recruit's breasts and take an overly fond interest in her. The captain could not bring herself to use the word *lesbian;* she referred to them as "Tootsie Belles." When a recruit ran across a Tootsie Belle, it was important to turn her in. It was for the recruits' own good and the good of the United States Navy.

Before the Vietnam era, indoctrination had been much more formal. In the Navy, for example, there was a designated time for women and men to hear specific lectures on homosexuality, modeled on lectures that had long warned sailors about venereal diseases. The formal indoctrination lecture was adopted in 1948. "You have read in the newspapers of fiendish and horrible sex crimes committed against men, women and ofttimes, small children," the lecturer told his captive audience. "Sometimes the bodies of these victims are horribly mutilated." Most instances of these sex crimes "can be related to homosexuality," according to the lecture, and frequently "the person who commits such an act is found to be homosexual."

A 1957 report on homosexuality in the Navy included the full text of the lectures used for all sailors and WAVEs. The document, forthrightly entitled "Indoctrination of Male Recruits on Subject of Homosexuality," warned of the dishonorable discharge a gay sailor would face if he was discovered, and just what that meant for one's future; and it assured that the homosexual "will eventually be found out." This is because gays "are constantly trying to involve normal persons in their acts, and once this is accomplished, the homosexual uses all kinds of pressure, including blackmail, to make them continue in these acts. . . . It is also a peculiarity of homosexuals that they will freely give all details of their contacts to the law enforcement officers when picked up for questioning."

A chaplain followed up this lecture with a talk citing "the sin of Sodom," and there was a further discourse by a psychiatrist explaining that homosexuals most certainly were not born that way but learned their behavior in ways that make it possible to seduce even the most healthy heterosexual male into their lamentable way of life.

For members of the WAVEs and WACs, such lectures presented no small anomaly, given the fact that through the 1940s and 1950s both corps were overwhelmingly lesbian. WAVE recruit Carol Owens was eighteen years old at her boot camp in Bainbridge when her petty officers delivered their stern indoctrination lecture on lesbians. It was confusing when she saw the same women out later at the lesbian bars. The message was: Hypocrisy is part of life. Say one thing, do another. Tell them what they want to hear. It would be years, however, before Carol discovered where their indoctrination ended and her own thinking began.

———————

By the time of the Vietnam War, indoctrinations were less formal but still apparent in many ways, often not verbal.

Disappearances, for example: A man would be in boot camp one day and be gone the next, his locker empty, his bunk stripped bare, as if he had never existed. Later, you heard that the missing recruit was queer. You began to accept the fact that queers just disappeared as part of the way things worked. They were strange people and strange things happened to them.

The indoctrination's effect went far beyond the confines of the military, ensuring that millions of young people received a grossly intolerant introduction to the issues of nonconforming sexual orientation. The young men who listened to the proscribed indoctrination of the Korean War era became America's military leaders and corporate executives of the 1970s. The men who saw sissies taunted and tormented during the days of the Vietnam War became the leaders of the 1980s and 1990s.

EVEN BEFORE THE DRILL INSTRUCTORS assembled the battalion for the weekend bivouac, Private Gilbert Baker knew what he would do. At the arsenal, he loitered behind the other guys and was the last man out the door, so that no one would see him leave without a gun. Once they were under way, his platoon noticed that Baker was not carrying his weapon, but it was not until they had ventured six miles into the rough country around Fort Leonard Wood that a drill sergeant noticed.

"You dumb ass, you forgot your gun," he shouted.

"No, I didn't forget it," said Baker. "I'm not carrying it. I'm not going to shoot it."

Baker was braced for a torrent of insults, but instead the sergeant stared at him curiously, then went to consult with the captain. The whole march ground to a halt in the middle of the road while the captain came back to the private without his M-16.

"We could kill you right now if this was combat," Baker recalls the captain saying. "This is treason. For that matter, we can kill you right now."

Baker replied that he would not carry a gun and that he wanted to file for conscientious-objector status. The captain ordered the battalion to drop to the road and start doing push-ups until the sissy got back into formation and marched with them. Under the blazing sun, Baker watched the bodies, one thousand of them, do push-ups around him.

He refused to move. "I won't do it," he said. "I won't touch a gun again."

The captain screamed at him for the next half hour, calling him a sissy and a fag, and the drill instructor called him a pussy and a turd. The whole battalion did push-ups, and Baker would not move. Finally, the captain sent him back to Leonard Wood in a water truck.

The next day, Baker's parents appeared at the base. His mother wept, shocked that Gilbert would bring such shame on the family. "How can you do this to us?" she asked. Both his parents made it clear they would never support his contention that he was a lifelong pacifist, something he would need to prove to be a conscientious objector.

"We're going to send you to Vietnam right now and put you on the front lines," a captain told him.

"You can, but I'm not going to carry a gun," Gilbert said.

Finally, the captain sent Baker to a grizzled master sergeant who was ready to cut a deal. Without his parents' support, he would never get to be a conscientious objector, the sergeant noted. But they could fix it so Baker could be a medic and never have to pick up a gun, if he would finish basic training without any more hassles. Baker agreed. He would not handle a gun, but another private shot for him on the firing range, so it looked as if Baker had the requisite marksmanship to pass basic. He went to San Antonio for his medical training and from there he was assigned to Letterman Army Hospital at the Presidio in San Francisco.

SEPTEMBER 1970
WESTOVER AIR FORCE BASE
CHICOPEE, MASSACHUSETTS

"I'M AS HORNY AS A TWO-DICKED GOAT. I go home; sometimes I bang the little woman three, maybe four times a night. I can tell you're horny, too. What do you do?"

Three months after Sergeant Rich McGuire had been brought in for his first interrogation, the Office of Special Investigations was still at it. No charges had been filed against him, and he was not even sure whether he was being processed yet for a discharge. The only thing he was sure of was the inevitability of these hours and hours of interviews with one agent behind him and one in front—one angry and confrontive, the other kind and understanding. And McGuire had never heard such obscene talk in his life as he heard from OSI agents who tried to goad him into talking about his sexual exploits.

"You're like me—you're a horny guy," said an OSI agent during one extended interrogation. "You must have been to bed with half the base. You can only jack off so much. Give us their names."

McGuire blew up. "I'm not like you at all," he said. "You're enjoying this. It's not just a job to you. How do you sleep at night?"

The agent just smiled.

Rich had no one to talk to about what was happening to him. The OSI agents swore he would see much bigger trouble if he dared whisper a word about the investigation. He spent the night of his twenty-first birthday alone at the Yankee Peddler Inn in Holyoke. After the surf and turf special, he ordered a Bloody Mary, his first mixed drink, but he gagged on it and left it nearly full on the table before going back to the barracks.

OCTOBER 1970
THE PRESIDIO
SAN FRANCISCO

THE GOLDEN GATE BRIDGE hovered over a fine layer of fog outside the window of the barracks on Crissy Field, not far from Letterman Army Hospital. After a life in the flat gray prairies of Kansas, San Francisco seemed like magic, with its green hills, shimmering blue bay, and the cool white fog rolling through the Golden Gate every afternoon. And not only that.

Private Gilbert Baker, fresh from his medical training in San Antonio, had met another private and he was in love for the first time. His work was gruesome; Baker was a surgical nurse. But after working all day alongside surgeons piecing together faces and limbs that had been blown apart in Vietnam, there was his boyfriend to explore San Francisco with.

Unfortunately, several weeks into the affair, Gilbert saw a problem; maybe it had been there all along. Gilbert liked to dress up for an excursion to the city. His favorite civvies were a pair of red, white, and blue bell-bottoms, platform shoes, and a tie-dyed T-shirt. But after a few weeks, his boyfriend had begun to mumble excuses about not going into the city, and then he began to be less and less available. The sex was still terrific—it was not that. Finally, when Baker insisted, his boyfriend told him why he did not feel comfortable going out together. Gilbert was just too femme. Everybody would talk. Couldn't he just butch it up some?

Baker reeled from the rejection. Over the next few days, the weight of the past six months fell suddenly on him. He was a fag, a sissy, no better than a girl. Nobody wanted anything to do with a femme like him. *You're nothing but a turd.* One afternoon, with the gray fog pushing through the bay outside, completely obscuring the Golden Gate Bridge, Private Gilbert Baker locked the door to his barracks room and pulled a single-edged razor from his toilet kit. He had had medical training now, so he knew how to do it right. No lateral cuts across the wrist; that was amateur stuff. A nice long cut up and down the arm. The blood pumped rapidly from his arm; Gilbert figured he had hit an artery. Satisfied that he had done the job, he lay back feeling slightly dazed and slowly began to lose consciousness.

— 14 —

Dykes and Whores

LOCATED NEAR THE Rocky Mountains in the scenic Pacific Northwest and sporting one of the most bucolic names of any military installation in the country, Mountain Home Air Force Base had long drawn airmen who envisioned verdant mountain meadows. What they got was a stretch of barren desert south of the mountain range, littered with dusty brown tumbleweeds.

The news that a contingent from the Women in the Air Force (WAF) was being assigned to the remote Tactical Air Command base in Idaho sent thrills through the enlisted ranks. Finally, some action. With her slim, athletic build, Airman Penny Rand proved an immediate hit with the guys. Before she had walked twenty feet from her car toward the barracks, one of the first thirty-five WAFs to be assigned to Mountain Home, three airmen were at her side, asking for a date. They seemed genuinely incredulous when Penny ignored them.

At chow, more enlisted men hit on Penny and the other WAFs. None of the women would go out with them.

"If you're not going out with me, who are you going out with?" one airman asked Penny.

Penny recalls saying she was not going out with anybody; she just did not want to go out with any of them.

"What's wrong with you?" another man asked. "You don't like men?"

Within days, the tone was more surly. "You're just a fucking dyke," an airman concluded.

And that was the word that went out among the 3,500 airmen, many of whom were profoundly disappointed. The WAFs were a bunch of dykes.

From the time women first entered the U.S. military during World War II, there was a truism among male GIs that classified all uniformed women into one of two camps: those who would provide for a man's sexual needs and those who would not. The former were whores; the latter were dykes. As the saying went, "They're either dykes or whores."

That aphorism, more than any other, was the malediction that military women faced as they began enlisting in larger and larger numbers from the 1970s to the 1990s. Though virtually all female service personnel suffered from the aspersions, it was worse for those women who did not accept traditional feminine roles. And for women who were, in fact, lesbians, life was very, very difficult.

Like most stereotypes, there was some truth behind the assumption that an inordinate number of women in uniform were lesbian. The military's stringent criteria for admitting its female members then ensured this. For twenty years following WWII, married women could not enlist and pregnancy ensured immediate discharge. This almost guaranteed huge numbers of WACs, WAVEs and WAFs whose sexuality leaned toward the nonbreeding side of the street. By some counts, albeit imprecise ones, lesbians comprised as much as 80 percent of the women who served in World War II. The highest-ranking women officers in the military services well into the 1980s came largely from this group. Until the late 1960s, when the first rumblings of the women's movement made nontraditional jobs attractive to women from all walks of life, women's military units tended to include a large proportion of lesbians.

The assumption became something of a self-fulfilling prophecy. Young lesbians sometimes joined up specifically because they expected to find other lesbians in the military. This was the major reason Penny Rand had joined the Air Force two months after graduating from Will Rogers High School in Tulsa, Oklahoma. Born into a working-class family, the daughter of a telephone lineman, Rand knew in junior high school that she was not like the other girls, that her friendships with her girlfriends were far deeper and more meaningful, crushes really. She did not have words for what she was or what her attractions meant. She did not even know there were words for it. She just knew she was different. She fulfilled her peers' expectations by dating men, although she always sensed that whatever long-term relationship she found would be with another woman.

When she was fifteen or sixteen and riding in her parents' car in Tulsa, they pulled alongside and then passed a woman alone in her car; she was wearing a blue uniform. Penny fantasized about the attractive, independent woman who, she dreamed, was like herself, and it struck her that she might meet other women like herself in the military. A recruiter promised opportunities that women were hard-pressed to find in the civilian world: equality and over 150 jobs to choose from. Penny signed on the dotted line.

From the first days of Penny's initial assignment in Idaho, it was clear that the Air Force, like the rest of society, had not understood what women's equality really meant. Yes, there were 150 different jobs women could choose from, but they were basically 150 different types of clerical jobs. Or you could be a cook or a nurse. Penny had wanted to go into photography or illustration, since she'd had some commercial-art training in high school, but these jobs were not open to her. Instead, she became a secretary in the office that handled the base's suggestion box. She spent her days typing the suggestions in triplicate and sending off little gifts—a toothpaste roller or a rubber jar opener—to the box contributors. During her lunch breaks and evenings, she fended off the sexual advances of the male airmen, who had taken to hooting and hollering at the small, frightened cluster of WAFs as they made their way around the base. At night, the women shoved broom handles through the push bars of their barracks doors to keep the men from breaking into their rooms.

It was around this time that Penny began to read about women's liberation. It was difficult not to read about women's lib, as prominent as it was in the media. Kate Millett, author of the best-selling *Sexual Politics*, was on the cover of *Time* magazine. The Women's Strike for Equality provided "Freedom Trash Cans" at demonstration sites across the country, where women could deposit their bras and lipsticks and other accoutrements of their cosmetic subjugation. Women should dress for comfort, feminists argued, not to please men. Their substantive demands were so elemental that, years later, it would be hard to imagine they were ever controversial: equal pay for equal work, a chance for traditionally male jobs, and more participation in the political decisions that shaped their destinies, such as abortion and contraception.

The message made a lot of sense to Penny. She saw the severely restricted Air Force job list as a preview of her life, and she was not enthusiastic. She was just eighteen years old, but she knew there would be no man supporting her later in life. Without a college degree or a family affluent enough to help her get one, she could look ahead to forty or fifty years of low-level jobs at pay more than 40 percent less than what a man would earn for the same work.

Rather than offer a solution, WAF seemed a part of the problem. As the size of the WAF contingent on the base grew, so did the seriousness of the problems with men, including rapes. Barracks meetings, however, consisted not of serious advice to help women cope with the pandemic sexual harassment but of makeup tips from a perky little lieutenant fresh from ROTC. It was important always to look one's best, she insisted.

Many women dropped out of the military rather than take the constant harassment. Penny's closest friend was one who went to her chaplain to confess she was gay and wanted out. The chaplain seemed understanding and referred the young woman to the Judge Advocate General's office. There, JAG lawyers asked her for the names of other lesbians, but she refused to give any.

While other women left, Penny rebelled. She stopped wearing makeup and, in the ultimate act of feminist defiance of that time, stopped shaving her legs. When she was counseled that WAF members shaved their legs to look feminine, she smiled warmly but refused to shave. When she was ordered to shave her legs, she disobeyed the order. No sooner had she gotten her promotion to airman first class, even before she had sewn on her stripes, than she was busted back to airman—for not shaving her legs.

These acts of insolence, her refusal to date male airmen, her outspoken belief that she deserved the same opportunities that men had, all contributed to certain suspicions. As it was, the other airmen were convinced *all* the WAFs were dykes, and they were not shy about saying so. Finally, the base commander decided to move. Rand recalls being called into the JAG office and being greeted by two young male lawyers, both captains. One opened by saying a terrible sickness was spreading among the women on the base, lesbianism. Lesbians had been harassing the other women, he said, and they wanted to put a stop to it.

Penny did not believe a word of it. She had seen plenty of sexual harassment all right, and it came from heterosexual males, not lesbians. Given the fact the women all lived in one barracks, she did not think there was much going on that she did not know about. But the lawyer said that, yes, it was happening, and he wanted to know who in the barracks was lesbian. "We're doing this to protect you," he said.

Penny said she did not know any lesbians.

She must know some, he said reasonably. All she had to do was give him their names. Nobody would ever know.

When Penny refused again, the other lawyer took over, in a far more severe tone than his colleague. "What about you?" he asked. "We have suspicions that you probably are, too."

Rand laughed.

"*Are* you a lesbian?"

Rand laughed again, without answering.

The second lawyer said that they would find out who the lesbians were, and they would get them all, and if Penny did not come out with it right now she would get a dishonorable discharge.

"You'll never be able to find a job," the first lawyer pressed. "You'll be the same as a felon in some states. You'll have no benefits, no rights."

Penny still refused to talk, and the lawyers finally let her go.

For all her bravado during the interrogation, she was terrified. She was only a few months out of high school, and she had already done something that could follow her the rest of her life.

And then, in the weeks that followed, one after another of her friends—heterosexual and homosexual, women who did not fit into traditional female roles, the ones who would not go out with the guys, the women's libbers—began disappearing.

THOUGH THE LESBIAN INVESTIGATIONS at Mountain Home Air Force Base in late 1970 and early 1971 garnered no publicity for either the gay or women's movements, it defined the shape of things to come, as greater numbers of women began joining the military. Even as the women's movement exploded into the national consciousness during these months, a palpable reaction grew against it. Though the backlash would not take a tangible political form for nearly a decade, it lay just beneath the whisperings about Penny Rand and other women's libbers at Mountain Home Air Force Base. . . . *They're all fucking dykes.* It was a suspicion that presented the new women's movement with its first crisis in the same weeks that Penny Rand's friends began to vanish at Mountain Home Air Force Base.

The summer and autumn months of 1970 were an exhilarating time for the feminist cause, whose roots may be said to go back to Abigail Adams. As an organized political movement, it dated back to 1848 at least, when Elizabeth Cady Stanton convened the first women's rights convention in Seneca Falls, New York. Except for the ratification of the constitutional amendment allowing women the right to vote in 1920, however, most of the demands set forth at the 1848 convention were still unmet come 1970.

With Millett's *Sexual Politics,* the feminist movement acquired a philosophical framework and a glossary of new terms, including *male chauvinism, patriarchy, male supremacy,* and the new honorific *Ms.* Its political demands were commonsensical enough to gain credence and consensus, at least in liberal circles. These were the days when abortion was still illegal in many states; and in many jurisdictions, married women needed written approval from their husbands in order to apply for credit or to incorporate a business. In legal terms, they were considered their husbands' chattel.

In 1970, the Equal Rights Amendment, first introduced to the House Judiciary Committee in 1923, made it out of the committee and onto the floor of the House of Representatives for the first time, although it was not passed. Electorally minded organizers were on the brink of forming their first grass-roots group, the National Women's Political Caucus. The momentum for women's rights was even greater than for that other social movement that had its nativity in 1970, the ecology movement, whose contemporary incarnation began with its Earth Day celebration earlier that year.

Feminist euphoria, however, came to an abrupt halt in late autumn when Millett was "zapped" at Columbia University, where she was speaking to a joint meeting of the feminist and gay liberation groups. She was supposed to talk about bisexuality, but her comments were interrupted by a member of the Radicalesbians. "Bisexuality is a cop-out," the woman said. "Are you a lesbian?"

Millett was married and had been photographed kissing her husband, but the aura of fashionable bisexuality was not altogether honest. She hesitated. As she later recalled the moment in her book *Flying,* "That word in public, the word I waited half a lifetime to hear. Finally I am accused."

"Yes," she said. "I am a lesbian."

Coming from the leading theoretician of the women's liberation movement, the acknowledgment confirmed every nasty suspicion antifeminists had about the burgeoning feminist cause. A maelstrom of controversy followed. *Time* magazine immediately issued a story, "Women's Lib: A Second Look," asserting that Millett's "disclosure is bound to discredit her as a spokesman for her cause, cast further doubt on her theories, and reinforce the views of those skeptics who routinely dismiss all liberationists as lesbians."

The controversy created a schism within the feminist movement that would last for years. Gloria Steinem, Susan Brownmiller, and a number of other leading lights of the movement rushed to Millett's side and released a strongly worded statement in her support. Other feminist leaders, most notably Betty Friedan, were profoundly homophobic and felt that the involvement of acknowledged lesbians in the feminist cause would undermine popular support for the movement in mainstream America.

Exacerbating the fear of antigay feminists was the reality that a substantial number of the early feminists were lesbian. Naturally, since they were women living without the support of a male on substandard female pay scales, they were among the vanguard who knew there was something inequitable about the status quo.

The women's movement continued to make remarkable strides in the next few years, beyond anything women had achieved during the past century. But feminists were always suspect from then on. And although the vast majority of women accepted the central tenets of women's liberation, such as the demand for pay equity, the right to abortion, and expanded job opportunities, most amended their allied opinions with the proviso, "I'm not one of those women's libbers, but . . ." What they meant was, "I'm not a lesbian, but . . ." The enemy of the women's movement would always be homophobia, as much as male chauvinism, although there were some who argued that you could never be quite sure where antigay prejudice ended and misogyny began.

It would certainly be a difficult distinction for women in the military to make. Feminist consciousness-raising groups on campuses across the country had discussed breaking into nontraditional jobs in a man's world, but it was in the military, more than any other arena of American society, that women actually did it. And those issues around which American women would soon rally—such as sexual harassment and dead-end jobs— were those that women in uniform confronted on a daily basis. There was also the added sting of homophobia. Just as women who asserted their rights in civilian society became suspect for being lesbian, women who protested sexual advances and job discrimination in the military were accused of being dykes. The difference was that in the civilian world, the lesbian issue pretty much stopped at the level of accusation; in the military, the accusation was only the beginning.

AT MOUNTAIN HOME, the lesbian investigations brought renewed efforts by base officers to help the women be more, well, feminine. The young lieutenant lectured on lipstick and eyeliner. The chaplain began conducting regular birth-control talks. Young women could not expect men to take responsibility for birth control, the chaplain said. That was up to the women themselves. He used slides to discuss the advantages of the pill over the condom or diaphragm. The women must keep in mind that GIs were unhappy being away from home and their wives. If nature took its course, WAFs needed to be prepared.

Meanwhile, the WAF's senior noncommissioned officer, a seasoned master sergeant who, Penny knew, lived with a female lover in Boise, gave the women practical advice. It goes easier on you, she said, if you wear skirts when you are in civilian clothes. The master sergeant was quick to scold any woman who lingered too long in another's room. The nonverbal message seemed to be: If you're careful, you won't get caught. Later, Penny understood that the woman was trying to be helpful, but at the time it seemed hypocritical to be making accommodations to an unjust system. Sisterhood might be powerful, but the master sergeant, Penny thought, was no sister.

———

IT WAS DURING THIS TIME that ANC Captain Mary Hall heard of a female lieutenant colonel who had become obsessed with the idea that lesbians dominated the Army Nurse Corps at the Walter Reed Institute of Nursing. The lieutenant colonel made up a list of every lesbian she could name in the ANC and handed the list over to military intelligence. The names of many of the highest-ranking women in the Army, even the name of a female general, appeared on the list, among the hundreds of other names from bases where the colonel had been assigned previously. According to Hall, most of the officers who knew her believed—and reported—that the colonel had been under strain and had simply cracked in recent weeks. The male military-intelligence staff had to agree she'd gone loony, since the allegation that lesbians permeated the entire ANC hierarchy was so outrageous. Not too much later, the lieutenant colonel was straitjacketed and shipped off to a psychiatric ward for treatment. Afterward, women who saw the list she had drawn up admitted that it was remarkably accurate.

WESTOVER AIR FORCE BASE
CHICOPEE, MASSACHUSETTS

THE END OF Rich McGuire's two-and-a-half-year career in the Air Force came quickly, so abruptly, in fact, that it was almost anticlimactic, after the drama of the previous four months. The word came directly from

Lieutenant General David Jones that McGuire be discharged immediately. Rich was so eager to leave Westover and never see the base again that he waived his right to a hearing. Everyone he worked with gave him glowing references, despite the nature of the charges. He counted on those recommendations and his outstanding record to earn him an honorable discharge—especially since no one had ever accused him of doing anything wrong. All the Air Force had on him was a copy of *After Dark,* a couple of nudist magazines, and his own confession to an incomplete sexual experience. In spite of this, General Jones issued McGuire the lowest kind of separation he could get without a formal court-martial. Rich read his name above big block letters that stated: UNDESIRABLE DISCHARGE.

Just why the Air Force kept Rich McGuire in for a full four months after learning he was gay is a matter of some conjecture. There are no records in his file to speak to the issue, though similar cases from that time and subsequent years make it seem as if the military investigative agencies just liked to keep suspected homosexuals around to interview again and again, until they were absolutely convinced there was nothing more to gain from them.

On the day his discharge orders came down, the Charge of Quarters called McGuire into his office and demanded he leave right away. Rich called his dad. Rich had not told his parents what was happening to him; he explained that the military was issuing "early outs" now that the Vietnam War was beginning to wind down. So Rich's dad rented an Econoline van and a U-Haul trailer and drove to Massachusetts. As dark clouds rolled over the Berkshire Hills to the west, they loaded up the last of Rich's possessions. From then on, McGuire would spend his life trying to forget what had happened to him in his twentieth year.

THE PRESIDIO
SAN FRANCISCO

WHEN A FRIEND, worried about Private Gilbert Baker's state of mind, knocked on his barracks door and got no answer, he immediately went to the CQ and suggested they force their way into his room. They found Baker lying dazed on the floor, in a large pool of his own blood. Once he was stitched back together again, Gilbert became a patient in the psychiatric ward of the hospital where he had worked the week before. When he assured the psychiatrists he would not attempt suicide again, they let him return to his work as a medic.

After work, he began to discover San Francisco and the city's nightlife. It was his salvation. In North Beach, he went to a club where a group called the Cockettes performed. These were campy guys in dresses and mustaches, and an overweight black drag queen named Sylvester who could really belt out a song. Gilbert had a feeling he was not in Kansas anymore.

As Gilbert watched them sing and dance, it occurred to him that here were homosexual people having fun. It was a startling concept to him that you could be gay and be happy. Once he got out of the Army, Gilbert thought, maybe he could be happy, too. He would stay in San Francisco and try, which is what he did. He would never hide again.

15

In Country

"ARE YOU A HOMOSEXUAL?"

It was the question Sergeant Leonard Matlovich had both dreaded and hoped for. He had dreaded the word for half his life; the hope was something recent, coming from an awareness that he would never have love if at some point he did not say aloud, "Yes, I am a homosexual."

He was twenty-seven years old and still had never made love. His Air Force career progressed; he had just received an Air Force Commendation Medal to go with his Bronze Star and Purple Heart. He was advancing rapidly in the Mormon Church, fulfilling the church's dictate of eternal progression. But Leonard's mind fixed on what he lacked the hope of attaining in his current circumstances: affection. The harder he tried to be like the other men, the more alienated he became. What acceptance he did gain was predicated on his lies, which only made him feel worse about himself.

It was during Matlovich's third tour of duty in Vietnam that someone first put the question to him. The war was beginning to phase down, and, as part of the Vietnamization process, Leonard was teaching civil engineering to South Vietnamese when he struck up a fast friendship with another Air Force NCO. They began spending all their free time together until, finally, the man said he had just one question for Leonard—but he did not want to come right out and ask. *Don't talk about it.* Matlovich thought he understood and he was not sure that he wanted it spoken aloud, either, so they agreed that the friend would write the question on a piece of paper and leave it in Leonard's top desk drawer. Then Leonard would write his answer on a piece of paper and leave it there for the friend to retrieve.

Though his friend's question was what Leonard expected, he was still stunned to see the words, stunned that someone had finally asked. And he felt something like relief when he scribbled out his one-word response: Yes.

Unfortunately, Matlovich was once again a victim of his poor judgment in choosing potential boyfriends. The friendship quickly collapsed. The friend moved immediately—to a different part of the vast base at Da Nang—and they soon stopped even running into each other. Once again, Matlovich was alone, his yearnings so strong, he thought he would explode.

———

SERGEANT LEONARD MATLOVICH's disheartening quest for love, played out largely during his three tours of Vietnam, said less about the overall chances of finding gay romance at war than about Matlovich's own bad luck and poor judgment in appraising potential boyfriends. By 1971, a vast gay subculture existed within the American military stationed in Vietnam. Six years of intense U.S. presence had been time enough to establish huge networks of gay servicemen throughout Southeast Asia.

By the time Air Force Captain Bill Oyler made it to Nha Trang Air Base above Cam Rahn Bay to fly with the Ninetieth Operations Squadron, gay airmen in the States had filled his address book with the names of scores of other gay pilots stationed there. Between Nha Trang and the larger Tan Son Nhut base near Saigon, Oyler knew about one hundred gay pilots. When he transferred to Thailand, he met between 150 and 200 more gay Air Force personnel.

Just as the heterosexual GI's quest for diversion had by now been institutionalized into a circuit of well-known bars and brothels, so had the homosexual search for a good time. Gay hangouts were so famous that *The Advocate* published an extensive list of gay hot spots in Saigon, including a review of which bases were best for making assignations. In the gay bars on Saigon's Tu Do Street, it was now not unusual to see muscular Marines dancing together in full camouflage to "Tears of a Clown," their Colt .45s bouncing on their hips. Nearby, the Asian Man Club, which was the Far Eastern answer to the Western Playboy Club, had one section for servicemen who liked women and another for soldiers who liked men. Eye contact among men at the Continental Hotel's bar had become so obvious that Tom Dooley's old hangout was becoming altogether notorious.

Libidinous GIs hardly had to leave the base for their adventures. The swimming pool at Tan Son Nhut, for example, had a reputation as one of the most active gay cruising areas that side of Fire Island. There were usually gay men available for dating among civilian personnel at the USO libraries. For gay soldiers, Sydney became a favorite R and R site—with those cheerful guys who could not seem to get enough of American men. Singapore also featured a rousing gay scene, although this tended to attract more gay Australian and New Zealand soldiers, who were in Vietnam as part of a multinational alliance. The in-country R and R center at Vung Tau was also known for wild gay partying. Discharges on the grounds of homosexuality still occurred in Vietnam, but there was growing tolerance of gay servicemen there, unmatched at stateside duty stations.

This phenomenon was not restricted to the American military: The Australian navy, which supported the U.S. war effort in Vietnam, had one ship, the HMAS *Swan*, that was so notoriously homosexual that when it pulled into Sydney harbor, sailors assembled on the decks of other warships to wave white hankies at the "poofters."

FOR MOST GAY SOLDIERS during the latter stages of the war Southeast Asia was a place they could go to escape the investigations and interrogations that were often a way of life in stateside duty. If military officers went lightly on gays in Vietnam, it was also in part because there were so many genuine threats to good order, discipline, and morale coming out of the war. It is a truism that society's problems flow into the Army, and this fact was never more clear than during the latter phases of the Vietnam War. Military personnel, like their civilian counterparts, were polarized.

There were stark divisions between blacks and whites, between juicers, who preferred beer and country music, and heads, who preferred cannabis and rock.

Dissatisfaction with the war also undermined discipline. The way the war had been handled disgusted both hawks and doves within the military. Hawks believed it was the civilian authorities' fault that they could not win the war decisively, because civilians would not allow the necessary hard-hitting attacks. Doves did not believe the United States had any business being there at all. It was no help when Assistant Defense Secretary John McNaughton said in 1971 that "the present U.S. objective in Vietnam is to avoid humiliation." Many GIs were not thrilled over the idea of being blown apart simply to assert the nation's manhood.

Soldiers no longer talked of winning the war; they talked of surviving it. Aggressive officers who took what enlisted men saw as unnecessary risks could find themselves "fragged." Fragging meant blowing up your commanding officer with a fragmentation grenade. That threat kept a lot of officers in line. AWOLs and desertions reached record levels. Between 1969 and 1973, one American soldier went AWOL every two minutes. One soldier deserted every six minutes. They were some of the darkest days the United States military had ever faced.

DID THAT AIRMAN really need to go to Vietnam?

Penny Rand thought not. Instead, she decided that the airman should go to Turkey and that the officious lieutenant who was supposed to be going to Turkey should go to Da Nang. Penny liked that idea and promptly typed the orders into the computer.

After a few hours more of changing orders, Penny decided she was bored with work. With a few artfully pressed buttons, the entire base computer crashed. "My God, what's happened?" she asked as officers went scrambling to try to get it back on-line. As she left the office, Penny pulled a stack of freshly written orders out of an in basket and tossed them in the trash.

Airman Rand figured her transfer to the personnel office was designed to make it easier to monitor her activities after all the fuss over her refusal to shave her legs. The investigation of lesbians continued. Although Penny had not shown much aptitude for adjusting to military life, she had quickly deciphered the meanings of various coded orders. Once she had figured the system out, she promptly took it upon herself to sabotage it at every turn.

Welcome to the Air Force of the 1970s. Welcome to the "GI movement."

The difficulties of maintaining military order in Vietnam were no less challenging than maintaining discipline at military installations in the States. Though the fierce campus protests against the war were winding down, the government faced fresh challenges from peace protesters who were moving their efforts away from colleges and to military bases across the country, to the very heart of the war machine they wanted to subvert.

The antiwar movement arrived at Mountain Home Air Force Base in late 1970 in the form of Mark Lane, the radical attorney who had gained fame a few years earlier with the book *Rush to Judgment,* a critique of the Warren Commission's report on the assassination of President Kennedy. Lane's antimilitary message resonated with Penny Rand, who was profoundly disaffected by the lack of equal opportunity for women in the Air Force. Lane brought with him a coterie who opened a coffeehouse for GIs in an abandoned theater downtown; they called it the Helping Hand. They held meetings that advised enlisted personnel how to assist the antiwar movement. They published an antiwar newspaper for the base, began counseling GIs on how to file for conscientious-objector status, and opened a small library of radical books. It was at Helping Hand that Penny realized what contributions she could make to undermine the war effort, right in her lowly job in the personnel office. The most significant connection she made, however, was not to the antiwar movement but to the new women's movement, and her most influential new ally was Lane's girlfriend, a radical feminist from Boston.

Penny and the few female airmen of an iconoclastic bent made an immediate bond with their new feminist friend and began holding informal rap sessions in which they shared what they were beginning to understand were their problems as women in a man's world. Although they saw eye-to-eye on militarism, the all-female consciousness-raising groups threatened the male antiwar organizers, who accused feminists of elitism, a major no-no in the collectivist-oriented theology of the New Left. The women ignored the name-calling and continued excluding the men. As she gained a theoretical framework for her intuitive self-reliance, Penny found it easier to tell the men at the base that she would not put up with their harassment anymore. She soon learned that the less tolerant she became of the harassment, the less they bothered her. It was an empowering message for Rand; and disempowering for the men with whom she worked.

Across the country, organizers from the new GI movement launched comparable efforts at other bases, lecturing on soldiers' rights, on how to refuse illegal orders, and how to resist war duties. Coffeehouses sprang up in every major base town. Some 144 underground newspapers were being published near military posts. There was even ambitious talk of unionizing the military. All this was anathema to military officials.

"Your discharge is on the way," Penny Rand's CO informed her when she showed up at work one morning—for her antiwar work, she was told. Since Rand did not want to stay in the Air Force anyway, she did not demand a hearing or attempt to fight the discharge.

"You can leave now," the CO said. "We want you off the base."

Penny packed and left Mountain Home Air Force Base. Her career in the Air Force had lasted eleven months. For Rand, there was no doubt what to do next; she did what tens of thousands of other politically committed young people did then. She went to work in the antiwar movement full time.

APRIL 24, 1971
WASHINGTON, D.C.
_____

AROUND THE WHITE HOUSE, past Congress, and spilling over the malls around the Washington Monument, hundreds of thousands of protesters marched through the streets against the Vietnam War. These were not merely the university students who had set campuses ablaze a year before: These were trade unionists, housewives, and snappily dressed professionals. By late afternoon, the news reports estimated the size of the March on Washington to be 750,000, the largest demonstration in the history of the United States. In San Francisco, another 300,000 paraded for peace in a companion demonstration.

Though the slogans were familiar, there was a new element emerging in other peace protests in New York and San Francisco, and now in Washington for the first time. Contingent after contingent of them took up the new chant: "One-two-three-four, we don't want your macho war."

Gay Liberation Front chapters proliferated in every major city and college town in the country, equaled only by the presence of the burgeoning women's movement as a new force at antiwar protests. In Washington, gay marchers came from as far away as Northwestern University and Michigan State. On the West Coast, the GLF announced its March Against War & Sexism and cheerfully shouted, "Vietnam for the Vietnamese/San Francisco for the gays!"

It was elemental: To be gay and an activist in 1971 meant to be against the war. When the subject of gay servicemen came up among gay activists, the discussion centered solely on how to get gays out of the military, never on how to help the ones who wanted to stay in. A growing number of gay periodicals across the country told horror stories of drill sergeants shouting *faggot* into the faces of new recruits. *Gay Sunshine*, among other radical papers, carried stories about gay sailors pushed overboard in the dead of night and gay soldiers being lynched by fellow GIs. The stories tended to be long on rhetoric and short on verifiable facts, but they served to confirm the fears of a movement rooted in the era's antimilitarism. Just as other veteran groups organized against the war, some gay Vietnam vets did, too. A former medic named Jess Jessop was key in organizing the Gay Liberation Front in San Diego, where he settled after his 1967 discharge from the Navy.

GLF chapters across the country took up with a passion military counseling geared to deprive the war machine of its human cogs, sometimes forming imaginatively named groups such as LISP, the Legal In-Service Project. The projects were propitiously timed, given the fact that the Army was doing all it could to skirt the gay regulations.

In a move that the government solemnly insisted was meant to protect privacy rights of inductees, the standard form for potential draftees suddenly dropped the question regarding "homosexual tendencies." If conscripts were gay, draft spokesmen said, it was their job to bring this to the attention of military doctors during their routine psychiatric exam. But psychiatrists allowed fewer and fewer gay deferments. In one case, for example, an Army psychologist told a federal court that he could not believe the inductee, an activist in the Orange County GLF, really was homosexual, because he seemed to be in good mental health.

"Haven't you ever seen a happy homosexual?" asked U.S. District Court judge Charles Carr incredulously. At the end of the court hearing, Carr granted the gay activist his deferment, and mused that he would like to be "the commander of a homosexual army. It would be the greatest fighting force in America."

The process of deciding who was or was not gay was only slightly more scientific than during World War II days when doctors sometimes put a tongue depressor deep into a recruit's throat to see whether he would gag. (If not, he must be a homosexual, the psychiatrists believed, apparently convinced that all gay men were blessed with an innate talent for deep fellatio.) During the Vietnam era, a letter from a psychiatrist and a few hours of a lawyer's time was sometimes enough to do the trick. This allowed the *Los Angeles Free Press* to quantify the cost of a gay discharge at $350. Even with such homosexual credentials, several gay men had to appeal to federal court to prevent their induction. One San Francisco man required the intercession of his United States senator and two congressmen before the Army would disallow him on the grounds of being an acknowledged homosexual.

The person with the most success in helping gay men stay out of the Army was the feisty Los Angeles gay activist Don Slater of the Committee to Fight Exclusion of Homosexuals from the Armed Forces. Slater did not subscribe to the antiwar movement, but he deeply opposed the barring of gays from the military. He also decided early on in his counseling that since homosexuality could in fact not be proved in any authoritative sense, he would not try. For each gay person about to be drafted, Slater wrote a form letter to the headquarters of the U.S. Army Recruiting Command on his organization's letterhead, noting his group's opposition to the gay policy and the fact that the Army had apparently agreed with his organization, given the fact that they were about to induct an acknowledged homosexual. "Fair play would seem to demand that the finding that he is 'acceptable' for military service should be reviewed in the light of your policy excluding homosexuals from the service, or that your policy should be reviewed in the light of your acceptance of him." Nearly six hundred men sought counseling from Slater, and he wrote hundreds of such letters, always succeeding in keeping his clients out.

Once in the Army, it was increasingly difficult to get out on grounds of homosexuality. For example, at Fort Polk, Louisiana, Army Specialist Five Mark Houston, working as an administrative clerk in the discharge section of the adjutant general's office, was ordered to make the discharge process as difficult as possible for anyone who claimed to be homosexual. Gay soldiers had to undergo repeated psychiatric evaluations in which they were ordered to prove that they were homosexuals by providing at least three letters from people with whom they had had sex. But merely having sex with another man was not enough; the letters must affirm that the man had actually swallowed semen in the process. While a typical discharge took several weeks to process, gay discharges took between six to eight months. The point of all this, Houston was instructed, was so anyone contemplating this way out knew it would be hell to pursue.

JUNE 1971
TACOMA, WASHINGTON

PERRY WATKINS HAD THOUGHT he was done with the Army when his
two-year hitch ended in 1970, and, indeed at that time, he had no intention
of returning. But Perry had a hard time readjusting to civilian life. He
knew he needed more education for any job he might want and he realized
he could get that education in the Army. So even as Gay Liberation Front
chapters chartered buses for the peace protests in Washington and San
Francisco, Perry was back at the recruiting center in Tacoma signing up
for Uncle Sam. And once again, Perry said he was gay. The recruiters
reviewed all his records, which indicated beyond a shadow of a doubt
that Watkins was, in the vernacular of the day, a practicing homosexual.
And once again, they swore him into the United States Army.

This time when Perry set out for the Army, he carried considerably
more luggage than when he had first joined three years earlier. This time,
he had packed for two: for Specialist Four Perry Watkins and for
"Simone."

Simone was born on a dull Wednesday night when a friend took Perry
to a downtown Tacoma gay bar called The Sand Box where a hefty drag
queen named Scarlett O'Hara hosted an amateur night for aspiring female
impersonators. A truck driver at the bar, whom Perry had known since
junior high, urged him to get onstage. Within a few minutes, Watkins
and Scarlett were singing a duet of "All I Need Is the Girl" from *Gypsy*.
Scarlett suggested Perry might want to try on a dress and work weekends
at The Sand Box.

The next day, Perry told his mother that he had had a job offer—
doing drag at a gay bar.

"That's a legitimate profession," Ola offered.

"I need to borrow your wigs," Perry said.

Happily, mother and son wore the same dress size, too. Then at the
Woolworth's makeup counter, as he stocked up on powder and blush,
Perry saw the brand name Simone on a compact case. He liked it better
than his first choice of a *nom de drag*, Tinkerbelle, and that was that.
Perry Watkins certainly was not going to let a little thing like the Army
get in the way of his show-business career.

At Sergeant Watkins's first duty station, a Pershing missile unit near
Frankfurt, West Germany, the unit's recreation coordinator asked Perry
what he had done before joining the Army.

"I was a female impersonator," Perry said. He showed the coordinator
a photo of Simone and explained his routines.

The coordinator, who was selecting acts for the unit's Organization
Day, was thrilled. Perry told him the unit commander would never approve his performing, but the coordinator took Simone's picture to the
commander anyway, and Perry later recalled being asked into his commander's office.

"Is this you?" the commander asked.

"Yes, sir, it is," he said.

"What do you do?"

Perry explained that he did some comedy, lip-synched to records, and could act as a master of ceremonies.

"Is this good for a family?" the commander asked.

"I did it in front of my mother," Watkins said, not adding that he would do just about anything in front of his mother.

On Organization Day, Simone was onstage and proved such a success that other units invited Perry to perform for them. He soon acquired an agent, who booked Simone in NCO and enlisted men's clubs throughout Europe. Ever since he was a kid with the Tacoma City Ballet, Perry had wanted to be an entertainer. Now he had finally achieved his dream, in the Army. As Simone.

16

Back to the World

WAS THERE A DEEPER REASON that Armistead Maupin and other veterans were returning to Vietnam? The reporter was very curious about this. Was there something these men wanted to atone for? A dark secret? An atrocity, perhaps?

It was something Maupin had gotten used to in the months since he had left the Navy; the gnawing suspicion that as an American serviceman stationed in Vietnam he must have killed a baby or two. Even when Maupin joined a group of nine other veterans to perform the inarguably altruistic task of building housing for disabled Vietnamese soldiers near Saigon, there were those questions about a hidden reason for their doing it.

Maupin's experience was not unique. The early 1970s was not a good time to be a veteran of the United States military.

Former Army Captain Jerry Rosanbalm could attest to that. One day at Columbia University, where he was a doctoral student, another student cornered him, thrust his jaw out accusingly, and said, "I understand you're a fucking baby killer."

"What does that mean?" asked Rosanbalm.

"You were one of those guys who was in Vietnam and you're proud of it," the other man said.

Rosanbalm said he was indeed, and the other man threw a punch in his face.

Most gay Vietnam vets, like their heterosexual counterparts, simply found it easier not to tell anyone what they had been doing for the past few years. Vietnam began to exist only in their memories—and their nightmares.

Danny Flaherty would wake up in the middle of the night screaming and writhing in his bed. Were the dreams of those piles of bodies being bulldozed into a ditch during Operation Cedar Falls? He could never remember when he awoke. It was a part of his life he had pulled a curtain over and sealed into the past.

ALL DURING THEIR TOURS of duty, GIs talked about going "back to the world," the expression for returning to the States. Invariably, coming home was a disappointment. Danny Flaherty, Armistead Maupin, Jess Jessop, and Jerry Rosanbalm had returned to a country that did not much want to hear about this war and did not much want to think about the young men who had died and been wounded in it.

A generation later, when the dead were largely forgotten and the debates about whether this was a justifiable war were no longer argued, the callous attitude toward Vietnam veterans was still remembered as one of the greatest injustices of the conflict. In the immediate wake of the war, it seemed as if popular imagination had declared that these young men *were* the war, and, by ignoring them, the nation could ignore this particular war's senselessness and, perhaps more significantly, the fact that it had ended in defeat—the first defeat the United States had ever endured on the battlefield. For it was clear by 1971 that though the American withdrawal was called Vietnamization and peace with honor, it was still a retreat. Better to forget it all, and to a large extent that meant forgetting *them.*

So young men like Jessop and Flaherty and Rosanbalm returned to a country that just didn't care. Not only did nobody want to hear about Vietnam; veterans got the message that most people blamed *them* for the government's foreign policy, and for the humiliation of defeat.

The stories of antiwar demonstrators spitting on veterans and of insults meted out by ideologues of the American Left were only part of the reality for veterans, and a smaller part of the reality at that. The harshest treatment came not from peace protesters but from the faceless bureaucracy of the United States government.

Wounded soldiers were assigned to Veterans Administration hospitals that were sometimes dilapidated. Returning Vietnam veterans received substantially lower benefits than those awarded to veterans of the two previous wars. Their educational benefits sometimes arrived so late that they had to drop out of school for lack of money. For the first time, being a veteran was not helpful in finding a job; it was an impediment. Many employers believed that Vietnam vets were drug addicts and refused to hire them. While the overall unemployment rate in the United States during 1971 was 5.3 percent, the unemployment rate for Vietnam veterans was 8.8 percent. Many Americans had a hand in degrading the Vietnam veteran.

AT CAT LAI, Armistead Maupin's trip into his past illuminated the road to his future. Far from a journey of atonement, going back to Vietnam was actually a political venture that had begun with a phone call a few months earlier. The Vietnam Veterans Against the War had garnered a huge amount of press by lobbying Congress for a withdrawal of all troops from Southeast Asia. President Nixon wanted to show there were prowar vets, too, and he had assigned Chuck Colson to mount a PR counteroffensive. Colson arranged for the ten veterans to build the cinder-block homes at Cat Lai that summer, under the watchful eyes of media, hungry for any new angle on the endless Vietnam story.

It was during this trip to Cat Lai that Maupin, who had been working for the *News and Courier* in Charleston since he had gotten out of the Navy, quizzed an Associated Press reporter covering the story about employment opportunities. No sooner was Maupin back in South Carolina than he received a job offer to work in the AP's San Francisco bureau. Maupin was driving cross-country in his Opel GT when he got a message from Bob Haldeman, the White House chief of staff, to say that the President wanted to meet with him and the other vets from the Cat Lai project.

Nixon appeared incredibly nervous during his forty-five minutes with the veterans. The only time he seemed to relax was when he talked about the girls in Vietnam—"those lovely little butterflies," he called them.

A week later, Maupin felt quite smug arriving at San Francisco's AP office and apologizing about being late, what with his personal visit to the President and all. Unimpressed, the bureau dispatched him to accompany a peace march across the city—an eight-mile march at that. San Francisco, he saw, was not Charleston. Being a confidant of Richard Nixon's was nothing anyone would brag about in public here.

There was another difference, which impressed Maupin the day he told the sister of a college friend, after three mai-tais and great hemming and hawing, that he was gay. The friend, who was heterosexual, took Maupin's hand, stared directly into his eyes, and said, "Big fucking deal."

Maupin began exploring San Francisco's gay subculture and came to realize that if others could accept him, he could accept himself. The song of the day was "Rocky Mountain High" by John Denver, about a man who "was born in the summer of his twenty-seventh year, going home to a place he'd never been before," and Maupin felt the song was about himself.

After he had settled into his apartment on Russian Hill, he received an award from the Freedom Foundation for his work in Vietnam, an honor arranged for by his old friend and mentor Jesse Helms, who was said to be contemplating leaving television commentary for a new field, politics.

It was about this same time that Danny Flaherty, strolling down Castro Street in San Francisco, met a long-haired man who was opening a camera shop. Flaherty managed a wicker-furniture store around the corner; he was aware that the older, more established merchants on the street were not happy with the influx of homosexuals into the neighborhood. The two men started to talk. The camera store's owner thought gays should fight back, organize their own gay merchants group, and encourage gay consumers to buy from them. "There's power in gay money and in gay votes," he told anyone who would listen. It had been seven years since Danny had been detained in a small room at Northern Illinois University and asked to name other homosexuals; seven years since he had experienced that utter lack of power. The years had not dulled that memory, and talk of building a power base struck a chord. Danny would not forget that first meeting, or the camera store owner's unusual name, Harvey Milk.

MEANWHILE, IN WASHINGTON, political trends and military necessities conspired to change forever the sexual makeup of the United States armed forces. President Nixon's goal of an all-volunteer military by July 1973 was in trouble. Despite pay increases, the Army did not have enough volunteers for its infantry and artillery units. Not only were adequate numbers of new recruits not appearing but retention rates of experienced soldiers were at their lowest since the Korean War. In 1971, fewer than 4 percent of Army soldiers reenlisted, about half the number who had re-upped just five years before. There were serious doubts as to whether the Pentagon could sustain enlisted ranks for any length of time without the draft.

There were also problems in securing new officers. Typically, the Army obtained half its officers from colleges' ROTC programs; the Air Force netted 35 percent of its officers from ROTC. With the military's popularity at a nadir on college campuses, ROTC enrollment had plummeted. Critics of a volunteer army pronounced it dead before arrival. And then it occurred to someone how to save the idea of a volunteer Army and to eliminate the draft: women.

In June 1972, a special House subcommittee on military manpower chaired by Congressman Otis Pike issued a key report: "We are concerned that the Department of Defense and each of the military services are guilty of 'tokenism' in the recruitment and utilization of women in the Armed Forces. We are convinced that in the atmosphere of a zero-draft environment or an all-volunteer military force, women could and should play a more important role." At the Department of Defense, personnel officials analyzed their recruitment numbers and arrived at the same conclusion. The head of the Pentagon's task force for a volunteer army ordered the Marine Corps to plan for a 40 percent increase in women by 1977, and for the Army, Navy, and Air Force to get ready to double their numbers of women. The Army launched an ambitious program to make up with WACs its shortfalls in male recruitment. Political pressure mounted on the services to open more job categories to women.

Meanwhile, the campaign for women's rights steamrolled through Washington with little organized opposition. Even the Department of

Labor signed on in support of the long-stalled Equal Rights Amendment, which would amend the Constitution to bar any discrimination against women. In October 1971, the House of Representatives had voted 354 to 23 in support of the ERA; in March 1972, the Senate had overwhelmingly voted its approval. Given the massive public support and the lack of any foes, ratification seemed inevitable.

Almost immediately, those congressmen who supplied the service academies with nominations for new students began calling for women to be allowed into West Point and the Naval and Air Force academies. The suggestion horrified senior Pentagon officials. The Navy was particularly aghast. "There are no facilities for women at the Academy," said Secretary of the Navy John H. Chafee, who also maintained that since federal law gave preference to "sons" of Naval personnel and "enlisted men," women should not be allowed. More and more federal rulings, however, indicated that the courts would force the integration of women at the academies under the equal-protection clause of the Constitution, whether the military liked it or not.

By 1972, two things were clear about the future of the United States military: Women would play an ever-increasing role in the armed forces and military men would do everything they could to stop it.

MARCH 10, 1972
BISMARCK KASERNE
NEAR FRANKFURT, GERMANY

ACTING ON A TIP from a "confidential informant," the investigators from the CID undoubtedly had the morning entirely scripted. Interrogations nearly always ran the same course: Make the accusation, listen to the impassioned denial, and, in the end, get exactly what you needed to know. Given the predictability of these sessions, the agents were clearly taken aback by the twenty-three-year-old black specialist four sitting in front of them.

Of course he was a homosexual, Perry Watkins said. You could read it right on his enlistment papers. And he would not give the CID names of other homosexuals on the base, nor would he give them names of people with whom he had been to bed. By now, he knew the regulations and knew he did not even have to talk to the CID.

When CID agents searched Watkins's locker, they found wigs and dresses, makeup and high heels, evidence that in normal circumstances would lead to the quick separation of the suspected homosexual. The CID investigators studiously took Polaroid photos of all the paraphernalia and marked the photos exhibits G through J in their investigation file.

In the days after Watkins's interrogation, the CID pulled in several other soldiers from the Bismarck Kaserne who confirmed that, by all appearances, Watkins was a homosexual and that he had made it known to several of the better-looking GIs that he was available for them if they needed anything. None of this news seemed particularly startling among the men of the Fifty-sixth Artillery Brigade. Just about everyone, it seemed, had seen Perry slipping into his Simone outfit at the barracks.

Two weeks into its investigation of Watkins as a potential sodomite, the CID called it off, not sure of what to do with a homosexual who admitted it. According to the official file, "This investigation is terminated due to the refusal of WATKINS to furnish any investigative leads."

Watkins was enjoying his celebrity status on Army posts in Germany. The *Stars and Stripes* published a glowing feature article on his act. In the States, the number-one TV show was "The Flip Wilson Show," on which the black comedian had popularized his own drag character, Geraldine. GERALDINE MEET SIMONE, the *Stars and Stripes* headline read. SHE MAKES THE 56TH ARTILLERY BRIGADE GUYS FLIP." Perry laughed to himself at the irony of it: He had made more guys flip than the Army would ever know. When Watkins as Simone competed with eleven actual women in an Army beauty pageant, she won.

Nevertheless, the investigation stung. It was the second adversity Perry had encountered since arriving in Germany. The first had been a drawn-out fight for security clearance to work at the classified Pershing missile site. The security officer had denied Watkins a clearance because he was a homosexual and could be blackmailed. Watkins challenged him: How could he be blackmailed for being a homosexual? He was making nightly appearances in an evening gown under the name of Simone. He was not exactly in a deep closet. It took several months for the wisdom of the argument to prevail; finally, Watkins was granted his security clearance.

Perry knew that many men did indeed get kicked out of the Army for being gay and he was always astounded that none of them ever fought back. Working in personnel, he saw it again and again, men waiving their rights to a hearing, quietly accepting less than honorable discharges, as if they had done something wrong. The mistake these guys were making, Perry thought, was certainly not that they were queer, and not even that they had gotten caught. Their mistake was that they were not fighting back.

After the CID investigation, Perry learned that married men in the platoon got a day off to spend with their wives on their anniversaries. He patiently waited for the day that marked a year since he had met his German boyfriend and then informed his platoon sergeant that he wanted the day off for his anniversary. The sergeant said he could not allow that.

"Sure you can," Perry said.

He got the day off.

AT ABOUT THE SAME TIME Perry Watkins arrived in West Germany, two sociologists, Drs. Colin Williams and Martin Weinberg, both from the

Institute for Sex Research at Indiana University, Dr. Kinsey's institute, released one of the first studies conducted on men receiving gay-related discharges from the military.

The researchers found that much of the military's own data on gay-related discharges was so incomplete as to be "worthless." But they were able to pick through the complicated regulations that defined the types of discharges given out to gays, and then they were able to discern the long-term effects of those discharges on gay soldiers. At that time, the services offered five levels of discharge: The honorable discharge allowed its recipient all rights and privileges due to veterans. The general discharge was less than honorable. An undesirable discharge was one step above a bad conduct discharge. And the lowest separation, called a dishonorable discharge, was only given after one was found guilty of a serious criminal offense at a military court-martial. Drawing from a study sample of more than four hundred gay veterans who had returned questionnaires, Weinberg and Collins found that among veterans who had received less than honorable discharges, 39 percent had gotten general discharges, 55 percent had received undesirable, and 6 percent had been given dishonorable.

Though statistics were difficult to unearth at the Pentagon, gays clearly comprised a huge share of all undesirable discharges handed out by the military. Commanders, who made the initial decisions regarding the type of discharge, sought the toughest possible punishment for gays, even if this conflicted with official military mandates for general or honorable discharges. In 1961, for example, fully 40 percent of all of the Navy's undesirable discharges had gone to presumed homosexuals. Nearly one in five undesirable discharges given to Marines that year had been for homosexuality. There was no indication that in the decade since then the quality of discharges had improved much for the approximately 2,700 gays who had been kicked out of the military each year on gay-related charges.

Perhaps the most intriguing part of the study, however, was the research indicating how gay soldiers got caught and what happened once they were under investigation. Only one in six of the discharged gay soldiers had been detected because he had committed an indiscretion that brought him to the attention of his commanding officers. Instead, 54 percent had been turned in by someone else, often someone under investigation himself. Another 29 percent had identified themselves as gay, almost always as part of a standard military interrogation.

During an investigation, the researchers found, "He is removed from his daily duties and set apart. Often frightened and confused, he is subjected to threats or promises on the part of investigating authorities who often have little evidence to secure a conviction. Under such pressure he is often willing to sign anything to stop the harassment and so cooperates. . . . Such threats and persuasions are usually enough to make the homosexual waive his rights and confess. The investigating authorities are tenacious, and in representing the situation to be other than it is, the accused often feels he has little alternative but to cooperate."

The two eminent sociologists came to the same conclusion as had Specialist Four Watkins at his Pershing missile site in Germany: People did not fight back. Of the soldiers sampled by the researchers, 81 percent had waived their rights to hearings on their discharges, virtually guaranteeing an undesirable discharge. "In our research we have no cases of people who demanded their rights and really made a fight of it," the researchers wrote. "Nor do we know the extent of those who are charged with homosexuality but later have the charges dropped. Both kinds of cases do exist but are small compared to the general reaction of servicemen accused of homosexuality. What evidence we have supports the belief of homophile organizations that the majority of homosexuals discovered by the military do not make a fight of it and in effect allow themselves to be discharged without honor."

The study further found that some 26 percent of those who had received less than honorable discharges felt "guilt and shame," while 12 percent reported "confusion and collapse" from the ordeal. More than half said the bad discharges affected their ability to get jobs—it was routine then for prospective employers to check all veterans' discharge papers. In the long term, most gay GIs managed to weather the significant psychological distress and recover. The researchers found that 58 percent of the veterans who had received less than honorable discharges had considered suicide in the aftermath of their investigations and release from the military. Those who succeeded obviously were not around to be interviewed.

A less formal study of employers taken some time later concerned the negative long-term effects of less than honorable discharges. According to a survey of major employers by U.S. Representative John Seiberling of Ohio, 41 percent admitted that they discriminated against veterans with general discharges, 61 percent admitted bias against undesirable discharges, and 73 percent said they would not hire anyone with a dishonorable discharge.

If there were any questions about what had sparked even an honorable discharge, employers could read the story in a set of obscure numbers the Department of Defense had typed onto every discharge paper it issued. The "spin" numbers—so-called for their official moniker, the Separation Program Number—designated at least four different kinds of gay-related discharge. For example, 46-D meant "unsuitability—sexual deviate"; 249 indicated "resignation on grounds of homosexuality"; 256 stood for "acceptance of discharge in lieu of board action on grounds of homosexuality." The numbers were presumably for internal use at the Pentagon only, but, in truth, most major employers kept a list of spin numbers to check against discharge documents. That was how a military accusation of homosexuality could become part of a person's permanent record.

JUNE 1972
NEWARK, DELAWARE

RICH MCGUIRE WAS NOT ALONE, but he could not tell who was with him. Then he caught a glimpse of them, the men with no faces. Silently, they led him into a quaint New England house and down a flight of stairs into a basement. He could smell its damp mustiness. In the center was a small cell with thickly padded walls. They had some questions to ask. He stared at them, but still he could see no faces, just forms of vague hostility.

Rich bolted upright in bed. His stomach was churning and his head reeled until he could reassure himself that he wasn't at Westover Air Force Base but at home, in his own bed, his parents sleeping a few rooms away.

He had been out of the Air Force twenty-one months. He had a good job engineering the morning news at WJIC radio in Wilmington, the kind of job he had held throughout high school. In many ways, it was as if he had never left and his Air Force career had never happened.

Rich believed what the OSI agents had told him, that if he ever spoke of his interrogations, he could go to jail. So he had never spoken about it.

17

Winners

JULY 14, 1972
DEMOCRATIC NATIONAL CONVENTION
MIAMI, FLORIDA

JIM FOSTER STRODE across the stage and took his place at the podium. As he began to speak, his sharp brown eyes scanned a crowd that was barely visible in the glare of the network television lights. But he was not really talking to the crowd or to the tens of millions of Americans watching his speech on TV. *Does your father know his son is a stinking little fairy?* Nor was he speaking for posterity, though the speech would be remembered as a turning point for the gay-rights movement. *Just give us the names of other queers. They did it to you. That's how we got your name.* Looking into the crowd, as he began his speech at the Democratic National Convention, Jim Foster looked into the eyes of Army Captain Walsh. He never knew his first name, just the surname on the tag above the pocket of the green uniform: Captain Walsh. Jim Foster was speaking to him.

"We do not come to you pleading your understanding or begging your tolerance," Foster began. "We come to you affirming our pride in our lifestyle, affirming the validity to seek and maintain meaningful emotional relationships and affirming our right to participate in the life of this country on an equal basis with every citizen."

There were cheers and there were murmurs as Foster launched into his speech. Conservative delegates, already stunned by George McGovern's liberal shenanigans, were dumbfounded that the presidential candidate's handlers had allowed this, a speech supporting a gay-rights plank for the national party platform, *a gay-rights plank* . . . on the night McGovern was giving his acceptance speech. Foster knew that discontent was rife in the convention, even among liberals sympathetic to his words.

But the McGovern people had a debt to repay, and so it was that Jim Foster addressed the convention and the nation on behalf of a movement that, for all practical purposes, did not even exist during the previous presidential election. As much as addressing the conventioneers about the movement's future, Foster was addressing his past.

ON A DAY IN JUNE 1959 when Foster was at work in his office at Fort Holabird, Maryland, three agents from the CID had appeared at his door.

"Who is Jim Foster?" one asked.

Foster identified himself.

"Pack your things and come with us right now," the CID agent said.

Foster was just over halfway through his two-year Army stint, having been drafted after he graduated from Brown University with a degree in English. His high test scores landed him at the military-intelligence command. Weekend trips to the Provincetown gay beaches on Cape Cod introduced Jim to other gay soldiers, including an intelligence officer from Fort Holabird who maintained a vaguely superior attitude toward everyone. Jim had not much cared for the fellow, and, recently, he had dropped out of sight, just disappeared. Nobody knew what had happened to him.

Foster was taken into a small room where he was interrogated by two CID agents. The way Foster later remembered the morning, one agent was fairly pleasant; the other was Captain Walsh.

"We know you're a queer," Walsh began. "You could end up in jail. Make it easy on yourself and admit it."

"He's right, Jim," the other agent broke in. "You could be in big trouble, and you don't really deserve that, do you? Just give us some names and we'll make sure you get a general discharge. We'll see that you're treated fairly."

"You stupid fagola," Walsh said when the softer tack didn't work. Jim focused on his name tag. "You stupid fairy. Your one chance to make it better for yourself is to give us names of other faggots. They'd do the same to you." Walsh grinned. "They already have."

The first four-hour round of interrogation went nowhere, and the agents next rifled through Jim's locker, seizing all his mail and his address book. Every day for the next two weeks, the two agents took Jim back to the little room and questioned him again. Walsh threatened to call Jim's father, a proud veteran of New York's Seventh Regiment, to testify against him. Did he know his son was a fairy? Jim's aunt was a retired WAC, a lieutenant colonel in the reserve. Did she know he was a queer?

Finally, Jim admitted that he was gay, hoping the questions would stop. Instead, they got worse. Captain Walsh thumbed through every page of Jim's address book and read each name aloud.

"Sarah Whiteside, is she a dyke?"

"That's my eighty-four-year-old great-aunt."

"And this one—is she queer, too?"

"That's my grandmother."

As Walsh continued reading names, Jim could see a smile underneath his fierce expression, a kind of relish that showed him that the captain really enjoyed what he was doing.

Jim had always considered being homosexual as something you did, not something you were. But in Captain Walsh's eyes, he saw hate for who he was. His year in military intelligence had shown Jim that the Army spent more time hunting homosexuals than Nazi war criminals. Now Jim understood why. To guys like Captain Walsh, Jim Foster was more despicable than a Nazi war criminal. Jim had never known such hatred. He had been raised in a solidly Republican family in the solidly Republican town of Manhasset, Long Island, and taught to believe America stood for good things. He could see now that America stood for Captain Walsh, and that the entire weight of the United States government stood behind Walsh and against Jim Foster.

It was during the fourteenth interrogation that Jim Foster finally gave Captain Walsh what he wanted, in return for the other agent's pledge of a general discharge. Jim knew a rabidly antigay private in his barracks who could never talk enough about how much he hated queers. Jim gave the CID that man's name. The interrogations ended then, and the next morning Foster watched Walsh and the other agent take the private away. When Jim received his discharge on July 15, 1959, he learned that the CID had lied to him about obtaining a general discharge. In huge black letters across the top of the page, his document read: UNDESIRABLE DISCHARGE.

Months later, Foster moved to San Francisco, where he hoped his disgrace would not follow him. He left home vowing to get back at Captain Walsh, to make the system change. Almost immediately upon arriving, he threw himself into promoting gay equality. He was among the founders of the Society for Individual Rights in 1964, a pioneering gay-rights group. Foster had grown up believing the way to change the country was to elect people who saw things your way, so he used his influence with the group to do something unimagined over the previous two centuries of the Republic: to question public officials about where they stood on gay issues, and then make endorsements. By 1969, a novice San Francisco politician named Dianne Feinstein credited her landslide election to the local board of supervisors in part to the gay community. A new voting bloc was in the making, in no small part due to Jim Foster's organizing. Feinstein repaid gay support by sponsoring an ordinance that, in April 1972, made San Francisco the first major city in the country to outlaw discrimination among city contractors on the basis of sexual orientation.

In 1972, as liberals rallied around South Dakota Senator George McGovern as a presidential candidate, Foster transformed the SIR political committee into the Alice B. Toklas Memorial Democratic Club, the city's first gay Democratic organization. Though named for the hashish brownie-baking lover of lesbian author Gertrude Stein, Foster immediately positioned the club as one of the most productive grass-roots political groups in the city.

Their first major test came in the Democratic primary, which was shaping up as the crucial showdown between McGovern and former Vice President Hubert Humphrey. McGovern's managers calculated that about 3 percent of the vote went to the candidate whose name appeared first on the ballot, which could be a decisive margin. First place went to the first campaign to turn in their candidate's qualifying petitions to the office of Secretary of State Jerry Brown. But campaigns could not begin collecting signatures until after midnight of the designated day. McGovern's people thought about throwing wine tastings that would last until midnight, at which time they could circulate the petitions. Foster had a better idea.

At precisely midnight, Toklas Club members poured through gay bars in San Francisco, rousting every registered Democrat they could find for McGovern. Within two hours, they had collected more than one-third of the signatures the campaign needed, thus ensuring the senator his top berth on the ballot. After McGovern won the primary and wrapped up the nomination, his managers appointed Foster one of two openly gay delegates to the convention.

The party's platform committee declined to adopt the comprehensive gay-rights plank Foster proposed, opting for a broadly worded statement that "Americans should be free to make their own choice of life-styles . . . without being subject to discrimination." Foster did garner enough support to present a minority report to the full convention, calling for an end to all sodomy laws and all forms of discrimination against gays. But the McGovern forces cringed at including such language in their platform and dispatched Ohio delegate Kathleen Welch to lead the charge against the minority report, claiming that such reforms would encourage child molestation and white slavery. "It would be a political disaster of monumental proportions for this party to adopt such a report," she said. Welch won the vote, but not before Foster was given the chance to speak.

It was thirteen years since he had received his undesirable discharge at Fort Holabird. He wore a garish plaid jacket that hung loosely off his tall, thin frame, and the TV lights glinted off a pate that had grown bald, but Jim Foster's years of public speaking had given him a classic oratorical style, enhanced by his rich baritone voice. Foster enumerated injustices against gays, including the "brutal and ruthless" purges of gays in the military and the $12 million the Civil Service Commission spent each year investigating gay civilian employees. If authorities enforced laws against heterosexual bars with the vigor they employed against gay establishments, Foster said, "there would not be jails in the United States big enough to hold all the prisoners." All this bred a terrifying fear, he said, leading to "the most devastating fear of all—the fear of self-acceptance."

He aimed his words as if he were aiming a gun. He hoped beyond all else that Captain Walsh was out there somewhere listening.

"These are not conservative or radical issues, these are human issues," Foster concluded. "Regardless of whether this convention passes this plank or not, there are millions of gay brothers and sisters who will say to the Democratic Party: We are here. We will not be still. We will not go away until the ultimate goal of gay liberation is realized, the goal that all people live in the peace, freedom, and dignity of who we are."

THAT FOSTER SHOULD BE STANDING before the Democratic National Convention just three years after the contemporary gay cause was conceived in a riot at the Stonewall Inn reflected how nearly effortlessly the early gains of the homosexual movement had come. In the same way that most reasonable people readily acceded to the many obviously sensible demands of the women's movement, there were also elemental truths in the language of the new gay movement that struck a chord with people of all sexual orientations. The right words needed only be spoken aloud, and there were people ready to listen.

Few disputed, for instance, that the government did not have any business telling people what to do in the privacy of their own bedrooms. "Legislating morality" was the phrase gay activists used in criticizing the laws that made "sodomy" or "unnatural sexual acts" a felony punishable in most states by prison sentences of five to ten or even twenty years. In some jurisdictions, a repeat offender could get a life sentence. Since the birth of the Republic until 1971, only one state, Illinois, had repealed such a law, but, beginning in 1971, sodomy laws began falling in state after state. Oregon became the second state, after Illinois, to do away with its sodomy law. In the 1972 and 1973 legislative sessions, Connecticut, Hawaii, Delaware, and Ohio also did away with their statutes banning the "crime against nature." In North Dakota, where the repeal passed the Republican-dominated state house of representatives by an 87 to 9 vote, legislation restricting the rights of teenagers to smoke in public proved far more provocative than the new rules allowing consenting adults to indulge in any form of consensual sexual activity they liked. Except in Idaho, where a huge population of Mormons pressured the legislature to rescind its 1971 sodomy repeal in 1972, the reforms caused barely a ripple of controversy.

In Congress, Representative Ed Koch of New York introduced legislation to amend the federal civil rights act to ban discrimination on the basis of sexual orientation. The campus radicals of the early Gay Liberation Front days came together with new organizers interested in more mainstream political endeavors. Their successes were modest by the standards of other minority groups, but they were nothing short of momentous considering the brief time in which gays had been organizing seriously. Their achievements convinced gay leaders that theirs were ideas whose time had come. There was some truth in that analysis, but perhaps a better reason the victories came so quickly was the fact that there was no organized opposition. Plenty of people disagreed with changing the sodomy laws and with granting any legitimacy to homosexuals, but these people had no spokesmen, no lobby, and no organization, so they were largely silent. Just because they were silent, however, did not mean they were not there.

GEORGE WASHINGTON HOTEL
WASHINGTON, D.C.

THOUGH SHE WAS STILL YOUNG and pretty, her show-business career had certainly known better days, it was clear. That undoubtedly was why she was dressed up in a cowboy hat, a satin cowboy dress with fringe, and had toy six-shooters strapped to her hips. Her husband hovered nearby, looking officious and shouting orders, but the woman looked lonely and a little sad sitting backstage knitting, waiting to appear. Everybody else knew Anita Bryant from her orange-juice commercials on television, but this was how Copy Berg always remembered her, looking lonesome and a little lost backstage at the George Washington Hotel.

It was one of the perks of being in the Glee Club of the United States Naval Academy that you got to meet celebrities wherever you went. This was how winners lived, and as he lined up with the other Annapolis cadets to back up Anita Bryant on her trademark song, "The Battle Hymn of the Republic," Navy Midshipman Copy Berg had no doubt that he was a winner.

Vernon E. Berg III was the eldest son of Navy Commander Vernon E. Berg, Jr., one of the most respected officers in the Navy's chaplain corps. The senior Berg had been equally revered in the civilian ministry, as a preacher who touched people's souls. His sermons changed lives, they said of Vernon E. Berg; he was charismatic, and no one could believe how much his namesake resembled his father. Their childhood photographs were indistinguishable. As young Vernon grew into his full five-foot-nine-inch frame and his hair turned sandy blond, he was still the carbon copy of his dad, right down to the deep blue eyes and second-tenor voice, which was why they called him Copy. And they were extraordinarily close, to the point that Copy knew what his father was thinking just by looking at him, as if they were the same person. They did virtually everything together until the commander went to Vietnam in 1967 to minister to the Marines.

Copy began establishing his own track record of being a winner then. He was not just another track letterman at Frank W. Cox High School; he was also student-body president. At Boy's State, he was not just a delegate, he was a candidate for governor. At Boy Scout Troop 422, he was not simply another Life Scout, he was Alowat Sikima, Chief of Fire, the top position of the elite Order of the Arrow fraternity for the entire Chesapeake Bay area. Whenever local chapters of the Lion's or Rotary or Optimist's Clubs needed a *good* teenager to speak, they trotted out Copy Berg.

There was a creative side to Copy, and he excelled in music and art.

Later, he regretted he did not apply to Juilliard to develop his artistic talent earlier, but Copy Berg lived in Virginia Beach, Virginia, one of the communities that circles the elaborate network of Navy installations centered around Norfolk. In Virginia Beach, nobody went to Juilliard; few had even heard of it. Winners went to the United States Naval Academy at Annapolis. In the Cox High class of 1969, a dozen graduates went, and Copy Berg was among them.

Only in his sexual attractions did his confidence waver. He liked women and had had plenty of sexual experiences with them in high school and after. But he also liked men. In Troop 422, he had begun a four-year relationship with another Boy Scout that endured through his senior year at Cox. They had good sex, too. He was not plagued by guilt over this, but he knew he was not supposed to be having these kinds of attractions and he also knew instinctively he was not supposed to talk about it. Commander Berg had a number of books about sexuality in his library, and one day Copy looked up homosexuality. The book offered "case studies of deviate sexual behavior," which relieved Copy. Homosexuals wore dresses and wanted to be women; Copy was not like that, so obviously he was not one of them.

But in the year he spent at the Naval Academy Preparatory School in advance of his first year at Annapolis, there were rumors. One friend finally asked, "Why is it everyone thinks you're a homo?"

"Because I'm thin," Copy said, which seemed reasonable enough.

On weekends, Berg went from the preparatory school to New York City, and occasionally had sex with men he met at Times Square or on the subway. But for him, these encounters were play; they did not comprise an identity.

Copy never wanted for dates with girls. He was active in the Annapolis drama program, where he met and began dating the daughter of Admiral William Mack, the superintendent of the Naval Academy. The admiral was pleased. Copy Berg was the kind of man you wanted your daughter to date. All this was diverting, but Copy sometimes felt that somehow, in his romantic life, he was missing the point. By the autumn of his sophomore year at Annapolis, he was thinking more about his identity and becoming aware that his attractions were drifting toward males. Lord knew, he could not expect to pursue a Navy career with such extracurricular activities; they threw people like that in the brig.

With no one to talk to about them, his conflicts grew. The Naval Academy did not offer many opportunities to explore one's feelings and Annapolis was not an environment that gave a twenty-year-old any venue in which to discuss his confusion over sexual identity. Any such discussion would be the end not only of a Navy career but the Academy's college education, as well. One night, standing at the head of the stairs in Bancroft Hall, the huge redbrick Academy dormitory, Copy Berg stared down the open stairwell toward the lobby, eight floors below, and wondered what it would be like to throw himself down.

WHILE COPY BERG STRUGGLED with his sexuality, the Navy was struggling with its first case of a sailor who, confronted with a homosexual discharge, had done something no other person had done in the history of the U.S. Navy: He fought back.

Petty Officer Third Class Robert Martin had an unblemished record when he wrote a former shipmate, Terry Fountain, about his latest sexual adventures at his current home port of Naples, Italy. Martin's exploits centered largely on women but also included several men, who, he wrote, always seemed attracted by those tight-fitting Navy bell-bottoms. Fountain had left the letter on his desk at work, where someone else read it and promptly turned it over to the Naval Investigative Service, the successor agency to the Office of Naval Intelligence.

According to an interview Fountain later gave to *The Advocate*, NIS agents told him that while he did not have to speak to them, he faced a court-martial if he failed to cooperate. This was not true, but Fountain did not know that. Facing the threat of jail time, Fountain signed a statement that had been written by NIS agents before he even began the interview. The statement alleged Fountain had had sex with Martin and accused Martin of various violations of both Navy regulations and the Uniform Code of Military Justice. Fountain later submitted a notarized affidavit saying the statement was "false, fabricated, inaccurate and generally written by" NIS agents, but the recantation did not move the administrative board hearing Martin's case, and they ordered the petty officer separated from the service with a less than honorable discharge.

In the tens of thousands of hearings since World War II where comparable actions had been taken on the basis of comparable evidence, the matter ended there, with the sailor skulking away in disgrace. Petty Officer Martin, however, went public with what had happened to him and swore to fight for an honorable discharge. What was more, he enlisted some powerful support.

Congressman Koch scolded Defense Secretary Melvin Laird that the discharge reflected thinking "cruelly out of date" and that it should be upgraded to honorable. In remarks he read into the *Congressional Record*, Koch said, "While it is apparent that the leaders of the military, in order to maintain discipline, feel it necessary to exclude homosexuals, there is no need to gratuitously punish them with an undesirable discharge." Congresswoman Bella Abzug, also of New York City, called on Secretary of the Navy John Chafee to personally intervene. Martin's attorney, meanwhile, went ballistic on the quality of the Navy's evidence used in the hearing. "No Nazi court ever acted on evidence of a lower standard," he said. "In six years of military law, I've never seen a case where concepts of 'due process' were so ignored."

The Marine Corps also saw their first case of a gay leatherneck fighting for his job at about the same time. Eighteen-year-old Jeffrey Dunbar, a high school dropout from Falls Church, Virginia, had joined the Marines hoping it would make him a man. Instead, the secret knowledge that he was gay cast him into deeper turmoil. Ultimately, he attempted suicide. Rifling through his belongings, the Marine Corps's Criminal Investigation Division discovered a love letter written to Dunbar from another man. An administrative board handed him an undesirable discharge.

Dunbar went public with his plight. Longtime Washington gay activist Frank Kameny lined up gay ex-Marines to testify at the young man's hearing. *The Washington Post* ran an editorial supporting an upgraded discharge, noting that Dunbar "was involved in no scandal and had brought no shame on the Marine Corps," and called the undesirable discharge "a strange and, we think, pointless way of pursuing military 'justice.'" The Washington Gay Activists Alliance staged a protest at the Quantico Marine Corps Base, where Dunbar was stationed. Other Marines grimly watched the protesters with their provocative signs: THE MARINE CORPS BUILDS CLOSET GAYS: ASK A MARINE, and YOUR DRILL SERGEANT COULD BE GAY. One gunnery sergeant muttered to a young *Post* reporter named Carl Bernstein who covered the demonstration, "I wish I had a grenade. I'd drop it right in the middle of them."

Though both the Dunbar and Martin cases generated substantial coverage in the gay press, they received little support from gay-movement organizations. Martin's defense fund raised only ninety-three dollars for his appeal. Because Martin was in the military, gay activists had a tough time getting enthusiastic about supporting him.

The publicity undoubtedly saved Martin from the undesirable discharge Navy prosecutors originally wanted to grant him. But it did not get him anything better than a general discharge and it did not save his career. In the end, the case was noteworthy because Robert Martin was the first sailor to fight the Navy's ban on gays.

Copy Berg would be the next.

THE 1972 DEMOCRATIC NATIONAL CONVENTION had marked a number of pivotal points for emerging constituency groups. There was the first, though unsuccessful, attempt to obtain a gay-rights plank to the party platform. Women, for the first time, received a substantial role in the proceedings, comprising 40 percent of the total delegates, compared to just 13 percent four years earlier. Though these advances were significant for gays and women, it must also be noted that the convention was a prelude to disaster for the Democratic party.

A political realignment took shape in the 1972 election, a shift that would define presidential politicking for the next two decades. Democrat McGovern based his campaign in large part on an extremely liberal domestic agenda and the promise to withdraw troops from Vietnam. The war, however, was fading as a campaign issue. Only fifty thousand American troops were still stationed in Vietnam by election day, and Secretary of State Henry Kissinger assured the public in the last days of the campaign that "peace is at hand." That left McGovern with a domestic agenda demanding more change from a public weary and fearful of all the changes that had been foisted on it in the past decade.

Many of the fears were unspoken, but Republicans were learning to play on them just the same. President Nixon talked about his opposition to school busing as a means of achieving racial integration in schools and about the need for law and order. To a public fearful of African Americans and of crime and economic dislocation, these were powerful code words. Jim Foster and Gloria Steinem did not speak to those fears; often they exacerbated them. And so the Republicans could paint the Democratic party as a radical fringe, outside the mainstream. Vice President Agnew called them the party of the three A's: acid, abortion, and amnesty for draft dodgers. Blue-collar workers, who had found a new spokesman on the wildly popular new television show "All in the Family," retreated into the nostalgic rhetoric of Archie Bunker and deserted the Democrats. Most crucially, the Republicans pursued a "southern strategy" of alienating conservative southern voters from their century-old alliance with the Democrats. All of this culminated in one of the largest landslides in American history, meaning that come January 20, 1973, Copy Berg and the Naval Academy Chorus would be singing for the inauguration of Richard Nixon to a second term as President.

———————

THERE WAS ONE RESPITE from Berg's growing personal turmoil at the Naval Academy: singing second tenor in the Glee Club. Every other month, the Glee Club toured to promote the Academy, and it was on one of these tours at a meeting of the International Truckers' Association that Berg saw Bryant in her cowboy outfit. Copy felt sorry for her, so he and a friend grabbed a vase of roses sitting on the side of the stage and passed them out among the entire Glee Club. One by one, the white-uniformed men walked up to the singer and handed her a rose. She seemed almost shy as she put aside her knitting and gave each of the cadets a kiss on the cheek as he handed her a blossom: for every rose, a kiss from Anita Bryant.

— 18 —

STRAC

DECEMBER 1972
EGLIN AIR FORCE BASE
VALPARAISO, FLORIDA

HIS FACE LATHERED, his razor in hand, Technical Sergeant Leonard Matlovich stopped abruptly and stared into his mirror. His reddish hair was thinning now; his hairline was receding. Nearly a decade in the Air Force had kept him trim, but he could see youth was leaving his face.

Matlovich had been sure his roommate was gay. Tim, a junior non-commissioned officer, was always doing these provocative things, like lying languidly on the couch in his underwear, pushing the top of a Coke bottle in and out of his mouth. Leonard had given him a rubdown one night and Tim had lain passively while Matlovich kneaded his strong, muscular back. But when Leonard offered to do it again a few days later, Tim declined, saying the episode had given him troubling dreams. Leonard could imagine the kind of dreams. At last, he had found someone like himself. Unable to contain himself, Matlovich confessed his secret to his friend. Five minutes later, Tim had his bags packed and was pulling out of the driveway.

Never had Matlovich felt so alone, so miserable, so dirty. The next morning as he began to shave, he stared at himself in the mirror with a loathing beyond any he had felt before. Years later, he recalled his feelings precisely. "Why, God, why me?" he asked the mirror. "What have I ever done to deserve this?"

He was nearly thirty years old and he had never been held by another person, never been kissed, never been loved. He wiped the shaving cream off his face and went to the hall closet, where he kept a shotgun. He checked its chamber to be sure it was loaded.

Tim's room was still in disarray from his hurried departure, empty dresser drawers left open, papers strewn about. On the wall was a poster he had left behind, of a kitten clinging to a tree branch, with the legend HANG IN THERE, BABY.

Leonard lay down on the bare mattress and pulled the shotgun to his side. What would it be like to pull the trigger? he wondered. He opened the chamber and unloaded the shell. He rested the cold steel barrel against his temple and reached down to squeeze the trigger. It took much less pressure to pull than he had imagined; the hammer fell quickly on the empty chamber. *Click.* It would be over that fast.

Leonard put the shell back into the shotgun, placed the barrel to his head, and reached toward the trigger. He was just about to fire when he heard a scratching at the back door. He had forgotten Ralph.

Like a zombie, Leonard pulled himself off the bed and let Ralph inside. Ralph was a mutt Leonard had rescued from the local animal shelter after his return from Vietnam. Ralph had a perpetually happy disposition and an intuitive sense of when something was wrong with his master. He sniffed Leonard suspiciously, lapped at his water bowl, and then returned to the door. He wanted to go outside again, but, when Leonard opened the door, Ralph would not leave without Leonard.

Leonard pulled on a jacket and followed Ralph into the scrubby Florida woods near their apartment complex. Winter was only a few weeks away; the trees had lost their leaves. In the barrenness of the December morning, Matlovich crumpled to the ground and began to weep. His unhappiness engulfed him, but Ralph intruded, pushing against Leonard, nuzzling his chest. Then, when Matlovich looked up, Ralph carefully licked the tears from his face.

ON JANUARY 27, 1973, at the Hotel Majestic in Paris, Secretary of State William Rogers and North Vietnamese representative Nguyen Duy Trinh took their seats across a huge round table. A hush fell over the room as each leaned down to sign his name to the peace treaty that ended the Vietnam War. Hours later in Washington, Secretary of Defense Melvin Laird announced that the military draft was ended. From that day onward, the United States would employ an all-volunteer armed forces, fulfilling the campaign pledge President Nixon had made five years earlier.

At the White House, staffer Pete Randell was surprised there was not more jubilation. The President had just won one of the most overwhelming landslides in American history; the long nightmare of Vietnam was finally over; the history of the next four years was theirs to write.

For all their successes, however, Nixon's senior aides continued to be a dour lot, obsessed with settling old scores and hypersensitive about any slight they perceived from the media. Pete got occasional glimpses of this pettiness, such as the time he was handed a list of critics of the Nixon administration, complete with notations about their offenses against the President. Pete was to type it up for very limited distribution in the White House. Later, the document became known as the "Enemies List." In early 1973, the White House was that kind of place.

Not that Pete Randell wished for one minute he was working anywhere else. Every morning, when he drove his Thunderbird through the gate outside the West Wing of the Executive Mansion, awe struck him. He had been brought up in the South, so poor that in the summer he did not wear shoes so his family could save money. Now he worked at the White House. He was only a little wheel, to be sure, but to be working there in any capacity was like a dream, an only-in-America tale that reaffirmed the old-fashioned patriotism he held dear.

Pete's road to success had been through the United States Army. His dad was an Army chief warrant officer who had left his son to be raised by his impoverished grandparents in a clapboard house across the railroad tracks from Columbia, South Carolina. Pete had not really considered college; four months after he graduated from high school in 1965, he was in the Army, where he excelled. Pete was very STRAC, the Army term derived from the fact that soldiers are to be "Straight, Tough, and Ready, Around the Clock." In Army jargon, this meant a soldier who had his spit-and-polish act together. Pete was five nine, athletic, and blond, and he looked good in his dress blue uniform, which is probably why he won a prestigious assignment to the unit in which his father had once served, the Old Guard. The guard was one of the most elite units in the Army, whose duties included the laying of wreaths at the Tomb of the Unknown Soldier, burials at Arlington National Cemetery, and ceremonial inspections by heads of state. The guard's main job was to look good and look military, and STRAC Pete Randell did both.

It was with the guard that Pete first went to the White House. He had met President Johnson, who called him by his first name, and Lady Bird. His familiarity with the Executive Mansion undoubtedly helped Pete two years later when, newly discharged from the Army, he applied for a job as a secretary in the Nixon White House. The new administration preferred male secretaries to female, it seemed, and with his upright demeanor and studied military bearing, Pete Randell was welcomed to the White House staff. He started out as a typist, for speech writer Pat Buchanan, among others. Later he took over the night watch, typing daily news summaries for the President and preparing executive orders and new legislation for the presidential signing ceremonies the next day.

Pete's strong attractions to other men had started in his teen years. He had done the usual amount of messing around with other teenage boys, to a degree that must have caused some suspicion, because, he recalled, his mother began leaving pamphlets around the house that warned about masturbation causing blindness. "You know if you ever do anything to disgrace our name, we'll have to disown you," he remembered her telling him one day. By then, Pete was well enough along in his Catholic education to know that what he did was also an abomination to God. Pete learned that he should start suppressing his urges, which is what he did.

In the Army, he became aware of other penalties for his kind of attractions. During basic training at Fort Jackson, Pete was awakened one night by a commotion in the showers. When he investigated the noise, he found about forty guys lined up eagerly near the latrine. The other recruits had realized there was a faggot in the barracks, and two of the bigger guys had pushed him down on his knees and held him in the shower while the entire platoon lined up for blowjobs. The next day, the soldier was gone, just disappeared, and the men all joked about how they had really shown that faggot what for.

Two years later, when Pete was a sergeant for the Old Guard, he heard another disturbance in the shower stalls of his Arlington barracks. When he arrived on the scene, two men were scouring an effeminate young soldier with stiff bristle brushes used to scrub the floor. "You're dirty, you little faggot," one of the men shouted. "We're going to clean you up." The soldier's legs were raw and bleeding, and he screamed for help. And although Pete was an NCO and could have stopped it, he turned and walked upstairs, afraid of what it might say about himself if he came to the aid of a queer.

Still, his longings persisted, and sometimes they erupted. Pete frequently bowled at the Fort Myer bowling alley after hours. He was contemplating a professional bowling career and knew he had to practice to keep his scores high enough for a corporate sponsorship. It was late one night at the alley that he met a second lieutenant, a Kentucky farm boy, from the company that did all the burials at Arlington National Cemetery. When the officer's hand brushed against Pete's thigh, Pete did not move. By 3:00 A.M., they were having sex in lane three of the Moonlight Bowl. When the lieutenant saw Pete a few days later, he upbraided him for not saluting fast enough.

Such incidents left Pete unprepared for how casual sex was among gay White House staffers. In the West Wing, there were plenty of small offices for out-of-the-way encounters. One story had it that President Johnson had stepped into an office where a male senior staffer was having sex with his male junior aide. Johnson turned, closed the door, and said nothing. Entertainers traipsed through the White House for visits or performances, usually with heavily gay retinues. Three doors down from the President's office in the Old Executive Office Building, a senior staffer for President Nixon was said to have consummated his affair with an aide from the White House correspondence section. The pair had to cavort there, the story went, because they were afraid that if they moved in together people would know they were queer.

For most gay White House aides, however, there were fewer fears. Most were married, which gave them the cover they needed for the security clearances and social obligations required in such top-level positions. In May 1972, Pete had married a phone operator who worked with his mother. They had met at a bowling alley three months earlier and had a whirlwind courtship. Pete knew getting married was what he was supposed to do.

To be honest, despite his occasional dalliances with men, Pete never considered himself a homosexual. He barely considered these encounters at all. Once they were over, he did his best to forget they had ever happened, and he pledged not to do it again. Being queer was not STRAC. His sexuality, however ill-defined, was more a distraction than a preoccupation. There were more important things to think about in early 1973, such as the new agenda for the next administration and what could be accomplished over the next four years. It was in those weeks, Pete later remembered, that the reportage on the previous year's break-in at Democratic National Committee headquarters in the Watergate became more relentless, and there were the first indications that there might be something bigger in the unfolding scandal than just a few newspaper headlines.

FEBRUARY 1973
UNITED STATES NAVAL ACADEMY
ANNAPOLIS, MARYLAND

COPY BERG'S WINDOW on a new world opened unexpectedly during his junior year when he tried out for the part of Senex in *A Funny Thing Happened on the Way to the Forum.* The part was outrageously campy and, since the twenty-one-year-old midshipman always had had more nerve than talent onstage, it suited Berg's disposition perfectly. It was during auditions that Copy met Lawrence Gibson, a private grade-school teacher who was choreographer and director for the play. Bald and bearded, not especially handsome, Gibson was fifteen years older than Copy. He was, by most accounts, a bit stuffy; he always wore a three-piece suit and was not what you would call, in the lingo of the day, laid-back. None of this mattered to Copy, however, because Gibson also was many things that Copy Berg had never seen before in another person, someone he had never met in base towns like Virginia Beach or among the squared-away, buttoned-down instructors at the Naval Academy. Gibson was the first person Copy had ever met who he knew was gay. Copy aggressively invited himself to dinner at Gibson's apartment and the two began an affair.

Lawrence Gibson introduced Copy to a new world. The older man knew about good wines and antiques, the latest books and theater. He was not married, nor did he have children, something Copy just assumed he would have to do one day, because he had no idea there was any other way to live. On trips to Washington, Gibson introduced Berg to a vast network of gay men. Berg, who was barely old enough to go to bars, had been vaguely aware that such a subculture existed, but he never considered it something that related to him. This was not the gay world of, say, the Gay Liberation Front or even the Mattachine Society. This was more like life in the play *The Boys in the Band,* full of shrewd one-liners, aging opera aficionados, and stuffy bureaucrats, all extremely closeted.

Although Gibson brooded over the flattering attention his handsome young midshipman drew, the pair quickly settled into a routine. During the day, Copy was Midshipman Vernon E. Berg III, the model Academy cadet; every weekend, he carted his homework to Gibson's antique-filled apartment on Franklin Street, where he could explore a new side of himself and contemplate a new future.

Meanwhile at the Academy, the hot subject was whether to admit women to Annapolis. The cadet corps was overwhelmingly opposed to the idea, but they had also viewed with deep suspicion President Nixon's establishment of diplomatic relations with Red China a year earlier. The United States Naval Academy was not in the vanguard of social change, which was what made the appearance there of feminist writer Gloria Steinem so remarkable. Her reception at the Academy was an indication of the growing rift between the military and the civilian world. In Congress, Steinem, who was launching a new magazine for women called *Ms.*, might be taken as an influential presence, but at Annapolis the cadets hooted and hollered at her. "Why did you come here?" somebody finally asked her. She answered, "I came here to find out why I was invited." It was clear that the military men had never thought seriously about the new women's movement and that the new women's movement had not thought seriously about the military.

Not all the cadets were opposed to women, however, and debate dominated the next forty-eight hours at Annapolis. In every corner of Bancroft Hall, midshipmen clustered in groups of eight and twelve, yelling at one another about what the presence of women would do not only to the Academy but to the Navy as a whole. "What's happening to tradition?" was a common refrain. Christ, before you knew it, they would be putting women on ships, some worried, although most cadets agreed that this would probably never happen in their lifetimes—not if they had anything to do with it.

SIMILAR DEBATES occupied much of the country that year as the women's movement continued to push its concerns to the top of the cultural agenda. The number-one pop song in the first months of 1973 was Helen Reddy's anthem, "I Am Woman." Five days before the end of the Vietnam War, on January 22, 1973, the United States Supreme Court voted 7 to 2 to overturn all state laws restricting the right to an abortion during the first three months of pregnancy. As feminist author Marcia Cohen wrote later of the *Roe* v. *Wade* decision, "The legalization of abortion. It all seemed— in those giddy triumphant days—nothing less than the natural course of events."

Rumor was never far from the women's movement, even in those early victory days. Feminist pioneer Betty Friedan sparked a new frenzy of lesbian baiting in 1973 when she wrote a *New York Times* op-ed piece asserting that lesbians were "both hurting and exploiting the women's movement to try and use it to proselytize for lesbianism because of the sexual practices of a few."

In no arena of American life, however, was the link between suspected lesbianism and the new progress of women in society more pronounced than in the military. This was an unfortunate situation, given the fact that by mid-1973 it was clear there were going to be many, many more women in the armed forces than anyone had previously anticipated. Six months after the end of the draft, there were not enough people volunteering for the Army. In May 1973, the Army's offer of a fifteen-hundred-dollar bonus for men volunteering for combat jobs drew about fifteen hundred takers—nine hundred fewer than the projected goal. Army Chief of Staff General William Westmoreland publicly called the end of the draft "premature." By August, the Army was 19 percent short of the numbers it needed; the Marine Corps was 17 percent short. The 1972 predictions about recruitment shortfalls were the realities of 1973. Politically, however, Congress could not reinstate the draft and face the potential of renewed antimilitary protests on campuses.

"I think young girls who are willing to go into the service should be encouraged," said crusty Mississippi senator John Stennis, the Democratic chairman of the Senate Armed Services Committee. "It seems to me that they should be given more and more places and used more and more by the services—especially the Air Force and the Army—but not for combat."

Opportunities for women exploded. The Army announced it would double the size of the Women's Army Corps by 1978. WAC uniforms would be restyled "to make them more feminine"; and the number of Military Occupational Specialties for which women qualified would increase from 139 to 436 out of the 484 MOS's in the Army. The Air Force more than doubled its jobs open to women, freeing up all but five of its 242 MOS's to WAFs. In January 1973, the Navy put its first woman in pilot training. And Admiral Elmo Zumwalt, the Chief of Naval Operations, stunned sailors nationwide when he said that if the Equal Rights Amendment passed, women would be allowed to serve on warships.

Though the military was changing, it was hardly a bastion of women's liberation. The Marines remained particularly resistant to opening MOS's to women. While 81 percent of jobs were now open to women servicewide, only 36 percent of Marine Corps jobs were available to females as of early 1973. Inequities remained in all the services. Women faced tougher entry criteria than did men. Unlike males, females needed a high school diploma to enter the military. While any man could receive dependent's benefits for his wife, a woman who wanted comparable benefits for her husband had to establish that she was responsible for more than 50 percent of his support. Most galling to women, however, was their continued exclusion from combat roles. But for all the inequities, the military still offered women more opportunities than much of the civilian world did, and the number of women enlisting soared. By 1973, the women in the Air Force program, for example, had grown to 17,000—compared with 7,000 just five years earlier.

By November 1973, the armed forces met its recruiting goals for the first time since the draft had been abolished; 9 percent of the new enlistees that month were women. Some 20 percent of the Army ROTC program's new college freshmen were female. Among the political leaders in Washington, there was talk that in time the separate corps in which women served—the WACs, WAVEs, and WAFs—would be abolished and women integrated throughout the military.

During that time, the Center for Women's Policy Studies filed a federal lawsuit to force the service academies to admit women, and it was clear from the growing successes women were having in federal courts that they would win.

———————

BY THE MIDDLE of Copy Berg's senior year, in December 1973, he had decided that he would not make a career of the Navy as his dad had. There was a free world outside the rigid confines of the Navy, one in which he did not have to hide. The past year had shown Copy how to navigate in those waters. On his summer cruise aboard the USS *Kennedy*, he had gone to Majorca and realized how easy it was to meet like-minded men.

Back in the United States there was also a palpable hostility toward anything military. Midshipmen were advised not to walk around the streets in their uniforms. When the Academy Glee Club toured other cities, people would shout out, "How many babies have you burned?" These Glee Club members were college students; they had not killed any babies. This was not the career for Copy. His future was clear to him. He would do the five years he owed the Navy for his education, then leave.

19

Politics and Prejudice
(Part I)

WHAT ASTOUNDED PETE RANDELL most about the Pentagon was the number of homosexual acts that routinely occurred in such a homophobic institution. In the bathroom on corridor 6, just inside the five-acre central courtyard, men literally stood in line outside the stalls during the lunch hour, waiting their turn to engage in some hanky-panky.

Gay sexual activity was only part of the libidinous goings-on in the huge complex that oversaw the nation's defense establishment. Pentagon offices hosted some of the wildest Christmas parties Randell had ever seen, with cases of taxpayer-purchased liquor flowing into the mouths of assembled generals and staff who cheered lustily while female strippers jiggled their wares from desktops. There were also plenty of secretaries who seemed to understand that some of their duties were to be performed horizontally for senior staff members.

Randell's move to room 5C-887 in C ring of the Pentagon, the section reserved for the administration of the United States Air Force, came in October 1973. And it had not been a day too soon. President Nixon had just executed what would become known as the "Saturday Night Massacre," in which he had fired the assistant attorney general and the special prosecutor who were investigating possible administration wrongdoing in the burgeoning Watergate scandal, after Attorney General Elliot Richardson refused to and resigned. The scandal had grown so large that the resignation of Vice President Spiro Agnew, for taking bribes during his tenure as Maryland governor, had been entirely overshadowed by the prospect of a presidential impeachment. This was not a White House in which there was much in the way of job security. When Randell requested a secure Civil Service position, he landed the Air Force assignment.

The Air Force Board for Correction of Military Records is one of those inscrutably named federal agencies that is both obscure and incredibly powerful. Comprised of civilians, the board has unlimited authority to "remove injustices" or correct errors in military records. The board has the authority to upgrade discharges, overturn any disciplinary action, and even reinstate airmen who it finds have been wrongfully separated. It could, in effect, rewrite history. Each branch of the service has such a board, which represents the highest level of administrative review for people who feel they have been unjustly treated by the military. Randell would work in the agency through the administrations of four presidents, starting as a records examiner but assuming greater responsibilities each year.

At the Pentagon, Pete settled into a life that was the lot of many gay government officials, keeping up appearances while sneaking a little sex on the side. Many military men picked up dates at LBJ Memorial Park across the street from the Pentagon's north parking lot, and the best spot to cruise in the Washington area, the Iwo Jima Memorial, was a short drive away, where both military men and civilians came. Most of the ranking military officers pursuing men at these various locations were, like Pete, married with children, playing by the rules heterosexuals had laid out for them generations earlier.

FEBRUARY 1974
EGLIN AIR FORCE BASE
VALPARAISO, FLORIDA

"IT'S RIGHT HERE in the newspaper—so-and-so, *a black woman*, killed her child yesterday in Pensacola."

Technical Sergeant Leonard Matlovich held up the newspaper story so the thirty young airmen in his class could see the article.

"But think about it," he said. "Very few black people in America are really *all* black. Most have some white blood from back in the slave days."

Assuming a confidential tone, Leonard put aside the paper and said, "I think it was the white blood in her that made her do it. I'm sure of it. That white blood coming through again."

The students shifted uncomfortably in their chairs. "Why the white blood?" somebody finally asked. It was what Matlovich had been waiting for. "Exactly," he said. "And that has to make you ask, Why does anyone think it would be the black blood, either? What does blood or race have to do with it at all? Nothing. But when you read the newspaper story and it says a black person did this or that bad thing, it seems natural enough, because that's how we're used to thinking about blacks. They do bad things. Start rearranging some of the words and say the same thing about whites and it's sort of irritating, isn't it?"

The all-white class mumbled its agreement. Lesson learned, Matlovich thought triumphantly.

Never in his almost eleven years in the Air Force had Matlovich found a job that excited him so much. After the racial tensions that had mounted in every branch of the armed forces during the Vietnam War, the military had launched an intensive program of racial-sensitivity classes for its members, with more advanced training in race awareness for NCOs and officers. The edict was very simple: Racial prejudice would no longer be tolerated in the U.S. military. And most observers agreed that the Air Force took this training more seriously than any other service.

As a child of the South, born into a military family during the time of segregated armed forces, Matlovich was an unlikely candidate to be a race-relations instructor. He had found it hard to discard entirely the words *jigaboo* and *pickaninny* from his vocabulary in his first years in the Air Force, and through much of his duty in Vietnam he had kept a Confederate flag over his bunk. But his experience in the military had itself begun to erode his racism. His experience with black airmen had taught him that any notions he had held about black inferiority did not pass muster. Blacks were among the most talented and dedicated Air Force members he knew.

In fact, Matlovich learned that everything he had been taught about black people from his earliest days in South Carolina was entirely wrong. Discarding his old ideas about blacks was a liberating moment in the life of Leonard Matlovich, akin to a born-again experience. He launched into his new job with almost religious fervor.

Matlovich's teaching methods were sometimes unconventional. Often, he divided his race-relations class into two groups, based on some characteristic over which they had no control, such as hair or eye color. One week, the brown-eyed group was superior, figuring out rules for the blue-eyed people and doling out privileges for themselves while denying rights to the others. It was strange to see that within a few hours of the exercise, both groups adopted the roles of oppressor and oppressed; the former sometimes seemed actually to enjoy its new prerogatives, while the latter accepted without challenge the most outrageous constraints.

Though Matlovich's evaluations had always been high, his evaluations from this period were packed with superlatives by officers who testified to his stellar performance in the new job. Airmen begged to get into his class. An astounding 93 percent of his students gave him a rating of eight or above on a scale of ten. As *The New York Times* later noted, military records themselves showed that Technical Sergeant Leonard Matlovich was one of the best race-relations instructors in the United States Air Force—possibly *the* best. By early 1974, his work won him an Air Force Meritorious Service Medal. Every day, he reminded his classes of the plea of his new hero, Dr. Martin Luther King, Jr., that they judge people by the "content of their character," not by the color of their skin. Slowly, week after week, the words sank in, not only to his students but to Matlovich himself.

THE RACE-AWARENESS education that the military began pursuing vigorously in the early 1970s represents one of the most laudatory and successful efforts against prejudice ever undertaken in the history of the United States. It also represents an extreme departure from the way African Americans had been treated throughout much of the previous history of the armed forces.

Black soldiers fought in the Continental Army during the American Revolution and in the War of 1812. During the Civil War, 25 percent of the Navy was African American, and 186,000 blacks fought in the Union Army. Four black regiments fought with distinction during the Indian wars; through the late 1800s, between 20 and 30 percent of sailors at various times were black, working in a fully integrated Navy. With the rise of Jim Crow laws in the early 1900s, the military establishment veered dramatically into full segregation. By World War I, only 1.2 percent of Navy enlistments were black. By the 1920s, the Navy was entirely white. The Army Air Force expressly forbade black participation. By 1940, blacks comprised only 1.5 percent of the Army and Navy.

Although newly formed civil rights groups had protested these policies since World War I, their protests escalated dramatically when the United States entered World War II. Even as manpower shortages forced the Navy, Marines, and Army Air Force to admit blacks, the rapid expansion of the military during that conflict saw the stubborn entrenchment of segregationist policies. For northern blacks, military service often marked their first experience with harsh southern-style segregation. The creation of new bases around the country to handle the millions of new recruits introduced federally mandated segregation to areas where it had never existed before. The Red Cross even segregated military blood supplies so that the blood of an African American would never be transfused into Caucasian veins.

Though the armed forces maintained that all soldiers were treated equally in the segregationist tradition of separate but equal, the distribution of jobs among the races argued against this assertion. All branches of the military were reluctant to allow blacks to serve in combat. In the Navy, blacks could not serve on ships. There were no African American Navy officers or WAVEs. Two-thirds of the Navy's 27,000 black sailors were stewards. A survey of job assignments among black Marines serving in the Pacific theater during World War II found that 85 percent were either menial laborers, stewards, or worked in munitions depots performing the most dangerous warehouse work in the military.

War Department officials occasionally let slip out-and-out racist comments to justify their policies. When pressed about why black soldiers were not allowed into combat, for example, Secretary of War Henry Stimson told congressmen that military studies had found that "many of the Negro units have been unable to master efficiently the techniques of modern weapons." Perhaps no soldier was as outspoken about segregation as Major General Thomas Holcomb, commandant of the Marine Corps, who maintained it would be "absolutely tragic" if blacks were integrated into the services. "If it were a question of having a Marine Corps of 5,000 whites or 250,000 Negroes, I would rather have the whites," he said.

With World War II and growing black political clout, however, times were changing and the Roosevelt administration felt obliged at least to pay lip service to notions of civil rights. This required new logic to justify the military's segregation—logic that did not rely on racist stereotypes. The military met this challenge by asserting that there was nothing about blacks that required segregation; it was needed because of white soldiers' attitudes toward African Americans.

The brass of every service adamantly insisted that military efficiency, good order, and morale demanded segregation. The Army Air Force's exclusion of black pilots, for example, resulted from the fact that pilots were officers, and integrated squadrons would mean that black officers might be giving orders to white enlisted men, a situation that, it was presumed, most white soldiers would find intolerable. It was believed that not only would white soldiers refuse orders from black soldiers but that no white GI would want to be in the same foxhole as a black man. To buttress their arguments, the Army conducted surveys that showed 88 percent of whites favored segregated armed forces, as did 38 percent of blacks.

The Navy convinced President Franklin Roosevelt, a former assistant secretary of the Navy, that it must be segregated because Navy personnel had to live and work under close conditions affording minimal privacy. As Roosevelt wrote Secretary of War Stimson, "If the Navy living conditions on board ship were similar to the Army living conditions on land, the problem would be easier but the circumstances . . . being such as they are, I feel that it is best to continue the present system at this time."

According to the defense establishment, it was not that the military endorsed racism; it merely acquiesced to reality. The military could not engage in social experimentation. In a speech before the Conference of Negro Editors and Publishers, Colonel Eugene Householder of the Adjutant General's Office explained, "The Army is not a sociological laboratory; to be effective, it must be organized and trained according to principles which will insure success. Experiments to meet the wishes and demands of the champions of every race and creed for the solution of their problems are a danger to the efficiency, discipline and morale and would result in ultimate defeat." In essence the military's refashioning of its policies toward African Americans had very little to do with black people themselves—it was a policy about white people.

There was only one problem with the argument that integrating the military would undermine military efficiency: There were few facts to back it up. As Army historian Morris J. MacGregor, Jr., documents in his exhaustive book, *Integration of the Armed Forces (1940–1965)*, substantial evidence mounted in the early years of World War II showed segregation was a very inefficient way to achieve military goals. The Air Force had to postpone deployment of black air squadrons because there were not adequate numbers of trained black men and policy did not allow black trainees into schools with white airmen. And as resentment built among black troops, race rioting erupted at several military bases in the United States.

In the end, though, what propelled the movement toward integration had little to do with military concerns and much to do with politics. Civil rights groups had agitated against segregation since the war's first days with their "Double V" campaign, seeking victory not only against the Axis powers but against a Jim Crow military. The 1944 presidential elections boosted their efforts: The Republican party, which never had any chance of carrying southern states, used the military issue to try to frustrate President Roosevelt's bid for a fourth term. After needling from Republican nominee Thomas Dewey, the first black units were introduced to combat. In October 1944, after Dewey assailed the Navy for its lack of black officers and WAVEs, Roosevelt hurriedly ordered the admission of the first black women into the Navy. The Navy also commissioned its first black officers, though they were not line officers with the potential for command responsibility. When pressed further by Dewey's campaigning, the Navy began to integrate its training schools.

The results of these first forays into expanded African American participation in the war effort were impressive. An Army survey found that 80 percent of officers and NCOs who worked with black units thought they performed "very well" in combat. More significantly, another study showed 77 percent of enlisted men reported their attitudes toward African Americans had changed for the better once they worked together. None reported a less favorable attitude toward blacks. Perhaps because the study did not conform to Army policy, however, Chief of Staff George Marshall sought to keep it secret.

The final push for an integrated military also had everything to do with politics. As historian MacGregor recounts, President Harry Truman faced an uphill battle for election in 1948. Conservative southern Democrats had split off from the party to attack Truman from the right, under the Dixiecrat banner. And Thomas Dewey was again campaigning for President on a Republican platform pledging to integrate the military, while Henry Wallace of the Progressive party courted the liberal vote by aggressively criticizing the armed forces' segregation. The only way Truman could win the election was by capturing the northern states, which meant capturing the increasingly restive black urban voters unhappy about federally mandated segregation of the military. Even as Truman sought to establish peacetime conscription, civil rights groups threatened a nationwide campaign of draft resistance if the armed forces were not integrated. Civil rights leader A. Philip Randolph even threatened an embarrassing election-year march on Washington over the issue.

It was in this environment that President Truman issued Executive

Order 9981 on July 26, 1948, calling for "equality of treatment and opportunity for all persons in the armed services without regard to race, color, religion or national origin."

Getting this order on paper, however, was the beginning, not the end, of a long process toward real racial equality in the military. Though the Korean War accelerated racial integration of combat units, the last all-black Army unit was not disbanded until 1954, six years after the executive order. It was not until 1963, fifteen years after the order, that the military moved against discrimination that dogged servicemen in their attempts to obtain off-base housing and public accommodations—by declaring that all segregated facilities would be off limits to military personnel.

According to MacGregor's account, even at this time the Army was the only branch of the service that included compliance with equal-opportunity regulations as an issue upon which an officer's performance could be rated. And though the first presidential advisory committee to recommend a desegregated military in 1948 had also called for education to combat racism in the services, it was not until after the Vietnam War that such education began, with classes such as those that Technical Sergeant Leonard Matlovich taught.

It had been a very long process, which said less about the military than about the glacial speed of any movement for social change in an institution as vast as the armed forces. Still, by 1974, the military had moved further toward guaranteeing the equality of its minority members than any other institution within American society. Strict enforcement of equal-opportunity compliance codes as part of officer and NCO evaluations ensured that officers would be *required* to stand by the services' rules. Intolerance would no longer be tolerated. Within the coming decade, the United States military would become the most advanced segment of American society in dealing with racial problems. In a relatively short time, one of the most conservative institutions in the United States would experience a sea change in attitudes that had been entrenched for centuries.

———

LEONARD MATLOVICH had always been determined to demonstrate his worth by saving those in distress. In his early days in the Air Force, his rescue fantasies had won him the Bronze Star in Vietnam. Now he rescued people from the prevarications of prejudice. No job had ever given him such satisfaction.

Before his race-awareness education, it had not occurred to Matlovich to question what he had learned from his teachers or his religious counselors or his government. Now, realizing that society had been wrong about black people, he understood that it could be wrong about other things, as well, most notably about homosexuals. He decided it was entirely possible that he was not the one who needed to change; it was society that did.

Matlovich had an easier time integrating these new ideas intellectually than behaviorally, so his first tenuous steps toward self-acceptance came not in the bedroom but in the arena where he grappled with the issues of prejudice, his classroom.

"What is the most discriminated-against group in America today?" he asked his class.

Students called out, "Blacks, Jews, Hispanics." Matlovich nodded his head at each, then walked to the blackboard and wrote *homosexuals*.

Most members of the class had not thought of homosexuals as a minority before, they admitted, although a number of snide comments demonstrated a profusion of prejudice. The next week, Matlovich introduced a guest speaker, an agent from the Office of Special Investigations, to explain the Air Force's policies against gays.

"Homosexuals are a threat to national security because they can be blackmailed," the OSI agent said. Matlovich asked whether the agent knew of any homosexuals who had indeed been blackmailed. The agent responded that he did not know any but insisted that homosexuals were security risks just the same. And, he added, the presence of homosexuals would undermine the good order, discipline, and morale of the Air Force. Nobody would follow orders from a homosexual officer. Nobody would want to serve in the same foxhole or live in the same barracks with one. Matlovich pointed out that these were the same arguments that had been used to justify a racially segregated military. Once put to the test, the dire predictions had proved to be incorrect.

Far from alienating the class, as Matlovich had feared, these new discussions intrigued his pupils, who began sharing personal stories of this or that friend who was homosexual and not so bad. Matlovich was amazed at how willing his classes were to entertain new ideas about homosexuality, far more willing than he had been. It was during one of these discussion groups that a student mentioned the Yum Yum Room in Pensacola. No sooner had the airman and his wife found a table, he said, than they were surrounded by fourteen-year-old waiters clad only in jockstraps. When the airman went to the bathroom, he reported, a whole crowd of men followed him and watched his every move.

Matlovich had heard about the Yum Yum Room for years but had never ventured near because of rumors that the OSI staked out the parking lot. Now, however, he had a legitimate excuse to check out the truth of his student's story. One Friday evening, he drove his pickup truck to Pensacola, parked it three blocks from the restaurant, and slipped in through a side entrance. There were no fourteen-year-old cocktail waiters in jockstraps and the bathroom was too small to hold more than one person at a time. When he scanned the smiling faces in the crowded bar, what he saw were not the furtive and frightened expressions of a haunted minority but a group of successful and well-adjusted people having a good time.

This is paradise, he thought as he stared across the room, according to how he remembered the night later. *This is incredible.*

Matlovich sat at the bar until closing time. He did not speak to anyone, but it did not matter. He felt as if a million pounds had been lifted from his shoulders. He did not have to be alone, after all. There were other people like him.

Every Friday and Saturday night thereafter, he drove to Pensacola and took a bar stool at the Yum Yum Room. Maybe he should leave the Air Force, he thought, and get a job where he did not have to worry about the OSI or a dishonorable discharge. One night, as he entertained these thoughts, he struck up a conversation with a middle-aged woman. Yes, she loved Pensacola, she said, but she worried about being seen here. She was the president of a local bank. She might lose her job. Matlovich put aside thoughts of leaving the military. Discrimination was everywhere. He had nothing to gain by leaving the only life he had ever known.

After three months of quietly perusing the crowd, Matlovich met another serviceman at the bar. They talked, danced, and then made a date to see each other again. Several days later, after dinner at Leonard's apartment, the other man embraced him. Leonard trembled. After all these years, now nearly thirty-one, he would finally make love with another person.

FEBRUARY 15, 1974
THE HAGUE, NETHERLANDS

THE ELECTION OF A NEW COALITION of centrist Christian Democrats and the more left-leaning Social Democrats had created the perfect environment for the Hague's new minister of defense, Henk Vredeling. Shortly into his new tenure, Vredeling issued a letter to the chairman of the Standing Committee on Defense of the Dutch Parliament explaining the changes he wanted to make concerning the admission of homosexuals into the Royal Dutch Armed Forces.

"The views of society concerning homosexuality are clearly changing," he wrote. "They are moving away from the notion that homosexuality is objectionable behavior with a strong stigma attached to it, via homosexuality as an illness, to the recognition of two forms of sexual orientation. This recognition arises from the fact that there are many people who, apart from their homosexual behavior, barely differ, if at all, as regards their contacts with their fellow human beings, their personality structure or their social behavior, from other people who do not feel ill, disturbed or who have no deviation. . . . The consequence of this should be that the diagnosis of 'homosexuality' as such cannot and should not be used exclusively as a reason for rejection from military service." The only grounds for dismissal based on homosexuality, therefore, would be in the case of a recruit who believed he could not cope with military service because of his homosexuality or the prejudice he might find against it.

The Dutch had been moving toward such reform for several years, with the Dutch Society for the Integration of Homosexuality, the nation's major gay organization, calling on the country to end all forms of discrimination. The government had launched a study of homosexuality in 1969 that concluded, like virtually every other study undertaken in modern times, that homosexuality is not a chosen lifestyle but an orientation determined by the time a person is very young, perhaps before birth and most likely not more than three or four years old. Given the fact that the presence of homosexuality has been recorded throughout history, it may be regarded as "normal," in the same way that left-handedness is deemed "normal," the study found, even though it does not represent the condition of the majority. As such, the Dutch determined gay people to be a minority like any other and deserving of civil rights protection.

Believing that laws and policies should be based on facts, Parliament had repealed its law banning sex between consenting adults, and the Social Democrats incorporated gay concerns into its party platform. Then came Mr. Vredeling's announcement about the military in February 1974. Three months later, the Swedish Federation for Sexual Equality announced that it would go to court in Stockholm to ensure that the Swedish armed forces stopped discriminating against gays.

State Secretary for Defense C. J. L. van Lent issued the official order to the commanders of the Royal Dutch Army, Navy, and Air Force on November 4: "You are requested to give effect to the new policy laid down in the memorandum concerned. If instructions and regulations have been issued by you in regard to this matter, they should be checked against the new policy and adapted where necessary."

Though there were muted complaints from some military quarters, the announcement caused very little controversy. The change in policy was less a radical departure than an official acknowledgment of reality in the field. In fact, some of the more disgruntled voices came from gay leftists who maintained that gays should not join the army at all, since doing so meant turning their backs on the pacifist agenda that they had championed since the 1960s.

Unfortunately, changing the official written policy on gays and guaranteeing genuine equality were two different issues. Five years later, the Dutch service academies still asked applicants whether they were homosexual. Ten years later, security-clearance investigators sometimes inquired about the sexuality of unmarried service personnel. But slowly, the changes percolated through the entire military and it became known through every level of the Royal Dutch Armed Forces that intolerance would no longer be acceptable.

MARCH 1974
CATHEDRAL STREET
WASHINGTON, D.C.

UNTIL 1959, DR. FRANKLIN KAMENY had been a happy, eccentric scientist performing his tasks in observational astronomy for the Army Map Service. He had a doctorate in astronomy from Harvard, and everyone agreed that he was very good at what he did, but this made no difference when his boss called him in and told him he was fired because he was a homosexual, since under the rules of the Civil Service Commission no homosexual could work for the United States government. Kameny had never demonstrated much of a political bent in the past, but as a man of science he was devoted to reason and could not fathom how his behavior in the privacy of his bedroom affected his job as a government astronomer. An intellectual, he was also not about to suffer fools gladly. Rather than quietly accept the termination and seek employment elsewhere, he decided to fight.

For the next two years, Kameny labored over his petition for certiorari, or a request of review by the Supreme Court. He developed legal arguments against the government's action and formulated his own ideas about what would later be called gay liberation. In March 1961, when the high court turned down his petition, he began to seek out organizations championing homosexual rights. He found only five or six of them in the country. He soon set up his own group, the Washington chapter of the Mattachine Society. From that moment on, he had three goals: to end the Civil Service's ban on gays working for the government, to end discrimination against homosexuals seeking security clearances, and to end the exclusion of gays from the military.

Over the following years, Kameny organized the first homosexual pickets of the White House, the State Department, and later the Pentagon. With FBI agents snapping photos and sending informers to every meeting, he cajoled Washington's mild-mannered homosexuals to get involved and start fighting back. The more militant posture of the post-Stonewall gay movement suited him much better than the trepidatious 1960s, and by the early 1970s he was pursuing his goals as leader of the Washington Gay Activists Alliance. The press quoted him frequently and every quote elicited a few phone calls from people who needed help with security clearances or discharge proceedings. This was why, one night in March 1974, a call from a nervous young man who said he was a technical sergeant in the United States Air Force seemed simply routine.

The Sunday editions of the *Family* magazine section in the *Air Force Times* had just run an article on gays in uniform. The story was culled from anonymous interviews with one hundred gay service people and was remarkably sympathetic to the plight of homosexual service members. It also quoted Kameny saying he was looking for a test case: someone with a model military record who had been kicked out of the military for being gay. He wanted to take the issue to the Supreme Court.

The caller spoke with a slight southern accent. He would not give his name, but he did say he was stationed at an air base in Florida and that he had a friend who might fit the qualifications Kameny was looking for. Kameny suspected that the caller might, in fact, be speaking for himself. He replied that he would like to talk to the caller's friend. The caller said he would see whether it could be arranged. But as he hung up, Kameny was not sure that he would hear from the man again.

At Eglin Air Force Base, as Leonard Matlovich shakily put the receiver back in its cradle, he was not entirely sure, either.

20

The Letter

JUNE 5, 1974
UNITED STATES NAVAL ACADEMY
ANNAPOLIS, MARYLAND

FOR MIDSHIPMAN VERNON "COPY" BERG, the graduation ceremony at the Naval Academy seemed somehow representative of the times. President Nixon, just two months away from resignation, was the commencement speaker. Copy's family photo album commemorated the day: There was Copy's sister in a black miniskirt, his younger brother in a Fu Manchu mustache, and Berg's lover, Lawrence Gibson.

His time together with Gibson seemed about to end. Copy had known for several months that his first duty station would be in Gaeta, Italy, with the Sixth Fleet. He had been excited about striking out on his own, but Gibson seemed crestfallen to him. Copy had ignored the older man's entreaties that he could not live without Berg, until the night before graduation, when he went to Gibson's apartment and found him dazed and stumbling, apparently suffering from what looked to Berg like a drug overdose. Years later, Gibson would not discuss this period of his past, but to Berg it looked as if he had attempted suicide. It was enough to make the twenty-two-year-old midshipman feel terrible about leaving Gibson behind.

Okay, Berg recalls finally agreeing, Gibson could join him in Italy the following year when Berg had completed his technical training in the San Francisco Bay Area. The next morning, Gibson joined Midshipman Vernon E. Berg III, Berg's father, the commander, and the rest of the family for the commencement at Annapolis.

Newspaper accounts of the graduation ceremony mentioned that the day reflected the tensions of the times. A month earlier, the House Judiciary Committee had begun hearings on whether to impeach Nixon. Already, a host of administration officials had been indicted, including two former Attorneys General. Calls for Nixon's resignation mounted. The President had long ago stopped making public appearances where he might encounter a hostile audience, which was just about everywhere in the country; now he spoke mainly in foreign countries or on military bases. If Nixon thought Annapolis would be an entirely friendly site, however, he was mistaken. Some midshipmen refused to stand for the Commander in Chief. When each company mounted the stage for the customary presentation of a gift to the commencement speaker, the President found himself accepting such items as a rubber lizard. Ignited by the unpopular war and accelerated by the distrust in public institutions that the Watergate scandal had caused, the questioning of authority that had begun years ago in the Summer of Love reached even here.

THE TOPIC THAT LOOMED larger even than President Nixon at the Naval Academy, however, was whether women should be admitted to Annapolis in years to come. In February, the United States Merchant Marine Academy on Long Island had enrolled its first two female "midshippersons." The first WACs had begun training to be military police; in August 1974, the Army opened its first coed barracks. Meanwhile, after Congress ordered it to admit women for the first time in its 184-year history, the Coast Guard was trying to figure out how to adapt what had always been an all-male service. As Chief Boatswain Mate Royce Jones, an eighteen-year veteran in charge of the new women recruits, told *The New York Times,* "We don't want to take the woman out of the women. Maybe you've seen movies of the old Marine women sergeants. This is not what we're looking for. We don't want them acting like a bunch of Russians. We hope we never have to have the women on the front lines in this country, but they certainly are nice to have behind you."

The other service academies were still adamant in refusing admission to women. Major General James Allen, the superintendent of the Air Force Academy, went on record as being firmly opposed to women cadets. West Point superintendent Major General Sidney Berry also vowed women would never attend the Army academy. At the Naval Academy, the idea that women might one day inhabit their beloved Bancroft Hall horrified Copy Berg's classmates.

Nevertheless, even as dissension echoed through the Pentagon, political trends forced changes. Six days after the Annapolis graduation ceremony, Senator Hugh Scott, a senior Republican solon, announced he would accept applications from females for all the service academies. Women seemed to be gaining on every front. In the 1974 elections, Connecticut voters elected Ella Grasso as governor, the first time in the history of the United States that a woman who was neither the widow nor the wife of a previous governor won the governorship. Voters elected eighteen women to the House of Representatives, a record number. Most significantly, 130 more women won election to state legislatures, bringing the total number of female state legislators to 600, nearly double the number of just five years earlier. For the military, such political realities meant that one year after vowing never to accept women at West Point, a senior officer at the military academy recalls Major General Berry summoning New York fashion designers to choose uniforms for the incoming female cadets.

———————

As years went, 1974 was not such a bad time to be gay in the United States military, at least in comparison with the other years that were to come. The armed forces were still struggling to maintain manpower levels in the new all-volunteer Army, so as few people as possible were being discharged unnecessarily. In fact, during calendar year 1974, the armed forces dismissed only 875 people for homosexuality, according to Pentagon statistics. The portion of discharges characterized as "Undesirable" had dropped precipitously, too, from 419 in fiscal year 1970 to 79 in fiscal year 1974. Taken together, the number of gay people drummed out of the military in 1974 was lower than it had been in the past twenty years, and almost as low as it would be for nearly the next twenty years.

Pressure mounted on the Defense Department to stop coding its discharges with "spin numbers," which had branded tens of thousands of veterans homosexual, even though most had honorable discharges and were not even aware that these numbers existed on their separation papers. When congressmen began complaining to the Defense Department, the end of spin numbers followed close behind. The change reflected an appalling new phenomenon with which the Pentagon suddenly had to cope: congressmen coming to the aid of homosexuals. It would have been unthinkable five years earlier. Where would it end?

JULY 1974
CATHEDRAL STREET
WASHINGTON, D.C.
———————

By the time Technical Sergeant Leonard Matlovich appeared at Frank Kameny's two-story brick house a half block from the Potomac River, he had already confided that he was indeed the "friend" for whom he had placed the phone call several months earlier. Kameny's enthusiasm built as Matlovich recounted his military résumé. The man held the Bronze Star, a Purple Heart, two Air Force commendation medals, and a recent Air Force Meritorious Service Medal, had done three tours in Vietnam, and had altogether eleven years of unblemished service. Central casting could not have provided a better test case to take to the Supreme Court. Kameny, however, was no lawyer. Fortunately, a former Air Force lawyer had already volunteered for the job.

David Addlestone had never thought much about homosexuality before his days in the Air Force. He and his wife had some older gay friends in college, but they were polite enough never to discuss the issue openly.

As a lawyer for the Judge Advocate General in the Air Force in 1967, however, Addlestone defended an enlisted man who had gotten drunk one night and made a pass at a younger airman. The Air Force wanted to give the man an undesirable discharge. Such treatment irritated Addlestone's civil-libertarian streak. The defendant, after all, had served the Air Force well. Whatever his transgression, it had occurred when he was off duty and had hurt no one. In researching the regulations, Addlestone discovered an odd clause in the Air Force's gay policy that allowed exceptions to the ban on gays. "Immaturity" or some other extenuating circumstance could excuse a suspected homosexual. The exception could not be invoked solely because an airman was drunk or solely because he had outstanding service or solely because of a one-time experimentation with homosexuality. (Some gays sarcastically called the policy the "Queen for a Day" rule.) At the administrative hearing, however, Addlestone argued that in this case all three of these circumstances applied to the accused, therefore he merited the exception to the policy. The administrative board agreed and refused to discharge the airman.

This outcome informed Addlestone of something he had long suspected. Most United States Air Force officers also believed, as he did, that the military regulations against homosexuals were draconian, if not altogether archaic. During his remaining years in the Air Force, the lawyer grew more deeply offended by a policy that was invoked only against that minority who were unfortunate enough to get caught. It was rank hypocrisy, Addlestone thought, and it needed to end.

Once he was out of the military and had started practicing law in Washington, Addlestone kept abreast of developments in military law and by 1971 had become a counsel at the Military Law Project of the American Civil Liberties Union. When Frank Kameny called him in early 1974 and said he believed he had the perfect test case to challenge the exclusion policy, Addlestone was eager to meet Kameny's Air Force sergeant.

While Addlestone's five-year-old son played on the floor in the same room, Matlovich explained that he could not stand the hypocrisy of teaching equal opportunity while working for an organization that would not extend the same equality to him. Addlestone was as enthusiastic about Matlovich's military record as Kameny had been, but he felt obliged to describe the repercussions such a case could have on Matlovich.

"Do you really want to throw away eleven years of service? You could retire in just eight years. You'll be losing all that," he said. And he warned that Matlovich might lose his relationship with his family. His father was a lifer. He might not appreciate his son battling the Air Force. "It's *your* life that could be ruined by this," Addlestone concluded. "In my opinion, we'll probably lose this case."

"I can't go on living like this," Matlovich said. "I can't be a hypocrite."

It struck Addlestone that after so many years of living in doubt, Matlovich at last was sure of something and would stick to his guns. Furthermore, the lawyer liked Matlovich immediately. They had both been raised in South Carolina and spoke with the same slightly southern drawl. Addlestone agreed to take the case, though when to force the issue remained to be seen. Normally, the government had the advantage of control. They made the charges; all the defense could do was react. It was a rare opportunity for the ACLU to choose the time and place of the disclosure. With Matlovich now assigned to Langley Air Force Base in Hampton, just a four-hour drive from Washington, Addlestone began his legal research with the confidence that they could afford to bide their time until the perfect moment.

———————

MATLOVICH'S DECISION to fight the military's exclusion of gays came as he settled into a new routine within the huge array of military bases around the Norfolk area, the region locals called Hampton Roads. At night military men with their telltale short haircuts and without the longish sideburns fashionable in the posthippie era packed the local gay bars. For the first time, Matlovich could socialize with other gay military people, but when he spoke of challenging the regulations he found that such talk genuinely frightened many of his new friends.

Matlovich would not be deterred, however, even though he dreaded both the moment when he would tell the Air Force he was gay and the inevitable aftermath of telling his parents. Still, he felt he had no other choice. For years, he had spoken about the need for the United States to attain justice and equality for all its citizens. Now, he had actually begun to believe it.

FEBRUARY 1975
FORT DEVENS
AYER, MASSACHUSETTS
———————

PRIVATE FIRST CLASS Tanya Domi knew it was going to be a horrible mistake the moment she heard that the two WACs were going to turn themselves in as lesbians. She could understand the pressure on them, of course. The fear among the WACs stationed at the post, the site of the Army's latest lesbian investigation, was almost palpable.

Fear had become an unwelcome subplot to the nineteen-year-old's year-long WAC career. She had been a card-carrying member of the National Organization for Women since she was sixteen. She was a committed feminist and supporter of civil rights causes when she was student-body president of her Catholic high school in Indianapolis, but she had not done well in college, and so she had joined the Army in January 1974. She had not known she was gay when she enlisted.

It was during her basic training at Fort McClellan, Alabama, where all the WACs were trained, that Tanya realized the Women's Army Corps was lesbian heaven. Not long after that, she got her first kiss. By the time she was assigned to Fort Devens in March, she did not hesitate when a group of WACs invited her to a gay bar, The Other Side, in Boston.

Within days of the trip, however, somebody informed on the group and Domi soon found herself being interrogated by military investigators. The way Tanya recalled the day, one was kind, the other hostile.

"Lesbians are disgusting," one said. "We find them repulsive. They have no place in the United States Army. We're going to do everything we can to get rid of all the lesbians." Meaningfully, he added, "We know you're a hard-core homosexual."

Since Domi had done no more than visit a gay bar once and steal two or three kisses in the laundry room at Fort McClellan, she did not consider herself a hard-core lesbian. She confessed to the kisses, insisted that she was not really gay, and her company commander called the investigation off, given the fact that her sexual experiences represented "an isolated experience."

But the larger investigation continued and by December 1974, the CID was rumored to have the names of between forty and fifty lesbians. Many of these women were heterosexual—any hug between two women was often interpreted to be lesbian lovemaking. The probe turned fierce. At a commander's call, a new hard-assed female captain announced, "If you're a lesbian, I'm going to get you." The WACs were pressured to make lists of other lesbians and everybody talked about the "buddyfuckers," as those who turned their friends in were called.

During this atmosphere of hysteria, a pair of lovers, Private First Class Barbara Randolph and Private Debbie Watson, both members of the honors platoon, decided that they would turn themselves in as lesbians. "They'll destroy you," Domi warned them. Everybody seemed hell-bent on self-destruction, she thought.

But the two women were adamant. They would not act as if they were ashamed of something that was perfectly natural to them. Maybe it was time to get out of the Army and start a life together. Soon, a third woman and then a fourth woman told Tanya that they were giving themselves up. More lists were in the making. A few weeks later, Tanya learned that her security clearance was being revoked; she would be charged with being a lesbian.

Tanya retreated to her room. While the other women around her seemed to be falling apart, she read *Atlas Shrugged* by Ayn Rand. She identified with the book's assertion of self-reliance and individualism; she read everything by the author, gaining strength and growing angry at what was happening. Then she called the Boston chapter of the American Civil Liberties Union, who referred her to the group that counseled gays in the military, the Legal In-Service Project, or LISP. She also talked to Frank Kameny, the Washington activist advising Matlovich. By the time the Army filed charges against her, Tanya had a civilian lawyer, to whom she had also referred Debbie Watson and Barbara Randolph.

If they really wanted to make a statement about the way the Army treated gays, the lawyer advised Watson and Randolph, they could go public with their case and fight their discharges openly. The women liked the idea. They preferred to stay in the Army, and this might be the only way they could. If they were on their way out, they had nothing to lose.

AMERICAN CIVIL LIBERTIES UNION
WASHINGTON, D.C.

ATTORNEY DAVID ADDLESTONE began to craft the legal arguments that he hoped would go all the way to the Supreme Court. He had no doubt that Technical Sergeant Leonard Matlovich's military record provided the perfect set of facts to argue in his court case; what he needed now were constitutional arguments. Though homosexuals had been making legal breakthroughs in state courts and on the lower federal courts in recent years, the nation's highest court had never agreed even so much as to hear a case relating to gay civil rights.

A few arguments were obvious. The Constitution's equal-protection clause of the Fourteenth Amendment, and the Ninth Amendment, had been interpreted to include a right to privacy. In rereading the Air Force regulations, Addlestone stopped again at the obscure subsection that allowed for exceptions in the overall exclusion of gays from the Air Force: "It is the general policy to discharge members of the Air Force who fall within the purview of this section. Exceptions to permit retention may be authorized only when the most unusual circumstances exist and provided the airman's ability to perform military mission has not been compromised." What constituted such "unusual circumstances" was not spelled out. It was a typical piece of have-it-both-ways regulating that let the Air Force keep whom it wanted and get rid of the rest.

But more than that, Addlestone knew that legally any government regulation must make it clear what constitutes a violation. If there were exceptions, these also had to be specified. Along with pursuing the constitutional arguments for Matlovich's case, Addlestone would challenge the legality of the regulation, based on its vague exceptions.

Matlovich made the drive from Hampton to Washington frequently to consult on the developing legal strategy. After months of research, Addlestone drew up the letter Matlovich would hand his commanding officer.

———

IT HAD BEEN A DECADE since the escalation of the Vietnam War had begun, that period that caused the reevaluation of so many tried-and-true American traditions. And it had been nearly six years since the riots at the Stonewall Inn in New York City, the event that had challenged the American ethos, the ideology of masculinity for which millions of Americans had altered their lives and aspirations in order to try to be people they were not. Now that was slowly changing.

Finally, the questions reached deep enough to penetrate the institution most wedded to tradition and resistant to social change, the military. In those first few months of 1975, the battle would be engaged for the first time, and from that moment on the challenges would never stop.

MARCH 6, 1975
TO: THE SECRETARY OF THE AIR FORCE
THRU: CAPTAIN DENNIS M. COLLINS
4510TH SUPPORT SQ. (T.A.C.)
FROM: T/SGT. LEONARD MATLOVICH, 463-76-2847

1. After some years of uncertainty, I have arrived at the conclusion that my sexual preferences are homosexual as opposed to heterosexual. I have also concluded that my sexual preferences will in no way interfere with my Air Force duties, as my preferences are now open. It is therefore requested that those provisions in AFM 39-12 relating to the discharge of homosexuals be waived in my case.

2. I will decline to answer specific questions concerning the functioning of my sexual life. . . . However, I will be glad to answer any questions concerning my personal life if reasons are given detailing how the questions relate to specific fitness and security concerns rather than the generally unconstitutional provisions of AFM 39-12 relating to the discharge of homosexuals. If more specific criteria other than the notion that homosexuals are morally unqualified for service in the Air Force can be shown as basis for questioning, I will answer the appropriate questions. . . .

In sum, I consider myself to be a homosexual and fully qualified for further military service. My almost twelve years of unblemished service supports this position.

Leonard Matlovich
T/Sgt., USAF

Matlovich read the letter again and again. It was a clear, crisp day in Hampton when he decided to deliver it. The Air Force was the only life he had known, and within minutes he would hand in the letter that would end it all. The thought opened a huge pit in the bottom of his stomach, but he remembered Rosa Parks, who would not move to the back of the bus, and the little girl whose family had filed the suit known as *Brown* v. *The Board of Education* that had resulted in the historic Supreme Court decision ending segregation in schools. He felt compelled to keep walking toward his boss's office.

When Matlovich entered, Captain Dennis Collins, a black officer in charge of race-relations instruction, was standing at his desk in front of a big poster that read I DON'T DISCRIMINATE—I HATE EVERYBODY. Collins never contradicted the oft-reported account of what was said next.

"Captain Collins, I have a letter I'd like for you to read," Matlovich said. "But I think you ought to sit down before you read it."

"I'll stand," Collins said.

"I mean it," Matlovich answered. "You'd better sit down."

"I'll stand," Collins said again, taking the letter.

Collins read the first few sentences and slumped into his chair.

"What does this mean?" he asked.

"This means *Brown* versus *The Board of Education*," Matlovich replied.

BOOK THREE

TRIALS

(1975–1976)

One person with courage makes a majority.

—Andrew Jackson

21

The Color Purple
(Part 1)

"UNDER THE PROVISIONS OF AFM 39-12, Chapter 2, Section H, paragraph 2-104b(1), I am initiating action against you with a view to effecting your discharge from the United States Air Force."

Technical Sergeant Leonard Matlovich received the neatly typed letter as he arrived for work. Until that day, Matlovich had done nothing to pursue publicity for his case. The ostensible point of his letter had been to convince the Air Force to allow an openly gay member to serve, and a small part of Matlovich actually believed that an exception might be made in his case. Within days of his request, however, it was clear that the Air Force would handle the case as a routine gay discharge. Agents from the Office of Special Investigations suggested that Matlovich might be faking homosexuality to make some political point. They demanded proof that he was gay, including confessions to specific sexual acts and the names of other gay airmen. Though Matlovich declined to name others, he did write a letter acknowledging "mutual masturbation, anal intercourse, and fellatio." The final OSI investigation included the admission, as well as evidence from another sergeant that "he suspected that you were homosexual." The official notification that discharge proceedings would begin jarred Matlovich and removed the final impediment to notifying the press. That afternoon, his civilian attorney, David Addlestone, called a *New York Times* reporter and arranged an interview.

Matlovich also needed a military lawyer, willing to launch a broad attack on a Department of Defense regulation. It would not be easy; many Air Force lawyers were unsympathetic to the cause, and even those with private sympathies were bound to be reluctant to go after the organization that issued their paychecks twice a month. After much investigation, Matlovich heard about one attorney among them who would not be afraid to buck the system. That was Captain Jon Larson Jaenicke.

Jaenicke had served four of the five years he owed the Air Force for financing his college education through the ROTC program. The twenty-eight-year-old attorney knew he was not going to make a career in uniform. Though he had grown up in South Carolina, his attitudes toward homosexuality reflected the fact that both his parents were from New York City and he had attended law school at New York University. He was cool, everyone told Lenny.

Both Sergeant Matlovich and Jaenicke remembered the afternoon when Matlovich walked into the legal office late on a Friday afternoon and handed Jaenicke the letter he had sent to the Air Force Secretary, admitting to homosexual acts.

"This is dumb," Jaenicke said. "Why did you do this? I could have gotten you out without anyone ever knowing you were gay. You shouldn't have told them."

"I don't think you understand," Matlovich said. "Read the letter again."

When Jaenicke did understand, he was intrigued. Matlovich was going to challenge the military's entire policy. That night, Jaenicke went home and mixed one martini for himself and another for his wife. Settling into his easy chair, he told her, "The next six months are going to be incredible."

THREE DAYS AFTER Leonard Matlovich received his notification of discharge proceedings, Staff Sergeant Rudolf "Skip" Keith raised his hand in a race-relations class at Dover Air Force Base near Washington. As an African American, Keith was certainly sensitive to the issues of racial discrimination, but, Keith asked, "What about discrimination against gays?" That question sparked a lively discussion during which somebody asked Keith whether he was gay.

Yes, he was, Keith said, adding that just as many negative stereotypes of blacks had evaporated once white people actually got to know and work with them, so would stereotypes of gays. The problem was that most gay people concealed their homosexuality. Therefore, heterosexuals lacked an accurate perception of the reality of who homosexuals were and what kind of people they were.

All of this was pretty heady stuff for what was normally a fairly predictable hour of antiracist indoctrination. Keith himself was surprised that most of the class seemed genuinely interested in the issue.

Keith's roommate was less receptive, however, and abruptly moved out of the apartment they shared when he heard of Keith's candid disclosure. There might be repercussions at work, Keith realized then, and the next day he called together his crew. After seven years in the Air Force, the twenty-five-year-old still loved his job. He had known since he was eight, growing up in the black neighborhoods of Washington, that he would serve in the Air Force, where he had become a jet maintenance specialist. At Dover, he was crew chief on a team that serviced the huge C-5A cargo planes. They consistently received top ratings for their work and they worked together like the pieces of a finely synchronized watch. Still, Keith knew that the OSI often assumed guilt by association and he did not want anyone on his crew to suffer for his remarks. He offered to transfer out if any of his crew was uncomfortable working with an openly gay man.

"Your personal life is your business," said one man, to general nods of agreement. Though he heard nothing from the Air Force about his disclosure, he girded for a possible confrontation. He resolved he would go to court to stay in if he had to.

At about the same time, Private First Class Barbara Randolph and Private Debbie Watson of the Women's Army Corps at Fort Devens, Massachusetts, had some unsettling news for their commanding officer. They were going public with their case, becoming the first women in the history of the military to challenge the regulation excluding homosexuals. The newspapers loved their story, since there was no question that both Randolph, twenty-two, and Watson, twenty, were very good soldiers. Randolph had only recently been Fort Devens's "WAC of the Month" and "Soldier of the Month." Both women had resolved they would go all the way to the Supreme Court to stay in if they had to.

Meanwhile, in the fashionable seaside city of Santa Barbara, California, the Navy was gearing up for its own homosexual battle. In early 1975, the state was in an uproar over legislation to repeal California's law banning sodomy. At a public meeting, Gary Hess, forty-four, a respected member of the community who was on the Santa Barbara County Board of Education and vice president of Santa Barbara Educational Television, argued with two local conservative politicians who spoke against the repeal. For normal citizens, asserting an opinion on a controversial issue was an inalienable right. However, Hess was also a commander in the United States Naval Reserve, with twenty-three years in active-duty and Reserve service. According to documents later filed in federal court, those conservative politicians whom Hess had challenged contacted the Naval Reserve. An investigation found evidence that Hess, a divorced father of four, was bisexual, and the Navy started proceedings against him.

Once again, the military faced an unfamiliar response. Hess went public with his case and resolved to go to court to stay in the Navy if he had to.

Meanwhile, in San Diego, a former Navy ensign named Jim Woodward filed his first papers in what would become a nearly two-decade-long battle against the military's antigay regulation. In late 1974, Woodward was on the USS *Constellation* during its WESTPAC cruise when he fell in with the ship's notorious "Connie Girls" and learned of the daily harassment of gay enlisted men. Though he had only recently come to grips with his own homosexuality, he wrote a letter to his commanding officer explaining that he was gay and that he wanted to continue serving in the Navy. Since the missive was obviously framed to instigate a court case, Woodward was not discharged but transferred to the inactive Reserve. Since technically he remained in the military, the move denied him a discharge that he could legally contest. Woodward resolved to fight the maneuver just the same, all the way to the Supreme Court, which is precisely where his case ended up.

Most remarkable about all these cases was that, though they were all percolating simultaneously at different bases throughout the country, none of the people contesting them knew of the others. These were all separate, spontaneous acts of insurgence. Ohio State University legal scholar Rhonda Rivera, a leading expert on issues of sexual orientation and military law, later noted that between the Korean War and this moment in 1975, the U.S. military drummed out between forty to fifty thousand people for being homosexual. Only a handful challenged their separations in court, and when they did, Rivera wrote, they "did not voluntarily admit their homosexuality and, in fact, all but one person consistently denied it." Furthermore, challengers argued against their discharges on procedural grounds of insubstantial evidence, improperly obtained evidence, or improperly placed burden of proof. None challenged the legality of the government's policy itself. In the first weeks of May 1975, however, a critical mass had been achieved and the old era had come to an end.

Notice of the new era appeared on page one of *The New York Times* on May 26, Memorial Day. Matlovich's challenge, the story reported, "was the opening round of a classic test case—a clear-cut challenge by a 'perfect' challenger. . . . At stake are major, possibly competing, issues and rights—the military's interest in having rules it deems necessary to maintaining an adequate armed service system; the homosexuals' constitutional rights to privacy and equal protection of the laws. Perhaps also at stake is the future of thousands of other service personnel."

Speaking for the Air Force, Major General Jeanne Holm, a champion of the right of women to serve in the military, became a champion against the rights of gays. The gay exclusion, Holm said, let young people going into the Air Force "know they aren't in the company of people who have what they consider aberrant behavior." Parents would surely object to gays in the military, she continued. "Can you imagine, for instance, being on a submarine, isolated, and being concerned about having homosexuals around preying on young people, or being leaders?" Holm asked. "I think it would be intolerable." Nobody would want to take orders from a homosexual; few would want to serve with them, she said, adding, "People don't like it."

Matlovich's phone started ringing the morning the story appeared, and it did not stop. Every news service wanted a quote. *Time* magazine was preparing a story. "CBS News" chartered a plane to fly to Norfolk to tape a piece for that evening's news. Still, Matlovich needed to tend to one unfinished piece of business. He had told his mother he was gay on the day he gave his letter to the Air Force. Mrs. Matlovich was not convinced that Lenny really was gay; she rather thought this was all part of his newfound crusade for human rights. But the two had grown so close over the years that even if he was a homosexual, she would not reject him. Matlovich had not told his father, however. On the morning of May 26, Leonard Matlovich, Jr., phoned home.

"We've got to tell Dad right now," he said.

It was not necessary, his mother answered. The *Times* story had appeared in their hometown newspaper. After reading the piece, Leonard Matlovich, Sr., had locked himself in his bedroom and cried. But the next time Lenny visited his parents in Florida, his father greeted him at the door, paused a moment, and then wrapped him in a bear hug, the first he had given Lenny since he was a kid.

JUNE 5, 1975
SUEZ CANAL
EGYPT

ENSIGN VERNON "COPY" BERG stood on the bridge of the USS *Little Rock,* snapping pictures of Egyptians berserk with joy. The Suez Canal, devastated by the Six-Day War in 1967, had been reopened at last. Thousands lined the banks, climbed up phone poles, piled into little boats, and waved from the roofs of buildings. The USS *Little Rock,* the flagship of the Sixth Fleet, in "full-dress ship," would lead all other ships through the narrow channel of water into the Red Sea.

The mid-1970s was not an ideal time to be part of the United States military stationed overseas. The Vietnam War had been even more unpopular in Europe than in the United States, and American ships found themselves unwelcome in the ports of such traditional allies as Greece, Spain, and France. The *Little Rock* was home-ported in Gaeta, Italy, near Naples, a pit of a town with no base or facilities. Morale among the sailors and their families was low. Of the five ensigns on the *Little Rock,* Berg was the only Academy graduate, which presaged jealousies. But his positive attitude saw him through his service, and he managed to have a pretty good time aboard the "Show Boat," as he called the *Little Rock,* though he formed no intimate relationships. There had been a close encounter when a journalist second class named Laurent John Crofwell showed interest. Crofwell even went to Berg's villa one night and was about to spend the night, but he left abruptly, before any physical contact, as Berg recalled. He thought Crofwell was struggling just as Berg had years earlier. He did not think much more of it and over the ensuing weeks the two resumed a normal working relationship on the *Little Rock.*

Meanwhile, Berg looked forward to Lawrence Gibson's imminent arrival. Gibson would arrive while the *Little Rock* was visiting Yugoslavia, so Berg left notes for his lover throughout the apartment. It was at about this time, while Berg was still in Yugoslavia and Gibson had not yet arrived, that Berg's sister came early for a visit. Another ensign's wife, a dour Mormon as it turned out, let her into Berg's apartment, where they found the little notes everywhere, with affectionate allusions obvious to anyone who saw them, all addressed to Lawrence.

By then, however, Berg was already under investigation, as he had been for several months.

JUNE 29, 1975
CENTRAL PARK
NEW YORK CITY

THE CROWD STRETCHED ON for blocks in front of the makeshift stage, here for the Gay Pride March commemorating the sixth anniversary of the Stonewall riots. Their placards promoted the slogans of the day:

HOW DARE YOU PRESUME I'M HETEROSEXUAL?

YOU CAN OVERCOME YOUR HETEROSEXUALITY

AN ARMY OF LOVERS CANNOT BE DEFEATED

AVENGE OSCAR WILDE

Leonard Matlovich surveyed the throng with wonder. Two years earlier, he had believed he was the only homosexual in the world. Now he was one among tens of thousands. How had he allowed so much of his life to be wasted in loneliness? A cheer rose from the crowd when Matlovich delivered the line he had used in every newspaper and television interview since his case went public. "The military gave me a medal for killing two men," he said, "but it wants to give me a discharge for loving one."

With Matlovich were the other heroes of the moment: Staff Sergeant Skip Keith in his blue Air Force uniform and Barbara Randolph and Debbie Watson from Fort Devens. When the four of them stood side by side at the microphone, waving to the crowd that billowed through Central Park, a huge ovation rose up and it felt as if their spirits had also lifted into the air and soared over the city's skylines. It was a moment Leonard Matlovich would cherish for the rest of his life.

"IF EVERY GAY PERSON turned purple, there wouldn't be any prejudice anymore."

Events a decade later would imbue this statement with an eerie irony, but, in the early 1970s, it was the central article of faith for young gay activists. They believed if people knew how many of their friends, family members, and acquaintances were homosexual—because, for example, they had all turned purple—the stereotypes would fall under the weight of their own fraud. For years, earnest activists had insisted at press conferences that the greater population of gay people remained in hiding. The assertion was problematic. All the public ever saw of such press conferences were wild-eyed, long-haired militants who did not look a bit like the average Americans for whom they claimed to be speaking. The appearance of Technical Sergeant Leonard Matlovich and other gay military personnel began to change that.

———————

THE PACE OF CHANGE had been so fast, it was hard for Roberto Reyes-Colon to believe it had been just six years since the Stonewall riots and, as he surveyed the thousands in Central Park, it was also hard to believe that the movement had grown so large. Like Matlovich, Reyes-Colon was living quite differently from how he had ever imagined he would when he cowered in the face of Air Force purges. After earning his college degree and serving two years in the Peace Corps, Reyes-Colon, now twenty-nine, had returned to New York City to teach grade school. But before he took the job at a school on West Ninety-first Street, he told the school board that he was gay. If they had any qualms about hiring homosexuals, he wanted to know it up front. When he became involved in neighborhood community-action groups, he also let everyone know, believing that attitudes toward gays would never change until every homosexual asserted himself or herself in this way. These were bold times, but Reyes-Colon was confident that with the changes coming so fast, antigay prejudice might be wiped out in four or five years. At *The Advocate*, the nation's leading gay newspaper, editors privately debated whether final approval for a federal gay-rights bill would come when the Congress convened in 1979 or whether it would be delayed until 1981.

The gay liberation movement of the early 1970s had become the gay-rights movement, focusing less on personal liberation and more on working within the political system to achieve gay rights. Though these more moderate leaders were under constant attack from radical factions of harder-line organizations, their patient lobbying was paying off in a string of heretofore-unimaginable successes. In statehouses across the country, legislatures took up gay-related issues. Nine legislatures were considering gay civil rights bills, and in three states the measures passed at least one legislative house. In 1975 alone, ten cities and three counties passed gay-rights ordinances. Scores of colleges passed policies banning discrimination by anyone recruiting employees or doing business on campus. There was even talk of organizing efforts for gay-rights laws in such conservative cities as Miami.

The day after the Gay Pride rally in Central Park, the state of Washington's legislature made that state the twelfth to repeal its sodomy law. Within weeks, the move was followed in such disparate states as California and Nebraska, where Christian fundamentalists dubbed the reform the "Child Victimization Act of 1975." By international standards, the legislation to repeal sodomy laws was not a remarkable occurrence. France, for example, had tossed out its sodomy laws in 1810. The United Kingdom repealed its "unnatural acts" statutes in 1967. Though tardy, the United States reforms represented an essential step toward equality, since the sodomy statutes, even if unenforced, had the effect of bestowing on all homosexuals the legal status of unapprehended felons.

The most significant legal breakthrough came four days after the Gay Pride March, on July 3, when the U.S. Civil Service Commission announced it would end its policy forbidding the employment of gay people in federal jobs. The decision followed a federal court decision that ruled that the Civil Service must assert a nexus, or a rational connection, between employees' conduct and the ability to perform their jobs. Since no connection could be found between homosexuality and job performance, the Civil Service was forced to open its 2.6 million positions to gays, removing those barriers that had been put in place by President Eisenhower at the height of the McCarthy era.

Another telling sign of the times from this period was the decision of the American Psychological Association to remove homosexuality from its list of mental disorders. Some psychoanalysts among APA members rebelled and led an unsuccessful attempt to recertify homosexuals as sick, but they were soundly defeated by a vote of the full membership and the change stuck.

The rapid remodeling of society's view toward homosexuality was felt in the military as well. Throughout the services, the number of gay-related discharges in fiscal year 1975 dropped to 937, the second lowest number since the Korean War—and the lowest number of any year to follow. At the National Security Agency, which was not covered by the Civil Service reform, there was even a move to allow gay employees. "To exclude an individual from employment purely on the basis of sexual preference . . . is considered discriminatory," one NSA official wrote in a private memorandum. Terminations of course continued, but in hundreds of other smaller moments, it was evident that the changes were seeping into the armed forces.

WHEN PETTY OFFICER First Class Jim Wagner came under investigation for homosexuality at Misawa Air Base in Japan, Naval Investigative Service agents contacted his base chaplain, coworkers, and other Navy friends. Most of these people knew Wagner was gay, but all of them insisted to NIS agents that he was heterosexual.

At the Presidio of San Francisco, a twenty-two-year-old Army medic named Bob Stuhr told his colonel that he was gay and wanted out. The colonel begged him to stay. According to Stuhr's memory of the episode, the colonel said he did not care whether Stuhr was gay; nobody did. He could have a good life in the Army, the colonel said. Everybody knew that a certain general in charge of one of the Army's most prestigious medical commands on the West Coast was gay and married to a lesbian officer. Stuhr turned himself in as a homosexual anyway, but the colonel delayed his paperwork; it took six months for the discharge to be processed.

————————

WHEN MILITARY HARD-LINERS later recalled the year 1975 and the evolution of attitudes toward gays in the military, they were far less apt to remember Leonard Matlovich at Langley Air Force Base than three enlisted men at Fort Sill, Oklahoma, a major Army artillery training center. On the same day Leonard Matlovich handed his letter to Captain Collins, court-martial proceedings had begun against the three men, all accused of sodomizing and then murdering Private Anthony Ray Jaurigui.

According to the story that unfolded in the courts-martial, the three men had been smoking marijuana and drinking with Jaurigui, a twenty-two-year-old private in their battery, when they decided to rape him. When Jaurigui started screaming, they stuffed paper in his mouth and then took turns holding their hands over his mouth and nose to keep him quiet. Jaurigui died of suffocation. The three privates, two eighteen-year-olds and a nineteen-year-old, concealed the body behind a panel in the recreational dayroom of their barracks and left it there. An unpleasant odor led to the corpse's discovery a few days later.

When all the macabre details came out in the young men's trials, officers assured one another that this was where admitting homosexuals to the armed forces led: to homosexual rapes and murders. Not believing gay-activist rhetoric, they did not buy the notion that even if these were gay men, they were aberrants, not typical of other healthy homosexuals who served in the military. As far as they were concerned, these three men were indeed homosexuals and they may well have been the only homosexuals at Fort Sill, Oklahoma. For years, in the artillery branch of the Army, the gay issue meant only rape and murder at Fort Sill.

The six-year-old gay movement had only barely nudged these beliefs. If some officers in the field showed a more laissez-faire attitude toward homosexuality, that was not the case in the upper ranks of the Pentagon. The Department of Defense became even more strident in its opposition to any loosening of attitudes toward gay soldiers. In a new official "rationale" for its ban on gay sailors, the Navy wrote, "Parents would be more than reluctant, to say the least, to permit their sons and daughters to join the Navy if the Navy had the reputation as a haven for homosexuals." Even almost twenty years later, former Secretary of Defense Melvin Laird would refuse to utter publicly one syllable on the issue.

The Air Force asserted that gays should be banned because they were prone to alcoholism, drug abuse, abduction, and child molestation. "By way of example, we have documented cases of homosexuals (former Air Force members) assaulting and even kidnapping individuals for the sole purpose of sexual gratification," wrote Colonel Ronald Skorepa to Congressman Fred Richmond, a critic of gay exclusion. "Within this area of deviant behavior, minors are often the target. . . . A team research study (also) concluded that homosexuals have a particularly difficult time coping with combat and group pressures."

Washington officials were even harsher. While discharge boards on the field level increasingly recommended honorable discharges, their decisions were frequently overruled at the Pentagon in favor of less than honorable discharges. A private review of pending gay discharges from the Navy in November 1975 revealed that the Chief of Naval Personnel had downgraded the discharge recommendations of administrative panels in four out of five cases, all of which involved sailors with records rated as either "excellent" or "outstanding." In Washington, it seemed that a discharge was used not to characterize a sailor's service but to punish him for being gay.

In Congress, the Navy helped buttress the opposition to gay civil rights legislation. Since the federal gay-rights bill was introduced by Congresswoman Bella Abzug in 1971, it had accumulated twenty-three cosponsors. An April 1975 memorandum from the head of the Navy's congressional liaison branch shows that the Navy prepared point papers and fact sheets for Congressman Bill Chappell "to refute the bill which Bella Abzug is preparing" and "to assist him in his efforts." According to the memo, released later under the Freedom of Information Act, the documents were passed to the conservative Florida congressman through a retired rear admiral on his staff.

JULY 1975
424 MARION ROAD
HAMPTON, VIRGINIA

LEONARD MATLOVICH was sound asleep when the first shot rang out. Three tours in Vietnam had taught him what to do at the sound of incoming fire. He dived onto the floor. Two more shots echoed in the humid night. He heard a car speeding away. Matlovich put on a robe and went outside. The three shots had ripped into his house. All of his neighbors were on their porches, too, in housecoats and robes, staring at the man whose name was in the local newspapers every day now.

For all of the genuine social change occurring across the country, back at Langley Air Force Base, Matlovich was still a target of intimidation. Since there was no evidence of any improper homosexual activity on his part, it appeared that the Air Force would try to manufacture some. They pulled Matlovich from his job as a race-relations instructor and put him in charge of a barracks full of young airmen. Soon after, a first sergeant appeared late one night and ordered Matlovich to conduct an inspection. Though such after-hours probes were contrary to Air Force policy, the sergeant then roused the sleeping airmen from their bunks and made them stand at attention, even though many were nude or dressed only in their underwear. Matlovich adopted his most professional demeanor. The point of the inspection, he felt, was to gain testimony that he stared longingly at the naked airmen.

It was also essential to rewrite the past whenever possible to justify the Air Force's course of action. The Air Force was arguing that a homosexual was not fit to serve, so it was necessary to show that Matlovich's service was unfit. In the military, the past could be altered. While Matlovich's supervisor, Captain Dennis Collins, had given him top ratings on his most recent evaluation, calling his job performance "outstanding," Lieutenant Colonel John Schofield interceded and reduced them after the sergeant became a cause célèbre, giving Matlovich a zero rating on a scale of ten in three categories. The lower evaluations were necessary to support the argument that the Air Force had decided to advance: Not only did it want to kick Matlovich out; it wanted to give him a less than honorable discharge.

Matlovich believed that the desire to accumulate evidence for a bad discharge lay behind the long delays in getting a separation hearing. By early July, four months after he had notified the Air Force of his homosexuality, no hearing had been scheduled. Even the *Air Force Times* commented that the delay represented "an unusually long time." And while a number of airmen and officers privately congratulated Matlovich for his stand and wished him success, a number of others wished that the Air Force would crack down harder on him. As Matlovich recalls his first sergeant bluntly telling him one day, "If I were in charge of this, I'd get rid of you in a week. We'd set you up so fast your head would swim."

A few weeks after the gunfire was aimed at his home, Matlovich received a phone call. The voice sounded concerned: "I'm not trying to scare you," it said, "but a group of men met last night and they're coming to get you. They're going to cut your tongue and your balls off and put lye in your eyes. They have surgical instruments to do it with and something to stop the bleeding, because they don't want you to die."

Before he hung up, the caller concluded, "I'm worried about you."

22

The Green Beret

SPECIALIST PERRY WATKINS'S EFFICIENCY amazed just about everyone with whom he worked. Therefore, when the job of mail clerk became open, it was agreed that Perry could do it along with his other duties as company clerk. The job did not require much—a daily drive to pick up the mail at Camp Red Cloud, a post made famous in the current television show "M*A*S*H," sorting, and distributing the mail. But the job did require a cursory check of records at the Criminal Investigation Division to ensure that a prospective mail clerk had never engaged in theft or mail fraud. When the check came back, Watkins's commander, Captain Albert J. Bast III, was troubled to find the records of the 1968 investigation into Watkins's homosexuality when he was assaulted at Fort Belvoir.

Bast was a tall, strapping man with thick dark hair and chiseled features. He reminded Watkins of Tyrone Power. Because of Bast's easy disposition, Watkins also counted him as one of the best officers with whom he had worked in his seven-year Army career. The admiration was mutual. As he would testify later, Bast considered Watkins one of the best clerks he had encountered in the United States Army and he had never heard of Perry making any untoward advances to other men. But as Bast read the CID report and reviewed Army regulations concerning homosexuality, he had to conclude that Perry Watkins, who had acknowledged being gay years earlier, should not be serving in the military. Bast did not really want Watkins out, but regulations were regulations. "I don't have any choice," he told Watkins.

No matter that the regulations were not enforced when Watkins was drafted in 1968, nor when he reenlisted in 1971. Perry respected Captain Bast and he did not bicker. He did insist, however, on doing all the paperwork himself. "I want to make sure it's done right," he said, and Bast agreed.

Watkins worked directly out of Bast's office; to relieve the captain of any potential embarrassment, Perry offered to work somewhere else until the discharge board began its machinations. Bast would not hear of it. Of course he wanted Watkins to remain in his office. Nobody was saying Perry Watkins was not good at his job.

JULY 29, 1975
ABOARD USS *LITTLE ROCK*
GAETA, ITALY

AS AN OFFICER, Ensign Copy Berg frequently interacted with agents from the Naval Investigative Service, so he did not consider it unusual when NIS Agent Parker called him into his office on a sunny day while the ship was at port. From Parker's office, Berg was escorted to an old apartment house that the Navy had converted into a warren of offices and classrooms. Once there, Parker introduced another NIS agent. "We're here to talk about your homosexuality," he said.

"What homosexuality?" Berg asked.

The NIS later said it could not locate Agent Parker for an interview, but the way Berg recalled the afternoon, the agents alternated their questions. One was confrontational and hostile; Parker was kind and understanding.

"You can tell us everything," Parker said. The NIS already had the names of all the Naval Academy officers, midshipmen, and faculty members with whom Berg had had sex and the dates when these assignations had taken place. They knew everything already, he said. He recited a long list of names. Berg recognized some as Academy faculty members, but he had never even met most of them. He refused to admit to anything.

The interview continued by the script, the good cop/bad cop dialogue, the crudely detailed questions about Berg's sexuality. When Berg still would not respond, the pair played their trump card.

"Mr. Gibson says that you did have sexual relations," the belligerent agent said, and then described a particular intimate act as Gibson had presumably described it to him. "Do you deny it?" he asked.

THAT MORNING, Lawrence Gibson had been removed from his classroom aboard the USS *Little Rock* as he prepared to teach his second class and was escorted to a small room where he met with two agents of the NIS.

According to Gibson's later account of the morning, one agent, who identified himself as R. W. Bartlett, was hostile; the other, S. I. Eisenson, was understanding. Neither Bartlett nor Eisenson were later made available to give their versions of what happened that morning, but Gibson said he held out for a while, through Bartlett's crude insinuations and impertinent questions, through Eisenson's assurances that anything he said about Berg would be held in the strictest confidence—they weren't after Gibson. He was Civil Service and the NIS had no jurisdiction over the Civil Service. They were simply trying to ensure national security.

Bartlett read Gibson a list of a dozen or more names from the Naval Academy—civilian teachers, midshipmen, senior officers—and said Ensign Berg had had sex with all of them, according to Gibson. Agent Eisenson asked Gibson how he had liked Annapolis. Wasn't it a beautiful setting? Bartlett wanted to know who fucked whom. Who was the "inserter" and who was the "insertee"?

Eventually, they broke Gibson down. He admitted that he was gay and that he and Berg were having a sexual relationship.

But this was not enough. Precisely when had they engaged in oral copulation? Anal copulation? How many times? When? The agents also wanted all correspondence between the two men. When Gibson refused, they asked him to sign a statement reiterating all he had told them. He refused again, pointing out that Agent Bartlett had taken copious notes all morning. He did agree to take an oath attesting to the truth of what he had said. They then asked him to sign a waiver allowing them to search his apartment. It was his "patriotic duty" to sign the waiver; Berg might have documents that would compromise national security. Gibson would not. Finally, he was permitted to leave.

THE NIS AGENTS told Berg what Gibson had said, including a number of specifics that convinced Berg that Gibson had indeed talked to them. Nothing Berg had learned at the Naval Academy had prepared him for this kind of interrogation. Gay issues had never even been discussed in his education. Now, with Gibson's confession, Berg saw no use in denying that he was gay. It seemed more significant that innocent names from the Naval Academy were being bandied about. It appeared that scores of careers were threatened. To define what was not true, Berg admitted to what was.

At the end of the interrogation, Berg figured his Navy career was over. He was very surprised, therefore, when he returned to the *Little Rock* and Vice Admiral F. C. "Fox" Turner's chief of staff asked him to replace the head of public affairs, who was going on vacation. They would sail for North Africa the next morning. Berg was to report aboard the *Little Rock* at 0730. There was no need to revoke his security clearance or to do anything "unusual" until further orders came from Washington.

It was the most responsible post Berg had ever held during his Navy career: managing public affairs for the fifty ships of the Sixth Fleet. But then, no one was questioning Berg's ability to do his job.

BERG WAS STILL NOT HOME when Gibson made his way back to the villa they shared. He was still waiting for Copy when Lieutenant Thompson appeared at the apartment door to summon Gibson to the office of the ship's executive officer, Commander Kent Siegel. Siegel ordered Gibson to pack up his books and get off the ship within a half hour, Gibson later recalled. "You're never to set foot on this ship again," he ordered and demanded Gibson submit his letter of resignation and return to the United States immediately. Gibson noted that he worked for the Civil Service, not the Navy, and that he would do nothing without talking to a lawyer first. He told Siegel that his "uncivil manners" were a discredit to the Navy, then left the stateroom.

The sun was blazing when Berg returned to the villa late in the afternoon. Blackness greeted him inside. Gibson had closed all the shutters and drawn the drapes. His bravado had been just that; he was convinced their lives were over.

But after all the years of hiding his homosexuality, Berg was ready to let the world know, if it really cared. The younger man went through the house pulling back the drapes, throwing open the shutters, letting the sunlight flood in. Just think, he said, they would not have to hide anymore. To Berg's eyes, Gibson did not seem reassured. Copy had long known that there was something in Lawrence that hearkened from generations past, from an era when it seemed as if homosexuals suffered almost eagerly to expiate their guilt. Copy had never felt particularly guilty and did not believe in suffering. In truth, he felt relieved.

The next morning, Gibson took Berg on the back of the couple's Vespa scooter down Mount Orlando and into Gaeta for the departure of the USS *Little Rock*. Gibson was grave. Berg was filled with optimism. He could get on with his life now, maybe move to New York and go to art school. His life was beginning again.

AUGUST 4, 1975
SPECIAL FORCES DETACHMENT, AIRBORNE EUROPE
BAD TÖLZ, WEST GERMANY

WHEN FIRST LIEUTENANT Joseph "Jay" Hatheway, Jr., lost his father shortly after his eighteenth birthday, the younger Hatheway was in his first semester at Claremont College, on a full four-year ROTC scholarship. He had been a straight-*A* high school student and National Merit Scholar. He always knew he would go to college, but his father's long struggle with heart disease had drained all the family's resources; ROTC had made his education possible.

Hatheway had been commissioned as an infantry officer in 1971 and promptly earned the silver wings of a parachute jumper before going on to advanced training with the Special Forces at Fort Bragg. Only at Fort Bragg did he discover the meaning of Special Forces—these were the famous Green Berets, the most macho of the Army's macho infantry units. *This is not going to be fun*, Jay thought, but by then he had been offered a European assignment, which was a plum. So he stuck around and went to Germany.

There was one perplexity. Physically, he fit in well enough. With dusty blond hair, blue eyes, and a muscular, compact body set on a five-seven frame, he looked the part of a fit warrior. But at least since college, he had had these attractions to other men. No one suspected he was gay. In his first Special Forces duty station in Germany, he had been too busy to think much about such things. In 1973, however, he had been reassigned from his Special Forces A-team to the battalion headquarters for the Special Forces in Europe. Though his work in an intelligence position kept him busy, he had more free time, and the leisure offered opportunities for encounters with other servicemen with similar interests.

Hatheway thought he was behaving discreetly, but in 1974 people started whispering *faggot*. When one young enlisted man got drunk in the NCO club and called him queer publicly, word got back to the Criminal Investigation Division, which began an investigation. In the process, Jay lost his security clearance, which meant he could not perform his intelligence job. In CID interrogations, he denied everything. Two months later, the probe concluded that Hatheway's record was "a clean slate," and he returned to work. The episode left Jay terrified. He knew he had to get out of the Army.

Bad Tölz was a strange place, anyway. The base was housed in what had been a headquarters of the Nazi SS. A number of former SS men now worked for the Army there, occasionally showing young officers a peek at their collections of Nazi memorabilia. It all gave Jay the creeps. He requested an early separation for August 1975, which would give him time to move back to Los Angeles and prepare for his fall term at UCLA. President Ford was downsizing the military anyway, so any voluntary resignation was usually accepted as part of the overall reductions in force. Hatheway got his early out.

By August 4, Hatheway had seven days left before his departure. His car and belongings had all been shipped to Bremerhaven for return to the States, except for the civilian clothes he could carry with him and his airline ticket home.

Perhaps he was unduly optimistic, perhaps it was his devil-may-care attitude, knowing his Army days were numbered. But on that afternoon in August, Jay accepted an invitation from Robert, a fellow Green Beret, for a good-bye drink in Robert's room. Unfortunately, Robert's roommate, who was to have been gone for the day, returned early. This occurred before the two had consummated their farewell but in time to elicit an "Oh my God" from the roommate, after which he turned on his heel and walked out.

The next morning, Jay received word to report to the commander's office. He figured the request meant one of two things: either a standard going-away talk from his boss or something very horrible was about to happen.

AT THE OPENING of the meeting, Jay Hatheway was being read his rights. He stood charged with violating Article 133 of the Uniform Code of Military Justice, the article forbidding "conduct unbecoming an officer and gentleman." Based on the statement of the interloper in the previous day's dalliance, Hatheway was also charged with violating Article 125 of the UCMJ, the provision outlawing sodomy.

Jay's commander asked him to sign an admission to avoid a court-martial. The Army later said it could not locate the commander or military judge in Hatheway's case, but, according to how Jay recalled the morning, he would receive a less than honorable discharge, of course, and lose all his VA benefits, which he needed in order to pursue his graduate degree at UCLA; if he signed, however, he would not embarrass himself, the Army, his parents, or his President. Jay decided he was not so embarrassed that he would give up his chance at a master's degree. He refused to sign.

The commander looked stunned. The JAG lawyer in attendance was astonished and started shouting, "Sign this. Sign this."

The next morning, Jay found a JAG lawyer in Munich, who called the charges "outrageous." The lawyer said he would certainly like to take the case but added, "In order to do it right, maybe I shouldn't."

Jay did not understand, so the military lawyer explained: He was not sure that he could mount an aggressive defense against the folks who signed his paycheck. Maybe Jay needed a civilian lawyer, he said, "in order to do it right."

The lawyer recommended a civilian counsel working with the Lawyers Military Defense Committee, an affiliate of the American Civil Liberties Union. That same day, Jay collected his paperwork and drove to Heidelberg to meet him.

"Welcome to the oppressed," Chris Coates commented after hearing Hatheway's story. A 1972 graduate of the University of North Carolina Law School, Coates had moved to Heidelberg with his wife in November 1974 to work with the ACLU. Defending enlisted men usually meant going up against officers and the hard-ass attitude of the military establishment. As an officer for the intelligence section of the hardest-ass branch of the Army, Jay Hatheway was everything Coates had been accustomed to fighting. But Coates was also intrigued with the case. The only other gay case Coates had defended was a specialist four whose mail had been opened by an Army captain. Reading romantic allusions in a letter to another man, the captain had promptly reported the enlisted man to the CID, which led to separation proceedings against him on grounds of homosexuality. All of this annoyed the libertarian in Coates, who moved not only to defend the officer but to press charges against the snoop. In the end, all the charges—including those against the suspected sodomite—were dropped. All this left Coates eager to challenge the more fundamental underpinning of the Army's gay policies.

"Given the merits of the case, you may be convicted in a trial," Coates told Jay. "But there's another issue here. We can begin laying the groundwork to challenge the constitutionality of Article One Twenty-five."

At issue here was not what Hatheway had been doing in Robert's bedroom, he said; the issue was what the Army was doing there. The case might go all the way to the Supreme Court.

Hatheway was not opposed to such a challenge, but he was much more concerned with getting this over with. He still had an airplane ticket to Los Angeles dated a few days hence. He did not really care about the Uniform Code of Military Justice and he did not really care about the Army anymore. He just wanted to get on with his life. He still hoped the Army would forget the charges and the whole mess would go away.

AUGUST 1975
ABOARD USS *LITTLE ROCK*
TUNISIA

TUNISIA IS A FRENCH-SPEAKING COUNTRY and there was only one person aboard the USS *Little Rock* who spoke any language other than English: Ensign Vernon Berg. Berg had already been honored by the Navy for his fluency in French, so he spent much of the tour translating for dignitaries and foreign press touring the ship, then returned to his office to translate French cables and telegrams for the admiral's staff. So much for being a threat to national security, he thought.

His future weighed heavily on his mind. He made several visits to the chief of the admiral's Judge Advocate General's staff, whom he had met in his days at Annapolis. As Berg later remembered, the attorney suggested that Berg should resign "for the good of the service." The most important thing was not to embarrass the admiral, he said, or the Navy, or Berg's family. Wasn't his father a Navy commander? Also, the lawyer added, if he resigned and behaved cooperatively, he would most certainly get an honorable discharge.

For his part, Berg was eager to get out of the Navy, anyway. His job did not challenge him, he did not like Italy, and he wanted to get on with his life. Putting aside the Navy's form-letter resignation, Berg wrote: "I truly feel that my own sense of duty is such that if I ever thought my private affairs or personal ambitions in any way endangered or conflicted with the United States, her Navy or the well-being of her ships at sea, I would have at that moment tendered my resignation."

In Gaeta, Gibson refused to resign his job. His boss promised to go to bat for him, muttering, "It's like something out of the Middle Ages." But shortly, she stopped returning his phone calls.

Under the new Civil Service regulations, Gibson could not be fired for being gay, of course. But he could be fired for not showing up at work; since he was no longer allowed aboard the *Little Rock* to conduct his shipboard classes, he lost his job.

AUGUST 10, 1975
SPECIAL FORCES DETACHMENT, AIRBORNE EUROPE
BAD TÖLZ, WEST GERMANY

LIEUTENANT JAY HATHEWAY was among three Special Forces officers slated to leave the intelligence command within a few days, and his co-workers had organized a going-away party weeks before. Word had not gotten around about Jay's possible court-martial and he wondered what people would say the next day when he was still on the post, even though he was supposed to be flying to Los Angeles.

His attorney, Chris Coates, had given him the bad news. He had not been able to make the charges disappear and the Army would proceed with a court-martial if Hatheway did not resign. Chris also said he had talked to his ACLU colleague David Addlestone in Washington, who was challenging the regulation against gays on behalf of another gay man named Leonard Matlovich. A dual challenge to the administrative regulation *and* the UCMJ statute against sodomy made sense to Coates; Addlestone agreed. How did Jay feel about it? Jay said okay. Getting on with his life, he realized, was going to take a while.

The going-away party was filled with good cheer and fond farewells. Jay received a plaque from his A-team and a hand-carved wooden statue of a Green Beret soldier with backpack and weapons. There was even the approximation of writing on the soldier's patch that bears the motto of the Special Forces: "*De Oppresso Liber*," "To Free the Oppressed."

23

Freedom

PETE RANDELL WAS in his office when his boss, the executive director of the Air Force Board of Correction of Military Records, gave him his new assignment, according to the way Randell later recalled the exchange.

"There's a queer case coming up here," he told Randell. "I want you to handle it, but you won't do anything without telling me or the Secretary of the Air Force first."

Randell had heard of the Matlovich case by then. The press was all over it. Matlovich was telling any reporter who would listen that he expected the whole matter to end up in the Supreme Court.

The director of the agency was not available to comment on the case years later and the Air Force declined comment on the board's actions. But the subsequent handling of the matter substantially corroborates Randell's recollection of events. From the start, his assignment communicated several things to Randell. First, it said that the fix was already on for Matlovich's administrative-board hearing, now slated for mid-September. The executive director could not know that the corrections board would be hearing Matlovich's appeal unless he also knew that Matlovich was going to be separated. Second, it told Randell that the fix was also going to be on at the Board of Correction of Military Records. That was why the Secretary of the Air Force had to be apprised of every move. And it would be Pete Randell's job to make sure the fix went smoothly.

From that day onward, Pete Randell read every report, legal opinion, and memorandum concerning Technical Sergeant Leonard Matlovich. As he oversaw efforts to ensure that Matlovich would lose, he secretly hoped he would win. Randell had no interest in being a crusader himself. He and his wife were expecting a child and he had the prospect of better jobs in the Department of the Air Force. Still, underneath, he was rooting for Matlovich.

AUGUST 30, 1975
NORFOLK, VIRGINIA

ENSIGN VERNON BERG and Lawrence Gibson arrived back in Virginia in the sultriest summer weather. Berg had hoped the Navy would move quickly for his separation, but, instead of ordering a hearing, it had transferred him to the staff of Rear Admiral Richard Rumple, commander of the Fifth Fleet in Norfolk. But no charges were pressed. All Berg could do was wait.

Time crept by. It was while he drifted in this netherworld that Berg wandered into The Cue, a gay bar in Norfolk, and saw a face that looked familiar. That was Technical Sergeant Leonard Matlovich, someone explained. He looked familiar because Leonard Matlovich in his crisp blue Air Force uniform was on the cover of *Time* magazine, over the bold headline I AM A HOMOSEXUAL. His picture could be seen at every checkout stand and magazine rack in the country.

It marked the first time the young gay movement had ever made the cover of a major newsweekly. To a cause still struggling for legitimacy, the event was a major turning point. For the general public, the interest in Matlovich reflected a deeper, almost unconscious fascination with the incongruities of his case. On one hand, Matlovich defied everything people believed homosexuals were. The substance of his case, however, pitted the gay movement, the ultimate affront to the ethos of American manhood, against the military, the last great bastion of male heterosexuality. At a time when sex roles were being called into question, the conflict was too archetypal for the media to resist.

Beyond what Matlovich meant for the gay movement, there was no place in society where his impact was felt more strongly than in the military. Even the most hardened homophobe had to take pause when he reviewed Matlovich's record. Credentials such as a Bronze Star, a Purple Heart, and twelve years of outstanding service meant something that civilians could barely imagine. As one wizened sergeant told Matlovich at Langley one day, "You can't have a Purple Heart and a Bronze Star and suck cock."

At military installations around the world, the merits of the gay policy were fiercely debated, in wardrooms and the enlisted mess, from the guard posts of the DMZ in Korea to Check Point Charlie in Berlin. Most veterans of that period recall that one vocal minority argued vehemently that all gays should be kicked out of the military; another minority argued equally vehemently for gays; the majority did not care one way or the other. Regulations were regulations, and no matter what the regulations were— or would be, one day—they would obey them. To this great mass in the middle, the group that was violently against gays was as suspect as those who were vocally for them. When the commander at Vandenberg Air Force Base ordered the manager of the base exchange to pull that week's

Time from magazine racks, he received a lecture on the First Amendment. The magazines stayed.

For others in uniform, Matlovich's message rang closer to home. One of these soldiers was Miriam Ben-Shalom, a twenty-seven-year-old single mother in Milwaukee, Wisconsin. For over a year, Ben-Shalom had spent every other weekend training with the Eighty-fourth Training Division of the Army Reserves. She was attending drill instructor's school and would soon begin her stint as one of the first female DIs in the division. When she saw the *Time* cover, she asked her commander, "Why don't they kick me out?" She was gay, too, and had been involved in lesbian-feminist groups for several years.

"Because you're a good NCO," the commander replied. He explained that the exercising of regulations was discretionary. This made sense to Miriam. As she continued her biweekly drilling, she formed a resolution that one day people should know they allowed open lesbians in the Army.

———

FOR MATLOVICH, his new status as a gay media star was a thrill. Speaking invitations poured in from across the country. Few of his gay audiences were accustomed to the "only in America" flag-waving tone. Matlovich had decided it was his flag too, and he could wave it just as hard as those people who wanted him out of the Air Force. He invariably pointed out that for all of America's faults, he could not launch this type of challenge behind the Iron Curtain.

On first hearing about his case, most gay activists called Matlovich brave. After he had made several appearances, organizers began calling him naïve. When a movie producer named Robert Weiner flew into Norfolk to speak to him, Matlovich was thrilled. He even took the producer to lunch at his favorite restaurant, the local McDonald's. There might be a movie here, Weiner said. All Lenny had to do was sign a paper, and Weiner could get him five hundred dollars!

With the stroke of a pen, Matlovich optioned away the rights to any film or dramatic presentations for his life story in perpetuity. The moment symbolized much of what was happening to Matlovich in those intoxicating months: He was signing away his life.

At the bar in The Cue, Copy Berg had introduced himself to Matlovich, and they talked frequently thereafter. Copy thought Leonard was one of the sweetest and most sincere people had ever met. But Copy's own life in a Navy family also allowed him to understand military lifers. Matlovich was a lifer, he could see, and he was about to lose his life. The gay movement expected a general, but Leonard Matlovich was a sergeant.

———

NOWHERE WAS THE DEBATE over Leonard Matlovich sharper than at Langley Air Force Base, where he was stationed. Younger officers and many senior enlisted people, most notably the African Americans on the base, were sometimes outspoken about Matlovich's right to stay in the Air Force. Senior officers, meanwhile, were just as vocal in defending the armed forces' obligation to throw him out.

Their concern with protecting the sexual morals of the Air Force held no small irony. By 1975, the sexual revolution had hit the United States military in full force, for homosexuals and heterosexuals alike. At Langley, as well as at other military installations, "key" parties had become a frequent pastime for married personnel who were into swinging. Revelers at such parties tossed their house keys into a basket and randomly drew from the pot, gaining access to alien bedrooms to dally with their colleagues' wives. Such activities, of course, represented a violation of the adultery statute in the Uniform Code of Military Justice. Moreover, any military man participating in an act of oral copulation during such activities would be guilty of the same UCMJ Article 125 proscription of sodomy under which gays were so frequently prosecuted. These military laws were rarely enforced against heterosexuals, however.

Matlovich's attorney, Captain Jon Jaenicke, had more immediate concerns. Something about the Air Force handling of this case smelled rotten to him. Jaenicke received a phone call one morning from a young enlisted man he had once helped out of a scrape. The young man had overheard two officers in the Judge Advocate General's office, which was prosecuting the case. The officers, he said, had been talking about the composition of the five-member administrative board that would decide whether to discharge or retain Matlovich.

"They're never going to buy it," one of the officers had said, according to the caller.

"If they ask," said the other, "just say you pulled the names out of a hat." Both men had laughed.

When the names of the proposed board finally crossed his desk, Jaenicke saw why the JAG officer did not think the Matlovich defense team would "buy" its composition. In three years of defending enlisted men at such procedures, Jaenicke had come to expect that administrative boards would include a major and a couple of captains, almost always assigned from the defendant's own base squadron. The proposed board for Matlovich's case, however, consisted of a full colonel, three lieutenant colonels, and a major. And a majority of the officers were from the Tactical Air Command's headquarters. The Air Force clearly wanted control of the hearing and was trying to stack the board with high-ranking officers, tightly under the thumb of the TAC's command.

In a tense meeting at the JAG office, Jaenicke fought the board. Faced with the prospect of even more unpleasant publicity, the Air Force withdrew its original slate and named another, but the whole experience left Jaenicke with the sinking feeling that he was playing against a stacked deck.

CAMP JACKSON
NEAR SEOUL, SOUTH KOREA

SPECIALIST FIVE Perry Watkins read the *Time* cover story on Leonard Matlovich with great interest, knowing that he, too, was on his way to an administrative separation hearing on precisely the same charges. Watkins dashed off a letter to Matlovich's ACLU lawyer, David Addlestone, but knew that stateside legal support was unlikely given the fact that he was several thousand miles away from the mainland.

The date of his discharge hearing was set for October, just weeks after that of Leonard Matlovich. As part of the legal research for Watkins's hearing, the Army's JAG office conducted a records search to check for Army precedents in the cases of other soldiers who had said they were homosexual and fought to stay in the Army. There were certainly plenty of men who had denied they were gay during such hearings, and plenty who had said they were gay when they waived their rights and accepted their discharges. But a search of all the legal records of the Pacific theater found that no person who had admitted to being gay had ever fought a discharge. The only comparable case was Matlovich's, but he was in the Air Force, so his case could carry no precedent for the Army.

When Watkins learned of the extraordinary conclusion to the legal records search, he matched it with his own experience of watching gay soldier after gay soldier quietly accept his discharge without a fight. Gays sometimes lost their freedom because heterosexuals wanted to rob them of it, he thought, but sometimes gays lost their freedom because they were willing to give it away.

SPECIAL FORCES DETACHMENT, AIRBORNE EUROPE
BAD TÖLZ, WEST GERMANY

AS ELSEWHERE in the military, the men at the Special Forces detachment in Germany hotly debated the Matlovich case, even while the base's own gay officer, Lieutenant Jay Hatheway, quietly prepared to fight his court-martial on sodomy charges. Many supported the antigay policies. Some rough-and-tough NCOs thought the regulation was so much bullshit. One crusty Special Forces sergeant observed to Hatheway, "Best sergeant major I ever knew in Nam only liked doing two things—shooting gooks and sucking cock."

As news of Hatheway's pending court-martial spread across the base, Jay stopped going to the officers' club and started socializing with noncommissioned officers, who tended to be more sympathetic to his case. But one afternoon, his neighbor, an Army captain, knocked on Jay's apartment door, asking to borrow a pen. The captain proceeded to force his way in, grab Jay by the throat, lift him up against the wall, and was about to start beating him when several neighbors, hearing Jay's screams, dashed into the room and tore the captain off him.

Afterward, Jay filed an affidavit requesting security. The way he remembers their response, he was told by base officers, "If you're going to play with fire, you're going to get burned."

Watching military justice in action was an experience that would forever rob Hatheway of his faith in his country. The frightened enlisted man with whom he had had the afternoon assignation at the onset of these proceedings had presumably decided to save himself from prosecution by insisting that Hatheway had raped him. According to the confession he gave to the CID, he was sleeping in his room when he awoke and found Jay fondling his genitals. He repeated this under oath at the preliminary hearing to determine whether enough evidence existed to put Jay on trial. But not even the prosecutors believed the confession, it seemed, and Hatheway was charged only with consensual sodomy rather than with the more severe charge of forced sodomy. The man who had cried rape then changed his story, admitting the encounter had been consensual, so that his statement would reflect the change in charges. This man, who by his own admission had already perjured himself twice, was the prosecution's only witness.

It was about this time that Hatheway learned he must undergo psychiatric testing to ensure that he was mentally capable of standing trial. His Army medical records show that he underwent psychiatric testing at the Army hospital in Augsburg. Jay recalls the psychiatrist explaining that it was essential to check him for neurological damage. This required an encephalogram. But instead of the normal paste-on sensors used for this test, the psychiatrist used pins to attach the sensors across Jay's brow, Hathaway recalls.

"It doesn't hurt," the psychiatrist said as he stuck a pin into Jay's forehead, just below the hairline. "Don't worry."

Small rivulets of blood started trickling down Jay's forehead. The psychiatrist seemed to become flustered, grabbing for tissues to wipe the blood away before continuing.

"Don't be scared," he said, pinning the sensors to the back of Jay's head.

Jay was in a large padded chair, like a dentist's chair, with a thick padded neck rest that held his head in place. As the pins dug into his flesh and the blood trickled down his face, he felt all control over his own destiny slip away. The doctor spun the dials on the machine, which whirred its needle over the graph paper, while the blood dripped down Jay's forehead, over his eyes, and down his cheeks.

He wanted to run away, but he could not move because he was wired to the machine. And he knew he could be ordered back, anyway. He was in the Army; he was their property. But it was more than just that. Suddenly, it struck him with utter clarity: He had no freedom. What the government wanted, it would get—by any means necessary.

For his entire life, Jay had thought of the United States as the land of the free. Now sitting in this chair, with the pins digging into his flesh and blood running over his face, Jay understood differently. The government would allow its citizens a certain measure of freedom when it was convenient, Hatheway realized. But when freedom ran counter to enforcing other conventions, such as those of sexual behavior, the government would discard democratic rhetoric and resort to totalitarian rule. That the government resorted to totalitarian tactics infrequently was completely irrelevant to Jay; what mattered was that the government kept dictatorial measures in its arsenal of options, to use when appropriate. Whether it was shooting students or intimidating homosexuals into surrendering their rights, it was all the same. Civics lessons about life, liberty, and the pursuit of happiness were simply classroom talk. For all Americans, Jay decided, freedom was a fraud.

The realization swept over him abruptly, not as a gradual awareness but as a fully formed thought. By the time the psychiatrist pulled the last pins out of Jay's head and mopped up the last drops of blood, the disillusionment possessed him completely. As Jay rose from the chair, he felt dazed, not sure of who he was. He no longer belonged to a country that was better than other nations; it was the same, and, for all its pretenses, perhaps a little worse.

SEPTEMBER 1975
NEWARK, DELAWARE

EVEN FIVE YEARS LATER Rich McGuire had never told another person about the threats that he could go to prison and his parents' home could be taken away, though the memory was never far from his thoughts or his nightmares. Whenever Rich applied for a job in the five years since he had left the Air Force, he froze at the question about his military service and the character of his discharge. Whenever he lied that he had obtained an honorable discharge from the U.S. Air Force, he worried that the shame of his military record would surface one day.

Rich was now the chief engineer at WNRK, a commercial radio station in Newark, and lived in a cottage in the artist colony of Arden, Delaware. He had just turned twenty-six, but his boyish face and perpetual grin made him look years younger. It was only in the wake of the *Time* magazine cover story on Leonard Matlovich and the news about people suing the military for reinstatement that Rich McGuire told someone for the first time about the ordeal of his interrogations and discharge from the United States Air Force in 1970. His confidant was a heterosexual friend, a law student at Rutgers University who could not get over the absurdity of the Air Force caring about its employees' sexual attractions. They cared, Rich told his friend; they cared big-time. And he proceeded to tell what had happened to him, trembling as he recalled the interrogation chamber in the musty basement of that charming New England frame house.

The law student was outraged. A few weeks later, when he ran into Rich, the law student said he had gone to the federal building in Springfield and taken out preliminary papers so he could file a lawsuit against the Air Force on Rich's behalf. He would ask for a $1 million judgment, he said, "just to get their attention."

McGuire was terrified. The Air Force would know he had told someone. He counted himself lucky that he'd escaped the Air Force without going to prison. Now the whole frightening process could start again.

Within two weeks, Rich quit his job at WNRK. Days later, he was packing his 240Z. He had friends who crewed on a fancy eighty-five-foot diesel yacht owned by a wealthy stock analyst. They agreed to sign him on as first mate if he could meet them in Norfolk, where the boat was in dry dock.

Worried that his parents might give away his whereabouts if questioned by the Air Force, Rich decided against giving them too many specifics about his new job, beyond saying that he was running yachts up and down the East Coast. The Air Force played rough, Rich knew, and he did not think his parents could stand up to the type of questioning he had endured. Nor did Rich explain to his friends why he had so abruptly decided to leave Delaware and go sailing.

He arrived at the Portsmouth yard of Norfolk Shipbuilding and Dry Dock on Wednesday, September 17, 1975, the second day of Leonard Matlovich's discharge hearing, which was taking place a few miles away at Langley Air Force Base.

24

The Mile-Wide Word

September 16, 1975
Langley Air Force Base
Hampton, Virginia

With sleek blue jet fighters roaring overhead and huge gray battleships sailing in and out of its choppy gray channels, Norfolk, Virginia, lay at the hub of the most sprawling military presence in the United States. The Norfolk region, called Hampton Roads by locals, was not so much one metropolitan area as a collection of military installations hugging every available bay and ocean inlet. The Marines had bases here, as did the Army, the Air Force, the Coast Guard, and even NASA. The Navy, of course, reigned supreme. The Hampton Roads area encompassed the greatest bastion of naval power in the world.

The region was steeped in U.S. military history. When General Douglas MacArthur died, Norfolk gave up its historic City Hall to serve as his tomb and memorial. A few miles down Highway 17 is Yorktown, where George Washington and Baron von Steuben defeated the British and gave birth to a new nation.

At 0900 hours on the rainy morning of September 16, 1975, a different kind of history was being made in Hampton. A horde of journalists had joined a group of tight-lipped Air Force officers on the staircase of a base building at Langley Air Force Base on their way to the administrative discharge hearing of Technical Sergeant Leonard P. Matlovich, Jr.

Matlovich was charged not with transgressing a criminal statute of the Uniform Code of Military Justice but with violating the administrative regulations that barred homosexuals from the service. This meant he would be subject to a fact-finding administrative hearing rather than a court-martial, which is a judicial process reserved for those who are charged with violating military criminal law. As a nonjudicial process, the administrative discharge board did not determine guilt "beyond a shadow of a doubt"; they established only that a "preponderance of evidence" existed that an administrative regulation had been violated. Since this was not supposed to be a trial, the prosecutor was referred to as a "recorder," and Matlovich was named a "respondent," not a defendant. But when the five-member administrative board took their seats at the front of the small hall and a silence swept through the room, it was clear to everyone that Leonard Matlovich was indeed on trial that day, as was the United States Air Force.

David Addlestone opened the hearing by asking each of the board's five members about his attitudes toward homosexuality. The members tended to answer tersely. Did homosexuals try to "recruit" young men to their lifestyle? Two said maybe; three did not know. Did homosexuals impair morale? Two said yes; three said maybe. Was homosexuality an illness? Two said no; one said possibly; two didn't know. According to writer Martin Duberman, who covered the hearing for *The New York Times Magazine,* half the questions concerning gay-related attitudes were answered with some variation of "I don't know."

Though the questioning was thorough, Addlestone had no intention of challenging board members. He simply hoped to mine some evidence of bias that would be documented in the hearing record. Even though Matlovich's Air Force lawyer, Captain Jon Jaenicke, had succeeded in revising the original board, Addlestone still saw the panel as a stacked deck. These board members were much higher in rank, and therefore potentially susceptible to command pressure, than a typical administrative board. The recorder was not a captain from the local base, as was usual, but a lieutenant colonel brought in from Nevada. All Addlestone could hope to do was create a strong record for the more crucial constitutional challenge to the issue that lay ahead.

Toward that end, Addlestone's associate, attorney Susan Hewman, immediately moved that the hearing be halted because the Air Force regulation against gays violated the constitutional guarantees to the right to privacy and equal protection under the law. The head of security for Langley Air Force Base, Lieutenant Colonel James Ramberger, seemed to bolster Hewman's argument when he testified that while his office did investigate all homosexual allegations, it never investigated charges of adultery or wife swapping. Though such activities were just as illegal as homosexual sodomy under Article 125 of the UCMJ, they were "minor sexual matters," he maintained.

"The regulation is a reflection of the Air Force's unlawful conduct in imposing the morality of the majority on its employees," Hewman argued. The prosecutor disputed this, saying the policy "is fairly related to the maintenance of military morals and is fairly related to the standards of the military organization." The board's legal adviser, who was appointed by the base commander, ruled against Hewman's motion.

THE JOB OF PROSECUTING Matlovich went to the hearing's recorder, Lieutenant Colonel James Applegate. Applegate had been a cannon cocker for the United States Marine Corps during the Korean War. He left the service to obtain his law degree from the University of Cincinnati; he joined the Air Force in 1960. By the date of the Matlovich hearing, he was only two years away from his retirement.

Friendly and casual in his manner, Applegate spoke with the slight drawl he had picked up from his childhood in the small hill towns of southern Ohio. As he saw it, there were specific scriptural prohibitions against homosexual practices. Homosexuality was wrong. Nor, on the more secular level, did Applegate doubt the legitimacy of the Air Force regulation he was bound to enforce. The presence of homosexuals would undermine military order, he believed. Still, he recognized Matlovich as a classic lifer and respected the service he had given his country. He held no personal animosity toward Matlovich; he was just doing his job for the Air Force and he believed the Air Force was in the right.

Applegate's first witness personified all that was problematical about enforcing the homosexual regulations, not only against Matlovich but against so many others who would follow him in the years ahead. The purpose of Sergeant Armando Lemos's testimony was to establish that Matlovich was homosexual and that he should be removed from the military. Lemos, who had served with Matlovich in Florida, told the board that Matlovich was gay, adding that the knowledge of Matlovich's homosexuality had not hurt their friendship and that he believed Leonard was an excellent race-relations instructor and a fine member of the United States Air Force. Air Force lawyers cringed when Lemos casually estimated that there were at least three hundred gay Air Force personnel at Hurlburt Field alone.

The next enlisted witness, Technical Sergeant Michael Marotta, was also supposed to buttress the government's case against Matlovich. Under cross-examination by Jaenicke, however, Marotta said that Matlovich's homosexuality did not make him a poorer instructor of race relations but an even more valuable one, because he had firsthand knowledge of discrimination. No, he didn't think the Air Force had any business booting him out.

What transpired next shocked Jaenicke. The senior member of the administrative board, Colonel David Glass, demanded a closed hearing, ejected the press, and then proceeded to castigate Applegate for his handling of the case. A second board member, Major Phillip Heacock, joined in. What was going on here? they demanded. These were supposed to be the prosecution witnesses and they sounded like defense witnesses.

Recorder Applegate appeared no less disturbed than the defense team. After all, the discharge boards were supposed to give at least the appearance of impartiality. Applegate knew that these statements would hurt the Air Force's case when the matter went to appeal, because it would show the panel's bias. For the first time he could remember in his fifteen years as an Air Force lawyer, Applegate demanded that Glass and Heacock be removed from the panel because of their prejudice against Matlovich. The board's legal adviser, who also appeared aghast at their behavior, complied and the pair were dismissed.

———————

THAT NIGHT, after the hearing, the defense team met with Matlovich to rehearse for the next day. Matlovich wanted to testify on his own behalf, but Addlestone warned him against his usual sentimental oratory for civil rights. Matlovich typically invoked Rosa Parks and Martin Luther King, Jr., to explain that homosexuality was another civil rights issue. The three remaining board members would not easily see it that way, Addlestone believed.

"Don't you understand what it is these people think?" Addlestone finally exploded. "They think you'll go into the showers and grab people by the genitals. They think you'll sneak around the barracks at night, that you'll be on your knees giving blowjobs in the latrine."

Matlovich was speechless. Addlestone tried to explain. "They've got all these fears. You've got to overcome their fears."

The next morning, when the hearing resumed, the rain had stopped and the air in Hampton was heavy with humidity. Matlovich took the stand and pleaded to be allowed to stay in the Air Force. He talked about growing up on Air Force bases around the world and the fears that had seized him when he began to be aware that he might be gay. With Addlestone's advice in mind, Matlovich told the board that he had "thought that to be gay I had to wear women's clothes, to go into the bathroom and watch people, to molest little children, all the stereotypes." Pausing, he added, "Well, I'm gay and I never wanted to do any of those things."

If the publicity over being homosexual troubled the Air Force, Matlovich said he would sign an oath then and there promising never to grant another interview or make another public statement if he was allowed to stay in the service.

In his cross-examination, prosecutor Applegate raised the ante. Applegate noted that every gay sexual act represented a violation of Article 125 of the UCMJ. "Sergeant Matlovich," Applegate said, "would you sign a contract never to practice homosexuality again?"

Matlovich blanched. Such a demand would never be made of a heterosexual, he knew. "No, I would not," he finally said. "That would be like making me a celibate for the rest of my life."

The final two days of the hearing were devoted to what was in effect a Homosexuality 101 course. Outside, a steady drizzle had cooled the air to the low seventies. Inside, with expert witnesses offering voluminous and sometimes arcane testimony, Addlestone and the defense team laid out the scientific basis of fact that would later be presented in federal courts to buttress the constitutional arguments against gay discrimination. A central question was how sexuality is determined. If being gay was something immutable, established at a very young age without reference to choice, then lawyers could reasonably argue that gays were a minority who were being systematically denied their civil rights. The issue also would bear on whether a homosexual serviceman could indeed "recruit" or influence other soldiers to his or her orientation.

Addlestone called in two leading sex researchers, Dr. Wardell Pomeroy, a coauthor of the Kinsey Institute's famous 1948 report on male homosexuality, and Dr. John Money, the head of psychohormonal research at Johns Hopkins University and the president of the Society for the Scientific Study of Sex. The best evidence suggested that sexual orientation was not a matter of adult choice but a disposition established in the first years of life, perhaps even by hormones released by the mother while a child was still in the womb, he said. "By adulthood, we don't have the potential any longer to be other than what we by then are— homosexual, bisexual or heterosexual," Money said. "Once the die is cast, it's impossible to turn the clock back." As far as what represented the "normal" or the "natural" course of sexuality, Money noted, "Anything that occurs in nature is 'natural' and homosexuality is recorded among all primates."

For his part, Pomeroy noted that his studies had shown that 40 percent of adult American males had had at least one sexual experience with another man to the point of orgasm. The defense used the expert's testimony to undermine the other dark stereotypes of homosexuals, including the notions that they might betray their country, and molest young children. It was not merely the regulation that was being disputed here; it was every bad thing people thought about homosexuals, because those attitudes were the basis of the regulations.

The data left the Air Force attorneys disconcerted. Prosecutor Applegate asked Pomeroy, for example, how Matlovich would respond if he were assigned to the South Pole with ten other men for a year. How would it be for him to shower with these men? he asked. "You don't understand," answered Pomeroy. "Well-adjusted people don't go around touching each other." Pomeroy then mentioned that he had an admiral in therapy who had adapted to very similar circumstances.

As for Matlovich himself, Money concluded, "Sergeant Matlovich is extraordinarily stable. He has a history of having stood up under pressure. He's just an unusually stable person." Even the Air Force psychiatrist who had examined Matlovich conceded that the sergeant was "fully capable of performing his duties." Another eleven race-relations instructors testified as character witnesses for Matlovich. In the end, the only testimony against him came from his commander, Lieutenant Colonel John Schofield, who argued that the sergeant's ability to do his job was now "totally impaired" and that his existence in the Air Force would project a bad image of American airmen everywhere.

MATLOVICH AWOKE EARLY the next morning and stared at the picture of Martin Luther King, Jr., on the wall across from his bed. He knew the hearing would reach its final moment that day and that the decision would come by nightfall. From the start, he had known that he would lose, but the past three days of testimony had reawakened his optimism. The facts were so plain. How could anyone dispute them? Outside, the sun broke through; it was going to be a beautiful day.

Back at the hearing, Addlestone closed his case by pleading with the board to note the clause in the Air Force policy that allowed for an exception to the gay exclusion rule in the "most unusual circumstances." There were two issues here, he said, whether the sergeant's homosexuality compromised his ability to serve effectively in the Air Force and whether "most unusual circumstances" existed in this case to allow the board to make an exception to its policy.

"No case has been made that his ability to serve has been compromised," Addlestone reminded the board in his closing arguments. He pointed out that of fifteen hundred students, 93 percent had rated Matlovich as the finest instructor they'd ever had. "The most unusual circumstances," Addlestone said, were "twelve years of unblemished service."

In his closing argument, prosecutor Applegate scoffed at the idea that Matlovich deserved such consideration. He had given Matlovich a chance to renounce his homosexuality, he noted, and the sergeant had refused a pledge of celibacy. No exceptional circumstances applied, Applegate said, "when Sergeant Matlovich says, 'I'm going to go out and do what homosexuals do.' " As for the lack of many witnesses to buttress the government's case, Applegate demurred, saying the Air Force had consciously refrained from "seeking to overwhelm you with indignant bigots who would rant and rave that we couldn't stand to have a man like Sergeant Matlovich in the Air Force."

After the arguments, the legal adviser to the board took pains to order the board that they had but one duty, to "apply" Air Force regulations. They were not to decide whether the regulations were just, and they most certainly were not to ponder constitutional issues. Matlovich's heart sank when he heard the words; he knew regulations would be obeyed and that he would lose.

The Administrative Discharge Board deliberated four hours and twenty-seven minutes before returning to the crowded room. Technical Sergeant Leonard P. Matlovich was "not considered a candidate for rehabilitation," and the board recommended that he be "subject to discharge for unfitness." Matlovich fought back tears while the word *unfitness* echoed through his mind. He was distracted to the point that the weightier implications of the next words were almost lost on him. The discharge board did not make the final decision on either dismissal or the character of discharge, but it would make a recommendation upon which the base commander and the Secretary of the Air Force would ultimately rule. And it was the recommendation of the Administrative Discharge Board that Matlovich not be granted an honorable discharge. Instead, he should receive a general discharge. He had known he might lose and be discharged, but he had never believed that the Air Force would claim he had not served honorably.

Matlovich had regained his composure by the time the hearing's formalities were completed. As he stepped outside into a bright sunny afternoon, a crowd of forty uniformed airmen burst into applause and cheers.

The reporters all wanted a quote for their stories, so Matlovich pulled a bicentennial half-dollar from his pocket and read the inscription. "It says 'two hundred years of freedom,' " he observed. "Not yet. Maybe someday. But not yet."

As Lieutenant Colonel Applegate watched Matlovich parry questions from reporters outside the building, he felt sympathy for the sergeant. Given Matlovich's outstanding record, Applegate had no doubt that he would have made chief master sergeant had he not launched this crusade against the homosexual regulation. Applegate believed that Matlovich was being used by the gay liberation movement.

FOR NEARLY THE NEXT TWO DECADES, when the homosexual-rights issue was debated, as it would be ever more ferociously, there would be few arguments posed for gays that had not first been lodged at the Administrative Discharge Board for Leonard Matlovich. On one side, an array of experts would present an impressive cornucopia of facts. The other side would argue, in effect, that this is the way it should be because this is the way it has always been. At issue were not the facts or the specifics of Leonard Matlovich in particular, nor of homosexuals in general. The true issue was about the limits of freedom in the United States.

JUST THREE DAYS AFTER the Administrative Discharge Board ruled that Leonard Matlovich should receive a general discharge from the United States Air Force, a gray-haired lady in a blue raincoat pulled out a chrome-plated revolver and tried to kill President Gerald Ford as he left the St. Francis Hotel on Union Square in San Francisco. Oliver Sipple, a husky ex-Marine, wrestled the gun from the woman's hand, probably saving the President's life.

Sipple pleaded with the Secret Service not to release his name to the press; he wanted to be anonymous, he insisted. When his name appeared on front pages anyway, it was read with great interest by Harvey Milk, who was then running what would be an unsuccessful campaign, his second, for the San Francisco Board of Supervisors. Milk had met Sipple over ten years earlier, when Sipple was fresh from the Marine Corps and frequenting the gay bars of Greenwich Village. Sipple had had an ill-fated affair with one of Milk's ex-lovers. Though Milk himself had remained firmly in the closet until he was forty-two years old, he was now of the opinion that all gays should be out of the closet, particularly those whose disclosure might help win a level of respect for gay women and men. Saving the life of the President qualified as that, so Milk mentioned to *San Francisco Chronicle* columnist Herb Caen that Sipple was gay. Caen printed the item and it was quickly picked up by papers across the country.

This presented a dilemma for President Ford. Normally, a man who saves the life of a President of the United States could expect a Rose Garden invitation and profuse thanks. Indeed, the President dutifully thanked the Secret Service agents who had pushed him into his limousine after the assassination attempt. The White House was mute on the matter of Oliver Sipple, however, because the word *homosexual* had been applied to him. It was only after several weeks, and many newspaper stories instigated by an irate Harvey Milk, that Ford penned a short thank-you note.

This little incident said everything about the place of the homosexual in America. The government did not want to thank Sipple for the same reason that the Air Force did not want to retain Leonard Matlovich. They were homosexual—the word was a mile wide in its meaning.

One by one, those service members who had announced their homosexuality in the heady early months of 1975 were discharged from the service. Sergeant Skip Keith was judged "unfit" for service five days after Matlovich was, and discharged. In back-to-back hearings, Private First Class Barbara Randolph and Private Debbie Watson faced administrative discharge boards. As would become routine, defense attorneys presented voluminous evidence of their good performance. Coworkers testified that they were "dependable" and "dedicated to their jobs." In her testimony, Randolph pleaded, "I want very much to be in the world to serve my country." But the discharge boards ruled they were "unfit" for the Women's Army Corps, and despite their outstanding records they received general, not honorable, discharges.

Altogether, seven women were ejected from the WACs as a result of the 1975 purge of lesbians at Fort Devens. Private First Class Tanya Domi survived the purge, in large part because of her audacious decision to fly to Washington and personally lobby her congressman about her case. Since a discharge hearing had still not been called, those efforts were enough. Within twenty-four hours, her case was dropped and she had new orders. Nevertheless, she would remember this close call nearly twenty years later when the President-elect of the United States asked her to develop new policies on gays in the military.

OCTOBER 14, 1975
CAMP MERCER, SOUTH KOREA

SPECIALIST FIVE Perry Watkins and Captain Albert Bast drove together from Camp Jackson to Camp Mercer, where Perry's discharge proceeding would be held. Watkins had been nervous, but he calmed down on the morning of his hearing and was once again feeling confident. Something told him he would win.

His discharge board, made up of two lieutenants, two captains, and a major, was clearly not stacked. Watkins's attorney offered copies of Perry's record, his award certificates, and the diploma he had recently received from the Eighth Army NCO Academy, all supporting his outstanding performance.

Testifying for the prosecution, Captain Bast said that Watkins was "the best clerk I have known," that he did "a fantastic job," and that "he has never approached other soldiers." But he explained that he had initiated the action against Perry because of his reading of the regulations. Watkins had admitted to being gay and the regulations said gays could not serve in the Army.

The second witness for the prosecution, First Sergeant Owen Johnson, said he knew that Watkins was gay but made no bones about the fact that he would work with him again. "Everyone in the company knows that Watkins is a homosexual," he said. "There have been no complaints or trouble."

The prosecutor, however, aggressively pressed his case, contending that Watkins was "guilty of committing homosexual acts."

"We don't have anything here saying he was guilty of homosexual acts," the chairman of the discharge board interrupted.

The prosecutor pointed to the statement Watkins had signed in 1968 after the attempted rape at Fort Belvoir. Nothing had come of that statement, however, because the CID had determined it could not be corroborated. Still, the prosecution maintained that it alone was enough to warrant his discharge now. The president of the board argued that the CID had not proved that the statement was true; the prosecutor countered that such proof was not necessary. Perry thought the prosecutor was missing the point.

"May I address the board?" Watkins asked. Permission was granted.

The crux of the matter, Perry began, was whether there was sufficient evidence to substantiate the CID confession. "Last night we both spent the night at the same installation," Watkins said to the prosecutor in his perfect enunciation. "If I walked in here saying that I had sex with you last night, the board would have insufficient evidence to prove or disprove it. If you want them to believe everything I say, do you want me to say that?"

The prosecutor blushed, leaving the board chairman to break the embarrassed silence. "Thank you, Specialist Watkins," he said. "That was a very good example."

The board took thirty minutes to weigh the evidence before voting unanimously to retain Perry Watkins in the Army. "There is no evidence suggesting that his behavior has had either a degrading effect upon unit performance, morale, or discipline, or upon his own job performance," it ruled.

The decision of this board, coming so close to Leonard Matlovich's, convinced Watkins that the military did not so much want to remove all homosexuals from their ranks as it wanted to be able to *say* it did not allow homosexuals. The board based its retention on whether Watkins had "intention" to commit homosexual behavior. He did not, they ruled. But neither had the defendants in several earlier cases. The board retained him; the Air Force would have kept Matlovich, too, Perry thought, if they could have done it without anyone knowing.

"I can't believe you won," Captain Bast kept repeating on the drive back to Camp Jackson.

Watkins reminded Captain Bast about a fifty-dollar bet they had made earlier. But officers weren't supposed to gamble, Watkins added. Bast could be in for some real trouble. Both men laughed.

That afternoon, Perry was back at work as company clerk in Bast's office and planning Simone's next USO appearance.

NOVEMBER 1975
NELLIGEN BARRACKS
STUTTGART, WEST GERMANY

SINCE HE HAD FIRST MET Jay Hatheway, attorney Chris Coates had spent the intervening three months working on constitutional arguments against Article 125 of the Uniform Code of Military Justice, the sodomy statute. Although he knew no military court was likely to throw the statute out, he wanted his arguments on the record at every level of the trial. He began by including them in a series of pretrial motions to be considered by the military judge who would preside over Jay's court-martial.

It was a time when optimism ran high about the ability of American courts to solve society's injustices. Coates was thirty years old and just three years out of law school; he shared that optimism and worked carefully to develop his case. He relied heavily on the nascent right to privacy, which the Supreme Court had been expanding for the past decade in its decisions to allow birth control, interracial marriages, and abortion. But Coates believed his strongest case lay in arguing that the enforcement of Article 125 in the military clearly violated the clause of the Fourteenth Amendment guaranteeing equal protection under the law to all Americans. Congress had enacted Article 125 to forbid sodomy among all military people. In practice, however, military officials enforced the law only against homosexuals, except in the most egregious circumstances. From where Coates stood, this practice was plainly unconstitutional and a violation of the equal-protection clause.

It was with this argument that Coates thought he might win, at least with the civilian judiciary, if not in military courts. He took the case very seriously and he hoped the military judge would take it seriously too, especially considering that Hatheway faced a federal felony conviction and prison time.

After Chris made his arguments, however, the judge, a colonel, called for a break in his chambers. Other participants in the proceeding, since lost in the military diaspora that rotates its players throughout the world, were unavailable to confirm Coates's memory, but nearly seventeen years later Coates said he could recall the judge's words precisely.

"I don't have anything against queers," the judge said, and added, smiling, "I've always heard a blowjob was as good from a man as from a woman—but I don't know about that."

Later, the judge ruled Article 125 constitutional.

25

Triangulates

NOVEMBER 1975
HAMPTON, VIRGINIA

WITH EVERY PASSING DAY, new invitations to speak, new awards, and new opportunities arrived at Leonard Matlovich's home on Marion Road. Every news organization in the United States, and many from outside the country, appeared at his doorstep demanding interviews. Not only had Matlovich achieved unparalleled status within the gay community; he had managed to capture the sympathy of the mainstream as well.

Even as he attained a level of celebrity heretofore unknown within the gay movement, his life was losing direction. The gay military friends he socialized with at The Cue wanted little to do with him now, fearing that the OSI was probably following him and that anyone associating with him would be implicated. An even greater loss came three weeks after his hearing, when he received a letter from the Norfolk Stake of the Mormon Church.

> *This is to formally advise you that the High Council Court of this Stake . . . took action to excommunicate you from the Church of Jesus Christ of Latter-Day Saints. . . . You have stated your intention to continue activism in a practice which is abhorrent to and in direct violation of the laws of our Heavenly Father. We cannot accept that you cannot change or be helped. It is our prayer that you may come to realize that you can indeed be changed and that you will seek such help as is necessary to accomplish it. . . . Our Heavenly Father loves you, brother Leonard, as we love and appreciate you. We are deeply concerned for your welfare and your eternal salvation, but our duty is clear. We urge you to study the scriptures and pray that you may come to know the* truth, *and to ignore the rising popular clamor for liberal practices in conflict with God's laws and eter-*

> *nal purpose. We believe that within your heart you know that*
> *the Gospel is true.*

Religion had always been one of the most significant aspects of Leonard's life. The excommunication robbed Matlovich of his religious foundation. For the rest of his life, he disavowed all organized religion. Though he wryly kept the excommunication letter framed on his wall for years, next to his *Time* cover and his discharge certificate, there was an unspoken despair in Leonard's newfound atheism. Those close to him understood that he rejected God in large part because he felt God had rejected him.

After his religious beliefs, Matlovich's faith in America had been the second most important point upon which he triangulated his identity. He truly believed, as he would for years to come, that the courts would eventually order his reinstatement in the Air Force. He hoped this would happen sooner rather than later so that he could get on with his military career. Days after his excommunication, however, Air Force Secretary John McLucas accepted the separation board's recommendation to oust the sergeant, though with an honorable rather than a general discharge. This was David Addlestone's first opportunity to take Matlovich's case to federal court. The Air Force planned on moving immediately to discharge Matlovich, he knew, so Addlestone asked a federal court in Washington for a temporary restraining order to block the separation.

The case went before Judge Gerhard Gesell, who made it clear that his sympathies lay with the gay sergeant. "I would simply comment that in this test case . . . involving a man of exceptional qualifications for the military, who has served his country well both in combat and in peacetime, that the Air Force is proceeding by the book when possibly a more compassionate view could have been taken of this situation pending the resolution of these serious and important issues."

Despite these sentiments, which he said he "felt quite strongly," Gesell ruled that no legal rationale justified halting the separation. Gesell noted "a clear but unfortunate trend" by the Supreme Court "strictly limiting the opportunity for servicemen in the modern Army to raise Constitutional issues." Given this, he wrote, "The chances of ultimate success in this particular matter are not great." Matlovich would have to be discharged and then seek normal redress through the courts, Gesell ruled. Gesell did allow the case to be put on a fast track, and he ordered the Air Force to come up with a justification for their policy of excluding gays. His orders left little doubt that he thought the policy could not be justified. Still, he maintained, Matlovich would have to leave the Air Force to fight the exclusion.

The next day, Technical Sergeant Leonard Matlovich drove into Langley Air Force Base for the last time, for his final processing out of the United States Air Force, his family for the past twelve years. A few hours later, he drove out again, Citizen Matlovich now.

On one level, he felt relieved that he had been able to weather the past eight months without the Air Force discrediting him or setting him up on some specious charge. And he still believed that one day he would be back. He would win.

COLUMBIA UNIVERSITY
NEW YORK CITY

A GAY CONFERENCE? It had never occurred to Ensign Vernon Berg that there were such things. His only experience with the gay community was what he knew through his older lover: Georgetown cocktail parties, where sly but vaguely bitchy witticisms were bandied about. But here at Columbia University were people like himself, *winners*, who were doing more than mouthing clever bon mots, who diligently pondered how to refashion the world and eliminate prejudice and discrimination.

Berg and Lawrence Gibson had come to New York City to see whether some of the gay activists there could help them with Copy's increasingly problematical relationship with the Navy. Somebody mentioned a gay symposium at Columbia University that weekend. The conference was a mélange of what was old and what was new in the burgeoning gay movement. In some rooms, participants engaged in "rap sessions" in which they discussed the traumas of coming out to families that could not understand. Every gay man, it seemed, had thrown out his battered copy of Gore Vidal's *City and the Pillar* and was now reading the new book in vogue, *Society and the Healthy Homosexual.* The new word of the hour, introduced in the volume, was *homophobia*, meaning an irrational fear of and prejudice against homosexuality. Every gay woman, meanwhile, had discarded the former lesbian Bible, the depressing *Well of Loneliness,* and was quoting from Rita Mae Brown's sassy *Rubyfruit Jungle.* Such sessions, throwbacks to the early movement's borrowing from feminist consciousness-raising, were now supplemented by new seminars favoring more prosaic political strategizing. What was the best way to lobby the legislature for sodomy repeal? What approach was most effective in getting a city council to enact a gay-rights ordinance? What legal strategy would best win civil rights guarantees in the state and federal courts?

Throughout the day, Copy Berg listened as the gay conference unfolded. For the past six months, he had considered his interrogation and pending discharge as a singular ordeal, something just between himself and the Navy. Suddenly, he understood that there was more to his case than his Navy career. His story had to do with the relationship of all gay people to the military, and, in a broader sense, with the question of where homosexuals fit into American life as a whole.

At the end of the conference, as the sun set across the Hudson River and a winter chill settled over Manhattan, in a crowded classroom where the subject of discussion was discrimination against gays in the military, Copy Berg stood and told the assemblage that he was in the process of being thrown out of the Navy for being gay. And then he said he had decided to fight it. The crowd burst into spontaneous applause. An attorney from a new gay advocacy group called Lambda Legal Defense and Education Fund slipped Copy his card; they would help him with a lawyer, he said. And Copy Berg, a Naval officer who was the son of a career Naval officer, knew that from that moment on his life would be very different.

IN JULY, BERG would have been happy enough to have had his resignation accepted and to have quietly left the service. Why the Navy did not immediately accept the resignation would become a matter of some conjecture. Perhaps it hoped to find evidence of a judicial offense for which it could prosecute Berg criminally. Perhaps the Navy simply wanted to make Berg's life difficult as their punishment for his being homosexual. Certainly the Navy believed it could decide Berg's fate in its own time and in its own manner. After all, no officer in the history of the United States Navy had ever picked a public fight over this issue before.

In the beginning, after his return to Norfolk from Italy, Copy had confidently taken weekend trips to New York and New Jersey to apply for jobs. He hoped to have a decent position waiting for him when he was discharged. The country was gripped by a recession, but Copy's Annapolis education made him an enviable catch for a number of corporations. Invariably, though, a prospective employer asked precisely when Copy Berg would be leaving the Navy, and since the Navy had still not set a date for a discharge hearing, Berg could not even guess.

Nor was there an easy answer for why, just one year after graduating from Annapolis, Berg was exiting so abruptly. Every employment application also asked about the character of discharge for an ex-military applicant. This was when Copy began to understand the long-term implications of even a general discharge. He needed an honorable discharge, and it was increasingly clear that the Navy had no intention of issuing such a separation. Copy's frustration had been mounting for months before the gay conference in New York. But he had certainly not gone expecting to make his case a cause célèbre. By the end of his first day in Manhattan, though, his impromptu announcement at the Columbia University conference had accomplished just that.

A few hours after Berg left the Columbia campus, he and Gibson were talking about the case with Bruce Voeller, executive director of the National Gay Task Force, at Voeller's apartment. Though many of the older hands of the gay movement had cut their political teeth in the antiwar movement and were reluctant to take up the cause of allowing gays into the military, Voeller had appreciated the potential influence of the issue from the start. But then Voeller's entrée to the gay movement had been unconventional. Voeller had worked for twelve years as a molecular biologist at Rockefeller University when his wife, a pediatrician, sued him for divorce in order to marry another doctor. Voeller had long struggled against what was then called "latent homosexuality," but he realized there might be another way to live when he saw a David Susskind show featuring a number of well-adjusted homosexuals such as himself. They were members of New York City's Gay Activists Alliance. A few weeks later, Voeller cautiously took his first steps into the church on Ninth Avenue where the group met.

That was in 1970, when Voeller was thirty-six. He was much older than the typical GAA member and extraordinarily articulate. He was also exceptionally good-looking, six feet tall, with white-blond hair and a model's face, which may have contributed to his rapid rise in the organization. By 1973, he was the group's president and pushing to change the focus from local issues to national concerns. With Washington activist Frank Kameny, Voeller aggressively lobbied both the American Psychiatric Association and the federal Civil Service Commission to make what would be historic changes in their antigay policies. He also began cultivating relationships with national news organizations, believing media exposure, not radical confrontations, was the better means of educating the country about gay injustices.

His actions antagonized those radicals who had long dominated GAA. All these meetings with reporters and psychiatrists and politicians put the gay movement in bed with the dreaded Establishment, they argued. That was so much blue-denim elitism, Voeller retorted, and it was scaring mainstream gays away from political activism. A schism developed. Voeller insisted that the gay cause would be best served as a mainstream liberal reform movement along the lines of the National Association for the Advancement of Colored People (NAACP); his militant detractors wanted a "liberation" movement to agitate not only against discrimination but for fundamental restructuring of the economic system. As the arguments became fiercer, Voeller and his supporters left GAA and formed the more moderate National Gay Task Force.

Gays such as Leonard Matlovich and Copy Berg were precisely the people for whom reformers like Voeller were scouting, responsible homosexuals with impeccable credentials. Though *Time* magazine had originally planned to use a photo of Voeller and his lover on the cover of its 1975 gay issue, it was Voeller himself who had argued for Matlovich's, sensing a stronger public-relations coup if a serviceman's image was used. The evening after Berg's dramatic announcement at the Columbia conference, Voeller was excited at what Berg's case might accomplish. But he did not minimize the problems or the risks.

Voeller described the custody battle he himself was fighting against his wife for visitation rights to his three children. Most state courts were so steeped in the notion that homosexuals were child molesters, he noted, that few would allow gays any form of parental rights, even to their own children. Voeller's lover, meanwhile, was the unnamed plaintiff in a lawsuit, *Doe* v. *Commonwealth's Attorney,* making its way through the federal courts. Already, a federal judge had decided that the Commonwealth of Virginia had every constitutional right to punish homosexuals with three years of prison every time they made love. No matter what changes had transpired in the past several years, acknowledged gay people could not expect meaningful redress against discrimination for many years to come, Voeller warned Berg.

Much to Voeller's relief, none of these arguments deterred Berg. As far as Berg was concerned, his life could not get any worse than it was now, his future clouded by the prospect of a less than honorable discharge. Lawrence Gibson, still indignant at his treatment by the NIS and Civil Service, was ready to fight, too.

Berg and Gibson spent the weekend at Voeller's refurbished brownstone on Spring Street and West Broadway, taking in the Manhattan gay scene, which still astounded Copy. They visited gay restaurants and gay discos crowded with thousands of successful young gay men. It was a world Berg had never imagined in his days as a lonely Academy student.

When Copy returned to Norfolk, he wrote a brief letter to the Chief of Naval Personnel, withdrawing his resignation and requesting a hearing on the matter of his separation. "I have compiled in my six years of service a record of which I am proud," he wrote. "I feel strongly that I bring to the Navy talents which are versatile and unique . . . Upon reflection on my actions I now feel that my submission of a letter of resignation was neither in the best interest of the naval service nor myself. My actions were completed naively with undue haste while under duress."

Two days later, Berg contacted a reporter for the *Newport News Daily Press.* The Navy would be forced to give him a fair hearing if they knew the media were watching, Copy thought, and he wanted the case to be scrutinized from now on. The *Daily Press* story immediately went over the Associated Press national wire. "Ensign Vernon E. Berg III, a homosexual, may be forced out of uniform," the story reported. "Berg, 24, a 1974 graduate of the U.S. Naval Academy, has become the latest serviceman—and the first officer—to fight the military's traditional ban on homosexuals."

After months of drifting aimlessly, Copy felt a new resolve, his optimism renewed. Though his lawyers cautioned that it would be unprecedented for an acknowledged gay officer to be retained, he believed that he could win a fair fight with the Navy on the issue. All he had to do was present the facts of his case. In a few months, he believed, his Navy career might be back on track.

DECEMBER 1975
SEATTLE, WASHINGTON

THE OVERFLOW CROWD in the hotel ballroom roared their approval when Leonard Matlovich began his speech with his famous epigraph about getting a medal for killing two men and a discharge for loving one. By now, he had logged tens of thousands of miles to give his speech scores of times. In truth, he had only modified his race-relations presentations to suit his new role as the chief spokesman for the gay-rights movement.

His new navy blue blazer hung loosely from Matlovich's lanky frame. Since departing from the service, he had not let his neatly trimmed red hair grow out even an eighth of an inch. He kept his mustache clipped, too, not like the bushy mustaches that were becoming de rigueur in gay bars. After all, Matlovich expected to be back in the Air Force before long. He exuded a calm professionalism and self-confidence in his appearances, characteristics commonplace in a military setting, but in a civilian world unfamiliar with military bearing it was something novel, and something quite unlike the angry gay spokesmen of years past. Matlovich was a hit with his audiences.

Rather than bemoaning oppression and homophobia and heterosexism, Matlovich spoke of the victories ahead. It was inevitable that gays would gain their civil rights, he said. It was the right and just thing, and in the end America always did the right and just thing. The only question was how many people would suffer before the heterosexual majority acquiesced to the actions its conscience would ultimately demand.

By December, three months after his board hearing, there was a barely discernible undertone of melancholy to his appearances. That it was heard by so few was only because so few wanted to hear it from someone who had come to symbolize homosexual wholesomeness. But it was there that afternoon in Seattle, where a crowd of eight hundred sat in light blue upholstered chairs finishing their Dijon chicken luncheon. It was time for Leonard to take questions from the audience.

"I know what the first question will be already," said Matlovich before anyone could raise a hand. "And the answer is no, but I'm looking."

The largely gay crowd laughed appreciatively. Matlovich's canned answer, of course, was a pitch for his availability. In almost every interview, he also talked about believing in monogamy and said that he was looking for that right man with whom to settle down.

Though Lenny was not movie-star handsome, he had a charisma that made him irresistible to some men, particularly so soon after he had been on the cover of *Time* magazine. Most of these men were not looking for long-lasting relationships, though it was years before Lenny understood the difference between fans and potential lovers. What he had in late 1975 were not boyfriends but fans, and lots of them. By the end of December, they had also left him exhausted and confused.

To make matters worse, Matlovich could barely keep up with the gay movement's growing demands. Almost every gay group in every city wanted to host a fund-raiser with Matlovich as its guest of honor. A string of volunteers working out of his small house was poorly coordinated and frequently scheduled him for appearances on different coasts for the same night. Some charlatans even announced events to feature Matlovich, without consulting him first. Meanwhile, other gay activists who had been jealous of his meteoric rise started muttering about his shortcomings. The old arguments against aiding gays in uniform resurfaced. Why should the movement support anyone who wanted to participate in a warmongering antigay military? We should be fighting to keep people out, some radicals said, not to keep them in.

It was during this time that *The Advocate*'s editor, John Preston, asked Matlovich how he was doing with all the celebrity and attention, and Matlovich started to cry. "No one," he said, "has ever asked me that."

DECEMBER 21, 1975
VIRGINIA BEACH, VIRGINIA

THE NAVY SET a January hearing date for Copy Berg's separation board. Copy assembled a team of five lawyers, including an Air Force lawyer from Langley Air Force Base who was familiar with the gay regulations from the Matlovich case, a Navy attorney, and E. Carrington Boggan, a gay ACLU attorney who had been brought on board by Lambda Legal Defense and Education Fund. There was one key piece to Copy's case that was not yet in place, however, even as the hearing neared. He wanted his father at his side, in uniform, during the hearing.

Four days before Christmas, during a monsoonlike rainstorm, Commander Vernon Berg, Jr., and his wife drove their camper van from Chicago, where the elder Berg served as senior chaplain for the Services School Command at the Great Lakes Naval Training Center. From the beginning, the commander had encouraged his son to fight the discharge, largely because he assumed Copy had been falsely accused. Copy had dated girls all through high school and through much of his Naval Academy career, his father knew, in spite of Lawrence Gibson, who he felt was obviously the cause of all Copy's problems. Meanwhile, Copy's mom wandered through the tiny house the two men shared, came upon the one bedroom with its one bed, and burst into tears.

When his parents left, nothing had been decided. Copy did not know whether his father would stand with him or not. Over the next days, Copy bore down on his case with his attorneys. The Navy planned to introduce new evidence in the hearing: a statement from Journalist Second Class Laurent Crofwell asserting that Berg had made a pass at him the previous February. Then on Christmas Eve, the NIS released a new five-page report indicating that it had used "confidential informants" to spy on Berg while he was aboard the USS *Little Rock*.

One informant, identified only as GAP-1 in the report, was clearly another officer, most probably another ensign. GAP-1 had told the NIS that he had noticed Berg writing numerous letters to Gibson before the latter's arrival in Gaeta and that he had actually read the letters and seen that they included "various romantic endearments." The fact that at least one other officer had read Copy's private correspondence was troubling enough, but the report also noted that GAP-1 was aware of "some additional letters further indicating a homosexual relationship between subject and Gibson," which told Berg that the ensign had rifled through his private residence to find evidence for the NIS investigators. Copy's lawyers moved to delay the hearing to investigate this breach, which again raised questions as to how the Berg probe had begun, but their request was denied.

While the attorneys dug into their law books, Copy worried about whether his father would make the trip to Norfolk when the separation hearing began. His lawyers were unanimously opposed to having the senior Berg appear. No one was sure what he would say. He could hurt Berg's case if he came down on the side of the antigay regulation.

Copy did not think his father would hurt his case. On one level, he appreciated the significance of walking into the hearing alongside his father, a career Navy man like those who would be judging him. This, however, was an almost trivial consideration in comparison with the main issue. He could stand losing his bond with the service, but he could not stand losing his father. It would be like losing a part of himself.

As the date of the hearing neared, he awaited word from Chicago; finally it came. When did the hearing start? Commander Vernon Berg asked Ensign Vernon Berg when he finally called. He wanted to be there.

— 26 —

Adjectives and Nouns

WITH ITS LACKLUSTER ARCHITECTURE and landscaping, Norfolk Naval Station had the nondenominational look of all military installations. Inside the gate, past the navy blue jet fighter that seemed to fly out of the ground on iron legs, were signs of a moment of glory that had touched the site once, when an exposition there had featured pavilions from every state in the nation. A two-third-scale reproduction of Independence Hall still stands from that time, not far from the stately row of admirals' homes. Other than this Colonial touch, there was little about the place that spoke of its role as the capital of the United States Navy.

On an unseasonably cold and windy January morning in 1976, however, it was clear by the number of reporters descending on the place that something important was happening. Uniformed guards politely directed members of the media to a two-story redbrick building, one of three identical buildings surrounding a dusty courtyard. Inside, under the fluorescent lights of a hearing room, an administrative board took up the case of Ensign Vernon E. Berg III, the first officer in the history of the Navy to say he was a homosexual and wanted to stay in the military.

The legal machinations were unsettling. Berg's Navy lawyer made it clear from the start that he believed homosexuality was immoral, though he did concede that everyone facing separation hearings deserved legal representation—"even a homosexual." Berg's decision to put an Air Force lawyer, Captain Wendall Smith, on the defense team was permissible under military regulations, but Berg knew the Navy would consider it a slap in the face. The appearance of a civilian attorney from a gay-rights group was necessary to lay the groundwork for the constitutional issues Berg wanted to appeal, but he knew it represented still another strike against him with the Navy board. Berg weighed all these matters carefully because he still thought that he might win at the board level.

Early legal maneuvering did not bode well for his optimism. *Voir dire* interrogation of the board members indicated that every one of them believed that all homosexuals should be ejected from the Navy in all circumstances. In one telling moment, attorney Smith asked board president Captain Robert Gibson whether the Navy "should investigate and eliminate heterosexuals that indulge in such things as adultery and wife swapping."

"I don't think the Navy condones that," said Gibson, a forty-three-year-old graduate of Officer Candidate School with twenty-one years of Navy service.

"Do you think the Navy should investigate and eliminate such persons?" Smith continued.

"No, I don't think so," Gibson said.

But Gibson conceded that wife swapping could be as injurious to a ship's morale as homosexuality, and Smith pressed Gibson as to why an adulterer, whose behavior violated both military law and Navy regulations, "should be treated any differently from a homosexual if all the problems of homosexuals are also present in heterosexual acts of adultery." Gibson said he couldn't "correlate" the question with the issue at hand.

Berg's civilian attorney, E. Carrington Boggan, asked that all the board members be disqualified because of their antigay attitudes. His motion was quickly dismissed. Captain Smith then formally requested more information about the Naval Investigative Service's "confidential informant" who had clearly broken into Berg's private apartment in Italy and read personal correspondence. If this information was the basis of the investigation, Smith pointed out, it represented "fruit of the poisonous tree," a legal doctrine that meant that ill-gotten evidence could not be used later to buttress a prosecution. "The constitutional rights have been so flagrantly violated that we need to probe into it," Smith said. For his part, Lawrence Gibson submitted an affidavit indicating that his NIS confession, which was central to Berg's own admission, was coerced and similarly inadmissible.

Captain Robert Gibson dismissed the objections and ordered the hearing to proceed. "This is not a court of law," he noted accurately, "and rules of evidence do not apply."

While the lawyers engaged in motions and objections, Commander Vernon Berg perused the NIS investigatory reports on his son. Though he had come to Norfolk with the intention of helping Copy, he still believed that his son had been put up to the legal challenge by his older lover. He had taught Copy to stand up for himself, but it did not seem he was standing up for himself so much as for this gay liberation movement. As he read the NIS reports, however, his own sense of outrage grew. He saw the evidence of the agency's deceptive tactics during the interrogations. Moreover, there were substantial indications that Copy's hearing was part of a broader investigation of gays at the Naval Academy. It rankled Berg—secret informants, coerced confessions, purloined mail, and endless investigations directed against people whose crime was a desire to serve their country. He loved the Navy, having devoted the past fifteen years of his life to its service. And he loved America. But what he saw in the NIS reports and what he heard at the unfolding discharge hearing was not the Navy he had known, not the America he had loved.

COPY BERG'S FIGHT against the Navy regulation bore one crucial difference from Leonard Matlovich's battle against the comparable Air Force rule. While Matlovich's case rested solely on his statement that he was homosexual, the Navy investigation had turned up allegations of sexual conduct on the part of Berg. Copy's accuser, Journalist Second Class Laurent John Crofwell, was the first witness to take the stand. As in the Matlovich hearing, however, it was hard to discern for which side the government's star witness spoke. Crofwell himself had warned prosecutors in pretrial questioning that he would prefer to be speaking for Berg's retention than for his separation.

In a soft voice, Crofwell told the board that his parents had died when he was seven years old and he had been brought up thereafter in an orphanage. He had joined the Navy in 1964 before finishing high school but consistently had difficulties fitting into military life. In fact, he admitted, his enlisted time had been marked by conflicts with Navy brass. Berg, he testified, was one of the only officers in his twelve-year Navy career who had taken what seemed like a genuine interest in whether he succeeded or failed, the only person who had ever encouraged him.

The hearing's recorder, or prosecutor, quickly directed Crofwell to describe the incident of a year earlier when he claimed Berg had made a pass at him. Crofwell said that he had stopped by Berg's apartment in Gaeta, uninvited and unannounced, had had some wine with Berg, and then decided to spend the night. When they were in bed together, Berg had pressed his hand briefly over his crotch, Crofwell said. When Crofwell had said, "Enough," Berg had stopped, he testified. Crofwell said he assured Berg that he would not tell anyone of the encounter. Later, however, he did mention the night to an ensign who subsequently informed others in the USS *Little Rock*'s chain of command.

Under cross-examination, Berg's attorney, Captain Smith, asked Crofwell whether he would have a problem serving with Berg on another ship after what had happened. The sailor struggled to answer honestly. "Personally, if I knew Ensign Berg to be a homosexual, it might inhibit my relationship with him if I did not know him. I think it is important that I know Ensign Berg and some of his personal preferences," Crofwell said. He was much clearer about whether he could work with Berg again. "That particular incident would not influence my working relationship with him at all," he said.

"Do you think homosexuals should be allowed to stay in the Navy," Smith asked, "and what about Ensign Berg?"

"Ensign Berg is not a homosexual," Crofwell said. "He is Ensign Berg."

The hearing prosecutor, Lieutenant J. Gregory Wallace, picked up the questioning, unimpressed by the distinction Crofwell was trying to make between whether *homosexual* was an all-encompassing noun or merely an adjective.

"Should [Berg] be retained?" he asked Crofwell again.

"Yes," Crofwell said meekly.

"No further questions," Wallace muttered.

Another important government witness, Commander Theodore Williams, chief of psychiatric service at the huge Portsmouth Naval Hospital a few miles from the Norfolk base, did not help the Navy's case much, either. Though he said he believed homosexuals should not be allowed in line duty in the Navy, he added that the gay policy was something of a lost cause. "I feel that it's probably just a matter of time before a homosexual is allowed to stay on active duty in the military," he testified.

THE WITNESS WHO GARNERED the most press strode into Building SP-64 on the fourth day of the Berg hearing. He was well known in the Navy— the honors awarded him during his decades of service included the Bronze Star, the Silver Star, and the Legion of Merit. Vice Admiral William P. Mack had retired from the Navy five months earlier with the pithy observation that both political and military leaders were responsible for the Vietnam debacle. Coming from a man who had served years in both the Pentagon—including a stint as Deputy Assistant Secretary of Defense— and on the battlefield—including a tour as Commander of the Seventh Fleet—the candid remarks had caused no small embarrassment to the military establishment. So would his comments at the Berg hearing.

Mack remembered Berg from the days when the midshipman had dated his daughter. He had personally commissioned Berg as an officer in the United States Navy in a private ceremony seventeen months earlier, and it was clear that even given the events of the past year he had no regrets about his action. Between his academic performance and his extracurricular activities, Berg had been in "the top ten percent" of Academy students, Mack testified. Though he understood that Berg now identified himself as a homosexual, he added that he did not believe his separation should be mandatory and that "each case should be determined on its own merits." As far as he was concerned, Ensign Berg still "was capable of performing as a Naval officer."

Board president Gibson pressed Mack about this conclusion. Mack admitted that he had never opposed the Navy's gay policies in the past and that the regulations being enforced against the ensign were no different from when he commanded the Seventh Fleet. That did not make them right, however, Mack said. "The country is changing," he said, "the Navy is not."

Berg next took the stand in his own defense. Just listing all his extracurricular activities at Annapolis consumed two hours. When prosecutor Wallace finally asked him about the crucial evening in his apartment in Gaeta, Berg said any contact between himself and Crofwell was "insignificant in consequence."

The climax of the eight-day hearing occurred the next morning when a sandy-haired Navy commander took the stand. His dress blue uniform only highlighted the striking resemblance the man bore to the defendant. On his chest, among all the other ribbons Commander Vernon Berg, Jr., had accumulated during the course of his career, was the Bronze Star he had won when he almost died ministering to Marines during the Tet offensive. In the middle of the red, white, and blue ribbon was the letter V—for valor. Berg's Navy lawyer, Lieutenant John Montgomery, asked the chaplain about his experiences with gay sailors.

"A person is a person," Berg began. "I really have felt strained in this whole hearing about people saying homosexuals have different problems. They have the same problems as anybody else. A homosexual can perform badly or spectacularly well. Homosexuals that I have known in the military have done extremely well, getting to extremely high ranks after I first met them."

"Are you saying that you know of homosexuals who are officers in the United States Navy today?" Montgomery asked.

"Certainly," the chaplain answered.

"Do you know any of them of the rank of commander?"

"Certainly."

"The rank of captain?" Montgomery asked.

"Certainly."

"The rank of rear admiral?"

"Yes, sir," Berg said. The room fell utterly silent while the chaplain continued. "Therefore, I would like to interject that I think it behooves all of us to look at what we do. We condemn blindly with prejudice and, you know, we must be careful whom we condemn."

When Montgomery asked about Berg's experience as a chaplain to Marine units in Vietnam, the commander said that at least once a week one or another Marine would come to him and admit to being gay. He also acknowledged, somewhat painfully, what he would have done not too long before if a commander had sent him a gay soldier.

"This week has been a learning experience for me," the elder Berg said, "and I'm sure it has been for all of us. I'm a product of Navy society also, and, sadly to say, years ago in 1960, '61, '62, I would have told him carte blanche, 'If you are a homosexual, you had better get out.' "

The world was changing, he added, looking toward his son. "We are advancing into an age of enlightenment. Hopefully, that will make such inquisitions unnecessary in the future."

Berg's statements about Marines clearly rankled the board's most junior member, Lieutenant Herbert Artis. Artis was a *mustang,* the Navy term for an enlisted man who later became an officer. At thirty-eight, Artis had twenty years in the Navy, including his thirteen years in enlisted service, and was the most outspoken board member against Berg. Copy thought it was ironic considering Artis was also the board's only African American member.

"Getting back to the Marines," Artis said to the commander. "You say you served with the Marines in Vietnam and it came to light that certain Marines were homosexuals and their buddies knew about them. From my experience, they were not accepted. They were sort of outcasts."

"In the Marines, we're talking about a Marine unit," Berg answered. "When one of those guys in that small unit finds their buddy is a homosexual, and if anybody else tells on him, watch out. They will protect him."

"Why?" asked Artis.

"Knowing Marines as I do," Berg said, "why would a given unit of Marines, once they know a man, live with him, fight with him, watch friends die with him, what do they care about what he does in his bedroom? It becomes unimportant, like color, or like male or female. Gosh, who cares? Sometimes, even in combat, I have had all sorts of men come to me and say, 'Gee, why can't the real world be like this? Why can't we all sit down and have communion together and drink wine together? Why can't we all love each other as human beings and accept each other as we are?' "

Another board member, Charles Erwin, interrupted Berg. "I'm having difficulty in trying to interpret homosexual behavior and tendencies," he said. "What is normal homosexual behavior that makes it identifiable?"

"When I hold a dying Marine in my arms and cry because he is dying, and I stroke his face and kiss him on the head, am I a homosexual?" Berg asked. Tears appeared in his eyes. He paused briefly while he brought his hands up to cover his face.

"Pardon me," he said. "When I talk about Vietnam, I get out of control. When I talk about Marines I get out of control, because I love them. Does that make me a homosexual?" He looked at the board. "What is a homosexual?" he asked. "Where does emotion and love stop and perversity take up?"

Lieutenant Artis cut the commander short. "The way I read the SEC-NAV instructions," Artis said, "it clearly states it is the policy of the Secretary of the Navy to dismiss homosexuals. It says, 'Prompt separation is essential.' "

The board had no more interest in listening to Chaplain Berg's musings. Before Berg could utter another word, the board president, Gibson, said, "Chaplain, you may be excused."

The elder Berg walked down the aisle of the hearing room as Lieutenant Artis began reading from the Navy's regulations on homosexuals again: "Under 'Policy,' paragraph four, it's very clear, very insistent, the way I read it. . . ."

The voice faded into background noise as Copy watched his father walk from the stand. Commander Berg had rarely discussed his Vietnam experiences, and now Copy could see why. A part of the chaplain still grieved for the dying Marines he had held in his arms. Copy had never seen his dad so emotional; he had never seen him so mortal; he had never loved him more.

When Copy focused again on the proceeding, he was consumed with resentment that the officers could so roundly ignore what his father had just said and so easily slip back into quoting SECNAV instructions. There were many things that would long anger Copy Berg about the hearing, but nothing more than a board that asked a man to resurrect the most painful moments of his life and then answered him with quotes from a rule book.

There was a second painful understanding Copy came to that day. He had learned for the first time what his father thought of homosexuals there, in a hearing room in answer to a lawyer's questions, because he had not had the courage to ask such questions himself.

PATCH BARRACKS
STUTTGART, GERMANY

A SHEET OF WHITE PAPER drifted down from the military judge's desk and wafted back and forth in front of the panel deciding Lieutenant Jay Hatheway's court-martial. From his seat at the defense table, Jay had seen the judge write something on the paper a few moments earlier, before a breeze from the window lifted it off his desk and sent it floating toward the floor. At last, it landed on the floor in front of the panel. Just four letters were scrawled across the sheet, but they were so large that they took up nearly the entire page: HOMO.

The entire court-martial was becoming a lesson on the worst aspects of military justice. While administrative separation hearings, such as the kind Leonard Matlovich and Copy Berg faced, were nonjudicial proceedings, a court-martial functions as a court of law, with far more stringent rules of evidence and due process, as well as the ability to mete out prison sentences. Its juries, also part of the military system, are chosen by the same authorities who initiate the action. In Jay's case, this meant that most of the jury was from the commanding general's staff. Even if there were no overt orders on how to rule—which, under military law, is banned as "illegal command influence"—Hatheway worried that career-minded officers would not be keen on siding with a homosexual.

Jay's attorney, Chris Coates, was able to disqualify one panel member after he said that "the only proper penalty" for a gay officer was jail, but the judge cut short the extensive *voir dire* questioning Coates sought. In one intriguing moment before testimony began, however, Coates asked the prosecutor whether he had ever performed sodomy, as defined by Article 125 of the Uniform Code of Military Justice upon which Jay was being tried that morning. The prosecutor refused to answer. Ultimately, the judge ordered him to. Yes, he said, he had.

Before the trial got under way, the Army had dropped all charges against Hatheway except for the one Article 125 count. The entire trial, therefore, rested solely on the testimony of the enlisted man who had engaged in sex with Jay the previous August and who had given wildly contradictory statements in the preliminary hearing and to Army investigators.

It was after his testimony that Jay began to notice inconsistencies in the psychiatric reports being given to the jury. The psychiatrist, Jay knew, had found him to be mentally stable; he had seen the report. But in the document the prosecutor turned over to the jury, there were several new paragraphs he had not seen. Under sharp questioning by Coates, it turned out an Army investigator working with the prosecutor had inserted on his own a few paragraphs of derogatory information into the reports. Coates stated that the reports should not be used as evidence. The judge, who in a court-martial does little more than rule on points of law, dismissed Coates's arguments. "So what?" he asked.

The reports were accepted as evidence.

It was about then that the judge doodled his note and a breeze came through the window and carried the paper to the floor, where it stared them all in the face: HOMO.

When it came time to argue Jay's punishment, the prosecutor took a ferocious stance. The jury would be tempted to be lenient, he said, but this was not the time to be permissive. There was only one appropriate punishment: prison.

JANUARY 25, 1976
NORFOLK, VIRGINIA

FOR THE NAVY, the first four days of Copy Berg's hearings were a public-relations disaster. The first public cracks in military support for the gay exclusion policy were apparent with the statements of retired Vice Admiral Mack and the testimony of Commander Berg. When the hearings entered the second week, the Navy launched its own counteroffensive against the gay ensign.

The first phase of the Navy's retaliation became apparent outside of the hearing room when Lawrence Gibson happened to run into Special Agent Parker of the Naval Investigative Service at the Norfolk Navy installation. Parker seemed embarrassed to see Gibson and hurried away. Gibson was stunned to see Parker, knowing that Berg's lawyers had pleaded that he be brought from Gaeta to Norfolk to testify in the hearings. His testimony could go a long way toward answering questions about the legality of the secret informant's search of Berg's apartment and the manipulated confession from Gibson. The Navy had refused to make Parker available. He was not in Norfolk to appear at the hearing; he was here to brief the press on the NIS investigation of Berg, reading to them from the extensive NIS files.

Such briefings are illegal. The NIS acts only as an investigatory agency for the Navy; materials from their probes are for release solely to Navy officials. Attorney Boggan moved that the charges against Berg be dismissed "on the grounds of the gross misconduct of the United States government." The motion was denied.

That afternoon, the Navy called the Norfolk base commander to testify at the hearing. His testimony seemed cursory; the commander merely reiterated support for the Navy's prohibition of gay sailors. All homosexuals, he said, should be kicked out. Just why he appeared to restate obvious Navy policy mystified Berg's lawyers—until Copy pointed out that the captain was also one of the board members' commanding officer.

To ensure that all board members got the point, the region's highest-ranking naval officer, Admiral Richard Rumble, appeared on television that afternoon to reiterate his position: The Navy should rid itself of all homosexuals. The comments of Vice Admiral Mack, he added, were "taken out of context," and any change in the gay policy "is going to be a long time coming."

The statement astounded Berg's attorneys. Rumble was the board's convening authority. He would make the first ruling on whether to accept the board's decision. Citing this fact, and the base commander's relationship with one of the board members, Berg's lawyers asked that the board be terminated because of unlawful command influence. The motion was rejected.

Perhaps the strangest incident occurred on the last full day of testimony when the prosecution announced that Journalist Second Class Laurent John Crofwell would testify again. While Crofwell had been an earnest and friendly witness during his first day of testimony, he appeared pale and dispirited when he walked into the hearing room again.

Under sharp questioning from Lieutenant Wallace, Crofwell said he had not told the whole story of his evening with Berg in Gaeta a year earlier. Berg had not only brushed his hand over his crotch, he said. He had also pulled down Crofwell's underwear and started to copulate with him orally. Only then had he said, "Enough," Crofwell told the board, and Berg had stopped.

Crofwell went on to say that after he left the bedroom, Berg had come down into the living room to talk to him, wearing a blue terry-cloth robe. It was an odd detail, Berg thought, given the fact that he had never owned such a garment.

As for his testimony that Berg could perform well as an officer on the USS *Little Rock* even after the revelations about his sexuality, Crofwell had reconsidered that, too. Although some of the enlisted men were initially sympathetic to Berg, he said, others had the attitude that "we've got to get that fag out of the Navy."

Copy listened. It seemed impossible to him not to conclude that the Navy lawyers had gone back to Crofwell and ordered him to revamp his testimony.

Berg's lawyers pointed out that this was different testimony from Crofwell's first statement to the NIS, and different from his testimony a week earlier. Which version was the truth? they asked. Crofwell answered weakly that all three were true, but that the new version was "more complete."

Further questioning revealed that Crofwell had failed two lie-detector tests. This did not mean his story was not true, the NIS polygraph examiner maintained. The first test was actually "inconclusive due to lung congestion," the examiner said. And while the second test showed that Crofwell was lying, it may have been because Crofwell was nervous talking about a sexual experience in which he could implicate himself as being gay. In fact, the NIS had cut off the polygraph questioning when Crofwell pleaded the possibility of self-incrimination.

Berg's attorneys argued that Crofwell had thoroughly impeached himself by offering multiple versions of what had transpired between them, which had led to a charge of sexual misconduct for Berg. Prosecutor Wallace responded that the discrepancies in Crofwell's testimony had to do with embarrassment at discussing a homosexual encounter. Crofwell was like a rape victim, Wallace said, who had a difficult time telling others about a sexual assault.

In final arguments that afternoon, attorney Boggan asserted that the Navy's gay policies violated the constitutional rights to privacy and equal protection under the law. Berg's military attorneys cited the discrepancies in Crofwell's statements, which were, in the end, the only evidence of misconduct presented. In his summation, prosecutor Wallace asked that Berg be separated from the Navy with an other than honorable discharge.

The next morning, the five-member board reconvened and announced its decision. Berg waited nervously with his attorneys at the table in the front of the room.

"After a review of the testimony and exhibits presented before this board, and due deliberations, it is the recommendation of the board that Ensign Berg be separated from the Naval service," Captain Gibson read.

"It is the opinion of this board that such separation should be under other than honorable conditions.

"This board is adjourned."

STUTTGART, GERMANY

THE JURY TOOK MORE than two hours to reach its decision as to whether Lieutenant Jay Hatheway was guilty or innocent of violating Article 125 of the UCMJ.

"Guilty."

But the jury had decided against prison time and ordered that Jay instead receive a discharge under less than honorable conditions.

The ruling stunned Hatheway. For attorney Chris Coates, the decision was a disappointment but not a surprise. The real fight, he knew, would be in the federal courts over constitutional issues that military panels were always loath to confront. Jay seemed more surprised at the unfairness of the system than most of Coates's clients, the lawyer observed. But then, most of his clients were enlisted people—many of them poor or from racial minorities. Therefore, they did not expect the system to work fairly and were not surprised when it did not. White male officers didn't expect the inequities, he thought, even if they did belong to a group that was clearly a despised minority.

ABOUT THE TIME that Jay Hatheway was court-martialed and Copy Berg faced his separation hearing, Sergeant Miriam Ben-Shalom graduated from drill sergeant's school in Milwaukee. Not only was it a very proud moment in her military career but it was also the time she had chosen for her "coming out," as the public acknowledgment of being gay was now called in activist circles. It was a time she had been moving toward since her conversation with her commander at the height of the publicity surrounding Leonard Matlovich. Later, her commander asked her again whether she was a homosexual.

"Sir," Shalom answered, "homosexual is an adjective."

"You know what I mean," he said impatiently.

Yes, she said, she was.

Now she had decided to let other people know about it, too, and she told reporters for the local gay newspaper that she would be graduating that night.

"How does it feel to be a lesbian in the Army?" a reporter asked her.

"It feels like everybody else," she answered.

Though her commander had been willing to accept a privately lesbian sergeant, he was not ready to retain a publicly gay one. A few days later, furious, he confronted her. "Why didn't you say, 'no comment'?" he asked. With that, he initiated discharge proceedings. Miriam Ben-Shalom knew that her performance evaluations documented that she was as good as any soldier in the Army Reserves, and a good deal better than most. She decided to fight such proceedings—all the way to the Supreme Court if she had to.

With that decision of the then-unknown substitute teacher in Milwaukee, the stage was set for the next fifteen years of legal maneuvering around the issue of homosexuals in the military. Until well into the 1990s, when people talked about the civil rights of gays in uniform, or, for that matter, the civil rights of gays in the United States, the names of those whose court cases would be most frequently cited were Matlovich and Berg, Ben-Shalom and Jim Woodward, Jay Hatheway and, within a few years, Perry Watkins. As these people began the arduous process of seeking redress through the federal court system, their names were reduced to the italics on the covers of legal briefs: *Matlovich* v. *Secretary of the Air Force*, *Ben-Shalom* v. *Secretary of the Army*, and so on. As they left the military, they would help define the legal limits of freedom for homosexuals in the United States.

BY THE TIME Commander Vernon Berg left Norfolk, his relationship with his son had been renewed and strengthened. There were to be repercussions, however. At the hearings, Copy had, of course, noted the presence of Commander T. J. Hilligan, Admiral Rumble's staff lawyer. Hilligan had sat through the entire proceedings and taken copious notes. Occasionally, a board member would glance his way before answering a question during the voir dire process. Even out of the courtroom, the admiral's men were never far away. Every time Copy or his father had talked to a reporter, a uniformed member of the admiral's staff seemed somewhere within earshot.

It was several years later, after Berg's attorneys had successfully obtained reams of memoranda under the provisions of the Freedom of Information Act, that Berg discovered that the reports Rumble's staff had forwarded to Washington each day contained notes on Commander Berg as well as on Ensign Berg. Two men, it turned out, saw their Navy careers end that week.

The Next Generation

FROM THE TIME Carole Jane Brock was eleven years old and saw the ocean for the first time, its mysteries and its power had tugged at something deep inside her and always drew her back. She was born in Great Falls, Montana, but her large family had moved to the San Francisco Bay Area in 1968, first to Oakland and then a few years later to San Jose. In high school, Carole and her friends drove down Highway 17, over the coastal mountains to Santa Cruz. Sometimes they visited the boardwalk, where rickety amusement park rides swooped them into the sky and down again toward the white sandy beaches. But Carole preferred the Natural Bridges State Beach a few miles north of the city. Here the beaches were desolate, and she could walk among the tide pools, marvel at the thousands of sea creatures that scurried about, and feel the power of the ocean.

Carole was five three, with short brown hair and hazel eyes. She was an *A* and *B* student and graduated in 1975 from Piedmont Hills High School, set among the working-class tract homes on the east side of San Jose. There would be no higher education. Her father, an auto mechanic, had committed suicide when she was fourteen; her mother supported Carole and her four brothers and sisters by working as a cook in retirement homes. Carole did not want to continue her education anyway. But eight months out of high school, her job at an electronics plant had grown tedious. She wanted out of it all, but she could not conceive how to escape. Then she thought of the Navy, a way to combine work with her love of the ocean, a way out of San Jose.

But Carole was also a well-informed eighteen-year-old who had been paying close attention to the travails of Sergeant Leonard Matlovich. His problems were of more than casual interest to her because several years earlier she had realized that she was gay. It was not a particularly traumatic realization, although she gathered the fact was best kept to herself. By her senior year in high school, several others had come out, so she had a circle of lesbian friends.

About the time Carole decided to enlist, she had heard not only about Leonard Matlovich but also about an acquaintance of hers who was being kicked out of the Navy for being a lesbian. These were cautionary tales but not enough to deter Carole. It would not be that different from civilian life, she thought. At the Navy enlistment center in San Jose, she hesitated at the question about engaging in homosexual practices and then checked *no*.

For the two months before she was formally inducted into the Navy, Carole looked ahead to a new life and opportunities far beyond what a woman could expect to attain in the civilian world. Though the Navy could not guarantee her field of training, her choice was aviation mechanics, not a traditional field for a woman then. But in the Navy, the advertisements said and the recruiters assured her, sex discrimination in nontraditional jobs was a thing of the past. And Carole believed it.

BY 1976, THE DETERMINATION of young women like Carole Brock to venture into fields long denied women was becoming a growing sociological trend. Though the political activism that marked the late 1960s and early 1970s had generally faded away, the burgeoning women's movement had lost none of its momentum. Changes were evident everywhere in American life. The American Broadcasting Company hired veteran broadcaster Barbara Walters as the first female coanchor in television news history, at an annual salary of $1 million a year. In December 1975, *Time* magazine had named twelve women as its Man of the Year. The Episcopal Church was on the brink of voting to allow the ordination of women.

Unlike the corporate world, the military operated entirely under the control of political forces that could mandate changes. In 1975, the services stopped forcing discharges on pregnant women. Weapons training was made mandatory for women, even though the combat exclusion remained in effect. Officer Candidate School initiated an integrated program and the Army opened 92 percent of its job categories to females. Plans were in the works to eliminate separate women's services such as the WAVEs, WACs, and WAFs in favor of a fully integrated military.

In 1976, the focal point of these changes were the service academies, which had been directed to include women in their fall classes. By late spring 1976, West Point had announced that 119 of its 1,480 new students that fall would be female. The Air Force Academy included 123 women among its 1,804 incoming freshmen, while Congress had authorized the Navy to admit 80 women to its freshman class of 1,250. Throughout all levels of the services, the numbers of women exploded. Between 1971 and 1975, the number of women in the Army tripled to 35,000, so that WACs comprised 4.5 percent of Army personnel.

Though women raced for the chance to enjoy new opportunities in the military, resistance to their growing presence was high. At the Air Force Academy, for example, the last all-male class adopted the motto Last Class with Bravado. Unofficially, the cadets understood that the motto's initials, LCWB, stood for Last Class with Balls. As the first coed classes of college ROTC programs graduated their first female officers, senior enlisted men found themselves under the command of women for the first time.

For all the sweeping changes, inequities persisted. There seemed to be an obsession with ensuring that military women behaved like ladies, given the suspicion that women who wanted to enter what had always been a man's world were not normal. In the Marine Corps, for example, female Marines attended classes on the proper application of nail polish and how to climb out of a car in a tight military skirt. At a number of bases, women were ordered to wear their skirts even in the most inclement weather rather than dress in more practical pants or fatigues. There was always an image problem. As *The New York Times* reported, "Back home, Army females are still regarded by many as heavies or lesbians, many female recruits said. . . . 'I was amazed,' said a male officer. 'You get a few Paulette Bunyan types, but most of these girls are really good-looking.' "

Sexual harassment also was pandemic. WAC Tanya Domi learned this in her first assignment after leaving Fort Devens in Massachusetts. Domi had survived the lesbian purge that had ended the careers of Debbie Watson and Barbara Randolph, only to be assigned to a new job as a petroleum laboratory specialist at Hunter Army Airfield in Savannah, Georgia. The Army had begun integrating women into their formerly all-male units, and Tanya was among the first women assigned to her unit. The problem was that a male noncommissioned officer was always fondling her. Tanya told him to leave her alone, but he persisted. Tanya complained to the female first lieutenant, who did not do anything; the same NCO was fondling her, too.

When an inspector general's team came through the base asking questions about sexual harassment, Tanya told them her problems. A few days later, her first sergeant grabbed her by the arm and took her to the battalion headquarters, according to Domi's recollections. "You're disloyal," he said, "you piece of shit." The battalion commander complained that she should have gone to him before complaining to the inspector general. He promptly transferred her to the motor pool. For the next eighteen months, she swept floors.

In the Navy, the new front against women's liberation was the issue of women at sea. Whatever changes were being made elsewhere in the services, the Navy was determined that women would not serve on ships. But for males as well as for females, going to sea was usually the prime reason for joining the Navy. Carole Brock knew about the prohibition against women at sea when she was sworn into the Navy in Orlando. But a year earlier, the Navy had said women would never attend Annapolis, either. Things were changing fast; her goal seemed within reach.

VANDENBERG AIR FORCE BASE
LOMPOC, CALIFORNIA

THE NEW GENERATION of the all-volunteer military not only drew growing numbers of women but also an increasing number of ethnic minorities like Adam Gettinger-Brizuela. Gettinger-Brizuela was stationed at Vandenberg Air Force Base, in the lush green hills of the central California coast halfway between San Francisco and Los Angeles. Though Adam's father was from German-Irish stock out of Tulsa, Oklahoma, his mother was Mexican, born in Sonora. Adam had his mother's dark hair, deep brown eyes, and the light brown cast to his skin that identified him as Mexican-American, particularly in his hometown of Spring Valley, California, a suburb of San Diego, where such distinctions were keenly observed.

Born in 1956, Adam had spent his childhood feeling embarrassed over his Mexican heritage. The role models offered him were Frito Bandito and Speedy Gonzalez. His favorite cartoon shows portrayed Mexicans as drunks, peasants, or bandits. In movies, one white cowboy could ride into a sleepy border town and single-handedly defeat scores of slovenly Mexicans. These were not images that did much for his self-esteem, and it was the same for others, such as those kids named Jesus who told everybody their name was really Jess. They were the *acomplejados,* those who accommodated.

The Chicano movement in the late 1960s instilled Adam with a new confidence and an entirely new personal identity. Its arrival coincided with his transfer from a suburban junior high to a school in San Diego where the Chicano kids were tough, good-looking, and did not accept trouble from anybody. If a white kid called you a beaner, the other Chicanos stuck up for you. You were in it together. Adam began to learn about Mexican culture. He became proud of his roots and added his mother's name to his father's Germanic surname, in the old Spanish style.

Being gay felt just as right to Adam as being Chicano, until the night his Anglo boyfriend said that he had more to lose than Adam if it was discovered he was gay. "You already are a minority," he told Adam. "It's different for you."

Once again, Adam saw, he did not fit in. He started dating girls, trying to conform, but he still gave in to other urges. He was confused and became more so. He started taking barbiturates and finally dropped out of school. Seeing his life spiraling out of control, he took the one route that he thought might restore stability and his manhood. Ten days after his seventeenth birthday, in October 1973, he enlisted in the United States Air Force.

It was a tense time to join the military. The first Arab oil boycott found automobiles snaking around gas stations across the United States, and the Air Force was put on a quiet alert in the event that President Nixon decided to take some decisive measures against the country's petroleum suppliers. Meanwhile, airmen had come back from Vietnam with a serious attitude problem toward any REMFs or stateside lard-ass officers who had not done any tough action overseas. A lot of these returning soldiers had gotten used to having sex with men, if only, they insisted, because they never knew what awful disease they might pick up from Saigon prostitutes. Adam had gone into the Air Force looking for his manhood, but there were all these opportunities for liaisons.

Adam was assigned to Mather Air Force Base near Sacramento in early 1974. He reaffirmed his commitment to be heterosexual until he met another young airman, also seventeen, and they became friends and roommates. Then they started sleeping together every night.

The growing numbers of WAF recruits also meant a growing lesbian presence on the base. Informal seventies-style segregation had relegated straight white women to the first floor of the women's barracks, straight black women to the top floor, and lesbians of both races to the second story.

Even as Adam dabbled in Sacramento's gay life, he was not sure he belonged there. This was not love, not in the pure romantic sense he had always wanted; it was just lust. He read some medical texts about homosexuality. Apparently, the condition could be reversed. People did change, the experts said, and Adam believed he might, too, if he got married. So he transferred to Vandenberg Air Force Base, the third-largest Air Force installation, and he married a young WAF he had met in his technical school. She was Chinese and Filipino; like Adam, she did not really fit in anywhere, either. She cried when Adam confided to her about his sexuality, but they resolved to stay together.

There was also a growing gay community at Vandenberg. Bolstered by the assertive ideology of the women's movement, a number of outspoken lesbians formed the community's hub there.

"You got a wedding ring—you got a lover?" one lesbian asked Adam a few weeks after they had met.

"I've got a wife."

"Honey," the WAF answered, "you may have a wife, but you're queer."

Adam liked their candor and their politics. He felt it was bullshit the way the military kicked gay people around, how everyone kicked gays around. The entire system was screwed up. You did not have to look much further than the headlines to see the corruption that permeated the government from the top down. There was a time when such disillusionment existed only among hippies in Haight-Ashbury. Nearly a decade after the Summer of Love, however, disenchantment had spread across the country, even to military bases. The Watergate scandal proved to growing numbers of disaffected citizens that they should fight the system because it needed fighting. The recent controversy over Leonard Matlovich had fueled gay dissatisfaction. At Vandenberg, the black lesbians were the most outspoken about gay people standing up for their rights.

Adam agreed. In fact, it was easier for him to relate to being gay on a political level than on a personal one. Personally, he did not want to be a pariah; he was torn between his desire to live an open life and the fear of the rejection he might face if he did. At some point, he knew, he'd have to make a choice.

ADAM HAD BEEN ON ASSIGNMENT at the Marine base at Camp Pendleton to cover the airlift of Vietnamese orphans for *Airman* magazine when he met a Marine Corps first lieutenant with whom he fell in love. The lieutenant was a Texan who was also married, but he said he would leave his wife if Adam would do the same. Adam might have left his wife, but by now they had a daughter, and he could never leave his daughter. He took a post office box so that he could correspond with the lieutenant, and he learned to express feelings he had not known he could have.

The affair reaffirmed Adam's sexual identity and that strengthened his friendships with the lesbian and gay community at Vandenberg. In his weekly column for the base newspaper, a man-on-the-street profile called "Airman in Green," Adam started featuring other gay airmen. Insiders joked that there was such a homosexual bias to his column that it should be titled "Airman in Lavender." Nor was he likely to run out of subjects anytime soon. Every new gay friend seemed to have other gay friends on military installations throughout California, just as Adam's Marine lover seemed to have uncounted gay military friends throughout the Southwest. All this gave Adam an idea: Maybe they should get organized. Within weeks, the Coalition of Gay Servicepeople was formed.

After the base newspaper was put to bed, Adam sometimes joined his gay friends in a barracks room to plan for their new group. When the hour grew late and it was time to turn the stereo down, they stayed together to talk about their hopes for the future. This all had to change, they agreed. And one day, they'd make a stand.

— 28 —

Transitions

EVER SINCE Ensign Berg had gone public about his fight with the Navy seven months earlier, he had been assigned the most obscure job the brass could find, which meant working in the Naval base's Civilian Personnel Office. His coworkers were largely civilians who had been extraordinarily supportive of him throughout the hearings. When the Navy set May 28 as the date of Copy's discharge, they planned a going-away party. Legal delays postponed the discharge for several days, but the party went on as scheduled. The secretarial pool awarded him a civilian shirt and a large sheet cake inscribed, "Good Luck, Copy! We'll Miss You."

It was odd to be partying, given the other than honorable discharge the Navy had handed him. This decision meant no benefits for his education. The Veterans Administration listed homosexuals in the same category as mutineers, spies, and convicted felons when deciding who should receive benefits. The Navy had also decided to withhold substantial back pay Berg had accrued from unpaid leave.

On June 1, Judge Gerhard Gesell refused to issue a temporary restraining order to bar Berg's discharge. As he had in Leonard Matlovich's case seven months earlier, Gesell made it clear he would hear arguments against the Navy's policy but that he could find no legal reason for obstructing that policy now. With that, the Navy ordered Copy Berg to be gone by midnight the next day.

As Berg was being processed out the next afternoon, a cluster of reporters gathered around him to ask whether he would continue to fight—he said he would—and to ask about his plans. A slight rain had begun to fall when Lieutenant Commander C. W. Albaugh broke through the circle of reporters and ordered Berg to remove the base sticker from his car. "Make sure I get it before you leave the base," Albaugh said.

The drizzle turned into a heavy downpour, many of the reporters scattered, and Copy Berg spent his last minutes in the United States Navy scraping the blue parking sticker from the rubber bumper of his station wagon. It was an automobile-age version of ripping the shoulder boards off a disgraced officer's jacket, one reporter joked. The ordeal delivered the desired humiliation. By the time he had returned the pulpy remains of a parking sticker to Albaugh and was ready to leave the base for the last time, Copy was soaked, his dress white uniform splattered with mud.

In the months that followed, Berg granted endless interviews and appeared on countless talk shows to advance his cause. There were two striking things about Copy's surge into media prominence during those months. First, he had the words to articulate ideas that he could barely have conceived of just a year earlier. Second, there were people ready to listen.

———————

COPY BERG'S EXPERIENCE was not singular. Across the nation in the second half of the 1970s, people were taking the gay-rights movement more seriously. It was not a widespread acceptance, to be sure, but gay demands were being discussed with earnestness in some quarters, which was a remarkable achievement considering that just a few years earlier gay activism had seemed an utterly fringe cause.

Former Navy Lieutenant Armistead Maupin was learning this was the case the same week as Copy Berg's going-away party in Norfolk. On May 24, Maupin's new column, called "Tales of the City," started appearing as a daily serial in the *San Francisco Chronicle*. The column included a panoply of San Francisco characters, such as a pot-smoking septuagenarian landlady named Anna Madrigal, an aspiring young career girl named Mary Ann Singleton, and her best friend, Michael Tolliver, a young gay man perpetually seeking romance. Maupin fashioned these characters' lives into a newsprint soap opera that was an instant sensation and made Maupin a national celebrity. He became the best-selling gay fiction writer in America, and from then on, no one could write honestly of life in urban America without including gay characters.

———————

MAUPIN'S WORK challenged the later consensus that nothing happened in the 1970s in American society. Much later, in his sixth best-selling book based on the "Tales of the City" characters, Armistead Maupin wrote that only heterosexuals assessed the decade that way because most certainly something did happen in the 1970s, and arguably the most important development was the growth of the gay movement. Though born from a riot at the very end of the 1960s, the new community that sprang up in major cities across the country was entirely indigenous to the 1970s. The gay and feminist movements were, in fact, the only new movements to emerge in that decade. Both movements shared one feature that lent them far greater power than was then evident to the politicians courting them or the media writing about them. More important than changing the way people thought, these movements changed the way hundreds of thousands of Americans lived. This was surely the most powerful kind of change.

The evolution in lifestyles was most obvious in major cities, where one of the most significant, though overlooked, urban migrations since the days of the Dust Bowl had occurred. Publicity about the burgeoning gay-liberation groups in the early 1970s had created gay meccas to which tens of thousands of young gay people, mostly men, streamed each year. In San Francisco, for example, later studies showed that gay refugees arrived at a rate of nearly five thousand a year through the late 1970s. Many of them were like Danny Flaherty from Spring Valley, Illinois, and Gilbert Baker from Chanute, Kansas, who were all at the Gay Freedom Day Parade on June 27, 1976. They were living in San Francisco in large part because their own hometowns were so entirely inhospitable to them. Because of refugees like this, within five years of that June day, gay men accounted for 40 percent of all single males in San Francisco. Other major urban areas were also sites of the new "gay ghettos," including New York, Los Angeles, Chicago, Houston, Philadelphia, Atlanta, Miami, and Seattle. More than mere gay neighborhoods, these were nascent communities with social institutions and newspapers. Typically the newcomers revitalized and spruced up older and sometimes rundown neighborhoods. A new word, *gentrification*, was introduced to the urban vocabulary.

Gay organizing continued to explode. Most major cities now saw the first meetings of gay businessmen. Gay Democratic clubs now existed in every major city in the country. Most significantly, one-quarter of the nation's college campuses had gay organizations by 1976, which meant that a whole new generation of gay organizers was being inculcated with the philosophy of the gay-rights movement. The National Gay Task Force estimated that by 1976 there were nineteen hundred homosexual organizations in the United States. A decade earlier, there had been a dozen at most.

The Democratic campaign for President in 1976 reflected the gains gays had made, at least among the opinion leaders of the more liberal political party. The gay issue was deemed serious enough that all but one of the ten Democratic presidential aspirants had position papers on the subject. Only Alabama governor George C. Wallace took no position and only conservative Senator Henry "Scoop" Jackson was forthrightly opposed to gay rights. The three most liberal candidates strongly endorsed federal gay-rights legislation; the five others were more comfortable with statements in support of "equal rights for all Americans" and vaguely opposed to "discrimination of all forms."

The man who broke out of the pack, former Georgia governor Jimmy Carter, claimed, "I oppose all forms of discrimination against individuals, including discrimination on the basis of sexual orientation. As President I can assure you that all policies of the federal government would reflect this commitment to ending all forms of discrimination."

But once it began to look as if Carter might be nominated, his campaign backed down: "I have never told anyone that I favor total equality," Carter later told *The Advocate*. As for the gay-rights bill, which he had earlier said he would sign, Carter now said, "I have not made up my mind on it. I do not feel that people should be abused because of their sexual preference, but I don't know how we could deal with the issue of blackmail in federal security jobs. But with that possible exception, I would probably support this legislation."

The Carter campaign wanted to downplay the whole gay issue as much as possible. At the 1976 Democratic National Convention in New York City, delegate Jim Foster found little support for a gay-rights plank to the platform. Instead, all he and the four-member gay caucus could get accepted was a vague promise to oppose "all forms of discrimination." The Democrats were intent on winning this time and were not going to allow McGovernesque fringe groups to take over the convention, Foster heard again and again. Foster and his colleagues in the national gay political leadership did not complain too loudly about this because it did appear that change was in the air again, after eight years of Republican administrations. The pendulum was swinging the other way, they assured themselves. There was plenty of time to push for their demands once the return to a progressive agenda was complete. Given the sweeping changes that had occurred in the seven years since the Stonewall riot, optimism seemed entirely reasonable.

For the gay community and for the nation as a whole, the late 1970s was a period of transition. Gays were evolving from a radical fringe group to something of a new ethnic minority. The rest of the country had emerged from a period of intense change and turbulence, ending with President Nixon's resignation, and seemed headed for a time of great reaction. The movement for greater rights for women and homosexuals advanced on the previous years' momentum. Meanwhile, careful observers saw the forces coalescing to create the more conservative epoch that lay ahead.

It was significant, for example, that Carter, a devout Southern Baptist, was the first presidential candidate in modern history to acknowledge publicly that he was a born-again Christian. When Carter emerged as the Democratic front-runner, the media suddenly discovered vast numbers of born-again Christians, particularly those in Carter's home turf of the Deep South. The phenomenon was discussed and written about endlessly. Even President Gerald Ford felt obliged to announce that he, too, was born-again, which was rather uncommon for an Episcopalian to claim. In 1976, in analyzing the impact of the southern born-again vote on the presidential election, the question was whether these people would vote for one of their own for chief executive rather than for any specific political agenda they expected one of their own to stand behind. Throughout the campaign, Carter kept his rhetoric vague to avoid alienating fundamentalists. Enough of them did vote Democratic that year to break the back of the Republican party's "southern strategy" and narrowly win Carter the presidential election.

The political phenomenon that was second only to the born-again vote in the 1976 presidential election was the surprising strength of former California governor Ronald Reagan in his challenge to incumbent Ford in the Republican primaries. The term *Reagan Republican* had for years been the political pundits' shorthand for right-wing extremist. In 1976, that very extremist came within a hairbreadth of unseating an incumbent President of his own party. It was the last time pundits would ever sneer at Ronald Reagan.

JULY 4, 1976
NEW YORK HARBOR
NEW YORK CITY

FROM A HILL at Owl's Head Park in Brooklyn, near the graceful Verrazano Narrows Bridge, Copy Berg, Lawrence Gibson, and a group of friends watched fireworks burst, flare, and flourish in red, white, and blue, celebrating the nation's bicentennial. Around them was spread a picnic of Virginia baked ham and fried chicken, deviled eggs, and three-bean salad. Though the harbor was crowded with extraordinary tall ships from fifty-five nations, Copy's attention focused on the USS *Kennedy,* from which President Ford was watching the largest pyrotechnic display in American history, and on all the other Navy ships that glided through the calm harbor. He knew the sizes and classifications of all of them, had served on one of every class during his summers at the Academy. But his civilian friends had little interest in the facts and figures he rattled off to them. Like most civilians, they felt a complete disconnection from the military. Copy watched the gray ships that had once been his home float past one another and a deep regret seized him. This was something he had once been a part of, but he was part of it no longer. He was, in fact, not much of a part of anything.

Copy was in the process of learning some painful truths about the gay community to which he had migrated. Although there were thousands of social activists devoted to changing the plight of homosexuals, there were millions who were indifferent. Many people wanted to meet Berg when he moved to New York, but to a large degree this stemmed from the fact that his picture had appeared in almost every gay publication in the nation and he took a very handsome picture. Berg met with people who he hoped would offer him a job, only to find that their interests resided elsewhere. Because of the publicity surrounding his case, there were no job offers from defense contractors. Berg tried for work as an illustrator in the heavily gay field of advertising. Gay advertising executives insisted that it was all right with *them* that he was openly gay, but if their clients knew they had hired an avowed homosexual . . . Berg, a graduate of the United States Naval Academy, pieced together an income by cleaning apartments and doing house painting when he could.

His deliverance from poverty came with the unexpected aid of an artist named Charles Bell, a man with a unique appreciation for what Berg had been through. Bell was a former Navy officer himself, having entered Officer Candidate School in the summer of 1957 after his graduation from the University of Oklahoma. He had known he was gay since he was very young and had first entered gay life when he had an affair with the artist Harold Stevenson. He fell into the Navy's discreet gay networks of the late 1950s, even as he earned a stellar service record.

It was on a routine cruise of the western Pacific that Bell went on a double date with a friend and two buddies—a thoroughly forgettable evening except for the fact that his friend's date got picked up by the Office of Naval Intelligence in a gay bar in San Diego some months later. After intense interrogation, this sailor named eighty-four other homosexuals in the Navy. They were then questioned and they named more. By the time ONI agents got to Charlie, they had evidence not only that he was gay but that he had fraternized with an enlisted man, his date from that night a few months before. Bell was told to resign or face a court-martial, so resign he did, resisting the ONI's assurances that things would be much easier for him if he provided a list.

Had he been heterosexual, Charlie Bell later recalled, he believed he might have ended up an admiral. Instead, he ended up disgraced with a discharge under other than honorable conditions. He moved to New York and took a corporate job as a systems controller at International Nickel, where his boss and mentor was a former Under Secretary of the Navy. Every time he received an unexpected call from this man, he steeled himself. The jig is up, he thought. They've found out. By the mid-1970s, he was launching what would be a very successful career as a fine artist, but he had not forgotten the shell shock he had felt over his separation. When he met Copy Berg and heard he needed a job, he hired him as an assistant. By the end of the year, Copy had decided to pursue his own career as an artist, and the next year he enrolled at Pratt Institute.

LEONARD MATLOVICH was having an even more difficult transition to civilian life. At the end of 1975, he had moved to Washington, D.C., hoping to work for gay civil rights. There were not many paying jobs in that field, however; Matlovich got by on paid speaking engagements. He never turned down an opportunity to speak, even if the groups couldn't pay his expenses. His life belonged to the gay movement now, and for the next three years he'd survive on an annual income of about $4,500.

The made-for-TV movie about him should have provided some income, but in signing away the rights to his story, Matlovich soon learned, he had also signed away the rights to all future income from any projects based on his story. And even though NBC wanted to produce the movie,

Robert Weiner was holding out for more money. Matlovich was appalled; he wanted his case to gain the wider exposure that a television movie guaranteed. At a tense meeting with Weiner and NBC executives in New York, he pleaded with the producer to let the network purchase the story.

"This is my life. I'm entitled to own it," he begged. When Weiner would not budge, he cried, "Give me my life back. I want my life back."

———————

ATTEMPTS TO NAIL DOWN specific times and places would be forever elusive, but it was probably at this time, during the summer of 1976, that something else of great import for the history of the gay community came to pass. Something new and frightening began to stalk gay men in America. It was a virus, but not an ordinary virus. It was uniquely insidious because it could lie dormant for many years. By the end of 1976, a small handful of gay men in New York and in San Francisco were already feeling a vague malaise that would later be traced to infection with this virus. There was a nightmare waiting to happen, but no one then could have known.

The Secret Report

JULY 1976
AIR FORCE BOARD FOR THE
CORRECTION OF MILITARY RECORDS
THE PENTAGON
ARLINGTON, VIRGINIA

THE FEDERAL COURT ruling on the case of Technical Sergeant Leonard Matlovich was only days away, Pete Randell knew. Judge Gerhard Gesell had indicated he would issue an oral opinion the same day as he heard arguments. That indicated that he already knew what he would rule. Randell knew Gesell to be a liberal judge with a maverick streak; he hoped that Matlovich would win—in spite of the fact that Randell himself had helped grease the skids for Matlovich's defeat at the Air Force Board for the Correction of Military Records.

Appeals to the board were typically doled out to small three-member review panels, each member chosen randomly from among the thirty civilians serving on the board. Board members could usually be counted on to follow the party line on controversial cases; a good share of them were themselves civilian employees of the Air Force. But in the case of Technical Sergeant Leonard Matlovich, several had already opined that if they had to review the Matlovich case they would rule for the sergeant. Such an outcome would be a major headache for the Air Force, given the fact that the board represented the court of highest appeal within their administrative processes. If the board reinstated him, the service would be hard-pressed not to accept its decision.

Even those members who did not support the gay airman believed that the government would lose if the case went to court. The record they created at the board, they also knew, would be part of what federal courts would review. Given all these complications, the Air Force decided nothing should be left to chance in Matlovich's review.

To make sure there were not any surprises, the board's executive director handpicked the review panel to ensure the vote against Matlovich. Randell called this practice "red lining," and it was a common procedure in gay-related cases.

The Secretary of the Air Force had already ordered that Matlovich receive an honorable discharge. In his appeal Matlovich asked that the board find the discharge to be invalid and that they reinstate him in the service. Matlovich's lawyer, David Addlestone, used the hearing to load the record with factual support that might be persuasive to federal courts in their later review of the case. He submitted thousands of pages of media stories and supporting affidavits and hundreds of letters from other gay service members. Everybody from lowly E-2's to two-star generals had written to Matlovich to say they were gay and had served honorably in the military. While the testimonials from higher-ranking officers tended to remain unsigned, their language and stilted military writing style indicated to Pete Randell that they were genuine.

For Pete, whose only contact with other gay people was an occasional encounter in Pentagon rest rooms, the Matlovich documents represented a crash course in gay sociology. In one story in *Parade* magazine, Matlovich talked about going to a gay discotheque in Washington and meeting scores of ordinary middle-class gay men such as himself, people who held responsible jobs in the military and government. Imagine that, Pete thought, entire bars filled with people like himself, ordinary people leading ordinary lives. But he did not allow his imaginings to go too far. His wife had just had their second child. He had his family to take care of. The decision Randell helped craft took gracious note of Matlovich's "outstanding" record in the Air Force. But this was not enough to invoke the clause of Air Force regulations that allowed for exceptions to the gay exclusion. "An outstanding military record without other unusual circumstances is not sufficient basis to compel a member's retention," the board concluded.

Even as Pete typed the opinion, he looked forward to the court appeals, which he believed would ultimately rule in the sergeant's favor. Just about everyone else in the Air Force, including key members of the service's top legal staff, believed Matlovich would win his case.

Elsewhere in the Pentagon, Navy officials fretted over the legal challenge to their gay regulations by former Ensign Vernon Berg III. Aware that the Navy's own delays in approving Berg's resignation a year earlier were responsible for the current court challenge, the Chief of Naval Personnel issued an order to all commands demanding that from then on Washington be notified whenever an officer "involved in alleged homosexual activity" had submitted a resignation. "Approval of the resignation would normally be appropriate under SECNAV [Secretary of the Navy] policy," the memorandum stated pointedly.

In another memorandum from the Chief of Naval Personnel to the Judge Advocate General later obtained under the Freedom of Information Act, the Navy tried to define a rationale for its gay policies:

(1) *An individual's performance of duties could be unduly influenced by emotional relationships with other individuals which would interfere with proper command relationship.*

(2) *Such an individual would be liable for court martial or civil punishment as a result of manifestations of homosexual tendencies.*

(3) *Such individuals might force their desires on others resulting in sexual assaults.*

(4) *Additionally, an officer or senior enlisted person who exhibits homosexual tendencies will be unable to maintain the necessary respect and trust from the great majority of naval personnel who detest/abhor homosexuality. This lack of respect and trust would most certainly degrade the officer's ability to successfully perform his duties of supervision and command.*

Then the memo posed a rhetorical question: "Does the Navy have any empirical proof that homosexuality among its members has an adverse effect upon the completion of its mission?" The office of the Chief of Naval Personnel answered, "No such empirical proof is known at this time."

———————

BY MID-1976, extensive digging through Navy back files had most certainly yielded empirical data concerning the role of homosexuals in the Navy. The problem was that the data did not support Navy policy. This was most dramatically evident in the 639-page document entitled "Report of the Board Appointed to Prepare and Submit Recommendations to the Secretary of the Navy for the Revision of Policies, Procedures and Directives Dealing with Homosexuals." Given its ponderous title, the document became more commonly known as the Crittenden Report, for Captain S. H. Crittenden, Jr., the chairman of the five-member board that wrote the document in 1957.

Rumors of such a secret report had long circulated among gay legal scholars, but the Defense Department had always denied its existence. Congressman Ed Koch, hearing the rumors, had specifically petitioned the Defense Department for it in July 1975. He received a brusque reply: "The Office of the Secretary of Defense is not aware of any studies that have been conducted in this area." The report's appearance, among reams of papers obtained by Copy Berg's lawyers under provisions of the Freedom of Information Act, was a coup. To be sure, the report did not call upon the Navy to end its policy of banning gay sailors. This was not because the panel's thorough investigation found anything about homosexuals that made them unfit for the Navy; it was because the authors concluded the time was not right for such a change.

"There is no correlation between homosexuality and either ability or attainments. Whether or not public opinion holds homosexuality to be synonymous with degeneracy, the fact remains that a policy which long remained contrary to public opinion could not but have an adverse effect on the Navy," the board wrote. Elsewhere, the panel concluded, "A nice balance must be maintained in changes of policy to ensure that public sensibilities are not offended in any attempt to promote a forward looking program in recognition of the advances in the knowledge of homosexual behavior and treatment, nor can there be any intimation that homosexual conduct is condoned. It is not considered to be in the best interests of the Military Departments to liberalize standards ahead of the civilian climate; thus in so far as practicable it is recommended that the Navy keep abreast of developments but not attempt to take a position of leadership."

That conclusion appeared on page six of the report. What followed was copious evidence to support that finding. Drawing on testimony from psychiatrists and personnel experts from every branch of the armed forces, the panel examined every argument posited against gays in the military.

"One concept which persists without visible supporting data . . . is the idea that homosexual individuals and those who have indulged in homosexual behavior cannot acceptably serve in the military," the report said. ". . . There have been many known instances of individuals who have served honorably and well, despite being exclusively homosexual." One reason for so many successful careers, the report conceded, was that pre-induction screening for gays was unsuccessful and "usually serve to eliminate only the more flagrant and exhibitionistic of the confirmed homosexuals."

The notion that gays were security risks existed "without sound basis in fact," the report concluded. "No intelligence agency, as far as can be learned, adduced any factual data" to support this conclusion. In fact, "There is some information to indicate that homosexuals are quite good security risks."

Statistical analysis of gay discharges in 1956 found that gays tended to be concentrated among hospital corpsmen. In fact, one in every 66 corpsmen received a discharge in that year for being gay, compared to one in every 1,145 in aviation jobs. The report also documented that the Navy discharged women for homosexuality at a rate four times higher than men. While one in every 450 expulsions for men were for homosexuality, the number was one in every 122 for WAVEs.

"It is to be noted that the rate of homosexual activity is much higher for the female than male as reflected in the statistics available to the board," the panel concluded. "Military service may be more attractive to females with latent homosexual tendencies. . . . Homosexual activity of female members of the military has appeared to be more disruptive of morale and discipline in the past than similar male activity." The board also remained uncertain as to how to define lesbian behavior. "Of concern, and interest to the Board, was the apparent need for a more definitive approach and analysis as to what constitutes homosexual activity among women," the report said, noting that women kiss, embrace, and sleep together "without any connotation of homosexuality."

In its conclusions, the report asked that gay discharges no longer be mandated to be "undesirable" or even "less than honorable," given the fact that the bad discharges did not appear to be a deterrent to homosexual behavior. The report also suggested the Navy "keep abreast" of social attitudes toward homosexuality, so its policies would be in synch with the rest of society.

The official reaction to the report was positive among Navy brass. The Chief of Naval Personnel wrote that the report was "a great forward step in handling an age-old problem," and that it would be "of inestimable value for years to come." Comparable praise came particularly from the medical branches of the Navy.

Despite its "inestimable value," the report was never circulated outside of the tightly controlled naval hierarchy. From the start, the Navy worried that publicity about even conducting such a study "would create a widespread impression that a substantial proportion of Navy personnel are homosexual." The report was kept secret until Navy attorneys ran across it during their search through Pentagon files in 1976.

The report's appearance inspired optimism among gays and led many of the Navy's top lawyers to share the same fears as the Air Force lawyers facing the Matlovich case. Gay lawyers would argue that gays were entirely fit to serve, that they posed no security risk, and that the only reason the policy existed was to assuage the prejudices of those who disliked gays. Now they could point out that the Navy had come to precisely the same conclusions—in 1957. The policy was doomed.

In March 1976, the Supreme Court gave its first indication as to how it would rule on the right-to-privacy arguments that were central to the appeals of both Matlovich and Berg. The watershed ruling came in the matter of *Doe* v. *Commonwealth's Attorney*, which challenged the constitutionality of the Commonwealth of Virginia's statute outlawing "crimes against nature."

Gay activist Bruce Voeller and gay legal strategists had organized the lawsuit after a private meeting with the court's most liberal associate justice, William O. Douglas, at Staten Island College several years earlier. This was just after the high tribunal had ruled that state abortion laws violated the right to privacy in its historic *Roe* v. *Wade* decision. Douglas felt that a challenge to the sodomy laws might succeed if plaintiffs could show that people were in genuine jeopardy as a result of these laws and lived in dread of their enforcement, even though they led otherwise impeccable lives. Voeller and gay activists found an anonymous person who had been prosecuted under the law, and Voeller's lover, who had ancestors on both sides of his family dating back to the establishment of the state's first white settlement in Jamestown in 1607, became another plaintiff, attesting to the contention that fear of the law's enforcement affected his life.

The case seemed ill-fated from the start. Scheduling problems precluded appointment of a normal federal appeals court panel in Richmond. Instead, two elderly judges were brought out of retirement to sit on the three-member panel hearing the case. Both voted in favor of the statute in the two-to-one ruling. The judgment said that Supreme Court precedents allowing right to privacy in birth control and abortion had to do with marriage and the sanctity of family life, issues that were not addressed in the sodomy laws. Rather than base their legal rationale solely on the Constitution, however, the judges invoked divine authority, citing both the Old and New Testaments, right down to specific verses from Leviticus.

By the time the matter made it to the Supreme Court, Douglas was gone and only three justices, Thurgood Marshall, William Brennan, and the newest justice, John Paul Stevens, would rule even to hear arguments on the issue. The six other justices voted simply to stand by the lower court's ruling without allowing debate or even writing an opinion. These justices included Harry Blackmun, Potter Stewart, and Lewis Powell, all of whom had voted in favor of extending privacy rights in *Roe* v. *Wade*. The Supreme Court's only statement on this matter was: "The judgment is affirmed." The court would not even say why.

The refusal to articulate a legal rationale infuriated the court's three remaining liberals. Marshall, the only black justice in the history of the court up until that time, was said to be outraged. Brennan posted a newspaper cartoon in his office depicting a couple in bed in a brick house called "The Rights of Individuals"—while a smiling Associate Justice William Rehnquist served on a wrecking crew that was demolishing the structure. "We were told they were 'strict constructionists,' " said the man in bed. According to one account, Brennan kept the cartoon on his office wall until Chief Justice Burger saw it.

Constitutional law experts were "astonished" and "thunderstruck" by the fact that the high court would make such a judgment without offering a legal rationale. Stanford University law professor Gerald Gunther called the summary decision "irresponsible" and "lawless." *The New York Times* editorialized that the decision was "retrogressive" and "bad news for the country and for the future." *Time* magazine noted that in upholding the law, the Supreme Court supported criminalization of sexual acts in which 80 percent of all American adults had engaged at least once, since the Virginia statute outlawed oral and anal sex between all people, heterosexual or homosexual.

For gay leaders, the fact that the Supreme Court would not deign to utter a syllable about homosexuality, even while assigning gays to the class of de facto felons, was, sadly, not surprising. They all remembered: *Don't talk about it.* Nevertheless, the ruling was devastating. Gay advocates had believed that change would come for gays as it had for African Americans, through federal court decisions that encouraged specific legislation. The *Commonwealth* decision, however, delivered a stunning setback to strategies that anticipated the Supreme Court riding to the rescue of the gay movement.

FOR ALL THE SOUND legal judgments to the contrary, Leonard Matlovich expected to be rescued on the afternoon of July 16, 1976, in federal judge Gerhard Gesell's courtroom. Gesell's reputation gave him cause for optimism. A protégé of the fiery William O. Douglas in the 1930s when Douglas headed the Securities and Exchange Commission, Gesell had been appointed to the federal court by Lyndon Johnson in 1967. Since then, he had been an indefatigable defender of individual freedom. In 1969, he had made one of the first federal court rulings holding that a woman had a constitutional right to an abortion. In 1971, he had denied President Nixon's request for a court order to stop publication of the Pentagon Papers. When Solicitor General Robert Bork fired the Watergate special prosecutor during the "Saturday Night Massacre," Gesell ruled the termination illegal. He was the very kind of judge whom Matlovich, the lifelong conservative, had criticized as a judicial activist. Now Matlovich worried Gesell would not be activist enough.

Matlovich studied the sixty-six-year-old jurist as he entered the courtroom, his long black robe set off by his thick white hair. Gesell paused briefly, looked toward Matlovich, and started reading. Citing the *Commonwealth* decision, Gesell ruled, "It is now clear . . . from recent cases, that there is no constitutional right to engage in homosexual activity." Other high court rulings had also allowed the services to "establish standards of acceptable behavior when conduct impinges directly or indirectly on discipline and the fullest achievement of military objectives." Having said that, Gesell then launched into an impassioned plea that the Air Force change its policy.

> Here is a man who volunteered for assignment to Vietnam, who served in Vietnam with distinction, who was awarded the Bronze Star while only an Airman First Class, engaged in hazardous duty on a volunteer basis on more than one occasion, wounded in a mine explosion, revolunteered, has excelled in the Service as a training officer . . . and has at all times been rated at the highest possible ratings by his superiors in all aspects of his performance, receiving in addition to the Bronze Star, the Purple Heart, two Air Force Commendation Medals and a Meritorious Service Medal . . . .
>
> This is a distressing case. It is a bad case. It may be that bad cases will make bad law. Having spent many months dealing with aspects of this litigation, it is impossible to escape the feeling that the time has arrived or may be imminent when branches of the Armed Forces need to reappraise the problem

which homosexuality unquestionably presents in the military context. . . .

Homosexuality is more prevalent than generally believed and takes many different forms, some overt and disruptive, some wholly private and of minimal significance under differing conditions.

In the light of increasing public awareness and the more open acceptance of what is in many respects essentially a matter of private sexual conduct, it would appear that the Armed Forces might well be advised to move toward a more discriminatory and informed approach to these problems, as has the Civil Service Commission in its treatment of homosexuality within the civilian sector of the Government . . . .

While the court has reached its conclusions, as a judge must do, on the law, I hope it will be recognized that after months of intense study of this problem, matters within and without the record, the Court, individually, for what it is worth, has reached the conclusion that it is desirable for the military to reexamine the homosexual problem, to approach it in perhaps a more sensitive and precise way.

It seems to the Court a tragedy that we must confront—as I fear we will have to unless some change takes place—an effort at reform through persistent, insistent and often ill-advised litigation.

There are many problems in this world that can't be resolved by litigation and can't be resolved by statutes. The Armed Forces have shown they can lead the way on matters of discrimination; and I simply suggest that this is an area that deserves its more intense and immediate study.

Matlovich stood, shaken, in the wood-paneled courtroom while Gesell continued to speak. How could a judge say that something was wrong *and* legal? Over the past few months, Matlovich had given enough flag-waving speeches for gay rights that his patriotism was all pumped up again. In America this just could not happen. He would be back in the Air Force; he knew it.

David Addlestone was less sanguine. No matter what the federal appeals court ruled, the Supreme Court would clearly not look upon the issue with favor. A high court's ruling against Matlovich, he feared, would engrave the policy in stone for many decades to come. This was not the time to take these cases to the Supreme Court, he warned. "If you lose this case, the headlines are going to read, COURT DECLARES QUEERS UNCONSTITUTIONAL."

Matlovich would hear nothing of these arguments. He was right, therefore he would win. He would certainly appeal Gesell's ruling. Though Addlestone and the American Civil Liberties Union withdrew from the case, E. Carrington Boggan, who was handling Copy Berg's appeal on behalf of the Lambda Legal Defense and Education Fund, took it on.

———————

AT THE AIR FORCE BOARD, Pete Randell was disappointed in the ruling but pleased by the judge's criticism of the policy. The Air Force lawyers were right. Higher courts would overturn it.

Back at the Pentagon, a number of top lawyers for the armed forces privately agreed with Randell. The unusually strong condemnation of the government's policies startled many senior attorneys both at the Pentagon and in the Attorney General's office. Federal judges did not usually talk that way. These military cases, the lawyers were beginning to realize, offered something that none of the other litigation advanced by gay activist groups could: clean-cut plaintiffs whose real desire was to serve their country. No matter what the legal facts of the case were, they could not win in the court of public opinion. Most Americans believed that serving one's country was an entirely commendable thing to do. Worse, each passing week seemed to bring a new legal challenge to the military's gay policies.

In June 1976, a federal appeals court in San Francisco demanded a temporary restraining order in the gay-related discharge of a Marine staff sergeant. It was the first such order to be issued against the military in eleven years. The order came in the case of Staff Sergeant Robert LeBlanc, a thirteen-year veteran with a Purple Heart, two tours in Vietnam, and sixteen combat ribbons. Though administrative boards had voted for his retention twice after he was charged with being gay, the Marine Corps commandant had ordered his separation, saying that the fact LeBlanc had been accused of being gay twice was in itself evidence of "homosexual tendencies." The court did not agree.

Meteorologist Dennis Beller, a Navy petty officer first class, with fifteen years of service and a record described as outstanding, was another federal court challenger. As in the Matlovich case, federal district court Judge George Harris ruled that the Navy's regulation met constitutional muster, even as he condemned the regulation. ". . . The Navy does itself and the public little good by removing an experienced and able serviceman from its ranks," Harris wrote, "and it should seriously consider what interest is furthered by its decision to do so."

At about the same time, former Army Lieutenant Jay Hatheway filed his suit challenging the constitutionality of the military law against sodomy.

In Washington, the collective effect of these court challenges was to convince the Attorney General's office that the courts would ultimately reject the gay exclusion policy. The most likely forum for that reform, federal lawyers thought, was Copy Berg's appeal. By late 1976, weeks after Jimmy Carter's election as President, the federal government offered

Berg a deal. The Navy would upgrade his discharge to honorable, making him eligible for VA benefits, if he would drop his appeal. Berg refused. Worried that Berg's other than honorable discharge would heighten judicial sympathy for him, the Attorney General's office told the Navy to upgrade the discharge, anyway. In early 1977, Copy Berg finally received his honorable discharge.

Government lawyers were still convinced their regulations would not stand up in court, given the lack of evidence supporting the policies' rationale. On March 4, 1977, a staff lawyer in the Attorney General's office bluntly wrote the Navy's Judge Advocate General, "The record in this case clearly supports [Berg's] allegations, and we believe the Court will rule adversely to the Navy based upon these facts." Such a ruling would "in all probability" lead to Berg's reinstatement in the Navy, the Attorney General's office decided. "We foresee that an adverse ruling . . . could seriously impede the Navy and other military services in discharging other homosexuals under existing regulations. Additionally, the Court's ruling may also act to reopen past cases in this area."

Given the sluggish pace at which cases moved through the federal courts, government lawyers also knew that such a decision was years away. Until that time, the government would stand firmly behind its policy, even as its own legal experts said its enforcement was nothing more than a holding action against the future.

———

YEARS LATER when lawyers and gay activists read the Crittenden Report, they frequently wondered what had inspired the Navy to engage in such a comprehensive review of its policies. Few of the top Navy brass from that era were even alive by the time these questions could be raised, and by then the Navy maintained that the documents commissioning the study had long since been lost. The best clue as to its genesis may well be internal Navy memoranda that show that planning for the board began in the summer of 1956—just weeks after the service's most famous member, a young lieutenant junior grade named Tom Dooley, was forced to resign because he was homosexual.

BOOK FOUR

THE FAMILY

(1977–1980)

The great purges involving thousands of people with public trials of traitors and thought-criminals who made abject confessions of their crimes . . . were special showpieces not occurring oftener than once in a couple of years. More commonly, people who incurred the displeasure of the Party simply disappeared and were never heard of again. One never had the smallest clue as to what had happened to them.

—George Orwell, *1984*

— 30 —

The Family

AFTER THE SURGE of the Coalition of Gay Servicepeople in late 1976 and the first months of 1977, Adam Gettinger-Brizuela was sure that the genie was out of the bottle for good. The CGS was refashioning the way that thousands of lesbians and gay military personnel at California bases lived. The fear and paranoia that had attended interactions among gays in previous years were falling away. Instead of worrying whether this or that gay airman or sergeant or lieutenant would turn you in during the next witch-hunt, you could look at him or her as a brother or sister. You were family now.

In an editorial on behalf of the CGS written for a Santa Barbara alternative newspaper, Adam wrote, "A 'Family,' as a group of gay GI's is known, has the potential for becoming a powerful social force. If a given member of a Family were to be busted for being gay (in private with another consenting adult) the group would come to his or her aid. . . . The world would be amazed, and maybe enlightened, to see gays standing up for their Brothers and Sisters. We could surprise everyone, and begin decreasing their bigotry, by showing a little concern, a little courage."

As lesbian CGS members traveled through the Southwest on the military's intramural sports circuit, they built enormous networks of gay service people. During championship tournaments, when large numbers of teams came together, the parties were massive. Sports events with military bands guaranteed larger attendance, since the bands seemed second only to the military's medical corps in their proportions of gay members. CGS organizers at different bases kept in touch via the military AUTOVON phone system. Even if the callers did not know one another, saying "I'm CGS" established rapport.

At Vandenberg, CGS members created their own old boy's network on the sprawling base. Family in the motor pool assured CGS associates the pick of the best vehicles. Other CGS members at the military police could tip off the Family if an investigation seemed about to begin. Hundreds of gay service people now came to Family parties, held discretely off the base at the suburban homes of CGS members' civilian friends. Every day at lunchtime, CGS members referring to one another as "girlfriend" and "Miss Thing" filled long tables in the enlisted mess hall. None of this was terribly subtle, but it seemed to Adam that few of the heterosexual enlisted people on base cared. They had their own problems. Besides, Adam figured, about half of the straight airmen smoked marijuana, which did not put them in a position to snitch on anyone else for being queer.

Still, organizing put CGS members in potential danger, so organizers took precautions. Every CGS participant had a code name, usually taken from the menagerie of Disney characters. Men took female names, women took male names; everyone wanted to be Bambi or Dumbo. In the end, there were not enough characters to go around. Adam was named for rock star Adam Ant and became the "Ant." In the CGS newsletter, *The Voice*, distributed late at night to all barracks, references to an upcoming party were amended by such comments as "Call Goofy and she'll tell you where." Base security officials tried vainly to figure out who was sneaking onto the base in the middle of the night to pass out *The Voice*, unaware that gay military police dropped off the bundles themselves during their routine rounds.

The group established several rules. First, no one should keep lists of other CGS members. Phone books should contain only the Disneyesque code names and there was to be no central phone list of CGS participants. In investigation after investigation, such lists had been gold mines for agents from the Office of Special Investigations. The golden rule was: Don't snitch on your brother or sister!—under no circumstances, even under the harshest interrogation.

The group also offered informal mediation for feuding gay friends. One of the least savory aspects of military witch-hunts was that they were often instigated not by heartless heterosexuals but by vindictive gay friends or lovers. To avert such reprisals, CGS teams visited both parties of an intragay dispute and conveyed a simple message: "Resolve this. It could affect us all."

As these ideas spread and gay service people throughout California and then the Southwest began referring to themselves as Family, Adam was thrilled at the implications. The CGS was building a homosexual utopia in the heart of one of the most antigay institutions in the United States. CGS was multiracial; its members were black, Chicano, and white. And while separatism was in vogue among lesbians in the civilian world, CGS was a model of cosexual integration. Even more significantly, Adam thought, by refusing to cooperate with interrogations and purges, gay people had at last said that they would no longer offer the military the sanction of the victim. That would make their subjugation infinitely more difficult, he knew; ultimately, it would end it.

Though he had been in the Air Force over three years, Adam was only twenty years old and still given to idealistic lapses. He talked about starting Operation TMT (Take Me, Too). According to this plan, when the OSI asked gay service people for the names of other homosexuals, gays would respond, "Take me, too." If every gay person in the military came out, he argued, then the investigations would have to end, because the military could not function if it truly kicked out all who were homosexual.

———

THOUGH THE CREATION of CGS marked a singular event in the late 1970s, it reflected the new phenomenon that was unfolding for lesbians and gay men in the U.S. military during the late 1970s: the creation of gay communities within the service. Networks of homosexuals had existed within the armed forces at least since World War I. Now, however, the military's gay members were connecting with one another not just for sexual reasons, but because they understood they shared a common bond and common dangers. The creation of gay communities at military bases throughout the world only mirrored what was happening to gay people in civilian society, as gays spent most of the late 1970s building up their neighborhoods and institutions in major cities across the nation. The big difference between civilian gays and their military brethren was that gays in the armed forces still needed code words to conceal themselves. They chose "The Family" for their new communities.

The military was as powerless to prevent this coalescence of "Family" on its installations as it had been in trying to stop the spread of African American pride among black service members in the 1960s or in trying to hinder a broader role for women in the 1970s. Changes in society inevitably flow into the military; officials could slow and frustrate the trend, often with great short-term success, but they could not halt it.

———

OPTIMISM CONTINUED to infuse the gay movement through those early months of 1977. Despite the previous year's setback at the Supreme Court, federal courts continued to deliver surprisingly strong decisions in favor of gay civil rights. In February, a federal district court judge in San Francisco ruled that the Navy's policy of mandatory discharges for gays was unconstitutional. The case in point was that of sailor Mary Saal. Saal, a Navy air-traffic controller, had come under investigation as a lesbian in 1973 but had gone to federal court to halt discharge proceedings. Before the court could grant a final ruling, Saal's term of enlistment expired. The Navy then dispensed with the matter by not allowing Saal to reenlist, citing the gay policy.

Judge William Schwarzer, however, ruled that Navy policies should be "free of any policy of mandatory exclusion." As for the Navy's contention that the presence of gays would create "tensions and hostilities" among heterosexuals and frighten parents away from allowing their children to enlist, Schwarzer ruled: ". . . The particulars specified could in each case be grounds for excluding others as well. Thus 'tensions and hostilities' could justify exclusion of members of minorities or other persons who may also be 'despised' by some. . . . Parents may become concerned over their children associating with Navy personnel who may gamble, use alcohol or drugs. . . . [The Navy] does not, and presumably could not, contend that such blanket exclusion of persons who engage in homosexual acts would eliminate or substantially reduce these problems. Yet those persons alone are classified as 'intolerable' and singled out for 'prompt separation.' "

Schwarzer's ruling did not order Saal's reenlistment but said her application should take into account her entire previous career and not be denied solely because she was gay. The Navy, he added, should strive to maintain its "traditional position in the vanguard of providing equal opportunities." The government promptly appealed, but attorneys were heartened by the ruling, which resurrected hopes for future court victories after the judicial battering gay rights had suffered a year earlier.

In Washington, fifteen gay leaders made their first official visit to the White House, meeting with four domestic-policy aides of the newly inaugurated President Jimmy Carter. Presidential staff went out of their way to insist that the meeting did not represent an endorsement of any gay agenda. White House press spokesman Jody Powell announced on television, "What I feel about gay rights or any other group doesn't have a thing in the world to do with it," but he said every American should have a right to talk to government officials. The meeting did not produce anything substantive beyond an administration pledge for further meetings. Nevertheless, gay leaders pronounced the two-hour encounter a breakthrough. A White House visit conferred legitimacy.

A Democrat in the White House also seemed to presage a more amiable bureaucracy, even if this did not herald sweeping changes in the government's attitudes toward gays. The most immediate impact for gays was the opportunity to upgrade gay-related discharges as part of President Carter's sweeping amnesty program for Vietnam-era draft evaders, deserters, and service members. The upgrade program drew the vitriolic opposition of such veterans groups as the Veterans of Foreign Wars, but for gays who had been haunted by undesirable or other than honorable discharges it was a godsend. One of the first to receive a new honorable discharge was Robert A. Martin, Jr., the radioman third class who in 1972 was the first sailor to publicly acknowledge being gay.

On a state level, progressive moves were being made in legislatures across the country. In February, Wyoming became the nineteenth state to repeal its sodomy law. Four more states were debating measures to decriminalize all sexual activity between consenting adults, and eleven legislatures were considering whether to amend their civil rights statutes to ban discrimination based on sexual orientation.

On the local level, forty cities had enacted gay civil rights ordinances. The most important breakthrough came in January 1977 when the Dade County Commission, the governing body for the Miami metropolitan area, voted five to three to enact a gay civil rights law, the first such ordinance to be enacted in a major city south of the Mason-Dixon line. The excitement over this victory at first overshadowed something new that arose from a Miami effort: organized opposition. In this case, the opposition came from a loud contingent of Southern Baptists on hand for the final vote on the gay-rights law. Their spokesman was a woman instantly familiar to anyone who had ever seen an orange-juice commercial on TV. In Miami, Anita Bryant was a local celebrity, and she was outraged. She would fight this ordinance, she said, and even go directly to the voters to have it repealed.

The notion that an orange juice–industry spokeswoman could offer a serious political threat seemed fairly outlandish, however, so not very many gay activists paid Anita Bryant much attention.

———————

EVEN WHILE GAY CIVILIANS savored their gains, gays in uniform began to experience a disquieting sense that a heavy hand might come down on them. An increase in gay-related discharges had begun slowly in 1975; by 1977, it was a discernible trend. The manpower exigencies of Vietnam no longer existed; though the all-volunteer military struggled to maintain its recruiting quotas, the times were not as desperate as during the height of the war. According to Department of Defense figures, all the services discharged 937 enlisted personnel for being gay in fiscal year 1975. That number rose to 1,296 in the following year and to 1,442 in 1977. The Carter years would prove to be even worse ones for homosexuals in the armed forces.

One of the broader investigations from the mid-1970s occurred at the Woman Marine Company at Camp Elmore, near Norfolk, Virginia. When news of the probe hit the newspapers, however, the Marine brass halted discharge hearings, which prompted a group calling itself the Committee Against Homosexuals in the Marine Corps to respond with anonymous letters of protest. This campaign led base officials to begin separation hearings. According to a spokesman for Atlantic Fleet Marine Force Headquarters, the investigation resulted in the discharge of five women. Two more women were denied reenlistment and several more remained under investigation. The one investigation had cut out about 10 percent of that installation's eighty-seven-woman company.

Several months later, a purge at Malstrom Air Force Base near Great

Falls, Montana, put forty gay servicemen under investigation. A dozen airmen lost their military careers, according to the last public accounting from Malstrom officials.

The Navy continued its record as the most enthusiastic distributor of gay discharges. In fiscal years 1976 and 1977, it gave out more separations for homosexuality than all branches of the military combined, 54 and 57 percent, respectively.

At Castle Air Force Base in Merced, California, a full-fledged purge was launched after an airman, discharged for homosexuality, took a group of gay Air Force friends to San Francisco's Golden Gate Park for his going-away party. The Office of Special Investigations heard of the party and used the threat of jail to pressure one of its only heterosexual guests, a female airman, to name the gays present. One sergeant who worked at the base personnel office at the time later recalled that those names led to still more naming until he counted twenty of the twenty-four beds at the base transient barracks filled with gay men awaiting separation.

The only thing new about all these investigations was the rising number of them. What was striking, in fact, was how old-fashioned they were, using the same techniques that the military had used to discover homosexuals since the days of Tom Dooley and the enthusiastic purges of the McCarthy era.

MARCH 1977
VANDENBERG AIR FORCE BASE
LOMPOC, CALIFORNIA
_____

AT VANDENBERG, senior enlisted personnel who had weathered years of witch-hunts and OSI interrogations warned the younger, more militant airmen that trouble lay ahead. Plans such as Operation TMT might look good on paper, but, when the whip came down, people would want to protect themselves. One lesbian master sergeant cautioned Adam Gettinger-Brizuela that he and his friends would be caught if they did not cool it. Somebody would confess and all hell would break loose, she said. But the CGS would hear nothing of it. Her warning only reflected the fear that had always kept gay people apart, Adam thought. In 1977, Adam capsulized his ideas in an essay that became the CGS manifesto.

> We are a legion that dares not speak its name.
> The military knows this. Their philosophy is one of public contempt and private tolerance. They say they want no gays, but in truth only drum them out very selectively.
> It is government policy to keep straights paranoid about gays and make gays afraid of each other. . . . If gays in the Navy, or any other service get to know each other and trust each other, there won't be any further reason to fear. If every

*gay man and woman in uniform knew that he or she was not
alone—a new day would dawn. . . .*

The essay was published in the *Santa Barbara News & Review* under the
signature of the Coalition of Gay Servicepeople. Adam considered it a
brazen challenge to the status quo of the United States Air Force and this
made him very proud. The CGS was on a roll; to its members, it seemed
unstoppable. Lately, members sometimes joked among themselves that
the OSI must be really stupid. They had founded and operated what was
becoming a national network of gay service members and the OSI had
not even noticed—or so it seemed.

31

Reaction

HAD HIS MESSAGE made no difference? Leonard Matlovich wondered, as he heard of the stunning majorities the opponents of the gay civil rights bill had tallied in virtually every neighborhood of Miami. Black neighborhoods were against gay rights; Jewish sections were against gay rights; the Cuban-American population represented an Iron Curtain–style majority against gay rights. Polls a day earlier had predicted that the election would be close; when the votes were counted, however, opponents of the gay-rights ordinance outnumbered supporters by a two-to-one margin.

"Homosexuals cannot reproduce, so they must recruit," Anita Bryant had repeated throughout the campaign. Homosexuals were not born that way. They chose to be gay, she said, and they could influence other young people to choose to be homosexual, as well. That was why they wanted gay-rights protection, so they could work at playgrounds and public schools and recruit young people to their way of life. They were flagrant lawbreakers and now they wanted "special privileges" of civil rights guarantees. One antigay pamphlet asked: "If homosexuals, who break Florida's law against unnatural sex acts every time they perform homosexual sex, can be granted special privileges, then what about other law-breaking sexual libertines—prostitutes, pimps and their ilk?"

Anita Bryant had no more credentials than status as a Miss America runner-up to address complicated matters of national importance. Nonetheless, she obviously touched a nerve with millions of Americans. She made the cover of *Newsweek* magazine and pushed the gay-rights issue to the front pages of every newspaper in the country.

On the other side of the debate were the gay activists, most notably

Leonard Matlovich. After Bryant and her anti–gay-rights group, Save Our Children, Inc., had gathered more than six times the signatures needed to qualify their referendum for the ballot and it was clear that their efforts should be taken very seriously, gay leaders called on Matlovich to serve as cochair of the Dade County Coalition for Human Rights. Matlovich's plan for success was similar to his plan for winning at his board hearing and in federal court. All you had to do, he believed, was educate people; tell it like it was; give people the facts and they would understand. It had worked when he had taught race relations.

Privately, Matlovich and other gay organizers were confident they would win because they believed the other side consisted of such buffoons. Who could take these Bible-thumping fundamentalist ministers seriously? Surely, it did not help that Bryant had received the endorsement of KKK Imperial Wizard Robert Shelton, who pronounced homosexuality to be one of the "three vast conspiracies," which also included socialism and Judaism.

In interview after interview, Matlovich had explained that homosexuals did not choose to be gay, that one's sexual orientation was determined at a very young age, probably at birth. Since no one chose to be gay, they could not influence others to make that choice. Civil rights were not special privileges.

What Matlovich did not realize was that persuading the electorate on issues of homosexuality was very different from teaching a military race-relations class. Air Force personnel were under orders not to be racist. This was a powerful motivation to accept the military's indoctrination. Civilians were under no such compunction. If anything, the mandate most citizens received, whether in the form of biblical condemnations of homosexuality from their churches or as laws against "unnatural sexual acts" from their secular authorities, was that they should be prejudiced against gays.

The forces against gay rights also had a motivator far more forceful than anything the gay side could muster: fear. Brochures from Save Our Children, Inc., featured copies of sixteen news stories about men molesting children. The lurid headlines included: FORMER SCOUTMASTER CONVICTED OF HOMOSEXUAL ACTS WITH BOYS; FOUR MEN ACCUSED OF ABUSING BOYS; and SEX CLUB LURED JUVENILES WITH GIFTS. The brochure copy warned: "Practicing homosexuals—both male and lesbian—would be free to become playground supervisors and welfare workers dealing with very young and impressionable people. . . . They may influence our children to adopt homosexuality."

The gay side countered with their own fear campaign, distributing leaflets with pictures of Joseph McCarthy, hooded Ku Klux Klansmen, and billboards advertising "Gentiles only" apartments. "Don't Be So Sure You Won't Be Next! It's Happened Too Many Times Before," their leaflets warned.

But Anita Bryant was not advocating taking civil rights away from blacks or Jews, which, everyone agreed, would be wrong. She was only talking about denying civil rights to homosexuals, which, most people in Miami agreed, was okay. And while the talk about early psychosexual development might be true, there were still these nagging fears. No one seemed to know for sure how homosexuals got that way, so just about any assertion made sense.

Anita Bryant had capitalized on the confusion, so that night she was at the Miami Beach Holiday Inn ballroom, under the surreal glow of klieg lights, pronouncing victory. "Tonight the laws of God and the cultural values of man have been vindicated," she said. "The people of Dade County—the normal majority—have said enough is enough is enough. . . . We will now carry our fight against similar laws throughout the nation that attempt to legitimize a lifestyle that is both perverse and dangerous to the sanctity of the family, dangerous to our children, dangerous to our freedom of religion and freedom of choice, dangerous to our survival as one nation under God."

Across town, Leonard Matlovich stood on the worn maroon carpeting at the front of the Hotel Fountainbleau's ballroom, trying to encourage a listless crowd. No one had expected the night to end in a landslide loss for gay rights. Lenny did not know what to say. His eye fell on a large American flag standing to the side of the ballroom stage. He removed it from its stand and held it up to the crowd and reminded them that America stood for justice and that justice would prevail. When the TV cameras rolled in for the obligatory visit to the campaign headquarters of the losing side, there stood Lenny Matlovich with the American flag, and the crowd in front of him joined hands, singing "We Shall Overcome."

———————

FROM THE BACK of the ballroom, Jim Foster thought it all looked a little pathetic. Foster had joined the legion of gay organizers who had come to Miami to work on the first gay-rights campaign that had ever garnered national media attention. Foster was schooled in serious politics and he knew that this was a major setback. There was nothing hopeful in a two-to-one margin of defeat. In the five years since he had addressed the Democratic National Convention, the gay movement had seemed to gain an unstoppable momentum. This, he knew, had been something of an illusion, due largely to the fact that the movement had never faced much in the way of organized opposition. It is hard to lose a campaign when you are unopposed. Those comfortable days were over now, he could see. Foster suspected that something new was happening here.

In fact, the crusade for gay rights would never be the same again. Forces of reaction were moving into place. From now on, everything would be a struggle.

JUNE 10, 1977
VANDENBERG AIR FORCE BASE
LOMPOC, CALIFORNIA

ADAM GETTINGER-BRIZUELA had never trusted Billy Mitchell, so he did not much miss him when he was gone. Billy was a dental technician at the Vandenberg hospital and hung out with the rowdiest airmen. He liked to party, and frequently showed up at work hung over, his eyes glazed. He also had a penchant for homeless teenage boys whose parents had thrown them out for being gay. Billy put such boys up and invited other airmen over to the party. Apparently, the police had become interested in the teenagers, which led them to Mitchell. Agents from the Office of Special Investigations took over then and were able to cut a deal. Billy would talk, and the Air Force would not prosecute him. Instead, he would receive an honorable discharge and not one on the grounds of homosexuality but, as he later told *The Advocate*, on psychiatric grounds.

Billy's discharge, three days after Anita Bryant's victory in Florida, came as official interest had piqued in the CGS organizing. Just days earlier, Adam's essay "Politics of Paranoia" had appeared in the local alternative paper, signed by the CGS and including a discussion of The Family. Indeed, subsequent OSI reports invariably referred to Billy, and later to others, as "a member of a group of hospital homosexuals who call themselves 'The Family.'" Before leaving Vandenberg, however, Billy had given the OSI a lengthy statement, the first of many he would give over the next four months.

Later, rumors spread that the OSI had paid him handsomely for his information, but Mitchell denied this. Records released fifteen years later under the Freedom of Information Act contain no reference to compensation, but they do reveal that the OSI had suddenly gained an extremely loquacious source. In various statements, this source named twenty-two other Air Force personnel, including many with whom he had been involved sexually. The statements contained everything he could recall about their lives—whom they dated and when they might have had sex, for example. The informer also named dates and places of Family parties over the past year. His most extensive statement led the OSI to another source, who in turn named fifteen more gay airmen.

The OSI did not move quickly to capitalize on the information it had received. Instead, it began methodically calling in lesbian airmen, one by one. OSI agents advised each woman that if she told anyone else about the interviews, she could be charged with obstruction of justice, so it was several months before anybody told. One by one, the accused began cutting their deals with the OSI. One by one, they disappeared.

Adam did not think of them as disappearances, however. In the military, people were transferred to temporary duty at other bases, often abruptly. Through the summer, life went on normally for The Family, with dance parties and raft trips on the nearby Consumnes River. All the while, they were being watched.

WITHIN A MONTH, it was clear that the loss in Miami was the most decisive event for the gay movement since the Stonewall riots eight years earlier. Support for sodomy-law reform and gay civil rights bills began to wane. In California, the gay-rights law's sponsor simply shelved the bill. In three other states, gay advocates shifted from an offensive to defensive posture and had to fight off attempts to enact antigay legislation. Once-vocal allies grew silent. Where gays had once pushed ahead, they now battled back antigay legislation. Nevada passed a bill decriminalizing all acts between consenting adults and then enacted new legislation making all sex between same-sex couples a felony punishable by one to six years in the penitentiary. After voting in favor of a gay-rights law, the Minnesota state senate reversed itself and defeated the bill. And that senate included an openly gay member.

The most surprising retrenchment came in three states, including California, which quickly passed laws banning gay marriage. The laws were designed to protect the institutions of marriage and family, their authors argued, because homosexuals were incapable of having meaningful long-term relationships.

That a state legislature would so casually ban homosexuals' life-long relationships was a measure of how little freedom gays truly had in the United States. Perhaps most surprising, such new laws provoked no comment from either heterosexuals or homosexuals. The California governor who signed the antimarriage bill into law, Democrat Jerry Brown, garnered almost unanimous gay support when he sought reelection the next year.

Across the nation, homosexual rights were no longer a popular social cause but a controversial political issue. Suddenly, the votes to be gained by championing gay rights seemed fewer than the votes a politician stood to lose. It would be nearly a decade before any state enacted a gay civil rights law.

Emboldened fundamentalist ministers campaigned for repeal of gay-rights laws in other cities. In the conservative stronghold of Orange County, California, an ambitious state senator named John Briggs promised a statewide referendum on whether gays should be allowed to teach in public schools.

The new ambivalence became evident in the popular media. Although episodes about gays had become a staple on situation comedies over the past three years and one of the nation's top-rated television shows, "Soap," featured a gay character played by a rising young comedian named Billy Crystal, the entertainment media now grew fearful of approaching gay themes. NBC had filmed its two-hour television movie *Sergeant Matlovich v. the Air Force*, but then shelved it.

Gay groups countered these setbacks with an explosion of activism unprecedented since the first Gay Liberation Front groups proliferated around the country in late 1969. No longer scruffy malcontents, the new activists came mostly from the affluent gay gentry that had migrated to major cities during recent years. These young professionals benefited from the tolerance engendered by the gay movement, but few had become involved politically. There had been little to protest in the comfortable life they had forged in the bustling gay meccas of the late 1970s. The defeat in Miami came as a startling wake-up call, prodding a whole new generation of gays into action. The streets of San Francisco, Los Angeles, and Greenwich Village were filled with marching protesters. They may have been angry, but they were also largely middle-class and inclined to work within the system. They began by raising money for campaign contributions with which to enter the political process. By November, this new activism had resulted in the election of the first openly gay public official of any major city: Harvey Milk won his campaign to sit on the San Francisco Board of Supervisors.

There were two very significant aftereffects of the Miami election. The vote marked the end of what homosexual organizers had long called "the conspiracy of silence." Not only had homosexuality been taboo but talking about homosexuality was off-limits as well. This had made it very difficult to advance a political agenda. More significant than what Anita Bryant said about homosexuals was the fact that she said anything at all. In truth, Anita Bryant had accomplished something that all the earnest gay activists of the past decade had failed to do. She had started people talking about gay rights. The love that dare not speak its name had become the love that would not shut up.

For opponents of gay civil rights, the election marked a turning point, too. Fundamentalists had been grumbling for several years about "secular humanism" sweeping across the nation, but the election in Miami marked the first time in recent history that conservative Christians had channeled their discontent into powerful political action. It was not that these born-again Christians represented a majority of the electorate; they did not. But on the issues dearest to their hearts, they could find enough sympathy among mainstream voters to win elections. Their victory said to fundamentalists for the first time that they could move their crusade out of the revival tent and into the political mainstream.

The issues that these Christians cared most about involved changes in traditional American life, especially changes involving the roles of men and women. The fundamentalists had campaigned against the Equal Rights Amendment in southern states, and, with Catholic groups, formed the foundation of the antiabortion movement. Even while average Americans might be prepared to allow choice for abortion or equal rights for women, they remained uncomfortable with the emergence of the new homosexual minority. With the gay issue, all the residual uncertainties about rapidly changing gender roles seemed to find a lightning rod, and it allowed conservative Christians to extend their support far beyond those who might agree with them on other issues.

Prominent among the new preacher-politicians was a television preacher from Lynchburg, Virginia, named Jerry Falwell. He soon went to work organizing a group called the Moral Majority. Across the South, its organizers realized that at last they had issues with which to battle the long-entrenched Democratic party there. After many years of so many changes, people wanted things to settle down again. People were afraid, and fear bred hatred. Among those candidates feeling the new political climate was the man who had once been Armistead Maupin's mentor, a television commentator named Jesse Helms, who was even then preparing his candidacy for the U.S. Senate in the 1978 elections.

SEPTEMBER 1977
VANDENBERG AIR FORCE BASE
LOMPOC, CALIFORNIA

FOR THE PAST YEAR, Adam Gettinger-Brizuela and his friends in The Family had believed that they had the power to change the military and even to change the world. But as the first days of autumn chilled the coastal air at Vandenberg Air Force Base, it was clear that the government held all the power, and in those difficult months the full power of the United States Air Force came down hard on the Coalition of Gay Servicepeople.

By October, a purge was in progress at the base. CGS members had sworn not to inform on one another, but, faced with threats of prison, many relented. The amount of information the OSI had collected about them was impressive. Hundreds of pages of OSI reports demonstrated an extraordinary campaign of surveillance. Notations and summaries of phone conversations indicated the use of wiretaps. Quotes from private correspondence peppered the OSI records, indicating surveillance of mail. Ostensibly confidential counseling sessions with base chaplains were duly noted for the record, along with names and phone numbers culled from individual address books. Agents subjected suspected homosexuals to lie-detector tests and arranged lineups of photographs from which heterosexuals identified homosexuals. The OSI also had pictures surreptitiously taken at The Family's parties. With leads from the successful interrogations at Vandenberg, agents contacted OSI offices at other bases around the world.

Gay life at Vandenberg suddenly changed from a utopian model to a daily nightmare. With his cover of marriage and children, Adam Gettinger-Brizuela was immune from investigators, but this did not protect him from the sense of fear that hung over the base. Longtime gay friends stopped speaking to him and to everyone else. Anyone could be talking to the OSI. Now if you saw another gay person walk into the mess, you looked the other way. Couples broke up. As the pressure mounted, friends began to exchange bitter accusations.

Lesbians blamed gay men, noting that none of the gay women had ever gotten involved with minors. At least two lesbians, desperate to remain in the Air Force, married men. One was impregnated by her gay brother's lover so her heterosexuality would not be questioned. Another lesbian friend of Adam's lost her young daughter after OSI agents informed the woman's mother that she was under investigation for being gay. "We'll raise her," the woman's parents said when they came to take the child away. OSI documents confirm that agents contacted the mother of another suspect and she subsequently gave a detailed statement and a list of her son's gay friends.

"It's your own fault," a lesbian master sergeant told Adam one day. "I told you this would happen. You don't belong in the military."

A number of the CGS members' heterosexual friends valiantly defended the gay airmen. Some straight men insisted in OSI interviews that they had dated the accused lesbians and added with a wink that they sure didn't act like queers. Supervisors volunteered to vouch for the heterosexuality of some of the most effeminate men on base. When called upon to name gays in the probe, many heterosexuals who knew better voiced disbelief that any such people could be stationed at Vandenberg.

Still, the number of dismissals mounted in the final months of 1977. By January 1978, Vandenberg officials acknowledged discharging a dozen airmen for homosexuality, but many more were let go on charges that were easier to make stick, such as marijuana use. Still others were denied reenlistment. Adam calculated that at least thirty airmen lost their jobs during the investigation. Gay civilian employees on the base also lost their jobs, after being named as people who socialized at Family gatherings.

The last months of 1977 also marked the last months of Adam's four-year term of service. He stayed in Santa Maria after his discharge, because his wife was still in the Air Force and he wanted to be near his children. But the daily disappearances of his old friends left him feeling desolate. He had believed that The Family would fight back. Their battles would overshadow even the struggles of Leonard Matlovich or Ensign Berg. In fact, only one of those charged, a sergeant with six years of service, hired a lawyer and fought his discharge. The rest cut whatever deals they could and quietly went away.

Adam did his best to stir the media; he wrote letters to the editor of the local alternative paper and tried to interest the Santa Barbara daily press. But Santa Barbara and Santa Maria were company towns of the United States Air Force and the mainstream press was not much interested in Adam's tips, though every one of his letters to the editor was quietly filed away in OSI folders; OSI agents even paid him a visit at home. Of course he wasn't in the Air Force anymore, but maybe he could help them with their investigation. Adam declined.

By February 1978, the investigation of homosexuals at Vandenberg came to an abrupt halt. There were a number of rumors as to why. The secretary of the colonel in charge of the Vandenberg base hospital told one serviceman that the colonel had put his foot down, saying, "If you kick out all the gays at this hospital, I won't have a staff left."

The Air Force's own files include three telling pages directly preceding the memo that ended the probe. The first is one of Adam's anonymous letters to a local newspaper; the others are copies of a story about the purge that appeared in the *Santa Barbara News & Review*. Military public-information officials had never understood civilian sensibilities with regard to such crackdowns, and the Vandenberg officers were no exception. When asked whether the probe was widening, for example, Vandenberg spokesman Major Richard Kline said it was not but told a reporter, "If you would like to supply us with the names of other suspected homosexuals on the base, we'd be more than happy to take you up on it." The reporter described the comment as "chilling." This story provoked countless phone calls from the gay press and word of the investigation spread in the civilian world. This news and the unsavory publicity about OSI interrogation methods created bad publicity, which, though minor, came to the attention of the Secretary of the Air Force.

On February 16, 1978, eight months after Billy Mitchell was discharged, a directive from the Secretary of the Air Force ordered "all separation processing should cease." The 1977 investigation of gays at Vandenberg Air Force Base was ended; so was the Coalition of Gay Servicepeople.

32

The Gayest Ship in the Navy and Other Stories

IN MAY 1978, Gene Barfield graduated from the Navy's nuclear training school, and he was given his first assignment aboard the submarine USS *Nathanael Greene*, where he was detailed to the blue crew and soon won the coveted silver dolphins of those qualified for submarine duty. Gene did his best to be extraordinarily discreet, given what he had heard about the Naval Investigative Service. Even as Gene concealed his sexuality, he registered the casual comments straight sailors sometimes made about this or that crew member who was gay or lived with another guy. Gene was struck not because the gay sailors were so well known but because the straight crewmates were not derisive or threatening in their conversations, just matter-of-fact.

Barfield was not sure what to make of this. Finally, he sought out a gay sailor about whom he had heard gossip. Before long, he had hooked up with a half-a-dozen other gay enlisted men on the USS *Nathanael Greene*. When the ship put in at Newport News, Virginia, for an overhaul, the Navy rented an apartment complex for the crew. Gene lived with two gay crewmen in a garden apartment surrounded by other shipmates. While the straight sailors lived like college students, with cinder-block bookshelves, secondhand furniture, and TV dinners, Barfield and his roommates tossed out the Salvation Army furnishings that had come with the apartment, redecorated in high *House & Garden* style, and took turns preparing gourmet meals for one another. At about five o'clock every weekend, their straight sailor friends started dropping by, knowing they could wangle an invitation to dinner.

Gene and his roommates got talked into hosting a Tupperware Party for the apartment complex. On the appointed Friday night, twenty-five sailors and their wives and girlfriends filed into Gene's apartment for a congenial mix of drinking and Tupperware demonstrations. As soon as the married sailors' wives got home, however, phones began to buzz. Those guys just *had* to be gay, they agreed. Their apartment was far too tasteful for them to be anything but. Within days, everyone knew about the gay apartment, but, as far as Gene could tell, it was not a problem. The next Monday the ship's captain called Gene into his office.

"I heard you had a Tupperware party on Friday," he said.

Gene was petrified. "Yeah, it was fun," he replied.

The captain had heard as much and was concerned that no officers had been invited and all the enlisted wives were talking about what a good evening it had been. After this, the captain said, he wanted invitations to go out to officers, too.

In the months that followed, Gene and his gay friends introduced their fellow sailors and their wives to the local gay dance bar. For dinner parties, enlisted wives usually issued invitations to a gay sailor with permission to bring a date—"as long as he's good-looking."

MANY GAY SAILORS throughout the Navy during this period enjoyed a comparable level of acceptance. On the aircraft carrier USS *Constellation*, the Connie Girls conducted their own shipboard socials, where they served little sandwiches and introduced new gay sailors to the old hands. It was at such a gathering that Petty Officer First Class Jim Frisbie met a gay member of the SEALs, the most prestigious unit with the most macho image in the Navy. Although the enlisted man's team members all knew he was gay, SEALs stuck together. Nobody turned him in. Aboard the USS *Ranger*, the Rangerettes typed up a regular newsletter and gay yeomen photocopied it on the ship's Xerox machine before the carrier pulled into a new liberty port. The newsletter informed sailors of the local gay bars and other points of interest, whether in Nairobi or Diego Garcia. When the *Ranger* docked in San Diego after a six-month cruise, the local gay discos were packed with young sailors in their Philippine-embroidered Rangerette jackets.

By 1979, there was a significant gay presence at the Navy installation on Diego Garcia, a remote island in the Indian Ocean that was used largely for refueling and bringing aboard new supplies. Within days of entering the base aboard the USS *Dixie*, Petty Officer Wayne Walls found a thriving gay underground at the First Class Club. There, a dental technician known as Tinker Belle worked part-time as a bartender. Everyone knew he was gay and nobody complained. The *Dixie*, a destroyer, had its own gay community. Wayne knew two gay corpsmen, and gay sailors, in the engine room and the personnel and supply departments. During their week-long stay on Diego Garcia, they might be found making assignations on the bucolic white sandy beach outside the First Class Club or sharing drinks with the ebullient Tinker Belle.

Even the Marine Corps was seeing the beginnings of gay awareness, as was evident at the Marine Corps Air Station in Beaufort, South Carolina, where Lance Corporal Art McDaniel had met three other gay Marines from the base at a gay bar in Augusta, Georgia. They called themselves the "Four Musketeers" and hung out at the Enlisted Club.

One night, after three of the Musketeers had spent a long evening playing "quarters" and imbibing far too many pitchers of beer, seven other beefy Marines came over to their table and announced they were going to "clean up the pansies." After several shouts of *faggot* and *queer*, a fight broke out. One of the Musketeers, a mechanic named Bud, was an experienced brawler and quickly laid out two of their assailants, breaking both their noses. Art was from a family of five brothers and had learned young how to fight dirty. He slammed a pitcher down on the head of one Marine and a chair into the chest of another. The third Musketeer knew karate. By the time the fight was over, the three had meted out a broken leg, a broken arm, two broken noses, two concussions, several fractured ribs, and numerous stitches. Art's commanding officer knew he was supposed to scold McDaniel over the fracas, but Art could see that his CO was secretly proud that he had won the fight when he had been outnumbered seven to three.

Bud, the brawling mechanic, was dating Danny, who performed in drag as "Danielle" in the gay bar in Augusta. Danny was a spectacular female impersonator with a waspish waist, small hands, and his own dark long hair cascading over his shoulders. No one would ever know he was a man unless they saw him in the morning when he needed a shave. It struck Bud that he could get subsidized housing off the base if he was married, so into the housing office he walked with Danielle in full drag, explaining that they were newlyweds and therefore qualified for married quarters. The Marine Corps complied and the happy couple moved into their Marine-subsidized love nest.

––––––––

THE SECURITY CLEARANCE investigation conducted on Specialist Five Perry Watkins in early 1978 also reflected the spirit of the times. Superior officers went to great lengths to ensure that the Army's only officially acknowledged gay soldier would be treated fairly. Perry had been transferred to the Thirty-third Field Artillery Detachment when the security clerk reviewing his records noted that Watkins had long ago said he was homosexual. The message went out to the command that "records indicate [Watkins] is an admitted homosexual" and was "not medically suitable for assignment" for a security-related job at the base.

Perry immediately went about appealing the disqualification. As had happened before, his superiors rallied to his defense. In pleading Perry's case, Captain Dale Pastian wrote that the "disqualification resulted from an erroneous, subjective ruling based wholly upon a cursory check of his medical records. This was not an adequate, nor just, evaluation and his reliability was misjudged." Pastian went on to praise Watkins's "outstanding professional attitude, integrity and suitability." Wrote Pastian, "He has, in fact, become one of our most respected and trusted soldiers, both by his superiors and his subordinates."

On June 18, 1978, word came down from Colonel Marvin Simmons at the headquarters of the Fifty-ninth Ordnance Brigade that Perry Watkins should be requalified for service in the program.

Watkins put the requalification in his own personnel file, right next to the letter he had received the previous year commending him for his "impersonation pantomimes" as Simone at the Noncommissioned Officer's Dining Out, a formal Army event. "Where comradeship is evident, so is high morale and good discipline which are the signs of a great unit," wrote Sergeant Major Walter Pederson. "The Dining Out could not have been a success without your full support, enthusiasm, initiative and imagination."

ONE IRONIC EMBLEM of the new tolerance for gays in the services were the problems soldiers had when they tried to get out of their enlistment contracts by admitting their homosexuality to superior officers. Aboard the USS *Nassau* in 1978, for example, two young enlisted men decided to leave the Navy to start a new life together. They went to the ship's Executive Officer to explain they were homosexual and therefore could not stay in the Navy. To the first sailor, the Executive Officer said, "What else is new?" To the second, he said, "So what." The two sailors stayed aboard.

OF ALL THE AIR BASES, naval installations, and Army posts in the U.S. military, there was one command that clearly had the highest proportion of gay personnel of any in the late 1970s: the USS *LaSalle*. By the account of nearly everyone who served on or near the intelligence ship, the *LaSalle* was the gayest ship in the Navy. A number of circumstances contributed to this distinction. First, the ship was permanently ported in the Persian Gulf emirate of Bahrain, which kept strict limits on how many Americans could be stationed there. No families could accompany servicemen, which meant that few married sailors wanted to be assigned to the ship. Second, as one of the military's chief intelligence stations in the increasingly turbulent Gulf, the ship drew its crew from the most specialized areas of military intelligence, which have historically been among the most predominately gay job categories. As the flagship for the Commander of Middle East Forces, the vessel housed a command staff who also tended to draw heavily from gay personnel. Speculation about the preponderance of gay personnel included suggestions that job detailers in Washington ensured the choice assignment for their gay friends. No matter why, gay officers and crew who served on the ship in the late 1970s and early 1980s later estimated that at least 60 percent of the five-hundred-member crew was gay. The ship was also one of the most continuously decorated vessels in the modern U.S. Navy, winning numerous awards and citations.

Of all the places in the Middle East for the USS *LaSalle* to set anchor, Bahrain was a particularly fortuitous port. A former British protectorate, the tiny island has few of the harsh restrictions on alcohol and socializing common among its Islamic neighbors. The island was a veritable playground for the Middle East jet set, where oil-rich sheikhs flew in on their private planes for weekends with Western airline stewardesses and American servicemen. Numerous *LaSalle* crew members tell stories of sexstarved Arabs offering them gold bracelets and substantial cash for a weekend of pleasure.

The best parties on the island were reputed to be those given by a prominent member of Bahrain's royal family, a notorious party animal given to an interest in both genders. Though most celebrated for his imaginative positioning of American airline stewardesses on glass-topped coffee tables, the prince hosted huge outdoor orgies, according to several *LaSalle* crewmen.

Early in the evening, the prince sometimes led a caravan of Land Rovers into the desert, near the emirate's legendary Tree of Life. According to legend, this was the site of the Garden of Eden. There, under the ancient tree, servants erected large tents and spread out huge Persian rugs and the prince would pass around a water pipe to relieve any inhibitions the *LaSalle* sailors might feel. After nightfall, countless sexual fantasies were realized in the desert, in the dark. The next morning, crewmen staggered up the *LaSalle*'s gangplank, usually a little richer for the experience. Just as heterosexual sailors had their favorite sex ports in the Philippines, the gay sailors on the *LaSalle* had Bahrain and long nights under the Tree of Life.

Painted white to deflect the harsh Middle Eastern sun, the *LaSalle* was distinctive as the only white ship in the U.S. Navy, leading to its official nickname: "The Great White Ghost of the Arabian Coast." Given the libidinous pastimes available in Bahrain, gay crew used their own sailorly variation: "The Great White Whore of the Arabian Shore."

JUNE 25, 1978
SAN FRANCISCO GAY FREEDOM DAY PARADE
SAN FRANCISCO

AN ESTIMATED 375,000 joined the march, making the parade the largest single demonstration for any political cause in the United States since the days of antiwar protests. Only the news helicopters hovering overhead could take in the full sight. Everywhere, huge flags the colors of the rainbow fluttered under a spectacularly blue summer sky. The rainbow flags had been the creation of a gay designer who had once served in the Army in San Francisco, a man from Chanute, Kansas, named Gilbert Baker. Baker's design became part of the official logo of the parade, a rainbow surrounded the Greek symbol lambda, long identified with the gay movement. But these were a chain of lambdas; collectively they looked like a long strand of barbed wire. Concentration-camp motifs were de rigueur for this year's parade.

The trend spoke volumes about the drift that had begun to separate the zeitgeist of the gay community and mainstream America. While the rest of the country enjoyed the carefree somnolence of the apathetic era, watching "Happy Days" and *Saturday Night Fever*, gays were beginning to see ominous signs. In the first months of 1978, fundamentalist Christians organized in city after city to repeal gay-rights ordinances. And they won every election. In California, voters faced an unprecedented attempt to stigmatize gays with a statewide referendum that would ban gays from teaching, as well as anyone who publicly endorsed homosexual civil rights. It was becoming an article of faith among gay activists that these fundamentalist campaigns would lead to barbed-wire concentration camps for homosexuals and that the Christian fundamentalists would ultimately seek their own final solution for the "homosexual problem." The more outspoken conservative preachers were already citing the Old Testament verse that recommended homosexuals be stoned to death.

In his speech to the huge crowd massed in front of San Francisco City Hall that day, Supervisor Harvey Milk recalled that Hitler had killed 300,000 homosexuals in his concentration camps; Milk invoked the potential of gay Buchenwalds arising in modern-day America. Another new symbol of gay liberation to appear that day was the pink triangle—the identifying patch that Nazi camp guards forced homosexuals to wear.

To many heterosexual observers, all this talk of death camps and extermination sounded paranoid. There was really not that much discrimination against gays, they argued. In fact, it had become a standard argument among moderate Republicans and conservative Democrats that they would vote against gay-rights bills not because they were for discrimination but because the legislation was not needed.

Gays, meanwhile, saw that the fundamentalists' successful national organizing was due in no small part to the emotional appeal of their antigay message. Gays saw that they were losing jobs. They also knew that the government spent millions of dollars in its investigations and purges of gays in the military. What was more galling than the antigay campaigns was the fact that so few heterosexuals rose to object. President Carter had made the principle that "Human rights are absolute" the centerpiece of his foreign policy. That sentence adorned a banner that led the San Francisco gay parade. Still, Carter refused to take a public stand on the antigay teachers' initiative, even though it had received a huge amount of international publicity, until the eleventh hour of the campaign, when the President appeared in Sacramento with Governor Jerry Brown. Carter had completed his speech and was about to leave the stage when a live microphone picked up Brown advising Carter to say he was against the initiative. "You'll get your loudest applause," Brown said. "Ford and Reagan have both come out against it, so I think it's perfectly safe." With the assurance that it was "perfectly safe," Carter weighed in against the referendum.

Five months after the parade, when Supervisor Milk and the city's liberal mayor George Moscone were assassinated by the city's most outspokenly antigay politician, former supervisor Dan White, the alienation grew. A jury on which no gays were permitted to serve declined to find White guilty of murder, instead convicting him of voluntary manslaughter, which meant that for two killings, he would serve only five years in jail. The verdict set off gay rioting, which caused heterosexuals to be outraged, again indicating the gulf that was coming to separate the gay and straight worlds. To gays, both the murder and the trial verdict were acts of homophobia, plain and simple. Straights were often reluctant to accept this assessment, leading gay people to mutter about the denial that appeared to envelope heterosexuals whenever they were forced to confront the fact that they had created a very prejudiced society. Denying a problem, after all, is easier than trying to repair it.

Such episodes had begun to drive a wedge between homosexual and heterosexual America, and the gay community's view of their place in the world began to diverge from that of the majority. The growing acceptance of gays in the military, after all, only reflected the comparable experience of gays throughout American society, but this acceptance came less because heterosexuals had changed their attitudes than because homosexuals were simply not willing to live the furtive lives they had before. When push came to shove, many heterosexuals really did not care that much one way or another about homosexuality, so there was a modicum of acceptance when gays asserted themselves, just as there was a modicum of acceptance for those antigays who were also asserting themselves. The two forces, however, were beginning to collide.

AFTER EIGHTEEN YEARS in the Navy, Commander Vernon E. Berg had been on a fast track to his admiral's star, but his promotions came to an abrupt halt when he testified on behalf of his son at the 1976 hearing. By July 1978, he received word that he had been passed over for promotion to the rank of captain for the second time. Berg knew the rules: Passed over twice, he would never be considered for promotion again. His career in the Navy was over.

In fact, it had been over since the day Berg took the stand. Officers who had once been friends had been giving regular reports to the Pentagon about Berg's activities ever since the hearing, in case he tried to start any further trouble. His comments about gay admirals and captains had other chaplains muttering that Berg had betrayed the sacred confidence chaplains should honor. In truth, none of Berg's knowledge of high-ranking homosexual brass had come out of his work as chaplain. He knew about the gay admirals because they had made passes at him. Though the Presbyterian Church was edging toward a position of moderate acceptance concerning homosexuality, there were still church officials who were embarrassed that a high-ranking Presbyterian clergyman in the military had countenanced a challenge to the military's homosexual regulations. Berg found little support in the church hierarchy.

Though only forty-seven, the older Berg was beginning to suffer health problems, a result of exposure to Agent Orange in Vietnam. Given his situation, it seemed wisest to take a medical discharge. Once he had believed in the Navy and the ideal of service to his country that it represented, but Berg no longer believed much in either anymore.

Once out of the Navy, Berg gave up the ministry, moved to Kitty Hawk, North Carolina, and cornered the market on duck blinds there. In the years that followed, he grew his hair long, wore a cowboy hat, lived on his retirement, and guided duck hunters to the choicest blinds. The bond he had developed with his son never lessened over the years, and Copy's admiration and concern for his father deepened. Copy saw that his dad had lost much: his belief that had translated as charisma, his friends, his service, his country, and even his church, and Copy hated the Navy for taking all this away from him.

About the same time Commander Berg left the Navy, an account of Copy's own tribulations was published. Penned by Lawrence Gibson, *Get Off My Ship!* faithfully recorded every twist and turn of the Berg hearing. Though the book received plaudits from some gay critics, several homosexual newspapers refused to review or even note its existence. These papers considered it inappropriate to support such a cause.

A mysterious coda attaches to the book's publication. Gibson had included excerpts from the long-suppressed Crittenden Report in his appendix. But the book was published without those excerpts. Neither the book's editor nor publisher nor printer could explain what had happened to those pages; they had apparently just disappeared from the printer's plates and were never run. Gibson's publisher destroyed the first twenty thousand copies of the book and ran off another twenty thousand under tight security. It was the first publication of the report that had been secret for two decades.

33

Women at Sea

NOVEMBER 1978
GREAT LAKES NAVAL TRAINING CENTER
GREAT LAKES, ILLINOIS

CAROLE BROCK ARRIVED at Great Lakes a week before Thanksgiving, just after the winter's first snow had blown in from Lake Michigan. Excitement was part of the assignment to any new duty station, but Carole was particularly exhilarated because she was here for the technical schooling that would qualify her as an engineman. After that, she would finally achieve the ambition that had drawn her into the Navy in the first place— to go to sea.

Now in the Navy for two years, Carole had already taken her exam for petty officer third class and had undergone a lot more training than her seaman recruit classmates. Still, in her first day in the school an instructor thought nothing of ordering her to fetch him a cup of coffee.

"I don't work the mess decks," Carole replied tartly. "Get your own coffee." The only reason new opportunities like sea duty were opening up for women was because they were standing up for themselves. It was the tone of the times.

Carole's recruiter had been explicit that women were not allowed at sea in the Navy, but Carole had been confident that the quick pace of change in the services would provide her the opportunity. She was right. In July 1978, federal district court judge John J. Sirica declared the federal law prohibiting women from serving at sea to be unconstitutional. The ban on women serving aboard all but hospital and transport ships represented unlawful discrimination, he said, because "sex is required to take precedence over individual ability." By the time Carole had unpacked her seabag at Great Lakes, the first eight women to serve aboard any non-hospital ship in the U.S. Navy had walked up the gangplank of the USS *Vulcan* in Norfolk.

Even before Sirica's decision, pressure had been building on the Navy, the service most resistant to expanding the role of women. Legislation was pending in Congress to mandate the rules that Sirica ordered from the bench. In 1977, Navy Secretary W. Graham Claytor, Jr., put the Carter administration's imprimatur on a proposal to allow some women on auxiliary ships. To a large extent, the new policies were a response to the Navy's own changing needs as much as to changing mores. With an aging baby boom generation and a pool of potential young recruits shrinking more each year, the Navy desperately needed a source for fresh enlistments. Women filled the gap. Secretary Claytor announced the Navy's Women at Sea program and started designating ships aboard which women would be allowed to serve. By 1984, the Navy planned to have 210 female officers and 5,120 enlisted women to fill approximately 25 percent of the crew billets on fifty-five noncombat ships. Once again, women would save the all-volunteer military.

The move to allow women on ships did not come without substantial controversy. The most outspoken source of opposition came from Navy wives who, like their husbands, were convinced that women in the military tended to be either lesbians or man-hunters. Unlike their husbands, however, the spouses tended to be far more concerned with the latter than the former. Old-time sailors simply opposed women because they didn't want them on their ships. As one old salt told *Newsweek*, "I'm not used to having a female telling me what to do." Given such resistance, the fact that the Navy finally broke with a 203-year tradition was revolutionary.

Such changes in policies regarding women were occurring throughout the military. The most significant development, which came in 1978, was the dissolution of the separate but equal all-female branches of the military through which all women recruits had been channeled since World War II. The change had been in the works for much of the 1970s, as senior female officers became outspoken in their resentment that women soldiers served as auxiliaries to the "real" armed forces. The office of WAVE director was abolished in 1973 after its director announced she would never again use the term *WAVE*, and the WAF director's slot was eliminated in 1976. A year later, the Marine Corps did the same, and the last vestige of the segregated women's military came to an end on October 20, 1978, when the Army officially "disestablished" the Women's Army Corps.

Though applauded by civil rights advocates as a necessary step toward assuring full equality for women in the military, the abolition of all-female services created new problems. It also meant an end to the support structures for women. Although their numbers had been rapidly growing in the past decade, women still represented a tiny minority of the military force. Only 4.3 percent of Navy enlisted personnel in late 1977, for example, was female. A brand-new woman soldier might find herself the only woman in her command. Female officers were always the first women to hold one or another job. Often, their assignment to a particular command represented the first time their subordinates had ever served under a woman. For a lot of men, this was not a welcome experience.

Sex discrimination was rampant. In 1978, for example, the Air Force routinely passed over women with outstanding evaluations in order to promote men with far lower evaluations. A male Air Force captain was twice as likely as a female to make the cut to major. The Air Force galled women's rights advocates further when it declared it promoted on the basis of the "whole man" concept, which meant factoring in service academy attendance and combat experience, things that no woman officer at that time could attain. The Marine Corps and Navy continued to mete out promotions on a separate basis for women and men. They would stubbornly adhere to this practice until December 1980. Top military brass were also obdurate in their opposition to having women in any combat positions, and successfully obstructed the Carter administration's efforts to integrate women throughout the military.

Resentment toward the growing presence of women expressed itself in a thousand smaller ways as female recruits grew in number. Many senior drill instructors made no secret of the fact that they resented having to train women in the new, all-integrated basic-training programs. Male recruits who could not keep up with their peers during the morning jog went to the rear of the formation—to run with the women. The practice taught male recruits that to be with women was to suffer an indignity.

Officially, discrimination was forbidden. On paper at least, a woman who could make a case for overt discrimination would have the support of her chain of command. There was another kind of discrimination, however, which was entirely acceptable: discrimination against lesbians. For harassment concerning suspected homosexuality a woman had no recourse, everyone knew, and much hostility that could not be directed against a woman on the grounds of her sex became expressed on the officially sanctioned grounds of her supposed sexual orientation.

At the New River Marine Corps Air Station in North Carolina, women recruits found themselves the objects of catcalls when they walked by the men's barracks on their way to the mess hall. "Hey babe, you want to get lucky?" the male Marines called. And if the women ignored them, other shouts followed: "What's the matter—you a dyke?"

If a woman wanted to complain, she had to go to an investigative service that itself took extraordinary interest in whether its new female recruits were lesbians. Most lesbian investigations focused on an arena that had long been the most productive mine for lesbian discharges—women's sports. An investigation of the women's softball team at a major NATO base resulted in the discharge of a dozen female Army personnel. As the colonel in charge of the base chuckled at the start of the investigation, "They're slurping it up over there in the women's barracks. We're going to get them." In the course of the year-long purge, every woman on the installation was interrogated about lesbianism because every woman was suspect. A lesbian investigation at the Navy's Officer Candidate School in Newport, Rhode Island, in late 1977 also saw every woman in the school interrogated by the Naval Investigative Service.

The suspicions cast a cloud over the careers of many military women. Though the Air Force could not prove charges of "lesbian tendencies" lodged against Mary Ann De Palo, they denied her reenlistment for "displaying poor judgment by . . . associating with known homosexuals." De Palo, who was stationed at Loring Air Force Base, went to federal court to try to force her reenlistment, but she failed.

Service investigative agencies also began to recruit informants among new female recruits. When Jill Waters, a radioman second class, was assigned to the Naval Security Group in the remote naval installation on Adak Island in the Aleutian Islands chain, the installation commander told her that a lot of women on the island engaged in homosexual behavior. Since it was Jill's first day on the base and she had no friendships there, he wondered whether she would be his "special informant." As Waters recalled the conversation, the commander said, "I want to clean up this island and get rid of this lesbianism that's going on. Keep your eyes open. I want you to write down anything suspicious." In return, Waters would receive special consideration for passes, leaves, and promotions.

The investigative tactics were often devious. In late 1977, for example, six women in basic training at Fort McClellan, Alabama, were detailed to the CID training school for the day. According to Julie Stonacek, then a private, agents asked them to role-play to help train the agents in the use of lie-detector machines. Once hooked to the polygraphs, CID agents asked, "Have you ever had relations with a person of the same sex?" This was not part of an investigation, they assured the women; it was just part of the agents' training. Male recruits, of course, were not subject to the same role-playing.

A mythology also sprang up concerning the presence of lesbians in the military, according to Army documents of the period. Stories spread among male officers that lesbians were victimizing young female recruits and luring them into their deviant lifestyle. An Army position paper on homosexuality in the military, prepared for use in a 1979 federal court challenge to the gay policy, advanced the notion that "gangs of female homosexuals inflict or threaten bodily harm to female heterosexuals."

To be sure, a large portion of the new female recruits were lesbian, particularly in those early days in the integrated military. Pentagon recruiting studies from the late 1970s and early 1980s showed that the idea of entering the military appealed to only a "narrow" segment of the female population. The gay image of military women became something of a self-fulfilling prophecy, leading young lesbians to join the military in hopes of finding a peer group. The intense scrutiny of all women in the military also meant that a lesbian in uniform was far more likely to be detected than her gay male counterpart. In 1979, for example, women received one in ten of the Navy's gay-related discharges, even though women comprised about one in twenty-five of Navy enlisted personnel. In the Army that year, women were six times more likely to be discharged on grounds of homosexuality than men.

CAROLE BROCK did not know the statistics, but after two years in the Navy she knew the dangers for women in the service, particularly for those women like herself who were both gay and had chosen a nontraditional job. Carole had watched a friend in San Diego go through an investigation and had by now heard all the horror stories about how the Naval Investigative Service conducted its purges.

A certain amount of caution was necessary to get by, but a camaraderie developed among her lesbian classmates. After school was out, Carole and her friends played in the snow and then retreated to the barracks for a hot shower and an evening in front of the TV. On weekends, they commuted to Chicago to dance at the gay clubs on the Near North Side.

Training came easily. Carole got along well with her classmates and performed well in the two advanced-training schools she needed before her shipboard assignment. In both classes, she was the only woman; in both classes, she was among the top half of the class. Toward the end of her program, the names of ship billets for the Women at Sea program were posted, listing the USS *Vulcan* and the USS *Dixon* and the USS *Norton Sound* in California, and Carole learned that she would be heading west to the *Norton Sound*.

DECEMBER 6, 1978
WASHINGTON, D.C.

THE DECISION from the United States Court of Appeals in Washington was as unexpected as it was dramatic. After having joined the appeals of Vernon Berg III and Leonard Matlovich into one case, the court ruled unanimously that the discharges were illegal.

Though attorneys had argued against the discharges on constitutional grounds, the court sidestepped these issues by ruling on the more narrow basis of administrative law. While the Air Force was the only service whose exclusion policy included exceptions in specific cases, Department of Defense attorneys had argued in federal court in 1974 that the Navy also allowed for exceptions to the policy of excluding homosexuals. This was not true, but it was a legally convenient argument to make in that specific case, so government lawyers asserted it. The legal problem with this allowance was that neither service could ever define what it took to qualify.

"The Air Force regulation expressly contemplates that exceptions can be made to the general policy of separating homosexuals, and the record shows that the Air Force has in the past retained members on active duty who had engaged in homosexual activity," the court ruled. "But what disturbs us is that it is impossible to tell on what grounds the Service refused to make an exception or how it distinguished this case from the ones in which homosexuals have been retained. . . . We are at sea as to the circumstances. . . . in which the Air Force makes exceptions to the policy of eliminating homosexuals and when it refuses to make an exception." The only apparent reason why a serviceman with Matlovich's "superior record" did not qualify for an exception, the court suggested, was perhaps his "going public with his homosexuality and the publicity surrounding his case." The court noted that such a consideration would be "blatantly improper."

As for Berg, the court said, "It is proper . . . to call upon the service for a fuller articulation of its policy on retention of homosexuals and the application of those standards to Berg's case."

The implication of the ruling was immediately clear. If the military must now state explicitly why it did not separate some gays, it must also offer a rationale for why it did separate others. As the court ruled, "We cannot escape the conclusion that in cases of this type, a reasoned explanation should be made for any detrimental action ordered."

Never before, in over thirty years of the military's formal ejection of homosexuals from its ranks, had a federal court at this level demanded that it cite reasons for its gay policies. The ruling did not reinstate either Berg or Matlovich and it did not mandate that gay-related discharges must end. Instead, the court remanded the issue back down to federal district court judge Gerhard Gesell to sort out the specific issues concerning military policies.

The next day, the Army, Navy, and Air Force confirmed to reporters that they had begun "major reviews of policies concerning homosexuals." Court challenges to the policy continued to mount. In San Diego, a former Marine Corps officer whose photo was once used on a recruiting poster filed a $12 million lawsuit against the Marine Corps, claiming his gay-related court-martial represented "malicious prosecution" ordered by a vindictive superior officer. New federal lawsuits against the policy had recently been filed in San Francisco and Denver.

An even more creative tactic to force change was taken in Washington, D.C., where a well-organized gay vote yielded substantial clout with local government. There, the local board of education was investigating whether to order the Junior ROTC program out of Washington public schools under the mandate of district policy that held that schools could not offer programs that discriminated on any basis, including sexual orientation. Since there was no question that the military discriminated against gays, gay activists argued that its curriculum should be dropped from public schools. Though the school board ultimately voted to keep the program, the issue, handled at no less a level than that of the Assistant Secretary of Defense, was but another example of the headaches the gay policy was causing the Pentagon.

IN HIS SMALL APARTMENT in San Francisco, Leonard Matlovich was thrilled at the news of the court decision. Once again, his hopes rose: He would return to the Air Force and his life would begin again.

Matlovich's desire to return was in no small part due to the fact that he had yet to find a niche for himself in the civilian world. Though he had lived three years in Washington, he never did find work. His idea of a foundation for civil rights had fallen through. He changed his political party registration to become a Democrat with the idea of running for city council, but he gained little support. The only job he thought he was right for was as a full-time civil rights activist, which was not all that different from what he had done as a race-relations instructor in the Air Force. In San Francisco, homosexuals could win public office, so, in late 1978, Matlovich decided to move there, where he thought he could once again become a Republican and begin a political career. In early 1979, he packed up his portrait of Martin Luther King, Jr., and his framed cover of *Time* magazine and drove his maroon Pontiac to San Francisco.

Though he was not the celebrity he had been a few years earlier, his stock had recently risen when NBC aired his life story. The made-for-TV movie had attracted a far lower viewership than Matlovich had hoped, largely because the network feared repercussions from well-organized conservative groups and therefore had run the film in the middle of the summer, a dismal placement assuring dismal ratings. Still, it represented the first nonfiction treatment of any gay-rights tale ever undertaken by network television, and it somewhat revived Matlovich's standing as the nation's major homosexual star. Perhaps in San Francisco, he would find his place.

———

PETE RANDELL made it a point to watch *Matlovich v. the Air Force* when he heard the movie was finally going to be shown. His wife and children were already in bed when he switched on the TV. The film opened with the statement from the Secretary of the Air Force ordering Matlovich out of the service. Randell knew the words precisely; he had written them himself.

———

FOR MILLENNIA, men who sail have spun legends to explain the strange and mysterious ways of the sea. If sharks follow a ship, someone will die aboard; an earring is protection from drowning; bad luck follows any ship whose name ends in the letter *a*. Sailors are the most superstitious of all military folk. And one sailors' myth supersedes all others in its authority: Women should not be on ships. The origins of this folklore are murky, but the way the usual story goes is that the sea is ruled by goddesses who are jealous of other women in their sailors' lives. The presence of women on ships is likely to raise the goddesses' ire and bring bad luck.

Sea duty had for untold generations been an exclusive private men's club. Now those days were coming to an end at the order of politicians in Washington. All this was very much on the mind of Petty Officer Second Class Carole Brock and the other sixty women who boarded the USS *Norton Sound* in the first weeks of the summer of 1979.

Named for an Alaskan inlet of the Bering Sea, the thirty-six-year-old, 15,000-ton vessel was a former seaplane tender that had been converted to a research and development ship in 1948. Since 1973, it had been testing the Navy's new Aegis missile system. The crew, who could deal with women as Navy nurses on land, were not sure what to make of the women who were coming on board as radiomen or mechanics. It just didn't seem right to a lot of them.

On the second night at sea, about fifty miles off the Southern California coast, Carole was awakened by an alarm sounding the ship to general quarters. Somebody had ignited a magnesium flare—the signal normally used to issue a distress call—in a rear passageway outside the back door of the female berthing area, which was now filling up with smoke. It was a difficult area to reach for the harried crew. Carole rushed to her duty station at the emergency diesel generator, which they would need in the event the fire damaged any of the boilers. After a tense hour, the flames were doused.

When she returned to the women's compartment, blowers were sucking out the last of the acrid smoke. By then, it was clear that the fire had not been an accident and that whoever had set it knew what he was doing. The women suspected it was an attempt to intimidate the new crew members. The episode reminded Carole that during their orientation a captain had noted that there would be men on board the ship who would not welcome them. "You'll have to stick together," he said.

Still, the evening also left Carole thrilled with the excitement of real-life drama. As the USS *Norton Sound* heaved under the azure blue Pacific swells, she could feel the power underneath, the hidden power of the sea.

— 34 —

Angry Gods

RUTH VOOR would probably never have ended up at Annapolis except for a Naval Academy coach she met one summer while she was at a high school basketball camp. With her thick mop of red hair, soft, reassuring voice, and warm, expressive smile, Ruth did not fit the standard image of a woman athlete. At five-six and 128 pounds, she was sometimes the smallest member of her team. But on the basketball court, she was a terror, excelling at defense, aggressively setting up plays, and methodically establishing the team's tempo. Making the team play as a team, with all the parts working together, was what Ruth loved about basketball. The Naval Academy's basketball coach noticed this immediately. Eager to fill women's slots with students who could bolster the school's athletic reputation, he called Voor at her home in Louisville to urge her to apply to Annapolis. She was vice president of her student body, basketball team captain, and a straight-A student; she was just the high-achieving kind of leader the service academies like to attract.

Ruth hesitated. She was not from a military family and the Navy was not a career she had ever contemplated. Her dad was a civil engineer, her mom a second-grade teacher. Ruth was one of six children and she knew her parents would have a difficult time paying for a college education, but she intended to go to college. No matter where she went to school, she would need a scholarship. Most of the other girls at Our Lady of Mercy Academy seemed happy enough in their typing and home economics classes, but Ruth wanted bigger things. In the end, Ruth applied, and was quickly accepted. In the first weeks of summer, she was sworn in as a midshipman at the United States Naval Academy.

Before the ceremony, everyone had been quite cordial, but the moment the swearing-in was completed, the upperclassmen began screaming at the top of their lungs at the midshipmen. It was the beginning of Plebe

Summer, the Academy's approximation of boot camp. As a first-year student, Ruth and the other freshmen spent the next two months receiving the taunts and orders that mark the first difficult months of military service. The spit-and-polish grind and daily humiliations handed down by upperclassmen had a purpose: to forge the class of 1983 into one unit, a team in which everyone would help one another out.

Team spirit dominated the first weeks of Plebe Summer, with men and women working together in a regimen that largely revolved around athletics. Considering that many of the complaints about the growing presence of women in the military centered on the men's fears that women would lower the services' physical standards, Ruth was surprised at the poor physical shape of many of the men. With her own strong athletic background she usually ranked among the top five plebes in her thirty-member unit. More than anything, she relished the team spirit the summer was designed to inspire. It was what she had loved about sports and what she was coming to love about the Academy.

But then the school year began and everything changed. Four thousand midshipmen returned. Ruth saw that the male plebes were getting new signals from their upperclassmen. If one of the guys spent too much time with a female midshipmen, he was taken aside. "What do you mean, you're friends with the women?" he was asked. Women didn't belong in the Navy and they didn't belong at Annapolis. The very first class that included women was only now entering its senior year, and a number of individuals took pride in asserting that no woman would ever graduate from their company, no matter what they had to do. Slowly, the younger men who had been friendly during June and July grew cool. They began repeating that women did not belong in the Navy and that they were destroying the traditions of Annapolis.

The Twenty-first Company, to which Ruth and five other women were assigned, took particular enthusiasm in its resolution that no woman would ever graduate from its ranks. To reaffirm its macho image, the company had adopted a logo that featured the profile of the Playboy Bunny. The company's nickname was "Playboy 21." When two of the six female plebes dropped out, the upperclassmen crowed, "Two down and four to go." As for the others, they predicted, "They'll either quit or be transferred." This made Ruth more determined to succeed. She was not a quitter.

The importance of sticking together became very apparent on the night of the Academy's Forrestal Lecture, the speech named in honor of the first Secretary of Defense. Admiral Thomas Hayward, Chief of Naval Operations, was one of the speakers that year and during the question and answer period after his lecture, one female midshipman asked whether he thought women should be at the Naval Academy. The issue was very much on the minds of women, given a controversial article just published by Annapolis graduate and Vietnam war hero James Webb. The article, entitled "Women Can't Fight," claimed the presence of women in the military academies was "poisoning" the institutions and had "sterilized the whole process of combat leadership training." After quoting a female midshipman who complained of wearing a different hat from men, Webb added, "Many women appear to be having problems with their sexuality. Part of it comes from male scrutiny: What kind of woman would seek out the Academy routine?" What did Hayward think about this controversy? the female student asked.

Hayward was candid in his reply. He couldn't see why they were there either. "I don't know," he said.

Male midshipmen broke into laughter at the answer. The women sat horrified. They had hoped for some word of support in what was becoming a very arduous process of integrating into the Navy. Instead, the top of the Navy's chain of command seemed to be weighing in against them.

Late that night, after the lecture, shouts went up in companies across Bancroft Hall: "Plebettes, ho." As female midshipmen stood at attention, braced against the wall, upperclassmen assumed their most aggressive in-your-face stance.

"Admiral Hayward says you shouldn't be here," an upperclassman shouted at Ruth, his face only two inches from hers. "You're not supposed to be here. James Webb says you shouldn't be here. Why don't you go home?"

Because it was so late, the company officers had gone for the night, so there was no one to stop the shouting. For three hours, the haranguing continued. Some upperclassmen even pulled out their copies of "Women Can't Fight" and brandished them in the faces of the stricken women.

"You don't belong here," they shouted again and again. "Why don't you go home?"

They wanted to make the women cry. Ruth's roommate did, but Ruth refused. She was angry that the Navy was not supporting them after having made the decision to allow them in the Academy, and she would be damned if any of these idiots would make her cry or make her quit. The male plebes with whom the women were to have bonded over the summer watched in silence. Their survival depended on getting along with the upperclassmen. Team spirit was essential, yes, but women were not part of the team.

In the Twenty-first Company, that night steeled the men in their resolve that no woman would ever graduate from their company. For the rest of the year, female midshipmen were met in the mess hall or barracks hallway with one question: "When are you going to quit?" The yelling in the mess hall was often so intense that some women simply skipped meals. When the third of the six women in the company resigned, many men were delighted.

Ruth had only one refuge from the seemingly endless harassment—

the basketball court. At practice, she was treated like a human being. Nobody called her plebette and there was the genuine team spirit she loved. The camaraderie gave her the confidence to return to Bancroft Hall and the men in Playboy 21. Because of the most recent departure, the three women left moved in together. As they reorganized their belongings, Ruth said, "We're not going to survive alone. We've got to stick together. The way to get back at them is to graduate."

———————

AT THE SAME TIME Ruth Voor was entering the United States Naval Academy, a twenty-one-year-old cadet named Dan Stratford was leaving the United States Air Force Academy, forced out because authorities had accused him of "associating" with known homosexuals. What had actually caused the dismissal, of course, was the suspicion that Stratford was gay himself, but the Air Force could never prove it, so instead he was pressured to resign for his "associations."

The investigation was a sign of the times. By the late 1970s, there were many gay cadets at the Air Force Academy, as in all the service academies. Across the country, gay people in their early twenties increasingly discarded the covert life of past eras for the gay communities springing up in every city; and it was the same for the youth of the nation's military academies. Gay cadets meant gay investigations, such as the type that had occurred at the Air Force Academy in early 1979. From this time onward, there would never be an academic year at any service academy in which there was not an investigation into the suspected homosexuality of one or more students.

This is not to say that homosexual investigations of the nation's service academies were new in the late 1970s. In the early 1960s, when General William C. Westmoreland was superintendent of West Point, a gay scandal erupted involving the manager of a Manhattan hotel who advertised cheap rates for cadets at his hotel in academy publications, and who chose his boyfriends from the young West Pointers who lodged there. The academy dismissed five cadets in that one investigation alone, but it took pains to keep the matter out of the newspapers, according to an officer assigned to the academy then. The pace of investigations increased in the following years. Throughout the early 1970s, there were always rumors of formal inquiries and secret dismissals from the Naval Academy at Annapolis.

That such investigations would increase during the 1970s and into the next two decades reflected a historical inevitability, given the changing times for gays. For the military, the presence of gays at its most prestigious centers of learning—and as the source of the major share of the next generation's military leadership—presented new and heretofore unimaginable difficulties. Though the 1979 Air Force Academy investigation centered on Stratford, investigators were also checking into the lives of his two best friends, one of whom, George Gordy, was one of the more outstanding students of the academy that year. An instructor also came under scrutiny—as did a 1978 graduate, who was by 1979 in pilot training in Texas.

The probe had started when Dan's roommate, suspecting he was gay, perused his desk for evidence. When he found an incriminating letter, he photocopied it and handed it over to the OSI, leading to a room search. The search gave the OSI many leads, from all the letters and names in Dan's address book, but the only evidence against the cadet remained the one letter that indicated the author, not Stratford, was gay.

Though the Office of Special Investigations attempted to threaten Stratford into resigning immediately and naming others, Stratford refused—unless he was assured that he would be awarded his diploma, which he was only weeks away from receiving. The Air Force at first did not want to allow him to graduate, relenting only after he threatened to file a lawsuit.

Stratford got his diploma and his honorable discharge. The instructor was also cashiered out of the military, though the other cadets survived. Perhaps the most enduring impact was not on the gay students, however, but on the entire student body, which learned lasting lessons from the ongoing gay purges at the service academies.

Cadets learned that rifling through another student's desk and reading his personal letters was justified if it resulted in the dismissal of a homosexual; that normal rules of justice did not apply; that homosexuals had no rights, only punishments; that no expense was too great to deter the enforcement of the ban on homosexuals; that merely "associating with a known homosexual" could be grounds for punishment; that it was in the natural order of things that homosexuals just disappeared. Even if some cadets did not believe this was right, and there were clearly some who did not, the events of the year showed that the system was set up in such a way as to be in accord with those who did and that it was best to hold one's peace.

These were the lessons taught to a very important audience: The people in the Air Force Academy in 1979 would be a large share of the officers in midlevel Air Force management in another ten years, majors making career decisions for others. Five years later, they would be lieutenant colonels and colonels in senior staff positions at the Pentagon, and, five years after that, the best of them would be earning their first generals' stars. Then they would work their way up to the Joint Chiefs of Staff, because that was where Academy graduates ended up; they would be the very people who would run the military through the first decade of the twenty-first century.

SEPTEMBER 29, 1979
ABOARD THE USS *NORTON SOUND*

FIERCE WINDS BLEW across the Pacific toward the coast of Washington State, rocking the *Norton Sound* as it sailed fifty miles offshore. Nobody thought much of it when Seaman Muriel MacBride politely asked a crewmate if she could borrow a coat. Winter was approaching and the first autumn storm was screaming out of the Gulf of Alaska. MacBride was a quiet woman. Though Muriel had a boyfriend, Carole Brock felt she might be a member of The Family. She did not socialize much with any of the gay networks on board or with the other women. It was only later that Carole reflected on how lonely Muriel must have felt, because the *Norton Sound* could be a lonely place for a woman who did not seek support among the other female sailors.

The men had not gotten over the novelty of having women aboard. When the ship pulled into port, seamen brought their friends on board to show them the women's berthing area, as if it were a zoo. One chief petty officer had decided that the women were in his department for his sexual gratification and had taken to grabbing their breasts and buttocks. As it was, overall discipline on the ship was at a nadir. A gang called the "Dirty Dozen" dealt drugs and engaged in loansharking on board. The ship's command seemed oblivious to all these problems, most notably those of the female crew members.

Fortunately, Carole was gregarious, smiled easily, and radiated self-confidence. Having grown up with brothers, she was accustomed to roughhousing and dishing it back when the men dished it out to her. Though she was the only woman in her shop, she overcame resistance by virtue of the fact that after three years of working with Navy engines she knew more about them than her male counterparts. If she made a mess, she cleaned it up herself rather than delegating the chore to some fireman's apprentice, as a lot of men in her rank would have done. After three months on the *Norton Sound*, when her shop supervisor was transferred to the mess deck, Carole was put in charge of her engine shop A-gang, over the head of a more senior-ranking engineman. In her new job, she reestablished a detailed maintenance system for all the auxiliary engines aboard the ship and reorganized the department's logbooks. Her evaluations showed that the Navy considered her an exceptional petty officer. At the end of the day, she and the men on her crew went out for beer together; she easily became one of them. She loved the Navy.

By late summer, Carole had also figured out who was gay among the women on the crew. A little less than a third of the women were gay by Carole's count, and several had started buddying around together. Some of the younger women even drove into the mountains north of L.A. for the "Gay Night" festivities at the Magic Mountain amusement park. On a typical weekend, the lesbian sailors, like their heterosexual peers, rented an eleven-dollar-a-night room at the Surfside Motel, bought a couple cases of beer, and spent the weekend watching TV together.

Still, there were moments when something ominous seemed to hang over the ship, and that was the case on the morning after Muriel MacBride had borrowed a coat to venture on deck. That morning, after the storm had passed, the coat was found neatly folded, next to a pair of shoes. MacBride was gone, presumably drowned in the icy waters off the Washington coast. Her body was never found.

DECEMBER 2, 1979
PHILADELPHIA, PENNSYLVANIA

IN THE JOHN F. KENNEDY MEMORIAL STADIUM, a standing-room-only crowd cheered Navy on to its crushing 31-to-7 defeat of Army. Midshipman Ruth Voor yelled lustily, as glad to be away from Annapolis as to be rooting for the winning side. It was her first trip away from the Academy since the start of the school year. After the game, Ruth and her friends from the basketball team went out, and she found herself drawn to one of her teammates. It was an attraction that excited and frightened her.

Our Lady of Mercy was an all-girls school and sex had not been a major issue in Ruth's teen years. Besides, she was frightened of getting pregnant. Her trepidations were a phase, she figured, that would end when she met the right guy. At times, when she contemplated the implications of her occasional attractions to women, she prayed, "God, please straighten this out." The weekend of the Army-Navy game, however, she was not sure she wanted her feelings taken away. That night, she and her new friend got drunk and before long they were kissing.

Ruth's friend, a sophomore, was the star of the women's basketball team and part of a company whose men were far more accepting of women than the Playboy 21. In fact, these men made it a point to say they wanted *everyone* in their class to graduate and *no one* to quit. As December turned to January, when the harassment within the Twenty-first Company grew too fierce, Ruth found herself going over to her new girlfriend's room.

News of Ruth's first affair spread quickly among the women on the basketball team, which caused no small degree of consternation, given the previous year's lesbian investigation of the women's volleyball team. Friends started visiting Ruth in her room and marched both her and her girlfriend to a psychiatrist's office. This psychiatrist was a lieutenant commander who bought neither the antifemale nor antigay rhetoric of Navy men. "Don't do anything stupid, like trying to get laid to show you're not a lesbian," he warned them. "If word of this gets out, you'll have a lot of people approaching you trying to save you."

When word got as far as their basketball coach, he ordered Ruth's teammates, "You figure out what the hell is going on and stop it. I can't go through this again."

During the next off-campus game, the chaplain appeared on the women's team bus and, before giving his prayer, intoned, "You have to be careful what you do. You can't embarrass the Academy."

Ruth got the message: Don't get caught.

But it did not seem to Ruth that this affair was that big a deal. She really did not believe she was a lesbian. She believed she was drawn to women because the men were always hassling her. It was a phase.

It was about this time that Ruth twisted her knee in a particularly grueling practice. The injury required surgery and put her on the sidelines; she ultimately retired from the team. Her relationship continued, however, and on weekends Ruth and her girlfriend and a few other women would leave the Academy to spend their time with a sympathetic faculty member who lived off-campus. The weekends were a welcome respite from the hostility of the male midshipmen and seemed to be the only way they would make it through. They had to stick together.

NOVEMBER 1979
SAN FRANCISCO CITY HALL
SAN FRANCISCO

LEONARD MATLOVICH had known he might not win when he announced his candidacy for the San Francisco Board of Supervisors. He had lived in San Francisco for only eight months. But he had not expected humiliation, which was what the voters were handing him tonight. After months of campaigning and shaking hands, Lenny had received only 410 votes, trailing far behind most of the other candidates in the race for the supervisorial seat held by Harvey Milk before the supervisor was assassinated a year earlier.

Though Matlovich was shocked at the outcome, it hardly came as a surprise to city political pundits. As a Republican candidate, he had appealed for conservative gay votes and sought endorsements from such mainstream groups as the Board of Realtors. In the most liberal of large U.S. cities, this was a recipe for disaster. From the point of view of the military, Leonard Matlovich may have been a radical; from the point of view of the typical gay politico in San Francisco, he seemed intransigently conservative and hopelessly out of touch with an increasingly militant and angry community. Few were impressed by his appearance on the cover of *Time* magazine, now four years old. Professional gay activists were not all that rare a commodity in San Francisco and his opponents vehemently denounced him as a carpetbagger.

Finally, Matlovich was beginning to know something about himself that his friends had seen years earlier: There were not many places where he fit in except the United States Air Force. He began to feel adrift; the only thing that sustained him was his conviction that he would receive his reinstatement in the Air Force once his case had wound its way through the federal courts.

Until then, he had practical problems to deal with, most notably his lack of funds. He had not had a real job since the Air Force. Matlovich set out one day to walk door to door through the Castro neighborhood to find work. A tile warehouse took him on for $4.25 an hour.

On weekends, after he cashed his modest paycheck, Matlovich would leave his small apartment on Eighteenth Street and venture into Moby Dick's or one of the other bustling gay bars in the neighborhood to look for that special someone who he was convinced awaited him. But he only met the occasional fan, wanting to add a night with Leonard to his list of San Francisco experiences.

NATIONALLY, POLITICAL WINDS were shifting in those weeks, directing a new course in American history. Days before Matlovich's defeat in the San Francisco election, Iranian militants had seized the American embassy in Tehran and taken ninety people hostage. An attempt to rescue the hostages failed when American military equipment malfunctioned in a sandstorm. Weeks later, the Soviet Army invaded Afghanistan, deposed its president, and seemed poised to advance on the Persian Gulf. Suddenly, the United States seemed impotent. For most of the decade, in the aftermath of the Vietnam War, the nation had been downsizing its military. According to his detractors, President Carter had overemphasized human rights and injudiciously deemphasized the nation's traditional use of military might to assert its prerogatives, resulting in America's inability to save the hostages or evict the Russians from imperialist designs in Afghanistan. To conservatives, the United States seemed to have grown weak. Liberals were also dissatisfied with Carter's cuts in social-welfare programs. Senator Edward Kennedy announced a liberal challenge to Carter for the Democratic presidential nomination, while former California governor Ronald Reagan announced his campaign against Carter from the right. Liberals hoped to recapture the momentum for social change they had known in the 1960s; conservatives hoped to propel their agenda into the next decade. Nineteen eighty would be the decisive year, when the forces of change and reaction would meet in a showdown and the period of transition would come to an end.

35

Memorial Day

"THERE ARE NO gays in the military," the Army officer said.

White House staffer Allison Thomas thought he was kidding and that he would start laughing in a moment. But there was no laughter and it dawned on Allison that the man was serious.

"C'mon, are you crazy?" Thomas asked.

According to Thomas's later recollection of the conversation, he explained, "We get rid of all of them. If we find them, we kick them out. There are no gays in the military."

As an assistant to Anne Wexler, director of the White House Office of Liaison, Allison Thomas was responsible for addressing concerns of various political constituencies, among them the gay community.

Wexler was much more liberal than the conservative Democratic Georgia "mafia" that dominated the White House. Since her office was likely to take up the causes of groups more liberal than the core support groups for President Carter, her office observed the mandate to keep out of the newspapers.

Allison Thomas was a twenty-two-year-old Californian who had always been comfortable around gay people. It had not occurred to her that there were people who were not comfortable around gays—until she called the Army agency in charge of maintaining the Tomb of the Unknown Soldier about a letter she had received from Washington gay organizer Frank Kameny. Kameny had been infuriated by the Army's refusal to let a Miami gay group lay a wreath at the tomb on the previous Veterans Day. He was determined that he and his group, the Washington Gay Activists Alliance, would lay their own wreath at the Tomb on Memorial Day, 1980, in memory of lesbian and gay soldiers who had given their lives for their country. The Army, which managed the Tomb, promptly denied Kameny's request. This led to his angry letter to the White House and Thomas's phone call to the Army. She thought it would be a simple matter to resolve.

The Army officials to whom Thomas talked, however, were determined in their refusal to allow Kameny's group to place a wreath. There were no gay veterans to honor; they had never allowed a homosexual organization any sort of commemoration at the Tomb before; they were not going to do so now.

It was the first time Allison saw firsthand how the military responded to the issue of homosexuals in the service, an issue that arose increasingly as President Carter fought off tough challenges for renomination from California governor Jerry Brown and Senator Kennedy, who was being advised on gay issues by a gay organizer named Jim Foster. Both Kennedy and Brown endorsed all of the important gay demands, including one for an end to discrimination against homosexuals seeking security clearances and those in the military.

Compared to the pledges of Brown and Kennedy, the White House's own list of accomplishments for gay voters looked anemic. The best the Carter administration could say was that it had met with gay leaders, even though it had adopted few of their proposals; under Carter, the IRS was beginning to allow tax deductions for contributions to gay charities and the Immigration and Naturalization Service was no longer asking visitors whether they were homosexual. In a meeting with gay leaders in December 1979, Anne Wexler said that a sweeping executive order to ban all bias against gays working for the government was "under active consideration," though it was clear that this ban would not apply to military personnel. In a private memo from Wexler and domestic policy adviser Stu Eizenstat, Carter was advised against even a limited executive order "because you would then be pressured to do so too early while other candidates would have no obligation to do so until they came into office." No executive order was issued.

It was a surprising record for a chief executive who was more outspoken about human rights than any President since Franklin Roosevelt. Though Carter's human-rights policies demonstrated compassion for *campesinos* in Central America and members of the African National Congress in Capetown, that compassion seemed not to extend to people with nonconforming sexual orientations in San Francisco or New York or, for that matter, in Camp LeJeune or Fort Ord. Purges of gays from the military, in fact, increased drastically during the Carter administration, far beyond anything seen during the two previous Republican administrations of Nixon and Ford.

Given this lackluster record, gay voters were deserting the Carter camp in droves. A poll by the National Gay Task Force found that while 67 percent of gay respondents had voted for Carter in 1976, only 16 percent planned to do so in 1980. In the primaries, this meant wholesale defections to the most viable Democratic alternative, Ted Kennedy. Though the gay vote had minimal effect in a national election, gays represented a key urban swing vote in such important primary states as California and New York. So suddenly the White House was taking note of gay concerns, responding through the Office of Liaison, where Allison Thomas worked.

The military always seemed to be doing something to gall gay activists. The Marine Corps, for example, had taken to cosponsoring "God Bless America" rallies with Anita Bryant. The rallies were largely fund-raisers for Bryant, who had founded the Bryant Ministries, which claimed to be able to convert homosexuals into heterosexuals. Only after White House pressure did the Marines withdraw their sponsorship. The White House had to intervene as well to persuade West Point not to let Bryant use their facilities as a rally site. Now there was the fracas over the Memorial Day wreath.

Through the Secretary of the Army's office, Thomas began her gentle campaign for the gay observance. Thomas understood that the Pentagon's obstinacy had to do with concern for its own constituencies. Groups such as the American Legion and the Veterans of Foreign Wars had immense clout with the Department of Defense and were known to be vehemently against gays in uniform. The Army responded to the White House's pressure by contacting a junior senator who could be counted on to oppose allowing homosexuals to lay a wreath or anything else on government soil. Jesse Helms from North Carolina immediately issued a condemnation of the White House interference. A spokesman for the Veterans of Foreign Wars weighed in, saying the wreath laying would violate "common decency." The ranking Republican member of the House Armed Service's Committee, Congressman William Dickinson of Alabama, accused the Carter administration of pandering to gay voters by allowing "this nauseating spectacle." The Army added a new argument—that the wreath was an attempt to change the military's policies toward homosexuals and that the Tomb of the Unknown Soldier was no place for a political demonstration. Besides, there were no gay soldiers to honor, the Army said.

SAN DIEGO HARBOR
SAN DIEGO, CALIFORNIA

ABOUT THE SAME TIME that Allison Thomas made her first phone calls to the Pentagon, Carole Brock had boarded the USS *Gompers* to borrow a flat-bottomed Liberty boat for the *Norton Sound*'s planned cruise to Mazatlán. The *Gompers*, a tender, was also part of the Women at Sea program, and Carole knew a number of the female crew members from her days at Great Lakes. When she saw a woman fireman she knew, she asked about a mutual friend.

"She's out," the woman said.

"Where'd she go?" Carole asked, surprised; her friend had been in only for a year.

"Kicked out," the fireman said. There had been an investigation of homosexuality among the women on the USS *Gompers*, she added. Ten had been kicked out or resigned under pressure. Their friend had gone home to Florida.

The news shocked Carole. She had heard of one or two people separated in an investigation, but never ten. The paperwork for these discharges had been processed with lightening speed, the fireman said, and within days they had all disappeared.

It did not cross Carole's mind that this could happen to her. She had just received a recommendation for her first Navy Achievement Medal and, according to her evaluation forms, she continued to excel on the job. Nearly four years in the Navy had taught her how to live the necessary double life, though she was aware that there were rumors she was gay. A crewmate had come up to her recently and congratulated her on marrying another woman on the crew the previous weekend. Carole was dating the woman, but there had been no marriage. In fact, Carole had spent the past weekend in bed with the flu. Believing it was a joke, she played along, answering, "Yeah, I had to marry her. She got me pregnant." She did not give it another thought.

The *Norton Sound* was having far more serious problems in other departments. A nineteen-year-old sailor newly stationed on the ship had gotten on the wrong side of the Dirty Dozen and been stabbed with a screwdriver while he lay sleeping in his bunk. A second sailor was stabbed shortly after that, and late one night someone tied shut the door to the cabin of the master-at-arms and started a fire outside it.

Fearing for his life, the first stabbing victim contacted his congressman, Robert Dornan, a very conservative Republican known for his outspoken support of defense spending. Dornan was slated to go on the House Armed Services Committee during the next congressional session, which meant that the Pentagon took his phone calls very seriously. The Naval Investigative Service was informed of Dornan's interest and an investigation was quietly begun.

MAY 1980
USS *NORTON SOUND*
PORT HUENEME

BY 1980, THERE WAS a joke about the Naval Investigative Service, told among Navy lawyers and judges and masters-at-arms. Call the NIS and tell them you've got a dead body and the agents may show up in the next week or so. Call and say you've got a dead body and you think the murderer was a homosexual and the agents will be there in thirty seconds. The NIS was an agency not merely preoccupied with homosexuality; the NIS pursuit of homosexuals was an obsession.

Just where the fixation came from remains murky. As an agency, the

NIS had existed in its present form for only fourteen years. In the conversion to an all-volunteer military in the 1970s, the Defense Department had mandated the transfer of nonmilitary jobs from uniformed personnel to civilians whenever possible. Although the Army and Air Force retained service members to staff their investigative agencies, the Navy had replaced the sailors with a largely civilian force of investigators at the Naval Investigative Service. Among Navy prosecutors who relied on NIS reports, the agency quickly fell into disrepute. The word was that the NIS agents were FBI rejects. While NIS officials credited their agents with a high level of professionalism, it was not a view widely shared, even among Navy brass. There, the NIS came to be thought of as Keystone Kops, or, as one top Pentagon official in the early 1980s said, "the gang that couldn't shoot straight."

It has been suggested that the NIS pursued gay investigations so avidly because such probes were so much easier to conduct than criminal ones. Homosexuals did not think like criminals; it was easier to extract confessions and lists of names from them. Homosexual investigations yielded results and netted discharges, the kinds of things you could write up on a productivity report to demonstrate that your agency deserved to exist. Though the ONI had once employed coercive tactics to obtain confessions and cull informants from among gays during the Navy purges of World War II and in the McCarthy era, the NIS had in a few short years elevated these stratagems to the level of a high art. And so it was in the early weeks of May 1980 that NIS agents began swarming into Port Hueneme. The story of the next three months on the USS *Norton Sound* became the story of the Naval Investigative Service.

Nothing ever came of the agency's first investigation into drug dealing, loansharking, and violence aboard the USS *Norton Sound*. On May 16 however, NIS agent Charles Page hit pay dirt when questioning Helen Teresa Wilson, a mess specialist third class, who delivered a four-page statement about lesbians aboard the ship. Wilson's statement labeled twenty-three of the sixty-one female crew members homosexual. Wilson had not actually seen anyone have sex on the ship or anywhere else, but she could tell they were gay just the same.

She stated, for example, one woman "likes to walk around the compartment in various stages of undress and enjoys watching the other women dress and shower. Since I have been aboard I have not seen [her] express any interest in men." Sailor Tangela Gaskins, she said, "likes to use endearing terms when talking to other women, especially the gays" and was therefore a lesbian. Another woman was a lesbian because she "is very masculine and shows open hostility toward any feminine women on the ship. [She] tends to side with the gays in disputes and harasses the non gays." Another was a lesbian because she had befriended a gay male sailor. Another woman was "extremely masculine and openly discusses her hatred of men and the fact that she would never have any children."

Wilson was particularly emphatic about black women on the ship, insisting that all but one of the crew's nine African-American female members were lesbian. "The black gays flaunt their power and authority over the other females on the ship," she swore to the NIS. "They are very open in their physical activities with one another and if anyone complains, they become very aggressive and threatening. . . . " She described one seaman as "a black female who stays pretty much with the other black females. [She] likes to watch the women dress and shower and is very affectionate. She likes to hug and hold other women." Wilson had observed Alicia Harris and Wendi Williams in a taxicab together once. "They were sitting very close together," Wilson's statement read, "and one of them had her arm around the other's shoulder."

There was another rumor, Wilson reported, that Engineman Second Class Carole Brock was a lesbian and had "married" another crew member a few weeks earlier. "[She] and Brock always go on liberty together and never sleep on the ship unless they have duty," Wilson said. "Brock is a leader and is very outspoken in defense of homosexuals if that subject comes up in conversation."

Once they had taken Helen Wilson's statement, the NIS called in the thirty-eight women not named by her, presuming they were heterosexual. These sailors received a roster of female crew members and were asked to put a check mark next to the name of anyone they thought might be gay. From these, the NIS accumulated the names of twenty-nine suspected lesbians, although no informant had ever seen anyone have sex. Now the NIS agents began the task of gathering more convincing evidence.

The sailor who came to get Petty Officer Lynn Batey told her she was going on a "secret mission" for the ship as he escorted her to an office with an NIS agent. Like most of the women aboard, Batey told the agent she did not know anything about homosexuality on the *Norton Sound*— only the rumors, to which Special Agent John Stevens warned that if she did not give him any evidence, she could be court-martialed for homosexuality herself, according to Batey's later testimony. Batey believed him and wrote out a statement accusing Carole Brock and three others of being lesbians.

Similar tactics resulted in a dozen statements against alleged lesbians. Once these statements were compiled, the NIS interrogated the suspects themselves. Their line of questioning was often salacious.

One NIS agent began his interview with sailor Barbara Lee Underwood by inquiring, "Did you lick her juices?" He then assured her they had all the proof they needed, so she might as well confess.

Another NIS agent told Tangela Gaskins, a petty officer with an outstanding record, that Underwood had identified her as a lesbian. Among other crimes the NIS had documented, the agent said, was that Gaskins had raped another woman with a broom handle. They had the evidence. She ought just to confess. When NIS agents searched her locker, they found convincing evidence of her lesbianism: copies of *Vogue* magazine. "Do you get off looking at their faces or at their bodies?" one agent asked, thumbing through pictures of fashion models. Another wanted to know, "Where do you buy your dildos and other tools of the trade?"

They told Wendi Williams that they had amassed thirty charges against her, all thoroughly documented. Maybe she should just confess now, the NIS agent said.

"If you've got thirty statements, you don't need anything from me," Williams answered.

One woman aboard had a number of tattoos on her body. The agent interviewing her asked about one she was rumored to have on the inside of her lower lip. The sailor was more than happy to comply, rolling her lip down to reveal the words *Fuck you*.

CAROLE BROCK had had a doctor's appointment on the morning the questioning of suspected lesbians began. By the time she got back to the ship, all her friends were talking about the investigation. A number of the accused women were decidedly heterosexual, Carole knew. It was clear that the NIS had little more than the rumors that always float around a ship about who is gay and who is straight. Nobody had buckled in to the threats, Brock learned, though she also heard that a number had been asked about two women on board who had gotten "married" a few weeks earlier.

Soon the master-at-arms came for Carole. The NIS agents were very solemn when they said that Carole's girlfriend had already talked to them and revealed that they had kissed. Carole knew that her girlfriend had not even been called in yet. She denied everything. When Carole was pressed to name others, she remembered the captain's remark: "You'll have to stick together." She told nothing.

On the Friday morning before the Memorial Day weekend, a captain's call was held on the rear fantail of the ship. All the sailors assembled. Carole stood with the woman she was dating and some other gay friends. Their captain, Commander James Seebirt, announced through the ship's loudspeaker system that an investigation had been launched of "homosexuality in the women's berthing area."

Carole shouted a question that was on the minds of a number of the female crew members—why was it only women being investigated?

If there were men to be investigated, Seebirt replied, give him their names.

Carole shouted out the name of a gay male sailor who had been trying to get out of his enlistment contract for months by telling anyone who would listen that he was homosexual. The Navy, however, would not let him go until he furnished photographs of himself having sex. Seebirt had no comment when Carole shouted this sailor's name to the captain's call.

The episode angered her. There was more to the investigation than a mere witch-hunt. This was, after all, one of the first Naval vessels to allow women aboard. Moreover, the investigation had begun when Commander

Seebirt was away on leave; it had been instigated by a top officer known to oppose the Women at Sea program. The investigation seemed aimed less at homosexuality per se than at the controversial program. It all put Carole in a fighting mood. She had heard about a women's group in Los Angeles that was lobbying for the Equal Rights Amendment. Maybe they could help.

Meanwhile, eight agents were now working full-time on the case of lesbians aboard the *Norton Sound* and warning women that they, too, might be accused of lesbianism if they refused to sign statements against their crewmates. Some withstood the pressure, but the NIS wrote up statements accusing others of lesbianism, anyway. These were signed not by the accuser but by the NIS agent, with the notation that the accuser "declined to execute a written statement."

On one of its last weekends in Port Hueneme before sailing to Long Beach harbor for repairs, the *Norton Sound* hosted a dependents' cruise for the families and spouses of sailors. Given the rumors concerning the gay investigation and Navy wives' strident opposition to women on ships, Carole had dreaded the day-long outing, fearing a spate of nasty confrontations. But the wives were among the most supportive people the accused women had yet met. The wives, it turned out, did not mind their husbands going to sea with women if those women were lesbians.

The Dirty Dozen, meanwhile, also weighed in behind the accused. Several of the group's girlfriends had made the NIS list as suspects. The group put out the word: Snitch, and you've got trouble. As the investigation deepened, the women became surprised at the support they received among petty officers and other enlisted personnel. Some had not wanted women on the *Norton Sound* earlier, but having worked with them, had gained a grudging acceptance of their abilities.

Toward the end of the dependents' cruise, sailor Helen Wilson, who had instigated the probe with her detailed accusations, came sputtering into the women's berthing area. Somebody had just called her a lesbian and she was furious at the charge.

"See what it's like?" Carole said.

MEMORIAL DAY, 1980
TOMB OF THE UNKNOWN SOLDIER
ARLINGTON NATIONAL CEMETERY
ARLINGTON, VIRGINIA

GAY ORGANIZER Frank Kameny had made it clear that if the Army did not grant permission to lay his wreath on Memorial Day, he would do it, anyway—even if he got shot in the process. But it was White House intervention and Allison Thomas's persistence that finally moved the Army to accede just days before the scheduled ceremonies.

On the morning of the wreath laying, three high-ranking civilian officials from the Department of the Army stood at the ready to make sure the gay activists did not instigate a subversive act, and a squad of armed military police waited out of sight in the tunnel complex beneath the tomb. At the appointed time, Kameny and a handful of other members of the Gay Activists Alliance stepped solemnly down the wide marble staircase to the broad plaza where the Tomb of the Unknown Soldier sits, its pilastered facade facing Washington. From the tunnels below the staircase, an honor guard in Army dress blues emerged with the wreath into the plaza.

This was not a great turning point in the history of the United States, Kameny knew, but it was a small victory. He had known gay men who had died for their country in World War II and in the Korean and Vietnam wars, and he would be damned if they would be denied this honor any longer.

Being a stickler for detail, however, Kameny also noticed the difference between the Gay Activists Alliance commemoration and the others. While every other group was announced before it placed its wreaths, no announcement was made for the gay activists. And Kameny noticed someone had placed a spray of flower petals to cover the word *Gay*, so their identifying ribbon read Activists Alliance. And although the wreaths remained on the tomb until it was time for the next ceremony, the gay wreath was gone by the time Kameny and his friends reached the top of the stairs on their way out.

Not long afterward, Kameny received a phone call from a stranger who asked whether he and his lover might pay Frank a visit. As the grand old man of Washington's gay community, Frank was accustomed to such cryptic requests, and when the couple arrived Kameny recognized one of them as part of the Old Guard that had handled the ceremonies that day. He was here to thank Kameny for the wreath. There were a lot of people in uniform that day, he said, who appreciated what Frank had done.

36

Glory Days

A MAJOR EVENT of every graduation week at the Naval Academy features a mad scramble of freshmen up Herndon Monument. According to Academy lore, the first midshipman who makes it to the top of the monument and grabs the sailor's cap perched there will be the first admiral to be commissioned from the class. The race was designed to show the team spirit that each class had forged during Plebe Year; the point was that only by working together and creating a solid pyramid could anyone make it to the top of the monument, which was thoroughly greased for the occasion.

Ruth Voor could not participate in her class competition because of her basketball injury, so she watched from the sidelines and saw the turn the annual event had taken now that it included female midshipmen. The plebes scrambled up the growing pile of freshmen bodies under the bright blue skies. As the pyramid grew and a handful of midshipmen began making their way toward the top, Ruth noticed that among the male midshipmen there was a concerted effort not only to be the first to reach the top but also to ensure that only men achieved the upper reaches of the class heap. Ruth had her eye on fellow freshman Laura Hinckley, athletic and wiry, who had climbed halfway up the pyramid before a hand reached out and pulled her down, allowing a male to finally grab the cap.

WITHIN AN HOUR of their arrival at Long Beach harbor, Carole Brock and six of her crewmates were at the Copper Penny, a restaurant on Ocean

Avenue known for its industrial-strength coffee. They were there to meet with the chair of the Lesbian Rights Task Force of the Los Angeles chapter of the National Organization for Women, Johnnie Phelps, the no-nonsense WAC sergeant who thirty-five years earlier had told General Dwight D. Eisenhower that if he wanted to get rid of lesbians in the Army, he had better start with her. Phelps had been out of the Army thirty-four years now, but as she heard the *Norton Sound* women tell the story of the NIS investigation she marveled at how little had changed for gays, particularly for lesbians, since World War II—right down to the lists and informants.

Unlike these women, however, when Johnnie had faced the same witch-hunts in World War II, she had had no sense that they were unfair. She had figured one had to accept the rules. These women were not willing to play by the old rules.

Johnnie was also struck by how young they were. Alicia Harris was eighteen years old. She had been in the Navy just months before the investigation had begun, and now she was accused of being a lesbian. Most of the others were nineteen or twenty. Carole Brock, who was among the most outspoken and experienced, was twenty-two years old. Looking at them, Phelps, now a crusty fifty-eight-year-old printer, was not sure they could stand the pressures of a full-scale investigation. The most important thing, she said, was not to turn on one another. No matter what the investigators said—and they would say almost anything—the women must stick together.

The women understood and nodded in agreement. When they left the restaurant, it was with some trepidation—not about fighting back but about what might lie ahead. They were going against not only the brass on the *Norton Sound* and the U.S. Navy but the entire government, it seemed. Could they really expect to win?

———————

"HEY, QUEER."

Carole had learned to ignore the catcalls that always followed her through the Long Beach Naval Shipyard. Word of the lesbian investigation had spread throughout the installation within days of the *Norton Sound*'s arrival. Since it was the only ship in the yard with women, other sailors assumed any woman in the yard was a lesbian.

"Hey, dyke. Want some of the real thing?"

"Too bad, you dyke. You got caught."

The *Norton Sound* had been in Long Beach only a few days when nineteen of its women received letters of dismissal from the Navy for "unsuitability . . . because of participation in homosexual acts." Because of the regulation under which they were accused, none was entitled to a hearing, they were told. If they quietly left, which was clearly what the Navy wanted them to do, they would be assured of an honorable discharge. Several of the women had as much as ten years of service and knew they would lose substantial benefits if they were given less than honorable discharges. Still, none of the women quit.

Fear had turned to anger by the time the *Norton Sound*'s executive officer called the accused women into a meeting. As the women recalled it, Lieutenant Commander R. Myer began his remarks by saying that the Navy already knew who would be discharged and who would be retained among them. The outcomes of the hearings, he implied, were preordained.

Carole sat directly in front of Myer. If they knew that, why were all nineteen women being subjected to this, she asked. Why were only women being charged with homosexuality? There were gay men on board the ship. Why weren't they being investigated?

"I don't have to answer that question," Myer said.

Why were nearly all the black women under investigation? another sailor asked.

"I don't have to answer that question," Myer said again.

At that, the black women in the room walked. They had an appointment with a representative of the NAACP to keep.

Trying to garner some sympathy, Myer told those who remained that the investigation was hurting everyone, even the officers. "We're being harassed, too," he said.

"Are they calling you a queer?" Carole shot back. Then she demanded to see the statements being used as evidence against them, to which Myer replied that the captain would be happy to show them. Carole marched directly to the captain's stateroom and asked for the statements.

"I don't have them all yet," Commander James Seebirt told her.

Carole was stunned by his admission. The brass had charged them before seeing evidence against them.

WHEN SUSAN McGRIEVY of the American Civil Liberties Union reviewed the NIS statements against the nineteen women of the *Norton Sound,* she was stunned, too. The ship seemed like some kind of Sin City. At best, she thought she might prevent discharges of six of seven of the women. A dozen were clearly going to be kicked out. McGrievy kept the news to herself when she talked to the nineteen women, one by one, in Johnnie Phelps's comfortable suburban home in the San Gabriel Valley.

The women were nervous, not sure whom they could trust, and as McGrievy talked to them individually it became clear that they did not represent a Matlovich-style challenge to the military's gay regulations. Only some of these women were lesbians, though all of them wanted to stay in the Navy. Carole Brock believed that the homosexual sailors should identify themselves and mount a direct assault on the gay regulation, but such a strategy would only result in their immediate dismissal, with the potential of reinstatement being years down the road, if ever. They must defend themselves on the facts of the case and save appeals about the constitutionality of the regulation for a later time.

Against the full weight of the Navy and government, the women had one potentially powerful ally: the press. More than almost any institution in the United States, the military loathed bad publicity, which interfered with everything from recruiting new soldiers to procuring funds from Congress. The women might not be able to win in a Navy hearing but they could win in the court of public opinion if they were willing to go public. This raised the question of what the women were willing to say about their sexuality. The other causes célèbres, Matlovich and Berg, had publicly announced their homosexuality; since not all of the nineteen *Norton Sound* women were lesbians, however, this would not be possible. It seemed clear that they must stick together, take a common stance. Together, they would ask to be judged on their job performance. They would not answer questions about their sexual orientation, they decided. Their sex lives were nobody's business but their own.

Thus prepared, the ACLU went public in a press conference on June 13, 1980, four weeks after Helen Wilson had made her first statement to the NIS. The ACLU said it would go to court if the Navy tried to proceed with its plan to discharge the nineteen women without hearings. The blast of publicity worked. Within a week, Commander Seebirt announced that charges against eleven of the women had been dropped. The remaining eight would be charged with misconduct, not unsuitability, which entitled them to an administrative hearing.

The criteria for deciding who would be charged was imprecise, to say the least. For some women reported seen kissing, for example, one partner would be charged with lesbian misconduct but not the other. Many of the charges, however, did not involve kissing or any type of genital sexual activity but, rather, allegations that several of the sailors had given one another hickeys. This led to much banter among the suspects about the impending "Great Hickey Trial." Later, when Carole asked Lieutenant Commander Myer how they had decided which eight sailors to prosecute, he told her that they had just gone through the NIS statements and charged the eight who were named as lesbians most often.

In examining the NIS statements closely, attorney Susan McGrievy noticed that many were not signed by the sailors presumably alleging their crewmates' homosexuality. McGrievy talked to five of the twelve women who had made statements against the suspected lesbians. All five denied making the charges the NIS had attributed to them. The NIS agents had twisted their words, they said, and sometimes tried to make them sign statements that were complete fabrications. They had refused to sign.

Then McGrievy heard about NIS threats against women who declined to talk. As an ACLU attorney specializing in gay rights, it was hard for Susan to be startled by mere discrimination. That was an everyday occurrence in America. But she was galled by the routine use of intimidation and coercion. She believed that even people who did not think gays belonged in the military would be appalled by such tactics, yet they were typical witch-hunt tactics; it was how the policies against gays were executed. But this time it would be different, because this time people were going to find out about it.

ANNAPOLIS MIDSHIPMEN spend the summer between their freshman and sophomore years on cruises, getting a taste of sea life. For men, that means tours on submarines or aircraft carriers traveling to exotic ports. For Ruth Voor, who was not allowed on vessels that might see combat, the cruise meant time spent in small yard-patrol boats patrolling the Chesapeake Bay Area. Ruth preferred a pragmatic education: learning practical navigation, how to drive a ship, give orders, and raise flags. It was like summer camp, and on weekends off she ventured into New York City.

The news about the investigation on the USS *Norton Sound* was unsettling. Slowly, Ruth was coming to believe that she was a lesbian, and talk of the attempt at a sweeping purge of women jarred her. They really don't want me here, she thought. She briefly considered quitting the Naval Academy and getting out of the military; the more she thought about it, though, the less sense it made. She did not believe she had done anything wrong, she could not see why she should not be in the Navy, and she saw no reason to disrupt her life to satisfy an archaic regulation. Nevertheless, the unfolding drama on the *Norton Sound* gave Ruth pause. The regulation had seemed so silly, it was easy to disregard. Now she understood how serious the Navy was about it.

JUNE 22, 1980
CHRISTOPHER STREET WEST PARADE
WEST HOLLYWOOD, CALIFORNIA

CAROLE BROCK, her girlfriend, and three other women from the *Norton Sound* had spent Saturday at Disneyland and decided to meet at the Los Angeles gay pride parade commemorating the Stonewall riots in New York. It was a perfect Southern California afternoon. They found Susan McGrievy from the ACLU in the crowd. As they walked down Santa Monica Boulevard, they were stunned to see a huge banner stretching the breadth of the avenue, coming toward them: FREE THE *NORTON SOUND* EIGHT—IT'S NONE OF YOUR BUSINESS, UNCLE SAM!

The marchers, part of a contingent from the National Organization for Women, each wore a Navy Dixie cup cap with one of the eight charged sailors' names written in black Magic Marker on each bill. Johnnie Phelps grinned broadly as Carole and the other *Norton Sound* women fell in line with the NOW contingent. She had worried that they would not be able to stand up to the pressures of the Navy when the going got tough.

Everything from her experience in the military told Phelps that in the end people buckled. Now she knew better. Times were changing.

Days later, the San Francisco Gay Freedom Parade invited the *Norton Sound* Eight to come north and be their parade's grand marshals. A native of San Jose, Carole was delighted at the prospect. "If you want to stay in the Navy, don't go," an attorney warned her, but Carole decided to go anyway. She had always wanted to fight the *Norton Sound* case as a gay-rights issue rather than a privacy-rights one; in a way, the parade gave her that chance.

A week later, under crystalline blue skies in San Francisco, Carole marched at the head of the parade. The festive rainbow flags that former Army private Gilbert Baker had designed for the gay parade two years earlier had become all but official symbols of the gay movement. For the week preceding the city's celebration, they fluttered from every lamp on Market Street, San Francisco's main thoroughfare. Carole had come to parades here before, but she was not prepared for such a day as this, when at the moment the Navy had hoped to cast her into disgrace she instead strode proudly in front of 300,000 spectators on the high holy day of the national gay movement.

After the parade, a crowd of 200,000 gathered in front of San Francisco's city hall. As grand marshal, Carole was introduced and then asked to speak. The twenty-two-year-old petty officer second class stared at the ocean of people before her, all applauding and cheering. Here and there, she made out this or that old friend from San Jose or Piedmont Hills High School, shouting out her name and waving. The last month had been such an isolating experience, during which she had masked so much anxiety with bravado, that Carole felt overwhelmed by the moment. She also felt vaguely embarrassed that she could not be perfectly honest: She could not say, Yes, I am a lesbian and this is a stupid policy that has to go. Tears had welled in her eyes as the applause rose up from the huge plaza. "I don't know what else to say except thank you for all of your support," was the best she could do. And then she was overwhelmed again and could say no more.

The number and diversity of the groups marching that day showed once again how far homosexuals had come in asserting themselves in the eleven years since the Stonewall riots. Leading the parade was a contingent of lesbian and gay delegates to the 1980 Democratic National Convention to be held in August in New York City. Seventy-six delegates and alternates made the gay caucus larger than the delegations of twenty states, a dramatic increase from the 1976 convention, in which there had been only four openly gay delegates. With a crucial election shaping up between President Carter and his conservative challenger, former California governor Ronald Reagan, gays were flexing more muscle in the electoral process than ever. In deference to that fact, Governor Edmund Brown, Jr., had issued a proclamation decreeing Gay Freedom Week in California. The Democratic platform committee had already written an endorsement of gay civil rights into the draft of the party platform—the first time any political party had directly addressed homosexual concerns. That such a statement provoked hardly any controversy measured the light-years gays had traveled since Jim Foster first broached the gay issue at the 1972 convention.

Foster's own political career in 1980 demonstrated how deeply gays had managed to involve themselves in the political process. As northern California campaign manager for Senator Edward Kennedy's campaign, Jim had helped rally the liberal votes that allowed the Massachusetts senator to overwhelm Carter in the California primary. "You guys give me a lot of talk," Kennedy later said to a group of political advisers at a political cocktail party as he warmly embraced Foster. "Jim Foster gave me California."

THESE WERE THE GLORY DAYS of the gay movement, the time before the era of political reaction and still-nascent virological horrors that would cast long, cold shadows over it. In the summer months of 1980, however, it seemed that everything was about to change for gay people in America, and in the military, too.

For example, in reviewing the 1976 discharge of Miriam Ben-Shalom from the Army Reserves, Judge Terence Evans ruled that the regulation barring gays from serving in the Army violated the First, Fifth, and Ninth amendments of the Constitution. "Constitutional privacy principles clearly protect one's sexual preference in and of themselves from governmental regulation," he wrote. Although a growing number of federal judges had made such rulings over the past several years, Evans went a step further in ordering the Army to reinstate the schoolteacher into the Army Reserves.

Unlike the cases of Leonard Matlovich or Copy Berg, Ben-Shalom's dismissal stemmed solely from her statements to the press that she was gay and not from any evidence that she had ever engaged in homosexual conduct. Judge Evans ruled, however, that even if the federal government could establish homosexual conduct by Ben-Shalom, it would then have to prove why such conduct made her unsuitable for the Army Reserves. Since the military had not provided such proof, the court demanded that Ben-Shalom be reinstated into the Army Reserves. Coming after the appeals courts' decisions in the Matlovich and Berg cases, the courts appeared ever nearer to recognizing the rights of gays to serve in the armed forces. As legal expert Dr. Rhonda Rivera later wrote of these months, "At that particular moment in history, gay rights in the military seemed within reach."

Pressure was also mounting on President Carter to make a dramatic gesture to end this particular government-mandated discrimination. Though changes in the Uniform Code of Military Justice would have to clear Congress, the regulation against homosexuals had never been approved by any legislature; they were, instead, Department of Defense administrative regulations, which could be changed with a stroke of the Defense Secretary's pen. Even after he narrowly defeated Kennedy for the presidential nomination, Carter continued to face gay voter antipathy. When Republican congressman John Anderson announced an independent presidential candidacy and included a sweeping endorsement of gay rights as part of his socially liberal but fiscally conservative platform, gays deserted the Democratic fold in droves to work on his campaign, particularly in states such as New York and California, which Carter needed to take if he was to win reelection.

Though the issue of admission of homosexuals to the military had never been at the top of gay leaders' political demands, it became the focus of increased lobbying because it represented a concession that Carter could grant without having to go to Congress. The Carter administration was intransigent on the issue of allowing gays in the military. In one crucial memo, the suggestion was dismissed with the observation that even if Carter did throw out the regulation by executive fiat, conservatives would be on the floor of Congress the next day to sponsor legislation permanently barring gays from serving. Such a law would have the effect of casting the regulation in stone, White House aides candidly told gay activists, delaying future reform even further. The administration promised to "study" reforming military policy, and, perhaps to compromise, White House domestic-policy representatives gave private assurances that a second Carter administration would consider ending the ban on gays receiving security clearances. Though such promises were never put into writing and never circulated outside a small circle of gay leaders, they were the payoff for gay Democratic votes. Their gentlemen's agreement also satisfied a key concern of the Carter camp—that the President did not have to declare himself for gay civil rights.

Carole Brock sensed something new in the air as she waved goodbye to her friends and prepared to fly back to Los Angeles from the San Francisco parade. Her cause was a national cause, she saw. With so much support, they could win. Newfound confidence steeled her resolve to make her hearing into a showcase for gay rights. She had been informed that she would be the last of the eight to go before the administrative separation board, so her testimony would not influence the board's ruminations on the other sailors. Their cases would already have been heard. Her mind percolated with ideas. Gay police officers were now being recruited by the San Francisco Police Department, she knew. Why not get the police chief to testify that gays were not undermining the good order, discipline, and morale of that paramilitary organization? There were a number of such arguments she could make, and gay activists in San Francisco were ready to help her. By the end of the gay parade, Carole Brock was optimistic. They might not win their cases, but they could change the world.

———————

THE TRUE FUTURE of the gay community, however, would be dominated less by the confluence of the activists in the 1980 parade than by a strange malaise felt that day by a handful of young men. There was, for example, a French-Canadian airline steward who watched the floats along Market Street and stopped for a while at the Civic Center Plaza. He had a small scar under his right ear where doctors had just removed a strange skin cancer. It was Kaposi's sarcoma, they said, a disease usually found in aging men of Mediterranean or Jewish extraction. They had never seen it before on such a young and healthy man. And there were others at the parade plagued by fevers of unknown origin and chronic fatigue. The lives of these people would determine the future decade of homosexual history more than any federal judge or administration official. For many bystanders at the parade, for people like Jim Foster and Danny Flaherty and Leonard Matlovich, the parade marked the last clear memory of the cheerful time *before*. The recent past had given these people triumphs beyond anything they had dared to imagine; the impending future would offer challenges beyond anything they had ever feared.

———————

AT THE LONG BEACH NAVAL SHIPYARD, the *Norton Sound* Eight were considered more infamous than famous. With their case receiving front-page coverage almost daily in Southern California, everyone on board felt obliged to take sides, and petty harassment of the women escalated. The words "Dykes Den" were spray-painted in the stairway leading to the women's berthing area. Pornography with lesbian themes was taped regularly to the berthing area's door. Other graffiti labeled the female mess area the "Dyke's Diner." Some of the enlisted crewmen were outspoken in support of them: their girlfriends had been among those accused.

The ship's command aggravated the women's problems by engaging in its own form of harassment. Armed guards were stationed around the clock in the female berthing area, presumably to prevent the nonstop lovemaking alleged by the NIS investigation. When the ship's entire crew assembled for morning quarters one day, the executive officer ordered all the sailors to avoid contact with the eight women charged with homosexuality. "Unless you have to work with them, don't have anything to do with these women," he commanded.

Carole had transferred off the ship to shore patrol, but even this did not deter daily catcalls from the men, and now Carole noticed men in three-piece suits had started following her whenever she left the base. She might go as far as San Diego or into Los Angeles, but there they'd be, not particularly hiding the fact they were watching her. It was so strange. Two months ago, she had been an enthusiastic member of the United States Navy and now, because of one word that had been applied to her, she was followed like a criminal. Other *Norton Sound* defendants noticed tails, too, and clicks on their telephones.

Navy officials had problems of their own. The dates of the discharge hearings were near and they still had not accumulated evidence that would pass muster, even in the "anything goes" format of nonjudicial administrative hearings. For this reason, they were particularly interested in Petty Officer Joyce Arnold, who had been named on at least one statement as a lesbian and was a mother involved in a custody suit for her two children. Any hint that she was a lesbian could cost her her children. NIS agents would not comment on whether she was threatened with the loss of her children, but defense attorneys advanced the notion that she was. Such intimidation was not unusual in gay-related cases in the years that followed.

For whatever reason, it was clear that both the NIS and the ship's executive officer had targeted Arnold as a sailor likely to inform on the other women. In one week alone, Arnold later testified, the executive officer called her into his cabin on four separate occasions to insist that she accuse other women of lesbianism. NIS agents also summoned her again and again, mentioning that she might be accused of being homosexual herself if she did not name other homosexuals. Finally, after two months of such pressure, Arnold made a statement of accusation. The NIS still did not let up, and Arnold provided a second statement and a third, until she had given five statements accusing other *Norton Sound* women, including a number of her close friends, of being lesbians. Word spread quickly on the ship.

As the hearings neared, the growing tension was particularly difficult for the youngest of the eight women: Alicia Harris, just months past her eighteenth birthday. She had been an honors student in her high school, college material, but she was also the youngest in a family of six children from Twenty-second and State streets on the impoverished South Side of Chicago. Her parents had signed for her to go into the Navy when she was seventeen, wishing her the job training and educational benefits that would let her escape from the dismal future that awaited so many other youngsters from her neighborhood. Now, after just a few months in the Navy, Alicia's name was in newspapers from coast to coast. Every day, she endured more harassment from the Navy and more catcalls from men. Harris lapsed into a severe depression. Learning how the NIS went about securing their "evidence" against her, she sometimes said weakly, "I'm still an American citizen, no matter what they say I did."

Finally, she thought she could not stand another day. She offered the acceptance of an immediate discharge. But the Navy would not let her out. Hoping to force a discharge, Harris did not show up at her regular 5:30 A.M. shift in the enlisted mess. This brought quick charges of insubordination and a penalty of three days in the brig. But there was no women's brig in Long Beach. Instead, Harris was escorted to a nearby federal prison to do her time. For most girls Harris's age, the most difficult dilemma is choosing a dress to wear to the high school prom. But Alicia Harris was in the United States military and accused of being a lesbian, so that meant the teenager was in a federal prison cell, where she was fed just bread and water for three days.

— 37 —

"Until After November"

AUGUST 4, 1980
USS *NORTON SOUND*
LONG BEACH NAVAL SHIPYARD
LONG BEACH, CALIFORNIA

PROTESTERS HAD GATHERED outside gate nine of the Naval facility at 8:30 A.M. and stretched a huge banner across the entrance: IT'S NONE OF YOUR BUSINESS, UNCLE SAM! Already the temperature had broken seventy degrees; it would be a hot day. A thirty-member contingent from the National Organization for Women chanted:

> Turn the Navy upside down
> Free the women of the *Norton Sound*

Johnnie Phelps was on hand to give interviews about comparable witch-hunts in the 1940s. She wore a green hard hat with the bumper sticker WE ARE FAMILY, although this anthem of gay military personnel was deemed "too disco" by some picketers. Instead, protesters chanted a refrain that alluded to charges that women had hugged each other in the women's berthing area:

> Dare to struggle, dare to win,
> Dare to snuggle, dare to grin.

The roster of the *Norton Sound* Eight reflected a cross section of the women to be found in the new Navy. One had already been named a "Sailor of the Quarter"; others had compiled records that included accelerated promotions and top grades at their training schools. They hailed from all-American places such as Pelican Rapids, Minnesota; Rumford, Maine; Orlando, Florida; and San Jose, California. The three black recruits came from the nation's centers of urban poverty: Chicago, the Bronx, and Newark. In an inelegant piece of staging, the Navy had, until the day of the first hearing, planned to try the three black women as one group. Only objections from their lawyers gained the three separate hearings. The three-member administrative separation board first took up the case of Petty Officer Tangela Gaskins.

Gaskins, twenty-five, had joined the Navy eighteen months earlier, hoping to earn an education that would lead to college and an accounting degree. She wanted to make enough money to send her eight-year-old son to private schools. Gaskins had risen from seaman to petty officer third class in seven months, an impressive feat. She was the first black woman to advance beyond the deck crew on the *Norton Sound,* an accomplishment that had stirred some jealousy among lower-ranking women. Strikingly attractive, with high cheekbones and a broad, easy smile, Gaskins was also the ship's fashion plate. She was suspected of being a lesbian, it seemed, because she rejected the passes of male crew members. The real reason for her refusal was that she had a civilian boyfriend with whom she spent nearly every night.

While protesters shouted outside the base gates, Gaskins's hearing came to order in a tiny stateroom aboard the USS *Norton Sound.* Despite the presence of a spacious courtroom only a few hundred yards from the ship's berth, the Navy had wanted the hearing to be held on board, perhaps to restrict the number of reporters who could fit into the room. Gaskins's attorneys were escorted on and off the ship under armed guard. Although the Navy lawyers led off with what they seemed to think was their strongest case, the evidence lodged against Gaskins was problematic.

The Navy's first witness, Seaman Tammy Knehr, said she had seen Gaskins and crewmate Wendi Williams giggling together on a bunk in the women's berthing area. She had not seen any sexual activity between the two because it was too dark, but the situation looked "queer" to her. Knehr's other bombshell was that while rifling through Williams's mail she had come across a card from Gaskins that was signed "Love, Tange." Said Knehr, "If someone said that to me, I would think they were queer."

The second witness against Gaskins was Seaman Yvonne Nedrick, who testified that Gaskins had once confided to her that she was gay. There were no witnesses to the conversation, nor had she ever seen Gaskins participate in any conduct that could be interpreted as homosexual. Joyce Arnold testified that she had once seen Gaskins reading a book about homosexuality. Gaskins, Arnold claimed, had once said she was bisexual. But she had never seen any lesbian behavior.

Seaman Apprentice Pamela Tepstein was the only person who claimed to have seen anything resembling physical contact between Gaskins and another woman. Gaskins had kissed shipmate Williams on the mouth, she said. In fact, Tepstein's statement accused a dozen *Norton Sound* women of engaging in brazen shipboard sex, providing the NIS with some of the only hard evidence it had accumulated in its exhaustive investigation. But Tepstein could not attend the hearing in person. She had been checked into the Navy hospital in Long Beach. When two Navy officers had gone to escort Tepstein to the hearing, she had yelled that she never wanted to step aboard the *Norton Sound* again, then took off screaming down a hospital hallway. Tepstein was then committed to the hospital for psychiatric testing. Not to be deterred, Navy prosecutors simply submitted Tepstein's statement in writing.

Tepstein's allegations against the dozen *Norton Sound* women were not unprecedented. In boot camp, she had accused an officer of being a lesbian, saying, "I just wanted some attention." As for her credibility, the ship's master-at-arms testified, "I wouldn't believe anything she said. . . . If Tepstein told me it was night outside, I would go out and check."

The defense produced a dozen witnesses: Gaskins's fiancé, a local college student, testified that they slept together five nights a week and that they planned to marry when he graduated from college. Another *Norton Sound* crewman testified that he had lived with Gaskins for two months before her engagement to the other witness. Both men were then asked to describe the quality of their sexual relations with Gaskins and to discuss any sexual problems they had had. Both said there were not any problems.

The most damning testimony concerned the tactics the NIS had used in securing their evidence against Gaskins and the others. Under cross-examination, Arnold, for example, testified that the NIS had falsified at least one statement against Gaskins and coerced her into providing others. "Agent [John] Stevens [of the Naval Investigative Service] said I could be labeled as a homosexual if I withheld evidence," she said. Petty Officer Lynn Batey testified that the same agent used similar coercion against her. "I told him all I knew was rumors. He told me if I didn't tell him any evidence, I could be court-martialed like the others." Frightened, Batey had given thirty names to NIS investigators.

Defense attorneys asked the Navy to produce the NIS agents to testify at the hearing about their tactics. Even one panel member, a reserve officer, said he would like to question the NIS agents himself. "I've had too much experience with NIS agents," he said pointedly. The senior board member, Commander Francis Knipe, however, ruled that the agents would not be obliged to appear. They were civilians, outside the jurisdiction of military subpoenas. As the agents' employer, the Navy, of course, could order the agents to appear, but such orders were not forthcoming.

On the fourth day of the hearing, the three-member administrative panel took thirty minutes to reach its decision. "Petty Officer Gaskins, the board finds there is no credible evidence the respondent engaged in homosexual acts and recommends retention," Commander Knipe said.

Gaskins fell weeping into the arms of attorney Susan McGrievy. "Thanks for believing in me," she said. Outside the hearing room, she remained bitter about the experience. Although she had won the case, she faced an even more crucial battle ahead. Her mother, who had been tending Gaskins's son, was horrified at the lesbian charges against her daughter and went to court to seize custody of the child. "The guys think there are only two types of females in the Navy," Tangela Gaskins said.

"You're either there to serve the men—you're a whore—or else you are a queer. They just discredited my name, myself, destroyed my life. I've been angry over it. I've cried about it. I've laughed about it. But it's no joke."

———————

THE VERDICT CONVINCED Carole Brock that the group had made the right decision when they had moved to go public. The Navy frequently succeeded in obtaining separations with evidence even less substantial than what had been offered in the Gaskins case. The only difference was that now people were watching. Seven years of an all-volunteer armed forces had dramatically changed the public's and the media's attitudes toward military regulations concerning off-duty conduct. For most of the 1970s, television advertising campaigns had promoted the military less as a patriotic calling than as a job with unparalleled training and educational benefits. As military work became viewed increasingly as a job like any other there were growing questions about regulations that did not relate specifically to a soldier's ability to do the work at hand.

Merciless publicity followed the Gaskins hearing. The *Norton Sound* was called the "Love Boat" and the "Lust Boat." One magazine article referred to it as the "Ship of Shame"; another called it "The Ship That Dare Not Speak Its Name."

The day after the verdict, CBS television commentator Bill Stout in Los Angeles loosed a stinging attack on the "shocking" treatment of the *Norton Sound* Eight. "All of those women already have been dragged through the mud of notoriety, their sex lives discussed in detail in public," Stout said. "All to counter charges consisting mainly of rumors and hearsay and whispered allegations—almost none of which would be allowed in even the most poorly run court of civilian law. That's the sordid farce the Navy is playing aboard the *Norton Sound*. . . . And if it all sounds like an echo from the years of anti-Communist witch-hunting—well, it is."

Despite all the press coverage, defense attorney McGrievy remained frustrated at the relatively minor focus on the coercive tactics of the NIS. Although the testimony concerning threats and intimidation was dutifully reported, McGrievy began lecturing reporters that this was the *real* story of the *Norton Sound*. Not that the military kicked people out for being gay but *how* they did it. Reporters, however, seemed strangely uninterested. Some were outright skeptical that such things really happened in the United States and avoided reporting on what they considered the rhetorical excesses of defense lawyers.

———————

ALTHOUGH THE OUTCRY over the *Norton Sound* case produced widespread criticism of the military's policy of excluding homosexuals, the pace of gay-related discharges accelerated on military bases across the country.

According to Defense Department figures, the four services ejected 1,966 enlisted personnel for homosexuality in fiscal year 1980, more than twice the number discharged five years earlier. Gay discharges *increased* during the Carter administration; in fact, the last year of this Democratic presidency saw more such separations than at any time since the McCarthy era. The Navy accounted for nearly one-half of the total, the Army's tally soared by more than 30 percent between 1979 and 1980, and Air Force gay discharges increased by more than 20 percent in that year. The rigid enforcement of the gay regulations was evident not only in statistics but in the brutality with which those under investigation, particularly women, were treated.

A purge of suspected lesbians at Goodfellow Air Force Base in Texas resulted in four discharges. Frustrated they could not gather more names, investigative agents subjected women to extraordinary harassment. Twenty-one-year-old Pam Burwell, for example, was told to remove every grass clipping from a field, but there were no rakes for the job, so she had to do it with her hands. It was August 1980. Texas was in the grip of one of the worst heat waves that region had seen in nearly a century, and she was ordered to rake fields with her hands.

One day as Burwell crawled through the field, a noncommissioned officer threw a canister of tear gas at her. Mindful that she might be shot if she tried to run away, she stumbled blindly toward the perimeter and tripped over coils of razor-sharp concertina wire that surrounded the field. More than a decade later, she still bore the scars.

Eighteen women came under investigation at the North Island Naval Air Station in San Diego in 1980. Another half dozen were charged in a lesbian purge at Fort McPherson and Fort Stewart in Georgia. Thirty gay airmen came under investigation at Malmstron Air Force Base near Great Falls, Montana, during the summer of 1980, and at least eight were discharged. At least two airmen had nervous breakdowns after OSI interrogations, according to a report in the *Gay Community News*. Still another investigation focused on the women's volleyball team at the United States Air Force Academy in Colorado Springs. This investigation followed a probe of the women's softball team at West Point.

At the Defense Language Institute in Monterey, California, an even larger purge was under way, focused on sailors with the Naval Security Group studying at the language school. Because DLI graduates go on to work in some of the most sensitive cryptographic posts in the military, the school had long been a site where homosexuals were pursued aggressively. Even by DLI standards, however, the investigation undertaken in the summer of 1980 was remarkable.

It began when two enlisted men confessed they were gay to their commanding officer in order to get out of the Navy. The Navy maintained it needed proof of their homosexuality, however, so the two men provided names of other sailors with whom they had had sex. Before the NIS interrogations were over, investigators had targeted between twenty-five and thirty-five suspected gay servicemen. According to the last public accounting offered by the Navy, at least seven were discharged in that investigation. Only one chose to fight; the others quietly accepted their walking papers. An Army spokesman told *The Advocate*, "We just cannot have any type of situation in any person's past or present that could cause them to have to divulge information. . . . It's not like a witch hunt."

Virtually all of the hundreds of service members dismissed for homosexuality during the summer months of 1980 waived their right to a hearing and left the service quietly. By declining to fight, gay service members themselves helped perpetuate the military's antigay regulation. Military commands throughout the country would have been virtually paralyzed if every person charged with homosexuality exercised his or her rights and demanded a hearing. But that did not happen.

AUGUST 11, 1980
CIRCUS DISCO
HOLLYWOOD, CALIFORNIA

CAROLE BROCK and her friends from the *Norton Sound* arrived at the fund-raiser early, but actor Ed Asner was already there and so was television producer Norman Lear. The stereo system blasted "Funkytown" and "Fame" and the Village People's "In the Navy," and ACLU lawyers introduced Carole and the other crew members to the celebrities who were there to raise money for the defense of the women of the *Norton Sound*. There was already talk about buyers for a movie deal based on the *Norton Sound* case. Accusations of homosexuality had once meant ignominy and suicide. Now, they meant press conferences, celebrity fund-raisers, and meetings with entertainment lawyers in Beverly Hills. Although most accused gay service members continued quietly to accept their discharges, for those people who were willing to fight, times were changing.

ON THE MORNING of the fund-raiser, a new board convened in Long Beach aboard the *Norton Sound* to take up charges against Seaman Barbara Lee Underwood. Shaken by the extensive publicity the first hearing had engendered in Southern California, the Navy countered by trying to muzzle the press, allowing no more than three reporters in the small hearing room aboard ship. Defense lawyers argued against the restriction, citing the constitutional guarantee to a public hearing, but the Navy was adamant.

More than any of the *Norton Sound* Eight, twenty-two-year-old Seaman Barbara Lee Underwood was desperate to stay in the Navy. She had grown up on the huge Navy training base in Orlando, the daughter of a retired chief petty officer, and had signed up with the Navy just eighteen months earlier.

The Navy apparently believed it had a strong case against Underwood, but one witness's testimony consisted of nothing more than his having heard his girlfriend say that "Puppy" Underwood was gay. Tammy Knehr, who had also testified against Gaskins, reported that Underwood had once told her she "went for women instead of men." Another witness said that Puppy had once wet two fingers and put them in her ear in an attempt to give her an "eargasm," proof for her that Underwood was a lesbian.

Underwood's attorneys presented fourteen witnesses, including four chief petty officers who testified that even if Puppy was gay, she was welcome on their crews anytime. The clinchers were two men with whom Underwood had gone to bed who stepped forward to give details of their sexual liaisons. One, a petty officer first class who was Underwood's supervisor, answered questions not only about the circumstances of their intercourse but about its quality. Underwood, he said, was a "responsive" lover who appeared to enjoy heterosexual sex.

Meanwhile, attorney Copilow managed to have entered in the record the *Norton Sound*'s executive officer's statement that the results of the administrative hearings were "preordained." This, even more than the poor quality of evidence against Underwood, put the panel on the spot. To find her guilty would make it appear as if they were merely carrying out their superiors' orders.

On the fourth day of Underwood's hearing, the panel took fifty-five minutes to reach a two-to-one decision that Underwood should be retained in the Navy.

It was only the press attention, Carole Brock felt, that had shamed the Navy into this second verdict. Under quieter circumstances, both Gaskins and Underwood would be in civilian clothes by now. But no matter how much they might want to end the publicity, after accusing twenty-nine women of being lesbian, she believed, Navy officials could not very well walk away now and say it had all been a mistake. They would have to hang somebody before they could quit.

Three thousand miles from the Long Beach Naval Shipyard, aides in the White House carefully watched the *Norton Sound* case. On August 15, one day after the Underwood verdict, after meeting with gay leaders working on the Carter campaign, a White House staffer drafted a memo on gay concerns. Under Part III, headlinéd SUBSTANCE, was the note: "Do something with the USS *Norton Sound*." In response, another presidential staffer had scrawled alongside, "Prevent future purges until after November."

— 38 —

Interregnum

AUGUST 16, 1980
PENNSYLVANIA AVENUE
WASHINGTON, D.C.

AT EQUUS, a new gay bar located down the block from the Marine Corps barracks, patrons were beginning to eye one another with greater earnestness. Closing time was approaching and the 1:00 A.M. compromises needed to be made soon.

While pool balls clicked in the back of the bar, a clamor began outside. Equus owner Rick Holloway turned toward the door to investigate the ruckus as a Marine burst into the bar shouting about "faggots" and floored Holloway with a punch in the face. More Marines rushed in behind him— a mob of 150 carrying sticks and shouting antigay slogans had surged from their redbrick barracks and raced down Pennsylvania Avenue to the bar.

"C'mon, faggots—too afraid to fight?" some yelled. Glass shattered as the Marines knocked out the windows.

It was the sixth attack on the bar in the four months since Equus had taken over the space from Barb's Place, a topless bar and favorite leatherneck hangout. Outside, Marines overturned trash cans and shouted for the faggots to come out and fight. Inside, their companions picked up bar stools and approached the men who cowered in the back of the bar.

A bartender began throwing beer mugs at the Marines, and then, from behind the pool tables, a muscular young man with closely cropped hair leapt forward and shouted, "Fall back and retreat!" He grabbed a pool cue, rushing toward the assailants. There was momentary confusion and then the wail of police sirens. The Marines turned and ran out of the bar, pursued by one angry gay ex-Marine. The mob fought the police officers who arrived on the scene but fell back to their barracks when reinforcements arrived.

The increase in gay investigations and prosecutions within the military during the summer of 1980 seemed to produce a corresponding surge in antigay violence by heterosexual GIs. Confrontations like the one at Equus were perhaps inevitable. Every investigation in every branch of the service had the effect of indoctrinating hundreds of thousands of young Americans to believe that violence toward homosexuals and disrespect of them were acceptable.

Although antigay assaults by military personnel occurred throughout the country, in no locale were they more pronounced than in Washington, D.C., where a large contingent of Marines handled government guard duties. Over the preceding few months in 1980, police had arrested several Marines after a series of stabbings and beatings of gay men at the Iwo Jima Memorial, a popular cruising spot in Arlington. Ironically, the soldiers' victims were sometimes military people themselves, engaging in furtive park cruising because they feared that going to gay bars would make them vulnerable to military witch-hunts. Months before the August attack, several Marines had thrown a tear-gas bomb into a lesbian bar. Even as Equus owners swept up broken glass from the Saturday night attack, platoons of Marine joggers were doing their daily runs past gay businesses near Barracks Row, repeating cadences shouted out by their platoon sergeant: "Stamp out fags. Stamp out fags."

No issue seemed too trivial for the Marines to take up against gays. Earlier in 1980, for example, one Marine detachment refused to accept a $2,500 donation for its annual Toys for Tots program because it came from gay donors. "Some of our regulations won't let us associate with any group that might reflect negatively on the Marine Corps," a Marine spokesman said. "We would prefer that they donate toys anonymously."

Though news of mobs of Marines attacking civilians would normally send military officials into an uproar, the commander of the Marine barracks in Washington was unperturbed about the Equus incident. "The publicity that has come out of this has blown the whole situation out of hand," Colonel John Monahan told *The Washington Post*. "I don't think they were up there to bother gays, but went up to have a good time." Monahan promised a "voluntary collection" to pay for damage to the bar, but, in fact, no reparations were made.

Down Pennsylvania Avenue at the White House, the Carter staff worried that the attack on Equus might alienate gays and worried that taking a position against such attacks might alienate an even larger voting constituency. So the administration that had defined itself by its commitment to human rights remained silent and the purges and hearings continued.

AUGUST 18, 1980
USS *NORTON SOUND*
LONG BEACH NAVAL SHIPYARD
LONG BEACH, CALIFORNIA

ALICIA HARRIS WAS ASKED to stand while the chairman of the administrative separation board read his decision: "The findings of the board are that the defendant has engaged in homosexual activity aboard the ship," the officer read. "It is the recommendation that she be given a general discharge under honorable conditions."

Four hours later, the discharge hearing for Wendi Williams began. The testimony against Williams was much the same as that against Harris. Their crewmate Yvonne Nedrick claimed to have seen them kiss. Under cross-examination, Nedrick admitted to four fistfights with Williams. She also said she would kill Williams if she had the chance but added that she would never lie about the sailor, so her testimony stood. Helen Wilson, whose statement had begun the investigation three months earlier, reported having seen Williams and Harris on a couch together late one night. They were fully clothed, she said, but it looked sexual to her.

Throughout the hearing, looking up only occasionally, Wendi Williams sat at the defense table drawing pictures of a small rubber Donald Duck doll she kept propped in front of her. She was going to be found guilty, she knew, because her defense, like that of Alicia Harris, lacked the component that had saved Tangela Gaskins and Barbara Lee Underwood. Neither she nor Harris had men to testify about any heterosexual relationships and to provide a positive review of the women's sexual performance.

"I would like—if this board decides to discharge me—to discharge me for stupidity, not for misconduct," Williams said softly to the board shortly before the panel went into deliberations. "My work in the Navy has been real good. Therefore, I must be real dumb—the dumbest nigger in the Navy—if I had let these things happen, to commit these acts in a room with sixty people where they could see me."

The unanimous verdict was returned on the afternoon of August 20. Williams listened emotionlessly, her chin set on her hand.

Wendi Williams, the panel ruled, was guilty of "one or more homosexual acts," and it ordered she be dismissed from the United States Navy with a general discharge under honorable conditions.

The Navy had their convictions. Now they could call the whole thing off.

The next day, Commander James Seebirt told Carole Brock that the pending charges against the remaining four women were being dropped for "insufficient evidence."

"I could have told you that three months ago," snapped Brock.

"It's over, it's done, it's through," he said.

"Maybe for you it is," Carole answered.

In a similar announcement to the other three defendants of the *Norton Sound* Eight, Seebirt stressed that he had no "personal hard feelings" toward any of them. Later that day, Carole drove into the Los Angeles ACLU office.

"Can I tell now?" she asked a lawyer.

The answer was no. If Brock was to come out now as homosexual, she would be charged again and the whole investigation might be resurrected. Her admission would also surely bring down Carole's girlfriend, who was still on the *Norton Sound* crew.

Hours later, Carole and Susan McGrievy spoke to a crowd of reporters at the ACLU headquarters. Johnnie Phelps watched from the sidelines, marveling at how little it took—just a handful of young women refusing to acquiesce—to bring the Navy to its knees.

The newspaper pictures from the press conferences that afternoon showed Carole Brock beaming at the victory they had achieved. But in fact, Brock was more angry than relieved—angry at the Navy for subjecting them to the three-month ordeal, angrier that she would never get her day in court. Even if she could not say she was a lesbian, she had wanted to tell what the Navy had done, how the Naval Investigative Service had coerced witnesses, fabricated statements, and then disappeared when the hearings started. With all the focus on this or that defendant, the totality of a lesbian witch-hunt had never been described. The whole story was still untold, and she was angry.

For its part, through press spokesman Lieutenant Mark Baker, the Navy said, "The decision was made after carefully reviewing all the facts and testimony that could conceivably bear on the remaining four cases." As they had throughout the investigation, Commander Seebirt and all other Navy officials refused to comment at all. Privately, Navy officers admitted that the evidence in the *Norton Sound* case was not any less sufficient than that commonly used in any discharge hearing. However, typically, nobody ever knew about it.

———————

TWO WEEKS AFTER THE CHARGES against the *Norton Sound* Eight were dismissed, Judge Gerhard Gesell delivered a stinging critique of the military's ban on gay soldiers and ruled that Leonard Matlovich be reinstated into the United States Air Force; reinstated at the rank he would have achieved had he never been dismissed in 1975 and with all back pay and with the condition that the Air Force not attempt to bar his later reenlistment.

It had been two years since the U.S. Court of Appeals had remanded the case to Gesell with the order that the Air Force clarify what would constitute an exception to its policy of banning all homosexuals. The Air Force had at first delivered a "declaration" that explained how the service processed discharges, but it did not define the criteria upon which it might make an exception to its policy. When that proved unacceptable, the service submitted several affidavits with different guidelines as to what might constitute an acceptable homosexual. After a while, it seemed clear that the Air Force was temporizing with these different drafts to keep Matlovich out of the Air Force, and the case bottled up at the level of the federal district court, where it would do the minimum damage to the legal status of the policies.

Judge Gesell condemned the stalling: The Pentagon, he ruled, had engaged in "perverse behavior" by offering these numerous and often contradictory explanations for their policy. Gesell's terse two-page ruling on September 9 ordered the Air Force to put Matlovich back in uniform by December 5, 1980. Since Copy Berg's case had been legally joined to Matlovich's appeal, the ruling also had the effect of reinstating Berg in the Navy. The order shook the Pentagon. Deputy Defense Secretary Graham Claytor, Jr., announced a task force of lawyers to study the ruling and recommend grounds for appeal.

The national commander of the American Legion commented, "Our enemies in the world must be very pleased with the court order."

In one last desperate effort to keep the nation's most famous homosexual out of the Air Force, the Pentagon offered Matlovich a cash settlement if he agreed not to return. No one at the Defense Department really expected Matlovich to take it. He was a crusader, someone who had declared he was gay specifically to make a test case. Few in the Pentagon believed he would stop short of the Supreme Court. And there were plenty of Defense Department attorneys who thought he might win. The settlement was simply a last-ditch effort. Even as the Air Force made their financial offer, orders were being drawn up to reinstate Matlovich at the rank of senior master sergeant. His duty station was being selected. Preparations were being made to admit him by the December 5 deadline.

In his office at the E-ring of the Pentagon, Pete Randell was elated. Although the ruling applied only to Matlovich and was not won on broad constitutional grounds, he knew the symbolic impact that just one openly gay airman would have. Once Matlovich was back in uniform, the services would never again be able to say that the presence of homosexuals would do irreparable damage to their good order, discipline, and morale. Matlovich would return to work and the sky wouldn't fall and the Air Force would do just fine. With one gay in uniform, it would be harder to stop a second, and a third, and then thousands more.

Randell had a new job—he was now executive director of the Air Force Board of Correction for Military Records. He'd just been selected as one of the Outstanding Young Men in America by the U.S. Jaycees. He had everything going for him.

AFTER THE HEARINGS were concluded, the USS *Norton Sound* left its berth in Long Beach to return to Port Hueneme. Carole Brock had taken leave time to drive back to the ship's home port by herself rather than sail. Her anger persisted. The end of the investigation had brought little relief.

Many issues remained unresolved and Carole could not stop reviewing them in her mind: During the course of the hearings, one petty officer had admitted to having sex with Barbara Underwood, a lower-ranking enlisted woman directly under him in the chain of command, and another officer had admitted to adultery. Under the Uniform Code of Military Justice, both offenses were punishable with prison sentences, but neither sailor was ever charged or even investigated. The investigation into the stabbings, drug dealing, and loansharking had also been long forgotten and no charges would ever be brought in those crimes. Though the commander of Cruiser-Destroyer Group Five had launched an investigation into the fitness of the *Norton Sound*'s command, it was less clear whether the probe was to uncover the investigations' excesses or the fact that the excesses had become public. Even more disturbing to Carole was the lack of concern about misdeeds by agents of the Naval Investigative Service. The whole episode had left the ship, a crucial testing vessel for the Navy's newest weapons systems, virtually dysfunctional for three months. They were glad to be done with it.

Angry as she was, Carole was also aware that the *Norton Sound* hearings represented a turning point. Once, the Navy would have held its position with righteous pride while the accused cringed at the idea that the public might find out. Today, it was the Navy that cowered, ordering the press from its hearing rooms, refusing public comment. By fighting the Navy, Carole was at least satisfied to know she had helped turn the tables. Between the *Norton Sound* hearings and the Matlovich ruling, it really seemed as if the antigay regulations were in their very last days.

39

Future Imperfect

"MAYBE I SHOULD take it."

It was a suggestion Leonard Matlovich broached only with his closest friends—and even then only tentatively, because he fully expected the wrath of the gay community to fall upon him if he followed his instincts and accepted the cash settlement the Air Force had offered. The alternative was that the Air Force would appeal the Gesell decision to the Supreme Court.

Matlovich's attorneys considered his chances of winning in the nation's high tribunal slim at best. President Carter was nearing the completion of a term that gave him the distinction of being the first President in eighty years not to appoint a single Supreme Court justice. The court was only going to get more conservative and disinclined to view gay-rights issues favorably. This was evident not only in the *Doe* v. *Commonwealth* decision but in the litany of gay-rights cases that the justices had refused to hear in the ensuing four years. Lenny could forgo the money and pursue the case, the lawyers said, but he would probably lose and end up with nothing. Besides, the case was not the constitutional challenge Matlovich had wanted. The U.S. Court of Appeals had dodged the broader issues and ruled only on whether the Air Force had capriciously violated its own policy that allowed for exceptions to the gay exclusion. Even a win would probably not provide the sweeping reform he sought.

These arguments were persuasive to Matlovich, although he harbored profound fears about how the gay community would react. From the start, many members of the national gay leadership had been less than enthralled with doing battle for gays in uniform, given the antipathy to the military that dated back to the antiwar protests of a decade earlier. Although immensely popular with the gay grass roots, Matlovich had never been embraced by gay activists, who eschewed his conservatism and could not relate to his old-fashioned patriotism. Taking a settlement, Lenny worried, would only give the activists new grounds on which to condemn him, and more than anything Lenny wanted to be liked.

By now he had moved up from his warehouseman's job to a sales position at a Ford dealership near the Castro Street neighborhood. It was a sign of the gay community's economic clout that car dealerships, accustomed to hiring sports stars, now used a gay activist to push Fairlanes and Broncos. But Matlovich lacked the requisite toughness to deliver the hard sell; he was just too gentle for the used-car business. Five years out of the Air Force, he worried that he might never have the chance to start a new life if he did not take the lump sum offered and launch his own business. With a business, he could buy that home with the white picket fence he had always wanted and maybe find the lover he had always dreamed of.

Given his stature as the gay movement's leading poster boy, Matlovich received most of the coverage. In New York City, however, Vernon Berg III had his own decision to make about possible reinstatement. But for Copy, it was simple. He didn't want to be in the Navy. He had pursued the litigation to make a moral point, not for any practical gain. Since then, he had received his master's degree from Pratt Institute and had launched his own career as an artist. His mentor, Charlie Bell, who had been cast out of the Navy for being gay in 1961, was emerging as one of the nation's foremost photo-realist painters, and Copy looked forward to distinguishing himself as a painter, as well. He would take the settlement.

ON OCTOBER 23, 1980, the U.S. Court of Appeals for the Ninth Circuit, meeting in San Francisco, delivered a stunning setback to opponents of the military's gay policies. In a ruling that took up the dismissals of three sailors accused of being gay, the judges reversed the district court's ruling for Mary Roseanne Saal and upheld those of Dennis Beller and James Lee Miller. The ruling, written by federal judge Anthony Kennedy, was particularly disheartening for gay-rights advocates because while it acknowledged some legitimacy to the claims of unlawful discrimination, it ruled that such discrimination was constitutionally permissible. "To many persons the regulations may seem unwise," Kennedy wrote, and the mandatory exclusion of all gays was "perhaps broader than necessary to accomplish some of [the policy's] goals." However, "upholding the challenged regulations as constitutional is distinct from a statement that they are wise."

Kennedy then attempted to explain why the "special circumstances" of military life might occasionally justify policies not permissible in civilian life. "The nature of the employer—the Navy—is crucial to our decision," he wrote. "While it is clear that one does not surrender his or her constitutional rights upon entering the military, the Supreme Court has repeatedly held that constitutional rights must be viewed in the light of special circumstances and needs of the armed forces. . . . Despite evidence that attitudes toward homosexual conduct have changed among some groups in society, the Navy could conclude that a substantial number of naval personnel have feelings regarding homosexuality based upon moral precepts recognized by many in our society as legitimate, which would create tensions and hostilities, and that these feelings might undermine the ability of a homosexual to command the respect necessary to perform supervisory duties."

In a harsh dissent, Judge William Norris, a Carter appointee, called Kennedy's ruling a "knee-jerk acquiescence" to military arguments that soldiers would not want to serve with gays. Norris noted that no federal court would allow such blanket discrimination against black or female servicemen, even though it could be asserted with equal validity that many would prefer not to have African Americans or women in the military. "Intolerance is not a constitutional basis for an infringement of fundamental personal rights," Norris wrote. "Yet intolerance or a presumption of intolerance is at the very root of each of the dangers which the Navy asserts is posed to its interests by homosexuals."

But Norris was in the minority and the Kennedy ruling, occurring in one of the most liberal federal jurisdictions in the country, gave Pentagon attorneys new confidence that their positions would be upheld by the Supreme Court. The *Saal* case had been viewed as "the most promising military case . . . to advance the civil rights of homosexual servicemen and women." Instead, it had turned into the most significant disaster.

On the heels of this ruling, the Army took an unprecedented step in its battle with Wisconsin reservist Miriam Ben-Shalom, the Milwaukee substitute teacher who had announced she was gay in 1976. In May, the federal district court had ordered her reinstatement. Though the Army had appealed the decision, it had reversed itself in November and withdrawn the appeal. The federal judge then lifted the stay of judgment. The Army was now under court order to put Ben-Shalom back in uniform. Rather than fight the order legally, the Army simply disobeyed it. This intransigence stunned legal experts—one arm of the federal government was refusing to comply with its legal duty. More than anything, the Army's defiance demonstrated again the lengths to which the armed forces would go to maintain its gay exclusion policy.

In Washington, meanwhile, word spread that the task force convened in September after Gesell's ruling in the Matlovich case had come up with new iron-clad regulations against gays. The Pentagon would respond to the legal questioning of its exceptions clause by rewriting the regulations so there were no exceptions.

"THE GAYS IN SAN FRANCISCO elected a mayor," intoned a somber voice over film of some of the lewder scenes from San Francisco's Gay Freedom

Day Parade. The film faded to a still photo of President Carter. "Now they're going to elect a President."

In the 1980 presidential election, the issue of gay civil rights finally became what homosexual advocates had long hoped for—a concern raised prominently in a presidential election. Unfortunately, the issue was raised not for the votes it might gain its proponents but because it could be used to deny votes to candidates who supported gay rights. This created an unhappy political scenario that would dominate American politics for the next three presidential elections. The fact that Democratic candidates, scrapping in major urban areas for primary votes, largely supported the homosexual agenda obscured a harsh political reality. National election results throughout the 1980s demonstrated undeniably that support for gay rights was a much greater political liability than an asset in a general-election campaign. As gender-related issues, such as women's rights and gay rights, moved to the forefront of social consciousness, the politics of polarization, first engineered by Richard Nixon in his 1968 presidential campaign, found a new national fear around which to mobilize voters: homosexuals.

From the beginning, the race for the Republican nomination seemed a contest to see which candidate could be the most staunchly antigay. In the New Hampshire primary, former Texas governor John Connally accused opponent George Bush's campaign staff of spreading the word that Connally endorsed gay rights. Connally denounced the rumor as "a self-serving, scurrilous piece of propaganda" and set about to put the record straight. While homosexuals should have legal rights "like every citizen," he said, gays should not be allowed to teach in elementary or secondary schools or serve in sensitive national-security jobs. For his part, Bush, positioned as the moderate Republican, declared, "I don't think homosexuality is normal behavior and I oppose codification of gay rights." With some equivocation, however, he added, "I wish the issue would just go away, but, of course, I know it can't." After a gay Republican club in Los Angeles held a straw poll that gave a majority to Ronald Reagan, the former California governor went out of his way to shun gay support. "An employer should not be subject to special laws, such as 'gay ordinances' passed in some cities, which in effect would compel him to hire a person because of that person's sexual preference," he said. "My criticism is that [the gay movement] isn't just asking for civil rights, it's asking for recognition and acceptance of an alternative lifestyle which I do not believe society can condone; nor can I." And then Reagan alluded to the Bible, "which says that in the eyes of the Lord, homosexuality is an abomination."

All this posturing provoked little public response because the national media generally deemed gay rights a marginal issue and reported on it in brief, if at all. News organizations' best journalists covered presidential campaigns, and serious reporters did not talk about homosexuals.

There were people talking about homosexuals, however, using gay rights as the key argument in their campaign against the reelection of President Carter. These people were the newly politicized evangelical preachers who were the spokesmen for the New Right. Although born-again Christians were first heard from in the Carter campaign of 1976, they had not fully mobilized politically until they emerged in the anti-homosexual crusades of the late 1970s. By 1980, they were a full-blown force on the political landscape, focused largely on opposition to the profound transformation in gender roles. A dramatic shift in sex roles and challenges to the conventional ideology of masculinity had shaped a social movement in the 1970s; in the 1980s, the reaction to this transformation would be a major social movement, as well.

In no document was the history of the gay movement and the women's movement for the next decade more clearly written than in the 1980 Republican party platform. In it the New Right incorporated virtually all of its challenges to both movements. The 1980 platform, for example, was the first Republican platform since 1940 that did not include an endorsement of the Equal Rights Amendment. Republican nominee Reagan not only opposed the ERA, but supported the "human life amendment," which, if enacted, would overturn the *Roe* v. *Wade* ruling and ban abortion. George Bush, although he campaigned on a prochoice platform during his bid for the nomination, adopted a strong antiabortion position when he was selected as Reagan's running mate. The Republican platform also endorsed the Family Protection Act, which included a list of legislative proscriptions designed to turn back the gains of the gay and women's movements. Under the proposed act, no federal funds could be used to buy textbooks that portrayed women in nontraditional roles or that supported programs to help women battered by their husbands. No federal money would be available to any nonprofit agency designed to provide services for the gay community. The bill was sponsored by Senator Paul Laxalt, Reagan's campaign chairman.

In the South, Reagan's most outspoken supporters took great pains to bring up the gay issue. The Reverend Jerry Falwell, who had recently formed a group called the Moral Majority, told the faithful, "President Carter has given undue recognition to homosexuals, to a perverted life-style, giving them unreasonable privileges. It is something the President does not have to do, popularizing the existence of this 'minority.' " To make sure nobody missed the message, groups such as the Moral Majority, Christian Voice, and Christians for Reagan spent millions of dollars on television ads in the Deep South in the final weeks of the campaign, focusing on the Democratic party platform's endorsement of gay rights and depicting Carter as the candidate of the homosexuals.

In races for the U.S. Senate, another organization, the National Conservative Political Action Committee (or NCPAC) pumped millions of dollars into television ad campaigns linking Democratic incumbents to gay-rights support. The great irony was that NCPAC's founder and director, Terry Dolan, was a handsome young man who frequented Washington's gay bars, as well as the gay resorts of the Russian River, north of San Francisco. Dolan himself never denounced gay rights, but he raised millions for candidates who did. His crowning achievement was securing the nomination and election of Ronald Reagan as President. By the end of 1980, Dolan had raised $10 million for Reagan's effort, more than any other individual. And some of that money paid for those advertisements in the South that attacked the Democratic platform's gay-rights plank.

Still, the antigay tenor of the Reagan campaign did little to dampen the enthusiasm of gay Republican organizations for the Reagan presidency. Reagan was from Hollywood, homosexual GOP organizers assured one another; he had to have gay friends who would work behind the scenes for their interests. In Ohio, legal scholar Rhonda Rivera scolded her gay conservative friends, saying that by voting for Ronald Reagan, they were electing not just a President but a Supreme Court that would have the final say on their civil rights until well into the next century. But few listened.

The final irony concerned Carter. Although his administration had shifted a handful of regulatory matters that had a marginal impact on gay concerns, Carter had shown little interest in gay issues, and the harassment of gays, particularly those in the armed forces, had in fact increased dramatically during his presidency. In the climate of reaction that dominated the 1980 campaign, his sin was not that he was progay but that he was not sufficiently antigay to satisfy the conservative religious movement. That did not mean, however, that the New Right reflected the way most Americans felt about shifting attitudes toward gender roles or sexual orientation. Support for the ERA and other women's issues continued to increase across the country. One poll showed that only 7 percent of Americans subscribed to the agenda of the Moral Majority. Polls by both Associated Press and the Roper organization in 1980 both demonstrated that more Americans than not favored a legal ban on discrimination against gays.

Just as gays held power in a handful of specifically defined areas, largely in coastal cities, the fundamentalists had their strongholds, largely in the South. Unfortunately for gays, the South was crucial for winning presidential elections, and therefore the antigay clerics had a disproportionate say in Republican campaign strategies. The fundamentalists had proved the critical edge of difference in winning the South. Two-thirds of white evangelists had voted for Southern Baptist Jimmy Carter in 1976, giving him the presidency; in 1980, two-thirds voted for Ronald Reagan, making the crucial difference in the electoral vote–rich Sunbelt. When Reagan was elected President on November 4 in a landslide, this also meant that the most strident adversaries of women's and gay rights would have a disproportionate say in the White House. The period of transition was over and the era of reaction had begun.

From then on, evangelical conservatives used the issue of gay rights to play upon fears over the confusing changes that had developed in the way women and men related to one another. Politically, gays were a convenient target because so few would dare defend them.

REAGAN'S ELECTION, more than any other development, clinched Leonard Matlovich's decision not to pursue his court case and to accept a settlement from the Air Force. His lawyers assured him that the Supreme Court would grow only more inhospitable to gay claims than it already was, making his chances of success less likely. Furthermore, the justices might even use his case to set the gay cause back further. It was possible that if he returned to the Air Force, the service would set him up on some phony charge and dismiss him again.

Matlovich's back pay to 1975 amounted to $62,500, which was the amount the Air Force first offered. Ultimately, his attorneys secured him the promise of a tax-free $160,000. Matlovich immediately wrote checks for a significant portion of that amount to various nonprofit gay groups, but, as he had feared, some gay newspapers accused him of accepting a payoff to sell out the gay movement. For his part, Matlovich told the *Air Force Times,* "It'll be another ten years before I know whether this was the right decision." He would still campaign for a change in the military policies, Matlovich said, and he pledged to be "around for a long time." Would he advise young gay people to join the military, given his experience? Matlovich did not hesitate to answer. Of course, he said, "because it's a good way of life."

In his only public statement on the subject, Air Force Secretary Hans Mark said, "The Air Force agreed to the settlement because we continue to regard homosexuality as fundamentally inconsistent with military service and wanted to avoid returning Matlovich to active duty. The appeals process would have been lengthy, and if we had not settled, we would have been forced to take Matlovich back by December 5 under the court's order."

MATLOVICH'S DECISION CAME as authorities were bearing down even harder on gays in uniform, abruptly ending the careers of those who a few years earlier had enjoyed relative acceptance in their military jobs.

At the Marine Corps Air Station in Beaufort, South Carolina, Art McDaniel, who had fought off seven Marines with his gay leatherneck buddies, the Four Musketeers, saw his career crash when one of the Musketeers was pulled into a small room and threatened with prison unless he named other homosexuals. Art would have received a general discharge under less than honorable conditions, but then he heard about the Matlovich settlement. "I'll accept an honorable discharge, and if you give me anything less, I'll call an attorney from the ACLU and you'll pay," he threatened, and the threat worked. McDaniel was the only one of the discharged Musketeers to walk away with honorable papers.

To many gay soldiers and sailors in those months, it seemed as if the sky was falling. And this was just the beginning.

PETE RANDELL was at his desk in the Pentagon when he heard about the Matlovich settlement. He collapsed back in his chair. Didn't Matlovich know how close he had been to winning? Didn't he know that the orders had been written for his reinstatement and assignment?

It had been a decade since Pete had gone to work for the White House—ten years in which he had observed the political tides shift away from the cause he secretly championed. The "strict constructionist" courts, the increasing conservative influence in Congress, the new administration—it added up to dark times ahead for the fledgling gay movement. He knew that most gays wouldn't notice right away. It took years for changes in the political establishment to seep into the daily life of most Americans. But his perch in the Pentagon gave Pete a different perspective, and he knew who would first feel the redirection in political influence in Washington: homosexuals in uniform.

The future fell before him in a string of sentences written in the future imperfect. There would be more witch-hunts; more people would go to prison; the fear would feed upon itself and grow.

BOOK FIVE

LESBIAN VAMPIRES OF BAVARIA

(1981–1985)

His mind slid away into the labyrinthine world of doublethink. To know and not to know, to be conscious of complete truthfulness while telling carefully constructed lies, to hold simultaneously two opinions which canceled out, knowing them to be contradictory and believing in both of them, to use logic against logic, to repudiate morality while laying claim to it, to believe that democracy was impossible and the Party was the guardian of democracy, to forget, whatever it was necessary to forget, then to draw it back into memory again when it was needed, and then promptly to forget it again, and above all, to apply the same process to the process itself—that was the ultimate subtlety. . . . Even to understand the word "doublethink" involved the use of doublethink.

—George Orwell, *1984*

40

Thoughtcrimes

JANUARY 1981
GUERNEVILLE, CALIFORNIA

WATCHING THE SKY and the river in the hills of rural Sonoma County was a particular responsibility of Cliff Anchor, the owner of KRJB-FM radio, which transmitted the clearest signal for miles around and therefore played a central role in alerting locals to potentially dangerous weather conditions. In the first weeks of 1981, as clouds drifted darkly toward Guerneville from the north, Cliff Anchor had this and former Air Force Sergeant Leonard P. Matlovich on his mind.

Though Anchor's interest in politics had lent his broadcasting a discernible political edge in the twenty years since he had first approached a radio microphone in San Francisco, he lived a discreet life in terms of his sexuality. Local meddlers might gossip that the local radio station's owner was "light in the loafers," but Cliff had not come out in public. He was deeply afraid that something dreadful might happen to him if he declared the words publicly. He struggled with this fear, and perhaps this was what made his attraction to Leonard Matlovich so strong. Cliff had enormous respect for Lenny's courage in standing up to the government and challenging the military's discrimination.

They had met two years earlier in San Francisco shortly after Cliff had accepted a commission as a major in the California State Military Reserve. Cliff had never heard of Lenny, but, by the end of the evening, Anchor felt he had found a soul mate. They saw each other in San Francisco when Cliff could get away from the station, which was rare because he was the station's announcer, newscaster, programmer, and repairman, as well as the owner. When Lenny finally said he was moving to Guerneville to open a pizza parlor, Cliff saw their futures running together into one stream at last.

There was only one other person Cliff had ever met who had attracted him this way, driven by inner hurt and public fearlessness. Later, he saw that the two men stood like bookends on either side of his adult life, his first lover and his last.

Cliff Anchor had first heard of Dr. Tom Dooley in 1959 when Dooley announced that he had cancer. Cancer was a word rarely spoken in those days; Dooley hoped that his public admission would diminish the stigma endured by those suffering from the disease. Privately, he also knew that his plight would help raise millions more for his hospitals, which it did. His cancer operation at Memorial Sloan-Kettering in New York City was even filmed and televised nationally on CBS, along with Dooley's solemn pronouncement that he was cured. By then, of course, everyone knew of Dr. Dooley's work in the jungle of Southeast Asia, all retold in books, four of which had made the best-seller lists by the time Cliff met him in December 1959, just days after the Gallup poll had rated Dooley as one of the ten most admired men in the United States, right after President Eisenhower and Pope John XXIII.

Young people all over North America were taking up Dooley's call to help the less fortunate of the world. This appealed to Anchor, but just as intriguing was Cliff's sense that Tom Dooley, like himself, was, well, artistic, as Cliff's mother might have delicately put it. Cliff was pleased when Dooley suggested they talk at his apartment at the Waldorf Towers. After an evening discussing the work Cliff could do for Dooley's foundation in Laos, Tom suggested Cliff not rush home. They soon became lovers.

As Anchor labored to secure the necessary visas to fly to Laos for Dooley's foundation, MEDICO, Dooley's condition deteriorated. Still, he continued to plot public-relations forays and fund-raising schemes. Sometimes, Anchor thought the work helped Tom remember what his life had been about; at other times, he thought it was helping him forget. For all Dooley's fame and celebrity, Cliff saw some damaged part of the man, some hurt that had never healed.

After Tom died, Cliff's plans to work in Laos were lost in the general chaos that engulfed MEDICO. Cliff moved to California to start a career in broadcasting. He always felt that fate had robbed him of his chance for a singular love with a truly remarkable person, so when Leonard told him he was moving to Guerneville, Cliff promised himself that he would not let such an opportunity elude him again.

JANUARY 16, 1981
THE PENTAGON
ARLINGTON, VIRGINIA

GRAHAM CLAYTOR'S OFFICE overlooked the grassy parade ground in front of the Pentagon's River Entrance. In the distance, across the Potomac, the dome of the Jefferson Monument rose above the barren branches of cherry trees. A few doors down the hall was the office of the Secretary of Defense, the only man whom Claytor called boss. The sixty-eight-year-old Claytor was Deputy Secretary of Defense, the Pentagon's number-two man.

The post capped forty-five years on the periphery of power in Washington, a career begun in 1937, when, fresh from Harvard Law School, Claytor served as a law clerk for the legendary Supreme Court associate justice Louis Brandeis. After many years as a railroad lawyer, including ten years as president of Southern Railway, Claytor had joined the Carter administration in 1977 as its first Navy Secretary. It was he who had signed the final order to discharge Ensign Vernon "Copy" Berg. After two years at the Navy Department, he was appointed Deputy Secretary of Defense; to him fell the nuts-and-bolts running of the nation's military establishment, which freed the Defense Secretary's time for less prosaic matters.

By this, the third week of January in 1981, most of the other Carter hands in the Pentagon had cleared their desks to make way for the appointees of Ronald Reagan, who was to be sworn in as President in just four days. But W. Graham Claytor, Jr., had a major piece of business to accomplish. The business was a two-page memo addressed to the Chairman of the Joint Chiefs of Staff and the secretaries of the Army, Navy and Air Force.

"I am promulgating today a change to DoD Directive 1332.14 (Enlisted Administrative Separations), including a completely new Enclosure 8 on Homosexuality . . ." Claytor wrote. "I have personally worked on this problem from time to time during most of the four years I have served in the Department. I firmly believe that the most important aspect of our policy is the ability to keep homosexuals out of the service and to separate them promptly in the event they are in fact enlisted or commissioned."

The new policy voided all clauses in military regulations allowing for the retention of anyone who could be discerned to be homosexual. It was these rules allowing exceptions that had proved so problematic for the Defense Department in the Matlovich and Berg cases. Now there would be no exceptions. The new posture, Claytor wrote, "should enable the Department to sustain its position in the courts."

Along with the ironclad ban on gays in uniform, the new policy had a second aim. Claytor ordered that "the mere fact of homosexuality" should not be grounds for a less than honorable discharge. As Navy Secretary, Claytor had pushed for an end to the use of less than honorable discharges as a punitive vehicle against gays, and in 1978 he had ordered that gay sailors guilty of no misconduct should receive honorable discharges. He wanted this position to be reflected in the policies of all services.

The rewriting of the regulations had been in the works since September 1977, when the Defense Department began a grueling review of its rules for the administrative separation of enlisted personnel. In 1978, a Defense Department study group proposed shifting gay discharges from the category "misconduct," for which commanding officers could give bad discharges, to "unsuitability," which would allow for honorable discharges in cases where there were no aggravating circumstances. "Although the subject of homosexuality and the question of whether or not homosexuality is a mental disease are controversial, the Study Group felt that by and large, homosexual acts were in the nature of non-volitional acts and therefore absent certain aggravating circumstances, individuals discharged for this reason should not be stigmatized with a less than honorable discharge," the report concluded. "While the language in the proposed directive may at first blush seem excessively liberal, it is not a significant departure from what the Services are already doing in this area."

To the top echelons of the uniformed military, the new language for the gay discharges did seem excessively liberal. When Claytor announced he was expediting his review of gay policies in the wake of the Matlovich ruling in late 1980, the Joint Chiefs launched a series of delaying actions. The closing weeks of the Carter administration saw a flurry of memos from the Joint Chiefs. More than a decade later, the Pentagon would still be censoring much of these memoranda, but those that were released indicated that the Joint Chiefs hoped they could stall Claytor's reform until the Reagan administration took office and hard-liners presumably ran the Defense Department again.

Air Force Colonel Harold Neely, Secretary for the Joint Chiefs of Staff, insisted that "homosexual acts committed by Service members are in violation of the Uniform Code of Military Justice as well as being service discrediting and prejudicial to good order and discipline. While administrative discharges have proven to be an expeditious means for separating the unfit or undesirable, these precepts must not be slighted." When Claytor was unmoved by this argument, the Chairman of the Joint Chiefs, General David Jones, formally wrote the Defense Secretary complaining that "The Joint Chiefs of Staff feel that, with an issue of this importance and long-term consequence, it is essential that the services complete their evaluation. In light of this, they request that the proposed policy revision be delayed until the Joint Chiefs of Staff make their recommendation on the issue." But any delay would have put the matter into the hands of the Reagan administration, so the appeals were ignored.

The essence of the new gay policy was to be found in a four-page statement that accompanied Claytor's letter. The new policy regarding the service of homosexuals in the United States armed forces was contained in three sentences, only 123 words:

> *Homosexuality is incompatible with military service. The presence in the military environment of persons who engage in homosexual conduct or who, by their statements, demonstrate a propensity to engage in homosexual conduct, seriously impairs the accomplishment of military mission. The presence of such members adversely affects the ability of the armed forces to*

*maintain discipline, good order and morale; to foster mutual
trust and confidence among service members; to insure the integrity of the system of rank and command; to facilitate assignment and worldwide deployment of service members who
frequently must live and work in close conditions affording minimal privacy; to recruit and retain members of the armed forces;
to maintain the public acceptability of military service; and to
prevent breaches of security.*

The policy was the rationale; the rationale was the policy. These 123
words had taken months to craft, reduced from a six-page memorandum
completed in September 1980. The earlier draft gave a much more detailed
explanation of the arguments so tersely summarized in the new policy,
and more deeply reveals its logic. "Surveys show that the vast majority
of Americans, in and out of the service strongly disapprove of homosexuality, and homosexuals are estimated to be a small percentage of the
population," the earlier draft read. "The inclusion within a military unit
of members of a group whose behavior in such a fundamental area is
viewed as deviant and wrong by the majority of the unit would frustrate
formation of close personal bonds and would fragment the unit. . . . Even
if a service member known to be homosexual were accepted by others in
a particular military unit, that acceptance would likely dissipate as old
members are transferred and replacements arrive or when the homosexual
is routinely transferred to another location or unit."

The only way to get around soldiers' fears of roving homosexual eyes
would be to install separate shower and toilet facilities for "heterosexual
males, known homosexual males, heterosexual females and known homosexual females," and this solution "would be costly and would fragment
small unit cohesiveness."

Central to the exclusion of gays were concerns about the continued
viability of the all-volunteer military. "Allowing known homosexuals to
be members of the Armed Services also would damage the image of the
military in the eyes of the American people, our allies, and our potential
adversaries and make military service less attractive," according to the
draft statement. "This impact on the military's public image would also
cause great difficulties in recruitment and retention of service members."

Gays in leadership ranks also posed a threat to good order, discipline,
and morale, it was argued, because the presence of gay commanders would
"increase the potential for improper fraternization among ranks, and improper sexual advances and sexual harassment by leaders."

Remarkably, the new policy had hardly anything to do with homosexuals or their fitness for service. Except for those words concerning
national security, nothing in any private or public Pentagon statements
suggested that homosexuals themselves were not fit to serve in the military.
Instead, the policy's justification rested solely on the supposed reaction
of heterosexuals if they had to serve with homosexuals—whether they

would take orders from, sleep in the same barracks with, or serve in the same Army with homosexuals. The new policy was not a statement about homosexuals but about heterosexuals.

In its fashioning of the military's gay policies, the Armed Forces was following the same path that it had in the early 1940s when it sought to justify the segregation of black and white soldiers. Since it was no longer politically tenable to argue that anything innate about African Americans made them unfit to serve, the arguments for segregation rested on the notion that whites would not want to serve with, take orders from, or sleep in the same barracks with black soldiers.

The distinguishing aspect of the regulations concerning gays was to be found elsewhere, buried in the sections that delineated how a homosexual would be defined for purposes of administrative separation. One clause stated that a homosexual was anyone who had ever engaged in a homosexual act at any time in his or her life. This included sexual acts performed before military service. Another way to identify a homosexual was if a serviceman attempted to "marry" a person of the same sex. Anyone who told another that he or she was gay could also be ousted from the military. This clause was added to cover servicemen such as Leonard Matlovich, who had come to the attention of military authorities not through any homosexual conduct but because he had said he was gay.

The most startling new clause in the Department of Defense regulations on homosexuality, however, was the simple declarative sentence: "Homosexual means a person, regardless of sex, who engages in, desires to engage in, or intends to engage in homosexual acts." Later, this language was refined to include people who by "their statements demonstrate a propensity to engage in homosexual conduct." There was no longer any talk in the regulations of "homosexual tendencies" or of having "homosexual associations." There would no longer be any need to establish that a suspect had ever engaged in homosexual behavior. Instead, the mere "desire" or "intent" to engage in a homosexual act at some unspecified time in the future, even if never acted upon, was enough to warrant separation from the armed forces. The military had, in effect, banned homosexual thoughts.

Meanwhile, commanding officers would do their best to circumvent the more merciful provision of the regulation. While the proportion of honorable discharges increased among those separated for homosexuality in the years that followed, commanders were still issuing less than honorable discharges to homosexuals a decade later, blatantly violating the Defense Department guidelines laid down in 1981.

FOR ALL THE EFFORTS of many governments to suppress homosexuality over the centuries, there had been only one other government in modern history that sought to punish those who harbored homosexual thoughts. In 1934, the Ministry of Justice of Germany's Third Reich ordered that homosexual behavior was not necessary to warrant punishment under the German laws against homosexuality. The "intent" to commit a homosexual act could result in imprisonment. Homosexual thoughts, one Nazi theoretician said, represented "abstract coitus."

The National Socialist party had always opposed a broader role for women in society, abortion, and gay rights. The Nazi's "profamily" program saw the suppression of feminism and homosexuality as inextricably linked. In fact, the Nazi campaigns against abortion and gay rights were mounted from the same agency, the Federal Security Office for Combatting Abortion and Homosexuality. By 1938, under the ban on homosexual thoughts, the Gestapo was already sending homosexuals off to death camps, where they were forced to wear the inverted pink triangles that distinguished them from the Jews, who wore yellow patches in the shape of a Star of David.

The National Socialists were also preoccupied with gathering lists of homosexuals. Their goal to make Germany *homorein*, or homo-free, was not possible without the lists. Arrested homosexuals were pressured to name other homosexuals, who were pressured to name more, and so on. Address books were culled for more names. German pamphlets distributed to the Hitler Youth included charts nearly identical to those in the U.S. Navy's Crittenden Report that recorded one homosexual's sexual contacts and his contacts' contacts. Though records are imprecise, Nazi documents chronicle the arrests of between 50,000 and 63,000 homosexuals from 1933 to 1944. Most of them were later exterminated.

The Nazis were also intent on ridding the German armed services of homosexuals. Charges of homosexuality were used to harass officers whom Hitler considered too timid. Even the commander in chief of the German armed forces, Baron Werner von Fritsch, once faced homosexual charges after the Gestapo claimed to have discovered a hustler who had had sex with the general. Primarily, the military focused on rooting out anyone in the enlisted ranks who had engaged in homosexual acts or who had demonstrated an intent or desire to be homosexual. This was no small task. As documented in Richard Plant's history of the German antihomosexual campaigns, *The Pink Triangle*, many younger gay men had decided to escape the mass arrests of homosexuals in the mid-1930s by volunteering for military service. Between 1940 and 1943, some five thousand German soldiers were indicted for homosexual acts.

When Allied soldiers liberated death-camp inmates, the handful of homosexual prisoners who had survived discovered that their liberators shared attitudes similar to those of the Nazis. Some British and American military jurists, for example, ruled that imprisoned homosexuals were criminals and were not to be automatically freed as the Jews were. As Plant writes, a homosexual who had served three years of an eight-year sentence in prison, and five years in a concentration camp such as Auschwitz or Dachau, would be returned to prison for five more years. Time spent in a concentration camp did not represent time spent fulfilling a

prison sentence. When asked about the pervasive persecution of homosexuals during the 1930s and 1940s, the typical response from the ordinary
German was the same as his or her response to the questions of persecution
of Jews: "We knew nothing about it."

MORE THAN A DECADE after W. Graham Claytor, Jr., issued his order
banning homosexual thoughts among military personnel, he characterized
the policy as a compassionate act meant only to ensure that homosexuals
were no longer stigmatized by a less than honorable discharge. "I felt it
should be treated like a disability," said Claytor, who in 1982 moved into
a new government post as president of the Amtrak railway system. When
an interviewer noted that gay soldiers were "kicked out" of the armed
forces during his tenure at the Pentagon, Claytor grew indignant. "We
didn't kick them out," he insisted, "we gave them an honorable discharge."

He was not aware, he said, that the new regulations would enable the
separation of thousands more homosexuals in the years that followed. He
did not know that his order to grant honorable discharges would be widely
ignored. As for the dramatic increases in the separation of homosexuals
from the military during his own years as the Pentagon's number-two
official, Claytor also pleaded ignorance. "I knew nothing about it," he
said.

BEYOND THE PROSECUTIONS and impressive purges of gays that followed
the new regulation, there was also the fact that the Department of Defense
now had a concise statement with which it could answer any question
concerning homosexuality. By late January 1981, every public-affairs office on every military base and installation in the world had received the
Department of Defense fact sheet, entitled "Homosexuals in the Armed
Forces," and for the next decade the 123 words of Department of Defense
Directive 1332.14 would be the only words spoken publicly by any Department of Defense press spokesman to defend the Pentagon's policies
on homosexuals.

— 41 —

Surrender Dorothy

PERRY WATKINS loved being stationed back in Tacoma, his home since the age of twelve. It was in Fort Lewis, on the edge of Tacoma's sprawling southern suburbs, that he had entered the Army nearly thirteen years before. His new barracks was right across the street from the barracks where he had lived during basic training, which were the same barracks his stepfather had lived in decades earlier. Although he took his nighttime college courses in business administration, Perry pursued his dramatic ambitions by performing belly dancing and female impersonation with a local dance theater.

Perry was thirty-three years old and had by now decided to stay in the Army for the seven additional years it would take to earn his pension. He had been promoted to staff sergeant a year earlier and was now in charge of fifteen enlisted men as supervisor for his battalion's personnel center. His Army career had become fairly routine—a routine that included occasional annoyances concerning his singular stance as an openly gay soldier.

The most recent nuisance had begun in late 1979 when Perry was stationed in Germany and was advised that his security clearance would be revoked because he had told the security interviewer that he was gay. This was the fourth time Watkins's security clearance had come under review since he had entered the Army in 1968. He submitted the necessary rebuttal letter, which received no reply. Perry heard nothing more until July 1980, when he was advised that he was denied a security clearance because of his work as a female impersonator and because he did "not deny that he is a homosexual." Watkins's "character deficiencies are incompatible with the criteria established as necessary for the possession of a personnel security clearance," the official notice read.

The revocation, Watkins knew, could have disastrous implications.

Without a clearance, he could not be promoted to the rank of sergeant first class. This would reduce his pension and impede the rest of his career. He was also angry because the Army consistently allowed him to remain in uniform while constantly erecting roadblocks to his advancement. He knew he would fight this latest obstacle, although the avenue of his appeal did not become clear until one afternoon when he answered an advertisement in the Fort Lewis paper to buy an officer's stereo system. The captain was being transferred to West Point, where he would be promoted to the rank of major and teach law, he told Perry. Perry mentioned that he was involved in a fracas over his security clearance.

"Why?" the officer asked.

"Because I'm gay," Perry said matter-of-factly.

The captain, it turned out, had once represented a young officer who had fought a gay-related discharge; he thought that the gay exclusion policy was absurd. Encouraged, Watkins told his whole story—that he had said he was gay when he was drafted in 1968, and had said so again when he reenlisted in 1971. He told the captain about his hearing in 1975, which concluded he could remain in the Army. The captain didn't believe Perry at first, but Perry assured him he had the paperwork to prove it.

"Contact the ACLU and get a lawyer," the captain said.

Perry had never heard of the ACLU. Though keenly aware of Army administrative regulations from his decade of work as a personnel clerk, he did not know much about the law. So the captain framed Perry's letter to the ACLU for him, and within weeks Watkins was consulting with Jim Lobsenz.

Lobsenz was twenty-eight years old and three years out of law school at the University of California at Berkeley. He had moved to Seattle two years earlier to take a job as a deputy prosecuting attorney in King County, Washington. Jim was tall, thin, and lawyerly, Perry thought, with the distinguished demeanor of Gregory Peck in *To Kill a Mockingbird*. The facts of Watkins's career fascinated Lobsenz. He was willing to bet there was not anyone like Watkins in the United States Army, and he thought the basic issue of fairness would ultimately prevail in court. Not many county prosecutors cared to spend their spare time working on gay-rights cases for the ACLU, especially not straight ones, but Lobsenz was intrigued by the constitutional issues the gay movement presented. Watkins thought it was propitious that the attorney was also a Quaker. The Quakers had been central players in the Abolitionist movement and underground railroad before the Civil War.

In February 1981, Perry appealed the revocation of his security clearance, arguing that it was hypocritical to take it away because of his female-impersonation act when he had been performing for years at military installations with the enthusiastic support of his commanders. Regarding his refusal to deny being gay, he wrote, "I submit that I have been consistently penalized for my honesty. I will always continue to admit my homosexuality in the future. The Army has seen fit, on numerous occasions, to decide that my homosexuality is no obstacle to my military career." Watkins added that he had retained an ACLU lawyer.

Perry waited for several months and heard nothing from security officials at Fort Meade. When Lobsenz called the agency, they said they had not received any letter from Staff Sergeant Watkins. Lobsenz noted that the letter had been sent by certified mail and that he had a signed receipt from the agency. Perhaps whoever signed for the letter had just thrown it away, an agency official said. Lobsenz mailed a second letter of appeal. When more months passed with no reply, he finally filed a lawsuit in federal district court in Seattle asking the court to reinstate Watkins's security clearance.

Filing the suit represented the Rubicon of Watkins's career. Perry had long ago noted that the true purpose of the military's gay policies was not actually to expel all homosexuals from the Army but to allow the Army to *say* that it did. Now, in a federal lawsuit and with the media attention that was bound to follow the case, it was a matter of record that the Army had gladly engaged the services of a very open homosexual named Perry Watkins, as well as his alter ego, Simone. The order proceeded like a shot from the Pentagon to Fort Lewis: Discharge Watkins.

Perry's two-page notification came from his commander, Captain Rodger Scott. "I am initiating action to recommend your discharge from the United States Army," Scott wrote, adding that Watkins might receive a discharge under other than honorable conditions.

Watkins knew that Army regulations prevented his going before a separation board a second time on the same charges he had faced at his administrative hearing in 1975. That would be double jeopardy. But the Army argued that there were new charges: Watkins had stated he was gay in his appeal letter. There was a new regulation now, number 1332.14, and this was a new admission. It was all the evidence the Army needed. Lobsenz immediately appealed to the federal court. U.S. District Court judge Barbara Rothstein weighed the matter but declined to intervene before Watkins actually faced a discharge hearing, saying the board might decide to retain the sergeant and make her ruling moot. One thing was clear, however: She was interested in the case and would take any appeal of a discharge very seriously.

The Army's legal department was incensed. The case promised to demonstrate something gays had long alleged, that the military had no problem retaining homosexuals when it was deemed to be for the convenience of the government. The Army's general counsel, Delbert L. Spurlock, Jr., issued this memorandum to Brigadier General L. J. Barker, chief of public affairs: "Military service policy regarding separation of homosexuals has been a controversial matter and the subject of much litigation during the past few years. . . . We are interested in insuring not only that this litigation is decided in the Army's favor, but that we avoid or at least minimize unfavorable publicity such as the Air Force received in the Matlovich case."

The high-level concern underscored the Pentagon's dilemma. Just when the Defense Department thought it had ended messy legal battles over its gay policy, a new one was beginning.

DURING THE 1980s, as soon as one threat to the military's gay policy was struck down, two more rose up elsewhere. Even as authorities launched purges to rid this or that base of gay soldiers, new communities were forming at other installations, larger and stronger than their predecessors. In the courts, this meant that no sooner was one legal issue resolved than several more arose. The newly worded policy did less to settle the matter than to raise more questions for endless debate in the years ahead. Perry Watkins was the first to go to court to challenge the Army's implementation of Department of Defense revised Directive 1332.14. For the Navy, the first challenge came from a twenty-one-year-old sailor named Mel Dahl at the Great Lakes Naval Training Center.

WHEN MEL DAHL first enlisted in late 1980, he told Navy doctors that he was homosexual, and his affirmative answer was recorded on his enlistment forms. The issue did not come up again until March 1981, just weeks after the new gay policy went into effect, when the Naval Investigative Service conducted a probe to upgrade Dahl's security clearance for his admission to cryptography school. After the routine questions about whether he had ever written a bad check or joined the Communist party, the NIS agent asked Dahl whether he had any gay friends. When Dahl said he did, the NIS agent asked whether one of these friends had ever made a pass at him. Dahl said yes. The agent then asked whether Dahl was gay, and Dahl said he was. The NIS agent terminated the interview, and days later Dahl was informed that he was being discharged under the new regulations, which allowed for the removal of anyone who said he was gay.

Dahl contacted local civil-liberties groups, none of which seemed eager to take up his cause; then he called the newspapers, which were. Mel became a cause célèbre, the sailor who said he would fight the Navy's ban on homosexuals in court. This did not win him points with his base commander at Great Lakes Naval Station. By the time the NIS had completed its investigation, the only evidence it had were Dahl's press statements—and a letter that he had written to Senator Paul Tsongas, the Senate's leading champion of gay civil rights, arguing against the ban on gays in the military. Since these represented nothing more than Dahl's legal exercise of his First Amendment rights, Dahl argued that the execution of the new policy represented an unconstitutional infringement on his freedom of speech. A Chicago gay-rights lawyer took the case and Dahl's legal battle against the policy began.

Dahl told a newspaper reporter that there were many gays serving at the base, which spurred the Navy to launch a purge of what they presumed to be a massive network of homosexuals at Great Lakes. In the course of their investigation, NIS agents made a startling discovery—that homosexuals sometimes referred to themselves as "friends of Dorothy." This code term had originated in the 1940s and 1950s and referred to Judy Garland's character in the film *The Wizard of Oz*. Ever since, gay men had identified themselves as "friends of Dorothy." The NIS, however, did not know the phrase's history and so believed that a woman named Dorothy was the hub of an enormous ring of military homosexuals in the Chicago area. The NIS prepared to hunt Dorothy down and convince her to give them the names of homosexuals.

In gay bars known to attract military personnel, Dahl learned that NIS agents were asking pointed questions about someone named Dorothy. When one unfortunate sailor acknowledged he was gay in order to get out of the Navy, NIS agents sat him down and told him that they knew all about Dorothy. What they wanted to know from him was how to find her. The sailor, who was too young to know the code, was baffled.

The search for Dorothy was just one of many subplots unfolding during the crackdown on homosexuals that began with the implementation of the Defense Department's rewritten gay policies. During fiscal year 1981, Defense Department figures, which tended to be conservative, recorded that 1,976 enlisted men had been routed from the military under the gay regulations. This marked a new record for gay-related discharges in the post-Vietnam era, and it meant a succession of purges from bases around the world. Since virtually all the sailors and soldiers caught up in the military's vast dragnet waived their rights and quietly left the service, few outside the affected bases were even aware that the investigations were going on. People simply disappeared.

The Navy, which meted out 55 percent of all the services' gay discharges, was particularly aggressive. In July 1981, for example, ten sailors were expelled from the Naval Training Center in Orlando after they were discovered in a "circle jerk," according to Matt Oler, who was in boot camp at the same time. The unfortunate recruits all hailed from the 191st Training Company, which became known among recruits as the "Fag Company" from then on. A purge of gays on the USS *Starrett* in Long Beach resulted in the dismissal of four enlisted men and two officers, all of whom had been seen at local gay bars by agents of the NIS.

In this highly charged environment, the mere suspicion of homosexuality was enough to end careers. During a purge of lesbians in early 1981 in San Diego, one informant told NIS agents about an unidentified woman in the personnel office whom the informant had seen leaving the home of an accused lesbian. The NIS decided this unidentified woman must be Petty Officer Joan Dowling, though they never showed the informant a photo of Dowling to confirm it. When an administrative board dismissed charges against Dowling because of skimpy evidence, the Reagan administration's new Navy Secretary, John Lehman, intervened and summarily ordered the eight-year veteran booted out of the service for the "convenience of the government."

An investigation at the Naval Academy resulted in the resignation of a midshipman and an officer there. The midshipman was from the Twenty-second Company, which instantly became known to other Annapolis students as the BUFU's, a military-sounding acronym for "butt-fuckers." Seven years later, it was the name that other companies still used for the Twenty-second.

The purges extended throughout the American military's worldwide network of bases. At NATO naval installations, NIS agents regularly showed up at the softball games of both Navy and Marines women's intramural teams and took pictures. It was now an article of faith among NIS agents that participation in women's sports was synonymous with lesbianism. The photos were later used in interrogation sessions in which subjects were pressured to identify other lesbians. A lesbian investigation at Sheppard Air Force Base resulted in the discharge of at least one member of the Air Force national women's basketball team.

At the Torrejon Air Base near Madrid, the Air Force Office of Special Investigations hit pay dirt when it caught a gay airman bouncing checks. According to the scuttlebutt around the base, the airman was offered a medical discharge with no notation of his homosexuality if he would name other gays. He did. Among those ousted as a result were a master sergeant with a superb record, a technical sergeant with eight years of exemplary service, and two other enlisted men who both received less than honorable discharges.

Even the crew of the carefree USS *LaSalle* found themselves embroiled in an intense investigation after an indiscreet sailor took eight rolls of photographs at a party in Bahrain at the home of two wealthy British schoolteachers. Several ships had been ported in Bahrain at the time and as many as 250 American sailors and Marines had danced until dawn, enjoying the hosts' hashish, lavish buffet, and their eight bedrooms. Between sixty and seventy *LaSalle* sailors came under investigation after the photographs surfaced.

Although a handful of those dismissed during these investigations launched lawsuits, a series of rulings throughout 1981 made it clear that the increasingly conservative federal courts would not look kindly upon such challenges. In June 1981, the Supreme Court let stand the previous year's decision to allow the dismissal of former Navy weatherman Dennis Beller, in spite of the federal courts' wildly conflicting rulings on the issue over the past months. One federal court in Milwaukee, for example, had ruled the gay exclusion unconstitutional and ordered the Army to reinstate Miriam Ben-Shalom, while other courts had upheld the policies. As the nation's highest court, the Supreme Court was responsible for resolving such contradictions, but the high court would hear nothing of it.

In October, the Supreme Court closed the books on another lawsuit challenging the military's policies by refusing to hear the appeal of former

Army Captain Jay Hatheway, the Special Forces officer who had been arrested and tried for sodomy in Germany. Unlike others who had challenged the administrative regulation barring gays, Hatheway had argued that the provision of the Uniform Code of Military Justice that made sodomy a felony was unconstitutional. But the Court of Military Appeals did not agree, and the Supreme Court, without commenting, did not agree, either.

THE CRACKDOWNS ON GAYS in early 1981 occurred at a time when official support for the antigay policies was waning. Secretary of Defense Caspar Weinberger did not speak publicly about the policies and declined to do so later, but Dr. Lawrence Korb, who joined the Pentagon in May 1981 as Assistant Secretary of Defense for manpower, reserve affairs, installations, and logistics, shared the new attitude. His job was one of the most crucial in the Defense Department; his responsibilities included managing 70 percent of the nation's military budget. As the Pentagon's top manpower official, he was also responsible for setting personnel policies.

Korb had a military background that included four years of active duty as a Navy flight officer and extensive Reserve service after that. He had retired from the Reserves as a captain and spent the decade before joining the Reagan administration teaching at the U.S. Coast Guard Academy and then at the U.S. Naval War College. Korb considered the ban on homosexuality the last barrier to genuine justice in the military, now that the barriers to African Americans and women had fallen. What preserved the barriers against gays, he strongly believed, was politics. It was not in the political self-interest of the President to change these policies, nor was the Congress likely to tackle the issue. In the end, Korb believed, the one institution that was not answerable to the voters—the courts— would change the military's gay policy by declaring it unconstitutional. That would allow the President and Congress to grumble a bit, but then they would get down to enforcing the decision and this bit of silliness would be over. It would happen sooner rather than later, he thought, and it would not happen one day too soon for him.

Even some among the highest echelons of the uniformed services privately deplored the policy. Opposition was particularly strong in the military's medical corps, where gays had always played a major role and where the generals tended to be better educated. When Captain Stan Harris, a gay Army psychiatrist, disclosed his homosexuality to officers in order to protest the Pentagon's revision of its gay policies, he wrote to Major General Floyd Baker, the commanding general of the Army medical corps, for support. "I wish that sexual orientation did not have to be a discriminator for military service," replied Baker. "Some day in the future it might not be; however, I think the change will come about by evolution, not revolution. . . . I cannot see that falling on my sword over the issue would accelerate the process."

Despite the growing deference to changing times, it would be inaccurate to portray the homosexual issue as one that preoccupied Pentagon policymakers. The problems of incorporating women were a much higher priority, as were the hundreds of other logistical matters involved in the massive buildup of military force that occurred in the first years of the Reagan administration. In fact, Korb never recalled the matter being discussed at all during his four years as the Pentagon's top personnel official. And though he privately opposed the policy, he did not bring the issue up himself, either.

Although the increasing numbers of gay-related discharges suggested that an official crackdown was in progress, the truth was that the policy evoked this response without any directives from Washington. The decisions were made in the field, at the individual command level, where the policy seemed to have a life of its own and the power of its own momentum. So in a government where support was slowly dissipating, the antigay policies were growing stronger than ever.

———————

THE MILITARY'S POLICIES were bound to influence the practices and attitudes of other government institutions. This grim reality was very much on the mind of a former Army lieutenant named Greg Baldwin in the latter months of 1981. Baldwin, thirty-five, was the tall, square-jawed assistant minority counsel on the Senate Permanent Subcommittee on Investigations. His boss was Senator Sam Nunn, the conservative Democrat from Georgia.

In 1970, while an infantry officer in Vietnam, Greg had been hit with shrapnel from a Vietcong rocket, which earned him a Purple Heart and a Bronze Star. He fervently believed that he had served his country to further its promise of freedom and justice for all. In 1981, Baldwin had the opportunity to move to a better job with the committee. The new job required a new security clearance. This would entail an investigation that Baldwin suspected would reveal that he was gay. He did not want this fact to come as a surprise to Nunn, so Greg mentioned it to his immediate supervisor, who did not think the senator would have a problem with it.

But the senator did have a problem with it. Baldwin's job interview was canceled and Senator Nunn asked to see him. At first Nunn's office would not respond to queries about the episode, but his subsequent statements confirm Greg's account of it. Baldwin recalls Nunn explaining that as a member of the Senate Armed Services Committee, military issues were a priority for him. He had asked Admiral Bobby Inman, who had just left the Central Intelligence Agency, about Greg's chances of getting a security clearance, given that he was gay. According to Nunn, although Inman did not personally think this way, he had said that Baldwin would automatically be considered a security risk. Homosexuality per se was evidence of security risk. Nunn said he knew that Baldwin was not a threat to the national security, but technically he was considered to be one. And if Nunn had a perceived security risk on his staff, the Pentagon could use that fact to withhold sensitive information from him.

Nunn did not want to hurt Baldwin's career, he said. He would not fire him. He would not ask him to resign. But he did hope he would look for another job. Nunn would gladly be a reference. Greg could take as much time as he needed.

Baldwin was stunned. He was not angry with Nunn, and voiced no animosity a decade later when he retold the story. He saw Nunn's dilemma. He respected the fact that the senator sat down and explained it personally. Most other senators would have sent an aide to fire him with excuses about budget cuts. Greg appreciated Nunn's honesty, and in the months ahead the senator applied no pressure on him to quit while he looked for another job. Still, he was angry that after all he had given to his country, the application of the word *homosexual* marked him a potential traitor.

What was even more irritating was that hardly anyone involved in the process really believed there was any merit to the notion that gays were security risks. Those at the CIA didn't really believe it anymore, and Senator Nunn didn't appear to believe it, either. But the policy was still there, disrupting and destroying lives.

SEPTEMBER 1981
FORT LEWIS
TACOMA, WASHINGTON

PERRY WATKINS'S BATTALION COMMANDER took him aside to give him the good news. There had been a meeting—at the home of Fort Lewis's commanding general—and it had been agreed that once Perry was separated, he would receive an honorable discharge.

Perry could tell that he was supposed to respond to the news with great relief. Instead, he was furious. He had not even been informed what day his administrative hearing would take place, and already the base's commanding general, the superior to any officer who would serve on the panel, had held this informal meeting to decide the character of his discharge. Obviously, it was a foregone conclusion that he would be discharged.

IT WAS DURING the summer months of 1981 that a new player in the drama of homosexuals in the United States made its first public debut, though it had long been waiting in the wings. In June 1981, investigators at the U.S. Centers for Disease Control announced that in Los Angeles in recent months they had detected five cases of *Pneumocystis carinii* pneumonia. All those diagnosed were gay men. Four weeks later, CDC announced it had detected twenty-six cases of an unusual skin cancer, Kaposi's sarcoma. Four of those cases also suffered from *Pneumocystis carinii;* others had even more bizarre diseases, all rarely seen in the United States. The twenty-six men were all gay. Toward the end of 1981, the numbers of gay men suffering from these diseases compounded at a startling rate, but the cause remained an enigma. By the early months of 1982, there were members of the military, too, who were feeling vaguely ill, and breaking into night sweats.

— 42 —

Railroading

HISTORICALLY, FOR THE STATUS inherent in it, the Office of Special Investigations relished the opportunity to add an officer's scalp to its belt. At base command, charges against officers—particularly charges of homosexuality—were pursued much more vigorously than against enlisted personnel. So the current had been flowing against twenty-four-year-old Lieutenant Joann Newak for some weeks, as court records later showed.

The investigation had begun in the spring with the arrest of a security policeman named Donna Ryan for drunk driving. The arrest had cost Ryan her job and to redeem herself she volunteered to become an OSI informant, offering information about a group the OSI was always eager to investigate: homosexuals. At a women's softball game, Ryan met Joann Newak, who she thought to be a lesbian. She befriended Newak and learned that Joann had a relationship with a senior airman named Lynne Peelman. Quietly, Ryan gathered more evidence. At a party in Newak's home, she saw people smoking marijuana. From Newak's dresser, she took a pill that Joann later said was an amphetamine. When the OSI finally informed Newak and Peelman that they were under investigation for homosexuality, both denied all charges.

The Air Force would have preferred that Newak resign and quietly slip away. But when Newak learned that she was to receive a bad-conduct discharge, she refused to resign. The Air Force tried to frighten her into submission with a laundry list of criminal charges. Laboratory tests revealed that the alleged amphetamine was not an illegal substance but an over-the-counter diet pill that could be purchased at any Walgreens; the Air Force, however, maintained that because Newak appeared to believe that it was an illegal drug, she could be charged with possession of narcotics. There could be other felony charges involving the possession of marijuana and multiple counts of sodomy. On top of everything, Newak could be charged with "conduct unbecoming an officer and a gentleman." Still, she would not resign. At a preliminary hearing in September, the Air Force had found there was enough evidence to proceed with a prosecution.

Captain Raymond Smith represented both Lieutenant Newak and Airman Peelman. Major Carlos Torres was the Staff Judge Advocate for Hancock Field. Air Force documents record an astonishing conversation between the two. Torres suggested providing Peelman the promise of immunity from prosecution if she would testify against Newak and charge that the two had committed acts of sodomy. As Peelman's lawyer, Smith knew that it would be best for his client to accept the deal; as Newak's attorney, he knew that if Peelman agreed to the deal, Newak could well end up going to jail.

Most lawyers negotiating immunity in exchange for testimony are guided by the apprehension that the testimony might undermine their client's credibility, but Smith had no such anxiety. As Newak's lawyer, Smith knew precisely what arguments she would offer the court to counter any charges made under immunity by Peelman. It was with this knowledge that Smith cut the deal with Torres that afternoon.

Later, when Smith explained the situation to Peelman, he warned her not to have anything more to do with Newak. She was "going down the tubes," he said—odd words from Newak's lawyer, but in this case a knowledgeable assessment.

Three days after his meeting with Major Torres, Captain Smith withdrew from representing Joann Newak in her court-martial, citing "conflict of interests." By then, however, the deal was done and the prosecution had the evidence it needed to send Joann Newak to jail.

WHEN IT WORKS PROPERLY, the military judicial system can be a model of fairness and justice. Some lawyers argue that sometimes it is even fairer than civilian courts. The reading of rights, for example, was required by military judges long before civilian courts mandated such warnings. Court-martial juries are made up entirely of officers, ensuring that the accused are judged by a panel made up entirely of college graduates, a rare occurrence in the civilian world.

But there is another side to military justice. As a system completely segregated within the uniformed subculture, military justice is vulnerable to a command structure that believes in higher priorities than the adherence to judicial principles. It is in such times that, as Clemenceau once observed, military justice is to justice what military music is to music.

In the 1980s, the high priority that military commanders placed on weeding out homosexuals created just such a situation. While military judicial and administrative procedures had never been kindhearted to homosexuals, they grew even more hostile during the ferocious efforts to rid the military of gays in this decade, engaging in appalling abrogations of the most rudimentary notions of evidence, fairness, and civil rights. At times, administrative boards became little more than kangaroo courts.

Checks existed within the military judicial system to correct these kinds of injustices, and, by the end of the decade, military appeals courts found themselves overruling many of the convictions of homosexuals meted out by courts-martial. One cruel twist in the military system, however, rendered such reversals hollow: Civilian defendants may retain their freedom while they appeal convictions, most military personnel must serve their jail time during the sluggish process of military appeals. Vindication does not usually occur until after the defendant is already out of jail and on parole.

OCTOBER 28, 1981
FORT LEWIS
TACOMA, WASHINGTON

THE ADMINISTRATIVE SEPARATION board meeting to decide whether Staff Sergeant Perry James Watkins should be discharged from the United States Army convened at 9:00 A.M. on a cold, drizzly morning. Days before the hearing, the Army informed Perry's lawyers that they would call two witnesses to testify that Watkins had made homosexual advances toward them. The federal judge had said she would not uphold a discharge without proven charges of homosexual acts, so the Army was going to produce them. But Perry had never heard of one of the witnesses, and the other was a private who had been in Perry's company but never an object of his affections.

Private First Class David Valley testified first. On his first day under Watkins's supervision, some eighteen months earlier, he said, the sergeant had asked him to move in with him. Watkins recalled telling the private he was free to move off base if he wanted to get away from the cramped barracks, but he was certain he had not asked Valley to move in with him. Perry was living with a boyfriend then and had no interest in a complicated threesome.

Perry's attorney asked Valley whether he had considered it a come-on when Watkins said he could move off base. Valley said no, nor did he give it any more thought until some of the other guys in the unit mentioned later that Perry was gay. Watkins's lawyer asked Valley whether he ever thought that Watkins wanted to have sex with him. Had he ever made a pass?

"No, I can't say that, sir," Valley said.

He added that he would have no problem working for Watkins again and that he did not think Perry's homosexuality interfered with his work performance. All Watkins had ever done, he said, was tell him he could move off the base, adding that sometimes, "He would stare at me and smile."

Meanwhile, Watkins's lawyer learned that Private Andrew Snook, the soldier Perry did not know, would testify that a black staff sergeant had picked him up hitchhiking on July 1, 1981, at Fort Lewis and had put his hand on his thigh. Since Watkins did not pick up hitchhikers, much less make passes at them, Perry suspected that the proposition might have been made to Snook by some other black staff sergeant.

Watkins's lawyers asked that Snook identify Perry from among a group of black soldiers in a lineup before they met in the courtroom. The prosecution argued vociferously against it, but the board agreed. During the lunch break, Perry stood in a lineup. Private Snook was not able to identify any of the men as the one who had made a pass at him.

Undaunted, the prosecutor, Captain James Larson, put Snook on the stand that afternoon and asked him directly whether Watkins was the man who had picked him up and put his hand on the private's thigh four months earlier. Again, Snook said he could not tell. In fact, he could not remember much about the incident except that the man was black, a staff sergeant, and driving a light-colored car with light-colored license plates. He could not remember what state the plates came from. To tell the truth, he had not even thought much of it at the time, but he had mentioned it to someone at work who was from Perry's company, and that man had mentioned it to Perry's supervisor, Captain Hugh Hansel Bryan.

Captain Bryan took the stand. No matter what Snook said, Bryan insisted, the man who had made a pass at him was Staff Sergeant Watkins. He had investigated the matter "thoroughly," he said, and "it was definitely Sergeant Watkins." Bryan added that he had also talked to Snook's company commander, who said Snook was a "very good soldier" and a reliable source.

At this comment Captain Walter Johnson, one of the three officers on Watkins's discharge board, stiffened. Had Bryan talked to Snook's commander on the telephone or in person? Johnson asked.

"It was in person, on a one-to-one basis in his office," Bryan said.

Johnson was perplexed because *he* was Private Snook's commanding officer, and he did not recall ever talking to Bryan about this incident.

"It was not yourself," Bryan admitted.

Furthermore, Johnson told the hearing that Snook was a "below-average" soldier and allowed that he would take anything the private said "with a grain of salt."

Under further questioning, Bryan admitted that there could be thousands of black staff sergeants stationed at the sprawling Fort Lewis and that among them there could be hundreds who drove light-colored cars. Then he had to admit that he had somehow thrown out the statement he had taken from Snook when the incident occurred several months earlier. Captain Palmer Penny, an Army lawyer with the post headquarters company, testified that when Bryan brought the Snook allegations to his attention in the summer, he had bluntly advised him, "This isn't going to hold up in court," that the evidence "wasn't sufficient." And Penny added that he remained personally "unconvinced" that the man who made the alleged advance on Snook was Watkins.

In fact, Watkins not only had an alibi but several thousand witnesses to it. Like just about every other able-bodied soldier at Fort Lewis, he had been on the parade ground on the afternoon that the alleged advance occurred, practicing for the post's Organization Day ceremonies.

In his defense, a series of character witnesses testified to Watkins's superiority as a soldier. One lieutenant colonel called Watkins an "excellent" soldier, adding that he would be welcome back into his command at any time, even if he was homosexual. One major testified that while it was his professional duty to support Army policy, "Personally, I support Sergeant Watkins." A sergeant major dismissed the whole hearing as nonsense, given the fact that people had known for years that Watkins was gay. "This is not some great discovery that just came about," he said.

Regarding the informal meeting at the commanding general's house where the character of Watkins's discharge had been discussed, another officer testified he could not recall any details of the evening.

In the end, the prosecutor entered as evidence the statement that Watkins had signed in 1968 admitting that he was gay. Ultimately, it was this statement and the admissions Perry had made during his preinduction physical in 1967 that represented the only evidence of his homosexuality.

Despite the weakness of the case, prosecutor Larson argued that Watkins should be separated immediately and denied an honorable discharge. He pleaded with the panel to consider the impressionable young recruit who might come under Watkins's supervision: "He's 17, 18, 19, maybe 20 years old. He's away from home, perhaps for the first time in his life. His family is a thousand miles, two thousand miles, perhaps even an ocean away. . . . He's at a critical stage in his physical and psychological development. . . . Gentlemen, do you want to entrust the development of that young soldier to Staff Sergeant Watkins? I don't think you do."

Larson also insisted that Watkins was indeed the soldier who had made a pass not only at Private Snook but probably at many others who might have been seduced into homosexuality by the staff sergeant. "How many more soldiers have accepted the proposition that may not have been homosexual?" Larson asked. "Again, your private, the young man who doesn't know; the young man who's curious, the young man who is away from home."

Jim Lobsenz advanced his constitutional arguments against the Pentagon's antigay policies, arguing that they violated Perry's right to free speech and privacy. Furthermore, he said, "If the Army makes a promise to a man that you can enter the Army, be a homosexual, you can still have a career with us, they cannot turn around some 14 years later and say we didn't mean it. Now that you've invested 14 years of your life in an Army career, we are going to go back on our word and throw you out for something that we've known all along."

Watkins's military lawyer, Lieutenant Joel Courtemanche, called

Snook's testimony a "farce" and dismissed the whole hearing as "a vicious attempt at railroading, gentlemen. Again, I use the term railroading. It's an Army term. If you want to get somebody out of the Army, you just make things so unbearable that you just wait for him to screw up. When he does, you got him and you nail him. That is what we had. They were trying to nail Staff Sergeant Watkins."

In a three-minute session at the end of the second day of the hearing, the panel chairman read the decision of the Administrative Discharge Board. "Staff Sergeant Perry J. Watkins is undesirable for further retention in the military service because he has stated that he is homosexual," he said.

The panel did not find that Watkins was guilty of any homosexual acts, only that he was indeed homosexual, as defined by the new regulations. Even that conclusion was confirmed by a vote of only two to one, with one panel member arguing that the prosecution had not established Watkins's "intent" to commit homosexual acts in the future. Lobsenz counted the ruling as a victory, since it meant that the Army had proven nothing new against Watkins beyond what it had already charged him with in 1975. It was a clear case of double jeopardy.

Two days later, federal judge Barbara Rothstein ruled just that, disallowing the Army from separating Watkins. To this, an Army lawyer responded that even if the Army did retain Watkins for now, they would simply deny him reenlistment when his current term was completed in 1984. Since the Army raised the issue, Rothstein said stiffly, perhaps the lawyers should prepare arguments on that eventuality now. Under Army regulations, if a soldier could not be administratively separated for a given reason, neither could he be denied reenlistment for that reason. Watkins would stay put.

The Army chose not to appeal Rothstein's order, and so on October 31, 1981, Perry Watkins continued to be the first openly gay man to serve publicly in the United States Army. The next morning Perry returned to work in the personnel office and life for Watkins and for the Army returned to normal.

MARCH 1982
HANCOCK FIELD
SYRACUSE, NEW YORK

JOANN NEWAK sat absolutely still.

She had known hard times; her dad, a TV repairman, had died of a heart attack when she was a girl, and her mother had raised Joann and her two sisters on the modest salary of a registered nurse. A cheerful disposition and a sunny smile seemed the antidote to adversity, and Joann held on to these and excelled in academics and athletics at her high school in Vandling, Pennsylvania, and made her way through Marywood College, a Catholic school in Scranton. She had graduated in 1979 with her bachelor's degree in physical education and a teaching certificate, then had joined the Air Force.

After Officers' Training School, assigned to the Twenty-first Air Division at Hancock Field, she had excelled at all she did for the service; she loved the Air Force and looked forward to a career in uniform. Her supervisors extolled her, as well; her officer evaluation forms were thick with superlatives and suggestions that she be promoted quickly. And then came the investigation, just two years into her service, and now she was sitting in a courtroom listening to the court-martial verdict.

"Guilty," said each of the four panel members: guilty of a total of eleven felonies. Joann was convicted of three counts of sodomy with Lynne Peelman, who had testified against her. Each crime had occurred off the base in the privacy of the women's own bedroom, between consenting adults, but each count represented a violation of Article 125 of the Uniform Code of Military Justice, punishable by five years at hard labor in prison. Donna Ryan's assertions convicted Newak of possession of marijuana and the transfer of marijuana. Someone had seen her pass a joint to someone else. Newak was also guilty of possession and the transfer of a narcotic, because of the amphetamine that was not illegal but that was counted as a narcotic because Newak mistakenly thought it was. She was guilty of conduct unbecoming an officer and a gentleman, as well.

Joann's civilian lawyer, Faith Seidenberg, had argued against a stern judgment, given that most of the charges against her client were no longer crimes in the state of New York. Smoking marijuana, for example, was no longer against the law. And state courts had thrown out the New York sodomy statute. No civilian court in the United States would convict a person of possession of a controlled substance that was not really a controlled substance just because they believed it was. In a state or even a federal court, the drug charges would have resulted in probation time at most, if charges were brought at all, which Seidenberg thought unlikely. But this was not a civilian court. This was the military, and Joann Newak was a convicted homosexual, and homosexuals were to be dealt with harshly.

The judge read Newak's sentence: seven years at hard labor in the military prison at the United States Disciplinary Barracks at Fort Leavenworth.

Within weeks, Joann Newak was transferred to Fort Leavenworth, the 120-year-old Army post overlooking the Missouri River, not far from Kansas City. Like all new prisoners, she was strip-searched, tersely advised of the prison rules, and taken to her cell, where the steel door slammed shut behind her.

— 43 —

Doreen

SEPTEMBER 1982
USS *ENTERPRISE*
IN THE SOUTH PACIFIC

A CHIEF PETTY OFFICER dressed only in his underwear grabbed the young sailor's head and pressed it between his thighs. The other men hooted their approval. This was better than last night's drag show, at which King Neptune's queen had been crowned with a coronet and enthroned beside his husband.

On the flight deck, meanwhile, older sailors, armed with mock shillelaghs, long strips of cut-up fire hose, had formed a gauntlet through which the younger initiates had to pass. They shouted "Wogs!" as they applied their lashes to the young backs and buttocks of their juniors. The whips slapped across the flesh and the men grinned and howled "Wogs!"

Once the wogs had made it past the gauntlet, they congregated on the fantail and stripped, then hurled their clothes, soiled and torn from hours of initiation, into the ocean. No one rushed back to his locker for new clothes. They joked and laughed and strutted around the deck. Their nudity was evidence of having passed the test.

The players in the games aboard the USS *Enterprise*—experimenting with transvestitism, simulated fellatio, sadomasochistic role playing and group nudity—were not gay. Rather, they were sailors participating in a time-honored Navy tradition, the "shellback" ceremony that marked the first time a sailor, referred to as a "pollywog" or just "wog," crossed the equator. After the crossing and the ceremonies, the sailor became a "shellback."

Different ships employed different versions of the shellback ritual. On smaller ships in the U.S. Navy, for example, the wogs were sometimes required to get on all fours while older shellbacks mounted them and simulated anal intercourse. Photographs of the hundreds of couples feigning the doggie-style copulation immortalized the event in the high school yearbook–style "cruise books" each sailor received at the end of a long voyage.

The essentials of the shellback ceremonies did not vary from ship to ship, however. They included crowning King Neptune's queen the night before the initiation, and the lucky winner was allowed to metamorphose from wog to shellback without any of the degrading ceremonies. The next morning, when shellback hazing began in earnest, it was ritual to soak the younger sailors with garbage and other unpleasant slime, followed by the gauntlet of makeshift whips, capped by the wogs kissing the olive-studded navel of the chief petty officer with the biggest belly. The kiss was usually a prelude to the chief pulling the wog's head down into his groin. Baptized in seawater, christened a shellback, the sailors concluded their initiation on the ship's fantail by disrobing.

As a Navy corpsman, Hospitalman Second Class Kelly Kittell experienced only an abbreviated version of the shellback ceremony. He was required on deck to take care of the broken bones and sundry injuries that always accompanied the hazing. So Kelly, standing tall in his dungarees, watched from the flight deck and marveled at the homoeroticism of the ritual.

The homosexual subtext of the armed forces was not unique to the Navy and was conspicuous in military jargon. Common Army slang for protecting oneself was the phrase "cover your ass," meaning protecting one's rear from a sexual assault. Currying favor was known as "sucking up," while the most common command of gruff senior noncommissioned officers was "get your ass over here." Homosexually charged rituals existed in regiments the world over. In Scotland, for example, one initiation rite demanded that highlanders lift their kilts with their penises.

For all the gay undertones to be found throughout the military, however, the service with the most pervasive homosexual subtext was the Navy, in which the level of veiled homoeroticism seemed directly proportional to the amount of time sailors spent at sea out of the presence of women. (Winston Churchill once barked to a British admiral lecturing him on naval tradition, "Don't talk to me about naval tradition. It's nothing but rum, sodomy, and the lash.") Submariners were notorious. At one of the nation's most popular submariner hangouts, the Horse and Cow bar near the Mare Island Naval Station base in Vallejo, California, the rule was that customers may not wear underwear, so there were regular "skivvy checks," during which sailors were stripped of their pants to make sure they complied. A patron discovered wearing underwear was summarily disrobed and his shorts torn off. "The dance of the flaming asshole" was another regular event. A male crewman was ordered to strip naked in the bathroom and a long strand of toilet paper was thrust into his anus and the trailing end lit. The sailor then raced out of the bathroom, leaped up on the bar and performed a brief jig, and tried to get back to the bathroom before the burning paper reached the tender spot between his buttocks. Such sports among submariners supported the old Navy cliché that a submarine leaves port with 120 crew members but returns with 60 couples.

Second only to submarine crewmen for the blatant homoeroticism of their customs were the sailors on aircraft carriers, like the USS *Enterprise* on this September day in the South Pacific. As with submarines, the gargantuan carriers were combat vessels, made long voyages, and carried no female crew members. With crews of five or six thousand men, they were also like small cities, which seemed to magnify the homoeroticism aboard ship. The sight of the gauntlet and of the naked young men on the fantail caused Kelly Kittell to wonder at how utterly unconscious heterosexuals could be about that part of their psyches that responded with such enthusiasm to this sexually charged contact among them.

It was ironic, especially because the United States Navy, more than any other service, was dedicated to purging itself of homosexuality. During the 1980s, as it had for decades, the Navy discharged more people for this reason than all other services combined. Of course, Kelly had not known that in 1978 when he was seventeen and enlisted in the Navy. His father had been a career Air Force enlisted man himself before he retired and moved the family to Reno, Nevada.

Kelly had known that he liked other boys since he was a kid. He had known when he was fourteen years old and had seen the *Time* magazine with Leonard Matlovich on the cover. Inside the magazine was a photograph of two men on a couch together, one with his head on the other man's lap. He would like to be one of them, he knew. He also knew not to talk about his longings with his family or with his Mormon friends.

While attending a fire-fighting school at the Alameda Naval Air Station in California, Kelly had decided to visit San Francisco. It was the last Sunday of June 1981, Gay Freedom Day. Kelly was astounded. He had never heard of such a thing as a gay parade. He had never known there were so many normal-looking gay people. Thereafter, he went into San Francisco whenever he could, and he discovered gay newspapers; he began to think he could lead a normal, well-adjusted life as a gay person. At the open-mike night at a gay comedy club called the Valencia Rose, Kelly even tried some stand-up comedy, basing his routines on being gay in the Navy. He told his audiences he had enlisted because of the Village People, and he assured them that life aboard the USS *Enterprise* was nothing like *Anchors Aweigh* with Frank Sinatra and Gene Kelly dancing the hornpipe. He performed a sketch about the very closeted chaplain with a high-pitched voice who fluttered his hands nervously when he denied he was gay. People laughed. Kelly felt very liberated. After the show, he drove back to Alameda and the USS *Enterprise,* worrying about witch-hunts and informants for the Naval Investigative Service.

By now, three years after his enlistment, Kelly had become part of a gay crowd on the *Enterprise*. Since the *Enterprise* was known as the "Big

E" or the "Big Easy," the gay sailors referred to themselves as the E-Girls, or, more commonly, the Easy Girls. He had not imagined that there could be such an open gay community on a Navy ship, but Kelly found gays in every department, particularly his own, the medical department. There were ways to tell. Kelly learned to drop the word *nelly* to see if it raised a glimmer of recognition; or the surefire standby of mentioning the word *Family*. At the top of the gay hierarchy was the "Mother," the senior enlisted crew member who doled out advice and warnings to younger or indiscreet seamen. By the time the summer of 1982 approached and preparations were in earnest for the annual western Pacific cruise, or WESTPAC, Kelly felt as if he was indeed part of a big family.

With their huge populations, aircraft carriers had the largest and best-organized gay communities. By now, gay cliques on board each carrier had dubbed their ships with their own campy nicknames, usually based on the name of the wife of whomever the ship was named for. The carrier USS *John F. Kennedy,* for example, was called the "Jackie O" by its gay crewmen. The USS *Eisenhower* was the "Mamie"; the USS *America* was the "Miss America."

The carrier communities had their own institutions; the USS *America,* for example, had its own secret drag contests for the gay community's Miss America crown. (The crown is handed out annually to this day, gay crewmen say, having eluded officers' attempts to ferret it from the locker where it has remained hidden for more than a decade.) The gays aboard the USS *Forrestal* had enjoyed their own gay disco since 1976, down in the storerooms where other sailors rarely went at night. On the 1982 WESTPAC cruise, the USS *Eisenhower* published its own gay newsletter, *Mamie's Pages,* passed covertly to gay sailors with the ship's official paper whenever the ship pulled into a foreign port. Included in *Mamie's Pages* were the Xeroxed pages of *Spartacus,* the authoritative international gay travel guide that advised sailors where they could find local homosexual hangouts. Toward the end of WESTPAC, sailors were distributing fifteen hundred copies of *Mamie's Pages* at every port.

On the eve of the 1982 WESTPAC cruise, while other *Enterprise* sailors were enjoying their last days of liberty, Kelly Kittell and several gay friends made a pilgrimage to San Francisco to see Armistead Maupin. Kelly had first discovered Maupin when his mom gave him a copy of Maupin's first book, *Tales of the City.* Since then, he had learned that Maupin had also served in the Navy, so Kelly and his friends had decided to make him an honorary Easy Girl. They had a certificate made up, looked him up in the phone book, and explained they were from the *Enterprise* and had something for him.

Maupin had weighty matters on his mind at the time. A good friend was slowly dying in New York City. His friend had been fine one day and the next was wasting away from what people were calling "gay pneumonia." But Maupin met with Kelly and the Easy Girls just the same, accepted their certificate, and exchanged stories about being gay in the military.

They talked about change and about how gay people themselves needed to step forward, to show who they were, to fight prejudice and discrimination. Armistead, then thirty-eight years old, would never be one of the politically correct who peopled the forefront of gay leadership, but he was adamant that gay people should come out. Over the past few years, he had been encouraging his friend Rock Hudson to let people know he was gay. Hudson seemed to grapple with the idea, understanding it was the right thing to do but still afraid of the repercussions. With each year, Maupin grew more assertive, believing that by staying in the closet one acquiesced to the notion that homosexuality was something shameful, something that people should not talk about, much less admit.

Maupin's observations came like words from on high to twenty-one-year-old Kelly Kittell, and they stayed with him when the *Enterprise* pulled out of its berth and made its way into the Pacific. But balancing that philosophy with Navy regulations was hardly possible. Still, Kelly could strengthen his "family," he thought, make it more like a community. He began publishing a newsletter for gay *Enterprise* crewmen, *The Family-Gram*. Hardly anyone came into the main medical office at night, where Kelly could type the letter on an IBM computer, hiding it amid other files that few of the computer-illiterate crewmen knew how to access. A copy of the newsletter was passed to key gay personnel in other departments on the ship, who Xeroxed copies for their friends.

The Family-Gram was written with great discretion; a straight sailor would be unlikely to decode its gay references. Pseudonyms were always employed. Kelly wrote his articles under the byline Doreen. Much of the newsletter was idle gossip about who was found in the head with whom and which departments were offering the best "traid," a code word for *trade*, meaning heterosexual men who had sex with gay men when there were no women around. There were letters to "Edna," the editor. There were also listings for gay bars in the upcoming ports of Singapore and Perth and recommendations as to which section of the Subic Bay enlisted men's club was most productive for cruising.

As the ship's only pharmacy technician, Kelly manufactured greatly appreciated supplies for the Easy Girls. In his pharmacy blender, Kelly mixed Vaseline, K-Y jelly, and a combination of ointments to produce his own sexual lubricant, which he called Easy Come, Easy Go. The lubricant became wildly popular on the ship, especially after Kelly added something to make it taste good. Then he started making his own lip gloss—Doreen's Blow a Kiss Lip Gloss. On each jar of gloss and lubricant, Kelly tied his own label with red ribbon: Doreen's—signed with a great flourish. Kelly advertised his products in *The Family-Gram*, saying they were available on a first come, first served basis.

For all the campiness of Kelly's efforts, his writing carried a strong political subtext. As he wrote in an October 1982 *Family-Gram*, "I'm so glad to see an air of militancy has pervaded this ship. Yes, what you have heard is true. The powers that be are scared of a revolt."

Kittell's subversive message was not lost on the ship's command, which seemed instantly aware of every new *Family-Gram*, as well as Kelly's extracurricular activities with the pharmacy blender. One day, the ship's executive officer, who served at the right hand of the *Enterprise* skipper, called Kelly into his office to ask about Doreen's cosmetics line. Kelly did his best to sound righteously indignant, explaining that as the ship's pharmacist it was his job to provide a salve for the crew's chapped lips. He did not mention that his lip gloss also contained color and thickener; fortunately, the executive officer did not ask. It was clear, however, that someone had informed the officers of Doreen's identity, and it seemed clear they were also aware that Kelly was the ship's *Family-Gram* publisher. He was being watched. They were all being watched. The ship's chaplain, the priest with the fluttering hands and high-pitched voice, told Kelly in effect to cool it.

The most direct blow to Kelly's growing gay pride came during preparations for the shellback ceremony. Gay sailors had been winning the drag contest that determined King Neptune's queen with greater regularity throughout both the Atlantic and Pacific fleets in recent years. The straight guys used "skag drag," a mop for a wig, a tablecloth for a dress, while the gay sailors had filled their lockers with authentic apparel, shaved their legs, and plucked their eyebrows. It took experience to know how to do drag right; the heterosexual sailors did not stand a chance. Shortly before the ceremony on the *Enterprise*, however, the crotchety chief of the Navy corpsmen had issued an order denying the medical department permission to participate in the competition. Kelly was convinced the chief hoped to spare his department embarrassment.

The order grated on Kittell. He loved being in the military, but he thought its treatment of gays was deplorable. Then it occurred to him that the military's policies excluding homosexuals worked only because gays participated by staying in the closet. If all the gay sailors stepped forward, the service could never kick them all out and still function. Even if gays were only 10 percent of the Navy—the percentage gays were thought to comprise in the general adult population—the service could never stand to lose so significant a number overnight. The policy would be doomed.

Kelly could not get the idea out of his mind: Gay people participated in their own oppression. He began seeing signs of it among other crew members. One day after a seaman named Demerest had had sex with an ostensibly heterosexual crewman, the "trade" returned to a group of his straight friends and then turned and mocked his tryst as he walked by. "Oh, Mrs. Demerest," the straight sailor called in a high-pitched voice. It was humiliating, but Kelly knew the gay crewman would go back to the straight guys for sex again. Kittell had always viewed the other gay crew members as his buddies, but as he grew more strident in telling them to show some self-respect and stand up for themselves, a schism started to develop between him and the others.

They had made their accommodations; they had figured out a way to navigate around the perplexing rules heterosexuals had created for homosexuals. Change seemed threatening, more threatening, in fact, than the status quo. So as the *Enterprise* steamed toward Mombasa, Kenya, Kelly felt alone and frustrated.

The entire USS *Enterprise* seemed seized by a sexual doublethink in which everyone denied the experience of their own senses. Heterosexuals denied the rights and humanity of homosexuals, even as they participated in rituals designed to release their own homoerotic energies during the periods in which there was no possibility of heterosexual activity. Homosexuals complained bitterly about homophobia but never challenged it. These bizarre contradictions were a logjam to change. Kelly promised himself that if the opportunity ever arose, he would challenge it.

OCTOBER 1982
GUERNEVILLE, CALIFORNIA

FROM THE START, Leonard Matlovich's Stumptown Annie's pizza parlor seemed ill-fated. He had not done much checking on permits and other such details before moving to the area. Only when he was about to open did he learn that because the tiny town had no sewage system and drained its wastes through septic tanks, he could not use a dishwasher. Instead, he would have to serve from paper plates and use plastic utensils—and the restrictions only started there. Sonoma County inspectors enforced local codes ferociously; Matlovich found himself quickly hemmed in by the governmental regulations his Republican sensibilities had always detested.

Worse was his disappointing affair with Cliff Anchor. Their romance had started out promisingly enough. Lenny was happy to make the trip up to Cliff's hilltop home, where they could watch the Russian River wind through miles of redwood groves toward the fog-engulfed Pacific. Cliff had two playful dogs, and the relationship had begun to look as if it might offer the "white picket fence" life that Lenny had sought in the seven years since he had told the Air Force that he was gay. To seal their relationship, Cliff even bought two gold wedding rings. On Wednesdays, Lenny broadcast a public-affairs talk show from Cliff's radio station; afterward, they would light a fire in the fireplace and spend the evening together.

When they were alone, they were contented lovers. But when Lenny suggested that he and Cliff do something as a couple, Cliff balked. He worried what people would think. He wanted to be more open about being gay—or at least not hide it—but he was concerned for his adopted teenaged son and how he might react. Lenny accepted this, but, as the months wore on and he realized that he would never have the kind of relaxed marriage with Cliff that he wanted, he grew frustrated. There was always going to be a reason to hide being gay, Lenny argued. If it was not Cliff's son, who Lenny thought knew anyway, it would be the business, or what the neighbors thought. It was just such reasoning that kept gay people where they were, Lenny insisted. As a conservative, Matlovich was big on personal responsibility; he lectured Cliff that if the gay cause was failing as a movement, one major reason was that gay people were still participating in their own subjugation.

Intellectually, Cliff agreed with him. When he drove down Main Street in Guerneville, however, and saw this or that old friend in a pickup truck or Jeep, he froze at the idea that they might discover his secret. Years later, he learned that his neighbors and business clients had known he was gay all along, as had his son, and it had never mattered. But this realization came too late. Although the two remained friends, Lenny and Cliff started drifting apart then.

Lenny fought loneliness by throwing himself into community affairs. Before too long, he was elected to the board of directors of the Russian River Chamber of Commerce and became a mediator between new gay businesses and local old-timers, who were still wary of the homosexual influx. He did raise eyebrows, though, when he invited the huge San Francisco Gay Freedom Day Marching Band to parade down the hamlet's two-lane Main Street to observe the Chamber of Commerce's annual awards dinner. He became involved in local Republican party politics and soon there was not a local controversy in western Sonoma County about which Matlovich had not taken a position.

His constant opinionatedness sometimes got on peoples' nerves, but Matlovich was such a gentle man and so eager to please, he could usually wrangle his way back into the affections of the most homophobically inclined Guernevillian. Every morning, people honked from their pickups and waved when Lenny went out to the corner of Main Street and Armstrong Woods Road to raise the Stars and Stripes outside his restaurant. It was his trademark in the little town, his flag and his flagpole. The flag and Lenny's belief in what it represented remained central to his faith that somehow everything would turn out all right for him and for other gays.

It was at this time that Lenny began noticing small articles that were appearing more regularly in the newspaper about "gay pneumonia," "gay cancer," and the more complicated immune-deficiency problems that presaged the development of those diseases, something that was being called "gay-related immune deficiency" or GRID. New York, Los Angeles, and San Francisco seemed to be the centers for these mysterious maladies, Lenny noted with some cockiness, thus assured that it was all part of the fast-lane gay bathhouse and drug culture in which he had never participated. It would not affect him. In October 1982, as his relationship with Cliff Anchor wound down, Lenny read a new name for the diseases that were being recorded with greater regularity around the country. Now, it was being called Acquired Immune Deficiency Syndrome, or AIDS.

By now, military doctors had quietly treated their first AIDS case. In March 1982, a sergeant had come to San Francisco's Letterman Army Medical Center complaining that he couldn't even walk up the hill to his apartment at the end of his workday. The doctor who examined him, a major, suspected he might be suffering from *Pneumocystis carinii*, the rare pneumonia that struck AIDS sufferers. He asked whether the man was gay. The sergeant vigorously denied it. Subsequent tests confirmed that the sergeant did indeed have *Pneumocystis carinii*. Treatments for the disease were very primitive then, and within three months the man lay dying. About to put a respirator tube down his throat, his doctor explained that the sergeant would not be able to talk. Fighting for breath and sweating profusely, the patient clutched the doctor's white lab coat and said, "I'm gay."

The doctor understood the patient's earlier reluctance at saying these words aloud, but he sighed when he realized that the sergeant clearly believed that telling him now would make a difference, that something could be done now that the facts were out. It could not. Those were the sergeant's last words. He died in July, the first known AIDS case in the military, and one of the first three hundred in the nation.

His doctor was conscientious and was among those to propose sending a case report to the journal *Military Medicine* so that military physicians could familiarize themselves with the syndrome. The reply was concise: "This is not pertinent to the practice of medicine in the United States military."

A few weeks after the sergeant died in San Francisco, Ray Orsini, an airman first class en route from Guam to Japan, finally went to see his Air Force doctors about the strange fevers and sweats that came over him every night. He was fine during the day, but when he tried to sleep, his temperature went up as high as 103 degrees. Perspiration soaked his sheets; he would change his sheets, but his sweat would soak them again. He had also lost ten pounds over the past several months. His doctors were stumped. His blood tests revealed strange abnormalities in his white blood cells, the organisms that provide immunity to disease. The symptoms were not like anything they had ever seen before; Orsini was the first diagnosed case of AIDS in the Air Force.

OCTOBER 1982
ABOARD USS *ENTERPRISE*
IN THE INDIAN OCEAN

WHAT SET KELLY KITTELL OFF on his last crusade was a memo that came down from the ship's skipper, congratulating the *Enterprise* crew for lack of prejudice on the ship. They should feel grateful to be part of an organization that did not tolerate discrimination, the captain said, and if anyone became aware of any type of discrimination on board the USS *Enterprise*, that sailor should report it directly to him. Intolerance would not be tolerated.

As he read the memo, Kelly felt his hackles rise. Here, they routinely kicked gay people out of their jobs, dispatched spies to monitor them, and even sent some to prison, all the while maintaining that they would not tolerate prejudice. And by remaining silent, Kelly would be tolerating the prejudice, too. In San Francisco, he had heard someone speculate about what would happen if every gay person turned purple and heterosexuals were forced to confront those people against whom they harbored so much prejudice. Kelly decided he could remain silent no longer, and he quickly dashed off a letter to the ship's captain.

> *Recently you asked department heads for information on any type of discrimination that may exist on board the USS* Enterprise. *There is one type that I am sure no department has mentioned, yet still exists. As a matter of fact the entire military system promotes this discrimination because the fear of what it's about poisons the minds of those serving.*
>
> *Those of us who are victims of this for the most part have no shared country or religion. We are both rich and poor, male and female, single and married, officer and enlisted. However, we do have one common tie—we are homosexuals.*
>
> *I would hazard a guess that there is not a single department that does not contain at least one of us. Since I have been on board, one has been selected* Enterprise *Man of the Month and you, yourself, have personally lauded another. We seem to be both your worst fears and your best workers.*
>
> *I will no longer be prey to the homophobic attitudes that blind the Navy's eye and transform an otherwise rational and temperate group of individuals into a pack of ravenous witchhunters intent upon "purifying" their own ranks.*
>
> *I will no longer live a second, secret life because the Navy has seen fit to adhere to an ante-diluvian, Judeo-Christian posture that no longer and never was congruent with social realism.*
>
> *I will no longer remain silent when I see or hear a homophobic attitude spewn as upright, moral and the "Navy Way."*
>
> *I am not asking equality or sanction for my gayness, or even tacit, albeit reluctant recognition for our minority status. I am asking that we be allowed dignity and pride in ourselves. I am asking that we be recognized as contributing and valuable members of the crew— equality as human beings.*
>
> *I sign myself committed to this cause,*
>
> Kelly Kittell
HM2, USN

The ship's legal officer was blunt when he met with Kelly later. As Kelly remembers it, his first words were, "You're in a lot of trouble." Then he mentioned the military prison at Fort Leavenworth. Of course, everything would go easier on Kelly if he would give them names of other homosexuals. Kelly thought it was odd that the brass believed he would turn on other gays after passing them a rather strident statement for gay liberation. They had obviously not gotten the point. He refused. Eventually, Kelly was removed from the *Enterprise* in a small jet and flown back to the United States, where he was discharged.

His last weeks on the *Enterprise* were disconcerting because of the lack of support he received from other gay crew members. Only one offered any encouragement. To the rest, Kelly was a pariah, someone to be shunned and even feared. The vast majority of gay people, he could see now, were not ready to challenge the prejudice that shaped their lives. What would it take? he wondered.

Kittell moved to San Francisco. Several months later, he received a phone call from an *Enterprise* officer who had been transferred to Treasure Island. After Kittell left, he said, a crackdown had begun on the *Enterprise*. The Naval Investigative Service had had an informer planted among The Family on the ship for some months; he had even had sex with the gay men. That was how the ship's officers had known all along that it was Kelly publishing the paper and manufacturing Doreen's products. Then, shortly after Kelly's departure, the informant had also left the ship. When NIS agents called sailors in for interrogation, the agents explained that Kelly Kittell had already told them everything and that they should make it easy on themselves by admitting to being homosexual. Many did.

Kelly had wanted to make a statement of pride and even insurrection with his letter; instead, they had made him out to be a traitor. They had had the last laugh, after all.

— 44 —

Lesbian Vampires of Bavaria

OCTOBER 1982
UNITED STATES NAVAL ACADEMY
ANNAPOLIS, MARYLAND

"A MIDSHIPMAN DOES NOT LIE, cheat, or steal."

That was the fundamental precept of the Honor Code of the United States Naval Academy. Though high-sounding, there is a practical rationale behind its rigorous enforcement. The Navy cannot afford the luxury of even the slightest mistrust among officers. Twenty-one-year-old Ruth Voor, now in her final year at the Naval Academy, believed in the honor code and was proud to serve on the Brigade Honor Committee, which supervised its enforcement among the entire Academy. The appointment earned her a third stripe on her sleeve, made her a midshipman lieutenant, and gave her a number of special privileges. By the autumn of 1982, it also created some personal conflicts.

Another lesbian investigation was under way at the school, and it promised to imperil the women's basketball team that Ruth had helped manage. The female students were frantic. Lists of suspected lesbians were being drawn up. Careers were on the line, just seven months before graduation. Word spread that a first-year midshipman had already been interrogated by agents from the Naval Investigative Service's Annapolis office, which had a reputation as one of the most aggressively antigay NIS offices in the country. It became Ruth's job to tell the midshipman to stand strong against the coercive tactics of the NIS.

Ruth had already taken notice of Karen Colton, the plebe at the center of so much concern. Karen was cute by anyone's standards, with blond hair and a trim build, but Ruth was most taken by Karen's blue eyes. "Do you believe in love at first sight?" Ruth had asked Karen's squad leader early in the school year.

"Don't even think about it," her friend had advised. "You want to graduate. Don't get in trouble.

Ruth told her not to worry. She was not stupid.

But in the weeks that followed, it was hard for Ruth to stay away. When Karen had watch, Ruth made sure to come by her post to pick up her mail and messages. She wangled regular invitations to sit at Karen's squad's table, and it was clear that she was interested. But Ruth assured her friends it was just harmless flirting. She never revealed herself to Karen; quite the opposite, she frequently mentioned a supposed boyfriend. When Ruth asked Karen to help her manage the basketball team, Karen felt flattered and agreed.

At eighteen, Karen was a product of her age group, which was beginning to enjoy the benefits of more than a decade of gay organizing. Karen was five years old when the Stonewall riots occurred, and thirteen when Anita Bryant thrust gay rights onto the front page of every newspaper, especially in Florida, where Karen was raised. The whole issue just did not seem scary to Karen. Her best friend in high school had a lesbian sister, and, by the time Karen was sixteen, she had gone to Saturdays, the gay bar in Melbourne, Florida. That was pretty much all she knew about gay life firsthand. She expected that one day she would get married like everyone else.

Karen began thinking of going to a military academy in 1976, when she read an article in *Seventeen* about the first women to enter the academies. What with her high grades and her many extracurricular activities, she was easily accepted to Annapolis. By the summer of 1982, she had become a part of the seventh Academy class to include women. From the first days, Karen excelled. She ranked second in her company at the end of Plebe Summer, and as the school year got under way she went to the top of her class in academics and physical fitness.

And she soon discovered what Ruth had learned three years earlier—that a lot of men at the Academy resented the presence of women there. They laughed at her desire to be a pilot, explaining that the combat exclusion policy would prevent it. That she wanted to work in nuclear power was even a bigger joke, since virtually all the Navy's nuclear-powered ships, mainly aircraft carriers, destroyers, and submarines, were also off-limits to female sailors. She would end up in some supply depot somewhere, her male classmates assured her.

Sexual harassment was pandemic. On the night of the Army-Navy game in Philadelphia, Karen got drunk and passed out on her hotel room's bed. Several male midshipmen came into her room, took pictures of themselves in sexually suggestive poses with her, and then passed the photos around the dormitory. Only when Karen threatened to turn the men in to Academy brass did they finally relinquish the photos.

By now, men had developed a pejorative vocabulary to describe female midshipmen. The standard uniform, for example, was called the WUBA, an acronym for working uniform blue alpha, but the guys snickered that females should be called WUBAs—women in uniform with big asses. Throughout the huge dormitory at Bancroft Hall, men wrote WUBA on doors where women were likely to pass.

Much of the hazing revolved around the presumed lesbianism of any woman who would invade the Academy's once exclusively male domain. Five years after the lesbian investigation of the women's volleyball team, male midshipmen still hooted at female volleyball players. Since all female athletes were presumed to be homosexual, lesbian jokes abounded following any women's sports events. When the Navy women's basketball team prepared to play the Army's team, one young midshipman from Company Twenty-one made a huge banner and hung it from the Bancroft Hall rotunda: LEZ BEAT ARMY. Karen tore it down herself.

Karen had been surprised that there were any gay people at all at Annapolis, let alone so many. Her first lesbian Academy friend, who played softball, too, filled her in and gave her a rundown on the most crucial agency with which gays needed to be concerned: the Naval Investigative Service. They'll call you into a room, the friend warned, and lie to you and tell you they already know you're guilty. "If it ever happens," she said, "deny everything."

It was an October morning when Karen's company officer asked to see her. When Karen tried to postpone the meeting because she had class and the officer said no, she knew something bad was about to happen. A half-dozen NIS agents interviewed her. The subject was Karen's friend on the softball team. She had told her roommate she was a lesbian, they said. Had she told this fact to Karen? Karen said she did not know anything about it. The agents said they had pictures of her friend with her girlfriends. Had Karen ever seen any of them together? Karen said no. "But you're her best friend," they countered. "Why would she tell other people and not you? She must have told you."

"I don't know anything," Karen said.

Karen Colton was terrified. Lying was an offense for which an Academy student could be expelled, and she was lying. Scarier than that were the questions and what they signified. Her friends were being watched; they could be watching her.

The news that the assistant manager of the women's basketball team was being interviewed by the NIS was no less chilling to the gay women at Annapolis. Everybody worried that the eighteen-year-old would crack under pressure. Nobody wanted a repeat of the 1978 investigation of the women's volleyball team and a reputation that would persist for years.

When Ruth went to talk to Karen on behalf of the rest of the basketball team, she was painfully aware of how it would it look if it came out that an Honor Committee member had advised a plebe not to cooperate in an investigation. But Ruth did not believe she was violating the Honor Code by warning Karen against the NIS. She did sometimes worry that failing to tell the Academy she was gay might be a violation, an error of omission. One time, the commandant had told them to confess anything they might be guilty of and not to wait for someone to ask them about it. But Ruth genuinely did not believe there was anything wrong with being a lesbian.

She would not counsel Karen to do wrong; she would tell her only to be wary.

Ruth could not bring herself to say the words, however. What if Karen was an NIS plant looking to ferret out lesbians? It had happened before. So she broached the subject tentatively. Did Karen know about the NIS? she asked. Yes, Karen said. Ruth talked about their tactics, that they lied about what they knew, claiming to know facts that they did not. And she told Karen she should be aware that she did not have to talk to them at all if she did not want to.

Karen seemed to understand, and Ruth left her room relieved, convinced that Karen was savvy and the team was safe. But their conversation made Karen look ahead to her years at the Academy with trepidation. From now on, she thought, it would not be safe to talk to anyone, not even a friend. Though this investigation blew over without any expulsions, Karen started avoiding the friend who had been suspected. It just seemed too risky.

The school year ending in 1983 was a busy time for lesbian investigations at the Naval Academy. In January 1983, another student, a junior, came under investigation when it was suspected she had taken a plebe girlfriend. Two months after that, some of the women on the basketball team made a list of suspected lesbians, which had been turned in to one of the brigade officers. Among those listed was Midshipman Lieutenant Ruth Voor.

THE HUNT FOR LESBIANS in the U.S. military in the 1980s was not merely a preoccupation, it was an obsession. As the presence of women became more pronounced in every service, an entire mythology evolved, imbuing lesbians with menacing qualities—far darker, in fact, than anything that had been attributed to gay men in recent years.

At about the same time Ruth Voor met with Karen Colton to talk about the NIS, for example, a young Army specialist four named Steve Robin was serving as a launcher specialist on a Lance missile crew in the rolling hills of Bavaria, two hours from the West German–Czechoslovak border. Early in Robin's tenure, a rumor swept his unit that the older enlisted women in the battalion were intimidating young female recruits to have sex with them. Afterward, the younger women became part of their lesbian clique and, once they were trusted, they were sent out to seduce the new batch of incoming women. That was how the lesbians' numbers kept expanding. To Robin, it sounded like a grade-B vampire movie. Still, sinister fables like this were widely accepted throughout every branch of the military.

As with any stereotypes, there was a germ of legitimacy at the bottom of the lesbian-vampire myth. First, there was inarguably a higher proportion of lesbians among women in the military than in the civilian world.

Many lesbians who have served in the armed forces over the past decade estimate that at least 20 percent and perhaps as many as 35 percent of military women were homosexual. But these numbers are meager compared with the old days when as many as 80 percent of WACs were thought to be "members of the church."

The military offered opportunities that assertive and confident women could scarcely find elsewhere. In theory, strength and independence were assets for women in the military, while they could be decided liabilities for civilian females. Military life relieved some of the pressure to find a husband, too, since women could plead their dedication to the service first, an evasion gay military men had been using for generations. Furthermore, as researcher Patricia Davis concluded, the services' reputation as a refuge for lesbians had become a self-fulfilling prophecy. One of the key reasons for homosexual women joining the military, she found, was the belief that they would meet other lesbians there.

This phenomenon had long been obvious to military men, who also noticed that younger women sometimes ended up in relationships with older women. But young Karen Colton, as an example, would have been lesbian with or without her subsequent relationship with Ruth Voor. The theory of the enticing older seducer was no more or less valid among lesbians than it was among heterosexuals. But this fact carried little currency in male circles, where darker interpretations and stories like that of the lesbian vampires of Bavaria were heard with increasing frequency.

This was intriguing because at the same time women were making dramatic inroads in the military. Between 1972 and 1982, the number of enlisted women in the Army had increased by nearly 550 percent, from 12,349 to more than 67,000. The number of female officers had nearly doubled from 4,400 to 8,650. Women now comprised 10 percent of the Army's officer and enlisted strength, and comparable increases were evident throughout the services. A female of flag rank, Rear Admiral Pauline Harrington, commanded the key Naval Training Center in Orlando.

The growing female presence in the military mirrored a similar development in society at large. In 1981, President Reagan appointed the first woman, Sandra Day O'Connor, to the United States Supreme Court. In 1982, the first female astronaut, Sally Ride, was scheduled to fly in the space shuttle *Challenger*. There were now female bishops and university presidents. In November 1982, 992 women were elected to state legislatures, triple the number of a decade earlier, and 21 women entered the U.S. House of Representatives, a record number.

In ordinary life, a decade of feminism had produced astonishing changes in the lives of millions of women. Nearly 53 percent of women were in the work force in 1982, compared with 38 percent two decades earlier. Though women still dominated in such traditional jobs as secretary, phone operator, and receptionist, better jobs were opening up. Between 1971 and 1980, the proportion of management positions held by women increased from 10.9 percent to 19.2 percent. To accomplish this, women were marrying later and postponing having children. Such trends indicated permanent changes in American life.

One of the most intriguing symbols of the vast cultural impact of women's new freedom appeared on a billboard in Times Square in 1982—a beautifully muscled young man, naked except for his Calvin Klein underwear. The advertisement marked a turning point in the relationship between men and women in the United States. For the benefit of commerce, men would be sex objects from now on. The trend showed the vast chasm between the goal and the outcome of the women's movement. The aim had been to create a society in which no one was a sex object. The outcome was that feminism had democratized sexual objectification. Now, everyone could be a sex object.

For many men, these changes were frightening. Reaction fomented against women's new place in society. The resistance became most clear on the political level when President Reagan advanced his antifeminist agenda. Within months of taking office, the administration shut down the Office of Domestic Violence, the agency aimed at protecting women from abusive husbands. The pro-family movement appeared to consider programs that interfered with wife-beating to be antifamily. The most significant setback came on the last day of June 1982, when the Equal Rights Amendment failed to pass, having fallen three states short of approval by thirty-eight legislatures, as required for ratification. In the desperate final years of fighting its approval in state legislatures, spokesmen like Phyllis Schlafly, who had a gay son, had employed such scare tactics as saying the amendment would advance homosexual rights, including gay matrimony, if it were passed. The pressure worked, even while every public-opinion survey showed that the overwhelming majority of Americans approved passage of the law. Opposition to abortion rights, meanwhile, became a virtual litmus test for appointment to the federal judiciary.

The most profound resistance to the encroachment of women on traditionally male terrain happened under ordinary circumstances and away from much public notice. In thousands of small ways, men tried to reassert the old roles while women were trying to adapt the new. Insidious sexual harassment resulted, especially in the workplace as women's numbers grew. Women also found that job success created a disconcerting double bind. An aggressive male employee was complimented as assertive; an aggressive woman was a bitch. One source of the resistance to strong women was a barely articulated fear of lesbians. It had become a cliché among women trying to succeed in traditionally male domains to assure colleagues, "I'm not a feminist, but. . . ." But of course the great majority of women did indeed subscribe to the feminist ideology; what they really meant was, "I'm not a lesbian. . . ."

The disclaimer was intended to salve men's anxieties. *Lesbianism* was a comparatively new topic of discussion for heterosexuals. Talk about homosexuality had almost universally been about gay men. That changed in the 1980s. Whether in a corporate boardroom or on an Army post, a man in conflict with a strong woman colleague was likely to mutter that she was a "dyke."

These were difficult times to be a heterosexual male. For centuries, heterosexual men had defined themselves by their relationships with women. Surrendering relationships with women and being identified as homosexual could destroy a man. This was the cultural imperative that heterosexual men had constructed when they decreed that homosexuals were damned in the eyes of God and potential traitors to their nation, no matter what the facts of their lives might be. By the 1980s, this cultural edict was becoming as constrictive to heterosexuals as to homosexuals.

The old moorings were slipping. Once women had simply been wives and mothers. Now they did not need men to define themselves; they had their own jobs. Women once dropped their own surnames for their husbands'. But now, growing numbers of women refused to define themselves as Miss or Mrs., words that announced what relationship with a man a woman did or did not have, and the designation became Ms. Some steps further along this feminist path, many men feared, lurked the women who represented the ultimate rejection of men: lesbians, who refused to define even their sexuality by their relationship to men, who did not need men for anything.

As such, lesbians were the sum of all fears for the confused heterosexual male of the 1980s. Lesbianism was the phenomenon that could deprive heterosexual men of women who would participate in the construction of their heterosexual identity. It was a frightening thought for those men who had created a society in which heterosexual identity—or, more accurately, the proof that one did not have a homosexual identity—was of paramount importance. At the same time, the new popularity of men as sex objects exacerbated anxiety, because heterosexual men for the first time faced the same dilemma that they had thrust upon women for so long—that they might not measure up physically.

Some men—many men—tried to force things back to the old ways. At work, they harassed women, not necessarily because they wanted sexual favors but because they needed women to reaffirm their heterosexuality and the old patterns. When glass ceilings were quietly slid into place in the corporate world, it was not because men perceived women to be any less qualified than themselves but because of a collective fear for manhood as they understood it. If a woman could perform even the most responsible jobs, what good was such work at defining manhood?

Such anxieties were most acute within the institution most devoted to the ideology of masculinity, the military. Sexual harassment ran rampant through the military in the 1980s, to an extent barely imaginable in the civilian world. Here, the presence and growing influence of women would create a paroxysm of paranoia about lesbians.

None of these problems were unknown in the civilian sector, of course. In the civilian world, for example, a female worker who brushed aside a colleague's sexual advance might not be promoted. She might even lose a job or be whispered about as a lesbian. But in the military, such whispers could lead to purges and even prison time, and in the 1980s, again and again, they did. All women suffered from the discrimination and harassment meted out by confused and insecure men, but no group suffered as much as lesbians, because no group so embodied male fears.

Not surprisingly, the first ship in the Women at Sea program to allow woman on board as crew, the USS *Vulcan*, also became an early target for a lesbian investigation. Ten women were put under investigation. The witch-hunt aboard the USS *Dixon*, a submarine tender ported in San Diego, received more public attention, however. The investigation began in 1982 after some heterosexual women on the crew turned over to the NIS the names of women they thought were lesbians. Using the customary threats of court-martial and a bad discharge, NIS agents were able to get one of the younger suspects to confess and provide a list of lesbians aboard the ship.

What most struck Bridget Wilson when she started advising the ten women under investigation was that virtually all of them held nontraditional jobs. There was a boatswain's mate, a machine-repair technician, an electrician, a fireman, and a hull technician under investigation—not a secretary or a nurse among them. Of these, six were charged with lesbian activity.

The *Dixon* women responded by going to the press and insisting, as the *Norton Sound* women had two years earlier, that their sex lives were nobody's business. Faced with the potential of unfavorable publicity, the Navy backed off. In the end, only three women were discharged.

The more successful witch-hunts were the ones nobody heard about, such as that of lesbians aboard the USS *Puget Sound*, a destroyer tender. Impressive purges of lesbians also occurred at the Memphis Naval Air Station in Millington. According to an account in the newsletter of the National Organization for Women, one Millington investigation netted seventeen discharges, while a later probe of twenty-two women at the same base resulted in nine ousters. At the Concord Naval Weapons Station near San Francisco, seven women were accused of homosexuality in a 1983 investigation. Five were quietly discharged in this purge; three were denied honorable discharges.

In Okinawa, the NIS conducted an investigation of the women's Marine Corps softball team. In Puerto Rico in 1983, twelve members of a Navy women's softball team were investigated and two discharged. The fear of lesbian investigations of sports teams inspired the women's softball team on the Pensacola-based USS *Lexington* to actively recruit heterosexual females for their team. "I don't know how to play," one of the token heterosexuals complained. "That's all right," she was told. "We'll teach you—here's your mitt." Organizers of team parties were always scrupulous about making sure that men attended.

The discharges sometimes struck down women who were pioneers in their military fields. Captain Katherine Martin was one of the first four female flight surgeons in the Army and the only one assigned to Europe when her name was turned over to the Criminal Investigation Division by two lesbians who had decided to turn themselves in as gay so they could get out of the Army. When CID agents decided to question Martin and found her in a dentist's chair undergoing a root canal, they searched her, had her handcuffed, and drove her to the CID office for interrogation. Under threats of a prosecution that could cost her her doctor's license, Martin agreed to resign. The government then made her repay the Army scholarships that had financed her medical education.

The massive lesbian investigations resulted in an intriguing statistical turnaround for military investigators. While the numbers of gay discharges continued to go up in the early 1980s, the numbers of investigations went down sharply. Between 1974 and 1978, investigations outnumbered discharges; between 1979 and 1983, discharges outnumbered investigations, because each individual investigation yielded so many more discharges. In fiscal year 1982, that number was 2,069 enlisted personnel forced out of the armed forces for homosexuality. The Navy had contributed the most to that total, with 1,134 gay discharges; the Army had only 473 discharges, the lowest per capita separation rate for homosexuality. Though antilesbian fever contributed to the unprecedented level of gay discharges, economic realities also made the dismissals easier for military brass. The nation was caught in the grips of the worst recession in a generation. Unemployment hovered at 10 and 11 percent. With few new jobs in the civilian sector, there were plenty of eager recruits. Keeping homosexuals in the services at this time was not for the convenience of the government.

DECEMBER 14, 1982
COURT OF MILITARY APPEALS

LIEUTENANT JOANN NEWAK'S ATTORNEY, Faith Seidenberg, had argued that Joann's right to counsel had been violated by the twisted conflicts of interest of her Air Force lawyer; that Newak could not be legally imprisoned for merely believing that she possessed amphetamines; and, from a commonsense point of view, that Newak's seven-year sentence was "cruel and unusual punishment," since no civilian would have been tried for her "crimes," much less sent to prison.

But the Air Force Court of Military Review unanimously rejected her argument. In a thirty-seven-page concurring opinion, Justice Edward B. Miller offered an exhaustive rationale for why Newak should be imprisoned. That document included a sweeping history of the nation's military law, supporting references from the Continental Congress and the first three Presidents, as well as citations of Supreme Court decisions dating back to 1858. In conclusion, Miller wrote, "Certainly, had the accused been tried on these identical charges in a civilian court, which would probably have been unfamiliar with the laws and traditions developed by the military during its long history, it is likely the court would not have had full capacity to recognize the complete impact of damage to the national security. . . . The accused was tried by a military court-martial that fully appreciated the seriousness of her offenses in a military context. Her sentence was entirely appropriate, in view of her offenses, and properly vindicated by the military's disciplinary authority."

In the weeks during which the appeals court reviewed the arguments over Newak's imprisonment, the public was beginning to hear about the case and the young lieutenant's draconian punishment. Writers Nat Hentoff of *The Village Voice* and Coleman McCarthy of *The Washington Post* both wrote eloquent condemnations of the Air Force handling of the Newak case, and their columns prompted other reporters' interest. Finally, Army authorities at the Disciplinary Barracks at Fort Leavenworth ordered that Newak could participate in no "face-to-face interviews." When Newak tried to reply to reporters' questions in writing, officials ordered that interviews of any kind "are not authorized under any circumstances." When Newak decided to write to reporters anyway, prison authorities searched her cell and confiscated letters in progress, to be held for "investigatory purposes," according to documents filed in federal court.

When pressed in court to explain why the military would not let Newak talk to reporters, Army spokesmen argued that conversations with the press could involve breaches of national security. Meanwhile, Newak appealed for clemency from the Air Force so that she could be released from prison. It was then that word reportedly came down that if Newak wanted clemency, she should stop talking to reporters. And she did.

JANUARY 1983
UNITED STATES NAVAL ACADEMY
ANNAPOLIS, MARYLAND

BY THE END of her first semester at the Academy, Karen Colton had heard enough from Ruth Voor about her supposed boyfriends. Over a long dinner one night, Karen finally got Ruth to admit what was obvious to both of them, and in the months that followed a relationship developed. Ruth settled into the relationship with confidence: She knew this was the one she had been waiting for and it would last the rest of her life.

Meanwhile, Ruth had the new lesbian investigation in which she was a suspect to worry about. This probe had started when one heterosexual basketball team member made a list of her teammates who she assumed were lesbians for her brigade commander, who passed the list on to other brigade officers.

The gossip had a bizarre effect at first. Suddenly, several male midshipmen wanted to date Ruth. Ruth did go out with a gymnast, but when she refused to make out at the end of the evening, he snarled that the rumors about Ruth were true. Another incident occurred late on a Saturday night when Ruth was studying with another midshipman, a former enlisted Marine deemed promising enough to be channeled into the Academy as a prelude to his future as a Marine officer. Once Ruth was inside the Marine's room, he stripped down to his underwear and announced, "I'm going to show you what it's like. It's really great."

Ruth was strong and able to fight him off, but he blocked the door and would not let her out. The watch station was right outside the door. Ruth said she would scream. The Marine ignored the threat. Instead, he started talking about the accusations going around about Ruth. They said she was a lesbian. He wanted to show her what it was like; he was doing her a favor. He pinned her arms to the wall and tried to kiss her.

Ruth did not scream. He knew she would not. If he accused Ruth of being a lesbian, she would be kicked out, just a few months short of graduation. She managed to break away and get out of the room. She was enraged but had no one to tell. If she said he had tried to rape her, he would say she was homosexual.

— 45 —
Straights

WHEN BRUCE DIAMOND took his oath to join the Air Force Reserve in 1980, he swore to protect the Constitution from all enemies foreign and domestic. When, as a first lieutenant, he called the reporter from the *St. Louis Post-Dispatch* to say there was a purge of gays unfolding at Scott Air Force Base, he thought that was what he was doing, defending the Constitution against its enemies.

Diamond, who worked weekends as a reserve chaplain, could not believe it was legal for the government to conduct such purges, employing the tactics it did. But when he saw the fear in the faces of nineteen- and twenty-year-olds who came to him and heard their stories of grueling interrogations, he saw that it was true. He believed he had no choice but to speak out.

He was not gay himself. In civilian life, he was the rabbi for a small Reform congregation in nearby St. Louis. He was thirty-four, married, with two children. He had never been a typical military man. He had joined the Reserves in 1980 during the controversy over the reintroduction of draft registration for eighteen-year-olds, thinking that if there had to be a military, it should include decent people who disapproved of war. He was surprised to be accepted, given his well-publicized arrests for such peacenik causes as the nuclear freeze.

His Reserve work as a chaplain was less than challenging, especially for a rabbi, since there were so few Jews in any branch of the military. The witch-hunt brought to his attention by two lesbian airmen, Darlene Chamberlin and Lillian Whitaker, was a challenge, however, and moved him to action. The homosexual airmen under investigation were too frightened to go to the press themselves, so he took it upon himself to advise the *Post-Dispatch* of the "medieval abrogation of American justice" occurring at the headquarters of the Military Airlift Command. Then he called other newspapers and television stations.

———————

THE INVESTIGATION at Scott Air Force Base had begun like so many others, with interrogators subjecting a frightened nineteen-year-old to an eight-hour grilling. They told him they had a letter implicating him in sodomy, according to what the airman later told his friends. He could go to prison for sodomy. He could be dishonorably discharged. Anyone who read the *Air Force Times* knew that was what had happened months before to that lesbian lieutenant in New York; she was in prison now. Finally, the young airman gave names. Those he named were questioned, and they gave names, too, until thirty people were under investigation at Scott. Of course the OSI had no letter implicating the nineteen-year-old, just a tip that he might be gay.

"The Family" had been comfortably settled into the base for several years, including men and women, blacks and whites. One African American drag queen had recently won the "Miss Faces" contest at a St. Louis drag bar of the same name. He could frequently be seen leaving his barracks room in wigs and long sequined gowns. When the new movie *Personal Best,* which touched upon lesbian themes, appeared at the base theater, one gay medical technician, known to all as "Trixie," calligraphed and hand-delivered personalized invitations to all Family members, who then sat together in the first two rows at the premiere. The easygoing nature of The Family at Scott made it possible for the OSI to come down hard in the final months of 1982.

Diamond's commanding officer called the rabbi when the first newspaper stories appeared and ordered him to return in uniform to the base. A roomful of colonels and wing commanders from the Military Airlift Command and a representative of the chaplain's office attended his arrival. The Air Force later denied having records of the Scott investigation or of meetings related to it, but Diamond remembers that particular meeting quite well. He was "interfering with an ongoing national security investigation," according to the Air Force. When Diamond asked what aspect of national security he was interfering with, he was told that homosexuals were susceptible to blackmail. As such, their elimination was essential to the national security.

"Adulterers are susceptible to blackmail," Diamond said. As a believer in national security, he would gladly turn over a list of fifty adulterers on base, so the OSI could really have at it.

"That's not relevant," he was told.

The orders came from the Secretary of the Air Force. Homosexuals needed to be eliminated from the Air Force and Diamond was interfering with that goal. It was clear that none of the officials addressing him relished cashiering out gays. It appeared to Diamond they were yielding to Pentagon concerns about gays on such a high-profile base. Despite their personal feelings, they could not allow Diamond to talk to the press about their "national-security investigations." He could be facing time in the stockade. They wanted his guarantee that he would not talk to the press again. Diamond agreed not to talk. He did not mention that he had already notified reporters of their meeting that day. When reporters called to follow up, Diamond obeyed his command and explained that he had orders not to talk about the homosexual purge. That demurral resulted in new stories about how the Air Force had muzzled the rabbi and was trying to shroud the gay investigation behind a cloak of secrecy.

By now, the news coverage had come to the attention of Secretary of the Air Force Verne Orr, rumored to be livid over the loquacious rabbi. The Air Force was not conducting a "witch-hunt," Orr told reporters. The investigation was "normal military procedure." Diamond was called in a second time for a high-powered dressing-down and his commanding officer was ordered to send him a letter of reprimand.

Whatever headaches his position caused Diamond personally, the publicity all but derailed the purge. Whitaker and Chamberlin, for example, had been warned earlier of possible sodomy courts-martial and less than honorable discharges. Now, they were handed their honorables. Though forty had been under investigation, in the end only four were booted out, a modest number in those times of mass purges.

UNTIL THE EARLY 1980s, many of the gains made by the gay movement could be attributed to one factor and one alone: that gays themselves would no longer tolerate a subservient place in society. Something different was happening in this decade, however, a trend that grew more pronounced as the years wore on: Heterosexuals were learning about the injustices done to homosexuals and they were trying to right them.

The new allies were most in evidence on college campuses. Because of painstaking organizing efforts by campus gay groups in the 1970s, a good portion of the nation's colleges and universities had added sexual orientation to the laundry list of conditions against which they would forbid discrimination. Once having made the statement that discrimination against gay people was wrong, college administrators then actually had to take action. The biggest problems arose with the purveyors of the most systematic discrimination against gays in the United States—the military. As it had during the Vietnam era, controversy settled on campus ROTC units and on military recruiters.

In August 1982, the University of Pennsylvania Law School banned military recruiters from the campus because they violated the school's ban on discrimination. Temple University faculty voted for a similar exclusion several months later. In late 1982, a faculty committee at Boston College Law School also voted to ban military recruiters, an unprecedented action for a Jesuit-run college at the heart of the city's Irish Catholic community.

In March 1983, the Northeastern University Law School said that military recruiters would be banned from campus until they stopped discriminating against gays.

A similar controversy erupted in Oregon at Portland State University in 1983. Roberto Reyes-Colon now worked for Portland's Metropolitan Human Relations Commission. Fifteen years had passed since Reyes-Colon had been kicked out of the Air Force during the purge at Lowry Air Force Base. It was fourteen years since he had thrown rocks at Stonewall. Reyes-Colon had come to understand that social change occurred in less dramatic forums as well, so he pointed out that the school's ROTC program violated the county's ban on gay discrimination adopted in 1981 and he prodded his alma mater to make good on its promise to forbid discrimination.

Two things surprised Reyes-Colon in his effort: the support he got from heterosexuals for his challenge and the opposition he received from gays. Most heterosexuals conceded that discrimination was wrong. They were not prejudiced so much as ignorant; once informed, they were ready to see the right thing done.

Many gay activists, on the other hand, were unsympathetic to the plight of gays in uniform. During the Portland State University debate, some wondered aloud why gays would want to join a patriarchal, homophobic organization like the military, anyway. But that was not the point, Reyes-Colon argued. Gay people had as much right to serve as anyone else.

Military counselors like Bridget Wilson noted that lesbian activists were taken aback when they finally met some of the hounded sailors and saw that these were not "amazons for peace" but fairly ordinary sailors whose preoccupations were drinking beer and chasing girls. In fact, gays in uniform tended to identify much more with the military way of life than with the gay community. They shared little common ground with activists. Though the antiwar movement had faded out nearly a decade earlier, many liberal gay organizers still saw their struggle for gay freedom not as an effort to allow all gay people to express themselves as they saw fit but as a movement to allow every gay person the right to be a homosexual leftist.

The gay military issue continued to escalate just the same. The courts were now buried in a deluge of lawsuits instigated by discharged soldiers. In October 1982, when the Army refused to reenlist Perry Watkins because of his admission that he was gay, a federal judge in Seattle ordered his reenlistment and Watkins continued to serve. In January 1983, Watkins, three crew members from the USS *Dixon,* and Mel Dahl, the sailor whose gay admission had prompted the NIS search for Dorothy, all pleaded their case on a segment of *60 Minutes* devoted to the issue. Dahl then took off for a cross-country walk across the United States to bring attention to his lawsuit against the policy. Since the Army National Guard still had not obeyed the 1980 court order to reinstate Miriam Ben-Shalom, the drill sergeant filed a contempt of court suit to force her reinstatement. Columnists Nat Henthoff and Coleman McCarthy continued to champion Joann Newak. An Air Force parole board denied her clemency appeal in April 1983, but Major General Thomas Bruton reduced her sentence by one-half, meaning Newak would serve three years at hard labor.

In the end, most of the collegiate moves against the military's policy came to nothing. Trustees at Temple University reaffirmed the right of the military to recruit on campus—after the Department of Defense threatened to withdraw millions of dollars in government contracts from the school. The University of Pennsylvania's president reversed his institution's decision to ban recruiters, declaring "the policies of the U.S. armed forces are not now illegal in Philadelphia or elsewhere." The affirmative-action director at Portland State also refused to push the military for reform, and the matter died quietly. Still, the flurry of activity from mainstream institutions served notice that in time there might be others than homosexuals fighting gay discrimination.

OCTOBER 1982
THE PENTAGON
ARLINGTON, VIRGINIA

IN 1981, AFTER the new gay policy was in effect, Diane Matthews asked her ROTC instructor whether she could miss a leadership class to attend a meeting of the University of Maine student senate. When her instructor asked why the senate session was so important, Matthews explained that she was arguing to fund the Wilde-Stein Club, a gay student group. Under further questioning, Matthews, who had previously served four years of Army enlisted duty, said she was a lesbian. When ROTC moved to disenroll her under the new gay regulation, she filed a suit in federal court and retained the assistance of Michael Asen, a cooperating attorney with the Maine Civil Liberties Union. In October 1982, Asen was at the Pentagon taking depositions.

Like many civilians from the counterculture days of the 1960s, Asen had always assumed that the Pentagon would be full of bumbling, inarticulate Army hacks. He was surprised to find a lot of intelligent and affable people employed there. One was a major general, director of the military-personnel management in the office of the deputy chief of staff for the Army, responsible for the development and promulgation of the Army policy regarding gays.

In his sworn deposition to Asen, Major General Norman Schwarzkopf characterized homosexuality as being "incompatible with military service" because it impaired good order, discipline, and morale. The general, a West Point graduate, said that twenty-six years in the military led him to conclude that "homosexuals are unsuited for military service."

After the deposition, Asen and the general went to lunch. Asen recalls that they talked more about the case, off the record. Although Schwarzkopf used the word *queers* in conversation, Asen understood he was using the lingo everyone else used in the Army. Over lunch, Schwarzkopf confided that although he would deny ever saying it if asked in court he really did not care whether or not gays ended up serving in the Army. He had known homosexuals who were fine soldiers. The policy was something that he had inherited, and it was a policy he had to enforce and defend. That was his job, but if the policy were thrown out tomorrow, he said, it would be fine with him.

Later, Schwarzkopf's on-the-record deposition was part of the evidence that prompted federal appeals courts to rule that the military's exclusion of gays was constitutional. When contacted about the conversation, a spokesman said the general denied ever saying it.

DECEMBER 1982
SCOTT AIR FORCE BASE
BELLEVILLE, ILLINOIS

AFTER THE SCOTT INVESTIGATION was over, Lieutenant Bruce Diamond became an outspoken defender of gay rights. When a gay bar in a German neighborhood of St. Louis was firebombed one night, Diamond went to the site, saw the broken glass lying all over the street, and noted to reporters that the bombing had happened on the anniversary of Kristalnacht, when Nazis had rampaged against Jews in Germany. The hatred directed against gays in St. Louis was like the hatred shown toward Jews in Germany, he said.

This analogy was not well received among the more conservative members of the local Jewish community. They worried that associating homosexuals with the Holocaust was bad public relations for Jews. They had long argued that the Holocaust was unforgivable because Jews did not deserve to be exterminated; to many, the jury was still out on what homosexuals deserved. Diamond began receiving phone calls late at night from callers who told him to leave town and called him a "fag-loving Jew." When the police traced the calls, they discovered the source of the calls was a local Orthodox rabbinical seminary.

MAY 4, 1983
UNITED STATES NAVAL ACADEMY
ANNAPOLIS, MARYLAND

RUTH VOOR had sworn in her senior year that by the time she graduated from Annapolis, her "Playboy 21" company would be renamed. She did not want the women coming up in the younger classes to have to put up with the harassment she had faced. By spring, she had won, and her company became "Blackjack 21."

The Playboy Bunny made one last, albeit brief, stand when, as tradition dictated, it was the company's day to decorate the Tecumseh Monument. The ritual is performed in the dead of night, so that the decoration appears as if by magic the following morning when the entire student body lines up in front of the monument for daily formation.

And so, on a predetermined midnight hour on the twenty-first day before graduation, the men of Company Twenty-one crept out of their bunks and decorated the monument with a sizable facsimile of the Playboy Bunny. Once the male midshipmen had returned to their room, Ruth and her two roommates sneaked out to the monument, washed off the Playboy Bunny, and replaced it with a goofy-looking rabbit with wilted ears. The caption read, "It's Been Real . . . Boys!" And there it appeared, as if by magic, the next morning.

Ruth could not serve as a line officer on a ship because of her knee injury, but she wanted to do sea duty, so she went into supply, which would allow her on board. Other duties would keep her at Annapolis for the next eight months, which was fine with her since Karen Colton was at Annapolis and the two remained a couple.

That summer, Karen was assigned to the USS *Norton Sound*. Karen had heard about the lesbian purge a few years earlier; she knew she had to be extra careful. On the voyage from Pascagoula, Mississippi, through the Panama Canal and to Port Hueneme, some of the enlisted women spoke about the investigation. Karen enjoyed sea life and saw that there were plenty of lesbians in the Navy, but the trip also gave her reservations. The Navy was serious about ousting homosexuals, particularly lesbians. She wondered whether she had made a wise choice to spend her first five years after the Academy in the service.

Ruth also worried about her future Naval career, but she felt she had received a very good education from the Navy, and in return she had promised to put in five years as an officer. She owed that time to the Navy and she never seriously considered getting out of that obligation by turning herself in. At the same time, she decided that if anyone asked her whether she was a lesbian, she would not tell a lie.

In the Midnight Sky

JUNE 28, 1983
LACKLAND AIR FORCE BASE
SAN ANTONIO, TEXAS

HE WAS NOT there to talk about his sex life, said Airman First Class Ray Orsini. But the panel pressed on, anyway. They had it right there in his medical records that Orsini had admitted engaging in "bisexual acts." Just what did that include?

Orsini was silent. The board members asked again.

Were these homosexual acts? Did he perform these acts in the service? Had he engaged in homosexual acts before he joined the Air Force?

Orsini refused to answer. He was feeling tired again; he was sleeping twelve to fourteen hours a day, but he was still exhausted. And he was confused; he was not always coherent anymore. And now this.

The purpose of this interview with the Air Force Formal Physical Evaluation Board was to determine whether Orsini was no longer medically able to serve in the Air Force and whether the disease that caused his unfitness had been acquired during his time in the service. If the answer was yes to both questions, he would be entitled to medical retirement, which meant permanent health care in the military's medical system and disability benefits.

Orsini had been diagnosed with AIDS three months earlier at March Air Force Base Regional Hospital, not far from Norton Air Force Base in San Bernardino, where Orsini was stationed. Orsini, who had joined the service in 1980, was the first diagnosed AIDS patient in the Air Force and among the first in the military. He was immediately flown to Wilford Hall Medical Center in San Antonio, the Air Force's premiere medical facility.

At first sight, the twenty-seven-year-old airman had seemed the picture of health: He was lean, muscular, and extremely handsome. But his medical tests showed he had salmonella, an intestinal parasite that caused him to lose weight rapidly and suffer with persistent night fevers. When doctors biopsied his lymph nodes, they found evidence of both cancerous lymphomas and Kaposi's sarcoma, the once-rare skin cancer that was suddenly appearing among AIDS patients. His blood showed plummeting levels of T-4 cells, the critical fighters in the immune system.

Medical records in the military are not shielded by confidentiality. Two sentences, therefore, came to the attention of authorities. First, "The patient had a past history of rectal (gonorrhea), incidentally," and later the doctor added, "Pertinent to the history is that the patient admits to bisexual contacts in the past."

After treatment for the salmonella, the fevers and diarrhea stopped. However, when doctors put Orsini back on a plane to Southern California, it was with diagnoses of Kaposi's sarcoma, undifferentiated lymphoma, and AIDS, any one of which was fatal. Together, in 1983, they were a virtual death sentence.

Orsini wanted to be medically retired with full medical benefits the way any soldier facing a comparable prognosis from any other disease might be. It was how all the branches of the service took care of their own when members faced serious ailments. When a panel called the Informal Physical Evaluation Board took up the matter of Orsini's retirement on June 2, it determined that because his salmonella had been treated Orsini was "asymptomatic" and therefore not eligible for medical retirement. Orsini appealed to the Formal Physical Evaluation Board.

The board met on a humid day at Lackland, the titular capital of the United States Air Force. By afternoon, the temperature had soared to ninety-four. Orsini was pale and thin and had to lean on a Houston gay activist for support as he shuffled into the hearing room. He was too tired to fight, yet he must if he was to have any medical care during the physical decline that was his future. The board seemed strangely uninterested in Orsini's personal plight, however, and far more interested in his sex life. They seemed to take his refusal to answer questions about his sexuality, because of the legal ban on self-incrimination, as evidence he had something to hide.

When Lieutenant Colonel Neal Boswell, the chief of Wilford Hall's hematology service, testified that Orsini's condition was indeed "severe" and that with three terminal diagnoses he could not be considered "asymptomatic," the board asked whether, given the fact that Orsini was not a hemophiliac or an intravenous drug user or a blood-transfusion recipient, was it not likely that he had contracted AIDS through homosexual activities? Boswell conceded that it was.

On the second day of the hearing, Colonel George R. Davidson, the board's president, issued the panel's ruling. "It is the Board's opinion that the Evaluee contracted AIDS through homosexual activities," Davidson wrote. "The Board finds that homosexuality and homosexual acts are incompatible with Air Force Service." The ruling excerpted parts of the 123-word Department of Defense policy on gays and concluded that because Orsini's disease was due to "misconduct," he was not eligible for medical retirement, and because he was homosexual, he should be discharged.

Orsini felt numb. Not only would he lose his job, he was about to lose his medical benefits, disability compensation, and, if discharged less than honorably as a homosexual, even the medical care he could hope for from the Veterans Administration. Orsini's Air Force lawyer, Lieutenant Colonel Thomas Alfsen, immediately appealed, complaining that the "board has abandoned its impartial fact finding role, and has become the guardian of Air Force morality. . . . What we have is a terminally ill young man whose prognosis is grim at best. At present it probably is the most fatal of all known diseases, and were it not for the homosexual overtones, it would generate nothing but sympathy and kindness. Regardless of how the condition was contracted, he will in all probability not survive the next two years. It is, as yet, not a violation of the law to show compassion and in this case the law dictates that this member be given disability compensation."

The Air Force, however, was not about to relent. The intent of the Air Force, as well as the other branches of the military at this time, was not to treat AIDS as a health problem but as a homosexual problem.

———

THOUGH THE AIDS issue first arose with Airman Orsini, it soon affected all of the services. One week after Orsini's hearing, the *Navy Times* reported the first case of AIDS in the Navy and the second in the Air Force. Within days, the Air Force announced its third case. There were, of course, many more already sick and thousands more infected with the yet-undiscovered virus that caused the disease. When it finally acknowledged the problem, the Navy responded to its early AIDS cases just as the Air Force had, by seeking to discharge AIDS sufferers for being gay. Even expressing concern about AIDS could start discharge proceedings. In February 1983, Petty Officer Second Class William Kerr, a Navy corpsman assigned to the Naval Regional Medical Center in Oakland, asked a Navy doctor for a T-4 cell test because he feared he might have AIDS. Navy records claimed that Kerr made a "straightforward admission" to being gay to the doctor, but, according to Kerr, he made no such statement, though the doctor accused him of being gay and told him his presence in the service was "dangerous" because other sailors might kill him. Kerr probably did not have AIDS, the doctor added, just psychosomatic symptoms related to the fact that he was a homosexual. He then sent Kerr off to a psychiatrist, with the opinion that he suffered from "homosexuality with associated personality disorders." It was the psychiatrist who diagnosed Kerr with hepatitis, which caused the fatigue that Kerr believed was a symptom of AIDS. Kerr was sent home for a month of recuperation. When he returned, he was told that he was being discharged on grounds of homosexuality.

A few weeks after Orsini's hearing, Petty Officer John Baskin went to the Naval hospital in Jacksonville, Florida, with chest pains and high fevers. He was diagnosed with AIDS. After doctors assured him that anything he told them would be kept confidential, he acknowledged being gay. The doctor informed officers and the Navy launched administrative discharge proceedings against him. Baskin went public with his case and fought the discharge. At his administrative hearing, his attorney argued that the Navy would have had no evidence without the doctor's statement, which was gained under false assurances of confidentiality. The board voted unanimously that since they had seen no evidence of homosexual acts, Baskin should not be administratively discharged; instead, his case should be referred to a Physical Evaluation Board for consideration as a medical retirement. As this hearing neared, however, the Secretary of the Navy ordered Baskin administratively discharged on the vague rationale that it was "in the best interests of the service." Only when Baskin's attorney threatened to go to federal court and get a restraining order did the Navy back down and give the sailor a medical discharge.

The Pentagon remained skittish about anything that might engender bad publicity. It was the fear of media response that ultimately gained Raymond Orsini his medical retirement. Recalling the publicity he had seen years earlier concerning the USS *Norton Sound,* Orsini contacted Susan McGrievy from the American Civil Liberties Union, who found a young gay attorney, John Heilman, to work with him. When Heilman promised to hold "a very big press conference," the final avenue of Orsini's appeal, the Air Force Physical Review Council, reversed all earlier recommendations and ordered that Orsini receive a "temporary" medical retirement with disability and medical benefits. The decision would be reviewed in eighteen months, the board said.

By then, of course, Orsini would be dead.

DURING THE SAME summer that Ray Orsini was struggling against his administrative separation, a doctor at Walter Reed Army Medical Center received an unusual assignment, one that would have vast impact on how the Defense Department would handle AIDS for many years to come.

Major Robert Redfield had never planned a long military career. The thirty-two-year-old physician came from a family of scientists. His mother had met his father in the late 1940s at the National Institutes of Health, where they worked on a research team unraveling the mysteries of DNA. Redfield's father died suddenly of a heart attack when his son was five years old. His mother continued working at the NIH, bringing her son with her to the laboratory on weekends, where he met some of the great scientists of the era.

After Redfield graduated from high school in 1969, he took an Army ROTC scholarship to pursue his undergraduate work at Georgetown University. He attended medical school there for the next four years, also on an Army scholarship. When he was commissioned in 1977, he planned on paying back his eight years to the Army and then returning to the civilian sector.

By 1983, however, Redfield knew he would make the Army his career. His mother had always admonished him to be a "real" doctor, not a bench researcher, and he liked the fact that the Army got things done. He respected the patience of basic researchers like his mother and father, who knew they might have to wait fifty years before any practical application was found for their research. But in the military, you could see the results of your efforts in five to ten years. You could see the lives you changed.

At Walter Reed, Redfield had become the Army's expert on viral diseases that might infect the military blood supply. He had worked extensively on studies of hepatitis B, a sexually transmitted blood-borne disease. That expertise served him well in late spring of 1983 when Redfield was ordered to Chicago to represent the Army institute at a meeting with researchers who believed they had discovered the cause of AIDS. They hypothesized that the infectious agent might be *Erlichia canis*, a virus that caused a deadly form of aplastic anemia in dogs. The disease had been common in Vietnam, which meant that Walter Reed had studied it extensively to ensure it would not be a threat to soldiers.

Like so many other leads in those early frustrating days of AIDS research, this one proved a dead end. After several months of study, Redfield concluded that the virus had no relationship to AIDS, but by now he was intrigued with the frightening new disease and asked his military colleagues to send him every AIDS patient they came across. By autumn, Redfield was convinced that the new disease was sexually transmitted. He also suspected it might be caused by a subgroup of viruses called retroviruses. A sexually transmitted viral disease could be a huge problem for the military, Redfield knew, given the fact that the services drew their personnel largely from adults in the prime of their sexually active years.

As Redfield saw more patients, he grew even more alarmed. By the end of 1983, he had studied the immune systems of three women who were married to military AIDS cases. Although none of the women had the symptoms that characterized an AIDS diagnosis, all three had swollen lymph glands and evidence of immune dysfunction. The conventional wisdom then was that AIDS was a disease of homosexuals or Haitians. From these three patients, Redfield deduced that you did not have to be homosexual to get AIDS; you only needed to be sexually active. At that point, Redfield ceased thinking of AIDS as a medical curiosity and began to see the enormous challenge it posed for the military.

He started tracking not only the medical histories of his AIDS patients but of their spouses to understand the natural history of the disease. He also began to warn anyone who would listen: A huge problem was coming down the pike, he said, and the Army should be prepared.

In various corners of the armed forces, the AIDS epidemic edged its way forward in 1983. A sergeant major handling public affairs for the invasion of Grenada started running high fevers, then came down with shingles and unexplained memory loss. When Ken Solomon, a crewman on the USS *Eisenhower*, died of AIDS a month later, word went out that his sexual contacts aboard the ship should report to authorities immediately. Most of the military, like most of civilian society, was refusing to come to grips with the threat posed by this mysterious new disease. As one colonel explained to an infantry captain during a "dining in" at Fort Benning, "AIDS won't be a problem for us. The Army doesn't have any gays." The captain to whom he made the remark was gay.

Overwhelmingly, uniformed personnel with AIDS were gay men. Drug screening had all but eliminated the problem of intravenous drug use among uniformed personnel; hemophiliacs were screened out of the service prior to enlistment; Haiti was not a prime source for military recruits. For the rest of the decade, the AIDS epidemic would present gay men in uniform with their greatest challenge—and the military establishment with compelling evidence that gays were not only a crucial part of every branch of the military but in the possession of some of the most sensitive of military jobs. For more than a decade, gay activists had speculated about what would happen if every gay person turned purple one morning, how that would change the world for gays because heterosexuals would then see the important role gay people played throughout society. With the advent of the AIDS epidemic, the disease would distinguish gays in a frighteningly literal way.

THE REACTION of the military to AIDS—as a homosexual problem—merely reflected the attitudes of the broader society. The federal government mounted a torpid research effort against the disease. Money was simply not available to scientists who hoped to probe its still-unknown cause, nor would it be under an administration committed to cutting back drastically on domestic spending. Threats to mainstream Americans were handled expeditiously, such as the panic over cyanide-laced Tylenol capsules, but not threats to homosexuals.

Only when the disease appeared to affect people who were not gay men did it garner any public concern. In the first months of 1983, while the Navy prepared charges against Petty Officer Kerr and the Air Force moved against Airman Orsini, the United States suddenly became preoccupied with the disease. Public anxiety intensified with the first reports that AIDS could be contracted through blood transfusions. Then came inaccurate and grossly sensationalized stories suggesting that the disease could be transmitted through routine household contact. Hysteria spread.

An early victim of the hysteria was a restaurateur in the tiny northern California town of Guerneville. Leonard Matlovich's pizza parlor was finally operating in the black when the fear struck. Suddenly, his heterosexual clientele disappeared. His profits evaporated and within months he was forced to close down. Another dream vanished. Matlovich returned to San Francisco and went back to selling used cars.

SINCE THE SERVICES were relying more heavily on group dismissals than individual investigations between 1982 and 1984, the tenor of the purges grew more aggressive and even cruel. And the litany of witch-hunts continued. Investigations at Fort Carson, Colorado, a mechanized infantry post, resulted in the discharges of fourteen enlisted personnel in 1982 and twenty-three in 1983, according to figures released by the post's public-affairs office. Nearly one-third of the dismissed soldiers were women. In early 1984, another investigation there resulted in the discharges of eight women for homosexuality. Fort Carson spokesman Major Terry Monrad commented that the investigations were not part of any "witch-hunt" and the discharged soldiers were treated "with great compassion."

At the same time, agents of the Office of Special Investigations convinced a twenty-one-year-old enlisted man at the Air Force Academy to name names. According to a story in the *Gay Community News*, one airman whose only transgression was having had lunch with an accused man was discharged for being gay. This investigation resulted in six discharges, which the Air Force claimed was not an unusually large number. They also denied conducting a witch-hunt.

A probe launched in November 1983 at Bolling Air Force Base near Washington targeted at least thirty-four Air Force enlisted men. Industrious OSI agents seized address books, personal letters, and, from one airman, a tape of the ballet *Swan Lake*. The military's willingness to use intimidation to enforce the antigay policy became even more evident as the 1980s progressed. The parishioners of the Metropolitan Community Church in Long Beach learned this after they noticed a green and white van with a lot of unusual antennae and a uniformed Army driver sitting outside the front of their church in 1983.

The van's point of interest was the church's pastor, Army Reserve Captain Carolyn "Dusty" Pruitt. Pruitt had done active-duty service in the WACs from 1970 until 1978 before attending divinity school and taking her post at the gay community's church. On active duty in the Army, she had told many of her colleagues she was a lesbian and no repercussions had ensued. But she was aware she was taking a chance in a 1983 interview with the *Los Angeles Times* in which she discussed being a gay clergywoman and an Army reservist. Just days away from her promotion to major, Pruitt was informed that she was under investigation; she immediately went to Susan McGrievy at the American Civil Liberties Union. Pruitt's case seemed an ideal challenge to the rewritten gay regulation since it was an example of a discharge based not on any misconduct or, for that matter, any homosexual conduct at all but, rather, on a possible violation of her First Amendment right to say she was gay in a newspaper article.

Perhaps it was the threat of the constitutional challenge that made the Army so eager to document homosexual conduct before it actually launched a discharge proceeding. An intense investigation commenced, which included the van surveillance. It was apparently wired to record Pruitt's Sunday sermon. When the assistant pastor invited the driver in for coffee, he drove away, but the van returned the following Sunday.

Around this time, Reverend Pruitt noticed a black Pontiac Firebird parked outside her apartment in the Signal Hill section of Los Angeles County. Inside, men with binoculars stared at her window. The car followed her, even when she went skiing in the Big Bear resort area. She noticed strange clicks on her telephone. Upon returning home one night, it was clear to Pruitt that someone had gone through her belongings, though nothing was missing. And agents of the Army's Criminal Investigation Division began phoning in the middle of the night with questions that could not wait until morning. For its part, CID officials deny engaging in illegal searches or intimidation of those under investigation.

In other cases, the military demonstrated uncharacteristic flexibility. In 1982, for example, Dr. Stan Harris, an Army captain stationed in San Francisco's Presidio, was so angered by the rewritten gay regulation that he decided to challenge it by informing his commanding officer that he was gay and asking that he be made an exception to the policy. Harris was a psychiatrist, and the Army had only a limited number serving at that time. They did not want to lose him. They threatened him with psychiatric hospitalization. When that did not work, the Army reluctantly began discharge proceedings that dragged on interminably. In the process, the captain remained on the list of those promotable to major and was given expanded job responsibilities. In the end, it took the Army nearly two years to discharge him.

The purges and individual separations yielded large numbers of gay discharges during these years. According to Defense Department figures, 1,809 enlisted personnel were discharged for being gay in fiscal year 1983, while 1,801 were so discharged in 1984.

MOST OF THE PURGES and discharges escaped public notice because few gays either fought their separations or sought help from gay organizations or civil-liberties groups that might publicize their plight. One exception in the public eye was the case of Lieutenant Joann Newak, who remained imprisoned at Fort Leavenworth.

On August 12, 1983, the Air Force Clemency and Parole Board, which had previously denied Newak's plea for clemency, ordered her release. Their official reason was that Newak had recently agreed to enter a drug-rehabilitation program. But Assistant Defense Secretary Lawrence Korb recalls that after he read a column by Coleman McCarthy pleading Newak's case in *The Washington Post*, he called the Secretary of the Air Force and asked for her release himself.

On August 17, after fifteen months in prison, the twenty-six-year-old was escorted by guards from her cell and through the giant metal doors of the military prison; she was free at last. In 1986, citing gross violations of Newak's civil rights, an appeals court overturned her conviction.

TO THE END, Raymond Orsini remained loyal to the Air Force, separating his treatment by the brass from the allegiance he still felt to the men with whom he had served in the Fifty-third Military Airlift Squadron. As his health failed, he wrote a sixteen-page account of his Air Force ordeal, ending it with a tribute to his colleagues in the Fifty-third. "I tried to be part of the few, the proud, and the brave," he wrote. "As you cross the ocean in the midnight sky, please remember me."

Airman Raymond Edward Orsini died on April 6, 1984, at Balboa Naval Hospital in San Diego.

— 47 —

Heroes

JOE MILANO had been in Beirut, and he and his friend Fidel Comacho had not been able to talk for months. They took the walk they had taken so many times before from Fidel's apartment near Camp LeJeune toward Friends Lounge, the local gay bar. Fidel had crossed the bridge near the bar when he realized that Joe was no longer walking with him. He turned and saw Joe was still on the bridge. Then the bridge was collapsing and Joe was waving good-bye.

Fidel woke up with a start. Joe was dead, he knew, and had appeared in his dream to say good-bye. Still groggy, Fidel heard somebody in the barracks say, "There's been an explosion. They bombed the barracks in Beirut."

Though in California for desert training with his Marine unit, Comacho, a Navy corpsman, had served in Beirut a year earlier and had stayed in the reinforced concrete building on the edge of Beirut International Airport that served as the barracks for the Marine Corps peacekeeping force. The Marines called it the Beirut Hilton, but it had made Fidel nervous from the start, sitting there so exposed. Now his worst fears had come true, and his friend, Navy corpsman Joseph P. Milano, was dead.

WITH 241 MARINES and Navy corpsmen dead, more American servicemen were killed on October 23, 1983, than on any other single day since the beginning of the Tet offensive more than fifteen years earlier. Among them were at least two gay Marines and a gay Navy corpsman, Joseph P. Milano. That afternoon, as the nation's flag dropped to half-mast, a Marine corporal half a world away walked into his barracks, where his buddies sat huddled around a television set.

"The shit's going to hit the fan," one said.

"Better clean our weapons," said another. "We're going to war."

The corporal stood dazed, staring at the set. Like Comacho, the corporal's thoughts went immediately to Joe Milano. He had met Milano three years earlier when they were both assigned to the same barracks in Jacksonville, North Carolina. Joe was nineteen years old then, a meticulous corpsman dedicated to his "jarheads," as sailors call the Marines; in return, his Marine unit revered him. Over time, Joe and the Marine corporal began a relationship.

Their different assignments often separated them, but they exchanged almost daily letters, artfully phrased so as not to betray them if their correspondence fell into the wrong hands. Joe had confided his misgivings about the Beirut assignment from the start. But at the end of the tour, he expected to return to Camp LeJeune, and his corporal was due to be stationed back in Jacksonville, too. Just weeks before the explosion, they had made plans to get an apartment together.

That night, Marines around the world paced through their barracks, eager for any word of this or that buddy, so Joe's lover was not conspicuous in his obsession. The next day, he read that Joe's unit had been in the heart of the blast. But when the *Navy Times* listed casualties a few days later, Joe's name was not on the list of dead but on the roster of the missing. The corporal still hoped—and still wrote, dispatching two letters a day to Joe's fleet post office address.

Finally at mail call, a letter from Joe arrived. The corporal was ecstatic until he saw the postmark: October 20, three days before the bombing.

Late one night, he called Bethesda Naval Hospital, where a gay corpsman who knew both him and Joe confirmed what the corporal had feared all week. Joe's name had finally appeared on the list of the dead.

MICHIGAN STATE CAPITAL
LANSING, MICHIGAN

JIM DRESSEL was a war hero, and that distinction had provided his entree to politics. Even before he had gone to Vietnam as a fighter pilot, he had known he would pursue a political career. Flying 210 combat missions in Vietnam was his way of punching his ticket to the legislature. By the 1980s, of course, this was a fairly old-fashioned way of designing a political career, but Jim Dressel's constituents hailed from one of the most old-fashioned locales in the country, Holland, Michigan, so it was successful.

Holland sits about halfway up the western edge of the state's mitten shape, on the shore of Lake Michigan. The area was settled by a staunchly conservative Dutch population a century before, and their traditional Christian Reformed churches shot their spires up throughout Ottawa County, a bastion of fundamentalist orthodoxy. Appropriately, the region's major crop was tulips, and tourism was a major industry—visitors came from all over the upper Midwest to enjoy the annual Tulip Festival and the town's Dutch ambience. Jim fit in. Though his paternal grand-parents were German immigrants, his mother's family was Dutch, and Jim looked Dutch, with his square jaw, pale blue eyes, lanky build, and light hair.

He attended Hope College and became fascinated with politics, mo-tivated in part by the book *Profiles in Courage,* the primer by John F. Kennedy about officials who destroyed their political careers by pursuing noble causes. Jim wanted to do noble things. His ideological inspiration was *Conscience of a Conservative* by Barry Goldwater, and he worked on the Arizona senator's 1964 presidential campaign. The most conser-vative county in Michigan, Ottawa was only one of two counties in the state to support Goldwater.

Jim became aware of his homosexuality in the 1960s, as well—an awareness that he remembered coincided with seeing *Advise and Consent,* the movie in which a gay senator shoots himself in the head with a pistol. This and the overall opprobrium of gays told Jim that if he wanted to go into politics, he must suppress this part of himself, especially if he planned to use a war record as a first stepping-stone; you could not get a war record if you were queer. Jim resolved never to act on his sexuality. He had other plans for his life, and they could not include homosexuality.

A week after he graduated from Hope College in 1967, Jim Dressel was commissioned into the Air Force. In 1970, Captain Dressel was as-signed to an Air Force base in Thailand where he flew F-4 fighter planes and bombed supply trucks heading from North Vietnam into South Viet-nam. His 497th squadron flew only night runs, so they called themselves the "Night Owls." Dressel earned the Distinguished Flying Cross and a dozen other medals. He was discharged in November 1971. Climbing up the ladder to his jet cockpit in his flight suit, he posed for a dashing photo, which he used as a publicity shot six months later when he ran for Ottawa County Commissioner.

Jim knocked on every door in his district. It helped that his two opponents were both Christian Reformed, which split up that church's vote and allowed Jim, a Methodist, to win the Republican primary in 1972. Since the county never elected Democrats, winning the primary was tantamount to winning the election. Three years later, Dressel was ap-pointed to fill the seat of the county treasurer and he handily won reelec-tion to that post. He also worked the small-town political circuit, serving as county Republican chairman and as a stalwart in the Rotary and Jaycees. In a close race, he gained a seat in the Michigan House of Representatives in 1978, winning the race as a moderate Republican and a fiscal conserv-ative, but one in favor of the Equal Rights Amendment, a fairly radical position to take in Ottawa County.

A few weeks after that election, Jim took a vacation in Los Angeles. He had read in *After Dark* magazine about a gay disco called Studio One. He had never been to a gay bar. In fact, to his knowledge, he had never talked to another homosexual in his entire life. Jim drove around the block many times before he finally walked in. He stood at the bar all night and just watched, speaking to no one. He went back again the next night and again the night after that. He felt like an adopted child who many years later finds his real parents at last. By the end of his vacation, at the age of thirty-five, Jim Dressel had made love for the first time.

Dressel earned a reputation as a good-government Republican in the legislature. As a conservative, he was opposed to frivolous spending, so he returned all the pay increases the legislature voted itself during his tenure. Neither was he parochial. When Detroit clearly needed this or that job-training program, he supported it; he was among the few rural Michigan legislators who did not automatically oppose spending for Detroit. During his first four years in the legislature, Dressel was exceedingly discreet in his personal life. He never went to gay bars in Michigan; he socialized only on Christmas vacations at gay resorts in Key West. His reputation remained spotless until October 1983, when Dressel agreed to serve as one of two principal sponsors for a gay civil rights bill.

The other sponsor was a liberal Democrat from Ann Arbor. Gay lobbyists could always get the liberal Democrats from college towns; what they needed was evidence that support existed elsewhere. Jim Dressel was handsome, forty years old, and a bachelor; gay activists assumed, therefore, he must be gay. It was worth approaching him at any rate. When asked, he agreed to sponsor the bill. The good-government Republican in him supported the legislation because it seemed the right thing to do.

There was another reason, of course. The bill was a way of starting to right an injustice that Dressel had painfully experienced himself. He began to believe he could make a difference for others like himself. If other Republicans saw that he supported this bill, maybe they would, too. Maybe the bill would pass and the repercussions be felt across the country. A ground swell could occur. It took only one courageous person, he believed, to make a difference.

In Holland, the shock waves spread quickly. In the *Detroit News* published on the day of the Beirut explosion, Dressel's unusual move in sponsoring the bill was a page-one story whose headline declared that in Ottawa County supporting such legislation was "a sin." Jim's advisers could understand him voting for such a bill as a matter of conscience; but no one could fathom why he would be a principal sponsor. Only one state in the country had ever enacted such a law—Wisconsin, a year earlier. The Christian Reformed realtor whom Jim had first defeated in the 1978 Republican primary quickly announced he would run against Jim in the next primary.

Mail opposing the measure flooded Jim's office. "Homosexuals do not reproduce. They recruit, and, as they recruit, they corrupt," wrote one correspondent. "Homos are so low that God destroyed the WHOLE WORLD because of them and their behavior," wrote another. One expressed the hope that Jim would die of AIDS. A columnist for an Ann Arbor newspaper wrote that sponsoring the bill was tantamount to Dressel looking "down into his open grave." When Dressel was asked about his own sexuality, as he frequently was both in his district and by the press, he refused to answer, saying it was not anyone's business.

Under the rotunda of the state capitol in Lansing, Jim gathered support for his bill, calling in every chit he had out among Republican legislators, as well as from the Detroit politicians for whom he had gone to bat in the past. As they had been able to do elsewhere, gay lobbyists mustered an impressive array of mainstream religious leaders to support the bill. Once the bill had twenty-two cosponsors, including three Republicans, it went before the House Judiciary Committee and won in a vote of eight to five. Jim grew optimistic that they could get the bill passed. After the years of anxious sublimation, he could help make history.

NOVEMBER 1983
FRIENDS LOUNGE
JACKSONVILLE, NORTH CAROLINA

DANNY LEONARD was an unlikely hero for Marines at Camp LeJeune. Danny owned the Friends Lounge, the only gay bar within sixty miles of the base, where he was better known as Brandy Alexander, an entertainer who donned elaborate wigs, high heels, and sequined evening gowns to perform every weekend under the Christmas tree lights that twinkled over the small Friends stage.

Danny had never thought much about political matters, much less about Defense Department personnel policies. The seventh of eight children from Lexington, North Carolina, Danny had grown up as the town queer. He started doing drag in 1964, when he was eighteen, and over the next fifteen years became a well-known female impersonator in the South, supporting his avocation through a hairdressing business. He heard about a gay bar for sale in Jacksonville during the 1981 Miss Gay America pageant. The bar was not much to look at, a run-down one-story white cinder-block building across LeJeune Boulevard from the Marine base, but Danny bought it.

One night after closing the bar, Danny discovered a young man with a Marine haircut passed out at the wheel of his idling car in his parking lot. At first, Danny thought the man was drunk; then he noticed the torn-out backseat and a hose running from the exhaust pipe, through the trunk, and into the car. He had just figured out he was gay, the young man explained haltingly as he recovered. He was a Marine, he said. What could he do? He had come to the bar, but it was after closing time. He had decided he was better off dead.

With that conversation, Danny Leonard believed he had found his destiny. He was in Jacksonville, across the street from the nation's second-largest Marine base, in order to give confused young Marines like this one a healthy environment in which to come out. He remembered his traumas as the town queer of Lexington and could only imagine what it must be like in a hostile environment like the Marine Corps. So he decorated his bar with the Marine Corps flag and insignia and put out the word that service personnel would be welcome—and safe—in his bar.

By November 1983, the Marine Corps had taken notice. One Friday night, local sheriff's deputies and military investigators riding with them as a "courtesy patrol" began stopping anyone driving out of the Friends Lounge parking lot who appeared to have the "high and tight" haircut of the Marines. If the driver produced military identification, he was handed over to NIS agents for questioning. Deputies had pulled over three cars by the time word got back inside. The Marines and sailors at the bar were as terrified of leaving as they were of staying.

With the sheriff's cars still idling outside, Danny closed the bar and told the servicemen they could spend the night. Eventually, the deputies would give up and drive away. By his count, 123 servicemen bunked down at Friends that night. The next morning, patrol cars were still outside the parking lot when Danny went out to a nearby Hardee's for 123 orders of biscuits and gravy. He then called local television reporters and invited them to the Friends to discuss the questionable legality of county taxpayers' money going to support harassment of our fighting men. The deputies and NIS agents sped away at the sight of the TV cameras; official spokesmen denied they were engaged in a "witch-hunting" operation against gays. Meanwhile, the gay servicemen made their escape.

The next weekend, Danny initiated an informal shuttle service for his military patrons. Since driving in or out of his parking lot was hazardous, he arranged for them to park at a shopping center a mile from the bar and call for a ride. Some military customers arrived via the woods behind the bar, carrying a change of clothes. Danny provided a storage room for changing and freshening up for the evening. Every six months or so, as his Marine clientele transferred out and new recruits came in, Danny delivered a lecture warning customers against giving strangers their real names or letting unfamiliar people know they were in the service.

When a judge tried to make Friends off-limits, Danny fought back. In court, when the judge suggested that he might subpoena Danny's membership and mailing lists, Danny informed him he would burn any lists before he let a government agency get its hands on them.

This impudent drag queen infuriated Marine officials. One night, someone lobbed a tear-gas grenade at the bar. Another time, fifteen Marines showed up with tire irons, shouting that they were going to beat up the queers. Danny dispatched a cadre of his beefiest nonmilitary patrons to challenge the group with pool cues. The Marines backed off. Shortly after that, however, Danny received an anonymous phone call. "I think you're overstepping your bounds," the caller said, and advised Danny to "back off or we'll burn your bar down."

It was in this anxious climate that Friends patrons waited for word of their buddies and boyfriends from the LeJeune-based Twenty-fourth

Marine Amphibious Unit, which had been assigned to Beirut. When word filtered back that three Friends regulars were among the dead, Danny did what local community groups were doing throughout that part of North Carolina and joined the effort to memorialize the fallen Marines and Navy corpsmen. When the Marines announced plans for a Beirut Memorial on LeJeune Boulevard, including a Vietnam Memorial–style wall inscribed with names of the dead, Danny Leonard's Friends Lounge raised two thousand dollars for its construction, more than any other business in Jacksonville. And one night in early 1984, Danny dedicated a plaque at Friends to memorialize Hospitalman Joseph P. Milano and the other servicemen who had died in Beirut.

AFTER A FEW WEEKS, the news of the Beirut explosion dropped out of the headlines and into the back pages, displaced first by the invasion of Grenada and then by the forthcoming presidential campaign. For one young Marine, however, the memory would not fade.

The Marine corporal lapsed into severe depression in the days after he heard of Joe Milano's death. His grief was especially painful because he could not betray its source. Grieving widows and buddies got sympathy; grieving homosexual lovers got interrogated by the Naval Investigative Service and discharged. The corporal constructed the lies that would protect him, telling friends that his girlfriend had just been killed in a car accident. Whenever he talked about the death and his grief, he had to monitor his every word, making sure he got the pronouns right. Within a few months, he transferred back to North Carolina, although he could not bring himself to live in Jacksonville. It was where he had planned to live with Joe Milano; he could not live there now without Joe.

THE DEBATE OVER the Michigan gay-rights bill reflected attitudes dominant in the early 1980s. On one side were people like Jim Dressel and his supporters, mainly Democrats, who maintained that the issue was only a matter of fairness and that people should not stand to lose their jobs because of other people's prejudice. Gays seemed born that way, supporters noted, and discrimination based on sexual orientation was as invidious as bias against people with any other predetermined condition. Even most mainstream religious denominations assured legislators that God did not abide prejudice and discrimination, even if the Bible condemned homosexual acts. Most legislators accepted these arguments, and Jim frequently said that if the vote was held in private, 70 percent of the legislature would endorse the bill.

On the other side were fundamentalist religious groups, including an array of increasingly outspoken coalitions, such as the fifteen-thousand-member Moral Majority of Michigan. This group's chairman, the Reverend David Wood, argued that homosexuals chose to be gay and were no more deserving of civil rights than "rapists and thieves," who also chose to violate the laws of God and man. "I have a tough time wondering why elected officials are asked to pass a law giving sanction to a criminal," said Wood, noting that Michigan continued to hand down criminal penalties for sodomy.

Two newer issues raised by opponents surfaced in Michigan. The first was the argument that the bill would undermine the institution of the family. This reasoning, the argument that anything that did not condemn gay people tore away at the fabric of the American family, had been gaining ground since the formation of profamily lobbies in the late 1970s. To Jim Dressel, whether heterosexuals could make their families work seemed an entirely separate issue from whether gay people should have civil rights. Yet this logic was almost universally accepted. Even in liberal San Francisco, religious leaders successfully persuaded Mayor Dianne Feinstein to veto a bill in 1982 allowing unmarried couples restricted recognition as "domestic partners," because the bill allegedly "repudiated" the "sanctity of marriage and family."

The second new tactic that worked against the bill involved invoking AIDS. Ever since the issue had exploded on the front pages of newspapers in early 1983 with the first cases among blood-transfusion recipients, organizers of the religious right had used the perceived potential for widespread AIDS transmission in its argument against gay rights. "Although AIDS is carried primarily by immoral homosexuals, AIDS can be transmitted to healthy moral Americans like you and me," wrote David Williams of the American Family Association. "Homosexuals don't care if innocent people die as a result of their grotesque disease. Yes, homosexuals are only concerned with themselves and maintaining their sick, disgusting lifestyles." A Holland constituent forwarded Dressel the fund-raising solicitation that included these statements, with the note that this was definitive rationale for rejecting the gay-rights bill.

Although most Americans rejected such rhetorical extremes, the appearance of the baffling new disease, whose cause had yet to be discovered, added to all the nagging uncertainties about homosexuality. Heterosexuals seemed able to accept individual gays; Congressman Gerry Studds, the first member of Congress publicly to acknowledge being homosexual, was in those very months on the way to a comfortable reelection. But on a more abstract level, the new disease bolstered old fears. For the first time in more than a decade, support for gay civil rights in public-opinion polls began to decline.

It was the wrong time to be sponsoring a gay civil rights bill, and Jim Dressel represented the wrong district to be taking up the cause. The Ottawa County Republican Party, which he had once chaired, publicly disassociated itself from both Dressel and his legislation. After favorable votes in the House Judiciary Committee, the bill floundered. When the matter came up on the House floor, the bill was sent back to committee, where everyone knew it would die.

The defeat hurt, but what hurt more was that in Holland, where Jim had spent his life, old friends and high school classmates suddenly stopped talking to him. Conversation ceased when he walked into a restaurant. For forty years he had been one of them; now he seemed to embarrass them. Everyone was whispering that he was gay, and Jim reinforced these suspicions by refusing to deny it. He would like to have said forthrightly that he was, but four decades of programming had instructed him to remain silent. Polls showed he was headed for certain defeat in his primary election.

Columnists throughout the state rallied to his defense, writing that he represented everything that was sorely lacking in politics—someone who stuck to his principles even in the face of political disaster. Even the Republican newspapers in Jim's district, in Holland and Zeeland, supported him, aggressively calling for his reelection and defending his integrity. More influential, however, was the word that went out informally from the Christian Reformed churches: Dressel had betrayed them; he must go.

Jim's service in the Michigan Air National Guard had become a respite from the pressures of the legislature. But now, as the controversy reached its peak, Dressel discovered that the other pilots, his friends at the National Guard base in Battle Creek, would barely speak to him. An article about Jim's sponsorship of the gay-rights bill was posted on the base's bulletin board. Jim could read the concern in the other pilots' eyes: He was forty years old and unmarried and probably gay. If one National Guard pilot was gay, others might be, too. His pilot buddies worried that their neighbors and families might suspect them and that they, too, might become strangers when they went back to their homes in Kalamazoo or Augusta or Galesburg. Jim had used the military as his door into politics; now that he was on his way out, it seemed time to leave the military. After sixteen years of service, he resigned his commission.

MARCH 30, 1984
PORTSMOUTH NAVAL HOSPITAL
PORTSMOUTH, VIRGINIA

OFFICIALLY, RETIRED COMMANDER Vernon Berg was dying of a lymphoma in the early months of 1984, and there were indications his cancer was caused by exposure to Agent Orange. But his son and namesake, Vernon Berg III, believed that part of his father's malaise was disillusion.

Copy helped care for his father at the end. He had plenty of practice; AIDS had hit New York City's gay community early and hard. Copy had watched seventeen friends die over the past three years. He sometimes worried for himself, as most gay men did in those anxious early years of the epidemic, before blood tests could determine who had made it safely through the community's virological gauntlet.

The older Berg struggled against his disease, less because he loved life, Copy thought, than because he hated death. Throughout his illness, he had insisted on treatment at home. If he went into a hospital, he feared, he would not come out alive. But by the last days of March, he had grown so ill that he was moved to the Navy hospital at Portsmouth, across the Chesapeake Bay from Norfolk. He died there on the night of March 30, the day before his fifty-third birthday.

— 48 —

Exiles

THE FIRST SERGEANT gave Perry Watkins the word at work. The federal appeals court in San Francisco had declined to hear his appeal: He was going to be discharged. It would take two weeks to complete all the paperwork, the first sergeant said, so he had time to pack and get organized for the move back to the States.

Perry was composed. The Army had said they were going to discharge him before, but his lawyer had always gotten a temporary restraining order. It was sixteen years, almost to the day, since he had first walked into the induction center in Tacoma and confirmed that he was a homosexual; surely after all this time, the Army was not really going to kick him out for it. From the first day he filed in federal court, Perry never doubted that he would win his case.

The next morning when Perry showed up at the personnel office for work, there were new instructions. Perry was to be on a 3:00 P.M. flight back to the States; he would be out of the Army within twenty-four hours. While Perry raced from one office to another for the necessary papers, his supervisor became angry at the swiftness with which the normally torpid Army was moving. Everyone overheard him shouting to a major: "They're treating him like a goddamn criminal. He hasn't done anything wrong." By afternoon, the first sergeant was in tears, as were several of Perry's colleagues.

Although Perry's appearances on network television had made him the most famous gay soldier in the Army, he had continued to hold responsible jobs. At the hospital, he was in charge of the personnel actions section and supervised his own staff. He had continued to earn outstanding reviews on his evaluations.

Watkins understood what was happening. The Army wanted him out and on the street before his lawyer could get back in court for a restraining order. The Army dispatched a specialist five to Ramstein Air Base to carry Perry's records on the flight back to the United States. The Army so desperately wanted to be rid of Watkins that when it happened that the military transport was one seat short, a young man whose father had just died was bumped off the plane so that there would be room for the specialist and Perry's papers. From McGuire Air Force Base, Perry was driven directly to nearby Fort Dix, New Jersey.

The next morning, clerks began processing his paperwork. There was an unresolved issue of forty days' leave that the Army owed Perry. He wanted to be paid for it; the clerks refused. He should have taken it, they said; it was not their fault he was being moved out so quickly. In that case, Perry said, he was entitled to forty days of terminal leave, a routine procedure in which unused leave is simply tacked onto the end of a soldier's service. Official discharge occurs only after the leave is over. One of the clerks called Washington. A few minutes later, he shouted across the office, "Tough shit. You lose it."

Perry understood the unofficial rationale; the Army did not want him around another forty days to file for a restraining order, even if it meant violating their own regulations.

They took Perry's military identification card, handed him his DD-214 form, and, after sixteen years, he was banished from the Army with two words still ringing in his ears: *Tough shit.*

PERRY'S DISCHARGE CONCLUDED the first phase of what would be nine years of legal action. Although his journey through American jurisprudence was not yet over, his travails reflected the changing complexion of the federal court system. Ever since Richard Nixon's election in 1968, Republicans had promised a more conservative judiciary. After twelve years of Republican Presidents, their judges were fulfilling that promise.

The conservative direction of the courts had been manifested six months earlier when a three-judge panel of the Ninth Circuit Court of Appeals reviewed Watkins's case. The Army had appealed Judge Barbara Rothstein's 1982 order that Watkins not only be retained but reenlisted into the Army. It was only "equitable," she maintained, that he be kept, since the Army had known for so long that he was gay. But the appeals court ruled for the Army. Federal courts, the panel said, "may not be used to force the military to disobey its own regulations." Only if there were constitutional grounds for challenging the Army's regulation could the courts halt the enforcement of the antigay policy and order the retention of Sergeant Watkins. As for constitutional grounds, the court was bound by the ruling made by the circuit's entire appeals panel in the *Beller* case in 1981. That ruling flatly supported the military's regulations.

"It is not our function to question the wisdom of those who changed Army regulations [in 1981] . . . the district court has no power to force Watkins' superiors to disobey them," the court declared. "The Supreme

Court has recognized that the broad powers the courts possess to regulate civilian life are to a large extent inapplicable to the military. Simply put, military and civilian life are regulated by two separate systems of justice, to some extent parallel but nevertheless distinct."

As had happened so often in the past, the judges seemed ambivalent even as they voted to uphold the military's antigay regulation. Higher-court precedents forced these decisions, they said, and they used their opinions to chastise the military. Though voting to discharge Watkins, Judge William Norris, a Carter appointee, wrote, "The Army rewarded Sgt. Watkins' years of outstanding service by destroying his chosen career. . . . Our nation has lost a fine soldier, and Sgt. Watkins has suffered a manifest injustice. . . . Our court [has] abdicated one of its primary duties: to safeguard individual rights against intrusions engendered by governmental insensitivity or bigotry. To me, the Army's current bias against homosexuals is no less repugnant to fundamental constitutional principles than was its long-standing prejudice against minority servicemen."

Such attitudes were echoed by federal judges across the nation. In April 1984, for example, D. Brock Hornby, a magistrate of Maine's Federal District Court, ruled that the Army had violated Diane Matthews's constitutional rights to free speech when it disenrolled her from ROTC because she had said she was a lesbian. The case was an early challenge to the new Defense Department regulation that called for the discharge of anyone who evinced an "intent" or "desire" to participate in gay sexual acts at some unspecified time. "Indeed, the Army seeks to exclude servicepersons for even harboring thoughts or emotions on homosexuality, regardless of expression. The Army must develop other, more narrowly drawn measures that leave some scope for First Amendment interests," Hornby ruled. As for the rationale that the gay regulation was necessary because the presence of gays would undermine the discipline and morale of heterosexuals in the service, the judge ruled, "The Army cannot rely on the negative response of others to justify a complete foreclosure of a serviceperson's First Amendment right on selective topics. . . ."

The more telling ruling, and the one that signaled why the Matthews decision would never be upheld in a higher court, came three months after Perry Watkins was discharged, when a federal appeals court in Washington ruled on the case of former Petty Officer James Dronenburg. The *Dronenburg* ruling not only had far-reaching implications for gay civil rights but offered insights into the future of privacy rights for all Americans on such related issues as abortion.

Jim Dronenburg was a twenty-seven-year-old Korean-language specialist who had a superb record before being caught up in the 1980 purge of gays at the Defense Language Institute in Monterey. Unlike the court cases of Mel Dahl, Diane Matthews, or Miriam Ben-Shalom, Dronenburg's case involved not only speech about homosexuality but actual homosexual conduct. Dronenburg admitted to having had sex twice with a nineteen-year-old seaman in the Navy barracks at Monterey. With lawyers from the San Francisco–based National Gay Rights Advocates, Dronenburg filed a challenge to the gay regulations in federal district court in Washington, D.C. The lawsuit promoted what had become a classic gay-rights argument. First, his lawyers contended that Dronenburg had a right to engage in any private consensual sexual conduct under the right to privacy, as articulated in the Supreme Court's earlier decisions allowing contraception, miscegenation, and abortion. The lawyers also argued that the military had never demonstrated how the antigay regulations fulfilled any pressing government interest. Moreover, though the military laws regarding sodomy were written to punish anyone who participated in oral or anal sex, they were enforced only against gays, meaning they violated the constitutional mandate that all Americans be afforded "equal protection under the law."

The twenty-one-page ruling by Appeals Court Justice Robert Bork rebuffed these arguments with a sweeping rationale for the preservation not only of sodomy laws but of regulations to proscribe homosexuality in every shape and form. "Private consensual homosexual conduct is not constitutionally protected," Bork wrote, stating that any judicial attempt to extend civil rights to include gays represented the invention of new civil rights. "We can find no constitutional right to engage in homosexual conduct and, as judges, we have no warrant to create one," the judge ruled. Bork took broad swipes at the Supreme Court justices who had extended privacy rights to allow abortion in their *Roe* v. *Wade* decision. Maintaining that the court had not offered a rationale when it "creates new rights," Bork ruled that previous privacy decisions had dealt with issues of marriage, procreation, and contraception, "family" issues that did not extend to homosexuals. The Supreme Court, Bork wrote, "has never defined the right [to privacy] so broadly as to encompass homosexual conduct."

As for the military's regulation, Bork said it was "plainly a rational means of advancing a legitimate, indeed a crucial, interest common to all our armed forces. . . . The effects of homosexual conduct within a Naval or military unit are almost certain to be harmful to morale and discipline. The Navy is not required to produce social science data or the results of controlled experiments to prove what common sense and common experience demonstrate." As evidence, Bork pointed to the fact that Dronenburg himself admitted to having had sex with another sailor in a Navy barracks. Just such episodes, he said, was evidence that allowing homosexuals to serve in the military would "enhance the possibility of homosexual seduction."

The unanimous decision by the three-member appeals panel was based firmly in the strict constructionist idealogy that maintained that any decisions should be grounded in the specific language of the Constitution or the intent of its framers. If rights are not to be found there, then they should be enacted not by courts but by legislatures. As Bork wrote in the

Dronenburg opinion, "If the revolution in sexual mores that appellant proclaims is in fact ever to arrive, we think it must arrive through the moral choices of the people and their elected representatives, not through the judicial ukase of this court."

The decision reflected the increasingly conservative temperament of federal courts. Even the rights to privacy that the Supreme Court had already established were viewed with deep suspicion; they were certainly not going to be extended. The Washington court of appeals was generally regarded as the nation's most influential federal appeals court. When the case was filed, it was among the most liberal appeals courts in the country; by now, it was becoming the most conservative. At that time, Bork was considered a likely nominee for the Supreme Court, as was another judge who signed the *Dronenburg* opinion, Antonin Scalia. The decision was seen by some as a way of advertising both their conservative credentials as magistrates who would be likely to overturn *Roe* v. *Wade*, a cherished goal of the religious right and a judicial priority of the Reagan administration.

Legal scholars saw the *Dronenburg* decision as a harbinger of things to come on all issues relating to privacy. Calling the ruling "a serious setback for the gay liberation movement," scholar Kelly Carbetta-Scandy, writing in the *Cincinnati Law Review*, said, "The *Dronenburg* decision is a disenchanting preview of the dim future that lies ahead for individuals who will seek constitutional protection under the fundamental right to privacy."

Gay-rights advocates were morose. Dr. Rhonda Rivera, an Ohio State University Law School professor and a leading homosexual legal scholar, did not understand why the case was advanced in the first place, given the sexual conduct implicit in its circumstances. In San Diego, military counselor Bridget Wilson began referring to future ill-fated cases as products of the "Dronenburg Syndrome," in which lawyers unfamiliar with homosexual military issues advanced the wrong cases with disastrous results. For his part, Leonard Graff, who represented Dronenburg, noted that government lawyers themselves never made much of an issue over homosexual conduct. Their contention was that they were entitled to eliminate gays just because of their orientation, conduct or no conduct. It was Bork who ran with the facts about sex.

The debate was no less acrimonious within the eleven-member appeals panel itself. When Graff filed a motion for the judges to hear the case *en banc*, or all together, the liberal judges offered a rare castigation of the Bork opinion. The refusal to apply the privacy precedents from *Roe* v. *Wade* and other cases was "particularly inappropriate," wrote Chief Judge Spottswood W. Robinson III. Bork was not applying the *Roe* decision because he did not agree with it, Robinson said, not because it was irrelevant. Bork had used the opinion "to throw down gauntlets to the Supreme Court," he wrote, adding, "We find particularly inappropriate the panel's attempt to wipe away selected Supreme Court decisions in the name of judicial restraint. . . . Surely it is not their function to conduct a spring cleaning of constitutional law. Judicial restraint begins at home."

Robinson also took Bork to task for accepting the government's rationale for the gay policy. The government, Robinson said, had presented a "patently inadequate justification for a ban on homosexuality in a Navy that includes personnel of both sexes and places no parallel ban on all types of heterosexual conduct. In effect, the Navy presumes that any homosexual conduct constitutes cause for discharge, but it treats problems arising from heterosexual relations on a case-by-case basis, giving fair regard to the surrounding circumstances. This disparity in treatment calls for serious equal protection analysis."

Bork dismissed Robinson's objections as "moral relativism," a major profanity in the vocabulary of the religious right. He said that Robinson's willingness to accept gays was hardly "the moral stance of a large majority of Naval personnel." And Bork was in the majority. When the final vote was taken on rehearing the case *en banc,* only four judges voted affirmatively. The precedent stood.

The rightward tilt of the courts was evident in every court case affecting gays in general and military gays in particular. When the Army appealed the decision ordering Diane Matthews to be reinstated into ROTC, an appeals court ruled for the government. When federal judge Barbara Rothstein took Perry Watkins's case under consideration to weigh the constitutional issues his challenge presented, she reluctantly decided against him. "In upholding the general constitutionality of regulations similar to those dictating the Army's decision, the [appeals] court recognized the possibility of harsh, unwise, even arbitrary results in an individual situation and ruled that review of individual decisions was not necessary. Therefore, no matter how irrational the Army's denial of reenlistment may be in the particular circumstances of plaintiff's case, 'we cannot under the guise of due process give our opinion on the fairness of [this] application of military regulation.' " Nevertheless, Rothstein added that she maintained an "abiding conviction that the plaintiff has suffered a grievous wrong for which there is simply no remedy at this juncture. . . . Furthermore, if one case could establish not only the lack of wisdom, but also the irrationality of the Army's policy of categorically barring homosexuals from its ranks, this would be it."

LEGAL SCHOLARS PONDERING the future of privacy law had to look no further than the latest Gallup polls. In the summer of 1984, Ronald Reagan was advancing toward reelection. The presidential campaign that year saw gay rights once again edging slowly toward prominence as an issue of national concern.

The race for the Democratic presidential nomination reaffirmed what had been learned in 1980, that hopefuls at least needed to pay lip service to gay rights in order to earn the Democratic nomination. Candidates such as the Reverend Jesse Jackson and former Vice President Walter Mondale all supported the federal gay-rights bill and pledged to sign an executive order banning discrimination against gays in all federal jobs, including the military. Hopefuls Gary Hart and Ernest "Fritz" Hollings had election-year conversions on behalf of gay rights, and both signed on as Senate cosponsors of the federal gay-rights bill. Only Senator John Glenn opposed the bill, adding that homosexuals should also be excluded from "sensitive positions" such as the military and intelligence agencies. This stance prompted a maelstrom of controversy and led to the resignation of his New York State campaign chairman. It was among the factors that derailed what many had thought would be a promising campaign.

Years of working at the grass roots level in urban areas was paying off. The 1983 municipal elections saw voters install openly gay city council members in Boston and Minneapolis. Traditional liberal interest groups were signing on to the gay agenda. The AFL-CIO approved a resolution supporting the federal gay-rights bill in October 1983. Such broad support among Democratic opinion leaders made the adoption of a gay-rights plank in the 1984 Democratic party platform almost routine.

The Republicans continued to move in the opposite direction, although they said they were opposed to discrimination. When asked at a press conference in June about a federal gay-rights bill, for example, Reagan said he could not endorse any specific legislation without the opportunity to study it, but he added, "I am opposed to discrimination, period." At the same time, the President reassured supporters on the religious right that he would never approve of homosexuality. In a statement released to *Presidential Biblical Scoreboard*, Reagan cited "the Judeao-Christian tradition" of marriage and family and decried that "the erosion of these values has given way to a celebration of forms of expression most reject. We will resist the efforts of some to obtain government endorsement of homosexuality."

The more enthusiastic denunciations of homosexuality were left to surrogates from religious groups. The Moral Majority's Reverend Jerry Falwell said, "The Democratic Party is largely controlled by the radical ideas of a dangerous minority—homosexuals, militant feminists, socialists, freeze-niks and the like." Republican partisans of all stripes took great pleasure in the fact that the Democratic convention was held in the nation's homosexual mecca, San Francisco. In repeated television appearances, GOP strategists dismissed their opponents as "the San Francisco Democrats," which, given the city's reputation, was a way of constantly linking Democrats to gays.

It was arguable whether this posturing did much to influence the election outcome, given the landslide President Reagan won in November. The candidates' various pronouncements on gay rights were rarely discussed outside the gay press. National reporters covering presidential elections dismissed such issues as trivial and esoteric. The AIDS epidemic also continued to be ignored by the national reporters, and was therefore largely ignored by the candidates, as well.

More pronounced than any gay politicking were the gender lines along which the two political parties were beginning to define themselves. Indeed, it was perhaps less insightful to describe the political parties as conservative and liberal than as embodiments of male and female principles: the Republicans assuming a male posture, promising a strong defense against foreign aggressors and a tough stance against crime at home; Democrats maintaining a more female outlook, promising nurturance and compassion. The female angle was underscored by the selection of Geraldine Ferraro as the Democrats' vice-presidential nominee, the first time any major party had put a woman on the ticket. The perception of the Democratic party as more female produced an electoral disaster. White male voters, many of whom were once loyal Democrats, deserted the party in droves, attracted to the Republicans in part by the party's appeal to their manhood. In this sense, the small role the gay issue assumed in the 1984 elections was part of the broader conflict being played out in the American psyche over gender.

President Reagan's reelection in November guaranteed one outcome of long-standing consequence. The courts, already conservative, would grow more hostile to privacy rights in the years ahead. This legacy would last well into the next century, given Reagan's astute appointment of young judges who were likely to serve thirty or forty years before retiring. Some of the forty-year-old federal judges appointed by President Reagan in the late 1980s are certain to be deciding gay-rights issues in the 2020s.

OTTAWA COUNTY, MICHIGAN

ALL SUMMER LONG, while Republicans and Democrats held their respective conventions, a smaller drama was taking place in the ninety-fifth legislative district in Michigan, where Jim Dressel struggled to save his political career. The Republican primary campaign provided Dressel with some of the most dispiriting moments of his life.

When Jim marched at the annual Coast Guard Festival Parade in Holland, people lining the streets shouted epithets, calling him a queer and a faggot. When the campaigning started, Jim's volunteers had doors slammed in their faces. Although more than twelve hundred supporters put Dressel lawn signs in their front yards, nine hundred were stolen or vandalized. Eight of Jim's fifteen billboards in the district vanished. He could not go anywhere without being mocked. In a restaurant, a man pointed at Jim and began lisping loudly to his friends, waving his wrist about limply.

The week before the primary vote, anonymous mailings appeared in mailboxes. The *Advocate* had selected Dressel as one of four hundred

Americans, both heterosexual and homosexual, who had most contributed to the gay movement. The unsigned mailing used the *Advocate*'s cover photo of a hunky man in a football jersey and superimposed Jim's face over the photo so it looked as if he were posing as gay beefcake.

Jim campaigned furiously. He outspent his nearest opponent four to one, raising $55,000, more than five times what he had ever spent before. Virtually every newspaper in the district endorsed him, even those who did not agree with his stand on gay rights. But on election day, Dressel still lost by an overwhelming 60 to 36 percent margin to realtor Alvin Hoekman, the man he had defeated six years earlier.

Dressel's loss became the top political story out of the state's primary election, and newspapers were effusive in their praise for him. Sponsoring the bill, one columnist wrote, "was both his downfall and his greatest triumph." The *Detroit Free Press* summarized the election in this headline: HE STUCK TO HIS PRINCIPLES AND LOST HIS JOB. Playing on Dressel's background as a fighter pilot, it said he had "the right stuff." A Grand Rapids newspaper read, "Voters' minds work in strange and mysterious ways. Perhaps to them the world is still a vast elementary school playground, where screams of 'Faggot!' could destroy a young boy's reputation for years."

In the months that followed his defeat, Jim quietly wrapped up his work in the legislature. His brother-in-law hired him to work for his energy-conservation firm, which did extensive contracting with state agencies. It was a job for which Dressel was well suited. He rented an apartment in Lansing and then put his house in Ottawa County up for sale. Though he had lived there for his entire forty years, it was no longer home to him.

As PART OF the Reagan administration's promise to rearm America and make it indisputably the strongest superpower in the world, the Navy recommissioned four World War II–vintage battleships in 1984. Significant controversy surrounded the move. There were fears about the explosives used in the ship's huge guns, for example. That type of gunpowder was not made anymore, so what the Navy used was from old stockpiles. Some dated from the years right after World War I; most came from the era between World War II and the Korean War. Since explosives can become unstable over time, there were fears that the new battleships might be prone to accidents.

Battleship backers, however, won the day. The Navy loved its battleships, primarily for what they symbolized. Battleships looked the way warships were supposed to look, with their long, sleek hulls and their big guns, a perfect metaphor for military potency. No ship in the history of navigation was better suited for showing the flag. Battleships also represented Navy tradition. Whenever a battleship pulled into port, lines of visitors formed. Everybody had an uncle or father or grandfather who had served on a battleship. There was never a shortage of sailors to staff them. To many sailors, particularly those who ran the show, battleships *were* the Navy.

With many old sailors' superstitions fading away, there were only a few old salts who nodded grimly at the name of one of the four battleships taken out of storage. Bad luck would befall any whose name ended in the letter *A*, they recalled, and one of the ships recommissioned in 1984 was the USS *Iowa*.

MAY 1984
TACOMA, WASHINGTON

PERRY WATKINS looked for a job all summer. He had never expected that it would be so difficult. He had earned his bachelor's degree through night courses several years earlier, and he had fifteen years' experience in personnel and administrative jobs in the Army. But Perry was also something of a local celebrity in Tacoma, having appeared on network shows such as *60 Minutes* and the local television news. Very often, interviewers would say, "You're the guy with the case against the Army." Once this was confirmed, they assured Perry it made no difference to them; they did not discriminate, of course. And then Perry would never hear from them again.

There were interviewers who were not aware of Perry's court case. They surveyed his résumé and asked the logical question: Why had he left the Army so few years before he was due to receive his pension? Those interviewers never called back, either.

The rejections undermined Perry's self-confidence. He could accept being refused a job if he did not qualify, but his qualifications and potential job performance had nothing to do with the rejections, just as they had had nothing to do with his dismissal from the Army.

His finances diminishing, Watkins took whatever job he could find. For two weeks, he sold insurance. He sold fire alarms door-to-door for a month. His spirits sank lower. He began to wonder whether maybe the Army had been right all along, that he was an undeserving human being. Then another thought arrested him: *Like hell.*

JUNE 24, 1984
HOLLYWOOD, CALIFORNIA

A FEW MILES AWAY, the annual gay pride festival was gearing up, but in a motel room on Highland Avenue a young man was preparing his own celebration. His neatly pressed Marine Corps uniform hung in the closet. On the television set, he had propped a picture of a handsome Navy corpsman standing on the edge of the sea in Beirut—Joe Milano. Beside the picture were two glasses, which the corporal filled with champagne. Standing alone, the corporal took one of the glasses and toasted Joe's picture. "To us," he said.

Later, he walked over to the festival commemorating the fifteenth anniversary of the Stonewall riots. He did not go to pick anyone up; he went there thinking of Joe. There had to be one day when the love they shared was something beautiful, not something condemned. The corporal promised himself that he would return every year to be there on that one day when gay people could be accepted, and he would remember the time when he and Joe had shared something special, before it was taken away.

— 49 —

Blanket Parties

As EXECUTIVE DIRECTOR of the Air Force Board for Correction of Military Records, Pete Randell led what seemed a perfect life. He had a staff of twenty at the Pentagon. Another dozen people worked for him at the Air Force personnel center in San Antonio. The band struck up whenever he stepped off the planes that ferried him around various bases where he lectured on his corner of Air Force bureaucracy. Over the past year, he had been awarded citations from the American Legion, the Veterans for Foreign Wars, Disabled American Veterans, and the American Red Cross. The Civil Service had just given him the Civilian Meritorious Service Award. His children were twelve and nine years old and the family lived in a comfortable brick ranch home on five acres of what was once a Civil War battlefield near Fredericksburg, Virginia. Randell had been the youngest executive director of any corrections board. Now he was certain that he was being groomed to be Assistant Secretary of the Air Force.

Still, under it all, were the yearnings Pete had suppressed for most of his adult life. He was thirty-eight years old now and edging closer to allowing himself one moment of freedom. The catalyst for his seeking out the gay subculture was a case that came before the board in 1984, during which a gay airman said that he could spot gay men just by looking at them. Pete wondered how this could be; he certainly could not. The thought stuck with him. There were other gay people out there. How many more? How could you tell? Over the years, he had stolen a chance encounter here and there, but these did not represent any systematic interaction with the gay community.

Then Pete recalled the copious documentation of gay life used in Technical Sergeant Matlovich's appeal almost a decade earlier. Pete ordered up box after box of the Matlovich files from the archives and began poring over the testimony and newspaper clippings. In a *Parade* magazine story,

Pete read Leonard's comments about going to a gay bar in Washington, a place called the Lost & Found.

Late one night in October 1984, with wisps of Indian summer still in the air, Pete drove to the bar. He parked on a side street. Here he was, at an establishment catering to sexual deviates, and he really thought he might be raped when he walked in the door. He anticipated furtive homosexuals, mincing men, transvestites and lesbians in male drag. So when Pete took his first steps inside, he was stunned to see a normal-looking crowd, cheerful, chatting, seemingly happy.

A week later, he picked up a copy of the *Washington Blade*, the local gay paper, and noted the locations of other gay bars. He met civil servants and soldiers and professionals like himself. Soon, he made the acquaintance of the manager of an exclusive eatery where the President and Vice President sometimes dined. The manager was well connected to the powerful gay underground. He began introducing him to the large homosexual Republican establishment in Washington.

Over the next months, Pete met an associate justice of the Supreme Court, several congressmen, a handful of general officers, and a senator, one of at least two gay Republican senators. By now, Pete was also learning about the gay generals who had managed to navigate their way around suspicion into top Pentagon jobs. An Air Force active-duty major general put the make on him in a Pentagon rest room. And, of course, he heard about the four-star Army general widely rumored to be gay. Another story making the rounds was that one branch of the service had claimed two bachelor generals, one retired and one on active duty, who were brothers and both reputed to be gay.

All this came as a revelation to Pete. Everything his parents had taught him about homosexuals was a lie. There were decent homosexuals, and some were making decisions about how to run the country. He felt a tremendous relief as the two warring sides of his nature, the secret and the respectable, came together. It gave him no impulse to become a crusader for gay rights. He had not been in a closet, after all; he had been in a vault. He decided to separate from his wife.

Pete Randell had never used his position to pursue an antigay agenda within the Air Force. On the contrary, he had put an end to the practice of "redlining," in which gay-related appeals went to only the most conservative panels. This was no small matter during the early 1980s, given the unprecedented numbers of gay-related discharges meted out under the new Defense Department regulations. At his presentations on Air Force bases, Pete always asked for a show of hands as to whether officers thought gays would eventually be allowed to serve in the Air Force. Usually, by more than two-to-one margins, audiences responded affirmatively, and 90 percent commonly agreed that homosexuals should be allowed to serve. At the senior NCO academies where Pete delivered his standard two-hour lecture, the response was the same.

The military's antigay regulations galled Randell, as much because they violated his conservative "get the government off our backs" ethos as because of their implications for his personal life. This was not an issue about which he was outspoken, however, even as he began the process of self-discovery.

Others in Washington's Republican gay underground were outspoken opponents of gay rights, including a gay rock-ribbed conservative United States senator from the most conservative New England state. John "Terry" Dolan, whose fund-raising with the National Conservative Political Action Committee had played a key role in President Reagan's 1980 campaign, was a regular at the more exclusive gay bars, as were a number of prominent Defense Department officials.

IN A SOCIETY that supported so many institutions enforcing social proscriptions against homosexuality, it was inevitable that many homosexuals themselves would be involved in perpetuating that discrimination, because homosexuals exist in every social institution. In late 1984, for example, Fairfax County police conducted a routine sting operation on a gay cruising area in the Belle Haven Marine in Old Town Alexandria, outside Washington. According to news accounts, one of those arrested was Albert B. Fletcher, a judge on the U.S. Court of Military Appeals. Fletcher claimed that he had been jogging near the public rest room and had stopped to talk to an ostensibly gay man in order to gather information that would assist him in deciding a gay-related case. The man with whom he decided to chat, however, was an undercover officer. According to Fletcher, the officer asked him to have sex. Though police said that it was Fletcher who propositioned the police officer, other attorneys representing other victims of the sting said police officers were indeed engaging in entrapment.

Accusations of entrapment frequently followed operations in which police staked out gay cruising areas. In the eight months before Fletcher's arrest, Fairfax County police had nabbed sixty-nine men in similar sting operations. In July 1984, an undercover operation in a Fairfax County shopping mall led to the arrests of nineteen men, including an Army major, an Air Force major, and a Seventh Day Adventist minister. In a throwback to the journalistic conventions of the 1950s, *The Washington Post* published the names and occupations of all the suspects.

Fletcher's arrest was particularly ironic, given his 1978 ruling upholding the Army's court-martial of Private Reginald Scoby on sodomy charges. Fletcher resigned his post shortly after his arrest.

NORFOLK NAVAL STATION
NORFOLK, VIRGINIA

NAVAL INVESTIGATIVE SERVICE agents were blunt at Linda Gautney's first interview. The NIS investigated homosexuals, one explained. Did Linda have any problem with that? Linda did not. As far as she knew, she had never met a homosexual. When she had attended the NIS academy in Suitland, Maryland, she sat through lectures that taught her that homosexuals were security risks and a threat to the good order, discipline, and morale of the Navy. These notions were presented as well-established facts that barely needed explanation.

By now, Linda was aware that the NIS itself was concerned about the possibility of having gays in its midst. Though governed by civil service regulations that forbade discrimination on the basis of sexual orientation, Linda learned from friends in her hometown that, in the course of a background check on her, NIS personnel had asked questions about whom she had dated and whether she had any "deviate sexual practices."

None of these questions troubled Linda, who had lived a thoroughly ordinary life for all her twenty-two years. She had not wanted to work in cotton mills her whole life like most of the other people in eastern Alabama, so she put herself through two years at the local community college and then through Troy State University, where she graduated summa cum laude with a degree in criminal justice in 1984. During her last year at school, Linda interned at the Federal Law Enforcement Training Center in Glenco, Georgia, where a number of federal agencies train their agents. That was where she became interested in the NIS. The Naval Investigative Service is the FBI for the Navy, NIS agents said. Linda applied and in August was assigned to the Norfolk Resident Agency.

Immediately, she began hearing about "queer cases," or "8-G's," after the case codes assigned to sodomy cases—code 8-G. In training, Linda never received specific instruction on how to handle 8-G's, although she learned other interesting specifics. One teacher in an interrogations class explained that once a gay male suspect admitted his homosexuality, his voice sometimes turned higher and he might become more effeminate, break down and cry. "It's like they become a woman right in front of your eyes," the teacher said. Regarding lesbians, they could be the meanest people in the world, but a jilted lesbian could be a treasure trove of names, since she was likely to "dime out" other gay women.

In Norfolk, Linda saw that many agents did not like working the queer cases—not that they thought it was wrong; nobody ever said that, but they seemed to think that such work was beneath them. The FBI didn't go peeking under beds; why should they? Senior agents preferred to avoid the work altogether, leaving the 8-G's to junior agents. And then it was important that 8-G cases did not undermine an agent's professional standing.

Gays were considered the easiest marks for NIS interrogations, and an agent who could not wrest a confession from an 8-G became the butt of some ribbing. Agents took professional pride in eliciting more information than the suspect needed to give. It was a badge of honor to leave an interview with both a confession and a list of fifteen other gays to investigate. When an 8-G interrogation was over, nobody ever asked, "Did you get a confession?" It was assumed the agent had. Instead, Linda noted, the question was always, "How many did you get?"

This was the first time Linda had ever been away from rural Alabama, and that, along with all the talk about 8-G's and queer cases, caused her to reflect on her own sexuality. She had lived a perfectly conventional life but was aware of less than conventional personal feelings. Now she understood she was a lesbian. And her feeling of being different did not dissipate in this environment where homosexuality was frowned upon. She made it a point to date male agents and not to strike up friendships with women in the office. Still, she began to worry: Would they notice?

The possibility that other agents might be gay was a matter of constant speculation in the NIS office. One female agent, for example, kept a file of three-by-five-inch index cards on which she had written the name of every suspected homosexual ever named in her interrogations. She claimed to know the name of almost every lesbian in Norfolk. This led some agents to wonder openly whether she had something to hide. There was also talk about an extraordinarily high official at the NIS headquarters in Washington who had never been married and who seemed to have an inordinately close relationship with another agent.

It was in this ambience of suspicion and countersuspicion that Linda began to realize she could not repress her feelings forever. She also wondered whether 8-G's were worth all the time and money the government spent to root them out. But she dared not speak such thoughts aloud—then she would be suspect. She could imagine it now. Agents would fan out in her hometown. They already knew Linda Gautney was gay, they would say. That's what they always told friends and relatives of 8-G's under investigation: They knew the suspect was homosexual—they just needed more information to nail it down. Even if information was not forthcoming, word spread in hometowns just the same. Linda imagined the agents in Valley, Alabama, and people nodding knowingly and remarking that Linda had always been a tomboy.

———————

AT THE SAME TIME Special Agent Linda Gautney was worrying about NIS agents in her hometown, Air Force Sergeant Jack Green was preparing for a serious discussion with the sergeant with whom he shared his room and his bed at Incirlik Air Base in Turkey. Jack was about to explain that he was an informant for the Office of Special Investigations. Though Green's duties had to do with Department of Defense efforts to rid the services of drugs, the OSI was also the agency that investigated homosexuality. Since Jack's boyfriend was an occasional pot smoker as well as gay, Jack figured he would be frightened when he learned that Jack was more than just a munitions specialist.

It had started innocuously enough in 1982 when Jack joined the

Thirty-fourth Tiger Fighter Group in Guam. The Reagan administration had enunciated a "zero tolerance" policy for drugs in the military, and all the services were using young servicemen as informants to break the drug suppliers that had long fed off military installations. Although Jack had served in the Air Force less than a year, he was twenty-two years old and more mature than most airmen. With a diploma from Tecumseh High School in Tecumseh, Oklahoma, and two years at Southern Bible College, he also had the small-town credentials that made him a reliable foot soldier in the war on drugs. Since he contemplated a career in law enforcement, working with the OSI seemed a good career move.

What could not be read on his résumé were the profound conflicts he had long experienced over his sexuality. In high school, Jack had assured himself that his attractions to men were just a phase. At college, he had spent endless nights on his knees pleading for God to change him. He had joined the Air Force to get away from homosexuality. Now he was amazed at the numbers of gays there were in the military.

It was during his assignment on Guam that he began meeting other gay airmen. Drug cliques sometimes overlapped with gay social circles, and in his round of partying he met a lesbian officer with whom he became friends. Later, his OSI handlers became keenly interested in their friendship. Was she a lesbian? they asked. No, Jack said. Toward the end of the assignment, Jack had a brief affair with an OSI agent who, like himself, was secretly gay.

In Turkey, Jack still struggled with himself. He could no longer deny that he was gay and could no longer believe that he was ever going to change, but he still did not want this destiny. Only in the summer months of 1984, when he began a relationship with his roommate, did he move toward accepting himself. At first, the roommate talked a lot about his girlfriend back in the States. After several weekends on the Turkish coast, the two men got drunk together and made love. On almost every weekend after that, they went away, had too much to drink, and then had sex. Neither spoke aloud about their nighttime activity. Neither ever admitted to the other that he was gay. Their relationship simply drifted wordlessly somewhere beyond the taboos they had broken.

By the autumn of 1984, Jack knew they had to speak. Word was out among the drug dealers he was investigating that there was an OSI informant among them. Jack figured it was just a matter of time before they found out who. He had to tell his roommate before someone else did.

As Jack had expected, his roommate was petrified. Jack assured him he would not turn him in for being gay, but he was opposed to drug use and warned him to stop smoking marijuana as long as he was in the service. It was not safe.

Being a drug informant, however, was not safe work, either. As the dealers tried to figure out who was informing on them, suspicions fell on a young airman. Before long, he was tossed from the third-story balcony of his apartment. When the OSI finally closed the case against the dealer, Jack's testimony being the crucial evidence in the court-martial, he figured he would be transferred away from Turkey, as he had been in the past after similar busts. Instead, he was retained at his job in the munitions shop—even though the shop was crowded with people whom the dealer had named as drug users. Green pleaded with the local OSI commander for a transfer. None came, though he was warned not to stand around any heavy machinery on the base, just in case there might be an accident. Even after Jack was cornered in a barracks bathroom and beaten up, the OSI did not issue the transfer.

Jack's relationship with his roommate did not last long after his revelation, but that was the least of the airman's problems. Jack's immediate task was survival.

WHEN OTHER JROTC cadets started talking about having a blanket party, seventeen-year-old Kevin Drewery knew right away who would be the guest of honor. It had been obvious since that afternoon when Drewery and his entire platoon were forced to do extra calisthenics because of some screwup by Bob, a mildly effeminate cadet.

Kevin's two weeks at Fort Knox were supposed to be the prelude to a military career. At the end of the summer, he was slated to attend Kemper Military College in Boonville, Missouri, on a full scholarship. He had launched himself in a military direction after becoming increasingly aroused during his junior high school gym classes back in Rockford, Illinois. Taking JROTC courses was a way to get out of physical education, and he hoped the military would rechannel his desires in more conventional directions: The Army would make a man out of him.

After two years at Kemper, he would be commissioned as an officer. By then perhaps he would not be queer anymore. It was a frightening thought, to end up being outcast and hated like Bob, the cadet for whom the blanket party was now being planned.

Bob was asleep inside the barracks while Kevin and six other platoon members had a pizza outside and complained about the extra exercises they had had to do. They were all in their twenties, had completed several years of college, and were about to be commissioned. And Lord, how they hated queers. Kevin was not sure who brought up the blanket party, but you could not be in JROTC and not know what a blanket party meant. Kevin was frightened that they would be caught but equally frightened that if he did not help the other cadets, he would end up under a blanket himself.

Late that night, the platoon sneaked inside the barracks, threw a blanket over Bob in his bunk so that he could not identify his attackers, and began working him over. Bob did not fight back for the fifteen minutes that the half-dozen men pummeled him. Kevin flailed away with the other cadets, knowing with every punch that he was every bit as queer as Bob and that they would all be beating him if they knew.

When it was over, the cadets retreated outside, laughing about what they had done, congratulating themselves. Bob never reported the attack.

———————

NOT LONG AFTER his first visit to the Lost & Found, Pete Randell asked his wife to meet him in a restaurant. He had never told her why they had separated. She had believed he was having an affair with another woman. When they met, Randell told her it was not another woman, he was gay.

Pete's wife did not take the news well. She wanted a divorce, which Pete was willing to give her. She also told Pete's parents. "You ain't nothing but a goddamn queer faggot," was Pete's father's response when he heard.

Pete was prepared for this. What he was not prepared for was his wife's telling agents of the Office of Special Investigations, which she did when they conducted their background check in December 1984 to renew Pete's security clearance.

Pete lost his clearance immediately, which required his removal as executive director of the Air Force records board. Under national security rules, Pete could not hold the job without a top-secret clearance and, as a practical matter, the Defense Department was loath to give such clearance to a gay man. Civil Service said Pete could not be dismissed from his job for being gay, but he could be demoted to a position for which a security clearance was no longer required. He was offered a job as a clerk/typist—in the office where, until a few weeks before, he had been executive director.

Of course, the Air Force wanted him to resign. Pete was uncertain. His pride would not allow him to become a typist, with everyone else in the office sniggering about him behind his back. He had worked in government for his entire adult life, however, and was not sure what else he would do. Facing an uncertain future, the talk about discrimination and oppression did not seem so unrelated to his life anymore.

———————

AFTER MONTHS of extraordinary tension, Sergeant Jack Green received his transfer to the Thirty-second Tactical Fighter Squadron at a U.S. air base in Holland. Early in his assignment, the Office of Special Investigations asked Jack to work again as a drug informant. He refused. He had been left hanging in Turkey and had grown frustrated with the uneven hand of military justice in drug offenses: Enlisted men caught with small amounts of marijuana seemed to draw heavy penalties, while genuine drug kingpins seemed always to walk away.

Jack's new assignment put him near Amsterdam, Europe's gay capital. On New Year's Eve, Jack took his first trip into Amsterdam, and, as firecrackers burst and revelers cheered, he welcomed in 1985 at a popular gay coffeehouse on Leidse Straat.

In the months that followed, Green grew more comfortable with his sexuality. In March, he met Albert Taminiau. By June, they were living together in an apartment on the outskirts of Amsterdam, about an hour from Jack's job at Soesterberg Air Base, an installation that would soon become very famous in the Netherlands because of Jack Green's assignment there.

— 50 —

Costs

JANUARY 1985
WURTSMITH AIR FORCE BASE
OSCODA, MICHIGAN

CAPTAIN DAVID MARIER'S MAJOR POINT, which he repeated again and again when he reviewed the events of 1985, was how much it cost the Air Force to train him. Though only twenty-nine years old, Dave Marier flew with the Strategic Air Command. Training required extensive piloting of an aircraft whose fuel costs alone were five thousand dollars an hour— and by 1985, Captain Marier had accumulated 212 flying hours on the KC-135As. Altogether, Dave had logged fifteen hundred flying hours. Though a good share of the time was spent in less expensive planes, he conservatively estimated that his training had cost the Air Force between $4 and $5 million. The statistic was not difficult to believe.

Dave's instruction had taken nearly two years, beginning with training Cessnas in his first Air Force days to training in T-37s and T-38s, and finally in the huge refueling planes he piloted with SAC. He had completed his parachute training and ejection-seat instruction and his survival courses, in which he was left alone in the remote wilds of Washington State and had to kill squirrels and eat ants to survive. The grueling instruction was part of an arduous winnowing process to select those few pilots who would be entrusted with the crucial SAC component of the national defense. Of the thirty-six officer candidates in his class of the Flight Screening Program, only half got their wings. Of twenty trainees in Dave's squadron at Officers' Training School, only three became pilots in the end.

None of this protected him, however, during the purge of gays at Wurtsmith Air Force Base in 1985. It began with the most inconsequential of moments. According to the scuttlebutt around the base, an effeminate airman had gotten into an argument with a civilian woman with whom he worked at the base mess hall. The woman called the airman a "fag"; the airman called the woman a "cunt." The woman marched over to the

Office of Special Investigations to report the airman as a homosexual. OSI agents were disinterested; they had already heard about the mess specialist.

"What about all the other gays?" the woman said. The airman knew lots of other gay Air Force personnel on the base, including some officers.

The OSI was very interested in this and began the usual round of interrogations and threats that led to the inevitable confessions and list making, which led to Dave Marier being called into a small room and asked whether he was a homosexual.

"Yes, I am," Dave said, his blue eyes never blinking.

It was the end of Dave Marier's Air Force career.

By then, the Air Force was losing many expensively trained personnel because of the investigation. One of the base's most expert navigators was on his way out, too. This captain's job entailed navigating so well as to enable dropping nuclear warheads on specific enemy targets, which required training estimated to cost the Air Force at least $8 million. Five other enlisted men whose training had cost in the hundreds of thousands of dollars were being jettisoned, too. Those were just the costs at Wurtsmith. In a desperate effort to get an honorable discharge, one airman had turned in a Marine and two Army soldiers at other bases, and they, too, were being separated. No one was able to track what other pilots and enlisted men were being swept away at other installations.

Keeping the services a for-heterosexuals-only club was a very expensive proposition. Captain Dave Marier hoped that the high cost, among other reasons, would help save his career.

———————————

DAVE MARIER had always known he would tell them he was gay if asked. He had known even before he signed on with the Air Force in 1979. He had been working as a bartender late one night in the summer of 1978 when, after much delay, the made-for-TV movie about Sergeant Leonard Matlovich aired. The fact that the attitudes toward gays in the military were so much like the attitudes toward blacks in the segregated armed forces of the early 1940s struck Dave profoundly. Those attitudes had changed once whites got the chance to work side by side with blacks; straights' attitudes would change once they worked side by side with gays. He believed that. All the Air Force needed was the example of some exemplary pilots who were gay and the old rules would fall, Dave thought, and he intended to be one of those pilots who helped make things change.

That Dave would go into the Air Force instead of the Army or Navy was not in doubt. His dad had served in the Air Force during the 1950s and had sometimes taken his son along on reserve weekends. After the service, the elder Marier took a job as a maintenance man at a trailer park outside St. Paul, Minnesota. His wife was a waitress at the little diner near the mobile home where the family lived. Dave was the third of six children, but, as the oldest boy, he handled the lion's share of chores. Though his family had always been poor, he knew he was headed in another direction, and he had absorbed the midwestern certainty that hard work would take him there. Dave delivered the *St. Paul Pioneer-Press* in the morning and milked cows by hand before going off to school. After school, he tended the garden and sold tomatoes and corn from a roadside stand to pay for school supplies.

His father walked away from the family when Dave was in ninth grade, so Dave's mom took two jobs while Dave worked nights in a pizza parlor. Still, he kept up his grades and earned a place in the National Honor Society. Like many other Middle American gay men, Dave had his first sexual experience on a Boy Scout camping trip. He thought he would go into farming, so he accepted scholarships to attend the University of Wisconsin in River Falls. Dave persevered in his studies, earned degrees in both agriculture and economics, and made the dean's list almost every quarter.

Before settling into a life of farming, however, Marier decided to serve time in the Peace Corps. In the Philippines, he met other gay people for the first time. He also realized his homosexuality was intrinsic to him. Hungry for more travel, Dave joined the Air Force in 1979.

He planned to be the best officer and the best pilot. When the Air Force knew he was gay, they would understand the folly of their ways and things would change. After Dave had finished his pilot training, he was assigned to the 920th Air Refueling Squadron at Michigan's Wurtsmith Air Force Base along the remote Lake Huron coast. The squadron was among those SAC wings kept on twenty-four-hour alert in the event it was necessary to launch a nuclear attack on the Soviet Union. Dave piloted the huge KC-135s, the refitted Boeing 707s that carried 20,000 gallons of fuel for refueling B-52 bombers.

Each flight remained on alert for a week, with its crews in perpetual rotation. This meant endless games of Trivial Pursuit among bored team members, lots of repeat episodes of "Fame," and plenty of time to do homework on graduate courses, which the more ambitious officers always took. Marier was enrolled in correspondence courses for the Squadron Officers School and was working on a master's degree. He used his courses to hone more carefully the arguments he one day planned to use against the Air Force's policy on gays. In 1983, he had studied the court cases of Vernon Berg III and Leonard Matlovich in order to write a paper, "Air Force versus Homosexuality." By then, some officers' wives were gossiping about him. He was so handsome and yet at twenty-nine he was not married, they noted, and he never seemed to date.

On leaves, Dave traveled to San Francisco and enjoyed gay life. When he met other gay military men on Castro Street, he asked them the details of their careers and honors, collecting more ammunition with which to challenge the gay exclusionary policy. By then, he had had a relationship with an airman first class at Wurtsmith and had been introduced to others in The Family at the base—the accused mess specialist, for one, and several other enlisted men who in the first few months of 1985 were bargaining with the Air Force for honorable discharges.

Evidence other than Dave's admission was sparse. The mess specialist said he had photographs of Dave participating in an act of sodomy, but no such photos ever surfaced. In a search of the apartment of Dave's old boyfriend, OSI agents found a photo Dave had signed. There was no sexual content in the inscription, but any expression of affection between men was considered homosexual by the OSI. In any case, none of this evidence mattered; Marier's admission of homosexual thoughts was enough.

Agents pressed him for names. Dave said he would not give any, and he told them he intended to go to the press. The interrogation ended abruptly. The Air Force put Marier on restriction and ordered him to stay away from his squadron and to speak to no one on his flight crew about what was happening to him.

The Air Force was in a bind. It wanted Marier out, but it did not want publicity. Since Marier would not resign quietly like everyone else, the military pulled out its ultimate weapon—the threat of jail time—and began putting together evidence to advance a sodomy court-martial.

The plans had been made at the highest levels of the Air Force. On December 31, 1984, Lieutenant General Kenneth Peek, Jr., commander of the Eighth Air Force, ordered that Airman First Class Marc Mione be granted immunity for his testimony against Marier and a navigator under investigation. A week later, Mione gave OSI agents a statement asserting that he had had sex with Marier on two occasions. The picture inscribed to Dave's former enlisted boyfriend became evidence for fraternization between the two.

The latter charge took some legal juggling to justify. Their relationship fell well outside the time limit proscribed by the statute of limitations for a fraternization prosecution. The Air Force argued that they *might* have had contact more recently, so their fraternization *could* be viewed as "a continuing offense" deserving of a felony prosecution—with a possible prison sentence of two years.

––––––––––

THE COST OF PURGES such as that at Wurtsmith Air Force Base was the issue of the moment in late 1984 and early 1985 because of a study conducted by the General Accounting Office, the independent and nonpartisan research arm of Congress. The report found that the policy of separating gays from the military cost the Department of Defense at least $22.5 million a year in lost training and recruitment expenses. In the course of a decade, that figure would approach a quarter of a billion dollars.

Although these were impressive numbers, the actual costs of ejecting two thousand soldiers a year for being gay—as the military had been doing throughout the late 1970s and early 1980s—were much higher. The

GAO arrived at its estimates through Pentagon figures designed to obfuscate the actual expense of the antihomosexual policy. The lost training costs, for example, were based on the Army's estimate that they spent $12,299 to train a soldier for his or her first duty station. The entire annual cost multiplied this figure by the 1,796 enlisted personnel whom the Defense Department ejected in fiscal year 1983.

By using the Army's numbers, the Pentagon went with the least-expensive branch of the service rather than with the more technical and expensive training to be found in the Air Force, for example. By including only the amount it took to get soldiers to their first duty stations, the Defense Department did not count the training expenses accrued as soldiers' careers developed. The typical soldier dismissed for homosexuality was not separated at his or her first duty station, but more than three years later, the study found. The costs of highly specialized training, such as piloting or translating, were altogether ignored.

The Pentagon's estimated expenses for investigating gay cases were so low as to be ludicrous. The Navy, for example, claimed to spend only $111 per gay investigation, a sum that would barely pay staff time for one interrogation. The Army claimed $365 per investigation; the Air Force said it spent $529. Given the common use of almost round-the-clock surveillance of suspected homosexuals, the truth had to be much different.

However, the GAO's report on the subject did offer a revealing glimpse into the enforcement of the ban against gays. Over the previous decade, the armed forces had separated 14,661 soldiers and sailors under the provisions of Department of Defense Regulation 1332.14. The report affirmed the arguments of gay activists that the Pentagon was relying increasingly on massive purges of gays. The statistics revealed that even though discharges were increasing in the early 1980s, the number of investigations was decreasing. Still, it was clear that the Pentagon was mounting impressive numbers of investigations. In 1983 alone, for example, the various branches conducted 1,619 gay probes.

Perhaps most striking were the statistics on officers separated for homosexuality. According to the Pentagon, all the branches of the service combined discharged only 191 officers in the ten years between 1974 and 1983, clearly only a fraction of the real numbers. Unlike enlisted men, who were subjected to discharges with the word HOMOSEXUALITY emblazoned across them, officers were allowed to resign without a notation of their offense. By underestimating the numbers of officers discharged for homosexuality, the Pentagon could substantially understate the expense of the antigay policy. An officer trained in ROTC, for example, might well cost the government as much as fifty thousand dollars before seeing a first duty station. The estimated cost for schooling an officer at one of the service academies was between $100,000 and $150,000. None of these numbers made it into the GAO estimates.

Though the reports of the expense of the antigay policy gave new ammunition to liberal congressmen who opposed the gay exclusion policy, it did little to deter its continued enforcement. This was the era of all but unlimited budgets for the military, a period that would be remembered for the Defense Department's $140 screwdrivers and $880 toilet seats. Money was no object. The purges that had begun during the last years of the Carter administration continued to mount through 1984, 1985, and early 1986.

———

As at Wurtsmith, the most bizarre situations could lead to an investigation and purge. In late 1984, Navy brass at the office of the Commander Ocean Systems Pacific at Pearl Harbor distributed an anonymous survey among enlisted personnel about their working conditions. Several sailors complained that there were too many gays in the office, so the Naval Investigative Service launched an investigation that resulted in four discharges.

In 1985, Petty Officer Third Class Darren Gomez was the object of unwelcome attention from a married crew member of the aircraft carrier USS *Carl Vincent*, who had decided that he was gay and in love with Gomez. When Gomez did not return the crewman's affections, the frustrated suitor went to the NIS with a long list of gays, hoping that Gomez would be among those kicked out—so that he and Gomez could then begin a life together. According to Gomez's account, that list resulted in sixteen discharges, though Gomez himself was not among them.

At about the same time, a dozen men were ousted from the Air Force during a 1985 purge of gays at another SAC installation, F. E. Warren Air Force Base in Wyoming.

Purges continued overseas, as well. A gay investigation started in the remote Naval base of Diego Garcia in the Indian Ocean after a cryptographer was caught in bed with the lead singer of a rock group on the island for a USO show. This led to more names being collected.

———

Purges were now occurring among the most elite and honored units of the armed forces. In 1985, Army officials launched a purge of suspected gays from the service's Old Guard, the unit that guarded the Tomb of the Unknown Soldier and performed ceremonial functions at the White House and Pentagon. This probe began when Specialist Lionel Esclovon was called in by investigators who had heard a rumor that he slept with someone named Theodore. Yes, Esclovon said, he did sleep with Theodore—that was what he called his teddy bear. Though that interrogation yielded no charges, Esclovon and at least six others became the subject of further investigation, according to the *Washington Blade*. At least four Old Guard members were discharged as a result of the investigation.

A similar drama occurred in late 1984 aboard the USS *Constitution*— Old Ironsides—the oldest commissioned Naval vessel in the world and one of the first ships in the U.S. Navy. Commissioned in 1798, Paul

Revere had cast its brass. It had fought the Barbary pirates off the shores of Tripoli and had sailed in the War of 1812. Its official name was resonant with the pride of the new Republic. As with other ceremonial units, the Navy personnel who conducted the *Constitution*'s tours were selected on the basis of good military bearing and personal appearance, qualities that distinguished many gay sailors. When crewman Derek Landzaat first boarded the *Constitution*, he counted ten gay sailors among the fifty on the crew—and those were only the ones he knew about.

The large numbers of gay crewmen came to the attention of the *Constitution*'s command in late 1984, and the NIS launched an investigation. Barracks rooms were searched; the entire crew was questioned. In the end, the probe netted at least three discharges, including Landzaat's and that of one of the most highly honored crew members.

———————

ALL THE INVESTIGATIONS resulted in broken lives and suicides. Petty Officer Second Class Phil Zimmerman did his duty at the Naval Air Station at Jacksonville, Florida, and knew a nineteen-year-old named Jamie being drummed out for being gay. Before the processing was complete, however, Jamie was found dead in his bathtub, with his wrists sliced open. Another unrecorded cost of Defense Department Regulation 1332.14.

Zimmerman's own career also demonstrates what it cost to eliminate an entire classification of people, regardless of their skills or performance. A native of Philadelphia, Zimmerman had shown an acuity for languages since he was a child. He had taught himself how to read ancient Egyptian hieroglyphics in high school—by which time he had also learned the complicated Arabic alphabet. After surviving the 1980 purge of linguists at the Defense Language Institute in Monterey—which cost the Navy some of its top Russian- and Korean-language specialists—Zimmerman went on to learn Arabic cryptology and the dialects necessary to break Syrian and Egyptian codes. Upon graduating, he delivered a final speech to the class entirely in Arabic.

Phil also studied Farsi, the language spoken in Iran. He helped avert an international incident in 1982 when he alone was able to decipher Iranian radio traffic. For this, he won the Navy Achievement Medal, an unusual accomplishment for someone with the lowly pay grade of E-3. In the next few years, Zimmerman was given meritorious promotion to petty officer second class and a Navy Commendation Medal for his work. In Navy lingo, Zimmerman was a "golden boy," a sailor likely to have a blessed career.

None of these accomplishments mattered to the NIS agents who pulled Zimmerman off his assignment at the National Security Agency to quiz him about his sex life. He got the full treatment—the usual threats of prison and informing his parents he was gay. The NIS also advised him that they could not guarantee his safety if he was sent back to the Navy barracks. "It's a fact that known homosexuals tend to have accidents," an agent said. So Zimmerman signed a statement acknowledging he was gay. One Navy captain, who commanded Zimmerman at the Naval Security Group Activity at the NSA headquarters, shook his head when he learned Zimmerman was being discharged. "It's not your loss," he said. "It's the Navy's."

The loss was more serious than anyone could imagine then. Zimmerman was only one of several Arabic linguists discharged from the services in the late 1980s for being gay. A few years later when the United States went to war again, the military found itself without enough Arabic-speaking personnel. National Security Agency officials actually contacted some of those gay interpreters who had been discharged in earlier purges to beg for their services.

DAVE MARIER MADE UP his mind to resign his commission after a preliminary hearing in April 1985, in advance of his pending court-martial. Marier's Air Force lawyer had argued an arcane legal issue that could have ended the proceeding immediately: Marier's commanding officer, Lieutenant Colonel Robert Ogden, Jr., had put Marier on restriction in October 1984. Under Air Force regulations for speedy trials, the military must then commence its court-martial within 120 days. Since the 120 days had long since expired, the Air Force had lost its ability to try Marier.

The law of the matter was so clear that Dave's lawyer was sure the hearing would end with the dismissal of all charges. Lieutenant Colonel Ogden took the stand, however, to say that while he had put Marier on restriction in early October, he had lifted the restrictions ten days later. Dave had not been on restriction for more than 120 days, he said, just ten.

The assertion angered Dave's lawyer, who had had personal conversations with Ogden indicating that Marier had indeed been restricted for months. Dave's lawyer then put himself on the stand, swore himself in as his own witness, and testified under oath as to what Ogden had told him on the phone. The military judges ruled against Marier, anyway. His trial would commence on June 6, 1985. With all the charges leveled against him, Dave faced twelve years at hard labor at Fort Leavenworth.

He was convinced he did not have a chance. Marier had hoped to challenge the regulation in civilian courts, but President Reagan's reelection and the prospect of an even more conservative judiciary had ended that dream. Dave had followed the gay-rights controversy that had cost Jim Dressel his career in the state legislature a few months earlier. If lawmakers would not support gay rights in a heavily Democratic state like Michigan, Dave doubted that he had much chance of success on the national level.

And he had begun applying for jobs at the airlines. An extended court case would hurt his chance for employment in those firms, where most management positions were held by ex-military officers who supported the Air Force's gay exclusion policy. In May 1985, Dave offered his resignation and it was accepted.

THE WURTSMITH AIR FORCE BASE purge of 1984 and 1985 offered an intriguing standard by which to judge the accuracy of the Defense Department estimates of the costs of the gay exclusion policy, as reported by the General Accounting Office. The Defense Department figures indicated that in all of fiscal year 1984, the entire cost of the policy was about $22.5 million. Yet in just this one investigation, the Air Force lost at least $12 million on two officers alone. Of course, since the pilot and the navigator were both pressured into resigning—threatened with many years at hard labor at Fort Leavenworth—their departures were counted as resignations and not as discharges due to homosexuality. Nor did these costs include the other $125,000 or so it took to train the five enlisted men who were also discharged during the investigation.

And the Wurtsmith purge was a rather modest witch-hunt by the standards of the day, certainly far smaller than many of the other investigations during the same period. Nor did it include the lost training dollars spent on those sailors and soldiers and airmen who decided that it was not worth the risk to stay in and who did not reenlist. Given all this, it is doubtful that the annual cost of the gay exclusion policy could be counted in the millions or tens of millions of dollars. The real cost probably exceeded hundreds of millions of dollars every year.

HTLV-III

WITH HIS THICK BROWN HAIR and chiseled features, Hospitalman Third Class Byron Kinney had been handsome once, but by that balmy morning in San Diego the purple lesions of Kaposi's sarcoma had stained his face and his Navy uniform hung loosely on his wasted body. Kinney was also terribly tired. He had been sick for fourteen months, always getting worse, never better. The doctors said perhaps he had four months to live—at most, ten months. But no matter how close to death he might be, the Navy appeared to have only one purpose: to punish Byron Kinney for being gay. That was why he was here that day, for the administrative board to separate him from the Navy.

This official posture came at a time when the armed forces could no longer procrastinate in deciding how they would cope with the growing numbers of AIDS sufferers. Three months earlier, the Food and Drug Administration had licensed the first blood tests for antibodies to the virus believed to cause AIDS. Scientists called it human T-cell lymphotropic virus—variant type III—or HTLV-III for short. Since the HTLV-III antibody test kits were only now coming off the production line, the test's use was largely restricted to blood banks, but, once it became more widely available in a few months, its presence could have staggering social implications, not the least of which was for the Department of Defense.

Already there were calls for screening all 2 million active-duty service members. This proposal led to the next question: What would the services do with soldiers who tested positive for HTLV-III? Military doctors had already pressed their case: If medical testing revealed a soldier was stricken with cancer or heart disease, that soldier was medically retired and allowed a pension and use of military medical facilities. This tradition dated back generations and reflected a covenant between the military and its members.

The military was a family, according to this covenant, and it took care of its own. It did not dump people when they needed help most.

But Acquired Immune Deficiency Syndrome would never be treated like just another disease in the United States, given the fact that its first cases were detected among gay men. Questions of how to handle AIDS would always merge with questions of how to handle homosexuals. Since this was not a nation that dealt with gay people kindly, it was not likely to deal with AIDS sufferers kindly, either. In the early years of the epidemic, this was certainly the case within the institution that had most formally codified society's attitudes against gays. Though the military's medical people called for compassion, some officers in the more conservative branches, especially in the personnel commands, would hear nothing of it. And as the civilian leadership of the Defense Department still floundered for official policies, individual commands began implementing their own. Which was why Byron Kinney stood, exhausted, before a separation hearing in San Diego that morning, and also why he was fighting his separation, so that other sick and tired people would not have to suffer as he was.

The crescendo had been building for the past year. Naturally, the service most dedicated to punishing homosexuals took the hardest line against service members with AIDS. In March, Hospitalman Second Class Bernard "Bud" Broyhill was diagnosed with Kaposi's sarcoma at his duty station in Puerto Rico. His Navy doctor insisted that it was essential for his diagnosis to know whether Broyhill had ever engaged in homosexual conduct. When the corpsman was reluctant to answer, the physician assured him that any answer would be held in the strictest confidence. Broyhill said he was gay. A few days later, the Naval Investigative Service informed Broyhill he was being charged with sodomy and homosexuality.

At about the same time, another San Diego–based sailor newly diagnosed with AIDS, Daniel Abeita, answered his doctors' inquiries about his sexuality by confiding that he, too, was gay. Rather than moving for a medical retirement, the Navy began processing Abeita for separation under the gay regulations. Without a medical retirement, Abeita's future would be seriously compromised. When Abeita said he would fight the discharge, the Navy put him on medical hold and refused even to give him leave to go home to Texas to see his parents. He would have to stay in San Diego until the Navy decided what to do with him, however long that took. Near death, Abeita gave in. "I have to go home to my family," he told military counselor Bridget Wilson, and she understood. He accepted his gay discharge and left.

The Navy had won, but one last affront remained. Navy regulations called for providing a separated sailor either a plane or bus ticket home. Though it was already mid-June and the weather was fiercely hot, the Navy would not buy Dan a seat on an airplane; he got a nonrefundable Greyhound ticket. In the end, Abeita's volunteer gay lawyer, Tom Homann, took money out of his own pocket to buy a plane ticket for the dying man.

For Byron Gary Kinney, his final skirmish with the Navy proved to be the last act of his short life. He had joined the Navy in 1977 at the age of twenty-one and trained as a medical corpsman. Not long after that, he came to grips with the fact that he was gay and made his first sorties to the gay scene of Washington, D.C., not far from his duty at the Bethesda Naval Hospital. After his first enlistment ended in April 1981, he worked a few laboratory jobs around Bethesda, but the economy was weak and he was soon unemployed. In December 1981, Kinney joined the Navy again. Question 35f on his enlistment form asked: "Have you ever engaged in homosexual activity?" Byron did what everyone else he knew did and responded no.

He was assigned to the Oakland Naval Hospital, across the bay from San Francisco. It was a very bad time to be a gay sailor on leave in San Francisco. Since neither the government nor the media talked much about "gay cancer," there was little warning of the deadly new disease. Byron took the virus with him to Okinawa in February 1984 when he was assigned as a senior corpsman with the First Marine Division. About two months later, he began having diarrhea.

By the time he reported to the base hospital in October, he had lost 10 percent of his weight, his mouth was spotted with lesions of oral candidiasis, and all his lymph nodes were swollen. His diarrhea was bloody now, and when doctors did a CT scan of his intestinal track they saw that his lower intestines and rectum were covered with lesions of Kaposi's sarcoma.

The first references to Kinney's sexuality were scrawled on his chart on October 23, 1984. "The patient became sexually active with men at age 21," the doctor wrote. Two weeks later when the AIDS diagnosis was made, another doctor noted, "The patient has a history of homosexuality and has had several partners." These notes did not prejudice the Navy captain and lieutenant commander who comprised the medical board that in December ruled Kinney qualified for medical retirement. They also deemed that Kinney was entitled to his base pay and continued medical treatment from the Navy. The entire matter might have ended there but for Rear Admiral David L. Harlow at the Naval Personnel Command. He insisted that Kinney not be medically retired but separated for homosexuality instead. Kinney's offense was not only that he was gay, but also that he had perpetrated an act of fraud against the Navy with his answer to question 35f. Because of the fraudulent enlistment charge, Harlow wanted Kinney to receive a general discharge rather than an honorable one.

By now, Kinney had been evacuated to San Diego. Though military personnel are not guaranteed confidentiality in their relationships with service physicians, the Navy doctors whose notes indicated that Kinney was gay were appalled at the Navy's moves against the dying man. Lieutenant Commander Fred Millard furnished a blistering memo for Byron's lawyers. "The information . . . was obtained from Byron with the understanding that it would be used purely for purposes of medical diagnosis and treatment," Millard wrote. "Any attempt to use this information for other purposes without Byron's permission represents an unconscionable breach of the principle of confidentiality between patient and caregiver."

Navy spokesman Lieutenant Stephen Pietropaoli countered: "Homosexuality is incompatible with military life. It is the Navy policy that all homosexuals be separated from the Navy. No punitive action is taken when someone has AIDS, that is a medical diagnosis. . . . There is only punitive action when a person is homosexual." For all their denials, admirals in the Pentagon were not reviewing the records of medical retirement boards for sailors with heart conditions or diabetes for evidence of homosexuality or fraudulent enlistment. They were doing so only for sailors with AIDS.

The Navy was signaling how it would treat sailors with HTLV-III by its treatment of sailors with AIDS, Bridget Wilson and other military counselors believed, which was what made Byron Kinney's case so crucial. Bridget and two key allies from the Military Law Task Force of the National Lawyers Guild, attorney Ted Bumer and counselor Kathy Gilberd, went to work on Kinney's case with every intention of pushing the matter into federal court if they lost the separation board hearing. It was not just Kinney's career but thousands of careers that were at stake that morning.

The Navy was aware of the stakes, as well. Lieutenant Nels Kelstrom was brought aboard to serve as the recorder, or prosecutor, for the hearing. A full commander, Joseph Vrbancic, served as legal adviser; they were not taking any chances.

At 9:12 A.M., with reporters and television cameras clustered outside, the hearing was called into session.

THE CONFLICT BETWEEN Navy doctors and the admirals in the Navy personnel command reflected a larger dispute being argued throughout the military. A principal battle zone in this confrontation lay behind the solemn redbrick walls of Walter Reed Army Medical Center in Washington. Within the military, medical chores are divided among the services. The Navy specialized in tropical medicine; the Air Force handled aerospace medicine. The Army was responsible for infectious diseases, which now included AIDS.

The Army's emphasis dated back to the days when Dr. Walter Reed performed the crucial epidemiological work that determined that mosquitoes spread yellow fever. The discovery had led to measures to prevent the deadly disease, an accomplishment of military significance given the new U.S. colonies in Cuba and the Philippines. In the years since, the

United States Army had accumulated one of the world's most impressive but underappreciated rosters of medical achievements. The Army had developed more vaccines than any other institution, so it was only natural that the primary responsibility for dealing with AIDS fell to the Army and to its leading medical research facility, Walter Reed; and so it happened that the doctors in charge of AIDS would be men uncommonly dedicated to the welfare of their patients.

Principal among them was Colonel Ed Tramont, chief of microbiology at the Walter Reed Army Institute for Research and the official adviser to the Army's Surgeon General about infectious diseases. The forty-six-year-old physician had signed up to work at Walter Reed in 1968, shortly after he finished medical school at Boston University and just as he was about to be drafted. He set up an infectious disease training program at Walter Reed and launched a research program to develop a gonorrhea vaccine. By 1980, he was a colonel. If he had been willing to punch his ticket at other appropriate commands, he certainly would have been on his way to the rank of general, but he knew the Army was better served by his work in the laboratory. He knew that he could have pulled a much heftier income in the private sector, but the Army provided a "rich uncle" to finance his research into sexually transmitted diseases and he could operate without the distractions of academic politics and corporate profits.

Tramont proved a particularly important ally of Major Robert Redfield, who had been studying AIDS since 1983. Both Tramont and Dr. Redfield aggressively counseled Army generals who attempted to do to its soldiers what the Navy was doing to Byron Kinney. Though their work between 1983 and 1985 gained little public notice, both men found themselves on military transports to various bases in Europe to reassure jittery generals that the newly diagnosed AIDS patient among their troops represented no threat to the health of his colleagues and that he should be treated the same as any other sick soldier. And usually the generals heeded that advice once the scientific facts about AIDS were laid out.

As he began to observe more patients, Redfield had begun developing a staging system for the disease. Until then, AIDS had been defined solely by the criteria employed by the U.S. Centers for Disease Control, which identified AIDS sufferers solely as those who had contracted one of the dozen fatal diseases associated with the most severe forms of immune suppression. At Walter Reed, however, Redfield could see that AIDS was not a dramatic terminal event but, rather, a long, gradual process of immunological deterioration. It was a realization that provided Redfield with one of the darkest moments he had experienced in his scientific career. Though some researchers optimistically predicted that perhaps only 5 or 10 percent of the HTLV-III infected would get AIDS, Redfield's studies indicated that all would eventually become ill and die, given enough time.

Much of AIDS research was based on a fallacy, in Redfield's opinion. By focusing only on those end-stage patients with deadly diseases, the

CDC definition—accepted nationally as the gold standard of AIDS no-menclature—missed the great bulk of the AIDS cases. Every other chronic disease had been staged, or defined, in terms of levels of illness, beginning with infection and ending with death, except AIDS, until Redfield came along. Eventually, he separated the continuum of AIDS infection into six distinct stages, all measurable through blood assays and specific symptoms, thus defining AIDS as a continuum of immune dysfunction rather than as a single end-stage diagnosis.

The staging system aided researchers internationally on a number of fronts. For the first time, AIDS doctors could speak a common language in describing precisely the physical condition of a patient. Redfield was also concerned with finding new markers to determine the effectiveness of treatments for AIDS. At that time, a drug's success was measured by how long it delayed the "end point" of the disease—meaning death. Redfield wanted to be able to assess a treatment's effectiveness without having to wait for the patient to die. A medication that delayed patients' going from Walter Reed Stage Three to Four, for example, would give researchers information much more quickly.

At first, the AIDS research establishment rejected Redfield's radical new staging system. When he submitted his proposal for publication in the prestigious *New England Journal of Medicine*, for example, his paper was turned down as offering far too grim an assessment of the ultimate prognosis of the HTLV-III infected. Within two years, however, the Walter Reed Staging System had become the new gold standard by which all other definitions were judged. The staging system also offered the criteria for aiding the military to decide what to do with AIDS-infected soldiers. His staging system clearly delineated that HTLV-III infected troops could be useful to the military until they reached serious immune suppression in stages five or six. Before then, their service presented no risk either to the Army or themselves.

The announcement that American researchers had isolated HTLV-III in April 1984 made clear that mass screening of all Army recruits might be imminent, and an incident that occurred two weeks after the an-nouncement showed why such screening might be necessary. In basic training, an otherwise-healthy nineteen-year-old recruit was inoculated for smallpox, using a vaccine that included live vaccinia virus. (The erad-ication of smallpox in the 1970s had ended large-scale smallpox vaccination of the general public. Since the affliction was considered a likely armament in germ warfare, however, the Army continued to protect its soldiers from the disease.) About three weeks later, the recruit developed a severe fever and night sweats. By the time he was transferred to Walter Reed, he had developed a constellation of AIDS symptoms and a potentially deadly case of cryptococcal meningitis. While he was being treated for meningitis, vaccinia sores began to break out all over his body. His doctors had never seen anything like it. Ultimately, the nation's entire supply of vaccinia-immune globulin was pumped into the patient before the disease began to recede.

The case led Army doctors to support massive screening of new Army recruits for HTLV-III. Civil libertarians had the luxury of debating whether it was ethical to force AIDS testing on recruits as a condition of employment, but, as physicians, Redfield and Tramont saw no choice. Military recruits received vaccinations against as many as fourteen diseases. With so little known about AIDS, doctors could not predict what it would mean to inoculate an immune-compromised patient against so many ailments. Surely it was unethical to do nothing and hope that everything worked out in the end.

These debates did not become urgent until the HTLV-III antibody test was licensed in March 1985. Meanwhile, other events conspired to force the Army to come to grips with the problem. An early case of transfusion-related AIDS, for example, was diagnosed in the wife of an officer who was a favorite of the Army Chief of Staff. That brought the disease home. And the number of cases was mounting. By 1985, the military was treating 195 patients officially diagnosed with AIDS or its less severe manifestation of AIDS-related complex, ARC.

The FDA approval of the blood test demanded the first hard decisions in early spring. Military hospitals would now be vulnerable to huge liability lawsuits if they did not begin to screen all blood donations for HTLV-III. Since the largest proportion of the military's blood supply was donated by active-duty personnel, this raised the question of what the Defense Department would do with donors of infected blood. On March 13, 1985, the Pentagon's Military Blood Program Office, run out of the Army Surgeon General's office, ordered all military blood programs to test for HTLV-III. As part of the program, the Army also ordered: "Military and civilian blood agencies collecting blood on military installations will provide positive test results for antibody to HTLV-III to the respective service military health agency. . . ."

Military blood was also collected by private agencies such as the Red Cross, which put civilian agencies in the uncomfortable position of turning over names of HTLV-III positive donors to the services. This undermined the blood banks' tradition of protecting donor confidentiality at all costs. Blood banks also came under pressure from groups such as the National Gay Task Force, which noted that the results of blood tests could be used to harass suspected gay soldiers.

The executive director of San Francisco's largest blood bank, the Irwin Memorial Blood Bank, was the first to announce that his facility would not comply with the Pentagon order. Blood bankers collecting donations in Maine and Massachusetts also said they would not turn names in to the military, and the two national blood banking associations announced they would launch negotiations to get the Pentagon to withdraw the order. Congresswoman Barbara Boxer and Senator Alan Cranston, both Californians with heavy gay constituencies, fired off a letter to Defense Secretary Caspar Weinberger asking him to rescind the order, noting that the release of test results "poses a risk of abuse of the information," given the military's policies on gays.

For its part, the Defense Department was indignant at the accusation that they would use the results of blood tests improperly. The Air Force announced it was seeking "mature, sensitive and assuring" doctors to counsel service members who tested positive. Pentagon spokesman Major Pete Wyro said no blood-test result would be used "for pointing a finger or initiating a disciplinary action. None of that information would go to a [service member's] commanding officer." Privately, Secretary Weinberger was said to be furious that blood banks would interfere with Pentagon policy.

Even as blood bankers balked at cooperating with the Defense Department, researchers such as Tramont and Redfield provided a powerful new argument against the summary dismissal of all HTLV-III positive soldiers: research. Because AIDS had been detected less than four years earlier, many of the most important facts about it remained unknown. What was its natural history? With a disease like diabetes or liver cancer, a doctor could explain every phase of the disease and express with some certainty what the patient's prognosis would be. Even with the preliminary description of Redfield's staging system, no such time line had been ascertained for AIDS. With the HTLV-III antibody test only weeks old, researchers were just about to get their first glimpse at the true extent of AIDS infection. Such a moment presented an ideal opportunity for study. It was not at all understood, for example, why some HTLV-III infected patients became sick very quickly while others appeared to live for years with no ill effects from the virus. Understanding what protected these patients could lead to medicines that might help all HTLV-III patients.

There were other unanswered questions. New evidence suggested that HTLV-III somehow affected the central nervous system, perhaps leading to brain damage. At what stage during the disease did this happen? This was no small issue for the Navy or Air Force, which had to decide how to handle HTLV-III positive pilots. The HTLV-III positive personnel presented unparalleled opportunities for research precisely because they were military. Once they had volunteered for studies, subjects would not disappear, as they so often did in civilian research. The Army knew exactly where their soldiers were every minute of every day. The Army also knew every intimate detail of their medical treatment, since soldiers went to Army hospitals. There would never be problems about getting time off from work to take a blood test or answer a questionnaire. Moreover, it was likely that many HTLV-III positive men would be detected early in the course of infection, certainly much earlier than in the civilian sector. No other population offered the chance to view the full course of HTLV-III infection, from start to end, than the military.

The argument that HTLV-III positive patients represented a chance for groundbreaking medical research aroused the vanity of the military's medical officials and ultimately helped enlist a powerful ally in the Pentagon, Dr. William "Bud" Mayer, the Assistant Secretary of Defense for Health Affairs. As the top civilian Pentagon official for health matters, Mayer soon became a spokesman both for military AIDS research and for a humane approach to dealing with HTLV-III infected soldiers. By May 1985, he was waxing eloquently to congressional committees about the research opportunities.

In his briefings with the Army Surgeon General, and ultimately the Army Chief of Staff and the Secretary of the Army, Dr. Tramont made the same case. There was a great potential for research—but, he stressed, it was also crucial that the information doctors collected be used for medical purposes only. If the military used a soldier's data collected for "inappropriate reasons," it would detract from the doctors' ability to do their job. Moreover, it would scare potentially sick and at-risk soldiers away from the medical system when they needed it most. Tramont found support among his medical colleagues and opposition from the line officers in the Pentagon. The matter was far from resolved on the morning of Byron Kinney's hearing in San Diego.

KINNEY COULD SIT UP for only some of his separation hearing. For much of the procedure, he lay on a bench in the rear of the courtroom while the lawyers argued among themselves. In his opening argument, Lieutenant Nels Kelstrom, acting on behalf of the Navy, announced that he would present no witnesses, because he did not have to. Kinney's records spoke for themselves, he said. "I believe that the evidence presented today will firmly establish that Petty Officer Kinney absolutely has no place in the Navy and should be discharged and that should be the vote of this Board," Kelstrom said.

Kinney's attorney, Ted Bumer, attempted to present the objections of the physicians to the use of their records in the hearing. Kelstrom argued against it, saying, "In the military, the patient-physician privilege [of confidentiality] does not exist." When Bumer pressed further, the matter was taken out of earshot of the board to the legal adviser. "They obviously want members [of the board] to hear that their doctor is outraged by the fact of the use of those statements," Kelstrom complained. Such statements are "irrelevant and inflammatory," he argued. Commander Vrbancic, the Navy legal adviser, ruled against Bumer and for the Navy.

Bumer brought in AIDS experts from the University of California at San Diego to testify how long they thought Kinney could be expected to live. Bumer's intent was to show that the Navy had little to lose in the way of good order, discipline and morale by allowing Kinney to have a medical retirement. Kelstrom was angered by the line of questioning and asked it be halted. "That is irrelevant; it is nothing but a confusion tactic," he said. "We're here to decide whether or not he engaged in homosexual acts and a fraudulent enlistment, and that's all we're here to decide at this juncture." Again, the Navy legal adviser ruled for the Navy.

Back in the courtroom, Lieutenant Kelstrom delivered his final summation. The errant behavior, he argued, might continue if the board did not move immediately to kick Kinney out of the Navy. "I don't know; I can't tell you whether the likelihood of continued homosexual practices exists, but I know that it continued for a five- or six-year period," Kelstrom said. "It continued even after he had denied previous homosexual practices when he joined the Navy, and he knew good and well what the Navy's policy was regarding homosexuals or he wouldn't have lied when he signed the enlistment application and contract. So what is the likelihood for continuation? Well, I submit that under the circumstances of this case it is probably unlikely, but should we take a chance? . . . I think that we cannot speculate that it won't happen; if anything, I think we should speculate that it would perhaps continue. Will he be a disruptive or undesirable influence in present or future duty assignments? I submit he will be."

Though Navy regulations called for an honorable discharge for gay sailors, Kelstrom argued against mercy for Kinney, saying the "fraudulent enlistment" charge outweighed "the positive aspects of his performance" while a Navy corpsman.

In his closing argument, Bumer begged the board to consider the impact a separation would have on the military's ability to deal with AIDS. Sailors would be afraid to talk to their doctors; doctors would be afraid to talk to their patients. Before Bumer could get far into his closing argument, however, Kelstrom objected. AIDS was not the issue, he said, only homosexuality and fraudulent enlistment. None of this was relevant, he stated. And the Navy legal adviser ruled against Kinney and for the Navy.

Byron Kinney was allowed to make an unsworn statement before the board. "I feel I've given seven years of service," he barely whispered, "and this wouldn't be happening if I wasn't sick." And then he was too exhausted to speak any longer.

The board recessed to consider its decision at 4:45 P.M. Kinney shuffled down the hall and found an empty room where he shoved several chairs together and put his head on his backpack. It was not sleep he wanted so much as an escape from the voices, the noise.

At 5:14 P.M., the board's senior member, Lieutenant Commander Nancy Price, read the panel's unanimous decision: "By a vote of three to zero, the Board recommends that the Respondent be discharged from the naval service due to procurement of a fraudulent enlistment by knowing false representations and deliberate concealment of pre-service homosexual activity and homosexuality . . . and that the discharge be a general discharge.

"The Board will be adjourned," she said.

Byron's lawyers shielded him from reporters, but when one journalist shouted, "What's he going to do now?" Kinney turned and said simply, "I'll continue to fight."

THE KINNEY CASE did not generate much publicity outside the gay press and the immediate San Diego area, but the bad publicity made the Pentagon cringe, as did the mounting protests over the Defense Department plan to force blood banks to provide names of HTLV-III positive military donors. Inside the Pentagon, the conflict between line officers and military doctors continued.

A week after the Kinney hearing, Assistant Defense Secretary Mayer announced that the Defense Department would delay implementation of its order to civilian blood banks. Mayer wanted to "review concerns expressed by civilian blood collection agencies" centering on privacy issues, a spokesman said. After the Kinney hearing, it was no longer meaningful for the Pentagon to argue that it would never use medical tests to punish service personnel.

Before Kinney's separation became final—and before it could be legally challenged—the board's conclusion had to be accepted by the Naval Personnel Command. Bridget Wilson, who had been advising Kinney, hoped that Byron might win at that level, forgoing the need to drag him through a long court fight. Just how much longer Byron might live was a major concern for Wilson, Bumer, and Kathy Gilberd. When Wilson talked to Byron and heard the betrayal he felt, and his worry as well as his fear that the Navy would betray thousands more if he did not win, she realized that Byron was not about to expire. He was angry and he was determined, and he was not going to die until this thing was won.

JULY 1985
THE PENTAGON
ARLINGTON, VIRGINIA

PETE RANDELL'S LAST DAY at the Air Force Board for the Correction of Military Records came in July 1985, after more than twenty years of continuous service to the United States government in the Army, at the White House, and in the Air Force. By now, the gossip had reached his office.

And then two agents of the Office of Special Investigations appeared in his office, flashing their badges and announcing they were following up on reports that he was homosexual. Who else in the Air Force was gay? they asked. What other homosexuals held government jobs? They had been following him for weeks, they added, and began listing some of the gay bars he had been to. One had go-go boys that danced on the bar. Did Randell want his parents to know that he went to such bars? What would his children think?

Pete did not tell the investigators anything, but now he knew he could not fight them. He did not want his children involved; he did not want his name in the newspaper. He understood now what gay-rights activists had been fighting for all those years. Suddenly, the United States did not seem to be the free country he had always believed it to be. The prospect of serving as a clerk/typist in an agency he had once run was too humiliating to contemplate, so Pete resigned, officially citing other career opportunities.

Along with losing his job, Pete had lost his home and virtually all his possessions in a bitter divorce with his wife. Soon he declared bankruptcy. His two children no longer spoke to him.

The only solace he had came from an affair he had begun with a young Chicano man he had met on one of his last official Air Force trips to San Antonio. He moved the young man to the Washington area, much to the chagrin of Pete's handful of gay friends, who warned him the youth was a hustler. Pete thought that a hustler was someone who played pool. Besides, he was in love for the first time and would hear nothing of it. Being new to gay life, Pete also did not hear the talk about safe sex that was spreading through the gay community. Ultimately, he found out that his friends were right and that his lover was a male prostitute. The youth pleaded he would change, and Pete believed him for a while. But ultimately, he ordered the young man out of his house. By then, it was too late.

— 52 —

Dykebusters

NOBODY AT ANNAPOLIS understood Karen Colton's decision to drop out of the Naval Academy at the end of her sophomore year. With Karen's 3.7 grade point average out of a possible 4.0, she excelled academically, and she was popular among classmates. Two years of daily harassment from male midshipmen, however, had taken its toll. The limitations to women's advancement meant there was no real purpose to their education. The hassle simply was not worth it to her.

A week before Karen left, a group of women officers from Washington came to Annapolis to talk about opportunities for women in the Navy. That might be the case in Washington, but not at Annapolis, where opportunities for women seemed remote. "Why aren't you *here*?" Karen asked angrily. In the past two years, she had never seen a female naval officer performing any real task in the Navy. These field trips by equal-opportunity types utterly detached from the daily harassment women midshipmen endured were galling.

Karen's close friends believed that she dropped out to live with Ruth Voor. Karen was stubborn enough to want to prove them wrong, so after leaving Annapolis she went to school for a year at the Florida Institute of Technology. After that, she realized what Ruth had known when they first met—that the two of them were meant to be together. In May 1985, she moved to San Diego, where Ruth was stationed, and began final work on a mathematics degree at the University of San Diego.

Lieutenant (junior grade) Ruth Voor had stuck with her plan to do sea duty. The combat exclusion policy that prevented her from serving aboard a ship that might see hostilities rankled Ruth to no end. Male classmates with far lower grades could have any assignment they wanted, while she struggled to find a ship assignment. After completing supply school, she finally did find a submarine tender, the USS *McKee,* and took over the food-service division.

Although Karen and Ruth led a settled lifestyle, the fear of exposure always hovered nearby. When Karen's mother learned that her daughter was moving in with Ruth, for example, she became convinced that Ruth had corrupted Karen. She threatened to write to Ruth's commander if Karen proceeded with her plan to move to San Diego. Karen was pretty sure her mother would not follow through on the threat, and she did not.

Another danger hung in the air in the autumn of 1985 when the *McKee*'s legal officer urged the captain to launch an investigation of homosexuals on the ship. Gays were a time bomb that could go off at any moment, he warned. The ship's chaplain later confided to Ruth that he had also visited the captain and advised him, "Captain, if you have a witch-hunt, you're going to lose some of your best people." The captain was looking to earn an admiral's star and was not interested in damaging his career, so he heeded the chaplain's advice.

It was a close call. From her days at Annapolis, Ruth knew that these investigations could take on a life of their own, especially when women were involved.

THE FIRST FOUR YEARS of the Reagan administration marked more difficult times for women in the military. Though female recruits had saved the all-volunteer military in the early 1970s, the uniformed services seemed intent on taking advantage of the conservative administration's antifeminist posture to roll back both the numbers of women recruited for the armed forces and to restrict the roles they could assume to a greater extent.

Even before Reagan's hand hit the Bible at his inauguration in 1981, the Army and Air Force had privately proposed to his transition team that the Carter administration's recruitment goals for women for the next several years be reduced. Two months later, Army deputy chief of staff Lt. General Robert G. Yerks suggested it was time to "idle our motors" and not enlist higher numbers of women until there were further studies on their usefulness. Though Congress balked, advocates for women in the military believed that the services were advancing a "hidden agenda" to turn the clock back on the gains women had made.

Though women by now represented 8.5 percent of the active-duty military, new recruitment dropped off. The Defense Department reduced by sixty thousand the number of women it intended to enlist by 1986. The Air Force reduced its female recruitment goal from 90,000 to 61,000; the Army from 87,500 to 65,000. The cutbacks came at a time when the Reagan administration had announced its intention to increase the standing military by 200,000 troops, or about 10 percent. Since this goal would be difficult to achieve without women, the Army General Staff submitted a proposal suggesting that the draft be reinstated so the services could meet their manpower needs—with men. Though Defense Secretary Caspar Weinberger rejected the proposal and Congress generally objected to the armed forces reducing their female recruiting goals, the suggestion alone reflected the deep antipathy that military brass still felt regarding the increased presence of women in their ranks. The period that women's rights advocates call "womanpause" had begun.

By the mid-1980s, the effects were evident in the numbers of women entering the armed forces. In 1979, during the Carter administration's buildup, for example, the number of women in the military increased by 13,300. In 1984, the number increased by 5,200. Total projections for the numbers of women the military planned to enlist by 1986 were decreased in early 1985 from the Carter administration's projected 265,500 to 215,000. Still, women made up 9.5 percent of the armed forces by 1985. In 1983 and 1984, they comprised 12 percent of recruits. The feminization of the armed forces was a trend that could not be halted; Congress would not permit it, and the Pentagon could not dramatically decrease the numbers of women without reinstating conscription, a politically unacceptable alternative.

What could be manipulated, however, were the jobs women would be allowed to have in the armed forces. Combat assignments would not be among them. That policy was rooted in a 1948 law specifically prohibiting women from flying combat planes in the Air Force and from serving as combat aviators or in any other position on warships in the Navy. The Army's exclusion was not based on any statute but on regulations the Army itself had authored to ban women from combat jobs. The trend during the Nixon, Ford, and Carter administrations had been to open up the maximum number of jobs to women and to whittle down the numbers of jobs that fell into the combat exclusion category.

During "womanpause" in the early 1980s, the armed forces began to reverse that trend and began adding new military occupation specialties to those from which women would be excluded. Under the Reagan administration, the various branches of the military announced studies to determine whether this or that MOS should be reclassified as a combat job. Not surprisingly, many of the studies concluded that women's roles should be further restricted. In 1982, for example, the Army added twenty-three MOS's to the list of jobs that would be defined as combat slots. By early 1985, after extensive "research," the Marine Corps announced that it was closing forty-one MOS's to women. These included such positions as handlers for marijuana-sniffing dogs used in barracks drug searches.

It was no longer clear by the mid-1980s whether the combat exclusion policy could be justified in military terms. Other nations grappling with the same issue began to reconsider their combat exclusion policies. By 1984, for example, Norway, Greece, and the Netherlands had announced they would allow women in combat positions. When similar debates erupted in the United States, however, the discussion among the nation's top military men revolved less around questions of military effectiveness than around a defense of manhood.

General Robert Barrow, a former Marine Corps commandant, explained in a congressional hearing, "War is man's work. Biological convergence on the battlefield would not only be dissatisfying in terms of what women could do, but it would be an enormous psychological distraction for the male, who wants to think that he's fighting for that woman somewhere behind, not up there in the same foxhole with him. It tramples the male ego. When you get right down to it, you have to protect the manliness of war." General William Westmoreland put it more bluntly when he said, "No man with gumption wants a woman to fight his battles."

The comments were intriguing not so much for what they said about the combat exclusion policy, which was never in serious jeopardy during the conservative 1980s, but for what they revealed about the military's general attitude toward women in its ranks. The issue of women in the military was never about women; it was about men and their need to define their masculinity. That, more than the fighting and winning of wars, appeared to be the central mission of the armed forces, at least for many men. That was why they sought to limit the role not only of women in the military but of gays, as well. These exclusions were, in this sense, all part of the same package, a defense of traditional masculinity in a changing world. The fact that the world was shifting made the defense all the more impassioned. In the difficult years ahead, as the changes became more pronounced, it would also make the defense more ferocious.

AGAINST THE MORE pronounced resistance of the military hierarchy, it is striking that women continued to make impressive inroads in the armed forces. *Minerva*, the authoritative magazine on women in the military, kept track of women's achievements in every branch of the service. Every MOS, it seemed, had its first female: the first security police chief master sergeant, the first female officer in the Army's Golden Knights parachute team, the first colonel in military intelligence, and the first Air Force tactical fighter wing for which all maintenance squadrons were supervised by female officers. A female Naval Academy graduate became the first woman ship's executive officer in 1984, though the ship was a tug and not in the active Navy but in the Naval Reserve Force's fleet.

A decade of increased recruitment had at last allowed growing numbers of women to join the ranks of the senior enlisted. Though the dissolution of the all-women's services had destroyed the old support networks, new networks were building. In July 1985, the Army appointed its first female Army general who came neither from the fields of nursing nor administration. At the same time, a female colonel was put on the list of promotable colonels to be the second female general in a combat support job.

The advancements came less from the deference of an obliging command as from the fact that so many of the military's women were so well qualified. This fact was in no place more obvious than at the service

academies, where, despite constant harassment, women increasingly graduated at the top of their classes. The Naval Academy class of 1984, for
example, was the first in which a woman ranked as its number-one graduate. In 1985, a female earned that distinction for the first time at the
Coast Guard Academy. In 1986, a female cadet was the top-ranked graduate of the United States Air Force Academy.

Even as women succeeded against incredible odds, females in the
military were learning a lesson that many women in the civilian sector
were learning, as well. Accomplishment did not always spell success, and
sometimes it bred suspicion. Former Air Force Chief of Staff Curtis
LeMay enunciated this fact when he told an interviewer in 1986 that
women did not make ideal Air Force personnel because in the end they
would want to get married and have children. He added, "If we have
women who don't want to do that, I don't know if we'd want them in
the Air Force or not. They're probably kind of queer or something and
psychologically not very suitable to carry on some of this important work.
I think we're running too many [women] through the Academy."

The military world only mirrored the civilian world. But in the military, the penalties for violating gender roles were more severe, especially
for those women who were nontraditional in both their occupations and
sexual orientation. In this way, military lesbians found themselves on a
dangerous front line of the gender wars in the 1980s.

MARINE CORPS RECRUIT TRAINING DEPOT
PARRIS ISLAND, SOUTH CAROLINA

"WE HAVE TO GET our drill instructor quota for the year," said an agent
from the Marine Corps Criminal Investigation Division in warning Renee
Mueller to lay low. Mueller was a military policeman in the provost
marshal's office at Parris Island, the only Marine Corps boot camp where
women were trained. Though homosexual investigations were handled by
the Naval Investigative Service, the Marine Corps CID, which handled
less serious criminal matters, had gotten wind of an investigation of suspected lesbian drill instructors.

These had become fairly routine affairs at Parris Island. No branch
of the service was as hostile to the growing presence of women as the
Marine Corps. And while the leathernecks could not legally move against
them for being women, they could move against them for being lesbians.
Suspicion fell most heavily on women in nontraditional jobs, which in
the Marine Corps meant those in the most macho job of all, that of drill
instructor, or DI. This MOS proved a fertile ground for investigations
because there were, in fact, so many lesbian DIs.

Just why so many homosexual women gravitated to DI positions
remained a matter of speculation. It is indelicate work, and some lesbians
argue that homosexual women are less concerned with maintaining fem-

inine affectations than are heterosexual females and are therefore better suited for the *Sturm und Drang* of the drill field. The work is also better suited to women without husbands or families: DIs routinely work their recruits through eighty-hour weeks. The field also attracts Marines with something to prove. The position is highly competitive; only the top 10 percent are even considered for the work. For whatever reason, the records of lesbian drill instructors purged from the Marine Corps during the numerous witch-hunts of the 1980s offer ample proof that lesbians have been among the most accomplished DIs. Their excellence and their high visibility, however, made them vulnerable to investigations.

Some of the younger Marines, such as Renee's friend in the CID, understood that the investigations were mainly for show, to demonstrate to the brass at Marine headquarters in Quantico that nobody at Parris Island was going soft on queers. Mueller understood that, too, and she appreciated the warning.

A particularly nasty purge of lesbians, begun in 1984, was just ending. Although the NIS was happy to collar any lesbian it could identify, there was much more status to be gained by going after officers—the higher-ranking, the better. These were "the big fish." The NIS had its sights set on a female lieutenant colonel who lived in a comfortable two-story home in a residential neighborhood off the Parris Island Marine base. The lieutenant colonel was believed to be having an affair with another captain, whom the NIS was also eager to nail.

To gather evidence, the NIS planted two women among the drill instructors at the headquarters company to gather information on the two officers, according to several women stationed at Parris Island then. Their break came when rumors spread that two enlisted female DIs had gotten "married." An NIS search of their home turned up a certificate from a local gay church attesting to their union and receipts for two wedding bands purchased at a Navy exchange. At first, the two women denied the charges, but under NIS pressure they agreed to turn in all the lesbians they knew in exchange for honorable discharges.

The two NIS informers performed all sorts of unpleasant tasks for the NIS. One invited a gunnery sergeant to her home and seduced her. Once the couple was in flagrante delicto, an NIS agent leaped out of the closet and arrested the sergeant. Altogether, at least a dozen women drill instructors were rounded up in this purge.

The machinations typical of military justice in such cases were soon a problem. One staff sergeant was appointed a lawyer only one hour before her hearing; when the attorney requested an extension so they could discuss her case, they received only one day to devise a defense. When boards ruled contrary to the brass, they changed the boards: A female lieutenant colonel chaired one board that found an accused lesbian innocent. The lieutenant colonel was promptly removed from the panel for future hearings and replaced by a full colonel who worked directly for the base's commanding general. No other women were acquitted.

The purge cost the Marine Corps some of its most outstanding female drill instructors. One ten-year veteran had the longest experience of any female drill instructor in the Marine Corps, and she had been the first woman from the Marine Corps to attend jump school, the first woman on the drill field for more than three years, and the first woman drum major of a Marine band. She had trained over one thousand recruits and received outstanding performance ratings. But at her hearing, she had a hard time finding character witnesses. The Marine Corps was the only service that segregated its training companies by sex, so only women could testify on her behalf; and few women would testify because if they spoke up for a suspected lesbian, they might be investigated, too. In the end, the staff sergeant was told she would receive an honorable discharge only if she named other lesbians. She refused and received a discharge under other than honorable conditions.

There were other discharges of sergeants and staff sergeants, and yet these hardly reduced the visibility of lesbians on the drill field. Most of the newly vacated positions were filled with new lesbian drill instructors, since they were the top performers and next in line for the promotion.

THAT LESBIAN INVESTIGATIONS were aimed more at getting women out of the services than merely eliminating gays is clear in stories such as that of the USS *Land,* a Norfolk-based submarine tender. When Bob Ledet was assigned to the ship in 1983, he was struck by the fact that the crew was very gay. Of a ship population between twelve and thirteen hundred, Ledet estimated that between two and three hundred were gay, and most of these were men. Among the ship's very highest officers was a patron of the gay after-hours clubs in Norfolk, whose boyfriend was an enlisted seaman on the USS *America.* When the *Land* was overseas, the officer rented hotel rooms and hosted huge parties for the ship's gay male crew members.

For all the conspicuous male homosexuality on board, when an investigation of the *Land* occurred in late 1984 it was only of the women. As Ledet heard it, the NIS put an undercover agent in the female berthing area to collect names of suspected lesbians. Almost immediately thereafter, the women disappeared. Altogether eight women lost their Navy careers in that investigation.

Most commonly, lesbian investigations began after some man's advances had been spurned. Lesbians were especially vulnerable to sexual harassment because commands rarely looked into females' complaints against men but would almost always investigate a male's accusation of lesbianism.

An officer assigned to a military police unit at Fort Polk, Louisiana, for example, came to the defense of some enlisted women who complained that a male supervisor was pressuring each of them to engage in a ménage à trois with him and his wife. The fact that the women refused inspired post authorities to investigate them for being homosexual, along with the officer who had spoken up for them.

Petty Officer Mary Beth Harrison faced a similar investigation at the Navy base in Keflavik, Iceland, when she rejected the sexual advances of a petty officer first class. The African American petty officer, a yeoman, had announced his intention to sleep with every white woman on the base, according to Harrison's recollection. "I'll get you for this, bitch," he had said when she refused him. The yeoman then convinced a woman who worked under him to accuse Harrison of being homosexual. The base's administrative officer felt the accusation was justified because Harrison could offer no evidence of dating Navy men while assigned to Iceland. This fact was considered enough to bring Harrison before an administrative separation hearing, which, citing the scant evidence against her, acquitted her.

The pressures on women were especially acute at overseas duty stations. In Germany, Army men often would not learn German and therefore were dependent on Army women for dates. Women who refused the advances of nineteen-year-old privates often became the subjects of lesbian rumors. At the Army post at Krabbenloch Kasern near Stuttgart, West Germany, frustrated young GIs fueled a frenzy of lesbian baiting in the mid-1980s.

Private First Class Jeanne Martin, who was assigned there then, believed that Krabbenloch had earned its reputation as a lesbian center because it was home to the Ninety-third Signal Brigade, which meant women filled such nontraditional jobs as cable installer and phone-line repairman. Although clerk/typists were as likely to be lesbian, they were rarely suspect; mechanics almost always were. Husky women were suspicious; petite women were not. Any woman who swore was also probably a dyke, since men did not like women who swore and any woman who did must not care what men thought of her.

The Family was well-established at Krabbenloch. With hostility mounting against lesbians, gays sat together in the mess hall and in the television lounges and took trips to town in groups. This caused the straight GIs to promote the notion that gays were a dangerous cabal, an Army within the Army that threatened them all; and the brunt of their hostility was aimed at women perceived to be lesbians.

Visual testimony to this occurred when a general visited the post in 1984 and the soldiers in A Company of the Thirty-fourth Signal Battalion strung a line of women's panties, out of which stuffed condoms protruded, across the sidewalk from the post's entrance. The message was presumably meant to indicate that the women there all acted like men.

In 1985, a number of the younger enlisted and noncommissioned officers organized a group they called Dykebusters. They wore T-shirts with two interlocking female symbols in a circle with a slash. At the enlisted club, they gathered around the jukebox, slugged back snorts of whiskey, and sang their own version of the theme song from the popular movie *Ghostbusters*. "There's something strange in the neighborhood. Who you gonna call? Dykebusters!" When the men got to the final re-frain—"I ain't afraid of no ghost!"—they belted out, "I ain't afraid of no dyke!"

Martin recalls that when she was assigned as a toolroom clerk, she was warned that she better give the men whatever tool they wanted, whenever they wanted. "If you get guys mad at you, they start rumors," a senior NCO told her. "You have to be a people pleaser here."

Women, both straight and lesbian, complained to one another about sexual harassment but were afraid to go to post authorities. If you com-plained, you might come under suspicion yourself and have to answer questions about whom you were dating and if you were not dating, why not. One woman who reported sexual harassment suddenly began failing inspections. Although all branches of the services had regulations that forbade sexual harassment, few commands enforced them with much vigor. For all the talk of women's combat exclusion in the 1980s, the more pressing issue of sexual harassment received little attention. And the re-lationship between sexual harassment and the antigay regulations was ignored altogether.

Female military personnel with children were the most vulnerable to investigatory pressures. By the mid-1980s, military investigators had adopted the tactic of harassing the children of suspected lesbians as a routine part of gathering evidence. In March 1985, when the Army's Criminal Investigation Division suspected a female enlisted woman of having an affair with a West Point cadet, they showed up at the sports field where the enlisted woman's children had soccer practice after school and asked the children about their mother's sex life. Mothers who had once warned children not to talk to strangers now warned their kids against talking to agents of the United States government.

SEPTEMBER 1985
WURTSMITH AIR FORCE BASE
OSCODA, MICHIGAN

CAPTAIN DAVID MARIER was ordered to peel the base stickers off his car, turn in his uniforms and flight suits, and prepare for his discharge from the Air Force in July 1985. His final papers announced an other than honorable discharge. For the next two months, he stayed in Michigan to follow up on the various airlines to which he had applied as a pilot. The character of the discharge had its intended punitive impact, however. When one major carrier asked Marier why he had not received an hon-orable discharge, he told them. Suddenly, Dave was no longer qualified to fly for them. Other airline job offers also dried up. Marier still hoped something would work out, but until it did he would return to his home in Minnesota. He could not afford to keep up the mortgage payments on the house he had bought, so he gave it up.

In the autumn, Dave granted a round of interviews to the gay press and newspapers around Oscoda. Eventually, his story even ran with the Associated Press, but it failed to ignite the indignation for which Marier had hoped. When he talked about the military's coercive tactics and threats of prison time and bad discharges, he could tell that many heterosexuals did not believe him. Not in this day and age, they were thinking; things like that don't happen in America.

Dave wrote to the "Phil Donahue Show" and 60 *Minutes,* but nobody wrote back. An organizer from the National Gay Task Force told him that all their energies had been diverted to AIDS. Gay groups had meager funding in the best of times, and these were not the best of times. Dave still hoped to pursue a legal challenge; but before he could do anything, he had to file his appeal with the Air Force Board for Correction of Military Records.

On his way back to St. Paul, Dave stopped in Lansing to meet another former Air Force pilot who might understand what he was going through. Dave and Jim Dressel, the Vietnam war hero and former state representative, engaged in usual shoptalk. In the Reserves, Jim had flown A-37s, as Dave had. Dave joked that he might have refueled Jim when he was flying with the Air National Guard. Jim seemed upbeat about his future, which encouraged Dave.

Back in St. Paul, Dave got a job as a waiter at a Red Lobster restaurant. He received the minimum wage, and he could eat there for half price. A year earlier, he had flown some of the most sophisticated aircraft in the history of aviation. Now he was twenty-nine years old; he had lost his job, his home, and his future; and the best he could do was to wait tables at a Red Lobster.

— 53 —

Friends of Helga

WHAT SAVED THEM—what helped prevent an astounding purge of gay men from the military—was the study being prepared for publication in those autumn days of 1985, when the AIDS epidemic had at last entered the public consciousness.

By scientific standards, the study, authored by Dr. Robert Redfield for the *Journal of the American Medical Association,* drew upon a small sample of subjects for its conclusions, just forty-one Army personnel and their dependents who were being treated for AIDS at Walter Reed Army Medical Center. The forty-one subjects included fifteen very special people: They said they were not gay men or intravenous drug users, the groups commonly afflicted with AIDS. Instead, they said they were heterosexual. Of these, five were women who had apparently contracted the disease from their HTLV-III infected spouses, a route of transmission already established. The other ten were the big news, because they were men whose only acknowledged risk behavior was sex with women, mainly prostitutes in Korea and Germany. The study seemed to show, for the first time, that men could contract the disease heterosexually.

The headlines trumpeted the news. That Major Redfield had discovered no fewer than 37 percent of the Army's AIDS cases were heterosexual (fifteen out of forty-one individuals) seemed to foreshadow a heterosexual explosion of the disease, along the lines of the exponential increase that had marked the spread of AIDS among gay men. Though cases of men who claimed to have contracted the disease from women accounted for only one-tenth of 1 percent of AIDS cases nationally, military doctors believed that their data were the truer presage of things to come. The heterosexual AIDS epidemic was beginning.

The study came at a decisive moment in the history of the epidemic and had profound repercussions not only for the development of HTLV-

III policies in the Defense Department but for the entire national debate over AIDS. For the first four years of the epidemic, few had paid much attention to the disease, even as thousands of gay men died and the government's own frantic researchers warned that death tolls would soon reach into the hundreds of thousands and health-care costs would mount into the billions. For America's celebrity-driven media, it took the announcement that actor Rock Hudson had AIDS to direct attention to the epidemic in a way that four years of death, suffering, and dire predictions had not been able to accomplish. Suddenly, every newspaper was running a five-part series on the epidemic and every local news affiliate had dispatched an Instant Eye or Eyewitness news team to the Centers for Disease Control.

Media attention mobilized the government, as well. Senators and congressmen who had ignored the disease now clamored for more government funding. Hopeful of a new source of research money and perhaps a Nobel Prize, scientists who had previously thought it beneath them to study a homosexual disease dashed off grant proposals. Even President Reagan spoke the word *AIDS* in public for the first time. (Not one to be overcome with zeal, it would be nearly another two years before he actually delivered a speech on the subject, by which time more than 25,000 Americans had died of the ailment.) For years, AIDS had been the disease that dared not speak its name. Abruptly, it had become the most discussed topic in the United States.

Just as civilian society finally focused attention on the disease, the military sprang to attention as well, making decisions that had been long delayed. The Defense Department tackled the easier issues first. On August 9, two weeks after Hudson's announcement, the Armed Forces Epidemiological Board met to consider whether new recruits should undergo HTLV-III testing before being allowed into the armed forces. The meeting brought new faces to the civilian advisory board that weighed military medical issues.

Jeff Levi of the National Gay Task Force was on hand to argue against the testing, maintaining that research was still inconclusive about what HTLV-III infection really meant. Would those who tested positive get sick for sure, and if so, when? No one knew. It would not be fair, he said, to exclude such a large number of people when so many factors were up in the air. AIDS researcher Dr. Mathilde Krim aired concerns over maintaining the confidentiality of HTLV-III test results.

The debate was resolved when Dr. Ed Tramont of Walter Reed asked Krim whether she would recommend inoculating an HTLV-III infected individual with live-virus vaccines. "No," Krim said, "I would not."

The board voted to recommend screening for all recruits, with the military rejecting anyone who tested positive. On August 28, Tramont briefed Deputy Defense Secretary William H. Taft IV on the recruit-testing proposal. Tramont explained that bleeding soldiers could infect their comrades on the battlefield. He cited direct soldier-to-soldier transfusions, though such transfusions were very rare and had not been commonly employed by the military for many years. More persuasive were the photographs of the nineteen-year-old recruit at the height of his nearly lethal reaction to the vaccinia virus. Taft was said to be moved by the pictures; two days later, he ordered the testing of all recruits, as well as all applicants to the reserves, ROTC, and the military academies, altogether about 25,000 a month. Testing would begin no later than October 1.

By August, the Defense Department had reached a compromise with civilian blood bankers over the Pentagon's earlier requirement that the names of all HTLV-III positive donors be turned over. The Pentagon agreed to allow military donors to sign an "informed consent" form authorizing the blood bank to pass on blood test results to military doctors. Soldiers who did not want their test results to go to the military "may leave the blood donation site without providing an explanation," according to the Defense Department order.

Although the compromise at least advised military donors that their doctors would be notified, it was far less a victory than blood bankers had hoped for. In a private memo to members of the American Association of Blood Banks, Grace Neitzer described their unfortunate choice "of either terminating existing constructive relationships with local military facilities or arranging to collect blood in accordance with the DOD directive." By threatening to ban uncooperative blood banks from bases, the Pentagon had played its trump card. As blood donors, military personnel were extraordinarily good citizens. In some heavily military areas, blood centers received as much as 18 percent of their donations from military installations. Nationally, 3 percent of the nation's blood supply came from donors in uniform. At a time when AIDS hysteria had drastically reduced blood donations, the industry could not afford to lose such a reliable source.

Meanwhile, a more significant battle was being fought over whether to test the 2.1 million active-duty military personnel. The debate again pitted the medical branches of the military against personnel commands. That there would be some form of mass screening was never in doubt. There were too many overseas duty stations in areas with high levels of endemic diseases that could endanger immune-compromised soldiers. Although it might be easy to care for an infected person assigned to Pearl Harbor or Lackland Air Force Base, where major medical centers were close at hand, remote duty stations in the Aleutians or Diego Garcia were not well equipped to handle an unexpected case of *Pneumocystis carinii* pneumonia or cryptococcal meningitis.

The key question was what would happen to those soldiers who tested HTLV-III positive once the mass screening began. The medical branches continued to argue that HTLV-III infected personnel be retained at least for stateside duty until their immune systems declined to the point at which continued work was detrimental. There was no medical reason to boot out otherwise productive soldiers, they maintained; they found allies in some manpower officials with pragmatic views of the expense of re-training HTLV-III positive soldiers. As one official told *The New York Times*, it took three years to train a military air-traffic controller. It did not make sense to throw that training away if an HTLV-III positive controller was still able to do the job. Their potential value as research subjects was another reason to keep infected personnel. As Lieutenant Colonel Ernest Takafuji, the disease-control consultant to the Army Surgeon General, told *Navy Times*, "Our feeling is that the military right now is sitting on a gold mine of information to help us get a better idea of the natural history of the disease."

Uniformed personnel brass continued to argue for immediate separation of HTLV-III positive soldiers. The Army Chief of Staff made no secret of the fact that he favored immediately screening all his troops and removing those who were infected. While the Army and Air Force now routinely issued medical retirements to HTLV-III infected soldiers rather than seeking to punish them for homosexuality, the Navy and Marine Corps continued to scan the paperwork of any serviceman seeking medical retirement with HTLV-III—for evidence of violations of sodomy or drug rules.

The Navy Military Personnel Command stood by its draconian posture in early August when it reaffirmed the separation board's ruling to discharge Hospitalman Byron Kinney for homosexuality and deny him a medical retirement. Kinney's attorneys promptly filed a lawsuit in federal court. His congressman had also entered the debate and had publicly taken up Kinney's cause against the Navy. Although Byron's health was rapidly deteriorating, he promised to fight the discharge to the end. Hospitalman Third Class Bernard Broyhill, whose health was also failing, continued to fight his gay-related discharge, as well.

The conflicts over the handling of AIDS-stricken sailors had reached the highest levels of the Pentagon. In response to questions about the Broyhill case, Assistant Defense Secretary Mayer released a statement saying he expected "military physicians will adhere to the ethics of the medical profession and honor the tradition of doctor-patient confidentiality to the absolute maximum consistent with national security." Navy Secretary John Lehman responded by saying that HTLV-III test results in themselves would not be used to punish sailors, but a spokesman quickly added that this did not mean that information gathered by Navy doctors concerning homosexuality would be ignored. Action would continue to be taken against acknowledged gays and their sexual contacts, the spokesman told *Navy Times*.

Pressure mounted for an end to the dissension. While officials debated, the *Air Force Times* reported that the Defense Department had imposed a gag order on officials regarding AIDS policy and research. Meanwhile, the military testing issue assumed geopolitical significance. In the Philippines, agitators against the huge U.S. military installations there used the AIDS threat to urge the government to quit leasing property to the U.S. military, saying that American sailors would surely spread AIDS among the massive population of prostitutes who surrounded the bases. Only assurances that all servicemen would be screened could allay these fears.

Similarly, Japan believed its population was only at risk for AIDS because of the substantial American military presence on its islands. Even liberal Costa Rica let it be known that it would not allow American troops within its borders unless they were certified to be AIDS–free. Although Costa Rica hosted no American bases, it was a likely staging area for any military actions against Nicaragua. At a time when so much of the Reagan administration's foreign policy was focused on overthrowing Nicaragua's Sandinista regime, the Costa Rican concerns were taken seriously.

IT WAS IN THESE TENSE DAYS of discord that word of Dr. Robert Redfield's studies made the military newspapers. Redfield had long predicted that the military would have to grapple with AIDS, and now people were ready to listen. Although all four branches of the services counted a total of only ninety-one cases of full-blown AIDS by September 1985, fifty of them in the Army, studies of civilian gay men had revealed that the largest proportion of those infected with HTLV-III were asymptomatic. These healthy but infected patients were the people who would comprise the six-digit AIDS caseloads predicted for the 1990s. There was no reason to believe that the larger share of the military's AIDS iceberg was not comparably concealed. Major Redfield's defense of the notion that AIDS should be viewed as a broad-spectrum disease process reaffirmed this suspicion.

Preliminary results from blood-donor screening in July, August, and September seemed to confirm those fears. Military blood bankers detected 44 HTLV-III positive personnel out of 62,200 military donors, or about 1 out of every 1,400. By comparison, civilian blood banks were reporting HTLV-III positive results in about 1 out of every 2,500 blood donors. Colonel Tramont predicted that within a year, the Army would find itself treating a thousand cases of AIDS and HTLV-III infection among soldiers and their dependents. The problem was going to be significant, Tramont and Redfield argued, and it was not merely going to be a homosexual problem.

Military doctors also had a new argument against those hard-liners who wanted to remove all HTLV-III positive personnel from the services. Most hawks supported discharges not on the basis of any genuine medical or military rationale; they did so on the assumption that infected soldiers were likely to be gay men. The Redfield study showed that, to the contrary, infected personnel were just as likely to be heterosexual men. More patients identified heterosexual sex as their risk behavior than sex with other men, according to Redfield's study. AIDS had little to do with homosexuality, at least in the military, the doctors argued. To treat the AIDS problem as a homosexual problem was inappropriate.

By effectively separating the issue of AIDS from the issue of homosexuality, the doctors succeeded in making compassion an acceptable feature of military policy on AIDS. There were other factors, too. The military's skittishness over bad publicity helped. The prospect of one thousand cases like Byron Kinney's and Bernard Broyhill's was a nightmare for the public-affairs specialists. Congressional Democrats had made it clear they were adamantly against using HTLV-III test results to purge suspected gay men in uniform.

In three days of private hearings, the Armed Forces Epidemiological Board met at Walter Reed in early September to map out the procedures for screening all women and men in uniform. By September 17, they had written proposals for Assistant Defense Secretary Mayer. Immediate testing of all 2.1 million active-duty troops was not advised "because of the limited availability of trained personnel and medical resources" to accomplish such a task. Instead, the Pentagon should start testing all personnel slated for overseas assignment. Then screening would commence for all 500,000 troops stationed overseas, as well as "deployable" troops, such as Marines in the continental United States who were likely to be quickly mobilized in a military emergency. In keeping with the medical branches' interest in advancing AIDS studies, the board also recommended "pertinent and longitudinal studies" of HTLV-III positive soldiers.

The fear voiced by gay activists—that the massive screening might lead to pogroms of military gays—was met with indignation by the epidemiological board as well as by military doctors. Dr. Theodore Woodward, civilian chairman of the board, insisted that the military followed the same ethical rules as civilians and would not give information gathered during doctor interviews to commanders interested in ferreting out gays. "I can assure you that this body will have nothing to do with any agency that doesn't adhere to those standards" of doctor-patient confidentiality, Woodward said.

ON OCTOBER 24, 1985, Defense Secretary Caspar Weinberger issued the order to begin ultimately the largest AIDS screening program in the world, which would ultimately include all troops in the United States military. Although Weinberger's order provided no time line for the testing, his priorities for AIDS screening generally followed those proposed by the Armed Forces Epidemiological Board a month earlier. The projected cost for the entire screening program was $20 million.

Each branch of the service would designate medical centers for detailed evaluations of soldiers who tested HTLV-III positive. Only those soldiers with evidence of AIDS or of severe immunological problems would be separated, and they would be medically retired so that they would receive pensions and care in military hospitals, as would the victims of any other disease contracted while on active duty. Those HTLV-III infected soldiers who did not demonstrate "progressive clinical illness" would be retained, Weinberger ordered, though they might be reassigned to units that would not be deployed overseas.

An early internal memorandum from the Pentagon indicated that no information from epidemiological interviews could be used "for punitive action against an individual," but two days later the Pentagon reversed itself. Over the objection of the Defense Department's health and manpower officials, Weinberger ordered that admissions of homosexuality could be used as evidence in discharge proceedings. Gay personnel would be processed out under regulations allowing the dismissal of service members "for the convenience of the government," Weinberger said. Robert L. Gilliat, a health-affairs specialist with the Pentagon general counsel, explained Weinberger's reversal as being "decided in light of the general policy that there's no place for homosexuals on active duty in the armed forces."

Jeff Levi from the National Gay Task Force predicted that the order "will guarantee that when people test positive they will not be honest with health officials about how they may have come in contact with the virus." Levi's observation explained why it was no longer necessary to debate what to do with HTLV-III infected servicemen who acknowledged being gay. Hardly any soldier or sailor would admit to homosexuality now. The enormous publicity over Dr. Redfield's study only ensured that military personnel would admit to sexual contact with a prostitute as their sole risk behavior for having acquired the disease.

Within months, few in the military's medical services doubted that the explanations were anything but apocryphal. Still, the HTLV-III infected GI's story of sexual contact with a prostitute became so routine that doctors and nurses at Walter Reed joked among themselves that there must have been one very busy HTLV-III infected prostitute at work in Berlin; they even named the industrious hooker who seemed to have infected so many soldiers. When a new HTLV-III positive soldier was admitted to the ward and claimed heterosexuality, one nurse would joke to another, "Someone else who went to bed with Helga." Gays had for decades hidden themselves by using such code phrases as "friends of Dorothy"; now they were friends of Helga.

ALONG WITH SPURRING media interest and government action, Dr. Redfield's study was used by AIDS activists to redefine entirely the scope of the AIDS problem within the American consciousness. The new line from AIDS organizations read: "Now, AIDS is everybody's problem." The assertion was not merely a statement that everyone should be concerned with AIDS; the activists advanced the idea that AIDS was everyone's problem because everyone would soon be getting the disease. At the height of the heterosexual AIDS frenzy, *Life* magazine ran a dramatic cover story with the headline NOW NO ONE IS SAFE FROM AIDS. The inside story, titled "The New Victims," featured a hemophiliac and his wife, the female sexual partner of a bisexual man, and children of intravenous drug users—all people from previously defined risk groups. The only new addition to the lineup of AIDS patients was the faceless picture of an anonymous soldier who said he had contracted the disease from one of his "scores" of female heterosexual partners.

There was a psychological allure to the new twist to the epidemic. The idea that a disease would stay in narrowly defined risk groups ran counter to the ideals of social democracy. There was almost poetic justice in the threat that AIDS might spread to everyone. It was in virtually no one's interest to argue otherwise. The notion of an impending AIDS pandemic quickly became the new orthodoxy of the epidemic—largely based on Dr. Redfield's contention that 37 percent of Army AIDS patients had contracted the disease heterosexually.

FEW STUDIES in the history of the AIDS epidemic would have such staggering ramifications or prove so controversial. The obvious question was whether a valid survey could be conducted by an institution that would discharge anyone who said he engaged in anything but heterosexual sex. Redfield acknowledged this problem in the study but dismissed it, saying, "Although military patients may be particularly reluctant to admit to certain risk behaviors, corroboration of patient information was obtained by interviews with family members and other acquaintances and by a physical examination, including a rectal culture for gonorrhea, before including these patients in the heterosexually acquired disease category." When asked again about the study in late 1992, Redfield reflected that perhaps two of the ten men who claimed heterosexual contact were not telling the truth, which left eight—or about 20 percent of the sample— who he believed were.

But the study was conducted at a time when the armed forces were quite publicly kicking out AIDS-infected soldiers who acknowledged to doctors that they were gay. The Defense Department itself had created a powerful incentive to lie. Young men also frequently concealed their sexual identity from their families, making corroboration from such sources unreliable at best. Some scientists were persuaded of the subjects' heterosexuality because several were married. By the mid-1980s, however, many gay soldiers were marrying lesbians to conceal their sexuality.

A substantial body of scientific evidence also undermined Dr. Redfield's assertions. European studies had yet to document many German prostitutes infected with HTLV-III. Testing of nearly two thousand registered prostitutes in Munich, Stuttgart, Berlin, Heidelberg, and Frankfurt had found only seventeen who were infected. Moreover, among the three hundred documented AIDS cases in Germany, not a single one could be traced to a man's sexual contact with a woman, much less a prostitute. If the tiny number of HTLV-III positive German prostitutes were giving men AIDS, they were doing it on a highly selective basis—to American servicemen only. German health authorities, in fact, became incensed when they learned that American military researchers were blaming their prostitutes for the military's AIDS problem. New York City health officials also noted that it was strange that while prostitutes in Germany seemed to be infecting soldiers willy-nilly, there was no evidence that prostitutes in New York City, with a much higher rate of HTLV-III infection, were similarly spreading the disease.

The most persuasive argument against Redfield's study were the current statistics about AIDS in the United States. Only eighteen of the nation's fourteen thousand AIDS cases could be traced to female-to-male sexual contact. And ten of these cases came from the armed forces.

Redfield pointed out, accurately, that AIDS would be unique among sexually transmitted diseases if it proved to be spread only from men to women. He also argued that the lack of many female-to-male cases could be expected for many more years—studies indicated that people were most infectious at the latter stages of their immunological decline. Since men had been infected with HTLV-III much earlier in the epidemic than women, it was to be expected that they were infecting women at a much higher rate than women were infecting them. The bi-directional infections would come later, he predicted. Indeed, under this scenario, it would not be possible to weigh the threat of female-to-male transmission accurately until the mid-1990s, when women infected in the mid-1980s reached their most infectious stages.

Researchers at the El Paso County Health Department in Colorado Springs remained skeptical of the Redfield data and reinterviewed twenty HTLV-III positive servicemen as part of its state's contact-tracing program that began on November 1, 1985. Seventy-five percent of the soldiers had told military doctors they had acquired the disease heterosexually; only four of the twenty had acknowledged being gay. To the county health department, however, fourteen said they were gay, three admitted to being intravenous drug users, and only three said they could not identify how they had contracted the virus.

Later interviews by this writer with nearly 150 AIDS-infected soldiers found 150 gay men who had all solemnly insisted to military physicians that their only risk behavior for getting the disease was contact with prostitutes in Germany, Korea, or the Philippines. None of these men were among the forty-one that Redfield studied, but it does reflect the extent to which lying about heterosexuality became routine in the aftermath of that investigation. In truth, Helga was actually Helmut. And the soldier who told his story to *Life* magazine was not a heterosexual who ran into the wrong woman but, rather, a gay man with a boyfriend in San Francisco's Castro Street neighborhood.

Despite the questions about the Walter Reed study, few doubts were raised publicly about its validity outside scientific journals. It seemed everyone had a stake in advancing the heterosexual AIDS story. Editors suddenly had a new angle on the epidemic at a time when AIDS stories were hot, and it was an angle that brought the issue home to the great majority of newspaper readers and television viewers, most of whom were neither gay men nor intravenous drug users. Since the imminent threat of a heterosexual pandemic would increase research budgets, the nation's most distinguished scientists now echoed their concerns. Seeing a possible end to government lethargy and media apathy, AIDS activists also cited the Redfield data to advance arguments for more prevention and public-education efforts.

Within the military, it was even more crucial that Redfield's data be accepted, since the armed forces' entire HTLV-III policies rested largely on the fiction that most military AIDS cases were not connected to homosexuality. As late as 1992, press officers from both Walter Reed and the Army Surgeon General's office would try to prevent Army AIDS researchers from talking to an author about homosexuality and its relationship to AIDS in the military. "We've been able to do a lot of good because the two issues [AIDS and homosexuality] are not linked," a public affairs official said. "It would be better if it stayed that way."

WHAT WAS MOST remarkable about the Redfield study was not its scientific value but the insight it offered into the depth of antigay prejudice in the United States. At the time it was published, nearly ten thousand gay men were dead or dying of AIDS, a fact that had engendered no interest in most of society. The fact that ten cases among heterosexual men could so electrify the country reflected the relative value a heterosexual life had over that of a homosexual. And most heterosexuals continued to deny that prejudice against homosexuals was a matter of major concern.

ALTHOUGH THE HTLV-III policies adopted in October 1985 resolved several crucial issues concerning how the military would handle its massive AIDS screening program, important questions remained unanswered. What exactly would the military do with soldiers who tested positive? Though the Pentagon had ruled to retain them, how and where would they be assigned? Would their confidentiality be protected? There were no plans to gear up military hospitals for the one thousand new patients that researchers expected to find during the screening, nor had it been determined exactly what the hospitals would do with HTLV-III patients once they began arriving for the comprehensive immunological evaluations that the Pentagon now required. Although doctors had begun to consider these questions in the final weeks of 1985, the mass screening was not slated to begin until well into 1986. They had time to prepare—or so they thought.

———————

JUST ONE DAY before Byron Kinney was to be discharged from the Navy for homosexuality, the Pentagon ordered that his separation be delayed. On October 16, 1985, word came from Washington that Kinney would not be discharged for homosexuality, but would be processed for the medical retirement his lawyers had sought. Bernard Broyhill was also notified that he would be medically retired and not discharged for homosexuality. "I feel great!" Kinney told a gay newspaper. "This is what I wanted. I hope this case has helped others."

The next day, Kinney was admitted to Balboa Naval Hospital in San Diego. Bridget Wilson had suspected that Kinney was clinging to life until his case was won—for himself and for others in the Navy. She was right. Four days later, on October 21, Byron Kinney died.

Bernard Broyhill died in November.

— 54 —

Where It All Begins

WHEN LANCE CORPORAL Barbara Baum arrived at the Marine base near Beaufort, South Carolina, she had heard nothing of the 1984 purges of female drill instructors. What happened to lesbians did not seem to be an issue for Baum because she certainly did not consider herself a lesbian. She had never even thought much about homosexuality at all, as was evident during boot camp when another recruit began speculating about which drill instructors were gay.

"You can't be in the military and be gay," Barbara said. They asked right on the enlistment forms, she noted. The other woman looked at her as if she wondered what planet Barb had come from.

Barbara's observation did indeed have a lot to do with where she had come from. Mishawaka, Indiana, is a factory town near South Bend, about 120 miles east of Chicago. Standing only five foot five, she was small and wiry, with brown hair and dark green eyes. Barbara Jean Baum spoke with a broad, plain Indiana accent that bubbled with Midwestern enthusiasm and more than a hint of small-town naïveté. The Baums were a blue-collar family. Barb's father had worked a route servicing vending machines at local factories and her mother waited tables. She had one brother, two years older than she. That Barbara possessed such a perky disposition was no small wonder, given her brother's disposition.

It came out later in the trial testimony—that her brother beat her day after day in their small one-story, three-bedroom house. Barbara often showed up at school with a black eye or a fat lip or a welt spreading across some part of her upper torso. Her parents appeared oblivious of her brother's assaults, and Barbara did not discuss them. Nor did she speak of the sexual assaults that she endured at the hands of her brother, his friends, and one of her cousins. When she mentioned it once in the fourth grade, the other students mocked her. Others did not seem to believe her, so she learned to remain silent.

The circumstances of Barbara Baum's childhood were less unusual than most Americans want to acknowledge. Some studies indicate that as many as one in four women have experienced some form of incest by their teen years, usually from a father, stepfather, or brother. After such trauma, many women develop an overriding need for an orderly environment; safety is a major concern.

The Marine Corps was not Barbara's original career choice. She was a straight-*A* student through high school and excelled in athletics. In her senior year, she placed tenth in track and field competitions for the entire state of Indiana. After graduating from Mishawaka High, she attended Indiana University. But college was more a way to get away from home than a door of opportunity. By then, she had discovered that drinking soothed the shame and pain that plagued her. Eventually, she dropped out of college. She thought she could learn to be a policeman in the military. It was also a safe and orderly environment, far from the site of her abuse in Mishawaka. In February 1985, Barbara signed up for a six-year enlistment.

She had always done well under pressure. She earned the highest scores of her platoon in boot camp and was meritoriously promoted to lance corporal. She graduated number one in her Military Police school. She was the platoon's honor graduate in basic corrections.

Barbara was not a very sexual person in those days. When she thought of sex at all, it was associated with assault, so she had simply put the subject out of her mind, as she had done with her past. Barbara met her first lesbian WMs—as women Marines are called—during her Marine Corps training. First, there was her very masculine roommate at MP school. Barb was not comfortable with the idea of a masculine woman, though she was more intrigued with lesbians than she wanted to admit to herself. Then she met Diane Maldonado and the pair formed a fast friendship. Like Barb, Diane was a gung ho Marine. It was Diane whom Barb called the night after her lesbian roommate moved in. What should she do? Barbara asked. The way Baum recalled the conversation, Diane said not to worry, to just let it be.

Barb's first orders would have dispatched her to the Marine base in El Toro, California, but, as the honor graduate from two of her training schools, she had the option of choosing her assignment. She chose Parris Island. She had loved boot camp and wanted to stay with other gung ho Marines; she was thinking about becoming a drill instructor. Parris Island was home to a lot of hard-driving, hard-drinking Marines like Barbara Baum; it was where she belonged.

On Christmas Day 1985, she was working sentry duty at the main gate of Parris Island. She loved the snap and pop of the job, snapping to attention and popping salutes in her crisp dress blue uniform. Two days later, her commanding officer told her that never in his experience had so many people commented on one MP as had mentioned the striking military bearing of the new sentry, Lance Corporal Barbara Baum.

A few days later on New Year's Eve, a female drill instructor invited Barbara to her room for a wine cooler. When the woman made a pass, Barb stopped her, and the woman apologized. By now, Barb knew it was important to avoid being around the wrong people. She took up running, as she had in high school. The Marine Corps was her chance at a new beginning. Every day on her morning runs, Barbara jogged under the sign that spanned across Boulevard de France just beyond the parade deck. It was the sign that greeted all Marine recruits who entered the camp. It read, WHERE IT ALL BEGINS.

UNITED STATES NAVAL ACADEMY
ANNAPOLIS, MARYLAND

THE DEFINING MOMENT of Midshipman Joseph Steffan's career at the Naval Academy—the scene that would replay countless times on television stories about him later—occurred on a brisk December afternoon when he sang "The Star-Spangled Banner" at the nationally televised Army-Navy football game. Joe had known two months earlier that he would have the honor and had worried about it that long, knowing that even the greatest singers had forgotten its archaic verses or missed its high top notes. The game was the high point of the year for the Naval Academy. Among the live audience of 35,000 at this game was President Ronald Reagan, and for this moment, it seemed, Joseph Charles Steffan was the center of the universe.

It was a formidable challenge, which was just what Joe Steffan loved about his career at Annapolis. Every year brought new challenges, and year by year he met them and proved to himself that he could compete and win on a national level. It was exhilarating for a man in his early twenties.

Few places in the United States were as remote from the nation's mainstream as Joe's hometown of Warren, Minnesota, a hamlet of two thousand about sixty miles from the Canadian border. His was a stable Catholic family that had experienced nothing of the social turmoil that rocked the rest of the country during the 1960s and 1970s. Vietnam was simply a history lesson by the time Joe reached his teen years, and the sixties seemed nothing more than a social anachronism. He was the third of four children, the only boy, and fiercely idealistic. Joe wanted to help shape the future of his country. And he wanted to make other people in Warren proud that they knew him.

Later, he wondered whether his concern about making others proud and his great drive to succeed might be rooted in his very deep awareness that there was something about him that might disgust people and prevent his success. The glimmering awareness that he was different went back a long way; for years, he had not known what the difference was, but in high school its connection with his sexuality became clear. His friendships with other young men tended to evolve into crushes. Knowing this could lead to unspeakable shame, Joe buried his awareness in a frenzy of activity.

When Joe's best friend was approached to attend the Naval Academy, Joe became interested, too. Joe liked science, and the Naval Academy offered a highly technical education, which suited him. With a high school grade average of 98.6 points, award-winning participation in his school's track and field team, and an eclectic number of extracurricular activities, Joe was everything the Naval Academy was looking for in a midshipman, and he was accepted.

Joe's friend got in, too, but dropped out five months into the Plebe Year. Joe stuck with it. Along with his academic schedule, he joined the Catholic Choir and the Glee Club. He kept his grades up, consistently ranking among the top ten midshipmen in his company. Days before the beginning of his Christmas vacation in 1985, at about the same time Barbara Baum arrived in Parris Island, the class officers for Joe's senior year were posted on a bulletin board at Bancroft Hall. He had been appointed regimental commander, which ranked him as one of the top three midshipmen in the Academy's class of 1987.

Joe's dream had been to prove himself on a national basis; he was doing that now. But his whole success was wrapped around the fiction of being heterosexual. Many Academy rituals were constructed to combine heterosexuality and the military ethos. A few months after Joe learned of his ranking, for example, he participated in the "ring dance," a Navy ritual that joins its seamen to God, country, and heterosexuality. In the ceremony, Joe's date wore his new class ring on a ribbon around her neck; then Joe removed the ring from her neck and submerged it in a bowl of water collected from all the world's seven seas, including water from an ice core drilled by Navy scientists from deep below the polar ice cap in Antarctica, presumed to contain water from the days of Christ. The couple stood reverentially while the ring was baptized, and then his date slipped the ring on Joe's finger.

By late 1985, Joe no longer denied to himself that he was gay, even if he did not act upon it. He did not feel bad about being gay as much as he felt frustrated that he could never let anyone know. Glee Club appearances in New York City and Washington had made him vaguely aware that an entire gay subculture existed somewhere beyond the redbrick walls of Annapolis. Though Joe had not made a vow of celibacy to himself, he knew that any attempt to explore this subculture would require him to construct a double life and he knew that would be risky.

At the Army-Navy game, Joe finished the national anthem, standing tall in his thick, full-length blue Navy coat. He had not forgotten the words; he had hit the highest notes. Afterward, everyone told him that he had done a great job.

FEBRUARY 14, 1986
GUERNEVILLE, CALIFORNIA

FOR FOUR DAYS, Cliff Anchor had watched the thick gray thunderheads sweep in from the Pacific, over the grassy headlands and into the redwood-studded valleys of the Russian River. The river's waters rose slowly, first washing out the summer bridge, then submerging the road to the virgin redwood grove a mile outside Guerneville.

In years past, these would have been frenetic days for Cliff, but a year ago he had grown exhausted from his round-the-clock broadcast hours and had sold his station to a company that had converted his eclectic community programming into an "oldies" station.

Cliff kept busy at his new post as a state military reserve public-affairs consultant to the commanding general of the California National Guard. It was a new reason to stay in the closet, as he explained to Lenny Matlovich, with whom he had remained in touch. It was never clear to Lenny, however, whether people stayed in the closet because the circumstances of their lives demanded it or whether they created circumstances that required them to stay in the closet.

In any event, the British-born Anchor was patriotic with the zeal of a convert. When his energy started to fail in 1985, he believed it was a result of overwork. He had had a brief bout with night sweats and unexplained fatigue, but that seemed to be going around. When Cliff visited Lenny in San Francisco, Lenny, too, confided feeling vaguely out of sorts. They were both getting old, they told themselves, never expressing the more troubling thoughts in words.

When the rain kept pounding and it was clear the river would flood, Cliff raced into town to stock up on groceries and bottled water. He made it back to his hilltop just as the waters crested over River Road, stranding him on his promontory. A few miles away in Guerneville, water filled the corner storefront where Lenny had run his pizza parlor. And still the rains came, and the river became a torrent, tearing up trees and ripping away homes from its banks. The flood, it seemed, would sweep them all away.

BOOK SIX

HOMOVAC

(1986–1990)

The old civilizations claimed they were founded on love and
justice. Ours is founded on fear and hatred.

—George Orwell, *1984*

55

Tom Dooley's
Undesirable Discharge

NAVAL ANNEX, THE PENTAGON
ARLINGTON, VIRGINIA

FROM THE FIRST TIME Diana Shaw attempted to retrieve Dooley's official Navy records, it was clear that the service had something to hide. The twenty-five-year-old writer had been hired by a Hollywood producer to research a possible film adaptation of Dooley's life. It did not take her long to find what had stopped any previous producer from launching such a project. A priest involved in the campaign to have Dooley named a saint delicately referred to it as "the gray matter." Tom Dooley was gay.

Armed with permission from Tom's last remaining survivor, his brother Malcolm's widow, Shaw went to the Pentagon to see Dooley's files, but Navy officials stalled, at first handing her only a one-page biography of Dooley that noted his contributions to Operation Passage to Freedom. The more Shaw pressed Navy officials for Dooley's full service file, the more adamant they became that she could not see it. It was only after she asserted her legal right under the Freedom of Information Act that she was led into an office downstairs in the Naval Annex, where two officers brought her Dooley's thick file.

Looking through the files, Shaw expected to find Dooley's original discharge papers. What she found instead stopped her cold. The original papers were missing. In their place was a page that stated that Dooley had received an honorable discharge from the United States Navy. Shaw also discovered that the weightiest part of Dooley's file was a report by the Office of Naval Intelligence on Dooley's sex life. She scarcely believed the lengths to which the Navy had gone to discern whether one of its members was gay. Moreover, she could not understand why the Navy would go to such lengths for an officer who had, by their own standards, served the interests of the Navy and the U.S. government so well. Every succeeding page of the report showed her a side of the government that she had not known existed, and it was frightening.

IN THE FIRST MONTHS of 1956, Tom Dooley's star had never shone brighter. The release of his book documenting his role in Operation Passage to Freedom, *Deliver Us from Evil*, was imminent, and his lawyers were negotiating for the movie rights to his story. The Navy, the Ford Foundation, and Pfizer Pharmaceutical company, which had donated supplies for Dooley's work in Vietnam, were jointly sponsoring a five-month lecture tour that would take the lieutenant to thirty cities. Meanwhile, he had been transferred to the Naval Medical Command in Bethesda, and as he awaited the beginning of his book promotion tour, he spent his days speaking to the National Security Council, to teams of Navy officers curious about Vietnam, even to White House aides. Except for a few World War II admirals, Lieutenant Tom Dooley was arguably the most famous officer then serving in the United States Navy.

The ONI files revealed that the anonymous tip advising the Navy that Dooley was a homosexual came in January. The matter went immediately to the attention of the Chief of Naval Personnel, Vice Admiral James Holloway. "It is requested that an appropriate investigation be undertaken in order to determine whether or not subject officer has homosexual tendencies," Holloway wrote to the Director of Naval Intelligence. "In [the] event the same is determined to be factual, it is requested that an attempt be made to determine the extent of his homosexual activities." And one other thing: Word should get out to no one, due to "possible embarrassment to the Navy inasmuch as Subject is receiving notoriety in connection with his lecture tour, i.e. newspaper, magazine, book, TV and radio."

From that day on, Dooley was the subject of the strictest surveillance. His hotel rooms and private phones were bugged, his conversations taped and fully transcribed. Anyone with whom he talked was later pulled aside by ONI agents and questioned. When he flew between cities, ONI agents followed him and reports were dutifully filed about hour-long layovers between connecting flights. Agents rifled through his baggage at airports and recorded what they found. His lunches with Francis Cardinal Spellman were noted, as was the fact that the young senator from Massachusetts, John Kennedy, had dropped by for a luncheon with Dooley and the New York prelate.

No detail was too minor to escape reporting by the ONI. Agents listened at the door of his Miami hotel room and noted hearing "soft music" after Dooley went into the room with another man. When he spoke in Denver, one informant managed some time alone with Dooley's briefcase and industriously photocopied fifty-three pages of documents, diary entries, letters, and schedules. The records of any servicemen Dooley spoke to were scanned for suggestions that they were gay.

The investigation quickly yielded results. One man whom Dooley had taken back to his hotel room was found to have been discharged from the Marine Corps station at Parris Island, South Carolina, for "psychological" reasons. Agents frequently followed Dooley to the Astor Bar in New York City, noted in Navy records as "a known meeting place of homosexuals." There, the young officer would strike up conversations with other men who would then return with Dooley to his hotel room. When the date left, the ONI had the help of New York City police officers, who would stop the date to obtain his name and place of employment. Several gave ONI agents surprisingly detailed statements about their trysts with Dr. Dooley.

To seal its case, the Navy hired informants who struck up conversations with Dooley to elicit information about his homosexuality. A transcript of one of these discussions records Dooley explaining that he never made passes at men when he wore his Navy uniform. "I don't and I never want to disgrace the uniform," he told the informant. "I like the Navy. I always wanted to be in the Navy."

On March 8, the ONI completed an exhaustive report on the previous six weeks of surveillance. Tom Dooley was homosexual, the report concluded. The next day, Captain G. S. Bullen, head of the Officer Performance Branch of the Bureau of Naval Personnel, wrote the Director of Naval Intelligence a terse note saying the Chief of Naval Personnel "directed me to request that steps be immediately undertaken to effect a resolution" of Dooley's case.

The Director of Naval Intelligence laid out his plan: On March 24, Dooley would be speaking in New York City. He should be confronted there with all the evidence against him. The intelligence director cautioned that secrecy was essential. "The information contained herein shall not be disseminated or made known to persons outside the Department of Defense, nor shall further transmission of the enclosure(s) be made to any other activities without permission of Director of Naval Intelligence," he ordered. The final plans for the confrontation were laid out days later. "The belief is that the Subject can be separated without unfavorable publicity to the Navy," one memorandum stated. "Subject, of course, is free to give any explanation he may desire regarding the reason for his discharge, which will be in the form of a resignation under conditions other than honorable."

After a speaking appearance in New York in late March 1956, Dr. Tom Dooley abruptly announced he was leaving the Navy in order to establish a network of hospitals in Southeast Asia.

The irony of the discharge was that it marked the beginning of a new phase of Tom Dooley's career, one in which he gained even greater fame. In the next three years, he built a vast network of clinics across Asia— three in Laos, two in Cambodia, others in Vietnam and Malaysia—and he coordinated support projects in Haiti, Peru, Afghanistan, and Jordan. He kept his clinics far from national capitals, serving the hundreds of thousands of rural people who had never seen a doctor. Internationally Dooley became known as America's answer to Dr. Albert Schweitzer, the humanitarian doctor in Africa who had won the Nobel Peace Prize.

To support his work, Dooley maintained a dizzying schedule, repeatedly returning to America to tour and to raise funds. Dooley's new books, *The Night They Burned the Mountain* and *The Edge of Tomorrow*, climbed the bestseller lists. The popular radio and television entertainer Arthur Godfrey adopted Dooley's foundation, MEDICO, as his favorite charity, and lavished Dooley with air time when the doctor returned to America. In Catholic schools, where Dooley was particularly revered, nuns often mentioned Dooley in their daily morning prayers. In 1959, the Gallup poll listed Tom Dooley as the seventh most admired man in the United States.

Dooley could still work a crowd like few others in the charity business—"Make them laugh, make them cry, and pass the basket," he would explain to friends—but his speeches contained less anti-Communist rhetoric than the suggestion that America could win the Cold War by helping the developing world meet its needs for food and medical care. The governments the United States supported often did little to help their own people, Dooley said, making communism a seemingly appealing alternative.

In private conversations with the CIA operatives with whom he sometimes talked in Asia, Dooley had a second cause—he wanted his undesirable discharge upgraded. He never told the agents why he had received the bad paper, but CIA records show that he repeatedly brought up the topic to government agents. In a region where he was revered, the fact that the Navy had given him a bad discharge could cause America great embarrassment, Dooley insisted. In their private memos to Washington, the agents expressed amusement at Dooley's pleas—everyone apparently knew why he had received the discharge—and there were occasional suggestions that the promise of an upgrade be used to persuade the doctor to undertake this or that project for the government. No one, however, recommended that the Navy actually make good on such promises.

Although Ted Werner, the old Navy friend Dooley had hired as pilot, knew that part of the basis of their friendship was the fact that they were both gay, the topic rarely came up for discussion between the two men. People did not talk openly about homosexuality in those days, not even other gay people. When the subject of Dooley's discharge arose, Ted noticed that a great blackness clouded his friend's normally sunny disposition. From these moments, Ted came to understand that Dooley spent most of his life in the jungles of Asia because he felt himself an exile, an undesirable American.

The discharge revealed the great contradiction in Tom Dooley's life. He had believed that America was the land of the free and had defended her against totalitarianism; yet Tom Dooley's own life was evidence that this promise of freedom was a sham. Dooley had loved the Navy and by just about everyone's account, including that of the Chief of Naval Operations, had brought great honor to the service. Still, just one word applied to him in an anonymous phone call had ended it all. Ted sometimes thought that every new clinic, every speech Dooley gave, was an effort to show his worth, to convince the Navy of its error so that he could have the honorable discharge he so desperately wanted.

Even in the difficult months of 1959, when it became clear that the thirty-two-year-old doctor was dying, Dooley held on to his dream of an upgrade. It became his ultimate goal to resolve the contradictions between his life's ideals and its substance. As the final months neared and the concern over his discharge mounted, Ted thought it an odd preoccupation—there were so many larger issues Dooley had to face.

Though Diana Shaw's research into the Navy's investigation of Tom Dooley was the most exhaustive of any researcher in the thirty years since his discharge, it also had the unintended effect of derailing the projected film. Like so many producers over the years, Shaw's employers had anticipated a film about a heroic young doctor saving the lives of thousands and then dying tragically young. They weren't interested in a homosexual subplot. When Shaw's research indicated that the issue could not be realistically ignored, the project, like all the others before it, was dropped.

———————

THE GREAT IRONY of Diana Shaw's research into the Navy's investigation and discharge of Tom Dooley in the mid-1950s is that precisely the same stories were occurring across America in the late 1980s. Not since the McCarthy days had the military launched so vehement a campaign against gays in uniform. The official statistics reveal a downward trend in the numbers of gays discharged from the service—from about 2,000 a year in the late 1970s and early 1980s, to about 1,500 a year in the late 1980s— but the official statistics obscure the truth. So many field officers had come to feel ambivalent about the gay policies that they increasingly cited other reasons for discharging sailors and soldiers. In 1992, the Defense Department and the General Accounting Office agreed that the true numbers of soldiers discharged for homosexuality was far larger than the number released in the late 1980s.

What could not be disguised was the ferocity of the campaigns against homosexuals. Prison sentences were meted out with greater regularity; the pace of massive purges quickened. None of this marked a departure from the tactics used in the days of Tom Dooley. Within the military, very little had changed.

The attitudes of the rest of the world toward homosexuality had changed, however, which meant that this last great frenzy of antigay hostility would not go unchallenged.

———————

IF THERE WAS one moment that would encapsulate all that was about to unfold for gays in the military, and would anticipate all that was about to unfold for gays throughout America, it was the day in late March 1986 when, for the first time, a case regarding homosexuality was fully argued before the nation's highest tribunal. Up to then decisions regarding gays were simply one-sentence affirmations of lower court rulings, made without legal argument or public discussion. At long last, nearly two decades after the Stonewall riots, the battle for equal rights was joined at the Supreme Court.

The debate centered on a twenty-nine-year-old bartender named Michael Hardwick, arrested by Atlanta police on the night of August 2, 1982. The police officer had knocked on Hardwick's front door to serve a warrant for public intoxication; a house guest pointed the officer toward Hardwick's bedroom door. The policeman opened the door and saw Hardwick engaged in oral sex with another man. When the policeman said he was serving his warrant, Hardwick explained he had already cleared the matter with the court and offered to show the officer his receipt. That no longer mattered, the policeman said, because he had found Hardwick engaging in a violation of the Georgia law that banned oral and anal sex. Hardwick and his companion spent the next twelve hours in jail.

The county prosecutor dismissed the charges, but by then Hardwick had been approached by the American Civil Liberties Union, which asked him to file a civil suit against the state. Because Hardwick had been arrested in the privacy of his bedroom for engaging in conduct that all agreed was entirely consensual, libertarians believed they had an ideal case to take to the Supreme Court.

When lawyers met in the imposing high court chambers on March 31, 1986, Georgia attorney general Michael Hobbs aggressively defended the state's right to ban homosexual activity. Striking down sodomy laws would open "a Pandora's box," he warned, and result in the repeal of laws banning polygamy, incest, prostitution, homosexual marriages, and adultery. He cited the writings of *Leviticus*, *Romans*, and St. Thomas Aquinas to support his assertion that homosexuality was immoral, and he noted that homosexuals had been considered heretics in the Middle Ages. The law was also needed to prevent the spread of AIDS, he said. Moreover, Hobbs reminded the court that homosexuality had been condemned for thousands of years and that the law was necessary to protect marriage, the family, and the "collective moral aspirations of the people."

Harvard law professor Laurence Tribe, one of the nation's foremost liberal legal scholars, countered that the case was not about morality but about the extent to which the government should be allowed to intrude upon citizens' private lives. Like many libertarians, Tribe believed that one's rights to privacy in sexual matters was a logical outgrowth of previous court rulings upholding the rights to privacy in decisions concerning abortion and birth control.

After the arguments, gay attorneys told reporters they felt the session had gone "spectacularly well." The end of the sodomy statutes, which were the legal basis for much of the codified discrimination against gays in America, seemed imminent.

The nine justices met in private session several days later to discuss the case. Justice Byron White, the Kennedy appointee who had turned conservative in his years on the court, was the most outspoken jurist in favor of the sodomy statutes, arguing that the Supreme Court had no business creating new privacy rights, particularly on an issue that had deep historic roots in the culture. Supporting White were Chief Justice Warren Burger and justices Sandra Day O'Connor and William Rehnquist. Justice Harry Blackmun, who had written the court's 1973 opinion asserting a woman's right to an abortion, argued that if the right to privacy meant anything, it surely allowed adults to conduct their sex lives in the privacy of their own bedrooms without interference from state power. Siding with Blackmun were justices William Brennan, John Paul Stevens, and Thurgood Marshall. Justice Lewis Powell was undecided.

According to later accounts of the meeting, Powell was reluctant to agree to Blackmun's sweeping arguments about the right to privacy. Nevertheless, he felt uncomfortable about sodomy laws in general, believing they were unenforced, unenforceable, and generally useless. Even if he did not entirely agree with Blackmun's legal rationale, Powell finally decided to vote with him, providing the crucial fifth vote needed to extend the right to privacy to gay people. Blackmun began writing his opinion, which would forever alter the legal status of homosexuals in America.

Then, days later, Powell notified his fellow justices that he had changed his mind. He was switching his vote. His new logic was that the State of Georgia had not actually enforced the law against Hardwick; had it done so, he would certainly vote to throw the law out. Because the matter was a civil suit and it could not be established that the law actually hurt anybody, Powell did not want to use this case to overturn all sodomy statutes. Some court observers said later that Powell had a less judicial concern when he changed his vote—he did not want to be known as the man who legalized homosexuality in America.

56

The Unquiet Death of
Michael W. Foster

JANUARY 18, 1986
WALTER REED ARMY MEDICAL CENTER
WASHINGTON, D.C.

THEY FOUND the body in the early afternoon. The twenty-six-year-old private had tied his bootlaces to the hydraulic mechanism of a door leading to a rarely used stairwell and hanged himself. The subsequent Army inquiry on the suicide of Private First Class Michael W. Foster at Walter Reed Army Medical Center determined "the individual was not mentally responsible at the time of the act which caused his death."

To anyone who had observed the first stages of the military's mass AIDS testing, the suicide could hardly have come as a surprise. Military doctors had hoped for time to prepare protocols and programs for soldiers and sailors who tested positive for HTLV-III antibodies, but because testing had started much sooner than anyone had anticipated, few preparations had been made.

Attempts to halt the testing proved unsuccessful. In December 1985, five newly recruited sailors who tested positive during their basic training went to federal court to challenge the Pentagon policy of retaining only those service members who tested positive after completing basic training and who were no longer in a recruit status. In San Diego, another nine sailors, also new recruits, contested their discharges in federal court. A federal judge in Washington issued a temporary restraining order, but the order was lifted within two weeks and the discharges—and the testing—proceeded.

The reason for the abrupt instigation of testing in the early months of 1986 was a matter of much speculation. According to one unconfirmed story making the rounds of gay sailors in the Pacific, a sailor on the USS *Midway* had died suddenly of AIDS in Japan, alarming Japanese authorities who worried about AIDS-infected sailors cavorting with local prostitutes. Calls for assurances that the U.S. Navy was AIDS-free led to the accelerated testing. Whatever the cause, the lack of policies and plans for handling service members at far-flung bases who tested positive proved a prescription for disaster.

SPECIALIST FOUR JEFF HERWATT was one of the first twenty-five soldiers in the United States Army to test positive for HTLV-III. Like growing numbers of the new generation in the military, the twenty-year-old Herwatt had known that he was homosexual when he enlisted in the Army in late 1983. A native of Pleasanton, California, a quiet suburban community across the bay from San Francisco, Herwatt had been a computer nerd without many friends in high school. He would take the BART trains to San Francisco whenever he could to wander around the gay neighborhood on Castro Street.

He left home at fifteen, earned his diploma through the General Educational Development test, and enrolled in the local community college and later the University of California at Berkeley. When he was seventeen he enlisted, attracted by the military's job opportunities, and his high aptitude test scores guaranteed him challenging work with computers and an assignment to Europe, which was where he was dispatched after being designated the honor graduate of his advanced training classes.

Jeff knew from his first days in the Army that he was suspected of being gay. His enlistment papers showed he had been living in San Francisco with another man when he entered the service. He had decided not to say he was gay, but he would not deny it either. He settled into his new job at the Army's European Command in Heidelberg, Germany, and fell into the well-established gay military network. They were all Family and Family took care of Family, as Jeff came to understand. Before long, he was partying in the cavernous gay discos in Frankfurt that catered to American military personnel, and he had established friendships with a group of lesbians who, like the gays he knew in San Francisco, had an assertive gay pride with which he identified.

In January 1986, Jeff married an American student at Heidelberg University who was having a hard time making ends meet. The marriage allowed him to move off base and obtain a $1,000-a-month housing allowance, which included a cost of living adjustment because of the dollar's deflated value. Jeff shared the allowance with his "wife." The marriage, he knew, also provided an edge of safety.

Jeff proved singularly capable in his job. He received glowing evaluation reports and rapid advancement.

These were tense times for the American military in Europe, with terrorist threats and heightened concern for base security. In February 1986, at the same time the Army was conducting its investigation into Private Foster's suicide, Jeff felt himself falling ill. A few days later he was coughing uncontrollably and running a high fever. When he finally went to the Army hospital for treatment, he passed out at the check-in counter.

He awoke with an intravenous drip in his arm and an oxygen mask over his face. His diagnosis was walking pneumonia, but it proved an especially stubborn pneumonia and was resistant to the normal treatment by antibiotics. Its persistence mystified doctors until finally they drew blood for an HTLV-III test, which came back positive.

Though Jeff had recovered by then, he was told he had AIDS and would die within three to six months. He was then locked in a padded cell with a large red ISOLATION sign on the door and BIOHAZARD warning posters around his bed. His food was served on paper plates with plastic utensils by nurses who dressed in what amounted to medical space suits and who would not talk to him. Doctors were not enthusiastic about providing medical care, since they believed he was on the verge of dying anyway. He had never been allowed to see a psychiatrist, but his medical charts were flagged with notations that he might be suicidal. He was not even allowed a newspaper.

It was during the interview with Captain William Buchanan, one of his Army doctors, that Jeff made an admission that would complicate his life even further. During the standard questioning about risk factors, he confided to Buchanan that he had had homosexual encounters, believing the admission would be held in confidence.

He did not think too much more about it; he was much more focused on his virtual imprisonment. This made him angry, which, he noted, made him feel better. Having lived in San Francisco's aggressive gay community, Jeff decided the best solution was to rock the boat. Before long, his congressman was asking the local command about the treatment of its HTLV-III positive soldier. Meanwhile, having persuaded a sympathetic orderly to leave his door unlocked, Jeff marched out of his room and straight into the office of his unit commander, a colonel. He wasn't sick anymore, Jeff said. He wanted to be released and put back at his regular duty station. The colonel threatened to call the military police; Jeff threatened to spit on him if he did. The colonel relented, and after some discussion agreed to allow Jeff to return to his unit.

This created new complications. His unit commander was truly sympathetic and worried about the rumors circulating through the unit because of Jeff's extended hospital stay. In order to stave off problems, the colonel called a general muster of the personnel command. And so it was that one morning Jeff found himself standing in front of fifteen hundred soldiers, with a colonel on one side of him and a general on the other, while the colonel explained that Jeff had AIDS. To make sure there was no hysteria, the colonel introduced a doctor who said that no one need fear contracting HTLV-III through casual contact or by simply working with Herwatt.

With Herwatt now a very well-known HTLV-III positive soldier, the *Stars and Stripes* newspaper contacted him for an interview, agreeing to conceal his identity. The story was well written and sympathetic, and the writer emphasized the fact that Herwatt was married. Although he was not named, the article made him even better known as an AIDS-infected soldier, which caused him still greater problems.

Not long after the story was published, a private assigned to a nearby duty station informed the Criminal Investigation Division that he was a homosexual and asked to be discharged. Part of the "evidence" the private submitted to prove his assertion was a statement that he had gone to bed with Specialist Four Jeff Herwatt. Herwatt had never heard of the private. Nevertheless, CID agents began interviewing Jeff's doctors.

According to CID files, Dr. William Buchanan told them that Jeff had admitted to at least ten homosexual contacts during his conversations with the doctor. This statement became evidence that Herwatt was gay. In the CID files, the potential charge against Herwatt was noted in all caps: SODOMY. The punishment: five years in prison.

———————

THROUGHOUT THE MILITARY, comparable stories of mistreatment and harassment of HTLV-III positive soldiers began to unfold as the pace of testing quickened during the early months of 1986.

Navy corpsman Wayne Bell's commander told him he was the first sailor in Japan to test positive for HTLV-III, and that he would be discharged, though he added, "I'm not sure how to do it." Handcuffs and a Marine Military Police escort seemed appropriate, however, as Bell was transported by truck to the brig, where he was to be locked up "for your own protection." In the back of the truck, the MPs beat him up, assuming that if he tested positive he was gay. Once in the brig, Bell's head was shaved. The next day, the officer in charge of the brig ordered Bell out of his cell, saying he should not be imprisoned if he had not committed any criminal offense.

Bell was then locked in a windowless barracks room. He was not allowed to leave even to go to the bathroom. MPs provided him with a pail. Three times a day, a silent guard brought food to his room. After six weeks' confinement, a guard neglected to lock Bell's door and the corpsman escaped to a nearby clinic, slipped into the pharmacy, and swallowed two hundred Valiums. When he awoke later in a hospital bed with a very bad headache, he learned that he was now on legal hold because he had stolen Valium from the Navy. Bell searched through his toilet kit, found a bottle of cologne, broke it, and slashed his wrists.

After he had been stitched up, he was told he would no longer be locked up—someone had finally checked Defense Department regulations. Instead he would be transferred to the Naval Medical Command, NW Region, also known as the Navy Hospital in Oakland, for more extensive tests.

Although the testing of servicemen like Bell and Herwatt was part of an overall program mandated by the Secretary of Defense, once military officials had the AIDS test, they soon found uses for it outside the previous October's order. Robert Plowman, a gay civilian employee of the Army at Camp Humphreys in Korea, for example, was beaten up by three soldiers on April 16, 1986. When blood appeared in his urine, he went to a military hospital in Seoul, where an Army doctor secretly ran an HTLV-III test on him. Plowman tested positive and the doctor ordered him to the military hospital for further tests. When he refused to go, the doctor said the Army would have to report that he had AIDS to Korean authorities and "they could get nasty." A few days later he was told to resign or face termination. If he did not resign, he would have to pay to get himself and his belongings back to the United States. He did resign and lost all his health benefits.

These incidents in military life only reflected the same sort of AIDS hysteria that was afflicting America at large. Three hemophiliac children with AIDS were burned out of their Florida home, for example. President Reagan said publicly that he would not want his children going to the same school as HTLV-III positive students. After all the harassment Wayne Bell had endured in the Navy, the corpsman called his parents in Oklahoma to explain his predicament and enlist their support—only to hear that, while they loved him, they would prefer it if he never came home again.

The difference between the military and civilian world was that the armed services forced people to take the HTLV-III test—and didn't know what to do with positive results. HTLV-III infected soldiers were supposed to get medical workups, that much was known, so they were shunted off to major military medical centers.

In the Air Force, infected patients went to Wilford Hall in San Antonio. One patient there had spent a weekend in New York City and come back with a fever that Air Force doctors could neither diagnose nor treat. Two days later, the man was dead of *Pneumocystis* pneumonia, one of the most common and most treatable of AIDS diseases. At that point, a nurse treating the patients threatened to call CBS News, noting, accurately, that in any civilian hospital treating AIDS patients, the pneumonia would have been easily diagnosed and treated and the patient would be alive.

Meanwhile, horror stories mounted at Wilford. Some orderlies refused to serve meals to AIDS patients and would instead leave the food trays outside their doors. Those doors were easy to locate because they all bore distinctive red infection control signs. Such stories can be told of many hospitals treating AIDS patients in the United States at that time, but military patients became virtual prisoners of the military's confusion over what to do with infected personnel.

Although such doctors as Major Robert Redfield and Colonel Ed Tramont had given Walter Reed an outstanding reputation for treating AIDS patients, their efforts had not prepared the hospital for the exploding numbers of military personnel with the disease. Safeguards for patient confidentiality were not in place, as Tramont learned when one hospital technician accessed the Walter Reed computers to learn who was HTLV-III positive in order to discover toward whom he could make advances, since he assumed all the infected patients were gay. Patients themselves needed behavioral guidelines, as became apparent when a nurse walked into a room and found two HTLV-III positive patients in flagrante delicto.

Military investigatory agencies also tried to take advantage of the HTLV-III tests. At Wilford Hall, agents of the Office of Special Investigations appeared one day to gather the names of infected patients, presumably to investigate them for homosexuality. An irate nurse ordered the agents out of the ward, leaving no doubt as to what the OSI could do with their plans for gay probes. The agents did not come back. Army CID agents began to push for AIDS tests of soldiers they were investigating for homosexuality. Some officers also sought to abuse the military's authority to test its personnel. After surviving an investigation for homosexuality, one Army mess specialist was told he would not be allowed back at work in the mess hall until he took an AIDS test. Since many commanders saw the HTLV-III test as an assay for homosexuality, they issued clearly prioritized lists of who should be tested first in their individual commands. A petty officer who tested HTLV-III positive recalls that aboard the aircraft carrier USS *Nimitz* the seamen who were ordered to take the HTLV-III test first were almost entirely those widely believed to be gay.

Many doctors proved ill suited for AIDS work. One Walter Reed physician, for example, felt obliged to quote the Bible's incantations against homosexuality when treating patients who tested positive, even citing scripture about Sodom and Gomorrah. Dr. Tramont chastised his colleague, insisting that their job as Army doctors was to manage medical, not moral issues, but the doctor ignored him.

Patients could be just as judgmental. The early weeks of 1986 saw growing tensions and tauntings of newly tested HTLV-III positive personnel by other patients at Walter Reed.

In retrospect, Tramont said, it seemed all the stars were lined up against Private First Class Michael Foster, who came to Walter Reed after he tested positive, just two months into his Army career. The young native of Marion, Alabama, did not have a particularly positive self-image to start with, and then he had to cope with lectures about Leviticus from the moralistic Army doctor to whom he had been assigned. Other noninfected patients were hostile. His future looked even darker than the present. It was a short walk to the deserted stairwell where he ended his life.

Virtually every other military facility treating AIDS patients at the time reported comparable problems with patients. Some experienced soldiers had gone to gay health agencies or public health clinics for anonymous tests before submitting to the military's test, but for many others, the military's test result was their first inkling that their lives had intersected with the deadly epidemic sweeping across the land. Some soldiers tried desperately to avoid the testing, but to no avail. Navy Petty Officer

Phil Nolan said that he would refuse to take the test; he was court-martialed and given forty-five days in the brig.

The younger recruits in particular were unprepared for news that their lives might end prematurely. The lack of any counseling programs only compounded their sense of isolation and despair. Doctors at Wilford Hall documented at least twenty-four suicide attempts in the first two years of HTLV-III testing, and those were merely the attempts they knew about. A detailed study of fifteen suicidal patients found that nearly one-third tried to end their lives within the first week of having tested positive.

Despite the problems, plans for expanded testing proceeded. The West Point graduates of 1986 had the distinction of serving in the first service academy class to be tested for AIDS. By the next school year, all academy students and ROTC candidates would be tested. Defense Secretary Caspar Weinberger was mulling over plans to order AIDS testing of all the Army's civilian personnel. This testing, as well as the accelerated testing of active-duty personnel, boded for even greater strains on the Army medical system. While Walter Reed had typically handled a dozen AIDS patients at any given time over the past two years, by the summer of 1986, doctors projected that between fifty and sixty a month would be trooping through the facility. And those projections proved to be exceedingly optimistic.

By the time of the unquiet death of Private First Class Michael W. Foster, it was obvious that the military needed plans and programs for the hundreds of personnel who were abruptly learning they were infected with the deadliest virus known to modern man.

———

SPECIALIST FOUR JEFF HERWATT found deliverance from his German purgatory through the intervention of a San Francisco AIDS organization, Project Inform, which was committed to providing information concerning AIDS treatments to the growing numbers of gay men who had tested positive for HTLV-III. After discussing Jeff's case with Jeff's mother, Joe Brewer, a codirector of Project Inform, notified the Army that his group would put Herwatt into AIDS drug studies if the Army assigned him to the San Francisco Bay Area. The congressman who had interceded earlier for Herwatt also wrote to the Army suggesting that Jeff be allowed a transfer under regulations allowing for compassionate reassignments.

All this came before Jeff's commanding general, an old-timer up for his third star, a promotion that required congressional approval. The general saw the wisdom of acceding to congressional requests, and approved Jeff's transfer to the Presidio Army base in San Francisco. Herwatt's ordeal was over, at least for the present.

57

Countertrends

APRIL 1986
BALBOA PARK
SAN DIEGO, CALIFORNIA

EVERY AFTERNOON promptly at 4:00 P.M., the British Airways 747 roared into San Diego's Lindbergh Field. Some skeptics asserted that the runway at the international airport was too short for such a huge plane. Indeed, the aircraft needed almost every available inch of runway to make its landing. Therefore every afternoon at four, as the plane streaked directly over the broad grassy swards of San Diego's Balboa Park, everything stopped for a moment and all the young men listened for an explosion. When seconds passed and the sound faded, and it was clear there would be no crash, conversations resumed.

Welcome to "social hour," every afternoon in Balboa Park, especially on weekends. Social hour, when hundreds of young men gathered along the well-manicured lawns to talk and cruise the park's boulevard. The scene was anything but furtive, though only seasoned locals would notice that these men—muscular, handsome, and tanned from the Southern California sun—were not only gay but were also sailors or Marines. Short-cropped haircuts that allowed for some length of hair in the back and the sides, though not enough to hit the collar, belonged to the Navy; men with hair shaved severely close on the sides of their heads were Marines.

Well-informed cruisers could even identify precisely where these social hour visitors came from by the base stickers tucked on the lower left-hand corner of almost every windshield. Red stickers for enlisted men, blue stickers for officers, the names of their bases written out plainly in capital letters. There were no attempts to conceal them.

San Diego, home to one of the greatest concentrations of military personnel in the United States, was also home to an extraordinarily open gay military subculture. Balboa Park had become something of an open-air community center for gay military men. Though there was some cruising—along Balboa Park Drive, which had become known as "The Fruit

Loop," and by the spacious fields alongside nicknamed "Queen's Green" by the young enlisted men—the ambience was more social than sexual.

After daytime socializing, the men could retreat to any number of gay bars that hosted large concentrations of gay military personnel. The West Coast Production Company, one of the nation's biggest gay discotheques, was always packed with men sporting telltale short haircuts. Nights were especially celebratory when an aircraft carrier returned from a long cruise, or at the end of the western Pacific, or WESTPAC, cruises that took thousands of gay sailors away from San Diego for six months at a stretch. It was not unusual to see stocky young Marines moonlighting as bouncers at the gay bars. The more handsome military men often competed in bar-sponsored beefcake contests. Three of the four contestants at the "Mr. Bulc 1988" competition at a popular San Diego leather bar were in the Navy, one an officer. Often, these contestants' pictures appeared in local gay newspapers. Although no one doubted that the Naval Investigative Service or other military investigatory agencies knew that hundreds of easily identifiable military men frequented the parks and bars, witch-hunts rarely focused on the area. Few among the local Navy officials, it seemed, cared.

Although the late 1980s saw a great number of gay people expelled from the military, it also saw the beginning of an even more significant countertrend: the acceptance of gay soldiers and sailors by large numbers of military field commands. Much of the gay military subculture was now only slightly under cover, when it was hidden at all. The trend was most pronounced outside the more conservative bases in the American South. In no area was it more evident than San Diego, where local commands seemed to adopt the live-and-let-live California outlook and only enforced gay regulations when it was absolutely necessary.

Adding to this more relaxed posture was the resolution of growing numbers of homosexual military personnel that if they were ultimately presented with a choice between a covert life-style in the military and an open one outside it, they would choose the latter. Although most realized they could not press the issue of homosexuality, they were also resolved not to live fearfully under its shadow.

Navy Lieutenant Ruth Voor, now three years out of the Naval Academy, was typical of the new breed. Karen Colton's decision to move in with her in San Diego was risky, Ruth knew. Other officers who had attended Annapolis with them would probably recognize that Colton had clearly moved to San Diego to be with Voor, since it was beyond coincidence that Colton would simply happen to end up in the same city as the woman with whom she had spent so much time in college.

But Ruth had decided that furtiveness was not worth the psychological toll, so she did not make a great effort to hide the fact that she and Karen were decidedly a couple. Both women went to local women's bars and were active in Dignity, the organization for gay Catholics. Karen marched in the San Diego gay parades and became involved in the local group that was fighting a statewide initiative campaign to require AIDS testing of California's food handlers and public school teachers. When Ruth went to work aboard the USS *McKee* on Monday morning and was asked what she did over the weekend, she did not hesitate to say that "Karen and I" did this or that. Ruth no longer bothered to fabricate boyfriends.

Most of the officers with whom Ruth worked seemed to recognize that Ruth and Karen were a couple, and no one apparently cared. At a dinner with officers from the *McKee,* the ship's chaplain asked Ruth why she had not brought her roommate. Thinking the chaplain meant the man with whom she and Karen shared their apartment, Ruth said, "He couldn't come." The chaplain corrected her: "No, I meant Karen." When Ruth's boss, a lieutenant commander, married, he invited Ruth to his wedding and amended his invitation with the comment, "You know, it's not just you who is invited. Karen is invited, too."

Comparable stories emerge from every branch of the military during this time. When NIS agent Linda Gautney was transferred from the Norfolk NIS office to London, she found her colleagues as enthusiastic as ever about investigating gays, particularly lesbians. When rumors made it back to the office that there were a number of lesbians working in a particular Navy command outside London, Gautney was dispatched to see if the commanding officer wanted the NIS to launch an investigation. Gautney never looked forward to gay probes, but she remained fearful that if she did not carry out these assignments, she might elicit the same harassment routinely doled out to gays. In this case, however, she found that the Navy commander with whom she met was as reluctant to investigate gays as she.

"Why should we want to investigate?" he asked her.

Linda halfheartedly repeated that gays were security risks and a threat to the good order, discipline, and morale of the United States Navy. The commander did not seem convinced. If the rumors were true, he said, and he did not appear to disbelieve them, then a lesbian investigation could cost him half the women in his command. And that would surely cause a far greater morale problem than just letting the women do their jobs and serve out their time.

"So let's just leave it alone," he said.

Similar logic curtailed other gay probes. At Balboa Naval Hospital in San Diego, when a new admiral suggested launching an investigation of gay corpsmen, another officer advised him, "Admiral, if we fired all the gays, we'd have to close the hospital." It became a joke among gay corpsmen that if the Navy conducted a genuine purge of gays at Balboa, the admiral would be the only one left.

Many other commanders seemed inclined to agree. When launching a lengthy WESTPAC cruise in the late 1980s, the commanding officer of the USS *Cape Cod* used his opening remarks to say that his crew's private life was its own business. He made it clear he would not tolerate drugs on his ship, but the remarks about private lives made it obvious to gay personnel that he would countenance no witch-hunts. Word spread a few weeks later that the ship's legal officer had suggested a lesbian investigation and had been harshly scolded and informed that there would be no gay probes while this captain was in charge.

Conversations with scores of gay military personnel from this period also yielded numerous stories of gay sailors or soldiers who attempted to get out of the service by telling their commanding officers that they were homosexual. More often than not, commanders told the malingerers to get back to work.

Some commanders voiced exasperation at the interest military investigators showed in homosexuality. When a New York state National Guard commander discovered that Army National Guardsman Ellen Nesbitt had acknowledged she was gay to an investigator doing research for her security clearance, Nesbitt's commander asked incredulously, "Why didn't you just lie?" San Diego military counselor Bridget Wilson recalls that when one commander learned that one of his top women was being investigated for homosexuality, he blurted out, "I don't care if she fucks with monkeys, she's a damn good sailor."

Increasingly, senior officers and noncommissioned officers involved in relationships chose not to conceal them. When Master Sergeant Paul Ribarich was transferred to Tampa to work in the Air Force recruiting office there, he introduced his lover Jack to his colleagues. Although Paul referred to Jack as his roommate instead of his lover, it quickly became clear that the pair was a couple. When Paul was invited to dinner, he was told to bring Jack. When the recruiters decided to hold a thirty-ninth birthday party for Paul, they called on Jack to help organize it.

Major John Evans had served sixteen years in the Air Force when he began a relationship with Joe Hoyer in 1982. Hoyer understood gay military etiquette from his service as an Air Force enlisted man in Vietnam. Neither sought to challenge openly the Air Force's gay policies, but neither changed his life to accommodate them either. When the officers' club at Evans's Davis-Montham Air Force Base held their casino nights, Hoyer was often asked to deal. The pair was open about the fact that they lived together, and fellow officers understood that if they invited Major Evans to a party they also invited Joe. When Evans had his retirement luncheon in 1986, his mother sat on one side of him at the head table, and Joe on the other. The presiding officer at the retirement ceremony traditionally hands the retirement certificate and a dozen red roses to the officer's wife in deference to the crucial role officers' wives play in their husbands' careers. When Evans's ceremony was over, Joe grabbed a flower out of the table centerpiece and announced to a staff officer, "I want my rose." No one argued that he did not deserve it.

Retirement ceremonies in the late 1980s increasingly became coming-out rituals for career military people leaving the service, with gay officers using the occasion to speak against the military's ban on gays. When a black E-9 of Evans's acquaintance left the Air Force, he hung a huge sign at the site of his retirement ceremony: "The bitch got away with it," it read.

———————

THE MILITARY'S growing acceptance of its homosexual members paralleled the emergence of an all but openly gay subculture. While military installations had had gay cruising areas since the Vietnam War, gay gathering places now became oriented more toward socializing than sex. On aircraft carriers, out-of-the-way storage rooms became informal gay discos. By 1987, such a disco on the USS *Eisenhower* had evolved into a sort of community center where as many as 200 sailors congregated every day. Even smaller ships had discos. The presence of numerous gay sailors on the USS *California*, including some of very high rank, made Thursday night a ritual, with as many as fifty sailors crowding into a lower warehouse and dancing to the latest disco songs, recalls Terry Ryder, an Arabic linguist detailed to the ship at that time.

Even the most remote bases had gay areas. Gays stationed at the Indian Ocean refueling station of Diego Garcia claimed their own stretch of beach, where "It's Raining Men" blared from a dozen separate tape decks. And the isolated Naval Air Station at Adak, Alaska, had its "gay bay" where lesbian and gay personnel gathered on summer weekends to swim. Just as gay sailors had long given campy monikers to their ships, soldiers now created gay nicknames for their posts. Fort Benjamin Harrison in Indianapolis became known as Fort Benita; Fort Sill, Oklahoma, was Fort Silly.

The increasing gay openness produced new twists on old Navy traditions. The "shellback" ceremonies to initiate sailors on their first crossing of the equator had always contained a homoerotic subtext, but by the late 1980s the tradition, particularly the competition to be King Neptune's queen, had taken on the trappings of overt gay burlesque. Gay sailors came aboard with duffel bags full of wigs, heels, and makeup. During the 1984 WESTPAC cruise, a particularly flamboyant contestant on the USS *Carl Vincent* concluded the talent portion of the competition by gyrating into a wild dance and plopping himself into the lap of an admiral, much to the delight and cheers of the other enlisted men.

The Family permeated even the highest-level security positions in the armed forces. Gay military personnel assigned to the super-secret National Security Agency lunched together at the NSA cafeteria at Fort Meade and called themselves the GMA, Gay Military Association. Air Force linguists—who had Air Force specialty code number 203—had become so preponderantly gay that people called them two-oh-she's.

The emergence of Family units at every base helped gays create their own old-boys' network. A gay detailer at a hospital would likely assign his best gay corpsman to work with a gay anesthesiologist. Family members in motor pools made sure compatriots needing a vehicle went to the head of the line. Gays sometimes even congregated together at their duty stations. In 1983, one airman counted fifteen of the thirty-two airmen in his squadron at Sembach Air Base in Germany as gay.

New conventions emerged. It became a custom among gay men to wear each others' dog tags to signify a "steady" relationship. This helped distinguish a gay soldier's genuine relationship from the "heterosexual" one symbolized by the wedding rings that were increasingly being worn by lesbian and gay service personnel.

Though Ruth Voor was less concerned with concealing her sexual identity than others, she entered into such a marriage, and she was such a convincing bride that the clerk who married her to her friend Joe looked at the couple and sighed, "You're such a happy couple. You're going to be forever."

The comment amused Karen Colton, who with Joe's lover, Petty Officer First Class Todd Quintenz, had served as "best couple" at the wedding. By now, Karen was married herself—to Quintenz.

The two couples had met at the gay Catholic group Dignity, in which all four were active. In the Navy since 1981, Quintenz had recently been transferred to San Diego after a stint as an instructor in the Navy's nuclear power training school in Idaho Falls. The two couples had decided to wed as a matter of convenience, and to gain the same benefits heterosexual couples enjoyed in the military. Joe wanted to be able to visit Quintenz on base, and take advantage of the bargains at the Navy commissary. Karen stood to enjoy the same benefits, as well as the health insurance benefits she would gain as a military spouse. Both Ruth and Quintenz would also receive the housing allowance for married couples. And, of course, the veneer of matrimony would protect them from investigation.

As partners in lawful heterosexual matrimony, Ruth and Quintenz were part of a marriage boom among gay military personnel in the late 1980s. The trend was in large part a response to the increased pressure on both lesbians and gay men stemming from the mounting ferocity of gay purges. It was an easy adjustment for gay military personnel, given that homosexual women and men in the military had generally avoided the separatism so common among their civilian counterparts. The Family was co-sexual on bases throughout the world.

"Contract marriages" were a new phenomenon different from past generations when gay men would marry heterosexual women without informing them of their sexuality. Family marriages tended to be very aboveboard, with prearranged agreements that spouses would testify for one another if either ever came under investigation. Couples composed of two military people could easily explain why they did not live together; military couples were frequently assigned to separate duty stations. And marriage allowed couples to move off base, away from prying eyes.

There was also the naïve heterosexual presumption that anyone married must be straight. This allowed wedded gays a level of protection. In fact, gay investigations during the 1980s were often followed by a flurry of gay matrimony. After the 1984 purge of lesbians at Parris Island, at least a half dozen lesbians married gay servicemen.

One journalist attending a Thanksgiving dinner with lesbian and gay Marines at Camp LeJeune in the late 1980s, for example, watched with amusement while guests took two sets of photos: photos for parents, in which everyone sat with their presumed spouses, and photos for personal photo albums, in which everyone rearranged themselves so they were sitting with their actual partners.

The marriages had their own risks. When sailor Michael Patton married a heterosexual female friend from his hometown of Baltimore, he wrote a prenuptial agreement as to precisely what their marriage would entail and not entail, since he did not want the ersatz nuptials to interfere with a relationship he was pursuing with another man. When the couple separated unamicably two years later, his wife sent their letters of agreement to the Naval Investigative Service, which opened an investigation that resulted in Patton's discharge.

The vogue of contract marriage paralleled a growing concern among homosexual service personnel over preserving their relationships against the pressures of military service. The fact that the Stonewall generation was entering its thirties suggests that this would have happened anyway, and the AIDS epidemic only sharpened the case for settling into long-term monogamous relationships. Since society's rules for homosexuality were constructed with an eye toward keeping it invisible, if not altogether nonexistent, protecting domestic relationships was a difficult task, and all the more arduous for gay military personnel. Increasingly, the difficulties in maintaining relationships with the pressures of investigations and discrimination were cited as reasons for leaving the service.

WITHIN A YEAR of joining the Navy in 1964, Dr. Mike Rankin, a psychiatrist, took his first gay referral from a chaplain, a young sailor confused about his sexuality. Rankins's compassionate response led to more referrals. Wherever he was assigned, word preceded his arrival that here was a sympathetic listener for anyone struggling with gay issues—or for gay sailors who wanted a psychiatrist's support in leaving the Navy. The higher in rank Rankin rose, the more it seemed that his colleagues understood he was gay and the less it seemed to matter.

About the time that Rankin was made captain in the Reserves, he decided to leave his native Arkansas for the greater freedom of living in San Francisco. As the Arkansas state mental health commissioner, he felt obliged to offer the governor a candid explanation for his moving. The governor tried to dissuade him. It did not matter that he was gay, Bill Clinton said, and he hoped Rankin would stay on as chief of the state's mental health programs. But Rankin did relocate.

After several years in San Francisco, Rankin fell into a fairly open gay lifestyle. He was president of the local gay synagogue and became active in AIDS organizations. The turning point in his career occurred when he rented his home to two gay men, who promptly trashed it. When Rankin evicted them, they notified the local office of the Naval Investigative Service. Rankin's commanding officer interceded on his behalf. Leading a gay congregation, he ruled, was simply an exercise of Rankin's freedom of religion. The NIS could "shove off," he said. Later, he asked Rankin to be the godfather to his infant son.

By now, however, rumors had spread that the psychiatrist was gay. When he was assigned to a frigate based at Treasure Island, he found his new command less accepting. One day in 1987, Rankin walked into the ward room to find his chair turned away from the officers' table. In Navy tradition, the turned chair is a request by the officers present for one's resignation. Rankin looked at the other officers in the room, turned his chair around, and sat down to eat.

It was now clear that after twenty-three years on active and Reserve duty in the Navy, Rankin's future was limited. Though he had been in line for an admiral's star and to serve as the senior medical officer of the local command, it was increasingly unlikely. "It's very hard for single men to make admiral," a rear admiral told him bluntly. The next year, Rankin retired.

One Navy fighter pilot learned the nuances of acceptance and discrimination in late 1985 when he was surprised by a fitness report that gave him good marks but did not cite him as one who should be rapidly promoted. The lieutenant had always enjoyed the most exemplary performance evaluations and went to his commanding officer to ask why he had been marked down. None of the officer's explanations made sense, and the pilot bickered with him until finally the commander turned away and walked to the window. "The report doesn't say anything about your girlfriends, does it?" the officer said, staring out the window. The pilot replied that there was no place on the report to discuss his romantic involvements. The captain continued staring out the window. "No," he said pointedly, "there's no place for it."

Apparent acceptance sometimes masked subtle discrimination. After one Navy psychiatrist assigned to Balboa Naval Hospital confided to a heterosexual colleague that he was gay, the colleague began calling on him to take over his shifts. The heterosexual psychiatrist never made an overt threat, but the gay doctor felt the subtext—if he did not accede to his colleague's demands, the other doctor might turn him in.

At any time, a change in command could transform an accepting environment into a hostile one. The leniency of some segments of the military reflected the reality that decisions about pursuing gay investigations were generally made at the field command level. Like their civilian counterparts, growing numbers of these commanders were simply not as antagonistic toward gays as their predecessors had been. However, a large share if not a majority of commanders remained opposed to gays in uniform, which meant that one officer's transfer or promotion could be the harbinger of malicious crackdowns and purges.

Therefore, there was still a danger in living an openly gay lifestyle in the heart of an institution that maintained draconian codes against gays. But the new generation of gay military people had learned to take their chances, and by the late 1980s, it was clear that the odds were in their favor. By then, being gay in the military was like hearing the roar of the 747 every afternoon in Balboa Park. You knew it might end in a great explosion, but usually it made a safe landing.

JUNE 30, 1986
UNITED STATES SUPREME COURT
WASHINGTON, D.C.

IF THERE WERE any questions about the degree of leniency the United States government would afford gays, these were answered decisively when the Supreme Court released its opinion in the case of *Bowers* v. *Hardwick*, the constitutional challenge to Georgia's sodomy law. The justices, voting five to four, issued a decision far more sweeping and far more malevolent than anything civil libertarians had feared.

Rather than take up the broad issue of whether the state had the right to regulate citizens' consensual sexual activities, the court had brushed aside the fact that the Georgia sodomy statute applied to both heterosexuals and homosexuals, and instead focused exclusively on whether the Constitution conferred upon citizens the right to engage in "homosexual sodomy." As if to express his distaste for the whole matter, Chief Justice Warren Burger used the phrase "homosexual sodomy" repeatedly in his concurring opinion. The court's majority also made it plain that their ruling was meant to single out gays and not confront the broader issue of state regulation of sexual conduct. "We express no opinion on the constitutionality of the Georgia sodomy statute as applied to other acts of sodomy," the court said.

The majority opinion was a fascinating work of jurisprudence. Writing for the majority, Justice Byron White ruled that the nation's sodomy laws had "ancient roots" and stemmed from "millennia of moral teaching." No relationship existed between the issues at hand in *Bowers* and those raised by previous decisions regarding abortion and birth control, Burger ruled, because those decisions related to "family relationships, marriage or procreation," and "no connection between family, marriage or procreation on the one hand and homosexuality on the other has been demonstrated. . . ." Exhaustive footnotes recorded when states had enacted their sodomy laws—Connecticut in 1791, Delaware in 1797, and Georgia in 1784—leading White to conclude that it was "facetious" to argue that the gay people's right to privacy might be "deeply rooted in our Nation's history and traditions." The fact that half the states had laws banning gay sexual acts argued against this, White said. Moreover, by saying gays had the right to engage in sodomy because they did so in the privacy of their own home could lead to judicial logic that would also enfranchise acts of incest if they occurred in private, White ruled.

In his concurring opinion, Chief Justice Burger drew far less from the Constitution than from the Bible. Gays had been subjected to punishment "throughout the history of western civilization," Burger wrote, noting that under Roman law, homosexuals could be put to death. He then quoted the famed legal scholar Blackstone, who said that "the infamous crimes against nature" had a "deeper malignity" than rape, and constituted "a heinous act the very mention of which is a disgrace to human nature." Burger concluded, "To hold that the act of homosexual sodomy is somehow protected as a fundamental right would be to cast aside millennia of moral teaching."

In his scathing dissent, Justice Harry Blackmun ridiculed the majority's "obsessive focus on homosexuality" and argued, "this case is about the most comprehensive of rights and the right most valued by civilized men, the right to be left alone." Blackmun mocked the notion that sodomy could be a criminal offense now because it had been for hundreds of years, saying such logic would leave the nation with "moribund" laws that were justified only because "they were in blind imitation of the past." Laws against miscegenation, abortion, and for school segregation had been on the books for generations too, though the Supreme Court had ruled later that they were unconstitutional.

Blackmun opined that homosexual orientation was not a matter of "personal election" but an aspect of a person that "may well form part of the very fiber of an individual's personality. The fact that individuals define themselves in a significant way through their intimate relationships with others suggests, in a Nation as diverse as ours, that there may be many 'right' ways of conducting those relationships, and that much of the richness of a relationship will come from the freedom the individual has to choose the form and nature of these intensely personal bonds."

In the most curious opinion of the day, Justice Lewis Powell, whose vote had changed the outcome of the case, wrote that although he would not rule the laws unconstitutional, he felt there might be an Eighth Amendment issue if someone was put in jail for a violation. Such prison time for private consensual sex would violate the Constitution's ban on "cruel and unusual punishment."

Libertarians compared the ruling to the *Dred Scott* decision in 1857 that upheld the Fugitive Slave Act with the logic that since African Americans were not "citizens" they could not be entitled to constitutional guarantees of freedom. "In the shadow of the *Bowers* decision, the Court will be, in effect, sanctioning discrimination against homosexuals," scholar Serena Novell wrote in the *Howard Law Journal*. ". . . Such action will effectively stop many homosexuals from enjoying the basic freedoms which other citizens enjoy daily." Burger's concurring opinion, asserted legal scholar Yvonne Tharps, "was virtually a primer on Judeo-Christian moral standards and is an inappropriate substitution for rational judicial deliberation." In his pro forma response to the decision, Laurence Tribe wrote that by focusing on Michael Hardwick's sexuality, the Supreme Court had missed the point. The issue was not what Hardwick was doing in his bedroom, Tribe wrote, but what the State of Georgia was doing in his bedroom.

Protests broke out in San Francisco, New York, Dallas, Cincinnati, and Washington within hours of the announcement of the decision. Gays were stunned by the vehemence of the ruling. Even homosexual Republican groups joined the denunciations.

Most heterosexual Americans seemed appalled. One Gallup poll showed that 57 percent did not believe the state should have the power to forbid sexual relations between gay people, while 34 percent approved of such laws. The fact that there was any surprise at the ruling illustrated the profound denial with which the heterosexual majority insulated itself from acknowledging the injustices they meted out to the homosexual minority. The Supreme Court, after all, had only delivered what President Reagan had said he wanted—a society hostile to privacy rights, whether a heterosexual woman's right to an abortion or a gay man's right to have sex. The ruling was less about gay sex than about the extent to which limits of freedom could be narrowed in the United States of America. For homosexuals, at least, they could be narrowed significantly.

Prospects for the future looked poor. By the time the *Bowers* decision was released, Chief Justice Burger had announced he was retiring, President Reagan had named Justice William Rehnquist, the court's most conservative and viscerally antigay member, to replace him, and had nominated Appeals Court Judge Antonin Scalia to take Rehnquist's seat. Scalia was one of the judges who had voted for the *Dronenburg* v. *Zech* decision in 1983, a ruling that had served as a rough draft for the arguments advanced by the Supreme Court in the *Bowers* decision.

Bowers v. *Hardwick* had a devastating impact on the future of all litigation pertaining to gay rights. From now on, whenever a federal court ruled on a gay employment discrimination case, judges hearkened back to *Bowers* as the one Supreme Court precedent on the issue. If homosexuals did not have the right to engage in sex, what right did they have to be exempt from employment discrimination? When gays in uniform appealed their jail sentences on constitutional grounds—and more gays than ever would be imprisoned in the years ahead—military courts invariably pointed to *Bowers* for judicial support to confinement. In thousands of ways every day in the years ahead, the liberties of gay Americans would be circumscribed by the words of *Bowers* v. *Hardwick*.

IN THE MONTHS after it was revealed that Justice Lewis Powell had provided the crucial fifth vote for the *Bowers* decision, a story made the rounds of gay legal scholars. Powell had discussed his decision with a law clerk, the story went, said that he could not see what harm the sodomy laws did since they were rarely enforced, and mentioned in passing that he had never met a homosexual. By all accounts, the law clerk was a gay man who could have quite succinctly explained just what disastrous impact sodomy laws had on gay people, conferring on them the legal status of unapprehended felons. But the clerk did not share this information, nor did he reveal to Powell that he was talking to a gay person. Powell cast his vote in ignorance. According to gay legal observers, the clerk was one of two gay law clerks who had worked for Powell in recent years.

In a discussion with New York University law students in 1990, Powell was asked if he thought he had made any mistakes while he served on the Supreme Court. Powell cited his opinion in the *Bowers* case. "I do think it was inconsistent in a general way with *Roe*," he said. "When I had the opportunity to reread the opinions a few months later I thought the dissent had the better of the arguments." The case was a very minor one, he added, and had occupied not more than thirty minutes of his time.

263 PRINSENGRACHT
AMSTERDAM, NETHERLANDS

THE THREE-STORY BROWN BRICK HOUSE on the edge of one of Amsterdam's most charming canals had been one of the city's prime tourist attractions since World War II. In their first months living together, Air Force Sergeant Jack Green of Soesterberg Air Base was dutifully taken there by his Dutch lover, Albert Taminiau. Jack knew the story of Anne Frank and her family's years in hiding. He had not known how sweeping the Nazi genocide was, or that it was directed at groups other than Jews.

Jack mounted the narrow staircase and entered the small museum on the second floor of the building where the Frank family had concealed themselves through most of the Nazi occupation. He stopped in front of a glass case that displayed various patches assigned to those whom the Nazis did not favor. There alongside the purple triangle for the Jehovah's Witnesses and the yellow Star of David for the Jews was the pink triangle used to mark gays. Jack contemplated the particular madness that would prompt a society to brand others so cruelly. It made him grateful to be from the United States where such a thing could not happen.

58

The Color Purple
(Part 2)

THE PREVIOUS WEEK had been one of the most discouraging in his life, but when Petty Officer First Class T. J. Sterbens walked onto the ninth floor of the Navy hospital in Oakland, he was even more disheartened. The floor was supposed to house the HTLV-III unit for one of only four Navy hospitals in the world designated to evaluate the growing numbers of sailors who tested positive, and yet it seemed as desolate as a ghost town. There was no furniture on the ward, not even wall lockers for sailors to store their belongings. The ward's residents lived out of their duffel bags.

Administrators were adamant that the patients could not leave the hospital, and yet the men were not sick and there was no treatment. There were no counseling programs. They were simply told they were HTLV-III positive and that they might be dead within six months. Then they were shipped to a hospital ward and warehoused until the Navy figured out what to do with them.

The other patients avoided the ninth floor, and cringed when the elevator door opened on it. Like many other HTLV-III positive patients, Sterbens began getting off the elevator on the eighth floor and walking up the last flight of stairs to his ward. One afternoon in the hospital cafeteria, a table full of Marines stared in his direction and began a pointed conversation about the faggots in the AIDS ward. When Sterbens approached the leathernecks to confront them, one told him to sit back down. Sterbens punched him in the face.

Many other patients, however, turning their frustration on themselves, responded to their predicament less straightforwardly. Some dropped all pretense and discretion, as if they had nothing left to lose. They had their military careers and their medical benefits to lose, but, believing they were about to die anyway, few cared. Some tried to hasten the end. One almost made it out of the window; another slashed his wrists; another tried to overdose on drugs. The ninth floor of the hospital commonly known as Oak Knoll seemed a special corner of hell, set aside for a largely gay cadre of military personnel. In those first months of HTLV-III testing there were only two things that would save the growing number of sailors bound for Oak Knoll—Petty Officer First Class Sterbens, and the training paradigm of the United States Marine Corps.

ALTHOUGH A NAVY MAN, Timothy James Sterbens, known to everyone as T.J., took great pride in the fact that he was more of a Marine than most of the Marines with whom he served. When he joined the Navy in July 1976, Sterbens, a native of Alva, Florida, was suffering great conflict over his sexuality. His six-year marriage was coming to an end; he was beginning to understand that his attractions to other men were not a passing phase. Even after he went into the Navy and edged slowly into the gay military subculture of San Diego, he yearned to prove his manhood with the Marines.

T.J. relished his assignment as a Navy corpsman to an elite special operations capable unit, and was thrilled at the chance to undergo the most rigorous training the Marines offered. He was determined to prove he was not a sissy Navy corpsman. As a medic for a reconnaissance unit, Sterbens would be expected to go wherever his Marine squad went, however they went. That meant he did the same training in parachute jumping and deep sea diving as his unit. And when it was done and he received his wings from jump school, he underwent the same macho hazing as the Marines. Silently, he stood against a wall while a Marine buddy bared the quarter-inch steel pins that attach the medal to a soldier's uniform and pounded them directly into Sterbens's pectoral muscle, causing bloody stains on his white sleeveless T-shirt. T.J. was now a Marine, although unofficially.

By early 1986, after nearly ten years as a Navy corpsman, Sterbens had hit his stride with the Third Reconnaissance Battalion in Okinawa. He had recently received a meritorious promotion to petty officer first class. His most recent evaluations marked him a 4.0 sailor—on a scale of 4.0—and credited him as being "the most respected corpsman" with skills that "surpassed most recon Marines." He was, the evaluations said, a "sterling example to emulate."

Then one day in March he was called into an office to meet with his chaplain, the executive officer, and a doctor. Everyone was noticeably uncomfortable. He had tested positive for HTLV-III, he was told. He would be transferred back to the United States. The news stunned T.J. Never again would he see his battalion, which included men with whom he had served for as long as seven years. He had given them their shots for the clap, and sewed their faces together after brawls, and suddenly he would never see them again.

On the flight from Okinawa to Travis Air Force Base, Sterbens tried to figure out what it all meant. He could never go diving again with his Marines, because he would not be allowed to share an air tank regulator. He was not sure if he even had a future in the Navy. Arriving at Oak Knoll, Sterbens felt as if he had been robbed of both his past and his future, while his present bore an eerie resemblance to limbo.

It seemed everyone had a horror story. Some sailors returned from learning of their HTLV-III infection to find that the news had preceded them back to their ships and their belongings had been dumped overboard. One sailor married to a Japanese woman was ordered back to the United States immediately and not given time to inform his wife and children that he was leaving. Some commands were so eager to dispatch their infected subordinates that they sent them off to military hospitals without the pay records necessary for them to draw their salaries, leaving them all but impoverished.

And then the military made the men's plight worse by putting them into hospital wards where they had nothing to do except ponder what seemed an extremely grim future. Ironically, the vast majority was very healthy. According to one study, 91 percent of the Navy and Marine Corps personnel who tested positive during the first two years of the Defense Department's AIDS testing had no visible signs of any AIDS-related disease.

T. J. Sterbens pondered ways to diminish the tedium of life on the ninth floor. He began prodding administrators for programs and assistance. They responded by making Sterbens the leading petty officer of the ward and put him in charge of the hospital's HTLV-III program.

Sterbens had no training in psychology, but he did have Marine Corps training, which instructed him that there was no problem that could not be solved by discipline and calisthenics. Convinced that half the challenge of motivating the other HTLV-III positive patients was to take their minds off their problems, Sterbens applied what he had learned in the Marine Corps and ordered daily 7:30 A.M. musters. They were in the military, he said. They needed to act like it. Every Monday, Wednesday, and Friday morning, T.J. drove his ward mates to a nearby ball field and led them in forty-five minutes of calisthenics.

Some men groused at the Marine Corps approach to their dilemma, but they participated. Then Sterbens enlisted sympathetic chaplains as counselors. Believing that the sailors could also provide each other with the best advice, Sterbens launched a peer counseling program with time specifically designated for sharing health-related anxieties. Slowly, the regimen of exercise and counseling pulled the men out of their collective depression. Some began to believe that they did have a future even with the HTLV-III virus in their bloodstream.

"How long do I have to live?" a sailor sometimes asked Sterbens. "For as long as you make up your mind to," T.J. would say. "You need to decide that for yourself."

AT ABOUT THE SAME TIME that Petty Officer Sterbens was leading his first calisthenics group in Oakland, Army AIDS researcher Robert Redfield was making a crucial presentation at the Second International Conference on AIDS in Paris. The previous year, Major Redfield had raised the ire of more staid scientists when he presented the Walter Reed Staging System with its premise that everyone infected with HTLV-III would eventually contract a serious AIDS disease. The past year of AIDS research had provided substantial evidence that Redfield's depressing prognostications were true, but this did not allay those critics who considered Redfield's new declarations about AIDS to be as outlandish as his last. Redfield's new idea was to commence research for an AIDS vaccine—not merely a vaccine to prevent AIDS infection, but one to use as medical treatment for people who were already infected.

Redfield had conceived the idea one night when he was reading to his children about Louis Pasteur and his controversial suggestion that vaccines could be used as therapy for sick people. Redfield had been thinking that the reason the HTLV-III virus seemed to have such a long incubation period—as long as ten years—was because the body was able to use some unknown mechanism to keep the virus in check. When that unknown mechanism finally failed, the virus rebounded and produced the immunological devastation that led to AIDS. Maybe a vaccine that contained some portions of an inactivated virus could replicate and prolong the body's resistance to HTLV-III.

Redfield had run into Dr. Jonas Salk, inventor of the polio vaccine, at the National Institutes of Health, and explained his theory. He had found an enthusiastic believer in Salk, who said that he was already working on a therapeutic vaccine for AIDS-infected people. But at the Second International Conference on AIDS in Paris, many scientists dismissed the idea. Many were outspoken in the belief that no effective treatments would ever be found for AIDS, much less a vaccine.

Redfield felt that such thinking would only ensure failure; no one would ever solve a problem if they thought from the onset that it was insoluble. Though most scientists disagreed with him, including many in the Army, he pressed on with the research plan he had outlined that day in Paris.

By now, the military's medical branch had enlisted extensive congressional support for AIDS research at the Department of Defense. Congress authorized Walter Reed Army Medical Center to be the Defense Department's lead agency in AIDS research. In order to allow the Army to hire researchers outside the stringent Civil Service guidelines, Congress had already authorized channeling AIDS research funds through the

Henry M. Jackson Foundation, a medical research group affiliated with the Army. By the late 1980s, AIDS studies had become the centerpiece of the foundation's work. The $40 million Congress appropriated for the Defense Department's AIDS studies represented a large share of the total federal AIDS research budget. With Redfield and Dr. Ed Tramont both assigned to the Jackson Foundation's programs, they were able to proceed at a much faster clip than they could have in the more ponderous academically oriented research establishments, most notably the lethargic National Institutes of Health.

The can-do orientation of military medical research, combined with the extensive clinical experience of the researchers, allowed the military scientists to forge significant breakthroughs to benefit AIDS patients. Redfield, for example, had noted that many of the most serious diseases that AIDS patients contracted also struck patients whose immune systems were artificially suppressed by chemotherapy treatments. So Redfield looked into what doctors treating leukemia patients did to help their patients and learned that they administered doses of antibiotics to help prevent the onslaught of *Pneumocystis carinii* pneumonia and tuberculosis, two of the great killers of AIDS patients. By 1986, Redfield was routinely giving his patients the same regimens of antibiotics to prevent pneumonia and TB.

The prophylactic treatments drew criticism from some doctors, who said Redfield should await the conclusion of long-term studies to see if the treatments were effective. Redfield knew that many of his patients would be dead by the time such studies were concluded and ignored the critics. In the end, his hospital saw remarkably few pneumonia and TB cases, while thousands of civilian patients continued to die prematurely because of the reluctance of civilian doctors to follow his lead. The prophylactic treatments for pneumonia were approved by the Food and Drug Administration in 1989 and became the standard of care for AIDS patients—three years after Redfield had begun offering the same treatments to his patients.

Such research successes bolstered the case medical officials had made for a compassionate response to HTLV-III infected soldiers. As Brigadier General Philip Russell told a Senate subcommittee in May 1986, infected military personnel "may be regarded as a unique research asset. For the first time, large numbers of cases will be identified in the initial stages of the disease. . . . We have a unique opportunity to observe the entire natural history of the disease in a basically healthy young population."

The research potential and the large sums of money being funneled into military AIDS research also engendered darker schemes that sometimes found a receptive audience among conservative military scientists. One San Francisco research group affiliated with the conservative Hoover Institution petitioned the military for $12.5 million to study whether AIDS could be transmitted through sweat, sneezes, and mosquito bites. If so, researchers supported "extreme public health measures" against HTLV-

III infected Americans, including "mandatory and overt identification" of AIDS carriers, possible quarantine, and perhaps branding of HTLV-III positive people, an option the study's authors referred to as "a Star of David concept." According to a story on the proposal in the *San Francisco Examiner*, the study's authors acknowledged that some of their measures would be "in direct conflict with the Constitution."

The proposal drew sharp criticism from both Congress and public health authorities. Virtually all the suggested experiments, it turned out, had already been conducted years earlier by federal health agencies, which had concluded that AIDS could not be transmitted through casual contact. The only group the study did not offend was the Army panel doling out research money. In fact, the study had already passed an initial screening by the Army's Medical Research and Development Command at the time it was made public. Outrage over the extraconstitutional policy recommendations quickly ended its chances for final approval.

Meanwhile, new battles were shaping up within the Pentagon over how to handle infected soldiers. Defense Secretary Caspar Weinberger's recommendations of October 1985 consisted of interim guidelines that were only to last for one year. As Pentagon officials began to rework the recommendations, those who had supported discharging of HTLV-III positive soldiers saw an opportunity to reverse the Defense Department's policy to retain them. At the annual Conference on Military Medicine in Bethesda, Navy Captain William McDaniel, commander of the naval hospital at Whidbey Island, Washington, called for the immediate medical discharge of anyone who tested positive.

Other line officers, including the Director of Naval Intelligence, wanted to use antibody test results to determine whether a service member should be allowed a security clearance. The medical officers continued to support retention of infected personnel, but their opponents within the military bureaucracy were outspoken as well. "Everybody on the force is supposed to be deployable," one Pentagon official told *The New York Times*, "and these people aren't."

The scientific terms used in the debates had changed by late 1986. At this time, researchers stopped referring to the suspected AIDS virus as HTLV-III and had given it a new name that stuck: the Human Immunodeficiency Virus, or HIV. As the squabbling over the military's future HIV policies continued into the autumn of 1986, it was not at all clear which side would win.

ONCE AGAIN, forces outside the Pentagon would determine the outcome of the bureaucratic battling. Data about heterosexual AIDS transmission and arguments for the research potential of HIV-positive soldiers had buttressed the case for retention of infected soldiers a year earlier; by 1986, another new phenomenon would help guarantee a permanent policy of retention. By late 1986, it was clear that the numbers of AIDS-infected men in uniform were far higher than scientists had expected, and that these soldiers included substantial numbers of high-ranking officers, including many in remarkably responsible and sensitive jobs.

With each month of testing, the numbers of HIV-infected soldiers grew. When the testing program began in late 1985, doctors predicted they would find 1,000 HIV-positive soldiers and dependents. By autumn 1986, however, testing had turned up 1,500 HIV-positive service members. By the time 62 percent of the military had been tested in February 1987, that number had risen to 2,139. Within a month, when 1.7 million of the military's 2.1 million members had been tested, 2,777 were found to be positive. By late 1987, at least 3,336 military personnel were known to be HIV infected. These numbers did not include dependents, family members, and civilian Defense Department employees.

Of these 3,336 cases, 1,074 were active-duty Army personnel and 387 were Air Force members. The service with the highest rate of infection was the Navy with 1,153 HIV-positive sailors, or an infection rate of 2.4 per 1,000 members, far above the Army's infection rate of 1.43 members per 1,000. Both Air Force and Marine Corps personnel were infected at a rate of 1.0 per 1,000 members.

More startling than the numbers was the fact that the infected soldiers existed at every level of the military. "Staggering" was the word several military doctors later used to describe the numbers of high-ranking HIV-positive officers. In the course of a three-month period, for example, one doctor at a major military medical center informed six active-duty colonels, including a colonel in Air Force intelligence, that they had been infected with HIV. At least five colonels at West Point tested HIV positive, according to one colonel who served at the academy in the late 1980s. The Director of Naval Intelligence expressed his concern in a private memorandum that "a significant percentage of personnel testing positive in the DoD AIDS testing program have security clearances with access to sensitive information."

There were also a large number of senior staff officers at the Pentagon who tested positive. These staff positions had long gone to the best and brightest among the protégés of rising admirals and generals, and these positions drew a disproportionate number of gay officers, who put their work ahead of traditional family concerns. This phenomenon had been a well-kept secret in Washington's gay subculture; with AIDS, the secret was out.

As it had in the civilian world, in the military culture the HIV epidemic fulfilled the twenty-year-old fantasy of gay activists in which all homosexuals become instantly identifiable, or, in the rhetoric of the 1970s, turned purple. The identification included those at the very top of the military command structure. Unconfirmed rumors had a rear admiral being secretly treated at Balboa Naval Hospital, where he later died. By the late 1980s, it was generally accepted among senior Army colonels that one of the Army's most illustrious four-star generals was suffering from AIDS, though the general maintained publicly that he had leukemia.

Navy Captain Art Pearson had just been selected for promotion to rear admiral and had been assigned to take over the command of the Charleston Naval Hospital in Charleston, South Carolina, when he fell ill with AIDS. Though Pearson had already sold his Oakland townhouse and packed for Charleston, he elected to stay at Oak Knoll for his treatment. There were a few doctors who cracked fag jokes at the captain's expense, but most treated the ailing doctor with great deference, putting him in the admiral's suite at the hospital. When Pearson's friend Commander David Derr, who had just been informed of his impending promotion to the rank of captain, was diagnosed with AIDS several months later, Pearson moved him into the admiral's suite as well.

Although some job categories, such as Navy corpsman, had inordinately high rates of HIV infection, no segment of the armed forces was immune from the epidemic. The infantry and airborne divisions at Fort Bragg had long considered AIDS and gays to be problems restricted to noninfantry, but substantial numbers of its own personnel were testing positive. One bisexual noncommissioned officer with the post's 82nd Airborne learned he was HIV positive when his wife gave birth to a baby infected with HIV. He was one of two to test positive in his unit alone. The large number of those testing positive, and the large number of those who were high-ranking military personnel, added weight to the argument for the retention of HIV-positive soldiers. What went largely unspoken was the public relations nightmare that would attend any attempt to weed out so many military men in important positions. The potential for embarrassing lawsuits and bad publicity and the fact that any wholesale purge of high-ranking infected officers could have a deleterious effect on the functioning of the Pentagon forced the military to abort plans to separate HIV-infected personnel.

———

WHILE THE DEBATES raged at the Pentagon, the impact of ongoing uncertainty over future HIV policies was being felt at medical centers throughout the military. In Oakland, when a thirty-three-year-old-lieutenant refused to answer questions about his risk factors for contracting HIV, a higher-ranking officer was called in to persuade him to answer.

It was not that the Navy expected the lieutenant to tell the truth, the commander said; they just needed the paperwork filled out. "We encourage you to lie," the commander said, "because we don't think it's right [to discharge sailors who admit to being gay]. But you have to answer the questions."

The lieutenant was incensed. "I'm wearing the uniform of a Naval officer," he said. "I will not dishonor that uniform by lying."

The commander gave up. The lieutenant did not answer. Three weeks later, however, he was put on report for his refusal. Finally, he agreed to answer the questions, although everyone understood that his answers would be false. Afterward, the lieutenant returned to his room, tore the shoulder boards from his uniform, and tried to jump out of his ninth-floor window. He remained on suicide watch for the next three weeks.

For Corpsman T. J. Sterbens, the drama of coaxing the lieutenant off his window ledge was just one of the complications created by the absence of a permanent policy guaranteeing the job security of his patients. Many counselors made it a point to assure patients that they had no intention of ever informing the Navy of personal information that might emerge during private discussions. As one Jewish chaplain said, "I have a very short memory."

Still, the lack of a clear policy from Washington increased tensions on the ward. One newly tested patient, Commander Mike LaBella, who had served as a Navy judge, became so enraged at the questions he was subjected to that he considered seeking a temporary restraining order to stop the interviews. When LaBella told a friend in the Navy Surgeon General's office about his plans, he was persuaded to hold off filing such a suit until the policy was clarified. Meanwhile, military doctors, including such prominent physicians as Admiral-select Art Pearson, lobbied their allies in Washington to maintain the year-old Pentagon policy.

Within weeks, word came to LaBella that his efforts had yielded results: The new policies to be issued by the Defense Department would call for the retention of HIV-positive personnel. In October, Congress stepped in to forbid the Defense Department from using any information collected during epidemiological interviews for any action against HIV-infected soldiers or sailors. Since the ban was written into the law, sailors and soldiers had the security of knowing any changes must now be enacted by Congress and could not be altered by changing attitudes at the Defense Department.

The new HIV regulations, which were formally adopted in April 1987, included several provisions supported by conservative line officers. HIV test results, for example, could be used in determining security clearances. All soldiers testing positive would be issued formal orders to inform all their sex partners that they were infected. Any failure to inform a sex partner might constitute the violation of a lawful order, a court-martial offense. On the whole, however, the permanent policies were viewed as a defeat for hard-liners. Although their assignment was restricted to the United States, HIV-positive soldiers were to be retained. The dissension that had rocked the armed forces since the days of the Byron Kinney and Ray Orsini hearings was at last resolved.

Moreover, the resolution left the Department of Defense with some of the most humane and progressive HIV guidelines to be found anywhere in the United States. Few civilian employers were willing to offer the guarantees of confidentiality and nondiscrimination that were now formal Pentagon policy. Even as Defense Department officials enacted their nondiscrimination policies, lawyers in the Reagan administration's Justice Department aggressively opposed enacting similar policies in other government departments. President Reagan went on record as being opposed to legislation that would offer employment protection to all HIV-positive Americans. Indeed, it was not until 1992 that the rest of Americans would enjoy the same civil rights that HIV-infected soldiers were guaranteed in 1987.

The policies also proved to be more than soothing rhetoric. Officers who violated a soldier's confidentiality could find themselves transferred and demoted, and many were over the next several years. Though some commanders attempted to use HIV information to discriminate against their subordinates, most infected personnel found the hierarchy intolerant of such actions if the soldier complained to his equal opportunity officer. HIV-infected soldiers discovered in the late 1980s what racial minorities had learned when the military committed itself to equal opportunities for all races—intolerance would no longer be tolerated. Once the new HIV policies went into effect, the military became a model of how employers could handle HIV-infected employees.

THE RESOLUTION of the divisive HIV policy issues coincided with renewed determination among military doctors to provide the best possible medical care for HIV-infected patients. At Walter Reed, the push for better care started with the suicide of Private Michael Foster, an episode that had proved extremely embarrassing for Walter Reed officials. Their mandate, after all, was to make their patients healthy again, not to make their lives so miserable that they would hang themselves. AIDS doctors used that argument to obtain approval for extensive training for doctors and nurses who worked with AIDS patients. Shortly after Foster's death, Walter Reed announced the establishment of a minimal care ward specifically for its HIV-positive patients. Comparable initiatives were undertaken in the Air Force, as well.

Throughout the services, there was a growing tendency among gay military physicians to gravitate toward AIDS work. Some uniformed gay doctors came to it by a chance assignment; others specifically sought out AIDS patients. At both Wilford Hall and Walter Reed, openly gay physicians, usually at the rank of captain or major, played an increasingly prominent role in the care of AIDS patients. In Naval hospitals, gay corpsmen, including many who were HIV infected themselves, volunteered to work on the HIV wards and became a mainstay of AIDS care.

The phenomenon was evidence of the reluctance with which commanding officers, particularly in the medical branches, were enforcing the ban on gays. Homosexuals were not supposed to exist in the military, so it was unthinkable that the forbidden orientation could be a factor favoring a soldier's assignment to this or that job. Yet this was precisely the case at hospitals throughout the military. For some doctors, who were officers and tended to be more discreet, the assignment to an AIDS ward some-times marked their first extensive networking with the military's gay subculture.

The Navy, however, continued to be inconsistent in its handling of HIV-positive patients. Balboa Naval Hospital in San Diego developed a high-powered HIV program that was generally considered among the best in the military. The HIV program at Oak Knoll had less support from hospital officials. While the San Diego effort was headed by two captains, one lieutenant commander who spent only one-third of his hours on the HIV ward was in charge in Oakland. Given such limitations, Oakland's HIV program remained largely the creation of corpsman T. J. Sterbens. As his efforts took hold, the mood shifted from the despair that had marked the first months on the ward. Incoming phone calls were likely to be answered, "AIDS are us," by one or another patient. Patients who had once cowered under the gaze of sailors in the elevator when they pressed the ninth-floor button had grown more secure in subsequent months. If one got a dirty look now, he might lapse into a fit of feigned coughing that tended to quickly clear the elevator of intolerant occupants.

A number of gay corpsmen volunteered to work on the ward, bringing with them their beefcake posters and a devil-may-care insolence toward the military's antigay atmosphere. As camaraderie grew, patients began referring to the top-floor ward as "the penthouse in the sky" or just "heaven." They joked that they were "the grand prize winners," since only people blessed with HIV infection got into the penthouse. At night, sailors signed themselves out to journey to "the promised land," the San Francisco skyline framed in the ward's large west-facing windows.

However, the official antihomosexual stance of the armed forces re-mained an impediment to AIDS care. Few military AIDS programs drew from the expertise of existing AIDS organizations, since virtually all those groups were based in the gay community and any dialogue might appear to countenance homosexuality. For that reason, Sterbens was denied per-mission to line up speakers from the San Francisco AIDS Foundation to counsel infected sailors about their future. Since virtually all public health brochures concerning AIDS also originated from such organizations, they were banned from the hospital, too.

The gay regulations also had a chilling effect on the doctors who volunteered to work on the disease. One military doctor who pioneered AIDS treatment for Air Force personnel came under investigation after two Air Force Academy cadets found an art project he had made of photographs he had taken of his AIDS patients. The cadets believed the photos were homoerotic and therefore the doctor must be gay. The doctor survived the probe and his photographs were later hung in New York City's Museum of Modern Art. When one military doctor helped organize a local AIDS support services facility, he found himself at loggerheads with gay militants who demanded that he march in the gay parade. When he declined to so jeopardize his career, some threatened to turn him in as gay to the military. The threat persuaded the doctor to discontinue his help in providing AIDS services to civilians.

Faced with a dearth of speakers for their HIV program, some patients themselves stepped in to fill the gap. At Oak Knoll, Captain Art Pearson spoke several times about AIDS. Sterbens gritted his teeth when the captain talked openly about being gay and about the opportunities the Navy offered gay sailors who were willing to devote themselves to the service. Sterbens worried that these disclosures would end in an administrative discharge hearing, but Pearson felt insulated from such discipline by his high rank. No one moved against him.

If there were lingering fears about disclosures of sexuality on epidemiological questionnaires, a new ritual evolved in the latter months of 1986 and the first part of 1987. The nurses or doctors administering the questionnaire now frequently began their interviews by assuring their subjects that they could answer any way they chose, that there was no way for the military to check the accuracy of any response, and that even if there were, they had no desire to do so. If these suggestions were not comforting enough, some interviewers openly advised the respondents to lie, which virtually everyone did. For this reason, military AIDS statistics continued to be loaded with personnel who claimed to have contracted the AIDS virus from prostitutes in Germany or the Philippines.

The problems confronting HIV-positive gays in the military mirrored those faced by HIV-positive gay men throughout the world. It was as if an entire generation was told that some time within the next five years or so they would be hit by a bus and die. In the meantime, they were expected to go on with the business of living. They could expect little sympathy from those around them, most of whom felt that gay men were to blame for their predicament. If solutions were to come, therefore, gays would have to find them themselves.

The ability of gay men to forge these solutions, at a time when they were simultaneously coping with one of the most brutal viruses in the history of medicine, remains one of the great untold stories of the 1980s. Faced with medical systems that were not equipped to provide support services for people with AIDS, the gay community simply created their own. Faced with public health agencies that were skittish about discussing gay sexuality, the gay community had devised their own AIDS prevention campaigns for "safe sex," which had produced remarkable changes in sexual practices in the gay community. Faced with a scientific establishment that was slow to provide treatments for AIDS patients, the gay community by the late 1980s had started its own research and supply networks for experimental AIDS drugs.

In the military, this phenomenon meant that the creation of HIV programs became the work of gay medics like T. J. Sterbens and the many gay military doctors who also enlisted in the fight against AIDS. Although the mainstream society tended to view gays as the core of the problem with AIDS, the truth was that gays were by now the most important provider of potential solutions for AIDS.

SEPTEMBER 15, 1986
SAN FRANCISCO, CALIFORNIA

LEONARD MATLOVICH had felt fatigued in recent weeks, but he had been working too hard. Then came a persistent cough—a chest cold, he thought. When he finally made it to a doctor, he got the bad news. He had contracted *Pneumocystis carinii* pneumonia; he had AIDS.

The case was mild and Matlovich took sulfa drugs for it on an outpatient treatment basis, but he developed a severe allergic reaction to the medication and within a week he was in the hospital. His infections proliferated. He lost forty pounds in a week. His friends feared he might be dying, but within a month he was better. In December, he was among the first patients to be given the new drug AZT. Too tired to work at the Ford dealership any longer, Matlovich went on disability and found a new cause—he would be an AIDS activist. With this resolve, Leonard Matlovich began what would be his final crusade.

— 59 —

At the Buccaneer Motel

AUGUST 1986
MARINE CORPS RECRUIT TRAINING DEPOT
PARRIS ISLAND, SOUTH CAROLINA

WHEN LANCE CORPORAL BARBARA BAUM first appeared at the gay bars around Parris Island, other lesbian Marines were suspicious. Baum was new to the base, and might be a plant by the Naval Investigative Service, a concern heightened by the fact that she was in the Military Police, an agency that sometimes worked closely with the NIS. Moreover, Barb openly denied she was a lesbian, which made people wonder exactly why she spent so much time with them.

Even the friend who introduced Barb to local gay life, Renee Mueller, assigned to the Marine Corps Criminal Investigation Division, sometimes worried that Barb might be an NIS plant. But Barb liked to party and Renee liked to party, so the pair struck a keen friendship. Slowly, Barb began to realize that some of her other friends were also gay, Barb later recalled. In April, after she had been on base for five months, her closest friend from technical school, Diane Maldonado, confided that she was in love—with another woman.

Diane had a boyfriend, Marine Sergeant Steve Davis, but he had been deployed to Okinawa, and she had been lonely. Diane worried that Barb would hate her now, but Barb said of course not. Meanwhile, Barb had taken a house off base with Lance Corporal Becky Feldhaus, a gay woman who was also becoming a good friend.

Concerns about lesbian purges influenced every major and many minor decisions of the women's lives on Parris Island. It was a significant reason why Barb and Becky had decided to rent together on Azalea Street in Beaufort. The nearest gay bar was The Who, forty-five miles away in Savannah, Georgia, where NIS agents were known to scout for lesbian Marines. With their nondescript government cars, dark suits, white shirts, and stern demeanor, the agents were easy to spot, however. When suspected agents entered The Who, the Marines raced to the bathroom and dispatched a civilian to ask the agents to identify themselves, which usually scared them away. But such encounters heightened anxiety. The women found it safer to socialize at private parties. Barb and Becky rented their three-bedroom house as much to have a place to be with friends as to live. And during the sultry summer weekends of 1986, as many as fifty women gathered there to drink beer, munch potato chips, and watch movies.

Barb still believed she was straight, but she was now very comfortable with lesbians, even as she began to appreciate how dangerous it was to be a gay woman in the Marines, particularly at Parris Island, where ferreting out lesbians was a major preoccupation. Renee Mueller was a victim in 1986 after she went on leave to San Antonio and loaned her car to a friend. Her car was impounded for expired tags. While the car was impounded, an MP searched it and found an intimate letter from Mueller's lover in the locked glove compartment. The MP took the letter back to his station, read it aloud and passed it around. A lesbian dispatcher in the MP station called Renee in San Antonio to warn her.

When she returned, a CID agent she knew took her into his office. Friend to friend, he said, he thought she should confess to being homosexual. Although she was only twenty-one, Mueller had served in military law enforcement and was not susceptible to the usual pressure tactics. The CID agent asked a few more questions, such as the nature of the relationship Renee had with the woman who wrote the letter. "Do you love her?" he asked. "I love her like a sister," Renee said. Before she left the interview, the agent asked her to sign the form on which he would type up their conversation. Renee signed.

The next time she saw that form, it was filled with inaccurate or incomplete assertions. The agent had noted that Renee said she loved her friend, but neglected to add "like a sister." The statement looked like a straightforward confession of homosexuality. Renee's career was over. The dispatcher who had phoned Mueller to warn her was herself court-martialed for "obstruction of justice," but was acquitted.

For all the dangers, it seemed inevitable that Barb would eventually establish an intimate friendship with one of her lesbian friends. That friend was Diane Maldonado.

In September, Diane's former boyfriend, Steve Davis, returned from Okinawa and was assigned to the Marine Corps Air Station in Beaufort. Davis, who later declined to comment on the case, was, according to testimony, cordial to Barb at first, but later wanted to know why she and Diane spent so much time together. What did they do together? he asked. Then Barb heard a rumor that Diane's roommate had turned her in to the NIS for being gay.

Davis, meanwhile, was becoming more unpredictable and confrontational. Diane confided to Barbara that she had heard stories about him, stories that he had held his last wife hostage for four hours in their home and had to be dragged out of the house in handcuffs. Davis had told her he had once shot at someone who was dating his girlfriend. (Davis later denied shooting at anyone, and said he had only told the story to impress Maldonado.) And there was the threat Davis made repeatedly to Diane: If he could not have her, no one would.

Diane was frightened for her life, and Barbara's. She went to the Marine Corps' Criminal Investigation Division to complain of Davis's harassment. Though CID agents said they would investigate, Maldonado heard later that they had told Davis not to worry, they were not going to interfere in his private business. The next day, Davis was back at Diane's barracks, wanting to see her.

Davis continued to spread rumors about Baum and Maldonado. By now, he had also contacted the local NIS office to share his suspicions. It was in such an atmosphere that Diane and Barb decided to get away from it all for a night, and took off for the Buccaneer Motel.

BARBARA BAUM'S CAPTAIN had already suggested that she grow her hair a little longer, maybe wear a little more makeup. She might also date some men, the captain suggested. "People might think . . ." the captain said, his voice trailing off.

"I don't care what people might think," Barb snapped back.

Like so many other women in the military during the late 1980s, Barbara Baum would suffer ferociously for not caring what people thought because this was a time when military men were thinking a lot about lesbians in uniform. Their concern seemed to grow in direct proportion to the incursion they felt women were making into their territory. With attempts at "womanpause" blocked by Congress, women now comprised record numbers of the post–World War II military. By September 1986, 217,430 women served in the armed forces, or about 10.1 percent of the nation's 2.16 million active-duty service members. Nearly 1,500 women were enrolled in the military academies.

The unprecedented numbers of women led to an unprecedented level of sexual harassment, a phenomenon intricately bound up with the harassment of lesbians. Mary Beth Harrison learned this lesson as the fifth senior woman aboard the USS *Grapple*, an auxiliary rescue and salvage ship commissioned in early 1986. Early on, Harrison noticed that many of the junior enlisted women spent too much time in their sleeping quarters during liberty. They were afraid to come out, she discovered. A male petty officer had been harassing them, one young woman in particular. Harrison confronted the man and informed him that he would be officially charged with sexual harassment if he continued to bother the women.

Harrison's stout defense of the junior women from male advances provoked the men on board to allege that she was lesbian and protecting the women so she could have them for herself. When another young woman refused the advances of several men, they accused her of having a relationship with Harrison. The rumors dogged Harrison for the rest of her Navy career, and led to her eventual discharge.

Senior women who defended other women from harassment often found themselves under comparable suspicion. At Fort Polk, Louisiana, an Army lieutenant was investigated for being a lesbian when she stood up for women who were being propositioned by the lieutenant's supervisor, who wanted the women to engage in ménages à trois with him and his wife. The lieutenant survived that investigation. Later, on a new duty assignment with a Military Police battalion in Germany, she saw a similar scenario play out when a male captain made a pass at an enlisted female, who complained to the battalion commander. When the captain was confronted, he insisted that the woman be investigated for being a lesbian. And so she was.

Female officers who angered enlisted men serving under them sometimes found themselves on the wrong end of a homosexual investigation. One soldier angry at his female Army captain informed the Criminal Investigation Division she was gay in early 1987. During the CID interrogation that followed, the captain was asked repeatedly to provide proof of her heterosexuality. "Do you have a boyfriend?" agents asked her. "Isn't there a man in your life?"

The fear of being branded a lesbian often made women acquiesce to harassment—and at times even rape. Navy Lieutenant Bonnie Clark was at a farewell party for another officer when an officer in her command began plying her with drink. After the party, he insisted that Clark was too drunk to drive, and offered to take her to his nearby home, make her some coffee, and help sober her up. Once there he became amorous, and although Clark protested verbally she was afraid to resist. She tried to think what a straight woman would do in her place. She had seen what happened to other women when they fell under investigation; she did not want it to happen to her. The man raped her, but Clark did not file charges. She knew being drunk would damage her credibility in a rape trial and was afraid the Navy would end up investigating her for being homosexual.

Those women who did press rape charges sometimes found a remarkable lack of concern among their superiors. Army reservist Pam Mindt was sexually assaulted by a Reserves sergeant while performing her weekend duty at Fort Riley, Kansas. When she complained, an Army investigator recommended the sergeant be brought up on charges. His command, however, disagreed, and allowed the reservist to retire from the Army with his full military pension. Mindt sued him for civil damages in a civilian court, and she was awarded $60,000 for her "emotional distress."

According to official Defense Department statements, the military had a "zero tolerance" policy toward sexual harassment, but this policy found expression in word more than deed. One study conducted at the time found that 70 percent of women in the armed forces said they had experienced sexual harassment. At an Army equal opportunity conference held in Europe, for example, Command Sergeant Major Karen Erickson, one of the four highest-ranking enlisted women in the Army, put the blame on officers "who fail or are incapable of stopping the kind of behavior that fosters sexual harassment . . . [those] who have the 'boys will be boys' attitude and use it as an excuse, a valid excuse, for things like harassment and discrimination."

In such a hostile environment, witch-hunts of lesbians proliferated throughout the military. Investigations continued to focus on women in nontraditional jobs, such as the Military Police. A 1986 investigation of women Military Police assigned to the United States Military Academy at West Point resulted in the discharges of eight women, or about one quarter of the females in the academy's MP detachment. Two of the women denied to reporters that they were lesbian, and said they had been named because agents for the Criminal Investigation Division threatened women with imprisonment and bad discharges if they did not name others. One thirty-one-year-old mother of two, who vehemently denied being homosexual, attempted suicide after her gay discharge.

The West Point investigation provoked local news coverage concerning the large presence of homosexuals at the academy. Newspapers ran stories quoting anonymous cadets and officers discussing the academy's gay subculture. The coverage made Army public affairs specialists apoplectic. "There are no known homosexuals in the corps of cadets or regular Army. None!" Colonel John P. Yeagley, West Point public affairs officer, insisted to reporters. As for the investigation, he added, "We're not on a witch-hunt. West Point is not a prison. It is not the KGB. People are treated with dignity and respect."

A purge of suspected lesbian Air Force personnel swept through Yokota Air Base near Tokyo in early 1987. Air Force Lieutenant Pam Lane came under investigation after the Office of Special Investigations interrogated a nineteen-year-old enlisted woman who had tested positive for marijuana. Offered a better discharge if she turned in gays, the woman said she had had sex with Lane twice. Basing its conclusions on the lesbian vampire stereotype, the Office of Special Investigations advanced the accusation that the twenty-three-year-old Lane was the leader of a lesbian recruitment ring at Yokota and was enticing younger women into the gay lifestyle.

Officials prepared charges of sodomy and indecent acts against Lane. Facing a court-martial and prison time, she wrote the ACLU and Congresswoman Patricia Schroeder, an outspoken supporter of both gays and women in the military. After Schroeder intervened, criminal charges were dropped and Lane was allowed to resign, though without an honorable discharge despite enthusiastic recommendations from her supervisor. According to Lane's count, at least four women were discharged from Yokota for being homosexual during that investigation. At about the same time, an investigation of the Marine women's volleyball team in Okinawa resulted in four more discharges of suspected lesbians.

The purges sometimes affected women in extraordinarily high ranks.

It was during this period that the woman in line to be the first female commanding officer of a Navy ship was quietly derailed from the assignment after rumors spread that she was gay. In the mid-1980s, one of the first female admirals was quietly processed out of the Navy when it was suspected she was a lesbian. According to a personnel man who saw the paperwork, the Navy officially cited "mental reasons" as the rationale for the separation.

The purges reflected the military adamancy about denying honorable discharges to accused gays, particularly lesbians. None of the eight women in the West Point probe received an honorable paper; all received general discharges. None of the women discharged during the Yokota investigation received honorable discharges. Of the 1,648 enlisted personnel officially discharged for homosexuality in 1985, more than 600 were denied honorable discharges, despite the 1981 regulations that mandated that all homosexuals receive honorable discharges unless there were allegations of misconduct.

THE IRONY OF the greater focus on homosexuals among military women was that the proportion of lesbians was actually decreasing. As the military became an increasingly acceptable career path for women, the armed forces began drawing from a broader spectrum. While military lesbians estimated that homosexual women comprised perhaps as many as 35 percent of females in uniform during the early 1980s, they calculated that by the late 1980s the percentage had dropped to 25. This trend paralleled increased tensions and disaffection between straight women and lesbians.

Heterosexual women accused lesbians of excluding straights. Lesbians responded that they were forced to be cliquish, because the pressures of ongoing investigations made them unsure of whom they could trust. Gay women resented that straight women with children could use that as an excuse to beg off hard duties or long hours. And they especially disliked women who succumbed to male sexual advances in order to curry favor with their superiors. Lesbians sometimes talked about heterosexual "zebras"—women who would lie down with men to get their stripes. To make matters worse, straight women sometimes turned in the names of women they suspected of being lesbians. These strains added a dangerous new element to the hazards lesbians faced in the military.

SEPTEMBER 30, 1986
BUCCANEER MOTEL
BEAUFORT, SOUTH CAROLINA

WHEN SERGEANT STEVE DAVIS went to the Parris Island barracks looking for Diane Maldonado, one of Diane's friends said she had gone to the Buccaneer, a one-story motel on a highway, next to a mobile home park.

When Davis arrived at the motel, the desk clerk denied that Maldonado was there, but Davis saw her name on the register and her room number.

Baum and Maldonado were lying in bed watching Johnny Carson when Davis burst in, tearing the chain lock out of the door and splintering the wooden door frame. The NIS was waiting for them outside, he shouted. Diane threw a chair at him. Davis grabbed Baum's car keys and her wallet from the dresser and ran out of the room.

Barbara went out after him. They talked in the parking lot; Davis was clearly distraught and wanted Diane back. He asked Barb to intercede for him. Barb said she would, if Davis would return her keys. He refused and Barb went back inside.

The two women decided to wait Davis out and watched movies all night on HBO. He was still there in the morning. Finally, Barbara called her roommate, Becky Feldhaus, who was famous for her temper and who promptly showed up and engaged Davis in a shouting match over Baum's keys. Feldhaus had heard the stories of Davis's violent past, and she concocted the most extreme threat she could. Davis should not mess with The Family, she warned him; they could have him hurt, they could even have him killed.

Davis responded that he would call the NIS about Barb and Diane. Feldhaus looked across the parking lot and saw a nondescript green car. Inside, a man wearing sunglasses was watching them. "I think they're already here," she said.

Indeed, they were.

UNITED STATES NAVAL ACADEMY
ANNAPOLIS, MARYLAND

WITH JUST SEVEN MONTHS until his graduation, Midshipman Joseph Steffan felt he was near the finish line. He had made it. As a battalion commander in charge of 600 midshipmen, and given the responsibilities that still rested on him as one of the three top-ranked midshipmen in his class, Steffan always looked forward to Glee Club trips away from the academy.

On one such trip, at a bar after a performance with a plebe member of the Glee Club, Joe, filled with camaraderie, confided for the first time that he was gay to another midshipman. He felt safe making the confidence to a plebe; he believed his rank protected him. The plebe did not seem shocked or disgusted and within a few weeks Joe had told a second classmate.

During Christmas vacation, the second midshipman to whom Joe Steffan had disclosed his homosexuality told his parents in rural Kentucky about it. And he mentioned it to his girlfriend, who told her parents, who, it turned out, knew a captain who was legal adviser to the Naval Academy's superintendent. Quietly, in March 1987, the Academy began an investigation.

BARB AND DIANE ended their relationship several weeks after the blow-up at the Buccaneer Motel. Barb was drinking a lot these days, and one night was arrested on a drunk and disorderly charge. This was about the same time her commanding officer told her that she was the subject of an NIS investigation into a "hotel incident." The captain appeared to be an ally. When the investigation dragged on with no resolution, he told Barb that he would personally ask the NIS to either press charges or halt the probe.

Two days before Thanksgiving, the NIS asked to see Diane Maldonado. The next day Barb was called in and told she was "suspected of homosexual activity." Both women refused to answer questions; both asked to see a lawyer.

Barb's drinking escalated. She quit once for three weeks, but then started again, waking up one Monday morning without the vaguest recollection of the past two days. It frightened her. Early in 1987, Baum enrolled in the Navy's alcoholism rehabilitation program, and the program seemed to work for her. When she got out, she was feeling on top of the world, and everything seemed fresh. Back at Parris Island, she drifted away from her old friends who partied hard and drank. Nor did she hear any more from the NIS. She put the matter out of her mind.

FEBRUARY 20, 1987
ABOARD USS *IOWA*
INDIAN OCEAN

WITHIN WEEKS of his assignment to the USS *Iowa* in November 1986, Gunner's Mate Third Class Kendall Truitt had found a best friend, Gunner's Mate Second Class Clayton Hartwig.

Both were single; both were better-read than most of the other sailors; both were interested in guns; both liked the same kind of music, like the dance group Depeche Mode.

When the *Iowa* pulled into ports, they preferred going to art museums and historical sites rather than socializing in bars. Both men spent their share of time with prostitutes, but their generally low-key demeanor set them apart from other sailors. This made their friendship stronger.

Like other best friends on ships, the two men sought shifts together when it was their turn to stand watch at night. Ken Truitt especially hated the tedium of the watch. On the night of February 20, he was bored and wanted to nap. Hartwig would hear nothing of such malingering, and told Ken so. Ken, who knew judo, started wrestling with Hartwig. Both men were big, Ken six-foot-three and Clay six-two; they were evenly matched for wrestling, but Ken had more experience and threw Hartwig to the deck, at which time another crewman who was taking soundings shone a flashlight on the pair.

The next day, the master-at-arms called Truitt and Hartwig into his office. "We have someone who saw you kissing," he said. "I don't think so," Truitt replied. Nevertheless, they were now formally under investigation for "indecent acts."

Both men signed statements saying they were not gay. Truitt explained what had happened and was written up for nonjudicial punishment for dereliction of duty, since he was supposed to be making rounds, not taking naps or wrestling on deck. Hartwig was ordered to take an HIV test. It came back negative. He was demoted one rank and warned not to wrestle again on duty.

That was where the matter officially ended, but gossip about the episode spread throughout the ship. During the *Iowa*'s long deployments, crewmen alternated as the butt of their mates' jokes. One gunner's mate was teased because he was fat, another because of his oversized glasses. Clay and Ken were ribbed for being fags. The jokes were good-natured but the suspicion was there nevertheless, both because of the wrestling incident and because of the pair's indifference to the usual sailorly carousing. It did not help that both were handsome—nineteen-year-old Truitt was blond with angular features; twenty-two-year-old Hartwig had dark, moody eyes and a strong cleft chin. In recent years in the military, as in civilian society, being handsome had come to be associated with being gay.

The teasing always passed when it became someone else's turn, and neither Truitt nor Hartwig took it seriously. It was just another shipboard rumor that would eventually fade into the ether, they believed, as shipboard rumors do, especially false ones. And that would have been the case, except for events that occurred two years later.

60

HOMOVAC
Prisoner Number 73343

PAUL STARR had believed his record would protect him. He was the youngest United States Air Force squadron commander in Europe. At an earlier assignment, he had been named Strategic Air Command Administrator of the Year, Junior Officer of the Quarter, and later Junior Officer of the Year, and Administrative Officer of the Year for his base in 1985. His proficiency reports routinely rated him among the top 2 percent of his peers. Moreover, he had a long record of civic activities before he joined the Air Force. He had served on the Governor's Commission on Youth in California when he was still in high school; he had founded a Search and Rescue team in his hometown of Pacifica, California, served on the board of directors for the March of Dimes, and received numerous awards in the Civil Air Patrol. With this background, Paul Starr could not believe the Air Force would send him to prison.

But here was the judge, Colonel Bryan G. Hawley, saying, "Captain Starr, this court-martial sentences you to forfeiture of all pay and allowances, to be confined for eighteen months, and to be dismissed from the service." With those words, Paul Starr became a convicted felon on his way to the military prison at Fort Leavenworth. Even when he heard the sentence, it was impossible to believe, and the twenty-eight-year-old captain told himself it was not happening.

The events leading up to that afternoon in Germany had begun more than a year earlier when agents from the Office of Special Investigations interrogated a frightened young airman and, with the usual threats of jail time and a bad discharge, persuaded him to give names of homosexuals. He named more than one hundred and twenty, according to the word around the base. Among them was Captain Paul Starr, who denied being gay when the OSI called him in.

The matter seemed to end there, until many months later when an acquaintance of Starr, a bisexual sergeant who socialized on the periphery of The Family at the medium-sized air base in southern Germany, was arrested and court-martialed on charges of beating his wife, perjury, and forcible sodomy. After he was sentenced to three years in prison, the sergeant was persuaded to help the OSI on other investigations for a reduction of his prison time. Soon afterward, the sergeant persuaded Paul Starr to hire his wife as a secretary. Thinking he was doing the man a favor, Starr did; nor did he think much of it later when the man's wife seemed interested in whom Starr was dating.

Shortly after one such conversation, however, OSI agents called Starr into their office and repeated the dialogue Starr had with his secretary verbatim. If she had not been wired, he thought, she had at least provided an extraordinarily accurate account of his social life. The information was so precise that Starr considered himself doomed. Thinking he could mitigate his losses, he told the OSI what was true and denied what was not.

Even when Starr heard that he would be court-martialed he did not believe it. Charges were filed all the time against officers and later dropped. His alleged crimes consisted of fraternization with an enlisted man and three charges of sodomy, one with a German civilian. Given the fact that on his base there were even marriages between officers and enlisted personnel, Starr did not think a prosecution of fraternization would stand, since the enlisted man whom he had dated was outside Starr's chain of command. The other charge was making false official statements—his denial to the OSI a year earlier that he was gay.

At the court-martial, Starr waived his right to a jury and asked that his case be heard by a single military judge, believing he would fare better. He was not prepared for the fierce arguments of the military prosecutor, Captain Lawrence Price. "When one man takes his penis and puts it in the mouth of another man, or in his anus, and ejaculates . . . that's a disgusting act." Price argued strenuously for prison time, saying, "Confinement is appropriate because confinement is really the only way . . . that you can tell the people of the community . . . that we're going to uphold the standards of the officer corps of the United States Air Force, that if somebody who's an officer . . . goes out and commits these kinds of despicable acts with enlisted folks, we're not going to just brush it under the door. . . . The reason we're asking for those three years of confinement is because we've got to send the message to anyone who fraternizes, to begin with . . . and who commits these kinds of blatant acts of homosexuality, deserves to be imprisoned and deserves to be punished."

In his statement to the judge, Starr said, "The crimes of sodomy and fraternization are not normally punishable in any other context. . . . I do not see myself as a criminal in the classic sense and consequently would implore this court to find that confinement would not be appropriate for a person who has worked as long and as hard as I have for the betterment of my society."

After a half-hour deliberation, the judge returned his verdict and Starr was escorted by Security Police to the bachelor officer quarters where he was allowed to pick up some belongings before being taken to the base Security Police Station, Building 18. The facility held only three cells; in the neighboring cell was the sergeant who had persuaded his wife to turn on Starr.

NEW YORK CITY

VERNON "COPY" BERG had maintained many friendships from Annapolis, and even did occasional work for the Academy, such as designing sets for school plays. Early in 1987, a friend on the school faculty and his wife visited Copy in New York and introduced him to Joe Steffan, who was traveling with them as part of the Academy choir.

Copy, who was enjoying some success as an artist, showed Steffan around the studio he shared with artist Charlie Bell. Berg found Joe to be exceedingly polite, pleasant, and undoubtedly heterosexual; he did not give their meeting any more thought. "Was I that straight when I was in Annapolis?" Berg asked his faculty friend at the end of the meeting. Yes, the friend said, he was.

UNITED STATES NAVAL ACADEMY
ANNAPOLIS, MARYLAND

MIDSHIPMAN BATTALION COMMANDER Joseph Steffan did not really believe he would be kicked out of the Naval Academy. He trusted that his accomplishments and his rank as one of the three top officers in his class would protect him. Steffan had believed in the Academy, and believed that the Academy believed in him, which was why he responded as he did when the commandant of midshipmen looked Steffan in the eye and asked if he was gay.

Though Steffan did not believe he would be dismissed, the interrogation that day was not entirely unexpected. He had learned he was being investigated from one of the two midshipmen he had confided in the previous autumn. That midshipman had told NIS agents that he did not know whether Steffan was gay; the other, however, said he was. Rather than wait for the Academy to move, Joe seized the initiative. Graduation was less than two months away. If he could not save his Navy career, maybe he could save his diploma. Steffan approached the captain of chaplains, and the chaplain talked to the Academy superintendent, who suggested that Steffan get a lawyer. He would not be allowed to graduate.

To appeal his case directly to the superintendent, a meeting had to be approved through Steffan's chain of command, which included Captain Howard Habermeyer, the captain of cadets. Just weeks earlier, Habermeyer had awarded Steffan a special commendation for "outstanding leadership." Habermeyer asked if the meeting Steffan sought concerned "the NIS investigation currently under way." Joe said it did. Habermeyer got straight to the point.

"Are you willing to state at this time that you are a homosexual?" he asked.

Joe hesitated. He could deny the charge and the matter might probably end there. But he had been denying he was gay all his life. He also remembered the honor concept, by which he had lived his whole Academy career: "A midshipman does not lie, cheat or steal."

"Yes, sir," Steffan said, "I am."

He still did not believe they would throw him out; he was confident he would have a fair hearing. That night a group of his friends loaded up all his belongings in a pickup truck and drove him off campus, so he could stay with a sympathetic civilian instructor and avoid the Annapolis rumor mill.

The next morning, rumors were already circulating. At 7:00 A.M., the brigade commander told his staff about Steffan's investigation, in order, he said, "to quell the rumors." At formation, the word spread. By 8:00 A.M., nearly every student at the Academy knew. As a battalion commander, Joe Steffan's portrait was displayed prominently in the main office at Bancroft Hall. By that afternoon, however, there was an empty space on the wall where it had hung.

The next afternoon, a performance board met to evaluate Steffan's academic performance, which had been outstanding. Under Academy rules, however, homosexuality was incompatible with good performance. An admission of homosexuality therefore automatically indicated bad academic performance, which if confirmed by an academic board would be grounds for dismissal. On his way into the board, the Academy's deputy commander offered Joe advice: Don't be adversarial, he said, you'll only make it harder on yourself.

The board chairman asked if Steffan was gay. Joe said he was. After sixty seconds of deliberation, the board recommended that Steffan receive an F in military performance.

Meanwhile, Academy officers attempted to widen the investigation. The brigade commander interviewed a friend of Steffan's named Rick for several hours. The commander knew there was a whole group of gay midshipmen, he said; he knew there were orgies. All Rick had to do was name the others, and he could be out of the Academy quickly, within a few hours. Rick denied knowing anything of the sort. In truth, Steffan was the only gay midshipman Rick knew.

Stories proliferated. According to one story, Steffan had been discovered having sex with a janitor in a closet. Other stories had it that he was caught with another midshipman, and that he had been seducing plebes all year. There were even Joe Steffan jokes. "What did Steffan say as he was leaving the Academy?" went one. "I sure hate to leave my buddies behind."

Other gay midshipmen watched with great fear. Although midshipman Orlando Gotay was in the same class as Joe Steffan, they were not friends; neither had suspected the other was gay. Just months before Joe's investigation, Gotay, a native of San Juan, Puerto Rico, had made his first trips to the gay bars in Washington, D.C., and had met a number of staff officers from the Pentagon, which informed him that there were many gay people in the military. It made him believe that he could slip by during his four year obligation to the Navy, but Joe's predicament made him wonder.

Two midshipmen Steffan had known at Annapolis told him in confidence that they too were gay and wished him the best. Other midshipmen sent messages of support through his friend Rick. Few were willing to voice an opinion for Steffan publicly.

Steffan thought about going public and challenging the discharge. He talked to the one person who might understand his predicament, the artist he had recently met in New York, Copy Berg. Berg warned Joe to be prepared for the Navy to be ruthless. The NIS would probably tail him, as it had followed Copy; Joe should not expect a fair fight. Joe's mother was adamant that Joe not go public. The family was going through enough with the discharge, she said. Don't make it any worse. Still, Joe was unsure and made an appointment with the ACLU lawyers who had been contacted by Copy.

Joe still hoped that he might be allowed to get his diploma when the academic board met to decide his future. Days later, a hearing was set. Joe decided to hold off on any decision until then.

———————

IT WAS DURING this period that a young midshipman in the Navy's ROTC program named Robb Bettiker was on a cruise to become familiar with Naval sea duty when a senior chief petty officer explained offhandedly what happened if a submarine crew discovered that one of its members was gay. The sub surfaced and a helicopter came in from the nearest aircraft carrier to take the homosexual away, he said. Bettiker had never heard of this procedure, but the older petty officer said the operation even had a name, reduced like every military term to an acronym: HOMOVAC, or homosexual evacuation.

The late 1980s was a period of many HOMOVACs from the United States military. The phenomenon was noteworthy less for the numbers involved—according to official Department of Defense statistics the services were discharging fewer people than previously for homosexuality—than for the growing reluctance of commanders to burden the discharged personnel with punitive paperwork. Even with this bureaucratic sleight of hand, the numbers of investigations and discharges were impressive. Between 1986 and 1990, military investigative agencies conducted 3,663 investigations on suspected homosexual service members, some of which involved scores of suspected gay soldiers. In that same period, 5,951 were officially discharged for homosexuality.

The HOMOVACs of the late 1980s were distinguished by their ferocity rather than their sheer number. Interrogations grew ruthless. During a purge of gays at Chanute Air Force Base in Rantoul, Illinois, one young airman, Steve Ward, was simply locked in a closet until he provided authorities with the desired confession. Locking suspected gays in closets became a popular interrogation technique during the 1980s, particularly in the Air Force. The purges became more sweeping, too, and the punishments increasingly draconian. It became more common to send a convicted homosexual to prison, and again and again courts-martial did.

Perhaps it was because everyone understood that the battle to preserve the homosexual regulations would ultimately be lost. The times were turning against the exclusion policy, and this would become even more apparent in the years ahead. Homosexual soldiers were also easier targets, because gays within the armed forces, like lesbians and gay men everywhere, were living more and more openly.

Later, Paul Starr realized he had been imprisoned so that the Air Force could make an example of him. The gay community at Spangdahlem was getting too visible; sending one of its highest-ranking members to prison would hammer it down, at least for a while. Toward this end, the Air Force gave Starr's court-martial very big play. News of it made page two of the European edition of *Stars and Stripes*, as well as coverage in the *Air Force Times* and Armed Forces Radio Network. Such cases had what military prosecutors referred to as "deterrent value."

MARCH 26, 1987
SOESTERBERG AIR BASE
SOESTERBERG, NETHERLANDS

COMFORTABLY SETTLED into his two-year relationship with a Dutch citizen, Air Force Sergeant Jack Green felt safe from the prospect of gay purges. In 1986, he had watched a gay witch-hunt unfold at his base outside Amsterdam. Nineteen men had been discharged in that investigation, Green heard. One day he saw five men being led around by two Security Police officers. "Those are the faggots," a coworker told him.

It was a little thing that proved Green's undoing. His lover, Albert Taminiau, had borrowed his car for the day. Across the lake near their home outside Amsterdam, Albert was stopped in a routine traffic check by Dutch police. The traffic checks are meant to monitor everything from drunk driving to stolen cars. When they stopped Albert, the police took great interest in the fact that his car had the special license plates designated for United States armed forces, which allowed the car's owner to avoid paying expensive Dutch road taxes. Dutch citizens like Albert were prohibited from driving cars with such plates. Albert showed police officials the car's registration papers and explained that it belonged to an American military friend. This explanation was not satisfactory, however, and the car was taken to a nearby police station, where it was impounded. Sergeant Green would have to pick it up himself, Albert was told.

Before the pair went to the police station, Albert called a lawyer to see if there would be any legal penalties if they simply acknowledged to the police that they were a couple and Green's loan of the car was a domestic matter rather than a matter of state interest. The lawyer assured them that they were protected under Dutch law, which banned discrimination of all forms against gays, and suggested it would be best to level with the customs officials and pay whatever fine was demanded.

That was just what the pair did. Jack explained that he and Albert were a couple, although he would appreciate it if authorities did not mention that to the Air Force. Customs officials said there would be a delay in returning the car. Shortly afterward, a customs agent came to Jack and Albert's residence with paperwork. Finally, he said, Green would have to pay $2,000 in import taxes in order to get the car returned. Green paid the fee and then heard it would be another two to three months before he could have the auto. Albert threatened to hire a lawyer. The threat appeared to rile customs officials.

One week later, Dutch military police came to the men's apartment while Green was at work, to search the apartment "by request of the American government." Albert was reluctant to permit it, but the Dutch MPs insisted. "There's a lot of things you would not want your neighbors to hear," they said. Albert acceded. The MPs were particularly keen on searching the bedroom. By now, of course, customs officials had informed American military authorities of the nature of the relationship between the sergeant and the Dutchman; the MPs knew what evidence they had to get.

When Green returned home and realized that the Dutch had informed the Air Force he was gay, he decided to go on the offense. The next morning, he went to the Dutch military attaché on the Soesterberg base. The attaché declined to say anything except that an agency of the United States government had asked the military police to investigate Green's living situation. Green knew enough about the Dutch abhorrence for prejudice against minorities to know that the military police would be in trouble if their participation in an American military investigation of gays became public.

The next day, Green's first sergeant told him that he was under investigation for homosexuality. The Dutch customs officials had tipped them off, the first sergeant said. Green was ordered to the Security Police office to be interrogated. He was urged to "make it easy on" himself and confess. He refused. The Security Police warned that if he did not confess, he could be punished "to the fullest extent of the law," which was five years at Fort Leavenworth. Green still refused.

Green immediately contacted Dutch gay-rights groups that put him in touch with Major Abel van Weerd, the Dutch army officer who headed the government-sanctioned organization for gays serving in the Dutch military. Van Weerd called the commander of the Dutch military police in Amsterdam. He thought he understood why the customs officials had called and the military police had assisted the Americans. Although the Dutch defense ministry had banned discrimination against gays in 1974, pockets of resistance to accepting gays remained in the armed forces, and the Dutch military police was among them. Nevertheless, since their actions were contrary to the nation's official policies of nondiscrimination, both van Weerd and they knew that the government stood to be embarrassed if the military police's action against Green ever became public.

Days after van Weerd's intercession, Green's commander called the sergeant into his office. The investigation was closed, he said, on one condition. Green must tell no one, especially in the Dutch media, what had happened. As Green recalled it, his captain said, "If I see one scrap of paper with your name on it, the investigation will be opened again."

Green's first sergeant was more blunt. "If you speak one word to the press," he said, "I guarantee you'll see jail time." On the official files concerning the matter, the first sergeant wrote that "the allegations have been determined to be unsubstantiated."

––––––

FEAR OF DISCOVERY, exposure, and disgrace reached into the top echelons of the military. In the end, it was his fear of exposure that drove one gay brigadier general not to allow his name to be put up for major general. It was a decision he made in the 1980s, and one that still haunted him years later.

He had joined the Army in World War II, and served as a young officer near London. He was introduced to gay life there when a group of officers from the Royal Air Force took him to the bar at the Ritz Hotel, which was crowded with other RAF officers. In the following months, they took the American lieutenant under their wing, and explained how one could live a discreet gay life without anyone knowing. He left the Army at the end of World War II as a lieutenant colonel and went into the Reserves, returning to active duty during the Korean War and becoming a general's staff officer. He survived the purges and even the terrors of the McCarthy era. It was a bad time to be gay in America and an even worse time to be homosexual and fall in love, which is what the officer did, with the manager of a Washington movie theater in February 1951; they moved in together in November.

Every two years, when a new security clearance investigation was required, there came a period of sleepless nights pondering whether this misstatement or that slipup in pronouns one day might end a career in its fourth decade. He survived it all, and when his name came up on the list of one-star generals selected for a second star, he knew he should be enthusiastic, even flattered, but at night, he tossed and turned at the thought of still another background investigation. *We see that you lived for years with another man. A single man. You've never been married. How would you describe your relationship?*

There were some people who could stand it. He knew a gay four-star general, the former chief of the United States Air Force in Europe, who had managed it all the years of his career, even with a handsome young colonel as his lover. But this brigadier general believed he was stretching his luck. He declined the rank of major general and retired.

Years later, speaking of the day he turned down a second star, his voice cracked. "It was the most difficult thing I've ever had to do," he said, "but I figured I had to quit while I was ahead."

THE MILITARY'S GAY POLICIES, like the overall social ambience from which they grew, affected all sorts of relationships. In the late 1980s, a young soldier went home to tell his father that he was gay. As he edged toward the subject, the older man stopped him. "Don't say anything that I may have to repeat if I ever have to testify against you," he said. The father wore the uniform of a major general; he knew what could happen. In his own way he was trying to protect his son, and the younger man understood this and changed the subject.

THE WHITE HOUSE
WASHINGTON, D.C.

THE POLICE WERE STANDING nearby. Leonard Matlovich knew that getting arrested while demonstrating at the White House was something a liberal would do. Already, his friends teased that he sounded like a Democrat, calling for more government action on the AIDS epidemic. But even his diagnosis with AIDS had not made him a radical, or even a liberal; he just wanted to live.

To dramatize the need for more funding and government action against the disease, Matlovich and a crowd of 350 gay activists had marched on the White House, while across town 6,000 AIDS researchers were meeting at the Third International Conference on AIDS. Leonard wore his Air Force jacket, covered with his various medals, and carried an American flag. After several indignant speeches, he joined the crowd that sat down in the middle of Pennsylvania Avenue, blocking traffic. The police, wearing long yellow plastic gloves to protect themselves from AIDS, moved in to arrest the group, prompting demonstrators to chant, "Shame on you—your gloves don't match your shoes."

For the first six years of the epidemic, the gay community had been a surprisingly passive population on the political front. Most of their energy was spent in establishing support services for AIDS patients, which made sense, since if gays did not perform such tasks themselves, no one else would. When they demonstrated about AIDS, however, the protests tended to be sentimental, candle-lit affairs with anguished pleas for help. By 1987, as HIV testing alerted tens of thousands that their lives were on the line, this changed dramatically, mobilizing staid figures like Leonard Matlovich, who would previously never have considered breaking the law.

Matlovich's new career as an AIDS activist gave him a purpose again. His entire life, it seemed, had been a struggle against one form or another of hatred; now society was not even going to let him die in peace, and he was going to fight that. When a Northwest Airlines ticket agent told Matlovich he could not fly the airline to a gay-rights march on Washington in October because he had AIDS, he left the airport—and returned with television camera crews and newspaper reporters to record the refusal. After several days of unfavorable publicity, Northwest announced it was rescinding its policy of banning AIDS patients from its flights.

A comparable fervor swept the gay community throughout the country. When he found out he was HIV positive, Copy Berg became involved with the Gay Men's Health Crisis and when a militant activist group called the AIDS Coalition to Unleash Power—or ACT-UP—was organized, he began attending their angry protests. Army Sergeant Jeff Herwatt, who had been locked up in Germany after his diagnosis with AIDS in 1985, also joined ACT-UP San Francisco in its formative days.

Herwatt and the other HIV-infected soldiers found themselves at the cutting edge of military AIDS policy, having to forge their own futures. When Herwatt sought advanced training, he was denied it, presumably because the Army did not want to pay for schooling for a soldier who might die soon. Herwatt fought the denial and won training not only for himself but for other HIV-positive soldiers. He was also among the first known HIV-positive soldiers to seek reenlistment, forcing the Army to decide how it would handle that. Lieutenant Colonel Jerry Roberts, another HIV-infected soldier, took Herwatt's cause to Washington and ultimately secured not only permission for him to re-up, but a policy decision that would ban HIV status from deterring reenlistment.

Military medical centers continued to navigate around the military's see-no-evil posture toward homosexuality. Doctors in the HIV ward at San Diego's Balboa Naval Hospital created a highly regarded program that included weekly support group meetings that earned the facility its nickname "the hug ward." Still, when speakers came from the gay community center, they were listed as representing the "Center for Social Services."

At Oakland Naval Hospital, daily battles with the Navy took its toll on corpsman T. J. Sterbens, who saw the level of his disease-fighting T-4 cells drop from a healthy 896 to 190 in just nine months. Knowing such low T-4 cell numbers put him on the brink of illness, Sterbens took his medical retirement from the Navy.

The epidemic hit hardest those young men who had come of age in the Vietnam era, in large part because they entered the gay community during the sexual heyday of the late 1970s. By 1987, the biggest provider of AIDS care in the country was the Veterans Administration, tending to more than 1,500 AIDS patients. By 1987, Danny Flaherty was taking care of his sick lover in San Francisco, Democratic party activist Jim Foster had buried his lover and was sick himself, Pete Randell's immune system was declining, and a former Navy corpsman named Jess Jessop was battling the disease in San Diego.

Several weeks after returning from the White House demonstration, Matlovich suffered a gallbladder attack. He survived that episode, but while in the hospital, he fell ill with pneumonia again and nearly died. He revived and set about working on another project, a memorial for the gay-rights movement in Washington.

UNITED STATES NAVAL ACADEMY
ANNAPOLIS, MARYLAND

DAYS BEFORE the academic board was to meet to decide Joe Steffan's future, word reached him through a faculty member: If Steffan decided to pursue legal action, the Academy would court-martial him. Another indication of the Academy's get-tough attitude occurred just as Steffan was about to walk into the academic board hearing and a major ordered him to go immediately to the school's tailor and have the four stripes removed from his shoulder board. He was no longer a battalion commander and was not entitled to wear the stripes. When Steffan explained that his hearing was due to start in five minutes, the major said it did not matter, they would wait. The stripes had to go. Now.

The board voted unanimously to dismiss Steffan immediately, refusing his request that he be allowed to graduate. An academy officer laid out his options. Joe could appeal the decision to the Secretary of the Navy, which would be futile, or he could resign, in which case his discharge certificate would read "voluntary resignation." If Joe appealed, his discharge papers would indicate that he had been dismissed for homosexuality. No matter what, he would be leaving the Navy.

Joe contemplated a court fight, but his mother argued strenuously against it and in the end this persuaded him. Days later, Joe Steffan packed his belongings into his car and drove away from Annapolis.

MARINE CORPS RECRUIT TRAINING DEPOT
PARRIS ISLAND, SOUTH CAROLINA

THE DEFENSE ADVISORY COMMITTEE on Women in the Service, or DACOWITS, had been organized in 1951 to monitor the concerns of military women. In the summer of 1987, the committee toured Navy and Marine bases in the western Pacific. Tensions were simmering between lesbians and straight women in the Marine Corps, particularly in Okinawa, where a group of heterosexual female Marines met privately with DACOWITS members. The straight women complained about being housed in barracks separate from men, claiming that the living arrangement promoted lesbianism. What was more, the Marine Corps did not enforce its regulations against lesbians as aggressively as it did against gay men. Lesbians, the straight women said, were tolerated. One barracks at Camp Butler, the women said, was so gay that they called it "Lessy Land," and the situation was tolerated by noncommissioned officers who, they implied, were gay themselves.

On August 26, DACOWITS chairman Dr. Jacquelyn Davis wrote a memo to Marine Corps General Anthony Lukeman that included the complaints about lesbians. The memo's reference to lesbians, although it comprised only a few sentences in the lengthy account of the DACOWITS trip, became the immediate focus of concern among the generals in charge of the Marine Corps.

Several weeks later, Corporal Barbara Baum and her roommate Lance Corporal Becky Feldhaus heard the rumor that heterosexual women in Okinawa had fingered not only lesbians serving in Japan but had complained about homosexual female drill instructors at Parris Island. Talk of an imminent witch-hunt spread.

Baum had heard such talk before, and did not take it seriously. Despite the best efforts of Steve Davis, attempts to open an NIS investigation on her had failed. Both she and Diane had slipped through, and Barbara was scheduled to be transferred to Hawaii in December. Her career seemed on track.

A few weeks after she heard the first rumors, she heard them again, this time from a friend who always seemed to know what was going on at Marine Corps headquarters in Quantico, Virginia. The service's commanding generals had had a meeting, Barbara's friend said, and decided that there were too many lesbians in the Marine Corps. They needed to be cleaned out. The generals did not care how it was done, only that it was done, completely. They even discussed specific lesbians they wanted discharged from Parris Island, right down to this gunnery sergeant and that lieutenant colonel. Be careful, Barbara's friend warned, all hell was going to break loose.

61

Foreign Affairs

THE AGENTS FROM the Office of Special Investigations had told Captain Paul Starr that they would take time off his prison sentence if he would give them names of other homosexuals. Starr knew gay colonels and one gay Air Force general, but he would not betray others as he had been betrayed and he refused to cooperate. After being held at the Mannheim military prison for more than two months until his commander approved his sentence, Starr was finally put on a plane bound for Fort Leavenworth.

Military planes flying prisoners into Fort Leavenworth used the civilian airport at Kansas City, unloading their prisoners at a civilian terminal. There, prisoners were handcuffed and shackled, and marched single file through the airport. For Paul Starr, that was the most memorable humiliation of his ordeal, seeing mothers pull their children away from him in alarm as he was escorted to a waiting military van.

For confinement purposes, prisoners were classified by the severity of their crimes, the danger they might pose to others, and whether they had committed offenses against people or property. Though Starr was imprisoned for having consensual sex with another adult in private, his crime, sodomy, was still considered a crime against another person, which categorized him as a danger to others and earned him maximum custody, where his cellmates were murderers and rapists.

After his first few days in his six-by-ten-foot cell, Prisoner 73343 had one priority—to get out, and as soon as possible. Starr became a model prisoner. He worked in the mental health department; he never caused problems.

THE STORY OF an unnamed gay airman who had been identified by Dutch customs officials for U.S. authorities first aired in a broadcast of "After the News," a show of investigative journalism like "Sixty Minutes" in the United States. Mindful of the promise that he would serve time in jail if he talked to the press, Sergeant Jack Green had done his best to keep the story quiet. Gay Dutch military personnel, however, had pushed it to reporters on national newspapers, and within two weeks it was on the front pages throughout the country.

Green was removed from his job in munitions and put to work on twelve- and sixteen-hour shifts at the base post office, six and sometimes seven days a week. His commander told Jack bluntly that he was going to jail. He was convinced Green had talked to the press and that, he said, was against the law. Homosexuality, he added, was good for five years at hard labor in Fort Leavenworth.

That Dutch military police had illegally turned over information to the U.S. military began to take the shape of a domestic political scandal. In Parliament, some members compared it to the Dutch police who helped round up Jews for the Nazi occupation army. Senator Marie Louise Tiesinga Autsema called for an investigation. The controversy makes it clear that in some countries, cooperating with American authorities to enforce their antigay regulations was considered embarrassing, if not politically disastrous. It was a mark of the United States' increasing isolation among Western nations due to its continued legal harassment of its homosexual citizens.

By 1987, sixty-four nations had legalized homosexuality. The trend was most pronounced among industrialized Western nations. The European Court of Human Rights ruled in 1981 that laws restricting private gay sexual acts by consenting adults were a violation of the right to privacy outlined in the European Convention on Human Rights.

The acceptance of gay people in the armed forces of most European countries paralleled a growing acceptance of gay civil rights throughout the continent. Gay sex was legalized in Norway in 1972 and in 1981 that country became the first in the world to pass federal legislation guaranteeing gay rights. In 1977, the military's Joint Medical Services circulated a letter to all Norwegian military doctors asking that they "shall do their best to protect homosexual persons from discrimination." Ireland dropped its gay exclusion provision at this time, in the same policy shift that allowed atheists and agnostics to serve in their military. In 1978, Denmark changed its regulations to allow gays to serve in their armed forces. Sweden dropped their exclusion of homosexuals in the military in 1980.

In Austria, gays were allowed to serve in the army, though they were to be punished if they had sex with a subordinate or in a military barracks. In Belgium, not only was discrimination against gays forbidden in the military, but military personnel were not allowed to ask questions "that could contain any infringement on the private life sphere." The 1985 law passed by the French National Assembly banning discrimination against gays throughout the country was interpreted by courts to allow the end of the ban on gays in the French armed forces. In 1984, Spain lifted its ban on gays when the Parliament repealed the article in its Military Justice Code that made homosexuality a punishable offense. Australia ended its exclusion of gays in 1992, shortly before the federal court of Canada lifted the ban.

In Germany, gays were allowed to serve as draftees but not as professional soldiers. Still, the German attitude toward the possibility that there might be gay officers even in its highest ranks was far more lenient than the American. In late 1983, for example, rumors surfaced that General Guenter Kiessling, a German four-star general serving as deputy commander of NATO, frequented gay bars in Cologne. Citing concerns that the bachelor general might be a security risk, the West German defense minister dismissed Kiessling, although he denied the charges. But the German Parliament rallied behind the general, eventually forcing Chancellor Helmut Kohl to reinstate him to his full rank. "Mistakes," Kohl said, had been made.

NATO's United States commanders became so sensitive about the possibility of a gay German general that Air Force General Richard Lawson, the Deputy Commander in Chief of the U.S. Military Command, took the unusual step of banning any mention of the general's homosexuality in the *Stars and Stripes*. The order, he said, was to protect "the good order, and discipline" of GI readers, who "work and train closely with their German allies." The ban was lifted after it provoked congressional criticism.

In Israel, the nation where defense issues are taken more seriously than almost any other issue, gays have also been able to serve openly since 1982. Before that, Israeli authorities took homosexuality into account when devising a potential soldier's "profile," the numerical score every recruit received before entering the Israel Defense Forces. Although homosexuality was not a disqualifying factor for service per se, in practice it reduced a profile number by so much that one would be unlikely to qualify. In 1982, in response to a query from an Israeli gay-rights organization, a military medical officer ruled that homosexuality was "not a medical topic," and would no longer be weighed in determining a soldier's profile. Though homosexuality was still weighed as a factor in denying security clearances, openly gay officers and noncommissioned officers served uneventfully in the Israeli Defense Forces from then on.

Israeli military personnel say there was one key factor in the decision to allow gays to serve. Since defense policies are a matter of the nation's survival, the Defense Ministry is historically allowed to determine its own policies without political interference, based on purely military considerations. Allowing gays into the military was deemed an effective policy shift for military reasons.

Gays were not universally accepted among Western armies, though virtually all those countries that still maintained antigay exclusion policies in the late 1980s were in some way related to one country—Great Britain. When the British Parliament legalized all sexual activity between consenting adults in 1967, the armed forces were exempted from this law. Military regulations still punished "disgraceful conduct," defined as conduct of an "indecent or unnatural kind," with two years of imprisonment. As in the United States, British military authorities exercised their prerogative to jail gays. Of 228 gay soldiers and sailors discharged from the British military between 1987 and 1989, 32 were court-martialed "with disgrace," and several were sent to prison, usually for sentences of three to five months.

The British regulations, like the American ones, led to allegations of abuses. In a 1987 lobbying effort to repeal the military's exemption from Britain's sexual reform laws, the Campaign for Homosexual Equality, one of England's largest gay-rights groups, surveyed former and current military personnel. The survey found that gay service members were subjected to long and repeated interrogations and a demeaning discharge process that led some to consider suicide. Though the reform effort gained support in the press and among Labor party members of Parliament, it was defeated by Conservative party members.

Nations with historic ties to Great Britain also maintained the exclusion of gays. New Zealand decriminalized gay sexual acts in 1986, but the law exempted the armed forces, whose penal codes still punished sodomy by up to seven years' imprisonment.

By the late 1980s, the only other nations where antigay policies seemed secure were the Union of Soviet Socialist Republics and the Union of South Africa, which maintained that homosexuality "is very undermining for any society or organization and is unacceptable for the South African Army."

———————

ABOUT A MONTH before police impounded Jack Green's car near Amsterdam, Captain Frans van Dorp, a thirty-two-year-old infantry officer in the Royal Dutch Armed Forces, told his general that he was gay. "No problem," the general said. "Your private life is your business."

The response was what Dutch generals were supposed to say ever since the Netherlands became the first nation officially to allow gays to serve in the armed forces in 1974. Though the abolition of the ban on gays in most European armed forces occurred uneventfully, general acceptance of the reform throughout the military took many years.

Not long after van Dorp informed his general, for example, a teacher in a military training course announced that he gave poor marks for "emotional stability" to any student he knew to be gay. When van Dorp confronted the instructor after class, the teacher admitted he knew such grading was not military policy, but that "it was for their own good." Two years earlier, during screening for a security clearance, van Dorp had filled out a form indicating among other things that he lived with an English man. The security investigator later asked a friend if van Dorp was gay.

Though such incidents also occur in the U.S. military, they are officially forbidden by the Dutch. When van Dorp learned of the security investigation, for example, he warned the investigator that he would report the incident if he did not receive his security clearance. He received the clearance.

Since 1980, a group of gay Dutch military personnel had actively pressed gay concerns for the Dutch armed forces. In 1984, the precursory group gained more prestige when Major Abel van Weerd, who had just come out as gay, took over its chairmanship, reformed it, renamed it by its acronym, the SH&K, and within a year had requested and been granted a meeting with the defense minister to discuss gay matters. In the years since then, van Weerd had worked with Parliament to obtain official government recognition and subsidies for the SH&K, and had made huge strides in educating military personnel about homosexuality. The SH&K gained a similar status to that of the unions representing various Dutch military personnel. This recognition meant that the group could meet with the defense minister twice a year and make personal contacts with the ministry in the event of an emergency.

Meanwhile, other military officers stepped forward to accelerate the glacial pace of change within the Dutch armed forces. When Lieutenant Colonel Rene Holtel became commander of a training company for noncommissioned officers and regular soldiers, he saw it as an opportunity to sensitize future soldiers to homosexual issues. In human relations classes, he said that he was gay, and took questions from his soldiers on that subject. The center's commander was not enthusiastic about Holtel's innovative training and gave him a low evaluation, writing that since Holtel was gay, he should not be promoted too fast. Holtel appealed the evaluation and won.

Not long after that, Holtel was selected to serve as a deputy director of material for the army. The job put him under a conservative brigadier general who made no secret about not liking gays. In fact, his boss only accepted Holtel as a deputy after being ordered to by a major general. The pair argued constantly until, after one blowup, the brigadier general appeared at Holtel's door at home, apologized, and suggested they try to get along. And they did. Later, when Holtel became chairman of the SH&K, the general became one of the group's unofficial advisers.

With prejudice still persisting throughout the military, gay military spokesmen such as Abel van Weerd seized upon the Jack Green episode as an opportunity to instruct all levels of the military that antigay attitudes would not be tolerated. This created outrage among military police, renowned for being antigay. At one point, the chief of staff for the military police, a general, called the major and warned him that "you'll harm yourself" pressing the investigation of the Jack Green case. "No," van Weerd replied, "I'll harm you." Van Weerd, who then worked in the logistics command in Amsterdam, told his own commanders about the phone call and his officers agreed to back him up.

In Parliament, meanwhile, defense officials were asked to explain why military police conducted house searches on behalf of American authorities investigating people's private sex lives. Relying on false information from the military police, defense officials simply denied it had happened.

Members of Parliament demanded to see the defense ministry's documentation of the case, which officials furnished and which contained factual inaccuracies. Through gay channels within the military, van Weerd obtained a copy of the original draft of the investigation marked with notes in red ink that read "change this" and "don't say that." Ultimately, van Weerd counted a dozen rewrites before the defense ministry finally released an accurate account of the story. Faced with new allegations of a cover-up, the secretary of state for defense issued orders for a formal investigation.

ALTHOUGH THE JACK GREEN incident would become the most embarrassing public clash with the Dutch government over the military's gay exclusion policy, the more liberal atmosphere in Europe had given American commanders headaches for years. In the early 1980s, one Air Force captain brought his male lover with him to Holland and introduced him as the au pair for his children. About the same time, Air Force investigators launched a probe to determine what was happening to the supplies of the Crisco shortening that were disappearing from the kitchens of an air base near Amsterdam. It turned out that a cook, an enlisted man, was selling the shortening, which was a popular sexual lubricant in the sadomasochistic scene, at leather bars in Amsterdam.

A corollary problem was the violence perpetrated by American servicemen against Europeans they believed to be gay. Men in southern European countries, for example, far less reticent than the North American male regarding physical contact, frequently walked down the streets holding hands, or with an arm around the other's shoulder. In the 1980s, this incited American servicemen to go into Naples and Rome to beat up homosexuals, which, by their definition, were any two men displaying physical contact. A lot of American military men were themselves beaten in the process.

OCTOBER 10, 1987
WASHINGTON, D.C.

THROUGHOUT WASHINGTON, the streets were crowded with the hundreds of thousands who had come for the March on Washington for Lesbian & Gay Rights. Every hotel was booked months in advance, as gay organizers used the gathering to advance a panoply of gay causes. Two thousand gay couples staged a massive wedding on the steps of the Internal Revenue Service to dramatize their demand for legally sanctioned marriages and the attendant benefits. Protesters on the steps of the Supreme Court denounced the previous year's *Bowers* v. *Hardwick* decision. A wreath honoring lesbian and gay veterans was laid at the Tomb of the Unknown Soldier. On the day of the march, as many as a half million walked to the Capitol to demand passage of a federal gay-rights law, more AIDS research, and an end to the ban on gays in the military. The march represented the largest protest of any sort in Washington since the antiwar demonstrations of April 1970.

For Leonard Matlovich, the most important moment came the day before the march, at the Congressional Cemetery, where he directed a ceremony dedicating a memorial to slain San Francisco supervisor Harvey Milk. Matlovich had come up with the idea of a gay memorial when he visited the Père-Lachaise Cemetery in Paris and saw the adoring graffiti on the graves of Oscar Wilde, Gertrude Stein, and Alice B. Toklas. He wanted a place for gays to pay their respect to their movement's fallen in the United States. From Milk's estate, Matlovich received a small portion of Milk's ashes for a memorial.

After the ceremony, many of those assembled walked down the gravel paths to the site where the Milk memorial would be erected. Nearby, there was an even more arresting sight, however, a black granite gravestone with two pink triangles engraved on it. The marker had no name except for the legend A GAY VIETNAM VETERAN. On the top was written the words NEVER FORGET, and under that, NEVER AGAIN. Most prominent, however, was the slogan Leonard Matlovich had ordered etched on the stone that would mark his grave: *When I was in the military, they gave me a medal for killing two men, and a discharge for loving one.*

ONE OF THE MOST POIGNANT moments of that weekend of protests occurred when San Francisco AIDS organizer Cleve Jones unfolded a huge quilt on the lawn near the Washington Monument. The quilt contained nearly two thousand panels commemorating those who had died in the first six years of the AIDS epidemic. Among the names were some of the celebrated: Rock Hudson and Liberace and Michael Bennett. Among the panels, however, were mementos of other Americans. Army jackets and Marine Corps shirts were sewn into some panels; there were commendation and achievement medals, Purple Hearts and Bronze Stars and even a Silver Star sewn onto other panels. Each panel was six feet by three feet, the size of a grave.

DECEMBER 1987
SOESTERBERG AIR BASE
SOESTERBERG, NETHERLANDS

ONCE THE DUTCH INVESTIGATION indicated that the military police had indeed turned over personal information about Jack Green to the American Air Force, the government of the Netherlands took the unofficial posture that it was responsible for Jack Green's difficulties and that it would play a role in resolving them. Green had kept government officials informed of his punishing work schedule and they worked behind the scenes, both to end the threat of punitive action against the sergeant and to allow him reinstatement in his munitions job. In December, those efforts succeeded and he was reinstated. The Air Force, however, refused to give him any work. He sat at a desk all day and did nothing.

After nine months, Green was psychologically devastated. He had begun to have trouble sleeping in October; by now, in December, he was barely sleeping at all. Though the publicity over the incident had died down in the Dutch press, Green still worried that it was only a matter of time before his commanders fulfilled their pledge to court-martial and imprison him.

His despair culminated at the end of a bitter cold weekend in early January 1988. It was 3:00 A.M. and he lay staring at the ceiling. He had had no sleep for the previous three days, and in four hours, he would have to be back at his desk in Soesterberg, in an office where no one would talk to him.

His lover Albert Taminiau found Green in a pool of blood, his wrists slashed, and rushed him to the hospital. After his release, Green was put under the care of a psychologist, who insisted that under no circumstances should he return to Soesterberg Air Base. His life was at stake now.

— 62 —

The Escape

SNOW WAS FALLING outside when the guard gave Captain Paul Starr his yellow checklist to complete before his parole. Starr's model behavior in prison had paid off; he was being released after serving nine months of his eighteen-month term. Though the parole board at Fort Leavenworth, headed by a tough Marine colonel, had ruled against parole, Starr had appealed to the Secretary of the Air Force, noting that his imprisonment had already served whatever deterrent value it might have. From Washington, his parole was approved.

Paul had found work in Sacramento, but as a federal prison parolee he was required to report to a local parole officer. Starr arrived before his formal paperwork did, so he had to explain to his parole officer that he had been imprisoned for consensual sexual activity with another adult in the privacy of his home. The parole officer did not believe him. When the papers arrived and the officer saw that there were indeed no children and no force involved in Paul's crimes, he assigned Starr to the lightest supervision possible, one visit every three months for the nine months of his parole. Starr had served nine months in federal prison and would forever bear the label of convicted felon and ex-con, but as far as the parole officer was concerned, Starr could not be considered a criminal and he would not be treated as one.

JANUARY 11, 1988
MARINE CORPS RECRUIT TRAINING DEPOT
PARRIS ISLAND, SOUTH CAROLINA

PETTY OFFICER THIRD CLASS Terry Knox was working at her first aid station for female recruits at Parris Island when she was summoned into the office of the Naval Investigative Service. Although the NIS would later decline to comment about what happened next, numerous court documents corroborated Knox's recollection of the interrogation, which was led by Special Agent Renea King.

Knox knew King, who she believed was having an affair with Knox's estranged husband. For weeks before the couple's recent separation, King had repeatedly called Knox's home to talk to her husband, who maintained to Terry that it concerned his application to join the NIS. Shortly before their final bitter fight, Knox's husband admitted the calls from King had to do with an investigation the NIS was launching of lesbian Marines at Parris Island. The investigation, he added, included a drill instructor, Sergeant Mary Kile, who was Terry's close friend.

Terry brushed aside King's suggestion that the sergeant was gay. She had met Kile a year earlier. Like Terry, she was involved in a crumbling marriage. Terry understood that her own marital problems had to do with her sexual identity; she had thought she was heterosexual, but she was attracted to Mary Kile and the pair had become inseparable friends. To complicate matters, Terry was pregnant, and determined to keep her baby.

Terry's husband had offered to interrogate Kile for the NIS and told Terry so one night, which led to an altercation. Fearful he would hurt her as he had before—Knox's attorney later recalled that the husband had broken one of Terry's fingers in a fight—Knox called Mary Kile, who came and drove her away. Shortly afterward, Terry moved into housing on base, and was living there when she gave birth to her daughter.

In the weeks that followed, Terry noticed that she was being followed by her husband and others. Sergeant Kile noticed that she was being tailed as well.

Between that and the rumors of an imminent crackdown, Knox was not surprised when she was called into the NIS office from her job at the Parris Island clinic at 6:30 A.M. She was disconcerted, however, when she saw her husband's car parked outside the office.

Upon entering an interrogation room, Renea King threw a pile of videotapes on a table and announced that the tapes included proof that Knox had committed adulterous homosexual acts. The NIS had it on tape and they had recordings of phone conversations between Terry and Sergeant Kile. Terry responded that she was full of shit. King pressed on: If Knox talked about her relationship with Kile, they could offer her immunity. Knox refused.

"Do you want your daughter growing up knowing her mother is a jailbird and went to jail for being a lesbian?" King finally asked. She then laid out the ultimate threat: If Terry did not cooperate, the NIS would move to have her daughter taken away from her. "In South Carolina, homosexuals cannot have children," she said.

Terry asked for a lawyer. King ignored that and badgered her further. When Terry asked to go to the bathroom, King followed her right into the stall. As the hours wore on, King became more specific. They had photographs of Terry and the sergeant sitting in front of the A&P supermarket in their car, kissing and embracing each other. Terry and Kile had embraced once in front of the A&P, Knox remembered, one day when her husband was following them, but they had certainly not engaged in sex in a supermarket parking lot.

After lunch, Terry was locked in a small room with her estranged husband. "They're going to throw you in jail," he told Terry, and they were going to take away her daughter. He would go to court to ensure that Terry did not have custody. Then King turned up the intensity of the interrogation. Knox's daughter would go to a foster home after Terry was sent to jail, she said. It might be a long time before Knox saw her. Terry asked for a lawyer again; King ignored her.

King would later be unavailable for comment, but Knox subsequently testified that occasionally King shoved Knox or threw a pen at her. Then Terry would hear a rustling in the next room behind the large one-way mirror, and another agent would come in and take King out. While King had been harsh and confrontational, this agent was warm and understanding, trying to coax a statement from Knox. When that did not work, King returned to threaten and accuse Knox. Several times more Knox asked for a lawyer and was ignored. Several times she asserted her suspicions that King was having an affair with her husband. Then King would glance at the one-way mirror and try to change the subject.

Finally, the Staff Judge Advocate, Colonel Kenneth Taylor, came in to offer Knox immunity. He called her "little lady," and assured her that the immunity would protect her. The visit was intimidating. Taylor was in effect the base commanding general's own lawyer.

After more than ten hours of interrogation, Knox finally broke down and admitted she had embraced Mary Kile in front of the A&P. She agreed to sign a statement to that effect. NIS agents typed up the brief statement, only a few lines long, and Knox signed it and was released. The next time she saw the statement, she barely recognized it. Someone had typed in additional paragraphs of entirely fabricated information above Knox's signature in what had been the blank portion of the page, accusing others of being gay, and having sex.

At the same time Terry Knox was being interrogated, Sergeant Kile was also taken to a small room and told that she too would go to prison if she did not cooperate. The NIS asked her repeatedly if she had sent flowers to a Marine Corps captain named Judy Gretch. The line of questioning seemed almost comical to Kile. Later, she would realize the agents were not joking. The Parris Island witch-hunt had begun.

MARINE CORPS CORPORAL Barbara Baum was packing for her pending transfer to Hawaii. Over the past two months she had been in training for track with Captain Laura Hinckley, on whom she had developed a massive crush. Hinckley, an Annapolis graduate from the same class as

Ruth Voor, said she was not gay, but Barbara thought otherwise. The pair became friends. By January, however, the friendship seemed as if it would fade—Barb's uniforms had already been shipped to Hawaii and she was about to take a thirty-day leave at home in Indiana before her transfer. On what was to be her last day at Parris Island, Barbara went to the Military Police headquarters to say good-bye to the people with whom she had worked for the past two years. Arriving there, she was told that agents from the Naval Investigative Service wanted to see her—right away.

An NIS agent explained that although Barbara was a good Marine, the NIS knew she was gay. They knew because they had almost caught her redhanded in bed at the Buccaneer Motel with Lance Corporal Diane Maldonado. Barbara could make it easy on herself if she would just answer some questions. As an MP, Barbara knew her rights: She asked for a lawyer and the interview was ended.

The word spread through Parris Island as more women were called into the NIS. One female drill instructor was taken off the drill field in handcuffs and brought into the NIS office, where she encountered a gay male Marine friend. "They've got us—they've got us," he said when she arrived. "You better talk to them." So she did, though it turned out that the friend who had urged her to make a statement was an NIS informant who had himself given a statement against her two months earlier. His presence at the NIS office was part of the setup.

No one knew who had talked and who had not. Suspicions flared. Friends stopped speaking to each other. Quietly, meanwhile, the NIS used jealousy among the women to nail down evidence. When Sergeant Cheryl Jameson, a drill instructor, began seeing a particular recruit, she enraged another whom she had once dated; a fourth female Marine became even more jealous when she realized that it was her girlfriend with whom Jameson was having an affair. All three of the women ended up giving statements and cooperating with the NIS in its investigation of Jameson. One of them, Staff Sergeant Bonnie Ferguson, named forty-five female Marines as lesbians in her statement, including a woman Marine Corps general, a colonel, three lieutenant colonels, a major, five captains, and three lieutenants.

Strange things began to happen that did not make sense at the time, but which carried great significance later. In February, for example, Staff Sergeant Ferguson made numerous phone calls to a civilian named Paula Berry who had once been a roommate, and who she knew to be a close friend of Captain Judy Meade. When Berry mentioned that Meade was stopping by her home, Ferguson showed up that very night in the company of Private First Class Jill Harris, another of the women involved in the jealous ménage that proved so fruitful for the NIS.

Meade's father had just died and she was on her way back to Camp LeJeune after the funeral. She was distraught and wanted to talk to Berry alone. The pair went back into Berry's bedroom, but Ferguson and Harris followed them there. According to Berry's recollection of the evening, Harris brought up the subject of who was lesbian among the Parris Island women. Meade warned her to stop spreading rumors; she could get in a lot of trouble.

From what Parris Island defendants later pieced together, Harris had been dispatched from Okinawa to help set up women at Parris Island. Meade's warning about not gossiping about other women became the basis of charges against her a year later. According to the Marine Corps, her statement had represented a threat. In the gathering darkness of the Parris Island purge, any remark could contain criminal implications; it could even send a person to prison.

Later, when Paula Berry tried to understand why her old friend Bonnie Ferguson would betray not only their friendship but the dozens of other women she had named, she recalled that Bonnie had mentioned her child. The NIS agents had told her if she did not cooperate, she could lose custody of the little girl.

———————

A WEEK AFTER her first interrogation, Petty Officer Terry Knox was called back into the NIS, where she was presented with a written promise of immunity if she would provide a statement against Sergeant Kile. The immunity papers were signed by the top of Terry's chain of command, Rear Admiral W. N. Johnson, commander of the Naval base in Charleston. Again, Special Agent Renea King was in charge of Terry's interrogation. During this four-hour interrogation, Terry would say only that she had given Kile a kiss of a nonsexual nature in front of the A&P. King was infuriated, according to Knox, and held out the paper that represented Terry's guarantee of immunity. "Terry, we're going to take away this immunity if you don't come clean now," she said. When Terry remained silent, she ripped the document into pieces and threw it at her.

Knox demanded an attorney, and the interrogation ended. As she was leaving the room, Knox says, King was still fuming. "I'm going to get you if it's the last thing I do," she said. "I don't care about the other dykes in the Marine Corps—if it's the last thing I do, I'll get you."

By now, the NIS had focused their efforts on three women: Sergeant Mary Kile, Sergeant Jacqueline Hickey, and Captain Judy Gretch. As an officer, Gretch was the big fish, and NIS files on the Parris Island purge were labeled the "Gretch case." By late January, all three women were informed that they were being charged with homosexuality and would face administrative hearings.

Kile was accused of the A&P kiss, and also accused of having a relationship with Captain Gretch. According to one story, Kile had sent Gretch flowers as a sign of devotion. The flowers had been delivered anonymously and Kile's role in it was mere gossip, but the gossip became the basis of charges against them both.

It seemed that every Marine who ever had a grudge against a lesbian stepped forward to offer the NIS a statement about this or that woman who might be gay. These statements led to new interrogations.

Barbara Baum was at home in Indiana when she received word that her orders to Hawaii had been revoked and she was to return to Parris Island. Back in South Carolina, Barbara went to the NIS. "It's not you we're after," an NIS agent explained. The NIS was hoping she could lead them to other people—the female Marines that the NIS really wanted. Barbara suspected they meant Captain Laura Hinckley, with whom she had once spent so much time. Barb had heard that the NIS had a statement that placed Baum's car at the captain's home.

Barb agreed to be interviewed by the NIS if she could tape-record their discussion. Major David Beck, a Marine Corps prosecutor, accused Barbara of "playing games." As an MP, he said, she should know better. Besides, she might play the tape for others, which would warn them of what to expect in an interrogation. The NIS agent said she absolutely could not allow a tape recording of the interview. Barbara requested a lawyer and the interview ended.

The idea that people were watching other people's apartments and reporting the license numbers of visitors gave Barbara a chill, but she still felt safe from the purge. She had had only one relationship, with Maldonado the year before, and did not have dozens of former girlfriends who might give statements against her. Although Baum and Maldonado were no longer dating, Barbara had called her several times to make sure they had their stories straight if they did have to talk to the NIS. According to the story they had agreed on, they had spent the night at the Buccaneer Motel in 1986 to get away from Steve Davis, Diane's violently jealous ex-boyfriend. They were not involved sexually; they were not gay; they did not know any gays.

JANUARY 18, 1988
AMSTERDAM, NETHERLANDS

AIR FORCE SERGEANT Jack Green had been AWOL for a week when Senator Marie Louise Tiesinga Autsema met with Colonel Rick Parsons of Soesterberg Air Base and his legal adviser, Captain Johan Muller of the Staff Judge Advocate's office. Tiesinga Autsema was a leader of the Democrats' 66, a liberal party in opposition to the government. Because she had good relations with U.S. officials in Holland, however, she was appointed to be the government spokeswoman and negotiator in the Jack Green matter. The Dutch senator explained that Green was under psychiatric care and that she hoped to work out an agreement with the Americans so that he could be quietly and honorably discharged without having to suffer prosecution from the Air Force for his homosexuality.

Parsons maintained that this was not a subject that could be discussed.

Green was expected to return to the base immediately. "Why can he not return?" he asked repeatedly.

Parsons was not available for comment on this matter. Later, Tiesinga Autsema, after a number of exchanges like this, finally blew up. "Quit acting like a robot," she said. "Talk like a human."

Parsons's attitude seemed to soften. The military was beginning to cut troops, he said. Perhaps they could work out an administrative discharge. However, Green would have to be examined by an Air Force psychiatrist.

The meeting was agreed upon, and Green and his Dutch psychologist and psychiatrist met with a Soesterberg psychiatrist, Colonel Ralph Johns, in Amsterdam. The Dutch explained that Green suffered from "acute reactive depression" and that they could not in good conscience suggest he return to Soesterberg or put himself under Air Force authorities again.

Colonel Johns, however, ordered Green to return to the Soesterberg base immediately. Green said that he understood the order, but that he would not go back. The colonel advised him that he could now be found guilty of disobeying a lawful order and of desertion. He could go to jail. At this, Green's Dutch psychiatrist told the colonel to shut up. "Don't threaten my patient," he said.

Senator Tiesinga Autsema made some headway at her next meeting with Colonel Parsons. The issue had by now become the subject of communications between the Dutch secretary of state's office, which included the defense ministry, and the American State and Defense departments. In a tense meeting with American officials, the Dutch achieved the concessions they sought. Green would be medically discharged from the Air Force with no punishment except for a general discharge. He could then return to Holland.

But in order to clear the medical discharge, the Air Force insisted that military doctors at the Air Force's 7100th Combat Support Wing Medical Center in Wiesbaden, West Germany, must examine Green. By now, Jack had been in hiding for nearly a month and was eager to resolve his conflicts with the Air Force. Still, he worried what might happen once he left the Netherlands. With much trepidation, Jack finally agreed to the plan. After all, the American government had given its word to the Dutch government.

On February 9, Green turned himself in to the American embassy in The Hague, expecting that within three days, as provided by the agreement between the Dutch and American authorities, he would be out of the Air Force, a free man. According to Air Force documents, Donald Brown, the embassy's military and political affairs officer, reassured Green while the sergeant was en route to Wiesbaden that the Air Force would not punish him.

From his first hours at Wiesbaden, everyone who interviewed Green focused on one issue: Was he gay? It was one of the first questions the admitting officer asked him before he was placed in a ten-bed psychiatric ward. Though Jack had been promised that he would be released within two to three days, it soon became clear that the Air Force was not in any hurry. It took two days for a doctor to make his way to Green's bedside, and the physician knew nothing of any agreement between the Dutch and American government concerning Jack's discharge. As far as he knew, Jack was at Wiesbaden for "observation and testing." Another doctor told Jack that he was going to be put up on charges of homosexuality; he might be going to jail.

Jack panicked. He asked to contact Dutch officials, but he was not allowed to make any calls. Then he heard that officers from Soesterberg would be arriving within a few days, with papers formally charging him with homosexuality.

Shortly afterward, Green did manage to contact a friend in Holland, and they laid their plans. His friend arrived at the hospital at noon on February 14, a Sunday, the most popular day for visitors at the hospital, claiming she was a doctor who had come to examine Sergeant Green. Since Jack would be in the company of a doctor, he was allowed to leave his second-floor room to walk in the courtyard. Once outside, the pair hurried to a nearby car driven by Jack's lover, Albert Taminiau. Albert drove a few blocks, where they switched vehicles in case anyone had seen them make their getaway.

Jack was wearing his Air Force green fatigues, but Albert had brought him civilian clothes. Jack changed in the car as the three drove toward the Dutch border. Since Jack did not have his passport, it would be impossible for him to cross from Germany to Holland, so shortly before they came to the border, they pulled alongside the road. Jack's rescuers pointed toward a windmill in the far distance. That windmill was in the Dutch village of Rhiemen, Albert said. They would wait for him there.

It was bitter cold as Jack made his way through the forest on the frontier between Germany and Holland. He knew that if he was captured by German border guards, he would be returned to American military authorities where he would most certainly face jail time. It was an eerie feeling, walking through the ash and linden trees, worrying that someone might see the vapor from his breath, worrying about border guards, knowing his liberty depended on being able to avoid U.S. officials. After a two-hour walk, fearful of every snap and rustle in the forest, Green made it to the windmill and his friends, and freedom.

— 63 —

Naming Names

AFTER SURVIVING the 1976 WAC purge at Fort Devens, Tanya Domi had served two more years in the active-duty Army before leaving to continue her college education. She stayed in the Army Reserves, however, and joined the ROTC program at Central Michigan State University, from which she was the Distinguished Military Graduate. In 1982, she reentered the Army, was commissioned a second lieutenant, and as a former enlistee who had achieved officer status, became known as a *mustang*, a rare distinction among women in the armed forces.

No matter how distinguished her awards or how high her officer evaluation reports, she was still a woman in a man's Army. Sexual harassment remained pandemic, even for Domi, who by 1988 had been promoted to captain. Once in her office, a male captain who bothered her frequently blurted out, "I ought to fuck you right here," a remark overheard by a lieutenant who supported Tanya's story when she took the matter to their major. The major gave a cryptic response: "Familiarity breeds contempt," he said. Shortly thereafter, an anonymous message appeared in the company's computer system accusing Tanya of being a lesbian.

At the same time, Domi's position was further undermined by a first sergeant who took great pride in the number of female military careers he had ended because he was able to convince authorities that they were lesbian. Two women whom the first sergeant had accused had managed to beat the charges and were transferred to the company of which Tanya had recently been made commander. When one of the women applied for Military Police school, the first sergeant called his company commander late at night to complain. When that complaint did no good, he called Domi to insist that her soldier not be allowed the MP training because she was a lesbian.

The call angered Domi. First sergeants had no business calling officers of other units to make demands about how soldiers are treated. Put simply, such matters were none of their damned business, and Domi told the first sergeant so.

Not long after that, agents from the Criminal Investigation Division called Domi into their office to say she was "suspected of lesbian activities" for having been overheard making love to another woman in the bedroom of her apartment. Domi denied the accusations, but told the CID about the first sergeant's interference in her work, as well as the captain's sexual harassment. When she spoke to CID agents again, they conceded that her allegations had been confirmed; however, no action was taken.

Domi knew that she would continue to be suspect and that no matter how much she excelled, her military career could end abruptly at any time. But she could not bring herself to resign her commission. She loved the Army and the rare opportunities it offered women to achieve genuinely responsible positions. She stayed in, but began suffering from stress-related health problems, such as colitis, even as she won greater honors.

When she was interviewed to be a tactical training officer for the history department at West Point, the interviewer warned her, "Our women have a much tougher time of it." It was the policy of administrators not to interfere with homosexual investigations, the interviewer said. She decided to forgo the appointment and she began to contemplate a career outside the military.

THE COMBINATION of sexual harassment and lesbian accusations, so prevalent since the sexual integration of the armed forces in the mid-1970s, grew more pronounced and more malicious as the 1980s wore on. At the same time the Parris Island women were being pulled into small rooms for NIS interrogations, women aboard the USS *Grapple* found themselves the objects of the sexual attention of their male crewmates. Petty Officer Mary Beth Harrison, one of the senior female petty officers, remembered one crewman who accused a woman of being a lesbian after she rejected his advances, and who slugged another woman who came to the defense of the first. The assault victim was afraid to press charges for fear that the crewman would accuse her of being a lesbian, too.

Another female crew member became pregnant by a crewman who demanded she get an abortion, which she did against her own desires, fearing that if she crossed him he would accuse her of lesbianism. Nor was the ship's command supportive of the women. The commander issued a "climate assessment" questionnaire for the crew that included questions to determine whether gays were undermining the morale of the ship. As tensions mounted along gender lines, male sailors hung signs that announced a new club called S.A.D.—or Sailors Against Dykes. Signs with the slash marks over the word "Dykes" in a circle became a common sight aboard the ship.

When Petty Officer Harrison complained about sexual harassment, the NIS began an investigation—not of the accused men but of the alleged lesbians. By the end of the year, Harrison was up on charges of being gay and on her way out of the Navy, one of at least three women from the *Grapple* discharged in that round of lesbian investigations.

The lack of command interest in sexual harassment had by now become a matter of public discussion. After a tour of European military bases discovered pandemic sexual harassment of women, the Defense Advisory Committee on Women in the Service wrote a scathing report to the Defense Department. The Pentagon responded by refusing to release the report until it was forced to do so under a Freedom of Information Act request from *The Washington Post*. Even Dr. Jacquelyn Davis, DACOWITS chairman, who was outspoken in asserting that she was *not* a feminist, complained of the top Pentagon officials, "They've just thrown up their hands and said there's nothing we can do about this."

Although feminist groups were denouncing sexual harassment, they were far less keen on addressing the special form it took against lesbians. One of the foremost experts on women in the military, Linda Grant DePauw, took feminists to task for this failure in a 1988 essay in *Minerva*, the magazine about women in the armed forces. On one hand, DePauw noted, radical feminist groups were opposed to women going into the military at all, because it was a "male patriarchal" organization; on the other, the groups that lobbied for women in the military, professional groups like the Federally Employed Women and the Women Officers' Professional Association, found the lesbian issue distasteful and would not confront it. This phenomenon, as well as the ambivalence that some national gay organizations still had toward the military, left lesbians with little support.

The association between sexual harassment and lesbian accusations continued to create a disproportionate rate of gay discharges for military women. In 1987 and 1988, for example, women comprised 10 percent of the armed forces, but accounted for 26 percent of gay discharges. The trend was most pronounced in the services most resistant to women, the Navy and the Marine Corps. While white females made up 3.1 percent of the Marine Corps in 1989, they accounted for 31 percent of gay discharges, a rate ten times higher than for men.

THE FIRST PUBLIC NOTICE of the investigation of lesbians on Parris Island was made on page one of the *Beaufort Gazette*, the hometown paper for the Marine base, to which three unidentified female Marine drill instructors had given a detailed interview. "The qualities and traits that we demand and are supposed to be training our recruits are the same traits that make us look homosexual," one woman complained. Parris Island officials declined comment on the story, which claimed at least ten women were being investigated. But a day later they released a statement confirming that Captain Judy Gretch and Sergeant Mary Kile were being charged with fraternization and "indecent acts."

Meanwhile, the interrogations continued. "You're going to spend time in jail," an NIS agent confidently told Lance Corporal Becky Feldhaus at the beginning of her interrogation. Becky had seen other female drill instructors escorted in and out of interrogation chambers. She and her friends had kept close tabs on who was being interviewed at the NIS office, and who was talking. Feldhaus was not intimidated by the NIS and said she wanted to see a lawyer. The agents were confident, nonetheless. "We have eyes and ears everywhere," one said.

The NIS would not tell Sergeant Jacqueline Hickey why they wanted to talk to her until they had her in a small, stuffy room with a one-way mirror. Then they explained that she would go to prison if she did not cooperate. The NIS wanted names of other homosexuals and a confession. After repeated interrogations, Hickey, who denied being gay, relented, waived her right to a hearing, and accepted a gay-related discharge.

NIS agents and base officials denied using coercive tactics. "It [Hickey's interrogation] was conducted in accordance with established military justice rulings," said public affairs officer Major Robert W. McLean after Hickey told her story to reporters. "The administrative and judicial discipline that has resulted [in Parris Island] is the logical and foreseeable consequence of people violating the Uniform Code of Military Justice," he said.

As February and March passed, new women came under investigation and new charges were filed. Sergeant Cheryl Jameson and Staff Sergeant Bonnie Ferguson were charged with indecent acts. At their Article 32 hearing, the military equivalent of a grand jury proceeding, Lance Corporal Carrie Prusa explained that her attraction to Jameson, her drill instructor in boot camp, had evolved into assignations in hotel rooms in Savannah and Atlanta.

The other jealous lover, former girlfriend Private First Class Jill Harris, also testified against the women, admitting under cross-examination that she was accusing them in part because she felt "betrayed and used" when she realized Jameson and Ferguson were having an affair. Under questioning from prosecutors, Harris began to describe a secret cabal that existed within the military, a group that called itself The Family.

The specter of this conspiracy of homosexuals was first raised in the Jameson hearings, but it quickly became a standard feature of all the gay prosecutions at Parris Island, and the rationale for the harsh punishments that were sought.

Unfortunately for prosecutors at the Ferguson and Jameson hearings, their witnesses could not keep their stories straight. In their courtroom testimony, both Prusa and Harris contradicted what they had told the

NIS; their stories even changed from day to day in the courtroom. Prusa, for example, denied to the NIS that she had ever had sex with Jameson; in one day of testimony at Jameson's Article 32 hearing, however, she said they did have oral sex; days later, she changed her story again and said they did not.

Despite the contradictions, defense attorneys believed the hearings were designed to reach a foregone conclusion. As Charles B. Macloskie, a civilian lawyer representing Ferguson and several other Parris Island women, told the proceeding, "I'm not under any illusion that I'm going to get any charges dismissed here." And he did not.

By the time Sergeant Mary Kile, the fourth woman charged, faced her Article 32 hearing in late March, there was another standard feature to the proceedings—accusations of NIS misconduct. When prosecutors presented Private First Class L. M. Miller with the three-page statement the NIS had provided for the trial, she denied under oath many of the statements attributed to her. The NIS, she said, had simply made them up.

Three recruits took the stand to say that NIS agents had "twisted" their comments and added paragraphs to their written statements without their knowledge. "Everybody's trying to put words in my mouth, sir," said Private Michelle Hodroskie, whom the NIS said had accused Kile of being gay. That allegation, she said, had been added to her statement without her knowledge.

When Petty Officer Terry Knox took the stand, she recanted her statement to the NIS, and said NIS agents had threatened to jail her, to take away her daughter, and had finally brought in her abusive, estranged husband to threaten her further. Neil Robbins III, the special agent in charge of the Parris Island NIS office, countered, "I have never browbeat a witness in my life." The Navy responded to Knox's recantation by putting her up on perjury charges. The statement she recanted, the Navy asserted, represented a false statement. Her court-martial date was set for June.

While servicewomen like Knox, Kile, and Jameson fought their discharges, others began to crack under the pressure. On the second day of Kile's hearing, Parris Island officials announced that two women had waived their right to hearings and accepted administrative discharges.

For her part, Lance Corporal Barbara Baum kept in regular contact with Lance Corporal Diane Maldonado, the one person whose testimony could bring her down. Diane's resolve held, but she was pregnant now by a man she had met after she broke up with Barbara.

One day in early February, Diane called Barbara for a ride to her Lamaze class. She was feeling very emotional lately, and she wanted to talk about the investigation. She did not plan to say anything to the NIS, she told Barb, but she added, "I *do* want to keep the baby—no matter what, I want to keep my baby."

MARCH 1988
AMSTERDAM, NETHERLANDS

EVEN BEFORE JACK GREEN was back in Amsterdam, the Air Force had
notified Dutch authorities of his escape. Senator Marie Louise Tiesinga
Autsema, who had negotiated the terms for Jack's earlier return to the
Air Force, was angry that the Americans had so flagrantly gone back on
their word. She was also distressed that Green had escaped.

Jack met with her four days after his return to Amsterdam. She promised to try to work out another agreement with them, and Jack returned
to his life in hiding, staying at the homes of various sympathetic civilians
as well as the apartment of the head of the Dutch gay military group,
Major Abel van Weerd, near the royal palace in Amsterdam.

Meetings with American officials, however, dragged on with little
progress. In late March, Jack's Dutch attorney and officials from the
American State Department met at the U.S. embassy with representatives
of the Air Force. No, the Air Force colonel said, he could not make any
decisions or promises regarding Green's future if he turned himself over
to the Air Force. It did not matter to the Air Force if this dragged on,
they could just deal with it by using the "Oriental treatment."

What was that? Jack's lawyer asked.

They could wait, just wait. Green was a deserter, and the longer he
was gone, the worse it would be for him.

Van Weerd, now a lieutenant colonel, recalls that it was at one of
these meetings that the Dutch pressed the Air Force to consider the feelings
in Holland on this issue, and an American colonel looked at them incredulously and said, "Holland? Holland is peanuts."

MARCH 15, 1988
MARINE CORPS RECRUIT TRAINING DEPOT
PARRIS ISLAND, SOUTH CAROLINA

IN NO SENSE COULD Corporal Barbara Baum be considered a lynchpin of
the lesbian community at Parris Island. There were intimations in NIS
reports that she was "the enforcer" for The Family at Parris Island. But
given Baum's petite stature—she was five-feet-five inches tall and weighed
120 pounds—this was difficult to assert publicly. Not even the prosecutor,
who asked that she be imprisoned for thirty-five years, had raised this at
her trial. It was perhaps precisely Baum's newness to the gay scene that
was responsible for her predicament by late March. Prosecutors had access
to her medical records, which showed that she had recently undergone
treatment for alcoholism, another sign that she might be vulnerable to
pressure. Since the object of the investigation was to purge as many lesbians
as possible from the Marine Corps, its success rested on getting names,

or, more accurately, getting lesbians to name names of other homosexual women.

There were three charges against Baum: that she had had a relationship with Lance Corporal Maldonado, that she had had a phone conversation with another Marine that indicated they were lovers, and that she had kissed another woman passionately at a private home. Only the first charge was true. The second was based on an overheard phone call in which Baum had allegedly said, "What time are you picking me up for dinner?" and her friend had replied, "What's for dinner?" This exchange sounded like a lesbian conversation to the person who overheard it, and she had reported it to NIS agents. Parris Island was getting to be that kind of a place now.

The fact that the Marine Corps was ready to discharge her on the basis of such scurrilous evidence angered Baum and she decided to fight the charges. Her Marine Corps lawyer was less than enthusiastic. "Where there's smoke there's fire," he said, philosophically. Baum asked what he meant. "If there's puddles everywhere and everything's soaking wet, you may not see the rain, but you know it rained," he said. Obviously, the attorney considered her guilty. He advised Barbara to make it easy on herself and do what the NIS wanted her to do, name names. That way she could get an administrative separation, maybe even an honorable discharge.

Baum refused. Since the only true charge against her involved her relationship with Diane Maldonado, Barbara checked back again with her former girlfriend. No, she had not talked to the NIS, Maldonado said, but she was still worried about losing her baby. Barb's lawyer had warned her repeatedly not to talk to Diane and both women worried that their conversations might be overheard, so they had worked out a system for talking discreetly when Barb was on duty. Diane would say, "This is Debbie from Fox Jewelers," and Barb would know to call Diane on a phone that was not likely to be tapped.

The three-month ordeal had taken its toll on Baum. In February she had started drinking again; she was frequently ill now, and the doctors said her health problems were due to stress. Moreover, she could see that no matter what happened in her current discharge proceedings, it could happen again and again; she would never be free from suspicion. There was a saying among the women Marines at Parris Island: One accusation of lesbianism means an investigation; two accusations equal proof.

Finally, toward the end of March, Barbara told her lawyer that she would not fight her discharge. She told Maldonado too; two days later, perhaps believing that it no longer made any difference, Maldonado met with NIS agents and gave them a statement about her relationship with Barb and their night together at the Buccaneer Motel.

The next Monday, when Barbara went to her Marine Corps lawyer to sign the statement that would waive her right to an administrative hearing and clear the way for her discharge, the lawyer was furious.

"You've been talking to Diane Maldonado—I told you not to talk to her," he said. "She made a statement and now you're going to jail."

Maldonado's statement offered the evidence for charges of indecent acts and sodomy. Maldonado's jealous ex-boyfriend Steve Davis, now a Beaufort County sheriff's deputy, also gave a statement about the night he had caught Diane and Barbara in bed at the Buccaneer Motel nineteen months earlier. There were also felony charges of "obstruction of justice," based on conversations between Barb and Diane about creating a cover story for NIS agents. The addition of such charges served prosecutorial purposes by making the accused appear to be a hardened criminal when in fact she was being prosecuted solely for being homosexual.

On March 29, Barb was informed that her Article 32 hearing would be held in two weeks; after that, she would face a court-martial. Barb's lawyer urged her to make a statement, to name names. There was particular interest in Barbara's relationship with Captain Laura Hinckley, who had been put on legal hold although no charges had been filed against her yet. As an officer and a Naval Academy graduate, Hinckley represented one of the "big fish," the most prized prey in lesbian purges such as this, and the NIS needed proof.

The NIS was also interested in a statement about Gunnery Sergeant Diane Edwards, a fourteen-year veteran of the Marine Corps. Barb recalled hearing about a meeting of Marine Corps commanding generals in Quantico citing this lieutenant colonel and that gunnery sergeant as lesbians who must be dismissed. It had seemed too strange to believe that generals would concern themselves with gunnery sergeants, but now Barbara suspected it was true.

Barb's lawyer urged her to make a deal, and all the charges might be dropped. Barbara, however, would not make a statement or name either the captain or Edwards or anyone else as a lesbian.

BARBARA BAUM WAS the fifth woman to be put up on charges during the Parris Island purge of 1988; the friend who had warned her the previous autumn about an impending witch-hunt became the sixth. After being implicated in Diane Maldonado's statement, Barb's roommate, Becky Feldhaus, became the next.

A week after Baum received notice of her charges, Captain Judy Gretch, one of the original targets of the investigation, faced her Article 32 hearing. The thirty-year-old commander of the Fourth Battalion's K Company was charged with conduct unbecoming an officer, fraternization, dereliction of duty, and indecent acts, among other charges. Testimony against her included such statements as the assertion that Gretch and Sergeant Kile were "too friendly," evidenced by the fact that they sometimes exercised together. One woman said she suspected the pair had a lesbian relationship because Kile "could walk in and out of Gretch's office whenever she wanted to." Under cross-examination the witness conceded that Captain Gretch had an open-door policy and that all the drill instructors in K Company could walk in and out when they wanted to.

Barbara Baum's Article 32 hearing convened on April 15 at the Law Center on the Parris Island base. The centerpiece of the prosecution was the statement and subsequent testimony of Lance Corporal Maldonado. With the guarantee of immunity from prosecution, Maldonado had by now named twenty other women Marines as lesbians, including a colonel and a captain. Barbara thought it was obvious that much of the statement was coerced, if not altogether fabricated. At one point, for example, Maldonado said Baum insisted she iron her fatigues, and treated her like a "wife." As a military policeman, Baum never wore cammies; it was the kind of detail few military people would miss, but one that would be over the heads of the civilian NIS agents.

Nevertheless, once on the stand, Maldonado, who was close to giving birth, testified about her relationship with Baum. Now that she was under oath, prosecutors spent much of the hearing asking not about Barbara but for the names of other lesbians. Statements obtained under oath can be used in other administrative hearings. Maldonado's testimony about Becky Feldhaus that day, for example, became the basis of her discharge three months later.

Every statement Barb had made to Diane about destroying their letters and sticking to their cover story became so much more evidence of obstruction of justice. Maldonado recounted that the heterosexual brother of a woman Marine had said someone should punch out Steve Davis, who had informed on Barb and Diane to the NIS. Since this statement was made in a conversation with Baum, this made Barb a participant in a conspiracy to obstruct justice, and guilty of "threatening behavior."

Maldonado also recalled that Barb had said "somebody should do something about" Davis, a statement that was the basis of the charge that Baum was "communicating a threat" against the former Marine. The threat that Becky Feldhaus made against Davis in the parking lot of the Buccaneer Motel, about The Family exacting revenge on him if he did not stop harassing Diane and Barb, also became evidence of a conspiracy to obstruct justice. Davis, after all, was assisting the NIS in its lesbian investigation; obstructing the investigation was obstructing justice. Baum's presence at the time Feldhaus made the threat made her party to a conspiracy to obstruct justice. Becky's remark also raised the specter that was central to the burgeoning Parris Island purge—the dark cabal of The Family.

When Barb's attorney attempted to get testimony from Maldonado about her NIS interview and what agents might have said to induce her lengthy statement, the prosecution objected, and the military judge ruled that she should not have to answer such questions. As in the other hearings, the conclusion was foregone. On April 18, Corporal Barbara Baum was ordered to face a court-martial for "indecent acts," sodomy, obstruction of justice, and communicating a threat. Altogether, the charges could earn her thirty-eight years in prison.

By now, Barbara had lost one military lawyer, who told her that he could not represent her if she would not do the reasonable thing and give the NIS what they wanted. Barbara's new Marine Corps lawyer, Joseph Codega, seemed more determined to fight the charges but he also presented Baum with the ongoing offer from the prosecution that she could escape the trial if she would provide names to the NIS. Once again, she refused. It did not seem possible that she would really go to jail just for being gay, not in the late 1980s, not in America.

ABOARD THE USS *IOWA*

"IF I DIE, you're going to be a rich man."

At first Gunner's Mate Third Class Kendall Truitt thought his friend Clayton Hartwig was joking. But then Hartwig explained that his dad and his Navy buddies in World War II had taken out insurance policies on one another, so they could all have a big party if any one of them died. Hartwig had decided to carry on the tradition, and when he was offered a $50,000 life insurance policy through the Navy credit union office in Norfolk, he signed up, and named his best buddy, Ken Truitt, as beneficiary. Both men were young and healthy, so Ken thought very little of the conversation after that night.

It was during the early months of 1988 that a nineteen-year-old seaman named Dave was assigned to the *Iowa*, his first assignment after only months in the Navy. Dave had told his Navy recruiter that he was gay, but the recruiter had signed him up anyway. Once on the *Iowa*, Dave, who requested even three years later that his full name not be used because his lover remained in the active-duty Navy, fell in with the substantial gay population aboard the battleship. In just two months, he met six officers, three chief petty officers, and twenty-three other enlisted crewmen who were gay.

Of course he heard the gossip that Clayton Hartwig and Kendall Truitt were gay, too. Attracted to Hartwig, Dave offered to give him a massage one night. Offering a massage had become a standard gay come-on on ships, but although Hartwig agreed to the massage he seemed oblivious to its sexual connotations. Instead, he talked about his level of stress because he had not seen his girlfriend in months. He even showed Dave his girlfriend's picture. When Dave suggested that Hartwig might want to loosen his clothes, the gunner's mate became uncomfortable and refused. Nor did he seem particularly comfortable having another man touch him.

After the aborted massage, Dave commented to one of his gay friends, "That's the straightest guy I've ever met in my life."

The Soesterberg Affair

MAY 1988
MARINE CORPS RECRUIT TRAINING DEPOT
PARRIS ISLAND, SOUTH CAROLINA

ON FRIDAY NIGHT of the Memorial Day weekend, Corporal Barbara Baum learned that she would go before a general court-martial two weeks later. That night she got drunk. In the days before the trial, the NIS increased pressure on her to make a statement. Major David Beck, reputed to be one of the Marine Corps' sharpest prosecutors, had come in to handle the lesbian cases. Beck was not available later for comment, but Baum recalled that he told her before the trial, "Go write a statement." Barbara actually considered it, but she did not know what she should write, so she pushed her paper aside.

When it was clear that she would not provide the Marine Corps with names of other lesbians, it was decided that her court-martial would proceed. Captain Laura Hinckley was taken off legal hold; the evidence against her, which prosecutors had hoped would come from Baum, was not about to appear. In one last attempt to derail the proceedings, Barbara wrote to the junior senator from her home state of Indiana. The letter she got back from Dan Quayle said that he would not involve himself in her case.

One of Barbara's civilian friends, Fran Cail, counseled her to contact gay-rights groups, go to the press, make a public scene. Cail had watched Parris Island witch-hunts for years, and always marveled at the loyalty the women felt for the Marine Corps, even while they were being ruthlessly railroaded out. By not going to the press, she argued, Barb was putting the Marine Corps' interest over her own. But Barb's own Marine Corps lawyer told her not to talk to reporters. Besides, friends assured Barbara that the threat of a thirty-eight-year prison sentence was just meant to frighten her. She would never go to jail.

Nevertheless, it was in these days that she began to have recurring nightmares in which she was handcuffed with her arms lashed to her sides, an armed guard on either side. The guards did not have faces. They took her to a cell, led her in, and the doors slammed shut behind her.

The Marine Corps feared one thing only: bad publicity. Except for the gay press, the purge had received little media attention outside the Beaufort area and the Marine Corps appeared to want to keep it that way. Later, when NIS statements were made public in hearings, they documented a careful accounting of women who had tried to gain media interest in the case. Among the names of those reported to be talking to journalists was the woman who would be singled out for especially harsh punishment, though she had told reporters not to use her name, and they had not. The Marine Corps knew that Barbara Baum was talking anyway.

AMSTERDAM, NETHERLANDS

BY EARLY JUNE, Jack Green was assured that negotiations were proceeding in earnest at the "highest levels" of the Dutch and American government concerning his release from the Air Force. Though the Air Force was content to wait Green out, the Dutch government was eager to resolve the matter before it escalated further.

Jack continued to stay with friends and acquaintances from the SH&K, though American agents were never far behind. Major Abel van Weerd, who hid Jack from time to time, began to notice strange clickings on his telephone, and an American military car parked outside his apartment. Senator Marie Louise Tiesinga Autsema also believed her phone was being tapped and noticed that she was being followed as well.

At any time, the United States government could demand extradition of Green as a deserter from the military, which complicated the situation. Although Holland would legally be required to turn Green over, it would be a difficult move for the government, given the popular sentiment against the policies for which Green was being sought. As a gay military organizer, van Weerd pointed out repeatedly on Dutch television that any move to force Green's return to American control was akin to turning Jews over to the Nazis, an accusation that had a special resonance for the Dutch. Jack's lawyer said that if the United States sought extradition, he would request political asylum for Green. Senator Tiesinga Autsema asked for five more days to work out a deal.

On June 8, American officials led by John Ras met with State Secretary J. van Houweligen, other Dutch state department officials, and Tiesinga Autsema. The Americans made the following promises: If Green turned himself in to American authorities, he would be honorably discharged from the Air Force and not subject to a court-martial. Once he turned himself in, he would be allowed twenty-four-hour contact with his Dutch attorney. To make sure everything went as agreed, Senator Tiesinga Autsema would accompany him. According to the agreement, Green would be out of the Air Force within four or five days.

The Americans had their demands as well. First, if Green agreed to turn himself in, he must do it quickly. Second, he would be processed out of the Air Force in Germany. The latter condition made Jack nervous. His presence in the Netherlands, he felt, was his only protection. But the Dutch state department and Senator Tiesinga Autsema assured him that these conditions represented a "state-to-state agreement" that was "guaranteed" to go smoothly. In the end, Jack felt he had no choice. To refuse meant alienating the Dutch government, his protectors. He agreed that he would turn himself in on June 9.

Within days, he believed, the ordeal would be over. By now, Senator Tiesinga Autsema had secured a resident's permit for Green once he was released from the Air Force. This was a relief to Green, and also served the Dutch government, which was torn between protecting Green from prosecution under the United States antihomosexual regulations and still safeguarding Holland's close alliance with the United States. As one Dutch newspaper wrote of the agreement, "The Dutch government and especially State Secretary van Houweligen seemed to be released from a difficult diplomatic problem and an international incident with an ally, the United States."

By now, Dutch gay activists were referring to Green's predicament as "The Soesterberg Affair."

MAY 1988
NORTH DAKOTA STATE UNIVERSITY
FARGO, NORTH DAKOTA

WHEN JOE STEFFAN returned to the Midwest from Annapolis, he felt as if the past five years and all that he had accomplished during them had never happened. Though Joe had been just weeks away from graduating at the time of his expulsion from Annapolis, North Dakota State University required that any student spend a full academic year at the institution to earn a degree. Since he was working a full-time job at a software company by day, this required that Joe take a full-time school schedule through night courses. Every night, after classes and several hours of study, Joe would fall exhausted into his bed and the hearings would begin replaying in his head. They had no right to do that, he lay there thinking. Why had he made it easy on them and resigned?

In Fargo, Joe began visiting the local gay bar, the only gay establishment in the state of North Dakota. These visits represented the first time he had ever had contact with the gay community as such, and he began to gain a sense of support and camaraderie. As his own self-esteem grew, his regret over having resigned began reforming itself into a resolve to rectify the situation. In late 1987, Joe again contacted Vernon "Copy" Berg, another Naval Academy alumnus who might understand what that would require.

Copy contacted gay civil liberties attorneys in New York City on Joe's behalf. Although the unusual circumstances of Joe's case intrigued them, particularly his high rank at the Academy, they were disheartened by the fact that Joe had resigned from the Academy, which made it more difficult legally to argue that he had been the victim of the military's antigay policy. The Lambda Legal Defense and Education Fund agreed to take the case, but before filing suit they set about researching the issue of Joe's resignation.

When he had first entered the Naval Academy, one expectation inspired Joe Steffan beyond all others: that he would be part of the mainstream, writing the future history of his nation. Back in Fargo, Steffan was far removed from the mainstream, but once his plans for the lawsuit were set, he began to think that he might still influence the direction of the country, although in a way that he could never have imagined as an eager young plebe just five years ago.

THE ONGOING INVESTIGATIONS of gays at the Naval Academy, now a regular feature of the school year, continued to keep Copy Berg occupied. Steffan's friend Rick had seen his Academy career end abruptly when he denied a female midshipman the lead role in the Academy production of *The King and I*, which Rick was directing. The aspiring actress, who had a crush on Rick's boyfriend, told a friend she wanted "to do something about it," and her friend agreed to send an anonymous letter to the NIS claiming that Rick was gay and that he had smoked marijuana.

A urine test confirmed the marijuana use. NIS agents spent the weekend before Rick's graduation ceremony interrogating other midshipmen about him, including everyone who had performed in a dramatic production with Rick. He had been slated to sing "Blue and Gold," the Naval Academy anthem, at the graduation ceremony, but was ordered to stay away from the commencement. Finally, he was offered immunity if he resigned from the Navy and accepted an other than honorable discharge and if he would testify against his boyfriend.

Rick resigned—and was presented with a bill for the $53,000 the government had paid for his Academy education. Since he had resigned before fulfilling his four-year commitment to the Navy, the government reasoned it was entitled to its money back. Rick moved to New York City, where Copy Berg helped him get a job as an accountant for his friend Charles Bell, another person who understood the special trauma of a gay discharge. Even as investigators bore down on Rick, the Academy announced that it had put two female midshipmen "on leave" for being homosexual.

Minutes before Barbara Baum's court-martial was to begin, Marine Corps prosecutor Major David Beck offered a new deal. For the next hour and a half, Barb's lawyer, Joseph Codega, negotiated the terms. Under the agreement, Barbara would plead guilty to all counts. Major Beck insisted that Barbara be sentenced to prison, but agreed to allow the sentence to be suspended.

The promise of no confinement was inviting, but Barbara suspected that Marine officials were still after Gunnery Sergeant Diane Edwards and Barb's friend Captain Laura Hinckley, the Naval Academy graduate. With a suspended sentence, the Marine Corps could continue to pressure her for a statement and could threaten her with new charges that might lift the suspension on her sentence, in which case she would go to jail anyway. Baum would not make a statement. Either she would face confinement or not; if the Marine Corps would not set aside Beck's demand that she be sentenced to jail, she would not cut the deal. So the court-martial began.

The proceeding had the air of a Roman holiday. Every Marine who had ever crossed swords with a Parris Island lesbian, it seemed, attended the court-martial, the first of many anticipated lesbian trials in the months ahead. Since the most outspoken antilesbian officers had also attended the Article 32 hearings, it was not easy to find an unbiased jury among officers on the base. And as the Court of Military Review would later rule, the Marine Corps did not even try.

There was the selection of a Sergeant Major Moore as a juror, for example. Moore had attended portions of Baum's Article 32 hearing and so had already heard evidence that was to be presented against her. Jurors are supposed to enter a court-martial with an open mind. They most certainly are not supposed to have already heard the case against the defendant.

Another questionable juror was Colonel Robert Nunnally, who admitted that he had discussed the ongoing lesbian investigations repeatedly with Neil Robbins, the special agent in charge of the Parris Island NIS office. Moreover, in staff meetings for the past several weeks, Nunnally had been outspoken in his opinion that lesbians had no place in the Marine Corps and that they should be routed out. Under questioning by attorneys, however, Nunnally, who later declined to comment on the case, denied making prejudicial statements against lesbians. As far as Baum was concerned, Nunnally had committed perjury, a belief shared by the military lawyers themselves, who later conceded to a military appeals court that he should never have been allowed on the jury. Even accepting Nunnally's denial, merely the admission of the discussions with the NIS should have been enough to disqualify him, Barbara's attorney argued at the court-martial. But this reasoning was unsuccessful with the military judge.

Other jurors had also been exposed to pretrial publicity about the case, which in most civilian courtrooms would have disqualified them from serving. Only two of the eleven jurors, in fact, said they had not been exposed to publicity about the case.

The testimony against Baum was essentially the same as in her Article 32 hearing, though there were some embellishments. A male sergeant testified that he had seen Baum passionately kiss another sergeant at a private home off base one night. The sergeant whom Baum was supposed to have kissed, however, testified that she had never even met the corporal and had no contact with her except to wave to her when she passed her guard post at the front gate, something a good share of the base had done. Later, when Baum reviewed her pay records, she saw that she had been on leave and not even in Beaufort on the day of the alleged kiss.

Diane Maldonado appeared in civilian clothes, on maternity leave. She covered the familiar ground about the couple's night at the Buccaneer Motel, their "indecent acts" together, and their collusion to keep the story of their relationship away from the NIS.

Steve Davis testified about that night at the Buccaneer, as did Neil Robbins, the NIS agent who had been waiting outside the motel. Robbins recalled hearing Feldhaus "exchange words" with Davis in Baum's presence, thereby substantiating the charge that the two women were involved in a conspiracy to obstruct justice by interfering in Davis's role as an NIS informant.

The Military Police with whom Baum worked were eager to line up as character witnesses for her. Their supportive testimony could have gone on for days, but the military judge stopped it when it became clear that most of her coworkers would only sing her praises.

In closing arguments, Major Beck put aside suggestions that the jury consider the fact that all of Baum's sexual activity occurred with consenting adults in the privacy of their own homes, away from military installations. "A Marine is a Marine, twenty-four hours a day, on-duty and off-duty," Beck said.

Barbara waited for the verdict in the office of her lawyer, Captain Joseph Codega. Codega advised her that if she was found guilty, she should try to gain the jury's sympathy during the final portion of the court-martial, which would decide her sentence. She should be ready to recount the story of the sexual and physical abuse that had blighted her childhood. Barbara rebelled at the suggestion. In her entire life she had told only a handful of people about it, and almost no one seemed to believe her. She would rather expose all the lies that had been spoken about her in the hearing and chastise the jury for its decision. Codega pointed out what a bad idea that would be, and Baum finally agreed to take his advice.

After two hours of deliberation, Corporal Barbara Baum was called back into the courtroom and asked to stand at attention while the verdict was read. Barbara's legs felt like jelly, but she stood erect, her head held high. She fixed her gaze at a point on the wall; nothing would move her, she decided. She was a Marine.

The judge read the first verdict.

"On specification one," he said. "Guilty."

And specification after specification, felony after felony, the word was the same: "Guilty." Of the eighteen charges lodged against her, she was found guilty of fifteen. The maximum possible sentence was thirty-five years in prison.

While Baum's jury had been listening to testimony, base public affairs officers had issued new announcements of the widening purge. Sergeant Mary Kile had accepted her administrative discharge in lieu of a court-martial. She was the third sergeant to leave the Corps so far. The charge that had focused suspicion on Kile was the rumor that she had sent flowers to Captain Gretch. Later, another woman confessed to having sent the flowers, but by then Kile was gone.

It was also announced that morning that administrative proceedings would begin against Baum's roommate, Becky Feldhaus.

Amsterdam, Netherlands

WITHIN AN HOUR of the beginning of Barbara Baum's court-martial, a Dutch government limousine picked Jack Green up at his safe house in Amsterdam. Senator Tiesinga Autsema and an official of the Dutch secretary of state's office were along to make sure that the Americans kept their side of the agreement this time.

A Dutch military plane flew the group to Sembach Air Base in Germany. Four base officials, including two colonels, were waiting for the plane when it touched down. One of the colonels advised Senator Tiesinga Autsema that the base commander wanted to greet her. The colonel ushered the Dutch government's representatives inside, leaving Green on the tarmac. As soon as the Dutch were out of sight, Security Police surrounded Green, handcuffed him, and took him to a jail cell.

Two hours later, Green was before a board hearing to examine whether charges should be filed against him. He had had only twenty minutes to talk to his Air Force lawyer, who knew nothing of his case or the agreement that had been so laboriously worked out between the Dutch and United States governments.

Addressing the board, the prosecutor explained that they knew Green was a homosexual but that they could not submit the evidence that the Office of Special Investigations had gathered as proof because that evidence had been obtained illegally by the Dutch military police.

What the Air Force could prove, however, was that Jack Green had deserted the military not once but twice, and that he had twice disobeyed a direct order to return. The prosecutor also told how the Dutch government had tried to influence the Air Force decision to prosecute Green. It would not work. Green, he said, should be court-martialed. Jack was ordered to Mannheim Confinement Facility at least until his Article 32 hearing.

When Jack was turned over to Army prison guards, it was clear they had been apprised of his case. "What are you—a faggot?" one said. Another taunted, "Who do you think you are, running away from the American government?"

Jack was marched into a maximum security cell. In one adjacent cell was a man who had just been convicted of murdering a child, in the other was a convicted rapist. They got beds, cigarettes, and clothing; Jack was ordered to strip down to his underwear and given no bed, just a blanket and a pillow.

The next day, Jack asked to talk to his Dutch attorney. The guards refused to allow him any calls, although his prosecutor had said that if Jack had anything to say to his counsel in Amsterdam, he would be happy to pass it along. Since conducting talks with his defense attorney through the prosecuting attorney did not seem prudent, Jack refused, but kept pressing his guards for a phone call to Holland.

On the third day at the Mannheim prison, Jack was allowed to make a phone call if he said nothing about the conditions of his imprisonment or how he was being treated. "If you do try to say anything, we'll disconnect you," an officer said. "And if you think you have it bad now, you could be in a straitjacket and chains in the cell." Jack talked with his lawyer for less than a minute when it became clear that someone was listening on another extension.

After the call, the officer asked about Jack's assertion that there had been an agreement between Dutch and American authorities concerning his treatment. When Jack outlined the terms that were to have been followed, the officer called him a liar. He would know about any state-to-state agreements concerning his prisoners, and he had heard nothing.

The next day, Senator Tiesinga Autsema called. Once again, Jack was ordered not to reveal anything about his treatment, and not to speak in a foreign language. Moments into the conversation, however, Jack started speaking Dutch and said, "I have no bed, I have no clothes." At that, the officer grabbed the phone from his hand and ordered, "You've got to speak in English. I'll give you one more chance." When the conversation resumed, Senator Tiesinga Autsema continued speaking in Dutch, telling Jack that she and the secretary of state were doing all they could to get him released. The phone was taken away and the senator was told she could talk to Jack no more.

Back in the Netherlands, the Americans' abrogation of their agreements with the Dutch government inspired outrage both in the press and in Parliament. Senator Tiesinga Autsema felt double-crossed.

The chairman of the Standing Committee for Defense in the Lower

House, MP Ad Ploeg, announced he would intercede to try to get Green released from prison and out of the Air Force. Other senators said they would call the secretary of state before the Parliament to answer questions about the government's handling of Green's surrender to the Americans.

The United States embassy responded through a spokesman that there had never been an agreement with the Dutch, and that no meetings to discuss Green's fate had ever taken place. "There is absolutely no promise," the spokesman said, adding, "That would be remarkable if it happened to a soldier who committed a penal offense twice, desertion." The next day, the embassy confirmed that Green was being court-martialed.

Dutch newspaper columnist Bert Steinmetz took up Green's cause in a series of columns, and felt obliged to explain the curious customs of the United States when it came to gays. "It is, defense experts say, difficult to imagine what a completely different world the American military society is, compared to the Dutch society. Homosexuality is not only formally forbidden, it is considered to be a very despicable thing. That is, according to these defense experts, the explanation why it is so difficult for the American authorities to comply to the Dutch pressure of releasing Sergeant Green without punishment."

WHILE JACK GREEN shivered in his cell at the Army's prison in Mannheim, Barbara Baum took the stand in the sentencing phase of her court-martial. For thirty-five minutes, she did as Codega had suggested, and told the grim story of her abused and battered childhood. The testimony embarrassed her profoundly. It was going to kill her family to have this in the newspapers, she thought, and she wasn't even sure it would help. Maybe it would look like she brought it up as a sort of excuse because she was in trouble.

Halfway through the emotional testimony, Barbara broke down and cried. In the rear of the courtroom, she heard someone break into laughter. In his summation, Codega asked for leniency and asked the court not to make Barbara "an example for an example's sake."

Prosecutor Beck told the jury they should sentence Baum to the maximum thirty-five years in prison to inform other Marines that homosexuality would not be tolerated in the Corps. As for her troubled background, she would have plenty of time to sort it out in jail, he said.

The jury took just forty-five minutes to decide that one year's confinement was appropriate. After she had served her time, Barbara would receive a dishonorable discharge from the Marine Corps.

When her fellow MPs handcuffed her to take her away, she wanted to cry again, but she stayed strong and did not. Codega had urged her not to talk to the press on the way out; doing so would only anger the Marine Corps, and there was the clemency request to consider now. So

Barb did not speak when the handful of reporters shot questions at her, until she was within earshot of Judge Colonel Taylor, who had tried the case, and then she said, "It's not over yet."

Before being transported to the Marine Corps brig in Quantico, Virginia, she spent the weekend at the detention cell at the Marine Corps Air Station in Beaufort. Among her visitors was Captain Codega, who said he had received a call from Major General Hoar, the commanding general of the base, offering a new deal. Hoar later declined comment on the Parris Island purge but Baum recalled that Codega said if she was willing to give a statement, "All the cards are on the table." Said Codega, "You could be free tomorrow." Baum told him "absolutely not." Codega said he would give her another day to think about it.

When Barbara's parents arrived from Indiana, her mother spoke to Captain Laura Hinckley, a key target of the Parris Island purge, and came away with the impression that Hinckley gave permission for Barb to make a statement. As long as Hinckley didn't mind, her mother encouraged her to save herself by talking.

For the rest of the weekend, a number of friends came by to lend their moral support. Of no small concern to many of the other lesbians at Parris Island was whether Baum would now crack and name names.

Gunnery Sergeant Diane Edwards was particularly anxious when she went to visit Baum at the Air Station that weekend. With fourteen years in the Corps, she would be a prize for investigators, but the NIS had no evidence against her. Edwards had not committed any of the indiscretions with recruits that had become the crucial evidence against Sergeant Cheryl Jameson. In fact, Edwards, like many other lesbian drill instructors, felt so strongly against becoming involved with recruits that she believed Jameson deserved her court-martial and whatever punishment she received. But the point of the Parris Island purge, she believed now, was not to eradicate inappropriate behavior among drill instructors, it was to root out lesbians, any lesbians, good or bad—the higher ranking, the better.

"What is it they want from you?" Diane asked Baum when they were alone.

Baum answered, "They want you."

JUNE 15, 1988
SEMBACH AIR BASE
KAISERSLAUTERN, WEST GERMANY

As THE FUROR in the Netherlands mounted over the Soesterberg Affair, American authorities had new concerns with which to contend. Jack Green's father told reporters in the United States that he would seek a congressional investigation of his son's case. In Parliament, the secretary of state was grilled by senators and promised that the government was doing all it could to secure Green's release. Senators announced that they would question the defense minister the following week. Perhaps most significantly, Jack Green's Dutch lawyer announced he had retained a German attorney, raising the possibility that the United States could face legal action in Germany. In the United States, Jack's dad told reporters he would fly to Germany to champion his son's cause.

The threat of more international wrangling over Green lit a fire under the Air Force. Guards rushed into Green's cell and removed him to Ramstein Air Base, where he was loaded onto an Air Force transport. An hour into the flight, however, the airplane developed mechanical problems and had to be diverted back to Rhine-Main Air Base. There, the plane was met by three Security Police cars, all waiting to escort Green back to a cell.

Jack overheard the SPs say they had never seen the brass jump the way they did when they heard that the sergeant would be coming to their base. One of Green's escorts said the orders had come from Secretary of Defense Frank Carlucci himself. (Carlucci later declined to comment on the case.) "It is of the utmost importance that he not escape," they were told, so Jack was put in leg irons and handcuffed with his arms chained to his sides. He felt like Al Capone. He was placed in a holding cell, and near midnight given a sheet and told to sleep on the floor.

At the first change of guards that night, Jack heard someone shout, "Where's the faggot?" Then several guards lined up in front of his cell to make degrading remarks. "All this trouble for one faggot?" one asked.

Early the next morning, Jack was flown to McGuire Air Force Base in New Jersey. When he was able to call Senator Tiesinga Autsema, she told him that the matter was being handled at the "very highest levels" of the Dutch government. The prime minister, Jack later learned, was trying to work out a new deal with Secretary Carlucci, and not long after that, he found out that his Article 32 hearing was being planned in advance of his expected court-martial on felony counts of desertion.

AFTER BARBARA BAUM told her attorney she would give a statement, she expected that she would not be taken to Quantico as planned, but that Major Beck would come to her cell in Beaufort and she would tell him what he wanted. But on Monday morning, Military Police came instead, handcuffed her, and then locked her arms to a black belt around her waist. She was paraded through Savannah Airport between two huge MPs, flown to Washington, and then driven to the Marine Corps brig in Quantico.

It was just like her dream of being marched into the prison, except the guards had faces. That night, Barbara dreamed about Buckwheat, a black-and-white cat she had adopted a year earlier. When she woke up, she expected to feel the cat purring at her feet, and see the inside of her own bedroom in her own home, but when she opened her eyes, all she saw were the bars of her jail cell.

65

Funerals

JUNE 22, 1988
WEST HOLLYWOOD, CALIFORNIA

BY APRIL, when Leonard Matlovich could no longer walk the three flights of stairs to his apartment on San Francisco's Castro Street, he packed up his few belongings and moved to West Hollywood to stay with a friend who would take care of him. Every week he came down with something new. Soon the Kaposi's sarcoma lesions that stained his skin spread to inside his digestive track, which made it impossible for him to absorb nutrients. He began to lose weight rapidly.

In those final weeks, Matlovich, long the calm and reasonable leader among gay activists, found his rage. His whole life had been hemmed in by prejudice. His childhood and early adult years had been haunted by nameless self-loathing; prejudice had ended his Air Force career; and now he was dying of a disease for which he believed there would certainly be medical solutions, except for the sluggish government response. Even in dying, it seemed, he could not escape the hatred.

Despair overwhelmed him; to friends, he was curt and sometimes angry. And he still yearned for that which he had never found, a lover. As he said in one of the last interviews of his life, with journalist Mike Hippler who was then working on Matlovich's biography, "I'd like to have a lover. I'd like to have that feeling once in my life—to love and be loved wholeheartedly."

Leonard's friend Ken McPherson, a veteran gay activist, had arranged for Matlovich to speak at a huge gay march in Sacramento; it would be his last public appearance. Lenny was very weak; when he spoke, even he noticed that his oratorical fire was gone. He told them at the end, "We've got to love each other."

Matlovich could no longer absorb water. He became severely dehydrated. He was hospitalized, but then released; the doctors gave him three weeks to live. Within a week, he was coherent only part of the time.

His family came for a last visit, completely devoted to Leonard, but still unaware of what he symbolized for many people. When McPherson told them that there would have to be a press announcement when he died, and a public funeral, his parents looked mystified. It had not crossed their minds that this was anything but a private drama.

In his last days, Lenny refused all medication, perhaps because it only prolonged his suffering and delayed the inevitable. Finally, he slipped out of consciousness, and his family watched as his breaths turned into long, deep sighs, and then into a regular pattern of shallow breaths. At 9:43 P.M. on June 22, 1988, two weeks before his forty-fifth birthday, Leonard Philip Matlovich, Jr., stopped breathing altogether.

LATER HISTORIES WILL RECORD these years as an era of death for the gay community. The largest regular features in local gay newspapers became the obituary pages, which were crowded with death notices of thousands of young men. Reading such pages was how one kept up with who was dead and who was still living. When someone ran into an old acquaintance he had not seen in some time, he might say it was good to see him, but what he meant was that it was good to see that he was still alive.

Gay organizing floundered as virtually an entire generation of gay male leaders, who had spent years achieving positions of influence within mainstream institutions, suddenly wasted away and died. The impact would be felt on the gay movement for decades; there were few to replace them. A new generation of lesbians began moving into many of the more prominent leadership positions. Their presence in the movement's top echelons was long overdue and many gained these positions through talent and competence, but at least some women rose to become prominent in local gay groups in large part because the male leaders had all died off.

The funeral became a central ritual in the lives of homosexual people, and this was no less true for gay men serving in the United States military. By the time Major George Gordy died, he had achieved unusual distinction among Air Force fighter pilots. Though he had been investigated in the same 1979 Air Force Academy purge that had claimed two other careers, he had gone on to become a much-decorated F-16 pilot, the winner of such prestigious Air Force honors as the Orville Wright Achievement Award. But he died of AIDS, and that implied that he was homosexual, which seemed incongruous with an illustrious career. So the Air Force Academy alumni newsletter reported that Major Gordy had died of cancer, and a two-star general flew in from Korea to deliver his eulogy.

Colonel Kenneth Wittenberg also found ignominy after his HIV-related death. Wittenberg was a signal corps officer who worked in a highly sensitive job at the military's White House communications center for several years. When his lover Kary Walker sought the military funeral for Wittenberg to which he was entitled, the local Army detail in LaCrosse,

Wisconsin, asked for a copy of Wittenberg's death certificate. When they saw that he had died of AIDS, the local detachment waffled about conducting services for him, and ultimately refused.

This was not always the case, however, and many victims of AIDS did receive the same dignities as those given any other soldier. This was so for retired Air Force Colonel David van Poznak, who was something of a legend among gay military personnel in the Washington area. In 1963, he had been a junior captain assigned to work on protocol in the White House. Succeeding First Ladies valued him and influenced their husbands to intercede so that the Pentagon allowed him to remain at this assignment rather than rotate out. Van Poznak stayed at the White House for fourteen years. His walls were adorned with photos of himself with Presidents and with other heads of state—French President Charles DeGaulle and Queen Elizabeth II, among others.

In one garrulous, animated moment, he had sat right down on a hysterical Soviet President Leonid Brezhnev's lap, and had his picture taken there. When he died, he was afforded full Air Force honors in Arlington National Cemetery.

Major Jeff Bircher, commander of the Air Force honor guard at Arlington National Cemetery, also received full military honors after he died of AIDS, and his coworkers thought well enough of him that they named one of their rooms in his honor.

As OF MID-1988, more than 2,200 of the nearly 6,000 soldiers and recruits who had tested HIV positive remained in the military, but there were still some quarters that would have preferred simply to discharge all of them. In December 1988, Colonel John Cruden, chief of the Pentagon's legislative division, wrote the Defense Department's general counsel that "Maintaining in the active duty force over 2,200 permanently nondeployable combat assets who are certain to progress to medical unfitness in a relatively short period of time is a very unwise personnel policy." The Pentagon now estimated that the cost of maintaining these "nondeployable assets" was $57 million a year.

Cruden had an ally in Deputy Defense Secretary William Howard Taft IV, who directed Army officials to devise a program to allow any HIV-positive soldier early medical separation or disability retirement. However, this change would require congressional approval. Although the Pentagon forwarded legislation to enable the services to discharge all their HIV-infected sailors, the bill went nowhere on Capitol Hill, effectively resolving the issue. The new HIV regulations issued in August 1988 offered no substantive changes in how the services should deal with HIV-infected personnel.

By late summer 1988, all the services had started their first round of retesting soldiers and sailors. The new testing showed that, as elsewhere in society, military members continued to become HIV infected. In the

Army, one out of 1,300 soldiers converted from HIV negative to HIV positive every year, according to the testing, making for about 600 new HIV-infected soldiers annually.

Some military doctors argued that the real numbers of HIV-positive service members was really much higher, and suggested that military officials obscured this fact, presumably for fear of alerting the public to the large presence of gays in the armed forces. In San Diego, for example, Dr. William Harrison, who had recently retired as a Navy captain, challenged the Navy's claim that 622 HIV-positive soldiers had been processed through the AIDS unit at Balboa Naval Hospital. This was about 37 percent of the 1,681 sailors and Marine Corps members who the Navy said had tested positive between 1986 and 1987. Of these, only 350 remained on active duty in the San Diego area, according to the Navy.

Harrison was in charge of Balboa's AIDS program and knew he had treated between 800 and 1,000 patients. Moreover, he said, between 650 and 900 were on active duty in the area. "The Navy is lying, manipulating the statistics," Harrison told the *San Diego Tribune*'s AIDS reporter Cheryl Clark. He pointed to another official military publication that reported that 2,187 sailors and Marines had tested positive.

The Navy did not allay suspicions when it ordered its San Diego epidemiologist not to discuss HIV statistics with the media, or when the Navy's AIDS coordinator at the Naval Medical Command declined comment altogether, and a spokesman explained it as such: "If people are reading about the numbers of HIV-positives in the military, it may raise some concern."

There were also inconsistencies in the numbers Defense Department officials reported to the press. While medical officials said the number of active-duty HIV-positive servicemen was 2,200, other Pentagon officials privately told the *Navy Times* in May 1988 that the true number was closer to 2,900.

Most HIV-infected personnel from this period reported fair treatment by their commanders, and an adherence to the official regulations guaranteeing confidentiality and nondiscrimination. When a pharmacist at the Reynolds Army Community Hospital, Fort Sill, Oklahoma, tried to embarrass an HIV-positive serviceman by calling out to him loudly in the crowded pharmacy that his AZT, an AIDS drug, was ready, the pharmacist was severely disciplined for violating the soldier's confidentiality. In San Diego, a Navy commander became leader of his aviation squadron *after* he tested HIV positive, an appointment that was personally approved by the Deputy Secretary of the Navy. HIV-positive soldiers and sailors routinely continued achieving positions that required the most sensitive security clearances.

The attitude toward HIV-positive soldiers, however, was sometimes hostile. At Fort Hood, Texas, the world's largest tank and artillery post, the commanding general, Lieutenant General Crosbie Saint, consolidated all HIV-positive soldiers in one barracks, which commonly became known as the "HIV Hotel." Saint maintained that the segregation was necessary to preserve the combat readiness of his other units. Saint executed his order by transferring all fifty HIV-positive soldiers on the base to the headquarters unit, where they would perform administrative tasks and not be deployable. On the same day, in April 1988, they were also moved to Building 21006, which even Saint referred to as "the leper colony."

The abrupt job transfers and barracks relocations immediately alerted the other 38,000 soldiers on the base as to who was HIV positive, which resulted in the harassment of anyone housed in the barracks. To make matters worse, the fifty soldiers were not allowed to leave the barracks at night; the HIV Hotel was more a prison than a hotel. Any infraction of the rules earned a disciplinary hearing.

Under mounting harassment on the job and off, HIV-positive Private John Brisbois went AWOL and sought psychiatric treatment at Lackland Air Force Base. Fort Hood authorities were contacted and Brisbois was put in shackles and leg irons and taken to the Fort Hood confinement facility. At the stockade, he was handed a bottle of insecticide shampoo that featured the word POISON on its label, and told to shower. He drank it, hoping it would kill him. After his stomach was pumped, he was thrown back in jail. Shortly after that, he received a less than honorable discharge.

The HIV Hotel shut down after *Newsday*'s AIDS reporter, Laurie Garrett, sneaked onto the post with a photographer and published a front-page exposé of the facility. Brisbois ultimately filed a complaint asking for an investigation by the Inspector General, which found that Army regulations had been violated. No disciplinary action, however, was recommended against the officers who had violated the regulations. By then, the unfavorable publicity had prompted officials to transfer the HIV-positive soldiers out of the headquarters unit and reintegrate them into post housing. Lieutenant General Saint was not chastened by the Inspector General's finding. When Saint received his fourth star and was assigned to be commanding general of the Army in Europe, he was overheard to boast, "I will have no trouble controlling the troops in Europe, after all, I ran the largest leper colony in the United States here at Fort Hood."

The most pivotal battle line regarding the treatment of HIV-infected personnel involved the enforcement of "safe-sex orders." Under them, any GI testing positive had to sign papers acknowledging that he had been ordered to inform all his sexual partners that he was HIV positive and to engage only in "safe-sex" practices.

The orders were a very military way to deal with a problem that the gay community had largely fumbled over the years: what to do about those who put others at risk for HIV infection. The military's solution was simple—order people not to do it and punish them when they did. The gay community had mainly ignored the issue, as it would for many more years. For their part, civil libertarians objected to the orders, suggesting they were meant to stigmatize further HIV-infected people in a way that carriers of other communicable diseases were not.

Gay worries that the safe-sex orders were designed to penalize homosexuality were appeased by the fact that they were enforced most aggressively against heterosexuals. In early 1988, Petty Officer John
Crawford became the first sailor to be charged with criminal charges
relating to unsafe sex. Navy officials accused the twenty-seven-year-old
of assault, adultery, and violation of an order for having unprotected sex
with his ex-girlfriend without informing her he was HIV positive. Crawford's attorneys contended that the Navy was using Crawford as "a guinea
pig, just to see how far they can go with this AIDS issue." They also
argued that the girlfriend was an unreliable witness, angry at Crawford
because he broke off their short engagement. A Navy jury acquitted
Crawford of the assault and adultery charges, but confined him to his
barracks for fifteen days because he had broken a Navy order by having
his tryst in his barracks room.

The potential antigay uses of the regulations became evident in the
case of Air Force Lieutenant Colonel David Eckert of McClellan Air Force
Base in Sacramento. Eckert flew a weather plane and was in his nineteenth
year in the Air Force, just one short of retirement. Though he had known
he was gay since he first signed up for officers' training in 1969, he had
kept his sexual orientation to himself, except for a few rare furtive trips
to a gay bathhouse before returning to his wife and two children. He was
introduced to the gay military subculture during a three-year assignment
to Clark Air Base in the Philippines. His wife had remained in the States,
and he developed a relationship with a twenty-three-year-old airman from
Georgia. Toward the end of his assignment, he was almost caught up in
an OSI investigation, but he refused to be interrogated and his lawyer
aggressively defended him. Ultimately, nothing happened.

By 1986, after his transfer to Sacramento, Dave Eckert wanted to
explore his gay identity outside his marriage. He and his wife separated
amicably and established residences two miles apart to afford their children
as close to normal parenting as possible. After his daily weather flights,
Eckert, a former seminarian, became involved in the local Metropolitan
Community Church and he planned to work in the gay church when he
retired in 1989.

In early 1986, the man Dave was then seeing took him aside to tell
him that his most recent boyfriend had just tested HIV positive. Eckert
went to a private hospital and found that he too was now infected. Eckert's
lover said he would stay with Dave, and the pair lived together for some
time in their Sacramento apartment until Dave discovered that the man
had been using his credit cards to the tune of many thousands of dollars.
Dave kicked him out of their home. Not long after, a woman friend of
the credit card thief called the OSI to report that Eckert made porno-
graphic movies with teenagers. Two weeks later, Dave's commander told
him he was being investigated for homosexual activity and, for reasons
that were never made clear, disclosure of classified information. He was
ordered to take an HIV test. When he tested positive, he was charged

with reckless endangerment for allegedly having unsafe sex, as well as with public sex with a minor, sodomy, and conduct unbecoming an officer.

Since a court-martial conviction could cost him both his freedom and the pension for which he had worked nineteen years, the forty-three-year-old pilot decided to go public and fight the charges. Bald, with a fringe of gray hair, Eckert looked like Dwight Eisenhower, but he had a booming, deep voice and impressive television presence. The case against him fundamentally rested on two facts, he asserted: that he was gay and that he was HIV positive. All the other charges grew out of assumptions about what gay AIDS-infected people did, and he was going to prove that those assumptions were false.

The media, even the military press, remained overwhelmingly supportive, particularly when it became clear that there was no evidence to buttress the Air Force charges. As columnist Michele McCormick wrote in *Navy Times*, "Officially, the charges against Eckert are not directly based on the fact that he is HIV positive. . . . But the fact remains that a person whose positive test becomes publicly known is a person who must endure an added handicap."

Eckert's lawyer, meanwhile, promised pickets and even more media coverage if a court-martial proceeded. Finally, Air Force Major General Trevor Hammond ruled that there was insufficient evidence to try Eckert on any of the court-martial offenses, although he did hand over evidence that Eckert was gay to the lieutenant colonel's commanding officer for administrative action. When asked to comment on the case, Hammond told reporters, "It's kind of nasty stuff that I don't like to talk about." In fact, the Air Force never did find any minor with whom Eckert allegedly had had sex, or any witness to any of the charges against him, except the admission of his ex-boyfriend that they had engaged in sodomy. Though Eckert no longer faced jail time, he once again risked losing his pension benefits, still being eight months from retirement. He and his lawyer managed to prolong the procedures, however, so that the administrative separation board could not be scheduled until August 2, 1989, one week after Eckert's twentieth year in the service, which enabled him to resign with full benefits.

Because of his rank and willingness to go public, Eckert had sidestepped a possible prison sentence or, at best, the loss of nearly twenty years of benefits. Others were not as lucky. By late 1988, the armed forces were prosecuting at least eight soldiers and sailors for violating their safe-sex orders, and as time went on those numbers grew.

WHILE THE MILITARY waged its war on sexually active HIV-positive soldiers, the quality of medical care for HIV-infected soldiers declined at some of the medical facilities mandated to handle the new cases of HIV-positive personnel. Walter Reed and the Air Force's Wilford Hall continued to receive excellent marks for their work with HIV-positive patients, but at outlying facilities, such as the Oakland Naval Hospital, complaints mounted. Without a strong advocate for AIDS patient care, such as Petty Officer T. J. Sterbens, or high-profile patients such as Admiral-select Art Pearson, who died in 1987, programs for the HIV infected deteriorated profoundly. At one point during a period of remodeling, hospital administrators were so detached as to tell the HIV patients to move their wards themselves. Meanwhile, the NIS office at the nearby Treasure Island Naval Station began nosing around the ward to find evidence that patients were homosexuals.

The champion of patients remained the feisty gay Navy judge Commander Mike LaBella, who had resided in the ward after his HIV diagnosis. LaBella served as unofficial legal adviser to the ward's patients. He also began traveling to Washington to lobby on HIV-related issues with his friends in the highest ranks.

It was during one of these trips that he first heard about a report concerning gays in the military that was being kept a closely guarded secret at the top echelons of the Pentagon. The reason for the secrecy, he heard, was that the report found gays were entirely capable of serving in the armed forces and that the policies against them should be abolished. That was all he could learn, however—that and the fact that it was the most fervent wish of the Department of Defense that no one outside the Pentagon learn that the report existed.

CORRECTIONAL FACILITY
MARINE CORPS COMBAT DEVELOPMENT COMMAND
QUANTICO, VIRGINIA

THE SAME DAY Leonard Matlovich died, Corporal Barbara Baum met with Major David Beck, the aggressive prosecutor of lesbians at Parris Island, and finally gave the statement that the Marine Corps had been seeking for six months. Barb was convinced that the two-week delay between her agreement to a meeting with Beck and his actual appearance was calculated to let her experience how awful imprisonment was, so she would be more cooperative. It worked. Barb hated prison. She had lost a great deal of weight. She could not eat or sleep. Her emaciation startled her attorneys, who said that she looked as if she had cancer. Prison psychologists worried that she might commit suicide.

Her Marine Corps attorney assured Barbara that the nightmare would end if she talked; he had promises from the base commanding general himself that if she named names, she would be freed.

On June 22 and 23, she spent fourteen hours with Major Beck and an NIS agent, telling them everything she knew. Her statement filled 178 pages. Beck had arrived with his own long list of suspected lesbians and quizzed Baum at length about each one. The NIS agent had a computer printout of names of alleged lesbians from throughout the Marine Corps, and he had questions about them. Most of the "evidence" Baum gave was hearsay; she said only that she had heard this or that woman was homosexual. Several of the responses that would later be used in administrative hearings against some of these women included such answers as "yes" or "I think so" to the question of whether this or that woman was lesbian. She did not claim to have any firsthand knowledge, either through her own sexual experiences or those of others, about any activities that could be the basis of charges for sodomy or indecent acts.

In the course of her statement, however, she provided the NIS with seventy-seven names of suspected lesbians and gave the "evidence" that would become the basis of discharge proceedings against several Marines, including Gunnery Sergeant Diane Edwards, the highly decorated veteran who was an early object of the probe, and Captain Judy Meade, a fourteen-year veteran who, Baum said, was "involved with" a civilian lesbian. For the Marine Corps, the statement was disappointing because it did not name as a homosexual Captain Laura Hinckley, the Naval Academy graduate. Baum's statements about their friendship gave the NIS enough evidence for a fraternization charge, but this, they knew, was unlikely to net the prison sentence that a prosecution for sodomy or indecent acts might produce.

The fact that she had talked so exhaustively to Beck and the NIS, however, made Baum confident that she would be released from jail any day. She began eating again, and began to gain weight. During her exercise period, she took up running, talking to God as she did her laps around the prison yard, praying that they would let her go tomorrow.

She waited for news of her expected release. And waited, and waited.

JULY 4, 1988
CONGRESSIONAL CEMETERY
WASHINGTON, D.C.

LEONARD MATLOVICH HAD KNOWN on precisely what day he wanted his funeral to be held: July 4, Independence Day. Ken McPherson remembered some of Leonard's old enthusiasm when the pair had met to discuss Matlovich's funeral. Matlovich had wanted the occasion to feature gay pride, the Air Force, and patriotism. He wanted flags and military honors and full deference to the notion that homosexuality should be talked about openly.

Lenny's grave site was in Washington, which made that city the logical place for a memorial service. Memorials for figures of less historical importance had drawn more than a thousand in San Francisco, so McPherson figured that with its huge gay community, Washington would offer up as large a crowd. From the start, however, every mainstream institution McPherson contacted threw up obstacles. Since Matlovich had died a confirmed atheist, he did not want a religious sendoff, but to comfort his parents he had decided that his memorial should be held in Washington's Christ Church, which was affiliated with Congressional Cemetery.

The minister at Christ Church concluded that that decision meant that in his last days, Lenny had returned to the fold. He ordered a service with full Episcopal communion. A Congressional Cemetery official, dressed in long, flowing robes, was to carry a gold crucifix at the head of the procession. Nothing Ken said could stop it. It seemed to Ken that the church had also decided to honor Matlovich as someone who was a noble soul *in spite* of being a homosexual, so there would be nothing political about the service. Ken fought to allow an outside public address system for the overflow crowd he anticipated; the church refused, saying it would not accommodate a "political circus."

For its part, the Air Force at first refused to participate at all; it would not provide an honor guard, bugler, or riflemen for the ceremony, all of which Matlovich was entitled to under Air Force regulations. Only the threat that the matter would become a newspaper story caused the Air Force to relent and allow the funeral detachment.

Ken had brought several leading spokespeople against the military's gay exclusion policy to attend the service—in uniform—and serve as pallbearers, including former Staff Sergeant Perry Watkins, whose case was still in the federal courts, and Ellen Nesbitt, a New York state National Guard officer who had recently launched her own federal case. When McPherson told the Air Force that these famous gay soldiers would hand the casket to the military honor guard for its transfer from the church to the graveyard, the Air Force again objected. They would not participate in any service with gays in military uniforms. In the end, McPherson had to give in, and Watkins and the others acted as escorts to the official honor guard, walking alongside them.

Ken plastered Washington's gay neighborhoods with posters featuring a photograph of Lenny's tombstone with its nameless epitaph for "A Gay Vietnam Veteran." On the morning of July 4, he believed that thousands would descend on the church, but they never came. The hundred-member Gay Men's Chorus comprised a majority of those in attendance; the leadership of the Washington-based national gay groups, sensing the passing of someone historic, made up the rest. Inside the church, the entire service was conducted without anyone mentioning that Matlovich, arguably the most influential gay activist of his generation, was gay, or that Lenny, who had spent his last years as an AIDS activist, had died of AIDS. *Don't talk about it*. The silent imperative that had so haunted his childhood and filled his early adult years with anxiety, the silence he had spent the last third of his life fighting, had descended once again.

Outside, there was more that would have been to Lenny's liking. His body was carried to the Civil War–style caisson, drawn by two black horses with plumes and braided manes. Marchers, carrying both the American flag and the rainbow flag that had become the symbol of the gay movement, surrounded the coffin and began the slow, mile-long march toward Congressional Cemetery with Washington police diverting traffic off Pennsylvania Avenue.

At the grave site, Perry Watkins spoke eloquently about the dream of equality Matlovich had advanced, and told how it had inspired him and a generation of others who had lived through those days before homosexuality was something one could talk about out loud, a time Leonard Matlovich had helped end irrevocably.

The Air Force had delivered a final indignity to the gentle man who had confronted it so publicly and boldly. When the manager from the caisson service began affixing the American flag to the top of Lenny's casket at the church, the head of the Air Force honor guard stepped in and ordered him to stop. The caisson manager objected, but if the Air Force was going to participate, there would be no flag on Leonard's coffin. And thus—during the procession, thirty minutes before the twenty-one-gun salute was fired for a fallen soldier and the last strains of taps drifted toward the Potomac—was Leonard Matlovich denied his flag-draped procession, the symbol he had held most dear in life.

On his way out of the graveyard, Ken McPherson walked up the gravel walkways past two other famous homosexuals who resided in the very same row as Leonard Matlovich: former FBI director J. Edgar Hoover, who was just eight grave sites down from Lenny, and his longtime companion, Clyde Tolson, who lay just several more graves from Hoover. It was Lenny's last little joke to be buried so close to them. Although the day had given Lenny some of what he wished for with its display of patriotism and gay pride, there was also disappointment for anyone who understood what Lenny had truly wanted. With its gap between expectation and outcome, Matlovich's death was like his life. As Ken walked out of the cemetery he heard the rumbling of the yellow bulldozers shoving the last sod over Lenny, now beneath the tombstone whose legend he had written, about a nameless veteran who had won medals for killing and a discharge for loving.

66

Malleus Maleficarum

ON THE SAME DAY that Leonard Matlovich died and Barbara Baum was talking to the NIS, Air Force Security Police told Sergeant Jack Green that he was being taken back to McGuire Air Force Base. It was only hours before his Article 32 hearing on felony desertion charges, and Jack had spent the previous night dreading that he would go to prison. The Security Police, however, had different news: He was being released, they said.

Two days later, Jack stood outside the base gate. He had no identification, no money, only the clothes on his back. Finally, his Dutch attorney arrived with his passport and he and his lawyer flew back to Holland, where Green was granted resident status. He would not be returning to live in the United States, a family spokesman explained; he wanted to live in a free country.

In its statement on the matter to the Dutch press, the United States embassy said, "The rapid solution of this case underlines the honesty and the rapid judicial process of military law in the United States."

The end of the Soesterberg Affair as an active political issue in the Netherlands did not stop the discussion of homosexuality in the military there. The treatment of Dutch gay soldiers became a topic of national discussion and policy review. More officers began acknowledging to their coworkers that they were gay. In 1988, one crucial disclosure came from Lieutenant Sylvan Benistant, who had entered the Royal Dutch Navy in 1967 as an enlisted man when he was seventeen years old and later became an officer. He had begun telling his coworkers he was gay in 1985, but did not go public until 1988. Benistant was the first naval officer to become involved with the SH&K.

At the time he joined the group, Benistant was about to be deployed on a six-month cruise. There was by now gossip that he was gay, so in the wardroom on the second night out, he told his fellow officers that he was homosexual and asked if anyone had any questions. Other officers admitted they had heard rumors, but there were no questions. In the weeks that followed, several took Benistant aside to ask what it was like to be gay, what about safe sex? Did he have a lover? Was it difficult in the macho naval environment? Benistant had expected a measure of hostility at his disclosure; instead, he found curiosity. He was the first openly gay officer in the Dutch navy and hardly anyone seemed to care. The next year, he was promoted to lieutenant commander.

At this time, in response to a question concerning the Soesterberg Affair, a Dutch admiral commented in an interview that the Royal Navy had no such problems, because there were no gays in the navy. Benistant suggested otherwise. Defense ministry officials therefore commissioned a study on the problems gay sailors faced in the navy and what the government could do to make military service more comfortable for them.

So in the same months that U.S. military authorities were jailing gays, the Dutch were launching programs to combat homophobia like those the United States had developed in the early 1970s to combat racism in the armed forces. The differences between the nations were obvious, as became clear to Major van Weerd when he spoke in 1988 at a Dutch military academy to Dutch and other Western military officers who were part of a NATO exchange. Though van Weerd's subject on this occasion was budgeting, he had received extensive coverage during the Soesterberg Affair, and when he began speaking, the two United States officers attending the briefing got up and walked out of the room.

CHARLESTON NAVAL STATION
CHARLESTON, SOUTH CAROLINA

PETTY OFFICER THIRD CLASS Terry Knox faced her Article 32 hearing for perjury, obstructing justice, and swearing an oath to a false statement largely stemming from the January interrogation in which she had given NIS agents her statement against Mary Kile. Her subsequent recantation had led to charges of perjury. The obstruction charge grew from her alleged interference with the Kile investigation. Virtually every woman now being charged at Parris Island had "obstruction of justice" or "impeding an investigation" added to her indictments. Lawyers considered the charges part of a strategy by prosecutors to make it appear the Marine Corps was interested in something other than merely rooting out lesbians: A long list of other charges made the women look more criminal.

Like a growing number of women from the Parris Island investigation, Knox had hired a civilian attorney, fearing that military lawyers would always owe their first allegiance to the service that signed their paychecks. He was Beaufort attorney Charles Macloskie, who had extensive experience in military law and was known as a maverick in local legal circles. When Macloskie heard about Knox's interrogation by the NIS, he immediately recalled a book he had perused in college, the *Malleus Maleficarum*. Written in 1484 at the height of the Inquisition by Fathers Jacobus Sprenger and Henry Kramer, the inquisitors for the German states, the book was a medieval manual for conducting real witch-hunts, as well as instructing how to interrogate suspected witches. The parallels between the strategies outlined in the *Malleus* were strikingly similar to those used by the NIS, so Macloskie inquired as to whether the Naval Investigative Service had a manual for conducting interrogations. Such a document would help determine whether the Knox interrogation had been handled within the agency's own guidelines.

When Knox's Article 32 hearing convened at Charleston Naval Station, Macloskie asked the NIS to produce its manual for interrogations. Neil Robbins, the special agent in charge of the Parris Island NIS office, denied such a manual existed. Once it became clear that it did indeed exist, the Marine Corps lawyer attempted to block its release to Macloskie. The Navy judge hearing the case, however, determined that such guidelines were relevant in a case where all the charges rested on one statement Knox gave during one interrogation session. He ordered the NIS to release the manual.

The NIS text varied little from the strategies first outlined four hundred years earlier during the Catholic Church's aggressive pursuit of witches. Where the NIS manual instructed, "It is considerably easier to successfully interrogate the anxious subject whom the interrogator observes is on the verge of losing self control, than the calm, collected individual who is in excellent self control," *Malleus Maleficarum* instructs inquisitors to keep "the accused in a state of suspense, and continually postponing the day of examinations."

The good cop–bad cop strategy was also prefigured by the *Malleus*, which suggested that one judge "shall use his own persuasion and those of other honest men zealous for the faith to induce her to confess the truth voluntarily; and if she will not, let him order the officers to bind her with cords, and apply her to some engine of torture; and then let them obey at once but not joyfully, rather appearing to be disturbed by their duty. Then let her be released again at someone's earnest request, and taken on one side and let her again be persuaded." The *Malleus* recommended extending promises of clemency, but to ensure that inquisitors did not have to deliver upon the promises, the judge should "afterwards disclaim the duty of passing sentence on her, deputing another Judge in his place."

There was one other important aspect to successfully interrogating a witch, according to the book—to ensure that "she supply evidence which will lead to the conviction of other witches."

It was amazing to Macloskie that the nation that considered itself the most advanced democracy in the world still employed tactics from the most discredited chapter of criminal proceedings. And it was all happening at Parris Island.

As the Article 32 hearing progressed, Macloskie noted all the parallels, as well as the fact that the NIS had never read Knox her rights when they interrogated her. Nor had the agency supplied her with an attorney when she asked for one. The Navy argued that the NIS was not obliged to read rights or allow Knox a lawyer because she had not been brought in as a criminal suspect, but as a witness. This answer did not explain why NIS agents threatened to send her to prison, but the Navy aggressively pursued the argument anyway.

The judge did not agree, and ruled that Knox's NIS statement was inadmissible. Since the statement was virtually the only evidence against Knox, the Navy was forced to drop its charges against her; the NIS's excesses had effectively ensured Knox's acquittal. Knox was the first woman to be entirely cleared in any of the Parris Island hearings.

AFTER BARBARA BAUM's hearing, in the first weeks of summer, the Parris Island purge was beginning to turn into a major embarrassment for the NIS. Attorney Vaughan Taylor faced five witnesses in one case who the NIS said had made statements against his clients, but when he put them on the stand all five testified that the NIS had lied. Two witnesses had never even heard the names of women whom the NIS said they had charged with being lesbians. When Taylor requested that NIS agent Renea King, who was accused of being one of the most aggressive interrogators, appear to testify at a hearing, the NIS claimed that she was "not available" to appear and, as a civilian, she could not be subpoenaed by the military.

Such episodes, particularly the interrogation of Knox, brought a measure of public attention to NIS tactics for the first time. When activists began organizing belatedly around the Parris Island issue, their concerns had less to do with the expulsion of gays per se than with the means used to achieve the expulsions. In this way, the story of Parris Island became the story of the NIS.

Even before Parris Island, the agency was held in low esteem by other federal investigatory agencies. In 1985, after the agency had bungled the Walker family spy scandal and been oblivious to the espionage involving Marines at the United States embassy in Moscow, U.S. Congressman Jim Bates called for the agency to be abolished. Though the proposal did not find widespread support, it did not mean that the NIS had many friends in the Capitol.

In the redbrick headquarters of the agency at the Washington Navy Yard, NIS officials bristled at the suggestion that its agents acted in a less than professional manner. Its 1,000 agents received the same training as agents for other federal law enforcement agencies, such as the Customs Service and the Secret Service, officials noted. If they were held in low esteem by some in Washington, this had not deterred Congress from appropriating a hefty budget for the agency: $135 million in 1989. By 1992, the budget would be $190 million.

Still, the entry-level pay at the NIS was not designed to attract top candidates. The agency paid about $25,000 to new agents, compared to the FBI starting salary of $34,000 a year. This meant a higher proportion— and, some said, a lower quality—of applicants were accepted, since the NIS did not get as many applicants as the more prestigious federal agencies. The NIS hired one in ten of those who applied, compared to one in fifty at the FBI. NIS applicants tended to have far less expertise in criminal justice than applicants at other agencies. Because the agency was held in low regard, there was heavy turnover. According to a *New York Times* investigation in 1990, about 69 percent of NIS agents had been on the job five years or less.

Three years after the end of the Parris Island trials, David Powers, head of investigations for the agency, dismissed accusations that the agency had behaved improperly in the probe as the complaints of people who had violated the law and resented being caught. He flatly denied that the agency would ever threaten a woman with the loss of custody of her children. As for other interrogation techniques, Powers noted, accurately, that no one is compelled to participate in an NIS interview; subjects can walk out of an interrogation at any time. If people interrogated by the NIS felt intimidated, he said, it was in large part because they gave permission for themselves to be intimidated.

———————

BACK AT PARRIS ISLAND, the hearings and courts-martial continued. Five weeks after the Baum trial concluded, Sergeant Cheryl Jameson, a nine-year Marine, was court-martialed for sodomy, indecent acts with other women, failure to obey an order, and obstruction of justice. Much of Jameson's hearing consisted of legal arguing over what constituted sodomy among women. At one point, the chief prosecution witness, Lance Corporal Carrie Prusa, took the stand and used a diagram of female anatomy from a medical textbook to describe the three episodes of oral sex she said she had with Jameson. The sodomy charge was eventually thrown out, and Jameson was convicted of indecent acts with other women, fraternization, and failure to obey an order. Like Baum, Jameson was sentenced to one year in prison, and received a dishonorable discharge.

Three days later, Colonel Robert Nunnally, who had served on Barbara Baum's jury, called Staff Sergeant Christine Hilinski into his office. Though she was a drill instructor, Hilinski had taken a six-month temporary assignment as a depot inspector, serving under Nunnally. Hilinski was aware of the colonel's strong feelings about lesbians: In his meetings every Friday morning, he frequently mentioned his dislike and his belief that they had no place in the Marine Corps. Hilinski had appeared as a character witness for Cheryl Jameson at her court-martial, and had testified that she was an excellent drill instructor. Hilinski expected some flak from Nunnally, but was still surprised when Nunnally told her that because of her testimony for Jameson, he had voided her Military Occupational Specialty, or MOS, effectively terminating her job as a drill instructor. Nunnally said he lacked confidence in her "judgment," given her testimony for an accused lesbian.

Staff Sergeant Gwen Gurule, who had also been a character witness for Jameson, was similarly rewarded, her MOS was voided, and she was removed from the drill field for reassignment elsewhere, which effectively relieved her. Just hours earlier, Nunnally had met with Staff Judge Advocate Kenneth Taylor and Base Chief of Staff Robert McInteer, fanning rumors that the orders to demote Hilinski and Gurule had come from the top. Over the next three days, various officers held informal briefings in which Gurule's and Hilinski's testimony was read aloud. People making similar testimony, officers warned, could face comparable discipline.

Lawyers for lesbians facing hearings complained that the demotions represented "illegal command influence," and were part of a coordinated strategy to keep character witnesses from testifying for accused lesbians. Parris Island public affairs officers denied it. "No one is being punished merely for testifying," said base spokesman First Lieutenant A. J. Kozloski. "They were relieved as a result of loss of confidence by their superiors based on the content of their testimony under oath in the Jameson case." Another base spokesman, Major Bob McLean, concurred: "It was clear they did not understand DoD policy on homosexual behavior." When pressed about his decision later, Nunnally said that he objected to Hilinski's opinion that she would not judge Jameson by her off-duty sexual activities. Echoing the prosecutor in the Baum trial, Nunnally said, "I believe you are a Marine twenty-four hours a day."

Parris Island officers made little secret of their interest in possible witnesses for the accused lesbians. A week after the end of the Jameson trial, attorney Taylor says, he advised Lieutenant Colonel John Busbey, the commander of the Fourth Battalion, that it was illegal to demote Hilinski and Gurule because of their testimony on behalf of Jameson. Busbey responded that he "did it all the time."

If the demotions were meant to have a chilling effect on lawyers seeking testimonials for other accused gays, they succeeded. When Captain Laura Hinckley, who expected to face charges at any time, asked her lawyer Vaughan Taylor to contact twenty Parris Island officers and noncommissioned officers to serve as character witnesses, he found none willing to stand behind her at first without reassurances that there would be no repercussions from their command. One captain told him, "The prosecution might get a hold of it and try to get rid of me too." A staff sergeant said, "I'm not going to put my career on the line for anyone else."

Even more than Barbara Baum's imprisonment, the Hilinski and Gurule demotions informed other women under investigation that there was no length to which Marine officials would not go to remove them from the Corps. Meanwhile, NIS agents took a photograph of Gunnery Sergeant Diane Edwards to the mobile home park where she lived and showed neighbors that photograph and others of women under investigation to determine if any had ever visited Edwards. Agents were denied the neighbors' permission to conduct a surveillance from the woods adjacent to another staff sergeant's private home, but still attempted to photograph a room in which the sergeant had a Jacuzzi, presumably in hopes of documenting lesbian activity.

Under the mounting pressure, many women waived their rights to a hearing and accepted their discharges, usually under less than honorable conditions, rather than fight their separations. Based largely on Baum's accusation, Gunnery Sergeant Diane Edwards, rated in the top one percent of noncommissioned officers in her evaluation forms, was charged with homosexuality and obstruction of justice, the latter charge because she had asked another woman what NIS agents had asked her during her interrogation. Edwards had planned to fight her separation, but after the demotions of Hilinski and Gurule, she believed she would never win. She took her administrative separation in late July. On the same day Edwards was discharged, four other women were processed out of Parris Island for suspected lesbianism, including Barbara Baum's roommate, Becky Feldhaus.

Feldhaus had chosen to fight her discharge at a separation board. The NIS continued to pressure her to name names, even promising her immunity from prosecution if she did, but Becky refused, so she was charged with obstruction of justice, communicating a threat (to Steve Davis at the Buccaneer Motel), and homosexuality. Becky asked for a hearing at another post; it was denied. She asked that a woman serve on her board; that was denied. She asked for a lawyer from another post; that was also denied. When she mentioned to her Marine Corps lawyer that she might go to the press, the lawyer said that was not a good idea. Feldhaus's hearing found her not guilty of the first two charges, and was not able to prove definitively that she was homosexual, so her separation was recommended because she associated with homosexuals. Such associations, the board said, were "not acceptable to the Marine Corps." She would receive a less than honorable discharge.

The afternoon Becky was being processed out, a captain appeared with the good conduct medal she had been awarded shortly before her administrative hearing. Becky could not help but laugh. "You all need to make up your mind," she said. By then, the investigation had separated seven women from the Marine Corps; seven more faced separation proceedings; two were in jail. Those, at least, were the separations that base spokesmen counted publicly. Others were leaving too. At least one female captain and one lieutenant quietly resigned after their names came up in NIS interrogations. One full colonel, a woman who had been "deep selected" for both major and lieutenant colonel and who was stationed outside Parris Island, managed to survive the purge, but the general's star that she had hoped for was lost to her forever, because she had been a suspected lesbian. In fact, in the course of the investigation, half the female drill instructors at Parris Island had been interrogated by the NIS.

After they were separated, Becky Feldhaus, Diane Edwards, and two other women discharged that day went to a fancy bar in the nearby resort town of Hilton Head to toast their civilian lives, and celebrate being out of the Marine Corps. Privately, however, they knew they would miss the Marines. For thirty-two-year-old Edwards, it was the only life she had known since she was eighteen years old. So as they laughed and celebrated publicly, each privately mourned her separation.

SEPTEMBER 1988
CORRECTIONAL FACILITY, MARINE CORPS
COMBAT DEVELOPMENT COMMAND
QUANTICO, VIRGINIA

THE MARINE CORPS brig is a sprawling tan brick building, surrounded by concertina wire, sitting on the base that serves as headquarters for the Marine Corps. Corporal Barbara Baum lived in a dorm in this brig, sleeping in an open bay. By late summer, she had finagled an administrative job in the personnel records department, which was better than knitting baby clothes for Navy Relief, her earlier job. But conditions remained severe. When Cheryl Jameson arrived in late July, for example, the two friends were not allowed to speak to one another. Jameson, in fact, received a long list of people she was not to talk to, including the woman who held the power of attorney for her affairs. When a search of her foot locker found a letter she had written anyway, Jameson was charged with "deception" and put in the segregation room for the night.

Barbara kept her spirits up with the hopes she had for achieving clemency. She had hired a civilian attorney who had put together an elaborate "clemency package," as the formal appeal for clemency is called. The document exhaustively outlined legal errors during her trial, most notably those inherent in the jury selection, as well as an argument that imprisonment was cruel and unusual punishment, given the fact that the "indecent acts" for which Baum had been imprisoned occurred in a private, consensual relationship. As for maintaining the good order and discipline of the Marine Corps, her lawyer said, Baum's imprisonment had already achieved its desired "deterrent effect."

Barb's military lawyer also submitted a sworn deposition that he had been led to believe that Baum would receive clemency if she talked to Major Beck and the NIS. Still, three months after she talked, and after several Marines had been discharged on the basis of her statement, Baum remained in jail.

The Marine Corps took every opportunity to frustrate Baum's appeal for clemency. The official transcript of her court-martial, for example, was a necessary component of the clemency package, and normally took a few weeks to obtain from military lawyers. After three months, however, the Marine Corps had still not furnished it to Baum's lawyer, and he eventually submitted the clemency package without it. Similarly, prison sentences were not made official until the convening authority of the court-martial, in this case the commanding general of Parris Island, had set a final sentence, which normally took a few weeks at most. For Barbara Baum, it took 176 days, during which time she sat in jail.

Surprisingly, Major David Beck, the aggressive prosecutor of so many lesbians at Parris Island, recommended that Baum be granted a measure of clemency. By then, however, Beck had a different job, and was no longer in charge of the Parris Island prosecutions. The decision for clemency would be made by others, in a process straight out of the *Malleus Maleficarum*. In October, Colonel Gerald Jones, the Parris Island Staff Judge Advocate, recommended against clemency. Rather than a detailed point-by-point response to the various legal issues Baum's attorneys had raised, his explanation consisted of one sentence: "No corrective action based upon trial error or the review procedure is appropriate." The final decision for clemency, however, would be made by the base commander.

When Baum's attorneys publicly denounced the Marine Corps for reneging on its promise to release Barbara if she gave a statement, Parris Island spokesmen simply denied ever extending such a promise. "If we had done so, we would honor it," said Major Robert McLean.

At Parris Island, Barbara Baum was either the most reviled woman or the most pitied. Those women whose careers had been ended by her statement believed that she had tried to save her own skin by taking them down with her. Others, such as Becky Feldhaus, believed that Baum, who had been battling alcoholism, was in a delicate psychological state to start with. Barbara knew of the debate among the women and felt profound guilt about turning over names. As it became clear that the Marine Corps would not keep its end of the bargain and release her, she also felt profound humiliation: She had sold out her friends for nothing.

In late September, a court-martial convicted another drill instructor, Sergeant Glenda Jones, of sodomy, indecent acts, obstruction of justice, and failure to obey an order. She was sentenced to fourteen months in prison and a dishonorable discharge, although eight months of the prison sentence were suspended.

The same week, Barbara Baum's friend, Captain Laura Hinckley, was charged with fraternization for her friendship with Baum, for conduct unbecoming an officer, and for failure to obey an order. Base spokesman McLean conceded "there are no direct charges of homosexuality," but the newspapers wrote up the charges as being part of the lesbian investigation anyway. In her Article 32 hearing, Hinckley pleaded for her career and conceded that her friendship with Baum "overstepped the boundaries between officers and enlisted." Still, the fraternization was with an NCO who was wholly outside Hinckley's chain of command; few heterosexuals would be prosecuted under similar circumstances. "I would never do it again," said Hinckley, as she broke into tears. "But this was never done with any criminal intent whatsoever."

Ironically, the woman who had been one of the original targets of the investigation, Captain Judy Gretch, had by now been cleared of all charges of lesbianism, due to "insufficient evidence."

ABOARD USS *YELLOWSTONE*
ATLANTIC OCEAN

THE INVESTIGATION ABOARD the USS *Yellowstone*, a destroyer tender, began like so many others, with long interrogations of women pulled from their bunks in the middle of the night, with threats of jail, and with jealousies and recriminations. As an early participant in the Women at Sea program, the *Yellowstone* had about 340 women among its 1,100-member crew and had been the site of several other purges in recent years, but they had been mostly quiet affairs in which women and men simply disappeared. In 1987, the ship's captain made it clear he would not enforce the gay ban. According to several sailors on the ship, the witch-hunts stopped, until the captain's reassignment in 1988.

It was clear from the beginning that the 1988 witch-hunt would be awe-inspiring, and especially frightening because it occurred while the ship was at sea, far from its home port of Norfolk. The plans had all been laid before the ship departed for Marseilles, as evidenced by the fact that before anyone had been interrogated, even before the women knew they were under investigation, newspapers in Norfolk were running accounts of the impending probe.

Two days after the ship pulled out of Norfolk for maneuvers with the USS *Kennedy* carrier group, all the women crew members were assembled on the mess decks. There were lesbians on board, officers told them, and if any of the women saw anything that looked suspicious, they were to report it to the officer's wardroom immediately.

Crew member Kim Wilson, a petty officer second class, recalled that the investigation escalated on August 21, when the ship was nearly three weeks out to sea, and she and a crewmate named Cindy were paged over the ship's public address system. Cindy, who had an unrequited crush on Wilson, was young, part of the lesbian network on the ship, and one of the most indiscreet people Kim had ever met. When Wilson reported to the master-at-arms, it was to be interviewed; NIS agents told Wilson she would go to jail if she did not admit to being a homosexual, but she refused to talk.

Meanwhile, women were pulled from their bunks at 5:00 A.M. for grueling interrogations with the ship's legal officer and the master-at-arms. There were locker searches. An inspection of Wilson's locker turned up some innocuous photos of women at a party, but there was nothing that indicated sexual activity. The next day, however, Cindy told Kim she believed they could escape serious charges if they admitted that they were gay, and so both women agreed to sign statements, which the ship's legal officer wrote out. Although Kim refused to initial those paragraphs that were inaccurate, the legal officer assured the women that they would be separated quietly once they arrived in Marseilles. Later, when Wilson saw her statement again, her initials appeared alongside every paragraph.

As more women cut deals with officers, paranoia mounted on the ship. From the middle of the Atlantic Ocean, there was no access to civilian attorneys or reporters or gay community support, and female crew members listened anxiously to the ominous public address system call for one after another lesbian crew member to see the master-at-arms.

At first there were twelve women under investigation. They became known as "The Dirty Dozen." Then there were thirteen, all of whom became pariahs, even among other lesbians, who feared that any association with them would reflect badly on themselves. One woman who had been scorned in a relationship turned in her ex-lover and a list of other lesbians. Some heterosexual women became agents for the ship's officers. They would loiter within earshot of any group of women, and then turn in names if they heard anything they deemed suspicious. Linda Subda, the thirteenth woman under investigation, had been caught when someone stole her diary from her bunk and turned it in.

The women's berthing area came under around-the-clock watch to ensure that no lesbian activities transpired there. As part of the Navy's antidrug program, there were numerous posters around the ship that featured a marijuana plant with a slash mark through it and the words, "Not on my watch, not on my ship, not in my Navy." Some crew members had written the word "Dyke" over the pot plant. Another poster appeared of a woman's torso clad in a bikini with her legs spread open, crossed by a slash mark, with the caption: "No Dykes Allowed." When Linda Subda complained to her chief petty officer, he said he would "take care of this," but a month later the offensive poster still hung on the wall of the mess deck.

Toward the end of the cruise, NIS agents began their interviews at midnight, and frequently kept all the women up all night for questioning. They wanted names of other lesbians. They pointed to a list of the women aboard the *Yellowstone* who participated in the Navy women's intramural softball and football teams. This was how the NIS had assembled its list of suspected lesbians.

By the time the *Yellowstone* arrived in Marseilles, eleven women had admitted to being homosexual and waived their rights to administrative separation boards in order to receive quick discharges. In Marseilles, the women were driven to the local airport and ordered to return to Norfolk— but not provided with plane tickets. One woman had to charge a half-dozen air fares to her credit card.

Once the group was back in Virginia, four of the women, including Kim, recanted the statements they had signed and asked for separation boards. Since the only substantive evidence against Wilson was the expressed opinion of some officers that she *looked* like a lesbian, she was cleared. One other woman was cleared as well; two were separated after board hearings. The total toll from the *Yellowstone* purge: nine women, including one officer with fifteen years in the Navy.

———————

THE NIS BECAME even more aggressive. During a lesbian investigation at Pearl Harbor Naval Station in August 1988, agents took a twenty-four-year-old sailor named Shelli Hurd into an office, told her she would go to prison, and showed her scores of photographs of herself going in and out of a local gay bar, playing softball, and even at her apartment complex. Her changing hairstyle in the photographs indicated that NIS agents had been following her for three months, apparently with great constancy.

Agents also presented her with copies of letters from a variety of friends, even her mother. The only way they could have obtained the correspondence, Hurd believed, was to have fished the letters out of her mailbox, a federal offense. Lengthy transcripts of her telephone conversations indicated that agents had tapped her off-base home phone. The NIS denied tampering with mail or using unauthorized phone taps. In any case, none of these efforts produced the desired intimidation. Hurd would not confess or name other lesbians, and eventually the investigation blew over.

These investigations, coming so soon after the Parris Island court-martials, sent shock waves through women in the military, particularly on the East Coast where there existed elaborate friendship networks among lesbians in uniform, and many women were likely to know someone who was under investigation. Though the investigatory tactics used so successfully against lesbians varied little from those used to pursue gay men, lesbians were far more vulnerable. The Marine Corps had fewer women than any other branch of the service, only 4.8 percent of its personnel, and being a smaller service where all the women trained together in one boot camp, lesbians tended to know each other.

Relationship patterns also aided investigators. While gay men could choose their partners from a vast network of gay male bars and community institutions, homosexual women had far fewer social options. Their partnerships formed from among immediate friends, and often from among ex-lovers of friends, which spawned all kinds of petty jealousies that could prompt women to turn on each other, a fact NIS investigators took advantage of. A lesbian who decided to turn in others could often offer investigators many, many names, given the tightly knit nature of the lesbian community. Moreover, the institutions with which lesbians most commonly became involved, sports teams, were highly visible, and offered investigators ready-made rosters of suspects.

One Navy officer that summer recalled that softball players played less aggressively if they believed an NIS agent was in the bleachers, as they sometimes were. On such occasions, it became essential for women ball players to throw "like a girl" and not display an inappropriate amount of athletic prowess. Some women stopped participating in sports altogether. More women saw the wisdom of marrying gay men. At Parris Island, three women under investigation became pregnant to avoid suspicion. Women with short haircuts let their hair grow.

In the Marine Corps just about every lesbian knew someone facing charges at Parris Island. Indeed, the very words Parris Island came to mean out-of-control antilesbian hysteria. "It's another Parris Island situation," one woman would say to another; no other words were necessary.

Some women considered desperate measures. One of the highest-ranking generals in the Marine Corps was widely believed to be homosexual. He had married at a late age and then only when it was clear that he would never achieve the top job he sought if he were unmarried. Rumors flew because the general did not conceal his regular trips on Marine Corps jets to Richmond, Virginia, where his reputed lover, a dentist, lived, and because the woman he had married was believed to be a lesbian whose lover lived in the guest house behind the general's official Marine Corps residence. His wife and his wife's lover appear in the background in a number of photographs of the general at official functions, sometimes with the reputed lesbian couple's dog. This particular general was also said to be rabidly misogynistic and the most influential advocate of the lesbian purge at Parris Island. Women like Fran Cail, a civilian who was a friend to many of the Parris Island drill instructors, urged them to expose the four-star general as homosexual. None would.

When it was clear that Captain Judy Meade would face charges, women at her home base at Camp LeJeune feared that the witch-hunt would travel there. Who might be making lists? they wondered. Who might talk? Everyone was on edge.

In September, Corporal Valaine "Val" Bode heard that she was under investigation. Bode had played in the All-Marine female softball team of 1986, the All-Marine volleyball teams of 1986 and 1987, and had been awarded the title of Marine Corps Sportswoman of the Year in 1987. She was always cheerful, friends later recalled, in spite of a recently discovered heart problem. But that was not what prompted her suicide, according to her friends. As a prominent female athlete, Bode was naturally suspected of being gay. When she got word that she was under investigation, she pulled her automobile into her garage in a quiet cul-de-sac near Camp LeJeune, closed the garage door, turned on the ignition, and within a few minutes was dead, another victim of the Parris Island witch-hunt.

BY LATE 1988, it became known that the Parris Island investigation, while encouraged by the purportedly gay general, was inspired by a memo written by Dr. Jacquelyn Davis, chair of the Defense Advisory Committee on Women in the Service, the group that was supposed to safeguard the interests of women in the military. In her public statement about the investigations, Davis said she had never intended to provoke a "witch hunt" with her memorandum. "Obviously, we don't want to go to the extreme of a witch hunt," she told *Navy Times*. "We want to make sure— whenever action is taken—that it is on the basis of well-documented facts."

Still, when pressed, Davis repeated her assertion that there was a "perception" that lesbians were dealt with more leniently than gay men, and that "Women who are of this [homosexual] persuasion appear to be more aggressive than the males are . . . in manifesting their behavior and approaching other people."

LAURA HINCKLEY HAD grown up poor; she was raised by a single mother. But she had talent, drive, and athletic ability, and in the Naval Academy, she was an All-American runner and a graduate in the top 10 percent of her class. The Marine Corps was her ticket to success, and she loved her service in it. By November, however, it was clear that she had no chance of surviving there. Because of the Hilinski and Gurule relievings, no one would testify in her favor at a court-martial, so she did what the Marine Corps wanted her to do, and resigned her commission.

When Ruth Voor, Hinckley's classmate from Annapolis, remembered Hinckley later, she recalled the day in May 1980 when the plebes built their human pyramid to reach the sailor's cap at the top of the Herndon Monument, and she had watched the boys pull Laura Hinckley down. They had cast her down on that day in 1980, and they had cast her down again, for one last time, in 1988. No woman would be allowed to succeed.

67

The Release of Prisoner Number 17

DECEMBER 1, 1988
CORRECTIONAL FACILITY
MARINE CORPS COMBAT DEVELOPMENT COMMAND
QUANTICO, VIRGINIA

PRISONER NUMBER 17 was working in the records department when her counselor summoned her to his office and told her she would be released in two weeks, which marked her sixth month in prison. Corporal Barbara Baum began weeping. "Thank God," she said, "it's finally over."

The timing of the clemency did not escape her. The Marine Corps had waited until it had discharged Laura Hinckley, until it no longer needed Baum's testimony or statements for any other hearings. With the Parris Island purge winding down, Barb was of no more use to the Marine Corps.

On December 12, three days earlier than she anticipated, the brig's commanding officer told her to pack. "You're not a prisoner anymore," he said. She had received three days' credit on her prison sentence for the time she had sat in jail in Beaufort. That afternoon, Barbara Baum, no longer prisoner number 17, heard the metal prison door shut behind her; she was free.

BY THE TIME BAUM was released from prison, the Marine Corps had officially acknowledged that eighteen women were administratively discharged during the Parris Island investigations. Three others had been imprisoned. The investigation deprived the Marine Corps of more than 10 percent of its female drill instructors.

The official tabulation of Parris Island victims underestimated the true impact of the purge. Officers were not counted, because they were usually allowed to resign rather than face administrative separation procedures. Many other senior enlisted had decided to leave the military themselves rather than be forced out later by a "Parris Island situation" and lose their veterans' benefits. Their numbers would never be officially tallied, but by one count, the Marine Corps lost some sixty-five women, largely women who simply decided not to reenlist, or officers who resigned.

The losses occurred at other bases as well. One officer whose evaluation forms designated her as "flag-rank potential" left the active-duty Navy for the Reserves. Senior officers left as soon as they reached twenty years; it was too risky to be a thirty-year Marine or Naval officer, however alluring the jobs might be.

FOR ALL THE IMPACT the Parris Island investigation had on women in the military, it remained largely unheard of, drawing serious press coverage only in South Carolina, where the story had local interest, and in the gay press. Indeed, even four years later, the only significant reports on the purge had appeared not in large newspapers or magazines, but in *The Progressive,* a relatively small liberal journal out of Madison, Wisconsin, and in the *Harvard Women's Law Journal.* The excesses of the Parris Island investigation, particularly the NIS tactics, however, promised that no such purge would ever be met with such inattention again, at least not if its victims were willing to go public and fight their separations.

What ensured this was the Gay and Lesbian Military Freedom Project, organized in November 1988 by leaders of the National Gay and Lesbian Task Force, the National Organization for Women, Women's Equity Action League, the Lesbian–Gay Rights Project of the American Civil Liberties Union and the San Diego–based Military Law Project of the National Lawyers Guild. The Military Freedom Project represented the first organized effort to protect the rights of gays in the military and to lobby for a change in gay policies since the Vietnam War. Until the group's formation, gay military cases were handled, or not handled, by this or that homosexual advocacy group, with no coordinated strategy for gaining press attention or pursuing legislative channels for a repeal to the antigay policies.

The project's goals were the rescision of Department of Defense Directive 1332.14, the repeal of the Uniform Code of Military Justice articles forbidding consensual sodomy and "indecent acts," and support for gay military personnel under investigation. Organizers attempted to draw attention to the Parris Island investigation, since two women, Cheryl Jameson and Glenda Jones, remained in jail, and Captain Judy Meade still faced an administrative separation hearing at Camp LeJeune. Activists released Defense Department statistics to the press showing that women were separated for homosexuality at a far greater rate than men, prompting a number of stories on the relationship between sexual harassment and the military's antilesbian investigations. Investigative columnist Jack Anderson ran a number of hard-hitting columns condemning both the Marine Corps and the NIS for their harsh interrogations and the handling of the Hilinski and Gurule demotions.

Publicity over the military's gay exclusion policy occurred as a number of federal court rulings were delivered that seriously undermined the government's position. The most significant and most short-lived ruling came in February 1988 in the case of *Sergeant Perry J. Watkins* v. *United States Army et al.* A three-member panel of judges from the U.S. Court of Appeals in San Francisco ruled not only that Watkins should be reinstated in the Army, but that the government had failed to show how their anti-homosexual regulations served any "compelling government interest."

The most significant portion of the two-to-one decision was its sweeping conclusion that homosexuals represented a "suspect class," in legal terminology, a group of people that has suffered a history of grossly unfair discrimination based on an "immutable characteristic." A member of a suspect class received a more rigorous standard of judicial scrutiny, and demanded strict review under the provisions of the Equal Protection clause of the Fourteenth Amendment. In the Watkins case, the appeals court decision had found sexual acts to be separate from sexual orientation, and focused on the aspects of military policy that excluded people solely for their orientation, whether or not they had ever expressed their sexuality in deed.

Designation as a "suspect class" had long been the dream of gay civil liberties lawyers, since inclusion in such a category would in effect legally forbid discrimination against gay people. The opinion, written by Judge William Norris, was the most sympathetic legal finding ever written on gay rights. "Discrimination faced by homosexuals in our society is plainly no less pernicious or intense than the discrimination faced by other groups," Norris wrote. He also believed that ultimately the *Bowers* decision would be tossed out.

"Laws that limit the acceptable focus of one's sexual desires to members of the opposite sex, like laws that limit one's choice of a sexual partner to members of the same race, cannot withstand constitutional scrutiny absent a compelling governmental justification," he ruled. Such justification did not exist with the military policy, he wrote, wholly dismissing the Army's claims that the rules were necessary to maintain morale among heterosexual soldiers. Norris wrote, "For much of our history, the military's fear of racial tension kept black soldiers separated from whites. Today it is unthinkable that the judiciary would defer to the Army's prior 'professional' judgment that black and white soldiers had to be segregated to avoid interracial tensions." To use comparable rationale to support an antigay policy, Norris noted, was to "illegitimately cater to private biases."

In his dissent, Judge Stephen Reinhardt agreed that, in his opinion, the military's gay policies violated the Constitution, but said that he could not vote to abolish the policy given the constraints set by the *Bowers* precedent, a ruling that he also called "egregious," comparable to the *Plessy* v. *Ferguson* decision of 1896 that had ruled segregation was constitutional, and he said was likely to be overturned by "a wiser and more enlightened court." As a federal judge, however, Reinhardt said he had to abide by *Bowers* and rule against Watkins at least until the Supreme Court could "undo the damage to the Constitution wrought by *Bowers*."

Gay rights lawyers called the decision "earth shattering"; it was also one of the most fleeting. Reagan administration officials quickly asked the Ninth Circuit Court of Appeals to hear the case *en banc*, meaning it would be redecided by eleven judges, rather than the three who had ruled on the case originally. In June 1988, on the second day of Barbara Baum's court-martial, the appeals court judges of the circuit, a majority of whom had been appointees of Republican presidents Nixon, Ford, and Reagan, voided the earlier ruling and set the stage for a new hearing on the case before eleven judges in October 1988.

The second case making its way toward the nation's highest court was Miriam Ben-Shalom's, the drill sergeant who had acknowledged her homosexuality in 1976, during the height of publicity around Leonard Matlovich's disclosure. In late 1987, the U.S. Court of Appeals in Chicago reaffirmed that the Army Reserves must reinstate Ben-Shalom, endorsing the 1980 federal district court ruling that her First Amendment right of free speech was violated when she was discharged because of her comment to a gay newspaper reporter that she was lesbian.

For seven years, the government had refused to reinstate her, contending that it was not sure how to interpret the earlier order to reinstate Ben-Shalom, which led the court to observe tersely, "We are baffled by the Secretary's [of the Army] asserted confusion over the word 'reinstatement' in the 1980 order. The district court specifically ordered that the Army 'reinstate [Ben-Shalom] as a member of the Army Reserves with all duties, responsibilities and privileges earned prior to her discharge.' The order could hardly be clearer."

When Ben-Shalom tried to reenlist in August 1988, however, Army officials told her that she could not, because of her admission that she was a lesbian. Senior federal judge Myron Gordon in Milwaukee issued another order to the Army demanding that they allow Ben-Shalom to reenlist, and threatened a $500-a-day fine for contempt of court if the Reserves did not comply. In September, the Army Reserves relented and reenlisted the acknowledged lesbian into the 5091st Army Reception Battalion for a six-year term, as ordered.

In January 1989, Gordon reviewed the earlier decision and pronounced that the military's policies against gays were "basically irrational" and violated the Constitution. "The elimination of all soldiers with homosexual orientations from the ranks of the Army is not rationally related to the advancement of any compelling Government interest," he wrote. The Army immediately announced, however, that it would appeal the federal court decision, ensuring that Ben-Shalom, like Perry Watkins, would have her day before the Supreme Court.

Even as the old lawsuits filed by veterans of the Vietnam era military made their final stands in the judicial system, new legal challenges to the government's antigay regulations were begun. On December 29, 1988, Joe Steffan, now a senior at North Dakota State University just one class shy of graduation, flew to Washington to file his lawsuit in U.S. District Court, asking the judges to declare the military's gay policies unconstitutional.

After formally filing the papers, Joe Steffan and his lawyers from Lambda Legal Defense and Education Fund met with reporters. Steffan made some of the more obvious arguments against the policy, as did his attorneys. Steffan was struck most by the number of reporters present, their intense interest in his case, and the fact that almost all seemed entirely supportive of his position. It had taken so long for Steffan to accept himself, he was unprepared that so many heterosexuals were able to accept his homosexuality.

Changes in the heterosexual world's acceptance of gays were a response to growing self-acceptance among homosexual men and women, as was demonstrated by the impressive team Steffan had assembled to aid him. Joe's principal lawyer was a young mergers and acquisitions attorney in Manhattan named Marc Wolinsky. During college, Wolinsky's first gay relationship had been with the son of an Army general, which gave him an understanding of the military's antipathies toward gays. Wolinsky had decided to perform pro bono work for gays in the military after he read in a gay newspaper about the investigation unfolding at Parris Island. When he met Joe Steffan at a Lambda fund-raising dinner, he considered the facts of the case so compelling it would easily make it to the Supreme Court. Wolinsky discussed it with his law partners, members of one of the most prestigious firms dealing with business mergers, and they agreed that the case would be appropriate for the firm to carry.

Later in 1989, Howard Bragman signed on to do pro bono public relations work for Steffan. Like Wolinsky, Bragman had thoroughly impeccable professional credentials. He had been a vice president of Burson-Marsteller before launching his own public relations business in Beverly Hills. His client roster included L.A. Gear, the trendy shoe manufacturer, and numerous entertainment celebrities. At thirty-three, he was also young enough to be comfortable being openly gay, and felt obliged to devote a portion of his time and talent to support the gay movement. In Steffan, Bragman saw a man much like himself, a gay professional rather than a professional gay, but someone also committed to diminishing the prejudice gays faced in their daily lives. By late 1989, largely due to Bragman's efforts, Joe Steffan would become the most visible gay person in America.

IT HAD BEEN nearly fifteen years since Leonard Matlovich's first challenge to the gay regulations, and still the gay political leadership maintained an ambivalent posture toward gays in uniform. Organizers of the Military Freedom Project argued as often with gay radicals, who did not support gays serving "patriarchal, homophobic" institutions, as with government lawyers.

And those people who personally fought the battles often found themselves in a lonely position. When Miriam Ben-Shalom addressed a gay pride march in Chicago in the summer of 1988, she observed a smattering of signs reading, "No G.I. Janes." Perry Watkins, still living in Tacoma, struggled to survive. He had not been able to find a decent job since his discharge from the Army years earlier, nor did he find the community support that Joe Steffan enjoyed. Watkins remained convinced that it was in part because he was an effeminate African American. The more radical members of his community, whom he might expect to eschew racism, were the very ones who were least likely to sympathize with his desire to return to the armed forces.

This remained an uncomfortable truth about the military gay issue, one that revealed the deeper intolerance that many gay radicals held toward anyone, heterosexual or homosexual, who did not subscribe to their rigid ideology. Just as the government said there was only one proper way to be a soldier, many gay radicals felt there was only one proper way to be a homosexual—their way.

LEGAL MANEUVERING IN 1988 again illuminated the importance of the federal judiciary, and of the man who appointed all federal judges, the President of the United States. Once again, all the major Democratic presidential candidates attempted to curry favor with the gay community, which remained a crucial voting bloc in the primary elections. A young senator from Tennessee, Albert Gore, Jr., had the most detailed and informed program to fight AIDS. Senator Paul Simon became an election-year convert to supporting gay-rights legislation and signed on as a co-sponsor to the federal gay-rights bill on the eve of his campaign.

By July 1988, the nomination went to Governor Michael Dukakis of Massachusetts, who had a more problematic record on gay issues. Although his state offered excellent AIDS services and policies, the Dukakis administration had a formal policy of placing children in heterosexual foster homes rather than homes with two partners of the same sex. The policy seemed to support all the stereotypes of homosexuals as being child molesters and infuriated Massachusetts gay activists. Moreover, during the campaign, Dukakis was the only major Democratic contender to refuse to pledge to sign an executive order banning discrimination on the basis of sexual orientation in federal jobs.

The Republican nominee, Vice President George Bush, had promised a "kinder, gentler nation" in his campaign, and gay Republicans assured the community that this meant he would turn away from the conservative antigay appointees to whom President Reagan had handed so many crucial federal jobs. In answering a questionnaire from the National Gay and Lesbian Task Force, Bush seemed to reinforce this intention when he answered, "I believe all Americans have fundamental rights guaranteed in our Constitution." Gay Republican organizations overwhelmingly endorsed Bush.

Once again, the federal election suffered from the ongoing tensions over gender roles. Early in the election, pundits insisted that the most crucial barrier the Republican nominee must overcome was "the wimp factor," the perception that Bush was not manly enough to be President. This became a subject for satire in the popular "Doonesbury" comic strip that accused Bush of putting his manhood in a blind trust during his eight years as Vice President. Meanwhile, the Republican campaign focused on masculine issues, most notably emphasizing a strong national defense, while the Democrats, in contrast, promoted domestic programs. Bush's aggressive campaign—some called it vicious—and Dukakis's weak response vanquished "the wimp factor." The Republican message was more appealing, particularly to white male voters who became the decisive margin that ensured George Bush's victory.

For four more years, a President committed to a strict interpretation of the Constitution that favored the prerogatives of government authority over individual rights would name the nation's federal judges, including members of the Supreme Court. Like President Reagan, Bush chose his appointees for life terms in part for their youth, so that they might issue federal rulings well into the next century.

THE NAVAL INSTALLATION AT CORONADO, CALIFORNIA

NAVY TRADITION ALLOWS the spouses of retiring officers to attend the retirement dinner for free. Lieutenant Ruth Voor expected, and received, the same courtesy for her partner, Karen Colton.

Ruth had lived her last years in the Navy with comparable probity, never announcing in the wardroom that she was lesbian, but not making much effort to conceal it, either. Her commander had gone to some lengths to convince Voor to stay in. She could be "deep selected" for accelerated promotion, he said, but Ruth told him no, the Navy did not want her. The commander understood her cryptic denial, shook his head, and sighed, saying, "I have to change that rule."

The commander's response was as accurate a reflection of the military's attitude toward gay people in the late 1980s as were the purges on Parris Island and the USS *Yellowstone*. With each year, the military services found themselves increasingly at odds concerning the enforcement of gay regulations. Some officers demanded imprisonment of gays, and others believed in complete acceptance. Although largely ignored by top Defense Department officials, this was a tension that could not be sustained indefinitely.

BARBARA BAUM ARRIVED in Tampa, Florida, on New Year's Day, 1989, eager to start over again in a warm climate and in a city where nobody knew who she was or what she had suffered in the past year. She thought she would open a lawn-tending business. She began to make friends. A few times she confided to a new friend that the government had put her in prison for six months for being a lesbian. She could tell that her civilian friends found it hard to believe.

— 68 —

Embarrassments in the Making

JANUARY 1989
DEFENSE PERSONNEL SECURITY RESEARCH
AND EDUCATION CENTER
MONTEREY, CALIFORNIA

SEVENTY-EIGHT-YEAR-OLD Ted Sarbin had spent a lifetime conducting psychological research both as an academic scholar and a government adviser. A professor emeritus at the University of California at Berkeley, his résumé was thirty pages long, listing copious honors and prestigious publications. In 1979, at the request of the Naval Post Graduate School, he had developed a long thesis on military deception that became the basis of a book on the subject. After the Walker and Moscow embassy spy scandals, when the Defense Department recognized that it needed to improve its security regulations, the Defense Personnel Security Research and Education Center (PERSEREC) chose Sarbin to serve as its senior civilian adviser, along with PERSEREC's psychiatrist, Dr. Kenneth Karols, a Navy captain.

For all the intriguing research Sarbin had conducted in his nearly six decades in academe, he still found the question he had been studying for PERSEREC since 1987 uniquely fascinating: Did homosexuals represent security risks? And if so, should they be screened out of positions requiring clearances, including the military?

Sarbin had spent much of his career developing elaborate theories of "social constructionism," or how societies interpret various phenomena. The phenomenon of homosexuality was a nearly perfect example of social interpretation overriding fact. Homosexuality, Sarbin concluded, was biologically determined, most probably in the human embryo, but certainly within the first years of life. The fact that homosexuality appears in all mammal species also indicated that the trait could not be considered "unnatural," at least in the strictly biological sense. There was no evidence that gays had a unique psychological predisposition to betray their countries, or were any less able to observe others' privacy, or to avoid inappropriate sexual advances; it was the social construction of homosexuality, not homosexuals themselves, that was responsible for such fears.

Sarbin began writing his conclusions as an official PERSEREC report. Current military policies succeeded in identifying only an "infinitesimal percentage" of gays who served in the military, he wrote. He also suggested that official fears about disruption in the military's "good order, discipline and morale" were unfounded: "The order to integrate blacks was first met with stout resistance by traditionalists in the military establishment," he wrote. "Dire consequences were predicted for maintaining discipline, building group morale, and achieving military organizational goals. None of these predictions of doom has come true. Social science specialists helped develop programs for combating racial discrimination. . . . It would be wise to consider applying the experience of the past forty years to the integration of homosexuals."

In their summary, Sarbin and Karols wrote: "Our analysis directs us to regard people with nonconforming sexual orientation as a minority group. Our nation has a long history of successfully dealing with minority groups, particularly ethnic minorities. . . . The social construction of homosexuals as minority group members is more in tune with current behavioral science theory than the earlier constructions: sin, crime, and sickness."

Early drafts of the report caused consternation and considerable gossip at the Pentagon for months. In December 1988, the final draft of the report, entitled "Nonconforming Sexual Orientations and Military Suitability," caused outrage. On January 18, 1989, Craig Alderman, Jr., from the office of the Under Secretary of Defense, fired off an angry memorandum to PERSEREC director Carson Eoyang. Studying suitability criteria for military service, Alderman wrote, "exceeded your authority." Moreover, the report's conclusion did not take into account "relevant court decisions" that supported the military's policies, which "suggest a bias which does justice neither to PERSEREC nor the Department."

In his response, Eoyang said that the study did fall within the purview of the agency's mandate and that the agency had forwarded "*all* information that was relevant to homosexuals and not just that which is supportive of [Defense Department] policy." PERSEREC stood by the report.

Defense Department officials had reason to be concerned with the study. Its conclusions could undermine Pentagon arguments in continuing litigation over the constitutionality of denying security clearances and military service to gays. Even worse, if the report got into the hands of liberal reporters or congressmen, it could further embarrass the Defense Department. As Alderman wrote in a February memo, "It most probably will cause us in Washington to expend even more time and effort satisfying concerns in this whole issue area both in Congress and the media, and within the Department itself." The prospect was worrisome.

A month later, Colonel Ted Borek, director of Pentagon legislation and legal policy division, proposed identifying the report as a "draft," rather than as a final official document. In that case, the Defense Department could deny that the report even existed, because it was only a draft and not a report.

"In our view, the draft study . . . has significant analytical and factual shortcomings and does not contain new or useful information that has not been considered over time in the formulation of the present DoD policy that homosexuality is incompatible with military service," Borek wrote. "We have no interest in expending further resources either to complete the draft study or to conduct additional research in this area at this time." The study, he wrote, "represents only the personal opinion of the authors."

Although the Pentagon hoped that knowledge of the report would never become public, rumors soon reached attorneys at Lambda Legal Defense and Education Fund, as well as Congressman Gerry Studds, the openly gay congressman who had taken an interest in the issue of gays in uniform after hearing of the Parris Island excesses. When Lambda lawyers filed a motion to release the report under a court order for documents relevant to its legal challenge to the Pentagon's homosexual policy, the Defense Department denied it existed. Studds requested the report, too. Again, the Pentagon said it had no such report.

There was a new truism in Washington in those days, that the Xerox machine had become the most powerful device working against government deception in the history of America. Just to maintain security on the document, PERSEREC had prepared only three copies of the report for Washington. However, it was during those months that someone at the Defense Department photocopied one of these copies, and one photocopy bred another, and gradually the study began circulating through the vast gay network at the Pentagon.

Studds's own involvement added a new dimension to the military issue. The harsh reality on Capitol Hill is that an issue is not really an issue until a congressman takes a personal interest—and is willing to devote staff time to it. Studds's emerging role gave gays in the military a champion of incalculable importance.

THE COURTS WOULD NOT reform the military's policies on homosexuals; neither would the new Republican presidential administration. What would accelerate the ultimate termination of these policies, however, were a series of extraordinarily embarrassing episodes relative to gay policy-making at the Pentagon during 1989 and 1990; these, more than anything, laid the groundwork for the policies' ultimate abolition. The PERSEREC report was one such embarrassment; gay students participating in the ROTC program would soon become another.

ABOARD THE USS *HYMAN G. RICKOVER*
ATLANTIC OCEAN

AROUND THE TIME the first memoranda about the PERSEREC report were flying between Washington and Monterey, Robb Bettiker, a twenty-one-year-old midshipman in the Naval ROTC program, was participating in an ROTC cruise in preparation for acceptance into the Navy's prestigious nuclear propulsion program. The cruise had conjured up deep fears in the young college student, who had recently admitted to himself that he was gay.

Robb had been a straight-*A* student, a member of the National Honor Society, class valedictorian, and Most Likely to Succeed when he graduated from high school in Ohio. He had a talent for science. The one asset he lacked was a wealthy family, so Robb took a Naval ROTC scholarship to pay for his tuition at MIT, with the full expectation of repaying the scholarship through his required four years of Navy service.

Bettiker had never had much interest in dating girls, and now he understood why. He had a massive infatuation with his new roommate and he was terrified. Like most young gay people of his generation, he knew about homosexuality mainly as being associated with the killer disease AIDS. And in spite of all the things that had changed in the world over the past twenty years, young men still feared that they were less than men if they were gay.

All through the fall semester, the conflict grew between Bettiker's knowledge of what he was and his expectations of what he should be. When the campus newspaper reported a series of suicides among MIT students, he secretly thought that at least their conflicts were over.

Robb's membership in the Naval ROTC program was another problem, he knew, but over the next month, as he began to accept his new knowledge of himself, he fantasized that he could prove the service and its policies were wrong, and be a great Naval officer. The test would be the required cruise on the *Rickover* during his semester break from ROTC in December 1988 and January 1989.

Early in the cruise Robb heard about HOMOVAC, and experienced a new sense of foreboding. He would have to be constantly on guard in the Navy, he realized, would have to watch every word and gesture. He was just beginning to free himself from twenty years of absolute repression; the prospect of still more self-denial in the years ahead was disheartening. Still, Bettiker noted that the fear did not seem so overwhelming to another ROTC midshipman, David Carney, a Harvard student who, like all Harvard ROTC students, trained with the MIT unit of ROTC. Carney had been audacious in saying that he thought the Navy's policies against homosexuals were archaic, and in writing to that effect in a letter to the *Harvard Crimson*. Robb suspected Carney must be gay, too.

Back at school for spring semester 1989, Bettiker continued to go through the arduous process of "coming out" as a gay person. He learned that two other fraternity brothers were gay. They talked until late at night about the path toward self-acceptance. By the end of the school year, Robb had a boyfriend, a student from Dartmouth, and he was beginning to think he might tell the Navy he was gay before he entered the service. He believed his ROTC commander might just tell him to keep it quiet and everything would be fine.

He even brought the matter up to a psychiatrist who had once practiced in the Air Force. What would happen if someone told the ROTC he was gay? he asked. The psychiatrist thought the student would probably be disenrolled and the military could seek to recoup tuition money they had paid for the student, although the psychiatrist believed the latter was unlikely. Robb hoped so. His tuition amounted to nearly $40,000. Besides, he was willing to serve. The issue was whether the Navy would let him.

Robb did not know that on campuses across the country, a number of other ROTC students were picking their way through the same quandary and coming to the same conclusion. Dave Carney from Harvard University was one. Carney had been pondering his Naval future ever since 1986, when during an orientation for the Naval ROTC, a new cadet had come to formation with a pierced ear. The ROTC instructor had ordered the student to stand at attention in front of the assembled cadets and shout, "I am a faggot! I am a faggot!" Carney, struggling with his own sexuality, was sickened at the display.

Another student deciding his future in the military was Jim Holobaugh at Washington University in St. Louis. Articulate and strikingly handsome, Jim Holobaugh was the ideal ROTC candidate; in fact, the Army ROTC had featured him in magazine advertisements promoting the program. Holobaugh's conflict over his homosexuality culminated after one of his fraternity brothers was discovered to be gay and Jim sat through a long debate over whether he should be kicked out of the fraternity. Some brothers took the young man's side; the majority were outspoken against him. Through it all, Holobaugh, who knew himself to be gay, was silent, and the brother was formally ejected from the fraternity. His own hypocrisy had hung heavily on Holobaugh since then, and by early 1989 he knew that if he was present for another debate over gay rights, he would not be silent again.

FEBRUARY 26, 1989
CAMP LEJEUNE
JACKSONVILLE, NORTH CAROLINA

THE ADMINISTRATIVE HEARING on charges against thirty-six-year-old Captain Judy Meade, who had served twelve years in the Marine Corps, was the last stemming from the Parris Island investigations.

The charges centered on the events of the night of February 25, 1988, a year earlier, when Staff Sergeant Bonnie Ferguson and her friend Jill Harris had appeared at Paula Berry's home in Beaufort and asked Meade about lesbians in the Marine Corps. In his testimony at the hearing, Parris Island prosecutor David Beck revealed that Harris had been flown to South Carolina to help gather information on lesbians. From the start, Meade had been a victim of a well-planned setup. But the scheme had not succeeded in developing any evidence that Meade was a lesbian, only that she knew lesbians. Therefore, the Marine Corps charged that Meade had committed "conduct unbecoming an officer" because she had gay friends.

Both Meade and Berry testified that Meade had retreated to the bedroom to get away from Harris's questions, and had fallen asleep watching television. Berry had not wanted to wake her and Meade therefore slept in Paula Berry's bed that night, though there was no evidence that carnal activity took place. Sleeping in the proximity of a gay person, however, was another offense against the Marine Corps.

A third charge was that Meade had patronized the Leatherneck Tavern in Jacksonville, long a hangout for Marines. A local sheriff's deputy testified that the Leatherneck was a gay bar, which it was not. The bar's owners testified that it was not a gay bar, and that they did not allow gays. In the hearing, however, the Marine Corps' assertion was accepted as fact.

Meade had asked for a court-martial, so that witnesses against her would have to face her and undergo cross-examination, but the Marine Corps assembled a board of inquiry instead, which merely read the statements of witnesses, most of which were written by NIS agents. Some witnesses, such as Barbara Baum, did not appear because they did not want to help the Marine Corps case. (Though Baum's statement about Meade was used as evidence against the captain, Baum had never even met her.) Other witnesses, like Ferguson and Harris, could no longer be located. By now, Harris had made six statements to the NIS, all different and conflicting, so the Marine Corps only presented the two that incriminated Meade. Meade's attorney, Vaughan Taylor, asked that the Marines furnish the NIS agents, particularly Renea King, as witnesses, but they refused.

Without witnesses to cross-examine, Taylor asked attorney Charles Macloskie on the stand to testify about the unscrupulous NIS tactics in other Parris Island cases. NIS agent King, he said, "is every reason rolled into one person why agents of the government cannot be trusted." The prosecution countered by putting prosecutor David Beck on the stand. Beck, recently promoted to lieutenant colonel after his fifteen successful prosecutions at Parris Island, declared that the NIS and Agent King had behaved in a thoroughly professional manner.

Perhaps the most ominous twist to the Meade investigation was that the NIS had obtained payment records from Paula Berry's home telephone—Berry was a civilian with no attachment to the military beyond having friends in the Marine Corps—and had submitted them as evidence that Berry and Meade had talked frequently after charges were pressed against Meade, thus conspiring to obstruct justice and squelch the investigation.

Evidence that might exonerate Meade was manipulated to incriminate her. As one of Meade's attorneys noted in his successful appeal of her case, subsequent to Ferguson's initial accusations against Meade, she asserted that Meade had never been involved in homosexual activity—and a lie detector test showed Ferguson was telling the truth. So an NIS agent changed the assertion: Meade was gay, according to Ferguson, he wrote.

In her favor, Meade had an assortment of character witnesses, including a colonel who had supervised her before his retirement and who described her as a "superb" officer with "moral courage and integrity in all her duties." Paula Berry, an engineer in an aerospace plant, testified for five hours during which time the prosecutor aggressively asked her to name other lesbians she knew in the Marine Corps. In a personal statement that made Meade's gay friends wince, Meade herself vehemently denied being a lesbian and said it was "totally against my morals and my upbringing." Homosexuality, she said, was "disgusting."

Throughout the four-day hearing, it appeared to some that the case had already been decided. One particularly outspoken board member, a female colonel, could not restrain herself from frequent bursts of "Jesus," and "Oh, my God," at some of Meade's alleged indiscretions. When Meade claimed she did not know that Berry was a lesbian when they became friends, a board member asked how that was possible. Berry played women's softball, the board member said, and everyone knew that the only women who went out for softball were lesbians.

In his closing arguments, though he could present no evidence that Meade was gay, prosecuting attorney Captain Chris E. Dougherty suggested she must be to know so many lesbians. "Is it just a coincidence all her friends and acquaintances in her life are lesbians?" he asked. "I submit that in fact, Captain Meade is part of The Family." As for Paula Berry, Dougherty said she was an obvious lesbian; everyone in the courtroom could tell by looking at her and Meade should have been able to do so, too. In associating with a lesbian, Dougherty said, Meade "has disgraced all the commissioned officers of the United States Marine Corps by her conduct."

The board of inquiry deliberated for six hours before ruling that no one with a gay friend may serve as an officer in the United States Marine Corps. Specifically, the board found Meade guilty of "engaging in a public association and long-term personal friendship with a known lesbian," "being in the presence or occupying the same dwelling with enlisted Marines whom Captain Meade suspected to be lesbians," "associating with lesbians, thereby giving the perception that she herself was a lesbian, which brought discredit to herself," and "habitually frequenting the Leatherneck Tavern, a bar known by her to have a questionable reputation." For this unbecoming conduct, the board recommended that Meade be discharged from the Marine Corps under other than honorable conditions.

While other defendants had avoided press attention, Meade had given interviews and her case received extensive local publicity. After the hearing, the Defense Department and the Marine Corps defended their policies. "We're not out there breaking doors down looking for homosexuals," said Major Ron Stokes, a Marine Corps spokesman in Washington. "But do we aggressively pursue these allegations which are made? We do. . . . I think we're in step with the general public. We have an obligation to those mothers and fathers who provide their daughters and sons to us to provide them with a healthy environment." Pentagon spokesman Major David Super added, "When homosexuals are found, they must be removed. Is that a witch-hunt? I guess it depends on who's looking at it."

———————

ATTORNEY VAUGHAN TAYLOR, who had represented seven of the Parris Island women, had come to his military law practice the same way as most specialists in his field, through military service as an Army judge. Uncertain of his own feelings toward the gay policy, the forty-one-year-old lawyer had begun asking friends in the military what they thought of the regulations. Some thought lesbians offered advantages as soldiers, because they did not get pregnant. One two-star general said he worried about combat romances between male soldiers. If one soldier was shot, he reasoned, it would affect two fighters instead of one; 25 percent casualties might mean 50 percent ineffectiveness.

Taylor also sympathized with the lack-of-privacy argument: Heterosexual men would not feel comfortable showering with other men who might be looking at them as sex objects. The military was not like other jobs, the argument went, because in the armed forces, you showered and slept where you worked.

Taylor continued to feel ambivalent about the policy, and finally decided that the regulation was appropriate, at least as long as most of society continued to feel uncomfortable with gays.

Taylor's wife and paralegal, Christine Sharron Taylor, however, found the hearings extraordinarily disconcerting. She had gay friends, and she tried to imagine what it would be like to be put on trial for her acquaintances; it seemed surreal. She was also struck by the fact that the military's persecution seemed reserved for lesbians. She had to believe it was a connivance to rid the Marine Corps of a gender they never wanted much anyway. After her husband had spent all of 1988 and the first two months of 1989 almost exclusively on Parris Island cases—Mary Kile's, Laura Hinckley's, Judy Meade's, and others—Christine asked her husband not to take anymore, at least for a while. They had left her feeling terribly depressed.

APRIL 19, 1989
ABOARD THE USS *IOWA*
ATLANTIC OCEAN

ONLY AT THE LAST MINUTE did Gunner's Mate Second Class Clayton Hartwig hear that he would be the gunner's captain that morning for the *Iowa*'s Turret Number Two.

It was an important day for the *Iowa*. A two-star admiral was aboard, and the gunner in Turret Two would be trying a different arrangement of explosives geared to improve the gun's accuracy. The presence of an admiral meant pressure on the crew, particularly the gun crews, who were to be the day's star attractions. And pressure was one thing this crew did not need. Along with being understaffed, the gun crew was very inexperienced. This was why Gunner's Mate Richard Lawrence, originally on the roster as supervisor for the day, had been replaced by the more seasoned Hartwig. Only a handful had the certification that, under Navy regulations, was required of a gunnery crew member.

Like a number of the *Iowa*'s sailors, Hartwig had forebodings about the ship, and especially about his job given the age of the gunpowder the crew was using; the explosives that morning dated back to the Korean War.

Recently, someone had posted the lyrics to a song by the popular group Metallica in Turret Two. The song, entitled "Disposable Heroes," was about soldiers being sent away and killed for the convenience of the government. To keep the half-century-old ship floating, with guns and technology so antiquated that even Navy officials conceded they could never be replaced if damaged, made them all disposable heroes in the opinion of some.

But being a gun captain was what Hartwig had always wanted to be, just like his dad, who had been a gunner's mate in World War II. It was his job, and he probably did not think much of the abrupt assignment as he climbed the six-story hardened-steel cylinder that housed the huge gun, along with fifty-eight other sailors who would man it that morning.

Hartwig's friend, Gunner's Mate Third Class Kendall Truitt, was in the bathroom when general quarters was sounded to man the guns, so he was late to his station on the bottom floor of Turret Two; he was among the last to enter. The friendship between Truitt and Hartwig had changed in recent months. Truitt had married, and Hartwig did not like his wife. The pair had not spoken for a period, but lately they were warming up toward each other again.

69

Explosions

APRIL 19, 1989
ABOARD THE USS *IOWA*
ATLANTIC OCEAN

"I HAVE A PROBLEM HERE. I'm not ready yet. I have a problem here. I'm not ready yet."

They were the last words anyone heard from the center gun of Turret Number Two. They came from the turret's main gun room, from Gunner's Mate Richard Lawrence, the cradleman.

The gun turret was nothing more than a big gun, like the inside of a hugely magnified pistol into which the crew dropped ninety-pound bags of gunpowder not much larger than basketballs to propel the gun's orange-tipped 2,700-pound bullets. The powder bags were hoisted from magazines at the bottom of the turret, carried into the gun room, and gently set into the end of the sixty-six-foot gun barrel. At the bottom of each powder bag were red patches containing explosive black powder to ignite the bags. Because burning embers left in the barrel from a previous firing could cause a premature explosion, the gun captain placed a foil packet between every two gunpowder bags immediately before firing. The packet contained chemicals for cleaning the barrel to make it safe for reloading. Then the gunner's captain would give the order to fire, and everyone in the gun room would leap behind a red line, to avoid the fierce recoil from one of the world's largest guns.

Moments before the gun should have fired, at about 9:55 A.M., an explosion tore out of the center gun on Turret Two. Artists later recreated that moment in drawings that could never accurately suggest the inferno that engulfed the turret that morning. The blast from the gun, imploding inside the ship, tore apart crewmen's bodies and sent a ghastly fireball rolling through the turret. Some men had time to try to run for the hatches, and that is where their burned and suffocated bodies were found.

From the bridge of the sleek ship, another crewman captured the moment on videotape. Turret Number One raised its guns and lowered them without firing; there had been a misfire. Turret Two was directed to shoot next. The guns lowered so they would be parallel to the sea during reloading. The first gun raised up and fired. On the middle gun, however, the tarp between the barrel and the turret suddenly swelled up like a balloon. Flames spewed from the gun barrel, shooting straight out; smoke billowed from the turret. The ship rocked with a fierce explosion.

The gunnery crew knew the rhythm of the loading, firing, and re-loading cycle as well as they knew the constant hum of the ship's engines. When Ken Truitt heard the explosion, he thought at first that the gun had fired early. "That didn't sound right," Ken said to a crewmate. His crewmate tried to radio the powder magazines; there was no response. Ken ordered the powder stored and stepped into the next room. The lights were out and three sailors were screaming. He opened the door to the powder flats, saw bags of explosives on fire, and shouted for someone to tell him what was going on. No one answered. "Evacuate," Truitt heard a crewmate shout. "There's gunpowder that's going to explode."

Truitt and other crewman on the bottom floor of the magazine leaped for their Oxygen Breathing Apparatus, which looked like scuba gear and was designed for such conflagrations. They would have to flood the powder magazines to prevent an even bigger disaster, but there was no way to tell if water was actually pouring in. Truitt ventured down the stairwell to see whether the huge cranks had turned to allow sea water in to douse the flames, all the while thinking, "I'm going to die. I've got gunpowder in here that's burning. I'm going to die." When he got to the magazines, he saw a door closed improperly, preventing flooding. He closed the hatch, water began to fill the room, and he returned to his magazine, where he met the ship's firemen. One asked if he had been to the gun room. No, he said. "They're all dead," a fireman said. Of fifty-nine crewmen in Turret Two, only twelve had survived.

Truitt and his crewmates worked in the turret when the fire was doused for seventeen hours. All around them lay body parts, pieces of friends, some decapitated, some burned so badly that they could only be recognized by a tattoo, others mangled beyond recognition. Though the Navy would tell grieving families that the sailors had died instantly, the placement of some of the bodies, piled on top of each other by the hatch doors, frozen in death like mannequins, testified to their final attempts to escape the holocaust. The men on the lower decks had died of asphyxiation, because the fire had pulled the air through the turret's ventilation system, literally sucking the oxygen out of their lungs. At one point, Ken thought he saw pieces of Clay, too, but he could never be sure.

THAT MORNING
ARLINGTON, VIRGINIA

ABOUT AN HOUR after the explosion aboard the USS *Iowa*, hours before anyone outside the Navy would know of the tragedy, a meeting was taking place. For the first time, forty-six years since the Defense Department began formally banning homosexuals from the military, the issue was being taken up by an official government body. The topic of discussion before the Defense Advisory Committee on Women in the Service was not homosexuality per se, but the relationship between the exclusion of gays and sexual harassment of women. DACOWITS had not planned even to discuss this subject when they met at the conference that morning. The Military Freedom Project had simply lined up speakers of their own, and then put them behind a microphone during a "public comment" period, when anyone could raise any issue to the committee.

Among those testifying were Darlene Chamberlin, who recalled the purge of gays at Scott Air Force Base in 1982, the investigation that had brought her assistance from Rabbi Bruce Diamond. "I have an eighteen-year-old sister who will be on active duty in the military this year," said Chamberlin. "Is her career over because she has a sister who is a lesbian? Will she be investigated for knowing someone gay?"

Captain Judy Meade, awaiting the final word from the Marine Corps on whether it would accept her administrative board's decision, also testified about being charged and discharged without the benefit of facing one's accusers. Petty Officer First Class Mary Beth Harrison, just months away from her final administrative discharge hearing, said that aboard the USS *Grapple* women who did not respond to male advances were called "dykes." When she held up a copy of a sign that had appeared on the *Grapple*, the sign with the word *Dykes* struck through with a slash mark, she provided photographers with the picture that would make the newspapers.

DACOWITS Chairwoman Connie Lee responded, "I'm not convinced that the system is not working." The military justice system already had mechanisms for handling sexual harassment, she said, "*if* we decide there is harassment here."

When a subcommittee met later that day to discuss sexual harassment, they studiously avoided the issue's lesbian component, until Kate Dyer, an aide to Congressman Gerry Studds, asked whether they would discuss it. The subcommittee chairwoman nervously said they would, but they did not. At the end of the day, the DACOWITS executive committee issued a recommendation that the military institute training sessions to curtail sexual harassment against women and "expand existing leadership training to include dealing with unfounded allegations of homosexuality against Service members."

In making this statement, DACOWITS was not saying lesbians should be allowed to stay in the military; only that the Defense Department be certain that the women it did eject from the service really were lesbians and not merely the slandered objects of unrequited advances. This was hardly a statement for gay liberation, but organizers of the Military Freedom Project, which made its public debut at the hearing, pronounced the DACOWITS hearings "historic" and called the recommendation "a good first step."

THE FACT THAT THE ISSUE of homosexuality came up only tangentially to a fairly obscure commission tucked deep in the military bureaucracy demonstrated how embryonic the lobbying efforts against Pentagon policies were. Though liberal gay activists complained that the policy was being preserved by the Republican administration, which was currying favor with religious conservatives, the fact was that the policies were protected by both Republican and Democratic politicians.

The Democrats who chaired the committees on armed services in the Senate and the House of Representatives had steadfastly declined to hold hearings on the issue of gays in the military. Senator Sam Nunn of Georgia was known to be hostile to the idea of allowing gays to serve. The more liberal Congressman Les Aspin was thought to be somewhat sympathetic, but he had never made any public statement or gesture, nor had the topic ever been discussed openly in his committee. The chairwoman of the house subcommittee on military personnel, Representative Beverly Byron of Maryland, was a conservative Democrat who was not interested in addressing the gay policy.

The lonely voices calling for reform belonged to Congresswoman Pat Schroeder, a ranking armed services member, and Congress' two openly gay members, Gerry Studds and Barney Frank. Congresswoman Connie Morella, a liberal Republican from Maryland, had recently weighed in on the issue by asking the Pentagon to investigate the "Gestapo tactics" used by military investigators during gay purges. Their voices, in a capital city where hundreds of issues competed for congressional and media attention, were not enough, and on Capitol Hill the subject remained a nonissue.

The presence of two acknowledged homosexual congressmen did occasionally create anomalous moments on the Hill. As chairman of the subcommittee on fisheries, Congressman Studds, who represented the important fishing port of New Bedford, supervised the U.S. Coast Guard. This was a position of no small influence, since the House originated all funding bills, making Studds the point man for any issues relating to the service. Though the Coast Guard was part of the Department of Transportation and not the Department of Defense, it rigidly adhered to the Pentagon's gay policies, because Coast Guard sailors could be called to serve in military situations. At a hearing during this period, Studds asked the Coast Guard to explain its gay regulations, which it did by claiming the importance of consistency with other military services. Studds noted that it was odd that he was a good enough man to be in charge of the Coast Guard for the House of Representatives but not good enough to swab decks on a Coast Guard vessel.

THAT AFTERNOON
CLEVELAND, OHIO

CLAY HARTWIG TOOK after his dad, Earl, not only in appearance, with his tall build, distinctive chin, and sleepy blue eyes, but in his quiet, even shy, disposition. Neither Clay nor Earl laughed aloud; they smiled or at most chuckled quietly. Clay's older sister, Kathy, took after her mother, Evelyn, who was garrulous and outspoken. Thirteen years older than her brother, Kathy had left home to marry when Clay was only five. Since then, she and her husband, an electrician at a local Ford plant, had had three children and moved into a small house in Cleveland. With children always under foot and Kathy Kubicina's gruff but humorous demeanor, friends were reminded of the blue-collar family in the popular new television show "Roseanne."

Kathy sat nervously on her couch that afternoon, her Cleveland Browns stadium blanket pulled up over her. She had heard the news of an explosion on the *Iowa* hours before. She spent the rest of that afternoon on her couch, drinking cans of Pepsi-Cola, smoking cigarettes, and watching the television, hoping for any word that her brother was alive. Late that night, she called Ken Truitt's wife. She knew that Clay had not liked Carole, but Kathy hoped she might know something. Carole, however, knew nothing of Clay, only that Ken had survived.

The next afternoon, Earl and Evelyn Hartwig opened the door to two Naval officers in their dress whites. Evelyn began to sob.

A few miles away in her living room, a local television news crew was waiting with Kathy when her parents called. "He's dead," she heard, and she started to cry.

Across the country, other Naval officers in dress white uniforms were making similar visits to the families of the forty-six other crew members killed in the worst peacetime Naval disaster in more than a quarter century. Like most of the enlisted men in the services, most of these men were born in 1967, 1968, or 1969. Less influenced by the countercultural sixties than the Reagan-era eighties, most had sought out their assignments on the battleships, the symbol of American Naval strength.

WHAT MOST VEXED the Navy in the first days after the accident, as officials attempted to come up with an explanation for the disaster, was that no one had lived to tell what really happened. Though critics had long questioned the wisdom of resurrecting such old ships, the Navy hated to admit that their antiquated mechanisms and antique explosives might have caused the tragedy. To admit this would be to admit that battleships were dangerous, and battleships were a most beloved vessel of the seagoing service. As it was, the Secretary of the Navy ordered that all the sixteen-inch guns on the four battleships be silenced until investigators determined what had caused the blast.

But there was a significant problem. Admiral Richard Milligan had ordered the turret washed out and thoroughly cleaned after the explosion, even before the ship pulled back into its home port of Norfolk. Much of the most important evidence had been washed overboard.

From the start, the explosion thrust twenty-one-year-old Ken Truitt into the limelight. His efforts in the turret, which had required no small amount of heroism, brought him to the attention of the ship's captain. Ken was intelligent and articulate, and a presentable role model for the Navy. The ship's officers put Truitt on center stage for press conferences. He became a veritable USS *Iowa* poster boy. There was hardly a story on the incident anywhere in the national press that did not include a poignant comment from Kendall Truitt. And his moment in the national spotlight was only beginning.

THE REMAINS OF CLAYTON HARTWIG had been transported to Dover Air Force Base, where military morticians had the grisly task of reconstructing and then identifying the bodies, largely through dental records. Notice that Clay was among the dead had come late, after much uncertainty. His body was the last to be found, and when it was carried off the *Iowa* to be flown to Dover, it became autopsy number 47.

APRIL 1989
NORFOLK NAVAL STATION
NORFOLK, VIRGINIA

KATHY KUBICINA HAD NOT PLANNED to go to Norfolk for the official memorial service for the dead *Iowa* crewmen. Their bodies were at Dover Air Force Base; Clay would not be in Norfolk. But the Navy had said it would fly her and her husband there, as well as Earl and Evelyn Hartwig, and Kathy thought she might learn something about the cause of the accident.

President George Bush, just three months in office, delivered a moving tribute to the *Iowa* crewmen, with his newly sworn-in Secretary of Defense, Richard Cheney, at his side. "They came to the Navy as strangers, served the Navy as shipmates and friends, and left the Navy as brothers in eternity," Bush said, and pledged an answer to the mysteries of the accident. "I promise you today, we will find out why—the circumstances of the tragedy," he said. Although some Navy officials later argued that it was not necessary to explain the accident to others, the remark sounded like an order from the Commander in Chief. From that moment on, an explanation was imperative, because the President had said so.

Kathy sought out Ken Truitt, and they talked over an early lunch together. It was Ken who told Kathy that Clay had taken out an insurance policy at the Navy credit union and named him as beneficiary. Knowing of their friendship, she was not shocked by this information, but it bothered her. She knew Clay and Ken had not been as close since Ken's marriage. She thought her parents, who lived on her father's railroad pension and meager Social Security checks, should be Clay's beneficiaries.

Back in Cleveland, she wrote her local congresswoman, Mary Rose Oakar, asking her to pass along to the Navy her request to change the name of the beneficiary on Clay's insurance policy in favor of her parents.

When the letter from Congresswoman Oakar arrived, the Navy's frantic search for the cause of the blast took an abrupt shift. That one male crew member had made another male crew member his insurance beneficiary read *homosexual* to Navy investigators. And the suspicion of homosexuality led to suspicions of all sorts of other diabolical behavior. The explosion might not have been an accident, the Navy mused, but a criminal act of one crewman against his shipmates. This required the expertise of an agency that knew much about homosexuals, the NIS.

APRIL 28, 1989
RESTHAVEN MEMORIAL GARDEN
AVON LAKE, OHIO

A PROCESSION of two hundred cars accompanied Gunner's Mate Clayton Hartwig to the cemetery, where he was buried with a twenty-one-gun salute, taps, and full military honors. His grave was covered in mounds of red tulips and white chrysanthemums, and his body was placed under a small white marble headstone:

> CLAYTON M. HARTWIG
>
> GMG2 US NAVY
>
> DECEMBER 29, 1964–APRIL 19, 1989

In the days that followed, Evelyn and Earl Hartwig experienced a terrible listlessness. They did not know what to do with themselves. They came to Kathy's house and sat. They did not want to be alone.

Meanwhile, Ken had become a minor celebrity. He had enlisted in the Navy from Marion, Illinois, so the Illinois State Senate invited him to address a session and receive a certificate of honor for his heroism on the day of the explosion.

ON MAY 3, KATHY received a phone call from a Navy captain who said the service would look into helping her, so when two agents from the NIS appeared at her door five days later, she was ready to greet them.

By way of an introduction, one agent explained that the NIS was "the FBI of the Navy." Neither made an effort to conceal their guns. One sported a Velcro ankle holster. At first they talked about the insurance claim, but then one of the agents took a strange tack, according to Kathy.

"Do you consider yourself a liberal person?" he asked.

Kathy said she did.

"Do you have any gay friends?" he asked.

Though mystified, Kathy said that she did.

"Do you think your brother might have been gay?" he asked.

Kathy told him that it wouldn't matter to her whether he was or not.

"I want you to sit down and explain to me why your brother left money to another man," the NIS agent said. "Draw me a profile."

Kathy could not understand why they needed a "profile" for an insurance policy probe. The agents said they would be back in touch.

Soon after, Kathy heard from Brian Hoover, Clay's best friend in high school, and she learned more about how the NIS conducted investigations. The NIS agents had told Hoover that Kathy and her parents had said that Brian was gay; they wanted to know if Clay was gay, too. When they saw that Hoover wore a Navy ring, they ridiculed him. "Were you lovers?" one agent said. "When you wear a Navy ring on your left hand, that means you're engaged."

At Earl and Evelyn Hartwig's home, the NIS agents found Clay's upstairs bedroom remained exactly it was before he left Cleveland for the Navy, with its ship models and books on Civil War and World War II history. Evelyn allowed them to go through the room, but asked them not to disturb his belongings. "Don't worry," an agent said. "It's not a criminal investigation. If it were, we'd be tearing this room apart with a fine-tooth comb."

The agents were lying. By then, the *Iowa* investigation was a criminal investigation with two major suspects, the reputed homosexual lovers: Clay Hartwig and Kendall Truitt.

The NIS interview with Ken Truitt was standard. "Tell us about Clay," one agent said. Ken said they were friends. "What do you mean by friends?" the agent pressed. Ken said they were best friends; there was nothing he would not have done for Clay.

The agents mentioned another friend of Clay's. "We know they were fucking each other," one agent said. They believed Ken was gay, too. "We're not on a witch-hunt, Ken," one agent said. "I've got gay friends. That doesn't bother me. You can tell us." Ken said that if he was gay, he would tell, but that he was not. The agents pressed on. Was Clay suicidal, might he have wanted to kill himself or others? Ken said he was not, and that if he had wanted to commit suicide, it would have been much easier to jump overboard or use a lighter in the powder magazines at night. The agents got back to their original tack: "Ken, we know you're gay. We know you and Clay were gay. We know you're lying to us."

"Did he love you, Ken?"

They were friends, Ken said.

"Did you love him like a brother?"

Maybe, Ken said.

The NIS agents liked that answer; now they had a statement that Hartwig and Truitt loved each other; therefore, they must be gay.

Because he had nothing to hide, Ken let the NIS agents search his home. They spent hours poring over every autographed entry in his high school yearbooks and his wife's high school yearbooks. They even pawed through Carole's underwear.

When Ken came home for lunch to find his wife in tears, he learned that NIS agents had interviewed her as well. In the course of two interviews, they had asked Carole Truitt such questions as, "Has [Ken] ever fucked you up the ass?" "Is he rough with you?" Did Ken ever have sex with Carole while Clay watched? Had Carole ever had sex with any of Ken's friends? Did she ever have sex with Hartwig? Did she ever have sex with other *Iowa* crew members? Wasn't Ken really gay? Did she marry him to provide a cover so no one would suspect? How often did she and Ken have sex? When the agents found pictures of the couple on their honeymoon, one agent asked if Clay had been with them and taken the photographs. That was when Ken Truitt called the NIS and told them to "get the fuck out of my life." He would no longer cooperate with them.

By then, however, the NIS agents had their first theory on the *Iowa* explosion. In a search of Ken's locker, they had found a burlap bag, the kind filled with powder during the firing of the big gun. Gunner's mates routinely picked up such items as souvenirs, or to use when teaching gunnery techniques to new sailors, but the agents believed Ken might have used such bags to make an explosive device to kill Hartwig, so he could collect the insurance money he knew was coming to him if Hartwig died. Added to Clay's dislike for Carole Truitt, the plot thickened with the possibility of a homosexual love triangle. The NIS now had a suspect in the *Iowa* explosion: Ken Truitt.

70

Mockingbirds

IN THE EARLY WEEKS of May, Kendall Truitt heard that NIS agents were interviewing every available crew member about him and Hartwig. Investigators reviewed the disciplinary action taken against them two years earlier when they had been found wrestling on the *Iowa* deck. Agents also interviewed every sailor who had been discharged from the *Iowa* for homosexuality in recent years, looking for proof that the pair was gay. They found none, only old gossip. The interviews did turn up new homosexuals who were then discharged, but they provided no proof that Hartwig or Truitt was gay, or that either man could have done anything to cause the blast.

It took little time for the rumors to reach the press, and on a hectic Friday night, Ken received a call from his executive officer telling him that both *The Washington Post* and the *Norfolk Star-Ledger* were trying to locate him for interviews. There was no need for Ken to talk to the press, the officer assured him. In fact, the Navy would give him time off if he wanted to get away to avoid their questions. Ken went to stay with his in-laws in Tampa. His officers told him to check in by phone regularly. He would not have to come back to Norfolk until the whole thing blew over.

In late May, Ken got a call from a friend with a satellite television dish who had tapped into an early feed of national network news. He warned Ken that NBC was running a story that night on the *Iowa* explosion, and the story all but accused him of being a killer.

THE DAY BEFORE this story aired, Fred Francis, NBC's Pentagon correspondent, called Kathy Kubicina to ask, "What would you do if I told you the NIS found pictures of your brother and another guy on the ship?" Why would Clay Hartwig make another man the beneficiary of his insurance policy? he asked. Did she think her brother was gay? Kathy said she did not. At the end of the conversation, Kathy asked if NBC was doing a story. Francis replied that he "did not have an angle yet."

The next evening, about fifteen minutes before the nightly news came on, Kathy received a call from NBC telling her that Francis was doing a story that night. Kathy asked if it was a good story or a bad one. The assistant said, "It's going to be interesting." (An NBC spokesman later said that Francis would not comment on the story.)

Kathy thought that the focus would be on the insurance policy. Instead, the story quoted unnamed Navy sources as saying Hartwig and Truitt were rumored to have a homosexual relationship. The accompanying visual at this point was separate photos of the two sailors, positioned so that it appeared the two men were staring at each other. A Hartwig family "spokesman" had confirmed that Clay was gay, the piece reported. And it mentioned the burlap investigators had found in Truitt's locker, and the insurance settlement Truitt would receive if Hartwig died.

Kathy dispatched a friend to their Seventh-Day Adventist Church, where her parents were attending a service. She did not want them to hear the news from anyone else. She met them in her driveway and told her mother as she stepped out of the car. They were saying on television that Clay was gay, Kathy said, and had been murdered by his best friend for insurance money. Evelyn collapsed in the driveway.

The next day, a series of equally damning stories appeared in major newspapers across the country. *The Washington Post* reported that, "The NIS probe is pursuing at least two angles: that Truitt may have triggered the explosion to claim the insurance money, and that Hartwig, despondent over a rift in their relationship, caused the blast in an attempt to kill himself and/or Truitt. . . . The NIS is investigating the possibility that Truitt may have tampered with one of the powder bags sent to the gun house where Hartwig normally worked." As if to endorse the suspicions, Truitt had been granted a leave from the *Iowa* because his shipmates might do him harm, the paper reported. "For his own protection, it was not prudent for him to be there," an official told the paper.

The portrait of Hartwig was as incriminating. He was a "sullen" child, the paper reported, who became "obsessed" with joining the Navy at an early age. "He seldom smiled," the paper reported, shunned sports, and had few friends. "In almost every family photograph—at Christmas, birthday parties or outings—Clay is sitting in the shadows reading a book or staring blankly at the floor."

Though the connection between mass murder and homosexuality was implicit in every news story, it never made sense to Kathy. Though she was miffed at Ken for getting her brother's insurance money, she did not believe he had anything to do with the explosion either.

Because she had been the family's spokesperson in the wake of the explosion a month earlier, reporters began calling Kathy as soon as the NBC story appeared. The next day, she received 117 phone calls; the day after, 80 more. Kathy called Fred Francis's office at NBC to try to press Clay's side of the story, but no one returned her calls. The Navy advised Kathy not to talk to the media. "Tell them you have no comment," they told her.

One of the calls she took early on the morning after Fred Francis's story was from NBC radio. It was still dark, but Kathy had not slept all night. "I need you to comment on his homosexuality," the reporter said. Kathy said she did not believe her brother was gay. The reporter wanted better confirmation, however. "Could you please tell me if your brother is available for comment?" he asked.

TAMPA, FLORIDA

KENDALL TRUITT had gone along with his officers' suggestions that he avoid the press. He wanted to join the Navy SEALS and did not want to alienate officials who might be deciding whether he merited the prestigious assignment. The rash of stories suggesting he might have killed scores of his shipmates made Truitt realize that he could end up in jail if he did not fight back. Of course, the Navy did not want him to talk to the press; they were in the process of using the press to frame him for murder. Ken's first impulse was to fly back to Norfolk and talk to local newspapers, but his father-in-law had found a lawyer in Miami, Ellis Rubin, who would take their case. They should fly to Miami immediately, he suggested, and meet the press there.

Ellis Rubin was the kind of showy lawyer who aroused the suspicion of more conservative attorneys for what they considered self-promotion. Since Ken Truitt was being tried in the press, however, a press counter-offensive seemed appropriate, and few attorneys were as experienced as Rubin in launching such a drive. Rubin and a gaggle of television crews were awaiting Ken and Carole when they stepped off their plane at Miami International. An impromptu press conference followed. With a grand gesture, Rubin turned to Truitt and asked, "Are you a homosexual?" No, Ken said, he was not. Rubin turned to Carole Truitt. "Is he a good lover?" he asked. Carole laughed and assured Rubin that Ken was.

Truitt aggressively denied any involvement with the explosion. "I think the Navy is at a loss," he said, "They're just looking for a scapegoat." Ken laid out the other factors that he believed could have caused the explosion: an undermanned and inexperienced gun crew, gunpowder that had been improperly stored at high temperatures the previous summer, the possibility that the gun was "over-rammed," causing a compression that exploded the gunpowder before the breech was closed. Rubin demanded an apology for the leaked stories implicating his client, and served notice on the Navy that continuing allegations against Truitt "would be answered in court."

Because of all the publicity, Ken was transferred off the *Iowa* to an administrative job in Mayport, Florida. When he went back to the ship to pack his gear, an escort accompanied him on board. "It's for your own protection," he was told. "Just in case."

It was about this time that Ken began hearing clicks on his telephone. In conversations with NIS personnel, agents would sometimes repeat verbatim observations he had made in phone calls the night before.

———————

BY THE FINAL DAYS of May, the case against Truitt had unraveled. From the powder magazine, Truitt and his crew had fed gunpowder to all three guns in Turret Two. When they loaded powder—with or without any explosive device—Ken would have had no way of knowing whether the powder was going to the left, right, or center gun, where Clay was. The fact that Ken would know that he was as likely to be killed in such an explosion as Clay also argued against his involvement. Sailors had died eight feet from where Truitt was working. He could not have been sure of his own safety, something that someone planning on collecting insurance benefits would undoubtedly consider.

From the Navy's point of view, there was another reason not to pursue the allegations against Truitt, particularly when there was no evidence that they were true. Ken's publicity offensive informed the Navy that he would fight back. Navy investigators now settled on a different suspect, one who could not fight back or hold press conferences: Clay Hartwig.

Two days after Ken Truitt's press conference in Miami, NIS agents, casting about for evidence to finger its new suspect, called in Seaman David Smith at his instigation. The interrogation was conducted over two days, the first day lasting over eight hours. As was often the case, the NIS did not allow Smith breaks for sleep, although transcripts indicated that new shifts of agents relieved one another in the interrogation chamber during the course of the questioning. The transcripts also show such interchanges as this:

Agent: "I feel there's something you're not telling me. Is there something you're not telling me?"

"I'm just tired," Smith answered.

"I know you're tired. Look at me. Don't go to sleep on me now."

"I'm probably just tired. I'm tired."

Later in the official transcript, the NIS elicited a startling admission from Smith. First that Clay had made a sexual advance to him the night before the explosion and that Smith had rebuffed him. Second, the transcript says, Smith had seen an explosive detonating device in Clay Hartwig's locker. The two facts were crucial to what the NIS would later advance as its hypothesis for the *Iowa* explosion: that Hartwig, a frustrated and despondent homosexual, had placed a detonating device in the big gun to kill himself.

What was not in the official transcript, according to Smith, was another conversation that NIS agents had with him. "We know [Hartwig] did it," they told him. "We're just trying to find the proof." If Smith withheld information about the explosion, he could be put up on criminal charges, NIS agents warned him. Each death was a separate crime: Smith could face forty-seven counts as an accessory to murder, as well as charges of perjury and obstruction of justice. Smith had heard other crewmates speculate that the Navy was looking for someone to hang in the explosion; he did not want to be the scapegoat. He told the NIS what they wanted to hear. They had said, after all, that they already knew that Clay was gay and had an explosive device in his locker.

That David Smith's statement might have been coerced had been implied even in the official NIS transcript. At the end of the interview, Smith was asked to make the routine disclaimer that he had made "this statement of my own free will and without any threats to me or any promises extended." At that point, the transcript records an agent saying, "What makes you laugh about that?"

Three days later, David Smith was reinterviewed by the NIS and he recanted the two most crucial revelations of his previous statement, that Hartwig had made an advance toward him, and that Hartwig had a detonator in his locker. Neither was true, he said.

The recantation was of little interest to the NIS. A week later, Fred Francis of NBC aired the news that a witness claimed Hartwig had shown off a $15 timer for an explosive device and spoken about how painless and quick it would be to die in an explosion on the ship. Francis also reported that the Navy claimed Hartwig was the last person to touch the gunpowder before it went into the gun, putting him in a unique position to insert an explosive device.

Before those accusations could be formally lodged, however, the NIS had much work to do. In a search of Hartwig's automobile, they found a car radio antenna, fuses, and wires, all of which he had purchased at Radio Shack the previous summer for $114.98. In an unsuccessful attempt to find evidence that Hartwig was gay, agents went to local motels, showed desk clerks pictures of the dead sailor, and asked if he had ever been seen going into rooms with other men. His high school classmates were interviewed.

Shipmates recounted every rumor they had heard about Hartwig. One crewman, who was gay, said he believed that Hartwig certainly was homosexual, because he exhibited a tendency toward excessive "tidiness." Another said, "It was common knowledge among the enlisted men that there was something 'funny' about [Hartwig and Truitt's] relationship." Another noted that when the two talked in the mess deck, they "would be leaning over the table toward each other, as couples would do in a restaurant." One of the crewman killed in the blast was gay, and had written his mother that one of the other gunnery crew members in Turret Two was also gay. He never identified who his fellow gay crewmate was, but NIS agents believed Hartwig was the homosexual in question.

To obtain a psychological profile of Hartwig in order to develop possible motives for his having killed his shipmates, the Navy contacted the Center for the Analysis of Violent Crimes at the Federal Bureau of Investigation, which specialized in such profiles. In their instructions, however, the Navy specified that the FBI should not even consider the possibility that the explosion was caused by an accident. The FBI should pursue three theories only: that Truitt had plotted the explosion to kill Hartwig, that Hartwig had caused the blast to kill himself and others, including Truitt; or that Hartwig was intent only upon suicide. Using statements provided by the NIS, the FBI went to work.

There was a series of stories that cast doubt upon the Navy's hypothesis from the start. Disciplinary actions had been taken against a lieutenant commander who had cleared "unauthorized experiments" with gunpowder on the morning of the explosion. These experiments were the reason the gun in Turret Two carried a different load of gunpowder from normal, although the Navy maintained that this did not contribute to the explosion.

In June, the *Norfolk Star-Ledger* ran a story about the Navy violating its own munitions storage rules the previous summer when the *Iowa* was in Norfolk for overhauling. Navy manuals specified that the powder decomposed at temperatures over 70 degrees Fahrenheit, and that this process "dangerously accelerated" at temperatures over 110 degrees, causing instability and the possibility of accidental explosion. In 1988, however, the Navy had stored gunpowder from the *Iowa* on barges sitting in the middle of the York River during the hottest months of the summer. An internal Navy report found that the temperature on the barges probably exceeded 110 degrees on sixty-six separate days.

THE *IOWA* INVESTIGATION took place against the backdrop of renewed purges of gay military men around the world. The largest in this period occurred in Okinawa, where the NIS secretly installed videocameras in a public restroom at a picnic ground at Camp Lester. On its official complaint forms, NIS agents described the investigation as "relating to sexual impurity." Their cameras documented an impressive amount of sexual activity among at least forty servicemen or civilian military employees. As of July 1989, an Air Force major, a first lieutenant, and a chief master sergeant awaited trial. A Marine Corps master gunnery sergeant pleaded guilty to "indecent acts" after three enlisted men pleaded innocent on charges of sodomy. Many others waived their rights to hearings and quietly accepted discharges.

An investigation at the Defense Language Institute in Monterey between May and August 1989 resulted in the discharges of at least five soldiers and sailors. In Germany, the investigations of gay Army personnel grew so fierce that the owner of the Nanu, a bar in Kaiserslautern frequented by many gay soldiers, required any unfamiliar soldier to French kiss another patron before he could enter to establish that the visitor was indeed gay and not a CID agent. And at least a dozen Air Force enlisted men were discharged in a 1988 purge of gays at Loring Air Force Base in Maine, according to Senior Airman Tim Jernigan, one of the men separated in that investigation.

Gay civilians sometimes aided military investigators. Navy Reserve Captain Bob Dockendorf believes he was turned in to the NIS by a prominent San Francisco gay leader who was angry because Dockendorf supported a liberal candidate the gay leader opposed for San Francisco mayor. Shortly after the Navy received a program for a gay fund-raising event in which Dockendorf's name appeared, two admirals took him out for lunch. "You were going to be our next flag officer," one said. The other told him that trying to dodge the Navy's gay regulations was like trying to run stop signs. "You can only run them so many times before somebody's going to catch you." When a staff officer began processing Bob's paperwork, he commented that he didn't agree with the gay policy, but "this complaint [against Dockendorf] came from your own community." Dockendorf was allowed to put in his retirement papers, after twenty-six years of service in active duty and the Reserves.

After Dockendorf's separation, one of the admirals who had previously brought him out to the lunch that ended his career asked him to do them a favor, to help them in their efforts to make San Francisco the home port for the USS *Missouri*. Some local gay activists opposed the idea because of the military's gay policies. Would Dockendorf help them persuade voters that they did not discriminate against gays? Dockendorf responded to the admiral by saying, "I don't think I can do that." Dockendorf was president of a local gay Democratic club leading the effort against home-porting the *Missouri*.

The period was not without small victories for gay organizers. In July, five months after Captain Judy Meade was recommended for discharge because she had a gay friend, a board of review at Marine Corps headquarters ruled that the evidence was "insufficient to justify her involuntary separation" from the Marine Corps. Her attorney, Charles Bumer, had shown that an NIS agent had lied about the polygraph test results. Meade would be retained. Though Meade won this battle, she lost the war. From this point on, her evaluation reports, which had once been excellent, turned sour. She was not recommended for advancement in any form and in time she was passed over for promotion to major, and then passed over again. Military regulations suggest that any officer twice passed over for promotion consider retirement, which is what Judy Meade did, becoming the final casualty of the Parris Island lesbian purge.

GAY REPUBLICAN ACTIVISTS had assured skeptical gay leaders that President Bush would prove to be a quiet friend of the gay community. There were indications at first that this might be true. Bush rejected the Reagan administration's fervent opposition to laws banning discrimination against people with HIV, and supported legislation that allowed violence against gays to be included in federal hate crimes statistics. Moreover, though the new Defense Secretary, Richard Cheney, was known to be conservative, he was not inclined toward the doctrinaire homophobia that characterized so many Reagan appointees.

The first public indication that any moderation toward gays would not apply to those who served in the armed forces occurred during the confirmation hearings of Christopher Jehn, the new Assistant Secretary of Defense for Manpower Affairs. When asked about the PERSEREC report, Jehn repeated the 123 words of Pentagon policy, and added, "I would expect the current policy to remain in effect. I do not plan to initiate further study on this issue."

CLEVELAND, OHIO

A STRANGER APPROACHED Earl and Evelyn Hartwig in a restaurant and announced, "Your son is the gay guy who blew himself up on the ship."

The blame laid on Clay Hartwig for the *Iowa* explosion, attributed to unnamed sources within the Navy, had a devastating impact on the dead sailor's family. In late July, NBC's Fred Francis reported that the Navy believed there was "a compelling circumstantial case" against Hartwig. Francis cited David Smith's statement as the most damning evidence, but did not mention that Smith had recanted the statement nearly two months earlier—even though Pete Williams, the Assistant Secretary of Defense for Public Affairs, had already taken Francis aside to warn him that Smith had withdrawn the allegations. Meanwhile, the FBI had developed a psychological profile of Hartwig that characterized him as "troubled," despondent over Ken Truitt's marriage, and prone to suicide.

The NBC stories led to a rare display of public bickering among news organizations over whether colleagues were reporting the story ethically. Writing in *The Washington Post*, Robert Zelnick and Mark Brender of ABC News said the NIS "seemed inclined to blame the disaster on two of the *Iowa*'s sailors on the basis of flimsy evidence, most of which already lies in tatters," and they noted that both ABC News and the *Post* had refused to disseminate the stories being featured on NBC. The journalists pointed to the inconsistencies in the hypothesis that Hartwig had killed his crewmates. In the weeks before the explosion, Hartwig had talked about how much he looked forward to a new assignment he expected in England. The Navy said this was evidence that Clay was delusional, because he had already been passed over for the assignment. Later, the Navy admitted that Hartwig's orders to England had not been canceled and were still pending at the time of the blast. "He loved the sea, his ship, his comrades. And he loved the United States Navy," Zelnick and Brender concluded. "In the authors' view, he deserves better treatment."

Still, the Navy seemed confident in the case it was building against Hartwig, so much so that in June it partially lifted the ban it had imposed on the big guns on the four battleships. Now they could be fired if necessary to carry out military operations.

Kathy Kubicina believed the Navy had decided to blame the explosion on her brother because he could not defend himself, and she saw her parents suffering over it. Clay might not be able to speak up for himself, she thought, but she could speak for him. She got a second telephone line installed in her home, purchased a facsimile machine, and began contacting reporters to plead Clay's side of the story.

Official Government Sources

THE NAVY'S REPORT on the cause of the *Iowa* explosion was due out the next day, and Rear Admiral Richard P. Milligan, who directed the investigation, planned a full-scale press briefing on its conclusions. In order to hear how a public relations expert might view the report, Milligan met with Pete Williams, the civilian who served as Assistant Secretary of Defense for Public Affairs. Milligan went over the basic conclusions of the report, pulling out the charts and graphs that he believed supported it. The *Iowa* explosion was not an accident, the probe concluded, but sabotage, a "suicidal act" most likely committed by Gunner's Mate Second Class Clayton Hartwig.

Williams was not convinced by the explanation that Milligan laid out, and told him it was "nuts." The information he had offered simply did not support the conclusion they had reached, Williams said. The entire investigation had left Williams uneasy. Already he had told Fred Francis that he should not be the conduit for the Naval Investigative Service's leak-of-the-day.

The *Iowa* report had been the center of Pentagon gossip for the past two months. Under Navy regulations, it needed to be signed not only by Milligan, the chairman of the investigation, but by an officer senior to him before it would be accepted as an official Navy report. For nearly two months, however, no officer would endorse it. Navy officers were privately telling reporters that the report was but another example of NIS bungling. The NIS could not determine the real reason for the explosion, they said, so they pinned the blame on a dead man and lent the tale an overtone of homosexuality. Privately, officials conceded that they still did not know why the gun blew up. "There is a lot of pressure to get this thing finished with," said one Navy official to *The New York Times* in

July. "But I can tell you that the report will not be definitive, because we don't really know what happened."

Williams agreed with this assessment, believing that the pressure to come up with an explanation, *any* explanation, had forced the Navy to a conclusion it would have difficulty defending.

If the conversation with Williams conjured up any private doubts, Milligan was not sharing them the next morning when he officially released the conclusions of the $7 million probe into the *Iowa* blast. The investigation had "ruled out" any accidental cause for the explosion, Milligan said. The blast was caused neither by burning embers in the barrel, premature primer firing, mechanical failure, procedural error, nor any instability with the explosives. Meanwhile, he said, optical and electron microscopy found "the existence of foreign elements not normally present in the 16-inch gun." These traces, investigators concluded, were left by a detonating device inserted into the gun while the breech was still open, most probably when the gun captain inserted the thin foil packet between two explosive charges.

Milligan drew a stark portrait of Hartwig. He was suicidal: In high school, he had once confided to a friend that he wanted to kill himself. As a teenager, he had experimented with "homemade explosives," Milligan said. He had "professional delusions," as evidenced by a high school photograph NIS agents had found in his bedroom in which he was dressed as a Naval captain. His violent streak was reaffirmed by the fact that he subscribed to *Soldier of Fortune* magazine, a publication that championed mercenaries. He was a sullen loner, according to the profile provided by the FBI, and he hoped to aggrandize himself by dying a hero's death, going out in a blaze of glory. Milligan even produced a letter in which Hartwig said he might end up under a small white cross in Arlington National Cemetery, more proof of his preoccupation with death and heroism. Clay was alienated from his family, the FBI character analysis had found; he had not spent Christmas with his parents in three years. There was also the song lyrics of "Disposable Heroes," posted in the G1/G2 berthing area, the Navy said, in Hartwig's handwriting.

There was even more damning evidence. Milligan held up a copy of a small yellow book found among Hartwig's possessions that, he said, proved the gunner's mate was capable of violent acts of vengeance. The book *How to Get Even Without Going to Jail* detailed how to extract revenge on your enemies with explosives, Milligan said. Even worse, the Navy had found the makings of a detonating device in Hartwig's car. The most crucial evidence was the statement from David Smith asserting that he had seen a crude explosive device in Hartwig's locker and that the night before the explosion he had rebuffed Hartwig's sexual advance. Milligan did not mention that Smith had withdrawn the statement months earlier.

As the Chief of Naval Operations wrote in his final summation to the report, "The combination of these factors leads me reluctantly to the conclusion that the most likely cause of the explosion was a detonation device, deliberately introduced between the powder bags that were being rammed into the breech of the center gun. . . . The most likely person to have introduced the detonation device was GMG2 Hartwig." This conclusion, he said, was endorsed by "the preponderance of evidence."

The investigation also ruled that the ship's skipper, Captain Fred Moosally, and his executive officer be ordered to go before an admiral's mast for allowing uncertified crewmen to man gunnery positions and for not properly scheduling gun crew assignments. The admiral's mast effectively ended both men's careers, although investigators also said that these actions did not contribute to the explosion.

THAT AFTERNOON
CLEVELAND, OHIO

AFTER CAPTAIN DOUGLAS KATZ walked into the living room of Earl and Evelyn Hartwig's home, he apologized for what he was about to say. It was "the most horrible thing I've ever had to do," he said. Then he laid out the conclusions that had just been announced in Washington. The couple's son, he said, had killed himself and forty-six other sailors.

Evelyn began sobbing and then blurted, "My son is not a killer."

As soon as Katz had left, Kathy and the elder Hartwigs boarded a limousine to take them to the airport, so that they could appear on the next morning's television news shows. The newspapers all carried Clay's picture on page one, and generally accepted the conclusions the Navy had set forth.

The *Los Angeles Times* news account, for example, reported, "Gunner's Mate Clayton M. Hartwig, who almost certainly caused the calamitous April 19 explosion aboard the battleship *Iowa*, was a lonely suicidal young sailor consumed by destructive fantasies, Navy officials have concluded after a four-month investigation." The paper quoted Vice Admiral J. S. Donnell III as saying Hartwig was "emotionally capable of committing suicide, probably with the intent of killing others also," and reported that the sailor "owned a handbook that offered explicit prescriptions for exacting violent revenge on one's enemies." Numerous newspapers wrote long, moody profiles of Hartwig, weaving together the threads offered by Navy investigators to paint a portrait of a sullen, psychologically troubled man.

Milligan had told reporters the allegations that Hartwig was gay were "unfounded," but most news accounts included information leaked earlier that Hartwig was probably homosexual and depressed at the rejections he suffered from Kendall Truitt and David Smith. The reports cited information leaked from the volumes of NIS interviews, and reinforced the earlier impression that the *Iowa* explosion was the work of a suicidal-homicidal homosexual. Some papers, such as the *Los Angeles Times* and

The Washington Post, included a paragraph about the antigay reputation of the NIS, as well as retorts from gay leaders decrying the conclusions. Most reports, however, did not.

From a journalistic perspective, the reportage was accurate, as it merely quoted what Navy investigators had concluded, supported by anonymous quotes from official government sources who embellished the tale with details about homosexuality. It was virtually an article of faith among other journalists who covered this story extensively that the leaks were supplied by the Naval Investigative Service, probably with the blessing of Navy brass.

Kathy was surprised at the lack of any skepticism on the part of most journalists covering the story. Since the days of Watergate, she had come to believe that reporters challenged the government. She could not believe that conclusions she viewed as transparently false could be reported with such little incredulity. The mere fact that they were advanced by official government sources, she thought, did not make them legitimate.

Though the Navy's conclusions appeared well documented at first blush, particularly its devastatingly detailed psychological portrait of Hartwig, it did not take long for Kubicina to chronicle numerous inconsistencies and outright falsehoods. For example, Clay's personal correspondence, which the FBI relied upon so extensively in drawing its psychological assessment, revealed that he was anything but suicidal. He was eagerly planning his future, something that was rare for a person contemplating the end of his life. Though he had drifted apart from Truitt in late 1988, his more recent correspondence showed they were friends again. A note written three weeks before the accident recounted how Clay and Ken, whom Hartwig called "my best friend," had stayed up talking until 2:00 A.M. the previous night. Kubicina later learned that Hartwig's body was found not near the breech of the gun, as the Navy alleged, but a floor below, which was why it was the last corpse discovered in the turret.

As for the notion that he was "alienated" from his family because he did not come home for three Christmases, Kathy noted that in two of those years he was stationed in Cuba and on the third he was on duty in the Persian Gulf. He had not come home because it was nearly impossible to get away from his assignments.

There were other false innuendos in the Navy report. The photograph of Clay in a captain's outfit and saber was not the product of any professional delusions. It had been taken at a Valentine's Day dance at Hartwig's high school in 1982. The dance theme was based on the then-popular television show "Love Boat," and because of Hartwig's determination to join the Navy, his classmates had asked that he serve as the Love Boat captain for the dance. The "homemade explosives" that the Navy accused him of using in his teenage years were actually M-80 firecrackers, items with which a huge portion of teenagers in the Midwest routinely play.

Subscriptions to *Soldier of Fortune* magazine are ubiquitous among U.S. soldiers and sailors throughout the world, and hardly the singular interest of a death-obsessed sailor.

Perhaps the most ludicrous "evidence" against Clay, Kathy thought, was the book prominently displayed in the press conference, *How to Get Even Without Going to Jail*. Had any of the reporters bothered to read the pamphlet, they would have found that the book contained no blue-prints for diabolical "explosive devices," as the Navy alleged. Instead, the book was a compendium of innocuous practical jokes to play on obnoxious mothers-in-law and neighbors' dogs.

Kathy spent the next days pleading her dead brother's case. "My brother was not a depressed, despondent suicidal murderer," she said repeatedly to reporters. Her quotes, however, were usually buried deep in the news stories, long after the reporters had woven together what appeared to be a compelling case convicting the sailor.

Kathy's father, Earl Hartwig, was less surprised at the report's con-clusions. From his own years in the Navy during World War II, he knew the service loved its battleships and that they would do anything to protect them. As far as he was concerned, that was what the Navy report was all about, protecting the battleships. Like Kathy, he resolved to do anything he could to clear his son's name.

IN MAYPORT, FLORIDA, that day, Kendall Truitt watched the televised news conference on the Navy's report with great interest. Investigators had definitively excluded him as suspect in any wrongdoing, and there was no longer any public talk of a suspected homosexual relationship between himself and Hartwig. Still, the report angered him.

Like the Hartwig family, he matched the evidence against Clay with what he knew of his close friend. First, he did not believe Hartwig had the physical dexterity to manufacture and then insert an explosive device into the gun. A year earlier, when Clay had purchased the parts to install a car stereo—the purchase that the Navy asserted was really for components of a homemade detonating device—Truitt had had to do the installation himself. Clay was all thumbs and incapable of the simplest mechanical tasks. Moreover, any device inserted in the foil packets would have to be extraordinarily small, since the packets themselves were only the size of a compact disc. Such a det-onator would require far greater skill to assemble than Hartwig had ever demonstrated.

The allegations that Clay had made a sexual advance to David Smith seemed extraordinarily improbable to Ken. First, Smith had been on the ship for only three weeks before the explosion, making it un-likely that the reticent Hartwig would confide that much trust in him. More persuasively, Ken felt he was much more physically attractive than Smith. If Clay were inclined to make an advance toward any other man, he felt he would more likely have been its recipient. Clay, however, had never indicated any such interest. The fact that Clay had no idea he would even be manning the gun until moments before general quarters was sounded on the morning of the explosion also argued against sabotage, Ken believed. Such a scheme required precise timing and planning, neither of which Clay had that day. The suggestion that Hartwig had written out and posted the lyrics to "Disposable Heroes" was patently false, Truitt knew. Another sailor had done that; Clay hated heavy metal music.

To Truitt, however, the most important evidence in Hartwig's favor were those final words that he had heard over the radio moments before the blast. "I have a problem here," said Gunner's Mate Richard Lawrence. "I'm not ready yet. I have a problem here. I'm not ready yet." Truitt had worked with Lawrence and knew him to be an excitable man. Yet the words were not spoken with agitation. They most certainly were not the words of someone who was watching his gun captain insert an explosive device into the breech.

Throughout the summer, Truitt had also been researching the explosives used in the gun. The studies made him realize how extensive were the violations of standard practices on the *Iowa*, both with the storage of gunpowder in profoundly destabilizing conditions and the ease with which such destabilized gunpowder can explode.

Like the Hartwig family, Truitt resolved not to let up until he had cleared his friend's name. He granted numerous interviews assailing the Navy for making his friend a "scapegoat" and suggested other accidental scenarios that could have caused the blast. At one point a reporter said to him, "You've kept to the same story ever since this started—how do you manage to do that?" Ken looked back at him in wonder. "Because it's the truth," he said.

―――――――――――

THE DAY AFTER the report was released, Kathy Kubicina and Earl Hartwig were on an airplane back to Cleveland after appearing on "Good Morning America" when a stewardess approached them with a note, hastily written on the back of an airline napkin. The sender did not want to identify himself, the attendant said, and when Kathy read the missive, she understood why. He was a gay man in the Navy, he said, and he felt that Clay Hartwig was being framed. "Fight this to the bitter end," he wrote, "or they'll get away with it."

―――――――――――

THE NAVY'S CONCLUSION had implications that reached far beyond the particulars of the USS *Iowa*, or the guilt or innocence of Gunner's Mate Hartwig. At stake in the conclusion was the future of the battleships and, more significantly, the safety of the crews who manned them. Finding an accidental cause for the blast would require the Navy to scrap the battle-

ships, or at least end the firing of their big guns, which amounted to the
same thing since the sixteen-inch guns were the raison d'être for the
battleships. By allowing a conclusion largely predicated on antigay prejudice—even if not officially so—the Navy was risking the lives of thousands of sailors on the three remaining battleships.

It was a peculiar vanity of heterosexuals at this time to believe that
homophobia could be ignored as trivial, that this prejudice could be countenanced because it did not directly affect them. The *Iowa* report was a
dramatic example of how antigay attitudes affected and even endangered
the lives of thousands more.

From the first days after the report was issued, it began to raise
skepticism in Pentagon circles. When Pete Williams briefed reporters on
Defense Secretary Richard Cheney's reaction to the report, his statement
on the conclusion was, "As to how the explosion happened, the question
is obviously not resolved. The investigating officer offered his best conclusions as required under the Navy's investigative procedures." When a
reporter asked Williams whether this statement meant that Cheney "does
not necessarily accept the findings," Williams answered, "The Secretary's
been briefed on the report and he is satisfied that the investigating officer
did as well as he could." When pressed further, Williams conceded, "I
said I don't think [Cheney] is offering an opinion about the conclusion
one way or another."

Pentagon observers thought the statements reflected Cheney's desire
to distance himself from the report. Many reporters thought Williams,
who often said more by what he did not say than by what he did, was
allowing Cheney to damn the conclusion through faint praise. His remarks
certainly offered no support for the Navy's conclusions. Williams was
said to be privately convinced of what he had told Milligan at their briefing
a week earlier, that the Navy had not proven its case.

OCTOBER 18, 1989
U.S. CAPITOL
WASHINGTON, D.C.

THE COPY OF THE REPORT by the Personnel Security Research and Education Center, or PERSEREC, had arrived at the office of Congressman
Gerry Studds only a day earlier. The source who leaked the study to
Studds's aide, Kate Dyer, was so concerned that the Defense Department
would trace the report's source through photocopy analysis that he asked
Dyer to copy the report on five different machines and throw away each
previous copy. Given the fact that Studds was gay himself and was now
championing the cause of gays in the military, he found the study to be
extraordinarily scintillating reading. One sentence stood out. "Our studied conclusion is that the military services will soon be asked by the courts
or the congress to reexamine their policies and practices regarding the

recruitment and retention of men and women whose sexual interests deviate from the customary. . . . The military cannot indefinitely isolate itself from the changes occurring in the wider society, of which it is an integral part."

Studds and Congresswoman Patricia Schroeder had already requested a briefing with the report's coauthor, Dr. Ted Sarbin, and Pentagon officials in charge of security matters, most notably Maynard C. Anderson, Assistant Deputy Under Secretary of Defense for Counterintelligence and Security. When Studds opened the meeting by asking about the report, Anderson explained that the report really did not contain anything new or present any arguments for gays that had not already been weighed at the Pentagon. It was "flawed and useless," he said, "a feeble, unreadable waste of taxpayers' money." As Anderson put it in his later summary of the meeting, the report "was not of value to our office," and had been rejected. When Studds pressed as to the implications the report held for allowing gays to serve in the military, Anderson repeated the 123 words of the Defense Department's homosexual policy; they did not rest solely on security issues, he said. Anderson was clearly becoming uncomfortable as Studds, his aide Kate Dyer, and Schroeder's aide, Andy Feinstein, began dropping key phrases from the report. The study was not supposed to have been released outside a tight circle of Pentagon officials—the strategy had been to deny that it even existed.

Studds then turned to Sarbin and said that he thought the report reflected a superior intellectual effort that was far more incisive than anything he had read in the field. Studds's aide, Kate Dyer, watched the Pentagon officials with great interest at this moment, aware that this was the first indication they would have that Studds had read the report. To her eye Anderson went pale. Then Studds said that he had his own copy of the report, and Anderson became even paler. When Studds said he was going to release it to the news media, Anderson went white.

Anderson argued against release of the report, saying it would undermine PERSEREC. He even suggested, according to his summary of the meeting, that "there are possibly homophobic personnel within the Department who might have attempted the demise of PERSEREC by causing release of a product that would be considered detrimental or embarrassing." When Feinstein wondered if the new draft of the report would be "suppressed," Anderson said no, the report had not been suppressed, it had been judged not to have the professional quality required for its release. He had no intention of allowing it to be released either, whether to congressmen, attorneys litigating against the gay ban, or the news media.

Kate raised the issue of the Parris Island investigation and the bullying tactics used by NIS agents. Anderson defended the investigators, saying if the Pentagon did not thoroughly investigate allegations of misconduct, they would be vulnerable to criticism from members of Congress.

After the meeting, Kate Dyer returned to her office in the Rayburn

House Office Building and began typing up a press release to go out with as many copies of the PERSEREC report as she could photocopy. Four days later, news of the report and its rejection by the Pentagon was on page one of *The New York Times,* as well as a number of other major newspapers around the country. Along with the report, Studds had obtained copies of the memoranda that had been written between PERSEREC officials and Pentagon administrators during the period that the Defense Department sought to suppress the study.

Virtually every other gay organization put together their own press statements about the report as well. "The Pentagon brass believed it was hiring a group of 'yes men' to uphold a prejudiced policy," said Robert Bray of the National Gay and Lesbian Task Force. "It's a classic case of the emperor with no clothes—we see the DoD stripped of its honor and integrity and the naked truth of bigotry revealed."

Though the Defense Department stood by its stance that the report had been rejected because it contained no new information of any value, the study became the source of profound embarrassment for the Pentagon. According to official policy, homosexuality per se was no longer supposed to be the sole basis for denying security clearances to gays, but in practice, security agencies routinely denied clearances to anyone who was homosexual, and questions about sexuality remained a routine part of interrogations for security clearances. Moreover, the first thing that happened to any military member who came under investigation for homosexuality was that his or her security clearance was revoked.

Since there were growing numbers of openly gay people who could argue that they had nothing to hide and therefore were not vulnerable to blackmail, the Defense Department developed a new strategy to deny clearances. While the subject of the security investigation might not be vulnerable to blackmail, government lawyers argued in court, it was possible that the homosexual in question might have a partner in the future who might want to conceal his or her homosexuality. Consequently, it was deemed prudent to deny any homosexual, even open ones, clearances since the government could not be assured what *might* happen *some day* in the future *if* the person took a covertly gay lover.

Even when information about homosexuality was not used to deny a clearance, Defense security agencies sometimes passed the information along to military agencies in order to derail the careers of homosexuals in uniform. The most dramatic example of this came in the case of Colonel Margarethe Cammermeyer, the chief nurse of the Washington National Guard.

Cammermeyer's military credentials were as singular as they were outstanding. She had signed up with the Army student nursing program in 1961 and was commissioned in the Army Nurse Corps in 1963. She volunteered for duty in Vietnam, hoping she would be assigned there with her husband. Her husband was transferred elsewhere, however, leaving Cammermeyer to be a nurse during some of the most intense fighting of the war, including the fierce Tet offensive of 1968. Her outstanding service won her a Bronze Star, a rare achievement for a woman in those days, and later a Meritorious Service Medal and the Army Achievement medal. Later that year, Cammermeyer left the Army because of her pregnancy, returning to the Reserves in 1972 when regulations changed allowing mothers to serve.

Cammermeyer's marriage had produced four sons, but by the 1980s, she was also aware that there was another side to her that needed exploring. She came to realize she was a lesbian. She lived in San Francisco for several years, appreciating the more accepting atmosphere for homosexuals, even while she stayed in the Army Reserves. In 1985, she was selected as Nurse of the Year from among all the nurses working at the Veterans Association.

In 1986, Cammermeyer, now a full colonel, returned to live in Washington state and in 1987 was selected the State Chief Nurse of the Washington Army National Guard. Soon, she learned that she might be considered to be the chief nurse for the entire National Guard of the United States. In order to be a candidate for this job, which would make her a general, Cammermeyer had to attend classes at the War College, which required a security clearance. In May 1989, when an agent from the Defense Investigative Service (DIS) who came to interview her asked her whether she was homosexual, Cammermeyer answered the way she knew she must. She never wanted to be vulnerable to blackmail, so she had long ago resolved to tell the truth about her sexuality if asked. The DIS agent attempted to get Cammermeyer to describe in detail precisely what she did in bed with other women, but the colonel refused. She did, however, sign a statement stating that she was homosexual.

The DIS passed along information about her sexuality to the Department of the Army, which began proceedings to withdraw her federal recognition as a military officer and Colonel in the Army, effectively ending her twenty-three-year military career. Her superior officers rallied to her defense. The governor of Washington, who was titular commander of the state's National Guard, even wrote Defense Secretary Cheney to plead Cammermeyer's case: he did not care what her sexuality was, he said, she was a valued member of the National Guard and he wanted her retained. None of this mattered, however, and slowly the Army moved against Cammermeyer.

From the onset of the initial threat to separate, she sought out lawyers from Lambda Legal Defense Fund to fight the separation. As with so many stories from this period, it would not be immediately clear who had the most to lose from the Pentagon's homosexual policy, gay soldiers or the Defense Department itself.

EVENTS DURING this same period raised questions as to whether gays were a threat to national security, or whether the greater threat to security came from the enforcement of regulations against them. This issue was the source of much consternation at the National Security Agency, where there continued to be a drain on the agency's supply of Middle Eastern linguists because of the gusto with which the Annapolis office of the Naval Investigative Service conducted investigations of gays. Already, the NSA had lost Phil Zimmerman, one of its leading Farsi linguists. In April 1989, the agency also lost the services of Cryptologic Technician Third Class Terry Ryder, one of the agency's most expert Arabic linguists, trained particularly in the Yemeni dialect. Ryder's five-year Navy career ended during his NSA assignment when his name came up on lists of homosexuals circulated during a probe of gay sailors in the Annapolis area. In the course of the investigation, the NSA lost another of its best Arabic linguists as well, according to Ryder.

When Ryder was under investigation, he asked an agent in the NIS office at Annapolis why the agency spent so much time chasing down homosexuals when they could devote their efforts into rooting out drug users or bona-fide criminals. He recalls the agent responded confidently, "This office's specialty is homosexuality."

As his discharge date neared, Ryder heard numerous complaints from civilians on the NSA staff that the NIS purge of Arabic translators was doing far more to harm national security than to protect it. Clearly, if the nation was ever called to go to war in the Middle East against, for example, Iran or Iraq, the lack of Arabic translators could have profound repercussions.

NOVEMBER 1989
CLEVELAND, OHIO

THROUGHOUT THE AUTUMN, Kathy Kubicina continued to press for a new investigation into the cause of the explosion aboard the USS *Iowa*. She persuaded her congresswoman, Mary Rose Oakar, to call for congressional hearings, which were scheduled for December. As she pursued various routes to gather more information about the explosion, the Navy stopped returning her phone calls and then stopped answering her letters. When she went to Norfolk to talk to other crew members about the explosion, she was quickly ordered off the ship, and the captain issued an order saying Kathy was not to be allowed on board, even though family members of other *Iowa* survivors were. When Kathy learned that David Smith had recanted his statement to the NIS, she attempted to meet him in Norfolk. She was not allowed on base; when she did figure out where he worked, she waited outside his office for three hours, but he never appeared.

Meanwhile, Hartwig's high school friend, Brian Hoover, gave an interview to the *Cleveland Plain-Dealer* complaining that his statements to the NIS had been manipulated to make Hartwig appear suicidal when he had never believed anything of the sort. It was upon Hoover that the

NIS laid its claim that Hartwig had long had a suicidal personality, and had told Hoover he wanted to kill himself in high school. Hoover denied saying any such thing. Hoover's statements became key evidence in the FBI's psychological postmortem, which asserted Hartwig had a suicidal personality. The NIS agents "had their version of what was true and their questions were directed at trying to get me to admit that," Hoover complained. He was trying to set the record straight.

Kathy was so relentless in pursuing the investigation and proving that the cause of the explosion lay with the old battleships that one master chief petty officer had a bumper sticker printed up: "Save the *Iowa*," it read, "Mothball Kubicina."

Kathy's major forum for redress was the news media, particularly broadcast news organizations, which tended to be more sympathetic to her crusade. A year earlier, her heart would have gone into palpitations if she had to speak in front of a dozen people, but by now she had become a savvy and articulate interview subject during her scores of television appearances. In an interview on the American Broadcasting Company's news-magazine show "20/20," Kubicina denied her brother was gay, but added, "If he was, so what? What's the connection between being gay and blowing up battleships?"

72

Hearings

NOVEMBER 1989
MASSACHUSETTS INSTITUTE OF TECHNOLOGY
CAMBRIDGE, MASSACHUSETTS

FOR MORE THAN A YEAR, ever since he had come to grips with the fact that he was gay, Midshipman Robb Bettiker had suffered over whether to leave the ROTC. He felt an obligation to return the time he owed the Navy in exchange for his college education, but he was also mindful of the Navy's stringent antigay policies. And the explanation of the HOMO-VAC procedure stuck in his mind.

Robb had also heard rumors that another student in the MIT-Harvard ROTC unit was being separated for being gay. In September he called David Carney, with whom he had served on the USS *Hyman G. Rickover* a year earlier. Like Bettiker, Carney had been accepted into the prestigious nuclear power program, which he was scheduled to begin after his graduation. Carney had also spent much of the past year becoming acclimated to the idea that he was gay, and fearful of what could happen to him if he pursued his Navy ambitions. Robb asked if Carney was leaving the ROTC. Carney said he was.

By November 1989, Robb had decided that he would tell the Navy he was gay; if they wanted to retain him, that would be fine, but if they demanded his separation, that would be fine, too. Part of him believed that the Navy might say, "Keep it quiet—just do your job." He still worried that the whole issue could take an unpleasant turn, though, so he carefully planned how he would inform his Naval ROTC commander.

First, he explained his predicament to MIT's dean of counseling. The dean then approached the ROTC commander and asked what would happen, hypothetically, if one of his cadets was to inform him that he was gay. He would be disenrolled from the program, the commander said, and the Navy might ask for its tuition money back. That was all. Confident that his commanding officer would not blow up and rant homophobically at him, Robb approached him on Election Day, 1989.

The commander was very cordial and said that it was good that Robb had come forward on his own. "These things have a way of catching up with you in the end," he said. Robb felt a surge of relief while leaving the commander's office. He would not have to lie any longer. He was free.

Shortly after that, Dave Carney also told his ROTC commander that he was gay. The commander was amiable, although he muttered that he had lost two of his best-qualified candidates for the nuclear power program within a week.

On December 7, 1989, Robb Bettiker faced a review board, which posed the simple question, "Are you a homosexual?" Robb said he was. The board recommended his discharge, but added that Bettiker had made no effort to deceive the Navy, and recommended that the Navy not attempt to recoup the tuition money it had already paid Robb.

Dave Carney's separation board came days later. Though Dave was embarrassed by the detailed questioning about his sex life, the board voted to separate him, and, as in Robb's case, not to seek recoupment of tuition.

ANOTHER TEST of ROTC policies occurred at Washington University in St. Louis, where Army ROTC cadet Jim Holobaugh, who had once served as a poster boy for the program, informed a captain that he was gay. He wanted to be commissioned, he said, but he did not want to go into the Army and end up being court-martialed. "I don't necessarily agree with this policy," the captain said, and he congratulated Holobaugh for coming forward on his own.

Questions about Jim's sex life dominated his separation hearing. When was the first time he had had sex? Under what circumstances? Holobaugh refused to answer the questions. He was disenrolled from the program, and in December 1989 he moved to New York City to take a job with the Federal Reserve Bank. It was during the holiday season that a friend introduced Jim to Marc Wolinsky, one of the attorneys representing Joe Steffan. When a notice arrived from the Army that Jim must repay the $25,000 in tuition, Holobaugh went from being a Young Republican to a gay activist in one day.

Holobaugh was aware that Washington University, like many other major universities, had a policy forbidding discrimination against gays by any employer doing business with the university. After receiving the recoupment order, Jim contacted university administrators and enlisted their help. Before long, a campaign had begun at the school to eject the ROTC program if it did not comply with university policy of nondiscrimination against gays.

While Robb Bettiker faced his separation hearing, an MIT literature professor, David Halperin, began a similar petition drive on the MIT campus. Years earlier, MIT had adopted a policy that employers who discriminated on the basis of sexual orientation should not be allowed on campus. Halperin, who was the adviser to the campus lesbian and gay organization, argued that the military in general, and ROTC in particular, was in direct violation of this nondiscrimination policy.

A similar campaign was also underway at the University of Wisconsin at Madison. As at MIT, lobbying was not instigated by an ROTC cadet, but by a gay activist, in this case by a law student named Rick Villasenor. Villasenor lobbied professors and faculty for nearly two years on the issue. For all the arguments he made about prejudice and discrimination, he found that the most persuasive document in his favor was the ROTC application form and its standard question as to whether the applicant was homosexual. Something about the question galled enough faculty members that on December 4, 1989, three days before Bettiker's separation hearing, the university convened the first full meeting of the faculty senate since the campus turmoil of the Vietnam War. At that meeting, the faculty voted 386 to 248 to order the ROTC program off campus in 1993 if it did not comply with the university's policy not to discriminate against gays.

The vote did not resolve the issue. University regulations required affirmation by the university's board of regents. But the vote, coming at one of the nation's largest universities, served notice on the military that a new front was opening in the war against the homosexual policy. Gay campus activists around the country also took notice, and efforts to remove ROTC from other campuses because of the policy began to spread to colleges across the nation.

COURT CHALLENGES CONTINUED to meet with mixed results. In August 1989, a federal appeals court ruled against Miriam Ben-Shalom, the Army reservist who had been battling her discharge since 1976. "The Army should not be required by this court to assume the risk, a risk it would be assuming for all our citizens, that accepting admitted homosexuals into the armed forces might imperil morale, discipline, and the effectiveness of our fighting forces," wrote Judge Harlington Wood, Jr., for the appeals panel in Chicago. As for Ben-Shalom's arguments that her dismissal for merely stating she was a lesbian represented a violation of her First Amendment rights, the court ruled, "She is free to advocate that the Army change its stance; she is free to know and talk to homosexuals if she wishes. What Ben-Shalom cannot do, and remain in the Army, is to declare herself to be a homosexual." The fact that she stated she was a lesbian, the judge found, offered "compelling evidence" that she had engaged in homosexual acts and would do so again. The next stop for Ben-Shalom's appeal: the U.S. Supreme Court.

ON NOVEMBER 8, Judge Oliver Gasch, the federal district court judge hearing the case of Joseph Steffan, dismissed Steffan's suit after Steffan refused to answer questions from government attorneys concerning his sex life. Attorney Wolinsky believed Gasch's ruling violated legal principles. It was as if the government, having no evidence of sexual misconduct by Steffan while he was at Annapolis, had decided to use court depositions to gather the evidence that they should have had when Steffan was discharged. A higher court would overturn the dismissal, Wolinsky was certain, but it would mean a delay of as long as a year in confronting the substantive legal issues the case presented.

Probably the most unsettling moment in that round of litigation occurred when government attorneys sat Steffan down in October to ask questions about his sex life. Under Wolinsky's direction, Steffan refused to answer. Then Assistant U.S. Attorney Kenneth Kohl, representing the Justice Department, asked for names of other homosexuals in the Naval Academy. Wolinsky was repelled that civilian attorneys would use a deposition to launch a military witch-hunt, but the lawyers were deadly serious. When Wolinsky objected to the line of questioning, Kohl insisted that it was necessary because "to the extent it can lead to the discovery of a homosexual relationship, especially one that is sexual in nature, [it] is very relevant." Wolinsky told Steffan not to answer the question. "You can get another witness if you want to conduct some sort of witch-hunt," he told Kohl. "And that is on the Record."

Steffan continued his full-court press in the news media, believing that his ultimate victory was less likely to come from the courts than from changing public opinion. The Defense Department continued to employ the strategy it had used to counter bad publicity over the gay policy for the past two decades—it stonewalled. The only statements from Pentagon spokesmen were the recitation of the official gay policy. When Steffan appeared on television and producers sought a Defense Department spokesman to provide balance, the Pentagon refused to provide any, apparently hoping that the lack of another side would derail discussion of the issue altogether.

By 1989, however, television producers had found alternative spokesmen against gays, most notably Congressman Bob Dornan, a conservative member of the House Armed Services Committee from Orange County, California, whose fondness for military projects had earned him the nickname "B-1 Bob." Like so many other spokesmen for the Pentagon policy over the next two years, Dornan did not do much credit to the Defense Department. In an appearance on the ABC News program "Nightline," for example, Dornan focused less on military issues to support the department's position than on recent Vatican statements condemning homosexuality. Putting gay soldiers in barracks, he said, "is like putting a man in a harem. If you put a lesbian woman in a female barracks, it's like putting a woman in the opposite of a harem." He then asked Steffan whether he would insist on a wedding in the Naval Academy's chapel if he fell in love with another midshipman.

Against such spokesmen, new opponents emerged. Dr. Lawrence

Korb, who had quietly disagreed with the policies when he was Assistant Secretary of Defense for Manpower from 1981 to 1985, went public in opposing the gay ban and began making media appearances to advance his arguments. Even the staid American Bar Association called for an end to discrimination against homosexuals in the military as part of an overall endorsement of gay civil rights legislation passed at its 1989 national convention. The American Psychological Association began to study whether it should allow the military to recruit psychologists through its official publications and conventions, given its policy prohibiting discrimination among job recruiters. The tide was beginning to turn.

DECEMBER 12, 1989
SENATE ARMED SERVICES COMMITTEE
U.S. CAPITOL
WASHINGTON, D.C.

THE FIRST ROUND of hearings to investigate the investigation of the explosion aboard the USS *Iowa* was the beginning of the end of the Navy's official explanation that the blast was caused by Gunner's Mate Clayton Hartwig. Although the FBI stood behind its psychological profile that Hartwig was suicidal and capable of murder, and the Navy stood by its conclusions, Senator Alan Dixon called the report "highly speculative" and said "it strains the intelligence of most people" to believe there was adequate evidence that Hartwig was guilty of such a heinous act.

The same day, the House Armed Services Committee held the first of its three days of hearings on the *Iowa*, which included testimony from Kendall Truitt and another crew survivor, both of whom assailed the Navy's report. "It's a big cover-up," Truitt said. "Clayton Hartwig was not the suicidal freak they make him out to be." The committee also asked the Navy to explain why it washed out Turret Two in the hours after the explosion, thus destroying evidence that might have led to a different conclusion about the blast.

The Navy defended its report, though it was forced to admit revision. The sabotage had not been caused by a timing device, after all, Rear Admiral Richard Milligan told the congressmen. The blast had been caused by a chemical detonator inserted in the gun. Nevertheless, Milligan insisted that the case against Hartwig would "stand up in a court of law." Hartwig, he said, was guilty "beyond a shadow of a doubt."

But inconsistencies abounded. The Navy claimed it had "conclusive evidence" of foreign material in the gun that could have come from a detonating device. The FBI, however, found no such conclusive proof. In fact, an FBI explosives expert said, "No components of explosives which could be associated with an improvised explosive device or initiator were located." Since the FBI conclusions did not coincide with those of the NIS, the Navy disregarded them. The NIS report on the explosion noted that the ship's chaplain had never talked to Hartwig. Testifying to the committee, however, the chaplain said he had indeed talked to Hartwig on a number of occasions, and he did not believe that the sailor had suicidal tendencies.

When congressmen pressed Milligan about David Smith's recantations, the rear admiral said that this did not seriously undermine the Navy's explanation, since Smith had recanted only two statements. Never mind that the two statements had represented virtually the entire underpinning for the Navy's allegations against Hartwig.

Robert Powers, the criminal investigations director for the NIS, denied that the NIS had coerced Smith, saying, "He could have terminated [the interviews] at any time." Powers was also asked why the NIS had told the FBI not to consider an accidental cause of the explosion, and to focus instead on a rationale for Hartwig's murdering forty-six shipmates. As for the investigation's obsessive focus on homosexuality, Powers said it was relevant "in regards to motive" for Hartwig's alleged actions.

Republican Congressman Larry Hopkins told reporters that the poor quality of the *Iowa* investigation led him to believe that such probes should be taken out of the hands of the Navy in the future. "If these hearings should provide evidence that the Navy is protecting itself at the expense of the truth," he said, "we may have to change the way they are allowed to examine themselves. . . . The Navy has virtually convicted Mr. Hartwig without a trial." The conclusion, he added, could well be a "misrepresentation by the NIS."

As for the analysis of Hartwig's personality by the FBI and NIS, House Armed Services Committee Chairman Les Aspin put the studies before fourteen psychiatrists and psychologists, only four of whom found merit in the FBI analysis. Said Aspin, "Not only does the underlying documentation fail to support many of the findings, but in many instances the Naval investigators' interpretation of the data is incorrect."

Kathy Kubicina was eager to speak, but she had been advised against testifying lest she become "too emotional." Kathy had never been to Washington before and she looked forward to a measure of vindication when she arrived at the hearing chamber with her parents. Listening to the testimony, she thought, "We're going to get those guys."

Dissatisfied with the Navy's conclusions, the Senate and House committees both pledged to hold their own investigations, and ordered up new tests to explore whether the *Iowa* explosion could have been accidental. The General Accounting Office, the nonpartisan investigative branch of Congress, took charge of the probe, and the highly respected Sandia Laboratories, a research institution within the Department of Energy, was ordered to conduct the technical testing.

DECEMBER 1, 1989
CARSWELL AIR FORCE BASE
FORT WORTH, TEXAS

THE PURGE OF GAY AIRMEN at Carswell Air Force Base, part of the air combat command, began like many others with a sequence of events that had absolutely nothing to do with homosexuality at all. A female airman wanted to get out of a lease agreement on her apartment, which she could do if she showed her landlord orders that she was being transferred. A gay enlisted man wrote up fake orders for her, which were subsequently discovered and led to the woman's court-martial. In exchange for lenient treatment, she said she knew the names of gays on the base and she would list them for investigators.

Sergeant Dan Bell learned he was under investigation at 6:30 A.M. on the morning of December 1, when he returned home from working sixty-three hours straight at the base hospital. He was to report directly to the office of Master Sergeant Lester Walker at the Security Police squadron. Walker later declined comment on the episode, but Bell recalled that Walker said he was authorized to grant Bell "limited immunity" if he cooperated with investigators. Bell would not talk. Walker would not excuse Bell to use the bathroom, and questioned the twenty-seven-year-old airman for four hours before he allowed him a beverage. After several more hours of interrogation, Bell relented and signed a paper waiving his right to a hearing and admitting to fraudulent enlistment by virtue of not having told the Air Force he was gay when he reenlisted.

Pleased with the progress they had made, the interrogators still did not let Bell leave. Instead, he was locked inside a small closet under a stairway. Master Sergeant Walker still wanted the names of other homosexuals and told Bell, "You'll be left here to think," as he locked the door. Bell remained there, forced to urinate in a corner, until 7:30 that night, when, although he had still not named other gays, he was allowed to go home.

At 1:30 A.M., Bell was called back to the base. Investigators said they needed clarification on his earlier statement. When he would not clarify anything, Bell was locked back in the closet until 6:00 A.M., when questioning resumed. At 3:00 P.M., nearly thirty hours after his interrogations had begun, Bell went home. Six hours later, he was called back for more questioning, and when he declined to cooperate, he was again locked in the closet. The little room stank.

Over the next nine days, Bell was repeatedly questioned for hours, and then, because he would not name other gays, he was locked into the closet that smelled like a urinal for five to ten hours at a stretch. Bell asked many times for an attorney, but his requests were denied. He was going to be court-martialed, he could even go to prison, he was warned, unless he cooperated. After ten days of this, Bell called several friends who had recently left the Air Force and asked them if he could give their names to investigators. Six friends agreed, and on December 10, Bell gave their names to security police.

The next day, Bell was called back to the Security Police office and told that if he would sign a statement investigators had prepared, all questioning would cease and he would receive an honorable discharge within ten to twelve days. The past eleven days had been very hard on Bell. He had developed nervous diarrhea, was unable to eat, and had lost sixteen pounds. He was so eager to be done with it and out of there that he signed the paper without reading it. Later he discovered that it contained numerous fabrications, most notably the inclusion of many names that Bell had not identified.

Investigators did not let up on Bell, as promised. Master Sergeant Walker called his mother and grandparents to interview them about Bell's history of "homosexual activity." It was at this time that Bell noticed clicks on the phone line in his off-base apartment. He called a repairman from Southwestern Bell, and the technician who worked on the problem told Dan, "I've taken care of your bug." The phone company confirmed that Bell's phone was being "monitored," and the next day, Sergeant Walker referred to comments Bell had made in a phone conversation with his father.

On January 3, 1990, a day before Bell was scheduled to be discharged, he was told that his separation was being put on "administrative hold" until he named every lesbian and gay man on the base. When he refused, he was locked back in the closet for another seven hours. "I'm not done with you yet," Master Sergeant Walker told him when he began pounding on the door and cursing. "Yes, you are," Bell stated, "the next time you see me, it's going to be with a band of lawyers."

When he was free, Bell contacted the Tarrant County Gay Alliance and the Texas Gay Veterans and informed them of the investigation at Carswell Air Force Base. By the time activists heard from Bell, eighteen Carswell airmen were under investigation, and eight had been discharged. Gay airmen, however, estimated that in truth fifty service members were under investigation. In mid-January, about fifty representatives of local gay groups protested at the Carswell gate, demanding an investigation into the gay investigation. "Witch Hunts Waste Tax Dollars," read some protest placards. Others read, "Get Out Of Our Bedrooms." They took up the shout: "Shame, shame, shame."

The purge, however, continued. By January 20, Air Force spokesmen admitted that a dozen alleged gay airmen had been discharged, while investigations continued on six others. By the count of gay activists, however, as many as forty airmen may have been discharged during the probe. When asked about the propriety of locking servicemen into closets in order to secure their confessions, Air Force Lieutenant Colonel Walter Washabaugh of the Office of Legislative Liaison responded to a congressman's inquiry by saying the Air Force had not violated any regulation. "This investigation was conducted in a professional manner with command attention at all levels," wrote Washabaugh. "The wing and base commanders as well as the Inspector General were involved throughout the investigation and were especially sensitive to proper investigative procedures."

JANUARY 31, 1990
MASSACHUSETTS INSTITUTE OF TECHNOLOGY
CAMBRIDGE, MASSACHUSETTS

THE LETTER FROM the office of the Secretary of the Navy said it had approved Robb Bettiker's separation from the Naval ROTC program, but there was a catch. Although the MIT ROTC board had recommended against attempting to recoup Bettiker's tuition money, Navy Secretary Lawrence Garrett III had ordered Robb to repay $38,612. Days later, Dave Carney received a similar letter ordering a $51,000 reimbursement.

Although both men had been ready to forget their involvement with the military and get on with their lives, the huge debts made that impossible. Neither Bettiker nor Carney felt any obligation to repay the money. Neither had believed he was gay when he entered the program, and both had expressed a desire to fulfill his commitments. It was the government that refused to allow them to do so.

The net effect of the recoupment orders was to create two more gay activists. For the military this could not have come at a less opportune time, coming as it did on the heels of the embarrassing publicity over the PERSEREC report and at a time when the controversy over retaining ROTC on numerous college campuses was heating up. Bettiker contacted one of the lawyers representing Joe Steffan, Sandra Lowe at Lambda Legal Defense and Education Fund. "Don't sign anything," she said. When the notice arrived asking Robb to sign a statement "acknowledging" his indebtedness to the government, he did nothing.

FEBRUARY 9, 1990
MAYPORT NAVAL STATION
MAYPORT, FLORIDA

GUNNER'S MATE THIRD CLASS Kendall Truitt still hoped to become part of the elite Navy SEALS, but when he put in his paper work for reenlistment, the Navy told him he would not be accepted. The service could not discharge him for talking to the press and defending Clayton Hartwig, but it could deny his reenlistment, which it did. On February 9, Ken Truitt became a civilian again.

Truitt's discharge began a disjointed time of life for the twenty-two-year-old. He had not planned on returning to civilian life so abruptly.

He moved to Tampa, his wife's hometown, but he could not forget the *Iowa* explosion. He could not give up questioning the Navy's conclusions, or the fact that the Navy had turned his crewmates' deaths into a smarmy tale of a homosexual love triangle, and robbed them of the dignity of having died with honor, serving their country. He knew most of the men who had died in that explosion, and they deserved better. Clay certainly deserved better, and if their positions had been reversed, and Ken had died while Clay lived, Ken had no doubt that Clay would have defended him as aggressively. Ken's efforts, however, strained his marriage, and after three months in Tampa, the couple separated. Alone now, Ken moved back to Illinois and continued to pursue his crusade to clear his friend's name.

FEBRUARY 15, 1990
TAMPA, FLORIDA

WHEN SHE RETURNED home from a medical appointment, Barbara Baum heard the news that the U.S. Court of Military Review had ruled that she had not received a fair trial. Her attorney explained that her conviction had been tossed out; a reporter told her she would even receive back pay from the Marine Corps. Her lawyers had been confident she would win, especially after Marine Corps lawyers themselves conceded in court documents that Sergeant Major Moore, who had witnessed her Article 32 hearing, should not have been allowed to sit on her jury. In the panel's seven-page decision, the Navy–Marine Corps Court of Military Review dismissed the "indecent acts" charge against Baum for lack of corroboration and ruled that the inclusion of Colonel Robert Nunnally on the panel also represented a violation of Baum's constitutional rights.

Technically, the ruling could have led to Baum's retrial, but Major General J. D. Lynch, Jr., the commanding general of the Parris Island Marine Corps Recruit Training Depot, believed that it was "impractible to conduct further proceedings against" Baum, especially "in view of the time that had elapsed since the incidents leading to the allegations against Baum occurred and the additional expense to the government which would have to be incurred by conducting a rehearing." There would be no new trial; Baum would receive an honorable discharge.

Barbara knew she should feel grateful, but she felt drained. She had lost her car and her career and six months of her freedom, only to be told that even the government recognized that she had been wronged. Even worse, she had lost virtually all her friends from the Marine Corps, because she had named so many of them in her statement to the NIS. They would never forgive her; she would never forgive herself. Although eager to begin a new life, she could not always put Parris Island behind her. Her anger rose unpredictably from time to time; she would fly into a rage over nothing.

February 20, 1990
Veterans Administration Medical Center
San Diego, California

Robert "Jess" Jessop battled AIDS valiantly, but in the final days his friends could only watch his life ebb away. His last months were filled with tributes and award dinners in his honor. In 1986, for a Veterans Day observance, he wrote his recollections of the day in Vietnam in 1967 when he had determined to prove his manhood, and wondered again whether his efforts had cost one of his Marines his life. Confused young men were still entering the armed forces to prove their manhood; the cultural imperative still held for millions.

Jessop died on February 20, 1990.

73

Holding Actions

FEBRUARY 26, 1990
UNITED STATES SUPREME COURT
WASHINGTON, D.C.

THE SUPREME COURT RULING on the policies excluding lesbians and gay men from the United States military came, like so many other homosexually related decisions from the nation's highest court, without any comment or legal rationale. Instead, on a chilly morning in February, the justices merely released a statement that they would let stand federal appeals court rulings upholding the discharges of Army Reservist Miriam Ben-Shalom and former Navy Ensign James Woodward. Though the refusal to hear the cases did not provide proponents of the Pentagon's policy with the full support of an articulated Supreme Court opinion in their favor, it signaled that this high court had no plans to challenge the military's ban on gays, or, for that matter, any form of discrimination against homosexuals.

As advanced by Solicitor General Kenneth W. Starr on behalf of the Bush administration, the issue at hand concerned not only gays in the military, but the broader issues raised for gay civil rights in the cases. Given the fact that the high court had already supported the legality of state sodomy laws, Starr had argued that "it is implausible to say that those with a proclivity to commit such acts constitute a group that deserves special protection from the courts under the Equal Protection clause." By allowing the Woodward ruling to stand, the court endorsed the lower court's argument that military regulations against gays "serves legitimate state interests."

Though the rulings were not surprising, given the profoundly antigay tenor of the *Bowers* v. *Hardwick* ruling four years earlier, they discouraged gay leaders, who were finally forced to accept the fact that civil rights for homosexuals were not destined to come from the courts—at least not for the next several years, if not the next several decades. The template upon which gay-rights advocates had drawn their hopes for legal change had generally followed the model used by women and African Americans, in which courts mandated specific civil rights that were then implemented by Congress and the President. The Ben-Shalom and Woodward rulings offered definitive evidence that this model would not be relevant for gays until the makeup of the federal judiciary changed. "We can win this issue in any one of three arenas: the courts, the Congress or the Defense Department itself," said Nan Hunter, director of the ACLU Lesbian and Gay Rights Project. "In the past, efforts have been concentrated only in the courts, but we believe that the future resolution of this issue may lie in Washington."

NEWS OF THE RULING swept through Family networks at military installations across the world. The tidings could not be openly discussed, since expressing interest in the ruling might raise suspicions. Instead, it was whispered between enlisted personnel as they changed shifts, or late that night in berthing areas, when other crew members were asleep. The news demoralized many gays in uniform. In the past military personnel could say, "I have my rights," when facing discharge, but the Supreme Court ruling of February 1990 said with certainty that they did not.

THAT AFTERNOON
MILWAUKEE, WISCONSIN

MIRIAM BEN-SHALOM was substitute-teaching at a Milwaukee high school when reporters began calling for comments concerning the Supreme Court's refusal to hear her appeal. "You lost your decision at the Supreme Court," the first reporter said to her. "How do you feel?"

Ben-Shalom dropped the phone; she felt as if she had been hit with a sledgehammer. Like many members of the military culture, Ben-Shalom was fiercely patriotic. She had never really believed that the United States would let her down. In America, she had thought, you got your day in court and you got your fair chance. Now she saw that it wasn't true.

WITH THE Ben Shalom and Woodward rulings, the litigation that had begun in the final days of the Vietnam era with the cases of Leonard Matlovich and Vernon "Copy" Berg had finally run its course. The only case still making its way to the Supreme Court was that of Perry Watkins, but his case no longer centered on the broad constitutional issues that had been raised by Ben-Shalom and Woodward. His would be decided only upon the nonconstitutional question of whether it was fair to discharge Watkins after he had been honest about being gay for so many years.

It was a measure of the glacial pace of judicial proceedings that these cases were not resolved until a full fifteen years after they had begun with Matlovich's challenge to the Pentagon's policies; it was a measure of the profundity of conservative influence on the courts that judges in 1975 tended to be more sympathetic to such challenges than the federal judges of 1990. The new court challenges were championed by new names, like Joseph Steffan and the Reverend Dusty Pruitt, though it now appeared that if change was to come from anywhere, it would be from the court of public opinion.

For the record, the Pentagon's only official response to the Supreme Court decision was to reiterate the 123 words of the gay policy. In less public forums, however, Pentagon legal officers candidly stated that the decision at best reflected a holding action against change; that the policy excluding gays was doomed. In August 1990, for example, a Navy senior enlisted man attended a workshop at Norfolk Naval Station on how to process administrative discharges. A civilian attorney for the Chief of Naval Personnel told the packed auditorium about processing out drug abusers and malingerers, and when the subject of homosexuals came up, he conceded that "the day is coming and it's coming fast" when lesbians and gay men would be allowed to serve in the military. The senior chief petty officers might complain, he said, but military attorneys in Washington were talking more about this issue than they ever had, and everyone agreed that the changes would occur faster than even the military's leadership understood.

Ironically, days after the Pentagon enjoyed its most important legal victory on the homosexual policy, the battle for public opinion became fully engaged again.

MARCH 1990
MASSACHUSETTS INSTITUTE OF TECHNOLOGY
CAMBRIDGE, MASSACHUSETTS

A MONTH AFTER the Navy demanded that Robb Bettiker repay his $38,000 in ROTC scholarships, the issue seemed no closer to resolution. Robb had hoped to apply to graduate school, but the Navy was threatening to send his bill to a collection agency and he was worried that now he would not be able to afford further schooling. Before he had even begun to start his life, it seemed as if the Navy was determined to confound his plans. Robb had never considered himself a political activist, but he now felt he had to stand up for himself or suffer dire consequences. When Kate Dyer suggested he talk to reporters, he agreed.

Robb's problems occurred within a broader context of simmering discontent with the military's policies on college campuses. By January 1990, opponents to the presence of ROTC on the MIT campus had organized their own group, called Defeat Discrimination at MIT, or D-DaMIT, and had collected 2,000 signatures of students advocating the ouster of the military because of its antigay policies.

On March 2, the travails of Robb Bettiker, Dave Carney, and Jim Holobaugh made *The New York Times*, and within days, every major television network was on the story. The stories, one after another, represented another public relations disaster for the Defense Department. On one side were bright, attractive, articulate students who comported themselves well in television interviews. Each one said he was prepared to serve his country. On the other side was an implacable institution that had first alienated and separated these young men and then insisted that they mortgage their futures to repay huge sums of scholarship money.

In answer to any question on the issue the Pentagon repeated the 123 words that began "Homosexuality is incompatible with military service. . . ." With such Pentagon strategy, media coverage was overwhelmingly sympathetic to the ROTC students.

University administrators rallied to the defense of the gay cadets and in opposition to the military's homosexual policy. The MIT provost, John Deutch, who had served as Under Secretary of Energy during the Carter administration, wrote a "Dear Dick" letter to Cheney predicting that "many universities will withdraw" from ROTC because of the Pentagon's gay policies. Harvard University President Derek Bok wrote Cheney that the policy should be reversed "not only because it discriminates against people solely on the basis of their sexual orientation but also because it is likely to weaken the national ROTC program by creating an increasing amount of antagonism toward ROTC on university campuses." On March 7, the university council of Northern Illinois University voted to eject ROTC from campus if the policy remained unchanged.

In Congress, even representatives who were sympathetic to the Pentagon's ban on gays were outraged at the recoupment demands. Congressman Gerry Studds easily persuaded thirty-five members of Congress to sign a letter of protest to Navy Secretary Lawrence Garrett III.

Gay groups on campuses around the country took up the cause in a ground swell of organizing. The United States military had created a new generation of gay activists who, with military bearing and self-confidence, became eloquent spokesmen against the policy. Joe Steffan made numerous public appearances, as did Bettiker and Holobaugh. Veterans with old grievances resurfaced. A former Special Forces officer, Jay Hatheway, joined Miriam Ben-Shalom as an outspoken advocate for the end of ROTC at the University of Wisconsin. When the ROTC debate came to the University of Delaware, a former Air Force sergeant named Rich McGuire, who worked as an engineer at the campus radio station, pulled aside a handful of friends to tell about his interrogation nearly twenty years earlier in the basement of the wood-frame house at Westover Air Force Base.

Sometimes, the protests turned bitter. University of Wisconsin Chancellor Donna Shalala would not endorse the expulsion of the program and refused even to authorize disclaimers in university brochures that ROTC discriminated against homosexuals. Sixty protesters staged a five-day sit-in at the board of regents office until they were dragged out by university police.

Even more embarrassing for the Defense Department were the ROTC administrators, who were openly unenthusiastic about the Pentagon's policy. Speaking about Dave Carney, Captain Robert W. Sherer, commanding officer of the MIT-Harvard ROTC program, said, "I think the Navy's losing a good man. . . . I was very pleased and proud to send someone like that to the Fleet." As the second-highest-ranked midshipman among the forty-one at the university, Carney, he said, was "one of our best." Sherer told Bettiker that he did not believe the policy would last another five years. Everything the Pentagon did to defend the policy until then was merely a holding action.

MARCH 1990
U.S. HOUSE OF REPRESENTATIVES
U.S. CAPITOL
WASHINGTON, D.C.

THE DAY AFTER news organizations began running stories about the plight of the gay ROTC cadets, another embarrassment arose for the Pentagon. In their report on the *Iowa* explosion, two subcommittees of the House Armed Services Committee delivered what most reporters called "a stinging rebuke" to the Navy. "The evidentiary materials are simply not present to permit the Navy to accuse . . . Hartwig of being a suicidal mass-murderer," the report concluded. The committee also said the FBI's psychological postmortem on Hartwig was "inadequate and unprofessional."

The House report castigated the Naval Investigative Service for selectively presenting only evidence that would appear to implicate Hartwig, and for continuing to rely heavily on David Smith's claim of seeing a detonating device in Hartwig's locker, even after Smith recanted the story. The report also criticized the NIS for an "excess of certitude" in blaming Hartwig, and investigating only the gunner's mate when there were scores of other crewmen in the turret. "The Navy should more properly have left the issue unresolved and the investigation open rather than attach its name to a conclusion grounded in evidence that is both limited and questionable," the report concluded.

Armed Services Committee Chairman Les Aspin said the FBI and Navy investigations of Hartwig represented an occasion when "thin gruel became red meat." Subcommittee chairman Nicholas Mavroules commented that, "The police investigation performed by the Naval Investigative Service quickly ceased to be a full-scale investigation and was converted into something of a fact-gathering effort for the Hartwig murder-suicide theory."

In a statement released from Washington, the Navy responded that it "stands by its conclusion that the explosion in Turret Two on board the USS *Iowa* was the result of a wrongful, intentional act most probably committed by Petty Officer Clayton Hartwig." The FBI also stood by its psychological analysis.

In Cleveland, Kathy Kubicina's neighbors brought over a sheet cake with the inscription "Congratulations Kathy and Clay." Kathy had been heartened by the conclusions, but she did not feel her brother had been vindicated, and she continued meeting with *Iowa* crew members when she could, looking for more holes in the Navy's stories. By March she had heard of a meeting the previous winter, which a number of top officers from the *Iowa* and the surface fleet had attended. For all the criticism of the Navy's reports, the officers had decided that they must stand behind its conclusions, because to do anything else would risk the continued use of the battleships. Said one captain, "The future of the battleships rises and falls on this story."

It was during these months that Kathy noticed clicking noises on her telephone. Some crew members claimed to have written to Kathy, but she had never received their letters, leading her to believe that someone might be intercepting her mail.

MAY 4, 1990
MASSACHUSETTS INSTITUTE OF TECHNOLOGY
CAMBRIDGE, MASSACHUSETTS

ROBB BETTIKER WAS UNPREPARED for the national attention his case received. The outpouring of support in Congress and on campus cheered him, even if it was not enough yet to persuade the Navy to rescind its order that he repay his ROTC tuition money. In the weeks since the issue first hit the newspapers, the gay controversy had become the most serious threat to the ROTC program on college campuses since the Vietnam War; it had spread to scores of campuses and received widespread support among faculty and administrators.

On May 2, the Harvard University Faculty Council voted to "deplore" Pentagon policy and said that if there continued to be "insufficient progress" toward eliminating the policy, the school should end its participation in ROTC within two years. Two days later, activists at thirty-seven colleges and universities held simultaneous rallies across the country, and they read identical statements of protest. Later that afternoon, the California State University faculty senate voted to phase out the ROTC programs from the system's twenty campuses if the Defense Department continued to bar homosexuals from serving. Four days later, the University of Pennsylvania's university council unanimously passed a resolution calling on ROTC to observe the university's nondiscrimination policy; and the University of Michigan Law School voted overwhelmingly to add sexual orientation to that school's nondiscrimination policy—specifically so that the university could prevent military recruiters from using the institution.

On May 14, the four leading college associations—the American Council on Education, Association of American Universities, National Association of State Universities and Land-Grant Colleges, and the American Association of State Colleges and Universities—jointly wrote to Cheney asking him to rescind the exclusion of homosexuals: "We note a growing doubt about the need for such a practice and about its relation to the interests of the military, especially in preparation of a corps of future officers." The presidents of the four groups requested a meeting with Cheney to discuss the policy. In reply, a captain assigned to the legislative affairs branch of the Pentagon wrote a terse note, quoting the 123 words. "We do not plan to reassess the department's policy," the letter concluded. "Accordingly a meeting with the Secretary to discuss the issue would not be productive at this time."

By June, the movement had spread to nearly fifty campuses, including such major colleges as the University of California at Los Angeles, University of Colorado, University of Minnesota, Ohio State University, and the University of Pennsylvania. Among the university law schools that moved to ban recruiting by the military, as well as by the CIA and FBI, were those at Harvard, Stanford, Columbia, Yale, and Northwestern.

Conservatives rallied to defend the exclusion. Patrick Buchanan called the coordinated national protests on May 4 the "outrage of the week." Army ROTC spokesman Lieutenant Colonel Cal Blake told the *Washington Blade* that the effect of the protests could be summarized in one word: "None." Said Blake, "We will continue to produce officers in the number and quality required by the Army."

Privately, Pentagon spokesmen complained that the ROTC issue was being addressed by lesbian and gay activists whose agendas had little to do with military personnel policies. These activists, military officials believed, wanted to advance their homosexual-rights agenda, and had only attached themselves to the ROTC cause because it was timely and in the news. As Major Doug Hart of the Defense Department's public affairs office said, the campus movement was "a new angle of attack" for the gay movement.

It was an accurate opinion. Though a handful of ROTC cadets like Bettiker, Carney, and Holobaugh had genuine concerns about military personnel policies, most activists rallied to their side because advancing homosexual rights in the military meant advancing the same rights nationally. The symbolic value of the military finally allowing openly gay soldiers and sailors to serve would go far toward asserting that homosexuals should be allowed employment rights in all jobs and full participation in every aspect of American life. The new slogan uttered privately among lesbian and gay leaders was, "Once we win in the military, we've won."

For its part, the military was not engaged in mere bravado when it said that the campaigns against ROTC would have little impact on the program's ability to produce adequate numbers of officers. For all the resolutions and faculty pronouncements against ROTC and the military's gay policies, very few institutions were willing to back them with action. After the faculty at the University of Michigan Law School voted to ban employers who discriminated against gays from recruiting at the school, the university allowed the school to ban discriminating private employers—but not federal agencies. Despite the overwhelming faculty vote against the ROTC program at the University of Wisconsin, the board of regents would not remove the program and instead passed a weaker resolution that the university would endeavor to change the military's policies by "working within the system."

One of the more resolute stands against ROTC was taken by MIT, but even that was indecisive. In October, the MIT faculty, with support from the school's president, provost, and board of trustees chairman, approved unanimously a resolution opposing the military's ban on gays. The resolution, however, provided for five years of lobbying to end the policy. If the policy was not rescinded by then, the school president would appoint a task force on ROTC, "with the expectation that inadequate progress toward eliminating the DoD policy on sexual orientation will result in making ROTC unavailable to students beginning with the class entering in 1998." By then, it was everyone's expectation that the military's homosexual policy would be abolished, so the university would never have to make good on its threat to oust ROTC.

The school's reluctance was understandable. MIT received between $3 and $4 million in scholarships annually from the ROTC program, but even more significant was the fact that the school received an estimated $47.9 million in research money from the Defense Department. Cutting itself off from the Defense Department could cut into its research money, a consequence the institute did not relish.

At universities across the country, regents and trustees similarly temporized the resolutions enacted by their faculty senates and university councils. Proposals to oust ROTC were turned into suggestions that the university lobby the Defense Department, with actions to take place at some time in the future. By the end of the year, only one college, Pitzer College, a small liberal arts college in Southern California, had actually eliminated the ROTC from its campus.

From the gay activists' perspective, this did not mean that the campaign was useless, even if it would never have the immediate impact on Pentagon policies that they sought. Every time the debate over ROTC was engaged on a college campus, no matter what the outcome, the military's policies on homosexuals were cast into the spotlight, usually an unfavorable one. The unrelenting publicity, coming so close to the release of the PERSEREC report and the antigay tenor of the *Iowa* investigation, continued to provide Pentagon public affairs officers with headaches. It seemed to them that the publicity over gays in the military would never end. Later, it would become apparent that, in those days, the publicity had barely begun.

74

Vindication

UNLIKE THE NAVY'S INVESTIGATION, which centered almost solely on Clayton Hartwig and Kendall Truitt, the Sandia National Laboratories focused on the technical aspect of the explosion aboard the USS *Iowa*, exploring whether the blast could have been caused accidentally.

From the Navy's earlier investigation, Sandia learned that the projectile had been forced twenty-one inches too far up the barrel of the sixteen-inch gun, meaning there had been an "over-ram." The Navy also claimed to have found "foreign elements" trapped in the copper-nickel band encircling the projectile. The three elements were a fragment of plastic, tiny fibers of steel wool that contained traces of chlorine and calcium, and three different chemicals found in brake fluid or antifreeze. The presence of those chemicals had prompted the Navy to change its assertion that Hartwig may have used a time detonator to the new version that he had used a chemical explosive. According to the Navy's investigation, the various "foreign elements" indicated that Hartwig could have created his chemical detonator from steel wool, brake fluid, and another chemical. Then, according to the Navy, Clayton Hartwig had ordered the intentional over-ramming of the powder, which he knew would lead to the explosion.

From the first weeks of the investigation, the Sandia researchers found major problems with the Navy's scenario. The chemicals, calcium and chlorine, that the Navy had found on steel wool fibers were present not only in the *Iowa*, but in the big guns aboard the battleships *New Jersey* and *Wisconsin*. The calcium and chlorine, investigators concluded, could have come from a chemical detonator, or from ordinary seawater inside the barrel—seawater contains copious amounts of both—or from a chemical routinely used to clean the inside of the gun barrels.

As for the plastic traces, which the Navy thought were the residue of a bag containing the chemical detonator, the Sandia scientists found similar residue in other big guns, and concluded that they could be traced to any number of other objects, including pens or buttons that might have fallen into the breech. Other foreign chemicals the Navy identified could also be traced to cleaning fluids. Not only were most of the "foreign elements" not part of a detonator, they were chemicals that would be expected in the barrel of a battleship gun—they were not "foreign" at all.

Sandia investigators then attempted to recreate the events of the morning to determine if the explosion might have been sparked accidentally. At first the tests yielded nothing. Upon further analysis, however, scientists discovered that the gun had been over-rammed not twenty-one inches but twenty-four inches. The difference would have consumed only fractions of a second, but the scientists theorized that the extra pressure required for the larger over-ram could have afforded the crucial moment for self-ignition.

On May 14, Senator Sam Nunn, chairman of the Senate Armed Services Committee, ordered the Navy to duplicate all the tests being conducted by Sandia Laboratories. Alerted to the Navy's earlier error in measuring the over-ram, Navy technicians at the Naval Surface Warfare Center in Dahlgren, Virginia, again simulated the conditions at the moment of the *Iowa* explosion, using the same amount of explosives and applying the same pressure that the gunner's mates would have used. Five bags of gunpowder were compressed under an 800-pound weight, and dropped thirty-six inches onto a steel plate.

The first recreations produced no accidental explosions. On the eighteenth attempt on May 24, with scientists from Sandia Labs on hand to observe, the Navy researchers tried again and a loud explosion erupted from their test site. The gunpowder had ignited, by itself, without any detonation device. The previous September, the Navy had concluded that there was no scenario in which the explosion could have occurred accidentally; the Navy scientists had now demonstrated there was. A high-speed over-ram of the gunpowder into the breech could have caused several of the gun's explosive pellets to spark, which could have ignited the entire explosion. It was what gunner's mates like Kendall Truitt and Earl Hartwig had suggested all along.

Scientists immediately called the Navy. The next day, Navy Secretary Lawrence Garrett III suspended all live firings from the big guns on all of the battleships. As a Navy officer had said six months earlier, the fate of the battleships rose and fell on the Hartwig story and now it had fallen. The battleship guns would be silent forever.

By COINCIDENCE, the Senate Armed Services Committee had scheduled hearings on the *Iowa* explosion on the day after the laboratory showed that the explosion could have been accidental. Navy Secretary Garrett announced the reopening of the Navy's investigation into the explosion, and not a moment too soon, as far as the scientists researching the explosion and the senators at the hearing were concerned. They saw two reports, one by Sandia and the other by Congress' General Accounting Office that day.

The GAO report also found that the "foreign chemicals" in the gun barrel could have been residue from chemicals normally found in the big guns, and concluded that there was "only a very remote" possibility that the explosion was set off by a chemical detonator. GAO assistant comptroller Frank Conahan reported that "A close evaluation of the way the Navy conducted its investigation indicates that too early in the investigation [the Navy] ruled out other possible or plausible causes of the explosion." Given the age of the battleships and of their explosives, Conahan suggested that the vessels "seem to be top candidates for deactivation."

On top of these assessments were remarks made three weeks earlier by the *Iowa*'s commander, Captain Fred Moosally, who used his retirement ceremony to speak frankly about the Navy's investigation. The investigation, Moosally said, was conducted by "people more concerned with 'getting it over with' " than finding the genuine cause of the explosion. Investigators put too much confidence in uncorroborated gossip, he said, without regard to who might be slandered. The investigators, he said, were "people who, in their rush to manage the *Iowa* problem, forgot about doing the right thing for the *Iowa* crew."

The senators were displeased with the Navy, and made no attempt to hide it. "The Navy's investigative effort was flawed," said Senator Sam Nunn, the committee chairman; and Senator Howard Metzenbaum noted, "The facts are catching up with the foolishness of the Navy." He called on the Navy to apologize to the Hartwig family. In a joint statement released that day, House Armed Services Committee Chairman Les Aspin and investigations subcommittee chairman Nicholas Mavroules declared, "Today's new test development further erodes the Navy's theory that Clayton Hartwig committed mass murder and suicide in the Iowa turret."

As SHE WATCHED the hearing from the gallery, Kathy Kubicina felt great relief. Still, the victory felt pyrrhic. It could all happen again, she knew. And no matter how much technical data showed it was far more likely that the explosion was accidental, there would always be a public doubt as to whether Clay Hartwig was a hero who had given his life in service to his country or whether he was one of the most infamous criminals in the history of the U.S. Navy. Her parents felt the same. When Evelyn Hartwig heard a Navy captain at the hearing still defending the Navy's conclusions, she rushed up to him after his testimony and scolded, "How could you say my son killed all those people?"

Reporters talked to Clay's father after the hearing. "The Navy has got an awful lot of apologizing to do to forty-seven families for the wrongful attitude they used," he told them, "and for what my wife and I have gone through for the last year, claiming my son did this. They just ruined his name."

MASSACHUSETTS INSTITUTE OF TECHNOLOGY
CAMBRIDGE, MASSACHUSETTS

ROBB BETTIKER WAS DOING an interview with NBC network news when the reporter handed him the letter from the Bureau of Naval Personnel that informed him, "the appropriate commands have been notified to cease recoupment actions." The camera recorded Bettiker's reaction. Robb's friends were convinced it was staged. It was a measure of the fact that the Pentagon was handling the issue solely as a public relations problem that the order to stop recoupment went to the news media before it was released to the subject of the proceedings. Within days, the other ROTC causes célèbres, Jim Holobaugh and Dave Carney, had received comparable notices.

THE DEFENSE DEPARTMENT's abrupt reversal indicated the private disfavor that had fallen on the gay exclusion policies at the Pentagon's highest levels. Pete Williams, the Assistant Secretary of Defense for Public Affairs, was not particularly circumspect about his opposition to the homosexual policy, and he may have shared his feelings with Defense Secretary Richard Cheney, with whom he had a close professional relationship. Cheney was no great admirer of the policy either and was particularly taken aback at what he considered to be a vindictive effort to recoup tuition money. At a meeting of the Joint Chiefs of Staff, Cheney had personally ordered the services to cease recoupment procedures, which resulted in the letters to Holobaugh, Carney, and Bettiker. At about the same time, Cheney delivered another order to the Joint Chiefs: He did not want the services to pursue massive purges of gay personnel. Word of witch-hunt tactics had reached him, according to Pentagon sources, and he would have no such goings-on on his watch at the Defense Department.

Word spread around the Capitol that Cheney was unsympathetic to the military's policies. In a corridor one day, Congressman Barney Frank buttonholed the Secretary, who had served with Frank in the House when he was a congressman from Wyoming. Frank pressed Cheney to rescind the military's policy excluding homosexuals. Cheney did not rally to the defense of the policy, answering instead, "I pilot a big ship. It takes a long time to turn it around."

DAYS AFTER LEARNING he would not endure recoupment proceedings, Jim Holobaugh faced a bevy of reporters on his graduation day from Washington University in St. Louis. Friends congratulated him, strangers were eager to meet him, some wanted his autograph. The attention embarrassed him, but he was relieved that his future was now unencumbered. Months earlier, when he had first contemplated going public against the recoupment, he had feared he would lose his friends, be disowned, and ruin his career by publicly acknowledging being gay. None of these things had happened, although he remained nervous about the consequences his actions might have on his future employment.

Like his peers, Holobaugh had spent months sending out résumés and applications for a job in structural engineering. He received three offers and accepted one in New York. Shortly before his first day on the job, he learned that his boss's daughter had been a schoolmate of his at Washington University. It was not unlikely his reputation would precede him. Nervous, Jim greeted his new employer on his first day at work, and received the man's unequivocal support. His daughter, it turned out, had told her father how proud she was of him hiring her university's famous gay cadet.

THE UNIFORMED SERVICES continued to resist civilian reform of its gay policy, and so continued to defy Secretary Cheney's order to cease all purges. While the highly publicized cases were resolved for the gay ROTC students, the services, particularly the Navy, continued to press for recoupment whenever possible. In the same week that the office of the Secretary of the Navy notified Robb Bettiker and Jim Holobaugh that recoupment proceedings were dropped, it delivered an ultimatum to another former ROTC midshipman who had been discharged for being gay, instructing him that if he did not pay, the Navy would take the matter to the U.S. Attorney General's office for collection.

In September, a comparable story emerged after the Navy discharged Lieutenant Orlando Gotay, the Annapolis classmate of Joe Steffan's. Because Gotay did not complete his five-year commitment for his academy education, the Navy informed him after his discharge that he owed the government $22,949. "Please write a check payable to the Treasury of the United States," the letter concluded. Gotay told his story to the *San Francisco Chronicle* on a day when Cheney was on his way to Asia and had a layover at San Francisco International Airport. He is said to have become enraged when he read the story, fuming, "Goddamn it, I've told the military departments not to hit people up for back tuition." Cheney dispatched Christopher Jehn, Assistant Defense Secretary for Manpower, to repeat his orders to both the Chief of Naval Operations and the Chief of Naval Personnel that purges and recoupment proceedings cease against gay military personnel.

By autumn, the policy direction for such issues seemed clear. Even while official Pentagon spokesmen claimed that it was now Defense Department policy not to pursue recoupment in gay discharges, the actual policy was to seek repayment from anyone who did not go to the newspapers or talked about it publicly. ROTC cadets and service academy students who were not willing to become causes célèbres would find themselves stuck with substantial bills, no matter what the civilians who were nominally in charge of the Pentagon ordered to the contrary.

MILITARY OFFICIALS PAID as little heed to Cheney's order that witch-hunts be halted as they did to his order that the military cease recoupment proceedings. At nearly the same time that Cheney ordered the Joint Chiefs to halt massive gay investigations, civilian HIV counselors at Fitzsimons Army Medical Center in Denver, one of the military's designated AIDS centers, heard about a witch-hunt being planned for the Colorado Springs area. One of the top officers at Fort Carson, the headquarters of the 4th Infantry Division, believed that his base was receiving too many HIV-positive soldiers because of its proximity to Fitzsimons.

Investigators got their break when agents from the Criminal Investigation Division learned that Captain Robin Kerr had written his phone number on a restroom wall at Ironhorse Park, a recreation area on the grounds of Fort Carson. A Military Police investigator called the number Kerr left and planned an assignation with him at an on-base temporary living quarters. Military Police arrested Kerr as he was about to have sex, according to documents filed in court, and then persuaded him to co-operate with them by identifying other officers. Kerr's lengthy statement named numerous other gays in uniform at local bases of both the Army and Air Force. Four enlisted men were discharged as a result. Of particular interest to investigators, however, was Kerr's identification of a full colonel whom he knew only as Ed, who worked as an oral surgeon and was one of the highest-ranking soldiers at Fort Carson.

Kerr did not know Ed's last name, but after he was assured immunity from prosecution, he took agents from the Criminal Investigation Division to the local gay bar, the Hide 'N Seek, and pointed Ed out. That night, the CID agents saw Ed commit several acts that became the basis of court-martial offenses. At one point in the evening, Ed placed his hand on the shoulder of his lover Ron, who sometimes performed as a female impersonator under the name of Veronica. At another point, Ed put his hand on Ron's back. Agents also learned that night that, at two AIDS fund-raisers, Ed had donned a wig and dress and performed briefly as "Carmen."

When eight CID agents raided the home Colonel Ed Modesto shared with his lover, their search yielded scores of gowns and wigs, which was not surprising considering that Ron was a professional female impersonator. Agents also found a photograph of Modesto smoking a cigar, which they supposed to be a marijuana cigarette, leading to charges against him of drug use, even though no drugs or drug paraphernalia had been found at the apartment. When agents told Ron that he could go to prison for six months and be fined $500 for every question he refused to answer, he told agents everything they wanted to know, including the fact that he and Modesto regularly engaged in violations of the sodomy provision of the Uniform Code of Military Justice.

For his cooperation, Kerr was spared serious charges, but Modesto was informed that he would be court-martialed. Prosecutors tallied a list of charges against the colonel, including the drug offenses and nine counts of "conduct unbecoming an officer" that could have resulted in a seventy-four-year sentence. Also at stake was the fact that Modesto, with eighteen years in the Army, was only two years away from retirement on a full military pension. The news media focused largely on Modesto's two appearances at AIDS fund-raisers in its coverage, with such headlines as TRANSVESTITE ARMY COLONEL IS FACING COURT-MARTIAL and ARMY NOT AMUSED BY DRAG-LOVING DENTIST.

At his court-martial, the drug charges were dropped against Modesto, given the utter lack of evidence to substantiate them, but he was found guilty of nine counts of conduct unbecoming an officer. For each guilty verdict, he was sentenced to one month in the military prison at Fort Leavenworth, where he became prisoner number 74985.

Though imprisoned, Modesto did not suffer the worst fate among those who came under investigation as a result of Captain Kerr's statement. One Army captain, inaccurately identified as a major by Kerr, did. The captain was the son of a full Army colonel and had once been married to the daughter of a four-star general who had headed the influential Training and Doctrine command. The captain's photographic memory had made him a valued staff aide. Before he was thirty, he had served as an intern to the Joint Chiefs of Staff and had briefed the U.S. Secretary of Defense and the assembled defense ministers of NATO on the intricacies of European defense strategies. In his most recent job, he had served as aide-de-camp for four-star General John Piotrowski, the commander of the U.S. Space Command. His last eight officer evaluation reports had been signed by four-star generals, all of which suggested that the thirty-three-year-old captain was going straight to the top of the Army. And that was where the captain wanted to be. Unfortunately he tested positive for HIV in the same weeks that the Fort Carson investigation began and then he was identified as gay by Captain Kerr.

These were jarring events for a man who had one day hoped to be Army Chief of Staff. Rather than face an investigation, the captain went to the Shooting Den, a local gun store, and purchased a revolver for $199.95. Two days later, he carefully opened a box of .357 Magnum bullets and loaded them into the revolver. The captain then walked into his bedroom, stretched out on the red-and-blue flannel sheets of his double bed, placed the blue steel barrel of the revolver next to the left side of his head, and pulled the trigger.

JUNE 1990
COLORADO SPRINGS, COLORADO

AS THEY HAD FOR MANY DECADES, the military's relentless purges of gays continued to have tragic repercussions for many who had considered themselves remote from the lesbians and gay men who fell victim to the Pentagon's policies. One such man was an Army colonel who was the father of the thirty-three-year-old captain who had shot himself in the wake of the Fort Carson investigation.

Colorado Springs police officer Paul Meeks found the body the afternoon of the shooting after a frantic call from the captain's landlord. Before ending his life, the young captain had neatly written out a five-page suicide note and set out twenty-one four-by-six-inch index cards with the names of people to be notified after his death. His father's card lay on the top of the stack.

With thirty-one years in the Army, the colonel was next in line in his branch for promotion to brigadier general. In the months after his son's death, he pieced together the story of the suicide. The note alluded to the captain's HIV-positive status. It was not difficult for the colonel to imagine what his son's future would have been in the Army. Although the military did not discharge people solely because they were infected with the AIDS virus, regulations also demanded that no HIV-positive soldier serve overseas or in a unit that could be deployed for combat. Therefore the captain would have looked ahead to a series of stateside dead-end jobs. His medical record would be held in the strictest of confidence—the Army did a good job of that—but it would not take long for experienced hands to figure out why the talented captain's career had suddenly left the fast track.

The revelation of his son's HIV status was only half the story. All the intimations his son had offered, particularly in the past year, began to make sense—for example, that the captain had told his wife, "I love you, but like a sister, not a wife." The colonel had put the incident out of his mind, just as he had not thought much about his son telling him that his marital problems were due to a lack of physical passion. Before, the colonel had believed that homosexuals were other people's sons; now he realized that one of them had been his own.

There had been rumors about homosexuals in the military swirling through Colorado Springs during those months. The colonel had read about investigations underway at military installations in the Colorado Springs area in the *Army Times*. But he did his own investigation, and determined that his son was not one of those under suspicion. (In fact, the captain had been identified as gay in Captain Robin Kerr's statement.) The suicide haunted the father. What did it mean to be homosexual? A devout Southern Baptist, he had always believed homosexuals were an abomination to God. When he had thought about the subject at all, which was not often, he had assumed that such people chose their lifestyle. It was what his church had told him and what everyone he knew believed.

Now, however, the father was hungry for more information. He began to read books about homosexuality, and ultimately he began to look for friends of his son, even the gay friends. To a man, they all said they believed they had been born that way. There was no choice, they said. After all, why would someone wake up one day and *choose* a lifestyle that would make him part of a despised minority? The colonel had to admit that it did not make much sense. He had believed otherwise because, in some fundamental way, he had never believed homosexuals were really people, people motivated by the same fears and hopes he had. That his son had.

The colonel thought about his son's last days. In the world his son had always known, lorded over by a God who offered only damnation and entrenched in a military system that offered only intolerance, there was only one way out. All that the colonel had ever believed, he realized, was part of the ideology that had led his son to kill himself that cool April morning in Colorado Springs.

Meanwhile, the colonel's wife was suffering greatly. The couple had already lost one child to a tragedy years before; that had nearly killed her then. Now the death of her beloved boy, a child who seemed singularly gifted to make a mother proud, had plunged her into despair. The colonel had carefully kept the suicide note from her, and had told her nothing of his own investigation into their son's homosexuality. She came from a sheltered southern background and would not understand.

Whenever someone called, with every letter that arrived to console the grieving family, the woman fell deeper into depression. To accept the promotion to one-star general, the rank the colonel had served his entire career to gain, would require a move to Washington and extensive traveling, which an Army counselor had suggested might devastate his wife.

She had moved thirty-three times during their marriage without complaint. It was what Army life meant. Each promotion of his was a demotion for her, leaving the friends she had made, moving to a new home on a new post where she knew no one and would have to start again. Through his two tours in Vietnam and other unaccompanied duty in Asia, she had raised their children alone. She had paid her dues. Now it was time to repay her. So in 1991, the colonel told the Army he would not take his general's star.

When a journalist began asking questions about his son's suicide, the colonel went to court to seal the coroner's record. He would do anything to protect his wife's privacy. Their son had died a hero in her eyes; he would remain so. Everyone in the small hometown where their son had once coached grade-school baseball and where he had taught Southern Baptist Sunday school believed he had died in a car accident. Let them live with those memories, the colonel pleaded. Only he knew the truth, and the knowledge confused even him.

———————

IN THE WEEKS AFTER the Senate received its two reports on the Navy's conclusions regarding the *Iowa* explosion probe, the weight of public opinion fell resolutely against the Navy and its earlier indictment of Clayton Hartwig. The news media was uncommonly critical of both the investigation and the NIS. "Sixty Minutes" was preparing an investigatory report that included an interview with David Smith explaining that NIS agents had threatened to imprison him as an accessory to murder if he did not fabricate a statement against Hartwig. Even before the Senate report, Defense Secretary Cheney had announced that he was retiring both the battleships *Iowa* and *Wisconsin* as a cost-cutting measure. With the guns silenced on the two remaining ships, it seemed likely that they too would be decommissioned soon, and the time of the dreadnoughts would be past.

The *Iowa* story told much about how dramatically the world had changed toward homosexuality in the past generation. On the one hand, it was hardly surprising that the Naval Investigative Service, with its fixation on homosexuality, would find that gay men were somehow to blame for an explosion of a battleship gun, nor were the heavy-handed tactics the agency employed to procure its "evidence." There was a time, not very many years earlier, when the suggestion that the tragedy had been caused by a homosexual would have been easily accepted, conforming as it did to the old stereotypes that gay men were inherently maladjusted sociopaths, given to irrational, even dangerous actions. If some had doubted it, few would show their doubt publicly for fear of appearing to be homosexual sympathizers.

But the world had changed, even if the Navy had not. Few in Congress, in the media, and even among many Naval officials were ready to accept the thin evidence and huge leaps of logic required to abide by the Navy's scenario. What was most remarkable was that the story found little support even among officials of a conservative Republican administration—and though Cheney had little interest in the social issues championed by the religious right, he remained a hard-bitten conservative. Gays had not yet found a full measure of social acceptance, but they were also no longer the pariahs they had been a generation earlier. Too many Americans, from the Secretary of Defense to the reporters chronicling the story, knew acknowledged gay people now, and understood that the old stereotypes could no longer be trusted. The world had been changing, almost imperceptibly, for the past generation, and only in episodes such as the *Iowa* investigation were the parameters of those changes visible.

The USS *Iowa* was decommissioned in October 1990; within a year, all the battleships had been decommissioned and consigned to Naval history.

75

The Fag Killer

JUNE 1990
NORFOLK NAVAL STATION
NORFOLK, VIRGINIA

KAREN STUPSKY HAD STRUGGLED with her sexual identity ever since her sophomore year at Harvard University, where she had been an ROTC cadet. By early 1990, after graduating magna cum laude from Harvard and being commissioned an ensign in the Navy, Stupsky realized that she was indeed homosexual, though she had never engaged in any physical intimacy with another woman.

She was assigned to the USS *Sylvania*, where she was one of the ship's first female officers. She loved her sea duty, but remained profoundly conflicted over the impact her homosexuality could have on her Navy life. She had followed the travails of the women aboard the USS *Yellowstone* closely during the 1988 investigation of that ship. She knew that at any time she could become engulfed in a witch-hunt; she could even go to prison.

In January 1990, Stupsky was invited to a chaplain's retreat where other officers broke into small groups to talk about their conflicts. They raised many harrowing issues, including their sexual abuse as children, their drug and alcohol problems, their marital difficulties. Tentatively, Karen asked if her small group represented a "safe space" where she could talk about anything without fear of repercussions. Everyone said yes, so Karen confided that she was a lesbian. She loved the Navy and wanted to stay in, but she was also afraid. Should she turn herself in? she wondered aloud. The other group members, all in the active-duty Navy, were supportive. The Navy policy was wrong, they said; she was a good person and a good officer; there was no reason to turn herself in. No one condemned her for being lesbian, or suggested she did not belong in the Navy.

The strong support convinced the twenty-four-year-old ensign that she could make more crewmates aware of her sexuality. She came out to other officers she had known in ROTC and had met in Navy training schools. All remained friendly. She told the ship's chaplain, who confided that this was the first time he had heard of a homosexual sailor wanting to stay in the service. Usually, they wanted out. Some friends were skeptical when she said that she had accepted herself as gay, even though she had never had sex with another woman. "I just know," Karen said.

Finally in April, in an effort to resolve her conflicts, she informed the ship's executive officer. He suggested she resign, and she agreed. The daughter of an Air Force major, she was accustomed to following the military way. But in the succeeding weeks, she read about Robb Bettiker, Dave Carney, and Joe Steffan. It struck her that there was no reason she should make her departure an easy task for the Navy. "My homosexuality does not negatively effect my abilities as an officer," Stupsky wrote in a letter withdrawing her resignation. "While adhering to regulations, my chain of command and shipmates responded with personal compassion and understanding. Though we were all initially afraid of possible negative or violent reactions, none materialized. I feel that I still belong on my ship, and am very optimistic about the potential for change in the Navy's treatment of gay personnel."

Aware that she might be in for a prolonged struggle, Stupsky also contacted Kate Dyer at Congressman Gerry Studds's office and attorneys who were working on the Steffan case. If the Navy wanted a fight, she would give them one. In June, she received word that the Navy had initiated discharge proceedings against her. Stupsky's case uniquely fulfilled the "thoughtcrime" provision of the 1981 revision in the Pentagon's homosexual policy. Her discharge substantiated the fact that one did not have to have had homosexual sex in order to be discharged for being gay.

Stupsky's public disclosure represented a new watershed for lesbians and gay men in the military. The policy against homosexuals had survived nearly a half century in part because so few gays had challenged them. Most performed their service quietly, keeping their homosexuality hidden, allowing military officials to pick and choose when they would enforce the ban on gays, and when they would not. Before 1990, a handful of gays had declared themselves to challenge the policy, sometimes in small ways like Kelly "Doreen" Kittell and sometimes in public gestures like Leonard Matlovich, but these challenges were rare.

Stupsky's acknowledgment was the beginning of a slow but steady stream of episodes of gay military personnel announcing themselves to their commanders. It presaged a new trend that would ultimately do more to change the military's policy than any other: Gay military personnel were withdrawing that which had long sanctioned the military's harsh treatment of gays, the sanction of the victim.

In San Diego, Jim Woodward, president of the gay San Diego Veterans Association, found that in the months after the Supreme Court ruling in his case, active-duty military personnel who had long been reluctant to talk to reporters about their plight suddenly expressed a willingness to help. They would not allow their names to be used, but neither would they duck Woodward's phone calls when he linked the service members to journalists. Like most gays, military personnel had assumed the courts would come to their rescue. Now they realized that establishing their emancipation would be their work, and they were willing to do it.

In May, Miriam Ben-Shalom established the Gay, Lesbian, and Bisexual Veterans of America to coordinate the efforts of gay veterans groups seeking to change the military's policies with uniformed military people who often needed advice during the hardships of a gay purge. The organization marked the first attempt to network homosexuals in the military with their supporters in veterans groups and civil liberties organizations.

Despite the setback at the Supreme Court, lower federal courts continued to provide optimism about future legal challenges to the military's policies. On May 4, an eleven-member panel of the U.S. Court of Appeals Ninth Circuit in San Francisco delivered its *en banc* ruling on the eight-year-old lawsuit seeking the reinstatement of former Staff Sergeant Perry Watkins. Despite the panel's increasingly conservative posture, it surprised legal observers by ordering the Army to reinstate him. The panel would not rule on the constitutional issues Watkins had raised, focusing instead on the fairness issue. By reinstating Watkins, Judge Harry Pregerson ruled, "it would simply require the Army to continue what it has repeatedly done for fourteen years with only positive results: reenlist a single soldier with an exceptionally outstanding record." The Army had "plainly acted affirmatively in admitting, reclassifying, reenlisting, retaining and promoting" Watkins throughout his career, the court ruled, and it was unfair to discharge him after that.

Only two judges voting for Watkins in the seven-to-four ruling tackled the broader constitutional questions. As he had in previous decisions, Judge William A. Norris advanced the argument that military rules violated Watkins's rights. "The Army's regulation violates the constitutional guarantee of equal protection of the laws because they discriminate against persons of homosexual orientation, a suspect class, and because the regulations are not necessary to promote any governmental interest." In a dissent opposing reinstatement of Watkins, Judge Cynthia Holcomb objected that the judges had engaged in an "unwarranted application of common law principles to matters within the military's expertise."

Though the ruling lacked the sweeping implications of a constitutional analysis, it still put the military in the uncomfortable position of having to admit an acknowledged gay soldier. Once this was done, as military lawyers understood, trying to keep the second or third out of uniform would become much more difficult. The Army appealed the decision to the Supreme Court.

In Tacoma, where Watkins worked as a telephone operator at the Social Security Administration, the former staff sergeant remained supremely confident that he would win at the Supreme Court as well. From the day he filed his lawsuit in 1982, he had always told the truth, and the truth, he believed, would win the case for him.

———————

IN JULY, THE LAST SUBPLOT of the Parris Island purge was played out at the Board for the Correction of Naval Records, which ordered that former Staff Sergeant Christine Hilinski be given a clean service record and $1,320 in salary she had lost because of her demotion in 1988. The action to deny her Military Occupation Specialty and cut her pay because she appeared as a character witness for Cheryl Jameson was illegal, the board ruled. The victory was more symbolic than real, given the fact that Hilinski, her record stained, had left the Marine Corps earlier that year, after eleven years of service.

In many smaller ways, cracks were becoming evident in the military's attitudes against gays. As they had been throughout the latter portion of the 1980s, enlisted personnel were leading increasingly open lives, telling their coworkers about their homosexuality and usually finding acceptance. When an enlisted man at the Sixth Battalion, Eighth Field Artillery, at Fort Ord told his first sergeant he wanted out of the Army for being gay, the sergeant answered, "Boy, this is the Army of the nineties and you don't get out for that anymore." When another enlisted man in the same unit requested a discharge on the basis that he was gay, his captain and commanding officer talked him out of turning himself in, according to an officer in the unit at that time.

The openness extended to the officers' ranks. A female admiral in Norfolk took a Navy enlisted man whom she supervised into her confidence, showed him photographs of her lover, and introduced him to a gay lieutenant commander who could show him around the local gay community. Increasingly, new officers, drawn largely from ROTC programs, were also open about their homosexuality. One officer commissioned in 1990, for example, had served as president of his campus gay group before he entered into the Navy.

———————

THE RELUCTANCE OF ship commanders to enforce regulations against homosexuals had become so widespread as to come to the attention of the commander of the Navy's Atlantic fleet. Vice Admiral Joseph S. Donnell issued this memorandum to the officers of the two hundred ships and forty shore installations under his command: "With the influx of women on our ships and throughout the Navy in general, it is necessary to address the sensitive issue of female homosexuality and ensure equal treatment of male and female homosexuals. . . ."

Of particular concern to the vice admiral were rumors that commanders were becoming lax in discharging suspected lesbians: "There is a perception by many that female homosexuality is somewhat tolerated, while male homosexuality is dealt with swiftly and sternly. Several possible reasons for this perception exist. Unless a woman admits to being a homosexual, it is often difficult to prove. Male homosexual behavior or activity in the Navy has long been unacceptable, and is usually quickly reported by peers or subordinates. The male homosexual who has been reported, recognizing his untenable position is then more likely to admit his homosexuality and accept administrative processing. This is not necessarily the case for women. Experience has shown that the stereotypical female homosexual in the Navy is more aggressive than her male counterpart, intimidating those women who might turn her in to the chain of command. As a result, the ability to obtain credible evidence during an investigation of female homosexuality is often stymied, and all that remains are unsubstantiated rumors leading to accusations of a 'witch hunt' as investigators unsuccessfully search for evidence.

"Experience has also shown that the stereotypical female homosexual in the Navy is hardworking, career-oriented, willing to put in long hours on the job and among the command's top professionals. As such, allegations that this woman is a homosexual, particularly if made by a young and junior female sailor with no track record, may be dismissed out of hand or pursued half-heartedly."

After explaining why lesbians make the best sailors, Donnell explained why they must be discharged, relying heavily on the lesbian vampire stereotype. "Particularly for young, often vulnerable, female sailors, subtle coercion or outright sexual advances by more senior and aggressive female sailors can be intimidating and intolerable. . . . We must recognize that women who are targets for female homosexuals experience a unique form of sexual harassment which can be even more devastating and difficult to cope with than the more traditional harassment from men. . . . Women must be assured they do not have to exist in a predator-type environment."

Ensign Karen Stupsky was still working in Norfolk, awaiting her discharge hearing, when a gay friend in the Combat Logistics Squadron showed her the memo and obligingly made copies for her, which Karen sent along to Congressman Gerry Studds and the gay attorneys with whom he worked. The memorandum's release to the news media created a sensation. "If it's the Navy's policy to root out top performers, what is going on here?" Studds asked when he released the memo. As with the PER-SEREC report nine months earlier, the military seemed to confirm what homosexual activists had said for years, that gays are not only adequate military personnel, but among the best.

EVEN AS THE policy seemed to be weakening beyond repair, the military continued to defend it staunchly and more desperately after each undermining revelation. Faced with an avalanche of negative publicity, military investigators attempted to crack down on anyone talking to journalists. In 1989, for example, investigators went to astounding lengths to determine the identity of an active-duty officer who had appeared behind a screen in a televised interview. As part of this effort, they requested manifests of all passengers who flew into New York on domestic flights on the day of the soldier's appearance. After *New York Times* reporter Jane Gross wrote a lengthy article about gays in uniform in April 1990, she learned that Navy investigators had labored assiduously to identify her sources from the vague identifiers she had used to describe anonymous personnel interviewed in the story. Gross considered this chilling enough—what was more chilling was the fact that the investigators were successful in discerning the identities of several of them. When the San Diego Veterans Association held a June 1990 protest against the military's policy, NIS agents were on hand to videotape the marchers—even though they were civilians and nominally outside the jurisdiction of military authorities.

The latter months of 1990 also brought the usual round of witch-hunts of homosexual service personnel. Another purge of gays at the Defense Language Institute in Monterey, California, resulted in the discharges of at least seven military personnel. Several more were discharged during an investigation aboard the USS *Constellation* in June 1990. A lesbian purge at the Whidbey Island Naval Air Station added more discharges, as well as accusations of NIS excesses. At least twenty service members came under investigation at the remote air base at San Vito in southern Italy. When Sergeant Jim Neal was investigated for being gay during his assignment at Grisom Air Force Base in Bunker Hill, Indiana, he heard about an effeminate-looking OSI agent who was frequently used as a decoy to lure Family members out of hiding. This agent, Neal was told, had the nickname of "the fag killer."

As it had throughout the Reagan and Bush years, imprisonments of gays also continued. First Lieutenant Steve Marose was court-martialed in July 1990 for one count of conduct unbecoming an officer because he had gone to a gay bar, another count of conduct unbecoming because he had an enlisted roommate, and three counts of sodomy. Although even the prosecutor in the case confided to Marose's lawyer that it should never have gone to trial and Marose should have been allowed to resign, he was court-martialed anyway, and served nearly sixteen months in prison.

The courts-martial and purges had their usual effect, inflaming the passions of young antigay men in the services, and informing them that their homophobic attitudes were entirely appropriate. In late June, a mob of Marines from the Marine Corps barracks in Washington attacked patrons of Remington's, a gay bar on the site of the Equus, the tavern Marines had attacked in 1980. Two gay men were knocked unconscious in the attack by young leathernecks, who shouted "Kill the fags," and "Go Marines." Colonel Peter Pace, the barracks commander, pressed charges of disorderly conduct against two of the Marines involved in the attack, but when gay leaders met with Commandant Alfred Gray to press for sensitivity training on gay issues for Marines, they were rebuffed.

Between the witch-hunts and the growing acceptance, the "fag killers" and the officers who no longer enforced the military's gay policies, the summer months of 1990 demonstrated all the incongruities that had marked the armed forces' treatment of gays for the past decade. And it might have gone on that way much longer, except for events far away, events that would have very little to do with homosexuality. In southern Iraq on the night of August 1, 1990, Iraqi President Saddam Hussein ordered his tanks to roll into the small emirate of Kuwait.

76

Convenience of the Government
(Part 2)

THREE THOUSAND WOMEN gathered under sunny skies in the shadow of the spectacular granite rock formations of Yosemite for a weekend of women's music and lesbian comedy. From the stage, comedian Robin Tyler, who organized the annual gathering, began her routine. "I love a woman in uniform—it saves me from putting it on in the bedroom," she joked, adding, "If homosexuality is a disease, call in sick to work."

The women laughed appreciatively. After decades of invisibility, a new lesbian community was coalescing, as interested in culture as the lesbian community of the 1970s had been in lesbian-feminist political rhetoric. At the same time, a contingent of sex-positive S/M enthusiasts challenged old-time feminist sensibilities, as lesbians began exploring their sexuality with the gusto that had marked the gay male experimentation of two decades earlier. Their more diverse interests drew different women together in ways that could scarcely have been imagined a decade earlier, and a cultural identity touched the lives of lesbians in a way political dialectics never could.

The women's festival of 1990 had an added, somber undercurrent: the possibility of a war. Saddam Hussein's troops had swept through Kuwait a month earlier and stood on the border of Saudi Arabia poised for what could be an effortless invasion, earning Iraq control of 36 percent of the world's petroleum reserves. The idea of a war over oil was a matter of great concern to a twenty-five-year-old Army reservist named Donna Lynn Jackson and her lover, Christie Carr. As a specialist with the Army's 129th Evacuation Hospital, Jackson would likely be mobilized for service in the Persian Gulf. Iraq's army was the fourth largest in the world, and military experts predicted that if war came, U.S. casualties would be heavy. Jackson's unit would be among the most essential.

During the year that they had been a couple, Christie Carr had not thought much about the potential repercussions of Donna's service in the Reserves. She had been surprised at how many lesbians served in the Reserves and active-duty Army—Donna estimated that a third of the women in her unit were lesbians, and now at the women's festival Christie began to think about what it would mean for her if Donna was called to war.

Christie, a professional photographer, had just snapped a picture of Donna and two friends who had come to the festival with them from San Diego, one of whom served in the same Reserves unit as Donna. This woman became agitated. Didn't Christie understand that a photo of an Army reservist at a lesbian gathering could be used against her in an investigation? Investigations, the woman explained, led to discharges, and sometimes even to prison. It struck Christie as ironic that if her lover was to serve in Saudi Arabia, she would have as much to fear from her own army as from the enemy's.

Stout, round-faced, and cheerful, Donna Jackson was a "Navy brat," who had enlisted when she turned seventeen and been discharged from the Army in May 1985 because she was three pounds over the Army's weight limit. But she was patriotic and liked the military, so a year later she enlisted in the Army Reserves. In December 1988, she was assigned to the 129th Evacuation Hospital, a mobile hospital to be stationed between fifty and one hundred miles behind the front lines of the Persian Gulf.

The hospital had a large number of women reservists, and like most of the military's medical units, a disproportionately high number of gays. Concerns about purges led other women to take Donna aside and suggest she grow her hair a little longer—it raised fewer suspicions. Donna kept her hair short, but was wary of other giveaways. She referred to Christie as "he," for instance, and told the male reservists who asked for a date that she was already engaged to a very nice man.

In October, Donna Jackson agreed to volunteer for service in Saudi Arabia. Several weeks later, her unit was notified that it would be on active-duty status by December. And Donna vowed that if she went to war, she would not hide who she was.

DURING THE SAME WEEK that Christie Carr and Donna Jackson attended the West Coast Women's Music Festival, the Department of Defense was drawing up orders to implement its "Stop/Loss" policy. The aim of Stop/Loss was to slow the numbers of discharges from the armed forces to ensure adequate manpower to fulfill whatever military missions a war in the Persian Gulf might require. On September 1, 1990, the Secretary of the Army ordered that the service suspend discharges of active-duty personnel who had "skills in short supply in the Army." This included certain language specialists and medical personnel. By November, the order was expanded dramatically to suspend virtually all discharges from the armed forces, except in cases of misconduct, disability, or on humanitarian grounds.

By late autumn, Miriam Ben-Shalom, in her new role as national chair of the Gay, Lesbian, and Bisexual Veterans of America, was beginning to understand the practical impact of the Stop/Loss policies. With mobilization of Reserves units more likely than at any time since the Vietnam War, Operation Desert Shield, as the Gulf mobilization had been named, had prompted many reservists to reconsider their involvement with the military. Some were frightened of the enemy's threat to use chemical and biological weapons; they wanted out. Others wanted to serve, but were afraid of the possibility of a witch-hunt or a court-martial in the isolation of Saudi Arabia, where there would be no civilian lawyers or publicity or gay community support. Reservists in both categories who turned to Ben-Shalom for advice had gone first to their commanders and admitted being homosexual, and their officers had said that they did not care—the reservists would be mobilized like any other soldier.

Now that the military seemed willing to discreetly accept openly homosexual soldiers, Ben-Shalom had an idea. There were thousands of gay service members who had been discharged from the military during the great purges of the 1980s. Many, if not most, were eager to be back in uniform. Ben-Shalom wrote to President Bush asking him to allow the creation of a gay battalion, along the lines of the Civil War's 54th Massachusetts Volunteer Regiment, the all–African American fighting force made famous in the film *Glory*. Wrote Ben-Shalom, "We are willing to go and serve where we are needed, even to the front lines in the Persian Gulf. Mr. President, let us prove our worth. Let us show we can do the job with honor, dignity and responsibility." Ben-Shalom herself attempted to join the Wisconsin National Guard, so she could be mobilized and sent to Desert Shield.

Ben-Shalom's plea for a gay regiment was carried widely in gay newspapers. Within weeks, she told reporters she had the names of 250 homosexual military personnel willing to serve in such a regiment, all of whom had been in the armed forces within the past five years, many of whom provided records of their various achievement medals, commendations, and Bronze Stars. Ben-Shalom calculated the typical volunteer would bring nearly $100,000 worth of military training—money that would not have to be spent training green recruits. Ben-Shalom never did receive an answer to her letter.

Some gay ex-soldiers were considering going to Canada, where homosexual discharges had been suspended for several years, to serve with that country's component of any multinational force that might be sent to the Gulf. A generation earlier, young Americans had gone to Canada to avoid service in the military; now they spoke of going to Canada to serve.

Though the military issue had acquired greater cachet in recent years, civilian gay activists remained profoundly divided over how to handle both the prospect of war and the issue of gays in the military. The National

Gay and Lesbian Task Force announced it opposed military intervention in the Gulf. "We are deeply concerned that this war will allow our political leaders to ignore the pressing problems faced by the lesbian and gay community," the group's official statement read, noting in particular that the money spent to finance just several days of the buildup dwarfed all the research funds spent for AIDS during the past decade. Most polls taken by gay newspapers, however, found that an overwhelming majority of gays, like an overwhelming majority of the American public, supported intervention.

But among the more ideologically inclined, ambivalence toward helping homosexuals in uniform persisted. At the first National Lesbian Conference in early 1991, organizers had planned two workshops on lesbians in uniform, which prompted outrage from the Arab-American lesbian caucus, as well as among pacifist women who opposed lesbians joining the military altogether. During one angry confrontation, one lesbian pacifist, who apparently believed in pacifism more as an ideal than a practice, punched a woman with the lesbian military contingent. When the veterans attempted to address the conference, they were not allowed to speak.

Jeff Herwatt, the sergeant who was among the first Army personnel to test positive for HIV, had been medically retired from the Army, but he remained passionate about the policies that excluded gays from the services. Like many other younger gays, Herwatt, who was twenty-five years old in 1990, joined a new, confrontational gay group called Queer Nation. Queer Nation was to more established homosexual groups like the National Gay and Lesbian Task Force what the Student Nonviolent Coordinating Committee, or SNCC, had been to the NAACP during the 1960s. As in the earlier era, the differences fell largely along generational lines, with younger gays far more impatient and angry than their elders. When Herwatt first suggested protesting the military's policies, he heard the same old arguments that genuine "queers," using the new vogue term among young gays, should not be in the military; that any queer in the military was a hypocrite. After much debate, Herwatt was able to generate enough interest to put together a special caucus—Homosexuals Ideologically Mobilized Against Oppressive Military, or HI-MOM—and the group conducted a small protest during the annual Fleet Week festivities in San Francisco.

Nationally, however, the issue did not catch fire among the young Queer Nationals, who preferred more theatrical protests, such as kiss-ins in suburban shopping malls. As with the homosexual radicals of decades past, the aim of Queer Nation was not a world in which gay people might express their humanity as they saw fit; instead, the goal seemed to be a world in which every gay person could behave like a member of Queer Nation.

NOVEMBER 5, 1990
TACOMA, WASHINGTON

AFTER THE U.S. COURT OF APPEALS in San Francisco had ordered Perry Watkins's reinstatement into the Army, the Bush administration had appealed to the U.S. Supreme Court to grant a writ of certiorari, meaning a review of the case. The court, which had one vacancy due to the retirement of Justice William Brennan, Jr., took no action for months, leading some legal experts to speculate that the court was evenly divided and could not reach a decision. Shortly after the appointment of Justice David Souter, however, the court delivered its opinion in one sentence: "The petition for a writ of certiorari is denied." The appeals court decision stood. In effect, the Supreme Court had ordered the reinstatement of Perry Watkins into the United States Army.

It had been more than twenty-three years since Watkins had first told an Army psychiatrist that he was gay. The appeals court decision was not made on the broad constitutional grounds of civil rights or equal protection, but on the nonconstitutional reasoning that a basic rule of fairness ought to apply to Watkins's service, since the Army had been content to use him for fifteen years, knowing full well he was gay, before moving to discharge him during the purges of the Reagan administration. The ruling would not have the effect of setting a precedent for other soldiers battling the antigay policies, but it was a historic turning point in that the nation's highest court had for the first time ordered the armed forces to accept an openly gay soldier.

Perry was at work in his job at the Social Security Administration in Tacoma when his attorney, Jim Lobsenz, called with the news. Perry grabbed his supervisor and began jumping up and down. "We won," he shouted. "We won!"

Even when legal experts had assured Perry that the Supreme Court would never rule in his favor, he had believed that he would win, and now he called the person who more than anyone else had encouraged him to tell the truth, no matter what the consequences. Sixty-two-year-old Ola Watkins was thrilled, sensing something historic in the Supreme Court decision, an increment of change that might affect life for millions of people, just as life had changed for African Americans since she had grown up in the segregated South of the 1930s. Ola was prouder of her son than ever before. His honesty had made a difference in the world.

The Watkins decision coincided with several other developments that made the future viability of the military's discrimination seem tenuous at best. Within days of the Watkins decision, the U.S. Court of Appeals in Washington, D.C., ruled that Joseph Steffan's lawsuit against the Naval Academy should proceed. The unanimous decision by a three-judge panel maintained that federal judge Oliver Gasch was out of legal bounds when he ordered Steffan to answer questions about his sex life. It was not the role of federal judges to order plaintiffs to provide proof of misconduct for which they have already been punished, the panel said. The ruling was a direct slap at Gasch, which was unfortunate because the suit would now return to him to rule on the broader constitutional issues it raised. However, the fact that the decision came from an appeals court that was among the most conservative in the nation indicated that judges were increasingly willing to allow legal challenges to the military's policies.

Nine days after the Watkins ruling, the Defense Department asked its general counsel to clarify policies regarding granting security clearances to lesbians and gay men. The Pentagon's top lawyers privately issued that clarification seven weeks later. To make policy consistent with recent court rulings, Assistant General Counsel Michael Sterlacci wrote that sexual orientation could be weighed as a factor in security issues only if they reflected "untrustworthiness, unreliability, or a lack of common sense judgment." Even in states where gay sex was legally forbidden, it would be difficult to justify a refusal of a security clearance unless the behavior "is indicative of poor judgment other than criminality such as involvement with minors or sex in public places." Moreover, Defense investigators should cease asking questions about specific sexual practices of gays, Sterlacci suggested. "Absent some compelling reason . . . it is prudent to treat homosexuals and heterosexuals the same with respect to the questions put to them about sex."

The legal recommendations did not have the force of new regulations, however. It was still the official Department of Defense policy that excluding gays from the military was necessary "to prevent breaches in security," and investigators from the Defense Investigative Service continued to pry routinely into the private sex lives of suspected gays who sought a security clearance. Still, the memorandum, which was kept a closely guarded secret in the Pentagon until it was leaked to gay organizers eight months later, indicated that even the Pentagon's own lawyers believed that the Defense Department's long-standing policy against gays having security clearances could not withstand legal challenge.

The maneuvering caused some public comment on the issue of gays in the military from defenders and critics of the policy. Newspapers were nearly unanimously calling for letting gays and lesbians serve. The Pentagon would not comment beyond quoting the usual 123 words, so defending the regulation was taken up by those who argued their case not in terms of the military per se, but in terms of manhood. As columnist Bruce Fein wrote in a guest column in *USA Today,* "The lifeblood of a soldier is masculinity, bravery and gallantry. The battlefield soldier is inspired to risk all by fighting with comrades whose attributes conform to his view of manhood. . . . And it is inarguable that the majority of a fighting force would be psychologically and emotionally deflated by the close presence of homosexuals who evoke effeminate or repugnant but not manly visions."

OCTOBER 1990
FORT ORD
MONTEREY, CALIFORNIA

WHEN ARMY RESERVIST DONNA LYNN JACKSON was asked if she would volunteer to serve in Saudi Arabia, she agreed. Soon she was told she would be deployed by the end of December. That was when she made her final decision—to tell her commanding officer that she was a lesbian. If she was going to risk her life for her country, she would do so openly as a homosexual person; she did not want a casket to be her final closet.

Specialist 4 Jackson was with her unit at Ford Ord awaiting deployment when she approached her colonel and explained she was a lesbian. According to documents later filed in federal court, the colonel had a quick response. "Don't worry about it—it's no big deal," he said. When Jackson presented this response to an Army lawyer, he explained that Jackson would be allowed to serve in Operation Desert Shield; when she returned, authorities would discharge her for being gay.

By now, similar stories were unfolding throughout the country. Some commanders even said in writing that they would in effect not discharge gays—at least until the conclusion of the impending war. Many openly gay soldiers were ultimately deployed, but Donna Lynn Jackson was not among them, because she went to the press. After the ensuing publicity, Jackson was ultimately separated, reaffirming the principle that Perry Watkins had noted fifteen years earlier. The point of the military's regulations was not to actually rid the armed forces of all gays, but to allow the military to *say* they ejected all gays. It was in this way that the story of gays in the military continued to echo with the past. It had always been this way—official denunciations and unofficial acceptance—and it would continue. From war to war, the more things changed, the more they stayed the same.

NOVEMBER 9, 1990
UNIVERSITY OF MINNESOTA
MINNEAPOLIS, MINNESOTA

GREG TERAN had never considered discrimination against homosexuals until he began filling out the required questionnaire for his admittance to the ROTC program at the Massachusetts Institute of Technology.

It was the question that asked if he was homosexual that stopped him cold. He had no doubts about his own sexuality; he was completely heterosexual, but the question rankled him because he saw it as the means for ROTC to exclude gays from the program. It was bigotry staring him in the face. It was wrong.

Teran had strong feelings about prejudice. His father had moved from Mexico to Arizona when he was twelve years old, and lived in a shed while he worked his way through high school and later the University of Arizona. Signs separating "colored" and "white" still hung on restroom doors when he moved to Texas.

Greg was born in 1970 and grew up pro–civil rights, and with a lot of his immigrant father's drive to succeed. He had been an outstanding high school student and was accepted to MIT, but the $14,000-a-year tuition would pretty well derail his sister's plan's for college. The ROTC program offered the solution, and a way to put his engineering training to immediate use with the Air Force. The gay question jarred his enthusiasm, and he became more troubled when the ROTC issue exploded on the MIT campus in early 1990.

As a cadet, he felt personally threatened—ROTC was the only way he could get the education he wanted. He also felt that ROTC served a useful purpose in a democratic society because it ensured that the military's officer corps would come from a broad base of society educated in the liberal arts, and not just from military academies. Nevertheless, Greg Teran saw the other side of the issue, as well. When other ROTC cadets privately accused Robb Bettiker of trying to cheat the government out of its scholarship money by saying he was gay, Teran made it a point to meet Bettiker, and concluded that Robb would surely have served in the Navy, given the chance.

Assigned to do a full briefing on any military-related issue for his class, Teran delivered a report to the fifteen other Air Force cadets and his unit commander arguing that the regulations banning gays should be rescinded. Among his audience not one man rolled his eyes or looked away in disgust. Several cadets were sympathetic; some asked about sharing foxholes with gays, some wanted to know whether handling bleeding gay soldiers could put them at risk for AIDS.

After the class, Greg's commandant asked to see him in his office. Greg expected a dressing-down for challenging policy; instead the commandant said it was the finest briefing he had seen in his career at ROTC, and awarded Greg the best grade he had ever given—100 out of a possible 100 points. "It will change," he said. "It absolutely cannot last."

But Teran found strong resistance to gays in other quarters. When his flight training officer assembled the cadets and asked them to state their goals for military service, Greg said his was to serve in an Air Force that did not discriminate on race, sex, or sexual orientation. The captain looked back at him somberly. "You might have to fall on your sword for that one," he said.

By November, Teran had made his decision, and was among the 150 others who attended "About Face," a national conference of organizers bent on ousting ROTC chapters from campuses, unless the Defense Department changed its antigay regulations.

That young men like Greg Teran had taken up the cause indicated that among a segment of the young heterosexual population was the dawning awareness that something was wrong in the way society treated gays, and that they must help do something about it. It was surely not a social phenomenon, but it suggested a future in which homosexuals would not be altogether alone in their fight for social acceptance.

With representatives from fifty campuses across the country, the About Face conference reflected the new mood that was emerging among younger gay activists. Like the Queer Nationals in major urban areas, the new generation of activists were less preoccupied with AIDS issues and more firmly focused on returning the emphasis of lesbian and gay organizing to civil rights. Many had adopted confrontational in-your-face tactics. A subject of great discussion was the practice of "outing," in which activists revealed the names of covert gay public figures. Around classroom tables at the University of Minnesota student union, where the conference was held, young activists argued whether outing should be adopted among gays in the military. In her remarks to the conference Miriam Ben-Shalom "outed" a prominent university administrator who had not implemented the resolution of her faculty senate to kick ROTC off campus. The administrator, Ben-Shalom said, was a lesbian, and a hypocrite for not moving more aggressively against ROTC.

One contingent from a small liberal arts college in the West knew that the daughter of one of the nation's top Defense Department officials was a lesbian who had been active in her campus gay group, had herself considered coming out publicly and discussed that possibility with her father. (According to an unconfirmed and perhaps apocryphal story, her father, who was popular among conservatives and frequently mentioned as a future presidential candidate, had said, "Do what you think is right, but remember I do have a constituency.") Activists hoped that by "outing" the daughter—or at least threatening to do so—they could move the father to influence a change in Pentagon policies. Others argued that such a threat amounted to little more than political blackmail and would probably only stiffen resistance to reform. In the end, organizers opted against the tactic, in large part because the daughter was so popular among her college classmates.

The conference included workshops on more traditional lobbying strategies, outlining efforts in courts and through legislatures and the media to change the military policies. Other workshops analyzed which strategies worked best at large colleges versus small colleges, or liberal arts and technical schools.

By formulating a national strategy to focus attention on the issue of gays in the military, the conference, the first of its kind dedicated solely to this issue, spurred renewed activities against ROTC across the country in the months that followed. By April 1991, more than 120 campuses participated in a National Day of Action against ROTC. Though few campuses moved to abolish their ROTC programs, the threat was deemed great enough that Congressman Gerald Solomon introduced legislation in Congress to deny federal funds to any school that did not allow ROTC or military recruiters on its campus. A similar bill in the Illinois legislature passed easily, but was vetoed by the state's governor, who was then overridden by the state's General Assembly. Legislators in other states announced plans to introduce similar laws.

At the end of the day-long conference in Minneapolis, a group of conferees assembled a modest picket line at the University of Minnesota's ROTC building and posed for newspaper photographs and television interviews. Nearby, small knots of ROTC cadets watched the protesters suspiciously. What would happen to their scholarships if ROTC was disenfranchised? they asked. Why should they be made to suffer for policies they had no role in implementing? When asked how they felt about serving with gays once they were commissioned, the cadets fell into two camps. Some were adamantly opposed to serving with gays. "I don't want them staring at me in the shower," said one twenty-year-old cadet. "This is not like a regular job—in the military, you live where you work." Some cadets seemed resigned that policy would change, even though they were not enthusiastic at the prospect. Once in the military, they said, their job would be to follow orders. If new orders came through on homosexuals, they would obey them. None evinced wholehearted support for policy changes.

This cross-section of cadets watching the protest that day indicated that resistance to reform among many of the next generation of military officers would be strong. Idealists like Greg Teran were the exception, not the rule. Most heterosexual males remained uncomfortable with the notion of homosexuality, less because of a particular dislike for gays than for a fear of what accepting homosexuality as a norm would mean to the entire structure of what was accepted as masculine. The ideology of masculinity had remained a strong cultural imperative in the United States despite the best efforts of the gay and women's movements, perhaps because nothing had come along to replace the psychological anchor that imperative provided young males. The old ways were receding, but new ways to assert manhood, or more accurately personhood, had not yet taken shape, and many young men were lost, clinging to the old as if to a life preserver.

It seemed clear, watching these University of Minnesota cadets earnestly debate whether they should serve with gays, that whatever happened to the military's antihomosexual policy, even a presidential order to allow gays into the military would not mark the end of the campaign for acceptance of homosexuals in the armed forces; it would only be the beginning.

PROMISES TO KEEP

Never doubt that a small group of committed people can change the world. Indeed, it is very often the only thing that does.

—Margaret Mead

77

Politics and Prejudice
(Part 2)

THE FOUR SOLDIERS EYED the sky for any sign of Scud missiles. Iraqi president Saddam Hussein had promised to use chemical and biological warfare against the multinational force of over 500,000 arrayed against him in Saudi Arabia, so these soldiers from the Headquarters Battery of the 6th Battalion, 27th Field Artillery wore suffocating protective suits and peered from their gas masks, suffering the swelter of the desert. The four men, all stationed at Fort Sill, Oklahoma, were friends, including a young medic who had long ago confided to the others that he was gay. The night was so dark that the men could not even see each other. To assure themselves that they were still there, still alive, each man kept a hand on the other—on a shoulder, a leg, a back. And none of the three heterosexual soldiers seemed to mind that there, in that foxhole, one of the men touching them was a homosexual.

In the first major armed conflict since the birth of the gay rights movement a generation earlier, the Persian Gulf War expressed the anomalies and contradictions in the military's posture concerning gays that had persisted for decades, and pointed the way toward the future. As in World War II and Vietnam, the armed forces, needing warm bodies for combat, suddenly gained a new tolerance for gays. Reservist Donna Lynn Jackson was only the first to be told that she could serve in the war and be discharged later. Similar stories came from every branch of the military.

Once again, the military seemed less determined to rid the services of gays than to make it appear that no homosexuals served. The soldiers who did successfully gain their discharges after self-disclosure were largely those willing to publicize the fact that they were being kept in the fighting forces. Sgt. Sam Gallegos, mobilized as part of the Colorado National Guard, told his commander he was gay before the troop buildup, but the commander waited three months—until the day he learned that Gallegos had decided to contact the media—to discharge him. PFC Michael Dull was kept in the California National Guard for six months before the brass moved to separate him—after he gave a newspaper interview about being gay in the military. Although military media spokesmen insisted that the antihomosexual regulation was being strictly enforced, the actual policy was that the Department of Defense would discharge any gay soldier who went to the press.

The phenomenon was particularly striking in job categories the armed forces had difficulty filling, such as the medical field. The president of San Diego's gay veterans group was asked to reenlist in the active reserves so she could serve as a nurse. One Seattle reservist, a highly trained medical technician, was told bluntly that he could not be discharged unless he was willing to have his name on the front pages of local newspapers. Fearing publicity, he went to Saudi Arabia.

Some indiscreet officers even put the covert policy in writing. The *Commander's Handbook* distributed to reserve officers shortly after President Bush ordered reserve mobilization, instructed that no discharges for homosexuality could be granted once a unit was informed that it was about to be deployed. The Pentagon subsequently denied any policy shift on gays. At McChord Air Force Base in Washington, a lesbian reservist in the 40th Aeromedical Evacuation Squadron told her commanding officer she was gay, and the Air Force insisted that she produce a marriage license designating a woman as her spouse to prove it. No jurisdiction in the United States, of course, recognizes the legality of homosexual marriages. The fact that no jurisdiction in the United States recognizes the legality of same-sex marriages was beside the point.

When a Marine reservist claimed homosexuality and asked to be discharged, the Staff Judge Advocate's Office of the Marine Corps Reserve Support Center wrote that "claimed sexual preferences do not constitute an exemption from the mobilization process"—despite the explicit regulation to the contrary. Reservist after reservist declared homosexuality. "They don't want a coffin to be their final closet," Miriam Ben-Shalom explained. The gay press hailed these men and women as heroes, while Pentagon officials complained that these dramatic acts of conscience had not occurred until it appeared that the reservists might actually go someplace where they could be hurt.

At the Walter Reed Army Medical Center's AIDS program, Dr. Ed Tramont received a number of phone calls from commanders requesting that the policy banning HIV-positive soldiers from combat be waived for this or that GI. Among these commanders were some who had argued hotly for the discharge of HIV-infected soldiers during the AIDS debates of the mid-1980s. A lot had changed in the intervening years, Tramont thought.

The earlier purges of gay linguists had also taken a toll on the nation's military preparedness. Now, the military found itself short of Arabic translators. At least two linguists discharged for being gay were contacted by the National Security Agency at this time and asked to work on the agency's war effort. Still bitter over the government's treatment of them, the two men declined.

Once in the Mideast, gay soldiers found varying responses to their presence. One Navy corpsman was assigned to the front with the 6th Marine Division. Rumors about him spread. After a grizzled sergeant promised that he would be "the first to die" once shooting started, officers transferred him to a different unit. Those Marines had also heard the rumors, but to less effect. His new Marines befriended him and even nicknamed him "Precious," after the miniature poodle in the film *Silence of the Lambs*.

In other quarters, fiercely antigay attitudes still flourished. Marine corporal Don Gaines of the 2nd Supply Battalion remembers one Marine had told officers he was gay before being deployed to the Persian Gulf. He was allowed to go, but after the war, his commanding officer called him out of formation to denounce him. "This person wants to get out because he likes to suck dick," the commander said. Later, the corporal was discharged.

Purges continued stateside as well. Five soldiers were discharged during an investigation at the Defense Language Institute. Five Army lesbians, most of whom were stationed at Fort Lewis, were separated. Meanwhile, Pentagon spokesmen vehemently denied that the armed forces ever engaged in "witch-hunt" tactics.

Gay and lesbian soldiers in the combat zone continued to take precautions against detection. Lovers changed their names on the letters they sent from home, so the return address would indicate the appropriate gender. Hearing the plea that Americans write servicemen who might not have correspondents, Gene Barfield, the veteran who had held the gay Tupperware party when he was in the Navy, addressed his letters not to "any serviceman" but to "any gay serviceman." Surprisingly, he received several responses from gay soldiers, one of whom wrote, "Being here is like being a Jew in Berlin in 1941."

At home, lovers of deployed soldiers waited nervously. Some Metropolitan Community Church parishes, particularly those in military towns such as San Diego, offered support groups for "Gulf widows" similar to those that heterosexual spouses attended. At the front, some soldiers wrote farewell letters to lovers and carried them in their shirt pockets. Friends were instructed to find them and send them home if anything happened. Being neither a legal spouse nor a family member, a gay lover would not be notified by the Army in case of injury or death.

At the Friends Lounge across the street from Camp LeJeune, drag queen Danny Leonard was doing his part for the war effort. A Navy corpsman with access to a military computer in Saudi Arabia was providing him with a neatly typed and cleverly coded newsletter with updates on gay personnel on the front. Leonard made copies and distributed them at his bar, so his patrons could remail them to their friends serving in the Gulf.

Lesbian and gay veterans groups all around the U.S. were heartened by the publicity the gay issue was receiving and reasoned that change in the military policy was imminent. Once fighting was over and the military started kicking out "heroes" from the popular war, the public would be outraged. And liberal congressmen were ever more aggressive in their attacks on the policy, activists noted. There was no going back.

Optimism also spread among the gay troops. On the USS *Independence,* sailor Stephen Krug listened with awe when social workers started discussing the problems war veterans would face upon returning home. One matter-of-factly started his talk by saying things might be difficult with "your wife, your girlfriend, or your lover."

In the six months after the war, however, more than 1,000 gays and lesbians in uniform were discharged, including many who had told their commanders before they were deployed and had been allowed to serve. And among them was Stephen Krug.

The activists' optimism lacked historical perspective. African Americans, for example, had believed their service in World War I would change racial attitudes in the U.S. Instead, they returned to the same Jim Crow laws and prejudice. The German researcher Dr. Magnus Hirshfeld records that many gays joined the Kaiser's Army in World War I hoping that their service would inspire support for repealing that country's sodomy law. They too were wrong.

IN THE MONTHS FOLLOWING the Gulf War, the gay military issue gathered momentum. Court challenges to homosexual discharges mounted. Former Annapolis midshipman Joseph Steffan's case enjoyed a burst of publicity when the federal judge hearing arguments nonchalantly used the expression "homos." Steffan's attorneys asked to have the conservative jurist removed from the case, but an Appeals Court panel maintained that calling someone a "homo" did not signify prejudice. Ultimately, the judge, Oliver Gasch, ruled against Steffan, though his opinion contained relatively few arguments advanced by the Pentagon. Instead, Gasch declared his own reasons, saying homosexual discharges were necessary for public health reasons, because gay soldiers might spread AIDS. It was an argument that the government had never made. Steffan's lawyers remained convinced that the Appeals Court panel in Washington would rule not only to reinstate Steffan, but declare the gay regulation unconstitutional. Their optimism was justified; that's precisely what the panel did in November of 1993, assuring the fact that the Supreme Court ultimately would decide the issue, perhaps as early as 1994.

In the first months after the 100-hour ground war, the U.S. reveled in self-congratulations over its easy victory in Iraq. After all, America had won a war, thus expunging the subliminal fear that dated back to the Tet Offensive, a fear that the country had become less than potent. President Bush seemed to confirm this when he said that the win had helped the nation get over "the Vietnam thing." The politicians and the news media tended to gloss over the fact that the U.S. won so easily largely because the poorly disciplined enemy troops declined to fight back.

In the orgy of national narcissism that greeted returning troops, were all the parades so conspicuously missing at the end of the Vietnam War. Brushfire debates erupted in a number of cities when gay veterans groups sought to participate. In Denver veterans groups said they would allow a gay contingent to march in their parade—but only if they did not carry a sign identifying themselves as gay. In San Diego the city's bus company would not allow advertisements welcoming back gay and lesbian soldiers. Reporting on the event was Adam Gettinger-Brizuela, the survivor of the 1978 Vandenberg Air Force Base purge, who was now a journalist in Southern California. When the Military Freedom Project sought to run an ad in the *Army Times* to welcome home gay Gulf veterans, the newspaper refused to print it. And in his hometown of Raleigh, North Carolina, Armistead Maupin led a welcome-home march for gay vets right past the monument to fallen Confederate soldiers, a statue his own great-grandmother had raised funds to build.

Gay Gulf veterans were tapped to lead gay pride marches across the country. Although most already had been discharged, Air Force captain Greg Greeley was only one day away from the end of his service when he marched at the head of the gay parade in Washington. He gave interviews to the press and his picture appeared on the front page of the *Washington Post*. The next day, agents from the Office of Special Investigations responded by telling Greeley that his discharge, scheduled for that day, would be delayed until he provided the OSI with names of other gay service members. The agents also promised to contact Greeley's family and disclose that he was gay if he did not cooperate.

Apparently it did not occur to these investigators that someone who had just had his picture on the front page of major daily newspapers leading a gay march would not be likely to betray his gay friends or terribly afraid that Mom and Dad might find out he was gay. In fact, Greeley went back to the newspapers, who put the story of his interrogation on the front page. Secretary of Defense Cheney personally ordered that Greeley be discharged immediately. Pentagon spokesmen denied that it was routine for military investigators to gather names of gays when discharging a gay soldier. This was an aberration, they said.

Two significant events in 1991 set the stage for the drama that would unfold around the issue of gays in the military over the next two years. In August, *The Advocate* ran a story "outing" a very high-ranking civilian Pentagon official. The official, generally referred to in the press as a senior spokesman for the Defense Department, had worked at the right hand of Secretary Cheney for many years, and few believed that Cheney was uninformed of the man's orientation before the story appeared.

The mainstream press generally declined to identify the man, eschewing the newly popular gay practice of revealing the sexual orientation of people who would prefer to remain hidden. But aggressive promotion by the gay magazine ensured that there were several stories about a certain unnamed official. This led to an unprecedented event in the history of gays in the military: A Secretary of Defense admitted that homosexuals did serve in the armed forces.

In fact, in numerous interviews Cheney acknowledged that gays had always served, often honorably, but he tried to draw the distinction between a civilian serving on his senior staff and a soldier serving in a military environment where issues of order, discipline, and morale came into play. Cheney's defense of the military policy was anemic, however, and he frequently referred to it as something he "inherited" from previous administrations. As for the notion that gays were security risks, Cheney called it "sort of an old chestnut." As Congressman Barney Frank told one interviewer: "If Cheney defended the United States the way he defended this policy, we would have been captured by now—by Cuba." Nevertheless, Cheney's comments marked the first time in nearly a decade that anyone in the defense establishment had advanced any argument for the policy beyond the usual 123 words.

What was most remarkable about the outing was what it said about shifting attitudes toward gays. The gay Defense Department spokesman kept his job. According to one senior Pentagon official, Cheney brought the matter up personally with President Bush, who approved the man's retention. And there was the marvel of a Republican Secretary of Defense from the conservative wing of his party saying he did not care about the private lives of his closest aides.

The second major development for gays in the military in 1991 came in September when a Democratic presidential hopeful, Arkansas Governor Bill Clinton, appeared at Harvard University's John F. Kennedy School of Government, where someone asked him what he thought about the issue. There was no indecisiveness, hedging, or equivocation in his response: America could not afford to waste the talents of an entire group of people, he said. As President, he would lift the ban on gays and lesbians in the armed forces. Outside of the gay press, the pronouncement received very little attention.

With the issue now slowly edging itself into public discourse, many lesbians and gay men in uniform began rethinking their position. Recalling the impact African Americans had during the 1950s, when they refused to sit in the back of the bus or drink from separate fountains, some decided they could no longer participate in a system that would happily employ them—but only if they kept quiet. Lieutenant (j.g.) Tracey Thorne, a Norfolk-based Navy fighter pilot, was among the first, appearing on "Good Morning America" in mid-1992 to announce that yes, he was gay and he wanted to stay in the military.

With each passing month, more lesbian and gay soldiers began stepping forward; for much of 1991 and 1992 it seemed one could not turn on a morning talk show or evening network news broadcast without some new soldier declaring his or her sexual orientation. This proved a significant trend. The discharge of Col. Margrethe Cammermeyer, the head nurse for the Washington National Guard, drew immense attention, with even her commanding general shedding tears, saying that the policy that forced him to move against the woman was contrary to his own wishes. The antihomosexual policy had succeeded for so long in part because gays so rarely fought back—the military had enjoyed the sanction of the victim. Now the sanction was slowly beginning to crumble.

ELECTION DAY
NOVEMBER 3RD, 1992

THOUSANDS POURED ONTO CASTRO STREET, cheering and hugging each other, climbing on the roofs of city buses, and dancing to the disco music blaring from the back end of a flatbed truck. It was too good to be true— Bill Clinton was going to be the next President of the United States. For the first time in U.S. history, the President would be a man who appeared to harbor no prejudice against lesbians and gay men. In fact, by election day Clinton had endorsed virtually the entire litany of gay political demands, including support for a federal gay rights bill and increased AIDS funding. Clinton had spoken at numerous gay fund-raisers and talked poignantly about the need for the country to cherish all its citizens. To many gay audiences he seemed to be the first politician to truly understand gay issues and to have worked out his own rationale for gay rights, rather than have it handed to him on three-by-five note cards prepared by some aide. Virtually every speaker at the Democratic National Convention included gays and lesbians among the traditional Democratic constituencies whose rights needed to be safeguarded.

CLINTON'S STRATEGY OF PURSUING the gay vote more aggressively than any other major-party nominee in history proved profitable. Gay politicos walked precincts in the crucial urban areas he needed to carry, especially in California, and gay men and lesbians donated $3 million to his campaign. Television exit polls of voters, which now included breakdowns of heterosexual and homosexual voters, just as they long had for other demographic groups, found that three-quarters of gay voters said they supported Clinton. And to the amazement of the gays dancing in the streets of San Francisco, New York, and West Hollywood, he had actually won. In this small way the promise of America, the pledge that the nation was committed to justice and equality that they had all learned in civic classes, seemed fulfilled.

There was a second component to the joyousness. It was not just that the Democrats had won; it was also that the Republicans had lost. This was important to gays because the GOP had developed a particularly nasty antigay streak in the 1992 election, as moderate voters shifted from Bush to Clinton, and Bush sought to shore up the one constituency he could count on—conservative religious groups.

At the Republican party's convention in Houston, speakers denounced "special privileges" being sought by the "militant homosexual lobby," a force that they described as something of a dark fifth column quietly seizing control of public policy. Nearly one-sixth of the GOP delegates were from Pat Robertson's Christian Coalition, a politically sophisticated organization that was emerging as a potent political force. At the convention, fundamentalist Christians dominated both the speakers platforms and state delegations. Administration officials usually left the most virulent attacks to speakers like Robertson and columnist Pat Buchanan, who claimed gays were on the other side of a "cultural and religious war" that was being waged in the U.S. Even Vice President Dan Quayle weighed in with his opinions on the etiology of homosexuality. Were gays part of a minority that deserved civil rights protection? he was asked. "It's more of a choice than a biological situation," he said. "I think it is a wrong choice."

The new Republican preoccupation was "family values," a code word that became for gays what "law and order" had been for blacks during the 1960s and 1970s. While conventioneers waved signs bearing slogans such as "Family Values, Forever—Gay Rights, Never," the conclave passed a platform specifically opposing gay civil rights laws at any level of government. "We must not remain neutral toward our Judeo-Christian heritage," the platform said. The contrast to the rhetoric at the Democratic convention could not have been starker.

Although gays were the subject of some of the most fiery bravado among Republicans, the elections also marked the culmination of a generation of cultural conflict over issues of gender. The two conflicting political trends—the theocratic inclinations of conservatives on one hand and the humanism of liberals on the other—were joined in direct battle at last. For Republicans, Hillary Rodham Clinton became the subject of intense scrutiny because she made it clear that she would be a working first lady who addressed serious social issues rather than the innocuous apple-pie causes usually taken up by presidents' wives. Even a television character named Murphy Brown came under family values fire when she decided to have a child out of wedlock. The immorality was being sponsored by the "cultural elite," the Vice President said. And the Republican party platform called for a constitutional amendment banning all abortions—even for women who were the victims of rape or incest. Even the most strident conservative politicians rarely had taken such an extreme stance.

Meanwhile, across the country, Republican as well as Democratic women who favored the feminist agenda grew more aggressive. Record numbers were running for public office, and women's political action committees were raising substantial sums to back them. After the rhetorical excesses of the Republican convention, affluent suburban voters, who had been content to vote their pocketbook in the 1980s, were ready to do more in the 1990s. An attack solely against gays might have proven politically successful, but when gay rights became entangled with critiques of Murphy Brown and teenage incest victims being forced to have babies, the attack proved a political liability. For voters who had supported Reagan and Bush largely because of the promise of low taxes, the rhetoric was unsettling and sounded extremist.

For gays, the tenor of the Republican campaign was thoroughly terrifying. When the networks began projecting a Clinton win in the early evening of Election Day, euphoric lesbians and gay men cheered.

The crowds had high expectations for the new President. Some of his promises on the gay agenda would have to be approved by Congress, which was not likely to happen. There were only a handful that could be accomplished solely by presidential fiat. Clinton could, for example, lift the ban on gays in the military by simply signing an executive order, and that, gay aides to Clinton maintained, was exactly what was going to happen, perhaps as early as Inauguration Day.

At the Clinton camp, top aides did not believe the reform would cause much of a ruckus. When one gay politico active in the Democratic campaign was asked about possible controversy over lifting the military ban, he said that the new President could simply slip the order into a stack of other executive orders on controversial issues, and it would not stand out. "It won't be a big deal," he said.

NOVEMBER 12, 1992
VETERANS DAY
LITTLE ROCK, ARKANSAS

BARELY A WEEK AFTER THE ELECTION, a reporter asked Clinton if he still planned to fulfill his campaign promise to allow gays to serve, and Clinton responded affirmatively. The fact that the holidays were approaching, the slowest news time of the year, ensured that the comment would achieve front-page status. Clinton's position had been no secret; he had repeated it at candidates' forums and media appearances for over a year. But national political reporters rarely took gay rights seriously, so they had paid it little attention. Politicians always made campaign promises they had no intention of keeping, and most pundits assumed that this would be one of them.

When it was understood that Clinton might actually keep the pledge, the news hit Washington like a hydrogen bomb. Not since General Douglas MacArthur challenged President Truman during the Korean War had there been such a brazen challenge by military leaders to the civilian political leadership in nominal control of the armed forces. Joint Chiefs Chairman General Colin Powell repeated his earlier antihomosexual position. His statements so precisely mirrored what white generals had said in support of racial segregation a half century earlier that some younger military officers believed he was being facetious. He was not.

According to some reports, Powell was planning to resign so as not to spend the last eight months of his tenure enforcing a liberalized homosexual policy. Two other members of the Joint Chiefs reportedly threatened to resign if the gay ban was dropped. Others predicted mass resignations of officers and senior enlisted personnel who would refuse to work with lesbian or gay soldiers. The threat of resignations was more bluff than real, but it made good copy. Retired colonel David Hackworth, a rabid opponent of allowing gays in the military and a frequent writer on military affairs for *Newsweek,* wrote that he had heard that if Clinton showed his face on certain military posts, he was likely to be shot.

The various military constituencies and lobbying groups sprang into action. Veterans organizations, such as the American Legion and Veterans of Foreign Wars, immediately denounced Clinton's intention. From the pulpit and on religious television shows, fundamentalist leaders urged their congregations to mobilize and lodge their complaints with Congress and the White House. Radio talk shows encouraged their listeners to do the same. The strategy worked. The Capitol received 400,000 phone calls a day on the issue—and they ran twenty-to-one against lifting the ban, although most public opinion polls showed a near even split on the issue among the general public.

The conservative rhetoric grew fierce. Most of the talk focused on the old saws: good order, discipline, morale, and whether the presence of gays would hurt recruiting. Supporters of the ban talked darkly of showers and bathrooms where gay men would seduce young recruits. The debate was a barometer of the persistence of the old stereotypes of gay men as sexual predators. Lesbians were hardly discussed at all.

At least one member of the Joint Chiefs distributed copies of the videotape *The Gay Agenda* to other generals. Produced by a new right religious group, the video included the most lascivious scenes from one of San Francisco's Gay Freedom Day Parades: naked men dancing on floats and sadomasochists parading their finest leather. This was what gays wanted to introduce to the military, New Right leaders warned. Conservative commentators Rowland Evans and Robert Novak wrote that the proposed reform represented "gay culture being imposed on the military by political edict."

A flurry of other events contributed to the drama of the moment. One was House Armed Services chair Les Aspin's appointment as Secretary of Defense over Sam Nunn, chair of the Senate Armed Services Committee. Having learned of former Army captain Greg Baldwin and another gay man, both of whom had been asked to leave Nunn's staff when the senator found out they were homosexual, gay groups had lobbied vigorously against Nunn. Although other factors undoubtedly came into play, Nunn had little fondness for the minority group that had helped him lose the job he long had coveted. It was conventional wisdom that no reform could pass out of the Senate without Nunn's support, and the senior senator from Georgia did not seem inclined to enfranchise gays.

Faced with a wall of opposition, Clinton began to falter. Aides feared what the reform might mean to Clinton's relationship with the Pentagon, already shaky because of the perception that he had been a draft dodger. The President-elect soon conceded that he would not sign an order until he had consulted with the Joint Chiefs. When gay leaders expressed concern, White House aides assured them that the talks would not be about whether to change the policy, but how. When his concession did not assuage ban supporters, Clinton suggested that gay troops might be segregated from other soldiers. No one from either side of the debate thought much of that idea, and it was quickly dropped.

Congressional pressure on Clinton increased. Senator Nunn began talking about sponsoring legislation to seal the ban into law. If Nunn decided not to, Senator Robert Dole, the Republican leader, pledged that he would. Senate Democratic majority leader George Mitchell estimated he could muster thirty Senate votes at best to support lifting the ban. Congressmen were eager to put the issue behind them. For its part, the Washington press corps quickly pronounced Clinton's plan a major blunder that was distracting attention from economic issues.

Still, gay organizers believed they could win one-third of Senate and House members to their cause, enough to block an attempt to sustain a presidential veto. But then the White House put out the word privately: President Clinton would not veto a bill banning gays from the military. Lesbian and gay lobbyists would now have to get the support of the majority of Congress if they were to win.

Meanwhile, more drama: Allen Schindler, a twenty-two-year-old gay sailor stationed on the USS *Belleau Wood* was murdered by two shipmates. His skull was crushed, all but two of his ribs were broken, and his genitals were mutilated. The motive: His shipmates had learned he was gay. Partisans on both sides of the issue seized on the case. Gay leaders said it demonstrated the net effect of a policy that indoctrinated heterosexuals to distrust and despise gays. Supporters of the policy said it proved that heterosexuals would not serve peaceably with gays. It became an article of faith during the next months of debate that allowing homosexuals in the military would lead to violence and more killings. There was a curious logic to using this as an argument to exclude gays. It indicated that military brass believed that soldiers with nonconforming sexual orientation were a greater danger than heterosexual troops who were potential murderers.

In December the Department of Defense asked the U.S. Supreme Court to overturn a pro-homosexual ruling in the case of Army captain Carolyn (Dusty) Pruitt. The Federal Appeals Court had required the Pentagon to provide a rational basis for the homosexual regulations. The

Defense Department maintained that the policy was only common sense and that no more than the 123-word explanation was necessary. The Supreme Court did not agree. The Pentagon must give the Appeals Court their rationale, the high court said.

On January 28, 1993, Federal Judge Terry Hatter, Jr., delivered another blow to the policy when he ordered the Navy to reinstate Petty Officer Keith Meinhold, a sonar operator who was among those to come out publicly in 1992. Hatter also ordered the Pentagon to stop enforcing the policy altogether, saying it was based on "cultural myths and false stereotypes."

In spite of this, fearful of the threat that Congress would quickly enact a gay ban, the administration hammered out a deal with House and Senate leaders. If Nunn agreed to hold off introducing a bill mandating homosexual exclusion, Clinton would delay his decision on the issue for six months. That gave the Defense Department until July 15 to issue a Pentagon policy on the issue. Meanwhile, recruiters were to stop asking applicants if they were gay, investigations would cease, and there would be no discharges based solely on a person's status as a homosexual.

Though neither side was happy with the "compromise," as it was called by both the administration and the media, Nunn agreed to it. Upon further examination, there was less to the concord than met the eye. Not asking recruits about their sexuality would make little practical difference since few applicants ever told the truth anyway. While discharges technically were halted, gay soldiers, if discovered, were transferred to the inactive ready reserve. They were still in the military, but in reality they had lost their jobs, their pay, their housing, and all their base privileges. Pentagon officials said this would probably be the shape of the final policy as well. They dubbed it "Don't Ask, Don't Tell."

The "compromise" quieted but did not quell the controversy. Senator Nunn began hearings of the Senate Armed Services Committee, which was overwhelmingly opposed to reform. While he promised a "fair and open" inquiry that would objectively hear both sides, it soon became clear that the hearings were hopelessly weighted in support of the homosexual ban. Opponents of gays outnumbered backers in all the testimony. Nunn's staff simply would not allow the gay faction's most persuasive speakers to testify. When former Senator Barry Goldwater, himself a former Armed Services chairman, requested that he be allowed to speak in favor of lifting the ban, he was told he could not be scheduled.

Perhaps the most farcical aspect of the hearings was Nunn's moving them to military bases and ships, ostensibly to hear the soldiers' side of the issue. Gays claimed that these hearings were so well choreographed that even the audiences were selected to ensure that all but a handful present were against allowing gays to serve. Of course, anyone with even a vague knowledge of the military understood that no junior enlisted man was going to tell a hearing or a reporter that he opposed the Joint Chiefs—

78

Tom Dooley's
Honorable Discharge

JANUARY 20, 1961
ST. LOUIS, MISSOURI

IT WAS A BITTER COLD DAY in St. Louis, but hundreds had come for the funeral mass. President Eisenhower had sent a message of condolence. The Pope had authorized a special pontifical requiem mass.

It seemed that all of America attended Dr. Tom Dooley in the weeks before he died. Newspapers published near-daily reports on the status of his health. Dooley himself issued optimistic statements that he was feeling fine, but in the last week he deteriorated rapidly. Cardinal Spellman was a frequent visitor in spite of his aides' discouraging the visits, warning of rumors that Dooley was a homosexual. There were rumors about the Cardinal as well.

Nevertheless, the two remained close friends. It was Spellman who had introduced Tom Dooley to John Kennedy, and Kennedy, citing inspiration from Dooley's work, would found the Peace Corps on March 1.

The Surgeon General of the Navy made an official visit to Dooley's bedside two days before he died to present him with what he had sought since he had been separated from the Navy years before—his honorable discharge. But most of his friends believed Dooley was too sedated to be aware of the largely symbolic gesture.

Dooley died on the day before John Kennedy's swearing-in as President of the United States. It is unclear whether he knew that his country had forgiven him at last.

Years later, Retired Lieutenant Commander Ted Werner recalled the last moments he spent with Dooley, saying good-bye at the airport in Vientiane, Laos. Werner knew that Dooley was returning to America to die; if his work had not required that he remain in Laos to fly for Dooley's group, he would have accompanied him.

It was a strange afternoon, Werner remembered, because Dooley, who rarely discussed his sexuality with anyone, confided in him about the disgrace he had felt when he was discharged from the Navy. It was a disgrace that had followed him ever since, he said, and he knew that if, after his death, it became known what he had been discharged for, then all the good that he had accomplished in his lifetime would be forgotten. "All they'll remember is that I was queer," he told Werner.

This was, after all, the message Dooley and millions of other homosexual Americans had heard for generations. No matter what good deeds he did, his God would damn him; no matter how well he championed patriotism, his country would disgrace him. This ultimately was the point of the armed forces' regulations—they had little to do with military goals and everything to do with a culture enforcing millennia-old taboos. No matter what the content of his character, Dooley, like millions of others, would always be identified as queer; they were unworthy.

As Dooley prepared to board the Pan Am flight that had been outfitted to receive him on a gurney, he said good-bye to Werner, and recited a part of his favorite poem to his friend:

"The woods are lovely, dark, and deep," he said,

"But I have promises to keep,
And miles to go before I sleep,
And miles to go before I sleep."

NOTES AND BIBLIOGRAPHY

NOTES ON SOURCES

Each book of *Conduct Unbecoming* will be treated as a separate entity. All cited materials included in more than one book will be completely cited at first appearance in any book. The majority of interviews cited herein were conducted between 1989 and January 1993; interviews were conducted both in person and by telephone. Interview references are cited once per chapter at first appearance, except when previously cited information on a specific event, person, or case is used in a different context or for a different purpose than in the original citation. Generally, neither date nor place of any anonymous interview will be given in order to protect my sources. Articles or a series of articles by a specific person are referenced by the author's entire name at first occurrence in any paragraph; subsequent references in the same paragraph are by last name only. Unless otherwise indicated, all unpublished sources are from The Randy Shilts Collection, to be donated to the Gay and Lesbian Archives of the San Francisco Public Library. Hundreds of books were used in researching this work, and many of the publications not cited in these source notes are listed in the bibliography. A listing of those people who were interviewed for background purposes may be found at the end of these notes. I'd like to acknowledge the contribution of Mike Hippler, whose book *Matlovich, The Good Soldier* provided me with a wealth of information on Leonard Matlovich's life and thoughts.

PROLOGUE: THE DANGEROUS DIFFERENCE (1778–1954)

Baron von Steuben. Wayne R. Dynes, Warren Johansson, William A. Percy, and Stephen Donaldson (editors), *Encyclopedia of Homosexuality* (New York: Garland Publications, 1990). John McAuley Palmer, *General von Steuben* (Port Washington NY: Kennikat Press, 1966). Jonathan Katz, *Gay American History: Lesbians and Gay Men in the U.S.A.* (New York: Thomas Y. Crowell Company, 1976).

Lieutenant Gotthold Frederick Enslin. National Archives Microfilm Collection: Revolutionary War Company Payroll of Malcolm's Regiment 1777–1778. The Muster Rolls for Malcolm's Regiment, December 1777–February 1778. Papers of Aaron Burr Microfilm Collection: Orderly book as commander of Malcolm's Continental Regiment, 3 March 1778. *Valley Forge Orderly Book of General George Weedon of the Continental Army under Command of General George Washington, in the Campaign of 1777* (New York: Dodd, Mead and Company, 1902). Francis B. Heitman, *Historical Register of Officers of the Continental Army during The War of the Revolution April 1775 to December 1783* (Washington DC: The Rare Book Shop Publishing Company, Inc., 1914). Charles H. Lesser, (ed.), *The Sinews of Independence: Monthly Strength Reports of the Continental Army* (Chicago: University of Chicago Press, 1976). James C. Neagles, *Summer Soldiers, A Survey and Index of Revolutionary War Courts-Martial* (Salt Lake City UT: Ancestry, Inc., 1980). Mark Mayo Boatner III, *Encyclopedia of the American Revolution* (New York: David McKay Co., Inc., 1974). Fremont Rider (editor), *The American Genealogical-Biographical Index to American Genealogical, Biographical and Local History Materials,* Volume 51 (Middletown CT: The Godfrey Memorial Library, 1965). Professor I. Daniel Rupp, *A Collection of Upwards of Thirty Thousand Names of German, Swiss, Dutch, French and other Immigrants in Pennsylvania from 1727 to 1776* (Baltimore: Genealogical Publishing Company, 1965).

Stephen Decatur. Irvin Anthony, *Decatur* (New York: Charles Scribner's Sons, 1931). James Fenimore Cooper, *Lives of Distinguished American Naval Officers* (Philadelphia: Carey and Hart, 1846). Susan Wheeler Decatur, *Documents relative to the claim of Mrs. Decatur, with her earnest request that the gentlemen of Congress will take the trouble to read them* (Washington DC: J.C. Dunn, printer, 1826). Charles Lee Lewis, *The Romantic Decatur* (Philadelphia: University of Pennsylvania Press; London: Oxford University Press, 1937). Helen

Duprey Bullock (senior editor), *Decatur House* (Washington DC: National Trust for Historic Preservation in the United States, 1967). Glenn Tucker, *Dawn Like Thunder: The Barbary Wars and the Birth of the U.S. Navy* (Indianapolis and New York: The Bobbs-Merrill Company, Inc., 1963). Samuel Putnam Waldo, *The Life and Character of Stephen Decatur; late commodore and post-captain in the Navy of the United States, and navy-commissioner: interspersed with brief notices of the origin, progress, and achievements of the American Navy* (Middletown CT: Clark & Lyman, 1821). Smithsonian Institution Document from the Museum of American History, Department of United States Naval History: The History of the Somers and Decatur Memorial Ring.

Civil War Gays and Lesbians. Katz, *Gay American History*, op. cit.

Major General Cleburne. Capt. Irving A. Buck (Assistant Adjutant General, Cleburne's Division, C.S.A.), and Thomas Robson Hay (editor), *Cleburne and His Command* (Jackson TN: McCowat-Mercer Press, Inc., 1959). John Francis Maguire, M.P., *The Irish in America* (London: Longmans, Green, and Co., 1868).

Mrs. Nash. Katz, *Gay American History*, op. cit.

Articles of War. Major Jeffrey Davis, "Military Policy Toward Homosexuals: Scientific, Historical, and Legal Perspectives," *Military Law Review*, Vol. 131, 1991.

"Recruiting the elements . . ." Jonathan Katz, *Gay/Lesbian Almanac, a New Documentary* (New York: Harper & Row, Publishers, 1983).

Newport RI Investigation. Lawrence R. Murphy, *Perverts by Official Order, The Campaign Against Homosexuals by the United States Navy* (New York: Harrington Park Press, 1988).

World War II and McCarthy. Allan Bérubé, *Coming Out Under Fire, The History of Gay Men and Women in World War Two* (New York: The Free Press, 1990). Allan Bérubé and John D'Emilio, "The Military and Lesbians During the McCarthy Years," *Signs: Journal of Women in Culture and Society,* Summer 1984, pp. 759–775.

BOOK ONE: THE SANCTION OF THE VICTIM (1954–1969)

1. *What Tom Dooley Really Wanted: A Prologue to Vietnam*

Thomas A. Dooley, M.D. *Doctor Tom Dooley, My Story* (New York: Ariel Books, 1962).

Edwin Bicksford Hooper, Dean C. Allard and Oscar D. Fitzgerald, *The United States Navy and the Vietnam Conflict Vol. 1.* (Washington DC: Naval History Division, Department of the Navy, 1976).

William Lederer Interview (Vermont, 1991).

Diana Shaw Interviews (Los Angeles CA, 1990–1992).

Ted Werner Interviews (Los Angeles CA, 1990–1992).

Dooley Document: Department of the Navy Memo, From: Director of Naval Intelligence, Chief of Naval Personnel, Subject: Lieutenant Thomas A. Dooley III, USNR.

CIA/FBI Opinion of Dooley. Diana Shaw, "The Temptation of Tom Dooley." *Los Angeles Times Magazine,* 15 December 1991, p. 43. Documents also from the FBI and CIA files.

Dr. Wayne McKinney Interview (Honolulu HI, 1990).

2. *Manhood*

Robert "Jess" Jessop Documents: "One Veteran's Remembrances," a speech given to the San Diego Veterans Association on 15 November 1986. U.S. Navy records including: History of assignments 21 November 1961–16 June 1967; reports of enlisted performance evaluation from 17 May 1964–16 May 1967; Good Conduct Award; certification as Hospital Corpsman, Pharmacy Technician, Field Medical Service Technician; Honorable Discharge from the U.S. Navy dated 20 November 1967. Jessop Letter: Fragment letter from Jessop to Pat Katka, his cousin, dated March 1967 re Vietnam firefight. Jessop Letter: From Mrs. Harry R. Lynn dated 12 July 1967 re how Jessop saved her son's life. Towson High *1957 Sidelights,* Jessop's high school yearbook. Correspondence with George A. Murphy, executor of Jessop's Estate; Pat Katka, Jessop's cousin; Kate Johnson for Lesbian-Gay Archives of San Diego.

"In a survey . . ." Richard G. Druss, "Cases of Suspected Homosexuality Seen at an Army Mental Hygiene Consultation Service," *Psychiatric Quarterly,* January 1967, pp 62–70.

"Among the causes . . ." Dr. Magnus Hirschfeld, *The Sexual History of the World War* (New York: Cadillac Publishing Co., 1941), p. 127.

"The gesture is . . ." from Jessop letter to Pat Katka, op. cit.

3. *Rules*

Danny Flaherty Interviews (San Francisco CA, 1990–1992). Danny Flaherty Documents: Northern Illinois University transcript, second semester 1964–65. FOIA request to Northern Illinois University and letter from Gary L. Shilts, an attorney in Aurora, IL.

Robert "Jess" Jessop Documents, op. cit.

Gay Cruising in Vietnam. Pax Vobiscum, "Gay life is there, Vietnam GI says, but you have to be careful," *The Advocate,* 26 May–8 June 1971, pp. 10, 19. Also, Vobiscum, "Those tough Green Berets: orgies with an S&M touch," *The Advocate,* 9–22 June 1971.

Dave Dupree Interview (Atlanta GA, 1990).

Gerald Rosanbalm Interviews (New York NY, 1990–1992).

Gary Milo Interviews (Brooklyn NY, 1990–1991).

Mary Hall Interviews (Rockwall TX, 1990–1992). Mary Hall Documents: U.S. Army Officer Efficiency Reports from 13 November 1966–12 November 1967.

4. The Spy

Danny Flaherty Interviews, op. cit.

Operation Cedar Falls. Edward Doyle, Samuel Lipsman, and the Editors of the Boston Publishing Company, *The Vietnam Experience: America Takes Over* (Boston: Boston Publishing Company, 1982), pp. 90–121.

"A decisive turning . . ." Doyle and Lipsman, *The Vietnam Experience: America Takes Over*, op. cit.

Jim Spahr Interview (Sonoma County CA, 1990).

FOIA Document: Memo from U.S. Navy Chief of Naval Personnel to Commanding Officer, Fleet Intelligence Center, Pacific, San Francisco, Subject: Eligibility for Security Clearance in the Case of an Identified Individual, 10 April 1967.

"I am absolutely certain . . ." Clark Dougan, Samuel Lipsman, and the Editors of the Boston Publishing Company, *The Vietnam Experience: A Nation Divided* (Boston: Boston Publishing Company, 1984), p. 127.

Gerald Rosanbalm Interviews, op. cit. Rosanbalm FOIA Documents including over 1,000 pages of personnel records, transfer records, medical records, interrogation records, CID reports, confiscated personal letters and other materials. Selected documents from this collection will be referenced where appropriate.

5. A Name on the Wall

Gerald Rosanbalm Interviews, op. cit.

Mary Hall Interviews, op. cit.

Tet Offensive. From contemporary accounts appearing in *Time, Newsweek,* and *The New York Times,* 25 January 1968–5 February 1968.

"The mighty U.S. . . ." "The Generals Gamble," *Time,* 15 February 1968, pp. 15–16, 22–32.

"A complete failure . . ." Max Frankel, "Johnson Says Foe's Raids Are a Failure Militarily," *The New York Times,* 3 February 1968, sec. 1 p. 1 col. 8.

Dougan and Lipsman, *The Vietnam Experience: A Nation Divided,* op. cit., p. 127.

Antiwar Sentiment. Lynda Rosen Obst (editor), *The Sixties* (New York: Random House/Rolling Stone Press Books, 1977).

6. Convenience of the Government (Part I)

Perry Watkins Interviews (Tacoma WA, 1990–1992). Perry Watkins Documents include over 500 pages of letters, military records, military citations, court records, and other related materials. Selected documents from this collection will be referenced where appropriate. Perry Watkins Document: Induction papers were found in Summary of Proceedings, Board of Officers, Unsuitability Hearing, Department of the Army, 44th Engineer Battalion, Camp Mercer, Korea, 14 October 1975.

Draft Statistics. Dougan and Lipsman, *The Vietnam Experience: A Nation Divided,* op. cit., pp. 29, 72–80.

"The presence of homosexuals . . ." Peter Bart, "War Role Sought For Homosexuals," *The New York Times,* 17 April 1966, p. 10.

Don Slater Telephone Interviews and Correspondence (1991–1992). Don Slater Letter: To Randy Shilts, Concerning homosexuals and the draft, 11 February 1991.

"Because of the growing . . ." Don Slater, "Homosexuals Secretly Admitted into the Armed Forces," Press Release from the Committee to Fight Exclusion of Homosexuals from the Armed Forces, Los Angeles, 28 February 1968.

"Overt feminine behavior . . ." "Homosexuality: The Draft and the Armed Forces," *Draft Help,* NOH Directions Press.

Hoaxosexual. "How Faked Faggotry Can Lead to Your Honorable Discharge," *The Realist,* August 1969, p. 11.

Chevy Chase. Sherry Gershon Gottlieb, *Hell No, We Won't Go* (New York: Viking, 1991), pp. 95–6.

"If you wish to serve . . ." "What Should I Do About the Draft?" Community Services Committee of the Society of Individual Rights, 1967.

Draft Statistics. Compilation of statistics by author from various sources.

Darryl West Interview (Los Angeles CA, 1991). Darryl West FOIA Document: Enlistment Record 29 June 1967. Darryl West Documents: DD214, 9 November 1969.

Dennis Seely. From a series of interviews conducted between 1991 and 1992 with the primary interview for this book having been conducted in San Francisco CA, 1991.

Herbert Lotz Interview (Santa Fe NM, 1991).

Walter Jeff Boler Interview (Honolulu HI, 1990).

Defense Department Regulations. *Draft Help,* op. cit.

Navy Statistics 1963–1969. FOIA Document: Memorandum for Colonel Lucy from G. H. Hood, Capt. U.S. Navy, Assistant Chief for Performance, Bureau of Naval Personnel, Subj: SECNAVINST 1900.9, 21 May 1971. Author's note: Statistical information for the years 1960–1969 are widely inconsistent. Reliable information is not available.

Allan Bérubé, *Coming Out Under Fire, The History of Gay Men and Women in World War Two* (New York, The Free Press, 1990).

Korean War Era Statistics. Martin S. Weinberg and Colin J. Williams, *Homosexuals and the Military: A Study of the Less Than Honorable Discharge* (New York: Harper & Row, 1971), p. 49.

7. Days of Future Passed

Gerald Rosanbalm Interviews, op. cit.

Cultural References. Obst, *The Sixties*, op. cit.

"I am very proud of . . ." Gerald Rosanbalm Documents: Letter from Lyndon Baines Johnson to First Lieutenant Gerald L. Rosanbalm, 8 March 1968.

Mike Hippler, *Matlovich, The Good Soldier* (Boston: Alyson Publications, 1989).

Leonard Matlovich Interviews, 1975–1988.

Mary Hall Interviews, op. cit. Mary Hall Document: Citation by the Direction of the President, The Bronze Star Medal is Presented to Captain Mary A. Hall, Army Nurse Corps, United States Army, For Service in Republic of Vietnam, November 1966–June 1968.

Danny Flaherty Interviews, op. cit.

8. Home Front

Perry Watkins Interviews, op. cit.

Roberto Reyes-Colon Interview (Portland OR, 1991).

Walter Jeff Boler Interviews, op. cit.

Perry Watkins Documents: Watkins induction papers, op. cit. Criminal Investigation Division Report of Investigation, Ft. Belvoir Field Office, 12th MP OP (CI), Ft. Belvoir VA, 10 November 1968–17 January 1969.

Ending the Draft. "Nine Senators Propose Bill to Abolish Draft," *The New York Times*, 23 January 1969, p. 1 col. 8. William M. Beecher, "New Study by Pentagon on Ending Draft Urged," *The New York Times*, 24 January 1969, p. 3 col 1. "Volunteer Army Opposed in Poll," *The New York Times*, 26 January 1969, p. 27 col. 1. Robert B. Semple, Jr., "Nixon Seeks Plan to Replace Draft with Volunteers," *The New York Times*, 31 January 1969, p. 1 col. 8.

ROTC. "Yale Faculty Votes to End Credit for ROTC Work," *The New York Times*, 31 January 1969, p. 1 col. 5.

Oak Room Incident & Women's Movement. Marcia Cohen, *The Sisterhood: The Inside Story of the Women's Movement and the Leaders Who Made It Happen* (New York: Ballantine Books, 1988), pp. 13–22.

Gerald Rosanbalm Interviews, op. cit.

9. The Sanction of the Victim

Gerald Rosanbalm. Gerald Rosanbalm Interviews, op. cit. Gerald Rosanbalm Documents: Report of Information, Munich Station, 766th Military Intelligence Detachment, 66th Military Intelligence Group, Major William E. Twitty (No Date). Request For Authorization to Conduct Subject Interview, Deputy Chief of Staff Intelligence, United States Army Europe, 66th Military Intelligence, Colonel Robert W. Williams, 18 March 1969. CID reports on same incident. Karel Rohan, Witness Statement, 16 May 1969. Return of an Officer to CONUS Under Exceptional Circumstances, 19 March 1969. "Subject's foreign service tour . . ." Gerald Rosanbalm Document: Document Between General McChristian and General Cassidy to 66th MI GP Munich Germany From Department of the Army Staff Communications Division.

"Because he has occupied . . ." Gerald Rosanbalm Document: Document From Commanding Officer 66th MI Group Munich Germany to CINCUSAREUR Heidelberg, Germany.

Armistead Maupin Interview (San Francisco CA, 1991).

Roberto Reyes-Colon Interview, op. cit.

Stonewall and Rise of Gay Militancy. All unattributed references and relative quotes, including gay antiwar statements, are from Donn Teal, *The Gay Militants* (New York: Stein and Day, 1971).

"They've lost that wounded look," Teal, *The Gay Militants*, op. cit.

Mainstream Cultural References, 1969. Obst, *The Sixties*, op. cit.

Matlovich in Vietnam. Mike Hippler, *Matlovich, The Good Soldier*, op. cit. Leonard Matlovich Interviews, op. cit.

Gay Liberation Front Signs. "Gay Liberation Peace March," *Berkeley Barb*, November 1969.

BOOK TWO: INTERROGATIONS (1969–1975)

10. National Security

Gerald Rosanbalm Interviews (New York NY, 1990–1992).

"Subject was proud to be . . ." Gerald Rosanbalm Documents: Agent Report, 66th MIGP Repository, 25 March 1969.

"Numerous interviews with coworkers . . ." Gerald Rosanbalm Documents: Priority to Thomas O. Hutchinson, 29 September 1969.

"Based on the assessment . . ." Gerald Rosanbalm Documents: Subject Rosanbalm, Gerald L. Cpt. To

Assistant Chief of Staff for Intelligence, Department of the Army from Deputy Chief of Staff Intelligence: William C. Jennings, Special Assistant CI Division.

Gerald Rosanbalm Documents: Letter to Richard Nixon, 4 September 1969.

"Concern here is if subject . . ." Gerald Rosanbalm Documents: Memo from Col. Downie, Director of CI, OACSI, DA to Col. Van Tassell, Chief of CI Div, ODSCI, USAREUR.

Civil Service Purges/McCarthy Era. Allan Bérubé and John D'Emilio, "The Military and Lesbians During the McCarthy Years," *Signs: Journal of Women in Culture and Society*, Summer 1984, pp. 759–775.

J. Edgar Hoover/FBI. From among the roughly 5,000 documents obtained under the Freedom of Information Act. Randy Shilts, "FBI Spied on Gay Groups for More Than 20 Years," *San Francisco Chronicle*, 21 September 1989, p. 1 col. 4.

Johnnie Phelps. Allan Bérubé, *Coming Out Under Fire*, and Johnnie Phelps Interview (Los Angeles CA, 1990–1991).

Frank Kameny Interviews (1976–1992).

Adams v. *Laird*, 420 F.2d 230 (1969).

Theodore R. Sarbin, Ph.D., and Kenneth E. Karols M.D., Ph.D., of the Defense Personnel Security Research and Education Center (PERSEREC), *Nonconforming Sexual Orientations and Military Suitability* (Monterey CA: PERSEREC, December 1988).

11. Endings

Armistead Maupin Interview (San Francisco CA, 1991).

Cultural References. Lynda Rosen Obst (editor), *The Sixties* (New York: Random House/Rolling Stone Press Books, 1977).

Gerald Rosanbalm Interviews, op. cit.

"This ofc interposes no objection . . ." & "Subject should be released from" Gerald Rosanbalm Documents: Case/Operational File Review Summary Sheet, March 1969–January 1970. Gerald Rosanbalm statement of retirement, 2 February 1970. Department of the Army Physical Review Council, Review of Proceedings of Physical Evaluation Board, 25 March 1970.

Richard McGuire Interviews (Boston MA, 1991–1992). Richard McGuire Documents including: Enlistment Contract Armed Forces of the United States, 6 April 1968; Cryptographic Access Certificate, 11 July 1969; Airman Performance Report, 4 June 1968–9 October 1969 (overall evaluation 8 out of 9); Airman Performance Report, 10 October 1969–9 May 1970 (overall evaluation 9 out of 9).

"We unanimously believe . . ." Robert Semple, Jr., "Nixon Panel Asks Volunteer Army by Middle of 71," *The New York Times*, 22 February 1970, p. 1 col 8.

Gerald Rosanbalm Document: Special Orders Number 85 Extract from Headquarters, Department of the Army, Washington D.C. from W. C. Westmoreland, 1 May 1970.

Kent State & 1970 Unrest. Clark Dougan, Samuel Lipsman, and the Editors of the Boston Publishing Company, *The Vietnam Experience: A Nation Divided* (Boston: Boston Publishing Company, 1984), p. 168–176.

12. Interrogations

Richard McGuire Interviews, op. cit.

Military Manuals on Criminal Investigations. All references from: Field Manual No. 19–20, *Law Enforcement Investigations Headquarters Department of The Army*, Washington DC, 29 April 1977. United States Army Criminal Investigation Command, *Criminal Operations, CID Operations*, Headquarters US Army Criminal Investigation Command, Falls Church VA, 1 November 1986.

Burchill, Offutt AFB Case. "AF Sergeant names 200–250 men, sets off homosexual witch-hunt," *The Advocate*, April 1970, p. 1. Ed Jackson, "AF Man Names Sgt. X in Suit, Fights Discharge," *The Advocate*, 9 April–12 May 1970, p. 7. Jackson, "Air Force Used Threats, Promises Then Broke Its Word, Sgt. X Says," *The Advocate*, 13–26 May 1970, p. 1.

Armistead Maupin Interview, op. cit. Armistead Maupin, "Last U.S. Sailor to Leave Cambodia Tells How With Soapsuds," *The News-Courier*, Charleston SC, 14 February 1971.

13. Indoctrination

Gilbert Baker Interview (San Francisco CA, 1991).

Bill Oyler Interview (Washington DC, 1991).

Carol Owens Interview (Guerneville CA, 1990).

Indoctrination Speeches on Homosexuality. Formal Name: Report To The Board Appointed To Prepare and Submit Recommendations To the Secretary of The Navy For The Revision of Policies, Procedures, and Directives Dealing With Homosexuals, 21 December 1956–15 March 1957. Author's Note: Also known as the Crittenden Report.

Richard McGuire Interviews, op. cit.

14. Dykes and Whores

Penny Rand Interviews (Seattle WA, 1990–1992).

Women in the military. Married women without children were allowed to enlist during World War II, and some women were given permission to marry while serving. After the war's end, requirements for enlistment changed: women were required to have high school educations and be unmarried, and women were, generally, no longer allowed to marry. During the Korean War, most remaining married servicewomen were phased out through a refusal to grant requests for reenlistment. In 1964, a successful lawsuit was filed against the Air Force that, beginning in 1972, again permitted married women and women with dependents to enlist in the military. Sources: Department of Defense. Maj. Gen. Jeanne Holm, USAF (Ret.), *Women in the Military: An Unfinished Revolution* (Novato CA: Presidio Press, 1982).

Women's Liberation. Marcia Cohen, *The Sisterhood: The Inside Story of the Women's Movement and the Leaders Who Made It Happen* (New York: Ballantine Books, 1988).

Kate Millett and the "Kate Is Great" News Conference. "Women's Lib: A Second Look," *Time*, 14 December 1970, p. 50. Judy Klemesrud, "The Lesbian Issue and Women's Lib," *The New York Times*, 18 December 1970, p. 47.

Mary Hall Interviews (Rockwall TX, 1990–1992).

Richard McGuire Interviews, op. cit.

Gilbert Baker Interview, op. cit.

"The Army gave me a medal . . ." Charles McCabe, "The Fearless Spectator," *The San Francisco Chronicle*, 3 May 1971, p. 3.

15. In Country

Mike Hippler, *Matlovich, The Good Soldier* (Boston: Alyson Publications, 1989).

Bill Oyler Interview, op. cit.

Gay Cruising & Hi-jinx in Vietnam. Pax Vobiscum, "Gay life is there, Vietnam GI says, but you have to be careful," *The Advocate*, 26 May–8 June 1971, pp. 10, 19. Vobiscum, "Those tough Green Berets: orgies with an S&M touch," *The Advocate*, 9–22 June 1971.

Australian Navy, "Poofters . . ." Interview Glenn Chandler (Santa Rosa CA 1991). Author's note: Chandler was in the Royal Australian Navy, 1967–1977.

Unrest in the Armed Services. Dougan and Lipsman, *The Vietnam Experience: A Nation Divided*, op. cit., pp. 150–151.

Penny Rand Interviews, op. cit.

March on Washington, 24 April 1971. Doug Beardslee and Jim Kepner, "Gay Lib marches in S.F.," and David L. Aiken, "Activists turn out in D.C.," are from *The Advocate*, 26 May–8 June 1971, p. 1.

Gay Liberation Front (GLF). Robert "Jess" Jessop Documents: Letter to Jess Jessop from Aunt Grace, 16 December 1971. Jessop letter to Aunt Grace, 3 February 1972. Also, "A Faggot Military Freak-Out," *Gay Sunshine*, No. 11, Feb 1972, p. 12. Additional articles from *The Advocate* (Los Angeles), *Gay Sunshine* (San Francisco), *Fag Rag* (Boston) and *Gay* (New York).

"Haven't you ever seen . . ." "Gay Army or No, Draft Case Dismissed," *The Advocate*, 14–27 April 1971, p. 14.

Draft Gag Rule. Allan Bérubé, *Coming Out Under Fire*, op. cit.

Don Slater. Telephone Interviews (1991–1992). Form Letter: Committee to Fight Exclusion of Homosexuals from the Armed Forces.

Mark Houston Interview (Oklahoma City OK, 1991).

Perry Watkins Interviews (Tacoma WA, 1990–1992).

16. Back to the World

Armistead Maupin Interview, op. cit.

Gerald Rosanbalm Interviews, op. cit.

Danny Flaherty Interviews (San Francisco CA, 1991–1992).

Vietnam Veterans. Dougan and Lipsman, *The Vietnam Experience: A Nation Divided*, op. cit., p. 179–183.

Cat Lai Trip. Karlyn Barker, "Vietnam Veterans Return to Help," *The Washington Post*, 23 September 1971, p. G4.

Volunteer Army. "A 2–Year Extension of Draft Is Voted By Panel in House," *The New York Times*, 17 March 1971, p. 49 col. 5.

"We are concerned . . ." From Maj. Gen. Jeanne Holm, USAF (Ret.), *Women in the Military: An Unfinished Revolution* (Novato CA: Presidio Press, 1982).

Increased Usage of Women in the Volunteer Army. Holm, *Women in the Military*, op. cit.

Equal Rights Amendment. Cohen, *The Sisterhood*, op. cit.

"There are no facilities . . ." "Navy to Keep Academy All-Male," *The New York Times*, 9 February 1972, p. 43 col. 6.

Perry Watkins Interviews, op. cit. Perry Watkins Document: CID Report of Investigation, Goeddingen Resident Agency, Second Region, USACIDC, 19 May 1972.

Studies of Gay-Related Discharges. Martin S. Weinberg and Colin J. Williams, *Homosexuals and the Military: A Study of the Less Than Honorable Discharge* (New York: Harper & Row, 1971).

Seiberling Study. "Gays still marked men in the Pentagon," *The Advocate*, 8 May 1974, p. 5.

Spin Codes. Ibid.

Richard McGuire Interviews, op. cit.

17. Winners

James (Jim) Foster Interviews (San Francisco CA, 1976–1991). James Foster Documents: Undesirable Discharge from the Armed Forces of the United States of America, DD258A, 15 July 1959. DD214 dated 10 July 1959. James Foster, Speech at the Democratic National Convention, *Vector*, August 1972, pp. 5, 36. Lawrence Spears, "SIR's Gay Delegate," *Vector*, August 1972, pp. 4–5.

Vernon "Copy" Berg III Interviews (New York NY, 1991–1992).

Robert Martin Case. "Naval Board Gives Martin General Discharge; Appeal Set," *The Advocate*, 12 April 1972, p. 4. Laurence Leve, "Major Test Seen in Navy Case," *The Advocate*, 26 April 1972, pp. 3, 10. "Pentagon Holds to Anti-Gay Stand," *The Advocate*, 24 May 1972, p. 3.

Jeffrey Dunbar Case. Carl Bernstein, "Homophile Is Ousted from Marine Corps," *The Washington Post*, 22 March 1972, p. C1. "Lawmakers Eye Marine Discharge," *The Advocate*, 26 April 1972, p. 3. "Marines Give Cpl. Dunbar 'Undesirable,' " *The Advocate*, 19 July 1972, p. 3. Frank Kameny Interviews, op. cit.

Cohen, *The Sisterhood*, op. cit.

18. STRAC

Hippler, *Matlovich, The Good Soldier*, op. cit.

Draft Ends. David E. Rosenbaum, "Nation Ends Draft, Turn to Volunteers," *The New York Times*, 28 January 1973, p. 1 col. 1.

William "Pete" Randell Interviews (Atlanta GA, 1990–1992).

Vernon "Copy" Berg III Interviews, op. cit.

Women's Movement. Cohen, *The Sisterhood*.

"Both hurting and exploiting . . ." Barbara Love, "Friedan Attack on Lesbians Hit," *The Advocate*, 11 April 1973, p. 9.

Volunteer Army. "Enlistments Lag for Combat Forces," *The New York Times*, 19 June 1973, p. 8 col. 4. Ben A. Franklin, "Lag in Volunteer Force Spurs Talk of New Draft," *The New York Times*, 1 July 1973, p. 1 col. 3. Drew Middleton, "Army Enlistments Fall Short of Goal for Seventh Month in Row," *The New York Times*, 12 September 1973, p. 24 col. 1. "Stennis Upholds Volunteer Army," *The New York Times*, 24 September 1973, p. 13 col. 1.

Women and the Volunteer Army. "Women's Army Corps to Grow With More Jobs and New Styles," *The New York Times*, 8 August 1972, p. 36 col. 1. Linda Charlton, "Almost All the NonCombat Jobs in Air Force Opened to Women," *The New York Times*, 23 November 1972, p. 38 col. 1. Charlton, "Navy Wives Irate at Idea of Women on Warships," *The New York Times*, 27 August 1972, p. 1 col. 1. "Military Idea of Equality: Some Women Wonder If It's a Forward March," *The New York Times*, 18 April 1973, p. 54 col. 1.

Recruitment Goals Met. "Army Passes Enlistment Target First Time Since End of Draft," *The New York Times*, 9 December 1973, p. 99 col. 4.

19. Politics and Prejudice

William "Pete" Randell Interviews, op. cit.

Hippler, *Matlovich, The Good Soldier*, op. cit.

Race Relations and Integration. Morris J. MacGregor, Jr., *Integration of the Armed Forces 1940–1965*, Defense Studies Series, Center of Military History (Washington DC: United States Army, 1985).

Dutch Military Reforms. Casimir Elsen, Report on the Legal Situation of Homosexual Men & Women in the Armed Forces, International Lesbian & Gay Association, 1987. (No pagination, see section on The Netherlands.)

Frank Kameny Interviews, op. cit.

Gays in Uniform Article. Marianne Lester, "Homosexuals in Uniform," *Air Force Times*, 27 March 1974, Family Section: pp. 4–9, 12–13.

20. The Letter

Vernon "Copy" Berg III Interviews, op. cit.

Admission of Women to the Academies. Joseph B. Treaster, "In 185th Year Coast Guard Goes Coed," *The New York Times*, 11 February 1974. "Women Cadets Opposed," *The New York Times*, 18 August 1974, p. 28 col. 4. "Women Gain Backer," *The New York Times*, 12 June 1974, p. 31 col. 4.

Cohen, *The Sisterhood*, op. cit.

Discharge Statistics, 1974. Enlisted Homosexual Administrative Separations (DoD Directive 1332.14).

End of Spin Number Coding. "Army will quit discharge coding," *The Advocate*, 24 April 1975, p. 5.

Hippler, *Matlovich, The Good Soldier*, op. cit.

Frank Kameny Interviews, op. cit.

David Addlestone Telephone Interview (Washington DC, 1991).

Tanya Domi Interviews (Washington DC, 1991–1992).

Watson and Randolph. "Lesbians Battle the Army," *Detroit Free Press*, 5 June 1975, p. 1-C.

BOOK THREE: TRIALS (1975–1976)

21. The Color Purple (Part I)

Mike Hippler, *Matlovich, The Good Soldier* (Boston: Alyson Publications, 1989)
Jon Jaenicke Telephone Interview (Los Angeles CA, 1992).
Rudolph "Skip" Keith. "Second Sergeant Comes Out," *The Advocate*, 13 August 1975, p. 9.
Randolph-Watson & Hess. "Military Gays Come Out," *The Washington Blade*, July 1975, p. 1.
Jim Woodward Interviews (San Diego CA, 1991–1992). Jim Woodward Documents: Coming out letter from James M. Woodward to the Chief of Naval Personnel dated 17 September 1974. *Woodward v. Moore*, 451 F.Supp. 346 (D.D.C. 1978).
Military Law and Sexual Orientation. Rhonda Rivera, *Hastings Law Journal*, March 1979, Vol. 30, p. 44.
Matlovich. Lesley Oelsner, "Homosexual Is Fighting Military Ouster," *The New York Times*, 26 May 1975, p. 1. col. 1.
Maj. Gen. Jeanne Holm, USAF (Ret.), *Women in the Military: An Unfinished Revolution* (Novato CA: Presidio Press, 1982).
Vernon "Copy" Berg III Interviews (New York NY, 1991–1992).
E. Lawrence Gibson, *Get Off My Ship, Ensign Berg vs. The U.S. Navy* (New York: Avon Books, 1978).
Roberto Reyes-Colon Interview (Portland OR, 1991).
U.S. Civil Service Commission. David L. Aiken, "Gay Is Now Okay in 2.6 Million Federal Jobs," *The Advocate*, 30 July 1975, p. 4.
American Psychiatric Association. Aiken, "Larel Wrong All Along, Says Author of Change," *The Advocate*, 8 May 1974, p. 2.
Discharge Statistics, 1975. Enlisted Homosexual Administrative Separations (DoD Directive 1332.14).
"To exclude an individual . . ." FOIA Document: Homosexuality as It Concerns Employment in NSA, U.S. Government Memorandum, 22 September 1975.
Jim Wagner Interview (St. Louis MO, 1991).
Bob Stuhr Interview (Los Angeles CA, 1990).
Fort Sill Murder. Series of stories from the *Lawton Constitution*, 25 November 1974–2 April 1975.
"Parents would be . . ." FOIA Document: Rationale For Regulations Concerning Discharge by Reason of Homosexuality, Department of Naval Personnel, April 1975.
"By way of example . . ." FOIA Document: Letter to Rep. Fred Richmond from Ronald J. Skorepa, Colonel USAF, Congressional Inquiry Division, 31 December 1975.
FOIA Document: Memorandum for the Assistant Secretary of the Navy (Manpower and Reserve Affairs), Service Policy in Regard to Homosexuality, Department of the Navy, 3 November 1975.
Navy's Congressional Liaison. FOIA Document: Rationale for Regulations Concerning Discharge by Reason of Homosexuality, U.S. Government Memorandum from R.V. Dalton, Capt. USN Liaison Branch, 17 April 1975.
Air Force Times Article on Matlovich. Ann Gerow, "Matlovich Case: No Action Vet," *Air Force Times*, 2 July 1975, p. 5.

22. The Green Beret

Perry Watkins Interviews (Tacoma WA, 1990–1992).
Vernon "Copy" Berg III Interviews, op. cit.
Gibson, *Get Off My Ship*, 1978, op. cit.
Jay Hatheway Interviews (Minneapolis MN, 1990–1992). Chris Coates Telephone Interview (Milledgeville GA, 1991).

23. Freedom

William "Pete" Randell Interviews (Atlanta GA, 1990–1992).
Vernon "Copy" Berg III Interviews, op. cit.
Gibson, *Get Off My Ship*, op. cit.
Matlovich Leaves the Air Force. Hippler, *Matlovich, The Good Soldier*, op. cit. Andrew Kopkind, "The Boys in the Barracks," *New Times*, 11 July 1975, p. 21. "Gays on the March," *Time*, 8 September 1975, pp. 32–43. Author's note: This is the issue with the Matlovich cover.
Miriam Ben-Shalom Interviews. Series of interviews 1976–1992 with the primary interview for this book conducted in Milwaukee WI, 1991.
Air Force Handling of Matlovich Case. Jon Jaenicke, op. cit.
Perry Watkins Interviews, op. cit.
Jay Hatheway Interviews, op. cit.
Richard McGuire Interviews (Boston MA, 1991–1992).

24. The Mile-Wide Word

Matlovich Hearing. Hippler, *Matlovich, The Good Soldier*, op. cit. Martin Duberman, "The Gay Sergeant: Leonard Matlovich's strange trial betrayed a profound shift in American attitudes—and not only toward sexuality," *The New York Times Magazine*, p. 14–17, 58–69. David Addlestone Interview (Washington DC,

1991), Jon Jaenicke Interview, op. cit. James Applegate Telephone Interview (1991). "Homosexual Soldier Asks Air Force That He Not Be Discharged," *The New York Times*, 18 September 1975, p. 12 col. 1. "Homosexual Sergeant Described By Doctor As No Risk to Security," *The New York Times*, 19 September 1975, p 15. "Air Force Sergeant Feels He's a Patriot Fighting for Freedom," *The New York Times*, 20 September 1975, p. 15 col. 1.

Oliver Sipple. Randy Shilts, *The Mayor of Castro Street, The Life and Times of Harvey Milk* (New York: St. Martin's Press, 1982).

Rudolph "Skip" Keith. "Air Force Discharges Homosexual Sergeant," *The New York Times,* 25 September 1975, p. 14 col. 1. FOIA Document: Extracts From AFM 39–12 Hearing of Staff Sergeant Rudolph S. Keith Jr., 10 September 1975.

Watson-Randolph. "Military Follow-up," *The Washington Gay Blade*, August 1975, p. 3.

Tanya Domi Interviews, op. cit.

Perry Watkins Interviews, op. cit. Perry Watkins Document: Summary of Proceedings, Board of Officers, Unsuitability Hearing, Department of the Army, 44th Engineer Battalion, Camp Mercer, Korea, 14 October 1975.

Jay Hatheway Interview, op. cit.

Chris Coates Interview, op. cit.

25. *Triangulates*

Hippler, *Matlovich, The Good Soldier*, op. cit.

Matlovich's Celebrity. Sasha Gregory-Lewis, "Cannibalization of a Hero," *The Advocate,* 31 December 1975, Vol. 180, p. 7.

Leonard Matlovich Document: Letter to Leonard Matlovich from the Church of Jesus Christ of Latter-Day Saints, Norfolk Stake Presidency, 7 October 1975.

Matlovich's Discharge. "Gay Sergeant's Discharge Upheld," *Sexualaw Reporter*, Sept/Oct 1976, p. 53.

Vernon "Copy" Berg III Interviews, op. cit.

Gibson, *Get Off My Ship*, op. cit.

Bruce Voeller Telephone Interviews (Los Angeles CA, 1990–1992).

Vernon Berg Press Release: Wire service reports, November 1975.

26. *Adjectives and Nouns*

Vernon Berg Hearing. Vernon "Copy" Berg III Interviews, op. cit. Gibson, *Get Off My Ship*, op. cit.

Jay Hatheway Interview, op. cit.

Chris Coates Interview, op. cit.

Miriam Ben-Shalom Interview, op. cit.

27. *The Next Generation*

Carole Brock Interviews (Sonoma County CA, 1990–1992).

Women's Movement. Marcia Cohen, *The Sisterhood: The Inside Story of the Women's Movement and the Leaders Who Made It Happen* (New York: Ballantine Books, 1988).

End of Separate Service. James P. Sterba, "Army Women Now Serve in Many Once-Male Jobs," *The New York Times*, 4 May 1975, p. 1 col. 2.

Women at Military Academies. "Woman Cadet Seeks to Leave West Point," *The New York Times*, 14 June 1976, p. 25 col. 5. "123 Women to Air Academy," *The New York Times*, 8 May 1976, p. 26 col. 2. "First 7 Women Named to the Naval Academy," *The New York Times*, 19 March 1976, p. 12 col. 4.

Last Class With Balls. Karen Newman, "Controversy Goes With Diplomas at Air Force Academy," *Rocky Mountain News*, 31 May 1979.

"Back home, Army females . . ." James P. Sterba, *The New York Times*, 4 May 1975, p. 1 col. 2.

Tanya Domi Interviews, op. cit.

Adam Gettinger-Brizuela Interviews (San Diego CA, 1990–1991).

28. *Transitions*

Vernon "Copy" Berg III Interviews, op. cit.

Gibson, *Get Off My Ship*, op. cit.

Armistead Maupin Interviews, op. cit.

Gay Culture and Migration Patterns. Shilts, *The Mayor of Castro Street*, op. cit.

National Gay Task Force. Bruce Voeller Interviews, op. cit.

1976 Election. Sasha Gregory-Lewis, "As the Hot Air Balloons Soar Let's Look at Where the Prexy Hopefuls Stand on Gay Rights," *The Advocate,* 10 March 1976, pp. 13–15. James (Jim) Foster Interviews (San Francisco CA, 1976–1991).

Charles Bell Interview (New York NY, 1991).

Hippler, *Matlovich, The Good Soldier*, op. cit.

29. The Secret Report

William "Pete" Randell Interviews, op. cit.

"Approval of the resignation . . ." FOIA Document: Memorandum for the Record, Notification Procedure for Certain Homosexual Cases Awaiting Disposition, F.S. Barnett ACND for Performance & Security USN, 11 June 1976.

"(1) An individual's performance . . ." FOIA Document: Litigation Involving the Navy's Homosexual Discharge policy, From Chief of Naval Personnel to Judge Advocate General, 2 August 1976.

"There is no correlation . . ." Crittenden Report. Formal Name: Report To The Board Appointed To Prepare and Submit Recommendations To the Secretary Of The Navy For The Revision of Policies, Procedures, and Directives Dealing With Homosexuals, 21 December 1956–15 March 1957. (Also can be found in Gibson, Get Off My Ship, op. cit.)

Doe v. Commonwealth's Attorney. Bruce Voeller Interviews (Los Angeles CA, 1992).

Media Reactions to Doe. Lesley Oelsner, "Justices Decline to Remove Curb on Homosexuals," The New York Times, 30 March 1976, p. 1 col. 8. Anthony Lewis, "No Process of Law," The New York Times, 8 April 1976, p. 37 col. 1. Editorial: "The Rights of Privacy," The New York Times, 31 March 1976, p. 40 col. 1. "A No to Sodomy," Time, 12 April 1976, Vol. 107 No. 15, p. 50.

Matlovich Decision. Hippler, Matlovich, The Good Soldier, op. cit. David Addlestone Interview, op. cit. Matlovich v. Secretary of the Air Force, 414 F Supp 690 (1976). "Gay Sergeant's Discharge Upheld," Sexualaw Reporter, Sept/Oct 1976, p. 53.

Robert LeBlanc. "LeBlanc vs. US Marine Corps," The Advocate, 14 July 1976, Vol. 193, p. 7.

Dennis Beller Case. References are from the overview of contemporary homosexual military cases found in Hippler, Matlovich, The Good Soldier, op. cit., p. 160–61.

BOOK FOUR: THE FAMILY (1977–1980)

30. The Family

Adam Gettinger-Brizuela Interview (San Diego CA, 1990–1991). Coalition of Gay Service People, "Politics of Paranoia: Persecution of Gay Service People," Santa Barbara News & Review, 17 June 1977, p. 25.

Mary Saal. Randy Shilts, "Navy Appeals Ruling," The Advocate, 1 June 1977, Vol. 216, p. 9.

Carter Administration, 1977. Neal Miller, "Carter Aides Pledge to Set Up Series of Meetings," Gay Community News, 9 April 1977, Vol. 4, No. 41, p. 1. "First Gay Naval Vet Gets Discharge Upgrade Under Carter Plan," Gaysweek, 17 October 1977, Vol. 35, p. 2.

Gay History. Randy Shilts, The Mayor of Castro Street, The Life and Times of Harvey Milk (New York: St. Martin's Press, 1982).

Discharge Statistics, 1975–77. Enlisted Homosexual Administrative Separations (DoD Directive 1332.14).

Lesbian and Gay Purges. "A Lesbian Purge?" The Advocate, 26 March 1975, p. 10. "Military Purge in Montana," The Advocate, 24 March 1976, p. 9.

"We are a legion . . ." Coalition of Gay Servicepeople, "Politics of Paranoia: Persecution of Gay Service-people," Santa Barbara News and Review, 17 June 1977, p. 25.

31. Reaction

Anita Bryant, Dade County FL. Mike Hippler, Matlovich, The Good Soldier (Boston: Alyson Publications, 1989). James (Jim) Foster Interviews (1976–1992). Shilts, The Mayor of Castro Street, op. cit. Pamphlet: "Save Our Children From Homosexuality" (Dade County FL: Save Our Children, Inc., 1977). Pamphlet: "Vote Against Repeal of Human Rights" (Miami FL: Dade County Coalition for Human Rights, 1977).

"Tonight the laws of God . . ." Joe Baker, "Miami," The Advocate, 13 July 1977, pp. 6–7.

Vandenberg Air Force Base. Adam Gettinger-Brizuela Interviews, op. cit. Elenore Pred, "Vandenberg Air Base Ousts Men," The Advocate, 22 March 1978, p. 11. FOIA Document: OSI Report of Investigation, Vandenberg Air Force Base, March 1977–March 1978. (Approximately 500 pages of interviews, surveillance records, and other reports relevant to the investigation.)

Sodomy Laws. Shilts, The Mayor of Castro Street, op. cit.

"If you would like to . . ." Jackson Weaver, "Outlawing Love at Vandenberg," Santa Barbara News & Review, 28 January 1978, p. 2.

32. The Gayest Ship in the Navy and Other Stories

Gene Barfield Interview (Barre VT, 1991).

Jim Frisbie Interview (San Diego CA, 1991).

Wayne Walls Interview (San Diego CA, 1991).

Art McDaniel Interview (Atlanta GA, 1991).

Perry Watkins Interviews (Tacoma WA, 1990–1992). Perry Watkins Documents: Request for Requalification, Letter to Commander 5th USA Arty GP, from Dale E. Pastain, Captain 33d USA Field Artillery Detachment, 22 February 1978. Letter of appreciation to Perry Watkins from Sergeant Major Walter Pederson, Ft. Hood TX, re Noncommissioned Officers Dining Out, 11 January 1977.

USS Nausau. Interview with anonymous reservist, 1991.

USS *LaSalle*. Tim LaCroix Interview (Vermont, 1991). Other accounts based on numerous interviews with anonymous former and current crew members.

Gay Freedom Day Parade, 1978. Gilbert Baker Interview (San Francisco CA, 1991). Shilts, *The Mayor of Castro Street*, op. cit.

Vernon Berg Post-Military Experiences. Vernon "Copy" Berg III Interviews (New York NY, 1991–1992).

33. Women at Sea

Carole Brock Interviews (Sonoma County CA, 1990–1992).

Women at Sea Program. Karen deWitt, "Women's Sea Duty Curb Rejected," *The New York Times*, 28 June 1978, sect. 2, p. 2. col 1. Melinda Beck, "Eight Bells," *Newsweek*, 13 November 1978, p. 75. "Navy Seeking to Send More Women to Sea," *The New York Times*, 1 May 1977, p. D17 col. 1. "White House Backs Plan on Sea Duty for Women," *The New York Times*, 28 May 1977, p. 8 col. 6. Maj. Gen. Jeanne Holm, USAF (Ret.), *Women in the Military: An Unfinished Revolution* (Novato CA: Presidio Press, 1982).

New River Marine Corps Air Station. Anonymous interview with female recruit.

Women's Softball Team. "They're slurping it up . . ." Anonymous interview with WAC.

Lesbian Investigation, Navy OCS. Anonymous interview with female officer candidate.

Mary Ann De Palo. Tony Domenick, "US Air Force Member Appeals Anti-Gay Enlistment Ruling," *Gay Community News,* 28 October 1978, n14, p. 3.

Jill Waters Interview (San Diego CA, 1991).

Julie Stonacek Interview (Seattle WA, 1991).

"Gangs of female homosexuals . . ." FOIA Document: Position Paper, Army Policy on Homosexuality, Prepared by Human Resources Development Directorate & The Judge Advocate General, August 1979. (W.F. Ulmer, Jr. Major General, GS Director of Human Resources Development).

Percentage of Women Discharged. "Army Dykes: 6X More than Gays," *Off Our Backs,* November 1980.

Berg-Matlovich Appeal. *Matlovich* v. *Secretary of the Air Force*, 591 F.2d 852 (1978). *Berg* v. *Claytor*, 591 F.2d 849 (D.C. Cir. 1978).

"Major reviews of policies . . ." Bernard Weintraub, "Military, After Appellate Ruling, Starts Review on Homosexuality," *The New York Times*, p. A1 col 5.

Marine Corps Lawsuit. "Ex-Marine Court-Martialed for Being Gay, Sues Corps for 12M," *Gaysweek*, 30 October 1978, p. 2.

Junior ROTC Program. Letter from James E. Brown, General Counsel, Board of Education, District of Columbia to Harold Brown, Secretary of Defense, 28 September 1979. Craig Howell, "GAA Blasts D.C.'s Jr. ROTC Program," *Washington Blade*, 19 July 1979, p. 6. Ted Wojtasik, "School Board OK's Jr. ROTC Despite Protests," *Washington Blade*, 2 August 1979, p. 5. Wojtasik, "GAA Advances Jr. ROTC Battle," *Washington Blade*, 27 September 1979.

William "Pete" Randell Interviews (Atlanta GA, 1990–1992).

34. Angry Gods

Ruth Voor Interviews (Tampa FL, 1991–1992).

"Sterilized the whole process . . ." James Webb, "Women Can't Fight," *The Washingtonian*, October 1979, pp. 144–147.

Gay Cadet Purge at Air Force Academy. Dan Stratford Interview (Los Angeles CA, 1992).

Gay Scandal at West Point. From conversations with former aides of General Westmoreland.

Naval Academy Purges. Greg Smith Interview (Norfolk VA, 1991–1992).

Carole Brock Interviews, op. cit.

Hippler, *Matlovich, The Good Soldier*, op. cit.

35. Memorial Day

Tomb of the Unknown Soldier. Documents including: memoranda, newspaper articles and correspondence by Frank Kameny to the Ceremonies and Special Events, Department of the Army, 14 May 1980–22 May 1980; and Letter to the White House from Frank Kameny, 4 November 1979. Frank Kameny Interviews 1976–1992.

Changes Under Carter. Statement of Kay Whitlock, Co-Chairperson, National Gay Task Force, Presentation of Executive Order Petitions, The White House, 19 December 1979. Memorandum for The President from Anne Wexler and Stu Eizenstat on the National Gay Task Force Questionnaire, 19 December 1979. Lou Chibbaro, Jr., "Carter's Efforts Not Enough Activists Warn," *Washington Blade*, 10 July 1980, p. 3. Bill Peterson, "Brown's Support for Gays Brings Cheers," *The Washington Post*, 28 November 1979.

National Gay Task Force Poll. Lou Chibbaro, Jr., "Carter's Efforts Not Enough Activists Warn," *Washington Blade*, 10 July 1980, p. 3.

Marine Sponsorship of Anita Bryant. Letter from the National Gay Task Force to Ms. Allison Thomas, 12 August 1980.

Carole Brock Interviews, op. cit.

Dirty Dozen. "Something amiss on Navy ship," *San Jose Mercury*, 10 July 1980, p. 10A.

NIS Formation. Pamphlet: *This Is The NIS*, The Department of the Navy. Lawrence Korb Interview (Washington DC, 1991).

USS *Norton Sound* Witch-Hunt. Randy Shilts, "The Ship That Dare Not Speak Its Name," *The Village Voice*, 24–30 September 1980, pp. 13–14, 16. Randy Shilts's USS *Norton Sound* Documents: Interviews and related documents, roughly 200 pages of information collected while conducting interviews in Port Hueneme, Long Beach, and Los Angeles in 1980. This collection will subsequently be referred to as '*Norton Sound* Documents' in these Notes. *Norton Sound* Documents: Statement to Naval Investigative Service from Helen Wilson to Charles Page, Port Hueneme CA, 16 May 1980. Statement to Naval Investigative Service from Lynn A. Batey to John M. Stevens, Port Hueneme CA, 20 May 1980. Series of 12 statements from *Norton Sound* crew members, 16–28 May 1980, five of whom declined to sign their statements. All eight *Norton Sound* women who faced charges and their lawyers were interviewed in 1980.

Barbara "Puppy" Underwood Interview (1980).

Tangela Gaskins. Shilts, "The Ship That Dare Not Speak Its Name," *The Village Voice*, op. cit. *Norton Sound* Documents, op. cit.

Wendi Williams Interview (1980).

Reaction to Memorial Day Ceremony. Lou Chibbaro, Jr., "GAA Seeks Apology from Army Secretary," *Washington Blade*, 10 June 1980, p. 4.

36. Glory Days

Ruth Voor Interviews, op. cit.

Carole Brock Interviews, op. cit.

Randy Shilts, "The Ship That Dare Not Speak Its Name," *The Village Voice*, op. cit. *Norton Sound* Documents, op. cit.

Johnnie Phelps Interview (Los Angeles CA, 1991).

Norton Sound Document: Statements from *Norton Sound* crew members, 16–28 May 1980, op. cit.

1980 Democratic Convention. James (Jim) Foster Interviews (San Francisco CA, 1976–1991).

Ben-Shalom v. *The Secretary of the Army* 489 F.Supp. 964 (E.D. Wis. 1980).

"At that particular moment . . ." Rhonda Rivera Interviews, (Columbus OH, 1990–1992).

Carter Memo. Memorandum for The President from Anne Wexler and Stu Eizenstat re National Gay Task Force Questionnaire, 19 December 1979. Allison Thomas interview, op. cit.

Joyce Arnold Statements. *Norton Sound* Document: Joyce Arnold Statements dated 2 July 1980, 9 July 1980 (declined to sign), 16 July 1980. Robert J. Gore, "Sex and Drugs on a Top Secret Ship," *San Francisco Chronicle*, 25 August 1980, p. 20.

Alicia Harris Interview (1980).

37. "Until After November"

Protest at Long Beach Naval Shipyard. Johnnie Phelps Interview, op. cit. Randy Shilts, "The Ship That Dare Not Speak Its Name," *Village Voice*, op. cit. *Norton Sound* Documents, op. cit.

Tangela Gaskins Hearing. Shilts, "The Ship That Dare Not Speak Its Name," *Village Voice*, op. cit. *Norton Sound* Documents, op. cit. Jill Stewart, "Hysterical witness refuses to testify aboard *Norton Sound*," *Long Beach Independent*, 6 August 1980, pp. 8–9. Robert J. Gore, "Accused Female Sailor's Fiancé Tells of Normal Sexual Acts," *Los Angeles Times*, 7 August 1980, pp. 1, 4. Patricia Wolf, "More Surprises at *Norton Sound*," *Los Angeles Herald Examiner*, 6 August 1980 (Evening Edition). "Navy Threat in Lesbian Case," *San Francisco Chronicle*, 6 August 1980. "Navy Acquits First Sailor of Lesbian Charges," *San Francisco Chronicle*, 8 August 1980. Jill Clark, "Navy Clears Gaskins of Homosexuality Charge," *Gay Community News*, 23 & 30 August 1980. Victoria Podesta, "*Norton Sound* Trial Ends," *National Now Times*, September 1980. Tangela Gaskins Interview (Port Hueneme CA, 1980).

Carole Brock Interviews, op. cit.

Bill Stout Comment. Bill Stout commentary transcript, 7 August 1980, Los Angeles CA, CBS affiliate.

Discharge Statistics, 1980. Enlisted Homosexual Administrative Separations (DoD Directive 1332.14).

Pam Burwell Interview (Blacksburg VA, 1991).

Other Purges. "Navy Continues Homosexual Hunt," *Washington Blade*, 7 November 1980, p. A-9. "Then Expels Lesbians From Georgia Bases," *Washington Blade*, 21 November 1980. "Military Discharging of Gays Continues," *Washington Blade*, 10 October 1980, p. A-9. David Morris, "Air Force Discharges Eight for Homosexuality," *Gay Community News*, 4 October 1980, p. 1. "California Sailors Vow to Fight Navy Purge," *The Advocate*, 27 November 1980, p. 10. "Booted by Navy, Gay Sailor Will Appeal," *The Advocate*, 5 March 1981, pp. 11–12.

Barbara Underwood Hearing. Barbara "Puppy" Underwood Interview, op. cit. Barry Copilow Interview (1980). Randy Shilts, "The Ship That Dare Not Speak Its Name," *The Village Voice*, op. cit. *Norton Sound* Documents, op. cit. "2nd Lesbian Hearing Told of Suspicions," *San Francisco Chronicle*, 12 August 1980. Patricia Wolf, "Defense rests in 2nd *Norton Sound* hearing: Male officer testifies he had sex with accused lesbian sailor," *Los Angeles Herald Examiner*, 14 August 1980. Bob Keefer, "Another sailor's verdict due today in lesbian case," *Long Beach Independent*, 14 August 1980. Molly Burrell, "2nd sailor 'cleared' in *Norton Sound* lesbian case," *Long Beach Independent*, 15 August 1980. "Defense claims the Navy already has decided homosexuality cases," *San Jose Mercury*, 15 August 1980.

"Prevent future purges . . ." Interview with anonymous White House staffer. Internal memo dated 15 August 1980.

38. Interregnum

Gays vs. Marines at the Equus. Lou Chibbaro, Jr., "Officials Condemn Equus Attack," *Washington Blade,* 21 August 1980, p. 1. Thomas Morgan, "The Battle of Capitol Hill: Gays vs. the Leathernecks," *The Washington Post,* 24 August 1980, sect. B1, p. 1. Lou Chibbaro, Jr., "Problems With Marines Continues," *Washington Blade,* 11 September 1980, p. A-4. Documents: Memorandum for Anne Wexler re Attack by Marines on Local Gay Bar, 21 August 1980.

Alicia Harris Hearing. Alicia Harris Interviews, op. cit. Carole Brock Interviews, op. cit. Randy Shilts, "The Ship That Dare Not Speak Its Name," *The Village Voice,* op. cit. *Norton Sound* Documents, op. cit. Victoria Podesta, *"Norton Sound* Trial Ends," *National NOW Times,* September 1980. Patricia Wolf, "Witness says she saw women sailors kiss on lips," *Los Angeles Herald Examiner,* 16 August 1980. *"Norton Sound* witnesses fire salvos at sex hearing," *Long Beach Independent,* 16 August 1980. Mary Neiswender, "Female sailor convicted," *Long Beach Independent,* 18 August 1980. Neiswender, "Sailor guilty of lesbianism," *Long Beach Independent,* 18 August 1980. Wolf, "1st *Norton Sound* guilty verdict to be appealed," *Long Beach Independent,* 19 August 1980.

Wendi Williams Hearing. Wendi Williams Interview, op. cit. Carole Brock Interview, op. cit. Randy Shilts, "The Ship That Dare Not Speak Its Name," *The Village Voice,* op. cit. *Norton Sound* Documents, op. cit. Patricia Wolf, "Navy opens case against fourth *Norton Sound* sailor," *Los Angeles Herald Examiner,* 20 August 1980, p. A3. "Second woman sailor guilty of lesbian acts," *San Jose Mercury,* 21 August 1985, p. 2F. Claire Spiegel, "2nd Sailor Guilty of Lesbian Acts," *Los Angeles Times,* 21 August 1980. Mary Neiswender, "2nd woman sailor guilty in sex case," *Long Beach Independent,* 21 August 1980.

"The decision was made . . ." "Navy drops charges against four sailors," *The Advocate,* 2 October 1980, pp. 10–11.

Matlovich v. *Secretary of the Air Force.* 591 F.2d 852 (D.C. Cir. 1978).

Hippler, *Matlovich, The Good Soldier,* op. cit.

"Our enemies in the world . . ." "Policy on Homosexuals Being Checked," *Navy Times,* 13 October 1980, p. 15.

William "Pete" Randell Interviews, op. cit.

39. Future Imperfect

Hippler, *Matlovich, The Good Soldier,* op. cit.

Matlovich v. *Secretary of the Air Force,* op. cit.

Vernon "Copy" Berg III Interviews, op. cit.

Beller v. *Middendorf* 632 F.2d 788 (9th Cir. 1980). David Morris, "Navy Can Eject Gays, Federal Court Rules," *Gay Community News,* 8 November 1980, p. 1.

Ben-Shalom v. *Secretary of the Army.* 489 F.Supp. 964 (E.D. Wis. 1980).

1980 Presidential Election. Susan Faludi, *Backlash, The Undeclared War Against American Women* (New York: Crown, 1991). "Bush, Connolly Squabble Over Gay Rights Statements," *San Francisco Sentinel,* 18 April 1980, p. 4. Wayne Friday, "Politics & People," *Bay Area Reporter,* 14 February 1980, p. 17. "Reagan Gives Mixed Messages on Gay Rights," *San Francisco Sentinel,* 18 April 1980, p. 4. Falwell Advertisement: Democratic State Committee, California, *Bay Area Reporter,* 23 October 1980, p. 8–9. Randy Shilts, *And the Band Played On: Politics, People, and the AIDS Epidemic* (New York: St. Martin's Press, 1987). Rhonda Rivera Interviews, op. cit.

Matlovich Settlement. Don Mace, "Matlovich Case Settled, Gay Issue Isn't," *Air Force Times,* 8 December 1980, p. 1.

Art McDaniel Interview, op. cit.

BOOK FIVE: LESBIAN VAMPIRES OF BAVARIA (1981–1985)

40. Thoughtcrimes

Cliff Anchor Interviews (Monte Rio CA, 1990–1992).

Mike Hippler, *Matlovich, The Good Soldier* (Boston: Alyson Publications, 1989).

Gallup Poll. James Monahan (editor), *Before I Sleep, The Last Days of Dr. Tom Dooley* (New York: Farrar, Straus and Cudahay, 1961), p. 50.

"I am promulgating . . ." FOIA Document: Memorandum for Secretaries of the Army, Navy, Air Force and Chairmen of the Joint Chiefs of Staff from Deputy Secretary of Defense W. Graham Claytor, Washington D.C., 16 January 1981.

"Although the subject of homosexuality . . ." FOIA Document: Report of the Joint Service Administrative Discharge Study Group (1977–78), Department of Defense, August 1978, Prepared for Assistant Secretary of Defense (Manpower, Reserve Affairs & Logistics).

"Homosexual acts committed . . ." FOIA Document: Memorandum for the Assistant Secretary of Defense (Manpower, Reserve Affairs & Logistics) from Harold D. Neeley, Colonel USAF, 5 December 1980.

"The Joint Chiefs . . ." FOIA Document: Memorandum for the Secretary of Defense. Subject: Policy for Processing Homosexual Cases in the Armed Forces, To Joint Chiefs of Staff from David C. Jones, General USAF, Chairman, Joint Chiefs of Staff, 17 December 1980.

"Homosexuality is incompatible with . . ." FOIA Document: Homosexuality, Department of Defense Directive 1332.14, 16 January 1981.

"Surveys show that . . ." FOIA Document: Rationale for Exclusion of Homosexuals from Military Service, Department of Defense, 29 September 1980.

Nazi Persecution of Homosexuals. Richard Plant, *The Pink Triangle: The Nazi War Against Homosexuals* (New York: Henry Holt, 1986).

W. Graham Claytor, Jr., Telephone Interview (1992).

41. Surrender Dorothy

Perry Watkins Interviews (Tacoma WA, 1990–1992). Perry Watkins Document: Revocation of Security Clearance, Watkins, Perry James To Commander 9th Infantry Division, Ft. Lewis WA, From Richard J. Backus, Colonel A.D., 10 July 1980.

Jim Lobsenz Telephone Interview (1992).

"I submit that . . ." Perry Watkins Document: Letter to Assistant Chief of Staff for Intelligence, HQ Department of the Army, Washington DC, From Staff SSG Perry J. Watkins, February 1981.

"I am initiating action . . ." Perry Watkins Document: Letter to SSG Perry J. Watkins. Subject: Separation Under the Provisions of Chapter 15, Ar 635–200, Homosexuality, From Roger L. Scott Captain, 17 September 1981.

"Military service policy . . ." Perry Watkins Document: Memo for BG [Brigadier General] L. J. Barker, Chief of Public Affairs, Subject: Recent Litigation Challenging Army Separation Policy on Homosexuality, From Delbert L. Spurlock, Jr., General Counsel, 7 October 1981.

Melvin Dahl Interview (Spokane WA, 1992).

Discharge Statistics, 1981. Enlisted Homosexual Administrative Separations (DoD Directive 1332.14).

Matt Oler Interview (Norfolk VA, 1991).

USS *Starrett.* Anonymous interview with a former crew member.

Joan Dowling. "Mistaken Identities," *Gay Community News,* 2 May 1981, p. 2.

Naval Academy Investigation. Larry Goldsmith, "Student, Officer Implicated in Naval Academy Sex Scandal," *Gay Community News,* 18 July 1981, p. 3. Orlando Gotay Interview (San Francisco CA, 1990).

Sheppard Air Force Base Purge. Interview with an anonymous female service member.

Torrejon Air Base Investigation. John Thibeault Interview (West Hollywood CA, 1991).

USS *LaSalle* Investigation. Tim LaCroix Interview (Vermont, 1991). Accounts from anonymous former and current crew members.

Jay Hatheway Interview (Minneapolis, MN 1991–1992).

Lawrence Korb Interview (Washington DC, 1991).

"I wish that sexual orientation . . ." Letter from Major General Floyd Baker, Ft. Sam, Houston TX, contained in a series of documents relative to the two year-long discharge proceedings against Dr. Stanley Harris.

Greg Baldwin Interview (Miami FL, 1991).

AIDS. Randy Shilts, *And the Band Played On: Politics, People, and the AIDS Epidemic* (New York: St. Martin's Press, 1987).

42. Railroading

Newak Case. Faith Seidenberg Telephone Interview (1991). *U.S.* v. *Newak* 15 M.J. 541 (AFCMR 1982). *U.S.* v. *Newak* 24 M.J. 238 (CMA 1987). *U.S.* v. *Newak* 25 M.J. 564 (AFCMR 1987). Rhonda Rivera Interviews (Columbus OH, 1990–1992). Nat Henthoff, "The Court-Martial of Lieutenant Joann Newak," *The Village Voice,* 12 April 1983, p. 8. Henthoff, "I'd Be Willing to Give Up My Life for My Country," *The Village Voice,* 26 April 1983, p. 6.

Perry Watkins Interviews, op. cit. Perry Watkins Document: Administrative Discharge Hearing, Ft. Lewis WA, 28 October 1981.

43. Doreen

Gay Culture in Navy. Kelly Kittell Interviews (San Francisco CA, 1991–1992). Kelly Kittell Documents: *The Family-Gram,* Lambda Press, 3 October 1982, First Issue. *The Family-Gram,* Lambda Press, 3 October 1982, Second Issue (Special Edition: "Doreen Speaks Out!!!!!!!!"). Armistead Maupin Interview (San Francisco CA, 1991).

USS *Eisenhower.* Matt Oler Interview, op. cit.

Hippler, *Matlovich, The Good Soldier,* op. cit.

Cliff Anchor Interviews, op. cit.

First AIDS Cases in the Armed Services. Robert Redfield Interview (Washington DC, 1991). Ed Tramont Interview (Baltimore MD, 1991).

Raymond Orsini Documents: Raymond Orsini, Press Release and Letter, 1983. Medical Records of Raymond Orsini, Dr. Frank Rhode, Captain USAF, Lackland Air Force Base, Texas, 17 March 1983.

Kelly Kittell Documents: Letter to Captain Spane from Kelly Kittell (no date).

44. Lesbian Vampires of Bavaria

Ruth Voor Interviews (Tampa FL, 1991–1992).

Karen Colton Interviews (Tampa FL, 1991–1992).

Steve Robin Interviews (Los Angeles CA and Oklahoma City OK, 1990–1992).

Women's Enfranchisement. Patricia Davis, "Uncle Sam's Lesbians: Power, Empowerment, and the Military Experience," Master's Thesis, Old Dominion University, Norfolk VA, 1991. Maj. Gen. Jeanne Holm, USAF (Ret.), *Women in the Military: An Unfinished Revolution* (Novato CA: Presidio Press, 1982). Marcia Cohen, *The Sisterhood: The Inside Story of the Women's Movement and the Leaders Who Made It Happen* (New York: Ballantine Books, 1988). Document: Women In the Army, by Women in the Army Policy Review Group, 30 September 1982. "Breaking Through—Women on the Move," *U.S. News & World Report,* 29 November 1982, pp. 51–57.

USS *Dixon* Investigation. Jill Waters Interview (San Diego CA, 1991). Anonymous interview with a former USS *Dixon* female crew member. Bridget Wilson Interviews (San Diego CA, 1990–1992). Uncle Sam Doesn't Want You," *Sixty Minutes* transcript, Volume XV, Number 17 as broadcast over the CBS Television Network, 9 January 1983.

USS *Puget Sound* Investigation. Anonymous Interview.

Memphis Naval Air Station purge. Chris Riddough, "Military Harassment of Gays Continues," *National NOW Times* (no date), p. 3.

Concord Naval Weapons Station Purge. Anonymous interview.

Okinawa Softball Team Investigation. Diana Higgs Interview (Orange County CA, 1992).

USS *Lexington* Softball Team Recruits Heterosexuals. Anonymous interview with female crew member. Interview with anonymous female service member (San Diego CA, 1992).

Discharge Statistics. Hippler, *Matlovich, The Good Soldier,* op. cit., p. 157. Enlisted Homosexual Administrative Separations (DoD Directive 1332.14).

Newak Case. Faith Seidenberg Telephone Interview, op. cit. *U.S.* v. *Newak* 15 M.J. 541 (AFCMR 1982). *U.S.* v. *Newak* 24 M.J. 238 (CMA 1987). *U.S.* v. *Newak* 25 M.J. 564 (AFCMR 1987). Rhonda Rivera Interviews, op. cit. Nat Hentoff, "The Prisoner Who Had to Be Kept Away From the Press," *The Village Voice,* 19 April 1983, p. 6.

45. Straights

Bruce Diamond Telephone Interview (St. Louis MO, 1991).

Darlene Chamberlin Interview (Elkton MD, 1990).

Lillian Whitaker Interview (Elkton MD, 1990).

ROTC. Marc Killinger, "Students Fight Military Over Campus Recruitment," *Gay Community News,* 20 November 1982, p. 1. Larry Goldsmith, "Faculty Vote Bans Military Recruitment At Boston Law School," *Gay Community News,* 4 December 1982, p. 1. Goldsmith, "Law School Bars Defense Recruiters," *Gay Community News,* 12 March 1983, p. 10. Roberto Reyes-Colon Interviews (Portland OR, 1991–1992). Killinger, "Universities Reinstate Military Recruiters," *Gay Community News,* 5 February 1983, p. 3.

Bridget Wilson Interviews, op. cit.

Perry Watkins Interviews, op. cit.

Melvin Dahl Interview, op. cit.

Miriam Ben-Shalom Interview (Minneapolis MN, 1991).

Perry Watkins. "Uncle Sam Doesn't Want You," *Sixty Minutes* transcript, Volume XV, Number 17 as broadcast over the CBS Television Network, 9 January 1983.

Diane Matthews, ROTC. Michael Asen Telephone Interview (1992). Tom Philpott, "Avowed Lesbian Sues to Remain in ROTC," *Navy Times,* 14 March 1983, p. 29. *Matthews* v. *Marsh,* 755 F.2d 182 (1985). Deposition: Major General H. Norman Schwarzkopf, 28 USC sect. 1246, 29 October 1982.

46. In the Midnight Sky

Raymond Orsini Press Release & Letter. Author's note: Orsini did not date his press release; it is from 1983. Raymond Orsini Documents: USAF Formal Physical Evaluation Board, Lackland Air Force Base, 28 June 1983. Medical Record, Narrative Summary, by Frank Rhode, Cpt. USAF MC, & David Henry, Maj. USAF MC, 18 March 1983, Lackland AFB.

First Case of AIDS in the Navy. "3 in Service Called AIDS Victims," *Navy Times,* 4 July 1983.

William Kerr. Randy Shilts, "Sailor's Trouble Over AIDS Inquiry," *San Francisco Chronicle,* 30 March 1983, p. 3.

John Baskin. Jim Ryan, "Gay Man With AIDS Wins Discharge Battle," *Gay Community News,* 10 March 1984, p. 1.

Robert Redfield Interview, op. cit.

Grenada Invasion. Anonymous Interview.

USS *Eisenhower.* Matt Oler Interview, op. cit.

"AIDS won't be a problem . . ." Anonymous interview with infantry captain.

Hippler, *Matlovich, The Good Soldier,* op. cit.

Ft. Carson Purge. Paul Kutche, "Gay Community Alarmed Over Military Discharges," *Gay Community News,* 17 December 1983, p. 1.

Bolling Air Force Base. Urvashi Vaid, "Military Steps Up Harassment of Gays," *Gay Community News,* 17 December 1983, p. 1.

Carolyn "Dusty" Pruitt Interviews (Long Beach CA, 1991–1992).

Stan Harris Interview (Los Angeles CA, 1990).

Discharge Statistics, 1983–1984. Enlisted Homosexual Administrative Separations (DoD Directive 1332.14).

Newak Case. Faith Seidenberg Telephone Interview, op. cit. *U.S.* v. *Newak* 15 M.J. 541 (AFCMR 1982). *U.S.* v. *Newak* 24 M.J. 238 (CMA 1987). *U.S.* v. *Newak* 25 M.J. 564 (AFCMR 1987). Rhonda Rivera Interviews, op. cit. Lawrence Korb Interview, op. cit. "Air Force Paroles Lesbian Jailed on Sodomy, Drug Charges," *The Advocate,* 29 September 1983, Vol. 377, p. 8.

47. Heroes

Fidel Camacho Interview (Jacksonville NC, 1991).

"The corporal stood dazed . . ." Anonymous interview with marine corporal.

Jim Dressel Interviews (Lansing MI, 1991–1992). Dressel personal collection of clippings and documents: "A Case Study: Public Opinion and the Defeat of Incumbent James Dressel in Michigan's 95th District," Alyson R. Bitner.

"Homos are so low . . ." Form Letter, From David A. Williams, Executive Director American Family Association, Washington DC.

Danny Leonard Interviews (Jacksonville NC, 1990–1991). Author's note: Danny Leonard is also known as Brandy Alexander.

"Although AIDS is carried . . ." Williams letter, op. cit.

Gay Civil Rights and AIDS. Shilts, *And the Band Played On,* op. cit.

Vernon "Copy" Berg III Interviews (New York NY, 1991–1992).

48. Exiles

Perry Watkins Interviews, op. cit. Perry Watkins Document: *Watkins* v. *Army,* 721 F.2D 687 (9th Cir. 1983), 555 F. Supp 212 (W.D. Wash. 1982), 541 F. Supp 249 (W.D. Wash. 1982).

Matthews v. *Marsh,* op. cit.

Dronenburg Ruling. *Dronenburg* v. *Zech* 741 F. 2d 1388 (D.C. Cir. 1984) rehearing *en banc* denied, 746 F. 2d 1579 (D.C. Cir. 1984). Kelly Carbetta-Scandy, "The Armed Services' Continued Degradation and Expulsion of Their Homosexual Members: *Dronenburg* v. *Zech*," *Cincinnati Law Review,* pp. 1055–1060. Rhonda Rivera Interviews, op. cit. Bridget Wilson Interviews, op. cit. Leonard Graff Interview (San Francisco CA, 1991).

1984 Election. "Reagan Would Not Ease Stand on Homosexuals," *The New York Times,* 18 August 1984, p. 8 col. 6. John J. Goldman, "Angry Homosexuals Meet with Glenn, Decry His Stand on Gay Rights." *Los Angeles Times,* 14 December 1984, p. 9 col 1. James M. Perry, "Convention Site Is Unconventional," *The Wall Street Journal,* 12 July 1984, sec. 2 p. 62.

Jim Dressel Interview, op. cit. Susan Ager, "He Fought for Fairness and Was Fired," *Detroit Free Press,* 12 August 1984, p. 1. "A 'Queer' Election Campaign," *Grand Rapids Tribune,* 18 March 1984, p. A13.

Interview with Anonymous Marine Corporal.

49. Blanket Parties

William "Pete" Randell Interviews (Atlanta GA, 1990–1992).

Washington DC Cruising Sting. Jim Marks, "Military Judge Accused of Soliciting Cop," *The Advocate,* 11 December 1984, p. 29. "Judicial Irony," *Gay Community News,* 24 November 1984, p. 2. Author's note: Judge Fletcher was also involved in the Joann Newak appeal.

Linda Gautney Telephone Interview (1991).

Jack Green Interview (Oklahoma City OK, 1991).

Kevin Drewery Interview (Greensboro NC, 1992).

50. Costs

David Marier Interview (Atlanta GA, 1991). David Marier Documents: Court-martial of Captain David F. Marier, Headquarters 8th Air Force, 16 April 1985. Also includes: job evaluations, OSI documents, and discharge documents.

GAO Report on Cost of Homosexual Discharges. Department of Defense response to General Accounting Office Review of Homosexual Exclusion Policy, Jerry L. Calhoun, Principal Deputy Assistant Secretary of Defense (Manpower, Installations & Logistics), 18 September 1984.

Pearl Harbor Purge. Pam Westbrooke Interview (Seattle WA, 1991).

USS *Carl Vincent*. Darren Gomez Interview (Aurora CO, 1992).

Warren Air Force Base Discharges. "Warren AFB, Wyoming," *The Advocate,* 24 December 1985, p. 27.

Diego Garcia Investigation. Anonymous Interview.

Teddy Bear Investigation. Lou Chibbaro, Jr., "Army Investigates Four Soldiers in Fort Myer's Elite Corps," *Washington Blade,* 12 December 1985, p. 1.

USS *Constitution* Investigation. Derek Landzaat Interview (Honolulu HI, 1991).
Phil Zimmerman Interview (Columbus OH, 1991–1992).

51. HTLV-III

Byron Gary Kinney Documents: Administrative Discharge Board Proceedings, Naval Station, San Diego, CA, 25 June 1985.

Bud Broyhill and Dave Walter, "AIDS Confidentiality in the Military," *The Advocate*, 26 November 1985, p. 12.

Daniel Abeita. Bridget Wilson Interviews, op. cit.

Byron Gary Kinney Documents (Medical History): Clinical Records, US Naval Hospital, Okinawa, Japan, 29 October and 13 November 1984. Report of Medical Board, US Naval Hospital, San Diego, CA, 10 December 1984. Memorandum from Fred Millard LCDR MC, US Naval Hospital, San Diego, CA, 20 June 1985.

"Homosexuality is incompatible . . ." Paul Smith, "Navy Forces Out Victims who Admit Homosexual Conduct," *Navy Times*, 26 August 1985, p. 4.

Colonel Ed Tramont Interview, op. cit.

Major Robert Redfield Interview, op. cit.

AIDS History. Shilts, *And the Band Played On*, op. cit.

Smallpox Infected Recruit. Robert Redfield, et. al., "Disseminated Vaccinia in a Military Recruit with Human Immunodeficiency Virus Disease," *New England Journal of Medicine*, 12 March 1987, pp. 673–676.

Blood Bank. Shilts, *And the Band Played On*, op. cit. Marcos Bisticas-Cocoves, "Military Seeks Test Results," *Gay Community News*, 4 May 1985, p. 1. Bisticas-Cocoves, "Pentagon Delays Policy on Military Blood Donors," *Gay Community News*, 3 August 1985, p. 1. Letter from Barbara Boxer, U.S. Representative, and Alan Cranston, U.S. Senator, to Caspar Weinberger, Secretary of Defense, Subject: Release of HTLV-III Names to Military, 15 May 1985.

"For pointing a finger . . ." Mark Scott, "DoD wants lists of military personnel who test positive for HTLV-III antibody," *Washington Blade*, 26 April 1985, p. 1.

William "Pete" Randell Interviews, op. cit.

52. Dykebusters

Karen Colton Interviews, op. cit.

Ruth Voor Interviews, op. cit.

Women and Reagan. Holm, *Women in the Military*, op. cit., pp. 382–392. "Utilization of Women Slows Under Reagan," *Minerva*, Spring 1985, p. 18. "Marijuana Detection, Dog Handler and Other 'Combat Jobs' Closed to Women Marines," *Minerva*, Spring 1985, p. 20. "Three NATO Nations Now Allow Women in Combat, NATO Conference Told," *Minerva*, Fall 1988, p. 49. "More Historic Firsts," *Minerva*, Winter 1983, p. 34. "Army Captain Honored by *Glamour* Magazine," *Minerva*, Spring 1985, p. 28. "Army Intelligence Center Has First Woman Commander," *Minerva*, Spring 1985, p. 29. "More Firsts for Women and F 165," *Minerva*, Fall 1985, p. 54. "Navy Assigns First Woman Ship Executive Officer," *Minerva*, Spring 1985, p. 31. "Cadoria is Army's First Female Combat Support General," *Minerva*, Fall 1985, p. 55. "Foote Will Be Army's Second Female Combat Support General," *Minerva*, Fall 1985 p. 56. "Married Air Force Women Lack Commitment and Single Ones are 'Queer' Says Curtis LeMay," *Minerva*, Fall 1986, pp. 29–30. Lawrence Korb Interview (Washington DC, 1991).

Parris Island Witch-Hunt, 1984. Renee Mueller Interviews (Indianapolis IN, 1991–1992). Diane Edwards Interviews (Beaufort SC, 1991–1992). Interviews with anonymous Parris Island women Marines.

Bob Ledet Interview (Norfolk VA, 1991).

Fort Polk Harassments. Interview with anonymous military police officer.

Mary Beth Harrison Interviews (Durham NC, 1990–1992).

Jeanne Martin Interview (Medford MA, 1991).

West Point Affair. Interview with anonymous enlisted woman.

David Marier Interview, op. cit.

Jim Dressel Interview, op. cit.

53. Friends of Helga

Major Robert Redfield Interview, op. cit.

Colonel Ed Tramont Interview, op. cit.

Lawrence Korb Interview, op. cit.

Heterosexual HTLV-III. Robert Redfield, et al., "Heterosexually Acquired HTLV-III/LAV Disease Epidemiologic Evidence for Female-to-Male Transmission," *Journal of the American Medical Association*, 18 October 1985, pp. 2094–2096. Shilts, *And the Band Played On*, op. cit.

Department of Defense AIDS Policy Development. Statement of Jeffrey Levi, Director of Governmental and Political Affairs, National Gay Task Force to Armed Forces Epidemiological Board, 7 August 1985. Letter to William Mayer, M.D., Assistant Secretary of Defense for Health Affairs from Jeffrey Levi, Director, Governmental and Political Affairs, National Gay Task Force, 13 August 1985. Dave Walter, "Military Officials Say HTLV-3 Test Should by Used to Screen Troops," *The Advocate*, 17 September 1985, p. 12. Letter to AABB Institutional and Associate Institutional Members, From Grace M. Neitzer, Subject: Joint

Statement on Blood Collections on Military Installations, 4 September 1985. Paul Smith, "AIDS Seen Bankrupting Military Medical System," *Navy Times*, 26 August 1985, p. 4. Smith, "Navy Forces Out Victims Who Admit Homosexual Contact," op. cit. Smith, "DoD Seeks Suggestions on Monitoring AIDS," *Air Force Times*, 12 August 1985, p. 1. Smith, "AIDS Should Not Trigger Hysteria, Researchers Say," *Navy Times*, 28 October 1985, pp. 36–37. Government Document: Department of Defense, Armed Forces Epidemiological Board, Memorandum for the Assistant Secretary of Defense (Health Affairs), The Surgeon General, Department of the Army, The Surgeon General, Department of the Navy, The Surgeon General, Department of the Air Force, Subject: Human T-Lymphotrophic Virus Type III (HTLV-III) Antibody Positivity, 17 September 1985. Government Document: The Secretary of Defense, Washington, The District of Columbia, Memorandum for Secretaries of the Military Departments, Chairman, Joint Chiefs of Staff, Assistant Secretary of Defense and General Counsel, Subject: Policy on Identification, Surveillance, and Disposition of Military Personnel Infected With Human T-Lymphotrophic Virus Type III (HTLV-III). Author's Note: Many of the documents and articles used to research this section were provided by Dr. Rhonda Rivera of the Ohio State University Law School.

Bridget Wilson Interviews, op. cit.

Jim Glaser, "Navy Board Recommends Ouster," *San Diego Gayzette*, 27 June 1985, p. 6.

Bridget Wilson, "Kinney: He Beat the Navy But Lost to AIDS," *San Diego Gayzette*, 24 October 1985.

Dave Walter, " 'Bud' Broyhill Succumbs," *The Advocate*, 7 January 1986, p. 23.

54. Where It All Begins

Barbara Baum Interview (West Palm Beach FL, 1991–1992).

Joseph Steffan Interview (Los Angeles CA, 1990).

Cliff Anchor Interview, op. cit.

BOOK SIX: HOMOVAC (1986–1990)

55. Tom Dooley's Undesirable Discharge

Diana Shaw Interviews (Los Angeles CA, 1990–1992).

Tom Dooley Documents: Department of the Navy Memo, From Chief of Naval Personnel, To Director of Naval Intelligence, Subject: Lieutenant Thomas A. Dooley, III, Request for investigation of Homosexual Tendencies, 26 January 1956. Office of Naval Intelligence Surveillance by ONI Special Agents of Dooley, New York, Philadelphia, New Orleans, Miami, Charleston WV, Dayton OH, Columbus OH, Tuckahoe NY, St. Louis, Denver, Phoenix, Oakland CA, San Francisco, etc., from January 1956 through March 1956, Specific Informant Interview. District Intelligence Office Memo, From District Intelligence Officer, Third Naval District, To Director of Naval Intelligence, Subject: Dooley, Thomas Anthony III, Lieutenant, Transcript of conversation between Dooley and stoolie (informant) that occurred on 1 March 1956 in a car ride returning to New York from a speaking engagement. United States Government Inter-Office Memo: To Op-92C, From Op-921D, Subject: Lieutenant Thomas A. Dooley, 9 March 1956. Department of the Navy Memo, From Head, Officer Performance Branch, To Director of Naval Intelligence, Subject: Lieutenant Thomas A. Dooley, USNR, 9 March 1956. Censored Government Memo To Op-92, Subject: LT Thomas A. Dooley, 15 March 1956. Author's note: These documents are from among a set of over 300 pages of surveillance notes by the ONI (Office of Naval Intelligence).

Ted Werner Interviews (Los Angeles CA, 1990–1992).

GAO Report. Defense Force Management, DoD's Policy on Homosexuality, June 1992.

GAO Supplemental Report. Defense Force Management, Statistics Related to DoD's Policy on Homosexuality, June 1992.

Bowers v. *Hardwick*, 106 S. Ct. 2841 (1986). Brief Amicus Curiae for Lesbian Rights Project, Women's Legal Defense Fund, Equal Rights Advocates, Inc., Women's Law Project, and National Women's Law Center, October Term 1985. Rhonda Rivera Interview, op. cit. Leonard Graff Telephone Interview (1991).

56. The Unquiet Death of Michael W. Foster

Foster Suicide, Lou Chibbaro, Jr., "Soldier Tested for AIDS Hangs Himself," *Washington Blade*, 24 January 1986, p. 1. FOIA Document: Report of Casualty, Foster, Michael, Death Certificate, 21 August 1986.

Herwatt AIDS Case. Jeff Herwatt Interview (San Francisco CA, 1991). Carmen Roides, "GI has AIDS and Hope, 'I'm Not Dying Yet!'," *Stars and Stripes* (no date). Jeff Herwatt Documents: Criminal Investigation Division Report of Investigation, U.S. Army Criminal Investigation Command, NEU ULM Resident Agency Second Region, 11 August 1986.

Wayne Bell Interview (Jacksonville NC, 1991–1992).

Robert Plowman Interview (New Orleans LA, 1991).

Wilford Hall. Anonymous Interview with Air Force officer. Laurie Garrett, "The Army's HIV Hotel," *Newsday*, 26 February 1989, pp. 5, 26–27. Laurie Garrett, "The Army's War Against AIDS," *Newsday*, 27 February 1989, pp. 6, 26.

Major Robert Redfield Interview (Washington DC, 1991).

Colonel Ed Tramont Interview (Baltimore MD, 1991).

USS *Nimitz*. Interview with anonymous crewman.

Jeff Herwatt Documents: Letter from Joseph Brewer, MA., Chief Investigator, Project Inform, Subject: Sergeant Jeffrey Herwatt Medical Treatment, 13 June 1986.

57. Countertrends

Ruth Voor Interviews (Tampa FL, 1991–1992).

Karen Colton Interviews (Tampa FL, 1991–1992).

Linda Gautney Telephone Interview (1991).

Balboa Naval Hospital. Jim Jennings Interview (San Diego CA, 1991).

USS *Cape Cod*. Interview with three anonymous female sailors.

Ellen Nesbitt Interview (Sonoma County CA, 1990).

Bridget Wilson Interviews (San Diego CA, 1990–1992).

Paul Ribarich Interview (Tampa FL, 1991).

John Evans Interview (Alexandria VA, 1991).

Joe Hoyer Telephone Interview (1991).

Terry Ryder Interview (Baltimore MD, 1992).

Diego Garcia, A Day in the Life. Anonymous Interview. Robert White Interview (San Francisco CA, 1991).

Adak NAS. Jerry Foshee Interview (San Francisco CA, 1991).

USS *Carl Vincent*. Darren Gomez Interview (Aurora CO, 1991).

NSA, GMA. Terry Ryder Interview, op. cit.

Sembach Air Base. Interviews with anonymous Air Force personnel.

Todd Quintez Interview (San Francisco CA, 1991).

Michael Patton Interviews (San Diego CA, 1990–1991).

Dr. Mike Rankin Interview (San Francisco CA, 1991–1992).

Vance Walker Interview (Boston MA, 1991).

Dr. Ronald Rae Interviews (San Diego CA, 1990–1991).

Bowers v. *Hardwick*. Serene Novell, "Constitutional Law: State Proscription of Private Consensual Homosexual Conduct—*Bowers* v. *Hardwick*," *30 Howard Law Journal*, 843 (1987). Tharpe, "*Bowers* v. *Hardwick* and the Legitimization of Homophobia in America," *30 Howard Law Journal*, 829 (1987). *Bowers* v. *Hardwick*, 106 S. Ct. 2841 (1986). Brief Amicus Curiae for Lesbian Rights Project, Women's Legal Defense Fund, Equal Rights Advocates, Inc., Women's Law Project, and National Women's Law Center, October Term 1985. Author's Note: Information on this decision provided by Dr. Rhonda Rivera. Peter Freiberg, "Poll Shows Americans Disapprove of Ruling," *The Advocate*, 5 August 1986, p. 11. Ethan Bronner, "Ex-Justice Says 1986 Vote On Gay Sex Was Wrong," *Albuquerque Journal*, 26 October 1990, p. 8.

Jack Green Interview (Oklahoma City OK, 1991).

58. The Color Purple (Part II)

T. J. Sterbens Interviews (San Diego CA, 1990–1991). T. J. Sterbens Documents: Enlisted Performance Evaluation Reports from November 1984 to August 1986.

AIDS, 1986. Major Robert Redfield Interview, op. cit. Colonel Ed Tramont Interview, op. cit. FOIA Document: Background Information on the DoD Experience with Human Immunodeficiency Virus (HIV), Office of the Assistant Secretary of Defense Health Affairs, Washington DC, 1 May 1987, Prepared by Lt. Col. Herblod. R. Redfield, D. C. Write and E. C. Tramont, "The Walter Reed Staging Classification for the HTLV III/LAV Infection," *New England Journal of Medicine*, 1986, Vol. 314, p. 131–132. "Officials See Research Opportunity in Testing Program," *AIDS Policy and Law*, 21 May 1986, p. 4. David L. Kirp, "Drastic Measures in Disputed AIDS Study," *San Francisco Examiner*, 9 February 1986, p. A1. Sharon B. Young, "AIDS Panel Recommends Early Medical Discharge," *Air Force Times*, 20 October 1986, p. 12. "Top Pentagon Official Backs AIDS Policy," *The New York Times*, 18 December 1986, p. 19.

Top Military Officials. J. David Derr, D.P.M. Interview (San Diego CA, January 1991). Jim Kehrer Interview (New Memphis IL, 1991).

Anonymous Interview with former member, 82nd Airborne.

Mike LaBella Interview (Seattle WA, 1991).

New AIDS Regulations 1987. Kathleen Gilberd, "Department of Defense Revised Policy on AIDS and HIV Antibody Testing," *On Watch*, May 1987.

Walter Reed Ward. David France, "Military Created Wards for HTLV-3 Positive Soldiers," *The Advocate*, 8 July 1986.

Air Force Art Program. Anonymous interview with Air Force officer.

Hippler, *Matlovich, The Good Soldier*, op. cit.

59. At the Buccaneer Motel

Barbara Baum Interviews (West Palm Beach FL, 1991–1992).

Renee Mueller Interviews (Indianapolis IN, 1991–1992).

Becky Feldhaus Interview (Tampa FL, 1991).

Womanpause Source. "Women Over 10% of Military," *The New York Times*, 4 April 1987, p. 7.

Mary Beth Harrison Interviews (Durham NC, 1990–1992).

Anonymous Interview.

Bonnie Clark Interviews (Durham NC, 1990–1992).

Erickson Harassment Study. "Sexual Harassment in Army Has Not Decreased Says CSM Erickson," *Minerva*, Spring 1987.

West Point Purge. James Feron, "Army Dismissed Eight Women on Sex Charges," *The New York Times*, 4 October 1986, p. 11. Rose Marie Arce and Robert O'Harrow, Jr., "Army Ousts 8 MPs as Homosexuals," *The Times Herald Record*, 2 October 1986, p. 3. Arce and Mary Hedglon, "Point 'Gays' Running Scared," *The Times Herald Record*, (no page or date).

Pam Lane Interview (San Francisco, 1990).

Barbara Baum Parris Island Documents (Buccaneer Motel Incident): Details taken from Article 32 Investigation (Court-martial) of Corporal Barbara J. Baum, U.S. Marine Corps, Headquarters and Service Battalion, Marine Corps Recruit Training Depot, Parris Island, South Carolina on 15 and 18 April 1988.

Joseph Steffan Interview (Los Angeles CA, 1990). Joe Steffan, *Honor Bound, A Gay American Fights for the Right to Serve His Country* (New York: Random House, 1992).

Kendall Truitt Interview (Aiken SC, 1992).

60. HOMOVAC: Prisoner Number 73343

Paul Starr Interview (Sacramento CA, 1991). Paul Starr Document: Verbatim Record of Trial (and accompanying papers) of Starr, Paul C., Captain, 52nd Supply Squadron USAF, Spangdahlem AB, Germany, by General Court-Martial, Tried at Spangdahlem Air Base, Germany, 2 March 1987.

Vernon "Copy" Berg III Interviews (New York NY, 1991–1992).

Joe Steffan Interview, op. cit.

Steffan, *Honor Bound,* op. cit.

Orlando Gotay Interview (San Francisco CA, December 1990).

Anonymous interview with former Naval Academy midshipman.

Robb Bettiker Interview (Washington DC, 1991).

Statistics of Discharges, 1986–1990. DoD Public Affairs, Homosexual Discharges 1982–1991.

Soesterberg Affair. Jack Green Interview (Oklahoma City OK, 1991). Jack Green Documents include approximately 35 pages of Dutch news clippings with translations.

Major Abel van Weerd Interview (Netherlands, September 1991).

Interview with anonymous brigadier general.

Interview with a major general's son.

Hippler, *Matlovich, The Good Soldier,* op. cit.

Jeff Herwatt Interviews, op. cit.

Hug Ward. Cheryl Clark, "The Military and AIDS," *San Diego Union,* 1 March 1987, p. B1.

T. J. Sterbens Interviews, op. cit.

VA and AIDS. Anne Laurent, "VA Hospitals Face Issues Raised by AIDS Cases," *Air Force Times,* 2 March 1987.

Danny Flaherty Interviews, (San Francisco CA, 1991–1992).

James (Jim) Foster Interviews (San Francisco CA, 1976–1991).

William "Pete" Randell Interviews, op. cit.

Robert "Jess" Jessop Documents: Interviews with Jessop's cousin, Pat Katka and estate executor, George Murphy.

DACOWITS History. *DACOWITS,* Department of Defense Publication, 1982.

Okinawa Lesbians and DACOWITS. Linda Grant De Pauw, "Gender as Stigma: Probing Some Sensitive Issues," *Minerva,* Spring 1988.

Barbara Baum Interviews, op. cit.

Becky Feldhaus Interview, op. cit.

61. Foreign Affairs

Paul Starr Interview, op. cit.

Soesterberg Affair. Jack Green Interview, op. cit. Senator Marie Louise Tiesinga Autsema Interview (Netherlands, 1993).

Other Countries and Their Policies on Homosexuality and the Military, Casimir Elson, Report on the Legal Situation of Homosexual Men and Women in the Armed Forces, International Lesbian and Gay Association, 1987. NATO General: Neil Roland, " 'Stripes' Ordered Not to Print Story on West German General," *Navy Times,* 27 February 1984, p. 33. Interviews with David Said and two other former members of the Israeli Defense Forces. Great Britain Documents: Select Committee on the Armed Forces Bill, Evidence Submitted by the Campaign for Homosexual Equality, January 1986.

Franz van Dorp Interview (Netherlands, 1991).

Major Abel van Weerd Interview, op. cit.

Lieutenant Colonel Rene Holtel Interview (Netherlands, 1991).

Hippler, *Matlovich, The Good Soldier,* op. cit.

62. The Escape

Paul Starr Interview, op. cit.

Terry Knox Interview (Denver CO, 1990). Parris Island Document: Statement by Terry Knox to Miss L. R. King, Special Agent of the Naval Investigative Service, Parris Island, SC, 11 January 1988. Mary Jo Miller, "Petty Officer Charged with Perjury," *The Beaufort Gazette*, 30 June 1988, p. 2-A.

Barbara Baum Interview, op. cit.

Statement of Bonnie Ferguson to Naval Investigative Service, Parris Island SC, January 1988.

Paula Berry Interview (Lady's Island SC, 1992).

Soesterberg Affair. Jack Green Interview, op. cit. Senator Marie Louise Tiesinga Autsema Interview, op. cit. Jack Green Documents: "Lawyer Annoyed by Military Homosexual Case," *Traow*, 13 June 1988. Theo Kline, "The Case of the Homosexual Sergeant and American Embassy Response," *de Volkskrant*, 14 June 1988.

63. Naming Names

Tanya Domi Interviews (Washington DC, 1991–1992).

Mary Beth Harrison Interviews, op. cit. Mary Beth Harrison Document: Letter to U.S. Representative Harold Volkmer from Mary E. Harrison, PN 1, US Navy, Combat Support Squadron Eight, Naval Amphibious Base, Little Creek, Norfolk, VA, 27 January 1989, Subject: Sexual Harassment of Women on USS *Grapple*.

DACOWITS and Harassment. "Pentagon Has Given Up on Ending Sexual Harassment Says Former DACOWITS Chair," *Minerva's Bulletin Board*, Summer 1989, pp. 6–7. Linda Grant De Pauw, "Gender as Stigma: Probing Some Sensitive Issues," *Minerva*, Spring 1988, pp. 29–43.

Lesbian Discharge Statistics. GAO Report: Defense Force Management, DoD's Policy on Homosexuality, June 1992. GAO Supplemental Report: Defense Force Management, Statistics Related to DoD's Policy on Homosexuality, June 1992.

Parris Island Witch-Hunt. "USMC Investigating Homosexuality at Parris Island," *Beaufort Gazette*, 22 February 1988, p. 1. "Two Marines Charged with Indecent Acts." *Beaufort Gazette*, 23 February 1988, p. 1-A. Mary Jo Miller, "Hearings Scheduled for Female Marines," *Beaufort Gazette*, 2 March 1988, p. 3-A. Miller, "2 More Marines Charged," *Beaufort Gazette*, 15 March 1988, p. 1-A. Miller, "Marine Describes Sexual Encounters," *Beaufort Gazette*, 17 March 1988 (no page). Miller, "Hearing Postponed for Marine Captain," *Beaufort Gazette*, 18 March 1988, p. 1-A. Miller, "Marine Hearing Set for Wednesday," *Beaufort Gazette*, 28 March 1988, p. 1-A. Miller, "Hearing Under Way at Parris Island Depot," *Beaufort Gazette*, 30 March 1988, p. 1-A. Miller, "5th Marine Charged in Sex Scandal," *Beaufort Gazette*, 31 March 1988, p. 1-A. Miller, "Husband Testifies at Hearing," *Beaufort Gazette*, 1 April 1988, p. 1-A.

Becky Feldhaus Interview, op. cit.

Barbara Baum Interviews, op. cit.

Terry Knox Interview, op. cit.

Soesterberg Affair. Jack Green Interview, op. cit. Senator Marie Louise Tiesinga Autsema Interview, op. cit. Jack Green Document: Henk Kool (Translated by Janne Tuijhman), "US Sergeant Handed over Contrary to Agreement," *NRC Handelsblad*, 11 June 1988. Major Abel van Weerd Interview, op. cit.

Parris Island Witch-Hunt. Mary Jo Miller, "Hearing for Marine Captain Postponed to This Afternoon," *Beaufort Gazette*, 5 April 1988, p. 2-A. Miller, "Gretch, Kile Too Friendly, Witnesses Say," *Beaufort Gazette*, 6 April 1988, p. 1-A. Miller, "Witnesses Speak Well of Captain," *Beaufort Gazette*, 7 April 1988, p. 1-A. "Hearing Dates Still to be Set," *Beaufort Gazette*, 12 April 1988, p. 3-A. Miller, "Female Marine Testifies About Homosexual Acts, *Beaufort Gazette*, 15 April 1988, p. 1-A. Miller, "Deputy Says That He Found Marines in Bed," *Beaufort Gazette*, 18 April 1988, p. 1-A. Miller, "Marines' Hearing Resumes," *Beaufort Gazette*, 22 April 1988, p. 1-A. Miller, "Marine Tells of Affair With Her DI," *Beaufort Gazette*, 25 April 1988, p. 1-A. Miller, "Defense Grills Lay Witnesses in PI Hearing," *Beaufort Gazette*, 26 April 1988, p. 1-A. "Ex-Marine Describes NIS Probe," *Beaufort Gazette*, 14 June 1988, p. 1-A. June D. Bell, "A Proud Career Ends in Disillusion," *The Sunday Times Leader* (Wilkes-Barre PA), 31 July 1988, p. 1.

Parris Island Barbara Baum Documents: Statement of Diana E. Maldonado, US Marine Corps, To Gary E. Smith of the Naval Investigative Service, Parris Island, SC. 25 March 1988. Article 32 Investigation (Court-martial) of Corporal Barbara J. Baum, op. cit.

Kendall Truitt Interview, op. cit.

USS *Iowa*. Interview with anonymous seaman.

64. Soesterberg Affair

Barbara Baum Interviews, op. cit.

Fran Cail Interview (Sheldon SC, 1991).

Soesterberg Affair. Jack Green Interview, op. cit. Senator Marie Louise Tiesinga Autsema Interview, op. cit. Jack Green Document: Henk Kool (Translated by Janne Tuijhman), "US Sergeant Handed Over Contrary to Agreement," *NCR Handelsblad*, 11 June 1988. (Translated by Janne Tuijhman), "Lawyer Angry Because of Case of Military Homosexual," *Troun*, 13 June 1988. "Ad Ploeg Steps into the Breach for 'Homosexual' US Soldier Green," *Telegraaf*, 20 June 1988. Bert Steinmetz, "Tug of War About Fate of Homosexual Sergeant," *Parool*, 13 June 1988. Steinmetz, "The Nightmare of Sergeant Green," *Parool*, 17 June 1988.

"Father Seeks Inquiry into Military Case," *The Philadelphia Inquirer,* 19 June 1988. Major Abel van Weerd Interview, op. cit.

Joe Steffan Interview, op. cit. Steffan, *Honor Bound,* op. cit.

Parris Island Witch-Hunt (Barbara Baum Court-Martial). Article 32 Investigation (Court-Martial) of Corporal Barbara J. Baum, op. cit. Mary Jo Miller, "Sexual Acts Trial Is Set for Marine," *Beaufort Gazette,* 3 June 1988. p. 1-A. Miller, "Third Sergeant to Be Discharged in Lesbian Case," *Beaufort Gazette,* 9 June 1988, p. 1-A. Miller, "Witness Denies Baum Kiss," *Beaufort Gazette,* 10 June 1988, p. 1-A. Miller, "Marine Corporal Gets 1 Year and Discharge in Lesbian Case," *Beaufort Gazette,* 13 June 1988, p. 1-A.

Diane Edwards Interview (Beaufort SC, 1991).

65. Funerals

Hippler, *Matlovich, The Good Soldier,* op. cit.

Ken McPherson Interviews (San Francisco CA, 1991–1992).

Wittenberg Story. Kary Walker Interview (Chicago IL, 1992). Author's note: The Names Project AIDS Memorial Quilt has a panel made in honor of Colonel Wittenberg.

Anonymous interview with friends of van Poznak.

HIV Retirement Policy. FOIA Document: Memorandum to General Counsel. Department of Defense, Attn: Director, Legislative Reference Service, Subject: Misc. 2196, Proposed Legislation "To authorize the armed forces to retire for physical disability members with human immunodeficiency virus," 12 December 1988, From John C. Crunden, Colonel, GS, Chief Investigations and Legislative Division. "Prevalence of Human Immunodeficiency Virus Antibody in US Active Duty Military Personnel, April 1988," *Morbidity and Mortality Weekly Report (MMWR),* 5 August 1988. "AIDS Infection Rate Drops in Services," *Navy Times,* 29 August 1988, p. 3. Vesta Kimble, "Taft Wants Ouster of Members with AIDS," *Navy Times,* 9 May 1986, p. 3. Cheryl Clark, "AIDS: Navy Figures on Testing Questioned," *The San Diego Tribune,* 30 April 1988, p. B-1.

Fort Sill. Anonymous Interview with HIV-positive soldier.

Anonymous Interview with naval aviator.

Fort Hood HIV Hotel. Laurie Garrett, "The Army's HIV Hotel," *Newsday* (Long Island NY), 26 February 1989, pp. 5, 26–27. Laurie Garrett, "The Army's War Against AIDS," *Newsday,* 27 February 1989, pp. 6, 26. Kathleen Gilberd, "Army HIV 'Quarantine Unit' Exposed," *On Watch,* March/April 1989, p. 10. "History Repeats Itself," *San Antonio Aids Foundation Newsletter,* January 1989, p. 1.

Safe Sex Orders. "HIV and Military," *The Advocate,* 16 August 1988, p. 1. "Navy Acquits Infected Sailor of Malicious Assault Charges," *AIDS Policy and Law,* 18 May 1988, p. 4. "HIV-Positive Soldier Guilty of Having Unprotected Sex," *AIDS Policy and Law,* 10 August 1988, p. 1.

Dave Eckert Interview (San Francisco CA, 1991). Steve Gibson, "Sodomy Court-Martial Rejected for AF Pilot," *Sacramento Bee,* 2 December 1988, p. B-1. Michele McCormick, "AIDS vs. Privacy: We All Have to Face the Question," *Navy Times,* 31 October 1988, p. 21.

T. J. Sterbens Interviews, op. cit.

Mike LaBella Interview, op. cit.

Barbara Baum Interviews, op. cit.

Perry Watkins Interviews, op. cit.

Ellen Nesbitt Interview (Sonoma County CA, 1990).

66. Malleus Maleficarum

Soesterberg Affair. Jack Green Interview, op. cit. Senator Marie Louise Tiesinga Interview, op. cit. Lt. Sylvan Benistant Interview (Netherlands, 1991). Major Abel van Weerd Interview, op. cit. "American Homosexual Sergeant Released from Prison," *de Volkskrant,* 23 June 1988.

Parris Island Witch-Hunt (Terry Knox Hearing). Terry Knox Interview, op. cit. Mike Macloskie Interview (South Carolina, 1992). *Department of Defense, NIS Investigative Manual For Training Special Agents* (Washington DC: Department of Defense, Rev. Ed. 1987). Vaughan Taylor Interview (Jacksonville NC, 1991). Lawrence Korb Interview (Washington DC, 1991). Mary Jo Miller, "Female Marine Charged," *Beaufort Gazette,* 6 July 1988, p. 1-A. Henry L. Kramer and Jacob Sprenger (translated by Rev. Montague Simmons), *Malleus Maleficarum* (Suffolk, England: John Rodker, Publisher, 1928), from part III, question 14. Cindi Ross, "Three Marines Given Discharges in Lesbianism Inquiry," *The State* (Columbia SC), 29 July 1988, p. 2-C.

Parris Island Witch-Hunt (Cheryl Jameson Hearing). Mary Jo Miller, "Female Marine Charged," *Beaufort Gazette,* 6 July 1988, p. 1-A. Cindi Ross, "Second Marine to be Court-Martialed Monday," *The State,* 7 July 1988 (no page). "Marine Court-Martial Postponed until Thursday," *Beaufort Gazette,* 11 July 1988 (no page). Miller, "Prison Sentence Imposed," *Beaufort Gazette,* 15 July 1988, p. 1-A. "Marine Sentenced to One Year," *The State,* 16 July 1988, p. 1-D. "6th Marine Charged in Lesbianism Admits She had Sex with Recruit," *The State,* 19 July 1988 (no page). Miller, "Marine Testifies in Sodomy Case," *Beaufort Gazette,* 18 July 1988, p. 1-A. Parris Island Document: Declaration of Christine R. Hilinski, 30 August 1989. Ross, "Corps Deters Witnesses, Attorneys Say," *The State,* 1 August 1988, B-1. "Corps Punishes Two Females Who Testified in Lesbian Case," *Daily News* (Jacksonville NC), 2 August 1988, p. 1-A. Jack Murphy, "Lesbian Cases Sent Chill Over Marines," *Washington-Star News,* 7 August 1988, p. 1-A. Parris Island Document: Affidavit of Christine Sharron Taylor, Jacksonville NC, March 1990.

Parris Island Witch-Hunt (Diane Edwards and Becky Feldhaus). Diane Edwards Interview, op. cit. Becky

Feldhaus Interview, op. cit. "Marine Corps Boots 3," *Beaufort Gazette,* 29 July 1988, p. 1-A. Becky Feldhaus Documents: Notification of Separation Proceedings, 3 May 1988. Recommendation for Administrative Discharge in the Case of Lance Corporal Rebecca L. Feldhaus, 10 May 1988. Report of Administrative Discharge Board in the Case of Lance Corporal Rebecca L. Feldhaus, 19 July 1988. Discharge of Lance Corporal Rebecca L. Feldhaus, 25 July 1988.

Barbara Baum Jailed. Barbara Baum Interview, op. cit. Christina Smith, "Parris Island Pogrom: Lesbian Marines Jailed," *Coming Up* (San Francisco CA), November 1988, pp. 18–19. Lisa M. Keen, "Woman Says Marines Backed Down on Pact for Clemency," *Washington Blade,* 18 November 1988, p. 1. Barbara Baum Document: General Court-Martial Petition for Clemency, 9 September 1988.

Parris Island Witch-Hunt (Jones, Hinckley, and Gretch). "Marine Captain Charged in Parris Island Probe," *Beaufort Gazette,* 7 September 1988, p. 12-A. John C. Williams, "2nd Officer Implicated by Marines," *Savannah Morning News,* 7 September 1988 (no page). Mary Jo Miller, "Hinckley Awaiting Outcome of Hearing," *Beaufort Gazette,* 9 September 1988, p. 1-A. Wendy Eden, "Marines and Investigation; Gretch Will Remain a Marine," *Beaufort Gazette,* 12 August 1988, p. 1-A.

USS *Yellowstone* Investigation. Mary Beth Harrison Interviews, op. cit. Harrison Documents, op. cit. Kim Wilson Interview (Norfolk VA, 1992). Linda Subda Interview (Florida, 1991). James Longo, "11 Who Admit Homosexuality Face Separation," *Navy Times,* 5 September 1989.

Shelli Hurd Interview (San Diego, 1991–1992).

USMC Gay General. Fran Cail Interview, op. cit., six USMC soldiers.

Bode Suicide. Richard F. Smith, "LeJeune Officials Mourn Death of Athlete," *Daily News,* 13 September 1988. Valaine Bode Case Document: Report of Investigation by Medical Examiner of Valaine S. Bode, 11 September 1988, Charles L. Garrett, M.D., Onslow County NC. Anonymous Interviews with friends in USMC.

Ruth Voor Interview, op. cit.

67. The Release of Prisoner 17

Barbara Baum Released. Barbara Baum Interview, op. cit.

Impact of Parris Island Witch-Hunt. Becky Feldhaus Interview, op. cit. Barbara Baum Interviews, op. cit. Diane Edwards Interview, op. cit. Also, anonymous interviews with Parris Island women Marines. Jim Lynch, "Witch-Hunt at Parris Island: The Marine Corps Targets Lesbians," *The Progressive,* 26 March 1989, pp. 24–27. Michelle M. Benecke and Kirstin S. Dodge, "Military women in nontraditional job fields: casualties of the armed forces' war on homosexuals," *Harvard Women's Law Journal,* Spring '90.

Gay and Lesbian Military Freedom Project Statement of Purpose, Gay & Lesbian Military Freedom Project, Washington DC, May 1989.

Perry Watkins Interviews, op. cit. *Watkins* v. *The Army* 847 F.2d 1329 (9th Cir. 1988).

Miriam Ben-Shalom Interview, op. cit. *Ben-Shalom* v. *The Army* 881 F.2d 454 (7th Cir. 1989).

Joe Steffan Case. Joe Steffan Interview, op. cit. Marc Wolinsky Interview (New York NY, 1991). Howard Bragman Interview (Los Angeles CA, 1990). Steffan, *Honor Bound,* op. cit.

1988 Election. Rick Harding, "NGLTF Releases Results of Candidates Survey on Gay, AIDS Issues," *The Advocate,* 1 March 1988, p. 14.

Ruth Voor Interviews, op. cit.

Karen Colton Interviews, op. cit.

68. Embarrassment in the Making

PERSEREC. Theodore Sarbin Telephone Interview (1992). Theodore R. Sarbin, Ph.D., and Kenneth E. Karols, M.D., Ph.D., *Nonconforming Sexual Orientations and Military Suitability* (Monterey CA: Defense Personnel Security Research and Education Center, December 1988). PERSEREC Documents: Memorandum for Director DoD Security Research and Education Center, Subject: PERS-TR-89-002, *Nonconforming Sexual Orientations and Military Suitability,* From Craig Alderman, Jr., Deputy Under Secretary of Defense, 18 January 1989. Memorandum for the Deputy Undersecretary of Defense (Policy), Personnel Security Research and Education Center (PERSEREC) Research on Homosexuality and Suitability, From Carson K. Eoyang, Director, 30 January 1989. Memo for Mr. Peter Nelson Through Mr. Maynard Anderson, Subject: PERSEREC Draft Report, Nonconforming Sexual Orientation, From Craig Alerman Jr., 10 February 1989. Memorandum of Deputy Director, Counter Intelligence and Investigation Programs, Subject: PERSEREC Report, From Ted B. Borck, Colonel, VAGC, USA, Director, Legislation and Legal Policy, Assistant Secretary of Defense for Military, Manpower and Personnel Policy, 28 March 1989. Press Release: Lambda Legal Defense and Education Fund, Inc., New York NY, 25 October 1989.

Robb Bettiker Interview, op. cit.

David Carney Interview (Los Angeles CA, 1991).

Jim Holobaugh Interview (Minneapolis MN, 1990).

Marine Corps Lesbian Witch-Hunts (Judy Meade Hearing). Christine Taylor Interview (Jacksonville NC, 1991). Vaughan Taylor Interview, op. cit. Paula Berry Interview, op. cit. Richard Smith, "Corps Set hearing on Homosexual Allegation," *Daily News,* 11 February 1989, p. 1-C. Smith, "Lawyer Says Accusers Are 'Proven Liars,' " *Daily News,* 23 February 1989, p. 1-B. Smith, "Meade Declares Innocence; Decision Due Today," *Daily News,* 24 February 1989, p. 1-A. Smith, "Board to Deliberate on Captain's Fate," *Daily News,* 26 February 1989 (no page). Smith, "Officer Ousted for Knowing Lesbian," *Daily News,* 27 February 1989,

p. 1-A. "Corps Spokesmen Deny Over Zealousness to Rid Lesbians," *Daily News,* 5 February 1989, p. 1-A. "Corps Lack Direction in Responding to Gays," *Daily News,* March 1989 (no page).

USS *Iowa*. Kendall Truitt Interview, op. cit. USS *Iowa* Document: Review of Navy Investigation of USS *Iowa* Explosion, Joint Hearings before the Investigations Subcommittee and the Defense Policy Panel of the Committee on Armed Services, House of Representatives, One Hundred First Congress, First Session, 12–13, 21 December 1989. Peter Cary, "Death at Sea," *U.S. News & World Report,* 13 April 1990, pp. 21–30.

69. Explosions

USS *Iowa*. Review of Navy Investigation of USS *Iowa* Explosion, Joint Hearings before the Investigations Subcommittee and the Defense Policy Panel of the Committee on Armed Services House of Representatives, op. cit. Kendall Truitt Interview, op. cit. Peter Cary, "Death at Sea," *US News and World Report,* 13 April 1990, pp. 21–30.

DACOWITS. Lisa M. Keen, "Congress' Pressure Against Military Witch-Hunts Grows," *Washington Blade,* 7 April 1989, p. 1. Keen, "DoD Panel Advises Training to Help Curb Gay-Baiting," *Washington Blade,* 21 April 1989, p. 1. "Defense Advisory Committee Brief Congress on Lesbian," *South Bay Times,* May 1989, p. 24. Dianne Chamberlain Interview (Elkton MD, 1990). Mary Beth Harrison Interviews, op. cit. Kate Dyer Interviews (Washington DC and San Francisco CA, 1990–1992).

USS *Iowa*. Kathleen "Kathy" Kubicina Interview (Cleveland OH, 1992). "Sailors' Families Get Wrenching News," *The San Francisco Chronicle,* 21 April 1989, p. A-19. "Battleship Disaster/Navy Silencing Its 16-Inch Guns, Probe," *The San Francisco Chronicle,* 21 April 1989, p. A-1.

Scapegoating of Kendall Truitt. Kendall Truitt Interview, op. cit. "*Iowa* Sailor Says Navy's Looking for 'Scapegoat,' " *The San Francisco Chronicle,* 27 May 1989, p. A-12. Jerald Posner, "The Navy's Scapegoat," *Penthouse,* January 1990. Molly Moore, "Sailor Denies Link to Blast Fatal to 47 Aboard USS *Iowa*: Truitt Says Navy Prober Seeking Scapegoat," *The Washington Post,* 27 May 1989, p. A-1.

70. Mockingbirds

Congressional Hearings on USS *Iowa* (Background Information). Review of Navy Investigation of USS *Iowa* Explosion, Joint Hearings before the Investigations Subcommittee and the Defense Policy Panel of the Committee on Armed Services House of Representatives, op. cit. Kendall Truitt Interview, op. cit. Kathy Kubicina Interview, op. cit. Molly Moore, "2 Shipmates Focus of *Iowa* Probe: Blast Killed One Spared the Other," *The Washington Post,* 25 May 1989, p. A-1. Moore, "Sailor Denies Link to Blast Fatal to 47 Aboard USS *Iowa*; Truitt Says Navy Seeks Scapegoat," *The Washington Post,* 27 May 1989, p. A-1. "*Iowa* Sailor Transferred in Sabotage Probe," *The San Francisco Chronicle,* 26 May 1989, p. A-8. "New Twist in Battleship Turret Blast," *The San Francisco Chronicle,* 3 June 1989, p. A-8. "*Iowa* Sails Tomorrow/Battleship Blast Still a Mystery," *The San Francisco Chronicle,* 6 June 1989, p. A-12. "Probe of Blast/Navy's Gunpowder Crack-down," *The San Francisco Chronicle,* 12 June 1989, p. A-3.

Other Purges and Probes. Okinawa Document: Naval Investigative Service, Report of Investigation, Sodomy, Command/MCB Camp Butler Okinawa, Japan, 18–20 April 1989. Sid Balman Jr., "2 Court-Martialed in Wake of Restroom Videotaping," *Air Force Times,* 9 October 1989 (no page). Lisa M. Keen, "NIS Uses Hidden Cameras," *Washington Blade,* 8 September 1989, p. 1. Tim Jernigan Interview (Ft. Worth TX, 1991). Bob Dockendorf Interview (San Francisco CA, 1991).

USS *Iowa* (The Hartwig Smokescreen). "Navy Inquiry Points to Suicide in Blast on *Iowa*, NBC Says," *The San Francisco Chronicle,* 19 July 1989, p. A-1. David Johnston, "Navy's Evidence Suggests Sailor Set off Blast to Kill Himself," *The New York Times,* 19 July 1989, p. A1 col. 4. C. Robert Zelnick and Mark Brender, "The *Navy* vs. *Hartwig:* Did Leaks From the USS *Iowa* Probe Smear a Sailor," *The Washington Post,* 2 July 1989, p. C-1.

71. Official Government Sources

Navy's Case Against Hartwig. Congressional Hearings (Background Information), op. cit. John M. Broder and Melissa Healy, "Navy Finds *Iowa* Explosion Was Result of 'Suicidal Act,' " *Los Angeles Times,* 7 September 1989, Home Edition: part I, p. 1 col. 5. Andrew Rosenthal, "Fatal Blast Aboard Battleship *Iowa* was Probably Intentional, Investigation Finds," *The New York Times,* 7 September 1989, sec. A, p. 16 col. 2. George C. Wilson, "Sailor Probably Sabotaged USS *Iowa*'s Gun, Navy Finds; Report on Fatal Blast to be Released Today," *The Washington Post,* 7 September 1989, p. A-1. Healy and Broder, "*Iowa* Sailor Seen as Lonely, Troubled; 4-Month Navy Inquiry Finds Hartwig Capable of Suicide," *Los Angeles Times,* part 1, p. 8 col. 1. "Excerpts From *Iowa* Blast Findings," *The New York Times,* 8 September 1989, sect. A, p. 11 col. 1. Healy, "*Iowa* Skipper Faces Cruel Business of Accountability; 'Admiral's Mast' Proceedings to Determine Navy Careers of Captain, Executive Officer," *Los Angeles Times,* 9 September 1989, part 1, p. 20 col 1. Kathleen Kubicina Interview, op. cit. Wilson, "The Different Faces of Clayton Hartwig: USS *Iowa* Sailor Called Competent, Troubled," *The Washington Post,* 10 September 1989, p. A-3. *How to Get Even Without Going to Jail* (Rosman NC: Frozen Creek Press). Kendall Truitt Interview, op. cit.

PERSEREC. Kate Dyer Interviews, op. cit. Ted Sarbin Interview, op. cit. Sarbin and Karols, *Noncon-forming Sexual Orientations and Military Suitability,* op. cit. Jacob Weisberg, "Gays in Arms," *The New Republic,* 19 February 1990. Press Release: National Gay and Lesbian Task Force, Statement of Robert Bray, Director, 20 October 1989.

Col. Margarethe Cammermeyer Interview (Seattle WA, 1992).
Phil Zimmerman Interview (New Jersey, 1992).
Terry Ryder Interview (Baltimore MD, 1992).
Navy's Case Refuted by Hartwig's Family. Kathy Kubicina Interview, op. cit. "Friend Denies Saying Hartwig Attempted Suicide," *Cleveland Plain Dealer*, 3 December 1989.

72. Hearings

ROTC Campus Unrest. Robb Bettiker Interview, op. cit. David Carney Interview, op. cit. Jim Holobaugh Interview, op. cit. Rick Villasenor Interview (Los Angeles CA, 1990). Press release: Memorandum to Lesbian and Gay Press From William B. Rubenstein, ACLU Lesbian and Gay Rights Project, Campus Activity Challenging ROTC Discrimination, 7 June 1990. Bill Peterson, "Faculty Seeks ROTC Ouster over Policy on Gays," *The Washington Post*, 5 December 1989, p. A-14.

Ben-Shalom Decision. *Ben-Shalom* v. *Marsh* 881 F.2d 454 (7th Cir. 1989). Miriam Ben-Shalom Interview, op. cit. "Homosexual Policy Lawsuit Dismissed," *Navy Times*, 27 November 1989.

Steffan Case, 1989. Joe Steffan Interview, op. cit. Steffan, *Honor Bound*, op. cit. *Steffan* v. *Cheney* 733 F.Supp. 1 (D.D.C. 1989). Marc Wolinsky Interview, op. cit. "Gays in the Military," *ABC News Nightline*, Transcript from Journal Graphics, New York NY, 30 October 1989, Show #2201.

Hearings on *Iowa* Explosion. "Captain Can't Agree With All of Navy's Findings in *Iowa* Blast," *San Francisco Chronicle*, 12 December 1989, p. A-11. Review of Navy Investigation of USS *Iowa* Explosion, Joint Hearings before the Investigations Subcommittee and the Defense Policy Panel of the Committee on Armed Services House of Representatives, op. cit. Kathy Kubicina Interview, op. cit. Kendall Truitt Interview, op. cit.

Carswell AFB Purge. Dan Bell Interview (Ft. Worth TX, 1992). Tom Rockman Interview (Ft. Worth TX, 1992). Lou Chibbaro, Jr., "Air Force Discharges Seven at Texas Base," *Washington Blade*, 5 January 1990, p. 1. Newsletter: Texas Gay Veterans, Ft. Worth TX, May 1990. Catalina Camia, "Gay Servicemen Say Carswell Is Forcing Them Out," *Dallas Morning News*, 5 January 1990, p. 1-A. Stefani Gammage, "7 Gay Airmen at Carswell Ousted," *Fort Worth Star-Telegram*, 5 January 1990, sect 1, p. 1. Camia, "Gay Groups Assail Carswell Inquiry," *The Dallas Morning News*, 6 January 1990, p. 33-A. Camia, "Groups Seek US Review of Gay Inquiry," *Dallas Morning News*, 11 January 1990, p. 21-A. Gammage, "Groups Protest Investigation of Gay Airmen," *Fort Worth Star-Telegraph*, 14 January 1990, p. 1-A.

Barbara Baum Vindicated. Barbara Baum Interview, op. cit. Barbara Baum Documents: United States Navy–Marine Corps Court of Military Review documents. Author's note: These documents include a series of appeals by Baum's attorneys based on errors in her hearings that violated her Constitutional rights to a fair trial.

Letter to Commander, United States Army, Second Region, United States Army ROTC Cadet Command, Fort Knox KY, From US Representative Gerry E. Studds, et. al (23 reps).

The Death of Jess Jessop. Interviews and correspondence with Jessop's cousin, Pat Katka and estate executor, George Murphy.

73. Holding Actions

Case Histories. *Ben-Shalom* v. *Secretary of the Army* 881 F.2D 454 (7th Cir. 1989). *Woodward* v. *United States* 871 F.2d 1068 (Fed. Cir. 1989); cert. denied, 110 s. Ct. 1296 (1990). David G. Savage. "High Court Lets Military's Ban on Gays Stand." *Los Angeles Times*, 27 February 1990, p. A-1. Miriam Ben-Shalom Interview, op. cit. Jim Woodward Interviews (San Diego CA, 1991–1992).

Administrative Discharge Workshop. Interviews with anonymous Navy senior enlisted man.

ROTC Dissension on Campus. Robb Bettiker Interview, op. cit. David Carney Interview, op. cit. Carney/Bettiker Documents: Letter to H. Lawrence Garrett III, Secretary of the Navy from US Representative Gerry Studds and 34 other Representatives. ACLU Gay and Lesbian Rights Project, ROTC, op. cit. Letter to Richard Cheney, Secretary of Defense from John M. Deutch, Provost, Massachusetts Institute of Technology, Cambridge MA, 10 April 1990, Subject: ROTC and Gay and Lesbian Students. Letter Richard Cheney, Secretary of Defense from Derek Bok, President, Harvard University, Cambridge MA, 1 June 1990, Subject: ROTC and Gay and Lesbian Students. Jay Hatheway Interview, op. cit. Richard McGuire Interviews (Boston MA, 1991–1992).

USS *Iowa* Fallout. Congressional Hearing's Documents: USS *Iowa* Tragedy: An Investigative Failure, Report of the Investigations Subcommittee and Defense Policy Panel of the Committee on Armed Services, House of Representatives, One Hundred First Congress, Second Session, 5 March 1990. Ray Nelson, "What Really Happened on the *Iowa*," *Popular Science*, December 1990, pp. 84–87, 120–121. Kathy Kubicina Interview, op. cit.

ROTC Dissension on Campus. Letter to Richard (Dick) Cheney, Secretary of Defense from Robert H. Atwell, President, American Council on Education, Allan W. Oster, President, American Association of State Colleges and Universities, Robert M. Rosenzweig, President, Association of American Universities, Robert L. Clodius, President, Association of State Universities and Land-Grant Colleges, 14 May 1990, Subject: ROTC discrimination by sexual orientation. Christopher Michaud. "Students Give ROTC the Boot over Anti-Gay Policy," *The Advocate* (no date) p. 42.

74. Vindication

USS *Iowa*: The Truth. Ray Nelson, "What Really Happened on the *Iowa*," *Popular Science*, December 1990, pp. 84–87, 120–121. Kathy Kubicina Interview, op. cit. Dirk Johnson, "Their Hearts Said Navy Erred About *Iowa* Blast," *The New York Times*, 27 May 1990, part 1, p. 18, col. 1.

Robb Bettiker Interview, op. cit.

Cheney Disclosures. From discussions with high-ranking officials in the Pentagon and Legislative Aide Kate Dyer.

Jim Holobaugh Interview, op. cit.

Orlando Gotay Interview, op. cit. Orlando Gotay Documents: Recoupment of Scholarship Funds from Reserve Officers' Training Corps (ROTC) Participants Disenrolled for Homosexuality from Christopher Jehn, 4 June 1990. ACLU News Release: Navy Demands Gay Sailor Repay Scholarship, 2 October 1990.

Col. Edward Modesto Court-Martial. Edward Modesto Interview (Denver CO, 1990). Ed Joe Garner, "Transvestite army colonel is facing court-martial," *Rocky Mountain News*, 6 July 1990. "Nude photos, women's wigs, in colonel's home, agent says," *The Denver Post*, 8 August 1990. "Army officer who performed as drag queen Carmen charged," *Sacramento Union*, 13 May 1990. Randy Shilts, "Army Colonel Could Be Jailed on Gay-Related Charges," *San Francisco Chronicle*, 18 October 1990, p. A6. Edward Modesto Document: Grant of Immunity and Order to Testify, *United States* v. *Robin R. Kerr*, March 1990. Interviews with Mike Duncan (Colorado Springs CO, 1990) and Walter Gerash (Denver CO, 1990).

Suicide at Ft. Carson. Anonymous interview.

75. The Fag Killer

Karen Stupsky Interview (Norfolk VA, 1991).

Kate Dyer Interviews, op. cit.

Jim Woodward Interviews, op. cit.

Miriam Ben-Shalom Interview, op. cit.

Army's appeal in Watkins's Case. Perry Watkins Interviews, op. cit. *Watkins* v. *U.S. Army* 875 F.2d 699 (9th Circ. 1989) *en banc.*

Parris Island, Final Chapter. Robin Kane, "Navy restores pay and record," *Washington Blade*, 24 August 1990.

Acceptance of Homosexuals Begins to Surface. Anonymous interviews with various active duty service members, both officer and enlisted.

Admiral Donnell Memo. Jane Gross, "Navy Is Urged to Root Out Lesbians Despite Abilities," *The New York Times*, 2 September 1990. Unclassified Document: Administrative Message, From Commander Navy Surface Fleet, Norfolk VA, to All Navy Surface Fleet, Subject: Equal Treatment of Male and Female Homosexuals.

Gross's Article. Jane Gross, "For Gay Soldiers, Furtive Lives of Despair," *The New York Times*, 10 April 1990, p. 1. Jane Gross Interview (1992).

Other Purges, 1990. FOIA Documents: Series of documents relative to the Defense Language Institute, Monterey CA, purge. Lesbian Purge at Whidbey Island NAS: Anonymous interview. Italian Witch-Hunt: Lou Chibbaro, Jr., "Gay 'witch-hunts' underway at U.S. air base in Italy," *Washington Blade*, 19 October 1990, pp. 1, 19. Grisom AFB/Fag Killer Investigation: Jim Neal Interview (Indianapolis IN, 1992). Steve Marose Interview (Tacoma WA, 1992).

Marines attack gay bar, again . . . Lou Chibbaro, Jr., "Marines charge two, but Gays still angry over anti-Gay attack," *Washington Blade*, 6 July 1990, p. 1.

76. Convenience of the Government (Part 2)

Lesbian Culture. Robin Tyler Telephone Interview (1992).

Donna Lynn Jackson Interview (San Francisco CA, 1991). Photo essay of Donna Lynn Jackson, *On Our Backs*, March-April, 1991. Christie Carr Interview (San Francisco CA, 1991).

Stop/Loss Policy. Steffan, *Honor Bound*, op. cit.

Miriam Ben-Shalom Interview, op. cit. Miriam Ben-Shalom Document: Letter to President George Bush from Miriam Ben-Shalom, Subject: All gay and lesbian regiment, 13 February 1991. Author's note: Bush did not respond to this letter. Ben-Shalom also attempted to rejoin the Wisconsin National Guard. Wisconsin has equal employment statutes that would have allowed Ben-Shalom to serve. Her request to join the Wisconsin National Guard was turned down based on national military policy.

Steffan, *Honor Bound*, op. cit.

Gay and Lesbian Backlash. National Gay and Lesbian Task Force Press Release: Task Force Opposes Persian Gulf War; Position Paper Released, Says Gays and Lesbians "Detrimentally Affected" by Conflict, 30 January 1991. Mindie Spatt and Hildie Kraus, "Military Gals," *San Francisco Bay Times*, June 1991, p. 18. Karen Stupsky Interview, op cit. Karen Stupsky, "First National Lesbian Conference," *Our Own Community Press* (Norfolk VA), p. 1.

HI-MOM. Jeff Herwatt Interview, op. cit.

Perry Watkins Interviews, op. cit.

Joe Steffan Case. *Steffan* v. *Cheney* 920 F.2d. 74 (D.C.Cir. 1990). Joe Steffan Interview, op. cit. Steffan, *Honor Bound*, op. cit.

Security Clearances. Government Document: Memorandum for Director, Administration and Management, Subject: Eligibility of Homosexuals for DoD Security Clearances, 9 January 1991.

Manliness. Bruce Fein, "Keep the military's ban on homosexuals," *USA Today*, September 1990.

ROTC Storm and Strife. Greg Teran Interview (Minneapolis MN, 1990).

About Face Conference, 1990. Interviews and personal observation by the author.

EPILOGUE: PROMISES TO KEEP

77. Politics & Prejudice (Part 2)

Persian Gulf War: Four in a Foxhole. Eddie Miller Interview (Fort Sill OK, 1991). Randy Shilts, "What's Fair in Love and War," *Newsweek*, 1 February 1993, pp. 58–59.

Stop-Loss Policy. Donna Lynn Jackson Interview (San Francisco CA, 1991). Sam Gallegos Interviews (Ft. Irwin CA and Denver CO, 1991–1993). Michael Dull Interview (Orange County CA, 1991). Clifford Krapf Interview (San Diego CA, 1991). Interview with anonymous reservist (Seattle WA, 1991). Letter from Carl Longshore, Head Administrative Actions Unit, USMC, Marine Corps Reserve Support Center, Overland Park, Kansas, to James A. Henderson, Attorney at Law, dated 29 January 1991, Subj: Refusal of client's request for separation on the basis of homosexuality. Randy Shilts, "Claim You're Gay, Avoid the Military," *New York Times*, 7 January 1991, p. 17. Shilts, "Military May Defer Discharge of Gays," *San Francisco Chronicle*, 11 January 1991, p. 19. Shilts, "Army Discharges Lesbian Who Challenged Ban," *San Francisco Chronicle*, 19 January 1993, p. 12.

Commander's Handbook. Wade Lambert and Stephanie Simon, "U.S. Military Moves to Discharge Some Gay Veterans of Gulf War," *Wall Street Journal*, 30 July 1991, p. 6.

Marriage license required. Paul Di Donato Interview (San Francisco CA, 1991). Bulletin to all NGRA Members and Supporters from Paul A. Di Donoto, Legal Director dated 5 April 1991, Subj: Update on military issue.

Ed Tramont Interview (Baltimore MD, 1991).

"Claimed sexual preferences do not constitute . . ." Interview with anonymous Marine sergeant (1991). Letter from Marine sergeant to Colonel Steven Ipson, USMC Naval Station at Long Beach dated 13 February 1991. Reply from Staff Judge Advocate, Marine Corps Reserve Support Center to Mary Newcombe, Esq.

Purge of gay linguists. Terry Ryder Interview (Baltimore MD, 1992).

"They don't want a coffin . . ." Miriam Ben-Shalom Telephone Interview (1991).

Gay medics in the Persian Gulf. Interview with anonymous Navy corpsman (1992).

Don Gagins Interview (Midway Park NC, 1991).

Stateside purges. Robin Claussen Interview (Seattle WA, 1991). Christina Black Interview (San Francisco CA, 1991). Kenneth Miller Telephone Interview (1991). Randy Shilts, "In the Wake of War, Military Again Targets Gays," *San Francisco Chronicle*, 5 August 1991, p. 1.

The homefront. Gene Barfield Interview (Barre VT, 1991). Rev. John Pridonoff, Ph.D., Interview (San Diego CA, 1991). Danny Leonard Interviews (Jacksonville NC, 1990–1991). Gary Hendricks Interview (Midway Park NC, 1991). Stephen Krug Interview (San Francisco CA, 1990). Randy Shilts, "Gay Troops in the Gulf War Can't Come Out," *San Francisco Chronicle*, 18 February 1991, p. 1.

Discharge statistics. "The Outing of Assistant Secretary of Defense," *The Advocate*, 27 August 1991, pp. 34–44.

Dr. Magnus Hirschfeld, *The Sexual History of the World War* (New York: Cadillac Publishing Co., 1941), pp. 128–129.

Joseph Steffan case. "Judge Criticized for Calling Former Navy Cadet 'a Homo'," *San Francisco Chronicle*, 9 March 1991. " 'Homo' Term Spurs Call for New Judge," *San Francisco Chronicle*, 12 March 1991. Randy Shilts, "Pentagon Memo Urged Reversing Ban on Gays in Military," *San Francisco Chronicle*, 15 June 1991, p. 2. "Judge Says AIDS Threat Justifies Navy Ban," *San Francisco Chronicle*, 10 December 1991, p. 2.

Parades. Sam Gallegos Interviews (Denver CO, 1991). Armistead Maupin Interview (San Francisco CA, 1991). Greg Lopez, "July 4 Parade Puts Limits on Group of Gay Veterans," *Rocky Mountain News* (Denver CO), 29 June 1991. Letter form Sam Gallegos to Operation Welcome Home Parade Committee, Subj: Withdrawal of application to march in July 4 parade. Adam Gettinger-Brizuela, "Rainbow of Response to Gay Vets Parade," GLBVA Newsletter, Summer 1992.

Army Times ad. ACLU news release, 15 July 1991, Subj: Denying Existence of Gays and Lesbians in the Military, *Army Times* Censors Ad Urging End to Anti-Gay Discrimination. Eric Schmitt, "Publisher of Military Newspapers Rejects an Ad About Gay Troops," *New York Times*, 17 July 1991.

Greg Greeley's discharge. Greg Greeley Interview (Washington DC, 1991). Patrice Gaines-Carter, "Gay Parade Leader Questioned," *Washington Post*, 25 June 1991, p. 1. Gaines-Carter, "Gay Parade Leader Granted Discharge," *Washington Post*, 26 June 1991, p. D1.

The Advocate "outing" story. "The Outing of the Assistant Secretary of Defense," *The Advocate*, 27 August 1991, pp. 34–44.

". . . we would have been captured by now—by Cuba." Barney Frank appearance on *Good Morning America* (August 1991).

Bush approves gay spokesman's retention. Interview with anonymous senior Pentagon official (Washington DC, 1991).

Tracy Thorne Interview (Virginia Beach VA, 1991). Randy Schilts, "Proposed Bill Would End Ban on Gays in Armed Forces," *San Francisco Chronicle*, 20 May 1992, p. 8. "Navy Aviator Challenging Pentagon's

Ban on Gays," *San Francisco Chronicle*, 20 July 1992, p. 7. Letter from Christopher Jenn, Assistant Secretary of Defense, to Gerry E. Studds, House of Representatives, Subj: Tracy Thorne's administrative separation processing.

Margrethe Cammermeyer case. Col. Margrethe Cammermeyer Interviews (Seattle WA, 1991–1992). Randy Shilts, "Ambition to Lead Derailed Her Career," *San Francisco Chronicle*, 5 August 1991, p. 12.

The gay vote 1992. John Gallagher and Chris Bull, "Washington's New Attitude," *The Advocate*, 26 January 1993, pp. 34–41. John Purnell, "Power, People, Parties, Platforms," *The Advocate*, pp. 42–43. John Gallagher, "Friend of No One?" *The Advocate*, 30 November 1993, pp. 48–51.

Republican Convention. Jeannine Guttman and James Cox, "Republicans on the Attack Against Gay Rights," *USA Today*, 18 August 1992. Jill Lawrence, "GOP Putting Finishing Touches on Combative Platform," *San Francisco Chronicle*, 13 August 1992, p. 8. Carl Irving, "GOP's tent full of anger," *San Francisco Sunday Examiner and Chronicle*, 23 August 1992, p. 9. Chris Bull, "Why George Bush Hates You," *The Advocate*, 10 October 1992, pp. 38–47.

"It won't be a big deal . . ." Telephone Interview with anonymous Clinton aide (Washington DC, 1992). The president-elect addresses the issue. "Clinton Vows Strong Military—Better Health Care for Vets," *San Francisco Chronicle*, 12 November 1992 (Veterans Day), p. 4.

The response. "Lifting the Gay Ban: No Easy Answers," *Army Times*, 11 January 1993, cover story. David Tuller, "Gays Say Debate Could Be Beneficial," *San Francisco Chronicle*, 28 January 1993, p. 3. "At Presidio, Many Agree Ban Should Be Lifted," *San Francisco Chronicle*, 29 January 1993, p. 4. "Gay Ban Will Go," *Army Times*, 1 February 1993, cover story. Hackworth, David H., "Rancor in the Ranks: The Troops vs. the President," *Newsweek*, 28 June 1993, pp. 24–25.

Clinton begins to falter. "Clinton Stands Firm on Gay Issue, but . . ." *San Francisco Chronicle*, 29 January 1993, p. 3. Ruth Marcus and Helen Dewar, "Clinton Compromise on Gay Ban," *San Francisco Chronicle*, 30 January 1993, p. 1. "Keeping Gays From Combat Under Study," *San Francisco Chronicle*, 1 February 1993, p. 3. "Gay Ban Round One," *Army Times*, 8 February 1993, cover story.

The Gay Agenda videotape. Art Pine, "Marines Circulate Graphic Gay Video," *San Francisco Chronicle*, 28 January 1993, p. 3.

". . . gay culture being imposed . . ." Rowland Evans and Robert Novak, "Joint Chiefs, Congress Fight Clinton's Pledge on Gays," *San Francisco Chronicle*, 27 January 1993, p. 15.

Captain Carolyn (Dusty) Pruitt case. "Court Rebuffs Pentagon Over Lesbian's Lawsuit," *San Francisco Chronicle*, 8 December 1992, p. 3.

Keith Meinhold case. David Tuller, "Military's Ban on Gays Illegal, Judge Rules," *San Francisco Chronicle*, 29 January 1993, p. 1.

Allen Schindler's murder. "Slain Gay Sailor Becomes Martyr in Fight to End Military Ban," *San Francisco Chronicle*, 15 January 1993, p. 9. "Navy to Bring Murder Charges in Gay's Death," *San Francisco Chronicle*, 4 February 1993, p. 4.

Congress. Carolyn Lochhead, "Nunn's Idea for Compromise on Military's Ban on Gays," *San Francisco Chronicle*, 30 March 1993, p. 1. Richard H.P. Sia, "Military Experts Call Gays OK—In the Closet," *San Francisco Chronicle*, 1 April 1993, p. 1. Lockhead, "Dellums Sets Hearings on Gay GI Ban," *San Francisco Chronicle*, 29 April 1993, p. 6. "Gays Called Threat to Armed Forces," *San Francisco Chronicle*, 30 April 1993. [Note: This editorial appeared in the 24 August 1992 issues of *Army Times* and *Air Force Times*, two independent military-related newspapers. This was the first time they commented on the issue in an editorial.] "Goldwater Opposes Ban on Gays," *San Francisco Chronicle*, 11 June 1993, p. 3.

Gay leaders on the hearings. Michelle Benecke Telephone Interview (1993). Howard Bragman Telephone Interview (1993). Tanya Domi Telephone Interview (1993). David Mixner Telephone Interview (1993). David Smith Telephone Interview (1993). Thomas Stoddard Telephone Interview (1993). Katy Butler, "Gays Threaten to Halt Donations to Demos Over Military Issue," *San Francisco Chronicle*, 29 March 1993, p. 4.

The reformers. Tanya Domi Telephone Interview, op. cit. Joseph "Jay" Hatheway Interviews (Minneapolis MN, 1990–1993). Vernon "Copy" Berg Interviews (New York NY, 1991–1992). Joseph Steffan Telephone Interview (1993). Cliff Anchor Interview (Monte Rio CA, 1993). Gerald "Jerry" Rosanbalm Telephone Interviews (1993).

Where are they now? Carole Brock Interview (Guerneville CA, 1993). Barbara Baum Telephone Interviews (1993). Ruth Voor and Karen Colton Telephone Interview (1993). Terry Knox Telephone Interview (1993). Richard McGuire Telephone Interview (1993). Jack Green Telephone Interview (1993). Kathy Kubicina Telephone Interviews (1993). Charles Thompson Telephone Interview (1993). David Marier Interview (Atlanta GA, 1991). Perry Watkins Telephone Interview (1993). William "Pete" Randell Telephone Interview (1992). Jeff Herwatt Interview (San Francisco CA, 1991). T.J. Sterbens Interviews (San Diego CA, 1991–1992). Perry Watkins Telephone Interview (1993). Terry Knox Telephone Interview (1993).

AIDS losses. Frank Bruni, "Sponsor of Gay Rights Bill Died of AIDS Complications," *Detroit Free Press*, 28 March 1992, p. 3A. Randy Shilts, "S.F. Gay Movement Founder Dies of AIDS," *San Francisco Chronicle*, 1 November 1990, p. A10.

78. Tom Dooley's Honorable Discharge

James Monahan (ed.), *Before I Sleep . . . The Last Days of Dr. Tom Dooley* (New York: Farrar, Straus and Cudahay, 1961).

Ted Werner Interviews (Los Angeles CA, 1991–1992).
Diana Shaw Interview (Los Angeles CA, 1991–1992).

BACKGROUND INTERVIEWS

Among the roughly 1,100 interviews conducted, well over 300 were with people—current and former members of the armed forces, civilian government employees, government officials and congressional staff members—who did not want their identity disclosed. In addition to the sources whose names appear in the text, the following people were also interviewed. Among these interviewees are many heterosexuals; the inclusion of any person's name on this list does not mean they are homosexual.

Caroline Ackerman (USMC); Jane Meredith Adams (Journalist); Robert Adams (Congressional Aide); Henry Agueros (USN); Cliff Arnesen (USA); Kelly D. Arnold (USAF); Fay Baim (USMC); Renalda "Ronnie" Bancroft (USAF); Erik Barker (USAF/USMC); Paul Bashline (USAF); Glenn Beardsley (USAF); Johnny Beck (USA); Mike Beckwith (USN); Wayne Bell (USN); Wayne Benitez (USAF); Christina K. Black (USA); Katherine Bourdennay; Barbara Boyd (USN); Jay Bradshaw (USA); Ryon Brame (USA); Mike Brantjes (Holland); Joe Brewer (AIDS Activist); Lea Brown; Randy Bruno (USN); Charlie Brydon (USA); Claire Burbank (USAF); Cheryl L. Burnett; Pam Burwell (USA); Ray Busbee (USAF); Frank Buttino (FBI); Dana Cagle (USAF); Rene Carroll (USN); Bartholomew Casimir (USA); Dave Christensen (USA); Robin Claussen (USA); Ted Comerford (USN); Joe Cook (USA); Bill Cordes (USAF); Alberto Cortes (USN); Eileen Covato; Tracy Cox (USN); Melissa R. Crick (USAF); Trisha Critchfield (Citizen Soldier); John Cunningham (USN); Joe Czuberki (USA); Jim Darby (USN); Karen Denman (USN); Bob Derry (USA); Michele Douglas (Canadian Defense Forces); Kevin R. Drewery (ROTC); Michael Dull (USA); Kathy Duncan (Army Reserves); Mike Duncan (Attorney); Steve Dwyer (USCG); Steve Earl (USA); Jim Early (USN); Gregory Eaton (USAF); Scott Echard (Navy Reserves); Dave Eckert (USAF); Gene Elder (Activist); Dean Ellerbusch (USA); Ed Ellington (USN); Greg Ellsworth (Naval Academy); Steve Endean (Human Rights Campaign Fund); Tod Ensign (Citizen Soldier); Phil Entwistle (USN); Richard H. Epson-Nelms (USN); Mario Estrada (USA).

Andrew Fal (USA); Jim Fickey (USAF); Scott Folkerson (USA); Louis P. Font (Attorney); Kay Ford (Activist); Jerry Foshee (USN); Don Francis (Centers For Disease Control); Abbie Frost (USMC); Scott Fulkerson (USA); Robert Fullmer (USN); Don Gaines (USMC); Alan Gamble (USAF); Steve Garner (USN); Richard Gayer (Attorney); Walter Gerash (Attorney); Lawrence Gibson (USN); Michael Gingrich (USN/USAF); Skip Godsey (USN); Donny Godwin (National Lawyers Guild); Jose "Joe" Gonzales (USA); Dave Gooding (USN); Ben Goodwin (USA); Scott Grasser (USA); Greg Greeley (USAF); Don Gregory (USAF); Stacey Grey (USA); Kirt Grubbs (USN); Leonard M. Grube (USN); Paul Gundlach (USA); Warren Gunter (USA); Stan Hadden (USAF); Harry Haines (USA); Wes Haley (Research Consultant); Phyllis J. Hanniver (USA); Paul Hardman (USN); Bob Harmon (Army Reserves); Mike Hedrick (USA); Dennis Heer (USAF); Gary Hendricks (USMC); Lee Henley (USAF); Diane Higgs (USMC); Alica Hill (ROTC); Leslie Horvath (USN); Mark Houston (USA); John Ingham (USN); Jim Jennings (USN); Michael Job (USMC, Veterans Speakers Alliance); Curtis Johnson (USN); Doug Johnson (USA); Ken Johnson (USAF); Ralph Judd (USCG); Palani Kahala (USA); Roman Kalinin (Soviet Army); Sergey Katz (Soviet Army); Vera Keller; Mike Kiraley (USN); Paul Kirby (MIT/Activist); Mary Kitson (USN); Kitt Kling (USA); Madeline "Fran" Knight (USN); Charlotte Knutson (USAF/USA); Nick Koras (USA); Bill Kosky (USA); Clifford A. Krapf (USA); Pat LaFleur (USAF); Peter Laska (Navy ROTC); Robert Lehman (USA); Murray Liddell (USAF); Marvin Liebman (USA); Marie Lininger (USCG); Herbert Lotz (USA).

Doug MacKinnon (USA); Heidi Macy (USA); Chuck Magness (USA); Mark Malloy (USAF); Erik Andres Markestet (USAF); Steve Marose (USAF); Jeanne Martin (USA); Diane H. Mazur (USAF); Tim McCarthy (USA); Gill McDonald (USAF); Roger McFarlane (USN); Tim McFeeley (Army Reserves); Wayne McKinney; Chuck Medina (USN); Keith Meinhold (USN); Richard Meiss (USA); Carey Mellot (USN); Michael Menendez (USN); Fred Mesch, Jr. (USN); Don "Smokey" Metzger (USAF); Michael F. Metzger (Army ROTC); Ed Miller (Brother of Army murder victim); Edward Miller (USA); Tom Mitchell (USN); Charles Molle (USN); Greg Monsona (USN); Enrique Montoya, Jr. (Activist); Cynthia Moree (USAF); Steve Morin (Congressional Aide); Bruce Mulraney (USA); Brian Muni (NIS); Michael Murphy (USAF); Ellen Murray (USN); Thomas Musemeci (USN); Roxanne Norris (USN); Donald O'Higgins (USAF); Alan Ochsenbein (USAF); David Orahood (USMC); Dan Otero (USAF); Thomas Paniccia (USAF); Ted Pearson, Jr. (USN); Mark Perras (USAF); Eric Peters (USA); Cyndi Phillips (USN); Mark Plumb (USAF); Randy Powers (USA); John Prentice (USAF); John A. Pridonoff, Ph.D. (Metropolitan Community Church (MCC)); Frank Provasek; Andy Quintez (USN); Ronald Rae (USN); Sheldon Ramsdell (USN, Founding Vice President Vietnam Veterans Against the War); Ron Rasmussen (USAF); Marjorie Reed (USN); Dick Rhodes (USA); Ann Richardson (USN); Eric Roberts (USA); Tom Rockman, Jr. (USAF); Renee Rogers (USA); Mitch Rosa (USN); John A. Rovenolt (USN); Paul Royea (USCG); Herman Ruiz (USMC); Alberto Rullode (USN); Tim Rump (USAF).

David Said (Israel Defense Force); Mykul Saijoo (ROTC); Ronald Sampson (USAF); Greg Sanchez (USAF); Jeffrey Sayles (USN); Michael Schectman (USN); Chuck Schoen (USA); Grayton Schultz (USMC); Rob Schwitz (Air Force ROTC); Roxanne Setser (USA); Lois Shawver (Psychologist); John Sheneman (USN/USAF); Donna B. Simone (USN); Ray Skola (USA); Dennis Slocum-Kisinski (USN); Greg Smith (USN); Klaas H. Soesbeek, M.A. (Holland); Julie Stonacek (USA); Shaun Stout (USN); Jon Strait (USA); Bob Stuhr (USA); Cleve Taylor (USN); Chris Terry (USN); John Thibeault (USAF); Donna Thompson (USA); Tracy Timmons (ROTC); Lawson Tinker (82nd Airborne, USA); Scott Tobin (USA); Jayson Tollefson (USMC);

Nina Tuller (USA); Ronald George Tullier (USAF); Frans J. M. Van Dorp (Holland); Wanda Ford von Kleist (Sociologist); Jim Wagner (USN); Wayne Walls (USN); Kenneth W. M. Warnock (USN); Max Watts (Australia); Dale Weddle (USAF); Darryl West (USA); Shannon West (USAF); Pamela Westbrooke (USN); Robert White (USN); Dana Wilhusen (USAF); Arch Wilson (Alexander Hamilton Veterans Association); Stephen Wilson (USN); Stanton Wonn (USA); Perry Wood (USN); Bill Woods (Activist); Robert Young (USA); Tim Young (USA); Andrew Zaluski (USAF); Dave Zeni (USN).

INTERVIEWEE DEMOGRAPHICS BY CATEGORY

Sex
Female	26%
Male	74%

Ethnicity
African American	7%
Asian/Pacific Islander	1%
Caucasian	80%
Native American	1%
Spanish Surname	11%

Civilian vs. Military
Civilian (no military experience)	10%
Present and Former Military Personnel	90%

Military Personnel: Branch of Service
USA	28%
USAF	20%
USCG	2%
USMC	9%
USN	36%
ROTC/Military Academy	3%
Foreign Military Personnel	2%

Military Personnel: Officer vs. Enlisted
Enlisted	80%
Officers (Total Number Interviewed)	20%
Officer (High Rank)**	6% of military personnel interviewed

** High Rank includes all USA, USAF, USCG, USMC, and USN members who are field grade officers and above.

SELECTED BIBLIOGRAPHY

Alband, Linda; Steve Rees; and Denni Woodmansee. "The GI Movement Today: The Volunteer Armed Forces and the Movement in the Ranks." *Radical America*, Vol. 10, No. 3. May–June 1976.

Alband, Linda and Steve Rees. "Women and the Volunteer Armed Forces." *Radical America*, Vol. 11, No. 1. January–February 1977.

Anthony, Irvin. *Decatur*. New York: Scribner's, 1931.

Barkalow, Carol with Andrea Raab. *In the Men's House: An Inside Account of Life in the Army by One of West Point's First Female Graduates*. New York: Poseidon Press, 1990.

Benecke, Michelle M. and Kirstin S. Dodge. "Military Women in Nontraditional Job Fields: Casualties of the Armed Forces War on Homosexuals." *Harvard Women's Law Journal*. Spring 1990.

Bernstein, Carl and Bob Woodward. *All the President's Men*. New York: Simon & Schuster, 1974.

Bérubé, Allan. *Coming Out Under Fire, The History of Gay Men and Women in World War Two*. New York: The Free Press, 1990.

Bérubé, Allan and John D'Emilio. "The Military and Lesbians During the McCarthy Years." *Signs: Journal of Women in Culture and Society*. Summer 1984.

Boatner III, Mark Mayo. *Encyclopedia of the American Revolution*. New York: David McKay Co., Inc. 1974.

Bronson, Fred. *The Billboard Book of Number One Hits*. Rev. and enlarged ed. New York: Billboard Publications, Inc., 1988.

Bullock, Helen Duprey, senior ed. *Decatur House*. Washington, DC: National Trust for Historic Preservation in the United States, 1967.

Burr, Aaron. Papers of Aaron Burr Microfilm Collection: *Orderly book as commander of Malcolm's Continental Regiment*. 3 March 1778.

Chapkis, W., ed. *Loaded Questions: Women in the Military*. Amsterdam, Washington DC: Transnational Institute, 1981.

Chapman, Bruce K. *Our Unfair and Obsolete Draft—and What We Can Do About It*. New York: Pocket Books, 1968.

Cohen, Marcia. *The Sisterhood: The Inside Story of the Women's Movement and the Leaders Who Made It Happen*. New York: Ballantine Books, 1988.

Cooper, James Fenimore. *Lives of Distinguished American Naval Officers*. Philadelphia: Carey and Hart, 1846.

Criminal Investigation CID Operations (CID Regulation CIDR-195-1). Headquarters, US Army Criminal Investigation Command, 1 November 1986.

Dascanzo, Janine M. and Neal A. May. "Cleaning out the Pentagon's Closet: An Overview of the Defense Department's Anti-Gay Policy." *The University of Toledo Law Review*. Winter 1992.

Davis, Major Jeffrey. "Military Policy Toward Homosexuals: Scientific, Historical, and Legal Perspectives." *Military Law Review*, Vol. 131. 1991.

Davis, Patricia. "Uncle Sam's Lesbians: Power, Empowerment, and the Military Experience." Master's Thesis, Old Dominion University, Norfolk VA, 1991.

Decatur, Susan Wheeler. *Documents relative to the claim of Mrs. Decatur, with her earnest request that the gentlemen of Congress will take the trouble to read them.* Georgetown DC: J. C. Dunn, printer, 1826.

Delton, Carol and Andrew Mazer. *Everybody's Guide to Non-Registration.* San Francisco: Regional Young Adult Project of Northern California, 1980.

Denneny, Michael, ed. *The Christopher Street Reader.* New York: Perigee Books, 1983.

Dooley, Agnes W. *Promises to Keep, The Life of Dr. Thomas A. Dooley.* New York: Farrar, Straus and Company, 1962.

Dooley, Thomas A., M.D. *Deliver Us From Evil.* New York: Farrar, Straus and Cudahay, 1956.

———. *The Night They Burned the Mountain.* New York: Farrar, Straus & Cudahay. 1960.

———. *Before I Sleep.* New York: Farrar, Straus and Company, 1961.

———. *Dr. Tom Dooley's Three Great Books.* New York: Ariel Books, 1960.

———. *Doctor Tom Dooley, My Story.* New York: Ariel Books, 1962.

Dougan, Clark; Samuel Lipsman; and the editors of the Boston Publishing Company. *The Vietnam Experience: A Nation Divided.* Boston: Boston Publishing Company, 1984.

Doyle, Edward; Samuel Lipsman; and the editors of the Boston Publishing Company. *The Vietnam Experience: Setting the Stage.* Boston: Boston Publishing Company, 1981.

———. *The Vietnam Experience: America Takes Over 1965–67.* Boston: Boston Publishing Company, 1982.

Doyle, Edward; Samuel Lipsman; Stephen Weiss; and the editors of the Boston Publishing Company. *The Vietnam Experience: Passing the Torch.* Boston: Boston Publishing Company, 1981.

Dyer, Kate, ed. *Gays in Uniform: The Pentagon's Secret Reports.* Boston, Alyson Publications, 1990.

Dynes, Wayne R.; Warren Johansson; William A. Percy; and Stephen Donaldson, eds. *Encyclopedia of Homosexuality.* New York: Garland Publication, 1990.

Elshtain, Jean Bethke and Sheila Tobias. *Women, Militarism & War: Essays in History, Politics, & Social Theory.* Totowa NJ: Rowan & Littlefield, 1990.

Encyclopedia of World Mythology. New York: Galahad Books, 1975.

Engelman, Rose C., Ph.D. and Robert J. T. Joy, M.D. *200 Years of Military Medicine.* Fort Detrick MD: The Historical Unit, U.S. Army Medical Department, 1975.

Enloe, Cynthia. *Does Khaki Become You? The Militarization of Women's Lives.* Boston: South End Press, 1983.

Faludi, Susan. *Backlash, The Undeclared War Against American Women.* New York: Crown, 1991.

Freeman, Jo, ed. *Women: A Feminist Perspective.* 2d ed. Palo Alto CA: Mayfield Publishing Company, 1979.

Gallagher, Teresa. *Give Joy to My Youth, A Memoir of Dr. Tom Dooley.* New York: Farrar, Straus and Giroux, 1965.

Gettleman, Marvin E., ed. *Vietnam: History, Documents, and Opinions on a Major World Crisis.* Greenwich CT: Fawcett Publications, 1965.

Gibson, E. Lawrence. *Get Off My Ship, Ensign Berg vs. The U.S. Navy.* New York: Avon Books, 1976.

Gottlieb, Sherry Gershon. *Hell No, We Won't Go.* New York: Viking, 1991.

Grimal, Pierre with translation by Patricia Beardsworth. *Larousse World Mythology.* New York: Putnam, 1965.

Groom, Winston and Duncan Spencer, *Conversations with the Enemy: The Story of PFC Robert Garwood.* New York: Putnam, 1983.

Gunston, Bill. *Combat Arms: Modern Helicopters.* New York: Prentice Hall Press, 1990.

Hay, Thomas Robson, ed. *Cleburne and His Command.* By Capt. Irving A. Buck. Jackson TN: McCowat-Mercer Press, Inc., 1959.

Heitman, Francis B. *Historical Register of Officers of the Continental Army during The War of the Revolution April 1775 to December 1783.* Washington DC: The Rare Book Shop Publishing Company, Inc., 1914.

Hippler, Mike. *Matlovich, The Good Soldier.* Boston: Alyson Publications, 1989.

Hirschfeld, Magnus. *The Sexual History of the World War.* New York: Cadillac Publishing Co., 1941.

Holm, Maj. Gen. Jeanne, USAF (Ret.). *Women in the Military: An Unfinished Revolution.* Novato CA: Presidio Press, 1982.

Hooper, Edwin Bicksford; Dean C. Allard; and Oscar D. Fitzgerald. *The United States Navy and the Vietnam Conflict Vol. 1.* Washington DC: Naval History Division, Department of the Navy, 1976.

How to Get Even Without Going to Jail. Rosman NC: Frozen Creek Press.

Just, Ward. *Soldiers.* The Atlantic. October 1970.

———. *Soldiers, Part II.* The Atlantic. November 1970.

Karnow, Stanley. *Vietnam: A Television History.* New York: Viking Press, 1983.

Kramer, Henry L. and Jacob Sprenger with translation by Rev. Montague Simmons. *Malleus Maleficarum.* Suffolk, England: John Rodker, Publisher, 1928.

Karst, Kenneth L. The Pursuit of Manhood and the Desegregation of the Armed Forces. *UCLA Law Review.* February 1991.

Katkas, Michael. *The Vietnam Veterans Memorial.* New York: Crown Publishers, 1988.

Katz, Jonathan. *Gay American History: Lesbians and Gay Men in the U.S.A.* New York: Thomas Y. Crowell Company, 1976.

———. *Gay/Lesbian Almanac, A New Documentary.* New York: Harper & Row, Publishers, 1983.

Keegan, John. *Six Armies in Normandy, From D-Day to the Liberation of Paris.* New York: Penguin Books, 1982.

———. *The Mask of Command.* New York: Penguin Books, 1987.

Lang, Andrew. *Modern Mythology.* New York: AMS Press, 1968.

Law Enforcement Investigations, Field Manual No. 19–20. Washington DC: Headquarters Department of The Army, 29 April 1977.

Lederer, William J. *All the Ships at Sea.* New York: W. W. Norton & Company, 1950.

Lederer, William J. and Eugene Burdick. *The Ugly American.* New York: W. W. Norton, 1968.

Leinwand, Gerald. *The Draft.* New York: Pocket Books, 1970.

Lesser, Charles H., ed. *The Sinews of Independence: Monthly Strength Reports of the Continental Army.* Chicago: University of Chicago Press, 1976.

Lewis, Charles Lee. *The Romantic Decatur.* Philadelphia: University of Pennsylvania Press, 1937.

MacGregor, Jr., Morris J. *Integration of the Armed Forces 1940–1965, Defense Studies Series.* Washington DC: Center of Military History, United States Army, 1985.

Maguire, John Francis. *The Irish in America.* London: Longmans, Green, and Co., 1868.

[Malcolm's Regiment] National Archives Microfilm Collection. *Revolutionary War Company Payroll of Malcolm's Regiment 1777–1778.*

———. *The Muster Rolls for Malcolm's Regiment, December 1777–February 1778.*

Mayer, Jane and Doyle McManus. *Landslide: The Unmaking of the President, 1984–1988.* Boston: Houghton Mifflin, 1988.

Monahan, James, ed. *Before I Sleep . . . The Last Days of Dr. Tom Dooley.* New York: Farrar, Straus and Cudahay, 1961.

Murphy, Lawrence R. *Perverts by Official Order, The Campaign Against Homosexuals by the United States Navy.* New York: Harrington Park Press, 1988.

Neagles, James C. *Summer Soldiers, A Survey and Index of Revolutionary War Courts-Martial.* Salt Lake City, UT: Ancestry, Inc. 1980.

Obst, Lynda Rosen, ed. *The Sixties.* New York: Random House/Rolling Stone Press Books, 1977.

Orwell, George. *1984*. New York: Harcourt Brace, 1949.

Phelps, J. Alfred. *Chappie, America's First Black Four Star General: The Life and Times of Daniel James, Jr.* Novato CA: Presidio Press, 1991.

Plant, Richard. *The Pink Triangle: The Nazi War Against Homosexuals*. New York: Henry Holt, 1986.

Palmer, John McAuley. *General von Steuben*. Port Washington NY: Kennikat Press, 1966.

Rider, Fremont, ed. *The American Genealogical-Biographical Index to American Genealogical, Biographical and Local History Materials, Volume 51*. Middletown, CT: The Godfrey Memorial Library, 1965.

Rupp, Professor I. Daniel. *A Collection of Upwards of Thirty Thousand Names of German, Swiss, Dutch, French and other Immigrants in Pennsylvania from 1727 to 1776*. Baltimore: Genealogical Publishing Company, 1965.

Sarbin, Theodore R., Ph.D., and Kenneth E. Karols, M.D., Ph.D. *Nonconforming Sexual Orientations and Military Suitability*. Monterey CA: Defense Personnel Security Research and Education Center (PERSEREC), December 1988.

Scheer, Robert. "Hang Down Your Head Tom Dooley." *Ramparts Vietnam Primer*. San Francisco: Ramparts Magazine. (No date, circa 1967).

————. *How the United States Got Involved in Vietnam*. Santa Barbara CA: Center For the Study of Democratic Institutions, 1965.

Shilts, Randy. *The Mayor of Castro Street, The Life and Times of Harvey Milk*. New York: St. Martin's Press, 1982.

————. *And the Band Played On: Politics, People, and the AIDS Epidemic*. New York: St. Martin's Press, 1987.

Steffan, Joseph. *Honor Bound, A Gay American Fights for the Right to Serve His Country*. New York: Random House, 1992.

Teal, Donn. *The Gay Militants*. New York: Stein and Day, 1971.

Truby, J. David. *Women At War, A Deadly Species*. Boulder, CO: Paladin Press, 1977.

Tucker, Glenn. *Dawn Like Thunder: The Barbary Wars and the Birth of the U.S. Navy*. New York: Bobbs-Merrill, 1963.

Waldo, Samuel Putnam. *The Life and Character of Stephen Decatur; late commodore and post-captain in the Navy of the United States, and navy-commissioner: interspersed with brief notices of the origin, progress, and achievements of the American Navy*. Middletown, CT: Clark & Lyman, 1821.

Webb, James. *A Sense of Honor*. Englewood Cliffs, NJ: Prentice Hall, 1981.

Weedon, George. *Valley Forge Orderly Book of General George Weedon of the Continental Army under Command of General George Washington, in the Campaign of 1777*. New York: Dodd, Mead and Company, 1902.

Weinberg, Martin S. and Colin J. Williams. *Homosexuals and the Military: A Study of the Less Than Honorable Discharge*. New York: Harper & Row, 1971.

INDEX